CURRENT RESEARCH IN PHOTOSYNTHESIS

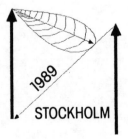

Current Research in Photosynthesis

Volume III

Proceedings of the VIIIth International Conference on Photosynthesis
Stockholm, Sweden, August 6–11, 1989

edited by

M. BALTSCHEFFSKY

Department of Biochemistry,
University of Stockholm,
Stockholm, Sweden

KLUWER ACADEMIC PUBLISHERS

DORDRECHT / BOSTON / LONDON

Library of Congress Cataloging in Publication Data

International Congress on Photosynthesis (8th : 1989 : Stockholm,
Sweden)
    Current research in photosynthesis : proceedings of the VIIIth
International Congress on Photosynthesis, Stockholm, Sweden, August
6-11, 1989 / edited by M. Baltscheffsky.
        p.   cm.
    ISBN 0-7923-0587-6 (set)
    1. Photosynthesis--Congresses.   2. Photosynthesis--Research-
-Congresses.   I. Baltscheffsky, Margareta.   II. Title.
QK882.I55   1989
581.1'3342--dc20   89-48127

ISBN 0-7923-0588-4 (Vol. I)
ISBN 0-7923-0589-2 (Vol. II)
ISBN 0-7923-0590-6 (Vol. III)
ISBN 0-7923-0591-4 (Vol. IV)
ISBN 0-7923-0587-6 (Set)

Published by Kluwer Academic Publishers,
P.O. Box 17, 3300 AA Dordrecht, The Netherlands.

Kluwer Academic Publishers incorporates
the publishing programmes of
D. Reidel, Martinus Nijhoff, Dr W. Junk and MTP Press.

Sold and distributed in the U.S.A. and Canada
by Kluwer Academic Publishers,
101 Philip Drive, Norwell, MA 02061, U.S.A.

In all other countries, sold and distributed
by Kluwer Academic Publishers Group,
P.O. Box 322, 3300 AH Dordrecht, The Netherlands.

Printed on acid-free paper

GENERAL CONTENTS

Volume I

Volume II

Volume III

Volume IV

CONTENTS TO VOLUME III

9. H^+-ATPases

VIII

11. Rubisco

XVIII

PREFACE

These four volumes with close to one thousand contributions are the proceedings from the VIIIth International Congress on Photosynthesis, which was held in Stockholm, Sweden, on August 6-11, 1989. The site for the Congress was the campus of the University of Stockholm. This in itself was an experiment, since the campus never before had been used for a conference of that size. On the whole, it was a very sucessful experiment. The outcome of a congress depends on many contributing factors, one major such factor being the scientific vigour of the participants, and I think it is safe to say that the pariticipants were vigourous indeed. Many exciting new findings were presented and thoroughly dicussed, indoors in the discussion sessions as well as outdoors on the lawns. For the local organizing committee it was very rewarding to participate in these activities, and to watch some of our younger colleagues for the first time being subjected to the impact of a large international congress. The stimulating effect of this event on the local research atmosphere has been substantial.

As was the case with the proceedings from both the 1983 and 1986 Congresses these proceedings have been compiled from camera ready manuscripts, and the editing has mainly consisted of finding the proper place for each contribution and distributing the manuscripts into four volumes with some internal logic in each. In this I have had the invaluable help from Dr. Åke Strid, to whom I am indeed very thankful. The professional and unfailing support of our publisher, Ir. Ad. C. Plaizier, is also gratefully acknowledged.

The scientific programme for the Congress was put together by the Swedish Organizing Committee, with important input from the International Committee on Photosynthesis, and I thank my fellow-organizers for their competent and valuable work. The practical arrangements for the Congress were very well handled by Congrex AB, and I would like to specially mention Anette Lifors and Christel Bomgren for their enthusiastic help. The Congress would not have functioned without strong local support, foremost that of Professor Bertil Andersson and Dr. Stenbjörn Styring from the Department of Biochemistry, but also from all the students who were most helpful in uncounted numbers of ways, before, during and after the Congress.

Finally I thank all those who financially contributed to the Congress. Without their support there would not have been any Photosynthesis Congress in Sweden.

Stockholm in October 1989   Margareta Baltscheffsky

ACKNOWLEDGEMENTS

The Swedish Organizing Committee wishes to thank the following sponsors for their financial Support of the Congress.

Sponsors

Astra AB, Sweden
Pharmacia AB, Sweden
Scandinavian Airlines System, Sweden
Sparbankernas Bank, Sweden
Stiftelsen Kempes Minne, Sweden
Stiftelsen Lantbruksforskning, Sweden
Strålfors AB, Sweden
Swedish Council for Forestry and Agricultural Research
Swedish Natural Science Research Council
The City of Stockholm
The Nobel Foundation, Sweden

Exhibitors

ADC. The Analytical Development Company Ltd, UK
BIOMONITOR SCI, Sweden
HANSATECH Ltd., UK
LI-COR Inc., USA
QA-DATA, Finland
SKYE INSTRUMENTS LTD, UK
TECHTUM INSTRUMENT AB, Sweden
WALZ, Mess-und Regeltechnik, FRG

Swedish Organizing Committee

Chairperson: Margareta Baltscheffsky, University of Stockholm

Per-Åke Albertsson	Lund University
Bertil Andersson	University of Stockholm
Carl-Ivar Brändén	The Swedish University of Agricultural Sciences
Petter Gustafsson	Umeå University
Anders Kylin	Lund University
Christer Sundqvist	Gothenburg University
Jan-Eric Tillberg	University of Stockholm
Tore Vänngård	Gothenburg University
Gunnar Öquist	Umeå University

International Committee on Photosynthesis

C. Arntzen	USA
M. Baltscheffsky	Sweden (Chairperson)
J. Biggins	USA
G. Farquhar	Australia
G. Forti	Italy
R. Van Grondelle	The Netherlands
H. Heldt	FRG
P. Horton	UK
R. Malkin	USA
P. Mathis	France
I. Ohad	Israel
K. Satoh	Japan
Y.K. Shen	PR of China
V. Shuvalov	USSR
R. Vallejos	Argentina

SPEECH HELD AT THE OPENING OF THE VIIIth INTERNATIONAL
CONGRESS ON PHOTOSYNTHESIS STOCKHOLM, AUGUST 6th, 1989

BENGT GÖRANSSON
MINISTRY OF EDUCATION, 103 33 STOCKHOLM, SWEDEN

I consider it a great honour to extend to the delegates to this
congress the greetings of the Government of Sweden. Welcome to
Sweden and welcome to our capital. I would like to take this opportunity to share with you a number of personal reflections.

Photosynthesis is a good example of a science which enjoys rapid
development and whose practical application extends to ever wider
areas. It provides, to my mind, evidence of the role which highly
qualified and at the same time highly theoretical research plays in
changing and developing our lives and our society. Earlier societies
were much more static in character, the individual relied on well
established patterns for economic activity and survival. Ways of
life, attitudes, values and interests all built on traditions established by earlier generations. Today we live more like the sailor
who when he sails on open sea, must rely on the discoveries made by
the researcher/navigator on the basis of his experience and knowledge.

The researcher is to a very great extent our navigator, our path-
finder. The fact that he is also more and more of a theoretician is
of no small importance - this makes for greater demands on basic
theoretical education. It also calls for greater effort in providing
the wider public with sufficient popularized knowledge in order to
ensure that the insights and directions developed by the theoretical
researcher can be usefully exploited.

I would like to be concrete on this particular point. With mounting
concern I have observed how here in Sweden, as in many other countries, while basic schooling for the majority of our citizens has
improved there has been an increase in various types of what can
only be described as occult trends. A lack of faith in the future
together with a strong mistrust not only in the political establishment but also in the intellectual establishment to which the world
of research belongs, - these are far from uncommon today. To put it

more provocatively I might say that only those who know next to nothing about the subject they express their opinions on, are accepted as authorities.

A lack of faith in the future is dangerous for mankind. It is dangerous because it is, paradoxically enough, often combined with an unlimited exaggeration of the level of development we now enjoy and of the capacity of the human brain that we judge ourselves to possess. Those who do not think that we can solve the different problems we face today with tomorrow's discoveries and with the help of tomorrow's people appear to believe that we in our own time, have reached the final frontiers of knowledge.

Just as dangerous is the naive belief in the future or in progress, especially that which is based on the belief that development is automatic, that we have no cause to worry. In reality development and change come about through the persistant pursuit of knowledge, through the demanding job of fitting together various bits of knowledge, of matching ideas to ideas. The foundations of a positive and productive belief in the future are to be found in the belief that there are always new possibilities combined with the hard work of winning new knowledge.

In creating a positive and productive belief in the future we have good reason to consider more closely the research being carried out in the field of photosynthesis. The experience gained in this field gives us hope that we will be able to solve the global problems affecting our environment, our future production of the necessities of life and the possibility of finding a cure for serious diseases. The global solutions will also be solutions to the problems faced by the individual. The importance of the results of research in the field of photosynthesis go far beyond the confines of the researcher's world. Those aspects of research on photosynthesis which have a bearing on the question of energy lead to an increased interest on the part of government bodies and of business interests. The nature of research calls for interdisciplinary cooperation and important contributions are made by such groups as programmers and technicians to the work of the researcher. This means that the need to promote the exchange of ideas and experiences, such as take place at congresses and conferences, is very great. The fact that representatives for science and research from university departments and research institutions all over the world meet and confer, becomes an event of decisive importance. I would therefore like to express my gratitude and appreciation to you all for attending this congress. I am of course delighted at the fact that our Swedish representives in this field of scientific research have been entrusted with the task of organizing the congress.

I would like to pursue my line of thinking further. In pointing to the paradoxical conflict between highly qualified and highly developed research on the one hand and the trend towards more occult interests on the other, I have done so because I think it is of vital importance that we combat the latter. Getting the researcher to step outside his isolation in the world of "interdisciplinary science" is not enough. It is vital that a broad section of the public should be given the opportunity to share the knowledge gained by research. A society in which the reseacher is isolated because of his research and knowledge and possibly regarded as a "deus ex machina", a wizard who can do things we others cannot do, such a society will never liberate itself from the threats posed by occultist movements. These threats are all the more dangerous because of the effects that they can have on wider relationships in society. A democratic social order rests ultimately on the fact that the citizens know enough about what happens in their community to feel secure. The ignorant and insecure citizen, who through lack of understanding is manipulated or feels manipulated becomes all too easily a victim of antidemocratic forces and campaigns. This gives me special cause to appeal to you as representatives for a highly specialized science, to give some consideration to what is often called popular science. I trust that the exchange of experience at the congress will in some way be made available for larger sections of the public. A quick glance through a Swedish school book shows that photosynthesis is far from being among the easiest of scientific topics and I regret to add that any student who satisfies himself with the contents of the school book will hardly broaden his knowledge of photosynthesis. What is important is that this broader knowledge is accessible to the average interested member of the public. (In this context it would be interesting to speculate on the causes of the chlorophyll hysteria of the nineteen fifties - you all remember the toothpaste with chlorophyll - was it in part due to a lack of understanding of man's own capacity in the field of photosynthesis?)

My personal wish, if you allow me to voice it, is that this congress and its work will stimulate popular education to take up popular science in the best sense of the term.

I would like to wish you all a fruitful congress week, a week that will benefit your scientific endeavours and ultimately, benefit humanity. It goes without saying, though I very much enjoy saying it - that I wish each and every one of you a pleasant stay in our summer clad Sweden and in Stockholm which I trust will show you the very best it has to offer the visitor from home or abroad.

Dear guests and congress participants!
I have used my privilege as invited minister by making these comments. I now turn to my official and ceremonial duty and declare the VIIIth International Congress on Photosynthesis opened.

MOLECULAR EVOLUTION OF PROTON-ATPases

HOLGER LILL AND NATHAN NELSON
ROCHE INSTITUTE OF MOLECULAR BIOLOGY, NUTLEY, NEW JERSEY
07110 U.S.A.

1. INTRODUCTION

Proton-ATPases can be divided into three classes: a) The plasma-membrane type, which operates via a phosphoenzyme intermediate and therefore is part of the P-ATPase superfamily. These proton pumps evolved from a common ancestor of the Ca^{++} and Na^+ pumps and are structurally distinct from the other two families of proton pumps (1-3). b) The eubacterial-type F-ATPases that are present in eubacteria, mitochondria and chloroplasts (3,4). c) The vacuolar-type V-ATPases that are present in archaebacteria and the vacuolar system of eukaryotic cells (2-6). F and V-ATPases are structurally and functionally related and have evolved from a common ancestral enzyme (3,4). This relationship was established from a wealth of sequence information regarding F-ATPases and by more recent studies on V-ATPases. The divergent pathways by which F and V-ATPases have evolved were recently elucidated by parallel studies in several laboratories (3). It is the purpose of this communication to discuss aspects pertinent to the evolution of CF_0-CF_1, which is the F-ATPase functioning in photosynthesis.

2. PROCEDURES

Genomic DNA of *Synechocystis* sp. PCC 6803 was isolated by equilibrium ultracentrifugation on cesium chloride gradients (7). The purified DNA was used to construct genomic libraries in YPN 1, a yeast - *E. coli* shuttle vector (H. Nelson, unpublished results). The oligonucleotide probe GGTCAAGCTGTCGAAGGGAT TGCTCGTCAGCCGGAAGCTGAAGGCAAAAT corresponding to a conserved region of the proteolipid gene from *Synechococcus* was used for screening the genomic library. Plasmid DNA was isolated from the positive colonies by the alkaline lysis method and further screening was performed by dot blots and Southern blots (8). A 15 kbp BamHI fragment was isolated from the positive clones. AvaI and RsaI fragments of this insert were subcloned into M13mp18 and sequenced using the dideoxy termination method (43). Overlapping deletions of the DNA fragments were obtained by digestion with exonuclease III (9). The nucleotide sequences were aligned and analyzed using DNAstar software.

3. RESULTS AND DISCUSSION

Like F-ATPases, V-ATPases are composed of two distinct structures (1-4,10,11): a catalytic sector that is hydrophilic in nature and a hydrophobic membrane sector which functions in proton translocation. The catalytic sector of both enzyme families is composed of five different polypeptides with a similar stoichiometry. The subunits of F-ATPases were denoted as α to ϵ and those of V-ATPases as A to E in the order of decreasing molecular weights. The active sites are situated on the β subunit of

M. Baltscheffsky (ed.), Current Research in Photosynthesis, Vol. III, 1–8.
© 1990 *Kluwer Academic Publishers. Printed in the Netherlands.*

F-ATPases and on the A subunit of V-ATPases (10-14). Sequencing of α and β subunits as well as A and B subunits from phyllogenetically diverse species revealed that all four genes encoding these polypeptides are related (5,6,14-18). As shown in Table 1, significant amino acid sequence homology exists among these four polypeptides. Therefore, it was concluded that subunits α, β, A and B evolved from a common ancestral gene (3,15,18,19). Close inspection of highly conserved regions of amino acids allowed theoretical reconstruction of the steps in the evolution of current polypeptides (3,4,19). A proposal for the evolution of genes encoding subunits α and β of F-ATPases and subunits A and B of V-ATPases is shown in Fig. 1.

TABLE 1. Percentage of identical amino acids among α and β subunits of F-ATPases and A and B subunits of V-ATPases

Subunits	% Identity
A to B	22-26
A to α	18-23
A to β	23-30
B to α	24-28
B to β	24-28
α to β	22-26

The main constituent of the membrane sector of F and V-ATPases is a highly hydrophobic polypeptide that binds DCCD, and on account of its solubility in chloroform/methanol was called proteolipid (20-23). In the F-ATPases and V-ATPases of archaebacteria the proteolipid is about 8 kDa and spans the membrane two times,

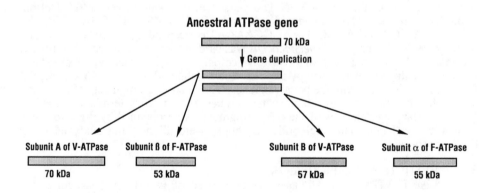

FIGURE 1. Gene duplication of a primordial ATPase gene led to the current genes encoding subunits α and β of F-ATPases and subunits A and B of V-ATPases.

while in the V-ATPases of eukaryotic cells the size of the proteolipid is about 16 kDa and probably spans the membrane four times (23). We think that it is no coincidence that the former enzymes can synthesize ATP at the expense of protonmotive force and that the latter serves exclusively as an ATP-dependent proton pump. Sequence information has revealed that the larger proteolipid of V-ATPases evolved by gene duplication of a common ancestral gene for the proteolipids of F and V-ATPases (23).

The symmetry of F-ATPases was addressed in several studies, the most comprehensive of which are those of McCarty, Hammes and their colleagues (24,25). It was clearly shown that despite its potential three-fold symmetry, the final structure of the chloroplast F-ATPase (CF_0-CF_1) is asymmetric. Fig. 2 depicts possible initial steps in the evolution of H^+-ATPases before the divergence of V and F-ATPases. It is proposed that the primordial proton pump was composed of two different polypeptides: a hexamer of an approximately 70 kDa subunit which formed the catalytic sector of the enzyme, and a hexamer of the proteolipid (8 kDa) which comprised the membrane sector. The reactions catalyzed by this enzyme with this symmetric arrangement were fully reversible; i.e., in response to the direction and magnitude of the protonmotive force it could catalyze the synthesis or degradation of ATP. Thus, the symmetry of the system rendered the pH of the environment a major factor in the capability of the cells to harvest energy.

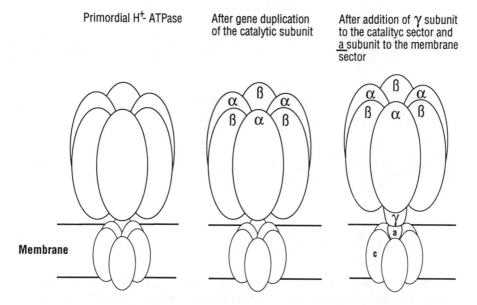

FIGURE 2. A proposal for the initial steps in the evolution of F-ATPases. A symmetric hexameric structure is proposed. The catalytic sector was comprised of six identical subunits which evolved to the current 3 α and 3 β structure following the gene duplication. The hexameric form of the proteolipid is based on the identification of a functional hexamer in F-ATPases (26-30). However, ten to twelve copies were reported in other studies (31,32).

```
                                                      M N R K I H V W F G K G L W N F G
Tobacco subunit I
Synechococcus b          M S S W I L L A H A E T S G F G L N L D L F E T N L I N L A I I I G
Synechocystis b    M L N T L F I L A A E A H E A G E G G F G I N L D F L E A N L F N L A I L L G
E. coli b                                        V N L N A T I L G Q A I A F V L F V L F -
```

```
K E W K N N L L S L S D L L D N R K Q R I L N T I R N S E E L R G G A I E Q L E K A R S R L R K
L L V Y A G R G F L G N L L S N R R A A I E A E I R E V E E K L A S S A Q A L S Q A Q T Q L K E
I I I Y Y A P K T L G K I L G D R R Q K I A D A I E E A E T R Q R K S A Q I L A E E E K K L A Q
C M K Y V W P P L M A A I - E K R Q K E I A D G L A S A E R A H K D L D L A K A S A T D Q L K K
```

```
V E S E A E Q F R V N G Y S E I E R E K L N L I N S T Y K T L E Q L E N Y K N E T I Q F E Q Q R
A E A E A A R L L V E A K A R A A A V R Q E I L D K A A A D V E R L K A T A A Q D V S T E Q Q R
A K A E A A R I V Q E A G Q R A E V A K Q E I A T Q T E A D L R R I E E A A A Q D L G A E Q E R
A K A E A Q V I I E Q A N K R R S Q I L D E A K A E A E Q E R T K I V A Q A Q A E I E A E R K R
```

```
A I N Q V R Q R V F Q Q A L R G A L G T L N S C L N N E L H L R T I R S N I G M L G T M K E I T D
V L D E L R R Y A V A Q A L S R V E T Q L S Q Q L D E A A Q Q R L I D R S L A T L
V I A E L K R R I A E Q A V A K A E A D L R D R L N E D T Q D R L I E R S I A Q L G G R
A R E E L R K Q V A I L A V A G A E K I I E R S V D E A A N S D I V D K L V A E L
```

```
Synechococcus b'    M N A W M I L A A E A V Q E A E G G L F D L D A T L P L M A V Q I L V L V F L
Synechocystis b'                              M F D F D A T L P L M A L Q F V V L A F L
E. coli b                                     V N L N A T I L G Q A I A F V L F V L F
```

```
L N A V F Y K P F G K V L D D R D Q F V R G G R Q D A K A R L A E V K A L T A Q Y E Q E L A A T
L N A I F Y K P M N K V L D E R A D Y I R T N E E D A R E R L A K A K A I T Q E Y E Q Q I T D A
C M K Y V W P P L M A A I E K R Q K E I - A D G L A S A E R A H K D L D L A K S A T D Q L K K A
                                                                              A
```

```
R K Q S Q A L I A E A Q T E A G R I A A Q Q L A E A Q R E A Q A Q R E Q A Q Q E I D Q Q K A V A
R R Q S Q A V I A D A Q A E A R R L A A E K I A E A Q R E S Q R Q K E T A A Q E I E A Q R Q S A
K A E A Q V I I E Q A N K R R S Q I L D E A K A E A E Q E R T K I V A Q A Q A E I E A E R K R A
```

```
L Q A L D Q Q V D A L S H Q I L D K L L A R A
L S S L E Q E V A A L S N Q I L H K L L G P E L I K
R E E L R K Q V A I L A V A G A E K I I E R S V D E A A N S D I V D K L V A E L
```

FIGURE 3. Conservation among the genes encoding subunit *b* of the bacterial membrane sector and the corresponding subunits in cyanobacteria and chloroplasts.

Reconstruction of the initial steps in the evolution of H^+-ATPases led to a proposal that one of the first molecular events in the development of the present enzymes was a duplication of the gene encoding the primordial catalytic subunit (3,4). This event led to an independent evolution of two genes which ultimately encode the A and B subunits of V-ATPases and the α and β subunits of F-ATPases (Fig. 1). The enzyme is characterized by a three-fold symmetry with three active sites on the A and β subunits and three allosteric sites on the B and α subunits of V and F-ATPases respectively. The allosteric sites provided a more flexible regulation of the enzyme responding to the nucleotide concentrations in the cell. The next step was the introduction of a novel polypeptide to both the catalytic sector and the membrane sector which interacted with each other to improve the communication between the two sectors (Fig. 2). The current equivalents of these polypeptides are the C and γ subunits of the catalytic sector of V and F-ATPases and the a subunits of the membrane sectors. As yet, we do not know if the corresponding subunits of the V and F-ATPases evolved from a common ancestor or independently from each other. Further molecular events, including the addition of several new subunits, completed the development of the current F and V-ATPases. One of the most important consequences of the addition of the new subunits was the deviation from symmetry. The molecular biology of subunits I and II of the chloroplast membrane sector (CF_0), provide the best example for the evolution of such structural changes.

The membrane sector of the chloroplast F-ATPase (CF_0) is composed of four different polypeptides denoted as subunits I, II, III and IV (25,33,34). The membrane sector of the enzyme from *E. coli* contains three polypeptides denoted as subunits a, b, and c with a stoichiometry of 1:2:6-12 (10,11). Subunit IV is homologous to the a subunit and subunit III is homologous to c which is also the DCCD-binding proteolipid. Cross-linking experiments revealed that subunits I and II of CF_0 are associated with the corresponding subunits of CF_1, sharing the function of binding CF_1 to the membrane (35). Recently it has become apparent that both subunits I and II of CF_0 are homologous to the b subunit of *E. coli* (33-36 and R. Herrmann, personal communication). Subunit II of CF_0 is the only nuclear gene product of the membrane sector, the other subunits are encoded on the chloroplast genome (33,37). Thus, these two subunits of the chloroplast membrane sector, one encoded in the nucleus and the other in the chloroplast, may assume the function of the two copies of the b subunit in *E. coli*. Recent sequencing of the operon encoding the various subunits of the F-ATPase in the cyanobacterium *Synechococcus* sp. provided an exciting clue for the evolutionary origin of subunits I and II in chloroplasts (38). We cloned and sequenced an operon encoding CF_0 subunits in the cyanobacterium *Synechocystis* sp. The arrangement of the genes in the operon is identical to that of *Synechococcus*. The homologous genes to the a and c subunits of *E. coli* are present as single copies, and in addition, two genes in the operon are homologous to the b subunits of *E. coli*. The translation products of these genes were designated subunits b and b'. Fig. 3 depicts the alignment of the predicted amino acid sequences of the polypeptides from cyanobacteria, chloroplasts and *E. coli*. The chloroplast encoded subunit I has higher homology to the b subunit from cyanobacteria. Similarly, the b subunit of the enzyme from *E. coli* also aligns more strongly to the b subunits of cyanobacteria. However, this polypeptide shows quite poor homology with the corresponding chloroplast subunit. It is apparent that gene duplication took place during the early evolution of the F-ATPases which functioned in photosynthesis, and after the development of the chloroplast one of the genes encoding the equivalent of subunit b from *E. coli* was transferred to the nucleus of eukaryotic cells. The functional significance of this development may be connected with breaking the symmetry of F-ATPases during their evolution (39).

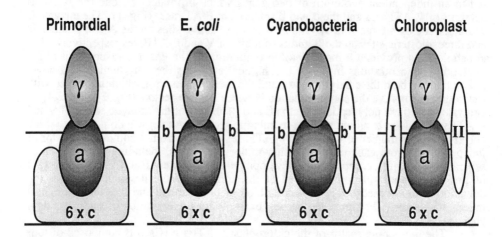

FIGURE 4. Structural consequences of the evolution of subunit *b* from eubacteria to chloroplasts.

The molecular events involved in this evolutionary step are depicted in Fig. 4. The initial is the duplication of the gene encoding the *b* subunit. Since the two gene products are identical, there are no structural consequences to this event. In the case of the primordial CF_0, the two gene products assembled randomly as the two copies of the *b* subunit in the enzyme from *E. coli*. However, the two genes are now free to undergo independent changes, and at the moment that an assembly of one copy of each gene product provided functional advantages they diverged onto separate evolutionary pathways. At this point in the evolution of the enzyme, the subunit structure deviated from the symmetry inflected by the two copies of different *b* subunits per enzyme. Advance in evolution caused further changes in the amino acid sequences as exemplified in the operon of the present cyanobacteria. When the eukaryotic cell evolved and the chloroplast was formed, one of the genes encoding subunit *b* was transferred to the nucleus and subunits I and II of the chloroplast CF_0 were formed. This step accelerated the evolutionary rate of the gene and gave the nucleus the possibility of controlling the assembly of the enzyme in the chloroplast.

Gene duplication has played a major role in the evolution of protein complexes involved in oxygenic and photosynthetic energy transduction. Subunits I_a and I_b of the photosystem I reaction center evolved by gene duplication of an ancestral gene, while the two major subunits of the bacterial and photosystem II reaction centers evolved through similar events (40-42). As discussed above, the crucial events in the evolution of proton pumps involved gene duplication. This type of mechanism was extensively employed in the development of hormones, receptors, carriers and enzymes in late stages of evolution. The gene duplications that occurred during the evolution of energy transducing systems are among the earliest events traced down to date.

4. ACKNOWLEDGEMENT

We would like to thank Dr. David Purvis for critical reading of the manuscript.

REFERENCES
1   Bowman, B.J. and Bowman, E.J. (1986) J. Membr. Biol. 94, 83-97
2   Nelson, N. (1988) Plant Physiol. 86, 1-3
3   Nelson, N. and Taiz, L. (1989) TIBS 14, 113-116
4   Nelson, N. (1989) J. Bioenerg. Biomemb. (in press)
5   Denda, K., Konishi, J., Oshima, T., Date, T. and Yoshida, M. (1988a) J. Biol. Chem. 263, 6012-6015
6   Denda, K., Kohishi, J., Oshima, T., Date, T. and Yoshida, M. (1988b) J. Biol. Chem. 263, 17251-17254
7   Williams, J.G.K. (1988) Methods Enzymol. 167, 766-778
8   Maniatis, T., Fritsch, E.F. and Sambrook, J. (1982) in Molecular Cloning: A Laboratory Manual, Cold Spring Harbor Laboratory, Cold Spring Harbor, NY
9   Henikoff, S. (1984) Gene 28, 351-359
10 Futai, M. and Kanazawa, H. 91983) Microbiol. Rev. 47, 285-312
11 Futai, M., Noumi, T. and Meada, M. (1989) Ann. Rev. Biochem. (in press)
12 Moriyama, Y. and Nelson, N. (1987b) J. Biol. Chem. 262, 14723-14729
13 Moriyama, Y. and Nelson, N. (1989a) J. Biol. Chem. 264, 3577-3582
14 Zimniak, L., Dittrich, P., Gogarten, J.P., Kibak, H. and Taiz, L. (1988) J. Biol. Chem. 263, 9102-9112
15 Bowman, B.J., Allen, R., Wechser, M.A. and Bowman, E.J. (1988b) J. Biol. Chem. 263, 14002-14007
16 Bowman, E.J., Tenney, K. and Bowman, B.J. (1988a) J. Biol. Chem. 263, 13994-14001
17 Manolson, M.F., Quellette, B.F.F., Filion, M. and Poole, R.J. (1988) J. Biol. Chem. 263, 17987-17994
18 Nelson, H., Mandiyan, S. and Nelson, N. (1989) J. Biol. Chem. 264, 1775-1778
19 Nelson, H. and Nelson, N. (1989) FEBS Lett. 247, 147-153
20 Sutton, R. and Apps, D.K. (1981) FEBS Lett. 130, 103-106
21 Uchida, E., Ohsumi, Y. and Anraku, Y. (1985) J. Biol. Chem. 260, 1090-1095
22 Randall, S.K. and Sze, H. 91986) J. Biol. Chem. 261, 1364-1371
23 Mandel, M., Moriyama, Y., Hulmes, J.D., Pan, Y.-C.E., Nelson, H. and Nelson, N. (1988) Proc. Natl. Acad. Sci. USA 85, 5521-5524
24 Richter, M.L., Snyder, B., McCarty, R.E. and Hammes, G.G. (1985) Biochemistry 24, 5755-5763
25 Nalin, C.M. and Nelson, N. (1987) Curr. Top. Bioenerg. 15, 273-294
26 Tzagaloff, A. and Meagher, P. (1971) J. Biol. Chem. 246, 7328-7336
27 Sigrist-Nelson, K., Sigrist, H. and Azzi, A. (1978) Eur. J. Biochem. 92, 9-14
28 Sebald, W., Graf, T. and Lukins, H.B. (1979) Eur. J. Biochem. 93, 587-599
29 Laubinger, W. and Dimroth, P. (1988) Biochemistry 27, 7531-7537
30 Lill, H. and Junge, W. (1989) FEBS Lett. 244, 15-20
31 Foster, D.L. and Fillingame, R.H. (1982) J. Biol. Chem. 257, 2009-2015
32 Fromme, P., Bockema, E.J. and Graber, P. (1987) Z. Naturforsch. 42c, 1239-1245

33   Westhoff, P., Alt, J., Nelson, N. and Herrmann, R.G. (1985) Mol. Gen. Genet. 199, 290-299
34   Hennig, J. and Herrmann, R.G. (1986) Mol. Gen. Genet. 203, 117-128
35   Rott, R. and Nelson, N. (1984) Proc. Int. Congr. Photosynth. 6th, 501-510
36   Bird, C.R., Koller, B., Auffret, A.D., Huttly, A.K., Howe, C.J., Dyer, T.A. and Gray, J.C. (1985) EMBO J. 4, 1381-1388
37   Nechushtai, R., Nelson, N., Mattoo, A.K. and Edelman, M. (1981) FEBS Lett. 125, 115-119
38   Cozens, A.L. and Walker, J.E. (1987) J. Mol. Biol. 194, 359-383
39   Nelson, N. (1988) in Plant Membranes, Structure, Assembly and Function (Harwood, J.L. and Walton, T.J., eds.), pp. 159-167, The Biochemical Society, London
40   Fish, L.E., Kuck, U. and Bogorad, L. (1985) J. Biol. Chem. 260, 1413-1421
41   Trebst, A. (1986) Naturforsch. 41c, 240-245
42   Barber, J. (1987) Trends Biochem. Sci. 12, 321-326
43   Sanger, F., Nicklen, S. and Coulson, A.R. (1977) Proc. Natl. Acad. Sci. USA 74, 5463-5467

CRYSTALLIZATION OF THE FUNCTIONAL β SUBUNIT FROM CF$_1$-CF$_0$.

Wayne D. Frasch and Jack P. Green
The Center for Early Events in Photosynthesis, Department of Botany, Arizona State University, Tempe, AZ, 85287 and
Department of Biology, University of Michigan, Ann Arbor, MI 48109

INTRODUCTION

The five polypeptides of chloroplast coupling factor one (CF$_1$) have a subunit stoichiometry of 3α, 3β, γ, δ, ε designated in order of decreasing molecular weight (1-3). Nucleotide binding and ATPsynthase/ATPase activity have been associated with the β subunit per CF$_1$ and evidence suggests that the three active sites are functionally linked (4). Purified CF$_1$ is a latent ATPase which can be activated to show specificity for Mg^{2+}(5-8) or Ca^{2+}(9-12).

Procedures that selectively remove subunits from CF1 have been developed to yield preparations that contain 3α,3β,γ,δ (13), 3α,3β,γ (14) and 3α,3β (15). Each of these preparations catalyzes high rates of Ca^{2+} dependent ATP hydrolysis but much lower rates of ATPase activity in the presence of Mg^{2+}. Activation of the Ca^{2+}-ATPase results from the exchange of disulfide bonds in the γ subunit (16) and/or the dissociation of the ε subunit from the enzyme (7-10). The Mg^{2+}-specific ATPase activity of CF$_1$ is increased by sulfite (10, 11), organic acids (12) or octyl-glucopyranoside (OGP) (12) by processes which appear to depend only upon the β subunit (17).

The β subunit has been purified from the coupling factors of several organisms (18-24). ATPase activity can be reconstituted by recombining the β and γ subunits or α, β and γ of the thermophilic bacterium PS3 (25, 26) or the α, β, and γ subunits from the F$_1$ of E. coli (27). The β subunit from the F$_1$-F$_0$ of *Rhodospirillum rubrum* can be selectively removed by a 1 M LiCl wash in a manner that allows the functional reconstitution of the subunit with the β-depleted chromatophores (21, 28-29). This protein has two nucleotide binding sites (29) and has been reported to catalyze ATP hydrolysis at about 0.1% of the rate attainable in the intact enzyme (30). The β subunit has also been purified from δ,ε-less CF$_1$ by incubation in NaClO$_4$ (22). Although this protein is incapable of binding nucleotides or hydrolyze ATP, it can reconstitute ATPase activity to β-less chromatophores of R. rubrum. Another preparation of CF$_1$-β, purified by high performance liquid chromatography, has been found to hydrolyze ATP very slowly over a 12 hour period (23, 24).

We recently reported the purification of the β subunit from thylakoid membranes by means of a 1 M LiCl wash (38). We have now examined the procedure with regard to factors that affect yield and purity and we present initial efforts to crystallize the protein.

METHODS

The β subunit of CF$_1$-CF$_0$ was solubilized from thylakoid membranes prepared as per (31) using a grind buffer that contained 0.4 M sucrose, 10 mM NaCl, 10 mM MgCl$_2$ and 50 mM Tricine, pH 7.3. To prevent proteolysis, the grind buffer and all other buffers used in the preparation contained 2 mM benzamidine, 2 mM ε-aminocaproic acid, 3 mM NaN$_3$ and 0.5 mM

M. Baltscheffsky (ed.), Current Research in Photosynthesis, Vol. III, 9–14.
© 1990 *Kluwer Academic Publishers. Printed in the Netherlands.*

phenylmethylsulfonyl fluoride. The pellet of thylakoids obtained in the last centrifugation step of thylakoid preparation was resuspended to a final concentration of 0.25 mg Chl/ml in resuspension buffer which contained 0.25 mM sucrose, 4 mM ATP, 4 mM $MgCl_2$, 50 mM Tricine, pH 8.0 and the proteolysis inhibitors described above. This suspension stirred at 4°C in darkness for 1 h then was pelleted by centrifugation at 3500 x g for 5 min. The thylakoids were resuspended to 1 mg of Chl/ml in resuspension buffer with 1 M LiCl then stirred at 4°C for 30 min in darkness. The thylakoids were removed by centrifugation at 3500 x g for 5 min and resuspended in the same buffer at 0.25 mg Chl/ml for an additional 30 min. After the thylakoids were removed by centrifugation at 32000 x g for 30 min, the supernatants from the two 1 M LiCl washes were combined and concentration to about 10 ml by pressure dialysis using a PM-30 membrane (Amicon), then centrifuged again at 32000 x g for 1 h to remove thylakoids that remained. The solution was diluted four fold in elution buffer which contained 4 mM ATP, 4 mM $MgCl_2$, 50 mM Tricine, pH 8.0 and the proteolysis inhibitors described. The solution was concentrated to about 1 ml by pressure dialysis with a PM-30 membrane. Final purification of the β subunit preparation was obtained by chromatography with a 1.5 x 78 cm column of Bio-Gel P-150 using elution buffer.

RESULTS

The major constituent of a 1 M LiCl wash was a 55 kDa protein which had the same mobility as the β subunit of CF_1 in an SDS-electrophoresis gel stained with Coomassie (Figs. 1 and 2A). Small amounts of 35 kDa, 9kDa and 6 kDa are also visible on this gel. Quantitation of the area under each peak by laser scanning densitometry showed that the 6 kDa protein comprised about 10% of the protein while the 9 and 35 kDa proteins each contained less than 5%.

Western immunoblotting against the anti-β as shown in Fig. 2C, verified that the 55 kDa protein was the β subunit of CF_1. In Figure 2B and D, Western blots were challenged with antibodies of the α and γ subunits, respectively. In these blots, CF_1 was loaded on the gels such that equal amounts of β subunit were present in the CF_1 lane (Lane 1) and the lane with the purified β subunit (Lane 2). A small amount of α subunit was revealed by immunoblotting. Since CF_1 contains equal proportions of α and β subunits, the fractional amount of α to β in the β subunit preparation is the same as the ratio of the amount of α subunit between Lanes 1 and 2 in

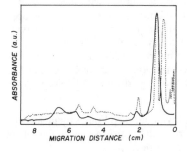

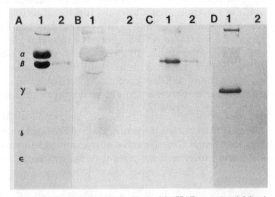

Figure 1. Densitogram of a Coomassie-stained SDS-PAGE gel to determine the polypeptide constituents of the 1 M LiCl extract from thylakoids after chromatography on Bio-Gel P-150 (—) or CF_1 (·····).

Figure 2. Western immunoblot analysis of the 55-kDa protein solubilized from thylakoid membranes with 1 M LiCl. A, Coomassies-stained, 12% SDS-PAGE; B,C,D, nitrocellulose blots transferred from gels as in A then challenged against anti-α, anti-β, and anti-γ (respectively). The amount of CF_1 loaded onto *Lane 1* contained equimolar amounts of the β subunit as the amount of the 55 kDa protein loaded onto *Lane 2*.

Figure 1B. The proportion of α to β subunits was estimated to be significantly less than 5% due to the observation that the 35 kDa protein comprises less than 5% of the protein whereas the α subunit is below the limit of detection by Coomassie staining.

As shown in Figure 2D, the γ subunit of CF_1 was not present in the purified β subunit preparation. The 35 kDa protein that is observed is apparently an extrinsic membrane protein that is unrelated to the β subunit but which is solubilized from the membrane at high salt concentrations. It is possible that this protein is the extrinsic 33 kDa protein (P_{33}) of photosystem II which is known to be removed by washes in 1 M $CaCl_2$ (39).

The elution profile of proteins from the P-150 column was determined by densitometry of SDS-PAGE gels loaded with equal volumes from successive column fractions (Figure 3). The fractions which contained the most highly purified β subunit eluted from the column first, while the latter fractions contained a greater proportion of the 6, 9 and 35 kDa proteins. The fraction which had the maximum amount of β subunit indicated that the protein eluted from the column with an apparent molecular mass of about 180 kDa. If the α subunit were present in stoichiometry amounts to the β subunit, the similarity in the size of these proteins (57 versus 55 kDa) would require that the α subunit comprise about one third of the total protein rather than the small amount observed. Thus, the preparation probably exists in solution as an aggregate of about three copies of the β subunit.

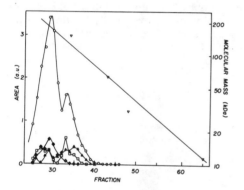

Figure 3.The abundance of each protein in successive Bio-Gel P-150 column fractions as determined by laser scanning densitometry. The proteins are the β subunit (O), the 35-kDa protein (▲), the 9-kDa protein (□), and the 6-kDa protein (◆).(▽) is a plot of apparent molecular mass vs elution volume for molecular weight standards.

Table I
Activation and inhibition of Mg^{2+}-ATP hydrolsis catalyzed by the β subunit preparation.

Treatment	40 mM OGP	−	+
		μmol ATP/mg β subunit • min	
Tentoxin[a]	−	0.403	0.389
Tentoxin	+	0.508	0.434
Na_2SO_3[b]	+	0.802	1.301
Anti-β[c]	+	0.547	0

[a]Prior to assay in 1 mM Mg^{2+}-ATP, 1.3 μM β subunit was incubated with 25 μM tentoxin for 90 min.
[b]Assayed in 10 mM mg^{2+}-ATP and 40 mM Na_2SO_3.
[c]The β subunit incubated with anti-β for 10 min prior to assay.

The yield of the β subunit and the composition of proteins eluted from the thylakoid membranes is significantly affected by the conditions of the 1 M LiCl wash. The yield of the β subunit increased significantly when the thylakoid membranes are subjected to two successive washes in 1 M LiCl. Decreasing the concentration of ATP during the 1 M LiCl wash from 4 mM to 0.1 mM decreased the amount of β subunit which was released from the membranes but did not alter the amount of the 35, 9 and 6 kDa proteins extracted. Washing the membranes in pyrophosphate buffer prior to incubation in ATP and solubilization in LiCl did not alter the yield of the β subunit but caused the release of several other proteins during the 1 M LiCl wash.

The purified β subunit preparation exhibited measurable rates of ATPase activity as shown in Table I. The rate of hydrolysis increased upon addition of sulfite which is known to stimulate the rate of Mg^{2+} ATPase of F_1 from several organisms (10, 11). The Mg^{2+} ATPase activity was also increased by octyl glucopyranoside (OGP) in a manner similar to that observed for CF_1 (12). Tentoxin decreased the activity of the purified β subunit by about 15% which was proportional to the extent of activation achieved by OGP. Although the concentrations of tentoxin used in this experiment are known to abolish the Ca^{2+} ATPase activity of CF_1 (32), this reagent only partially inhibits the CF_1-Mg^{2+} ATPase and, depending on the aqueous concentration of Mg^{2+}, can stimulate the latter activity (33). However, antibody to the β subunit was an effective inhibitor of ATP hydrolysis of the purified β subunit preparation. Although the rate of Mg^{2+} ATPase activity catalyzed by the β subunit preparation (V_m=1.86 and 3.36 in the presence and absence of OGP, respectively) is small compared to the Ca^{2+} ATPase activity of CF_1 (8), it is comparable to the Mg^{2+} dependent ATPase activity of CF_1 as well as to CF_1 preparations that lack the ε (13), the ε,δ (14) and the ε,δ,γ subunits (9).

Calcium was not an effective cofactor for this reaction since the Ca^{2+} ATPase activity was 100 fold lower than the rate observed with Mg^{2+}. In fact, treatments known to activate the Ca^{2+} ATPase activity of soluble CF_1 (10-12) were either ineffective or inhibitory to the catalytic activity of the ε,δ subunit preparation. This lack of Ca^{2+} ATPase activity is consistent with experiments that link the activation of Ca^{2+} dependence in CF1 to changes in the α,γ and/or ε subunits (13, 16, 34, 35).

The purified subunit was examined for the ability to bind ADP after subjecting the protein to extensive size exclusion chromatography to remove tightly bound nucleotides. The Scatchard plot in Figure 4 shows the presence of a high affinity and a low affinity binding site for Mg^{2+}ATP on the purified β subunit with dissociation constants of 15.3 and 202 μM, respectively. Negligible amounts of nucleotide binding were observed in the absence of the cation.

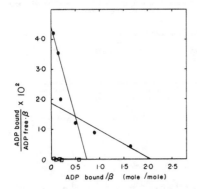

Figure 4. Scatchard plot of the binding of [3H]ADP to the β subunit in the presence (*circles*) or absence (*squares*) of Mg2+.

Figure 5. Silver-stained SDS-PAGE of crystal of the β subunit (*Lane 2*).purified β subunit preparation (*Lane 1*)

Crystals of the β subunit preparation were grown at room temperature by vapor diffusion (40) using ammonium sulfate. The crystals appeared in approximately 8-10 days and grew to full size in two weeks. A crystal of about 0.08 mm per side was found to diffract x-rays from a Mo source. After the crystal was redissolved, the protein constituents were determined by SDS-PAGE as shown in Figure 5. The silver-stained gel showed that the crystal was composed only of the β subunit.

DISCUSSION

The three-dimensional structure of F_1 from rat liver mitochondria has been calculated to 9 Å resolution (41, 42). However, problems which apparently result from the asymmetry of the smaller subunits of this enzyme have hindered the calculation of a fully interpretable map of the structure. The results presented here show that the β subunit of CF_1 is solubilized from the other subunits of CF_1-CF_0 by a 1 M LiCl wash in a manner that retains the ability to catalyze Mg^{2+} ATPase activity. This preparation elutes from a gel filtration column as a 180 kDa protein which suggests that it exists in solution as an aggregate of about three copies of the β subunit. The same stoichiometry (i.e. 3α, 3β, γ, δ, ε) is found in CF_1 and studies strongly suggest that the 3 active sites, presumably on each of the β subunits of CF_1 are functionally linked (36, 37). The preparation described here may exhibit ATPase activity because the association of β polypeptides and, thus, active sites have been preserved. The preliminary attempts to crystallize this preparation of the β subunit reported here suggest that it may ultimately be possible to obtain more highly resolved structural information of the active site of the ATPase by x-ray diffraction than previously possible.

ACKNOWLEDGMENT

This work was supported by Grants 83-CRCR-1-1334 from the United States Department of Agriculture-CRG and 0188 HF from the Herman Frasch Foundation of the American Chemical Society (to W.D.F.)

REFERENCES

1. Moroney, J., Lopresti, L., McEwen, B., McCarty, R., and Hammes, G. (1983) *FEBS Lett* **158**, 58-62
2. Merchant, S., Shaner, S. L., and Selman, B. R. (1983) *J. Biol. Chem.* **258**, 1026-1031
3. Yoshida, M., Sone, N., Hirata, H., Kagawa, Y., and Ui, N. (1979) *J Biol. Chem.* **254**, 9525-9533
4. Kohlbrenner, W. E., and Boyer, P. D. (1983) *J. Biol. Chem.* **258**, 10881-10886
5. Hochman, Y., and Carmeli, C. (1981) *Biochemistry* **20**, 6293-6297
6. Anthon, G. E., and Jagendorf, A. T. (1983) Biochim. Biophys. Acta **723**,358-365
7. Pick, U., and Bassilian, S. (1982) *Biochemistry* **24**, 6144-6152
8. Nelson, N., Nelson, H., and Racker, E. (1972) *J. Biol. Chem.* **247**, 6506-6510
9. Vambutas, V. K., and Racker, E. (1965) *J. Biol. Chem.* **240**, 2660-2667
10. Selman-Reimer, S., Merchant, S., and Selman, B. R. (1981) *Biochemistry* **20**, 5476-5482
11. McCarty, R. E., and Racker, E. (1968) *J. Biol. Chem.* **243**, 129-137
12. Farron, F., and Racker, E. (1970) *Biochemistry* **9**, 3829-3836
13. Richter, M. L., Patrie, W. J., and McCarty, R. E. (1984) *J. Biol. Chem.* **259**, 7371-7373
14. Mitra, B., and Hammes, G. G. (1988) *Biochemistry* **27**, 245-250
15. Deters, D. W., Racker, E., Nelson, N., and Nelson, H. (1975) *J. Biol. Chem.* **250**, 1041-1047
16. Nalin, C. M., and McCarty, R. E. (1984) *J. Biol. Chem.* **259**, 7275-7280
17. Yu, F., and McCarty, R. E. (1985) *Arch. Biochem. Biophys.* **238**, 61-68
18. Yoshida, M., Sone, N., Hirata, H., and Kagawa, Y. (1977) *J. Biol. Chem.* **252**, 3480-3485
19. Hou, S. Y., Senda, M., Kanazawa, H., Tsuchya, T., and Futai, M. (1984) *Biochemistry* **23**, 988-993
20. Dunn, S. D., and Futai, M. (1980) *J. Biol. Chem.* **255**, 113-118
21. Philosoph, S., Binder, A., and Gromet-Elhanan, Z. (1977) *J. Biol. Chem.* **252**, 8747-8752
22. Richter, M. L., Gromet-Elhanan, Z., and McCarty, R. E. (1986) *J. Biol. Chem.* **261**, 12109-12113
23. Roux-Fromy, M., Neuman, J.-M., Andre, F., Berger, G., Girault, G., Galmiche, J.-M., and Remy, R. (1987) *Biochem. Biophys. Res. Comm.* **144**, 718-725

24. Berger, G., Girault, G., Andre, F., and Galmiche, J.-M. (1987) *J. Liquid Chromatogr.* **10**, 1507-1517
25. Yoshida, M., Okamoto, H., Sone, N., Hirata, H., and Kagawa, Y. (1977)*roc. Natl. Acad. Sci. U.S.A.* **74**, 936-940
26. Yoshida, M., Sone, N., Hirata, H., and Kagawa, Y. (1977) *J. Biol. Chem.* **252**, 3480-3485
27. Futai, M. (1977) *Biochem. Biophys. Res. Commun.* **79**, 1231-1237
28. Khananshvili, D., and Gromet-Elhanan, Z. (1982) *J. Biol. Chem.* **257**, 11377-11383
29. Gromet-Elhanan, Z., and Khananshvili, D. (1985) *Methods Enzymol.* **126**, 528-538
30. Harris, D. A., Boork, J., and Baltshefsky, M. (1985) *Biochemistry* **24**, 3876-3883
31. Saha, S., Izawa, S., and Good, N. E. (1970) *Biochim. Biophys. Acta* **223**, 158-164
32. Steele, J. A., Uchytil, T. F., Durbin, R. D., Bhatnagar, P., and Rich, D. H. (1976) *Proc. Natl. Acad. Sci. U.S.A.* **73**, 2245-2248
33. Conrad, R. L., Conrad, R. M., and Durbin, R. D. (1981) *Energy Coupling in Photosynthesis* (Selman, B. R., and Selman-Reimer, S., eds) pp.175-178, Elsevier/North Holland, Inc., New York
34. Nelson, N., Nelson, H., and Racker, E. (1972) *J. Biol. Chem.* **247**, 7657-7662
35. Moroney, J. V., and McCarty, R. E. (1982) *J. Biol. Chem.* **257**, 5910-5914
36. Boyer, P. D., and Kohlbrenner, W. E. (1981) *Energy Coupling in Photosynthesis* (Selman, B. R., and Selman-Reimer, S., eds) pp.231-240, Elsevier/North Holland, Inc., New York
37. Grubmeyer, C., and Penefsky, H. S. (1981) *J. Biol. Chem.* **256**, 3728-3734
38. Frasch, W. D., Green, J. P., Caguiat, J., and Mejia, A. (1989) *J. Biol Chem.* **264**, 5064-5069
39. Ono, T., and Inoue, Y. (1983) FEBS Lett. 164, 255-260
40. Davies, D. R., and Segal, D. M. (1971) *Methods Enzymol.* **22**, 266-269
41. Amzel, L. M., and Pedersen, P. L. (1978) *J. Biol. Chem.* **253**, 2067-2069
42. Amzel, L. M., McKinney, M., Narayanan, P., and Pedersen, P. L. (1982) *Proc. Natl. Acad. Sci. U.S.A.* **79**, 5852-5856

UNI-SITE CATALYSIS BY THE RECONSTITUTED ATP SYNTHASE FROM CHLOROPLASTS

Peter Gräber[1], Petra Fromme[2], and Ulrike Junesch[2]

[1] Biologisches Institut, Universität Stuttgart,
Pfaffenwaldring 57, D-7000 Stuttgart 80, FRG
[2] Max-Volmer-Institut, Technische Universität Berlin,
Straße des 17. Juni 135, D-1000 Berlin 12

1. INTRODUCTION

The ATP Synthase from chloroplasts catalyzes ATP synthesis / hydrolysis coupled with a transmembrane proton transport. The enzyme contains several nucleotide binding sites and it is assumed that three of them (located on the β subunits) have catalytic properties (1,2). The presence of several catalytic sites raises immediately the question whether they work independently or cooperatively.

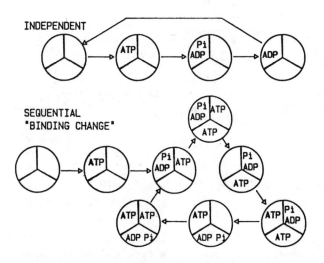

Fig. 1. Scheme of site interaction in CF_0F_1.
Each triangle represents an αβ-pair with one catalytic binding site.
Top: independent sites; bottom: sequential mechanism

M. Baltscheffsky (ed.), Current Research in Photosynthesis, Vol. III, 15–21.

This is schematically shown in Fig. 1. It sites work independently, each site binds ATP, splits it into enzyme-bound ADP and P_i and releases the products. Each site contributes one third of the maximal rate and the events on different sites are not correlated. In a cooperative mechanism ATP hydrolyis on the first site can occur only after binding of an another ATP to the second site and product release only after ATP binding to a third site (3). Of course the scheme shown in Fig. 1 is not the only way of cooperativity: binding to one site might influence either the binding, the hydrolysis or the release of product at other sites.
In isolated mitochondrial F_1 it has been found that ATP is hydrolyzed very slowly when only one site is occupied but the rate of ATP hydrolysis is increased by orders of magnitude when additional ATP is bound to a second (and third) site (4).
In this work we describe single site, single turnover ATP hydrolysis catalyzed by the reconstituted, reduced, and active ATP synthase from chloroplasts.

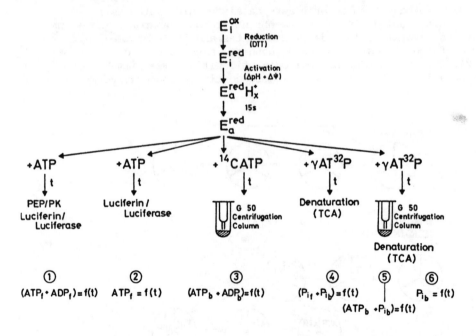

Fig. 2. Experimental protocol for measuring free and enzyme-bound substrates and products during single site hydrolysis catalyzed by by reconstituted CF_0F_1.

2. PROCEDURE
The ATP synthase was isolated from chloroplasts and reconstituted

into asolectin liposomes (5). Then, the reconstituted enzyme was reduced by dithiothreitol and activated by a $\Delta pH/\Delta\Psi$ transition. ATP (20 nM) and NH_4Cl (10 mM) were added 15 s after the activation. Under these conditions different experiments have been carried out as outlined in Fig. 2:
1) Measurement of free (ADP + ATP); 2) Measurement of free ATP; 3) Measurement of enzyme-bound (ADP +ATP) with ^{14}C-labeled ATP using centrifugation columns for separation of free and enzyme bound nucleotides; 4) Measurement of the sum of free and enzyme-bound P_i with γ-[^{32}P]-ATP; 5) Measurement of the enzyme-bound ATP + P_i with γ-[^{32}P]-ATP using centrifugation columns; 6) Measurement of enzyme bound P_i with γ-[^{32}P]-ATP using centrifugation columns. After starting the reaction by addition of ATP samples are taken at different times and the concentration of the different species is determined as a function of time as indicated in Fig. 2.

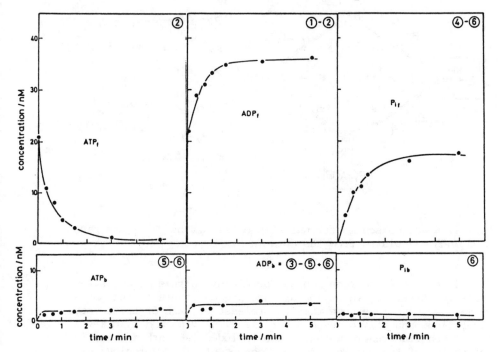

Fig. 3. Time course of concentration of free and enzyme-bound products during single site hydrolysis of ATP

3. RESULTS AND DISCUSSION
Fig. 3 shows the result. At the top the time course of the free species is shown. At the bottom the enzyme-bound species are depicted. A rapid decrease of the free ATP can be seen. The enzyme-bound ATP is hydrolyzed to enzyme-bound ADP and P_i, and both products

are released. Measurements with ^{14}C-labeled ATP showed that the released ADP originates from the newly bound ATP; the same was found for the P_i. (The ADP present at t=0 is a tightly bound nucleotide released during activation; the increase of the ADP concentration afterwards reflects the ATP hydrolysis. The $P_{i,f}$ indicates the P_i released during hydrolysis, the total P_i is 5 mM in this experiment.) The concentration of enzyme-bound P_i is about 1 nM, that of enzyme-bound ADP is 3 nM and that of enzyme-bound ATP is about 2 nM. The ratio of enzyme-bound P_i to ATP might represent the "equilibrium constant" between enzyme-bound substrates and products. As an average from different experiments we obtained $K_2=0.4$.

The rate constant for ATP binding was calculated from the second order plot of the free ATP, and the rate of constants for P_i and ADP release were calculated from the respective rates and concentrations of the species.

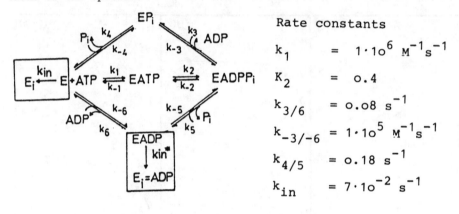

Rate constants

$k_1 \quad = \quad 1 \cdot 10^6 \ M^{-1} s^{-1}$

$K_2 \quad = \quad 0.4$

$k_{3/6} \quad = 0.08 \ s^{-1}$

$k_{-3/-6} = 1 \cdot 10^5 \ M^{-1} s^{-1}$

$k_{4/5} \quad = 0.18 \ s^{-1}$

$k_{in} \quad = 7 \cdot 10^{-2} \ s^{-1}$

Fig. 4. Reaction scheme for uni-site catalysis by CF_0F_1 and rate constants calculated from the data in Fig 3.

Fig. 4 shows the reaction scheme for ATP hydrolysis at one site. For a quantitative evaluation of the rate constants of the ADP and P_i release we have to assume that the release of each of these species occurs independently of each other, i. e. $k_3 = k_6$ and $k_4 = k_5$. In the reaction scheme we have also included two pathways for in-activation of the enzyme, one is independent of ADP binding, k_{in}, and the other depends on ADP binding, k_{in}^*. With this scheme and the rate constants, the kinetics of the single-site hydrolysis can be described completely. The data indicate that the reconstituted CF_0F_1 in its reduced form is able to catalyze under the experimental conditions a complete catalytic turnover. The comparison with the data from MF_1 (4) shows that the rate constant of ATP binding and the "equilibrium constant" on the enzyme are similar whereas the rate constants of ADP and P_i release are two to three magnitudes higher for CF_0F_1. Wherefore the concentrations of the enzyme-bound

species are much smaller then found for MF_1.
Since the rate constants are rather small it is doubtful whether this
site represents a normal catalytic site. In order to investigate
this, we have performed the following experiments (Fig. 5).

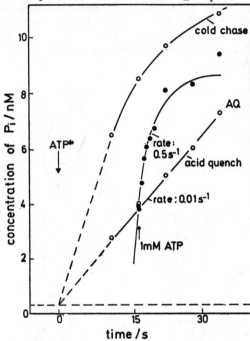

Fig. 5. P_i release in an acid-quench and a cold chase experiment.
The arrows indicate the addition of γ-[^{32}P]-ATP and the cold ATP.

The first binding site was loaded with γ-[^{32}P]-ATP and ATP hydrolysis
was measured by the amount of $^{32}P_i$ (free + enzyme-bound). After 15 s
1 mM cold ATP was added. This had two effects:
1) The binding of further γ-[^{32}P]-ATP was stopped immediately
because of the high isotope dilution. This implies that after the
addition of cold ATP we observe only the reactions of ATP which was
already bound to the enzyme.
2) All the other ATP binding sites are filled. If the γ-[^{32}P]-ATP
bound at the first site is involved in a sequential mechanism, it is
expected that $^{32}P_i$ is formed with the maximal rate, i. e. 100 s^{-1}.
The data in Fig. 5 indicate that the rate of ATP hydrolysis in this
"cold chase" is 0.5 s^{-1}, i. e. it is far below the expected rate.
On the other hand the rate has increased in the cold chase from
0.01 s^{-1} to 0.5 s^{-1}. We believe that this is only an apparent
acceleration: before the cold chase the rate of hydrolysis is
limited by the rate of ATP binding. When cold ATP is added their is
no further ATP binding and we observe ATP hydrolysis on the enzyme,

i. e. the rate constant k_2.
We conclude from these results that the catalytic site which we have
investigated here is not immediately involved in a sequential three
site mechanism.
In the scheme shown in Fig. 4 the different protonation states of the
enzyme have been omitted for the sake of clarity. It is, however,
clear that ATP hydrolysis is coupled with different protonation
states. In Fig. 6 a simplified scheme is shown where different
protonation states are included.

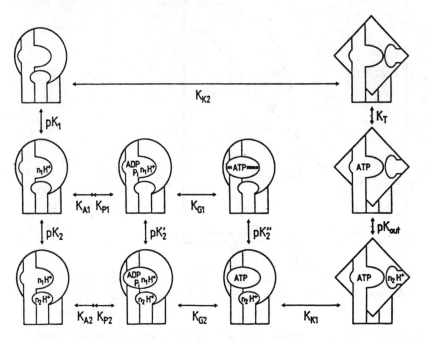

Fig. 6. Reaction scheme for one catalytic site including protonation / deprotonation steps.

This (minimal) mechanism works as follows: the (active reduced)
enzyme exists in two different conformational states symbolized
by the circular and the quadratic form. The quadratic form binds
first ATP and then protons from the outsite are bound (pK_{out}).
These protons are now transported to the inside (K_{K1}). After that,
there are two pathways: either first ATP is hydrolyzed (K_{G2}), P_i
and ADP are released (K_{A2}, K_{P2}), and then the protons are released
(pK_2) or first the protons are released (pK_2'), then ATP is hydrolysed (K_{G1}), and P_i and ADP is released (K_{A1}, K_{P1}). Finally, in
both cases the chemically produced proton from the catalytic center
is released (pK_1) producing the spherical nucleotide-free form,
which is in equilibrium with the quadratic form (K_{K2}). All steps are

reversible.
The model accommodates several experimental observations. The
different constants can be taken from the literature data and the
ΔpH-dependence of ATP synthesis and hydrolysis can be described.
It also illustrates kinetic analysis both theoretically and experimentally; even in such an oversimplified scheme where several
events are described by one constant (e. g. the threefold protonation or ADP and P_i binding) the number of enzyme species becomes
very high. Furthermore, no cooperativity between different sites
has been taken into account. However, one can use such a scheme
as a guide line for further experiments.

Acknowledgement: This work has been supported by the Deutsche
Forschungsgemeinschaft (Sfb 312).

REFERENCES

1. Kironde, F. A. S. and Cross, R. L. (1986) J. Biol. Chem. 261,
12544 - 12549
2. Girault, G., Beyer, G. and Galmiche, J. M. (1988) 5th EBEC report
247
3. Boyer, P. D. (1977) Trends in Biochem. Sci. 2, 38 - 41
4. Grubmeyer, C., Cross, R. L. and Penefsky, H. S. (1982) J. Biol.
Chem. 257, 12092 - 12100
5. Schmidt, G. and Gräber, P. (1985) Biochim. Biophys. Acta 808,
46 - 52

LIGHT-DRIVEN INORGANIC PYROPHOSPHATE SYNTHESIS IN PHOTOTROPHIC BACTERIA

Pål Nyrén, Beston F. Nore, Gaza F. Salih and Åke Strid
Department of Biochemistry, Arrhenius Laboratories, University of Stockholm, S-106 91 Stockholm, Sweden

1. INTRODUCTION

It is well known that inorganic pyrophosphate (PPi) is formed during biosynthesis of cellular constituents such as proteins, polysaccharides, nucleic acids and lipids. However, PPi can also be formed by oxidative phosphorylation in mitochondria from different sources and by photophosphorylation in some phototrophs, such as Rhodospirillum rubrum.

In R. rubrum there are two photophosphorylating reactions occurring in parallel: ATP and PPi synthesis (Fig. 1).

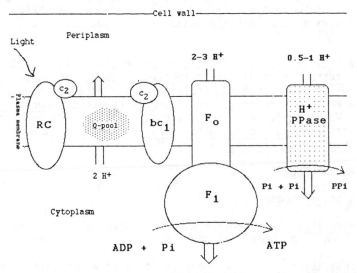

FIGURE 1. A schematic view of the two photophosphorylating reactions occurring in the plasma membrane of R. rubrum.

M. Baltscheffsky (ed.), Current Research in Photosynthesis, Vol. III, 23–28.
© 1990 Kluwer Academic Publishers. Printed in the Netherlands.

Both reactions are multistep processes that occurs in the inner membrane, i.e. the plasma membrane, of R. rubrum. Both ATP and PPi synthesis are coupled to the cyclic electron transport by a chemiosmotic process. The light energy, which is absorbed and transferred to the reaction centre by the antenna pigments, is converted to a proton gradient across the membrane probably by a Q-cycle mechanism. The complexes taking part in this process are the reaction centre, the cytochrome bc_1-complex, the cytochrome c_2 and an ubiquinone-pool. For each electron passing through the Q-cycle, two protons are extruded from the cell. The proton motive force created drive both the phosphorylation of ADP to ATP by the F_0F_1-ATP synthase and the phosphorylation of Pi to PPi by the reversible membrane bound proton translocating PPase (the H^+-PPase). For each ATP formed between two and three protons are transported inwards, whereas for each PPi formed only one proton is taken up.

The H^+-PPase has an orientation in the membrane similar to the F_0F_1-ATP synthase with the catlaytic part of the enzyme exposed to the interior of the cell. However, the enzyme seems to be simpler and more hydrophobic (1), than the F_0F_1-ATP synthase and lacks a structure similar to the F_1, which sticks out far into the cytoplasm and which can easily be separated from the membrane part, the proton-conducting F_0, either by sonication in the presence of EDTA or by chloroform extraction. The H^+-PPase is a reversible enzyme. It works either as a primary or a secondary transport system and couples the movement of protons across the membrane to the hydrolysis or the generation of PPi. Hydrolysis of PPi can support a number of energy-dependent processes such as ATP-synthesis, NAD^+-reduction, and transhydrogenation.

Despite the fact that photosynthetic PPi formation only has been revealed in R. rubrum it is plausible to suggest that other phototrophic bacteria would be capable of catalyzing PPi synthesis. Thus a membrane bound PPase has recently been found in Rhodopseudomonas palustris (2,3). We have also examined the possibility of PPi synthesis in chromatophores from Rhodopseudomonas viridis, Rhodopseudomonas blastica and Rhodobacter capsulatus.

2. EXPERIMENTAL PROCEDURES

2.1. Materials and methods

2.1.1. Materials: All materials were of reagent grade and obtained from commercial sources.

2.1.2. Preparation of chromatophores: Cells were harvested and chromatophores were prepared as in Ref. 4, except that cells from Rp. viridis and Rp. blastica were passed twice through the Ribi Cell fractionator.

2.1.3. Assay of ATPase and PPase activity: The method use was a modification, previously described (5), of the Rathbun method (6).

2.1.4. Measurement of continuous photophosphorylation: Continuous monitoring of ATP and PPi syntheses were carried out as described earlier (7).

2.1.5. Measurement of flash-induced PPi and ATP synthesis: The ATP and PPi syntheses were determined as described earlier (8).

3. RESULTS

3.1. The monitoring of PPi synthesis in continuously illuminated Rp. viridis chromathophores is shown in Fig. 2. The steady-state rate of PPi synthesis under continuous illumination was 0.15 µmol PPi/(min · µmol BChl). This rate is about 15% of the steady-state rate of ATP synthesis under the same conditions. We could not detect any PPi synthesis activity at all with chromatophores from Rp. blastica and Rb. capsulatas.

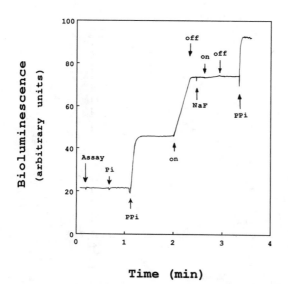

Time (min)

FIGURE 2. A typical trace from the measurement of photophosphorylation of Pi to PPi during continuous illumination of Rp. viridis chromatophores. The following additions were made: 20 pmol PPi, 10 µmol fluoride.

Table 1 gives a summary of the effects of the different compounds tested on the PPi synthesis. The PPi synthesis was inhibited by the uncoupler FCCP, the electron transport inhibitor
myxothiazol and the PPase inhibitor fluoride, but not by the
F_0F-ATPase inhibitors oligomycin and venturicidin.

TABLE 1. The effect of various agents on photosynthetic PPi formation
in Rp. viridis.

Additions	μmol PPi formed/ (min · μmol BChl)	Rate of PPi formed (% of control)
Control	0.15	100
Oligomycin (1 μg/ml)	0.15	100
Venturicidin (1 μg/ml)	0.15	100
FCCP (1 μM)	0.05	33
Myxothiazol (1 μM)	0.0	0
Na-Fluoride (10 mM)	0.0	0

3.2. As demonstrated in Fig. 3, the chromatophores of Rp. viridis
were also competent in catalyzing a flash-stimulated PPi synthesis. The amount of PPi formed after a 1 ms light flash was
approximately equivalent to 1 μmol PPi/500 μmol BChl. This value
can be compared with the yield of ATP after one flash, which was
1 μmol ATP/1000 μmol BChl.

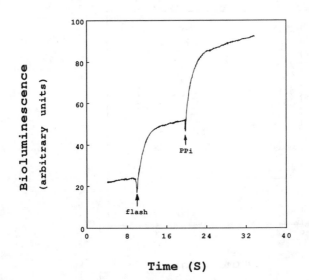

Time (S)

FIGURE 3. A typical trace from the measurements of PPi formation
after a single 1 ms flash in Rp. viridis chromatophores.
1pmol PPi was added where indicated.

3.3. The Rp. viridis chromathophores, but not the Rp. blastica or the Rb. capsulatus chromatophores, catalyzed the hydrolysis of PPi. The rate of PPi hydrolysis was 1.0 µmol PPi hydrolyzed/(min · µmol BChl) (Table 2).

TABLE 2. The rate of PPi and ATP synthesis, and PPi and ATP hydrolysis in four phototrophic bacteria

Activity	Bacteria studied			
	Rp. viridis	R. rubrum[a]	Rp. blastica	Rb. capsulatus
PPi synthesis[b]	0.1	1.2	0.0	0.0
ATP synthesis[b]	0.5	10.0	2.8	2.9
PPi hydrolysis[c]:				
Control	1.0	6.0	0.0	0.0
+ 1 µM FCCP	1.2	12.0	0.0	0.0
ATP hydrolysis[c]:				
Control	1.3	1.0	0.8	n.d.
+ 1 µM FCCP	1.5	8.0	1.4	n.d.

[a]Ref. 5; [b]µmol PPi or ATP formed/(min · µmol BChl); [c]µmol PPi or ATP hydrolyzed/(min · µmol BChl).

DISCUSSION

In Table 1 are summarized the results of the experiments on four different phototrophic bacteria taken from this and earlier studies (5). Of the four bacteria studied, only R. rubrum and Rp. viridis catalyzed photophosphorylation of Pi to PPi. Both the highest PPi synthesis and the highest PPi hydrolyzing activity were obtained with R. rubrum chromatophores. No hydrolyzing or synthesizing activity was observed in chromatophores from Rp. blastica or Rb. capsulatus. The large difference in PPi synthesis activity between R. rubrum and Rp. viridis can be explained mainly by a difference in coupling activity. This is indicated by the low uncoupler stimulation of both the PPase and the ATPase actiivties in Rp. viridis chromatophores and also by the low ATP synthesis activity (0.5 µmol ATP formed/(min · µmol BChl) in Rp. viridis (see also Ref. 9) compared to 10 µmol ATP formed/(min· µmol BChl) in R. rubrum. The planar structure of the intracytoplasmic membranes of Rp. viridis is hardly compatible with the formation of well coupled vesicles. This fact explain the differences in rate observed between the membrane preparations from the two bacteria.

The present results show that the phototrophic bacterium R. viridis contains a membrane bound PPase, which is able to couple the energy liberated from light driven electron transport to synthesis of PPi. Both continuous illumination and short light flashes are possible energy sources for driving PPi synthesis. We have shown in this study that R. rubrum not is unique among phototrophic bacteria in being able to couple light driven electron flow to the synthesis of PPi. Why some, and not all, phototrophic bacteria contain a membrane bound PPase is not easily explained.

However, it must be energetically more advantageous for a cell to be able to make use of the ΔG liberated during PPi hydrolysis in the form of a proton motive force driving other energy-linked processes than it is to waste the energy as heat.

ACKNOWLEDGEMENTS

This work was supported as a grant by the Swedish Natural Science Research Council (NFR) to P.N. We are grateful to Dr. Baz Jackson for the Rb. capsulatas culture (strain N22).

REFERENCES

1. Nyrén, P. (1985) Doctoral thesis, Univ. of Stockholm, Stockholm, Sweden.

2. Knobloch, K. (1975) Z. Naturforsch. 30c, 342-348.

3. Schwarm, H.-M., Vigenschov, H. and Knobloch, K. (1986) Biol. Chem. Hoppe-Seyler 367, 127-133.

4. Shakhov, Yu.A., Nyrén, P. and Baltscheffsky, M. (1982) FEBS Lett. 146, 177-180.

5. Nyrén, P., Nore, B.F. and Baltscheffsky, M. (1986) Biochim. Bio-phys. Acta 851, 276-282.

6. Rathbun, W.B. and Betlach, V.M. (1969) Anal. Biochem. 28, 436-445.

7. Nyrén, P., Lundin, A. (1985) Anal. Biochem. 151, 504-509.

8. Nyrén, P., Nore, B.F. and Baltscheffsky, M. (1986) Photobiochim. Photobiophys. 11, 189-196.

9. Kerber, N.L., Pucheu, N.L. and Garcia, A.F. (1977) FEBS Lett. 80, 49-52.

EXAFS ANALYSIS OF THE STRUCTURE OF MN.NUCLEOTIDE BOUND TO LATENT AND ACTIVATED CF_1-ATPASE.

C. Carmeli[1], A. Lewis[2] and A. T. Jagendorf[3]. Departments of: Biochemistry, Tel Aviv University Tel Aviv, Israel[1]; Applied Physics, Hebrew University, Jerusalem[2]; Plant Sciences, Cornell University, Ithaca, N. Y. USA[3].

1. INTRODUCTION

The catalytic sector of the chloroplast H^+-ATPase (CF_1) is composed of five types of subunits (1) having a stochiometry of $3\alpha, 3\beta, \gamma, \delta$ and ϵ. ATP binding studies and affinity labeling with ATP analogues indicated that at least three but possibly up to six binding sites were located on the β or at the interface of the α and β (2, 3) subunits of CF_1. Metal cofactors were also used as probes for the active site (4) in the last years. It was found that the optimal ATPase activity of CF_1 was a function of the divalent metal ion -ATP complex rather than one of its components, indicating that the entire complex is the true substrate (4). From nonequilibrium binding studies it was found that CF_1 contains one tightly bound Mg^{2+} ion which probably has a structural role (5-7). Equilibrium binding measurements indicated three loose noninteracting and three tight Mn^{2+} binding sites which interact cooperatively (7). Based on correlation between binding and kinetic constants of stimulation and inhibition (4, 7) we have suggested that this cooperativity is a result of interaction among the three active sites of the enzyme. Indeed convalent modification of a single arginine residue by naphthylglyoxal, which inhibited ATPase activity (8) also prevented this interaction (7). In previous studies (9) the structure of Mn^{2+} bound to three interacting binding sites in latent CF_1 was determined by extended x-ray absorption fine structure (EXAFS) analysis. In Mn^{2+} bound to latent CF_1 only a first shell of atoms could be measured. On addition of stochiometric amounts of ATP to the CF_1.Mn a second shell appeared indicating a formation of a ternary complex between the CF_1, Mn^{2+} and ATP. The three phosphorus of ATP were indirectly ligated to bound Mn^{2+} via hydrogen bonds of the metal hydration shell. The rather large distance between the Mn^{2+} and the phosphorus could be one of the reasons for the latency of the enzyme. In the present work, the structure of Mn.nucleotide complex in activated CF_1 was measured. The results indicated that the phosphates of ADP and ATP are directly bound to Mn^{2+}. Thus the phosphorus atoms are subjected to a strong electrophilic effect by the metal in the activated enzyme.

2. PROCEDURE

2. 1. Sample preparation

CF_1 was prepared from lettuce chloroplasts as previously described (7). The enzyme was incubated in 1 mM ATP for 1h at 25 C or activated by 15 h incubation with DTT and a short tryptic digestion and then freed from ligands by two passage through Sephadex G-50 centrifugation columns. CF_1 was concentrated by ultrafiltration to a volume of 50-150 ul bringing the enzyme concentration to 1.7-5 mM. X-ray absorption was measured in 50 ul sample, 1mm thick, in a solution containing 40 mM HEPES-NaOH, pH8, 100 mM mannitol and $MnCl_2$ in a concentration which was calculated to obtain Mn^{2+} binding to three interacting binding sites on the enzyme assuming Kd of 14.7 uM and 5.7 uM in the absence and presence of ATP respectively (7) leaving only 2-5% free Mn^{2+}.

2. 2. X-ray absorption and fluorescence measurements

X-ray measurements were made at Cornell High Energy Synchrotron Source (CHESS) on the focused A-3 beam between 6.4-7.0 KeV at 3 eV intervals at 4s/point. Scans were taken for a total of 10 h beam time with the diluted enzyme samples at 20 C as previously described (9). Data reduction followed standard procedures using the University of Washington package. The method consists of edge determination, deglitching, pre-edge background removal, edge normalization, post edge background removal, extraction of EXAFS signal, Fourier transformation and inverse transform isolated EXAFS contribution from a selected shell in real space. Each of the selected contributions were fitted by a single scattering formula . Phase shift and backscattering amplitudes of model compounds was used for the fit to the experimentally obtained filtered Fourier transformed EXAFS data.

3. RESULTS AND DISCUSSION

3. 1. Absorption spectra of Mn.nucleotides complexes in solution and fluorescence spectra of enzyme bound Mn^{2+} complexes.

The structure of Mn^{2+}.nucleotides complexes was determined from their x-ray absorption spectra in solution. The K-edge of Mn.ADP, Mn.ATP and Mn.AMPPNP was at 6543 ev which was at the same energy as the edge of Mn^{2+} (9). The same manganese complexes when bound to CF_1 were measured by x-ray fluorescence as their concentration was 50 fold diluted and required the use of the more sensitive method for detection. The fluorescence spectra had the same edge energy as that which was measured by absorption indicating that Mn^{2+} valency did not change on binding of the metal complex to the enzyme. Otherwise x-ray absorption and fluorescence can be similarly analyzed for EXAFS determinations.

3. 2. EXAFS analysis of Mn.nucleotides complexes in solution and bound to CF_1.

The determination of the structure of the substrates at the three active sites of activated CF_1 (ACF) required the use of nonhydrolyzable nucleotides. Therefore ADP, the product of hydrolysis, and adenylylimidodiphosphate (AMPPNP), a nonhydrolyzable analogue of ATP, were used. The analysis of the x-ray absorption spectra of the Mn.nucleotide binary complexes in solution and the fluorescence spectra of the ACF.Mn.nucleotide ternary complexes were used for extraction of the background subtracted EXAFS data. The EXAFS data obtained for Mn.AMPPNP bound to the trypsin and DTT activated CF_1 were Fourier transformed. Two distinguished peaks were observed. The first peak was between 0.7 - 2.2 A^O and the second between 2.2 - 3.0 A^O. The first peak was assigned for Mn-O pair and the second to the Mn-O pair.

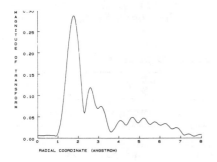 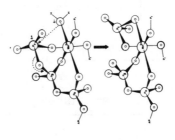

Fig. 1. Fourier transformed EXAFS spectrum of Mn^{2+}, and AMPPNP bound to activated CF_1 (ACF.Mn.AMPPNP).

Fig. 2. Hypothetical mechanism for ATP hydrolysis based on a model for Mn^{2+}.ATP bound to activate CF_1 determined from EXAFS analysis.

However the determination of the exact distances and the number of ligands was obtained from a fit of the backtransformation of the contribution of each of the shells of Mn.ATP to those of the unknown compounds. In these fits the previously determined (9) backscattering amplitudes, the phase shift and the Debey – Waller (SS) factors obtained from the EXAFS analysis of Mn.ATP complex were used. Similar procedures were used for the other compounds.

3. 3.Number of ligands and their distances from Mn^{2+}

In all the compound whether free in solution or bound to the activated enzyme the first shell of Mn^{2+} ion contained 6 ligands and their average distance was at 2.13 - 2.14 A^O (Table 1) . The second shell of Mn.ATP and Mn.AMPPNP had 3 phosphorus atoms and that of Mn.ADP had 2 phosphorus atoms at a distance of 3.31 - 3.37 A^O. Although the Mn-P distances are similar when the complex are free in solution or bound to the activated enzyme they are greatly different from the structure of Mn.ATP bound to the latent CF_1. In the latent CF_1 the Mn-P distance of 3 phosphates was 4.95 A^O indicating that the phosphate oxygens of the ATP are indirectly ligated to the metal probably through hydrogen bridges of first shell hydration molecules. From the number and the distance of the phosphorus atoms it is apparent that 3 of the oxygens in the first shell of the Mn.ATP and Mn.AMPPNP complexes were contributed by the phosphate oxygens of the nucleotides while from the data of the Mn.ADP complex it is likely that 2 of the oxygens were contributed by the phosphates. Normally Mn^{2+} ions has a hexagonal configuration. For example in aqueous solution the ion is ligated to 6 water molecules coordinated through their oxygens. As 3 of the ligands are contributed by the phosphate oxygens the other 3 coordinates are occupied by oxygens of the first shell of hydration in Mn.AMPPNP complex in solution. In the enzyme bound Mn.AMPPNP 3 of the first shell coordinates of the metal are also ligated to the three phosphate oxygens. The fourth ligand is contributed by a water molecule as one exchangeable water molecule in the first coordination shell of this complex was detected by NMR measurements (7). Under some conditions two exchangeable water molecules were observed (10) thus, the other one or two ligands are probably contributed by the protein. These might be oxygens of amino acid residues however they

Table 1. The number of ligands and their distance from Mn^{2+}.

	Oxygen			Phosphorus		
	No	Distance A^O	SS.10^{-3}	No	Distance A^O	SS.10^{-3}
Mn.ATP	6.0 ± 1	2.14 ± 0.1	3.0	3.0 ± 1	3.36 ± 0.1	5.0
Mn.AMPPNP	6.1 ± 1	2.14 ± 0.1	0.4	3.2 ± 1	3.35 ± 0.1	8.0
Mn.ADP	5.1 ± 1	2.14 ± 0.1	4.0	1.9 ± 1	3.36 ± 0.1	0.5
Mn.ATP.CF	6.6 ± 1	2.16 ± 0.2	0.4	4.2 ± 1	4.95 ± 0.2	2.0
ACF.Mn.AMPPNP	6.5 ± 1	2.14 ± 0.1	0.3	2.9 ± 1	3.37 ± 0.1	0.3
ACF.Mn.ADP	6.2 ± 1	2.13 ± 0.1	0.1	2.0 ± 1	3.31 ± 0.1	0.5

could also be nitrogens as it is impossible to distinguish between oxygen nitrogen or carbon by the analysis. Activation causes a change in the structure of the substrate displacing the phosphate atoms of ATP 1.6 A^O closer to the Mn^{2+} ion in the active site. It is suggested that as a result of the strong electrophilic effect induced by the metal the phosphorus of ATP becomes more susceptible to nucleophylic attack by water (Fig. 2). Exchangeable water molecules detected at the inner hydration shell of the CF_1 bound Mn.ATP are good candidates because of their proximity and their superior nucleophilic properties.

Acknowledgment: Supported by BSF Grant 86-00233.

5. REFERENCES
1. Racker, E., Hauska, G.A., Lien, S., Berzborn, R.J. and Nelson, N. (1971).
2. Bruist, M.F. and Hammes, G.G. (1981) Biochemistry. 20, 6298.
3. Zhixiong, X., Zhou, J. M., Melese, T., Cross, R. L. and Boyer, P. D. (1987) Biochemistry. 26, 3749-3753.
4. Hochman, Y. and Carmeli, C. (1981) Biochemistry. 20, 6287.
5. Girault, G. and Galmiche, J.M., Lemaire, C. and Stulzafz, O. (1982). Eur. J. Biochem. 128, 405-411.
6. Hiller, R. and Carmeli, C. (1985) J. Biol. Chem. 260, 1614-1617.
7. Haddy, A.B., Fresh, W.D. and Sharp, R.R. (1985) Biochemistry 24, 7926-7930.
8. Takabe, T., de Benedetti, E. and Jagendorf, A.T. (1982). Biochem. Biophys. Acta, 682, 11-20.
9. Carmeli, C., Huang, J. Y., Mills, D. M., Jagendorf, A. T., Lewis, A. (1986). J. Biol. Chem. 261, 16969-16975.
10. Haddy, A. E., Frasch, W. D. and Sharp, R. R. (1989) Biochemistry 28, 3664-3669.

On the Structure of the ATP-Synthase from Chloroplasts

B. Böttcher[1], U. Lücken[1], E.J. Boekema[2] and P. Gräber[3]

[1]Fritz-Haber-Institut, Faradayweg 4-6,1000 Berlin 33, FRG
[2]Biochemisch Laboratorium, Rijksuniversiteit Groningen,
Nijenborgh 16, 9747 AG Groningen, The Netherlands
[3]Biologisches Institut, Universität Stuttgart,
Pfaffenwaldring 57, 7000 Stuttgart 80, FRG

INTRODUCTION

The H^+-translocating ATPase ("ATP-synthase") from chloroplasts is a membrane-bound enzyme which can couple a transmembrane proton transport with ATP synthesis/hydrolysis.
The enzyme has a hydrophobic, membrane-integrated part,
CF_o, which is supposed to act as a proton channel through
the membrane and a hydrophilic part, CF_1, which contains
the nucleotide-binding sites. The CF_1 part contains five
different subunits with the stoichiometry $\alpha_3\beta_3\gamma\delta\epsilon$, the CF_o
part contains four different subunits with the stoichiome-
try I,II,III_{12},IV. However, there is no general agreement
about the subunit stoichiometry up to now.
The structure of CF_1 has been investigated by electron
microscopy of negatively stained samples. It was shown
that the large α- and β-subunits have a hexagonal arrangement with an alternating sequence of α- and β-subunits
(1,2). With computerized image analysis of 3000 CF_1 molecules, the signal-to-noise ratio was drastically increased
so that the individual subunits could be distinguished
clearly. The small subunits are located in the center of
the molecule and, presumably, are split into two parts δ
and $\gamma+\epsilon$ (3).
The shape of CF_oF_1 has been investigated by electron
microscopy of detergent-solubilized enyzme after negative
staining (4). The hydrophobic F_o parts have a strong tendency to aggregate and form string-like structures, where
the F_1 parts are arranged in alternating positions along
the string. The F_1 parts are connected to the F_o parts by
a stalk (length 3.7 nm, diameter 2.7 nm). Image analysis
does not lead to significant improvement of the signal-to-
noise ratio and, thus, does not reveal the arrangement of
the subunits within CF_oF_1. Possibly, this is due to the
presence of detergent. In this work we use two different
approaches to clarify the structure of CF_oF_1.

RESULTS

With single CF_oF_1 molecules - even after image analysis -

M. Baltscheffsky (ed.), Current Research in Photosynthesis, Vol. III, 33–36.
© 1990 *Kluwer Academic Publishers. Printed in the Netherlands.*

the arrangement of the different subunits in the enzyme could not be determined. Therefore, we have tried to generate ordered two-dimensional aggregates, i.e., two-dimensional crystals of CF_oF_1. The enzyme was prepared as described elsewhere (5) and samples containing 2-4 mg/ml protein were used for crystallization. The samples were treated with phospholipase A2, and the detergent and the lipids were slowly removed. After about five days, the samples were diluted with water and stained negative with 2% uranyl acetate. Electron micrographs were taken in a Philips EM 300 at 70,000-fold magnification. Fig. 1A shows

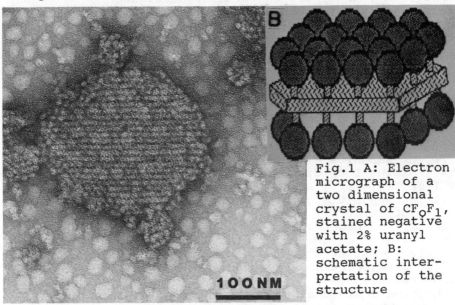

100 NM

Fig.1 A: Electron micrograph of a two dimensional crystal of CF_oF_1, stained negative with 2% uranyl acetate; B: schematic interpretation of the structure

an electron micrograph of an ordered two-dimensional aggregation of CF_oF_1. The top view shows the ordered CF_oF_1. The two-dimensional crystal has a three-layer structure as indicated in the scheme of Fig. 1B. The upper and lower layers are built from CF_1, the central layer is the aggregated CF_o. This implies that half of the CF_o is oriented in the opposite direction from the other half. This is similar to the orientation in the one-dimensional strings observed earlier (4). Main evidence for this structure derived from experiments in which the sample is tilted by 52° in the electron microscope. This allows detection of the central layer and the CF_1 in the lower layer.

Image analysis and image reconstruction has not yet been carried out with these two-dimensional crystals, since the long-range order is not sufficient for a successful analysis.

For a high contrast in the electron micrographs, the sample
was stained negative with uranyl acetate. This leads to
denaturation of the enzyme, and this might be connected
with considerable changes of shape and structure of the
protein. In order to avoid these problems, cryo-electron
microscopy of frozen-hydrated samples has been applied,
similar to that carried out with F_oF_1 from E.coli (6).
CF_oF_1 was reconstituted into asolectin liposomes. These
samples were rapidly (ms range) frozen in liquid ethane at
-192 °C. Under these conditions, water does not crystalize
in the ice structure but the structure of liquid water is
frozen. This is called the "frozen hydrated" state. These
samples are then investigated in the electron microscope at
liquid nitrogen temperature. The sample is only 30-400 nm
thick so that the electron beam can penetrate it. The
contrast of the image is, in this case, merely a phase
contrast of the electron waves that result from slight
differences in velocity of electrons in water, protein and
lipid. Electron micrographs were taken with a low dose kit
in order to minimize radiation damage.

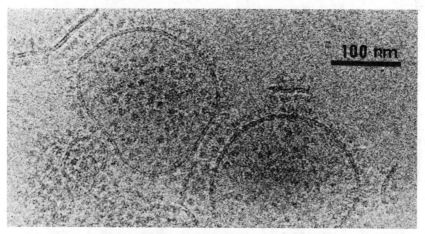

Fig. 2 Electron micrograph of reconstituted CF_oF_1 in the
frozen hydrated state.

Fig. 2 shows an electron micrograph of reconstituted CF_oF_1
in the frozen hydrated state. One can recognize the bilayer structure with attached CF_1. In order to increase
the signal-to-noise ratio, 34 images of the reconstituted
CF_oF_1 were selected and digitized. Then, they were oriented
with regard to a symmetrized reference image and added.
Fig. 3 shows the result. As can be seen, the CF_1 part is
connected with the membrane-integrated CF_o part by a small
stalk. This is in accordance with the result from negatively stained CF_oF_1 (4) and it is also in accordance with

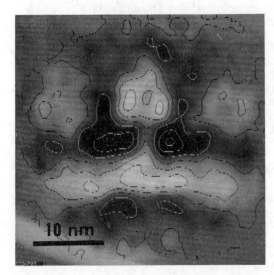

Fig. 3
Average image of 34
oriented images of
reconstituted CF_oF_1 in
the frozen hydrated state

the result obtained with EF_oF_1 in the frozen hydrated state
(6). Thus, we can exclude the possibility that the stalk
is an artefact of the staining procedure. It seems that
the F_1-stalk-F_o-structure is a general property of the F_oF_1
ATPases (7). Two further preliminary results can be taken
from Fig. 3: (1) There is only very little mass of the CF_o
part on the membrane side opposite to the CF_1 part; i.e.,
we have to conclude that the CF_o part practically does not
extend into the inner aqueous phase. (2) In the CF_1 part,
there is no indication of a groove parallel to the membrane. However, there is an indication of a groove vertical to the membrane. If this result is confirmed by a
higher number of molecules, one must conclude that the α-
and ß-subunits have an elongated shape and that they are
not spherical.

REFERENCES

1 Tiedge, H., Schäfer, G. and Mayer, F. (1983) Eur. J.
  Biochem. 132, 37
2 Tiedge, H., Lünsdorf, H., Schäfer, G. and Schairer, M.V.
  (1985) Proc. Natl. Acad. Sci. USA 82, 7874
3 Boekema, E., van Heel, M. and Gräber, P.(1988) Biochim.
  Biophys. Acta 933, 365
4 Boekema, E., Schmidt, G., Gräber, P. and Berden, J.A.
  (1988) Z. Naturforsch. 43C, 219
5 Fromme, P., Boekema, E. and Gräber, P.(1987) Z.
  Naturforsch. 42c, 1239
6 Gogol, E.P., Lücken, U. and Capaldi, R.A. (1987) FEBS
  Lett. 219, 274
7 Amzel,L.M.and Pedersen,P.L.(1983) Ann.Rev.Biochem.52, 801

Uni-Site ATP Hydrolysis Catalyzed by the ATP-Synthase from Chloroplasts

A. Labahn[1] and P. Gräber[2]

[1]Max-Volmer-Institut, Technische Universität Berlin, Str. d.17. Juni 135, 1000 Berlin 12
[2]Biologisches Institut, Universität Stuttgart, Pfaffenwaldring 57, 7000 Stuttgart 80, FRG

INTRODUCTION

The ATP-synthase from chloroplasts, CF_oF_1, catalyzes reversibly ATP synthesis/hydrolysis coupled with a transmembrane proton transport. The hydrophilic CF_1 part is composed of five different subunits with the stoichiometry $\alpha_3\beta_3\gamma\delta\epsilon$. The ß-subunits contain the catalytic nucleotide-binding sites, and from the stoichiometry it follows that there should exist three catalytic binding sites. This raises the immediate question whether these catalytic sites work independently or cooperatively. It has been proposed that there exists a "binding change" mechanism; i.e., the release of products from one site occurs only after binding of a substrate to a second site (1). With isolated mitochondrial F_1 it was found that ATP hydrolysis on a single site is very slow, but binding of ATP to a second site increases the rate by orders of magnitude (2). In this work, we have measured ATP hydrolysis under single site conditions with the active, reduced ATP-synthase from chloroplasts.

MATERIALS AND METHODS

Chloroplasts have been prepared from spinach. The ATP-synthase was brought into the active, reduced state by illumination in the presence of thioredoxin and dithiothreitol. Washing of the chloroplasts drastically reduced the content of endogeneous ADP and ATP. Then, the ATP-synthases are activated by a $\Delta pH/\Delta\varphi$-jump so that at the beginning of the experiment all enzymes are in the active, reduced state and contain no enzyme-bound ADP and only one enzyme-bound ATP per CF_oF_1. The maximum rate of ATP hydrolysis (at 1 mM ATP, pH 8.2) is about 100 s^{-1} before and after the washing. The enzyme remains in the active state for about 450 s (half-life time). All following experiments are carried out with such chloroplasts preparations.

To measure the kinetics of ATP-binding and hydrolysis, 15 s after the activation γ-[^{32}P]-ATP and NH_4Cl was added. The final NH_4Cl concentration was 6 mM, ATP concentration was changed between 3 nM and 1,5 mM. From the reaction mixture samples are taken at different times and treated differently. Acid quench: the samples are denatured by addition of trichloroacetic acid; cold chase: 1 mM cold ATP is added at t_x and 10 s later the samples are denatured. The rate of ATP hydrolysis is calculated from the slope of the acid quench curves.

RESULTS

In order to investigate the kinetics at a single site of the enzyme, the concentration of the enzyme was 3- to 10-fold higher than that of ATP.
Fig. 1 shows the result of one set of experiments. CF_oF_1 concentration was 20 nM, ATP concentration at the beginning of the experiment was $[ATP]_o = 4$ nM. A nearly linear in-

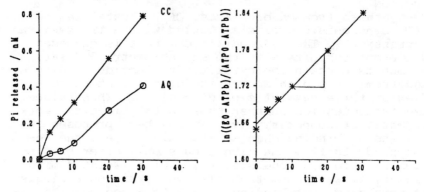

Fig. 1 (A) P_i released in an acid quench experiment, AQ, and a cold chase experiment, CC, as a function of time. The difference reflects the concentration of enzyme-bound ATP; enzyme concentration was 20 nM. (B) Second order plot of ATP binding to the enzyme.

crease of the concentration of $^{32}P_i$ released is observed. The $^{32}P_i$-concentration in the acid quench represents enzyme-bound and free $^{32}P_i$; i.e., $[AQ] = [P_{if}] + [P_{ib}]$. The concentration in the cold chase represents additional enzyme-bound ATP; i.e., $[CC] = [P_{if}] + [P_{ib}] + [ATP_b]$. Since all $^{32}P_i$ originates from the initial $[(^{32}P)-ATP]_o$, the concentration of free ATP can be calculated, i.e., $[ATP_f] = [ATP]_o - [CC]$. From the data in Fig. 1A the free ATP has been calculated and is shown in Fig. 1B as a second- order reaction plot. As an average from three measurements a second-order rate constant of $k_1 = 3 \cdot 10^5$ M^{-1} s^{-1} resulted for ATP binding.
Fig. 2A shows the concentration of free ATP, enzyme-bound ATP and P_i (free and bound). In the initial stage of the reaction practically no P_i is released; i.e., the data represent only the enzyme-bound P_i. In Fig. 2B the ratio

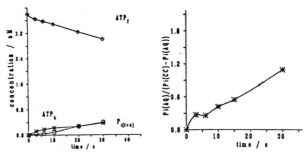

Fig. 2 (A) Concentration of free and enzyme-bound ATP and the sum of free and enzyme-bound P_i as a function of the reaction time. Data from Fig. 1A. (B) Ratio of $^{32}P_i$ obtained by acid quench to enzyme-bound ATP obtained by the difference, CC-AQ.

between enzyme-bound P_i and enzyme-bound ATP is plotted. As long as this ratio is constant, it might representthe equilibrium constant on the enzyme. It results $K_2 = 0.2$.

$$k_1 = 3 \cdot 10^5 \ M^{-1}s^{-1}$$
$$K_2 = 0.2$$
$$k_2/4 = 0.6 \ s^{-1}$$
$$k_{in} = 1.5 \cdot 10^{-3} \ s^{-1}$$

Fig. 3 Reaction scheme of ATP hydrolysis/synthesis at one nucleotide binding site. The measured rate constants are indicated.

Fig. 3 shows the reaction scheme for single site ATP synthesis/hydrolysis and the rate constants determined above. These rate constants are similar to the corresponding effective rate constants measured with the reconstituted CF_oF_1 (3) and with chloroplasts (4).

Measurements at such low substrate concentrations are difficult. Therefore, we have increased ATP concentration. Fig. 4 shows the rate of ATP hydrolysis as a function of the ATP concentration. One can see a linear increase of the rate up to about 7 nM. From the slope of the curve a second order rate constant of $k_1 = 1 \cdot 10^5 \ M^{-1}s^{-1}$ is calculated. At concentrations >7 nM a supralinear

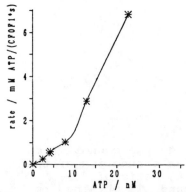

Fig. 4 Rate of ATP hydro-
lysis as function of ATP
concentration

increase of the rate is found. This indicates the involvement of a second ATP-binding site in ATP hydrolysis. (This
second site might be either a regulatory site; i.e., it increases the rate of hydrolysis on the first site without
ATP hydrolysis on the second site, or it is itself a
catalytic site which gives rise to higher rates, e.g. by a
binding change mechanism.)

DISCUSSION

The ATP-synthase from chloroplasts carries out single site
ATP hydrolysis, when the enzyme is in the active, reduced
state. The reaction mechanism can be described by the
scheme shown in Fig. 3, which is similar to that obtained
for mitochondrial F_1 (2,5). However, the rate constants
differ significantly: for CF_oF_1 ATP binding is slower and
the product release (P_i and ADP) is faster. This implies
that the concentration of the enzyme-bound species is always much lower than for MF_1. The rate of ATP hydrolysis
depends supralinearly on the ATP concentration. This indicates that even at low ATP concentrations a second ATP-
binding site plays a role in ATP hydrolysis. The function
of this site is now under investigation.

REFERENCES

1 Boyer, P.D. (1977)Trends Biochem. Sci. 2, 38-41
2 Cross, R.L., Grubmeyer, C. and Penefsky, H.S. (1982) J.
  Biol. Chem. 257, 12101-12105
3 Fromme, P. and Gräber, P.(1989) Biochim. Biophys. Acta
  (in press)
4 Fromme, P. and Gräber, P. (1990) Biochim. Biophys. Acta
  (in press)
5 Cunningham, D. and Cross, R.C. (1989) J. Biol. Chem. 263,
  18850-18856

ISOLATION OF THE CATALYTIC (β) SUBUNIT OF THE CHLOROPLAST ATP SYNTHASE IN A HYDROLYTICALLY ACTIVE FORM

Sashi Nadanaciva and David A. Harris
Department of Biochemistry, South Parks Rd., Oxford OX1 3QU (U.K.)

INTRODUCTION

The soluble, extramembrane segment of the chloroplast ATP synthase, termed CF_1, will hydrolyse ATP rapidly by a mechanism involving the cooperation of all three of its active sites - the 'alternating site' mechanism. In the case of mitochondrial F_1, kinetic analysis suggests that, in the absence of cooperativity, this enzyme still possesses an intrinsic ATPase activity, but that in this mode each subunit turns over independently - 'unisite' catalysis [1]. We have confirmed that CF_1 can also operate in a similar manner [2].

It is difficult to study unisite catalysis directly, since it is some 10^4 times slower than multisite catalysis. One approach has been to prevent cooperation in F_1, either by working at very low ATP concentrations (when only one catalytic site is occupied) or by adding a specific inhibitor of cooperative interactions such as azide [3].

Alternatively, it is possible to abolish cooperation by removing the catalytic subunit from its environment in the enzyme complex - providing that this can be accomplished while maintaining the subunit in an active conformation. This approach has been successful in the case of the β subunit from the F_1 of *Rhodospirillum rubrum* [4]. We show here that the β subunit of chloroplast F_1 can also be isolated pure in a form capable of ATP hydrolysis. The hydrolysis rate observed is of the same order as other estimates of unisite ATP hydrolysis. Properties of this isolated subunit are described.

M. Baltscheffsky (ed.), Current Research in Photosynthesis, Vol. III, 41–44.
© 1990 *Kluwer Academic Publishers. Printed in the Netherlands.*

METHODS

Isolation of the catalytic subunit from CF₁

CF₁ (10mg) was dissociated by freeze-thawing in the presence of 400mM NaClO₄, 50mM Tris-succinate, 0.5mM dithiothreitol, 0.5mM ATP (pH 5.9) and subjected to chromatography on hydroxylapatite, essentially as described in [5]. This yielded a solution containing β and δ subunits of CF₁ (2-3mg). The mixture was rechromatographed on a column of ATP-agarose, prepared by coupling periodate-oxidised ATP to aminohexyl (AH-)Sepharose, followed by borohydride reduction of the complex [6]. All added protein bound to this column in 25mM Tricine, 0.5mM dithithreitol, 1mM EDTA (pH 8.0); the subunit and other contaminating proteins eluted at [ATP] < 3mM, while pure β subunit eluted at 10-11 mM ATP. The yield of β was 15-30% of the expected value.

Gel permeation hplc

Gel permeation (size exclusion) hplc was performed on a Waters Protein PAK 300SW column, in a buffer containing 100mM sodium phosphate (pH 7.0). 5μg of protein was injected. The flow was driven at 0.5 mg/ml by a Beckman 110B pump and controller, and the eluate monitored at 220nm using a Beckman 165 flow-through spectrophotometer.

ATPase activity was measured using [³²P]ATP as previously [4].

RESULTS AND DISCUSSION

Solution properties of the β subunit preparation

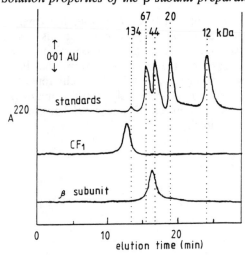

Figure 1. *Gel permeation hplc of CF₁ and affinity purified β subunit. Upper curve: standard proteins (cytochrome c, soybean trypsin inhibitor, ovalbumin, and bovine serum albumin, monomer and dimer)*

The β subunit preparation, as isolated from the affinity column, was >95% pure as judged by SDS-PAGE (data not shown), and gave a single band on gel permeation hplc (Fig. 1). This band moved with a molecular weight corresponding to 50kDa, close to the predicted molecular weight of the subunit. Thus this preparation comprises β subunit in the monomeric state. This is different from β preparations isolated from CF_1-CF_o [7] or *R. rubrum* membranes [4] by LiCl extraction, in which the subunits are aggregated. Interestingly, if the temperature of the affinity purified β is allowed to rise above 20°C, aggregation (followed by precipitation) does occur (data not shown).

When ATP (10μM) is included in the column buffer, the elution of the subunit is considerably delayed. This indicates that a conformational change occurs when ATP binds to the subunit - possibly leading to a more open , or more elongated, form of the protein.

ATP hydrolysis by the isolated β preparation

ATPase activity has recently been observed, by other workers, in a β subunit preparation from CF_1, but quantitation was not attempted in this work [8]. Our β subunit preparation has an intrinsic ATPase activity with V_{max} = 0.8 nmol/min/mg protein (10^{-3} s^{-1}). This value is an order of magnitude lower than the turnover of the β subunit isolated from *R. rubrum* F_1 [4]. However, it is very similar to the ATPase activity of CF_1 at limiting azide inhibition; the residual, azide insensitive ATPase of CF_1 lies around 0.6 nmol/min/mg [2]. This suggests that the activity of the isolated β subunit is equivalent to its activity within CF_1 when cooperative interactions are abolished i.e. it indicates that the intrinsic activity of this subunit is unaltered on isolation.

TABLE I   *Differential sensitivities of CF_1 and its β subunit*

| Preparation | MgATPase activity relative to control | | | | CaATPase |
	no addition	+ ethanol (15% v/v)	+ sulphite (5mM)	+EDTA (5mM)	MgATPase
CF_1	100*	1400	470	17	11.7
subunit	100*	96	145	7	3.8

100% values = 3nmol/min/mg (CF_1) and 0.8nmol/min/mg (β)

Clearly, this interpretation of such a low ATPase activity requires a demonstration that the observed activity is not due to contaminating CF_1 or other phosphatases. This possibility is investigated in Table I. The MgATPase activity of CF_1 is stimulated several fold by both ethanol and sulphite; the activity of the β preparation is hardly affected. In addition, the CaATPase/MgATPase activities of the two preparations are very different. Thus activity observed in the preparation cannot be due to contamination with CF_1. The sensitivity of the ATPase activities to EDTA suggest that a true ATPase, rather than a phosphatase, is involved. It is concluded that the isolated β subunit does indeed possess an ATPase activity, and that this activity is similar in nature and magnitude to unisite turnover in holo-CF_1.

REFERENCES

1. Gresser, M.J., Myers, J.A. and Boyer, P.D. (1982)
     J. Biol. Chem. 257, 12030-12038
2. Andralojc, J.A. and Harris, D.A.   submitted for publication
3. Harris, D.A. (1989)   Biochim. Biophys. Acta 974, 156-162
4. Harris, D.A., Boork, J. and Baltscheffsky, M. (1985)
     Biochemistry 24, 3876-3883
5. Richter, M.L., Gromet-Elhanan, Z. and McCarty, R.E. (1986)
     J. Biol. Chem. 261, 12109-12113
6. Barker, R., Trayer, I.P. and Hill, R.L. (1976)
     Methods Enzymol. 34, 479-491
7. Frasch, W.D., Green, J., Caguiat, J. and Mejia, A (1989)
     J. Biol. Chem. 264, 5064-5069
8. Roux-Fromy, M, Neumann, J.M., Andre, F., Berger, G., Girault, G.
     Galmiche, J.M. and Remy, R. (1987)
     Biochem. Biophys. Res. Commun. 144, 718-725

ISOLATION OF AN ACTIVE β SUBUNIT FROM CHLOROPLAST CFoF1-ATP SYNTHASE

SHLOMO AVITAL AND ZIPPORA GROMET-ELHANAN, Department of Biochemistry, The Weizmann Institute of Science, Rehovot, Israel

1. INTRODUCTION

A number of active β-subunits have been isolated from various F_1-ATPases after their complete dissociation into individual subunits (1-3). Two of these isolated β-subunits, the *E. coli* F_1-β subunit(Ecβ) and the chloroplast CF_1-β subunit ($CF_1β$), were shown to form hybrid F_oF_1-complexes upon their reconstitution into β-less *R. rubrum* chromatophores (3,4). These hybrid complexes restored a high Mg-ATPase activity, but very little ATP synthesis, in the inactive β-less chromatophores. On the other hand, reconstitution of the native *R. rubrum* F_1-β subunit ($Rrβ$), that has been removed from the chromatophore membrane-bound F_oF_1-ATP synthase by extraction with LiCl (5,6) led to full restoration of both coupled ATP synthesis and hydrolysis by the β-less chromatophores.

The above described difference in restoration of coupled ATP-linked activities could be due, either to the very different isolation procedures of the native $Rrβ$ as compared to the foreign $Ecβ$ and $CF_1β$ or to their inherent different interactions with all other RrF_oF_1-subunits in the reconstituted complex. Close interactions between the F_1-β subunit and other F_oF_1-subunits are a basic parameter in all recent models for the mechanism of ATP synthesis by the H^+-translocating F_oF_1-ATP synthase (7-9).

We have therefore applied the LiCl extraction procedure on coupled spinach thylakoids, in an attempt to isolate $CF_1β$ by the method used for $Rrβ$ and compare their activities. In the following experiments the composition and activities of the chloroplast LiCl extract and of a $CF_1β$ enriched fraction are described.

2. MATERIALS AND METHODS

Spinach thylakoids were thoroughly washed to remove large quantities of ribulose-1,5-bisphosphate carboxlase, that appear in the LiCl-extract and interfere with the identification of $CF_1β$ (10). The washed thylakoids were extracted for 30 min at 4° with 2M LiCl in buffer containing 0.25M sucrose, 1mM DTT, 4mM $MgCl_2$, 4mM ATP and 50mM Tricine, pH 8.0 and centrifuged for 1 hr at 200,000 x g. The supernatant was recentrifuged for 1 hr. SDS-PAGE and its western immunoblot analysis were carried out as described in (10). Reconstitution and assays of photophosphorylation and Mg- or Ca-ATPase activities were carried out as described in (3). The 2M LiCl-extract was dissociated and applied to a hydroxyapatite column according to (3) with minor modifications.

M. Baltscheffsky (ed.), Current Research in Photosynthesis, Vol. III, 45–48.
© 1990 *Kluwer Academic Publishers. Printed in the Netherlands.*

FIGURE 1:
Western immunoblot analysis
of the peptides extracted
from spinach thylakoids by
2M LiCl. In lane 1, 2μg
protein of the 2M LiCl-extract
and in lane 2, 2μg CF$_1$
protein were applied on SDS-
PAGE, transferred to
nitrocellulose and challenged
with antibodies against
the indicated CF$_1$ subunits.

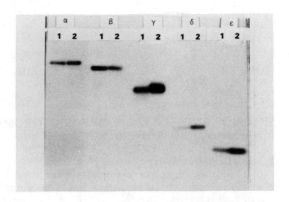

3. RESULTS AND DISCUSSION

Extraction of thoroughly washed spinach thylakoids with 2M LiCl in presence of Mg·ATP, under the conditions developed for complete extraction of Rrβ from coupled *R. rubrum* chromatophores (5,6), led to 95% inhibition of their photophosphorylation activity. Fig. 1, lane 1 illustrates that in the 2M LiCl-extract, when compared with the same amount of CF$_1$-ATPase protein (Fig. 1, lane 2), there is for each extracted CF$_1\beta$ also about 80% of CF$_1\alpha$ and less than 30% of CF$_1$-γ, δ, and ϵ. This 2M LiCl-extract restored up to 30% of the photophosphorylation activity of the extracted thylakoids (10). The 2M LiCl-extract could reconstitute β-less *R. rubrum* chromatophores and restored their Mg-ATPase activity as effectively as the native Rrβ (Table 1) and much more efficiently than the CF$_1\beta$ isolated from a dissociated CF$_1$-ATPase (3). It should be emphasized that the CF$_1(-\delta\epsilon)$ from which this CF$_1\beta$ has been isolated did not bind to the β-less chromatophores (3). It is therefore clear that, although the 2M LiCl-extract contains a mixture of CF$_1$-subunits, it does not contain a fully assembled $\alpha_3\beta_3\gamma$ complex.

TABLE 1: Restoration of Mg-ATPase acitivity in β-less *R. rubrum* chromatophores reconstituted by Rrβ and various thylakoid preparations[a]

Chromatophores	Reconstituted preparation	Mg-ATPase in presence of	
		no addition	tentoxin
		(μmol Pi released/min per mg Bchl)	
control	none	771	802
β-less	none	29	21
β-less	Rrβ	380	353
β-less	2M LiCl-extract	390	46
β-less	enriched CF$_1\beta$	458	35

[a]Reconstitution and Mg-ATPase assay were carried out with a protein/bacteriochlorophyll (Bchl) ratio of 1. At this ratio the restored activity is linearly correlated with the concentration of the reconstituted protein (3). The ATPase assay contained also 20 mM Na$_2$SO$_3$.

In an attempt to isolate from the 2M LiCl-extract an enriched $CF_1\beta$ fraction we have dissociated it by freezing in buffer containing 0.4M $NaClO_4$, and applied the dissociated mixture on an hydroxyapatite column as described in materials and methods. The peak eluted in presence of 30 mM sodium phosphate is enriched in $CF_1\beta$, and δ as compared to the 2M LiCl-extract (10). It still contains about 10% of the $CF_1\alpha$ present in the extract but no CF_1-γ or δ. This enriched $CF_1\beta$ restored a very high rate of Mg-ATPase activity upon its reconstitution into β-less chromatophore (see Table 1).

Both the 2M LiCl-extract and the enriched $CF_1\beta$ preparation, although they restored very efficiently ATP hydrolysis, could restore only trace amounts of ATP synthesis in reconstituted β-less chromatophores. In this respect they are rather similar to the $CF_1\beta$ isolated from a dissociated CF_1 complex (3). The inability of all these hybrid complexes to carry out coupled ATP synthesis and hydrolysis suggests that this is not due to their different isolation procedures.

Frasch *et al.* (11) have recently reported the isolation of a $CF_1\beta$ preparation, that has been extracted by 1M LiCl and shown to be a β_3 aggregate. This β_3 was shown to have a rather low Ca-ATPase activity but high Mg-ATPase activity, of about 1.8 μmol/min per mg, which was not sensitive to tentoxin. On the other hand, the results summarized in Table 1 indicate that the Mg-ATPase activity, restored in β-less *R. rubrum* chromatophores upon their reconstitution with either the 2M LiCl-extract or the enriched $CF_1\beta$ preparation, is fully sensitive to tentoxin.

We have therefore tested the Mg- and Ca-ATPase activities and tentoxin sensitivity of all our thylakoid preparations (Table 2). In CF_1 both ATPase activities are sensitive to tentoxin. Incubation with 3μM tentoxin inhibits 85% of the CF_1 Ca-ATPase and 75% of its sulfite stimulated Mg-ATPase activities (Table 2). The 2M LiCl-extract exhibits also both activities, but they are not sensitive to tentoxin, and are thus similar to the activity reported by Frasch *et al.* (11) for their β_3 aggregate. Our enriched $CF_1\beta$ preparation has no measurable ATPase activity.

TABLE 2: Tentoxin sensitivity of the Mg- and Ca-ATPase activities of CF_1, the 2M LiCl-extract, and the enriched $CF_1\beta$ preparation

Preparation	Mg-ATPase[a]		Ca-ATPase[b]	
	(-)	(+)	(-)	(+)
	(μmol Pi released /min per mg protein)			
CF_1	3.1	0.8	1.3	0.2
2M LiCl-extract	0.5	0.6	0.3	0.3
Enriched $CF_1\beta$	0	0	0	0

[a]Mg-ATPase was assayed in presence of 20mM Na_2SO_3 and 10mM of $MgCl_2$ and ATP. (-) and (+) were incubated for 10 min in the absence or presence of tentoxin.
[b]Ca-ATPase was activated by trypsin and assayed with 4mM ATP and 8mM $CaCl_2$.

Kagawa *et al.* (12) have recently isolated an $\alpha_3\beta_3$ complex of the thermophilic ATP synthase. It had an ATPase activity of 0.5 μmol/min/mg, that dropped upon dilution, but was stabilized and increased to 1.9 μmol/min per mg on addition of enough γ subunit to form a full $\alpha_3\beta_3\gamma$ complex. Moreover their β subunit by itself exhibited a very low ATPase activity of 1 to 2 nmol/min per mg, that is beyond the limit of detection of our assay. Our data (table 2) clearly corroborate those of Kagawa et al. (12) but not those of Frasch et al. (11).

4. CONCLUSIONS

A. The spinach thylakoid 2M LiCl-extract contains besides $CF_1\beta$, also 80% of the $CF_1\alpha$ together with <30% of $CF_1\gamma$, δ, and ϵ (Fig. 1). From it an enriched $CF_1\beta$ fraction, that contains traces of α and some δ has been isolated. Both the extract and the enriched $CF_1\beta$ restore a tentoxin sensitive Mg-ATPase in β-less chromatophores (Table 1).

B. The 2M LiCl-extract has by itself Mg- and Ca-ATPase activities which, unlike the CF_1-ATPase, are not sensitive to tentoxin, but the enriched $CF_1\beta$ has no measurable ATPase activity (Table 2).

C. Our results indicate that tentoxin sensitivity is dependent on presence of $CF_1\beta$, since $Rr\beta$ is completely resistant. But for expression of the inhibitory action of tentoxin interaction of $CF_1\beta$ with other subunits in an assembled F_1 complex is required. The other subunits could, however, be from a different, even completely tentoxin-resistant, source.

ACKNOWLEDGEMENTS

This work was supported in part by the Minerva Foundation, Munich, West Germany. Antibodies against $CF_1\alpha$ and β were a gift from Dr. S. Gepshtein; against $CF_1\gamma$ and δ- from Dr. R. Nechustai; and against $CF_1\epsilon$- from Dr. N. Nelson.

REFERENCES

1. Yoshida, M., Sone, N., Hirata, H. and Kagawa, Y. (1977) J. Biol. Chem. 252, 3480-3485
2. Futai, M. (1977) Biochem. Biophys. Res. Commun. 79, 1231-1237
3. Richter, M.L., Gromet-Elhanan, Z. and McCarty, R.E. (1986) J. Biol. Chem 261, 12109-12113
4. Gromet-Elhanan, Z., Khananshvili, D., Weiss, S., Kanazawa, H. and Futai, M. (1985) J. Biol. Chem. 260, 12635-12640
5. Philosoph, S., Binder, A. and Gromet-Elhanan, Z. (1977) J. Biol. Chem. 252, 8747-8752
6. Gromet-Elhanan, Z. and Khananshvili, D. (1986) Methods Enzymol. 126, 528-538
7. Gresser, M.J., Myers, J.A. and Boyer, P.D. (1982) J. Biol. Chem. 257, 12030-12038
8. Cox, G.B., Jans, D.A., Fimmel, A.L., Gibson, F. and Hatch, L. (1984) Biochim. Biophys. Acta, 768, 201-208
9. Mitchell, P. (1985) FEBS Lett. 182, 1-7
10. Avital, S. and Gromet-Elhanan, Z. (in preparation)
11. Frasch, W.D., Green, J., Caquiat, J. and Mejia, A. (1989) J. Biol. Chem. 264, 5064-5069
12. Kagawa, Y., Ohta, S. and Otawara-Hamamoto, Y. (1989) FEBS Lett. 249, 67-69

PROPERTIES OF THE BETA SUBUNIT OF THE CHLOROPLAST ATP SYNTHASE

Denise Mills and Mark L. Richter, Dept. of Biochemistry, University of Kansas, Lawrence, KS 66045 USA.

1. INTRODUCTION

The F_1 portion of the ATP synthase has three copies of the β subunit which is thought to contain the nucleotide-binding/catalytic sites of the enzyme. We recently described a procedure for isolating this important subunit from spinach chloroplast coupling factor 1 (CF$_1$) and showed that it was able to restore both ATP hydrolysis and a low rate of ATP synthesis to chromatophores of *Rhodospirillum rubrum* which lacked the native β subunit[1].

We have examined the state of aggregation of the isolated CF$_1$-β subunit in solution, together with its nucleotide-binding properties. We were unable to observe nucleotide binding to isolated β using the centrifugal column filtration technique which succesfully identified two nucleotide-binding sites on isolated β from *R. rubrum* F$_1$[2]. We were, however, able to observe binding of the nucleotide analog trinitrophenyl-ATP (TNP-ATP) to isolated chloroplast β. The results indicated the presence of one low affinity nucleotide-binding site per CF$_1$-β.

2. PROCEDURES

2.1 Isolation:

CF$_1$ was prepared from spinach. The β subunit was isolated from CF$_1$ as described elsewhere[1] and concentrated either by ammonium sulfate precipitation or by ultrafiltration. When necessary glycerol or salts were removed by centrifugal column filtration [3].

2.2 Analytical procedures:

Analytical ultracentrifugation was performed in a Beckman E-664 ultracentrifuge with Schlieren optics at 20^0C. The β subunit was concentrated in 25mM Tricine-NaOH (pH 8) with 1mM ATP.

Gel filtration was performed through a Sephadex G-200 32x2cm column at 4^0C.

Protein concentrations were estimated using the Lowry[4] and Bradford[5] methods.

2.3 Nucleotide binding:

Unbound ATP/ADP or other nucleotides were removed by passing β through Sephadex G-50 centrifuge columns. Any bound nucleotides were

M. Baltscheffsky (ed.), Current Research in Photosynthesis, Vol. III, 49–52.

released from β by the addition of TFA to 10% (v/v). Denatured protein was removed by centrifugation for 5 minutes in a Beckman airfuge. Supernatants were lyophilized and examined by HPLC. Controls contained bovine serum albumin instead of β subunit.

2.4 TNP-ATP binding:
TNP-ATP (from Molecular Probes) was purified and desalted as described elsewhere[6]. The β subunit was dialysed against 50mM Tricine-NaOH (pH 8) with 5% glycerol and concentrated with Aquacide II (Calbiochem.). The reaction mixture in a final volume of 1.5ml contained 50mM Tricine-NaOH (pH 8) with 5μM β. TNP-ATP was added in aliquots of 1ml with manual stirring at room temperature. Fluorescent measurements were recorded using a Beckman MPF-44B spectrophotometer with the excitation wavelength at 415nm and emission at 550nm.

3. RESULTS

3.1 Aggregation number:
The β subunit sedimented as a single sharp band with $S_{20,w}=$ 3.54 +/- 1.9% (not shown). Using the diffusion coefficient and partial specific volume calculated for *R.rubrum* $β^7$, a molecular weight of 45,000 was calculated which suggests that the β subunit (molecular weight 54,000) exists as a monomer in solution. This is supported by the fact that β coeluted with BSA (molecular weight 66,700) after gel filtration.

3.2 Nucleotide binding:
HPLC analysis of protein-bound nucleotides showed the absence of any nucleotides on the isolated β subunit (Figure 1). The BSA control showed less than 200 picomoles of each of AMP, ADP and ATP. This negative result is in contrast with that seen for isolated CF_1 which contains a tightly bound molecule of ADP.

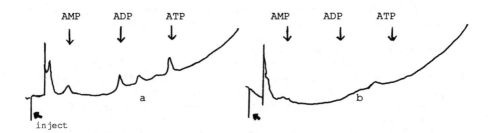

Figure 1 HPLC profile of protein-bound nucleotides. A Whatman Partisil 10 SAX anion exchange column was used. Mobile phase A: 7mM KH_2PO_4, pH 4, 7mM KCl B. 250mM $KH2PO4$, pH 5, 500mM KCl.
Gradient: 10-100% B in 30 mins. Detection: 254 nm
a: BSA control   b: β sample

3.3 TNP-ATP binding

Binding to the nucleotide analog (TNP-ATP) was detected giving an apparent K_d of 8×10^{-7}M with close to 1 mole TNP-ATP binding to 1 mole of β (Figure 2). Added ATP effectively competes for the TNP-ATP binding site (not shown).

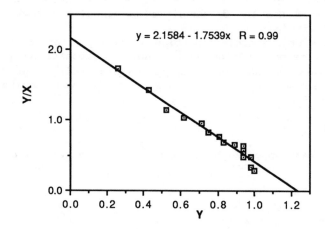

$$y = 2.1584 - 1.7539x \quad R = 0.99$$

Figure 2 Scatchard plot of TNP-ATP binding. Y= $F - F_o$/ F_{max} where F_o is the background fluorescence of TNP-ATP in buffer in the absence of protein and F is the observed fluorescence of TNP-ATP with protein fluorescence subtracted. X is the total μM concentration of TNP-ATP added.

4. DISCUSSION

Another method for isolating CF_1-β was recently described[8] using a 1M LiCl wash of thylakoid membranes to release β from the membrane-bound ATP synthase. The β apparently purified as an aggregate of three β subunits which showed two Mg^{2+}-dependent ADP binding sites per trimer, one high affinity site and one low affinity site. The aggregate also exhibited a low ATP hydrolytic activity in the presence of Mg^{2+}.

Our preparation, although reconstitutively active, does not hydrolyze ATP to an appreciable extent nor does it exhibit high affinity binding of ATP or ADP. In these respects it is very similar to the β subunit isolated from *Escherichia coli* [9] which is also reconstitutively active. In contrast, the β subunit of *R. rubrum* is unable to hydrolyze ATP but binds two molecules of nucleotides per monomer[2]. The different properties of these β preparations may be attributed to differences in the isolation procedures although they are difficult to reconcile with the known nucleotide-binding properties of the F_1 enzymes.

The ability of our isolated $CF_1-\beta$ to bind TNP-ATP in an approximately 1:1 ratio suggests that there is at least one low affinity nucleotide- binding site on this isolated subunit. A similar low affinity site was identified on isolated $CF_1-\beta$ using an HPLC method[10]. Isolated *E.coli* β subunit also contains a low affinity TNP-ATP-binding site[9].

Examination of the nucleotide-binding/catalytic properties of β subunits during reconstitution with other F_1 subunits should be a particularly interesting approach to understanding the factors governing the asymmetric distribution of nucleotide-binding sites found in native CF_1[11].

ACKNOWLEDGEMENTS

This work was supported by grants from The University of Kansas General Research Fund (#3009) and the National Science Foundation (#DMB-880548).

REFERENCES

1.   Richter, M.L., Gromet-Elhanan, Z. and McCarty R.E. (1986) J. Biol.Chem. 261, 12109-12113.
2.   Penefsky, H.S. (1979) Adv. Enzymol. 49, 223-280.
3.   Gromet-Elhanan, Z. and Khananshvili D. (1984) Biochemistry 23, 1022-1028.
4.   Lowry, O.H., Rosebrough, N.J., Farr, A.L. and Randall, R.J. (1951)J. Biol. Chem. 193, 265-275.
5.   Bradford, M.M. (1976) Anal. Biochem. 72, 248-254.
6.   Grubmeyer, C. and Penefsky, H.S. (1981) J. Biol. Chem. 256, 3718-3727.
7.   Philosoph, S., Binder, A. and Gromet-Elhanan,Z. (1977) J. Biol. Chem. 252, 8747-8752.
8.   Frasch, W.D., Green, J., Caguit, J. and Mejia, A. (1989) J. Biol.Chem. 264, 5064-5069.
9.   Rao, R., Al-Shawi, M.K. and Senior, A.E. (1988) J.Biol. Chem.263, 5569-5573.
10. Girault G., Berger G., Galmiche J-M. and Andre F. (1988) J. Biol.Chem. 263, 14690-14695.
11. Leckband, D. and Hammes, G.G. (1987) Biochemistry 26, 2306-2312.

Dissociation of Subunit III from Chloroplast ATP synthase after Modification with EITC

Enno C. Apley and Richard Wagner

Biophysik, Fachbereich Biologie/Chemie, Universität Osnabrück, 4500 Osnabrück, West Germany

Introduction

We were aiming in obtaining informations on the topological organisation of the membrane part of the chloroplast ATP synthase. For this we investigated the rotational mobility of EITC labelled CF_0CF_1, which was reconstituted into liposomes.

The rate of rotational motion can be used to deduce information on the size of the »rotating unit«, provided the dynamical friction opposing the motion is known. This we have previously achieved by measuring the rotational diffusion of EITC labelled lipid molecules in the membrane of azolectin liposomes (1).

Our results show that the CF_0 oligomer is rather unstable, since the proteolipid, after chemical modification with EITC, dissociated into the monomeric form. However, after dissociation of the proteolipid the remaining parts of the ATP synthase appeared to be still bound to the liposome membrane.

Materials and Methods

CF_0CF_1 was purified from spinach thylakoids as described in ref. (24). Labelling of CF_0CF_1 with EITC was performed after partial purification of the enzyme as described elsewhere (8). Protein was determined according to Sedmak and Grossberg (26) and stoichiometry of the bound eosin was determined spectrometrically using an extinction coefficient of $8.35 \cdot 10^4$ $M^{-1}cm^{-1}$ for the dye (2). Incorporation of the purified CF_0CF_1 into azolectin liposomes and determination of the ATP synthesis yield was followed by the luciferin/luciferase assay after an acid/base transition as described (4). The principles and instrumentation of measuring the rotational diffusion of proteins with extrinsic triplet probes under photoselection are given in detail elsewere (1,6).

Results and Discussion

Labelling and reconstitution of CF_0CF_1. Preparation of the ATP synthase complex was performed as described in detail by Fromme et al. (2). With this procedure the entire CF_0CF_1-complex was obtained as a water soluble micelle.

Figure 1, left lane, shows a SDS-PAGE gel after silverstaining of a typical CF_0CF_1 preparation. All subunits except negatively stained subunit α and subunit IV are clearly visible and no other contaminations were observed. Therefore the preparation appeared to be essentially pure. Probably due to its low staining intensity the band of subunit IV is not visible . In order to proove the structural and functional integrity of the purified ATP synthase, it was reconstituted into liposomes using the dialysis technique (4,8) and the ATP synthesis driven by an artificially imposed ΔpH across the membrane was measured (5). For different CF_0CF_1 preparations in liposomes containing ~0.3 mg protein/ml, we obtained an ATP yield between 40-50 $ATP/CF_0CF_1 \cdot s^{-1}$, which is in the same order of magnitude as observed by Schmidt and Gräber (5).

As previously described (1,6), we used eosinisothiocyanate (EITC), covalently attached to different sites in CF_0CF_1, as a triplet probe for measuring the protein rotational diffusion via absorption anisotropy. CF_0CF_1 was labelled after

M. Baltscheffsky (ed.), Current Research in Photosynthesis, Vol. III, 53–56.
© 1990 *Kluwer Academic Publishers. Printed in the Netherlands.*

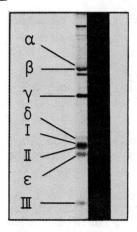

Figure 1. *Subunit distribution of the EITC accessible lysine residue in CF0CF1.*
Left lane : SDS-PAGE of purified EITC labelled CF0CF1 with a 12% separating gel run on the Pharmacia Phast system. 0.1 g CF0CF1 in 0.3 ml standardbuffer (Pharmacia) were applied. The identity of the individual bands is indicated.
Right lane : Fluorescence gel of EITC labelled CF0CF1. Labelling of the CF0CF1 detergent micelle was performed as described in (8). 8 mol EITC were bound per mol CF0CF1. SDS PAGE was carried out with a discontinous buffer system according to Schägger, H. and von Jago, G. (1987) Anal. Biochem. 166, 368-379.

solubilisation and partial purification of the enzyme. In this case, the crude CF_0CF_1 complex was labelled in the micelle and, after the labelling procedure, further purified to the final state.

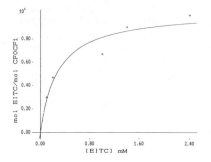

Figure 2. *Binding of EITC to CF0CF1.*
Labelling of the CF0CF1 detergent micelle and determination of the amount of bound EITC was performed as described in the »Materials and Methods« section. Each point is the average of 2 independent determinations.

Figure 2 shows the amount of EITC bound to CF_0CF_1 as a function of the incubation concentration. As obvious from this figure the binding of EITC to CF_0CF_1 followed a typical binding isotherm. Saturation of EITC binding was reached at about 10 mol EITC/mol CF_0CF_1. Interestingly, the binding of EITC to subunit III of CF_0 seems to saturate at about 10 mol EITC/mol CF_0CF_1. Considering that binding of EITC on subunit III occurs only at a single site (Lys 48), this result would indicate, that there exists 10 copies of subunit III/CF_0CF_1. The labelled CF_0CF_1 complex was subjected to SDS-gelelectrophoresis and protein bands containing bound EITC were monitored by fluorography. When CF_0CF_1 was labelled in the micelle, almost exclusively subunit III, the proteolipid, was labelled (figure 1, right lane).
The labelling of subunit III, at first sight, was a surprising result, since the hydrophobic subunit III should hardly be accessible for the EITC label from the water phase. However, under the applied conditions always and almost exclusively the proteolipid was labelled. Apparently, one part of the proteolipid in the CF_0CF_1

micelle must be easily accessible from the bulk phase. With liposomes containing CF_0CF_1 labelled in subunit III, even at a load of only 1 mol EITC/mol CF_0CF_1 ATP synthesis driven by an acid/base transition (5) was completely inhibited.
Rotational diffusion of subunit III labelled CF_0CF_1 in the bilayer membrane. The ATP synthase complex labelled in subunit III was incorporated into liposomes using the dialysis technique and the rotational diffusion was measured.

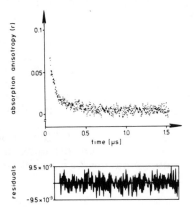

Figure 3. *Time course of the absorption anisotropy for the EITC labelled CF0CF1 reconstituted in liposomes.*
Liposomes containing subunit III labelled CF0CF1.
The sample was contained in a buffer with 10 mM Tricine-NaOH, 2.5 mM MgCl2, 0.25 mM dithiothreitol, 0.2 mM EDTA. Measurements were performed at a time resolution of 2 ns/adress at 30° C. The shown trace is the average of 100 single laser flashes.

Figure 3 shows a typical curve obtained for the decay of the absorption anisotropy. The shown measurement was performed at 30° C and the proteoliposomes were contained in aequous buffer solution ($\eta \approx 1$ mPa·s). In all measurements with subunit III labelled CF_0CF_1 in liposomes the decay of the absorption anisotropy could only be fitted by two exponentials according to equation 1 (Materials and Methods section).
As shown elsewere (7) the observed decay of the absorption anisotropy can be attributed to anisotropic rotation of the protein in the bilayer membrane. The mathematical analysis of the curve shown in figure 2 according to equation 1 yielded the following parameters : initial anisotropy $r_0 = 0.17$; $a_1 = 0.045$; $a_2 = 0.12$; $\Phi_1 = 200$ ns; $\Phi_2 = 50$ ns.
We measured the temperature dependence of the absorption decay and obtained at temperatures above 30° C always a factor of 4 for the ratio between the two rotational correlation times (see equation 1, data not shown). This factor strongly suggests that at temperatures $\geq 30°$ C, where the liposome membrane is in the liquid cristalline state, the rotational diffusion of CF_0CF_1 labelled in subunit III in fact may be regarded as restricted and uniaxial rotation about the bilayer membrane normal according to the model of Saffman and Delbrück (9). The rotational correlation time observed for uniaxial rotation of subunit III labelled CF_0CF_1 in the membrane was $\Phi = 200 \pm 20$ ns at 30° C. This rotational relaxation time for uniaxial anisotropic rotation of the labelled protein can be related to the size of the »rotating unit«
(1,6,9) : $\Phi = (k \cdot T)/(4 \cdot S_p \cdot h \cdot \eta_2)$
where S_p is the crossectional area of the protein cylinder in the membrane, h is the thickness of the membrane and η_2 the »effective viscosity« in the membrane, a quantity used to describe the dynamic friction in the membrane (9). For bilayer membranes identical in composition to the one used in the present study we have previously determined the friction in the membrane by measuring the rotation of lipid molecules (1). When the rotational diffusion of two different entities, which

»experience« the same effective friction in the membrane are related to each other by equation 5, one obtaines (1) : $\Phi_p/S_p = 2 \cdot \Phi_l/S_l$
where Φ_p and Φ_l are the rotational correlation times of the protein (Φ_p) and the lipid (Φ_l), and S_p, S_l the corresponding crossectional areas of the two entities. With the rotational correlation time of 200 ns at 30° C for subunit III labelled CF_0CF_1, the measured lipid rotation time of $\Phi_l = 20$ ns at 30° C (1) and the known crossectional area of the lipid molecules $S_l = 0.78$ nm^2 (10), one obtains $S_p \approx 3.9$ nm^2 or, since $S_p = \pi \cdot r^2$, a radius of 1.1 nm for the protein cylinder in the membrane. From this values we can exclude that we observed the rotational diffusion of the entire CF_0CF_1 complex in the liposome membrane.

The observed »rotating unit« in the membrane is probably composed of transmembrane α-helices. A single α-helix reveals a radius of r≈0.5 nm; therefore the observed »rotating unit« should contain not more than 2 transmembrane helices. From secondary structure predictions a »hairpin« like secondary structure, two transmembrane α-helices interconnected by a hydrophilic loop, has been postulated for the proteolipid (13). This proposed structure fits well with the above calculated size of the observed rotating unit.

Our results therefore strongly indicate that we observed the rotational diffusion of the monomeric proteolipid. It appears that, after reconstitution into the liposome membrane, the EITC labelled subunit III probabley due to binding of EITC at Lys 48, dissociates from the other subunits of the CF_0CF_1-complex.

Acknowledgements

Financial support by the Deutsche Forschungsgemeinschaft SFB 171/B2 is gratefully acknowledged. Skillful preparation of the figures by H. Kenneweg is very much appreciated.
We thank Prof. W. Junge for generous support.

Abbreviations

EITC : eosin-5-isothiocyanate
CF_0 : membrane part of the ATP synthase (proton channel)
CF_1 : soluble part of the ATP synthase
SDS-PAGE : sodium dodecyl sulphate polyacrylamid gel electrophoresis
Pam$_2$GroPEtn : L-α-dipalmitoylphosphatidylethanolamine

References

1. Wagner, R., Apley, E.C., Gross, A. and Flügge, U.I. (1989) Europ. J. Biochem. 182, 165-173
2. Fromme, P., Boekema, E.J. and Gräber, P. (1987) Z. Naturforsch. 42c, 1239-1244
3. Sedmak, J.J. and Grossberg, S.E. (1977) Anal. Biochem. 79, 544-552
4. Cherry, R.J., Cogoli, A., Oppliger, M., Schneider, G. and Semenza, G. (1976) Biochem. 15, 3653-3656
5. Schmidt, G. and Gräber, P. (1985) Biochim. Biophys. Acta 808, 46-51
6. Wagner, R. (1985) in Recent Advances in Biological Membrane Studies
7. Sebald, W. and Hoppe, J. (1981) Current Topics in Bioenergetics, 12, 1-64 (Packer, L., ed), Plenum Publishing Corp., New York
8. Apley, E.C. and Wagner, R. (1989) BBA, in press
9. Saffman, P.G. and Delbrück, M. (1975) Proc. Natl. Acad. Sci. USA 72, 3111-3113
10. McDaniel, R.V., McIntosh, T.J. and Simon, A. (1983) Biochem. Biophys. Acta, 97-108

IDENTIFICATION OF C-TERMINAL RESIDUES OF CF_1 δ AS PART OF
THE EPITOPE OF INHIBITING ANTIBODIES

Werner Finke and Richard J. Berzborn

Dept. of Biology, Ruhr-Universität, P.O.Box 102148,
4630 Bochum 1, F.R.Germany

SUMMARY: Antibodies, by reacting with some C-terminal residues of $CF_1\delta$, accessible and thus exposed in situ
on the thylakoid membrane, inhibit the PMS mediated cyclic photophosphorylation.

PROBLEM, EXPERIMENTAL, RESULTS and DISCUSSION:

**CF_1 δ should be accessible in situ, i.e. partially exposed
within the quaternary structure of CF_0CF_1 on the membrane**

- size (in solution) is 30 x 100 Å [1,2]
- anti δ sera agglutinated thylakoids [3]
- spinach $CF_1\delta$ contains many charged residues dispersed
  along the sequence [4]
- in homologous systems:
  - bovine OSCP and E. coli $F_1\delta$ part of "stalk" [reviews]
  - mitochondrial membrane absorbes anti OSCP [5]
  - Trypsin digests $F_1\delta$ on E. coli membrane [6]

**BUT: CF_1 δ seems inaccessible in situ, i.e. shielded
within CF_0CF_1**

- anti δ sera yield immuno precipitation rockets with
  CF_0CF_1 only after dissociation, by DOC [3]
- agglutination by anti δ sera, used earlier, was due to
  crossreaction with CF_1 β [7]
- no absorption of anti δ by δ within CF_0CF_1 [8]
- no monoclonal ab would react with δ within CF_0CF_1 [9]
- monoclonal ab 39D5, directed against $L_{162}VDMSVKK_{169}$ of δ,
  reacts only after resolution of CF_1 from CF_0 [9]
- no reconstitution of photophosphorylation of EDTA treated
  thylakoids by $CF_1(-\delta)$ and δ, if δ added last [10]
- Trypsin does not digest δ on the thylakoid membrane, as
  analyzed on SDS gels [11] and - more specifically - on
  Western immuno blots [9], i.e. all 12 lysines and 6 argi-

nines of δ, especially Arg_7, Lys_{161} and Lys_{169} are not susceptible to trypsin digestion of δ in situ.

- Aminopeptidase M does not digest δ in situ [7]
- Staphylococcus aureus protease V_8 does not digest δ in situ next to Asp_{53}, Glu_{61}, Glu_{94} and Glu_{106}, digestion sites on δ in solution [7]
- isolated δ binds to CF_0 [3,9] and reconstituted structurally [12]
- subunit δ is part of central mass within CF_1 [13]
- no Lys-spec. label on homologous E.coli $F_1\delta$ in situ [14]

However, CF_1 δ is not completely sandwiched between CF_0 and CF_1, but partially exposed, because

- monospecific anti δ serum 306 agglutinates thylakoid suspensions [7]

The exposed epitope(s) of δ seem situated underneath the barrel of the large CF_1 subunits, i.e. close to the CF_0 (stalk) subunits, because

- the agglutination is increased 10 fold by a 2nd antibody (goat anti rabbit IgG) [7]

With an antibody attached to the exposed epitope(s) CF_1 δ cannot perform its function - in photophosphorylation - any more, since

- anti δ serum 306 inhibits PMS mediated cyclic photophosphorylation [7]

Now: The inhibiting antibodies against the epitope(s), exposed in situ, can be absorbed from serum 306, separated and recovered by their affinity to thylakoids. They are positive in Western blots of thylakoids with 21 kDa δ, [8] and table 1.

Table 1: Apparent mol. weights of products of proteolytic digestion of CF_1 δ in situ, decorated in Western blots with antibodies from anti δ serum 306 (ab 306 abs. = residual antibodies after absorption of serum 306 with thylakoids; ab 306 affi. = absorbed antibodies from serum 306, separated and recovered by their affinity to thylakoids)

	ab 306 abs.	ab 306 affi.
control thylakoids	21 kDa	21 kDa
after protease V8	20 and 19 kDa	none
after protease CP-Y	20 kDa	none

Antibodies - from serum 306 - inhibit PMS mediated cyclic photophosphorylation by reacting with some C-terminal residues of δ, accessible in situ, since

- Staph. aureus protease V8 cuts δ in situ next to Glu_{173} and Glu_{179}, shown by sequencing oligopeptide Ile_{174} - Glu_{179} and by the stepwise decrease in molecular weight of δ in Western blot, [8] and table 1.
- Carboxypeptidase Y, digesting δ in situ, takes off about 5-10 residues, [8] and table 1
- in both cases: No reaction any more with the separated inhibiting antibodies (agglutination and blot, table 1)

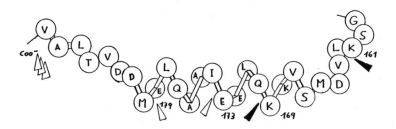

fig. 1: Scheme of amphipathic C-terminal α-helix of δ

Finally: Secondary structure calculations of spinach $CF_1\delta$ (and of homologous sequences) predict an α-helix, starting at Val_{167}. The helix and its strong amphipathic character, [8] and fig.1, is conserved in the δ-sequences of 12 species available (10 in table 2).

Table 2: Homology of the C-terminal amino acid sequence of CF_1 δ from spinach with respective sequences

		d	a	d	a	ref.
Saccharo.	ATPase5	G D K T V D L S I S T K I Q K L N K V L E D S I				[16]
Bos.pr.	OSCP	G E K Y V D M S A K T K I Q K L S R A M R Q I L				[17]
Sp.ol.	$CF_1\delta$	G S K L V D M S V K K Q L E E I A A Q L E M D D V T L A V				[4]
Syn.6301	$CF_1\delta$	G S Q V L D A S L R G Q L K R I S I S L A A				[18]
Ana.7120	$CF_1\delta$	G S Q V I D S S I R G Q L R R L S L R L S N S				[19]
Rps.bl.	$F_1\delta$	G S T M I D T S V K S K L A S L Q N A M K E V G				[20]
Rsp.ru.	$F_1\delta$	G S R M V D S S L S T K L K R L Q L A M K G V G				[20]
E.coli	$F_1\delta$	G D M V I D G S V R G R L E R L A D V L Q S				[21]
PS 3	$F_1\delta$	G N R I Y D G S V S G Q L E R I R R Q L I G				[22]
Bac.mega.	$F_1\delta$	G N R I Y D G S I S S K L E T I H R G L L A H R S				[23]

Thus: The hydrophilic face of the C-terminal α-helix of CF_1 δ comprises within the quaternary structure of CF_0CF_1 part of the surface, accessible to antibodies and proteases. The hydrophobic face of this amphipathic helix of CF_1 δ, cp. heptade in table 2, may be directed towards CF_1 subunits or towards binding structures on CF_0 subunits.

In contrast the N-terminal amphipathic α-helix of δ seems burried in the ATPsynthase complex [15].

This work has been supported by a DFG grant to RJB.

REFERENCES

1. Schmidt,U.D. and Paradies,H. (1977) B.B.R.C. 78, 1043- 1052
2. Wagner,R., Apley,E.C., Engelbrecht,S. and Junge,W. (1988) FEBS Lett. 230, 109-115
3. Roos,P. and Berzborn,R.J. (1982) in: Sec. EBEC Reports (C.N.R.S. ed.), pp. 99-100, Lyon-Villeurbanne
4. Hermans,J., Rother C., Bichler,J., Steppuhn,J. and Herrmann,R.G. (1988) Plant Mol.Biol. 10, 323-330
5. Archinard,P., Godinot,C., Comte,J. and Gautheron,D.C. (1986) Biochem. 25, 3397-3404
6. Gavilanes-Ruiz,M., Tommasino,M. and Capaldi,R.A. (1988) Biochem. 27, 603-609
7. Berzborn,R.J. and Finke,W. (1989 a) Z.Naturforsch. 44c, 153-160
8. Berzborn,R.J. and Finke,W. (1989 b) Z.Naturforsch. 44c, 480-486
9. Finke,W. (1988) Thesis, Ruhr-Universität Bochum
10. McCarty, (1987) pers. commun.
11. Moroney,J.V. and McCarty,R.E. (1982) J.Biol.Chem. 257, 5910-5914
12. Engelbrecht,S. and Junge,W. (1988) Eur.J.Biochem. 172, 213-218
13. Boekema,E.J., van Heel,M. and Gräber,P. (1988) B.B.A. 933, 356-371
14. Aggeler,R., Zhang,Y-Z. and Capaldi,R.A. (1987) Biochem. 26, 7107-7113
15. Berzborn,R.J., Finke,W., Otto,J. and Meyer,H.E. (1987) Z. Naturforsch. 42c, 1231-1238
16. Lee,M., Jones,D. and Mueller, D.M. (1988) Nucl.Acid Res. 16, 8181
17. Ovchinnikov,Y.A., Modyanov,N.N., Grinkevich,V.A., Aldanova,N.A., Trubetskaya,O.E., Nazimov,I.V., Hundal,T. and Ernster, L. (1984) FEBS Lett. 166, 19-22
18. Cozens,A.L., Walker,J.E. (1987) J.Mol.Biol. 194, 359-383
19. McCarn,D.F., Whitaker,R.A., Alam,J., Vrba,J.M. and Curtis,S.E. (1988) J.Bact. 170, 3448-3458
20. Falk,G., Hampe,A. and Walker,J.E. (1985) Biochem.J. 228, 391-407
21. Walker,J.E., Saraste,M. and Gay,N.J. (1984) B.B.A. 768, 164-200
22. Ohta,S., Yohda,M., Ishizuka,M., Hirata,H., Hamamoto,T., Otawara-Hamamoto,Y., Matsuda,K. and Kagawa,Y. (1988) B.B.A. 933, 141-155
23. Brusilow,W.S.A., Scarpetta,M.A., Hawthorne,C.A. and Clark,W.P. (1989) J.Biol.Chem. 264, 1528-1533

IDENTICAL TOPOGRAPHY OF SUBUNITS CF_0II and CF_0I IN SPINACH
CHLOROPLASTS SUGGESTS SIMILAR FUNCTION: BINDING OF CF_1

Joachim Otto and Richard J. Berzborn

Dept. of Biology, Ruhr-Universität, P.O.Box 102148
4630 Bochum 1, F.R.Germany

PROBLEMS:

1. Is CF_0II an additional subunit of the chloroplast
   ATPsynthase?
2. What is the topography of CF_0II and of CF_0I?
3. What is the function of CF_0II and of CF_0I?
4. To which subunit of other ATPases is CF_0II homologous?

STATEMENTS, SUPPORTING RESULTS and DISCUSSION:

1. 16 kDa polypeptide II is a unique subunit of CF_0CF_1.

·   Amino acid protein sequencing of 32 N-terminal residues
of polypeptide CF_0II, isolated by preparative gel electrophoresis, yielded a new sequence [1], (cp. table 1), which
shows no homology to any chloroplast polypeptide.
·   Monospecific polyclonal antisera against 16 kDa CF_0II
do not crossreact with any other thylakoid polypeptide
(Western immuno blot and ELISA [6]).

table 1:
Alignment of N-terminal amino acid sequences of CF_0 subunits I (as determined by us) and II [1]
from Spinacia oleracea and subunit b from E.coli [2] and PS3 [3] with homologous sequences
deduced from open reading frames for F_0 b and b' from Synechococcus sp. 6301 [4] and Anabaena
sp. 7120 [5].

```
CF o II    E E I E K A S L F D F N L T L P I I M A - E F L F L M F A L D - - - - K I ···
Syn b'  ··· V Q E A E G G L F D L D A T L P L - M A V Q I L V L V F L L N A V F Y K - - - - P ···
Ana b'  ··· K V A K E G G L F D L D A T L P L - M A I Q F L L L A L I L N A T L Y K - - - - P ···


E.c.b             V N L N A T I - L G Q A I A F V L F V L F C M - - - - K Y V W P P ···
PS3 b         E A A H G I S G G T I - I Y Q L L M F I I L L A L L R - - - - K F A W Q P ···


CF o I        G S F G F N T D I L A T N - L I N L S V V L P V L I F F G - - - - K G V L S D ···
Syn b   ··· S G F G L N L D L F E T N - L I N L A I I I G L L V Y A G - - - - R G F L G N ···
Ana b   ··· G G F G L N T N I L D T N - L I N L A I I I T V L F V F G - - - - R K F L G N ···
```

M. Baltscheffsky (ed.), Current Research in Photosynthesis, Vol. III, 61–64.
© 1990 *Kluwer Academic Publishers. Printed in the Netherlands.*

- Therefore CF_oII is not a degradation product of another thylakoid polypeptide.
- A sandwich-ELISA shows that CF_oII and $CF_1\beta$ are components of the same protein complex [6].

2a. CF_oII seems to be anchored in the thylakoid membrane by a hydrophobic span, like CF_oI.

- Hydropathy plot of N-terminus of CF_oII suggests a span.
- No loss of CF_oII - and of CF_oI - into supernatant upon EDTA or NaBr treatment of thylakoids is observed (Western blot of supernatant and ELISA with pellet ([6] and table 3).

2b. CF_oII is accessible to antibodies, i.e. exposed at the matrix side of thylakoids, as is CF_oI.

- PMS mediated cyclic photophosphorylation is inhibited to 25% by an antiserum against CF_oII.
- Anti CF_oII is absorbed by thylakoids, as is anti CF_oI (residual antibodies determined in ELISA [7]).

table 2:

Percent residual O.D.$_{450\ nm}$ in ELISA of antisera (anti-II; anti-I) after absorption with thylakoid membranes, EDTA-treated membranes and EDTA-treated membranes reconstituted with CF_1 (normalized to the absorption with thylakoid membranes)	membrane type 90 μg chl.	μg CF_1 added	% O.D. of anti-II	% O.D. of anti-I
	thylakoid	-	100	100
	EDTA-treated	-	66	65
	EDTA-treated	5	69	64
	EDTA-treated	15	82	71
	EDTA-treated	30	84	73
	EDTA-treated	45	87	85
	EDTA-treated	60	90	89
	EDTA-treated	75	91	94

2c. Part of the hydrophilic surface of CF_oII, at the matrix side, is shielded by CF_1, as is part of CF_oI, i.e. partially inaccessible to antibodies and not susceptible to proteolysis.

- After EDTA treatment <u>more</u> antibodies are absorbed from antisera against both subunits ([7] and table 2).
- After reconstitution with CF_1 <u>less</u> antibodies are absorbed from both antisera ([7] and table 2).
- After EDTA treatment a strong increase in susceptibility of CF_oII and of CF_oI to digestion in situ by trypsin ([6] and table 3) and Staph. aureus protease V8 [6] is observed.

3. **We suppose that the function of CF_oII, together with CF_oI, is binding of CF_1, or even in addition H^+ conduction.**

- The topography of CF_oII and CF_oI suggests this function.
- Proteolytic digestion of CF_oII (and of CF_oI) in EDTA treated membranes impaires CF_1 rebinding (ELISA of residual and rebound CF_1, table 3), correlated with the decrease in amounts of CF_oII (table 3) and of CF_oI (Western blot, [6]).
- Rebinding of CF_1 to EDTA treated thylakoids is diminished by IgG against CF_oII, or against CF_oI (ELISA of rebound CF_1, [6]).
- IgG of an anti CF_oII inhibited H^+ efflux from EDTA treated membranes and stimulated photophosphorylation by these membranes [8].

table 3:

Percent residual amount of $CF_1(\alpha)$ and $CF_o(II)$ after proteolytic treatment and subsequent reconstitution with CF_1 (normalized to amounts in untreated thylakoid membranes) After solubilisation of the different samples with Tx-100, dilution with carbonate buffer and coating to an ELISA-plate the amount of detectable antigen was determined with an anti-α- and an anti-II-serum.

membrane type	$\mu g/ml$ trypsin	$\mu g/ml$ CF_1	% $CF_1(\alpha)$	% $CF_o(II)$
thylakoid	-	-	100	100
thylakoid	3	-	70	95
thylakoid	300	-	11	54
EDTA-treated	-	-	17	105
EDTA-treated	3	-	11	23
EDTA-treated	300	-	4	4
EDTA-treated	-	22	30	96
EDTA-treated	-	133	102	97
EDTA-treated	3	22	10	27
EDTA-treated	3	133	24	29
EDTA-treated	300	22	3	6
EDTA-treated	300	133	3	5

- Our conclusion does not entirely exclude the speculation by N.Nelson [9], still cited [10], that CF_oII may function as an organizer subunit preventing the dissociation of the multiple copies of CF_oIII.

4. Both CF_oII and CF_oI show sequence homologies to F_ob.

- The aligned N-terminal residues of CF_oII and CF_oI, as determined by automated Edman degradation by us [1,6], show that CF_oII is homologous to cyanobacterial F_ob' (13 identities and additional conservative replacements), and CF_oI to cyanobacterial F_ob (15 and 16 identities and additional conservative replacements, cp. table 1).
- The homology of CF_oII to cyanobacterial F_ob and CF_oI, and the homology of CF_oI to cyanobacterial F_ob' and to CF_oII is about 15% each (cp. table 1).
- Both CF_oII and CF_oI show about 16% homology to E. coli subunit F_ob (cp. table 1).

CONCLUSION and SPECULATIONS:

- Both CF_oII and CF_oI of photosynthetic ATPsynthases are homologous in <u>structure and function</u> to F_ob of ATPases in heterotrophic organisms. The gen encoding for subunit b was dublicated during evolution of cyanobacteria to yield the open reading frames b and b' [11]. We concluded [7] that the cyanobacterial subunit b has developed into CF_oI and b' into CF_oII, to optimize further the protein interactions within CF_oCF_1. This diversification may also facilitate the regulation of enzymatic activities of the photosynthetic CF_oCF_1 complexes.

This work has been supported by a DFG grant to RJB.

REFERENCES:

1. Berzborn,R.J., Otto,J., Finke,W., Meyer,H.E. and Block,J.(1987) Biol. Chem. Hoppe-Seyler 36, 351-352
2. Walker,J.E., Saraste,M. and Gay,N.J.(1984) Biochim. Biophys. Acta 768, 164-200
3. Ohta,S., Yohda,M., Ishizuka,M., Hirata,H., Hamamoto,T., Otawara-Hamamoto,Y., Matsuda,K. and Kagawa,Y.(1988) Biochim. Biophys. Acta 933, 141-155
4. Cozens,A.L. and Walker,J.E.(1987) J. Mol. Biol. 194, 359-383
5. McCarn,D.F., Whitaker,R.A., Alam,J., Vrba,J.M. & Curtis,S.E.(1988) J. Bact. 170, 3448-3458
6. Otto,J.(1989), Thesis, Ruhr-Universität Bochum
7. Otto,J. and Berzborn,R.J.(1989) FEBS Lett. 250, 625-628
8. Klein-Hitpaß,L. and Berzborn,R.J.(1984) in: Adv. in Photosynthesis Res. (C.Sybesma,ed.) Vol. II, p. 563-566, Martinus Nijhoff/Dr.W.Junk Publ., The Hague
9. Nelson,N., Nelson,H. and Schatz,G.(1980) Proc. Natl. Acad. Sci. USA 77, 1361-1364
10. Hudson,G.S. and Mason,J.G.(1988) Photosynth. Res. 18, 205-222
11. Curtis,S.E. (1988)Photosynth. Res. 18, 223-244

STUDY OF THE SIMULTANEOUS BINDING OF ADP AND ATP ON COUPLING FACTOR
CF1 BY A MODIFICATION OF THE HUMMEL AND DREYER METHOD

G. BERGER, G. GIRAULT and J.-M. GALMICHE. Service de Biophysique,
Département de Biologie, CEN Saclay 91191 Gif-sur Yvette Cedex, France

1. INTRODUCTION

The study of the binding of a ligand on a macromolecule is carried
out by different methods which fall into two categories : those for
which the bound ligand is measured in presence of the free ligand
and those which involve previous separation of the two forms.

In the latter case, separation can be achieved by different means
(centrifugation, filtration, size exclusion chromatography, etc...)
and it is assumed that the equilibrium state is not modified during
the separation step. This condition is not necessarily fullfilled,
especially when the dissociation constant is sufficiently high.
Separation techniques must then be extremely rapid in the case of
loosely bound complexes.

The methods which do not require separation are not submitted
to this constraint. They include physical methods such as fluorescence
emission (1,2), ultraviolet absorption (3), or circular dichroism
(4), which have been used in binding studies with ATPases. However
these methods are often difficult to relate the signal amplitude with
the fraction of bound ligand. Another method which is theoretically
suitable in every situation, particularly for low affinity systems,
is equilibrium dialysis.

In this work, we have used the chromatographic method of Hummel
and Dreyer (5) and modified it in order to study the simultaneous
binding of ADP and ATP on coupling factor CF1. In the original method,
a known quantity q of macromolecule is injected on a gel filtration
column which is preequilibrated with a fixed concentration (A) of
ligand.

In the case of reversible binding of the ligand with n_i
independent sites of class i, of respective binding affinity
constants K_i, the quantity of bound ligand is :

$$q \sum_{i=1}^{i=m} \frac{n_i K_i (A)}{1 + K_i (A)}$$ where m is the number of site classes (6).

This quantity is withdrawn from the solvent and migrates with
the macromolecule since the size of the complex is not significantly
different from that of the macromolecule. There is then a local
decrease of the ligand concentration of the solvent which migrates
with the same rate as the ligand. It can be detected at the column
outlet as a negative peak in the ligand concentration.

Hummel and Dreyer have proposed an internal calibration (5),

M. Baltscheffsky (ed.), Current Research in Photosynthesis, Vol. III, 65–68.
© 1990 Kluwer Academic Publishers. Printed in the Netherlands.

based on the measurement of the ligand peak : the same quantity of macromolecule is injected together with increasing quantities of ligand. The size of the negative peak decreases progressively and eventually it becomes positive. Its surface varies linearly with the excess of injected ligand over the quantity contained in the same volume of eluent. The intersection with the x axis occurs when the bound ligand quantity exactly compensates what has been added to the solvent. The advantage of the method is that the complex does not dissociate during chromatography, even if it lasts a long time and if the affinity constant is low, since the complex is always in equilibrium with the free ligand.

In a precedent work (7) we have applied it to the fixation of ADP and ATP on chloroplast coupling factor CF1 and on some of its subunits. This protein is a part of a proton translocating multisubunit enzyme found in photosynthetic membranes and is able to hydrolyse and synthesize ATP. We have shown by this method that CF1 possesses six binding sites : two high affinity sites for ADP or ATP (K_D=1-5 10^{-6}μM) in addition to one site where endogenous not exchangeable ADP is bound, and three low affinity sites binding ADP or ATP with a dissociation constant of 15-20 10^{-6}μM, responsible for the catalytic activity.

In the original method, the separation between the free ligand and the complex is based on the difference of size. When there is simultaneous fixation of two ligands of similar molecular weights, separation by gel filtration is difficult or impossible. The respective concentrations of each ligand can be determined if they have different optical characteristics or if one of them is radioactive. In the particular (but frequent) case of an ADP-ATP mixture, the situation is unfavourable : same optical spectra, similar sizes. In order to avoid important levels of radioactivity, we have adapted the Hummel and Dreyer method by using anion exchange separation of the protein and of the two nucleotides.

2. MATERIALS AND METHODS

Coupling factor is extracted from spinach chloroplast by sucrose-chloroform treatment, then adsorbed on a batch of DEAE cellulose (Whatman DE 52) (8) and eluted by 0.4M NaCl. CF1 is further purified by HPLC on a Protein Pak 5 PW Waters column, eluted with ammonium sulfate gradient in 20 mM Tris pH 8 (9). For storage, CF1 is precipitated with 50% saturation ammonium sulfate. Before use, it is dialysed over night against adequate buffer.

1 to 2 moles ADP/mole of CF1 are firmly bound and resist to ammonium sulfate precipitation and dialysis. They are released by acidic treatment (0.5 N HCl) which precipitates the protein, separated, after neutralisation, by HPLC on an anionic TSK DEAE 2SW column, with 70 mM PO_4H_2K and 300 mM NaCl as eluent, and measured by absorption at 260 nm.

In addition to endogenous ADP, nucleotide binding to CF1 is measured according to Hummel and Dreyer, with a gel filtration TSK SW 2000 (30 cm x 0.75 cm) column, and in the modified method, with an anion exchange TSK DEAE 2SW (25 cm x 0.46 cm) column. Eluents are ADP or ATP solutions, from 0.5 to 10 10^{-5}M in 0.075M Tris sulfate pH 8.5, 1.10^{-3}M MgCl$_2$. A constant volume (50 μl) containing 1 to 2 nmoles of CF1 and variable quantities of ADP or ATP is injected on the column. Nucleotide concentration of the eluent is recorded by absorption spectrophotometry at 260 nm.

3. RESULTS AND DISCUSSION

3.1. Comparison of the gel filtration and the anion exchange methods

The binding of ADP alone is quite identical when measured by the gel filtration method or the anion exchange separation (fig.1). The total number of sites (respectively 6.04 and 5.87) and the dissociation constant of low affinity sites (45 and 52 μM) are similar in both cases (fig.2). That means that the binding of CF1 on the DEAE column does not perturb the nucleotide fixation on CF1.

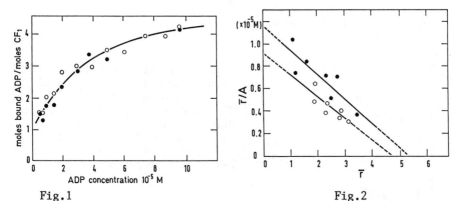

Fig.1   Fig.2

Fig.1 : ADP binding on CF1 in function of free ADP concentration, measured by gel filtration (●) or by anion exchange separation (○). The content of CF1 in endogenous ADP has been included.

Fig.2 : Scatchard plots of ADP binding on CF1 obtained by gel filtration (●) or by anion exchange chromatography (○). r̄=number of moles of ADP bound per mole of CF1, A=free ligand molar concentration. The dissociation constants for low affinity sites, measured by the two methods are respectively 45 and 52 μMoles, and the total number of sites are 6.04 (5.3, extrapolated from the Scatchard plot + 0.74, endogenous ADP) and 5.87 (4.72 + 1.15).

The same comparison between gel filtration and anion exchange has been performed with ATP. Scattering of the data precludes a precise determination of the dissociation constant but it is clear that it is greater than that corresponding to ADP (∿125 μM).

3.2. Measurement by anion exchange chromatography of simultaneous ADP and ATP binding

When the eluent contains a mixture of ADP and ATP (here in approximately equal concentrations) the injection of CF1 alone leads to the observation of two negative peaks. This is

interpreted as the simultaneous binding of both nucleotides.
The extent of binding of each nucleotide is measured by adding
known amounts of one of them. One negative peak decreases and
eventually becomes positive. It is null when the bound quantity
is equal to the excess of injected nucleotide over that of the
same volume of solvent.
The average numbers of bound ADP and ATP per molecule of CF1
have been determined as a function of free nucleotides
concentrations. Fig.3 shows that the increase of ADP binding
is equal or slightly greater than that of ATP. This indicates
that the affinity of CF1 for both nucleotides is nearly the same,
up to a total occupancy greater than four sites. However, the
endogenous ADP which is initially bound to CF1 does not exchange
with ATP, so that the total amount of bound nucleotides includes
more ADP than ATP.

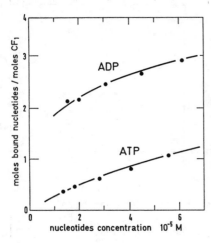

Fig.3 : Simultaneous ADP and ATP
binding on CF1, in function of
free nucleotide concentration.
The contents of CF1 in endogenous
ADP (1.88 mole/mole) and traces
of endogenous ATP (0.19 mole/mole)
have been included. Injected
CF1 : 1.55 nmole in 50µl.

REFERENCES
1 Girault, G. , Galmiche, J.M. (1978) FEBS Letters 95, 135–139.
2 Girault, G. , Galmiche, J.M. (1977) Eur. J. Biochem. 77, 501–510.
3 Hisabori, T. , Yoshida, M. , Sakurai, H. (1986) J. Biochem.
  100, 663–670.
4 Girault, G. , Galmiche, J.M. , Michel Villaz, M. , Thiery, J.
  (1973) Eur. J. Biochem. 38, 473–478.
5 Hummel, J.P. , Dreyer, W.J. (1962) Biochim. Biophys. Acta
  63, 530–532.
6 Scatchard, G. (1949) Ann. N. Y. Acad. Sci. 51, 660–672.
7 Girault, G. , Berger, G. , Galmiche, J.M. , André, F. (1988)
  J. Biol. Chem. 263, 14690–14695.
8 Binder, A. , Jagendorf, A. , Ngo, E. (1958) J. Biol. Chem.
  253, 3094–3100.
9 Berger, G. , Girault, G. , André, F. ,Galmiche, J.M. (1987)
  J. Liquid Chrom. 10, 1507–1517.

pH-DEPENDENT CHANGES IN ATP AND ADP AFFINITY FOR THE TIGHT NUCLEOTIDE-
-BINDING SITE OF THE CHLOROPLAST COUPLING FACTOR CF_1

A.N.MALYAN, O.I.VITSEVA, Inst. of Soil Science and Photosynthesis,
Acad.Sci.USSR, 142292 Pushchino, Moscow Region, USSR

1. INTRODUCTION
      The ATPase complex of chloroplasts (H^+-ATPase, ATP-synthase) carries
out synthesis (hydrolysis) of ATP coupled with transmembrane transport
of hydrogen ions. This complex consists of a hydrophylic catalytic part
called coupling factor CF_1, and a hydrophobic part, CF_0, the function
of which is to translocate protons towards CF_1. CF_1 can bind as many as
six nucleotide molecules /1/. After CF_1 precipitation by ammonium sulfate with subsequent gel filtration, the enzyme retains about 1 mol of
tightly bound nucleotides consisting mainly of ADP /2/.
      Recently, data on probable direct participation of the tight ADP-
binding site in the catalysis of ATP-synthase reaction have been reported /3/. To approach investigation of properties of this site, we studied
kinetics of exchange of nucleotides bound to it as well as pH effect on
its specificity for ADP and ATP.

2. MATERIALS AND METHODS
      CF_1 isolation from spinach leaves and its purification were perform-
ed according to /4/. The protein concentration was determined according
to Bradford /5/. After CF_1 had been re-precipitated in 2M $(NH_4)_2SO_4$ solution and depleted of loosely bound nucleotides by gel filtration one
mol of it contained 0.9 ± 0.1 mol of ADP and less than 0.05 mol of ATP,
as followed from the luciferin-luciferase assay. The enzyme was incubated in the medium containing 20 mM Tris-MES-acetate, 50 mM KCl, 1 mM
EDTA, as well as $[^{14}C]$ ADP and $[^{14}C]$ or $[^{32}P]$ ATP. To determine the
quantity of tightly bound nucleotides, 0.2 ml aliquot was applied to a
Sephadex G-50 column (superfine, 0.9x4.0 cm). The protein was eluted
with the same medium, except for ADP and ATP. After 2 min incubation
at 100°, the eluate, 20 to 60 mm^3, was separated on a chromatographic
plate (Kieselgel 60 F_{254}, Merck). Nucleotide-containing sections were
excized, placed in scintillation liquid, and their radioactivity was
determined. When determining the total content of labeled (free+bound)
nucleotides we excluded gel filtration. The quantity of free nucleotides was calculated as a difference between total and tightly bound
$[^{14}C]$ AD(T)P.

M. Baltscheffsky (ed.), Current Research in Photosynthesis, Vol. III, 69–72.
© 1990 *Kluwer Academic Publishers. Printed in the Netherlands.*

3. RESULTS AND DISCUSSION

A possibility, in principle, of exchange between free nucleotides and those tightly bound to isolated CF_1 was described in a number of publications /2,6/. When choosing experimental conditions we took into account data reported by /6/ according to which Mg^{2+} exclusion from the medium resulted in a more rapid equilibration of free and bound nucleotides and in a lower extent of ATP conversion.

As shown in Fig.1a, at pH 8.0, it takes less than 10 min of incubation to attain half-maximal inclusion of radioactive nucleotides into CF_1, and this corresponds to an exchange rate of about $10^{-4}s^{-1}$. At pH 6.0, the exchange is more rapid. During 2 h incubation the hydrolysis rate decreases from 2.2×10^{-5} s^{-1} to 6.5×10^{-7} s^{-1} (at pH 6.0, it is still lower) and becomes less than 0.005 of the exchange rate (Fig.1b). The obtained data allow to conclude that with an incubation period of 2 hours or longer, the distribution of nucleotides between the water phase and the enzyme is typical for the equilibrium state.

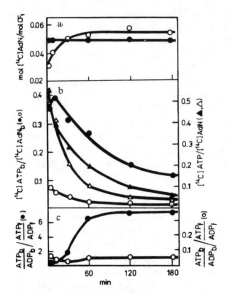

FIG. 1   Kinetics of nucleotide exchange and ATP hydrolysis at pH 6.0 ($\bullet,\blacktriangle$) and pH 8.0 ($\circ,\triangle$).
A. Inclusion of $[^{14}C]$ AdN into tightly bound nucleotides.
B. A change in the $[^{14}C]$ ATP content in tightly bound nucleotides ($\bullet,\circ$) and in the reaction medium (including tightly bound uncleotides) ($\blacktriangle,\triangle$).
C. Distribution of ATP and ADP between free and tightly bound nucleotides. 1.6 to 2.1 uM CF_1 was incubated with 0.05 uM $[^{14}C]$ ADP and 0.08 uM $[^{14}C]$ATP, 20 mM Tris-MES acetate, 50 mM KCl, and 1 mM EDTA at pH 6.0 ($\bullet$) or pH 8.0 ($\circ$).

It must be noted that throughout incubation, in tightly bound nucleotides, the $[^{14}C]$ ATP/$[^{14}C]$ADP ratio is a few times higher at pH 6.0 as compared to pH 8.0. To find whether this difference results from pH-dependent changes in the enzyme affinity for ADP and ATP or from different extents of ATP conversion, we used the parameter:

$$\frac{[^{14}C]ATP_{bound}}{[^{14}C]ADP_{bound}} \Big/ \frac{[^{14}C]ATP_{free}}{[^{14}C]ADP_{free}} = R.$$

It is easy to show that under equilibrium conditions $R = K_d^{(ADP)}/K_d^{(ATP)}$.

As follows from Fig.1c, at pH 6.0, tightly bound nucleotides get gradually enriched with ^{14}C ATP, and by the end of the experiment, the $[^{14}C]ATP_b/[^{14}C]ADP_f$ ratio attains a level which is 7.5 times higher than that in the water phase. At pH 8.0, the $[^{14}C]$ ATP content in tightly bound nucleotides reaches a value of more than 20 times lower as compared with free nucleotides. The calculated values of dissociation constants are: at pH 6.0, $K_d(ATP)=0.2$ uM, $K_d(ADP)=1.5$ uM, at pH 8.0, $K_d(ATP)=8.4$ uM, $K_d(ADP)=0.4$ uM. It follows from comparison of these constants that pH varying from 8.0 to 6.0 causes a 150-fold rise in ATP affinity for the enzyme as compared with the ADP affinity. The shape of a curve plotted in Fig.2 allows to believe that at lower pH values the ATP affinity for the enzyme will be still higher. However, denaturation of the enzyme at such pH values makes the experimental verification difficult.

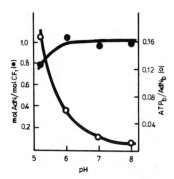

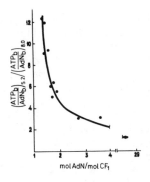

FIG. 2 Dependence of the tightly bound ATP content (1) and the total tightly bound nucleotides (2) on pH of the incubation medium. The ratio between ATP+ADP (free+ +bound) and CF_1 is equal to 1.3. incubation time is 3 h.

FIG. 3 pH-effect on ATP fraction in tightly bound nucleotides as dependent on the ratio between nucleotides (free+bound) and CF_1. 3.3 to 5.2 uM CF_1 was incubated for 3 h in the incubation medium containing $[^{14}C]ADP$ and $[^{32}P]ATP$, at pH 5.2 or pH 8.0.

In the above experiments the total amount of nucleotides per mol of the enzyme did not exceed 1.3. Within the pH range 6.0-8.0, the content of tightly bound (labeled+unlabeled) nucleotides was about 1 mol/mol of CF_1 (Fig.2). At pH below 6.0, the content decreased and the medium became slightly turbid due to partial denaturation of the enzyme. When the AdN/CF_1 ratio exceeds 1, the experimental results (Fig.3) show that the pH effect on the ATP content in tightly bound nucleotides decreases. Although the obtained data do not allow an unambiguous interpretation of the decrease, it is still very likely that, as a result of interaction of two nucleotide-binding sites, an increase in affinity of one of them for ATP can be accompanied by a higher affinity of the other for ADP. With AdN/CF_1 approaching 1, the second site remains vacant, and the obtained relationship reflects properties of only one nucleotide-binding site.

A sharp growth in affinity of the studied site for ATP at decreasing pH cannot be explained by different extents of nucleotide protonation because as follows from published data /7/ the difference between their pK$\acute{s}$ does not exceed 0.3 unit. The character of pH-dependence of the tightly bound ATP suggests that the growing affinity for ATP is caused by protonation of specific acid-base groups of the enzyme with pK $\leqslant$ 5.7 which affect the structure of the nucleotide-binding site.

The described above properties of the tight nucleotide-binding site are of particular interest when considered together with data on its ability to catalyze hydrolysis (Fig.1b) and synthesis /3,8/ of ATP. A probable mechanism of ATP synthesis including interchanging affinities of the enzyme catalytic site for ADP and ATP coupled with protonation--deprotonation of specific acid-base groups, has been proposed earlier /9/.

4. REFERENCES
1. Xue, Z., Zhou, J.M., Miller, C.G., Boyer, P.D. (1987) FEBS Lett. 223, 391-394
2. Carlier, M.-F. and Hammes, G.G. (1979) Biochemistry 18, 3446-3451
3. Feldman, R.I. and Sigman, D.S. (1982) J.Biol.Chem. 257, 1676-1683
4. Binder, A., Jagendorf, A. and Ngo, E. (1978) J.Biol.Chem. 253, 3094-3100
5. Bradford, M.M. (1976) Anal. Biochem. 72, 248-254
6. Bruist, M.F. and Hammes G.G. (1981) Biochemistry 20, 6298-6305
7. Rosing, J. and Slater, E.C. (1972) Biochim. Biophys. Acta 267, 275-290
8. Wu, D. and Boyer, P.D. (1987) Biochemistry 25, 3390-3396
9. Malyan, A.N. Dokl. Akad. Nauk SSSR (Russ.) (1986) 291, 1015-1018

PROPERTIES OF THE NUCLEOTIDE–BINDING SITES ON ISOLATED CF$_1$

Hidehiro Sakurai[1], Tetsuya Hosoda[1], and Toru Hisabori[2]

Dept. Biol., Sch. Educ., Waseda Univ., Nishiwaseda, Shinjuku, Tokyo 169[1], and Dept. Biol., Yokohama City Univ., Kanazawa-ku, Yokohama 236[2], Japan

1. INTRODUCTION

Isolated CF$_1$ has about 6 adenine nucleotide (AdN) binding sites. Feldman and Sigman (1) reported that externally added ADP was not a substrate for CF$_1$–bound ATP formation. We have found that some organic solvents (methanol, ethanol, acetone, and propanediols, but not dimethylsulfoxide nor glycerol) greatly enhanced CF$_1$–bound ATP formation. In the presence of methanol, externally added ADP was required for the enhanced ATP formation (2). We will report here that different results on the ADP requirement originate in part from the differences in bound AdN content of CF$_1$. Under appropriate conditions, IDP and GDP can be substrates for CF$_1$– bound nucleoside triphosphates (NTP) formation. The roles of the nucleotide (Nd)–binding sites will be discussed.

2. MATERIALS AND METHODS

Nd–depleted CF$_1$: The precipitate of CF$_1$ recovered from 50% saturated ammonium sulfate was dissolved in 10 mM Tricine (pH 8.0). The CF$_1$ solution was passed twice through Sephadex G–50 centrifuge columns equilibrated with 50 mM Tris–maleate–5 mM phosphate–5 mM pyrophosphate–1 mM EDTA (pH 7.0) and finally one equilibrated with 10 mM Tricine (pH 8.0) allowing more than 20 min between each centrifugation. The final preparation contained 0.5–0.9 AdN/CF$_1$. Nd–filled CF$_1$: CF$_1$ solution in 10 mM Tricine was passed twice through centrifuge collumns equilibrated with 10 mM Tricine (pH 8.0) allowing 20 min between centrifugation steps. The final preparation contained 1.0–1.2 AdN/CF$_1$. Preparation of CF$_1$ (2) and ATP determination (3) were as described.

3. RESULTS AND DISCUSSION

Fig. 1 shows that not only bound ADP but also externally added IDP were phosphorylated by [^{32}P]–Pi in Nd–depleted CF$_1$.

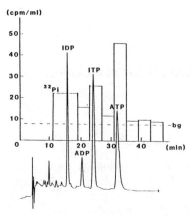

Fig. 1 [^{32}P]–ITP and –ADP formation from externally added IDP and bound ADP. CF$_1$ was incubated at 25°C with 100 μM IDP, 20 mM [^{32}P]–Pi, 50 mM MES–KOH (pH 6.0), 2 mM MgCl$_2$, 2.5 μM A$_2$P$_5$ and 30% (v/v) methanol. After 20 min, the reaction was quenched by 3% perchloric acid. Nds were analyzed by HPLC (Toso, DEAE–SW, Tokyo). Lower part: A260. Upper part: ^{32}P.

Under appropriate conditions, up to 0.09 mol ITP/mol CF$_1$ was formed. GDP also was the substrate, but CDP and UDP were not (to be published). These Nd specificities agree well with those in photophosphorylation by chloroplasts (4) and in ATP hydrolysis by isolated CF$_1$(5). Feldman and Sigman (1) reported that externally added ADP was not a substrate for CF$_1$–bound ATP formation. On the other hand, we found that the NTP formation was greatly enhanced by externally added ADP (2) as well as by IDP (Fig. 1). We later realized that these discrepancies arise from the difference in quantities of bound AdN in CF$_1$ preparations. In one experiment with Nd–depleted CF$_1$, about 45% of the total ATP formed came from externally added [^{14}C]–ADP. In Nd–filled CF$_1$ (AdN/CF$_1$=1.1) also, externally added ADP greatly enhanced ATP formation in 30% methanol (Table 1). However, [^{14}C]–ATP accounted for only 15–20% of the total ATP formed. Although a prolonged reaction time from 1 min to 10 min increased the total amount of ATP to 3–fold, the percentage of the labeled ATP was not increased. It should also be noticed that although the CF$_1$ contained more than 1 AdN, incorporation of [^{14}C]–ADP into ATP occurred to an insignificant extent. The reason for this is not clear at the moment.

Table 1 ATP formation from bound ADP and added [^{14}C]–ADP

[^{14}C]–ADP added (μM)	Reaction time (min)	ATP formed (mol/mol CF$_1$) total ATP	[^{14}C]–ATP
0	1	0.05	
	10	0.08	
2	1	0.08	0.016
	10	0.24	0.036

The reaction mixture contained Nd–filled CF$_1$, 25 mM MES–KOH (pH 6.0), 2 mM MgCl$_2$, 2.5 μM A$_2$P$_5$, 40 mM phosphate, 30% (v/v) methanol and [^{14}C]–ADP as indicated.

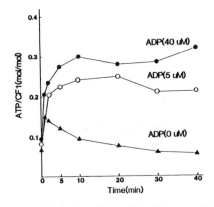

Fig. 2 Time course of ATP formation by Nd-depleted CF_1 in methanol

The reaction mixture contained 50 mM MES-KOH (pH 6), 20 mM Pi, 2 mM $MgCl_2$, 1 μM A_2P_5, 30% (v/v) methanol, Nd-depleted-CF_1 and ADP as indicated.

In studying the effects of methanol on the bound ATP formation, we found that methanol has denaturing effects in addition to enhancing effects on Nd-depleted CF_1 (Fig. 2). When no ADP was added, the ATP formed was the highest at 1 min after the beginning of the reaction and the level was steadily decreased thereafter to a lower-than-the-original (time zero) level. As 5 μM ADP efficiently protected CF_1 against the denaturation, the affinity of ADP for the binding site committed to this protection should be very high as reported in (3). The maximal ATP formation at 5 μM ADP was more than 80% of that at 40 μM ADP.From equilibrium dialysis, binding analyses and UV difference spectroscopy, Hisabori et al (3,6) found that CF_1 has about 6 Nd-binding sites: Site A, a hardly dissociable site at which no exchange of Nd was detectable in the presence of $Mg2^+$ even after 12h's incubation; Site B,C, exchangeable and high-affinity sites, to which not only ADP but also IDP, GDP, CDP and UDP can bind, and binding of these Nds induced difference absorption spectrum characteristic to each of them (7) (Fig. 3); several (probably three) low affinity sites, whose functions are unknown (Fig.4). We first thought that Site A is not a catalytic one, because even

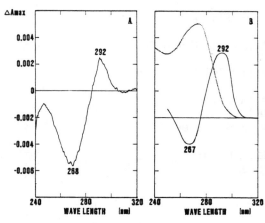

Fig. 3 Difference spectrum induced by binding of CDP to CF_1

Left: Difference spectrum obtained by mixing 3 μM CF_1 (AdN/CF_1=1.2) with 8μM CDP as in (3). Right: Spectrum of CDP itself and the difference spectrum obtained by shifting the former by 10 nm to a longer wavelength.

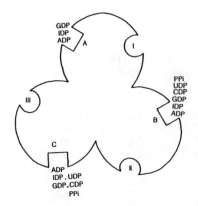

Fig. 4 A model of AdN binding sites on isolated CF_1

Site A: tightly binding and catalytic site
Site B,C: high–affnity non–catalytic sites, binding of Nds induces difference UV spectra characteristic to the respective Nds.

in the presence of 20% methanol which enhances ATPase of isolated CF_1, almost no exchange of Nd at site A was detectable (3). However, since Site A was shown to be directly involved in the bound NTP formation and its Nd spcificity was the same with that of the catalytic reactions, we now conclude that Site A is the catalytic site. The slow exchange of Nd at this site may be somehow related to the hysteretic behaviours of CF_1 (8). Based on the binding change hypothesis, Zhou et al (9) proposed that the high affinity sites (presumably Site B and C) are committed to catalytic turnover. This proposal is not acceptable, because the exchange rate of Nd at these sites are rather low ($t_{1/2}$ 30 s), and CDP, UDP and PPi which are not substrates of CF_1 can bind and interfer with the binding of ADP to these sites (3,6,7).

REFERENCES
1 Feldman, R.I. and Sigman, D.S. (1982) J. Biol. Chem.
   257, 1676–1683.
2 Sakurai, H. and Hisabori, T. (1987) in Progress in
   Photosynthesis Research III (Biggins, J., ed.) pp.13–16.
3 Hisabori, T. and Sakurai, H. (1985) Plant Cell Physiol.
   26, 505–514.
4 Krall, A.R. and Purvis, M.R. (1961) Arch. Biochem.
   Biophys. 94, 14–19.
5 Vambutas, V.K. and Racker, E. (1965) J. Biol. Chem. 240,
   2660–2667.
6 Hisabori, T. and Sakurai, H. (1984) Plant Cell Physiol.
   25, 483–493.
7 Chiba, T., Suzuki, H., Hisabori, T. and Sakurai, H.
   (1981) Plant Cell Physiol. 22, 551–560.
8 Feldman, R.I. and Boyer, P.D. (1985) J. Biol. Chem. 260,
   13088–13094.
9 Zhou, J.M., Xue, Z.X., Du, Z.Y., Melese, T. and Boyer,
   P.D. (1988) Biochemistry 27, 5129–5135.

CHARACTERIZATION OF NUCLEOTIDE BINDING SITES ON ISOLATED CHLOROPLAST
ATPase BY MODIFICATION WITH 7-CHLORO-4-NITRO-BENZOFURAZAN

S. Bickel-Sandkötter and P. Strümper, Institut für Biochemie
der Pflanzen, Heinrich-Heine-Universität Düsseldorf,
Universitätsstraße 1, D-4000 Düsseldorf, FRG

1. INTRODUCTION

The nucleotide binding sites on CF_1 have been widely studied. Catalytic
sites as well as "tight" binding sites are found to be located on the
β-subunits of CF_1 or between α- and β-subunits (1). Binding of ADP (ATP)
involves two recognition areas: One on the phosphate chain (2) and the
other one on the base moiety, which includes the C^2, N^1, C^6-region of
the base (3). Essential residues like the aminogroup of lysine (4) or
arginine take part in recognition of the negatively charged P_α of the
phosphate chain. The hydroxyl residue of tyrosine most probably forms an
H-bridge to the base N^1.

The F_1-ATPases from a variety of sources are inactivated by the tyrosyl
group-directed reagent NBD-Cl, which forms a Meisenheimer complex on C^4
with the tyrosyl oxygen atom (5). Modification of a single tyrosin residue per F_1 with NBD-Cl is sufficient to inactivate the enzyme completely.
For MF_1, the labeled tyrosine was determined as β-Tyr-311 (6), the one
identified to be labeled during photoinactivation of MF_1 with 8-azido
ATP. The homologous tyrosine in CF_1 is neither the one proposed to belong
to the non-catalytic binding site, which was identified by covalently bound
2-azido ATP, nor the one proposed to belong to the catalytic site (identified by covalently bound 2-azido ADP derived from 2-azido ATP). Our
results, however, indicate an important role of the tyrosine modified by
NBD-Cl, in the catalytic process, which may be functional or structural.

2. EXPERIMENTAL

Chloroplast-F_1 was isolated and stored by reported methods. Before use,
CF_1 was desalted in Tris/EDTA pH 7.5. After addition of NBD-Cl at the
indicated concentrations, the reaction was followed spectrophotometrically. The reaction with NBD-Cl was terminated by precipitation with
amonium sulphate. After centrifugation, the redissolved protein was
passed through a Penefsky column and analyzed spectrophotometrically.
The amount of bound NBD was calculated using the extinction coefficient
of 11600 M^{-1} cm^{-1} (385 nm) (7). Alternatively the loss of activity with
time was measured by assaing trypsin-activated Ca-ATPase. ATPase-activi-
ty was measured in a medium containing 20 mM Tris pH 8, 5 mM $CaCl_2$,
5 mM ^{32}P-labeled ATP and 10 µg modified CF_1.

M. Baltscheffsky (ed.), Current Research in Photosynthesis, Vol. III, 77–80.
© 1990 *Kluwer Academic Publishers. Printed in the Netherlands.*

3. RESULTS AND DISCUSSION

Addition of NBD-Cl to isolated CF_1 at pH 7.5 leads to time-dependent in-activation of CF_1. This process is accompanied by formation of a new chromophore with an absorbance maximum at 385 nm which belongs to a tyrosine-NBD adduct (7). In Fig. 1 an experiment is shown, in which bin-ding of NBD (increase in absorbance at 385 nm) and inactivation of CF_1 (inhibition of ATP-hydrolysis) have been measured simultaneously. The slopes are nearly identical, the reaction was completed after about 30 minutes.

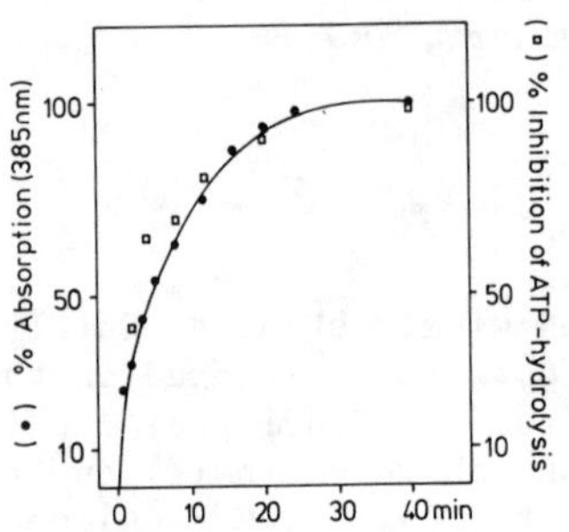

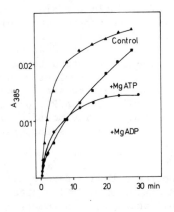

FIGURE 1. Time-course of modification of CF_1 at pH 7.5 and simultaneously measured inhibition of Ca-ATPase acti-vity. 1.5 μM CF_1 was incubated with 0.4 mM NBD-Cl. At various times, aliquots of the mixture were taken for determination of ATPase activity. 100% activity: 220 μmol $^{32}P_i$/mg protein·h.

Modification at pH 7.5 as a function of time is biphasic, showing an initial rapid and a slow kinetic component (Fig. 2).

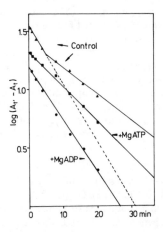

FIGURE 2. Time course of modification of CF_1 at pH 7.5 in the absence and presence of 2 mM ATP (ADP), 5 mM $MgCl_2$, and 10 mM phosphate. 1.4 μM CF_1 was incubated with 0.4 mM NBD-Cl.
FIGURE 3. Guggenheim plots of the data of Fig. 2, indicating a biphasic (control) and a monophasic time course of binding (+ nucleotides).

Analysis of the rapid and the slow phase in terms of two superimposed exponential processes (Fig. 3) yields the first order rate constants of 0.2 min^{-1} (rapid phase, 35% of bound NBD) and 0.06 min^{-1} (slow phase, 65% of bound NBD). After 30 minutes, 1.6 NBD/CF$_1$ could be found, using a value of 11600 M^{-1} cm^{-1} for the molar coefficient of the tyrosine-0-NBD derivative and a molecular weight of 4000 000 for CF$_1$. These results indicate two possible reaction sites per CF$_1$. A slow modification of a third β-tyrosine can not be excluded.

As only one single tyrosine (Y$_{311}$, bovine MF$_1$) has been found labeled with (^{14}C)NBD on MF$_1$ (6), we may assume, that three identical tyrosines, each of them on one of the three β-subunits, can react with NBD. One of these tyrosines then must be more exposed than in the others and therefore, be able to react faster.

Addition of excess ADP (Fig. 2) resulted in reduced amount of bound NBD, a monophasic absorbance increase with time, and a rate constant of comparable order to that of the initial rapid phase (Table I). Addition of ATP in presence of MgCl$_2$ did not reduce the maximal value of bound NBD, but resulted in a monophasic increase in absorbance, comparable to the slow phase of the initial curve (Table I).

TABLE I. Formation of 0-tyr-NBD-CF$_1$ in absence and in presence of different substrates

addition	k_1 (min^{-1})	$t_{1/2}$ (min)	k_2 (min^{-1})	$t_{1/2}$ (min)
–	0.196	3.5	0.062	11.1
MgCl$_2$	0.202	3.4	0.063	11.0
ADP	0.138	5.0		
ADP/P$_i$	0.153	4.5		
ADP/P$_i$/Mg^{2+}	0.203	3.4		
ATP	0.078	8.8		
ATP/P$_i$	0.153	4.5		
ATP/P$_i$/Mg^{2+}	0.060	11.5		

This result suggests a non-catalytic nucleotide binding site as a target of NBD in the first fast phase of the reaction, as isolated CF$_1$ contains one binding site on a β-subunit which binds ATP in presence of Mg^{2+} tightly, and which has no catalytic activity (8). Inhibition by ADP of the following slow phase might be related to interaction at a catalytic site of CF$_1$.

However, reaction of only one NBD-Cl per CF$_1$ is sufficient for complete inactivation of the ATPase activity (Fig. 4), which is certainly an additional indication for the strictly cooperative working manner of the three β-subunits.

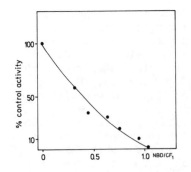

FIGURE 4. Inhibition of Ca-ATPase as a function of bound NBD/CF_1. The amount of bound NBD was calculated from absorbance increase at 385 nm. Control activity: 350 µmol $^{32}P_i$/mg protein·h.

The result, that not only ADP, but also MgATP is able to protect the ATPase partially against loss of activity (Table II) suggests a role of the non-catalytic MgATP site in the catalytic process, may be a structural one.

TABLE II. Ca-ATPase activity of isolated CF_1 (3 µM) pretreated with 80 µM NBD-Cl at pH 7.5 in the presence or absence of nucleotides (2 mM). Incubation time was 20 minutes.

conditions	µMol P_i/mg CF_1·h	% inhibition
control	538.5	0
+NBD	41.8	92
+NBD, +ADP	353.0	34
+NBD, +ADP	372.6	31

However, the experiments shown here, can not exclude the possibility of two different tyrosines on one β-subunit. Experiments to determine the modified tyrosine(s) on chloroplast F_1 are in progress.

REFERENCES
1 Xue, Z., Zhou, J.M., Melese, T., Cross, R.L. and Boyer, P.D. (1987) Biochemistry 26, 3749-3753
2 Bickel-Sandkötter, S. (1985) Biochim. Biophys. Acta 809, 117-124
3 Schlimme, E., de Groot, E.J., Schott, E., Strotmann, H. and Edelmann, K. (1979) FEBS Lett. 106, 251-256
4 Bickel-Sandkötter, S. and Gokus, M. (1989) Biochim. Biophys. Acta 974, 30-35
5 Sutton, R. and Ferguson, S.J. (1984) Eur. J. Biochem. 142, 387-392
6 Andrews, W.W., Hill, F.C. and Allison, W.S. (1984) J. Biol. Chem. 259, 8219-8225
7 Ferguson, S.J., Lloyd, W.J. and Radda, G.K. (1975) Eur. J. Biochem. 54, 127-133
8 Leckband, D. and Hammes, G.G. (1987) Biochemistry 26, 2306-2312

CATION CHANNELS BY RECONSTITUTION OF CF_0CF_1 AND BY SUBUNIT III OF CF_0

Althoff,G., Schönknecht,G., Lühring,H., Apley,E., Wagner,R. and Junge,W.
Biophysik, Universität Osnabrück, 4500 Osnabrück, West Germany

INTRODUCTION

CF_0, the channel portion of the ATP-synthase in the thylakoid membrane has a very high proton selectivity and a proton conductivity in the pS-range (1,2,3). Single-channel H^+ currents through the membrane part of CF_0CF_1 have been reported for the ATP-synthase incorporated into lipid bilayers (3). The thylakoid membrane has proved difficult to be inquired by patch pipettes, except, so far, in giant chloroplasts of *P. metallica*, where a voltage-dependent chloride channel has been detected (4).

For a further electrophysiological inquiry of the ATP-synthase we used the strategy of Tank and Miller (5): CF_0CF_1 and subunit III of CF_0 were isolated and reconstituted into lipid vesicles which were then fused to form large liposomes suitable for single-channel recordings (Fig. 1). At membrane voltages exceeding 40 mV cation channels were observed which were still sensitive to Venturicidin (as is CF_0) but had lost proton selectivity.

MATERIAL AND METHODS

CF_0CF_1 was purified and reconstituted into azolectin vesicles using the dialysis technique. The integrity of the preparation was tested by measuring ATP synthesis driven by an artificial pH-gradient (6). From dialysis vesicles large liposomes were formed by a dehydration/rehydration procedure (7). Subunit III of CF_0 was isolated by electroelution from SDS-gels (8) and added to lipid vesicles prior to dehydration. Single bilayer inside-out patches were isolated and single-channel recordings performed as in (9). All potentials given refer to the pipette.

THYLAKOID MEMBRANE   DIALYSIS VESICLES   INSIDE-OUT PATCH

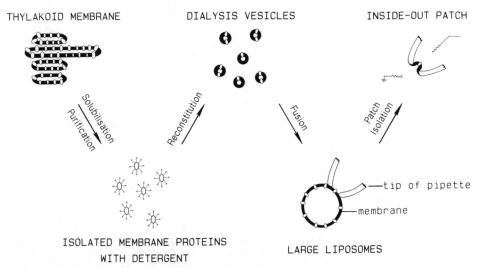

ISOLATED MEMBRANE PROTEINS
WITH DETERGENT

LARGE LIPOSOMES

tip of pipette

membrane

Fig. 1: Schematic diagram: From membrane protein purification over reconstitution into dialysis vesicles to patch clamp technique (adapted from ref. 5).

M. Baltscheffsky (ed.), Current Research in Photosynthesis, Vol. III, 81–84.
© 1990 *Kluwer Academic Publishers. Printed in the Netherlands.*

RESULTS

After forming an inside-out patch a potential difference was applied and with an induction period of a few ten seconds we observed the voltage-dependent onset of single-channel activity. Under aysmmetrical KCl concentrations, the reversal potential of the single-channel currents shifted in direction of the Nernst potential for potassium, as expected for a cation channel. Liposomes reconstituted with CF_OCF_1 showed most frequently channel openings with a conductance of about 13 pS (in 100 mM KCl). A detailed analysis showed 3 subconductance levels (10 pS, 13 pS and 18,5 pS) (Fig. 2). 1 μM Venturicidin (a blocker of CF_O) decreased the open probability (P_{open}) of these cation channels by more than a factor of 2 (Fig. 2). Additionally single-channel currents with an open channel conductance of 60 pS were observed with reconstituted CF_OCF_1 (Fig. 3).

Subunit III of CF_O was electroeluted from SDS-gels, either from the 8 kD band (monomer) or the 48 kD band (hexamer (10)) and incorporated into large liposomes. They showed no differences in electrophysiological behaviour. Aside from a conductance level of about 13 pS (in 100 mM KCl) at least two further conductance levels (of about 21 pS and 33 pS) were detected. They showed ohmic behaviour between +100 mV and -100 mV (Fig. 5). EF_O, the homologous channel portion of the ATP-synthase of *E. coli* (11) yielded similar single-channel activities (Fig.4).

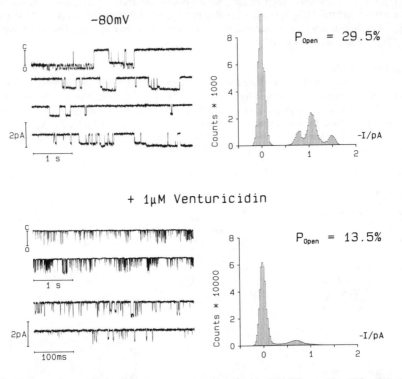

Fig.2: Single-channel recordings of liposomes reconstituted with CF_OCF_1 at -80 mV in 100 mM KCl, 5 mM $MgCl_2$, 10 mM Tricine/KOH pH 7.9. Single-channel traces (left) and correspondig total amplitude histograms (right). The histogram shows the amplitude relative to the baseline of each digitized point of a 85 s (top) / 45 s (below) record. After perfusion of 1 μM Venturicidin to the same patch channel gating was dramatically changed. Even digitized at a rate of 100 μs instead of 1 ms channel openings were hardly resolved.

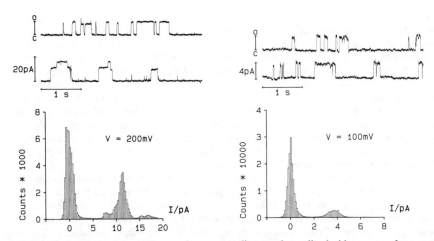

Fig.3 (left): Single-channel recordings and corresponding total amplitude histogram of reconstituted CF_OCF_1 in 100 mM KCl, 2 mM $CaCl_2$, 10 mM Tris/KOH pH 7.5.
Fig.4 (right): Single-channel recordings of liposomes reconstituted with EF_O in 100 mM KCl, 5 mM $MgCl_2$, 20 mM Tris/Tricine pH 7.8 and total amplitude histogram.

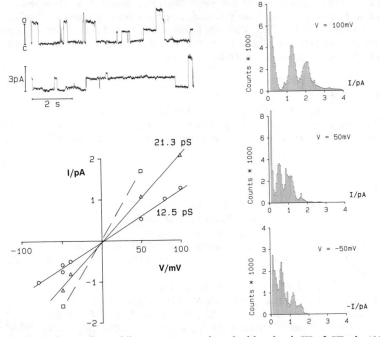

Fig.5: Single-channel recordings of liposomes reconstituted with subunit III of CF_O in 100 mM KCl, 5 mM $MgCl_2$, 20 mM Tris/Tricine pH 7.8. Top: Single-channel records at $+100$ mV and the corresponding total amplitude histogram (Record length: 8 min / Digitization rate: 2 ms). Right: Equivalent histograms for $+50$ mV (8 min / 2 ms) and -50 mV (6 min / 2 ms). Lower left: Current-voltage relationship of open channels. Data points were derived from total amplitude histograms.

CONCLUSION

In liposomes, reconstituted with CF_OCF_1, we observed potassium channels. This was surprising, as it is known, that the intact enzyme conducts protons only (12,13), and even in CF_1-depleted thylakoid membranes, proton conductance is dominant during the first 100 ms after flash induced generation of a potential difference (1,2). Dialysis vesicles containing CF_OCF_1 were competent to synthesize ATP in an acid-base jump and showed single-channel currents carried by H^+ when incorporated into a lipid bilayer (3). To explain the lack of H^+ specificity in our patch clamp experiments it was conceivable, that some CF_OCF_1-complexes had disintegrated during the dehydration/rehydration procedure and their components gave rise to cation channels. The dominance of proton conductance in CF_1-depleted thylakoid membranes (during the first 100 ms after a saturating flash of light) may be due either to the still intact structure of CF_O-complexes or to a time lag in channel formation (from CF_O-subunits) after the onset of a membrane potential.

Venturicidin, a highly specific CF_O blocker, decreased the channel open probability significantly (Fig.2). Therefore it was likely, that the described cation channels did not arise from contaminations in purified CF_OCF_1. Compared to the intact ATP-synthase, where 0.5 µM Venturicidin completely abolish ATP synthesis, the K_i seemed to be higher. Venturicidin is assumed to bind to subunit III of the channel portion of the ATP-synthase (14). In experiments with purified subunit III of CF_O (Fig.5) cation channels with conductance states and gating behaviour similar to CF_OCF_1 were observed. These results implied that subunit III (liberated from CF_OCF_1-complexes) was responsible for the formation of cation channels.

A closer look at the single-channel recordings obtained with CF_OCF_1 (Fig. 2 and Fig. 3) and with isolated subunit III of CF_O (Fig. 5), revealed some differences. With subunit III we hardly observed only one type of channel for a longer time period, and we never detected pronounced subconductance levels as shown in Fig. 2 for CF_OCF_1. Obviously, subunit III alone had channel forming ability. Yet it might be that in the presence of the other subunits of CF_O (as in liposomes with CF_OCF_1 incorporated), channel formation by subunit III was modified.

ACKNOWLEDGEMENT

Purified EF_O was a friendly gift of Dr. G. Dekkers-Hebestreit. We thank Dr. R. Hedrich and Dr. W. Hanke for introducing us into patch clamp electrophysiology, and H. Kenneweg for photographs. Financial support by the Deutsche Forschungsgemeinschaft (SFB 171 / B2 and B3).

REFERENCES

1 Lill,H., Althoff,G. & Junge,W. (1987) *J. Membrane Biol.* **98**:69-78
2 Althoff,G., Lill,H. & Junge,W. (1989) *J. Membrane Biol.* **108**:263-271
3 Wagner,R., Apley,E. & Hanke,W. (1989) *EMBO J.* in press
4 Schönknecht,G., Hedrich,R., Junge,W. & Raschke,K. (1988) *Nature* **336**:589-592
5 Tank,D.W. & Miller,C. (1983) *in* Single-Channel Recording (Sakmann,B. & Neher,E. ed.) pp. 91-105, Plenum Press, New York
6 Schmidt,G. & Gräber,P. (1985) *Biochim. Biophys. Acta* **808**:46-51
7 Keller,B.U., Hedrich,R., Vaz,W.L.C. & Criado,M. (1988) *Pflügers Arch.* **411**:94-100
8 Hanke,W., Andree,J., Strotmann,J. & Kahle,C. (1989) *Europ. Biophys. J.* in press
9 Hamill,O.P., Marty,A., Neher,E., Sakmann,B. & Sigworth,F.J. (1981) *Pflügers Arch.* **391**:85-100
10 Lill,H. & Junge,W. (1989) *FEBS Lett.* **244**:15-20
11 Schneider,E. & Altendorf,K. (1984) *Proc. natn. Acad. Sci. U.S.A.* **81**:7279-7283
12 Senior,A.E. (1988) *Physiol. Rev.* **68**:177-231
13 Junge,W. (1987) *Proc. natn. Acad. Sci. U.S.A.* **48**:7084-7088
14 Galanis,M., Mattoon,J.R. & Nagley,P. (1989) *FEBS Lett.* **249**:333-336

CORRELATION BETWEEN BUFFERING CAPACITY AND PROTON EFFLUX IN BACTERIAL CHROMATOPHORES

M.P. Turina, G. Venturoli and B.A. Melandri
University of Bologna, Department of Biology, Bologna, Italy

1. INTRODUCTION

The total amount of protons stored in the chromatophore vesicles after a period of illumination is related to the ΔpH and to the buffering capacity of the vesicle interior. The decay kinetics in the dark of the established proton gradient depend on the membrane permeability for protons and on the concentration and proton affinity of the internal buffering groups. A model based on these assumptions, developed by J. Whitmarsh (1), has been applied to the experimental results in order to obtain a quantitative evaluation of these parameters.

It is considered that
(a) the external proton concentration (H_o) remains constant due to the buffering of the external phase;
(b) no electric potentials arise, that is, ions other than protons and hydroxyls are sufficiently permeant and concentrated;
(c) the efflux of protons is diffusion limited and proportional to the transmembrane difference of proton concentration through a permeability constant, P_{H^+} = $V/S\ k_m$, where V and S are the volume and surface of the vesicles and k_m is the first order kinetic constant for the proton efflux;
(d) the flux of protons, J_{H^+}, is much greater than the flux of hydroxyls, J_{OH^-};
(e) the internal buffer is close to equilibrium with the internal protons at all time.

With these assumptions the following differential equation is deduced:

$$1)\qquad \frac{dH_i}{dt}\left[1 + \sum_r \frac{K_j\ A_j}{(H_i + K_j)^2}\right] = -k_m\ (H_i - H_\bullet) \qquad J = 1, n$$

where n is the number of internal buffers and A_j, K_j are the concentration and the dissociation constant of each buffer. The amount of protons taken up at internal concentration H_i

M. Baltscheffsky (ed.), Current Research in Photosynthesis, Vol. III, 85–88.
© 1990 Kluwer Academic Publishers. Printed in the Netherlands.

and external proton concentration H_o can be calculated as follows:

$$2) \quad h(\text{tot}) = V \cdot \left[H_i - H_o - \sum_j A_j \left(\frac{H_i}{H_i + K_j} - \frac{H_o}{H_o + K_j} \right) \right]$$

2. RESULTS AND DISCUSSION

2.1 Use of the probe: The pH decay kinetics has been followed in a suspension of pre-illuminated chromatophores of Rh. capsulatus in the presence of 9-aminoacridine (9AA). The signal of fluorescence quenching during preillumination has returned to its initial value in about 5min dark or has been maintained at a constant value in different moments of the decay firing trains of flashes at various frequencies. The pH gradient has been evaluated by means of an empirical calibration of the 9AA signal, as described in (2). The values of log $Q/(100-Q)$ fitted quite satisfactorily a straight line with the slope of 1 (2,3). This straight line has been extrapolated from $\Delta pH = 2.6$ (the maximal possible experimental point of the calibration) up to ΔpH 3.3, the maximal quenching value obtained in continuous light.

The kinetic competence of this probe, up to a response time of 100 ms, was demonstrated by the possibility of stimulating the decay rate of the quenching more than 2,000 times with nigericin.

2.2 Inclusion of the electric potential into the model: The assumption (b) of the Whitmarsh model could not be satisfied in our system. Despite the presence of 2 μM valinomycin and 50 mM KCl, an electrochromic signal of carotenoid was still induced by illumination and the decay in the dark was comparable to that of pH. Therefore, equation (1) has been used in the form:

$$3) \quad \frac{dH_i}{dt} \left[1 + \sum_j \frac{A_j K_j}{(H_i + K_j)^2} \right] = -k_m \frac{\Delta \bar{\psi}}{e^{\Delta \bar{\psi}} - 1} \left(H_i e^{\Delta \bar{\psi}} - H_o \right), \quad \Delta \bar{\psi} = \frac{F}{RT} \Delta \psi$$

and the integration has been performed with numerical techniques in which each value of the $\Delta \bar{\varphi}$ decay, measured as a given carotenoid shift signal, gave its contribution to the function value.

2.3 Evaluation of the km: Due to the fact that $\sum_j \frac{A_j K_j}{(H_i + K_j)^2} \gg 1$ A_j and K_j are in a proportional relationship in eq.(3), which makes a resolution of both parameters impossible. An independent evaluation of the k_m has been approached by superimposing an active inward flux to the passive efflux during the decay, in such a way as to maintain the fluorescence signal constant. Under these conditions is

$$4) \quad \frac{S}{V} J_{H^+}^e = k_m \frac{\Delta \bar{\psi}}{e^{\Delta \bar{\psi}} - 1} \left(H_i e^{\Delta \bar{\psi}} - H_o \right)$$

where $J_{H^+}^e$ represents the active inward proton flux.
By firing flash trains at the appropriate frequency, it
has been possible to obtain this stationary state at
different values of H_i and to build a plot as presented
in Fig.1. The value of $J_{H^+}^e$ is related to the
frequency

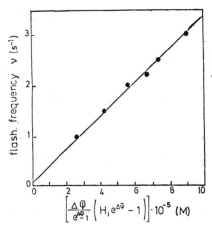

Fig. 1 Flash frequencies
plotted vs. x-axis values
calculated with the H_i and
$\Delta\varphi$ of the corresponding
steady states.

$$\left[\frac{\Delta\overline{\Psi}}{e^{\Delta\overline{\Psi}}-1}\left(H_i e^{\Delta\overline{\Psi}}-1\right)\right]\cdot10^{-5}\ (M)$$

by a proportionality constant which includes the
accepted stoichiometry of 2 H^+/e^- in bacterial
chromatophores and the surface density of the electron
transfer chains, as estimated by spectroscopic
measurements and literature data. The best fit of eq.
(4) has given $k_m = 19\ s^{-1}$, corresponding to a
permeability coefficient of 2e-5 cm s^{-1}. The results
in this figure also suggest the validity of point (c)
of the model in the whole range of the tested internal
proton concentration.

2.4 Fitting of the H_i decay: Eq. (3) with the evaluated k_m
value has been fitted to the H_i decay traces by
optimizing the number of the buffers and the values of
each buffer. Two different buffers were found to give
a much better fit than a single one; on the contrary,
more than two buffers failed to inhance the quality of
the fit as well as change the course of the function.
One of the best fits is shown in Fig. 2 with the
corresponding best fit values in the legend.

2.5 Steady state experiments: A completely independent
approach to the evaluation of these parameters is shown
in Fig. 3. These are the results of simultaneous
measurements in a poorly buffered medium of the
quenching of 9AA and of the signal of a glass electrode
under continuous illumination. The extent of the
steady state $\Delta\mu_H^+$ has been varied by titrating with

Fig. 2 A digitalized decay trace is shown with the numeric integral of eq. (3). Best fit values were: A_1 = .253 M, K_1 = 2.6e-4 M, A_2 = .012 M, K_2 = 2.0e-7 M.

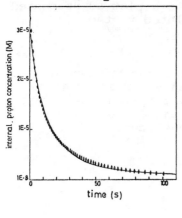

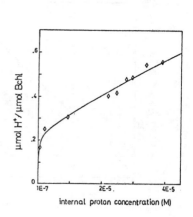

Fig. 3 Proton uptake vs. the internal proton concentration of the corresponding steady states

increasing nigericin. This parallel evaluation of both the H_i and the proton uptake values has given the possibility to apply eq. (2). The plotted function is actually eq. (2), in which the values of the buffer parameters are those of Fig. 2 and the value of V is 10 μl/μmole BChl, which is very close to the true osmotic volume measured with the ESR probe tempone at the same osmolarity of the present assay, as reported in (4).
The best fit values for the buffer capacity are clearly to be considered "formal" values, being a more realistic hypothesis the presence of a large number of buffering groups endowed with continuously variable proton affinity properties. The "summation" of these single values could give the values reported above.

REFERENCES
1 Whitmarsh, J. (1987) Photosynth. Res. 12, 43-62
2 Casadio, R. and Melandri, B.A. (1985) ABB 238, 219-228
3 Schuldiner, S. et al. (1972) Eur. J. Biochem. 25,54-63
4 Melandri, B.A. et al. (1984) ABB 235,97-105

DIURNAL PATTERN OF CHLOROPLAST COUPLING FACTOR OXIDA-
TION KINETICS IN LEAVES OF INTACT SUNFLOWER.

D.M. Kramer and A.R. Crofts.
Biophysics Division, U. of Illinois,Urbana, Ill. 61801 U.S.A.

In green plants light energy is stored in the form of redox free-energy and a proton gradient generated by light driven electron transport. The proton motive force (*pmf*) across the thylakoid membrane, in turn, drives the phosphorylation of ADP to ATP catalyzed by the CF_1-CF_0-ATP synthase or coupling factor (ATP-ase). The regulation of the chloroplast ATP-ase is important since this enzyme can catalyze not only the synthesis of ATP from ADP and P_i, driven by a *pmf* across the membrane, but also the reverse reaction, hydrolysis of ATP with the formation of a *pmf* (1) to passive dissipation of ΔG_{ATP} as protons across the thylakoid membrane. Work on this regulation using isolated systems has been summarized by a model presented by Junesch and Graber (2). Briefly, this model states as follows. The ATP-ase is not enzymatically active until a *pmf*, either as a ΔpH or as $\Delta \psi$, or their sum, is imposed across the thylakoid membrane. In addition, regulation is governed by the redox state of a pair of sulfhydryl groups on the -subunit of the ATP-ase. Both the oxidized and reduced forms of the enzyme apparently have the same maximal catalytic rate, but the magnitude of the *pmf* required to activate the reduced form is less than for the oxidized form.

We have recently studied this regulation in intact plants through the used of a highly sensitive portable kinetic spectrophotometer to observe the slow decay component of the flash-induced 515 nm change (3). The rate of decay of the electrochromic change should reflect the flux of ions across the membrane down the proton gradient. Under physiological conditions, the major part of the flux reflects the activity of the ATP-ase, since the proton flux through the ATP-ase accompanying the synthesis of ATP is the main physiological pathway for dissipation of the *pmf*. When the ATP-ase is inactive, the *pmf* can only decay by slower routes. Thus, we are able to use the extent of the slow phase of the decay of the electrochromic shift to indicate the amount of oxidized ATP-ase. These results of these intact plant studies were generally in agreement with the model presented by Junesch and Graber (2). They also show that the activation of the chloroplast ATP-ase through the thioredoxin system occurs at levels of illumination less than 0.2% of normal actinic intensities, and that this process is never limiting for photosynthesis. In addition, we found that the reoxidation kinetics of the γ-subunit of the ATP-ase showed a lag time which was dependent on the amount of light adaptation, and a recovery which did not appear to be dependent on the amount of light adaptation. Since the lag is associated with the continued presence of activated ATP-ase, we may assume that the γ-subunit sulfhydryl groups remained in the reduced state

M. Baltscheffsky (ed.), Current Research in Photosynthesis, Vol. III, 89–92.
© 1990 *Kluwer Academic Publishers. Printed in the Netherlands.*

during this time. The simplest explanation for this behavior is that, in the intact leaf, the redox state of the γ-subunit sulfhydryls reached equilibrium with a large buffering redox pool with a somewhat lower midpoint potential. Reduction of a relatively small fraction of this pool by a relatively small number of actinic flashes would reduce a large fraction of the γ-subunit sulfhydryls. During dark-adaptation, the buffering redox pool would become oxidized by oxygen or by turnover of oxidizing pathways. However, a large fraction of the pool would have to be oxidized before a significant fraction of the γ-subunit sulfhydryls would begin to be oxidized, causing a time lag between oxidation of the redox pool and the decrease in activity of the ATP-ase. We suggested that reasonable candidates for the redox buffering pool should include the $NADP^+/NADPH$ ($E_{m,7}$=-0.32 V) and the gluta-thione couple ($E_{m,7}$=-0.34 V).

This two redox pool model can explain the reoxidation kinetics of the ATP-ase sulfhydrils when fully dark-adapted plants are given relatively small amounts of light. Deviations from this simple model occur when plants are measured after exposure to full sunlight, when the plants are taken directly from the growth chamber at midday (600-800 μE $m^{-2}s^{-1}$) or when dark-adapted plants are light-adapted for more than 15 minutes under saturation illumination. In these cases, the recovery of the slow phase follows more complex kinetics. This paper describes the reoxidation kinetics of the ATP-ase over the course of a diurnal cycle and attempts to explain the data in terms of a modification of the two-redox-pool model described in ref 3.

MATERIALS AND METHODS Cucumber plants (*Cucumis sativus* L. cv. Ashley) were raised from seed in a soil/peat/vermiculite mixture, watered daily and fertilized weekly. The plants were grown in a controlled environment chamber (600-800 μE $m^{-2}s^{-1}$, 14 hour photoperiod, day/night temperatures of $23^oC/20^oC$) as described in Martin and Ort, 1985 (4). Attached leaves which had reached almost full expansion were used for the experiments. The instrument used to measure the kinetics of the electrochromic changes in intact leaves is described in Kramer and Crofts (5). The design of the spectrophotometer is based on an instrument developed by Joliot and Joliot (6), and achieves very high signal-to-noise ratios (noise levels of less than 10^{-5} A) by utilizing differential optics, and a xenon flash for the measuring beam in place of the conventional continuous measuring beam. The degree of saturation of the actinic flashes given by the spectrophotometer was about 50% (3). We used the amplitude of the electrochromic shift at 120 msec after the actinic flash to indicate the level of slow phase since at this time, the fast phase had essentially completely dissipated whereas the slow phase remained.

RESULTS AND DISCUSSION Figures 1 a-j show the diurnal pattern of reoxidation kinetics. Intact leaves were introduced into the spectrophotometer at different times during the day and the decay of the flash-induced electrochromic shift was monitored at a series of times during the dark-adaptation. The growth chamber light turned on at 8:00 a.m. and off again at 8:00 p.m. After a few minutes growth chamber light (Fig 1a), the reoxidation kinetics of the ATP-ase are as seen for the dark-adapted leaf given several hundred actinic flashes as in Fig 1b and ref (3). However, a cycle of complex kinetic patterns was seen during longer illumination times. In early morning, reoxidation of the CF had sigmoidal kinetics: a lag and oxidation phase of 12 min. each. From 0.5-5 hrs illumination (Figs. 1b-e), the kinetics become more complex; a shorter lag (about 6 min.) was followed by two phases of oxidation, one about 6 min and a much longer phase of about 2 hrs.

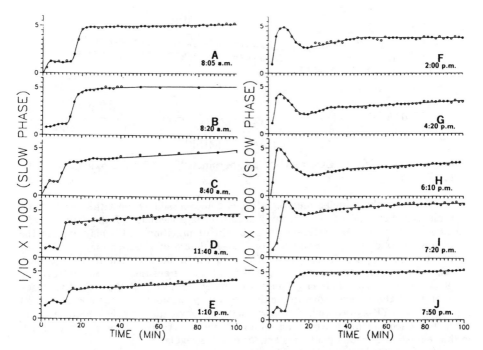

Figure 1. Diurnal pattern of the kinetics of reoxidation of the chloroplast ATP-ase in the dark. The *y-axis* represents the extent of the slow decay phase of the flash-induced electrochromic shift which is used as a measure of the fraction of ATP-ase in the oxidized form. See Text.

From 5-11 hrs illumination (Figs. 1 f-i), the lag phase was replaced by a transient, rapid and almost complete oxidation, followed by a partial rereduction and a subsequent slow reoxidation, also on the order of hours. At about 1 hr before dark, the kinetics gradually became similar to those of the early morning. It is noteworthy that no changes in light intensity occur until the chamber dark-transition.

This cycle appears remarkable consistent. For example the large transient oxidation consistently appears between 5-6 hours of illumination. Tomato plants exhibited similar phenomena, though we have not extensively studied these. Preliminary data from greenhouse and field plants showed similar effects, though the gradual return to the oxidation kinetics seen in the morning occurred earlier with the afternoon reduction in light intensity (data not shown).

Assuming that the four-state model of Junesch and Graber holds true for these cases, the following interpretations can be made. In the fully dark-adapted leaf, the redox pool(s) responsible for the "two-pool" behavior are kinetically isolated from (not in equilibrium with) other large redox pools in the plant. Under extended illumination with high intensity light, the enzymes involved in the Calvin cycle will become activated and the levels of intermediates of this pathway will change. A rapid turnover of the Calvin cycle may be expected to increase the rate of oxidation of PSI acceptor pools and therefore the ATP-ase as seen after 0.3 hours of illumination. The redox state of the large metabolite pools might come into equilibrium with that of the γ-subunit of the ATP-ase. The altered kinetics of recov-

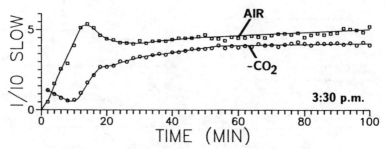

Figure 2. The effect of CO_2 removal on the kinetics of ATP-ase oxidation in the dark. See text.

ery of the slow phase under these conditions could possibly reflect the deactivation of these enzymes, and/or the changing levels of intermediates of the Calvin cycle which are expected to be different under bright illumination. This may explain the very slow reoxidation phases seen from 0.5-10 hours of illumination. The rapid transient oxidation seen in the early afternoon might be expected if a large percentage of the assimilatory power at the time of dark transition was in the form of a phosphate potential. This large phosphate potential may pull the reductive reactions of the Calvin Cycle forward, oxidizing the photosystem I acceptor pools and therefore the ATP-ase as well. The fact that the reoxidation kinetics become similar to those seen in the morning may indicate the functioning of a circadian clock in the regulation of redox pool sizes and/or enzyme regulation.

To test the hypothesis that the altered oxidation kinetics are related to turnover of the Calvin cycle, plants were removed from the growth chamber at 3:00 p.m. and placed for 30 min. in a plastic glove bag and illuminated at 600 $\mu Em^{-1}sec^{-1}$. The glove bag was filled with air (control) or 20% O_2 in N_2 (no CO_2). The results of this experiment are shown in Figure 2. Although the kinetics of the control plant differ from those of plants measured directly out of the growth chamber at the same time, there is clearly an effect of removing CO_2 from the plants atmosphere. The rapid transient oxidation seen at this time in the control plant was completely abolished by removing CO_2. This supports the hypothesis that the the altered reoxidation kinetics are related to the onset of CO_2 fixation.

The results in this paper can be interpreted with a modification of the model previously proposed (2) as adapted for the intact plants by ourselves (3). In this modified scheme, Calvin cycle enzymes and intermediates alter the rate of reoxidation of the redox pool in equilibrium with the ATP-ase. This study suggests that measurements of the electrochromic shift in intact plants with the type of instrumentation used here may become an important tool in the study of the energetics and biochemistry of the intact plant.

Supported by U.S. Dept of Energy. D.M.K. is supported by McKnight Foundation

1 Mitchell, P. (1961) Nature 191, 144-148.
2 Junesch, U. and Graber, P. (1987) Biochim. Biophys. Acta. 893, 275-288.
3 Kramer, D.M. and Crofts, A.R. (1989) Biochim. Biophys. Acta. In Press.
4 Martin, B. and Ort, D.R. (1985) Photosynth. Res. 6, 121-132.
5 Kramer, D.M. and Crofts, A.R. (1989) Photosynth. Res. In Press.
6 Joliot, P., and Joliot, A. (1984) Biochim. Biophys. Acta. 765, 210-218.

Single Channel Proton currents in CF_0CF_1 Proteoliposomes

Wagner, R., Apley, E.C. and *Hanke, W.
Biophysik, Universität Osnabrück, Barbarastr. 11, 4500 Osnabrück (FRG)
*IBI, Kernforschungsanlage Jülich GmbH, Postfach 1913, 5170 Jülich (FRG)

Introduction

We were aiming in obtaining information on the energy coupling in the proton translocating ATP synthase of chloroplasts (1). For this, the purified chloroplast ATP synthase (CF_0CF_1) was reconstituted into azolectin liposomes from which bilayer membranes on the tip of a glass pipette (»dip stick technique«) and planar bilayer membranes were formed. The chloroplast ATP synthase (CF_0CF_1) facilitated ion-conductance through the bilayer membranes.

The observed single channel currents were carried by H^+ through the isolated and reconstituted chloroplast ATPase. We demonstrate that it is the intact enzyme complex CF_0CF_1 and not the membrane sector CF_0 alone that constitutes a voltage-gated, proton selective channel with a high unit conductance of 1-5 pS at pH 5.5-pH 8.0. The open probability P_0 of the CF_0CF_1 channel increased considerably with increasing membrane voltage (from $P_0 \leq 1\%$ ($V_m \leq 120$ mV) to $P_0 \leq 30\%$ (120 mV $\leq V_m$ 200 mV)). In the presence of ADP (3 μM) and P_i (5 μM), wich specifically bind to CF_1, the open probability decreased and venturicidin (1 μM), a specific inhibitor of H^+ flow through CF_0 in thylakoid membranes, blocked the channel almost completely.

Our results which revealed a high channel unit conductance, and at membrane voltages <100 mV low open probability with concominant mean open times in the μs range suggest a gated mechanism with channel openings in the μs time scale (<100 μs) for the energy supply in the enzyme complex.

Materials and Methods

CF_0CF_1 was purified as described (2) and reconstituted into azolectin liposomes. ATP synthesis in the proteoliposomes driven by an artifical pH gradient (3) was used to assess the integrity of the preparation. Partial CF_1 depletion of CF_0CF_1 proteoliposomes was performed as described in ref.4.

CF_0CF_1 and CF_0 were incorporated into lipid bilayers formed on the tip of a glass

M. Baltscheffsky (ed.), Current Research in Photosynthesis, Vol. III, 93–96.
© 1990 *Kluwer Academic Publishers. Printed in the Netherlands.*

pipette as described (4).

Voltage activated single channel currents were recorded and analysed as given in detail elsewere (6,7).

Results and Discussion

Electrophysiological measurements using the dip stick (6) and patch clamp technique (7) were performed with three different preparations of proteoliposomes. Liposomes containing the entire CF_0CF_1 (4), liposomes containing mainly CF_0 where most of CF_1 was removed by NaBr treatment (4) and liposomes containing subunit III which had been recovered from SDS gels (4,8).

Measurements with bilayers formed on the tip of a glass micropipette (»dip-stick bilayers«) using dialysis liposomes were accomplished as previously described (4). For patch clamp measurements, giant liposomes were formed from the dialysis liposomes using the dehydration/rehydration technique (5).

With dip-stick bilayers formed from CF_0CF_1 liposomes at membrane potentials exeeding 100 mV, single channel currents were observed. This channel is described in more detail elsewere (4) and here we depict only some of their main features.

Figure 1

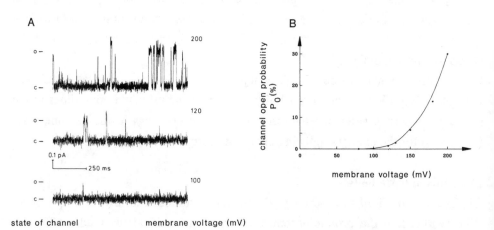

Figure 1A shows the voltage dependence of channel gating from CF_0CF_1 containing dip-stick bilayers at the indicated membrane potential. Measurements were performed at pH 6.8 with 200 μM Tris-HCl at both sites of the membrane. In figure 2B the channel open probability as calculated from the corresponding peaks of the total amplitude histogram of current fluctuations is shown (7). The estimated conductance of the open channel was 3 ± 2 pS (4). One of the most interesting features of the observed channel gatings was the extrem low open probability of the channel at membrane potentials below 100 mV. At membrane potentials < 100 mV the channel open probability was already below 1 % (see figure 1B) and the extrapolated open probability of the channel at more physiological potentials (~30 mV) was ~10-4 and the concomitant mean open time was > 200 μs (4). Therefor at physiological membrane potentials not only the amplitude of the channel currents is to small to be resolved, but also the mean open time is to short to be well resolved with single channel recordings.

CF_1 was removed from CF_0CF_1 proteoliposomes and the proteoliposomes containing mainly CF_0 were incorporated into dip-stick bilayers (4). In this bilayers the channel conductance, selectivity and gating behaviour changed drastically. Current fluctuations could already be observed at 40 mV where the channel open probability of the CF_0CF_1 complex was far below 1 % (see figure 1B). Moreover the uniform size of the open channel conductance and the H^+ selectivity disappeared. The observed channels revealed the reversial potential for monovalent cations and open channel currents up to ~18 pA at 200 mV (90 pS), in symmetrical solutions with 120 mM NaCl, 10 mM Tris pH 6.8, 1 mM $CaCl_2$, were observed.

In patch clamp measurements with giant CF_0CF_1 liposomes which were formed from the dialysis liposomes by dehydration/rehydration, the same type of channels (conductance states, selectivity) were observed as with the NaBr treated liposomes in dip stick bilayers (5).

Together our results (4) indicate that NaBr treatment, which had been employed to remove CF_1 from CF_0, and dehydration/rehydration, employed for preparation of giant liposomes, both destroy the CF_0CF_1 complex. In both cases, the H^+ selectivity observed for the whole CF_0CF_1 in dip stick bilayers dissappeared. We have shown previously by rotational diffusion measurements (9) that the membrane part of the chloroplast ATP synthase is rather unstable in liposomes. After chemical modification, subunit III dissociates completely into its monomeric form, however even the monomeric form was able to form ionic channels. From our experiments with lipid bilayers it appears as if CF_0 alone is not capable to form a proton selective channel, possibly because it desintegrates into its subunits. When CF_1 is detached from the membrane, the components of CF_0 seem to form various kinds of cation channels. These channels can be formed either by subunit III alone or in combination with the other subunits. Their physiological significance remain to be investigated.

Acknowledgements

We thank Mrs. Hella Kenneweg for the photographs. Financial support by the Deutsche Forschungsgemeinschaft (SFB 171, B2/C11) is gratefully acknowledged.

References

1. Maloney, P.C. (1982) J. Membr. Biol. 67, 1-2
2. Fromme, P., Boeckema, E.J. and Gräber, P. (1987) Z. Naturforsch. 42c, 1239-1244
3. Schmidt, G. and Gräber, P. (1985) Biochim. Biophys. Acta 808, 46-51
4. Wagner, R., Apley, E.C. and Hanke, W. (1989) EMBO J. -in press-
5. Althoff, G. et al. (1989) -in preparation-
6. Hanke, W. (1985) Crit. Rev. Biochem. 19, 1-44
7. Colquhoun, D. and Sigworth, F.J. (1983) in »Single Channel Recording«, Sackmann, B. and Neher, E. eds., Plenum Press, New York, 191-263
8. Hanke, W., Andree, J., Strotmann, J. and Kahle, C. (1989) Europ. J. Biophys. -submitted-
9. Apley, E.C. and Wagner, R. (1989) Biochim. Biophys. Acta -in press-

THE EFFECT OF PYRIDINE ON THE ONSET LAG OF PHOTO-PHOSPHORYLATION: NO EVIDENCE FOR "LOCALIZED COUPLING"

ANDREAS BORCHARD and WOLFGANG JUNGE, Abteilung Biophysik, Fachbereich Biologie, Universität Osnabrück, Postfach 4469, D-4500 OSNABRÜCK, FRG

1. INTRODUCTION

For the protonic coupling mechanism in photophosphorylation it is still under debate whether protons are pumped into the aqueous lumen which serves as a reservoir for all ATP synthases ("delocalized coupling", eg. Mitchell, ref. 1) or whether protons are released within the membrane and travel in special intramembrane ducts to the ATP synthase ("localized coupling", eg. Williams, ref. 2).

While several more indirect lines of evidence for localized coupling was now considered as inconclusive, there have been no convincing counterarguments against the interpretation of certain key experiments for localized coupling by Dilley and coworkers (3). These authors have found that addition of the buffer pyridine to thylakoids, prepared under low salt conditions ("low salt thylakoids"), fails to enhance the onset lag of photophosphorylation upon firing a series of light flashes, while in "high salt thylakoids" enhancement is observed. This has been taken as evidence for "localized coupling" in the former and "delocalized coupling" in the latter case.

We reproduced these observations for pyridine, but we found also another buffer, tris(hydroxymethyl)aminomethane (tris), which enhanced the onset lag in *both* types of preparations. Interestingly, when pyridine was added on top of tris, it again failed to further prolong the onset lag in "low salt" but not in "high salt thylakoids". This behaviour was paralleled with the ability or failure, respectively, of these buffers to decrease the extent of flash induced pH-transients in the lumen as indicated by absorption changes of neutral red. The reported pyridine effects are therefore compatible with the delocalized coupling scheme in contrast to the interpretation by Dilley and coworkers.

2. MATERIAL AND METHODS

Thylakoids were freshly prepared from 10 to 12 days old pea seedlings by the method of Ort and Izawa (4). The final medium for resuspension of pelleted thylakoids at typically 3 mM chlorophyll contained 200 mM sucrose, 5 mM Hepes-KOH pH 7.5, 2 mM $MgCl_2$ and 0.5 mg/ml bovine serum albumin (BSA) in the case of "low salt thylakoids". For "high salt thylakoids" 200 mM sucrose was replaced by 30 mM sucrose and 100 mM KCl. For most experiments thylakoids, equivalent to 10 μM chlorophyll, were placed in a reaction medium with 50 mM Tricine-KOH, 3 mM $MgCl_2$, 1 mM KH_2PO_4, 5 mM dithiothreitol (DTT), 100 μM methylviologen, 300 nM valinomycin and 1.3 mg/ml BSA. pH-transients in the lumen were obtained as differences between transient absorption changes after one exiting flash (wavelength > 630 nm) with 13 μM neutral red and without this pH-indicating dye, for details of the method see (5, 6, 7). ATP synthesis caused by a train of 90 to 120 flashes (4 Hz, wavelength > 630 nm) was measured by luminescence of luciferin. The content of one vial ATP monitoring reagent (LKB) was dissolved in 1,5 ml distilled water and 10 µl of this solution was added per ml of reaction medium. 40 µM of purified ADP (8) and 5 µM diadenosin pentaphospat was also added. Luminescence was calibrated by adding aliquots of ATP standard (LKB).

3. RESULTS AND DISCUSSION

As control we reproduced the data of Beard and Dilley (3). Fig. 1 shows measurements of ATP synthesis in dark adapted "high salt" (top traces) and "low salt thylakoids" (bottom traces). Without any buffer (trace a) the first rise of luminescence appeared typically after 24 to 30 exciting flashes in "high salt thylakoids" and some flashes before in "low salt thylakoids". After addition of 5 mM pyridine (trace c) the onset lag of photophosphorylation was only enhanced in the "high salt" case. So we found the same type of pyridine effect as Dilley and coworkers, though to somewhat smaller extent - in our experiments with "high salt thylakoids" the lag was prolonged by 5 to 8 flashes instead of 10 to 20 flashes in theirs. Possible reasons are the different nature of the starting material, spinach leaves there and pea seedlings here, or different contamination of media with $CaCl_2$ (see ref. 9 about the effect of Ca^{2+}).

Figure 1: The effect of 5 mM pyridine (trace b), 10 mM tris (trace c) and 5 mM pyridine together with 10 mM tris (trace d), respectively, on the onset lag of ATP formation in "high salt" (top traces) and "low salt thylakoids" (bottom traces). Trace a shows the control without buffer. Thykakoids were prepared as in material and methods. The pH of the reaction medium was at 8.0. A train of 90 flashes (250 ms intervalls) was started 8 s after begin of the measurement.

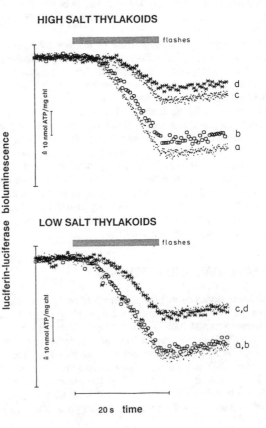

HIGH SALT THYLAKOIDS

LOW SALT THYLAKOIDS

20 s time

In some experiments we saw not only a enhancement of the photophosphorylation onset lag but also a slow down of the ATP synthesis speed. This would be expected, if pyridine had also uncoupling properties (data not shown but see the same behaviour eg. in ref. 9, fig. 1).

We repeated the experiment with another buffer to see whether the preparation dependent effect was particular to pyridine. We found that the onset lag was enhanced more drastically by addition of 10 mM tris but now in both preparations (10-15 flashes more, fig. 1, trace b). The question arose whether tris caused a switch from "localized" to "delocalized" behaviour. If that was the case then there should be no difference in the answer to additionally added pyridine between the two preparations. Trace d in fig. 1 shows ATP synthesis in presence of 10 mM tris and 5 mM pyridine. In "low salt thylakoids" the onset lag was the same compared to addition of 10 mM tris only, but it was furthermore enhanced in "high salt thylakoids". Added pyridine caused the same effect, selective to the preparation medium, with and without tris-buffer. This implied that tris had not caused the switching from a "localized" to a "delocalized" behaviour.

The above observations seemed to indicate that pyridine had different access to the thylakoid lumen dependent on the preparation medium. We checked the results obtained by luciferase assay by using neutral red as indicator of pH-transients in the lumen. Fig. 2 shows pH_{in}-indicating absorption changes of neutral red in "high salt" (top traces) and in "low salt thylakoids" (bottom traces) after one exiting flash. The fast phase of the signal was attributable to the rapid deposition of water-derived protons (half-rise time ~1 ms) and the slower phase to the release of plastoquinol-related protons (half-rise time ~20 ms, see also reference 10).

Figure 2: The effect of 10 mM pyridine (trace b) and 5 mM tris (trace c) on the pH_{in}-indicating absorption change of neutral red in "high salt" (top traces) and "low salt thylakoids" (bottom traces). Trace a shows the control without buffer. Thykakoids were prepared as in material and methods. The pH of the reaction medium was at 7.6. The flash frequency was 0.08 Hz, 20 samples were averaged.

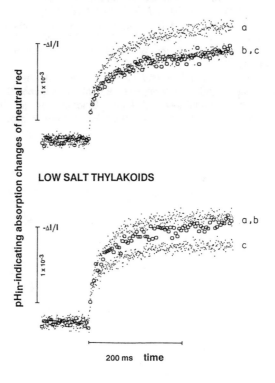

HIGH SALT THYLAKOIDS

LOW SALT THYLAKOIDS

200 ms time

In presence of 10 mM pyridine (trace c) the signal decreased significantly only in "high salt thylakoids" compared to the control (trace a). On the other hand, 5 mM tris-buffer decreased similarly the neutral red signal in both preparations (trace b).

Since buffering by pyridine was absent in "low salt" thylakoids, we suggest that either pyridine was nearly impermeant in the "low salt" case over a time range of at least five minutes or the "very narrow thylakoid lumen" prevented worth mentioning increase of the internal buffer capacity by this buffer. Investigations on this more complicated question are in progress. Notwithstanding, the failure of pyridine to prolong the initial onset lag of photophosphorylation in "low salt thylakoids" corresponded to the failure of pyridine to decrease the extent of the flashlight induced pH-jump in the lumen of "low salt thylakoids". This sheds doubt on the claim of this effect by Dilley and coworkers as evidence for "localized coupling".

ACKNOWLEDGEMENTS

We thank N. Spreckelmeier and H. Knebel for electronics and H. Kenneweg for photographs. Financial aid was provided by the Deutsche Forschungsgemeinschaft (Sonderforschungsbereich 171, Teilprojekte A2 und B3).

REFERENCES

1 Mitchell, P. (1961), Nature 141, 144-148
2 Williams, R. P. J. (1961), J. Theor. Biol. 1, 1-17
3 Beard, W. A. and Dilley, R. A. (1986), FEBS Lett. 201, 57-62
4 Ort, D. R. and Izawa, S. (1973), Plant. Physiol. 52, 595-600
5 Ausländer, W. and Junge, W. (1975), FEBS Lett. 59, 310-315
6 Junge, W., Ausländer, W., McGeer, A. and Runge, T. (1979), Biochim. Biophys. Acta 546, 121-141
7 Hong, Y. C. and Junge, W. (1983), Biochim. Biophys. Acta 722, 197-208
8 Shavit, N. and Strotmann, H. (1980), Meth. Enzymol. 69, 321-324
9 Chiang, G. and Dilley, R. A. (1987), Biochemistry, 26, 4911-4916
10 Förster, V. and Junge, W. (1985), Photochem. Photobiol. 41, 183-190

STUDIES ON THE ROLE OF THYLAKOID MEMBRANE-LOCALIZED PROTONS IN ATP SYNTHESIS

Li Youze, Ma Zhengping and Wu Shaolong, Shanghai Institute of Plant Physiology, Academia Sinica, Shanghai 200032, China

1. INTRODUCTION

In most cases, the rate of photophosphorylation (PSP) is dependent on the proton electrochemical potential ($\Delta\mu H^+$). One of the exceptions is that nigericin and NH_4Cl at low concentrations stimulate PSP in steady state but decrease the $\Delta\mu H^+$ (1,2,3,4,5). These phenomena are difficult to be explained by the chemiosmotic hypothesis. Our results indicated that there is an alternative mechanism of coupling between the photosynthetic electron transport and ATP formation.

2. MATERIALS AND METHODS

Chloroplasts were prepared from fresh spinach leaves grown in phytotron. The methods of preparation and measurements of Δ pH, 515nm absorption change, ATP formation and electron transport were as previous (6). See also Laszlo, J.A. et al (7) for the measurement of localized protons.

3. RESULTS

3.1. Effects of nigericin and NH_4Cl on PSP and electron transport. At low concentrations, nigericin ($<3\times10^{-8}M$) and NH_4Cl ($<10^{-4}M$) stimulated PSP in steady state obviously but had no such effects under us flashes (Fig.1a,b). At these concentrations (not uncoupling concentrations) NH_4Cl also enhanced coupling or basal electron transport (Fig.1c), nigericin had similar effect (data not shown).

3.2. Effects of nigericin and NH_4Cl on $\Delta\mu H^+$ and localized protons. ΔpH in steady state or $\Delta\Psi$ under flashes was not increased by nigericin or NH_4Cl at low concentrations which was not the cause of stimulating effects of nigericin or NH_4Cl on PSP (Fig.2). The 9AA fluorescence of dark-adapted chloroplasts in which internal and external bulk phase pH had been balanced was increased by adding nigericin in the dark at low concentrations which were corresponded to those with stimulating effects on PSP. It indicated the release of certain localized membrane protons by nigericin. NH_4Cl had no such effect (Fig.3).

M. Baltscheffsky (ed.), Current Research in Photosynthesis, Vol. III, 101–104.
© 1990 *Kluwer Academic Publishers. Printed in the Netherlands.*

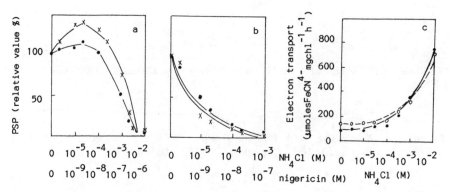

Fig.1 Effects of nigericin or NH$_4$Cl on PSP or electron transport
    a. PSP in steady state   b. initial PSP   × nigericin   • NH$_4$Cl
    c. FeCN reduction   ∘ coupled   • basal

3.3. Nigericin and NH$_4$Cl had different effects on PSP coupled with
    different electron transport systems such as H$_2$O→MV (PSI+PSII),
    H$_2$O→PDox+DBMIB (PSII), DPIPH$_2$+DCMU→MV (PSI). Nigericin at low
    concentrations stimulated PSI PSP obviously but not PSII, while
    NH$_4$Cl stimulated PSII PSP but not PSI (Fig.4). Under condition
    of high salt concentration (300 mM KCl), these stimulating effects
    were diminished or even eliminated (data not shown).

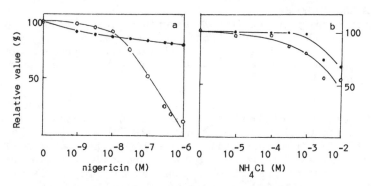

Fig. 2 Effects of nigericin or NH$_4$Cl on ΔpH or Δψ
    a. Nig   ∘ ΔpH   •Δψ b. NH$_4$Cl   ∘ ΔpH   •Δψ

3.4. Preillumination of chloroplasts with presence of 5mM DTT activated
    CF1 on the membrane and then increased the PSP activity. The ef-
    fects of nigericin on those pretreated chloroplasts were diminished
    remarkably or even eliminated which were similar to those on chlo-
    roplasts from preilluminated spinach leaves (Fig.5) and the effects
    of NH$_4$Cl were not eliminated (data not shown). In the presence
    of TPT (5x10^{-7}M) which mainly acted as an inhibitor of proton
    channel, nigericin stimulated PSP only at much lower concentrations
    which was quite different from those of control (Fig.6).

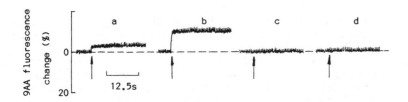

Fig.3 Effects of nigericin or NH_4Cl on protons release of dark-adapted
chloroplasts
a. 1% ethanol b. Nig 1×10^{-8}M c. H_2O d. NH_4Cl 5×10^{-5}M

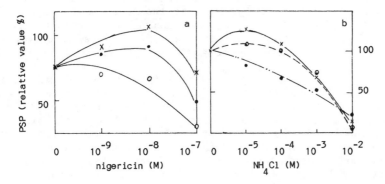

Fig.4 Effects of nigericin or NH_4Cl on PSP linked with different
photosystems
× $H_2O\rightarrow MV$ (PSI+PSII)   ○ $DPIPH_2(+DCMU)\rightarrow MV$ (PSI)
• $H_2O\rightarrow PDox(+DBMIB)$ (PSII)

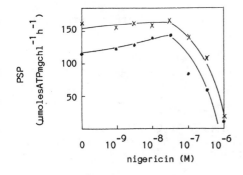 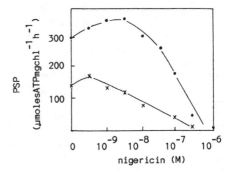

Fig. 5 Effect of nigericin on PSP in
chloroplasts after light-DTT
activation   • control
× light-DTT activation

Fig. 6 Effect of nigericin on PSP
in the presence of TPT
• control
× TPT 5×10^{-7}M

4. DISCUSSION

Effects of localized membrane protons on ATP formation were observed from the stimulating effects of nigericin and NH_4Cl at low concentrations on PSP in steady state.

It seemed that the stimulating effect of nigericin at low concentrations on PSP could be explained by its effect on the release of localized membrane protons since the effective concentrations of nigericin in these two reactions were in such a correspondence. The stimulation of PSI PSP by nigericin may implied that there is close connection between the localized membrane protons and the protons generated by PQH_2 oxidation. The diminished or even eliminated stimulating effect of nigericin at low concentrations on PSP in the presence of TPT and that of light-DTT pretreated chloroplasts with higher PSP activity indicated that the localized membrane protons released by nigericin at low concentrations may directly affect on the conformation of CFo-CF1 and change CF1 from inactive form into active form and then promote the catalytic activity of H^+-ATP synthase.

Analyzing the effects of NH_4Cl on PSP ($H_2O \rightarrow MV$), it stimulted PSP coupled with PSII but not PSI PSP and had no effect on the release of localized membrane protons and so on. The stimulation of PSII PSP by NH_4Cl implied that the protons generated by water oxidation were also localized. Nigericin and NH_4Cl at low concentrations enhanced electron transport from H_2O to MV which could be coupled with localized proton formation in different domains. Nigericin (lipophilic) and NH_4Cl (hydrophilic) had different characteristics and effects. They promoted the utilization of localized protons in different domains to ATP formation distinctively. Their different effects also indicated that the protons generated by water oxidation and PQH_2 oxidation were localized and reached CFo-CF1 through different pathway.

Although the detailed pathway of localized protons in different domains to CFo were still vague, there may exist different mechanisms of the energy coupling between electron transport and ATP formation. The localized membrane proton force may be one form of high energy states contributing to ATP formation.

* This work was supported by NNSF of China.

REFERENCES
1 Research Group I, Department of Photosynthesis, Shanghai Institute of Plant Physiology (1977) Acta Biochimica et Biophysica Sinica 9(2): 159-167
2 Giersch, C. (1982) Z. Naturforsch 37c:242-250
3 Giersch, C. (1983) Biochim. Biophys. Acta 725:309-319
4 Giersch, C. (1984) in Advances in Photosynthesis Research (Sybesma,C., ed.) Vol II pp 403-406 Martinus Nijhoff/Dr. W. Junk Publishers Dordrecht. The Netherlands.
5 Pick, U. and Weiss, M. (1988) Biochim. Biophys. Acta 934:22-31
6 Laszlo, J.A., Baker G.M., and Dilley, R.A. (1984) J. Bioenerg. Biomem. 16:37-51
7 Li Youze, Du Ziyun and Ma Zhengping (1988) Acta Biochimica et Biophysica Sinica 20(4):371-378

ATP SYNTHESIS BY ISOLATED CHLOROPLAST COUPLING FACTORS, INDUCED WITH pH-SHIFT

MICHAEL G. GOLDFELD AND VASAK D. MIKOYAN, INSTITUTE OF CHEMICAL PHYSICS, Ac.Sci., MOSCOW, 117 977 USSR

1. INTRODUCTION

It is commonly accepted that the coupling of the energy-donating electron transfer in membranes of chloroplasts, mitochondria and bacteria with the energy-accepting reaction of ATP synthesis the major role belongs to the proton. This implies that at least some steps of the H^+-ATPsynthase catalysed reaction are controlled by the deprotonation and protonation of several groups of the enzyme substrate complex (1,2). Therefore, it is quite natural that the attention of investigators is for more than 20 years attracted to the experiments of Jagendorf and Uribe (3), who revealed the ATP synthesis on the transfer of chloroplasts from acidic to alkaline media. We have attempted now to use this experimental approach to isolated protein coupling factors. The reaction of single-event ATP synthesis in solution, induced with acid-base shift, is treated as an "elementary act" which is multifold repeated with the alkaline shift in the suspension of thylakoid membranes. The protein which catalyses the direct (synthesis of ATP) and the reverse (hydrolysis) reactions occurs in the essentially different states.

2. EXPERIMENTAL

The studies were performed on CF_0-CF_1 complex is isolated according to (4) and on soluble protein CF_1 obtained according to (5) from bean chloroplasts. After the thermal activation (6) the latter had the ATPase activity about 30 μmol ATP/mg protein per minute (7). The pH shift was obtained by mixing equal volumes of solutions A and B. Solution A: A mM NaH_2PO_4, pH 4.5; 4×10^{-8} protein, 1 mM $CaCl_2$ (for CF_1) or 1 mM $MgCl_2$ (for CF_0-CF_1) and 10^{-6}M ADP. Solution B; 0.1 M Tricine-NaOH, pH 8.4. ATP was determined by bioluminescence using the immobilized luciferase from Luciola mingrelica (8). The yield ATP amounted to about 2% of the initial ADP.

3. RESULTS AND DISCUSSION

Acid-base shift in the solution of CF_0-CF_1 complex in the interval pH 4.5 - 8.4 induced the formation of ATP with the yield of about 6 mol ATP per mol of protein (mol. wt. 435 kDA). The plots obtained on the variation of initial (Fig. 1A, curve 1) and final (curve 2) pH values remind the curves of acid-base titration. For the variation of final pH value, the inflection point correspond to the effective value pK 7.3

Close results were obtained for the soluble protein CF_1 (Fig. 1B). However, the observation of ATP synthesis with CF_1 was possible under two conditions. Firstly, the synthesis of ATP required the addition of ascorbate or dithiothreitol in the protein incubation

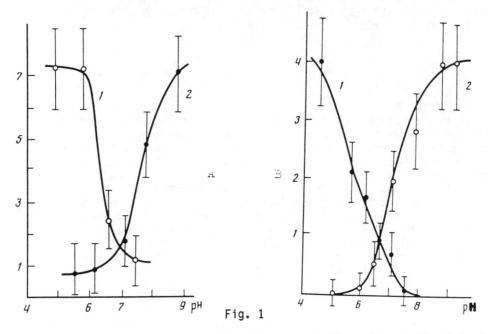

Fig. 1

ATP yield, mol ATP per mol CF_0-CF_1 (A) or CF_1 (B), as function of the initial (curves 1) or final (curves 2) pH values in acid-base shift experimental.

medium. It was essential that these reductants were introduced prior to the addition ADP, no matter this last was added to the initial acid solution or to the final alkaline phase. Once ADP was introduced in the incubation medium before ascorbate, no ATP formation was observed, irrespective of the subsequent addition of ascorbate. Secondly, the synthesis of ATP was observed even in the absence of both ascobate and dithithreitol if ADP was added to the final alkaline phase. The above observations can be explained, assuming that the oxidation of some gropus in the protein facilitates the transition of CF_1 into the conformation which hinders the binding of ADP. At the same time, the binding of ADP by protein in the absence of external reductants stimulated the irreversible oxidation and prevents from the subsequent ATP synthesis.

Without loss of generality, we may assume that the acidification induces the conformational transition of enzyme-substrate complex

accompanied by the formation of ATP. This transition develops in
time, with the kinetics shown in Fig. 2. These experiments were

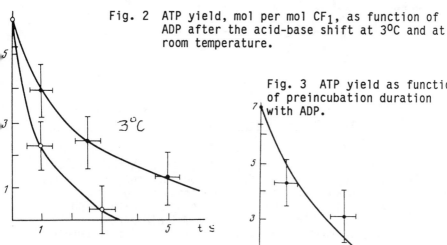

Fig. 2   ATP yield, mol per mol CF_1, as function of
ADP after the acid-base shift at $3^{\circ}C$ and at
room temperature.

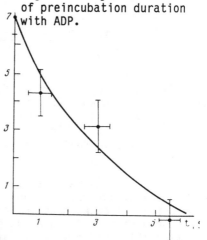

Fig. 3   ATP yield as function
of preincubation duration
with ADP.

methodologically similar to those
described above, but ADP was introduced in the mixture with some delay (up to 10 s) after acid-base
shift. The yield of ATP was observed
to decrease. The rate constant of the transition of protein to the
equilibrium state (corresponding to alkaline medium) evaluated from
these experiments was ca. 1 s^{-1} at room temperature and ca. 0.4 s^{-1}
at $3^{\circ}C$. The transition into inactive (not capable of the subsequent
ATP synthesis) state which is suppressed by the reductants, also
allows kinetic description. Fig. 3 shows a decrease in the ATP yield
for the acid-base shift vs. the duration of preincubation of CF_1
with ADP. At $3^{\circ}C$, the complete inactivation is achieved in ca. 5 s.
ADP-dependent inactivation, prevented by the reductants, is not
affected by the presence of phosphate and calcium in the mixture.
However, if all the components of the substrate mixture, ADP, P_i
and Ca, are introduced in the final alkaline phase and hans no preliminary contact with the protein (before the alkaline shift), no
ATP was formed. In the presence of ascorbate, the preliminary incubation with ADP has no effect on the ATP yield. (Fig. 4)

Fig. 5 ATP yield as function of ADP concentrations (pH 4.5 - 8.3).
The results presented in Fig. 4 can be considered from alternative
point of view: whether the synthesis of bound ATP occurs isoenergi-
cally, with the subsequent separation due to the alkaline shift, or
the condension is a direct effect of this shift involving the free
ADP. The data of Fig. 4 allow two possibilities. Firstly, the iso-
energetic ATP synthesis proceeds at a high rate and is completed
in less than 1 s; Secondly; the isoenergetic process is insignificant, and the major part of ATP is formed as a direct response to

Fig. 4 ATP yield, mol per mol CF_1, as function of preincubation duration with ADP in the presence of ascorbate. pH shift from pH 4.5 to pH 8.4.

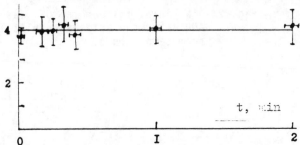

the alkaline shift producing an "energized" state with the life-time of ca. 3s (in the absence of substrate). We believe the first assumption to be hardly probable and the more so, considering that the iso-energetic synthesis of bound ATP on CF_1 protein (with no pH changes) with the final yield of less than 1 mol ATP per mol protein is characterized by an essentially greater half-time (of the order of 10 s) (9).

All our experiments were carried out on the background of very low ADP concentration (below 10 µM), which was initially intended to avoid the effect of background luminescence due to the admixture of ATP in ADP preparation. The dependence of the ATP yield on the ADP concentration (Fig. 5) shows that the amount of freshly formed ATP decreases two times when the initial ADP concentration is reduced

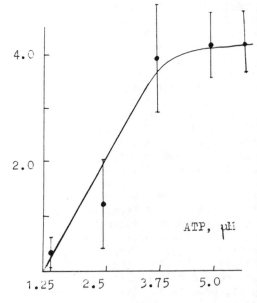

Fig. 5 ATP yield (mol per mol CF_1) as function of ADP concentration pH 4.5 - 8.4.

to 2.5 µM. The observed drop in the ATP yield agrees with the assumption that the synthesis of ATP results from the interaction of ADP present in the solution with the state of CF_1 protein changed due to the alkaline shift. The limited life-time of this state (of the order of 1 s, see Fig. 3) leads to the situation when the decrease in the ADP concentration, starting from a definite value, reduces the probability of ADP meeting with the stressed conformational state so strongly that a partial relaxation of the protein occurs prior to the collision. Thus, these data also disagree with the concept of slow synthesis of bound ATP preceeding the alkaline shift.

The main result of the above described experiments consists in the possibility of non-stationary synthesis of ATP from ADP and P_i in homogeneous solutions of the coupling factors of chloroplasts at acid-base shift, with the yield of about 6 mol ATP per mol protein in the absence of any asymmetric membrane structure.

The driving force of ATP synthesis in these systems is, eventually the evolution of free energy in the reaction of proton neutralization, whereby the dependence of ATP yield on the initial and final pH values allows us to conclude that the reaction mechanism includes as the working step, the deprotonation of molecular groups of the coupling factor with pK 7.3. It should be noted that a slow growth of pH within the same limits produced no ATP synthesis. In other words, the appearance of stressed state requires the practically simultaneous deprotonation of several acidic groups of the enzyme-substrate complex.

Putting aside the problem of the nature of various intermediate steps of the energy conversion on phosphorylation, it is nevertheless possible, on the basis of these results, to propose that the determining step in the normal membrane phosphorylation also is the ionization of some weakly acidic groups of the coupling factor, for example, of sulfhydrylic groups. Quite probably the transformation of SH-groups into disulfide groups excludes the pathway of conformational relaxation of ATP synthase, specifically coupled with the ATP synthesis, and affects the relative affinity of this protein to adenine nucleotides. The hydrophobic CF_0 part of this complex stabilizes to some extent the native conformation of CF_1, as result there is no need for reductants, when the reaction proceeds with CF_0-CF_1 preparation, in contrast to CF_1.

Within the framework of the concept of conformational relaxation as the general pathway of energy conversion in ADP phosphorylation (10), the "primary macroerg" is represented by a protein molecule not relaxed to a new conformational state and possessing several "extra" units of negative charge appearing due to the OH^--shock. It can be suggested that any other way of modification of the charged state would lead to the same result (e.g. the change in the pK of the protein groups). The shift of equilibrium in the deprotonation reaction can be induced, for example, by a change of the electrical potential of the membrane surface with the built-in ATP synthase complexes. The shift of pK of the surface groups induced by the variation of electric potential was studied in a number of model systems, including micelles of detergents, etc. and reached several pH units (11). The appearance of local charges on the sites close to the "essential" groups of ATP synthase due to electron transfer reactions also may be the direct physical reason for the energization of the enzyme and the subsequent ATP synthesis.

Thus, the energetics of the reaction is proposed to be determined by the deprotonation of acidic groups of the protein, EH_n E^n + nH^+ whose equilibrium is shifted on the addition of alkali. Usually the energy released on the deprotonation of low-molecular compound is dissipated instantly via the vibration relaxation. However, the deprotonation of the "essential" group of the coupling factor may lead to the long-living non-equilibrum states of the protein. The energy stored in this state is consumed only along the selected modes, coupled with the ATP synthesis. This is the essence of the concept of the "protein-machine" (10,12). The results of experiments on the ATP synthesis by isolated coupling factors from chloroplasts, and of similar studies with some other H^+-ATPases (13,14), allow a new approach to the experiments on phosphorylation induced by pH-shift in the suspension of thylakoid membranes. This approach is considered in accompaning paper (17). Some results described in this paper have been published in Russian earlier (15,16).

RERECENCES
1 Boyer, P.D. (1987) Biochemistry 26, 8503-8507
2 Galmiche, J.M., Girault, G. and Lemaire, C. (1985) Photochem. and Photobiol. 47, 707-713
3 Jagendorf, A.T. and Uribe, E. (1966) Proc. Nat. Acad. Sci. 55, 170-177
4. Pick, U. and Racker, E. (1979) J. Biol. Chem. 254, 2793-2799
5 Strotmann, M., Hess, H. and Edelman, K. (1973) Biochim. Biophys. Acta 314, 202-214
6 Farron, F. and Racker, E. (1970) Biochemistry 9, 3829-3834
7 Goldfeld, M.G., Koltover, V.K., Major, P.S., Mikoyan, V.D., Dmitriev, P.I. and Shapiro, A.B. (1986) Molek. Biol. 20, 120-127
8 Ugarova, N.N., Brovko, L.Ya., and Kost, N.V. (1982) Enzyme Mircobiol. Technol. 4, 224229
10 Blumenfeld, L.A. (1983) Physics of Bioenergetics Processes, Springer Verlag, New York
11 Gutman, M. (1984) In Methods of Biochemical Analysis, vol. 30 pp 1-103
12 Chernavsky, D.S., Chernavskaya, N.M. and Yagushinsky, L.S. (1982) Biofizika 27, 114-119
13 Blumenfeld, L.A., Malenkova, I.V., Kormer, S.S., Serejenkov, V.A. and Mileykovskaya and Davydov, R.M. (1986) Doklady AN SSR, 288, 1494-1496
14 Serejenkov, V.A., Malenkova, I.V., Talybov, M.T., Kapreljanz, A.S., Davydov, R.M. and Blumenfled, L.A. Biofizika, 31, 972-975
15 Blumenfled, L.A., Goldfeld, M.G., Vozyshaeva, L.V., Solovjev, I. and Blumenfeld, L.A. (1988) Biofizika 33, 254-257
16 Mikoyan, V.D., Goldfeld, M.G., Vozvyshaeva, L.V., Solovjev, I. and Blumenfled, L.A. (1988) Biofizika 33, 254-257
17 Goldfeld, M.G., Lobysheva, I.I. and Mikoyan, V.D., this volume

NON-LINEAR EFFECTS AT PHOSPHORYLATION INDUCED BY ACID-BASE SHIFT IN THYLAKOID MEMBRANES

MICHAEL G. GOLDFELD, IRINA I. LOBYSHEVA AND VASAK D. MIKOYAN
Institute of Chemical Physics, Ac.Sci., Moscow, 117977 USSR

1.   INTRODUCTION

Examples of oscillatory processes in membranes, arising as a result of modification of the transport properties of the membrane by the flow of a penetrating substance, have long been known in the physical chemistry (1-3).

When we go from model lipid membranes over to biological ones, the situation becomes drastically more complicated, since biological membranes not only perform barrier functions but they also constitute the medium, matrix, into which membrane enzymes are built asymmetrically and where vectorized enzymatic processes occur. Some of the membrane enzymes themselves make up ionic permeability channels. In particular, hydrophobic fragment CF_o of the coupling factor CF_o-CF_1 synthesizing ATP in chloroplasts, and homologous proteins in the membranes of mitochondria and bacteria, make up a protonic channel (4).

In this paper the behavior of H^+-ATPase/synthase in the membranes of chloroplasts under the conditions of artificially created transmembrane gradient of proton concentration (Δ pH) is considered. This approach was developed by Jagendorf and Uribe (5). We have turned to their approach in connection with our recent results (6,7), which demonstrate that isolated protein coupling factor CF_o-CF_1 or CF_1 from the chloroplast membrane is also capable to synthesize ATP in a homogeneous solution, in the absence of any asymmetrical structures, under the conditions of alkaline shift of pH. Experiments have shown that ATP synthesis is the result of deprotonation of some groups of the coupling protein, with pK~ 7.3, and may be regarded as a consequence of relaxation of the enzyme-substrate conformation which became stressed in the course of deprotonation as a consequence of appearance of excess bound negative charges. The specific character of H^+-ATPase as a "molecular machine" is that this stress does not become dissipated into heat but it relaxes along the singled out mechanical mode corresponding to the synthsis of ATP from ADP and P_i (8). Single turn-over synthesis of ATP by isolated CF_1 protein in the case of alkaline shift may be regarded as an "elementary act" of longtime phosphorylation by thylakoids in suspension, subjected to a similar pH shift. Here the role of the membrane consists in

M. Baltscheffsky (ed.), Current Research in Photosynthesis, Vol. III, 111–120.
© 1990 Kluwer Academic Publishers. Printed in the Netherlands.

closing the catalytic cycle, in ensuring multiple, cyclic functioning of the membrane protein (9).

In the present study it is shown that in the case of low concentrations of the substrate (ADP) the alkaline shift induced oscillatory changes of the value and sign of the activity of the membrane ATPase/synthase, with a period of about 10 s. These oscillatory changes are not connected directly with changes of the phosphate potential, i.e. with the energy characteristics of the system; apparently, they are defined by changes in the proton flux across the thylakoid membrane. In the model proposed on the basis of the experimental data obtained it is assumed that the proton flow across the membrane is also nonuniform, passing through the stages of accumulation of excess protons in the membrane and of their subsequent discharge into the external medium. These changes in the state of the membrane are the factor controlling the state of the membrane H^+-ATPase/synthase. Some preliminary results have been published in (10-12).

2. EXPERIMENTAL

Chloroplasts were isolated from the leaves of beans and spinach and were subjected to a hypotonic shock. The alkaline shift was carried out essentially by following the procedure described in (5): 0.175 ml of the suspension of chloroplasts was incubated for 1 min in an acidic medium comprising 13 mM sodium succinate, 3.6 mM $MgCl_2$, 1.6 mM Na_2HPO_4, 14 µM diuron, ADP (concentration is varied), pH 4.2, on ice. Then the suspension was rapidly mixed with an alkaline solution (0.1 M tricine/NaOH, pH 8.4). The final pH value of 8.1 was established. The concentration of chlorophyll in the medium was 0.01 mM. After the alkaline shift the phosphorylation reaction was stopped after definite time intervals (from 2 to 60 s) by way of 125-fold dilution with a solution comprising components of the liciferin-luciferase system and ATP concentration was determined by the bioluminescence technics.

3. RESULTS AND DISCUSSION

Fig.1 illustrates the kinetics of changes in the ATP concentration in the suspension of thylakoid membranes after the alkaline shift from pH 5.0 to 8.1. With a sufficiently low ADP concentration in the incubation medium damped oscillations of the ATP level were observed after energizing the membranes by the alkaline shift with a period of about 10 s. Amplitude of the oscillations varies within 1-3 uM ATP. In 30-40 s the ATP concentration reaches a quasi-stationary level which decline

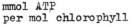

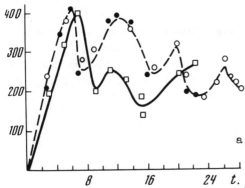
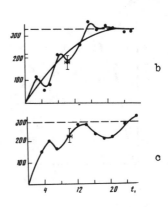

Fig.1. Changes in ATP concentration in suspension of thylakoid membranes after acid-base shift. ADP content in the medium was: (a)
12 uM; (b) 24 uM; (c) 48 uM. Curve 1 and b,c two preparetions
of bean chloroplasts. Curve 2 – spinach chloroplasts.

vary slowly because of a low ATPase activity of the preparations. The
main condition for the oscillatiry changes in the ATP yield seems to
be a sufficiently low concentration of ADP. Indeed, as is seen in Fig.
1, the depth of the oscillatory modulation of the kinetic curve dimini·
shes as the value of $[ADP]_o$ grows, and above $[ADP]_o = 50$ µM the kinetics degenerates into a normal monotonic function which has been already obtained in the studies of other authors(5,13). Within the same
limits the total yield of ATP grows and reaches saturation at $ADP_o = 25$–30 µM.

The appearance of oscillations correlates with a high initial
rate of ATP synthesis (Fig.2), which reaches its maximal value of abou
120 mmol ATP per mol of chlorophyll per second at $ADP_o = 10$–15 uM
but declines to 30 mmol/mol as $[ADP]_o$ increases further.

A consideration of the oscillatory kinetic curve suggests that in
the course of the experiment the activity of the membranes is switched
over from the ATP synthesis (during odd half-periods) to hydrolysis
of the accumulated product (during even half-periods).

In attempt to interpret these effects the first idea to be

V$_o$, mmol ATP per mol chlorophyll
    per s.

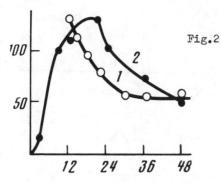

Fig.2. Initial rate of ATP formation
after acid-base shift as function
of ADP concentration. Chloroplasts
from bean (1) and spinach (2)

verified is that the activity of the membrane ATPase/synthase is regulated by changes of the phosphate potential, i.e. actually by changes
of the ATP/ADP ratio (in view of excess of phosphate whose concentration may be regarded to be constant). Variation of the initial ATP
concentration within 0.5-2.5 µM at constant $[ADP]_o$ = 12 µM (the phosphate potential changing from 42.4 to 47 kJ/mol) did not affect the
total yield of the newly formed ATP or the initial rate of phosphorylation, or, else, the oscillatory character of the kinetics. Thus, the
experimental data obtained cannot be explained within the framework o.
thermodynamic approach. Moreover, from Fig.3 it follows that the oscil.

V$_o$, mmol ATP per mol chlorophyll per s.

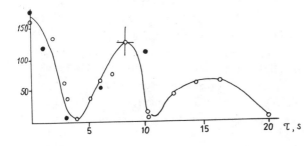

Fig.3. Net ATP yield
after acid-base shift
in suspension of thyla-
koid membranes from bea.
leaves as of ADP delay

latory changes induced by the alkaline shift characterize the intrinsic state of the thylakoid membranes, synchronized by the alkaline shift, and they are not connected specifically with the course of the phosphorylation reaction: the total yield of ATP upon ADP introduction after a definite period of time following the alkaline shift ("delay of substrate") also changes in an oscillatory manner. In other words, the state of the enzyme, determining the activity in relation to the ATP synthesis/hydrolysis, is a decreasing quasi-periodic function of time after the alkaline shift even in the absence of the substrate.

Insofar as the oscillatory effects are not determined by changes in the phosphate potential and, moreover, changes in the membranes are oscillatory even in the absence of the substrate, one has to admit that these effects are controlled by the sole process triggered by the alkaline shift in the absence of phosphorylation: by the leakage of protons. Apparently, this process proceeds non-uniformly, for instance, in such a manner that first in some domains of the membrane the protons (or at least some their fraction) are accumulated and then they are discharged cooperatively into solution on the other side of the membrane. In other words, the protonic permeability of the membrane is inhomogeneous in time and space and, thus, this hypothesis closes up with the ideas of local barriers for the transfer of protons (for instance, at the membrane boundaries), of the existance of local proton channels, et (14-17) In some studies pathways are discussed, along which the proton necessary for the ATP synthesis get into the channel of the ATPsynthase (18,19). It is believed that these are not necessarily completely delocalized protons in the volume of solution around the membrane, that the protons may get into the channel, by taking a shorter pathway than through solution, from the nearest cytochrome b_6/f-complex, becoming free on oxidation of plastohydroquinone, or from the water splitting system. Here we shall discuss the data on the effect of uncouplers on phosphorylation induced by the pH shift; we believe that these data also reflect this spatial inhomogeneity of the transport of the protons essential for the phosphorylation.

Fig. 4 illustrates the dependence of the yield of ATP in the phosphorylation induced by the alkaline shift in the thylakoid membranes on the concentrations of a number of uncouplers eliminating transmembrane gradients of pH. Irrespective of the mechanism and nature of the uncoupling action, the concentration dependence is essentially nonmonotonous in all the cases. In the range of small concentrations an

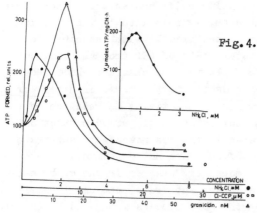

Fig. 4. The effect of uncouplers on
ATP yield (rel.units) at
acid-base shift in suspensio
of thylakoid membrane from
bean chloroplasts.
Inset: NH_4Cl effect on photophosphorylation according
to (20).

increase of the phosphorylating activity is observed. The concentrations ensuring maximal activity of phosphorylation are specific for
each of the substancees. They correlate with the efficiency of each of
them as the uncoupler and amount to 0.5 mM for NH_4Cl, 6 µM for Cl-CCP,
10 nM for gramicidin D. It should be noted that each of these concentrations is about 30% of the concentration corresponding to about two
fold suppression of the phosphorylation. In our experiments the degree
of stimulation reached 250%.

A qualitatively close effect was found earlier (20,21) for photophosphorylation in the presence of uncoupling amines. The concentrations stimulating the photophosphorylation coincide with those stimulating the phosphorylation in the case of alkaline shift, though the
stimulating effect in the light-induced reaction did not exceed 20-30%.
In (20) it is suggested that the activation is caused by acceleration
of the basal transport of the electrons in the presence of uncouplers
which remove kinetic limitations. However, the effect was observed by
us in the absence of any transport of the electrons, in darkness, in
the presence of diuron inhibiting the electron transport in thylakoids.
It should be noted that the effect of stimulation of the phosphorylatio
by the uncouplers, as well as oscillatory effects, were observed at lo₩
concentrations of ADP, but it declined (concurrently with the growth o:
the total yield of phosphorylation) with an increase of ADP_o.

A characteristic feature of the action of the uncouplers under

the conditions of alkaline shift is the absence of complete inhibition
of the ATP synthesis at the saturating concentration of the uncouplers
The residual,uncoupler-insensitive yield of the ATP, is about 6 mol
per mol of the membrane coupling factor, this corresponding a single
turnover phosphorylation induced by the alkaline shift in homogeneous
solutions of the isolated coupling factor protein (6,7), with respect
to which these uncouplers are ineffetive. This fact is consistent with
our interpretation of phosphorylation on the protein due to deprotonation of acidic groups as an "elementary act" of phosphorylation according to Jagendorf and Uribe.

In our interpretation of the stimulating effect of the uncouplers
we proceed from their ability to eliminate spatial pH gradients betwee)
the areas separated by membrane barriers. Apparently, this function is
actually dominant when the uncoupler concentrations are high. Nevertheless, some data point to the presence of local barriers for the
proton transfer: between the protons in the volume and in the protonic
channel of ATPsynthase, between the protons released in conjugation
with different redox reactions in the chloroplasts (in the system of
water oxidation and in the oxidation of plastohydroquinone on the
cytichrome complex). It may be supposed that the uncouplers taken in
small concentrations eliminate, first of all, just these local barriers, facilitating the access of the protons into the channel of ATPsyn·
thase. This eventually leads to stimulation of the ATP synthesis. The
degree of stimulation will, apparently, be dependent on the ratio of
the local and fully delocalized fluxes of the protons. In the case on
nonstationary phosphorylation induced by the alkaline shift the total
rate of the reaction, apparently, is kinetically limited by the local
barrier between the volume of solution and the ATPsynthase channel.
This is the cause of the very strong stimulating effect produced by th(
uncouplers (up to 250%). In steady-state phosphorylation this limitation is partly removed by lateral fluxes of the protons, directly,
without full delocalization over the intrathylakoid space, transferred
into the ATPsynthase channel. As a result, stimulation by the uncouplers is weakly pronounced.

Let us consider the oscillatory effects once again. The main qualitative result consists in periodic reversals of the sign of activity
of the H^+-ATPase/synthase in the thylakoid membranes, induced by the
alkaline shift at low ADP concentrations.

We assume that after the $\triangle$pH has been established the leakage of

the protons proceeds nonuniformly; first, the protons are accumulated
in some domains of the membrane, for instance, because of the permeability of the internal surface being greater than that of the external
surface. After a certain intramembrane concentration has been reached,
the ratio of the permeabilities of the internal and external surfaces
is changed for the opposite and a rapid discharge of the protons outward occurs. The possibility of such a nonuniform transfer of the
particles, leading to oscillatory changes in the state of the membrane
has been considered theoretically in (22). For the oscillation to appear we must assume three states of the membrane to be possible at Δ p
0: two conditionally stable states and one unstable state, whereas at
Δ pH=0 there is only one stable state. Let, further, the state of the
membrane determines and modulates the catalytic properties of the
ATPase/synthase which may also be in one of the three states. Two of
them are conditionally stable and catalytically active in the reaction
of ATP synthesis (1) and hydrolysis (2). State (3) is catalytically
inactive, it is stable at Δ pH=0 and unstable at Δ pH$\neq$0.

The analysis of this problem carried out in collaboration with
prof. D.S.Chernavsky, leads to the following equations described in
detail in (23):

$$\frac{dx}{dt} = y - \mathscr{H}z_0 \qquad (1)$$

$$\frac{dy}{dt} = x - x^3 - \delta y$$

or $\ddot{x} + (z_0 + \delta)\dot{x} + (\delta z_0 - 1)x + x^3 = 0$

Here the dimensionless variable x characterises proton concentration
within the membrane, y reflects proton permeability of the outer and
inner membrane surfaces, all other symbols standing for some adjustabl
parameters.

This equation describes the oscillations of the ball of unit moss
in the two minima potential under weak friction. The phase picture of
this system (at constant Δ pH and $z_0=0.3$, $\delta =0.3$) is shown in Fig.5.

The thick lines are the separatrices which separate areas of at-
traction of the two states: $x_1= -\sqrt{a/3\beta}$ (state (1)) and $x_2= \sqrt{a/3\beta}$
(state (2)). The areas of attraction of state (1) are hatched. Apparently, on substrate (ADP) addition simultaneously with pH-shift the
phase trajectory of the system gets into the area of attraction of
state (2), corresponding to the ATPsynthase activity $(x_2=\sqrt{a/3\beta})$(unhatc
ed area). The ATPase activity corresponds to state (1) of the membrane

$x_1 = -\sqrt{a/3\delta}$. The area of attraction of this state in Fig.5 is hatched.

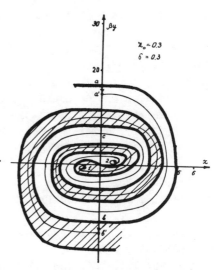

Fig.5. The phase picture of the
system (1) for the para-
meters $z_0 = 0.3$, $\delta = 0.3$; prepared by the program (23).
The thick lines are separatrices. The region of attraction of the state (1) is
hatched.

As Δ pH diminishes points (1) and (2) slowly approach one another
tending to symmetrical state (3). The ATP synthesis ceases and net
ATP yield is defined by the conditions and the phase trajectory of the
point.

To explain the behaviour of the system upon delay of the substrat
after the alkaline shift, we had to assume additionally that the ADP
influences but slightly the protonic permeability of the membrane (for
instrance, that it only weakly increases y_2). Then, if ADP is introduced immediately after the pH shift, point a shifts towards a' by
Δy. It remains in the area of attraction of state (2), where the ATP
synthesis predominant. After a half-period the point a moves along the
phase trajectory to position b. Addition of ADP at this moment increases y_2 and also shifts the point by Δy down, but now this brings the
point over to position b', i.e. to the attraction area state (1),
where the ATP hydrolysis is predominant. On addition of ADP after a
period when the point is in position c, the shift by the same value
Δy leaves the system in the attraction area of state (2) (ATP systhe
sis), etc. Only qualitative description is discussed at this stage.
A more detailed treatment taking into account slow changes in some
parameters of the model will be carried out later.

REFERENCES

1. Teorell, T. (1956) Disc.Faraday Soc. 21, 9-26
2. Langier, P., Page, K.R. and Wildner,G. (1981) Biophys.J. 36, 93-10'
3. Yoshikawa, K., Fujimoto, T., Shimooka, T., Terada, H., Kumazawa,N. and Ishii, T. (1988) Biophys.Chem. 29, 293-299
4. Boyer, P. (1987) Biochemistry 26, 8503-8507
5. Jagendorf, A.T. and Uribe, E. (1966) Proc.Nat.Acad.Sci.55, 170-177
6. Blumenfeld, L.A., Goldfeld, M.G., Mikoyan, V.D. and Solovjev,I.S. (1987) Molek.Biol. 21, 323-329
7. Mikoyan, V.D., Goldfeld, M.G., Vozvyshaeva, L.V. and Blumenfeld,L.. (1988) Biofizika 33, 254-257
8. Blumenfeld, L.A. Physics of Bioenergetic Processes, S(1983) Spring Verlag, New York
9. Blumenfeld, L.A. (1977) Problems of Biological Physics, Nauka-Pres: Moscow
10. Lobysheva, I.I., Goldfeld, M.G. and Mikoyan, V.D.(1988) Biofizika 33, 886-888
11. Lobysheva, I.I., Mikoyan,V.D. and Goldfeld, M.G. (1988) Biofizika 33, 888-889
12. Lobysheva,I.I., Mikoyan, V.D. and Goldfeld, M.G. (1987) Biofizika 32, 530-532
13. Yamamoto, T., Tonomura, Y. (1975) J.Biochem. 77, 137-146
14. Horner, R.D. and Moudrianakis, S.N. (1983) J.Biol.Chem. 258,11643-11647
15. Ort D., Dilley,R.A. and Good, N. (1976) Biochim.Biophys.Acta 449, 108-124
16. Williams, R.J.P. (1978) Biochim.Biophys.Acta 505, 1-44
17. Kell, D. (1979) Biochim.Biophys.Acta 549, 55-99
18. Kouchkovsky,Y.de, Sigalat, C. and Haraux, F.(1987) In Progress in Photosynthesis Research, Biggins, J., ed., v.3,pp.169-172 Dordrecht, Martinus Nijhoff Publishers
19. Beard. V.A. and Dilley, R.A. (1987) ibid, pp 165-168
20. Giersh,Ch. (1981) Biochem.Biophys.Res.Comm.100, 666-674
21. Giersh, CH. (1982) Z Naturforsch. 37c, 242-250
22. D'Alba, F. and Di Lorenzo,S. (1986) Bioelectrochem.Bioenerget. 15, 505-511
23. Goldfeld, M.G., Lobysheva, I.I., Mikoyan, V.D. and Chernavsky,D. (1989) Non-Linear Biology, in press

$\Delta\mu H^+$-DEPENDENT ACTIVATION OF THE THYLAKOID H^+-ATPase AND INITIATION OF CATALYSIS

D. LOHSE and H. STROTMANN, Institut für Biochemie der Pflanzen Heinrich-Heine-Universität Düsseldorf, F.R.G.

1. INTRODUCTION

Physiological activation of the H^+-translocating ATPase requires thylakoid membrane energization. With relaxation of the electrochemical proton gradient, the demodulated enzyme is rapidly inactivated, whereas deactivation of the thiol-modulated ATPase under certain experimental conditions is slow. Upon addition of ADP, however, inactivation occurs within a few seconds. This reaction is related with tight binding of 1 ADP per CF_1 to one of the three β subunits. Upon reactivation by membrane energization, the tightly bound ADP is transferred into a loosely bound form and finally released or exchanged (for review see ref. 1). Hence in illuminated chloroplasts in the steady state, the equilibrium between active and inactive ATPases and the equilibrium between enzyme molecules with tightly bound and loosely bound ADP depends on $\Delta\mu H^+$ when ADP is present at saturating concentration (≥ 10 µM). In the first part of this paper, steady state enzyme activities and levels of tightly bound ADP were investigated as function of ΔpH (at $\Delta\psi = 0$). Evaluation of these results permits conclusions about the number of protons translocated for activation of one ATPase molecule.
Upon reillumination release of tightly bound ADP is strongly accelerated by medium ADP and P_i. In the presence of both substrates, the initial rate of ADP release is identical with the initial rate of ATP formation (2). In the second part of this report, stimulation of release was analyzed as function of medium ADP and P_i concentration. The results show two different affinities for each of the two substrates. These reactions are interpreted to indicate pre-steady state processes at catalytic sites involved in the transition of the activated ATPase into the catalytically working enzyme.

2. EXPERIMENTAL

Thylakoids were isolated from spinach leaves by reported methods. Measurements of steady state ATPase activities and levels of tightly bound ADP were carried out in a fluorometer cuvette while fluorescence of 9-aminoacridine as measure of ΔpH was continuously recorded (3). In order to avoid generation of $\Delta\psi$, the reactions were performed in the presence of valinomycin + K^+. The fluorescence signal was calibrated as in ref. 4. After thiol modulation (2 min preillumination at ΔpH of about 3.6 in a medium containing 10 mM DTT), 10 µM ADP was added together with atte-

M. Baltscheffsky (ed.), Current Research in Photosynthesis, Vol. III, 121–124.

nuation of light intensity to yield different ΔpH values. After further 2 min equilibration time, ATPase activity was assayed by measurement of the initial rate of ATP-hydrolysis following addition of a mixture containing $(\gamma-^{32}P)$ATP, PEP, pyruvate kinase and nigericin as an uncoupler. For determination of steady state levels of tightly bound ADP, 10 μM $(8-^{14}C)$ADP was employed. After 2 min the reaction was quenched by isotope dilution combined with uncoupling (3).

For kinetic measurements of light-induced release of tightly bound ADP, thylakoids were preloaded with $(8-^{14}C)$ADP (4). The release reaction was carried out in media containing different concentrations of unlabeled ADP and P_i. Immediately after the light pulse (10 - 1000 ms) the reaction was quenched (see above). The released (^{14}C)ADP was measured in the supernatant after centrifugation.

3. RESULTS AND DISCUSSION

At first approximation, the process of ΔpH-dependent ATPase activation may be described by the reaction equation:

$$E_i + n\ H^+_{in} \underset{k_{-1}}{\overset{k_1}{\rightleftharpoons}} E_a + H^+_{out} \tag{1}$$

For the equilibrium state the following relationship (Hill equation) can be derived:

$$\log E_a/E_i = n \cdot \Delta pH + \log k_1/k_{-1} \tag{2}$$

Hence equilibrium measurements of the ratio of active to inactive enzymes versus ΔpH permit determination of the reaction order (= number of protons translocated for activation of one enzyme molecule). Equilibria between enzymes with loosely bound ADP (E·ADP) to those with tightly bound ADP (E=ADP) may be treated correspondingly. The results of measurements of enzyme activities and levels of tightly bound ADP as function of ΔpH in the presence of 10 μM ADP are plotted as Hill diagrams in Fig. 1. The results allow two important conclusions: (i) both, activation and nucleotide release exhibit positive cooperativity with regard to the protons translocated; (ii) the extent of cooperativity is different for the two reactions (n = 2.2 and 1.4, respectively). As the Hill coefficients give minimum numbers, extrapolation to 3 H^+/ATPase for activation and 2 H^+/ATPase for ADP release may be justified.

Recently Boyer's group has shown that tightly bound ADP of an inactive ATPase resides in a modified catalytic site (5). Earlier measurements have suggested that in the inactive state the catalytic sites are inaccessible to medium substrates (6). Assuming a number of altogether 3 catalytic sites per CF_1 (one per β subunit) the process of activation may be explained by successive opening of the occluded sites brought about by internal protonation/external deprotonation of the three β subunits in a defined sequence. The second step is the one which opens the ADP containing site; this explains the necessity of 2 H^+ for the conversion of a tightly bound to an exchangeable ADP. In order to obtain an active enzyme, however, the third site has to be opened, too. The single reaction steps are depicted in the upper part of Fig. 2.

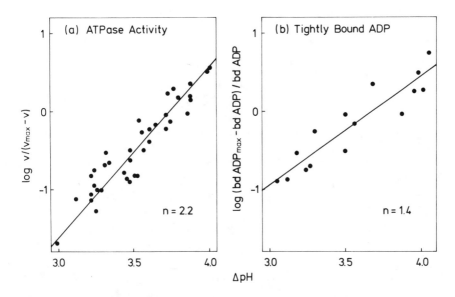

FIGURE 1. Hill plots of the steady state ATPase activity and the steady state level of tightly bound ADP as function of ΔpH in the presence of 10 μM medium ADP.

Upon illumination with short saturating light flashes, an active enzyme state with loosely bound ADP is generated within less than 10 ms (4). Initial release of the loosely bound ADP originating from tightly bound ADP is accelerated by a factor of about 10, if ADP plus P_i is present in the medium (2,4), indicating a negative cooperative effect of the substrates interacting with free sites on the ADP-containing site. While ADP is ejected, the first ATP is formed from medium ADP and P_i (2,4). Acceleration of release was investigated as function of ADP concentration in the absence and presence of P_i and as function of P_i concentration in the presence of ADP. The apparent K_d values are generally lower than the K_m values obtained in steady state photophosphorylation. In all cases two different affinities could be settled (Table I). The maximal

TABLE I. Apparent dissociation constants for medium ADP and P_i at free binding sites as measured by acceleration of light-induced release of tightly bound (^{14}C)ADP from preloaded thylakoids

	K_d(ADP) (μM)		K_d(P_i) (μM)	
	(1)	(2)	(1)	(2)
absence of P_i	0.2	10		
presence of 5 mM P_i	0.2	3		
presence of 10 μM ADP			30	250

I. ACTIVATION

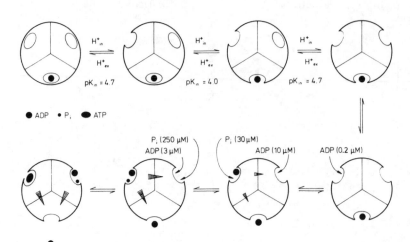

II. INITIATION OF CATALYSIS

FIGURE 2. Model of ΔpH-dependent activation of the thylakoid ATPase (upper part) and initiation of the catalytic process (photophosphorylation) (lower part). Apparent pK_{in} values (at an external pH of 8.0) were estimated by computer modelling of the data of Fig. 1, as described in detail in ref. 3

negative cooperative effect on the ADP occupied site therefore seems to require successive interaction of ADP and P_i at two non-occupied sites. Substrate binding to the first decreases the affinities for ADP and P_i at the second site as well as the affinity for ADP of the former "tight site". Substrate binding and the resulting cooperative influence between the sites are interpreted in the lower part of Fig. 2. These reactions may be regarded as pre-steady state processes following ΔpH activation, which are necessary to establish the functional order of the catalytic centers for steady state turnover.

REFERENCES
1 Strotmann, H. and Bickel-Sandkötter, S. (1984) Annu. Rev. Plant Physiol. 35, 97-120
2 Strotmann, H. (1984) in Advances of Photosynthesis Research (Sybesma, C., ed.) Vol. II, pp. 477-484, Martinus Nijhoff/Dr. W. Junk, N.V. Publ., Dordrecht
3 Lohse, D., Thelen, R., and Strotmann, H. (1989) Biochim. Biophys. Acta 976, in press
4 Lohse, D. and Strotmann, H. (1989) Biochim. Biophys. Acta 976, in press
5 Zhou, J.M., Xue, Z., Du, Z., Melese, T. and Boyer, P.D. (1988) Biochemistry 27, 5129-5135
6 Bickel-Sandkötter, S. (1983) Biochim. Biophys. Acta 723, 71-77

The H+/ATP Coupling Ratio at the H+-ATP-Synthase of Spinach Chloroplasts is Four

Bernd Rumberg, Karsten Schubert, Frank Strelow and Tuan Tran-Anh
Max-Volmer-Institut, Technische Universität Berlin,
D-1000 Berlin 12, FRG

1. Introduction

The importance of the H+/ATP ratio, i.e. the number of H+ which have to be translocated across the ATP-synthase for each ATP molecule being synthesized or hydrolysed, has its origin in the treefold aspect of
(1) mechanistic consequences with respect to the coupling process,
(2) energetic consequences with respect to the attainable excess of ATP above ADP,
(3) stoichiometric consequences with respect to the overall process of CO_2 reduction.
In this paper two complete independent experimental approaches, namely the kinetic approach realizing H+ flux measurements and the energetic approach realizing transmembrane ΔpH measurements, prove the H+/ATP ratio at the chloroplastic ATP-synthase to be four.

2. Experimental Procedure

2.1 Materials and Methods.

The experiments were performed with suspensions of envelope-free chloroplasts isolated from spinach at 20 °C temperature. The initial pH was 8.0 and did never deviate more than 0.05 units. The intensity of the actinic light was 300 Wm^{-2} unless otherwise stated. Changes of external pH (by glass electrode measurement) and of fluorescence (from the added indicator of internal pH) were monitored simultaneously. Changes of the ATP concentration were obtained from the change of external pH (0.94 H+ consumed per ATP formed). Light-induced electron flow (in the presence of ferricyanide as electron acceptor) was obtained from the decrease of external pH (1 H+ liberated per electron transported). Transmembrane ΔpH was obtained from the fluorescence quenching of N-(1-naphtyl)ethylenediamine (NED) or from the external pH jump after a pulse of 50 µM imidazole. The H/e determination was performed as described in [1].

2.2 Specification of the Suspension Medium.

H+ flux measurements: 10 mM KCl, 3 mM MgCl$_2$, 1 mM tricine, 1 (or 0.1 as specified in the Table) mM Mg ATP, 2 µM NED, and chloroplasts containing 10 µM chlorophyll. Additionally 100 µM benzylviologen, 3µM thioredoxin, 500 µM DTT for activation of ATP hydrolysis, which were replaced by 100 µM ferricyanide for realization of the e$^-$-flow measurements. Addition of DCMU, uncoupler, and tentoxin as specified in the Table.
Measurement of energy balance: 50 mM KCl, 3 mM of free MgCl$_2$, 1 mM tricine, 2,5 µM di-adenosinepentaphosphat, and chloroplasts containing 10 µM or 60 µM chlorophyll. The

M. Baltscheffsky (ed.), Current Research in Photosynthesis, Vol. III, 125–128.
© 1990 *Kluwer Academic Publishers. Printed in the Netherlands.*

e--cofactor was 20 µM pyocyanin or 100 µM benzylviologen. Agents for activation of the ATP-synthase were 5 mM DTT (preillumination 5 min) or 3 µM thioredoxin, 500 µM DTT (preillumination for 70 s). Phosphorylation substrates were varied between 100 µM and 3 mM for ATP, 20 µM and 1 mM for ADP, 20 µM and 2.5 mM for phosphate.

3. Results
3.1 H$^+$/ATP from Flux Measurements
We realized a two-step experiment. In the first instance we measured simultaneously the rate of ATP hydrolysis and the fluorescence quenching of NED which gives information on the transmembrane ΔpH. Then we replaced the agents for activation of the ATPase, namely benzylviologen, thioredoxin and DTT, by ferricyanide and measured simultaneously the rate of light-induced e--flow and again the fluorescence quenching of NED. By addition of DCMU the electron transport system was forced to produce just the same value of fluorescence quenching as in the case of ATP hydrolysis. Both experiments were performed under conditions of identical H$^+$ permeability of the thylakoid membrane, and therefore the H$^+$ fluxes are identical, too.
If additionally the H/e ratio is determined, the proton flux is calculable from the e--flow and the H/e ratio and may be compared to the rate of ATP hydrolysis. The results presented in the Table and Fig. 1 clearly demonstrate a H$^+$/ATP ratio of four, irrespective of the change of the rate of ATP hydrolysis produced by addition of different uncouplers, addition of the ATPase inhibitor tentoxin or by the use of different ATP concentrations.

No	Uncoupler nM	ATP mM	Tentoxin nM	V_{Hy} mmol/ mol Chl . s	$\Delta F/F_o$	DCMU nM	V_e mmol/ molChl . s	H/e	H/ATP	No. of exps.
1	-	1	-	11.47	0.40	226	17.58	2.57	3.94	15
2	Nig, 20	1	-	29.7	0.33	107	46.7	2.5	3.93	3
3	Gram, 10	1	-	37.5	0.31	-	77.2	2.0	4.12	4
4	Gram, 20	0,1	-	28.3	0.22	60	58.0	2.0	4.1	1
5	Gram, 20	1	-	40.7	0.28	27	79.9	2.0	3.93	4
6	Gram, 20	1	400	29.5	0.23	54	62.0	2.0	4.2	1
7	Gram, 20	1	660	19.3	0.16	112	37.0	2.0	3.8	1

Table
Data of the rate of ATP hydrolysis on the one hand, of e--flow and H/e ratio on the other hand for conditions of identical transmembrane ΔpH measured by fluorescence quenching $\Delta F/F_o$ of NED. ATP hydrolysis has been initiated by preillumination for 70 s in the presence of benzylviologen, thioredoxin, DTT and e--flow was induced by steady illumination in the presence of ferricyanide. The light intensity was 200 Wm^{-2}.

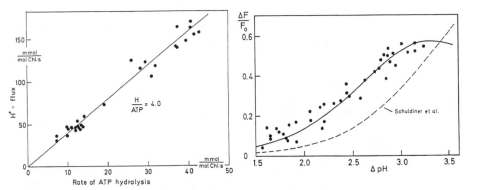

Fig. 1, left H$^+$-flux in dependence on the rate of ATP hydrolysis. The different experimental conditions are outlined in the Table.

Fig. 2, right Fluorescence quenching $\Delta F/F_0$ of NED in dependence on the light-induced transmembrane ΔpH as determined by the imidazole method. The chlorophyll concentration was 10 µM. ΔpH was varied by addition of gramicidin and DCMU. Deviation from the calibration curve according to Schuldiner et al. [6] is indicated.

3.2 H$^+$/ATP from Energy Balance

Equilibrium at the H$^+$-ATP-synthase is obtained, if the phosphorylation potential, ΔGp, and the electrochemical potential of H$^+$, $\Delta\mu_H{}^+$, are related to each other according to ΔGp + n $\Delta\tilde{\mu}_H{}^+$ = 0
where n is the H$^+$/ATP coupling ratio, ΔGp = ΔGp$^\circ$ + 2.3 RT lg [ATP/(ADP·P)], and - $\Delta\tilde{\mu}_H{}^+$ = 2.3 RT ΔpH + F$\Delta\Psi$. By comparison of ΔGp and $\Delta\tilde{\mu}_H{}^+$ the H$^+$/ATP ratio is determinable. The crucial problem is the determination of $\Delta\tilde{\mu}_H{}^+$. In the case of high salt concentration, which is realized here, the contribution of $\Delta\Psi$ during steady state conditions is negligible [2]. Trustworthy results on ΔpH are obtainable by both the electron transport method put forward by us twenty years ago [3] and the amine distribution method as realized by use of imidazole, introduced by Pick et al. [4]. A critical evaluation is outlined in [5]. The fluorescence quenching method introduced by Schuldiner et al. [6] is most easily handy but suffers from the wrong theory offered (for critical discussion see [5]). Fluorescence quenching has to be calibrated with respect to ΔpH by means of other methods (see Fig. 2).
Examples of finding out the equilibrium state at the ATP-synthase are given in Fig. 3. If such equilibrium state data are analysed it comes out that lg [ATP/(ADP·P)] correlates linearly to ΔpH (Fig. 4). From the slope a H$^+$/ATP ratio of four is read out. The intersection at the ordinate gives a ΔGp$^\circ$ of 31,2 kJ/mol in full agreement with the value determined by Rosing and Slater [7].

4. Discussion

H$^+$/ATP ratios as determined hitherto culminated in values around three. In our mind three reasons account for the deviation from the value of four reported here: (1) As far as H/e ratios have been taken as a basis [8] H/e values of two have been used instead of more reliable higher ones as shown in [1].

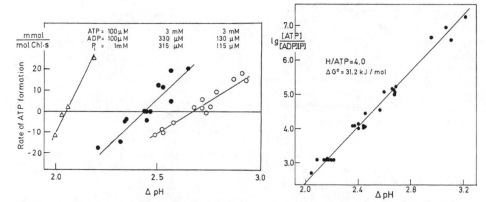

Fig. 3, left   Rate of ATP formation (consumption, respectively) in dependence on the light-induced transmembrane ΔpH for different substrate concentrations as indicated. ΔpH was varied by change of the light intensity and determined by the fluorescence quenching of NED using the calibration curve in Fig. 2.

Fig. 4, right   Logarithm of ATP/(ADP · P) in dependence on the light-induced transmembrane ΔpH for equilibrium conditions at the ATP-synthase.

(2) As far as ΔpH measurements have been taken as a basis [9], overestimation of ΔpH has been arisen from the use of a false fluorescence quenching interpretation. (3) Direct H^+ flux measurements during ATP synthesis [10] may have suffered from a limited response time of the experimental setup for pH change measurement.

With respect to mechanistic consequences of the H^+/ATP ratio of four we refer to a recent coupling model described in [11]. With respect to the overall process of photosynthesis we have to accept that on the basis of the H^+/ATP ratio of four, taken together with the probable H/e ratio of 2.5 (see [1]), linear electron transport alone does not produce enough ATP to drive CO_2 reduction.

5. Literature

[1]   Schubert, K., Liese, F., and Rumberg, B (1989), this Proceedings
[2]   Huber, H.L., Rumberg, B., and Siggel, U. (1980), Ber. Bunsenges. Phys. Chem. 87, 1050-1055
[3]   Rumberg, B. and Siggel, U. (1969), Naturwissenschaften 56, 130-132
[4]   Pick, U. and Avron, M. (1976), Eur. J. Biochem. 70, 569-576
[5]   Vu-Van, T., Heinze, T., Buchholz, J., and Rumberg, B. (1987) in Progress in Photosynthesis Res., Vol. III, pp. 189-192 (J. Biggins, ed.) Martinus Nijhoff Publishers, Dorchrecht
[6]   Schuldiner, S., Rottenberg, H., and Avron, M. (1972), Eur. J. Biochem. 25, 64-70
[7]   Rosing, J. and Slater, E.C. (1972), Biochim. Biophys. Acta 267, 275-286
[8]   Davenport, J.W. and McCarty, R.E. (1981), J. Biol. Chem. 256, 8947-8954
[9]   Strotmann, H. and Lohse, D. (1988), FEBS Lett. 229, 308-312
[10] Rathenow, M. and Rumberg, B. (1980), Ber. Bunsenges. Phys. Chem. 84, 1059-1062
[11] Strelow, F., Tran-Anh, T., and Rumberg, B. (1989), this Proceedings

A POSSIBLE MECHANISM FOR ATP SYNTHESIS AND ATP HYDROLYSIS BY THE F_oF_1 ATPase OF CHLOROPLASTS

JÜRGEN SCHUMANN
Institut für Biochemie der Pflanzen, Heinrich-Heine-Universität, D-4ooo Düsseldorf 1, Fed. Rep. Germany

On F_oF_1 ATPases, three catalytic nucleotide sites with different properties were found. Following hypotheses for ATP synthesis (1,2) these properties change for each site in an alternating or a cyclic process. In Boyer's hypothesis (2), tight binding of ADP and phosphate leads to formation of ATP; energy of the proton gradient is necessary for ATP release. Binding of ADP and phosphate to a second site accelerates this process ("dual site" mechanism).

Although energy-independent ATP formation was found under certain conditions, energy-dependent release of this ATP was not shown. For kinetic reasons, tightly bound nucleotides should be released at the rate of catalysis (3,4); it was reported, however, that exchange of nucleotides bound to the "tight nucleotide site" (site A; Ref. 5) is slower than the rate of ATP synthesis or hydrolysis (5-9).

It is therefore likely that mainly the site with lower affinity for nucleotides (site B; Ref. 5) is involved in rapid catalysis, while the "tight" site A has a high affinity for nucleotides but low catalytic activity. The affinity of site A remains unchanged upon transition from light to post-illumination conditions.

The dramatic change in the affinity of site B for ATP upon light-to-dark transition (1o) together with other indications (5,11) support the assumption that enzyme forms in the light and in the dark after illumination are different. On the basis of Hammes' hypothesis (12), a model was developed for ATP synthesis and hydrolysis as well as for nucleotide exchange reactions.

It is assumed that reversible conversion between the energized and the deenergized, active enzyme forms is coupled to the translocation of three protons. Formation of ATP starts from the energized enzyme form *E (predominant in the light) while ATP hydrolysis starts from the deenergized

M. Baltscheffsky (ed.), Current Research in Photosynthesis, Vol. III, 129–132.
© 1990 *Kluwer Academic Publishers. Printed in the Netherlands.*

form E (present in the dark after illumination) (Fig. 1).
During ATP synthesis and hydrolysis, the energized enzyme
with ADP and phosphate bound is at equilibrium with the deenergized form with bound ATP (step 5 ↔ 9). In this step,
conformational energy of the enzyme is reversibly converted
into chemical energy of ATP. ATP synthesis is favored by a
high proton concentration in the thylakoid lumen: enzyme
species 5 is withdrawn from the equilibrium. ATP hydrolysis
is favored by a low proton gradient, and species 9 is present in reasonable amounts (Fig. 1).

This model does not include tightly bound nucleotides in
the catalytic cycle; those nucleotides might be dead-end
products during deenergization. It is assumed that the inactive ground form with tightly bound ADP on site A is activated by protonation from the lumen without H^+ transport
(allosteric activation). Due to the high affinity of the
"tight" site for nucleotides, it is likely that this site is
occupied by loosely bound ATP during ATP synthesis (Fig. 2).
During deenergization, this ATP becomes tightly bound. Formation of "tightly" bound ATP at the rate of overall ATP
synthesis (3) is therefore explained as follows: ATP loosely
bound to site A is released during binding of substrate ADP
and P_i to site B (negative cooperativity). Formation of ATP
on site B (step 9a ↔ 5a) is then followed by protonation
and the formation of the energized enzyme species 14b. Since
the catalytic site B has a 1000fold lower affinity for ATP
than the empty "tight" site A, a rapid transfer of ATP from
site B to site A is likely (step 14b → 13a in Fig. 2).

REFERENCES

1   Mitchell,P. (1985) FEBS Lett. 182, 1-7
2   Boyer,P.D. (1987) Biochem. 26, 8503-8507
3   Smith,D.J., & Boyer,P.D. (1976) Proc.Natl.Acad.Sci.USA
      73, 4314-4318
4   Rosen,G., Gresser,M., Vinkler,C., & Boyer,P.D. (1979)
      J.Biol.Chem. 254, 12109-12113
5   Schumann,J. (1987) Biochim.Biophys.Acta 890, 326-334
6   Feierabend,B., & Schumann,J. (1988) Biochim.Biophys.Acta
      933, 351-357
7   McCarty,R.E. (1979) Ann.Rev.Plant Physiol. 30, 79-104
8   Aflalo,C., & Shavit,N. (1982) Eur.J.Biochem. 126, 61-68
9   Fromme,P., & Gräber,P. (1988) Abstracts 5th European
      Bioenergetics Conference, Aberystwyth, p. 245
10 Franek,U., & Strotmann,H. (1981) FEBS Lett. 126, 5-8
11 Schumann,J. (1984) Biochim.Biophys.Acta 766, 334-342
12 Hammes,G.G. (1982) Proc.Natl.Acad.Sci.USA 79, 6881-6884

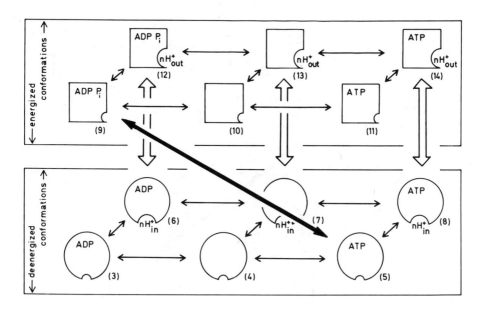

FIGURE 1   Reaction scheme for ATP synthesis and hydrolysis
by membrane-bound chloroplast ATPase

A square represents the energized, active conformation of
the ATPase with its H^+ sites facing the stroma, and a
circle represents the deenergized, active conformation with
its H^+ sites facing the lumen. Nucleotides shown in the
figure are loosely bound to the main catalytic site B;
nucleotides loosely bound to the "tight" nucleotide site A
are omitted. The inactive ground form with tightly bound
ADP is not shown.

Outlined vertical arrows indicate reversible conformational
changes with H^+ sites occupied by three protons. The bold
arrow between the energized enzyme species with ADP and P_i
bound (species 9) and the deenergized species with ATP
bound (species 5) indicates the "catalytic" equilibrium
reaction. During this reaction, the H^+ sites are deproton-
ated. Illumination withdraws species 5 from the catalytic
equilibrium; the reaction sequence 5 → 8 → 14 → 13 → 1o → 9
re-establishes the enzyme species competent in ATP synthesis.

When ATP is bound to the deenergized enzyme species 5, and
the proton gradient is low, the equilibrium form 9 becomes
protonated; the protons are then transferred into the lumen
via the reaction sequence 4 → 5 → 9 → 12 → 6 → 3 → 4.

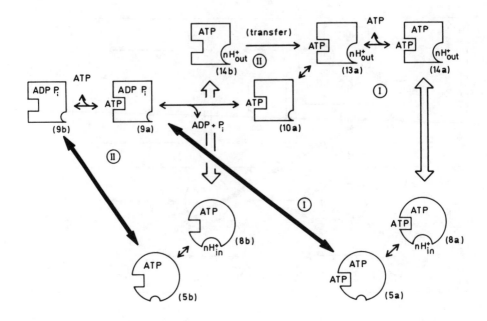

FIGURE 2 Nucleotide exchange between site A and site B
during catalysis

In this figure, both the main catalytic site B (with lower
affinity for nucleotides; upper part of the symbols) as well
as the "tight" nucleotide site A (with higher affinity for
nucleotides; left side of the symbols) are shown. Binding
of nucleotides is freely reversible; forms with tightly
bound nucleotides (i.e., inactive forms) are not shown in
this figure. Other explanations see Fig. 1.

The catalytic equilibrium reaction (step 9 ↔ 5) might occur
with or without ATP loosely bound to the "tight" site (way
I or II). ATP formation on the main catalytic site is possible via the reaction sequence as in Fig. 1 (way I) without
exchange of ATP bound to the tight site. Alternatively, ATP
synthesis might follow way II including the exchange of
bound ATP. In the latter case, binding of ADP and P_i to
enzyme species 1oa induces the release of ATP from the
"tight" site (steps 1oa → 9a → 9b). After formation of ATP
(9a ↔ 5a), the proton sites become protonated from the
lumen, and the energized enzyme species 14b with ATP bound
to the main catalytic site is formed. Since the empty
"tight" site has a 1ooofold higher affinity for ATP than
the catalytic site, newly formed ATP will be transferred to
the "tight" site (step 14b → 13a).

THE SINGLE CHANNNEL CONDUCTANCE OF CF_O

Gerd Althoff, Holger Lill & Wolfgang Junge
Biophysik, Universität Osnabrück, 4500 Osnabrück, West Germany

INTRODUCTION

Proton translocating ATP-synthases of eubacteria, chloroplast and mitochondria are composed of a membrane embedded channel portion, F_O, and an extrinsic portion, F_1, which carries the nucleotide binding sites. In photosynthesis membrane-bound proton pumps and ATP synthesis are coupled by cyclic proton flow (1). Despite of detailed genetical and biochemical informations on F_O (2,3), proton conduction mechanism of this channel (i.e. by hydrogen bonded chains (4,5)) and proton access to the coupling sites are still under discussion. Reported turnover numbers of exposed F_O from mitochondria and bacteria are in the range of 10 - 100 $H^+/(F_O \cdot s)$, which have been inferred from reconstitution experiments (*see* (3)). They have been in contrasts to 1200 $H^+/(CF_O \cdot s)$ determined for the turnover number of the integral, coupled enzyme (6,7). In spectrophotometric measurements with partial CF_1-depleted thylakoid membranes the single channel conductance of CF_O has become accessible (8). Here, the turnover number was found to be $2 \cdot 10^5$ $H^+/(CF_O \cdot s)$ at 30 mV driving force (equivalent to a conductance of 1 pS). This has established CF_O as the kinetically competent low impedance proton access to the coupling site between CF_O and CF_1.

We investigated the single channel conductance of CF_O as function of the medium composition (ionic strenght, pH, pD (isotopic substitution), altered water and/or membrane structure and temperature). Thylakoid preparation, CF_1 depletion and vesicle forming was carried out as described in (10). Excitation of the vesicle suspension with short flashes of light generated an electric potential across the thylakoid membranes (about 30 mV) and a protonic charge pulse (about 0.06 pH-units) inside the vesicles. The relaxation of the voltage, due to ion fluxes across the membrane, was measured by electrochromic absorption changes of intrinsic pigments. It was compared with the proton fluxes which were determined by pH-indicating dyes in the lumen and in the medium. CF_1 depletion accelerated the relaxation of the transmembrane voltage and of the transmembrane pH-difference. CF_O related proton flow was discriminated against currents through other pathways by its sensitivity to established F_O-type blockers, such as DCCD, Triphenyltinchloride and Venturicidin.
Since there were only very few active conducting CF_O per vesicle (on the average between 1 and 2) the time averaged single channel conductance, G, of CF_O became accessible by evaluating the decay of electrochromic absorption changes in terms of the following equation:

$$U_{app}(t) = U_0 \exp(-n) \exp(n \exp(-Gt/C)).$$

This equation has only two fit parameters, n, the average number of active channels per vesicle, and G, the time averaged single channel conductance. The initial value, U_0, was obvious and the vesicle capacitance, C, could be inferred from a calibration experiment with gramicidin as a channel with known properties (8).

M. Baltscheffsky (ed.), Current Research in Photosynthesis, Vol. III, 133–136.
© 1990 *Kluwer Academic Publishers. Printed in the Netherlands.*

RESULTS

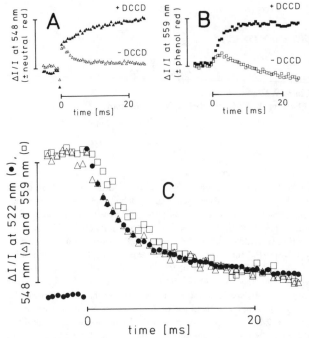

1. On the selectivity of CF$_O$ for protons.

The proton is the major charge carrier admitted by CF$_O$. The selectivity of CF$_O$ for protons over e.g. Na$^+$ is greater than 10^7.

Fig.1: Complete tracking of proton flow.

(A) Measurements with pH-indicating dye neutral red at 548 nm, indicating lumenal acidification after a flash of light. Open triangles: CF$_1$-depleted tylakoids. Filled triangles: same material, but after incubation with DCCD. The bar indicates relative change of transmitted intensity, $5 \cdot 10^{-4}$.

(B) Measurements with pH-indicating dye phenol red at 559 nm, indicating pH-changes in the suspending medium. Open squares: CF$_1$-depleted tylakoids. Filled squares: same material, but after incubation with DCCD. The bar indicates relative change of transmitted intensity, $1 \cdot 10^{-3}$. (C) Time course of the electrochromic absorption changes at 522 nm (filled circles) compared with the kinetics of proton displacement as viewed from the lumen (neutral red, ±DCCD, open triangles) and from the stroma (phenol red, ±DCCD, open squares).The relaxation of proton displacement follow the same time course as the relaxation of the transmembrane voltage. Extending these studies we found that variation of the concentration of several monovalent cations between 1 mM and 300 mM and of divalent cations from 100 μM to 30 mM did not influence the coincidence between proton and charge displacement.

2. Conductance of CF$_O$,G, as function of pH and H$^+$/D$^+$ substitution.
Between pH 5.6 and pH 8.0 the protonic single channel conductance of CF$_O$ did not vary as function of the medium pH, but was lower in D$_2$O by a factor of 1.7.
Fig.2: The time averaged single channel conductance of CF$_O$ plotted as function of pH and pD in the suspending medium. Circles indicate the single channel conductance ,G, triangles the ratio of G measured in H$_2$O and in D$_2$O at equal molal activities.

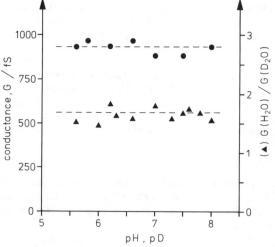

3. Effect of increased glycerol concentration on the conductance of CF_O.

The data suggest, that the conductance of CF_O might be limited by events before or at the mouth of the channel.
Fig.3: Results were obtained by fitting transients of electrochromic absorption changes as recorded in glycerol/H_2O mixtures (circles) and glycerol/D_2O mixtures. The triangles indicate G as measured with 5% and 10% dextran (wt/wt) in the suspending medium plotted at points of equal viscosity. Addition of glycerol lowered the measured single channel conductance of CF_O, G. The isotope effect of D^+ over H^+ disappeared at about 50% glycerol in solution. No effect was observed with dextran.

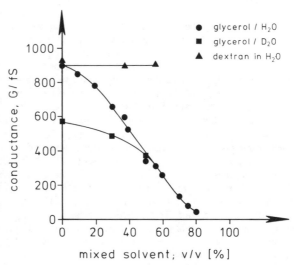

4. The temperature dependence of conductance of CF_O.

With 42 kJ/mol the activation energy of proton conduction by CF_O is intermediate between the lower one for a pore and the higher one for a mobile carrier.

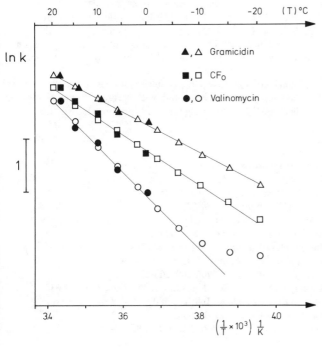

Fig.4: Temperature dependence of proton conductance by CF_O (squares), and ion conductance by gramicidin (triangles) and valinomycin (circles).
Arrhenius plot of the decay rates of electrochromic transients. The decay rates for gramicidin and valinomycin were observed in the same membrane after closure of CF_1-depleted CF_O with DCCD. Filled symbols refer to measurements in aqueous suspension, open symbols to experiments with 30% ethylene glycol (v/v) in the suspending medium. The activation energy of proton translocation through CF_O is 42 kJ/mol in H_2O and 47 kJ/mol in D_2O (not shown), 30 kJ/mol for ion transport by gramicidin and 65 kJ/mol for valinomycin.

DISCUSSION

Unlike suggested by the older literature CF_O is kinetically competent to serve as a low impedance access ("proton well") to the protonic coupling site in the integral ATP-synthase, CF_OCF_1. The analysis of measured decay curves in terms of the above equation yielded a time averaged single channel conductance of 1 pS which is equivalent to a turnover number of $2 \cdot 10^5$ $H^+ s^{-1}$ at 30 mV driving force. CF_O is distinguished by an extremely high selectivity for protons (H^+, OH^-, hydronium cation) over other cations and anions (greater than 10^7). A facultative behaviour of F_O with respect to H^+ and Na^+ which might be exist in *P. modestum* (11) can be excluded.

Which is the mechanism of proton conduction enabling CF_O to this high turnover rate and extreme selectivity?

Concepts for proton transport in water and ice along hydrogen bonded chains have been applied to proton transport across biological membranes (4,5,12). The passage rate through a hydrogen bonded network can range up to 10^5-10^6 $H^+ s^{-1}$. This is compatible with our findings for the turnover rate of CF_O, its selectivity for protons and even its activation energy of 42 kJ/mol. The rate of a reaction with an activation energy of 42 kJ/mol can be estimated, using Eyring's equation, to be about 10^6 s^{-1}. Clearly, there is no carrier-like conduction mechanism in CF_O.

Although, in this case, not the passage of protons across the membrane, but the supply of protons to the channel mouth may be rate limiting. According to (5) and (13) there are two reaction pathways for protonation of the channel "entrance" group: binding of proton in the acid pH-range or hydrolysis of water in the alkaline pH-range. Figures for both on-reaction and off-reaction in the range of 10^5 s^{-1} are possible only in the pH-range below pH5 and above pH9, respectively. This is in contrast to the measured pH-independency. The absence of a pH-dependency suggests that the rate limiting step is not governed by a titratable group. Hence, the question of how proton condution through CF_O occurs may be turned into: How is the supply rate for protons to the channel mouth of CF_O enhanced (large mouth, short selectivity filter, drag force in the coulomb cage, neighbouring buffers)?

If the environment of the channel mouth is disturbed (as in glycerol buffer) the supply of protons to the channel readily may become rate limiting. The H^+/D^+-isotope effect suggest rate limitation by the transit of a proton from one site to another one. The observed factor of 1.7, however, is small compared to published figures for such reactions between small acid-base molecules in solution. This may indicate a secondary isotope effect.

It is conceivable, though, that the full conduction cycle in CF_O comprises at least two extremely fast reactions in series, one unknown "proton supply" reaction regulated by the protein surrounding of the channel mouth and a "membrane crossing" reaction, comprising the highly proton selective filter.

REFERENCES

1   Mitchell,P. (1961) *Nature (London)* 191:144-148
2   Hoppe,J. and Sebald,W. (1984) *Biochim. Biophys. Acta* **768**:1-27
3   Schneider,E. and Altendorf,K. (1987) *Microbiological Reviews* **51**: 477-497
4   Nagle,J.F. and Tristram-Nagle,S. (1983) *J. Membrane Biol.* **74**: 1-14
5   Brünger,A., Schulten,Z. and Schulten,K. (1983) *Z. Phys. Chem* **136**: 1-63
6   Junesch,U. and Gräber,P. (1985) *Biochim. Biophys. Acta* **809**: 429-434
7   Junge,W., Rumberg,B. and Schröder,H. (1970) *Eur. J. Biochem.* **14**: 575-581
8   Lill,H., Althoff,G. and Junge,W. (1987) *J. Membrane Biol.* **98**: 69-78
9   Althoff,G., Lill,H. and Junge,W. (1989) *J. Membrane Biol.* **108**: 263-271
10 Lill,H., Engelbrecht,S., Schönknecht,G. and Junge,W. (1986) *Eur. J. Biochem.* **160**: 627-634
11 Laubinger,W. and Dimroth,P. (1987) *Eur. J. Biochem.* **168**: 475-480
12 Schulten,Z. and Schulten,K. (1985) *Eur. Biophys. J.* **11**: 149-155
13 Kasianowicz,J., Benz,R. and McLaughlin,S. (1987) *J. Membrane Biol.* **95**: 73-89

A VOLTAGE-DEPENDENT CHLORIDE CHANNEL IN THE THYLAKOID MEMBRANE

G. SCHÖNKNECHT*, R. HEDRICH+, W. JUNGE* and K. RASCHKE+
+Pflanzenphysiologisches Institut, Universität Göttingen, D-3400 Göttingen;
*Biophysik, FB Biologie/Chemie, Universität Osnabrück, D-4500 Osnabrück, FRG

INTRODUCTION

The light driven net uptake of protons into the thylakoid lumen is electrically balanced by the motion of other ions [1]. Earlier studies indicated that Cl^- influx into the thylakoid, or Mg^{2+} efflux, or both [2] may be involved. So far no ion channel has been identified in thylakoids other than the proton channel of the ATPsynthase [3] although charge balance would call for one.

During patch-clamp measurements on osmotically inflated thylakoids of *Peperomia metallica* we observed the activity of a voltage-dependent anion-selective channel [4], which would allow compensatory Cl^- and NO_3^- currents to pass the thylakoid membrane and thereby prevent the formation of a large $\Delta\phi$ resulting from electrogenic proton pumping.

MATERIAL AND METHODS

In a first step protoplasts were isolated from leaves by enzymatic digestion. These protoplasts were osmotically shocked. This caused the rupture of the plasma membrane, the vacuole, and the chloroplast envelope. Within 15 min swelling thylakoids emerged from the chloroplasts as large spherical vesicles ('blebs') with up to 40 μm diameter. High-resistance seals were formed [Fig.1] between the tip of patch pipettes and blebs. They allowed single-channel recordings either in the thylakoid-attached configuration or, after withdrawal of the pipette from the vesicle, in the inside-out patch configuration [5] with the intrathylakoid membrane face exposed to the bath [see Fig.1]. Potentials were measured with reference to the intrathylakoid space. For further details see ref. 4.

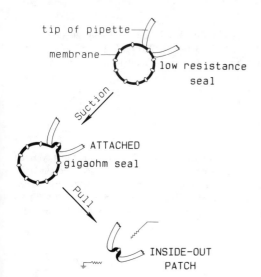

tip of pipette
membrane
low resistance seal
Suction
ATTACHED
gigaohm seal
Pull
INSIDE-OUT PATCH

Fig. 1 Schematic diagram of the patch-clamp technique [5]: A heat-polished glass pipette (tip diameter in the order of 1 μm) is pressed against a clean membrane surface. Upon slight suction a high resistance seal (> 1 GΩ) forms between the tip of the pipette and the membrane. This high seal resistance and the small membrane area reduce the background noise in such a way, that it becomes possible to measure currents (< 1 pA) passing through a single ion channel protein. The mechanical stability of the seal between pipette and membrane allows the isolation of the membrane patch encircled by the pipette: The withdrawal of the pipette in the attached configuration results in an inside-out patch.

M. Baltscheffsky (ed.), Current Research in Photosynthesis, Vol. III, 137–140.
© 1990 *Kluwer Academic Publishers. Printed in the Netherlands.*

RESULTS
     The patches drawn had an area of about 10 μm^2; almost each of them contained one or more channels. To determine the ion selectivity of the channels the reversal potential of the single-channel current was measured in asymmetrical KCl solutions [Fig. 2a]. It followed the Nernst potential for chloride, indicating a high selectivity for this anion [Fig. 2b].

a

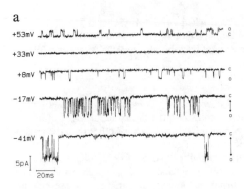

b

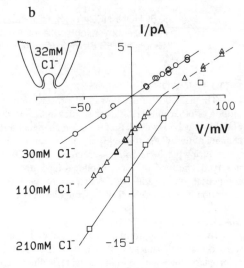

Fig. 2 Selectivity and current-voltage relationship of ion channels in the thylakoid. **a,** Single-channel recordings of chloride channels in inside-out patches (the intrathylakoid membrane side faced the bath solution) under asymmetrical KCl concentrations: 20 mM KCl, in the pipette and 100 mM KCl in the bath (background 5 mM MgCl$_2$, 2 mM MOPS/KOH pH 7.2 plus 1 mM CaCl$_2$ in the pipette). Upward current deflections represent Cl$^-$ influx into the thylakoid, whereas downward deflections represent Cl$^-$ efflux. **b,** Currents-voltage relationship of the open channel at three different KCl gradients : Starting at 20 mM KCl, the concentration in the bath was raised to 100 or 200 mM KCl (other ions as in a). The curves were fitted by linear regression.

     Raising the Cl$^-$ concentration on the intrathylakoid side led to the following single-channel conductances: 30 mM, 65±3 pS (n=14); 110 mM, 110±4 pS (n=4); 210 mM, 141 pS and 126 pS. Assuming saturation behaviour these data pointed to a maximum single-channel conductance of 152 pS and a Michaelis constant, K$_m$, for chloride of 42 mM.

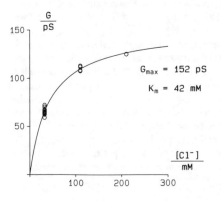

Fig. 3 Saturation of ion flux through the thylakoid channel. Single-channel conductance versus Cl$^-$ concentration. The data points were fitted by a non-linear regression analysis program (ENZFITTER) assuming Michaelis-Menten behaviour of the channel.

The relative permeability for NO_3^- with respect to Cl^- was determined by replacing KCl by KNO_3 in the bath. The reversal potential of the single-channel currents shifted to positive potentials, indicating a slightly higher permeability for NO_3^- than for Cl^-. Single-channel conductances were about 25 % higher in the presence of NO_3^- than in the presence of Cl^- (data not shown). The current-voltage relationship of the channel was ohmic between +80 and -80 mV in symmetric and asymmetric KCl and KNO_3 solutions.

Under bright light the thylakoid lumen acidifies by up to 3 pH units. We found that variation of the pH at the intrathylakoid side (between 7.8 and 5.9) did not effect the amplitude or the reversal potential of the single-channel current.

Channel gating showed a marked voltage dependence. Under voltage-clamp (constant potentials) the highest channel activity was observed at about +40 mV (inside the thylakoid). Quick changes of the holding potential elicited additional channel openings. These transient channel openings were most pronounced at voltage jumps to +40 mV [Fig. 4], a membrane potential comparable to that caused by a single flash of light [1].

Besides the main conductance state, subconductance levels were found [Fig. 5], showing the same ion selectivity. Generally, channel openings occurred in bursts [Fig. 5] and channel activity declined within 15-30 min after seal formation. Because of this complex gating behaviour, it was not yet possible to study of the kinetic properties of the chloride channel in more detail.

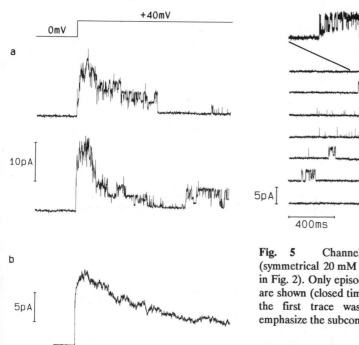

Fig. 5 Channel activity at +57 mV (symmetrical 20 mM KCl further conditions as in Fig. 2). Only episodes with channel openings are shown (closed times of up to 9 s). A part of the first trace was enlarged (twofold) to emphasize the subconductance levels.

Fig. 4 Single-channel kinetics in response to voltage steps. **a,** From a holding potential of 0 mV the potential was repetitively stepped to +40 mV for 3 s. With the onset of the +40 mV puls single-channel activity rapidly increased (up to six channels opening simultaneousely). **b,** Average of 28 traces as shown in a. The half-rise time was less than 100 ms and the half-decay time was in the order of 1 s.

CONCLUSION

As in earlier experiments with impalement microelectrodes [6,7] giant chloroplasts of *P. metallica* were used. The thylakoid membrane was osmotically inflated to form large blebs, accessible to patch pipettes. The thylakoid origin of the bleb membrane was established by chlorphyll fluorescence (not shown). Blebt thylakoid membranes show photochemical redox reactions sensitive to external electric fields [8], as well as light-driven [9] and electric field-driven ATPsynthesis [10].

As reported for chloride channels in animal tissues [11], the permeability of the thylakoid channel for NO_3^- was higher than for Cl^-. With about 5 mM Cl^- and 5 mM NO_3^- in the stroma [12], a single-channel conductance of 30 pS would result. Because of the strong voltage-dependence most of the channels would be closed during steady state. Only during changes in the net proton uptake resulting in the rise of an electric field thylakoid channels open so that the electric field decays.

As we were not able to observe K^+ or Mg^{2+} channels in thylakoid membranes exposed to solutions containing 5 mM $MgCl_2$ and up to 200 mM KCl, it is anion flow through the Cl^- channel we describe here, that would allow a rapid, voltage-dependent electric compensation of the light-driven net proton uptake into the thylakoid lumen [Fig. 6].

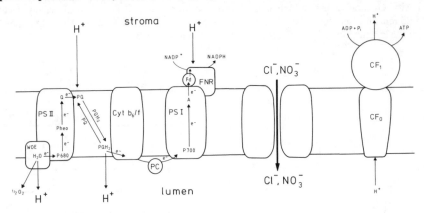

Fig. 6 Schematic view of ion fluxes across the thylakoid membrane.

ACKNOWLEDGEMENT: We thank I. Baumann for technical help and H. Kenneweg for photographs. Financial support was provided by the Deutsche Forschungsgemeinschaft Ra 122/11 and SFB 171 TP B3.

REFERENCES
1   Junge, W. (1982) *Curr. Top. Membrane Transp.* **16**, 431-465
2   Hind, G., Nakatani, H.Y. & Izawa, S. (1974) *Proc. natn. Acad. Sci. U.S.A.* **71**, 1484-1488
3   Lill, H., Althoff, G. & Junge, W. (1987) *J. Membrane Biol.* **98**, 69-78
4   Schönknecht, G., Hedrich, R., Junge, W. & Raschke, K. (1988) *Nature* **336**, 589-592
5   Hamill, O.P., Marty, A., Neher, E., Sakmann, B., Sigworth, F.J. (1980)
     Pflügers Arch. ges. Physiol. **391**, 85-100
6   Bulychev, A.A., Andrianov, V.K., Kurella, G.A. & Litvin, F.F. (1972) *Nature* **236**, 175-176
7   Vredenberg, W.J. (1974) *Proc. 3rd Int. Congr. Photosynthesis* 929-939
8   DeGrooth, B.G. & van Gorkom, H.J. (1980) *Biochim. biophys. Acta* **589**, 299-314
9   Campo, M.L. & Tedeschi, H. (1985) *Eur. J. Biochem.* **149**, 511-516
10   Gräber, P., Schlodder, E. & Witt, H.T. (1977) *Biochim. biophys. Acta* **461**, 426-440
11   Bormann, J., Hamill, O.P. & Sakmann, B. (1987) *J. Physiol.* **385**, 243-286
12   Schröppel-Meier, G. & Kaiser, W.M. (1988) *Plant. Physiol.* **87**, 822-827

TWO TYPES OF DEACTIVATION PROCEDURES FOR THE THIOL-MODULATED CHLOROPLAST ATP-HYDROLASE

PAULE BIAUDET [1,2] , FRANCIS HARAUX [1] , HEINRICH STROTMANN [2]
1) Biosystèmes membranaires, U.P.R. 39, C.N.R.S. 91198 Gif-sur-Yvette, France. 2) Institut für Biochemie der Pflanzen der Heinrich Heine Universität, Universitätsstrasse 1, D-4000 Düsseldorf, F.R.G

1 INTRODUCTION

Activity of the chloroplast $H^{\pm}$ATPase is controlled by activation of the enzyme and energization by the proton gradient ΔpH. Activation itself is a complex process depending on the redox state of the enzyme and involving protonation steps and nucleotide binding events. It is well known that release of tightly bound ADP in the presence of ΔpH converts the inactive form into an active one and that suppression of the proton gradient leads to tight binding of ADP and inactivation. Some previous results [1] have suggested two types of deactivation processes, one linked to tight binding of ADP, the second one independent of nucleotide binding. This hypothesis is here investigated.

2. MATERIALS AND METHODS

2.1 Materials

Envelope-free chloroplasts were extracted from spinach or lettuce leaves; they are either directly used or prereduced respectively .

2.2. Hydrolysis-rates measurements.

ATP-hydrolysis activity is monitored either by acidification of the medium according to [2] or measured with γ- ^{32} P-ATP [3]. After a preactivation time in the absence (prereduced thylakoids) or in the presence of 10 mM DTT (native thylakoids), the ΔpH is rapidly collapsed by injection of $2\mu M$ Nigericin when turning off the light. The substrate, ATP mixed with other constituants (ADP, PEP+PK, see text), is injected at the indicated deactivation times.

M. Baltscheffsky (ed.), Current Research in Photosynthesis, Vol. III, 141–144.

3. RESULTS
3.1 Kinetics of deactivation in fully uncoupled conditions

Fig. 1 shows one kinetic of deactivation of the hydrolysis activity obtained in fully uncoupled conditions and in the absence of added nucleotides in the medium. The initial rates of ATP-hydrolysis are in this case measured in the presence of pyruvate kinase (15 U/ml) and PEP (0.5mM) to recycle the new - synthesized ADP. In these conditions the deactivation process is biphasic with half times of $17 < t_1 < 30$ s for the rapid phase and $217 < t_2 < 360$ s for the slow phase.

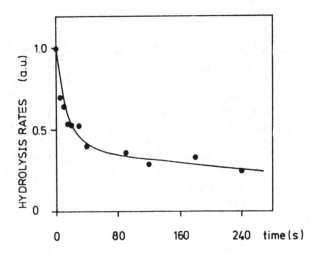

FIGURE 1. Kinetic of deactivation of the hydrolysis activity in fully uncoupled conditions and in the absence of exogenous nucleotides.

When phosphate 5mM is present in the medium, the same type of biphasic kinetic is observed and the mean values of half times for each phase are not significantly different from those obtained in the absence of phosphate.

On the other hand, if the hydrolysis rates are measured in the absence of the regenerating system, the rapid phase is notably accelerated with a half time of $\sim 10s$.

3.2. Effect of phosphate on fast binding of externally added ADP.

We have shown [1] that when the ATPase deactivates 10s in the absence of ΔpH and exogenous nucleotides, the affinity for ADP as inhibitor increases when compared to that found when ADP is added concomitantly with ATP and uncoupling. In this case hydrolysis rates were measured in the absence of the regenerating system. Fig.3. shows such inhibition curves: ADP at variable concentrations is added with ATP (500 μM) after 10s of deactivation in fully uncoupled conditions. One can observe that increasing the phosphate concentration protects the enzyme against ADP inhibition at least in the small concentrations range (0-10μM).

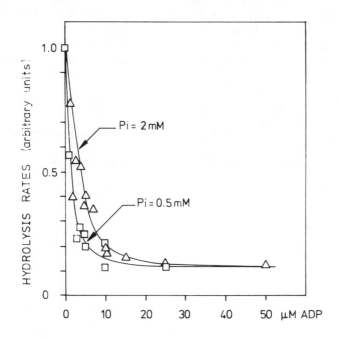

FIGURE 2. Protection by phosphate against fast inhibition by externally added ADP. Hydrolysis rates are measured on prereduced thylakoids by the pH-metric method.

4. CONCLUSION

The results presented here can be can be explained as follows:

In the absence of ΔpH and exogenous nucleotides the "active energized " state E_a^* deactivate rapidly in a second active state E_a wich itself turns to the inactive form E_i , all forms being ADP-free. These different active and inactive forms could represent the different states of protonation of the enzyme.

When during hydrolysis the new-synthesized ADP can interact with the enzyme, additional active and inactive forms occur containing ADP. Binding of this ligand accelerates the process of deactivation.

Phosphate seems not able to affect deactivation of the ADP-free forms, at least concerning the kinetic constants. But it can protect the active form whith a high affinity for ADP (which occured after 10s of deactivation) against inhibition.

Otherwise, the deactivation constants calculated here are relatively slow with regards to the dissipation of ΔpH. As they are thought to reflect the protonation-deprotonation events, this should indicate that the 'activating protons' are not easily exchangeable and remain a long time burried in the enzyme.

REFERENCES
1 Biaudet, P., de Kouchkovsky, F. and Haraux, F. (1988) Biochim. Biophys. Acta 933,487-500
2 Nishimura, M., Ito, T. and Chance, B. (1962) Biochim. Biophys. Acta 59, 177-182;
3 Avron, M. (1960) Biochim. Biophys. Acta 40,257-272

KINETIC CONTROL OF COUPLING FACTOR ACTIVITY

Donald R. Ort, Patricia A. Grandoni and Kevin Oxborough. USDA, Agricultural Research Service & Department of Plant Biology, University of Illinois, Urbana, IL USA

1. INTRODUCTION

Under non-energized conditions the coupling factors (CF_1) of dark-adapted thylakoid membranes are catalytically inactive and therefore incapable of even the thermodynamically favorable hydrolysis of ATP. Although the energetic requirement for activation of CF_1 has been recognized for almost two decades, recognition of the physiological relevance of redox modulation of the enzyme complex is relatively recent (e.g. 1,2). For instance, we have shown that the energetic requirement for activation is equivalent to about 2.6 pH units after reduction of CF_1, about 0.3 units lower than the ΔpH required when CF_1 is oxidized (3).

The work summarized here focuses on investigations of further effects that reduction of CF_1 has on the catalytic properties of the enzyme complex. We show that not only does the release of ADP tightly bound to CF_1 begin at lower levels of membrane energization after reduction but also that the 'steady-state' level of activated enzyme is greater. At high ΔpH values induced by increasingly large ΔG_{ATP} values, we found that the ATP flash yields declined and that the ATP flash yield of reduced membrane preparations declined more sharply than when CF_1 was oxidized. A six state model for CF_1 activation is proposed that includes as a new feature an activated state of the enzyme, induced by maximal ΔpH values, that conducts H^+ without the concomitant production of ATP.

2. RESULTS AND DISCUSSION

2.1. Effects of reduction on the release and rebinding of $[^{14}C]ADP$.

In dark-adapted thylakoid membranes, CF_1 has a tightly-bound ADP whose energization-induced release is associated with catalytic activation of the enzyme (4). With nonactin and K^+ present to prevent the formation of an electric potential, the release of the tightly-bound $[^{14}C]ADP$ from the DTT-reduced membranes (Fig. 1, ◆) could be observed after as few as 6 flashes and complete release was achieved by about 50 flashes. Nearly twice as many flashes were needed to induce ADP release in oxidized membranes (□) and thereafter the flash number dependence of the release was more gradual.

M. Baltscheffsky (ed.), Current Research in Photosynthesis, Vol. III, 145–148.
© 1990 *Kluwer Academic Publishers. Printed in the Netherlands.*

Eventually oxidized membranes released the same amount of [^{14}C]ADP as membranes with CF$_1$ prereduced. However, because rebinding of unlabeled ADP can occur undetected, this procedure does not provide information about the proportion of the CF$_1$ population that is active. In order to investigate the effects of reduction on the 'steady-state' level of activation we measured the rebinding of [^{14}C]ADP by rapid quenching methods. Figure 2 shows that, following 150 saturating flashes (10 HZ), 30% more CF$_1$ were active in the reduced (□) than in the oxidized preparation (◆).

2.2. Effect of high ΔG_{ATP} values on ATP flash yield.

Whereas CF$_1$ reduction enhances the efficiency of flash-induced ATP formation when the ΔpH is near threshold values (3), Figure **3** illustrates that ATP flash yields are actually lower for reduced preparations under conditions in which the ΔpH reaches high values. In this study conditions favoring the formation of large transmembrane pH differences were created by manipulating the free energy requirements for net ATP synthesis (i.e. ΔG_{ATP}). In oxidized

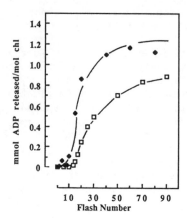
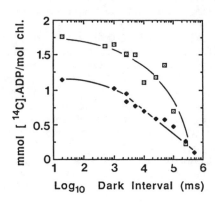

Figure 1. Flash-induced release of tightly-bound [^{14}C]ADP from oxidized (□) and DTT-reduced (◆) spinach thylakoid membranes. The sample contained thylakoids (100 nmol chl) prelabeled with [^{14}C]ADP (47 C$_i$/mol). The reaction temperature was 4°C.

Figure 2. Rebinding of [^{14}C]ADP to oxidized (◆) and DTT-reduced (□) thylakoid membranes following 150 saturating flashes. After a dark interval of between 20 ms and 500s, samples were mixed with an equal volume of reaction medium containing 50 uM [^{14}C]ADP, using a rapid quench device (Update Instruments). The reaction temperature was 4°C.

thylakoid membrane preparations (●), the amount of ATP synthesized per flash was maintained near 1.0 mmol ATP/mol chl/flash with the ΔG_{ATP} value set between 8.8 and 12 kcal/mol. At ΔG_{ATP} values exceeding 12 kcal/mol, the ATP flash yield decreased about 0.2 mmol ATP/mol chl/kcal. The ATP flash yield of DTT-reduced preparations was sensitive throughout the range of ΔG_{ATP} values investigated decreasing about 0.15 mmol ATP/mol chl/kcal. Since flash-induced electron transfer and proton accumulation were constant over the range of ΔG_{ATP} conditions used (5), these decreases in flash yield represent true declines in the efficiency of ATP formation. Furthermore, from an extensive examination of the ATP hydrolytic activity of CF_1, we were able to establish that these declining flash yields were not the result of increased hydrolysis of ATP (5).

2.3. Six state model for CF_1 activation.

A model summarizing current thinking about the regulation of coupling factor activation (6) proposes four potential 'states' of the enzyme complex: both active ($E_o{}^a$) and inactive (E_o) oxidized CF_1 as well as active ($E_m{}^a$) and inactive (E_m) reduced enzymes. A seemingly undesirable side effect of the increasing electrochemical potential that accompanies high ΔG_{ATP} values is the unexpected loss of phosphorylation efficiency (Fig. 3). Our data indicate that once CF_1 is activated a ΔG_{ATP}-dependent, leakage pathway is evident under conditions where very large driving forces are formed. In Figure 4

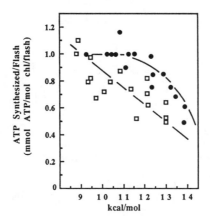

Figure 3. Effect that increasing ΔG_{ATP} values has on flash-induced ATP yields in DTT-reduced (□) and oxidized (●) membranes. The flash-yields are taken after the initiation of ATP formation and after a linear dependence of ATP synthesis on flash number has been established.

we propose additional activated 'states' of CF_1 that are induced by large ΔpH values and undergo turnover and the translocation of H^+ without the formation of ATP. If this line of thinking is correct, then it may show a provision within the catalytic and regulatory mechanism of CF_1 for permitting continued turnover of the proton/electron transport reactions when substrates for ATP formation are in short supply, that is, when the ΔG_{ATP} is high.

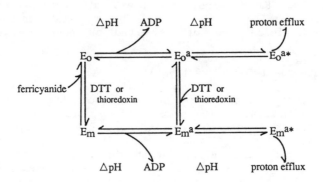

Figure 4. Six state model for CF_1 activation.

REFERENCES

1 Shahak, Y. (1982) Plant Physiol. 70, 87-91
2 Mills, J.D., Mitchell, P. and Schurmann, P. (1980) FEBS Lett. 112, 173-177
3 Hangarter, R.P., Grandoni, P. and Ort, D.R. (1987) J. Biol. Chem. 262, 13513-13519
4 Strotmann, H., Bickel-Sandkotter, S. and Shoshan, V. (1979) FEBS Lett. 101, 316-320
5 Grandoni, P. (1989) Thermodynamic and kinetic regulation of coupling factor. Ph.D. thesis, Univ. of IL., Urbana, IL USA
6 Junesch, U. and Gräber, P. (1985) Biochim. Biophys. Acta 809, 429-434

ATP-SYNTHESIS AND ATP-HYDROLYSIS IN WELL-COUPLED PROTEOLIPOSOMES
INCORPORATING RHODOSPIRILLUM RUBRUM F0F1.

Luit SLOOTEN and Saskia VANDENBRANDEN, Vrije Universiteit Brussel,Fac.
Sciences, Lab. Biophysics, Pleinlaan 2, B-1050 BRUSSELS, Belgium.

1. INTRODUCTION.

We have previously published a method for the preparation of well-coupled proteoliposomes incorporating R. rubrum F0F1 [1,2] . The size of these proteoliposomes is about 20-30 nm [2] . Because of this small size, such vesicles sustain $\Delta\tilde{\mu}_{H^+}$ -driven ATP-synthesis for only a few seconds. For the same reason, Gräber et al. used stopped-flow equipment to determine initial rates of ATP-synthesis in F0F1-proteoliposomes [3] . We have used luciferase luminescence to obtain, in a single experiment, a complete time course of $\Delta\tilde{\mu}_{H^+}$ -driven ATP-synthesis. Corrections had to be applied for a lag in the response of luciferase after ATP-addition, and also for a slow lipid-activation of luciferase after addition of proteoliposomes [4] . Here we present some results concerning the $\Delta\tilde{\mu}_{H^+}$ -dependence of ATP-synthesis, as obtained with this method. It is shown that in proteoliposomes $\Delta\Psi$ and ΔpH are equivalent as driving forces for ATP-synthesis, in contrast with earlier conclusions [3] . The origin of the threshold $\Delta\tilde{\mu}_{H^+}$ for the onset of ATP-synthesis (90 mV) is also dicussed. Finally we present some data concerning a differential lipid-specificity of ATP-synthesis and ATP-hydrolysis in these proteliposomes.

2. MATERIALS AND METHODS.

Unless indicated otherwise, partially purified [5] soya lecithin (Sigma, type IV-S) was used. F0F1 was isolated from R. rubrum as described [1] . Proteoliposomes were formed by incubation of F0F1 in the presence of lipid and cholate, followed by centrfugation through Sephadex G-50 columns in order to remove the cholate [1,4] . A molecular weight of 545 kDalton was assumed for R. rubrum F0F1 [2] .

ATP-synthesis was measured in a reaction medium containing 50 mM KCl, 10 mM Na-phosphate, 3.2 mM $MgCl_2$, 0.2 mM EDTA and 10 mM glycyl-glycin. 2.45 ml of this medium was supplemented with 0.1 mM ADP, 2 µg/ml luciferase, 50 µM luciferin and 0.1-0.2 µM valinomycin. ATP-synthesis was initiated by addition of 30-40 µl of acidified proteoliposomes (see below); the external pH, after this addition, was 8.0. The time course of ATP-synthesis was monitored by the increase of luciferase luminescence. After cessation of ATP-synthesis, 0.4-0.5 nmole of ATP was added as an internal calibration. Initial rates of ATP-synthesis were calculated as described [4] . The calculated initial rates were in most experiments 40-80 % higher than estimated on the basis of the slope of the recorder tracings.

Prior to this assay the proteoliposomes were acidified to the desired pH by incubation in a medium containing 50 mM succinic acid, 30 mM MES and

M. Baltscheffsky (ed.), Current Research in Photosynthesis, Vol. III, 149–152.
© 1990 *Kluwer Academic Publishers. Printed in the Netherlands.*

30 mM MOPS. The latter two impermeant buffers were present at the same concentration in the interior of the proteoliposomes.

ATPase was assayed in a medium containing 25 mM Na_2SO_4, 3 mM $MgSO_4$, 10 mM glycylglycin, pH 8. The reaction was started by addition of 3 mM ATP and was stopped after 10 min by addition of phosphate reagent [6].

3. RESULTS AND DISCUSSION.

Fig. 1 shows the ΔpH-dependence of the initial rate of ATP-synthesis. In these experiments the K^+ -diffusion potential (positive inside) was varied by the presence of the indicated concentrations of K^+ in the internal volume of the proteoliposomes; the external concentration was 50 mM. In the absence of a K^+ -diffusion potential (triangles) ATP-synthesis was observed when the ΔpH exceeded a threshold value of 1.5, corresponding with a $\Delta\bar{\mu}_{H^+}$ of 90 mV.

No ATP-synthesis was induced by a K^+ -diffusion potential alone (open circle at ΔpH=0), not even if the internal K^+ -concentration was zero (not shown); raising the internal buffer concentration (glycylglycin) in the proteoliposomes had no effect in this respect. The maximal turnover rate was approx. 200 mol ATP/mol F0F1.s, and the highest ATP-yield was approx. 200 mol/mol F0F1 (not shown). Thus, R. rubrum F0F1 is highly active after incorporation into proteoliposomes, not only during ATP-hydrolysis [1,2], but also during ATP-synthesis.

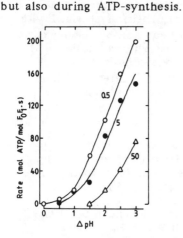
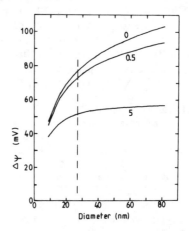

FIG. 1 (LEFT). ΔpH-dependence of the initial rate of ATP-synthesis. The media used for cholate incubation, column centrifugation and acid preincubation (see "Methods") contained 30 mM MES, 30 mM MOPS, the indicated concentration (in mM) of KCl (x), and (50-x) mM NaCl. Acid preincubation was carried out at pH=8-ΔpH.

FIG. 2 (RIGHT). Calculated dependence of the K+ -diffusion potential on the internal diameter of the proteoliposomes. The calculations were based on an external K+ -concentration of 50 mM. The initial internal K+ -concentration (in mM) is indicated in the Figure.

Fig. 1 shows that the curves obtained with 0.5 and 5 mM K^+ in the internal volume were displaced by only about 0.35 pH-units, or approx. 21 mV from one another. This is due to the effect of the membrane electrical capacitance on the distribution of K^+ at equilibrium [4,7]. We used the method of Apell and Bersch [7] to calculate equilibrium values of the K^+-diffusion potential after addition of proteoliposomes with a known internal K^+-concentration to a medium with 50 mM K^+, in the presence of valinomycin. Fig. 2 shows the dependence of these diffusion potentials on the internal diameter of the proteoliposomes. The dashed line in Fig. 2 shows that with proteoliposomes of 27 nm internal diameter, the K^+-diffusion potential obtained with an initial internal K^+-concentration of 0.5 mM is only 21 mV higher than the one obtained with an initial internal K^+-concentration of 5 mM. The diffusion potential obtained in the latter case is 52 mV. These diffusion potentials correspond with ΔpH-values of 0.36 and 0.88 units, respectively. This is in good agreement with the results shown in Fig. 1, and the required internal diameter of 27 nm is in good agreement with electron-microscopic and other evidence on the size of the proteoliposomes [2]. Furthermore, Fig. 2 shows that vesicles of this diameter generate a K^+-diffusion potential of only 77 mV even if the initial internal K^+-concentration is zero. Since ATP-synthesis was observed only above a threshold $\Delta\bar{\mu}_{H^+}$ of 90 mV (Fig. 1), this explains why a K^+-diffusion potential alone did not elicit ATP-synthesis. Thus our data are entirely consistent with the notion that $\Delta\Psi$ and ΔpH are equivalent as driving forces for ATP-synthesis in F0F1-proteoliposomes (contrast [3]).

We have shown that in chromatophores the membrane-bound F0F1-ATPase is inacive, and must be activated by an artificially applied -, or light-induced $\Delta\bar{\mu}_{H^+}$ [6,8]. Thus one might argue that in proteoliposomes the threshold $\Delta\bar{\mu}_{H^+}$ of 90 mV for the onset of ATP-synthesis is a reflection of this activation requirement. However we have shown that in proteoliposomes the F0F1-ATPase activity was activated to nearly the maximum extent by application of a K^+-diffusion potential of 77 mV [2]. Thus at least in our system the activation requirement of the enzyme does not explain the threshold $\Delta\bar{\mu}_{H^+}$ of 90 mV for the onset of ATP-synthesis. As suggested by Brune et al. [9], the reason for this may be that the rate of ATP-synthesis is determined by the rate of proton efflux across the membrane. This rate in turn was found to exhibit an exponential dependence on the transmembrane $\Delta\bar{\mu}_{H^+}$.

Table I shows some data on the lipid-specificity of ATP-synthesis and ATP-hydrolysis. Here we compared proteoliposomes with either soya lecithin (SL), or egg phosphatidyl choline (PC). During ATP-hydrolysis, CCCP was used as an uncoupler; it was added at the optimal concentration for both types of proteoliposomes (2 μM). It should be noted that similar results were obtained with other types of uncouplers, e.g. valinomycin plus ammonia [1]. During ATP-hydrolysis, both types of proteoliposomes exhibited comparable activities; the coupling ratio (i.e. the ratio of activities with and without uncoupler) was admittedly about 2 times higher in SL-proteoliposomes than in PC-proteoliposomes, but this ratio was in PC-proteoliposomes still higher than in the original system, i.e. chromatophores [6]. However the rate of

TABLE I. LIPID-SPECIFICITY OF ATP-SYNTHESIS AND ATP-HYDROLYSIS IN
FOF1-PROTEOLIPOSOMES. Proteoliposomes without K+ were used.
N.A., no additions.

| Lipid | ATP-HYDROLYSIS | | | ATP-SYNTHESIS') | |
| | rate'') | | coupling | initial | |
	N.A.	+ CCCP	ratio	rate'')	yield*)
SL	6.20	122.2	19.7	89.7	62.8
PC	8.70	72.8	8.36	2.97	200.6

°) ΔpH=3, $\Delta\Psi\approx$77 mV.   '') mol ATP/mol FOF1.s   *)mol ATP/mol FOF1

ATP-synthesis was in SL-proteoliposomes about 30 times higher than in PC-
proteoliposomes, although the ATP-yield was in the latter system about 3
times higher than in the former. We envisage two alternative explanations
for these results:
        (1). Uncouplers may abolish the lipid-specificity of FOF1-activities. Thus,
in PC-proteoliposomes FO may be shielded at the inside by a barrier of low
proton conductivity. During ATP-synthesis, protons moving outward would
have to cross this barrier before entering FO. However during ATP-
hydrolysis protons leaving FO and moving inward may be intercepted by
uncoupler and transported outward before entering the barrier.
        (2). In E. coli, only FO-subunits, and none of the F1-subunits are in
contact with the membrane lipids [10] . Hence a reversal in the direction of
catalysis may be accompanied by a reorientation of FO-subunits [11]. This
may result in a change in electrostatic and/or hydrophobic interactions of
FO-subunits with the lipids, which in turn would affect the rate of proton
conductance through FO.

4. REFERENCES.

1. Slooten, L. and Vandenbranden, S. (1987), in Proceedings of the 7th
        Internatl. Congress on Photosynthesis Research (Biggins, J., ed), Vol. III,
        pp. 95-98. Martinus Nijhoff Publ., Dordrecht.
2. Slooten, L. and Vandenbranden, S. (1989) Biochim. Biophys. Acta 975,
        148-157.
3. Schmidt, G. and Gräber, P. (1987) Biochim. Biophys. Acta 890, 392-394.
4. Slooten, L. and Vandenbranden, S. (1989) Biochim. Biophys. Acta 976,
        in press.
5. Kagawa, Y. and Racker, E. (1971) J. Biol. Chem. 246, 5477-5487.
6. Slooten, L. and Nuyten, A. (1981) Biochim. Biophys. Acta 638, 305-312.
7. Apell, H.-J. and Bersch, B. (1987) Biochim. Biophys. Acta 903, 480-494.
8. Slooten, L. and Nuyten, A. (1981) Biochim. Biophys. Acta 638, 313-326.
9. Brune, A., Spillecke, J. and Kröger, A. (1987) Biochim. Biophys. Acta
        893, 499-507.
10.Aggeler, R., Zhang, Y-Z. and Capaldi, R.A. (1987) Biochem. 26, 7107-7113.
11.Schneider, E. and Altendorf, K. (1987) Microbiol. Rev. 54, 477-497.

DOES THE CHLOROPLAST ATPase HAVE A VARIABLE AFFINITY FOR ADP ?

Yaroslav de KOUCHKOVSKY, Tania BIZOUARN and Francis HARAUX
Biosystèmes Membranaires, CNRS (UPR 39), 91198 Gif-sur-Yvette, France

1. INTRODUCTION
    The membrane-bound ATP(synth)ase 'affinity' (Michaelis constant K_m) for its substrates was found quite variable: for ADP, from less than 1 μM (1) to almost 200 μM (2). In fact, this was predictable (3), inasmuch as the chemiosmotic mechanism of phosphorylation makes that, as soon as ADP is added, the proton channels open, the proton gradient $\Delta\tilde{\mu}_H+$ lowers, and consequently the catalytic constant and/or the enzyme number, because of their $\Delta\tilde{\mu}_H+$-dependent activation (4), decrease. That is, V_m is not constant in the kinetic determination of K_m.
    It is therefore necessary to stabilize $\Delta\tilde{\mu}_H+$ during the experiment, which was achieved here by temporarily buffering $\Delta\tilde{\mu}_H+$ with hexylamine trapped in the lumen (5). The results showed that indeed K_m varies with energization and suggested that a key control is exerted by diffusion-limited local substrate concentration (Bizouarn et al., submitted). If this effect is minimized, K_m seems to level off at $\sim$ 3 μM.

2. PROCEDURE
    Thylakoids were extracted from Lettuce and experiments run at 20° C as described in (5). The usual conditions were: 20 μM chlorophyll, slightly buffered medium at pH 8.2 (2 mM Tricine + 2 or 8 mM phosphate, P_i + 50 mM KCl + 5 mM $MgCl_2$), supplemented with 50 μM pyocyanine to catalyse System-I H^+ translocation and, except for some controls, with hexylamine, usually at 300 μM. The proton gradient was estimated by ΔpH (50 to 250 nM valinomycin present) measured with 4 μM 9-aminoacridine, 9-AA. These values were calibrated against 'phosphate potential' in 'static head' conditions (5,6). The phosphorylation rate Vp was given by the medium slight alkalinisation due to 'scalar' H^+. After 1-2 mn illumination with variable red light to reach the 'basal' steady-state ΔpH, ADP was injected and the immediate pH-shift recorded ($\rightarrow$ initial Vp). 9-AA fluorescence levels, taken at zero-time of Vp, measure energization in quenching or ΔpH terms.

3. RESULTS AND DISCUSSION
    A priori, the simplest way to minimize the ΔpH drop upon ADP addition is to create sufficient H^+ leaks so that their additional escape through ATPases becomes negligible. Fig. 1 shows that this cannot be attained, because when ΔpH is sufficiently lowered by nigericin, the pyocyanine loop is no more regulated and cannot

M. Baltscheffsky (ed.), Current Research in Photosynthesis, Vol. III, 153–156.

compensate the phosphorylating H⁺ flow. The alternative was therefore to damp the ΔpH lowering by the capacitive effects of buffers. But a problem was that, superimposed to the scalar H⁺ uptake, a transient vectorial flux occurs due to the 'awakening' of ATPases by ADP, rendering unmeasurable initial Vp (another reason to reject the nigericin approach). Paradoxically therefore, one has to use amines of high pK both to stabilize ΔpH (see insets of Fig.1) and to hidden the transient medium acidification (5).

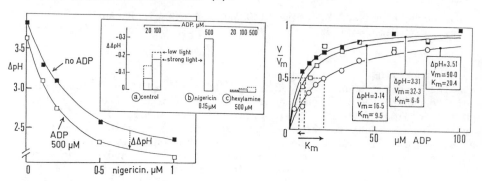

FIGURE 1. ADP-induced ΔpH drop (main) and hexylamine buffering of this ΔΔpH (inset). ADP added in light: a, c or in dark: b, main. P_i 2 mM.

FIGURE 2. Normalized phosphorylation rate vs. ADP concentration. P_i 8 mM, hexylamine 300 μM. The lines are computed hyperbolas (see text).

We could now trace saturation curves of the type shown Fig. 2. The lines drawn are theoretical Michaelian hyperbolas with V_m and K_m obtained by several regressions (5). Two facts appear: whereas V_m monotonously rises with ΔpH (cf. Fig. 6b in (5)) —more enzymes are active and/or turn faster— K_m first decreases with ΔpH then increases (see also Fig. 4 below). Another point, not seen Fig.2 made at 8 mM P_i, is that at high enough concentration, ADP clearly acts as an inhibitor, especially with low P_i (7): inset of Fig. 3. More precisely, this inhibition, expressed as the ratio of measured Vp to that extrapolated from a theoretical Michaelis hyperbola, is ΔpH-dependent (main Fig. 3). Considering that, at the present highest ΔpH, not all enzymes are activated (V_m may reach $\sim$ 400 mmol ATP mol⁻¹ Chl s⁻¹ (4)), that the activation is a stochastic process and that native, non-thiol reduced, ATPases have a very short lifetime when depolarized, this could mean that some deactivation may proceed without significant ADP binding to its inhibitory site. The stronger inhibition at lower ΔpH supports this view, insofar as the statistically longer time between two activated states of the enzyme allows then the strong ADP binding to occur.

The full (2 mM P_i) and dotted (8 mM P_i) curves on the left side of Fig. 4 show how steeply K_m rises with ΔpH above a critical value. One may think of a regulatory effect of energization on the enzyme affinity for ADP, but a reasonable alternative is that, at high ΔpH, ADP is

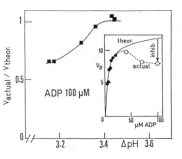 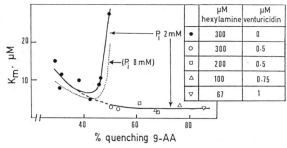

	μM hexylamine	μM venturicidin
●	300	0
○	300	0.5
□	200	0.5
△	100	0.75
▽	67	1

FIGURE 3. ΔpH-dependent ADP inhibition of phosphorylation rate Vp. The theoretical V is extrapolated from computed Michaelis curve. ΔpH varied by light, P_i 8 mM, hexylamine 300-500 μM. Inset: direct illustration of inhibition (only closed symbols are used to draw Michaelis curves).

FIGURE 4. Variation of K_m (ADP) with membrane energization, given by 9-AA fluorescence quenching. Curve traced by varying light, hexylamine and venturicidin, at 2 mM P_i (dotted line: 8 mM, from (5)): see text.

utilized faster than it can diffuse from the medium (cf. (8)). To test this hypothesis, one should decrease Vp, yet preserving high ΔpH, which may be obtained by blocking some ATPases with F_1 (tentoxin, phloridzin) or F_0 (DCCD, venturididin) inhibitors. As expected, raising the venturicidin concentration, keeping about constant ΔpH by light adjustment, not only diminishes V_m -the average number of functional enzymes is lower- but also K_m: see Table 1. The prolonged curve on the right side of Fig.4 shows, in addition, that K_m levels off, considering the large energization span, and to a low value: ∿ 3 μM. (Note that partial inhibition of ATPase allows to use less hexylamine without

TABLE 1. Effect of venturicidin on the kinetic parameters of phosphorylation (V_m in mmol ATP mol^{-1} Chl s^{-1}, K_m in μM ADP). Hexylamine 300 μM, P_i 2 mM. ΔpH adjusted by light.

Venturicidin (μM)	% quenching 9-AA	ΔpH	V_m	K_m
0	49	3.51	68.5	27.6
0.15	50	3.53	14.9	6.0
0.5	50	3.53	3.7	3.1

changing the overall picture). Finally Table 2 summarizes the effect of different inhibitors at comparable ΔpH. Phloridzin and venturicidin lower K_m probably because, being mobile inhibitors, all ATPases on the average slowly turn over, allowing a good renewal of consumed ADP. Tentoxin would not change K_m because its irreversible binding to some ATPases simply removes them from the active population, the remaining enzymes being fully active and creating their proper substrate depletion. The DCCD case is more complex and various considerations lead us to propose that a single molecule binding, yet irreversible, only partially restricts the H^+ flow (Bizouarn et al., submitted).

TABLE 2. Effect of ATPase inhibitors on its apparent Michaelis constant for ADP (K_m, μM). Hexylamine 300 μM, P_i 2 mM. ΔpH adjusted by light.

Inhibitor: (diff. prep.)	Tentoxin 1 μM	Phloridzin 1 mM	Venturicidin 0.25 μM	DCCD 16 μM
ΔpH: control	3.59	3.62	3.61	3.71
+ inhibitor	3.60	3.61	3.62	3.71
K_m : control	19.1	25.4	24.3	45.5
+ inhibitor	19.1	9.6	4.2	11.5

4. CONCLUSION

One cannot do enzymology if, while studying the parameters of one substrate (ADP), the other varies ($\Delta\tilde{\mu}_H{}^+$). Without an experimental 'trick' or a -constraining- graphical analysis (9), the case of ATPase would have remained unsolved. Yet, it is important to determine the kinetic constants and to study how they may vary, as this reflects molecular mechanisms. Another difficulty with membrane-bound enzymes is the existence of an unstirred layer where diffusion phenomena may become limiting. Our approach allows to investigate all these domains.

Mainly based on the comparison of how light (H^+ influx) and nigericin (H^+ efflux) affect K_m (10), it has been suggested that the redox chain directly interacts with ATPase (2,10). In fact, these experiments were made at unknown and uncontrolled proton gradients. We have established, using the hexylamine method, that actually no significant differences exist (unpublished). This was made possible because hexylamine not only stabilizes but also delocalizes ΔpH (11).

REFERENCES

1 Takabe, T. and Hammes, G.G. (1981) Biochemistry 20, 6859-6864
2 Loehr, A., Willms, I. and Huchzermeyer, B. (1985) Arch. Biochem. Biophys. 236, 832-840
3 Quick, W.P. and Mills, J.D. (1987) Biochim. Biophys. Acta 893, 197-207
4 Gräber, P. (1987) in Bioelectrochemistry (Milazzo, G. and Blanks, M., eds.), Vol. 2, pp. 379-429, Plenum Publishing Corp., New York
5 Bizouarn, T., de Kouchkovsky, Y. and Haraux, F. (1989) Biochim. Biophys. Acta 974, 104-113
6 Strotmann, H. and Lohse, D. (1988) FEBS Lett. 229, 308-312
7 Selman, B.R. and Selman-Reimer, S. (1981) J. Biol. Chem. 256, 1722-1726
8 Aflalo, C. and Shavit, N. (1983) FEBS Lett. 154, 175-179
9 Heinen, G. and Strotmann, H. (1989) Z. Naturforsch. 44c, 473-479
10 Vinkler, C. (1981) Biochem. Biophys. Res. Commun. 99, 1095-1100
11 Sigalat, C., de Kouchkovsky, Y., Haraux, F. and de Kouchkovsky, F. (1988) Biochim. Biophys. Acta 375-388

Functional Studies on the Reaction Pattern of the H$^+$-ATP-Synthase in Spinach Chloroplasts

Frank Strelow, Tuan Tran-Anh, and Bernd Rumberg
Max-Volmer-Institut, Technische Universität Berlin
D-1000 Berlin 12, FRG

1. Summary

Steady state kinetics of both ATP synthesis and hydrolysis in dependence on all substrate species, i.e. ADP, ATP, phosphate, internal and external H$^+$, have been measured and analysed. A functional model is derived which gives a unified description of both catalytical function and regulation of the enzyme. The main features of this model are:
(1) Conformational changes in CF$_0$ induced by H$^+$ translocation are strictly coupled to those in CF$_1$ which switch over between loose and tight nucleotide binding (indirect coupling mechanism).
(2) Conversion between ADP + P$_i$ and ATP + H$_2$O occurs spontaneously in the tightly bound state.
(3) Regulation processes are integral constituents of the catalytic reaction cycle.
(4) The H$^+$/ATP coupling ratio is four.

2. Materials and Methods

The experiments were performed with envelope-free chloroplasts isolated from spinach. The temperature was 20 °C, the initial pH was 8.0 and did never deviate for more than 0.05 units. The intensity of the actinic red light was 400 Wm^{-2} unless otherwise stated.
Changes of external pH (by use of the glass electrode) and fluorescence changes of N-(1-naphtyl)-ethylenediamine (NED) were monitored simultaneously. Changes of the ATP concentration were obtained from the external pH change (0.94 H$^+$ consumed per ATP formed). The internal pH was obtained from the fluorescence quenching of NED by use of the calibration curve published and discussed in [1]. The experiments were performed under conditions of modified ATP-synthases. This was achieved by preillumination for 5 min in the presence of DTT.
The suspension medium contained 50 mM KCl, 3 mM of free MgCl$_2$, 1 mM tricine, 5 mM DTT, 20 µM pyocyanine, 2 µM NED, and chloroplasts equivalent to 10 µM chlorophyll. The substrate concentrations normally were 500 µM ADP, 20 µM ATP, 1 mM phosphate for ATP synthesis, and 50 µM ADP, 3 mM ATP, 1 mM phosphate for ATP hydrolysis. Deviations are indicated in the figures.

3. Results

3.1 Steady State Kinetics of ATP Synthesis

We measured the steady state rate of ATP production in dependence on all substrate parameters independent from each other. The increased internal H$^+$ concentration was produced by light-induced H$^+$ pumping and adjusted by different amounts of gramicidin added after the modification period. The

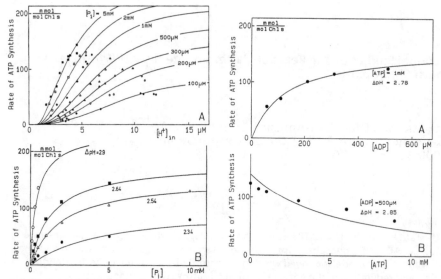

Fig. 1, left Rate of ATP synthesis in dependence on the internal H$^+$ concentration in the presence of different phosphate concentrations (A) and in dependence on the phosphate concentration at different clamped internal H$^+$ concentrations (B)

Fig, 2, right Rate of ATP synthesis in dependence on the concentrations of ADP (A) and ATP (B) under conditions of clamped internal H$^+$ concentration.

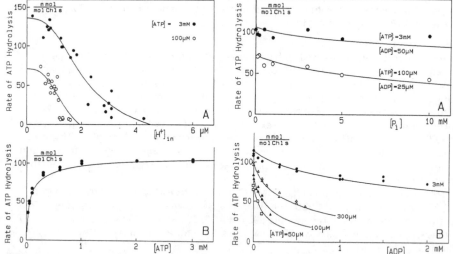

Fig. 3, left Rate of ATP hydrolysis in dependence on the internal H$^+$ concentration at two different ATP concentrations (A) and in dependence on the ATP concentration in the presence of 1 μM gramicidin for discharge of H$^+_{in}$ (B).

Fig. 4, right Rate of ATP hydrolysis in dependence on the ADP concentration in the presence of different ATP concentrations (A) and in dependence on the phosphate concentration at two different ATP concentrations (B). The measurements were performed in the presence of 1 μM gramicidin for discharge of internal H$^+$.

results are presented in Figs. 1, 2. The most interesting findings are: the synergistic interrelation between internal H^+ and phosphate, documented in Figs. 1A, B and the high K_i value for ATP, documented in Fig. 2B.

3.2 Initial Kinetics of ATP Hydrolysis

We measured the rate of ATP hydrolysis at the beginning of the dark period, i.e. after decay of the light-induced ΔpH but before decay of the hydrolysis rate due to desactivation of the ATP-synthase. $H^+{}_{in}$ was adjusted by different amounts of gramicidin or nigericin added at the moment of light-off. The results are presented in Figs. 3, 4. The most interesting findings are: the sigmoidal decay of hydrolysis in dependence on the internal H^+ concentration documented in Fig. 3A (in this respect we rectify our results published in [2]), the extreme high K_i value for phosphate, documented in Fig. 4B, and the competitivity between ADP and ATP as well as between phosphate and ATP, documented in Figs. 4A, B.

3.3 Determination of the Fraction of Active ATP-Synthases

The fraction of active ATP-synthases as dependent on the ΔpH required for activation may be read out from the rate of ATP hydrolysis if obtained under conditions of completely discharged ΔpH. This is achieved by uncoupler injection at the moment of light-off. The results are shown in Fig. 5. We determine a ΔpH of 2.2 for half-value activation.

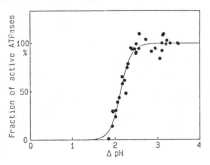

Fig. 5 Fraction of active ATP-synthases in dependence on the transmembrane ΔpH during activation. The results were obtained from hydrolysis measurements as explained in the text. The ΔpH was varied by use of different light intensities.

3.4 Elaboration of a Functional Model of the ATP-Synthase

The model we proposed in [2] no longer holds because of incompatibility with the refined hydrolysis data presented here. The main feature of a model which fits all the data presented here is the assumption of conformational changes in CF_0 induced by H^+ translocation and strictly coupled to those in CF_1 which switch over between loose and tight nucleotide binding (indirect coupling mechanism). With this respect we make use of ideas put forward by Boyer [3] and Penefsky [4]. A scheme of the model is presented in Fig. 6. E and E* stand for two conformational states of CF_1. In state E the substrate binding sites are in contact with the aqueous phase, in state E* this contact is excluded. T_0 and T_i stand for two conformational states of CF_0 which expose specific H^+ binding sites alternatively to the outer and inner aqueous phase, respectively. One reaction cycle runs through 6 steps, numbered 1 to 6 for direction of ATP synthesis (see Fig. 6). Steps 3 and 5 are assumed to be strictly coupled to the changes from T_0 to T_i and T_iH_n to T_0H_n, respectively. Reversed step 7 is assumed to occur accidentally in analogy to step 5 if E is occupied by ADP instead of ATP. E*ADP is an inactive state and in this respect regulation processes of inactivation and activation are integral constituents of the catalytic reaction cycle.

Table   Complete set of fitted rate constants

reaction step	$k_\rightarrow$	$k_\leftarrow$	$K = k_\rightarrow/k_\leftarrow$
(1) binding of P	$2.5 \cdot 10^6$ M^{-1} s^{-1}	$1.0 \cdot 10^4$ s^{-1}	(4 mM)$^{-1}$
(2) binding of ADP	$1.0 \cdot 10^7$ M^{-1} s^{-1}	$4.0 \cdot 10^2$ s^{-1}	(40 µM)$^{-1}$
(3) conf. change (k^o)	$2.6 \cdot 10^6$ s^{-1}	$1.5 \cdot 10^5$ s^{-1}	-
(4) conversion	$4.0 \cdot 10^2$ s^{-1}	$2.0 \cdot 10^2$ s^{-1}	2
(5) rev. conf. change (k^o)	$3.0 \cdot 10^6$ s^{-1}	$1.4 \cdot 10^5$ s^{-1}	-
(6) dissociation of ATP	$1.2 \cdot 10^3$ s^{-1}	$4.0 \cdot 10^6$ M^{-1} s^{-1}	300 µM

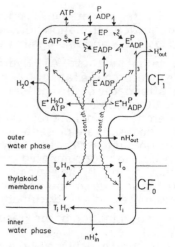

Fig. 6, right Reaction pattern of the H$^+$-ATP-synthase. The waved lines designate coupling by conformational changes.

Mathematical handling of the model is realized as follows:
(1) Definition of fast protonic equilibria with respect to T_o and T_i on the assumption of n equivalent and independent H$^+$ binding sites (dissociation constants K_o and K_i, respectively).
(2) Evaluation of the joint rate constants for the coupled conformational changes. k_3 is defined as the product of k_3^o and the probability that all n binding sites of T_o are free of H_o^+. k_5 and k_7 are defined as the products of k_5^o and k_7^o respectively, and the probability that all n binding sites of T_i are occupied by H_i^+. The two prabability factors are given by $K_o^n/(K_o + H_o^+)^n$ and $H_i^{+n}/(K_i + H_i^+)^n$, respectively. Equivalent relations hold for the reversed directions.
(3) Formulation of 7 independent steady state equations which solve for the concentrations of the 7 intermediate species of the reaction cycle by use of a computer matrix program.
(4) Fitting of all constants in order to produce harmony with the experimental results.

All curves inserted in the figures are direct computer graphs. The following constants did fit: $n = 4$, $K_o = 4$ nM, $K_i = 4$µM, $k^o_{-7}/k^o_7 = 0.02$ and the rate constants as given in the Table. The quantitative evaluation leads spontaneously to the following most significant evidences:
(1) The value $n = 4$ means that the H$^+$/ATP ratio is four. This agrees with our own very recent results of direct H$^+$/ATP determination [1].
(2) The value of 2 for the equilibrium constant of step 4 means that the conversion of ADP + P to ATP + H_2O at the level of E* occurs spontaneously.
(3) E*ATP and E*ADP turn out to be states of extreme high probability in the absence of ΔpH and may be specified as states of tightly bound nucleotides.

4. Literature
[1]   Rumberg, B., Schubert, K., Strelow, F., and Tran-Anh, T. (1989) this Proceedings
[2]   Tran-Anh, T. and Rumberg, B (1987) in Progress in Photosynthesis Research Vol. III
       (J. Biggins, ed.) pp. 185-188, Martinus Nijhoff Publishers, Dordrecht
[3]   Boyer, P.D. and Kohlbrenner, W.E. (1981) in Energy Coupling in Photosynthesis
       (Selman, B.R. and Selman-Reimer, S., eds.) pp. 231-340, Elsevier, Amsterdam
[4]   Penefsky, H.S. (1985) J. Biol. Chem. 260 13735-13741

INHIBITION OF ATP HYDROLYSIS IN ISOLATED CHLOROPLASTS BY LIPOPHILIC TERTIARY AMINES AND THE MECHANISM OF 'SELECTIVE UNCOUPLING'

HENRIK LAASCH AND JÜRGEN SCHUMANN
BOTANISCHES INSTITUT, HEINRICH-HEINE-UNIVERSITÄT,
UNIVERSITÄTSSTR. 1, D-4000 DÜSSELDORF 1, FRG

1. INTRODUCTION

Lipophilic, tertiary amines (t-amines) are effective inhibitors of ATP synthesis (1-3). Following light-dependent 9-aminoacridine (9-AA) fluorescence quenching and (14C)-methylamine uptake, inhibition of ATP synthesis is correlated with a decline of the light-induced transthylakoid proton gradient (ΔpH). In this, t-amines resemble 'classical' uncouplers. Nevertheless, deliminating from uncoupling is the absence of t-amine effects on the proton-dependent control of electron flux (3). In the presence of t-amines, flux control may be strong even when 9-AA and (14C)-methylamine indicate a low ΔpH (1,2). Considering this, the effects of t-amines resemble energy transfer inhibition. Evidence that protons still mediated flux control in the presence of t-amines came from the observation that flux control was released by addition of a 'classical' uncoupler plus dibucaine. t-amines at concentrations required for an inhibition of ATP synthesis and ΔpH do not inhibit electron transport per se (3). With regard to the selective inhibition of ATP-synthesis, t-amines were termed 'selective uncouplers' (1).

In order to cast further light on the mechanism underlying 'selective uncoupling', we here investigated in more detail to what extent inhibition of the phosphorylation reaction and a dissipation of ΔpH may be involved in the effects of t-amines. A model for mechanism of action of t-amines is presented.

2. PROCEDURE
2.1. Materials and methods

Broken chloroplasts were isolated from spinach, cv. Monatol, as described in ref. (5). The isolation of chloroplast coupling factor (CF1) was performed as in ref. (6). ATP hydrolysis was followed by liberation of (32P)-phosphate from (32P)-labelled ATP (7). Dibucaine (2-butoxy-(N-2(diethylamino)ethyl)-4-quinolinocarboxyamide) and chlorpromazine (2-chloro-10-(-3-dimethylaminopropyl)-phenothiazine) were used as t-amines.

3. RESULTS AND DISCUSSION
3.1. ATP hydrolysis by isolated CF1 and CFO/CF1

Isolated CF1 shows a Ca-dependent activity of ATP hydrolysis in the presence of 20 % ethanol (7). Under these conditions, the amines tested had no significant inhibitory effect on ATP hydrolysis (data not shown). The coupling factor apparently is no target for t-amine ef-

M. Baltscheffsky (ed.), Current Research in Photosynthesis, Vol. III, 161–164.
© 1990 *Kluwer Academic Publishers. Printed in the Netherlands.*

fects. When thylakoids are treated with 33 % methanol, the integrity of the membranes is lost. However, the assembled CFO/CF1 complex exhibits Mg-dependent ATP hydrolysis. When dibucaine was added under these conditions, there was only a minor decrease in the rate of ATP-hydrolysis, indicating that the phosphorylating enzyme is not a major target for this amine. In contrast, chlorpromazine severely inhibited the enzyme complex (not shown).

3.2. T-amine effects on light-triggered ATP-hydrolysis

The ATPase complex of intact membranes was activated by preillumination of thylakoids in the presence of the reducing agent, dithiothreitol. In the following dark period, ATP was hydrolyzed in the presence of Mg^{2+}. If dibucaine was added in increasing concentrations without an uncoupler added, the rate of ATP hydrolysis was slightly increased (Fig 1). Addition of a low uncoupler concentration (0.2 μM nigericin) increased the rate of hydrolysis in the absence of dibucaine. Dibucaine further increased the rate of hydrolysis (Fig 1). With a higher uncoupler concentration (0.6 μM nigericin), dibucaine first led to an increase of hydrolysis, but then ATP hydrolysis was reduced. The latter effect may be produced by uncoupling, as well as by energy transfer inhibition: if Δ pH is reduced by an uncoupler, the rate of ATP hydrolysis first increases, while at stronger uncoupling, previously activated ATPase becomes inactivated and the rates of hydrolysis decline (Fig. 2). Effects of 'energy transfer inhibitors' may not be distin-

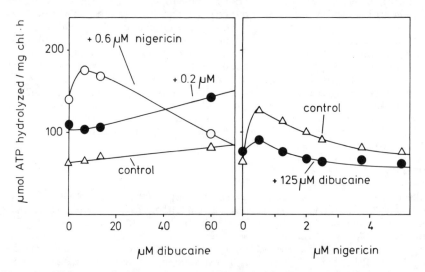

Fig. 1: Effects of dibucaine on ATP hydrolysis by light-triggered ATPase (left). Thylakoids at a Chl concentration of 125 μg/ml were preilluminated in the presence of 5 mM dithiothreitol for 30 s. After further 10 s in the dark, 1 mM (32P)-ATP was added, if required, together with nigericin and dibucaine as indicated. Hydrolysis was terminated after 60 s by addition of 0.3 M $HClO_4$.
Fig. 2: Titration of the activity of ATP hydrolysis with nigericin (right). The experimental conditions were as in Fig. 1.

ghuished from deactivation of the enzyme. In a similar experiment using
chlorpromazine instead of dibucaine, we observed no increase of ATP
hydrolysis in controls. In the presence of 0.6 µM nigericin inhibition
occurs after only a small initial increase of the rate of hydrolysis
(data not shown).

Since isolated thylakoids may be partly uncoupled in dependence of
the leaf material and the isolation procedure, an optimal activation of
hydrolysis by uncouplers demands for the titration shown in Fig. 2. The
nigericin concentration was varied from zero to 5 µM, the maximum activity was observed at 0.6 µM. When 125 µM dibucaine was added in addition to nigericin, the rates of hydrolysis increased up to about 0.6 µM
nigericin, then declined. In the presence of dibucaine alone, hydrolysis increased. Chlorpromazine showed a similar effect.

3.3. CONCLUSIONS

The t-amines tested apparently do not inhibit the thylakoid CF1.
Dependent on the t-amine used, the assembled CFO/CF1 complex may be
partly inhibited, indicating that an inhibition of the phosphorylating
enzyme is not obligatory for 'selective uncoupling'. The effects of
t-amines on light-triggered ATP-hydrolysis by intact membranes turned
out to be complex. A strong increase of hydrolysis in the presence of
dibucaine points to a release of the Δ pH, produced during ATP hydrolysis (Fig. 1). Nevertheless, the maximum rates of hydrolysis , as obtained in the presence of an optimal uncoupler concentration (see Fig. 2),
are not obtained under the influence of either of the amines tested. A
contribution of energy transfer inhibition, located on the membrane
level rather than at the enzyme complex, to the phenomenon of 'selective uncoupling' has to be considered. Depending on the nature of the
t-amine used, uncoupler-like effects or energy transfer inhibition may
be predominant. An intriguing feature of this type of energy transfer
inhibition, nevertheless, is the observed effect on 9-AA fluorescence
and (^{14}C)-methylamine uptake (1,3).

Based on the data presented here and previously (1-3,8), we propose the following mechanism for 'selective uncoupling' (Fig. 3): Protons, pumped during electron flow may be free in the lumen, thereby
creating a thermodynamically active proton potential, or bound to negative surface charges of the thylakoids (9,10). The lateral transport
from the sites of proton release to the synthase complex may proceed
either through the lumen or via repeated binding and unbinding to negative surface charges (Fig. 3). Lateral transport normally is not limiting for ATP synthesis (9). When t-amines are added, uncharged amine
(A_O) enters the lipid phase of the thylakoids (A_M) and on this way the
lumen (A_I). Protonated amine (AH_I, AH_O) is formed. AH_I and AH_O may bind
to negative charges of the membrane which become surface exposed during
membrane energization (10). The concentration of binding sites (S) and
the equilibrium constant of binding (K) have been determined recently
(8). AH_I may act as a lipophilic shield of the inner negative surface
charges and thus prevent proton binding to the membrane. Under these
conditions, the proton buffering capacity of the thylakoids is decreased. The observed inhibition of ATP synthesis, in the framework of
this model is created either by a hindered lateral transport of protons or by a decrease of the proton motive force due to shielding of
surface charges. The latter mechanism would be in agreement with the

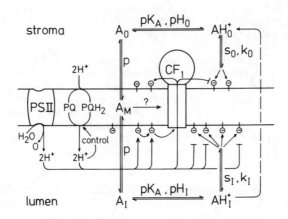

Fig. 3: A model for the mechanism of 'selective uncoupling' by t-amines. The symbols denote: p, partition coefficient of the t-amine; pH_0 and pH_I, proton potentials in the stroma and in the thylakoid lumen; PQ, plastoquinone. Negative charges are shown as ⊖ . For further explanations, see text.

model of 'energy transduction', as proposed by Kraayenhof et al. (10). Finally, inhibition may be brought about by a direct interaction of A_M with the CF_0 complex. A contribution to 'selective uncoupling' of an amine-related proton shuttle over the membranes has to be considered. We are aware, that the proposed mechanism of t-amine action in part is not easily to be reconciled with the hypothesis of a delocalized proton motive force in the thylakoid lumen. Nevertheless, at present we see no mechanism to explain the effects of 'selective uncoupling' in terms of the classical hypothesis of a fully delocalized proton potential as a driving force for photophosphorylation.

REFERENCES
1 Laasch, H. and Weis, E. (1988) Biochim. Biophys. Acta 936, 99-107
2 Laasch, H. and Weis, E. (1989) Photosynth. Res., in press
3 Laasch, H. (1989) Planta, in press
4 Siggel, U. (1974) In: Proc. 3rd Int. Congr. on Photosynthesis, Avron M. ed., 645-654, Elsevier, The Hague
5 Strotmann, H. and Bickel-Sandkötter, S. (1977) Biochim. Biophys. Acta 460, 126-135
6 Schumann, J., Richter, M.L. and McCarty, R.E. (1985) J. Biol. Chem. 260, 11817-11823
7 Schumann, J. (1987) Biochim. Biophys. Acta 890, 326-334
8 Günther, G. and Laasch H. (1989) In: Proc. 8th Int. Congr. on Photosynthesis, Martinus Nijhoff Publ., Dordrecht, in press
9 Junge, W. and Polle A. (1986) Biochim. Biophys. Acta 848, 265-273
10 Kraayenhof R., de Wolf, F.A., van Walraven, H.S. and Krab, K. (1986) Bioelectrochem. Bioenerg. 16, 273-285

THE CHARACTERIZATION OF A POTENT, NATURALLY OCCURRING, ATPase INHIBITOR (SIF) ISOLATED FROM THE HALOTOLERANT ALGAE DUNALIELLA

Susanne Selman-Reimer and Bruce R. Selman, Department of Biochemistry, University of Wisconsin-Madison, Madison, WI 53706, USA

1. INTRODUCTION

The in situ regulation of the catalytic activity of the chloroplast coupling factor ($CF_0 \cdot CF_1$) appears to be quite complex, involving protomotive force (μ_p)-induced conformational changes (1). These conformational changes are manifest in (i) the exposure of buried proton exchangeable groups in CF_1 to the aqueous medium (2), (ii) the exposure of buried reactive amino acid residues to hydrophilic chemical modifiers (3), (iii) large magnitude changes in the dissociation constant of CF_1 for its ligands (4), and (iv) an increased susceptibility of a disulfide bridge on the γ-subunit to reduction by dithiols (5). Stabilization of the in situ activated form of the ATPase is apparently achieved by the reduction of the exposed γ-subunit disulfide bridge to vicinal dithiols by dithiol reagents [e.g., dithiothreitol (DTT) in vitro (6) or thioredoxin in organello (7)], enabling on to measure an active ATPase in the subsequent dark period. In the absence of μ_p, reoxidation of the vicinal dithiols to the disulfide causes a rapid inactivation of the induced ATPase activity (8). Although the nature of the in vivo reductant has been postulated to be thioredoxin (7), the in vivo oxidant remains elusive (9). This mini-manuscript summarizes some of our work towards the isolation and characterization of a potential factor required for the negative regulation of the in vivo activated ATP synthase.

2. PROCEDURES

2.1. Material and methods

2.1.1. Analytical methods: Detailed methods for (i) culturing Dunaliella salina (10), (ii) the isolation of the Dunaliella CF_1 (11), (iii) measuring the various induced ATPase activities (12), (iv) measuring and activating the D. salina CF_1 ATPase activity in vivo (13), and (v) the partial purification and a preliminary characterization of an inhibitory factor (SIF) (14) have all previously been described.

2.1.2. Purification of SIF: A detailed purification of the inhibitory factor SIF will appear elsewhere. In brief, the extract from concentrated lysed cultures was heated to 95°C for 5 min followed by centrifugation to remove denatured

M. Baltscheffsky (ed.), Current Research in Photosynthesis, Vol. III, 165–168.
© 1990 *Kluwer Academic Publishers. Printed in the Netherlands.*

material. The extract was made 75% (v/v) in EtOH,
centrifuged to remove debris, concentrated, and applied to
a Dowex 1 x 2 - 400 column. The column was developed with
a linear HCl gradient (0 to 0.05 N) and active fractions
were pooled and chromatographed on a Bio Gel P2 column
developed isocratically in H O. Active fractions were
again pooled and applied to a silica gel column (Bio Sil
A). The column was again developed isocratically in H_2O.
Active fractions were pooled and concentrated.

3.   RESULTS AND DISCUSSION
3.1. Biological properties of SIF: Using the cell wall-less,
halotolerant alga Dunaliella as our test system (13) and source of
material, we have previously reported (14) the partial
purification of a factor, SIF, that has all of the above stated
properties. (i) SIF is highly polar. (ii) The ability of SIF to
inhibit the activated in situ ATPase is prevented if it is first
treated with and presumably reduced by DTT. (iii) SIF is
effective in micromolar concentrations. And, (iv) SIF does not
inhibit the octylglucoside-activated Mg^{2+}-dependent ATPase
activity of the soluble CF_1.

Although we have yet to work out an HPLC method for the
complete purification of SIF, by incorporating silica gel
chromatography, we have greatly improved (based on UV and NMR
spectroscopy; see below) our initial purification. Fig. 1
demonstrates the ability of the active fraction, eluted from a
Biol Sil A column, to inhibit the in vivo light-triggered ATPase
activity of the D. salina CF_1. As was the case for the partially

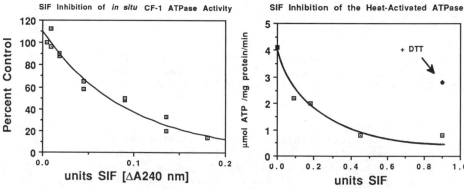

Figure 1 (Left): The ATPase activity of CF_1 in vivo was activated by
illumination (13). The cells were lysed in hypotonic medium containing
varying amounts of SIF and incubated for 5 min prior to the initiation
of the ATPase assay (14).
Figure 2 (Right): The heat-activated, Ca^{2+}-dependent ATPase activity
of the D. salina CF_1 was prepared and assayed as described (11) in the
presence of varying amounts of SIF. Where indicated (triangles), SIF
was first pretreated with 1.0 mM DTT.

purified factor (14), pre-reduction of the purified factor by DTT
completely prevents its inhibition of this ATPase activity (not
shown here). SIF does not inhibit the octylglucoside-activated,
Mg^{2+}-dependent ATPase activity of the soluble CF_1; however, as
shown in Fig. 2, SIF is a potent inhibitor of the heat activated,
DTT-requiring, Ca^{2+}-dependent ATPase. Furthermore, as
demonstrated in Fig. 2 (diamonds), the prior treatment (reduction)
of SIF by DTT prevents it from inhibiting the ATPase.

3.2. <u>Chemical properties of SIF</u>: Although concentrated samples of
purified SIF have a yellowish color, SIF has only a broad
nondescript absorption in the blue end of the spectrum. In its
oxidized form, SIF has a shoulder at about 224 nm and a peak at
about 264 nm (Fig. 3). Reduction of SIF by the addition of DTT
(Fig. 3), $NaBH_4$, or 2-mercaptoethanol, shifts the maximum to about
240 nm with a shoulder at about 288 nm, the isobestic point. The
reduced-oxidized difference spectrum shows an almost symmetrical
peak at about 240 nm (Fig. 3 insert). Because SIF cannot be
reduced by ascorbate (not shown), we estimate that the mid-point
potential for SIF is between 100 to 200 mV.

   Titration of SIF by DTT at 240 nm yields an extinction
coefficient of about 6/mEquivalent/cm. Gravimetric analysis,
based on the titration of SIF by DTT, brackets the molecular
weight of SIF between 400 to 800. This is consistent with the
ability of SIF to pass through molecular filters with a cut-off of
about 1000.

   From ^{1}H-NMR spectroscopy in D_2O, we know that SIF has (i) a
probable aromatic proton (7.75 ppm), (ii) either an N-CH_3 or

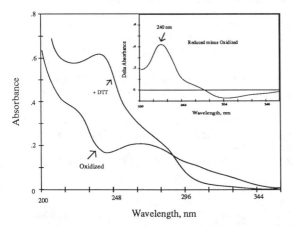

Wavelength, nm

Figure 3: The UV
absorption spectra of
SIF were measured in
a Gilford recording
spectrophotometer.
Where indicated, 1.0
mM DTT was added to
the sample cuvette.
Inset: The reduced
minus oxidized
difference spectrum
of SIF.

O-CH_3 group (3.65 ppm), and (iii) an "ABX" set with the "X" proton
at about 3.6 ppm and the "AB" protons at 2.75 and 2.55 ppm. The
ratio of these protons in the oxidized form of SIF are 1:3:1:1:1.
Upon reduction with $NaBH_4$, an additional proton appears at about
3.6 ppm. ^{1}H-NMR spectroscopy in DMSO-$\delta6$ indicates the presence of
an additional 6 to 10 OH groups in the region 5 to 8 ppm; however,

we cannot yet be certain whether or not these protons are part of SIF or arise from carbohydrate contamination.

From ^{13}C–NMR spectroscopy, an attached proton test, and ^{1}H–^{13}C COSY, we know that SIF contains a carbonyl (177 ppm), three aromatic carbons (131 and 134 ppm) only one of which is protonated (142 ppm), a CH group (64 ppm; the "X" proton), and a methylene group (at 35 ppm) which interacts with the aromatic carbons and is coupled to the CH carbon, and a methyl group at 26 ppm. The nature of two other carbons has not yet been resolved. Altogether, we can discern nine different kinds of carbons.

The presence of a carbonyl group is consistent with weak IR absorbances at 1620, 1586, and 1509 cm^{-1}.

Inductively coupled plasma emission heavy metal analyses indicates the complete absence of As, Cd, Cr, Cu, Fe, Mn, Mo, Ni, Pb, and Zn. These date are consistent with the observation that passage of SIF through a metal chelating ion exchange resin, Chelex 100, has no effect on its ability to inhibit the activated, in situ ATPase activity of CF$_1$.

Unfortunately, to date we have not been able to obtain any useful mass spectroscopy data, either from FAB or EI spectroscopy using either the modified (silated) or native factor.

4. ACKNOWLEDGEMENTS

This work was supported in part by grants from the University of Wisconsin–Madison, College of Agricultural and Life Sciences, and the National Institutes of Health (GM 31384). The authors are extremely grateful for the assistance provided by Mr. Roy Duhe and Mr. Brian Stockman in measuring and interpreting the NMR data. Both have continually provided intriguing suggestions for the structure of SIF.

REFERENCES
1   Shavit, N. (1980) Ann. Rev. Biochem. 49, 111–138
2   Ryrie, I.J. and Jagendorf, A.T. (1971) J. Biol. Chem. 248, 3771–3774
3   McCarty, R.E. and Fagan, F. (1973) Biochemistry 12, 1503–1507
4   Bickel-Sandkoetter, S. and Strotmann, H. (1981) FEBS Lett. 125, 188–192
5   Nalin, C.M. and McCarty, R.E. (1984) J. Biol. Chem. 259, 7275–7280
6   Ketcham, S.R., Davenport, J.W., Warncke, K., and McCarty, R.E. (1984) J. Biol. Chem. 259, 7286–7293
7   Mills, J.D., Mitchell, P., and Schuermann, P. (1980) FEBS Lett. 112, 173–177
8   Shahak, Y. (1982) Plant Physiol. 70, 87–91
9   Shahak, Y. (1985) J. Biol. Chem. 260, 1459–1464
10 Finel, M., Pick, U., Selman-Reimer, S., and Selman, B.R. (1984) Plant Physiol. 74, 766–772
11 Selman-Reimer, S., Finel, M., Pick, U., and Selman, B.R. (1984) Biochim. Biophys. Acta 764, 138–147
12 Selman-Reimer, S. and Selman, B.R. (1984) FEBS Lett. 171, 262–266
13 Selman-Reimer, S. and Selman, B.R. (1988) FEBS Lett. 230, 17–20
14 Selman-Reimer, S. and Selman, B.R. (1988) FEBS Lett. 230, 21–24

ISOLATION, PURIFICATION AND CHARACTERIZATION OF COUPLING
FACTOR ATPASE FROM ANACYSTIS NIDULANS

HIROSHI NEMOTO[1], YOSHINORI OHTA[1], TORU HISABORI[2], KENJI
SHINOHARA[3], and HIDEHIRO SAKURAI[1]
[1]Dept. Biol., Sch. Education, Waseda Univ., Shinjuku, Tokyo 169,
[2]Dept. Biol., Yokohama City Univ., Kanazawa-ku, Yokohama 236,
[3]Forestry and Forest Products Res. Inst., MAFF, P.O. Box 16, Tsukuba Norin Kenkyu
Danchi, Tsukuba 305, Japan

1. INTRODUCTION

F_1s, the ATPase sectors of the ATP synthases (F_0F_1), have been isolated from
various organisms. F_1s are composed of five kinds of subunits, and a striking homology
exists among the corresponding subunits. Although cyanobacteria are considered to be
more feasible to molecular biological studies than eukaryotes, preparation of
cyanobacterial F_1 especially from mesophilic ones have been rather rarely reported
(1,2).

We report here the isolation and the properties of F_1 (AF_1) from a cyanobacterium,
Anacystis nidulans (Meyer's strain). The purified AF_1 preparation could restore
photophosphorylation when added to AF_1-deficient thylakoid membranes from
A.nidulans and CF_1-deficient ones from spinach.

2. MATERIALS AND METHODS

A.nidulans (Meyer's strain) cells autotrophically grown at 25°C by bubbling air were
harvested, washed by centrifugation and treated with lysozyme in 0.6 M sucrose-20 mM
Tricine-NaOH (pH 7.8) with a slight modification of the previous method (3). After
disrupting the cells with a French pressure cell (400 kg/cm^2), the thylakoids were
collected by centrifugation at 104,000 x g for 30 min at 4°C. For AF_1 extraction, the
membranes were suspended in 20 mM Tricine-NaOH (pH 7.8)-0.75 mM EDTA-1 mM
ATP to a final concentration of 0.1 mg chl/ml at 23°C. After 20 min stirring with a
magnetic stirrer, the mixture was centrifuged at 104,000 x g for 30 min at 23°C. The
supernatant containing AF_1 was concentrated by pressure dialysis (PM-30; Amicon).
AF_1 was then purified by the gel-permeation chromatography with a Sepharose CL-6B
column (1.5 x 80 cm) equilibrated with the buffer A (20 mM Tricine-NaOH-2 mM
EDTA-1 mM ATP (pH 7.8)) containing 10% (v/v) glycerol at 23°C. The peak fractions
of ATPase were concentrated and applied to the second CL-6B column. The peak
fractions were concentrated again, and subjected to sucrose linear density gradient
centrifugation (10-30% in the buffer A, 6 tubes, 5ml each) at 100,000 x g for 14 hr at
20°C.

For the measurement of photophospohorylation activity, the thylakoids were
prepared from the lysozyme-treated cells using a French pressure cell (400 kg/cm^2) and
centrifugation. The thylakoids containing 10-40 µg chl in 50 mM Tricine-NaOH (pH

M. Baltscheffsky (ed.), Current Research in Photosynthesis, Vol. III, 169–172.
© 1990 *Kluwer Academic Publishers. Printed in the Netherlands.*

8.0)-10 mM NaCl-2 mM $MgCl_2$-20 μM PMS-25 μM DCIP-1 mM ascorbate-0.75 mM $[^{32}P]$-Pi (20,000cpm/ml), 0.2 mM ADP in a total volume of 1.0 ml were illuminated by 30,000 lux white light filtered through a sheet of red cellophane for 5 min at 30°C. The reaction was terminated by adding 2 ml of 8% TCA , and $[^{32}P]$-ATP formed was determined with a liquid scintillation counter after removing unreacted $[^{32}P]$-Pi from the acid-molybdate solution with isobutabol-benzene. For reconstitution experiments, thylakoids (2 mg chl/ml) were incubated with 2 M NaBr in 0.6 M sucrose-20 mM Tricine-NaOH (pH 8.0) for 30 min at 4°C to inactivate AF_1 and collected by centrifugation at 104,000 x g for 20 min. The washed thylakoids containing 25 μg chl were incubated with 50 μg AF_1 or CF_1 (total volume 1.0 ml) for 20 min at 15°C and then assayed for photophosphorylation.

Unless otherwise indicated, ATPase assay was performed for 20 min at 37°C in a reaction mixture containing 50 mM Tricine-NaOH (pH 8.0), 2 mM ATP, 20% (v/v) methanol (MeOH), 0.75 mM $MgCl_2$ and AF_1. Preparation of CF_1 and chloroplasts from spinach were as described (4,5). Protein was determined by the Lowry-Folin method.

3. RESULTS AND DISCUSSION

Table 1 shows a typical purification step of AF_1 starting with 13 g wet cells. On SDS-PAGE analysis of the purified AF_1, it was found to be composed of 5 kinds of subunits: 54, 52, 37, 19 and 15 kDa. These values were very similar to those of F_1 subunits of Synechococcus 6301 deduced from the DNA sequence analysis by Cozens and Walker: 54, 52, 34, 19 and 14 kDa (6).

In order to test if the AF_1 preparation was reconstitutively active, AF_1- and CF_1-deficient membranes were prepared by NaBr-treatment, and after the addition of AF_1 or CF_1 to the deficient membranes, the recovery of photophosphorylation was measured (Table 2). The addition of AF_1 to the NaBr-treated thylakoids from A. nidulans resulted in recovery of more than 80% of the photophosphorylation of the non-treated particles. CF_1 from spinach restored photophosphorylation to the AF_1-deficient membranes although to a lesser extent than AF_1. The reverse was true when the coupling factor activities were tested in CF_1-deficient thylakoids from spinach.

ATPase activity of AF_1 as prepared was latent as that of CF_1 from spinach. Various treatments which activate CF_1 ATPase were tested to see whether they also activate AF_1 (Table 3). MeOH present in the reaction mixture stimulated (4) the Mg^{2+}-ATPase activity rather strongly and Ca^{2+}-ATPase activity slightly. Trypsin was a rather poor activator of Mg^{2+}-ATPase, but a moderate activator of Ca^{2+}-ATPase. On the other hand, neither the heat treatment nor the dithiothreitol (DTT) treatment significantly activate the both ATPase activities.

TABLE 1 Purification of ATPase from A. nidulans

Purification step	Protein (mg)	Specific activity	Total activity	Yield (%)
EDTA-extract	13.2	0.5	6.6	100
1st CL-6B	3.2	0.7	2.2	33
2nd CL-6B	1.5	0.9	1.4	21
Sucrose density gradient	0.6	2.0	1.2	18

ATPase activity was assayed by the standard method in the presence of Mg^{2+} and MeOH (20 %).

TABLE 2 Reconstitution of photophosphorylation in NaBr-treated
A.nidulnas thylakoids or spinach thylakoids with AF_1 or CF_1

Thylakoid source treatment	Addition	Photophosphorylation (μmol ATP/ mg chl/hr)	
		A. nidulans	spinach
Non-treated	none	54.7 (100 %)	160 (100 %)
NaBr-treated	none	0.1 (0.2%)	8 (5%)
NaBr-treated	AF_1	45.0 (82 %)	98 (61 %)
NaBr-treated	CF_1	13.2 (29 %)	142 (89 %)

The purified AF_1 or CF_1 (2μg protein /μg chll) were
incubated with NaBr-treated membranes for 15 min
at 15°C in the presence of 50mM Tricine-NaOH
(pH8.0), 25mM $MgCl_2$, 0.6M sucrose.
Reconstituted membranes were assayed for
PMS-dependent photophosphorylation activity
for 5 min at 30°C.

TABLE 3 Activation of ATPase by various treatments

Treatment	Specific Activity (μmol/mg/min)					
	AF_1				CF_1	
	Exp. 1		Exp. 2			
	Mg^{2+}	Ca^{2+}	Mg^{2+}	Ca^{2+}	Mg^{2+}	Ca^{2+}
none	0.09	0.09	0.08	0.09	0.1	0.4
MeOH[a]	2.2	0.21	–	–	5.1	3.5
trypsin	0.20	0.51	–	–	2.2	5.4
heat (64°C 5min)	0.05	0.07	–	–	1.4	7.6
DTT (25°C 2hr)	–	–	0.11	0.14	1.3	3.2

[a]20% (v/v) in an ATPase assay mixture.
Trypsin activation was accomplished by adding trypsin to AF_1 (trypsin:AF_1
= 1:50, w/w) in 50 mM Tricine-NaOH (pH 8.0)-2 mM EDTA and the mixture was
incubated for 15 min at 25°C. The digestion was terminated by adding
three-fold (w/w) excess of trypsin inhibitor. Heat activation was
performed for 5 min at 65°C in the presence of 50 mM Tricine-NaOH (pH 8.0)-
2 mM EDTA-30 mM ATP, and stopped by cooling on ice. DTT activation was
carried out for 2 hr at 25°C in the presence of 50 mM Tricine-NaOH
(pH 8.0)-2 mM EDTA-30 mM DTT. ATPase activity of AF_1 was assayed for
20 min at 37°C in a reaction mixture containing 50 mM Tricine-NaOH
(pH 8.0)-2 mM ATP and 0.75 mM $MgCl_2$ or 6 mM $CaCl_2$ unless otherwise indicated.

MeOH concentration dependency of the Mg^{2+}- and Ca^{2+}-ATPase activities is shown in Fig 1. Both activities were maximally stimulated by about 20% (v/v) MeOH. The optimum pH was 8.5 for both activities (data not shown).

The nuclotide specificity of the Mg^{2+}- and MeOH-stimulated activity was tested. ATP was the most preferred substrate followed by ITP and GTP (2.2, 1.5 and 1.4 µmol/mg/min, respectively). CTP and UTP were hardly hydrolyzed.

The effects of divalent cations on ATPase activity were compared at 2 mM in the presence of 20% MeOH (Table 4). We found that Mg^{2+} and Mn^{2+} were effective as with CF_1. However, Ca^{2+} was not so effective as with CF_1. The optimal concentration of $MgCl_2$ was 0.75 mM and that of $CaCl_2$ was 6 mM.

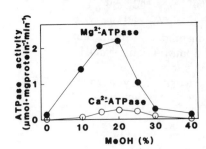

FIGURE 1
MeOH concentration dependency of Mg^{2+}- and Ca^{2+}-ATPase activity of AF_1. The reaction mixture (0.1 ml) contained 3ug AF_1, 50 mM Tricine-NaOH (pH 8.0) 2 mM ATP, 0.75 mM $MgCl_2$ or 6 mM $CaCl_2$ and the indicated concentration of MeOH % (v/v). The assay was carried out for 20 min at 37°C.

TABLE 4 Effects of divalent cations on ATPase activity of AF_1 and CF_1 stimulated by MeOH

cation	(µmol/mg/min)	
	AF_1	CF_1
none	0.00	0.0
Mg^{2+}	0.43	1.4
Ca^{2+}	0.15	3.7
Cu^{2+}	0.00	0.0
Zn^{2+}	0.00	0.3
Co^{2+}	0.07	2.8
Sn^{2+}	0.02	0.0
Mn^{2+}	0.41	1.5

The reaction mixture (0.1 ml) contained 3 µg AF_1 or CF_1, 50 mM Tricine-NaOH (pH 8.0), 2 mM ATP, 20% (v/v) MeOH, and 2 mM divalent cation as indicated. The assay was carried out for 20 min at 37°C.

REFERENCES

1 Binder, A. and Bachofen, R. (1979) FEBS Lett. 104, 66-70.
2 Hicks, D.B. and Yocum, C.F. (1986) Arch. Biochem. Biophys. 245,220-229.
3 Kojima, Y., Niinomi, Y., Tsuboi, S., Hiyama, T. and Sakurai, H. (1987) Bot. Mag. Tokyo 100, 243-253.
4 Sakurai, H., Shinohara, K., Hisabori, T. and Shinohara, K. (1981) J.Biochem. 90, 95-102.
5 Shinohara, K. and Sakurai, H. (1980) Plant Cell Physiol. 21,75-84.
6 Cozens, A.L. and Walker, J.E. (1984) J. Mol. Biol. 184, 359-383.

F_0F_1-ATPase CONTENT IN CHROMATOPHORES OF RHODOSPIRILLUM RUBRUM AND STOICHIOMETRY OF OLIGOMYCIN BINDING

BIRGITTA NORLING, ÅKE STRID, CHRISTOS TOURIKAS and PÅL NYRÉN
DEPARTMENT OF BIOCHEMISTRY, ARRHENIUS LABORATORIES FOR NATURAL
SCIENCES, UNIVERSITY OF STOCKHOLM, S-106 91 STOCKHOLM, SWEDEN

INTRODUCTION

In the F_0F_1-ATPase of mammalian and yeast mitochondria, the oligomycin sensitivity conferring protein (OSCP) is one of the subunits of the enzyme complex, and is needed for inhibition of ATP hydrolysis by oligomycin (1). The amino acid sequence of OSCP from beef heart mitochondria is homologous to the amino acid sequence of the δ-subunit of the F_1-ATPase from E. coli, 26.4% (2), chloroplasts, 25.3% (3), and Rhodospirillum rubrum, 28.9% (2). However, only R. rubrum is sensitive to oligomycin (4). It has also been shown that R. rubrum F_1-ATPase, with the β-subunits substituted with β from E. coli, is not oligomycin sensitive when reconstituted to depleted membranes (5). Thus it is obvious that also the composition of the β-subunit is crucial for oligomycin sensitivity. The homology between the β-subunits from beef heart and the other three sources is (2): E. coli 71.8%, tobacco chloroplast 69.0%, and R. rubrum 76.2%. Both the δ- and the β-subunit of R. rubrum thus show stronger homology with the same subunits from bovine heart mitochondria than do the subunits from chloroplasts and E. coli.

It has been shown for bovine heart F_0F_1 that binding of 1 mol oligomycin per mol of enzyme is enough to inhibit catalysis completely (6). For the yeast enzyme, however a large excess of oligomycin has to be added for maximal inhibition (7).

MATERIALS AND METHODS

Preparation of chromatophores from R. rubrum and purification of F_1-ATPase were done as described in ref. 8.

Antibodies against purified F_1-ATPase were raised in rabbit and used in Western blotting according to the method of Towbin et al. (9). ATP synthesis was measured by the luciferin/luciferase method (10) and ATPase activity by recording NADH oxidation in an ATP regenerating system (8).

M. Baltscheffsky (ed.), Current Research in Photosynthesis, Vol. III, 173–176.
© 1990 Kluwer Academic Publishers. Printed in the Netherlands.

RESULTS AND DISCUSSION

Antibodies against R. rubrum F_1-ATPase are used for quantification of the protein in the chromatophore membrane by the Western blotting technique. As seen in Fig. 1, there is a linear relationship between the amount of F_1 added and the area of the peaks for the α- and β-sub-units obtained in the recordings of laser scans of the autoradio-graphs. From four samples of chromatophores the mean value of F_1 present in the chromatophores could be calculated to 3.5 μg F_1 (nmol BChl)$^{-1}$. If 383 kDa (2) is used as the Mw of F_1, the chromatophores contain 9.1 nmol F_1 (μmol BChl)$^{-1}$ and 13.8% of the protein content is F_1-ATPase. Only a few F_0-moieties seem to be avoid of F_1 since the chromatophores are well coupled. ATP synthesis exhibited high rates, 9 μmol ATP (μmol BChl)$^{-1}$ and the ATPase activity was stimulated 3-4 fold by uncouplers. Thus it is assumed that the F_1-content is equal to the F_0F_1 content.

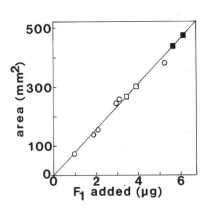

Fig. 1. Quantification of F_1 in chromatophores from R. rubrum by the Western blotting technique. SDS-polyacrylamide gel electropho-resis (11) was performed with iso-lated F_1-ATPase from R. rubrum (o) and with chromatophores (0.95 nmol BChl, □; 1.9 nmol, ■). Western blotting was performed as described in ref. 9. A laser scanner (LKB) was used to determine the optical density of the dots for the α- and β-subunits on the radioautograph. The area of the peaks of the recor-ded traces is plotted vs the amount of F_1.

The content of BChl per R. rubrum chromatophore has been determined to 790 (12). From the present work the number of F_0F_1-ATPases per chroma-tophore (60 nm in diameter) can be calculated to 7. Furthermore, the turn-over of the F_0F_1-ATPase in R. rubrum chromatophores has been determined. The chromatophores showed a rate of ATP synthesis of 9 ATP (μmol BChl)$^{-1}$ min^{-1}, which corresponds to a turn-over for the enzyme of 17 ATP sec^{-1}. Interestingly, the turn-over rate of ATP synthesis in rat liver mitochondria is similar, 16-27 ATP sec^{-1} (13,14). Turn-over rates for ATP hydrolysis in chromatophores was 2.0 ATP sec^{-1} in the absence of uncoupler and 7.0 in the presence of 1 μM FCCP. Furthermore, it was found that Mg-ATP hydrolysis of purified F_1-ATPase has a similar turn-over, 9.6 ATP sec^{-1}, whereas Ca-ATP hydrolysis is strongly stimulated by solubilization (77 ATP sec^{-1}). Thus the so cal-led "latent" Mg-ATPase activity of isolated F_1 seems to correspond to the native Mg-ATPase activity.

Inhibition by oligomycin of the ATP synthase and ATPase activities of chromatophores from R. rubrum was studied by incubating chromatophores at different concentrations of BChl with increasing amounts of oligomycin (Fig. 2). ATP synthase and ATPase activities are equally sensitive to oligomycin. By extrapolating the first part of the curves the amount of oligomycin required for total inhibition could be determined. A minimum value of 16 nmol oligomycin added per µmol BCh was required for complete inhibition, or 1.8 molecules of oligomycin per F_0F_1-complex.

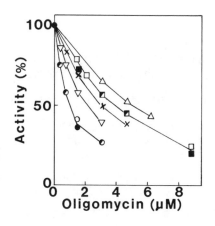

Fig. 2. Inhibition of ATP synthesis and ATP hydrolysis by oligomycin at different concentrations of chromatophores. Chromatophores containing 0.05 mM (o,●); 0.10 mM (▽); 0.19 mM (x); 0.40 mM (□, ■) and 0.5 mM (Δ) BChl were incubated with the indicated concentrations of oligomycin for 30 min at 22°C. Samples were withdrawn and the ATP synthesis rate (●, ■) and the ATPase activity in the presence of 1 µM FCCP (o,▽,x,□,Δ) were determined.

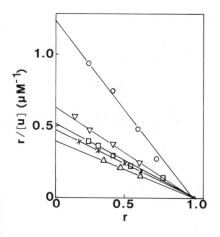

Fig. 3. Scatchard plots for the binding of oligomycin to chromatophores from R. rubrum at different concentrations of BChl. The results shown in Fig. 2 were used to construct the Scatchard plots. r denotes the fraction of inhibited F_0F_1 and [u] denotes the free inhibitor concentration. The same symbols were used as in Fig. 2 for the different concentrations of BChl during incubation with oligomycin.

The values obtained in Fig. 2 were used in a Schatchard plot. The concentration of free oligomycin was calculated from the concentration of added oligomycin minus the concentration of bound, assuming that one molecule oligomycin bound to each F_0F_1-complex causes complete inhibition. In Fig. 3, $\underline{r}$ denotes the fraction of F_0F_1 that is inhibited and [$\underline{u}$] denotes the concentration of free oligomycin. For all concentrations of BChl employed during incubation with the inhibitor, straight lines are obtained. They intercept the X-axis at an $\underline{r}$-value equal to 1 indicating one binding site per F_0F_1. The lines have different slopes, which indicates different values for the dissociation constant ($\underline{K}_d$) for the oligomycin-enzyme complex ranging from 0.8 to 2.5 µM. The reason for this difference is not clear, since repetition under exactly the same condition also gave variation in the $\underline{K}_d$. However, the intercept always gave an $\underline{r}$-value equal to 1.

RERERENCES.

1   Senior, A.E. (1980) Physiol. Rev. 68, 177-231
2   Falk, G., Hampe, A., Walker, J.E. (1985) Biochem. J. 228, 391-407
3   Hermans, J., Rother, Ch., Bichler, J., Steppuhn, J. and Herrmann, R.G. (1988) Plant. Mol. Biol. 10, 323-330
4   Baltscheffsky, M. and Baltscheffsky, H. (1960) Acta Chem. Scand. 14, 257-263
5   Gromet-Elhanan, Z., Khananshvili, D., Weiss, S., Kanazawa, H. and Futai, M. (1985) J. Biol. Chem. 260, 12635-12640
6   Glaser, E., Norling, B., Kopecký, J. and Ernster, L. (1982) Eur. J. Biochem. 121, 515-531
7   Norling, B., Hamasur, B. and Glaser, E. (1987) FEBS Lett. 223, 309-314
8   Norling,, B., Strid, Å. and Nyrén, P. (1988) Biochim. Biophys. Acta 935, 123-129
9   Towbin, H., Staehelin, T. and Gordon, J. (1979) Proc. Natl. Acad. Sci. USA 76, 4350-4354
10 Strid, Å., Karlsson, I.-M. and Baltscheffsky, M. (1987) FEBS Lett. 224, 348-352
11 Schägger, H. and von Jagow, G. (1987) Anal Biochem. 166, 368-379
12 Kakuno, T., Bartsch, R.G., Nishikawa, K. and Horio, T. (1971) J. Biochem. 70, 79-94
13 Schwerzmann, K., Cruz-Orive, L.M., Eggman, R., Sänger, A. and Weibel, E.R. (1986) J. Cell. Biol. 102, 97-103
14 Nelson, B.D., Kabir, F., Kolarov, J., Luciakova, K., Kuzela, S., Latruffe, N. and Lindén, M. (1984) Arch. Biochem. Biophys. 234, 24-30

INTRINSIC UNCOUPLING OF THE F_oF_1-ATPase DEPENDENT ON WHAT
DIVALENT CATION IS USED.

ÅKE STRID AND PÅL NYRÉN, Institutionen för Biokemi, Arrheniuslaboratorierna för Naturvetenskap, Stockholms Universitet, S-106 91 STOCKHOLM, SWEDEN

INTRODUCTION
    The presence of divalent cations is a prerequisite for
ATP hydrolysis or ATP synthesis to be catalyzed by F_oF_1-
ATPases. Mg^{++} is generally recognized as the physiological
cation. However, other divalent cations, such as Ca^{++} and
Mn^{++}, are also capable of promoting at least ATP hydrolysis.
    Recently, it was shown that Ca^{++} induces intrinsic un-
coupling of the F_oF_1-ATPase from chloroplasts (1). In this
communication we examine the effect of Ca^{++} upon the activities of the F_oF_1-ATPase of Rhodospirillum rubrum chromatophores and also the possibility of intrinsic uncoupling
by other divalent cations. The effect of these ions on the
ATPase activity of purified F_1-ATPase is also examined.

EXPERIMENTAL PROCEDURES
    Colorimetric assay of ATP hydrolysis, fluorimetric
assay of proton pumping and measurement of ATP synthesis by
a discontinuous luciferin/luciferase method have been described elsewhere (2).

RESULTS AND DISCUSSION
    Uncoupler-stimulated ATP-hydrolytic activity is exhi-
bited in the presence of Mg^{++}, Cd^{++}, Co^{++}, Mn^{++}, and Zn^{++},
whereas no stimulation by carbonyl cyanide p-trifluoromethoxyphenylhydrazone (FCCP) occurs in the presence of Ca^{++}
(Table 1). Furthermore, ATP-induced proton pumping also
occurs in the presence of Mg^{++}, Cd^{++}, Co^{++}, Mn^{++}, and Zn^{++}
(Table 2). No proton pumping is seen when Ca^{++} is the
choice. However, Ca^{++} does not inhibit light-induced or Mg-
ATP-induced proton-pumping (not shown).
    ATP synthesis is apparent when the divalent cation is
Mg^{++}, Co^{++}, Mn^{++}, or Zn^{++} (Table 3), but not Ca^{++} or Cd^{++}.
    The isolated F_1-ATPase has no or very small activity
in the presence of Mg^{++}, whereas a substantial rate is

TABLE 1. Results of the assay of the hydrolytic activity of
Rhodospirillum rubrum chromatophores. The assay
medium consisted of 0.1 M glycylglycine-NaOH, pH
7.4; 2.5 mM ATP; 0.8 µM bacteriochlorophyll (BChl)
and additions as indicated below. The concentrations of cations are those giving optimal activity, see Ref. 2.

Cation	Hydrolysis rate (µmol ATP/µmol BChl/min)	
	control	+ 2 µM FCCP
1.5 mM Mg^{++}	1.1	3.3
5.0 mM Ca^{++}	1.4	1.0
2.0 mM Cd^{++}	2.0	2.5
2.0 mM Co^{++}	0.8	1.8
2.0 mM Mn^{++}	1.2	2.9
2.5 mM Zn^{++}	1.6	4.4
2.0 mM Ba^{++}	0	0
2.0 mM Sr^{++}	0	0

TABLE 2. Results of the qualitative measurements of
9-amino-6-chloro-2-methoxyacridine quenching.
Quenching is indicated by (+), strong quenching by
(++), and no quenching by (-). The medium consisted of 80 mM glycylglycine-NaOH, pH 7.4; 50 mM
KCl; 0.4 µM 9-amino-6-chloro-2-methoxyacridine
(ACMA); 2.5 µM valinomycin; 0.2 mM Na-succinate;
0.8 µM BChl; 0.25 mM ATP and additions as indicated below.

Source of energy	Quenching
Light	++
Ca-ATP (0.5 mM Ca^{++})	-
Cd-ATP (0.2 mM Cd^{++})	+
Co-ATP (0.2 mM Co^{++})	++
Mg-ATP (0.15 mM Mg^{++})	++
Mn-ATP (0.2 mM Mn^{++})	++
Zn-ATP (0.25 mM Zn^{++})	+
Ba-ATP (0.2 mM Ba^{++})	-
Sr-ATP (0.2 mM Sr^{++})	-
Me-ATP + FCCP	-

TABLE 3. Results of discontinuous measurements of the ATP synthesis rate by chromatophores from <u>Rhodospirillum rubrum</u>. The assay medium contained 0.1 M glycylglycine-NaOH, pH 7.4; 0.9 mM Na-succinate; 0.5 mM ADP; 1 mM NaP_i; 0.8 µM BChl and additions as indicated below.

Cation	Synthesis rate (µmol ATP/µmol BChl/min)
1.5 mM Mg^{++}	7.4
1.5 mM Mg^{++} + 2 µM FCCP	1.2
5.0 mM Ca^{++}	0.2
5.0 mM Ca^{++} + 2 µM FCCP	0
2.0 mM Cd^{++}	1.1
2.0 mM Co^{++}	6.1
2.0 mM Mn^{++}	4.9
2.5 mM Zn^{++}	3.9
2.0 mM Ba^{++}	1.0
2.0 mM Sr^{++}	1.0
No divalent cation added	1.8

TABLE 4. Results of the assay of the hydrolytic activity of purified <u>Rhodospirillum rubrum</u> F_1-ATPase. The assay medium consisted of 50 mM Tris-Cl, pH 7.5; 3 µg protein; 2.5 mM ATP and additions as indicated below.

Cation	Hydrolysis rate (µmol ATP/µmol BChl/min)	+50 mM HCO_3	
	no addition		+ 20 µM DES
1.5 mM Mg^{++}	0	0.12	0.79
5.0 mM Ca^{++}	2.2	2.4	0.36[a]
2.0 mM Cd^{++}	0.72	0.54[a]	0.15[a]
2.0 mM Co^{++}	0	0.13	0.94
2.0 mM Mn^{++}	0	1.4	1.6[a]
2.5 mM Zn^{++}	0.03	0.12[a]	0.30[a]
5.0 mM Sr^{++}	0	0	0
5.0 mM Ba^{++}	0	0	0

[a]In the presence of HCO_3^- some precipitation occurred which presumably lowered the activity. However, the results in the presence and absence of DES should be qualitatively applicable.

attained with Ca^{++} as the cation. Also, no ATP hydrolysis occurs in the presence of Co^{++}, Mn^{++}, and Zn^{++}, whereas some activity is seen with Cd^{++} (Table 4). The hydrophobic compound diethylstilbestrol (DES), which strongly inhibits Ca-ATP hydrolysis and parallelly stimulates the Mg-ATP hydrolysis (3,4), also enhances ATP hydrolysis in the presence of Co^{++}, Mn^{++}, and Zn^{++}, but inhibits the Cd-ATPase activity (Table 4).

We propose to group the divalent cations into two groups, a "Mg^{++}-group" containing Mg^{++}, Co^{++}, Mn^{++}, and Zn^{++} in the presence of which the F_oF_1-ATPase exhibits the well-known coupled activities and the F_1-ATPase is unable to hydrolyze ATP without activators, and a "Ca^{++}-group". When Ca^{++} is present, intrinsic uncoupling of the enzyme is evident. Furthermore, the F_1-ATPase is able to hydrolyze ATP in the presence of Ca^{++}. Cd^{++} is suggested to fall in between these two groups. We also would like to propose that the ionic diameter is determinant for the effect: the ions of the "Mg^{++}-group" has an ionic diameter of between 0.65 and 0.80 Å (5), Mg^{++} being the smallest, whereas Cd^{++} and Ca^{++} have ionic diameters of 0.92 and 0.95 Å (5) respectively. Larger ions, such as Ba^{++} and Sr^{++}, cannot be used as promoters of the activities of the F_oF_1-ATPase of Rhodospirillum rubrum chromatophores.

ACKNOWLEDGEMENTS
    This work was supported by grants to P.N. and to Prof. Margareta Baltscheffsky from the Swedish Natural Science Research Council (NFR).

REFERENCES
1. Pick, U., and Weiss, M. (1988) Eur. J. Biochem. 173, 623-628.
2. Strid, Å., and Nyrén, P. (1989) Submitted to Biochemistry.
3. Strid, Å., Nyrén, P., and Baltscheffsky, M. (1988) Eur. J. Biochem. 176, 281-285.
4. Strid, Å. (1989) Doctoral thesis, Univ. of Stockholm, Stockholm, Sweden.
5. Hägg, G. (1979) In Allmän och oorganisk kemi, Almqvist & Wiksell, Stockholm, Sweden.

THE PURIFIED F_1-ATPase OF RHODOPSEUDOMONAS BLASTICA IS A Ca^{++}-ATPase.

ÅKE STRID AND PÅL NYRÉN, INSTITUTIONEN FÖR BIOKEMI, ARRHENIUSLABORATORIERNA FÖR NATURVETENSKAP, STOCKHOLMS UNIVERSITET, S-106 91 STOCKHOLM, SWEDEN.

1. INTRODUCTION

The genes for the catalytic part of the F_oF_1-ATPase from two different phototrophic bacteria have been sequenced: Rhodospirillum rubrum (1) and Rhodopseudomonas blastica (2). The sequence of the genes for the F_o of R. rubrum is also known (3). The atp1-operon of the latter bacteria encodes the five subunits found in the preparations of the enzyme (Walker, J. E., Falk, G., and Strid, Å., unpublished results) as judged by N-terminal analysis. The atp-operon of Rps. blastica also contains a sixth gene, termed X. The F_1-protein has not previously been prepared from Rps. blastica. Some characteristic properties of a pure preparation of the enzyme is compared to the properties of the R. rubrum F_1.

2. EXPERIMENTALS

The F_1-ATPase from R. rubrum (4) and Rps. blastica was prepared by a modification of the method described for rat liver mitochondria (5). The preparations revealed five and six bands on SDS-gel electrophoresis (6), see also Table 1, for the R. rubrum and Rps. blastica enzymes respectively. The sixth band in the Rps. blastica-preparation either correspons to the X-gene or is an impurity.

3. RESULTS AND DISCUSSIONS

A comparison between some of the properties of the ATP hydrolytic activity of the F_1-ATPase purified from the two organisms and between the properties of the ATPase activity of the chromatophores from the same organisms is shown in Table 2. It is evident that both preparations of F_1 show the highest activity with Ca^{++} as the divalent cation. HCO_3^- is an activator in both cases, and for both preparations, diethylstilbestrol inhibits the Ca^{++}-promoted activity but

TABLE 1. The molecular weights of the polypeptides of the preparations of this study compared with the molecular weights calculated from the genes. 107 kDa was used as the mean molecular weight of the amino acids.

Molecular weights (kDa)					
	Rps. blastica			R. rubrum	
Calc. from	Ref. 2	This study	From Ref. 1		This study
55.2	(α)	59	55.0	(α)	60
51.3	(β)	53	50.8	(β)	55
31.0	(γ)	32	32.4	(γ)	33
28.8	(X)	20.4	19.5	(δ)	18
19.5	(δ)	13.9	14.3	(ϵ)	16
13.9	(ϵ)	12.5			

TABLE 2. Comparison between the ATPase activities of different preparations from Rps. blastica and R. rubrum. 2.5 mM ATP was present in all experiments. The hydrolytic activities are expressed as μmol ATP (mg protein)$^{-1}$ min^{-1} and μmol ATP (μmol bacteriochlorophyll)$^{-1}$ min^{-1} for the solubilized F_1 and the chromatophores respectively. DES stands for diethylstibestrol.

Additions		Rps. blastica	R. rubrum
F_1	5 mM Ca^{++}	2.1	3.8
	5 mM Ca^{++} + 50 mM HCO$_3^-$	3.8	4.1
	5 mM Ca^{++} + 50 mM HCO$_3^-$ + 20 μM DES	2.3	0.6
	1.5 mM Mg^{++}	0.4	0
	1.5 mM Mg^{++} + 50 mM HCO$_3^-$	0.8	0.2
	1.5 mM Mg^{++} + 50 mM HCO$_3^-$ + 20 μM DES	1.2	1.4
Chromatophores	5 mM Ca^{++}	0.16	1.4
	5 mM Ca^{++} + 2 μM FCCP	0.19	1.0
	1.5 mM Mg^{++}	0.32	1.1
	1.5 mM Mg^{++} + 2 μM FCCP	0.45	3.9

increases the Mg-ATPase. The Mg-ATP hydrolysis in chromatophores from R. rubrum is strongly stimulted by carbonyl
cyanide p-trifluoromethoxyphenylhydrazone (FCCP). On the
other hand, the same preparation from Rps. blastica is only
slightly stimulated. This probably reflects the fact that
the intracellular membranes continuous with the plasma membrane in Rps. blastica are lamellar, whereas the corresponding membranes are spherical or tubular in R. rubrum. Thus,
it is likely that the chromatophores from the former bacterium are not closed to the same extent as the vesicle
preparation from the latter.

In accordance with the case in R. rubrum, oligomycin and
venturicidin inhibit the ATP hydrolysis in chromatopores
from Rps. blastica (not shown).

4. ACKNOWLEDGEMENTS

This work was supported by a grant to P. N. from Natur-
vetenskapliga forskningsrådet (The Swedish Natural Science
Research Council).

REFERENCES

1. Falk, G., Hampe, A., and Walker, J. E. (1985) Biochem.
   J. 228, 391-407.
2. Tybulewicz, V. L. J., Falk, G., and Walker, J. E. (1984)
   J. Mol. Biol. 179, 185-214.
3. Falk, G., and Walker, J. E. (1988) Biochem. J. 254, 109-
   122.
4. Norling, B., Strid, Å., and Nyrén, P. (1988) Eur. J.
   Biochem. 176, 281-285.
5. Fisher, R. J., Liang, A. M., and Sundstrom, G. C. (1981)
   J. Biol. Chem. 256, 707-715.
6. Strid, Å., and Nyrén, P. (1989) Acta Chem. Scand. in
   press.

MEMBRANE PROPERTIES OF *RHODOPSEUDOMONAS PALUSTRIS*
University of Erlangen, Institute of Botany and
Pharmaceutical Biology, Staudtstr. 5, D-8520 Erlangen, F.R.G.

KARL KNOBLOCH, BIRIGT PIRNER and HORST MÜLLER

Among purple bacteria, energy transformation rates are rather low in
Rhodopseudomonas palustris (ATCC 11168) due to a weakly membrane-bound
RpF_1-ATPase. Cell breakage by high pressure or sonication treatment resulted in a crude chromatophore preparation with a lag phase of about
6 h where no energy induced H^+ uptake or phosphorylation rate could be
observed (Fig.1), caused by RpF_1-solubilization and passive H^+ flow
through the RpF_1-leaks (1). The light-induced H^+ uptake could be restored by N,N'dicyclohexylcarbodiimide (DCCD) which seals the RpF_1-leaks.

A 100% depletion of RpF_1 from washed chromatophores could be achieved
by sonication in the presence of EDTA and washing the membranes again
(Tab.1). The totally depleted chromatophores did not perform any
ATPase activity or phosphorylation rate. – Depleted chromatophores re-
coupled the isolated and purified RpF_1-ATPase protein, and thereby restored light-induced H^+ uptake (in the presence of cytochrome $\underline{c}$) by
90% and photophosphorylation by 75%. NADH-dependent oxidative phosphorylation was reconstituted by 65%.

Optimal conditions for recoupling were obtained in the presence of 10
mM Mg^{2+} at a ratio of RpF_1-ATPase/depleted membrane protein = 1/6 for
photophosphorylation, and 1/16 for oxidative phosphorylation, respectively. Minimal concentrations of RpF_1-ATPase protein, needed to start
ADP-phosphorylation in depleted chromatophores, were 1 RpF_1-CF/200 depleted chromatophore protein units for the light-induced, and 1/400 for
the NADH-dependent phosphorylation.

Photosynthetically grown (red) as well as heterotrophically in the dark
developed (white) membranes from *R. palustris* undergo "respiratory control" (2) by influencing the electron flow rates, when substrate is
present in excess, upon the addition of ADP, P_i and Mg^{2+} (3). This acceptor control by phosphorylating substrates resulted in a retardation
of electron transport in chromatophores, whereas the flow rate was stimulated in white membranes from *R. palustris* (Fig.2). However, even in
totally RpF_1-depleted chromatophores an acceptor control by ADP, P_i and
Mg^{2+} can be observed (Tab.2) with an acceptor control index (4) of 1.6.

REFERENCES
1 Müller, H., Neufang, H. and Knobloch, K. (1982) Eur.J.Biochem. 127,
  559-566
2 Chance, B. and Williams, G.R. (1955) J.Biol.Chem. 217, 409-427
3 Knobloch, K. (1975) Z.Naturforsch. 30c, 342-348
4 Boyer, P.D., Chance, B., Ernstner, L., Mitchell, P., Racker, E. and
  Slater, E.C. (1977) Ann.Rev.Biochem. 46, 955-1026

M. Baltscheffsky (ed.), Current Research in Photosynthesis, Vol. III, 185–188.
© 1990 *Kluwer Academic Publishers. Printed in the Netherlands.*

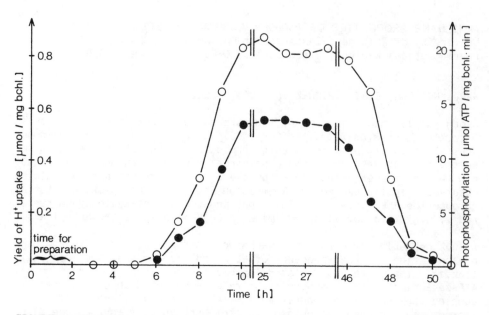

FIGURE 1. Photophosphorylation activity and yield of H⁺ uptake by chromatophore preparations from *R. palustris* upon illumination, determined
in intervals of 1 h after membrane preparation. Open circles (O-O)
correspond to yield of H⁺ uptake and the closed circles (●-●) to photophosphorylation activity. See also Tab.1. bchl = bacteriochlorophyll.

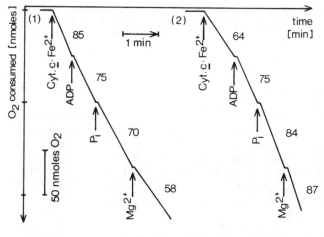

FIGURE 2. Acceptor control by phosphorylating substrates du-
ring cytochrome $\underline{c}$-in-
duced O_2 consumption
in chromatophores from
R. palustris. — (1)
Non-treated, (2) de-
pleted chromatophores.
Where indicated by ar-
rows, the respective
substrates were injec-
ted. Reaction mixture,
total volume 3ml, con-
tained 0.05 M glycyl-
glycin, pH 7.75, 1 mg
membrane protein, 100 μ of 10 mM reduced cytochrome $\underline{c}$, and final conc.s
of 0.2 mM ADP, 1 mM P_i, and 5 mM MgAc. — Numbers joining the traces indicate amounts of nmol O_2 consumed/mg protein · min.

TABLE 1. Photophosphorylation and light-induced pH changes in chromatophores from various purple bacteria as a function of chromatophore treatment.

Treatment of chromatophores	Method of measurement	R. palustris	R. sphaeroides	R. capsulata	R. acidophila	R. rubrum
None	Photophosphorylation	13.4	16.4	16.2	15.7	18.8
	Initial rate of H⁺ uptake	3.3	3.9	3.9	3.8	4.3
60 s sonication in the absence of EDTA	Photophosphorylation	4.8	13.5	13.1	11.8	15.8
	Initial rate of H⁺ uptake	1.2	3.2	3.1	2.7	3.6
150 s sonication in the absence of EDTA	Photophosphorylation	0	10.7	10.2	9.6	12.8
	Initial rate of H⁺ uptake	0	2.6	2.6	2.4	2.9
150 s sonication in the presence of 1 mM EDTA	Photophosphorylation	0	1.0	0.7	0.6	1.1
	Initial rate of H⁺ uptake	0	0.3	0.3	0.2	0.4
350 s sonication in the presence of 1 mM EDTA	Photophosphorylation	0	0.1	0	0	0.1
	Initial rate of H⁺ uptake	0	0.02	0	0	0.03

The chromatophore suspensions were submitted to the indicated treatment, followed by centrifugation at 144 000 x g for 100 min. The resulting pellet was washed in 20mM glycylglycine for assay of photophosphorylation or in 0.3 M NaCl for assay of light-induced pH changes. Prior to the measurements the washed chromatophores were resuspended in the corresponding medium. Numbers of photophosphorylation were expressed as µmol ATP formed per mg bacteriochlorophyll and per min, numbers of the initial rate of H⁺ uptake as µmol H⁺ taken up per mg bacteriochlorophyll and per min. – Rates of phosphorylaion were determined as described in (1). H⁺ uptake was followed in anaerobiosis, using light shorter than 720 nm, and starting at the same initial pH level of 6.5 ± 0.01 under calibrated conditions; the standard reaction mixture in a final volume of 6 ml contained 0.3 M NaCl and chromatophores corresponding to 20 µg bchl./ml.

TABLE 2. Respiratory control by phosphorylating substrates in *R. palustris* chromatophores, induced by NADH-dependent processes in the dark.

Membrane fraction	Additions	ADP-phos-phorylation [nmol ATP/mg prot. · min]	O_2-uptake [nmol O_2/mg prot. · min]	Membrane potential $\triangle \psi$ [mV]	H+ gradient $-z \cdot \triangle pH$ [mV]	Proton motive force $\triangle p$ [mV]
chromato-phores	–	0	6.0	118	104	222
	ADP	0.5	5.5	107	110	217
	ADP, Mg^{2+}	0.6	5.4	107	109	216
	ADP, P_i	–*	5.0	100	115	215
	ADP, P_i, Mg^{2+}	17	4.7	90	117	207
depleted chromato-phores	–	0	5.0	100	35	135
	ADP	0	7.4	105	30	135
	ADP, Mg^{2+}	0	7.9	105	31	136
	ADP, P_i	–*	7.8	109	25	134
	ADP, P_i, Mg^{2+}	0	8.2	117	15	132

*No result due to Mg^{2+} content of luciferin-luciferase reagent.

For experimental conditions see also Tab. 1 and Fig. 2; the membrane potential was estimated by NADH-induced carotenoid band shifts in the presence of 0.3 mg membrane protein/ml in 0.1 M cholinchloride, pH 7.0. Generation of NADH-dependent H+ gradient was startet at pH 7.0 with 1 mg membrane protein/ml. – Final conc.s of 0.2 mM ADP, 1 mM P_i and 5 mM MgAc were applied.

TRANSCRIPTION OF GENES CODING FOR SUBUNITS OF THE F_0 MEMBRANE SECTOR OF ATP SYNTHASE IN RHODOSPIRILLUM RUBRUM

Gunnar Falk
Department of Biochemistry, Arrhenius Laboratories, University of Stockholm, S-106 91 Stockholm, Sweden

1. INTRODUCTION

Genes coding for bacterial ATP synthase subunits are arranged in operons (Fig. 1). Transcription of the nine genes of the Escherichia coli unc (or atp) operon proceeds from a single promoter (1). The six genes of the Rhodpseudomonas blastica atp operon are transcribed predominantly from a single site although some transcription also appear to arise from a second site within the operon (2). Rhodospirillum rubrum is the only known example where the genes coding for F_1 and F_0 sectors are divided precisely into two separate operons (3,4). This finding may also support the view that these represent evolutionary modules which later became associated. Transcription of the Rsp. rubrum atp 1 operon (coding for F_1 subunits) occur from a single site, upstream of the initiation codon of the gene for the δ subunit (5).

Sequences on the 5'-side of the transcriptional start sites in the Rps. blastica atp operon are not apparently related to E. coli promoter sequences. However, the Rsp. rubrum start sites does contain sequences resembling the canonical E. coli promoter (Fig. 2). Presumably this indicates a divergence in the structure of the promoter binding factor of RNA polymerases in these photosynthetic bacteria.

Transcriptional termination of the atp operon in E. coli, Rps. blastica and Rsp. rubrum occur in all cases at sequences that could form stable hairpin-loop structures, followed by runs of thymidylate residues. These features are in E. coli characteristic of rho-independent transcriptional termination signals (6) and appear to be conserved in the two photosynthetic bacteria.

2. MATERIALS AND METHODS

Sources of chemicals, method of RNA preparation, making of single stranded probes, mapping with S1 nuclease and primer extension analysis have been described (5).

M. Baltscheffsky (ed.), Current Research in Photosynthesis, Vol. III, 189–192.
© 1990 Kluwer Academic Publishers. Printed in the Netherlands.

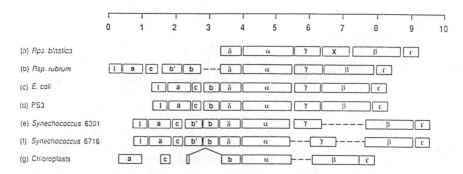

Fig. 1. Organisation of genes encoding ATP synthase subunits in bacteria and plant chloroplasts.

The scale is in kilobases, the letters a, b, c, α, β, γ, δ and ε indicates the ATP synthase subunit encoded in the gene. The letters I and X indicate genes of unknown function (1,2,7 and H.S. van Walraven, J.E. Walker, unpublished results). Chloroplast c subunit (prime tertron) is also known as subunit III and chloroplast b as subunit I; b contains an intron (8); b' is a duplicated and diverged form of b. The dashed line signifies that the gene clusters are at least 15 kilobases apart and are separately transcribed.

3. RESULTS AND DISCUSSION

3.1. Location of 5'-end of atp 2 (F$_0$) operon

The site of initiation of transcription of the Rsp. rubrum atp 2 operon was determined by two independent methods, mapping with S1 nuclease and primer extension analysis. The result of the S1 mapping experiment using probes no 1 and 2 (Table 1) indicated a 5'-end around nucleotide 620 (see Ref. 4 for nucleotide numbers in sequence). Primer extension analysis were then performed with probes 3 and 4 (Table 1). They extend from nucleotides 880 and 829 respectively to the SacII restriction enzyme site at 640. They were annealed with Rsp. rubrum RNA, and after extension with reverse transcriptase gave products extended by 21 nucleotides upstream from the SacII site. This corresponds to a 5'-end for the Rsp. rubrum atp 2 operon mRNA at nucleotide 620, thus supporting the result obtained by S1 nuclease mapping. The DNA sequence upstream of this site contain -10 and -35 regions similar to those of E. coli promoters (Fig. 2).

3.2. Termination of the atp 2 mRNA

Probes 5 and 6 (Table 1) covering a region of DNA beyond the 3'-end of the gene for the b subunit were used to map the 3'-end of the atp 2 operon mRNA. The protected fragments in the S1 nuclease experiment corresponds to a termination site at nucleotide 3615. This nucleotide falls in a region with self-complementary DNA sequences and a run of thymidylate residues, both characteristic of a transcription termination signal in E. coli (Fig. 3).

Table 1. Probes used for transcriptional mapping with S1 nuclase and for primer extension analysis

Probe No.	Start*	Restriction enzyme site	Length# (bases)
1	880	XhoI, 446	482
2	829	XhoI, 446	431
3	880	SacII, 640	288
4	829	SacII, 640	237
5	3560	PvuI, 3369	239
6	3632	PvuI, 3369	311

*Position in nucleotide sequence given in Reference No. 4.
#All probes include an additional 48 nucleotides derived from the primer (17 nucleotides) and M13 DNA adjacent to the SmaI digestion site (31 nucleotides).

```
                                    5'                                         3
Rsp. rubrum   atp2  (Fo)   TTCCTCCTTGACACCCCTCGCCACGCTCCGTATTTTGCCCGCGATT

Rsp. rubrum   URF4          ACTTACACCCATAGGTGGTGTTTATCGGAATATAAACCAGCACTCG

Rsp. rubrum   atp1  (F1)   TTCAGGTGGACGTGGACCCCATTTCCTTTCTATAGTCCGCGCCGTC

E. coli       consensus     [TTGACa]<------15-20----->[TAtAaT]<-1-8->[Pu]

                            "-35 box"                 "-10 box"   start
```

Fig. 2. Transcriptional promoters in Rsp. rubrum
The boxed E. coli consensus promoter sequence is from Reference No. 9. The dashed double arrow and the numbers between boxes indicated the number of intervening nucleotides. The site of initiation of transcription of the Rsp. rubrum atp operons are underlined.

The sequence of the Rsp. rubrum atp 2 operon has non-coding segments of 101 and 218 nucleotides upstream and downstream respectively of the c subunit gene. The possibility that this region harbours a secondary promoter in the operon is currently investigated. This together with a Northern blot analysis will give a more detailed picture of the transcription of the Rsp. rubrum atp 2 operon.

ACKNOWLEDGEMENTS

This work was supported by a grant from the Swedish Natural Science Research Council (NFR) to GF.

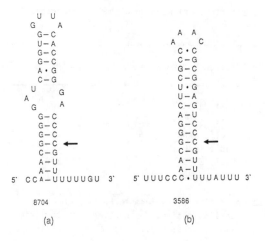

Fig. 3. Possible stem-loop structures of mRNA on the 3'-end of Rsp. rubrum atp operon which resemble E. coli transcriptional terminators.
(See Reference No. 10). (a) atp 1 operon (b) atp 2 operon. The transcriptional termination sites are arrowed.

REFERENCES

1. Walker, J.E., Saraste, M. and Gay, N.J. (1984) Biochim. Biophys. Acta 768, 164-200.

2. Tybulewicz, V.L.J., Falk, G. and Walker, J.E. (1984) J. Mol. Biol. 179, 185-214.

3. Falk, G., Hampe, A. and Walker, J.E. (1984) Biochem. J. 228, 391-407.

4. Falk, G. and Walker, J.E. (1988) Biochem. J. 254, 109-122.

5. Falk, G. and Walker, J.E. (1985) Biochem. J. 229, 663-668.

6. Pribnow, D. (1978) in Biological Regulation and Development, vol. 1 (Goldberger, R.F., ed), pp. 219-277, Plenum Press, New York.

7. Cozens, A.L. and Walker, J.E. (1987) J. Mol. Biol. 194, 359-383.

8. Bird, C.R., Koller, B., Auffret, A.D., Huttly, A.K., Howe, C.J., Dyer, T.A. and Gray, J.C. (1985) EMBO J. 4, 1381-1388.

9. Hawley, D.K. and McClure, W.R. (1983) Nucleic Acids Res. 11, 2237-2255.

10. Rosenberg, M. and Court, D. (1979) Ann. Rev. Genet. 13, 319-353.

EXPRESSION OF THE CHLOROPLAST *atp*B GENE OF *CHLAMYDOMONAS REINHARDTII* IN *E. COLI*

SARAH BLUMENSTEIN, STEFAN LEU, EAHAB ABU-MUCH, DUDY BAR-ZVI, NOUN SHAVIT AND ALLAN MICHAELS   BIOLOGY DEPARTMENT, BEN GURION UNIVERSITY OF THE NEGEV, BEER SHEVA, ISRAEL

1. INTRODUCTION

Energy derived from electron transport in mitochondrial, chloroplast thylakoids and bacterial plasma membranes is transduced to form ATP by the $F_1 \cdot F_0$ proton translocating ATP synthases[1]. These enzyme complexes are composed of an intrinsic membrane protein complex, F_0, which mediates H^+-translocation, and a peripheral protein complex, F_1, which catalyzes the terminal step of synthesis of ATP from ADP and P_i. F_1 is composed of five different polypeptide chains designated α–ε in order of decreasing M_r with a subunit stoichiometry of $\alpha 3\beta 3\gamma\delta\varepsilon$. The binding sites for ADP and ATP are located on the α and β subunits and the catalytic sites are thought to be on the β subunits. Isolated CF_1 is a latent ATPase which can be activated by a variety of means to exhibit a Mg^{2+}- or a Ca^{2+}- dependent ATPase activity (1). Subunits α, β and ε of CF_1 are encoded in the chloroplast DNA (2, 3). The gene *atp*B from chloroplast DNA of *Chlamydomonas reinhardtii*, encoding for subunit β, was isolated and sequenced (4). We have subcloned the *atp*B gene into pT7-2 from plasmid pB7 (a gift from Dr. N. Gillham). RNA from this plasmid was transcribed and translated *in vitro*. The β subunit synthesized *in vitro* was shown to assemble into CF_1 (5).

We expressed subunit β from the cloned *atp*B gene, in a system designed for inducible expression of genes under control of the T7 RNA polymerase promotor. *E. coli* strain BL21 contains the gene for T7 RNA polymerase integrated into its genomic DNA, under the control of the Lac UV 5 promotor (6). This strain was transformed with the plasmid pT7-2 containing the *atp*B gene. Here we describe the optimisation of the induced gene expression and the partial purification of the target protein.

---

[1]Abbreviations used: $F_1 \cdot F_0$, H^+-translocating ATP synthases from mitochondria, *E. coli* plasma membranes, plasma membranes of the thermophilic bacterium PS3 and chloroplast membranes; CF_1, chloroplast coupling factor one; ATPase, CF_1 E. C. 3.6.1.3; SDS-PAGE, polyacrylamide gel electrophoresis in the presence of sodium dodecyl sulphate; IPTG, isopropyl β D-thiogalactopyranoside.

M. Baltscheffsky (ed.), Current Research in Photosynthesis, Vol. III, 193–196.

2. MATERIALS AND METHODS

The *atp*B gene was resected from plasmid pB7 with the restriction endonucleases HindIII and KpnI and ligated directionally into pT7-2. The resulting clones were analysed with restriction endonucleases for correct insert and orientation. Competent BL 21 cells were transformed with pT7-2 -*atp*B plasmid. Ampicillin resistant clones were selected for inducibility by IPTG (7). Clones were grown in LB (200 μg / ml ampicillin) and aliquots were plated onto LB plates in the presence of ampicillin (0.5 mg / ml) or ampicillin and IPTG (0.5 mg / ml; 0.4 mM). Cells containing a functional promotor did not grow in the presence of IPTG, and therefore the number of cells containing a functional promotor could be estimated from the percentage of colonies growing in the presence of IPTG. To enrich for cells containing functional promotors, a negative selection procedure was developed. Growth of inducible cells was arrested with IPTG, then D-cycloserine was added to lyse cells that continued to grow. After this treatment clones were again screened for functional promotor.

For expression of the *atp*B gene, clones screened or enriched for a functional promotor were grown to 0.7 OD_{600} and induced by addition of 0.4 mM IPTG. Time dependent accumulation of subunit β of CF_1 was monitored by SDS-PAGE (7) and staining with coomassie blue. For optimal expression of subunit β, D-cycloserine (450 μg / ml) was added two hours after the induction to suppress overgrowth with non inducible cells.

The β subunit of CF_1 expressed in *E. coli* was solubilized after the cells were disrupted by ultrasonication and fractionated into supernatant and pellet by centrifugation (10,000 x g; 5 min). Pellets were washed several times and solubilized in a buffer solution containing: Tris·HCl, 50 mM, pH 8.0; Triton-X-100, 1 % and EDTA, 5 mM. The different fractions were analyzed by SDS-PAGE. The β subunit was identified by Western immunoblot analysis using antibodies raised against subunits α and β from CF_1 of *Chlamydomonas* .

3. RESULTS AND DISCUSSION

BL21 transformed with pT7-2-*atp*B were analyzed for functional promotor. About 10 - 20 % cells formed colonies in the presence of IPTG and did not contain functional promotor. Analysis of induced cells showed some synthesis of β subunit of CF_1. The content of induced protein decreased with time due to overgrowth with cells not containing functional promotors. Therefore, we reduced the amount of non-inducible cells with the negative selection procedure. Clones were grown to 0.7 OD_{600} and induced with IPTG (0.4 mM) for two hours. D-cycloserine selection eliminated most of the non-inducible cells.

The β subunit was found in the pellet of the cell homogenate. After removal of cellular proteins by several washes with buffer solution the β subunit was solubilized in 4 M urea. The content of β subunit in this fraction, as determined by densitometry of stained gels (Table 1) was estimated as 62 % of the total protein content. The identity of the protein was established by Western immunoblot analysis. The 52 kD protein induced by

TREATMENT		% STAINED PROTEIN
Sonicated cells	0 hours	0
	2 hours	6
	6 hours	13
Pellet	6 hours	18
Supernatant	6 hours	0
Pellet after washing in 1% Triton		53
Pellet after washing in 4 M urea		0
Supernatant after washing in 4 M urea		62

Table 1. Amounts of β subunit obtained after induction of transformed BL 21. Cells were disrupted by ultrasonication and the β subunit was partially purified as described. The % of total stained protein in the gel was determined by densitometry.

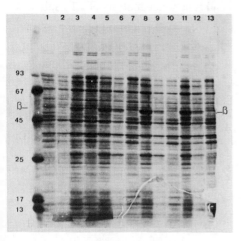

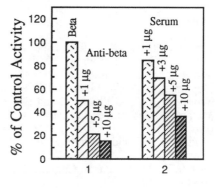

Figure 1: Protein pattern of *atp*B induction
1) untransformed BL21.

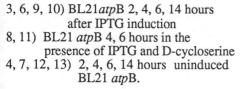

3, 6, 9, 10) BL21*atp*B 2, 4, 6, 14 hours
        after IPTG induction
8, 11) BL21 *atp*B 4, 6 hours in the
        presence of IPTG and D-cycloserine
4, 7, 12, 13) 2, 4, 6, 14 hours uninduced
        BL21 *atp*B.

Figure 2: Inhibition of Mg^{2+}-dependent ATPase activity of partially purified β subunit by β specific antiserum or control serum

IPTG gave a strong signal with the antibody, while no signal was detected in non-induced cells at comparable protein load. Cross-reaction with *E. coli* α and β subunits occurred at higher concentrations.

The induction time for optimal expression of β subunit was six hours. However, non inducible cells contributed to the total protein amount and thus diluted the content of β subunit. To prevent this overgrowth, D-cycloserine was added two hours after the induction. This resulted in production of β subunit amounting to 13% of the total protein of the culture (Table 1 and Fig. 1).

This partially purified preparation of β subunit catalyzed a measurable rate of ATP hydrolysis. The ATPase activity depended on the presence of Mg^{2+} but not Ca^{2+} and was detectable in the absence of known activators of ATPase in isolated CF_1. The activity was destroyed by heating the protein and was inhibited (Fig. 2) by an antiserum specific to β subunit of *Chlamydomonas* CF_1. A Vmax of 0.41 μmol ATP hydrolyzed per mg β subunit per minute and a Vmax/K_M of 288 were calculated for the Mg^{2+}-ATPase activity detected with the partially purified preparation. The ATPase activity of our preparation is thus similar to that recently reported by Frasch et al (8).

The expression system described will be used to express other CF_1 subunits. This will allow reconstitution of CF_1 activities and functional analysis of CF_1 subunits by site directed mutagenesis.

REFERENCES

1. Shavit, N. (1980) Ann. Rev. Biochem. 49, 111 - 138
2. Marder, J. B. and Barber, J. (1989) Pl. Cell and Envir. (in press)
3. Woessner, J. P., Masson, A., Harris, E. H., Bennoun, P. Gillham, N. and Boyton, J. E. (1984) Plant Mol. Biol. 3, 177 - 190.
4. Woessner, J. P., Gillham, N. and Boyton, J. E. (1986) Gene 44, 17 - 28
5. Michaels, A., Weinberg, D. and Leu, S. (1989) Proc. Int. Congr. Photosynth., 8th, (this issue)
6. Studier, F. W. and Moffatt, B. A. (1986) J. Mol. Biol. 189, 113 - 136.
7. Laemmli, U. (1970) Nature, 227: 680 - 685.
8. Frasch, W. D., Green, J., Caguiat, J. and Mejia, A. (1989) J. Biol. Chem. 264, 5064 - 5069.

ACKNOWLEDGEMENTS

This work was in part supported by a grant from NSF (to A. M.) and by a grant from the Bertie I. Black Foundation, Great Britain (to N. S.). We thank Dr. Gillham for supplying the plasmid pB7 and Dr. J. M. Galmiche for a gift of β *Chlamydomonas* antiserum.

SOME SIMILARITIES AND DIFFERENCES BETWEEN BACTERIAL CHROMATOPHORE, SPINACH CHLOROPLAST AND YEAST MITOCHONDRIAL INORGANIC PYROPHOSPHATASES

MARGARETA BALTSCHEFFSKY, ALAUDDIN PRAMANIK, MARIA LUNDIN, PÅL NYRÉN AND HERRICK BALTSCHEFFSKY

DEPT. OF BIOCHEMISTRY, ARRHENIUS LABORATORIES, UNIVERSITY OF STOCKHOLM, S-106 91 STOCKHOLM, SWEDEN

1. INTRODUCTION

Membrane bound inorganic pyrophosphatases (PPases) appear to play a role in energy metabolism (1,2). PPases are present in bacterial, plant and animal cells and cell organelles. Membrane bound PPases have been found in chromatophores (2), mitochondria (3) and chloroplasts (4). The membrane bound PPase from Rhodospirillum rubrum chromatophores can synthesize PPi (inorganic pyrophosphate) at the expense of light energy (1) and has been described in some detail (2). Mitochondrial membrane bound PPase has been reported to produce PPi as a result of oxidative phosphorylation (3). (Genes encoding soluble PPases of E. coli (5) and yeast (6) have been cloned and characterized). We have studied some similarities and differences between chromatophore, chloroplast and mitochondrial membrane bound PPases.

2. MATERIALS AND METHODS

2.1. Preparation of chloroplasts and yeast mitochondria

Chloroplasts were prepared from leaves of fresh spinach as described in (7) and washed 3 times. Mitochondria from yeast were prepared according to (8) and washed twice. As for R. rubrum chromatophores, see below under assays.

2.2. Assays

The inorganic pyrophosphatase activity was assayed colorimetrically according to (9) in a reaction mixture containing 5 mM $MgCl_2$, 0.2 mM $Na_4P_2O_7$, 0.8 ml 50 mM L-histidine-HCl, pH 7.2, chloroplast/mitochondrial suspension and H_2O, in a total volume of 1 ml. The assay mixture was incubated at 30°C for 10 min and the reaction was terminated by adding 0.1 ml 2.4 M $HClO_4$. In blanks $HClO_4$ was added before the

M. Baltscheffsky (ed.), Current Research in Photosynthesis, Vol. III, 197–200.
© 1990 Kluwer Academic Publishers. Printed in the Netherlands.

sample. Chromatophores were prepared and chromatophore PPase assays were carried out according to standard procedures in this laboratory (10-12).

3. RESULTS AND DISCUSSION

NaF, a specific inhibitor of PPase activity, inhibits the activity in chromatophores, chloroplasts and yeast mitochondria (Table 1). As is seen in Table 1, the presence of FCCP, which collapses the electrochemical potential difference of H^+ across the membrane, leads to stimulation of the PPase activity in all three organisms. Also valinomycin and nigericin in the presence of 15 mM KCl stimulate the enzyme activity from chromatophores, chloroplasts and mitochondria (Table 1). Valinomycin collapses the membrane potential by making a membrane permeable to K^+ which is translocated outward in response to the inward translocation of H^+ and nigericin dissipates ΔpH by forming an uncharged complex with K^+, which works as an exchanger for H^+. FCCP, valinomycin and nigericin stimulate the enzyme activity of these three PPases to a similar extent. These stimulations are taken as an indication that the pyrophosphatases are membrane bound and regulated by the $\Delta\mu H^+$.

Effects of Dio-9 and equisetin on membrane bound PPase activities from chromatophores, chloroplasts and mitochondria are given in Table 2. Both Dio-9 and equisetin strongly stimulate the chloroplast and

Table 1. Stimulation by uncoupler, ionophore and protonophore on the membrane bound chromatophore, chloroplast and mitochondrial PPase activities. 1.5 µM FCCP, 10 µg/ml valinomycin and 10 µg/ml nigericin were used for chromatophore activity. 5 µM valinomycin and 5 µM nigericin were used for chloroplast and mitochondrial activities. 1 µM FCCP - for mitochondrial PPase and 5 µM FCCP - for chloroplast PPase activity. The concentration of NaF, when added, was 10 mM. In the case of valinomycin and nigericin 15 mM KCl was added to the assay medium.

Additions	PPase activity (% of control)		
	chromatophores[a]	chloroplasts	mitochondria
FCCP	135	130	130
Valinomycin	124	130	140
Nigericin	146	143	145
NaF	16	6	8

[a]Data are taken from ref. 10.

Table 2. Effects of Dio-9 and equisetin on the membrane bound chromatophore, chloroplast and mitochondrial PPase activities. 30 µg/ml
Dio-9 was used for chromatophore PPase, 25 µg/ml Dio-9 for chloroplast PPase and 60 µg/ml Dio-9 for mitochondrial PPase. Concentration
of equisetin was 80 µM.

Additions	PPase activity (% of control)		
	chromatophores	chloroplasts	mitochondria
Dio-9	60[a]	189	200
Equisetin	25[b]	150	230

[a]Data are taken from ref. 11. [b]Data are taken from ref. 12.

the yeast mitochondrial PPase activities whereas they inhibit the
chromatophore PPase activity. Dio-9 inhibits H^+-ATPase in chloroplasts (13) and H^+-PPase in R. rubrum (Table 2) whereas it stimulates
the chloroplast and mitochondrial PPases (Table 2). Therefore its
effect on the chloroplast PPase is an uncoupling one compared not
only to the chloroplasts ATPase coupling factor but also to the PPase
coupling factor from R. rubrum. Dio-9 and equisetin appear to act
directly on the membrane components of the enzyme complex. So their
effects may well reflect structural modification of the enzyme systems. Similar stimulation by Dio-9 and equisetin on chloroplast and
yeast mitochondrial PPases may indicate structural and evolutionary
relationships between these PPases. However, the structural properties of the PPases causing these similarities are still unknown.
The different effects by Dio-9 and equisetin on the chromatophore
PPase indicate that the membrane bound chromatophore PPase is structurally different from the others.

ACKNOWLEDGEMENTS

This study was supported by the Swedish Natural Science Council, the
Swedish Institute and Wenner-Grenska Samfundet.

REFERENCES

1   Baltscheffsky, H., von Stedingk, L.V., Heldt, H.W. and Klingen-
    berg, M. (1966) Science 153, 1120-1121

2   Baltscheffsky, M. and Nyrén, P. (1984) in Bioenergetics (Ernster,
    L., ed.) pp. 187-2205, Elsevier, Amsterdam

3   Mansurova, S.E., Shakhov, Yu.A. and Kulaev, S.I. (1977) FEBS
    Lett. 74, 31-34

4   Gould, M. and Winget, D. (1973) Arch. Biochem. Biophys. 154, 606-613

5   Lahti, R., Pitkäranta, T., Valve, E., Ilta, I., Kukko-Kalske, E. and Heinonen, J. (1988) J. Bact. 170, 5901-5907

6   Kolakowski, Jr.L.F., Schloesser, M. and Cooperman, B.S. (1988) Nucleic Acids Res. 16, 10441-10452

7   Whately, F.R. and Arnon, D.I. (1963) Methods Enzymol. (Colowick, S.P. and Kaplan, N.O., eds.) vol. 6, pp. 308-313, Acad. Press, N.Y., London

8   Lundin, M., Pereira da Silva, L. and Baltscheffsky, H. (1987) Biochim. Biophys. Acta 890, 279-285

9   Shatton, J.B., Ward, C., Williams, A. and Weinhouse, S. (1983) Anal. Biochem. 130, 114-119

10 Shakhov, Yu.A., Nyrén, P. and Baltscheffsky, M. (1982) FEBS Lett. 146, 177-180

11 Nyrén, P., Hajnal, K. and Baltscheffsky, M. (1984) Biochim. Biophys. Acta 766, 630-635

12 Nyrén, P. and Strid, Å. (1989) Arch. Biochem. Biophys. 268, 659-666

13 McCarty, R.E. and Racker, E. (1968) J. Biol. Chem. 243, 129-137

DISTRIBUTION OF INORGANIC PYROPHOSPHATASE (PPase) ACTIVITY IN CHLOROPLASTS

HERRICK BALTSCHEFFSKY, ALAUDDIN PRAMANIK, MARIA LUNDIN AND
BERTIL ANDERSSON

DEPT. OF BIOCHEMISTRY, ARRHENIUS LABORATORIES,
UNIVERSITY OF STOCKHOLM, S-106 91 STOCKHOLM, SWEDEN

1. INTRODUCTION

PPases are widely distributed in animal, plant and bacterial systems (see ref. 1,2). PPase has been detected in chloroplast (3-5). Thylakoid bound PPase is also found to exist (6,7) and may well be energy linked (A. Pramanik and H. Baltscheffsky, to be published). Soluble PPase has been partially purified from chloroplasts (4,5). The distribution of PPase between stroma (87%) and cytosol (13%) has been estimated (8). It seems that PPase can play an important role in controlling metabolism in leaf cells. PPase may also function in the regulation of CO_2 fixation during photosynthesis of C_4 plants (4). In view of these findings we decided to investigate the PPase enzyme with respect to chloroplast compartmentation.

This communication will describe the distribution of PPase within chloroplast compartments following osmotic shock of purified intact chloroplasts.

2. MATERIALS AND METHODS

2.1. Preparation of intact chloroplasts and thylakoids

Intact chloroplasts were prepared from leaves of fresh spinach and purified using an aqueous polymer two phase system (9). Thylakoids were made from purified intact chloroplasts as reported in (10).

2.2. Assays

PPase activity was measured as described in (11). Native polyacrylamide gel electrophoresis was carried out by the procedure described in (12). The activity staining of the gel for PPase was performed as follows. To localize the PPase activity the gel was incubated for 30 min at room temperature in a solution identical with that utilized for the assay of the enzyme activity, rinsed with H_2O, and immediately immersed in the triethylaminemolybdate reagent of Sugino and Miyoshi (13), which specifically precipitates Pi. Within a few min in the gel sharp, discrete bands appeared, corresponding to the PPase activity.

3. RESULTS AND DISCUSSION

3.1. PPase activity within chloroplast compartments

Distribution of PPase within chloroplast compartments must be estimated with intact chloroplasts of maximum intactness and free from extra chloroplast contamination. In order to obtain such material intact chloroplasts were prepared using a two phase polymer system (9) where broken chloroplasts and extra chloroplast materials partition to the upper phase and purified intact chloroplasts partition to the lower phase. Total PPase activity was measured in intact chloroplasts, osmotically shocked thylakoid (pellet) and stroma (supernatant). As is shown in Table 1, about 25% activity is present in the first thylakoid pellet and about 75% in the stroma fraction.

TABLE 1. Distribution of PPase activity within chloroplast compartments following osmotic shock of intact chloroplasts. Total PPase activity in intact chloroplasts is taken as 100%, corresponding to 7.9 μmoles Pi/mg Chl·min. Total Chl in preparation was 0.45 mg.

	Total PPase activity[a] %		
Intact chloroplasts	Thylakoids (pellet)	Stroma (supernatant)	Yield %
100	26	68	94

[a]Average activity from 4 experiments.

3.2. Effect of washing on thylakoid PPase activity

To check whether the PPase found in the thylakoids is peripherally or integrally bound to the thylakoid membranes or simply adsorbed stromal PPase, thylakoids were washed at different pH. As the extrinsic proteins are easily released at alkaline pH (10), our osmotically shocked thylakoids were washed several times in buffer with pH 6.5 and 8.5. The total PPase activity was then determined in all subsequent supernatants and in the last pellet. As shown in Table 2 the washings release PPase into the aqueous solutions, but the extent of release of PPase from the membrane is about the same whether the washings are performed at pH 6.5 or pH 8.5. About 2% of the PPase activity remained in the final thylakoid pellet.

TABLE 2. PPase activity in supernatants and pellet after washing in buffers at pH 6.5 and 8.5. The washing solution contained 330 mM sorbitol, 30 mM tricine and 5 mM $MgCl_2$. S0, S1, S2, S3-supernatants after osmotic shock, 1st, 2nd and 3rd washings respectively. Total PPase activity in intact chloroplasts is taken as 100%, corresponding to 7.7 μmoles/mg Chl·min at pH 6.5 and 8.5. Only the last pellet was analyzed for PPase activity. Total Chl in preparation was 0.45 mg.

	Total PPase activity %	
	pH 6.5	pH 8.5
Intact chloroplasts	100	100
S0 (stroma)	68	70
S1	17	14
S2	6.8	7.0
S3	3.8	4.1
Thylakoids	2.0	2.1

3.3. PPase study in chloroplasts by native gel electrophoresis

Intact chloroplasts, pellet and supernatant from osmotically shocked intact chloroplasts were loaded on a native gel and the electrophoresis was run under low current in a cold room. After separation the gel was treated for activity staining. As shown in Fig. 1 the PPase activity from supernatant (stroma) formed a single band, whereas the PPase activity from pellet and from intact chloroplast formed two bands. The well washed thylakoids mainly show the lower band.

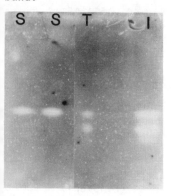

FIGURE 1. Native gel activity staining for PPase from intact chloroplasts, thylakoids and stroma. Activity staining was done as described in Methods. I - intact chloroplasts; T - thylakoids and S - stroma fraction.

The single band from the supernatant clearly corresponds to the upper band from the intact chloroplasts, indicating that these bands originate from stromal PPase. The lower band from intact chloroplasts is missing in the supernatant but corresponds to the lower band from the pellet, confirming that it originates from a thylakoid PPase. When the pellet from osmotically shocked intact chloroplasts is washed and subsequent supernatants are checked by electrophoresis, these supernatants show bands corresponding to both stromal and thylakoid PPases (not shown). This observation indicates that after the washings part of the released PPase (Table 2), was membrane bound and part is adsorbed stromal PPase.

Several washings of thylakoids at pH 6.5 and at pH 8.5 release most of the PPase into aqueous solution but the membrane bound PPase activity is also found in the subsequent supernatants, indicating that the thylakoid PPase is rather loosely bound to the outer surface of the membrane. In preliminary experiments we have observed that PPase activity can be seen in both inside out vesicles (grana thylakoids) and right side out vesicles (stroma thylakoids).

In conclusion we have shown that chloroplasts contain two different kinds of PPases - one soluble in the stroma and one extrinsically bound to the thylakoid membrane.

ACKNOWLEDGEMENTS

This study was supported by the Swedish Natural Science Council, the Swedish Institute and Wenner-Grenska Samfundet.

REFERENCES

1   Baltscheffsky, M. and Nyrén, P. (1984) in Bioenergetics (Ernster, L., ed.) pp. 187-205, Elsevier, Amsterdam
2   Lahti, R. (1983) Microbiol. Rev. 47, 169-179
3   Jensen, R.G. and Bassham, J.A. (1968) Biochim. Biophys. Acta 153, 219-226
4   Forti, G. and Meyer, E.M. (1969) Plant Physiol. 44, 1511-1514
5   Schwenn, J.D., Lilley, R.McC. and Walker, D.A. (1973) Biochim. Biophys. Acta 325, 586-595
6   Gould, M. and Winget, D. (1973) Arch. Biochem. Biophys. 154, 606-613
7   Rubtsov, P.M., Efremovich, N.V. and Kulaev, I.S. (1976) Dokl. Akad. Nauk., SSSR 230, 1236-1237
8   Weiner, H., Sitt, M. and Heldt, H.W. (1987) Biochim. Biophys. Acta 893, 13-21
9   Larsson, C. and Andersson, B. (1979) in Plant Organelles, Methodological Surveys (B) in Biochemistry (Reid, E., ed), Vol. 9, pp. 35-49, Ellis, Horwood, Chichester
10 Andersson, B. and Anderson, J.M. (1985) in Modern Methods of Plant Analysis, New Series Vol.1, Cell Components (Linskens, H.F. and Jackson, J.F., eds.) pp. 231-258, Springer-Verlag, Berlin, Heidelberg, New York, Tokyo
11 Shatton, J.B., Ward, C., Williams, A. and Wienhouse, S. (1983) Anal. Biochem. 130, 114-119
12 Davis, B.J. (1964) Ann. N.Y. Acad. Sci. 121, 404-427
13 Sugino, Y. and Miyoshi, Y. (1964) J. Biol. Chem. 239, 2360-2364

GENERATION OF MEMBRANE POTENTIAL FROM DIFFERENT ENERGY-LINKED REACTIONS IN PHOTOSYNTHETIC BACTERIA

BESTON F. NORE, YOKO SAKAI AND MARGARETA BALTSCHEFFKY

DEPARTMENT OF BIOCHEMISTRY, ARRHENIUS LABORATORIES, UNIVERSITY OF STOCKHOLM, S-106 91 STOCKHOLM, SWEDEN

1. INTRODUCTION

The protonmotive force Δp is composed of both a chemical component (ΔpH) and an electrical component ($\Delta\Psi$) according to the relationship [1]:

$$\Delta\tilde{\mu}_{H^+} = \Delta\Psi + Z\ pH \quad ; \text{ where } Z = 2.3\ RT/\ F$$

The proton electrochemical potential ($\Delta\tilde{\mu}_H^+$) difference across the coupled (energetically linked) plasma membrane in phototrophic bacteria plays an essential role in photophosphorylation and solute transport into bacterial cells. Therefore, the exact measurements of these quantities are required for studies of the mechanism of energy transduction. It was, for example, shown that *R.rubrum* chromatophores, associated with a phospholipid-impregnated filter, generated a photoelectric current by uptake of TPB^- anions upon oxidation of NADH by oxygen, by reverse transhydrogenase reaction and by ATP or PPi hydrolysis [2]. ATP and PPi act as energy generators in *R.rubrum* and in *Rps.viridis* chromatophores [3,4]. Recently, it was shown that chromatophores isolated from *Rps.viridis* have a membrane-bound PPi synthesis activity coupled to cyclic electron transport [5]. In this paper we report the membrane potential generation from energy-liberating reactions in native chromatophores from *R.rubrum* and *Rps.viridis*.

2. MATERIALS AND METHODS

2.1. Chromatophore preparations

R.rubrum (S1) and *Rps.viridis* (DSM 133) were grown anaerobically [5] and chromatophores were prepared as in Ref.[5,6]. Bacteriochlorophyll from *R.rubrum* and *Rps.viridis* was determined by using the in vivo extinction coefficient of $\varepsilon_{880nm} = 140\ mM^{-1} * cm^{-1}$ and by extraction with acetone/methanol (7:2) using $\varepsilon_{790nm} = 75\ mM^{-1} * cm^{-1}$ [7] respectively.

2.2. Membrane potential measurements

The $\Delta\Psi$ was determined from the uptake of TPB^- ions measured with TPB^- selective electrode [8] using the Nernst equation and an attempt was made to correct the unspecific

M. Baltscheffsky (ed.), Current Research in Photosynthesis, Vol. III, 205–208.
© 1990 *Kluwer Academic Publishers. Printed in the Netherlands.*

TPB⁻ accumulation, according to the model of Lolk´ema et al. [9]. The internal osmotic volume of the chromatophores was taken to be 1 µl per 20 nmol BChl [10].The assay medium contained: 1 µM TPB⁻; 0.1 µM TPP⁺; 50 mM Na-glycylglycine (pH 7.5); 0.1 mM Na-succinate and 25 mM NaCl. The reaction was started either by illumination or by addition of 0.5 mM ATP; 0.5 mM PPi or (0.5 mM NADPH + 0.5 mM NAD⁺). Chromatophores were added to the assay in a small volume to give a final concentration corresponding to 10-15 µM BChl.

3. RESULTS AND DISCUSSIONS

3.1. Light-induced potential

Fig.1 illustrates a typical trace of the light-driven membrane potential generation in *R.rubrum* and *Rps.viridis* chromatophores. In *R.rubrum* chromatophores the size of the membrane potential ($\Delta\Psi$) generated by light-driven cyclic electron transport was 110 mV (fig.1) whereas the corresponding $\Delta\Psi$-induced in *Rps.viridis* chrom-atophores was 50 mV (fig.1).

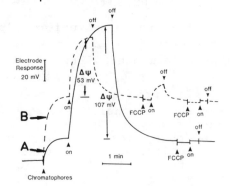

FIG. 1 A typical trace of the light-induced $\Delta\Psi$ in *R.rubrum* (A) and *Rps.viridis* (B) chromatophores.

Different light-induced $\Delta\Psi$ values were observed in *R.rubrum* chromatophores by different methods, ranging from 60 to 110 mV [see ref.10]. There are no data on $\Delta\Psi$ generated by *Rps.viridis* chromatophores in the literature. The light-induced membrane potential were sensitive to inhibitors of the cyclic electron transport, uncouplers and also Orthophenanthroline, an electron transport inhibitor of the reaction center (not shown).

3.2. PPi induced membrane potential

In this study the absolute value of the membrane potential formed upon PPi hydrolysis was measured. These measurements were our central point to get the extent and also the size of energy donated by PPi in comparison with other energy generator reactions. The addition of 0.5 mM PPi to a suspension containing *R.rubrum* chromatophores induces a membrane potential of about 50 mV (fig.2). The corresponding value of *Rps.viridis* chromatophores was only 15 mV (fig.3).

The PPi induced $\Delta\Psi$ could be blocked in the presence of the PPase inhibitor, fluoride (10 mM)(fig.2A,2B). The PPi generated potential can be abolished by FCCP and S-13 but the response was not sensitive to electron transport inhibitors or oligomycin (not shown).

3.3. ATP induced membrane potential

The maximal ATP induced $\Delta\Psi$ in *R.rubrum* and *Rps.viridis* chromatophores was 60 mV and 30 mV respectively. The $\Delta\Psi$ generated by ATP hydrolysis is higher than the $\Delta\Psi$ generated by PPi hydrolysis in both *R.rubrum* and *Rps.viridis* chromatophores. This is in contrast to earlier published results, where PPi appears to give a higher membrane potential compared with ATP [2,11]. All these experiments were performed in the presence of a high concentration of Mg^{2+} when the ATP hydrolysis rate was partially inhibited. The maximal $\Delta\Psi$ induced by ATP in *Rps.viridis* and *R.rubrum* chromatophores was 75% and 55%, respectively, of the $\Delta\Psi$-induced by light. The $\Delta\Psi$ generated by ATP was abolished by oligomycin and uncouplers (not shown).

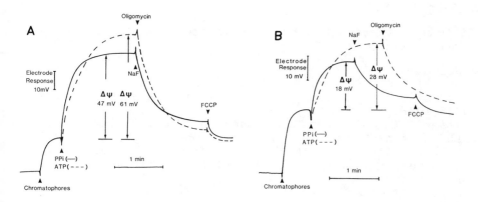

FIG. 2   A typical trace of and PPi induced $\Delta\Psi$ generation in *R.rubrum* (A) and *Rps.viridis* (B) chromatophores.

3.4. Reverse transhydrogenase induced $\Delta\Psi$

It has been shown that the reverse transhydrogenase reaction works as an energy generator [2]. *Rps.viridis* chromatophores [12] has an active transhydrogenase which is coupled to cyclic electron transport as in the *R.rubrum* chromatophores [2]. The reverse trans-hydrogenase induces a $\Delta\Psi$ of 25 mV and 33 mV in *Rps.viridis* and *R.rubrum* chromatophores respectively (not shown). The $\Delta\Psi$ was 50% and 30% of the light-induced $\Delta\Psi$ in *Rps.viridis* and *R.rubrum* chromatophores respectively. The reverse transhydrogenase driven $\Delta\Psi$ was sensitive to FCCP.

4. EPILOGUE

The steady-state membrane $\Delta\Psi$ were studied in chromatophores from; *R.rubrum* and *Rps.viridis*. The $\Delta\Psi$ generated by light was estimated to 110 mV and 50 mV in *R.rubrum* and in *Rps.viridis* chromatophores,respectively. In the dark,PPi,ATP and reversed transhydrogenase generated membrane potentials in *R.rubrum* and *Rps.viridis* chromatophores of 50,60 and 35 mV and 15,35 and 25 mV respectively. The potential induced in *R.rubrum* chromatophores is higher than that in *Rps.viridis* chromatophores because the membranes of *Rps.viridis* are not as well coupled as the membranes of *R.rubrum*. The data introduced in this report shows the contribution of potentials induced from PPi and ATP hydrolysis and the reverse transhydrogenase reaction in two different photosynthetic bacteria. The $\Delta\tilde{\mu}_H{}^+$ from these energy-linked processes probably has an importance to the cell.

ACKNOWLEDGEMENTS

This work was supported by a grant from the Swedish Natural Science Research Council to MB.

REFERENCES
1. Boyer, P.D., Chance, B., Ernster, L., Mitchell, P., Racker, E. and Slater, E.C. (1977) Ann. Rev. Biochem. 46, 955-1026.
2. Isaev P.I., Liberman E.A., Samuilov V.D., Skulachev V.P. and Tsofina L.M.(1970) Biochim. Biophys. Acta 216, 22-29.
3. Baltscheffsky M. and Nyrén P.(1984) in Bioenergetics (Ernster, L.,ed) pp. 207-219, Elsevier Scientific Publishing Co., Amsterdam.
4. Jones O.T.G. and Saunders V.A. (1972) Biochim. Biophys. Acta 275, 427-436.
5. Nore B.F., Nyrén P., Salih G.F. and Strid Å. (1989) Submitted for publication.
6. Shakhov, Yu.A., Nyrén, P., and Baltscheffsky, M. (1982) FEBS Lett. 146, 177-180.
7. Clayton R.K. (1963) in Bacterial Photosynthesis (Gest H., San Pietro A. and Vernon L.P., eds.), p. 495-500, Antioch Press, Yellow Springs, Ohio.
8. Kamo N., Muratsugu M., Hongoh R. and Kobatake Y.(1979) J. Membr. Biol. 49, 105-121.
9. Lolk´ema J.S., Hellingwerf K.J. and Konings W.N.(1982) Biochim. Biophys. Acta 681, 85-94.
10 Schuldiner S., Padan E., Rottenberg H., Gromet-Elhanan Z. and Avron M. (1974) FEBS Lett. 49, 174-177.
11 Azzi A., Baltscheffsky M., Baltscheffsky H. and Vaninio, H. (1971) FEBS Lett. 17, 49-52.
12 Ostroumov S.A., Samuilov V.D. and Skulachev V.P. (1973) FEBS Lett. 31, 27-30.

DETERMINATION OF THE INTRACELLULAR CONCENTRATION OF
INORGANIC PYROPHOSPHATE IN RHODOSPIRILLUM RUBRUM

Gaza F. Salih and Pål Nyrén
Department of Biochemistry, Arrhenius Laboratories, University of
Stockholm, S-106 91 Stockholm, Sweden

1. INTRODUCTION

Rhodospirillum rubrum is a purple, non-sulphur phototrophic bacterium. This organism is capable of catalyzing the synthesis of inorganic pyrophosphate (PPi) upon illumination. The phosphorylation
of Pi to PPi is catalyzed by the membrane bound proton translocating
inorganic pyrophosphatase (the H^+-PPase) (1). PPi is also formed
during the biosynthesis of cellular constituents such as proteins
and nucleic acids. Beside the H^+-PPase there is also a soluble PPase
in R. rubrum (soluble PPases are found in all types of cells). The
soluble enzyme only catalyze the hydrolysis of PPi not the synthesis.
When PPi is hydrolyzed by the soluble PPase, the energy liberated
upon hydrolysis of the anhydride bond is lost.

To understand the physiological role of the H^+-PPase in the metabolism of PPi in R. rubrum it is important to study the steady-state
situation concerning the concentrations of ATP, PPi and phosphate
under different growth conditions. Knowledge about the values of the
different parameters can be used to define the course for the different activities under different conditions.

In experiments reported here, the concentration of PPi and ATP in
R. rubrum cells, grown anaerobically in light, have been determined.
We have also estimated the H^+/PPi ratio in R. rubrum chromatophores.

2. EXPERIMENTAL PROCEDURES

2.1. Materials and methods

2.1.1. Materials: All materials were of reagent grade and
obtained from commercial sources.

2.1.2. Preparation of cells and chromatophores: Cells were
grown (in 50 ml flasks) and harvested, and chromatophores were prepared as in Ref. 2.

M. Baltscheffsky (ed.), Current Research in Photosynthesis, Vol. III, 209–212.
© 1990 Kluwer Academic Publishers. Printed in the Netherlands.

2.1.3 <u>Extraction and assay of PPi and ATP</u>: At the time of sampling 14 ml of the culture was taken for protein and cell
density determination and 14 ml 1 M KOH was rapidly mixed
with the rest of the culture under continuous shaking.
After 30 min at room temperature the sample was put on
ice, 14 ml ice-cold 20% tri chloroacetic acid (TCA) was
rapidly mixed with it and, after standing 5-10 min at
0^oC, the cell debris was separated from the medium by
centrifugation at 6000 rpm for a period of 10 min. The
supernatant was diluted ten times with 0.1 M glycylglycine, 2 mM EDTA (pH 7.75) and 10 µl was taken for PPi and
ATP determination as described by Nyrén et al. (3). For
estimation of intracellular concentrations of PPi and ATP
an intracellular volume of 1.5 µl/mg protein was used
according to Ref. 4.

2.1.4 <u>Determination of the steady-state level of PPi in chroma-
tophores</u>: The assay was peformred at room temperature, in
a reaction mixture containing 0.2 M glycylglycine, pH 7.4,
0.1 mM succinate, 1-10 mM $MgCl_2$ and chromatophores corresponding to 23 µM BChl. The mixture was illuminated for
20 min. The reaction was terminated by addition of 0.2 ml
20% TCA. 10 µl from a 10 times diluted reaction mixture
was taken for PPi determination as described above.

3. RESULTS

The phosphate potential and H^+/PPi ratio in chromatophores.

According to Moyle and Mitchell (5) the stoichiometry for the
PPi-driven proton translocation is one proton transported inwards
per two PPi hydrolyzed. They determined the stoichiometry by measuring the pH change induced in a chromatophore suspension, by a
known amount of PPi in the presence of valinomycin and KCl. The
stoichiometry can also be determined from the relationship between
the proton motive force (ΔP) and the energy stored in PPi at steady-
state phosphorylation, if it is assumed that the PPase reaction is
poised against the proton motive force. The relationship is expressed in eqn. 1:

$$\Delta p = \Delta Gp/nF \qquad\qquad [1]$$

where F is Faradays constant and n the number of protons translocated across the chromatophore membrane for each PPi hydrolyzed. The
level of PPi attained at steady-state in the presence of 7 mM phosphate and 10 mM $MgCl_2$ was 42 µM. From these values and a value for
$\Delta G^{0'}$ of -4.0 Kcal/mol (6), $\Delta G'$ was calculated to -3.9 Kcal/mol by
using eqn. 2:

$$\Delta Gp = \Delta G^{0'} + RT \ln [Pi]^2/[PPi] \qquad\qquad [2]$$

The reported values for ΔP varies around 180 mV (7,8). Using this
value for Δp, n was calculated to be 0.95. The value of n is higher
than the stoichiometry of 0.5 reported in Ref. 5.

The intracellular concentration of PPi and ATP in R. rubrum

According to our experiments the level of PPi and ATP in R. rubrum cells grown anaerobically in light were 65 and 5 nmol/mg protein, respectively, which is equivalent to intracellular concentrations of 43 and 3.3 mM, respectively, if there is 1.5 µl intracellular water/mg protein (4). The steady-state level of PPi in illuminated chromatophores, at 7 mM phosphate, was low (42 µM).

DISCUSSION

The above presented results indicates that the H^+-PPase mainly functions as a proton pump (hydrolyzing PPi). However, most of the PPi in the cell must be precipitated (perhaps in the form of Mg-Ca-granules) or bound so the concentration of free PPi in the cell is probably much lower than 43 mM. Most of the PPi in the cell is probably formed during biosynthesis of cellular constituents, but it is not ruled out that some of it might be formed by photophosphorylation. In Fig. 1 a model is presented to illustrate a possible role for the H^+-PPase in the cell. According to this model PPi might be stored in the form of granules and function as an energy buffer, which can be utilized by the H^+-PPase under low energy conditions to maintain a minimal proton motive force.

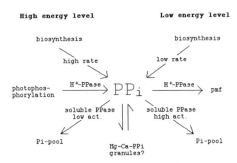

FIGURE 1. A proposed model for the role of the H^+-PPase in the PPi metabolism in R. rubrum.

ACKNOWLEDGEMENTS

This work was supported as a grant by OE och Edla Johanssons Foundation to Pål Nyrén.

REFERENCES

1. Nyrén, P. (1985) Doctoral thesis, Univ. of Stockholm, Stockholm, Sweden.

2. Shakov, Yu.A., Nyrén, P. and Baltscheffsky, M. (1982) FEBS Lett. 146, 177-180.

3. Nyrén, P. and Lundin, A. (1985) Anal. Biochem. 151, 504-509.

4. Schuldinger, S., Padan, E., Rottenberg, H., Gromet-Elhanan, Z. and Avron, M. (1974) FEBS Lett. 49, 174-177.

5. Moyle, J., Mitchell, R. and Mitchell, P. (1972) FEBS Lett. 23, 233.

6. Flodgaard, H. and Fleron, P. (1974) J. Biol. Chem. 249, 3465-3470.

7. Leiser, M. and Gromet-Elhanan, Z. (1977) Arch. Biochem. Biophys. 178, 79-88.

8. Bashford, C.L., Baltscheffsky, M. and Prince, R.C. (1979) FEBS Lett. 97, 55-59.

THE SLOW P515 SIGNAL IN RELATION TO THE STATUS OF INNERMEMBRANE PROTON DOMAINS.

Jaap J.J. Ooms, Pieter H. van Vliet and Wim J. Vredenberg
Department Plant Physiological Research, Wageningen Agricultural University, Gen. Foulkesweg 72, 6703 BW Wageningen.

1. INTRODUCTION

In the flash-induced electrochromic bandshift measured at 518 nm four different components can be distinguished in intact chloroplasts [1]. Figure 1 shows an illustration of the different components. Reaction 1/RC reflects the primary charge separation in the reaction centra, it has an instrument limited rise-time of 0.5 ms and a single exponential decay with a half time of 50-100 ms. Reaction 1/Q reflects an electrogenic secondary charge separation due to a Q-cycle with a rise time of 10-20 ms and decay kinetics equal to those of reaction 1/RC. Reaction 2, the third component, reflects a non-electrogenic phenomenon. It has been suggested that reaction 2 is associated with the liberation and stabilization of protons in inner membrane domains [2,3,4]. The fourth component is the gramicidin insensitive component and is discussed by Vredenberg et al. [5].

In the experiments presented here we adopted methods to manipulate the state of proton domains as characterized by Dilley and coworkers [8,9]. We monitored the kinetics of P515 signals in a flash train and in parallel experiments the activity of the ATP-ase.

It is known that the activity of the chloroplast ATP-ase strongly influences the decay kinetics of the P515 signal [6,7]. Reaction 2, greatly determining the over-all decay of the P515 signal, is suppressed after one to three preïlluminating flashes and under conditions where the ATP-ase is active. This suggested a correlation between the state of the proton stabilizing domains and ATP-ase activity.

However it is shown that the distinct acceleration of the over-all P515 signal, caused by the suppression of reaction 2 in the second and following flashes of a 1 Hz flash-train is not related to ATP-ase activity. Nevertheless in these flashes, there is a good correlation between the upcoming activity of the chloroplast ATP-ase and the enhanced decay of the P515 signal, which in the absence of reaction 2 is mainly determined by reaction 1/RC.

As mentioned above reaction 2 has been suggested to be associated with stabilization of protons in inner membrane domains. We found no convincing evidence for a correlation between the proton domains as identified by Dilley's group and reaction 2 amplitude and kinetics.

2. MATERIALS AND METHODS

Broken pea chloroplasts were isolated according to a modified procedure used for spinach chloroplasts [1]. Chloroplast were resuspended in 2 mM $MgCl_2$, 0.5 mg/ml BSA and 5 mM HEPES/KOH pH 7.5 with either 200 mM Sorbitol (low

M. Baltscheffsky (ed.), Current Research in Photosynthesis, Vol. III, 213–216.
© 1990 *Kluwer Academic Publishers. Printed in the Netherlands.*

salt chloroplasts) or 100 mM KCl (high salt chloroplasts). Low salt chloroplasts showed localized proton gradient responses as recorded by pyridine effects on the lag in the onset of ATP formation [8,9]. High salt stored chloroplasts showed delocalized coupling responses. ATP formation was followed measuring luciferine luciferase bioluminescence (LKB ATP-monitoring kit). Flash-induced absorbance changes at 518 nm were carried out as described before [1]. The assay medium for ATP and P515 measurements contained 10 mM sorbitol, 3 mM $MgCl_2$, 1 mM KH_2PO_4, 50 mM tricine/KOH pH 8.5, 5 mM DTT, 5 µM diadenosine pentaphosphate, 0.1 mM methylviologen, 0.1 mM ADP and 200 µl luciferine-luciferase. Luciferine luciferase was omitted in the P515 experiments. Final assay volumes 2 ml, with 10 µg Chl/ml for the ATP assay and 20 µg Chl/ml for the P515 assay. For CCCP/BSA (0.4 µM, 1 mg/ml) and BSA/CCCP (1 mg/ml and 0.4 µM) treatments, chloroplasts were incubated with the first component for 30 seconds and 150 seconds after addition of the second component the flash train was started.

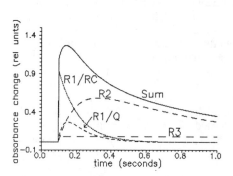

Figure 1: Illustration of different components in the flash-induced P515 signal of intact chloroplasts.

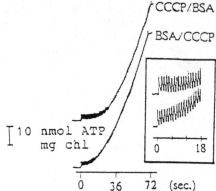

Figure 2: Flash-induced ATP production in broken low salt chloroplasts, treated with BSA/CCCP and CCCP/-BSA respectively. 1 Hz flash train started at t=0. Insert, start of the flash train on an expanded scale.

3. RESULTS AND DISCUSSION

Using broken low salt chloroplasts, it has been shown that addition of CCCP followed by BSA sets proton domains in an unprotonated state [9]. Addition of BSA followed by CCCP sets the domains in a protonated state. The unprotonated state of the CCCP/BSA, relative to BSA/CCCP treated chloroplasts is illustrated by the delayed flash-induced activation of the ATP-ase (fig 2). Under the same experimental conditions, we recorded P515 signals of the flash-train. These signals are shown respectively for CCCP/BSA treated chloroplasts in the presence of ADP (fig 3A) and for BSA/CCCP treated chloroplasts in the presence and absence of ADP (fig 3B and C). In the second flash the P515 decay is definitely accelerated, this is caused by the suppression of reaction 2 due to its saturation in the preceding flash [1,2,3]. This suppression of reaction 2 is independent of the ATP-ase activity, as it occurs in the presence as well as in the absence of ADP (fig 3B and C).

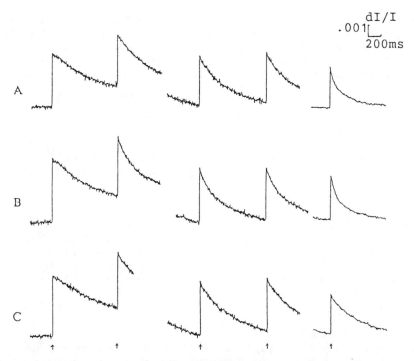

Figure 3: Flash-induced P515 signals in broken pea chloroplasts monitored during a flash train. Shown are P515 signal of flashes 1, 2, 3, 4 and 60. A: CCCP/BSA treated low salt chloroplasts, with ADP in the assay medium. B and C, BSA/CCCP treated low salt chloroplasts with and without ADP in the assay medium respectively.

Moreover the apparent acceleration of the decay is seen after the first flash whereas the first ATP-ase activity is only recorded after the second and twelfth flash for respectively BSA/CCCP and CCCP/BSA treated chloroplasts (figure 2). The P515 signals from the 60th flash show in the presence of ADP an acceleration in the decay, relative to the signal of the third or fourth flash (figure 3A and B). This acceleration of the over-all P515 signal is achieved during the 1 Hz flash train after the suppression of reaction 2 in the first two flashes. Figure 4 shows the correlation between the ATP-ase activity and the half decay times of reaction 1/RC from various flashnumbers in the flash-train.

Comparing the first flashes in fig 3A and 3B, it is clear that the kinetics of P515 and consequently of reaction 2 are hardly, if at all influenced by the protonation state of the domains as reflected by the onset lag time of ATP production. We further checked whether the localized or delocalized coupling mode of the chloroplasts, influences the appearance of reaction 2. Figure 5 shows recordings of P515 signal in the first flash in low salt (localized coupling) and high salt chloroplasts (delocalized coupling), respectively. The difference between these signals is minimal and suggests no major influence of the coupling mode on the appearance and kinetics of reaction 2.

From these results, we conclude that the kinetics of reaction 2 are independent of the protonation state or coupling mode of the domains as identified by Dilley et al [8]. The suppression of reaction 2 is not related to the ATP-ase activity, whereas the decay of reaction 1/RC, the main component after suppression of reaction 2 shows a good correlation with the ATP-ase activity.

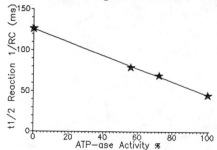
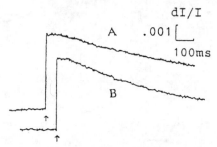

Figure 4: Correlation between the flash-induced ATP-ase activity and T1/2 of reaction 1/RC in untreated low salt chloroplasts. Results obtained from parallel experiments (see fig 2 and 3).

Figure 5: Flash-induced P515 signals from low salt chloroplast (A) and high salt chloroplasts (B). Averages of 5 sweeps with 20 seconds dark period.

ACKNOWLEDGMENT
This research was in part supported by the Stichting Scheikundig Onderzoek Nederland (SON), financed by the Nederlandse organisatie voor Wetenschappelijk Onderzoek (NWO).

REFERENCES
1 Ooms, J.J.J., Vredenberg, W.J. and Buurmeijer, W.F. (1989) Photosynth. Res. 20, 119-128
2 Schapendonk,A.H.C.M. and Vredenberg, W.J. (1979) FEBS-lett. 100, 325-330
3 Vredenberg, W.J. (1981) Physiol. Plant. 53, 598-602
4 Schreiber, U. and Rienits, K.G. (1982) Biochim. Biophys. Acta 682, 115-123
5 Vredenberg, W.J., Versluis, W. and Ooms, J.J.J. (1989) this meeting
6 Morita, S., Itoh, S., and Nishimura, M. (1982) Biochim. Biophys. Acta 679, 125-130
7 Peters, R.L.A., van Kooten, O. and Vredenberg, W.J. (1985) J. of Bioenerg. Biomembr. 17, 207-216
8 Dilley, R.A., Theg, S.M. and Beard, W. (1987) in Ann. Review of Plant Physiol. (Briggs,W.R., Jones, R.L. and Walbot, V., eds), vol. 38, pp 347-389
9 Theg, S.M., Chiang, G. and Dilley, R.A. (1988) J. of Biol. Chem. 263, 673-681

Proton Efflux and Phosphorylation in Flash Groups

P. Bogdanoff[1] and P. Gräber[2]

[1]Max-Volmer-Institut, Technische Universität Berlin, Str.
d.17. Juni 135, 1000 Berlin 12
[2]Biologisches Institut, Universität Stuttgart,
Pfaffenwaldring 57, 7000 Stuttgart 80, FRG

INTRODUCTION
When thylakoid membranes are illuminated by single turnover
flashes, transmembrane redox reactions in photosystem I and
II lead to the rapid generation (>1 ns) of a transmembrane
electric potential difference, $\Delta \varphi$. This $\Delta \varphi$ can be detected
by the electrochromic absorption changes which can be
measured at 524 nm (1). Whereas the generation of $\Delta \varphi$ is
due to a transmembrane electron shift, the decay represents
different events: in the absence of phosphorylation, it is
due mainly to the movement of ions, e.g., K^+, Cl^-, etc.
Under phosphorylating conditions, an additional H^+ efflux
coupled with ATP synthesis is observed (2). The kinetic
analysis of the electrochromic absorption changes permits
calculation of the phosphorylation-coupled proton efflux.
If the amount of synthesized ATP is measured simultaneously
the H^+/ATP ratio can be calculated (3). When the ATP-synthase is in the oxidized state, H^+/ATP = 3 is obtained (3).
We have carried out similar measurements with the ATP-synthase in the ative, reduced state (4).
MATERIALS AND METHODS
Chloroplasts were prepared from spinach. The ATP-synthase
was activated and reduced by illumination in the presence
of thioredoxin and dithiothreitol. After a dark time of 2
minutes, photosynthesis was excited by groups of single
turnover flashes (2 ms dark time between flashes, 5 s dark
time between groups). The electrochromic absorption changes were measured at 524 nm and simultaneously ATP synthesis
was measured with the ^{32}P method.
RESULTS
Fig. 1A shows the flash-induced absorption changes at 524
nm. The curve(-ADP) represents the $\Delta \varphi$ decay in the absence, (+ADP) shows the $\Delta \varphi$ decay in the presence of phosphorylation. As with the oxidized enzyme a faster decay
of $\Delta \varphi$ is observed under phosphorylating conditions. These
data have been fitted with non-linear regression by a

M. Baltscheffsky (ed.), Current Research in Photosynthesis, Vol. III, 217–220.
© 1990 *Kluwer Academic Publishers. Printed in the Netherlands.*

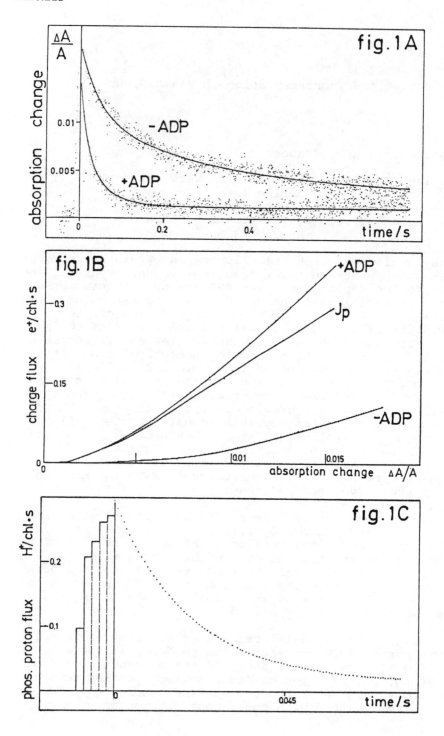

Fig. 1 (A) Absorption change at 524 nm in a flash group in the absence (-ADP) and presence (+ADP) of phosphorylation. The solid lines represent the fitted curves. (B) Current-voltage relation calculated from the data in Fig. 1A. J_p is calculated as the difference of the flux (+ADP) and the flux (-ADP). (C) Phosphorylation-coupled proton flux as a function of time. Data calculated from Fig. 1A and B.

sum of exponential functions. These fitted curves are indicated by the solid lines in Fig. 1A; wheras, the points represent the measured absorption change. Since the amplitude of these curves represents the transmembrane $\Delta\varphi$ and the slope indicates the transmembrane current, these signals can be converted into current-voltage graphs. Fig. 1B shows the current-voltage relation under basal (non-phosphorylating) and phosphorylating conditions. It is assumed that the total flux is the sum of the basal flux and the phosphorylation-coupled proton efflux; i.e., $J_t = J_p + J_b$. From this relation the phosphorylating flux is calculated and also shown in Fig. 1B. Then, this phosphorylating flux is plotted as a function of time as depicted in Fig. 1C. In addition, we have taken into account the proton efflux between the different flashes of the group. Numerical integration of this curve then leads to the amount of protons translocated across the membrane due to ATP synthesis, H^+_p. The amount of ATP synthesized was measured simultaneously in the same cuvette, using flash groups between two and eight flashes per group. The resulting H^+_p was calculated for each experiment and plotted versus the amount of ATP. This is shown in Fig. 2. For calibration of H^+_p we have assumed that in a single turnover flash two protons are

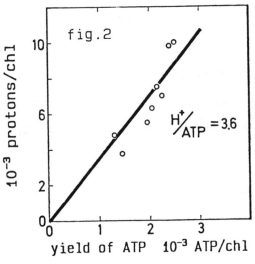

Fig. 2
Amount of phosphorylation-coupled protons translocated through the membrane as a function of the amount of synthesized ATP. The slope of the curve gives the H^+/ATP ratio.

translocated across the membrane per electron transport
chain. The number of chlorophyll molecules per electron
transport chain was measured by the oxygen yield per flash
in single turnover flashes. It resulted for the preparation used in this work 515 Chl/e-chain. With this calibration the absolute values in Fig. 2 are obtained. From the
slope in Fig. 2 it resulted $H^+/ATP = 3.6$.

DISCUSSION

Earlier measurements with the same method resulted in
$H^+/ATP = 3$. The measurements reported above differ in two
respects: (1) The proton efflux between the different
flashes of the group was not taken into account. This increases the phosphorylation-coupled proton efflux by nearly
30% in some experiments. (2) The ATP-synthase was in the
active, reduced state at the beginning of the experiments,
whereas the enzyme was in the inactive, oxidized state in
the experiments by Junge et al.(3). It has been shown that
reduction and activation of the ATP-synthase shifts the
functional dependence of the rate of ATP synthesis to lower
ΔpH values (4). Likewise, the funtional dependence on $\Delta\varphi$
is shifted to lower values, when the enzyme is reduced. In
particular, practically no threshold is observed in our experiments. Our results show that the H^+/ATP is 3.6 under
these conditions, and this might indicate that the true
H^+/ATP is 4, as has been concluded from completely different experiments (5).

ACKNOWLEDGEMENTS

This work has been supported by the Deutsche Forschungsgemeinschaft (Sfb 312).

REFERENCES

1 Junge, W. and Witt, H.T. (1968) Z. Naturforsch. 23b, 244-
  254
2 Rumberg, B. and Siggel, U. (1968) Z. Naturforsch. 23b,
  239-244
3 Junge, W., Rumberg, B. and Schröder, H. (1970) Eur.J.
  Biochem. 14, 575-581
4 Junesch, U. and Gräber, P. (1987) Biochim. Biophys. Acta
  893, 275-288
5 Gräber, P., Junesch, U., Thulke, G. (1987) in Progress in
  Photosynthsis Research (J. Biggins, ed.), Vol. III,
  pp.2.177, M. Nijhoff, Dr. W.Junk, Publishers, Dordrecht,
  The Netherlands

THE CHLOROPLAST *b* CYTOCHROMES: CROSSLINKS, TOPOGRAPHY, AND FUNCTIONS

W. A. CRAMER, P. N. FURBACHER, A. SZCZEPANIAK, AND G.-S. TAE, DEPT. OF BIOLOGICAL SCIENCES, PURDUE UNIVERSITY, WEST LAFAYETTE, IN 47907 U.S.A.

1. *Heme cross-linking of membrane cytochromes as a structural principle: cytochrome b-559, b_6, and cytochrome oxidase.* After the M_r 9,000 protein of cyt *b*-559 was purified and its NH_2-terminus sequenced (1), its *psb*E gene and the downstream *psb*F gene located and sequenced on the spinach chloroplast genome (2), an intermolecular heme cross-linked dimeric structure of cytochrome *b*-559 was proven by the findings that (a) each polypeptide contains only one histidine (2), (b) the *psb*E and *psb*F gene products are present in the purified protein in a 1:1 stoichiometry (3), and (c) the heme coordination is *bis*-histidine (Fig. 1a; ref. 4). Thus, a dimer would be required to provide two His residues for heme coordination. There are several reasons, including the 1:1 stoichiometry, for believing that the heme-binding unit is an α-β heterodimer (5), but this has not been rigorously proven.

Spectroscopy also indicated that the coordination of the cytochrome *b* of b_6-*f* and *b*-c_1 complexes is *bis*-histidine. The realization that the sequence of the chloroplast cytochrome contains the bare minimum of the four His residues in hydrophobic domains needed to coordinate the two hemes of the cytochrome b_6 protein provided the identity of these heme ligands in chloroplasts (6), as well as in mitochondria (6,7), photosynthetic bacteria (8), and cyanobacteria (9), where these His residues are quasi-conserved or conserved (recent summary of sequences in ref. 10). It was found that the distribution of hydrophobic residues in these *b* cytochromes is mathematically conserved (6,11). The recognition of pair-wise organization of the His residues (i) on each of two *trans*-membrane hydrophobic α-helices, and (ii) on opposite sides of the membrane bilayer implied that the two membrane-spanning helices are heme-linked on each side of the membrane. The two heme planes were predicted to be oriented perpendicular to the membrane plane, with a center-center distance of 20Å (6,7) [Fig. 1b]. The same kind of intramolecular linking by hemes of *trans*-membrane α-helices has been inferred for heme *a* in subunit I of cytochrome oxidase (12). The latter subunit contains the two hemes, *a* and a_3, of cytochrome oxidase. Heme *a* has two His ligands and was proposed to link two *trans*-membrane helices, VI and X, near the cytoplasmic side of the membrane. Heme a_3 that binds O_2 would bind only one His residue near the center of the bilayer in helix VI or X. It is not known when the heme is inserted into the apocytochromes during the assembly process. Presumably, it occurs when the protein is in an unfolded or partly unfolded state at the surface of the membrane or partially inserted into the bilayer. It is plausible that heme cross-linking as illustrated in the three examples presented here is necessary for the proper folding of intrinsic membrane cytochromes. The arrangement of the two hemes in the cytochrome b_6-*f* or *b*-c_1 complexes that span a large fraction of the membrane bilayer also provides a structural framework for their redox function (section 3a).

M. Baltscheffsky (ed.), Current Research in Photosynthesis, Vol. III, 221–230.
© 1990 *Kluwer Academic Publishers. Printed in the Netherlands.*

(a)   (b)

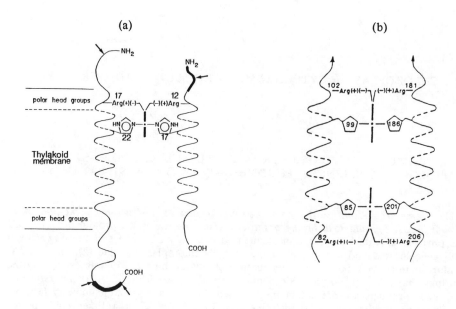

FIGURE 1. Heme-linked (a) intermolecular dimer of cyt b-559, assumed to involve
the α and β subunits (13) [epitopes for peptide-directed antibodies (bold
segments) and sites for trypsin (↑) are shown], and (b) intramolecular
connection of helices II and IV of cyt b_6, as well as cyt b (b-c_1) [6,7],
using the sequence of spinach b_6 (10) and a 4 helix model [see 2(b)].

2. *Topographical probes of membrane protein structure: (a) Cytochrome b-559.*
Predictions from sequence and hydropathy can never determine by themselves the orientation of a protein in the membrane. The cytochrome b-559 subunits are an example of a situation where inspection of the sequences, showing a single hydrophobic
span of 26 and 25 residues, respectively, in the α and β subunits, was sufficient to infer that each subunit would span the membrane once (2-4). This inference, and the
orientation of the α subunit in the thylakoid membrane, has been corroborated using
biochemical probes of topography. Information on the identity of exposed segments or
loops of intrinsic membrane proteins of known sequence and their orientation can be
obtained through (i) binding of peptide-directed antibodies to one side of the membrane using inside-out and right-side-out membranes (14), and antibody that is iodin-
ated (15) or labeled with gold and visualized by electron microscopy (16). (ii) Thylakoids or RSO and ISO membranes can be probed with residue-specific proteases (e.g.,
trypsin, V8 protease) together with subsequent (a) identification and sequencing of the
products from the gel, or (b) immunoidentification with peptide-specific antibodies
(13); (iii) specific residues such as lysine (17) or tyrosine (18) can be labeled in the
case that these residues appear on only one side of the membrane. (iv) For endogenous proteins, or those from cloned genes, that reside in the cytoplasmic membrane of
Gram-negative bacteria, the topography can be inferred from the pattern of fusions
with alkaline phosphatase (AP) resulting in high AP activity, since AP is active only
on the periplasmic, and not the cytoplasmic, side of the membrane (19). (v) In the
case of cyt b (b-c_1), topography and orientation has been inferred from the pattern of
inhibitor-resistant mutants for inhibitors that are believed to act specifically on the n-

or p-side of the membrane (20-23).

The orientation of the *psb*E gene product (α subunit) was determined by techniques (i) and (ii) above, using an antibody to a tridecapeptide epitope near the COOH terminus of the 82 residue protein that is bordered by trypsin-sensitive Arg residues (Fig. 1a). Trypsin added to thylakoids and RSO membranes cleaved the α subunit close to the NH_2-terminus, probably after Arg-7, while not removing the epitope near the COOH-terminus (13). This epitope was removed by trypsin added to non-sealed PSII complexes or ISO membranes, and binding of anti-α antibody to ISO membranes was visualized by electron microscopy (16). It was concluded that the NH_2- and COOH-termini of the cyt b-559 α subunit, are on the stromal and lumenal sides of the membrane, respectively, and that this polypeptide with a central hydrophobic domain of 26 residues spans the bilayer once. Most of the thylakoid membrane proteins have their NH_2-termini on the stromal side, notable exceptions being cytochrome f which has a leader peptide and the proteolipid DCCD-binding subunit of the ATPase. Preliminary data using antibody directed to a decapeptide epitope near the NH_2-terminus of the β subunit (Fig. 1a) indicate that it has the same orientation as the α subunit (Tae and Cramer, unpubl.). Because each b-559 subunit contains a single heme-binding histidine, the orientation of the polypeptide subunits determines the position of the heme in the membrane bilayer. Thus, His-22 of the b-559 α subunit is close (~5 residues) to the stromal side of the bilayer which is punctuated by Arg-17, and it is likely that His-17 of the β subunit has the same position relative to its Arg-12. Thus, if the PSII reaction center contains two hemes, as found in studies by seven different groups summarized in refs. 13,24 [however, see (25)], it is likely that both hemes are on the stromal half of the membrane bilayer, although only one of the two hemes can be photoreduced (in ~100 msec) by PSII (26). With the hemes on the stromal side, it is somewhat surprising that removal of the OEC 23 kDa polypeptide on the lumen side of the membrane affects the E_m of cyt b-559 (27). The proximity of the cyt b-559 subunits to those of D1-D2, as well as that of the b-559 heme(s) and the DCMU binding site to the stromal surface of the membrane, may explain the ability of DCMU to prevent an E_m shift of b-559 caused by protonation of acidic groups (28). The stromal-side location places some constraints on proposals for the functions of this cytochrome. That is, it is unlikely to participate in reactions that occur in the lumen (e.g., oxidation of Mn, ref. 5), and it is not optimally situated to participate with high efficiency in redox reactions near the lumen-side aqueous interface. It is known that cytochrome b-559 can be photooxidized by $P680^+$, which may be close to the bilayer center (29), when the H_2O donor pathway is blocked. Oxidation of cyt b-559 by $P680^+$ at low temperatures appears to proceed through a Chl intermediate, perhaps to keep this Chl reduced in the presence of the very positive E_m of P680 (30). It has been proposed that one function of the cytochrome is to function in reactions linked to stress (e.g., heat, loss of Mn, O_2, strong oxidant) response in photosystem II (5,30). This may be associated with a cyclic electron transport pathway around PSII. In addition to a role in chloroplast photoreactions, the possibility should be considered that some of the electron transport carriers, including cyt b-559, have a role in chloroplast metabolism. Components of the electron transport chain may use the membrane structure not only to accomplish energy transduction, but may also may fulfill functions needed to maintain the structure (see below, section 3b).

Cytochrome b-559 Lumen-Skeletal Structure. Measurement of the rate of trypsin proteolysis of the COOH-terminal epitope of the cytochrome b-559 α subunit under conditions where the OEC extrinsic polypeptide are selectively removed (1.0 M NaCl, -16-23 kDa; 0.9 M $CaCl_2$, -16, -23, -33 kDa polypeptides; 0.8 M Tris, -16, -23, -33 kDa, -Mn). The sensitivity of the b-559 COOH-terminus to trypsin was markedly increased upon removal of the OEC 33 kDa polypeptide (CaCl$_2$ treatment), and removal of the Mn in addition by Tris treatment did not seem to further sensitize the cytochrome (Tae and Cramer, unpubl.), implying that the COOH-terminal domain of the b-559 α subunit is specifically shielded by the OEC 33 kDa protein. It is known that the 33 kDa protein can be used as a ligand on an affinity column to purify a D1/D2/cyt b-559 reaction center complex (31). Because the psbB gene product, the so-called CP47 polypeptide, can also be cross-linked to the OEC 33 kDa polypeptide (32), and the OEC proteins shield the D1 polypeptide from antibody binding (15), it is possible that the cytochrome b-559 COOH terminus is shielded by other polypeptides in addition to the OEC 33 kDa. The shielding by the 33 kDa protein of the b-559 α subunit COOH terminal domain suggests that the latter, which contains 4 Glu, 2 Asp, 1 Gln, 1 Asn, 5 Ser, and 2 Thr residues per subunit and twice as many of these residues in two α subunits/reaction center, could participate in the ligation or binding of the OEC Mn.

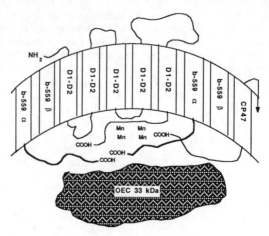

FIGURE 2. Photosystem II reaction center emphasizing polypeptide interactions on the lumen side of the membrane, including the shielding of the COOH-domain of the cyt b-559 α subunit by the OEC 33 kDa protein, and the coordination and shielding of the 4 Mn of the OEC. Each D1-D2 *trans*-membrane unit symbolizes 2 α-helices, one for each protein. Together with 2 copies of cyt b-559 α-β, and 1-2 other small polypeptides, the PSII reaction center core is predicted to contain 15-16 *trans*-membrane α-helices.

2(b). *Molecular genetic and biochemical probes; refinement of the folding pattern of cytochrome b_6.* The sequence and cross-correlation hydropathy analysis of the b cytochromes of the b-c_1 complex and that of the spinach chloroplast cyt b_6 of the b_6-f complex predicted the heme-cross linked structure discussed above (Fig. 1b), defined the smaller cyt b_6 protein as the heme binding domain, and predicted that subunit IV of the b_6-f complex contained at least one function of the COOH-terminal half of cyt b (b-c_1) [6]. One such function is quinone binding since photoaffinity azido-quinone analogs bind at a 'p' site to subunit IV (33). However, the prediction of refs. 6,7 that "helix IV" was *trans*-membrane appears to be wrong. The orientation of cyt b (b-c_1) was defined from the characterization of inhibitor-resistant mutants of yeast (20,21) and mouse (22) mitochondria, and photosynthetic bacteria (23), using inhibitors that are believed to compete for specific quinone binding sites on the 'p' or 'n' side of the membrane. The inhibitors known to act on the n side of the membrane in the b-c_1 or b_6-f complex in (i) mitochondria, (ii) chromatophores, and (iii) chloroplasts are (i) antimycin A, DCMU, and possibly HQNO, (ii) antimycin A, and (iii) no known inhibitors. The greater number of inhibitors acting on the p-side of the cytochrome complexes in these membranes include (i and ii) mucidin, myxathiazol, stigmatellin, and UHDBT, and (iii) DBMIB, DNP-INT, and stigmatellin. The position of mutants resistant to DCMU and antimycin A near the NH_2-terminus of the mitochondrial cytochrome established that the NH_2-terminus is on the n-side of the membrane. The conclusion that the fourth helix predicted in refs. 6,7 was not *trans*-membrane followed from the isolation of inhibitor-resistant mutants at about a half-dozen loci in yeast (DCMU^r-225, anti A^r-228, muc^r-256, and muc^r-275) and mouse (HQNO^r-231 and Stg^r-294) mitochondria for which the correct sidedness of n- and p- would not be preserved unless helix IV of refs. 6,7 is removed from the membrane (34). The approximate distribution of these mutations in the mitochondrial cyt b polypeptide is shown in Fig. 3. The effect of the removal of the fourth helix of cyt b_6 from the membrane bilayer would be to remove two negatively charged residues, Asp-155 and Glu-166, that were in the bilayer in the five helix model. Such residues were originally considered possible H^+ carriers, as found for the light-driven H^+ pump of bacteriorhodopsin (35). The absence of such residues of cyt b_6 in the bilayer region would be consistent with our inability to label cyt b_6 in the membrane with DCCD (Widger and Cramer, unpubl.).

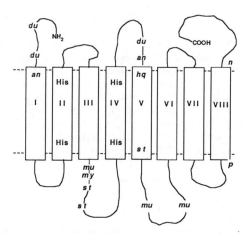

FIGURE 3. Summary of loci of inhibitor-resistant mutants in yeast (20,21) and mouse (22) mitochondrial cyt b. an, antimycin A; du, DCMU; hq, n-heptyl-4-hydroxyquinoline-N-oxide, HQNO; my, myxathiazol; mu, mucidin; st, stigmatellin.

Because of (i) some important differences in structure and function of cyt b_6 compared to cyt b (b-c_1) [36], (ii) the small degree of inhibitor resistance in the downstream mutations in the mouse cyt b (22), and (iii) the absence of an n-side inhibitor and a comparable map of inhibitor-resistant mutants in cyanobacteria, it was decided to use protease and peptide-directed antibodies to probe the *in situ* topography of cyt

b_6. The three epitopes chosen, for which synthetic peptides were synthesized as antigens, were: (i) Asp-5—Gln-14 (NH$_2$-D-W-F-E-E-R-L-E-I-Q-COOH) near the NH$_2$ terminus, (ii) Ile-205—Leu-214 (NH$_2$-I-R-K-Q-G-I-S-G-P-L-COOH) at the COOH-terminus, and (iii) Ala-146—Asp-155 (NH$_2$-A-V-K-I-V-T-G-V-P-D-COOH) that would be in the questionable helix IV (37,38).

The epitopes near the NH$_2$- and COOH-termini would be located on the same side of the membrane in a structure with an even number (e.g., 4) of helices, and on opposite sides in one with an odd (e.g., 5) number. The accessibility of these epitopes in thylakoid and ISO membranes was probed with trypsin. Cytochrome f and the OEC 16 kDa and 33 kDa proteins were used as markers for the lumen side of the membrane. The epitopes at the NH$_2$- and COOH-termini, as well as those for the entire cyt b_6, were much more sensitive in thylakoids than that to cyt f, and somewhat more sensitive than those to the highly charged extrinsic OEC polypeptides (37). In ISO membranes, the OEC proteins were more sensitive to trypsin than the epitopes of the cyt b_6 NH$_2$- and COOH-termini (37). The antibody to the entire cyt b_6 appears to have epitopes on both sides of the membrane since it is also more sensitive in ISO membranes than the epitopes from the cyt b_6 termini. These experiments thus provided (a) direct biochemical support for a four helix model of cytochrome b_6, with the two pairs of His residues on parallel helices II and IV (new notation). As noted in the papers on the inhibitor-resistant mutants in cyt b (b-c_1) [20-23], the orientation of the two His residues in the new helix IV is reversed from that originally proposed (6,7). In addition, the protease probe experiments also showed (b) that cyt b_6 is shielded on the stromal side of the membrane by the COOH-termini of other thylakoid proteins, since prior treatment of the membranes by carboxypeptidase A (CpA) increased the accessibility of cyt b_6 or sensitized it, but not cyt f, to trypsin (38). The CpA had no effect by itself on cyt b_6, although as previously shown, it cleaved a short segment from cyt f (39). (c) An interesting aspect of the lumen-skeletal structure is that cyt b_6 is more sensitive, and probably more accessible, to V8 protease on the lumen side of the membrane than cyt f (38), especially since cyt f has approximately seventeen Glu residues on the lumen side compared to the two predicted for cyt b_6, one each in the peripheral segments linking helices I-II and III-IV. This is somewhat surprising since the soluble part of cyt f on the lumen side of the membrane is usually depicted as an exposed structure because it must be accessible to plastocyanin.

Length of trans-membrane helices. The length of the single hydrophobic *trans*-membrane domain of cyt f near its COOH terminus is 20 residues, compared to 23, 19, 23, and 23 residues predicted for the four helices of cyt b_6, 25-26 residues for cyt b-559 α, β, 23-24 for bacteriorhodopsin (35), and an average of approximately 26 for the photosynthetic reaction center (e.g., ref. 40). The shorter length of the predicted *trans*-membrane span of cyt f and b_6 may be a result of assuming that all charged residues are excluded from the bilayer.

3. *Function of the b Cytochromes: (a) cytochrome b_6*: The many structural similarities of cyt b_6 with cyt b (b-c_1) discussed above and elsewhere (e.g., ref. 36) might imply that the functions of the b_6-f and b-c_1 complexes are the same. There are sequence and structure differences (36), however, including the greatly shortened cyt b_6 polypeptide, that may account for the relative homogeneity of the spectral (visible and EPR) and redox properties of the two b_6 hemes and the loss of antimycin A reactivity of b_6-f complex. The loss of cyt b_6 sensitivity to antimycin A has been specifically attributed to the Gly→Leu substitution at amino acid position 38 (22). Other differences that relate to function are (i) the presence of ferredoxin and the pathway of PSI phosphorylation, (ii) the non-electrogenic electron transport through the b_6-f complex in the steady-state (41), and (iii) the ATP/2e$^-$ ratio (~0.6) associated with the plasto-

quinol-plastocyanin oxidoreductase that is ~2/3 that of the mitochondrial ubiquinol-cytochrome c oxidoreductase.

There is substantial evidence to support a Q cycle mechanism of electron transport and H^+ translocation for the b-c_1 complex in chromatophores and mitochondria (e.g., ref. 42). The basic elements of the Q cycle are oxidant-induced reduction of heme b_p (b-566 in mitochondria and chromatophores) by QH_2 resulting in deposition of $2H^+$ on the p-side of the membrane, fast interheme transfer across the membrane bilayer from heme b_p to heme b_n, and reduction of quinone associated with H^+ uptake on the n-side of the membrane by transfer of two such electrons from heme b_n (42). It has been thought that the b_6-f complex, by analogy, should support a Q cycle mechanism for H^+ translocation. A Q cycle mechanism in chloroplasts was supported by (i) kinetic correlation of the slow electrochromic phase (43) with turnover of the b_6-f complex (44-46), (ii) pre-steady state H^+/e values of 1.7-1.9 for the complex (47), with transfer of the extra H^+ thought to be obligatorily coupled to electron transfer (48), only coupled under conditions of low $\Delta\tilde{\mu}_{H^+}$ (49,50), or with a variable facultative H^+/e ratio dependent on $\Delta\tilde{\mu}_{H^+}$ (51), (iii) reconstitution of electrogenic H^+ translocation with H^+/e $\simeq$ 2 (52,53); (iv) the increase in amplitude of cyt b_6 flash reduction by NQNO, proposed to act as an analogue to antimycin A (54). Two comments on data (i-iii) are that (a) they do not exclude other mechanisms, e.g., a H^+ pump; (b) it is generally agreed that some modification has to be made to the Q cycle model under reducing conditions (45,46,55).

Site of Action of NQNO. The inability of NQNO to inhibit non-cyclic electron transport at the same concentration at which it stimulates the flash-induced reduction of cyt b_6 (56) implies that its action is not analogous to that of antimycin A, and/or the Q cycle is not obligatory in non-cyclic electron transport. Furthermore, NQNO stimulation of the amplitude of cyt b_6 flash reduction is not affected if heme b_n is selectively reduced by NADPH-ferredoxin before the flash, showing that a site of action of NQNO, unlike that of antimycin A, is at heme b_p (57). The amplitude of the flash-induced reduction [0.6 ± 0.09 hemes/600 Chl] was not affected by prior reduction of heme b_n, further implying that the single flash predominantly reduces heme b_p (57). The amplitude of the flash reduction of cyt b_6 is not increased by multiple successive flashes, in the presence or absence of NQNO, so that it was not possible to observe the successive reduction of hemes b_n and b_p that is specified by the Q cycle and that has been observed in chromatophores in the presence of antimycin (58). One could argue that inhibition of electron transfer through heme b_p by NQNO prevents the b_p→b_n electron transfer. However, rapid reoxidation of heme b_p in the presence of NQNO is observed when heme b_n is first enzymatically reduced. Thus, the ability of NQNO to stimulate the flash reduction of heme b_p does not seem to be caused by inhibition of its oxidation, but perhaps by an NQNO-induced increase of approximately 90 mV in the E_m values (59). In summary, evidence for interheme transfer cannot be obtained based on the proposed site of action of NQNO at a quinone binding site near heme b_n because NQNO affects the flash reduction of heme b_p. The conclusion that NQNO affects heme b_p, and possibly heme b_n as well, is somewhat at variance with the claim that the shorter chain analogue HQNO has a "minute" effect on only heme b_n (b-562) in mitochondria (60), but it is consistent with the lack of effect of NQNO on H^+ uptake from the n-side of the thylakoid membrane (61). It is possible that NQNO also affects heme b_n, as implied by an increase in E_m of both hemes (59), but that the effect cannot be observed in the absence of interheme electron transfer. It is also possible that interheme electron transfer cannot be observed because (i) b_6 reduction is small in the absence of inhibitors, (ii) in addition to increasing the amplitude of heme b_p flash reduction, NQNO perturbs the hemes so as to preclude interheme transfer, and (iii) interheme transfer would be observed if an inhibitor could be found to act in oxygenic photosynthesis in a manner exactly analogous to the mode of action of antimycin A in mitochondria and chromatophores. It is our opinion that the direct evidence supporting a Q cycle in chloroplasts is not conclusive, and other mechanisms for electrogenic H^+ translocation at low $\Delta\tilde{\mu}_{H^+}$ should be considered.

Other functions of cytochrome b_6; PSI cyclic electron transport. The rate of reoxidation of cyt b_6 after a flash is increased by a factor of 4-5 if heme b_n is reduced prior to the flash (57). This suggests a mechanism for PSI cyclic phosphorylation that incorporates the oxidant-induced reduction of heme b_p concomitant with reduction of heme b_n by PSI and ferredoxin, possibly through a quinone site (62). The oxidation of the two hemes by plastoquinone would be cooperative, as implied by the effect of b_n reduction on the reoxidation rate. The proposal of a quinone niche near the center of the bilayer that could oxidize both hemes resembles the semiquinone cycle model (63). One confusing aspect is the action of antimycin A which inhibits PSI cyclic phosphorylation (64). Because this compound is a classic n-side inhibitor of the mitochondrial cyt b, it would be expected to act on cyt b_6, but there is no clear spectrophotometric effect. The slow reduction of cyt b_6 mediated by ferredoxin in the dark (65) may be a problem for this model, although this would be explained if the reduction of cyt b_6 as well as its oxidation is cooperative.

(b) Function of cytochrome b-559 in the pathway of fatty acid desaturation. Chloroplasts have a high content of unsaturated fatty acids (66). The precedent of cytochrome b_5 in fatty acid desaturation in animals and plants (67) suggests the possibility of an analogous function for one or both of the chloroplast b cytochromes. It is known that 16:0 and 18:1 fatty acids are desaturated to 16:3 and 18:3 products by membrane bound desaturases whose identity is not known (68). One soluble 18:0-ACP desaturase has been isolated (69). One set of substrates for these saturases are glycerolipids that are produced by a prokaryotic pathway (69). Therefore, the role of chloroplast redox carriers in fatty acid desaturation could be tested by adding palmitoyl-CoA or stearyl-CoA to chloroplasts, and assaying for concomitant O_2 uptake and redox changes of the electron transport chain. Such changes have been observed using intact CO_2-fixing chloroplasts (Tae, G.-S., and Cramer, W.A., unpubl.). The peak of the cytochrome redox difference spectrum obtained for the addition of palmitoyl-CoA, in preliminary experiments, is close to 559 nm, implying that this cytochrome may function in the pathway of fatty acid desaturation. A correlation of PSII, in particular, has been noted in *Euglena* between competence for O_2 evolution and the degree of unsaturation of chloroplast galactolipids (70). Cytochrome b-559, and perhaps other carriers in the intermediate electron transport chain, including cyt b_6, may have a dual role: (a) in photosynthetic electron transport and energy transduction, and (b) in the metabolic and biosynthetic reactions required to maintain and renew the structure of the organelle.

Acknowledgment. These studies were supported by NIH GM-38323. We thank Profs. F.L. Crane and R.A. Dilley for helpful discussions, Janet Hollister for painstaking work on the manuscript, and Gabrielle Cramer for Figs. 2,3.

REFERENCES

1 Widger, W.R., Cramer, W.A., Hermodson, M., Meyer, D., and Gullifor, M. (1984) J. Biol. Chem 259, 3870-3876

2 Herrmann, R.G., Alt, J., Schiller, B., Widger, W.R., and Cramer, W.A. (1984) FEBS Lett. 176, 239-244

3 Widger, W.R., Cramer, W.A., Hermodson, M., and Herrmann, R.G. (1985) FEBS Lett. 191, 186-190
4 Babcock, G.T., Widger, W.R., Cramer, W.A., Oertling, W.A., and Metz, J.G. (1985) Biochemistry 24, 3638-3644
5 Cramer, W.A., Theg, S.M., and Widger, W.R. (1986) Photosyn. Res. 10, 393-403
6 Widger, W.R., Cramer, W.A., Herrmann, R.G., and Trebst, A. (1984) Proc. Natl. Acad. Sci. 81, 674-678
7 Saraste, M. (1984) FEBS Lett. 166, 367-372
8 Davidson, E. and Daldal, F. (1987) J. Mol. Biol. 195, 13-24
9 Kallas, T., Spiller, S., and Malkin, R. (1988) J. Biol. Chem. 263, 14334-14342
10 Hauska, G., Nitschke, W., and Herrmann, R.G. (1988) J. Bioenerg. Biomem. 20, 211-228
11 Shiver, J.W., Peterson, A.A., Widger, W.R., Furbacher, P.N., and Cramer, W.A. (1989) Meth. Enzymol. 172, 439-461, Academic Press, Orlando
12 Holm, L., Saraste, M., and Wikström, M.K.F. (1987) EMBO J. 6, 2819-2823
13 Tae, G.-S., Black, M.T., Cramer, W.A., Vallon, O., and Bogorad, L. (1988) Biochemistry 27, 9075-9080
14 Åkerlund, H.E. and Andersson, B. (1983) Biochim. Biophys. Acta 725, 34-40
15 Sayre, R.T., Andersson, B., and Bogorad, L. (1986) Cell 47, 601-608
16 Vallon, O, Tae, G.-S., Cramer, W.A., Simpson, D., Hoyer-Hansen, G., and Bogorad, L. (1989) Biochim. Biophys. Acta 975, 132-141
17 Ortiz, W. and Malkin, R. (1985) Biochim. Biophys. Acta 808, 164-170
18 Markwell, M.K. and Fox, C.F. (1978) Biochemistry 17, 4809-4817
19 Boyd, D., Manoil, C., and Beckwith, J. (1987) Proc. Natl. Acad. Sci. 84, 8525-8529
20 diRago, J.-P. and Colson, A.M. (1988) J. Biol. Chem. 263, 12564-12570
21 diRago, J.-P., Coppee, J.-Y., and Colson, A.M. (1989) J. Biol. Chem. 264, in press
22 Howell, N. and Gilbert, K. (1988) J. Mol. Biol. 203, 607-618
23 Daldal, F. (1987) in Cytochrome Systems: Molecular Biology and Bioenergetics (Papa, S., et al., eds.), pp. 23-34, Plenum Press, New York
24 Dekker, J.P., Bowlby, N.R., and Yocum, C.F. (1989) FEBS Lett., in press
25 Miyazaki, A., Shina, T., Toyoshima, Y., Gounaris, K., and Barber, J. (1989) Biochim. Biophys. Acta 975, 142-147
26 Whitmarsh, J. and Cramer, W.A. (1978) Biochim. Biophys. Acta 501, 83-93
27 Larsson, C., Jansson, C., Ljungberg, U., Akerlund, H.E., and Andersson, B. (1984) in Adv. Photosyn. Res, I., (Sybesma, C., ed.), pp. 363-366
28 Horton, P., Whitmarsh, J., and Cramer, W.A. (1976) Arch. Biochem. Biophys. 176, 519-524
29 Innes, J.B., and Brudvig, G. (1989) Biochemistry 28, 1116-1125
30 Thompson, L.K. and Brudvig, G. (1988) Biochemistry 27, 6653-6658
31 Gounaris, K., Chapman, D.J., and Barber, J. (1988) FEBS Lett. 234, 374-378
32 Bricker, T.M., Odon, W.R., and Quierolo, L.B. (1988) FEBS Lett. 231, 111-117
33 Doyle, M.P., Li, L.B., Yu, L., and Yu, C.-A. (1989) J. Biol. Chem 264, 1387-1392
34 Crofts, A., et al. (1987) in Cytochrome Systems: Molecular Biology and Bioenergetics (Papa, S., et al., eds.), pp. 617-624, Plenum Press, NY.
35 Khorana, H.G. (1988) J. Biol.Chem 263, 7439-7442
36 Cramer, W.A., Black, M.T., Widger, W.R., and Girvin, M.E. (1987) in The Light Reactions (Barber, J., ed.), pp. 447-493, Elsevier, Amsterdam
37 Szczepaniak, A. and Cramer, W.A. (1989) these Proceedings and submitted for publication
38 Szczepaniak, A., Black, M.T., and Cramer, W.A. (1989) Zeit. für Naturforsch. 44c, 453-461

39 Willey, D.L., Auffret, A.D., and Gray, J.C. (1984) Cell 36, 555-562
40 Yeates, T.O., Komiya, H., Rees, D.C., Allen, J.P., and Feher, G. (1987) Proc. Natl. Acad Sci., U.S.A. 84, 6438-6442
41 Graan, T. and Ort, D.R. (1983) J. Biol. Chem 258, 2381-2386
42 Crofts, A.R. (1985) in The Enzymes of Biological Membranes (Martinosi, A., ed.), IV, pp. 347-382, Plenum, New York
43 Joliot, P. and Delosme, R. (1974) Biochim. Biophys. Acta 357, 267-284
44 Velthuys, B.R. (1979) Proc. Natl. Acad. Sci., U.S.A. 76, 2765-2769
45 Joliot, P. and Joliot, A. (1986) Biochim. Biophys. Acta 849, 211-222
46 Moss, D.A. and Rich, P.R. (1987) Biochim. Biophys. Acta 894, 189-197
47 Hangarter, R.P., Jones, R.W., Ort, D.R., and Whitmarsh, H. (1987) Biochim. Biophys. Acta 890, 106-115
48 Rich, P.R. (1988) Biochim. Biophys. Acta 932, 33-42
49 Bouges-Bocquet, B. (1981) Biochim. Biophys. Acta 635, 327-340
50 Hope, A.B. and Mathews, D.B. (1987) Aust. J. Pl. Physiol. 14, 29-46
51 Rich, P.R. and Moss, D.A. (1987) in The Light Reactions (Barber, J., ed.), pp. 421-445, Elsevier, Amsterdam
52 Hurt, E.C., Hauska, G., and Shahak, Y. (1982) FEBS Lett. 149, 211-216
53 Willms, I., Malkin, R., and Chain, R.K. (1988) Arch. Biochem. Biophys. 263, 36-44
54 Selak, M. and Whitmarsh, J. (1982) FEBS Lett 150, 286-292
55 Girvin, M.E. and Cramer, W.A. (1984) Biochim. Biophys. Acta 767, 29-38
56 Jones, R.W. and Whitmarsh, J. (1988) Biochim. Biophys. Acta 933, 319-333
57 Furbacher, P.N., Girvin, M.E., and Cramer, W.A. (1989) these Proceedings and Biochemistry 28, in press
58 Hladik, J., Snozzi, M., and Bachofen, R. (1987) Biochem. Biophys. Res. Comm. 148, 170-177
59 Clark, R.D. and Hind, G. (1983) Proc. Natl. Acad. Sci. 80, 6249-6253
60 Von Jagow, G. and Link, T.A. (1986) Meth. Enzymol. 126, 253-
61 Hope, A.R. and Rich, P.R. (1989) Biochim. Biophys. Acta 975, 96-103
62 Davies, E.C. and Bendall, D.S. (1987) in Prog. Photosyn. Res. (Biggins, J., ed.), 2, 2185-2188
63 Wikström, M.K.F. and Saraste, M. (1984) in Bioenergetics (Ernster, L., ed.), pp. 49-94, Elsevier, Amsterdam
64 Moss, D.A. and Bendall, D.S. (1984) Biochim. Biophys. Acta 767, 389-395
65 O'Keefe, D.P. (1983) FEBS Lett. 162, 349-354
66 Gounaris, K., Sandby, C., Andersson, B., and Barber, J. (1983) FEBS Lett. 156, 170-174
67 Koudelka, A.P., Kambadur, N., Bradley, D.K., and Ferguson, K.A. (1983) Biochim. Biophys. Acta 751, 121-126
68 Browse, J., Kunst, L., Anderson, S., Hugly, S., and Somerville, C. (1989) Plant Physiol. 90, 522-529
69 McKeon, T.A. and Stumpf, P.K. (1982) J. Biol. Chem. 257, 12141-12147
70 Constantopoulos, G. and Bloch, K. (1967) J. Biol. Chem. 242, 3538-3542

MOLECULAR BASIS OF RESISTANCE TO INHIBITORS OF THE CYT BC$_1$ COMPLEX IN PHOTOSYNTHETIC BACTERIA

Fevzi Daldal and Mariko K. Tokito

Department of Biology, Plant Science Institute, University of Pennsylvania, Philadelphia PA 19104-6019, USA.

1.   INTRODUCTION

The ubiquinol:cytochrome c oxidoreductase (or the cyt bc_1 complex) is a membrane-bound redox-driven proton pump present in mitochondria of eukaryotes and in many prokaryotes, including photosynthetic bacteria.   A similar complex, cyt b_6f, is also present in plant chloroplasts (1,2,3).   During respiration and photosynthesis, these evolutionarily well-conserved energy- transducing complexes catalyze electron transfer from lipid soluble quinol derivatives, ubiquinol and plastoquinol, to water soluble electron acceptors, cytochrome c and plastocyanin.   in general, they always contain two b-type cytochromes, of different spectroscopic and thermodynamic properties (cyt b_L and b_H), carried by a single polypeptide of approximately 40 kDa, a c-type cytochrome of about 30 kDa, and a 2Fe2S cluster containing protein of about 20 kDa (1,3).   The structural genes of the three redox-active subunits of the cyt bc_1 complexes of various bacteria have been isolated and their nucleotide sequences have been determined (4,5,6,7).   In *Rhodobacter capsulatus* these three genes are clustered and named *fbc* (4) or *pet* (5), with their 5' to 3' order being *petA* (*fbcF*) (Rieske FeS protein), *petB* (*fbcB*) (cyt b) and *petC*   (*fbcC*) (cyt c_1).

Mechanistically, the cyt bc_1 complex is thought to contain two distinct catalytic domains located on each side of the membrane (8,9,10).   The quinol oxidation site (called Q_z in bacterial and Q_o in mitochondrial systems) is on the outer side of the membrane.   It converts a quinol molecule to a quinone by transferring an electron to the Rieske FeS center and another to the lower potential cyt b heme (b_L).   This second electron is subsequently transferred to the cyt b_H which then reduces a quinone trapped at the quinone reduction site (called Q_c in bacterial, Q_i in mitochondrial systems) located in the vicinity of the inner negative face of the membrane (8,14).   Several classes of inhibitors are known to affect the reactions catalyzed at these active sites o f the cyt bc_1 complex (11).   Myxothiazol, mucidin and stigmatellin interfere with the electron transfer between ubiquinol, Rieske FeS protein and cyt b_L at the Q_z site (28).   Although stigmatellin also affects the Photosystem II of

M. Baltscheffsky (ed.), Current Research in Photosynthesis, Vol. III, 231–238.

chloroplast (12) its effect on quinol oxidation is similar for both cyt bc_1 and b_6f complexes (13). On the other hand myxothiazol has no inhibitory effect on chloroplast cyt b_6f complex (14). The inhibitors like antimycin, funiculosin and HQNO affect the electron flow from cyt b_H to quinone at the Q_c site (11). If indeed these chemicals act at defined sites to inhibit the function of the cyt bc_1 complex then the study of a collection of inhibitor resistant (Inh^R) mutants may reveal information about the binding of the inhibitors to, and the catalysis of quinone by, this complex. We have reported earlier the isolation of *R. capsulatus* mutants resistant to these inhibitors (15), and here we present the determination of the molecular basis of these mutations. We also correlate the natural inhibitor sensitivity and resistance of cyt bc_1/b_6f complexes with the differences in the amino acid sequences of a small region of cyt *b* from bacteria, mitochondria and chloroplasts.

2.   MATERIALS AND METHODS

R. capsulatus strains were cultured by respiration (aerobic, dark) or by photosynthesis (anaerobic, light) on PYE medium containing 2 mM of $MgCl_2$ and 2 mM of $CaCl_2$ (MPYE) and supplemented with antibiotics when appropriate, as described earlier (16). Spontaneous mutants resistant to cyt bc_1 inhibitors were selected under photoheterotrophic growth conditions on plates containing appropriate amounts of inhibitors dissolved in ethanol. They were derived from strain MT1131 (*crtD121*, Rif^R), a "green" derivative of SB1003 (17), and the plasmids used were related[i] to pRK404 (18). *E. coli* transformation and triparental matings with *R. capsulatus* were as described earlier (16). Recombinant DNA techniques were performed according to (19) and single strand (using the phage M13 derivative *mp10*) or double strand (using the plasmid pRK404 derivatives) DNA sequencing used the commercial "Sequenase" version of T7 polymerase according to the instructions provided by UBS Corp (Cleveland, Ohio). Myxothiazol was purchased from Boehringer-Mannheim and stigmatellin and mucidin were generous gifts of Drs. G. Hofle (Gesellshaft fur Biotechnologische Forschung, Braunschweig, West Germany) and V. Musilek (Institute of Microbiology, Prague, Czechoslovakia), respectively.

3.   RESULTS AND DISCUSSION

3.1   Isolation, characterization and classification of *R. capsulatus* mutants resistant to quinol oxidation (Q_z)-inhibitors.

Spontaneous mutants resistant to myxothiazol, mucidin and stigmatellin at final concentrations of 5×10^{-6} M, 5×10^{-5} M and 4×10^{-6} M, respectively, were selected under photosynthetic growth conditions on MPYE using MT1131 as a parental strain. To detect different possible classes among these mutants their cross-resistance to various Q_z-inhibitors were determined and shown in Table 1. Mutants exclusively resistant to myxothiazol (Myx^R) (MXT103) or to stigmatellin (Stg^R) (STG1 and STG3) were readily distinguished from those resistant to both myxothiazol and mucidin (Myx^R, Muc^R) (MXT101 and MUC21) or to myxothiazol and stigmatellin (Myx^R, Stg^R) (MXT102 and STG10).

Table 1. Phenotype, genetic linkage and basepair, and deduced amino acid, changes in the Q_z-Inh^R mutants of *R. capsulatus*.

Group	Strain	Phenotype	Cotr. fre.[a] with *ins171*	AA and bp change	Cyt *b* domain
I	MXT 101	Ps$^+$, Myx^R, Muc^R	9	G152S^b ($G_{1773}A$)	Q_z I
II$_a$	MXT 102	Ps$^+$, Myx^R, Stg^R	10	F144L ($T_{1749}C$)	Q_z I
II$_b$	MXT 103	Ps$^+$, Myx^R	9	F144S ($T_{1750}C$)	Q_z I
III	STG 1	Ps$^+$, Stg^R	21	V333A ($T_{2317}C$)	Q_z II
IV	STG 3	Ps$^+$, Stg^R	8	T163A ($A_{1806}G$)	Q_z I
V	STG 5	Ps$^+$, Stg^R	0	not in *pet*	--
VI	STG 10	Ps$^+$, Myx^R, Stg^R	8	M140I ($G_{1739}A$)	Q_z I
VII	MUC 21	Ps$^+$, Myx^R, Muc^R	7	L106P ($T_{1636}C$)	?
--	R 126	Ps$^-$	9	G158D ($G_{1792}A$)	Q_z I

[a]The average cotransduction frequencies (%) correspond to the number of inhibitor sensitive colonies found among at least 200 Kan^R transductants tested in each case.

[b]the numbers indicate the position of the amino acid residues of cyt *b* and the basepairs of the *pet(fbc)* operon (Davidson and Daldal, 1987)

To determine whether the inhibitor resistance is due to mutations in the *pet(fbc)* operon the Inh^R mutations were mapped with respect to the silent insertion *ins171::kan* linked to the *pet (fbc)* operon (16). The "Gene Transfer Agent" (17) produced by the strain R121-I171 (16) was used as donor in these crosses. As shown in Table 1, all of the Myx^R and Muc^R mutants were linked to *ins171::kan* with cotransduction frequencies of 8 to 10%. A similar cotransduction frequency (approximately 9%) was also observed for the *aer126* mutation of R126 which impairs specifically the Q_z site of the cyt *bc$_1$* complex (20) (Table 1). On the other hand, three distinct classes of mutations were detected among the Stg^R mutants: The first group of mutants (i.e., STG3) showed a cotransduction frequency of about 8%, a number similar to that observed with the Myx^R and the Muc^R mutants. A second group of mutants (i.e., STG1) were more tightly linked to *ins171::kan* (with a cotransduction frequency of approximately 20%) indicating that they were located closer to the 3' end of the *pet(fbc)* operon than the first group of mutants. Finally, the third group of mutants (i.e., STG5) were not linked to *ins171::kan* suggesting that they were not located within the *bc₁* cluster (Table 1). These results, together with inhibitor cross-resistance patterns indicated that at least eight different classes of mutants existed in our Inh^R mutant collection.

3.2 Molecular basis of the Q_z-Inh^R mutations, and their comparison to similar yeast and mouse mitochondrial cyt b mutations.

The *pet (fbc)* operons of various Inh^R mutants were cloned into the broad host-range plasmid pRK404 by digestion of the chromosomal DNA of their Kan^R derivatives with appropriate restriction enzymes that cut outside of the *pet-kan* cluster. These Kan^R pRK404 derivatives were conjugated back to a cyt bc₁$^-$ mutant, MT-CBC1, and the transconjugants obtained were tested for photosynthetic growth in the presence, and absence, of the Q_z-inhibitors. As expected, with the exception of STG5 and R126, all of the plasmids obtained yielded Tet^R, Kan^R merodiploids which grew photosynthetically and which had Inh^R phenotypes identical to those of their haploid parents (Table 1). The mutant *pet (fbc)* operons thus cloned were sequenced either directly from the plasmids, or after cloning their 2.2 kb (containing the *petA (fbcF)* and the NH₂-terminal part of *petB (fbcB)*) and the 2.0 kb (containing the COOH-terminal part of *petB (fbcB)* and the *petC (fbcC)*) long *Sma*I fragments into a phage M13 *mp10* derivative. The data, recapitulated in Table 1, indicated that Inh^R phenoytpes were due to single basepair changes in *petB (fbcB)*, encoding cyt *b*. Resistance to myxothiazol was conferred by the T_{1750} --> C (F144S), to stigmatellin either by the A_{1806} --> G (T163A) or the T_{2317} --> C (V333A), to both myxothiazol and mucidin by the T_{1636} --> C (L106P) or the G_{1773} --> A (G152S) and to both myxothiazol and stigmatellin by either the G_{1739} --> A (M140I) or a T_{1749} --> C (F144L) basepair substitutions. Furthermore, in the case of the non photosynthetic mutant R126 the G_{1792} --> A mutation yielded a glycine to an aspartic acid replacement at position 158 of cyt *b* (Table 1).

The Q_z-Inh^R mutations described here are not distributed randomly. Six of these are located in a very small segment of cyt *b*, spanning the region from the amino acid residues 140 to 163, called Q_zI. The clustering of several Inh^R mutations around the non-functional *aer126* mutation of the strain R126 suggested that this region is involved in the formation of the inhibitor-binding/quinol-oxidation (Q_z) domain of the cyt *bc₁* complex. Of the two remaining mutations the V333A substitution was found in another region (called Q_zII by analogy to Q_zI) located toward the COOH-terminal end of cyt *b* which is homologous to the subunit IV of the cyt *b₆f* complex of chloroplast (25). Finally, the L106P substitution that confers resistance to myxothiazol and mucidin was found to be located in the middle of helix II (21,22) which contains the two universally conserved histidine residues (H97 and H111 in *R. capsulatus*) thought to be the axial ligands of the two heme groups (b_L and b_H) of cyt *b*. The overall distribution of the Q_z-Inh^R mutations obtained in this study indicated that at least seven different amino acid residues at three distinct parts of cyt *b* may be mutated to affect the resistance or sensitivity of the cyt *bc₁* complex to Q_z-inhibitors. Only one class of mutation was not linked by genetic and molecular biological evidences to the cyt *bc₁* gene cluster. Although the exact location of this latter class of mutation is currently unknown it may also affect the cyt *bc₁* complex since it conferred resistance to stigmatellin and hypersensitivity to myxothiazol.

Cyt *b* mutations similar to those described here have also been obtained in yeast (23) and mouse (24) mitochondria, and a comparison of their location indicated that while mutations yielding resistance to stigmatellin were found in two distinct regions of bacterial and mouse mitochondrial cyt *b* they were confined only to one single region (QzI) in yeast cyt *b*. This may be due to the natural presence in yeast cyt *b* of the M140I substitution providing in bacteria low level resistance to stigmatellin. Conversely, while mutations yielding resistance to myxothiazol were found in two distinct regions of yeast (23) or mouse (24) mitochondrial cyt *b* no such mutation was obtained in the QzII region of bacteria perhaps due to the presence of the natural L298F substitution. Similar interspecies comparisons indicated that in general the nature of the resistance observed depended on the position of the residue in the cyt *b*, the nature of the substitution at this position and the context provided by the overall structure of cyt *b* of the organism studied. For example in *R. capsulatus* while the F144S substitution yielded resistance to myxothiazol only the F144L substitution conferred resistance to both myxothiazol and stigmatellin but in yeast the F144L substitution provided resistance to myxothiazol only (23).

3.3   The QzI region of cyt b subunit of the cyt bc₁   complex.

The Q_zI region of cyt *b* subunit of the cyt *bc₁* complex has an interesting primary structure, and a comparison of the amino acid residues of this region from bacterial, mitochondrial or chloroplast origin is shown in Figure 1. The amino acid residues at positions G146, Y147, P150, Q153 and W157 are well conserved in all cyt *b* sequences. Further, many other sequence positions (T/F142, A/G143, F/V144, V/S148, G/D152, S/G155, G/A158, A/V159, T/K160, V/I161, I/V162, T/S163, N/G164 and L/V165) are substituted only by one or two other, often conservative, amino acid residues. Although there are several differences in the primary sequences of the Q_zI region (positions 140, 141, 145, 149, 151 and 156) of mouse, yeast and *R. capsulatus* (Figure 1), interestingly, the same positions (F144, G152, G158 and T163) conferred resistance to the same inhibitors. The F144, G152 and G158 residues, which are well conserved in both bacterial and mitochondrial cyt *b* proteins but not in chloroplast cyt *b₆* are targets for mutations providing resistance to myxothiazol and mucidin. These inhibitors are potent on both bacterial and mitochondrial cyt *bc₁* complexes but they are without effect on cyt *b₆f* complexes of chloroplasts (14). It was observed that a glycine to an alanine replacement at the position equivalent to G158/143 in mouse mitochondrial cyt *b* provided resistance to myxothiazol (24). Similarly, in *R. capsulatus* the identical substitution, either engineered via site-directed mutagenesis or selected as a spontaneous revertant of G158D mutation also provided resistance to this inhibitor (unpublished data). Further, the systematic replacement of the *R. capsulatus* residues G152 and F144 by other amino acid residues has revealed that an aspartic acid and a valine at these sites, respectively, conferred resistance to myxothiazol (unpublished data). Considering that the G158/143A, G152/137D and F144V substitutions confer resistance to myxothiazol either in mouse mitochondrial (24) or in bacterial cyt bc_1 complexes the molecular basis of the natural resistance of cyt b_6f complexes to myxothiazol may be the natural presence of the G158A, G152D and F144V substitutions in cyt b_6 (Figure 1). In agreement with this idea, the T163 residue which is conserved both in mitochondrial and bacterial cyt b and chloroplast cyt b_6 is associated with resistance to stigmatellin, a quinol oxidation inhibitor that affects similarly both the cyt bc_1 and b_6f complexes *in vitro* (13).

Figure 2. **Homology around the Q_zI domain of cyt b from various cyt *bc/bf* complexes of mitochondria, bacteria and cloroplasts.**

MITOCHONDRIA

```
               125            135           145        150
Consensus:     - - T A F - G Y V L P   W G Q M S F W G A T   V I T N L
                     •                           •           • •
  Mam.  H:   ᵃM A T A F M G Y V L P   W G Q M S F W G A T   V I T N L
        B:    M A T A F M G Y V L P   W G Q M S F W G A T   V I T N L
        M:    M A T A F M G Y V L P   W G Q M S F W G A T   V I T N L
        R:    M A T A F M G Y V L P   W G Q M S F W G A T   V I T N L
  Amp.  T:    M A T A F V G Y V L P   W G Q M S F W G A T   V I T N L
  Ins.  D:    M G T A F M G Y V L P   W G Q M S F W G A T   V I T N L
  Fun.  Y:    I A T A F L G Y C C V   Y G Q M S H W G A T   V I T N L
        N:    M A T A F L G Y V L P   Y G Q M S L W G A T   V I T N L
        A:    M A T A F L G Y V L P   V G Q M S L W G A T   V I T N L
  Pla.  M:    I V T A F I G Y V P P   W G Q.M S F W G A T   V I T S L
        W:    I V T A F I G Y V P P   W G Q M S F W G A T   V I T S L
        O:    I V T A F I G Y V L P   W G Q M S F W G A T   V I T S L
  Par.  T:    I I I A F I G Y V L P   C T M M S Y W G L T   V F S N I
```

BACTERIA

```
               140            150           160        165
Consensus:     M G T A F M G Y V L P   W G Q M S F W G A T   V I T G L
               •       •                       •           •   •
        Pc:    M G T A F M G Y V L P   W G Q M S F W G A T   V I T G L
        Rs:    M A T A F M G Y V L P   W G Q M S F W G A T   V I T G L
        Rc:    M G T A F M G Y V L P   W G Q M S F W G A T   V I T G L
               •       •                 •                •   • •
```

CHLOROPLAST

```
Consensus:     - S F G V T G Y S L P   W D Q - G Y W A V K   I V T G V
  Cya.  N:     V S F G V T G Y S L P   W D Q V G Y W A V K   I V S G V
  Pla.  L:     V S F G V T G Y S L P   W D Q I G Y W A V K   I V T G V
        T:     A S F G V T G Y S L P   W D Q V G Y W A V K   I V T G V
        S:     A S F G V T G Y S L P   W D Q I G Y W A V K   I V T G V
```

ᵃThe amino acid sequences are taken from (25) and the numbering of the positions is according to that of *S. cerevisiae* (23) (mitochondria) and *R. capsulatus* (bacteria). The dots correspond to the positions where the Q_z-Inh^R mutations were observed, and the well conserved residues are underlined. Abbreviations are as follows: Mam., mammals; H, human; B, bovine; M, mouse; R, rat; Amp., amphibian; T, toad; Ins., insect; D, *Drosophila melanogaster*; Fun., fungi; Y, *S. cerevisiae*; N, *neurospora crassa;* A, *Aspergillus nidulans*; Pl., plants; M, maize; W, wheat; O, oenothera; Pro., protozoa; T, *Trypanosoma brucei*; Pc, *Paracoccus denitrificans*; Rs, *Rhodobacter sphaeroides*; Rc, *Rhodobacter capsulatus*; Cya., cyanobacteria; N, *Nostoc*; L, liverwort; T, tobacco and S, spinach.

Secondary structure prediction analyses (26,27) indicate that the Q_zI region is between the putative transmembrane helices III and IV, in the close proximity of the universally conserved histidine residues 97 and 198 (21,22). We have noticed that if the amino acid residues extending from 140 to 163 were to be modeled as an hypothetical "kinked helix" due to the presence of the conserved P150 instead of the proposed "helix-linker-helix" structure (26) then the residues M140, F144, G152, G158, I162 and T163 that are targets for mutations providing resistance to Q_z-inhibitors may be accommodated on one side of this "kinked helix" structure while the well-conserved residues G146, Y147, P150, Q153 and W157 may be partitioned on the other side. Although the significance of this imaginary structure is not clear it may be important to keep in mind that this region may have a local architecture which is well-conserved phylogenetically.

4. CONCLUSIONS

A major short-coming of the analysis of Inh^R mutants is that inhibitor-resistance cannot be obtained by destruction of determinants essential for chemical catalysis or for assembly of a multisubunit complex. Therefore, it can only reveal globally the areas of importance for inhibitor-binding and/or quinol oxidation. The accurate definition of the residues essential for catalysis ultimately requires a three dimensional structure for the cyt bc_1 or b_6f complex, which is presently unavailable. Nonetheless, in its absence molecular genetic analyses of the $Q_z\text{-}Inh^R$ mutations indicate the presence of at least two essential regions, Q_zI and Q_zII, predominantly related to quinol oxidation catalyzed by the cyt bc_1 complex. Furthermore, the observed differences in the primary amino acid sequence of the QzI region of cyt b may be correlated with the known inhibitor resistance or sensitivity of the cyt bc_1/b_6f complexes of bacterial, mitochondrial and chloroplast origin. The specific roles of the sidechains of the amino acid residues in these two regions of cyt *b* now need to be examined in detail to better define their contributions to quinol oxidation and inhibitor-resistance.

ACKNOWLEDGEMENT

The work in this laboratory was supported by PHS grant 38237 from the National Institute of Health to F.D. We acknowledge the participation of E. Davidson to the initial steps of this work.

REFERENCES

1. Prince, R. C. (1986) In *Encyclopedia of Plant Physiology*, New series, (Staehelin. L. A. and Arntzen, C. J., eds) vol 19 pp.539-546. Springer-Verlag, Berlin.
2. Cramer, W. A., Black, M. T., Widger, W. R. and Girvin, M. E. (1987) *In The Light reactions* (J. Barber, ed) pp. 447-493. Elsevier Science Publishers, Amsderdam.
3. Malkin, R. (1988) In ISI Atlas of Science: Biochemistry pp. 57-64.
4. Gabellini, N. and Sebald, W. (1986) Eur. J. Biochem. 154, 569-579.
5. Davidson, E. and Daldal, F. (1987) J. Mol. Biol. **195**, 13-24.
6. Kurowski, B. and Ludwig, B. (1987) J. Biol. Chem. **262**, 13805-13811.
7. Thony-Meyer, L., Stax, D. and Hennecke, Hauke. (1989) Cell, **57**, 683-697.
8. Crofts, A. R. and Wraight, C. A. (1983) Biochim. Biophys. Acta. **726**, 149-185.
9. Rich, P. (1986) J. Bioener. and Biomem. **18**, 145-155.
10. Robertson, D. E. and Dutton, P. L. (1988) Biochim. Biophys. Acta **935**, 273-291.
11. von Jagow, G. and Link, T. A. (1986) In *Methods in Enzymology* (Fleischer, S. and Fleischer, B, eds.) vol 126, pp. 253-271.
12. Oettmeir, W., Godde, D., Kunze, B. and Hofle, G. (1985) Biochim. Biophys. Acta **807**, 216-219.
13. Nitschke, W., Hauska, G. and Rutherford, A. W. (1989) Biochim. Biophys. Acta **974**, 223-226.
14. Rich, P. (1984) Biochim. Biophys. Acta **768**, 53-79.
15. Daldal, F., Davidson, E., Cheng, S. Naiman, B. and Rook, S. (1986) In *Microbial Energy Transduction* (Youvan, D. C. and Daldal, F. eds) pp. 113-119. Cold Spring Harbor Press, Cold spring Harbor, NY.
16. Daldal, F., Davidson, E. and Cheng, S. (1987) J. Mol. Biol. **195**, 1-12.
17. Marrs, B. (1981) J. Bacteriol. **146**, 1003-1012.
18. Ditta, G., Schimdhauser, T., Yacobson, E., Lu, P., Liang, X-W, Finlay, D., Guiney, D. and Helinski, D. R. (1985) Plasmid **13**, 149-153.
19. Maniatis, T., Frisch, E. F. and Sambrook, J. (1982) *Molecular cloning, a laboratory manual*. Cold Spring Harbor Laboratory, Cold Spring harbor, N Y.
20. Robertson, D. E., Davidson, E., Prince, R. C., van den Berg, W., Marrs, B. L. and Dutton, P. L. (1986) J. Biol. Chem. **261**, 584-591.
21. Widger, W. R., Cramer, W. A., Hermann, R. G. and Trebst, A. (1984) Proc. Natl. Acad. Sci. USA **81**, 674-678.
22. Saraste, M. (1984) FEBS Lett. 166, 367-372.
23. di Rago, J. P., Coppee, J-Y, and Colson, A-M. (1989) J. Biol. Chem, in press.
24. Howell, N and Gilbert, K. (1988) J. Mol. Biol. **203**, 607-618.
25. Hauska, G., Nitschke, W. and Herrmann, R. G. (1988) J. Bioener. and Biomemb. **20**, 211-228.
26. Rao, J. K. M. and Argos, P. (1986) Biochim. Biophys. Acta **869**, 197-214.
27. Brasseur, R. (1988.) J. Biol. Chem. **263**, 12571-12575.
28. von Jagow, G. and Ohnishi, T. (1985) FEBS Letters **185**, 311-315.
29. Kallas, T., Spiller, S. and Malkin, R. (1988) Proc. Natl. Acad. Sci. **85**, 5794-5798.

ELECTRON AND PROTON TRANSFER MECHANISMS OF THE bc_1 AND bf COMPLEXES: A COMPARISON

P.R. RICH, GLYNN RESEARCH INSTITUTE, BODMIN, CORNWALL, UNITED KINGDOM

1.   INTRODUCTION
     The electron transfer and proton translocation mechanism of the mammalian and bacterial bc_1 complexes is now relatively well understood. Their catalytic Q-cycle can occur in the monomeric enzyme and is always coupled to a net proton translocation. The key step is electrogenic electron transfer through the haems b from a site of quinol oxidation to one of quinone reduction. Associated (de)protonations are probably non-electrogenic but result in net proton translocation [1].

     The chloroplast bf complex proteins have great similarities of primary amino acid sequences, of predicted secondary structure and of redox centres, although the E_m value of cytochrome f is approx. 100mV higher, and the two b haems each around 100mV lower, than their bc complex counterparts. The enzyme has been shown to function electrogenically under some conditions with electron transfer behaviour and quinone reaction sites similar to those of the bc complexes. Despite such similarities, it is widely believed that the bf complex functions non-electrogenically under most conditions. In addition it has been suggested that it is functionally a dimer [2], possibly with proton translocation occurring only in the dimeric reaction cycle [3]. Experiments addressed at testing such possible differences of the bf complex are described in this report. It is concluded that such differences are not bourne out by presently available data.

2.   MATERIALS AND METHODS
     Pea plants were grown in a growth chamber at 20-25°C, in an 8/16 hour light/dark regime. The illuminance was about 50 μmol quanta.m^{-2}.s^{-1}. Class C chloroplasts were prepared as already described [4] and stored in liquid nitrogen in resuspension medium plus 5% dimethylsulphoxide, or kept on ice for more immediate use. There was little difference in results from either source of chloroplasts. bf complex was prepared by a modification [5] of the method of Hurt and Hauska [6]. Measurements of proton uptake, cytochrome kinetics and carotenoid bandshift were as in [7].

3.   RESULTS AND DISCUSSION
3.1.   Monomer or dimer operation?
     In the case of the mitochondrial bc_1 complex, most workers now agree that the monomeric enzyme is capable of a complete catalytic electron transfer cycle and experiments to the contrary have not

generally withstood the test of time. Moody and Rich [8] further
showed with intact beef heart mitochondria that the monomeric
reaction cycle is fully coupled to proton translocation. In
contrast, Graan and Ort [2] found that only one DBMIB/dimer was
necessary for full inhibition of the chloroplast *bf* complex and a
role of a dimeric reaction cycle in proton translocation is still
currently considered possible [3]. We therefore reinvestigated the
stoichiometry of DBMIB binding by two different methods. In the
first (Fig 1.a.), the duroquinol → MeV reaction in continuous
illumination was titrated. The results were consistent with a
requirement of 1 DBMIB per monomer and a K_D of 10^{-9} M. In the
second, the rate of cytochrome *f* rereduction after a single
turnover flash was titrated with DBMIB. However, it was found
surprisingly that stoichiometric concentrations of DBMIB were
without effect on this reaction (Fig. 2, top). This discrepancy
with the previous experiment was resolved with the finding that,
at low DBMIB concentrations, inhibition was only achieved after
several turnovers of the enzyme so that only after a brief
preillumination could maximal inhibition be observed (Fig. 2).
Hence by looking at the inhibition of cytochrome *f* rereduction
after 2 seconds of continuous illumination, rather than after a
single flash, it was possible to titrate the DBMIB inhibitory
effect (Fig. 1.b.). The results were again consistent with a
requirement of 1 DBMIB per monomer and a K_D of 10^{-9} M.

The nature of the dark recovery from DBMIB inhibition is not
known, but a decreased binding to reduced cytochrome *f* or FeS
seems unlikely in that the rate of cytochrome *f* rereduction in the
dark was much faster than that of recovery from inhibition (Fig.
3). I have previously suggested that the bound form of DBMIB in
the inhibited complex is the semiquinone or quinone form [9].
Recovery may involve slow reduction of these to the noninhibitory
quinol form under these conditions. Regardless of this problem,
however, it seems likely that the *bf* complex is functionally
monomeric from these data, although the reason for discrepancy
with previous data is not clear. It was found in these experiments
that progressive inhibition with DBMIB took the form of a
decreased rate constant for reduction of all of the cytochrome *f*,
rather than an inhibition of a fraction of the population. This
effect has already been noted by Jones and Whitmarsh [10] who
interpreted it in terms of rapid exchange of DBMIB between *bf*
complexes. The present work shows that this is not possible and
instead the effect must arise from rapid (< 1ms) electronic
equilibration between the high potential centres of the *bf*
complexes caused by plastocyanin.

3.2. A facultative quinone reduction site, Q_r?
It has long been thought that the *bf* complex is able to turn over
without being coupled to a net proton translocation. This largely
arose from early experiments which failed to detect a slow
electrogenic reaction or proton uptake associated with turnover of

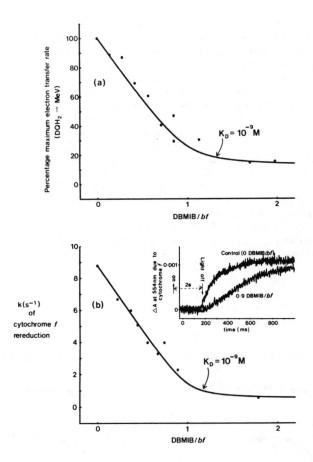

FIGURE 1. Estimation of the DBMIB/*bf* ratio in pea chloroplasts. In a) the activity of duroquinol → MeV was titrated with DBMIB. The reaction was monitored by light-induced oxygen consumption of broken chloroplasts (50μg/ml; 33 nM *bf*) in 330mM sorbitol, 50mM HEPES, 10mM KCl, 1mM EDTA, 5mM MgCl$_2$ and 5mM KPO$_4$ at pH 7.8 and 23°C and containing 0.5mM MeV, 3mM NH$_4$Cl, 10 μM DCMU, 10 μM ATP and 0.25mM duroquinol. In b) cytochrome *f* rereduction after 2 seconds red (RG635) preillumination was titrated with DBMIB. Reaction mixture was broken chloroplasts (75μg/ml; 67 nM *bf*) in 160mM sucrose, 40mM KCl, 0.8mM EDTA and 10mM potassium phosphate at pH 7.25 and containing 0.5mM MeV, 0.5mM duroquinol, 10 μM DCMU, 1μM gramicidin and 0.1 μM nonactin. Cytochrome *f* rereduction was approximated to a first order process for rate constant fitting. In both cases a theoretical curve for 1 DBMIB/monomer with K$_D$ = 10^{-9}M is plotted. DBMIB stock solutions were calibrated with an ϵ mM^{-1}.cm^{-1} in methanol of 13.7.

electrogenic reaction or proton uptake associated with turnover of the complex, especially under oxidising conditions in which the quinol is generated by photosystem II. Associated with this is the notion that the quinone reduction site is facultative; only when it operates is the enzyme protonmotive. It is widely assumed that under most conditions the site is not operative and that a different, nonprotonmotive, catalytic cycle functions.

An important further contribution was made with the introduction of NQNO and HQNO [11], compounds which were shown to promote oxidant-induced extra reduction of the b haems. Because of the analogy with the effect of antimycin A on the bc complexes, this was justifiably taken to indicate that they inhibited the Q_r site of the bf complex [11]. The finding that steady state flux through the enzyme was unaffected by NQNO [10] appeared to be further confirmation of the facultative nature of the Q_r site. Because of these considerations, a further investigation of the action of NQNO and HQNO was made.

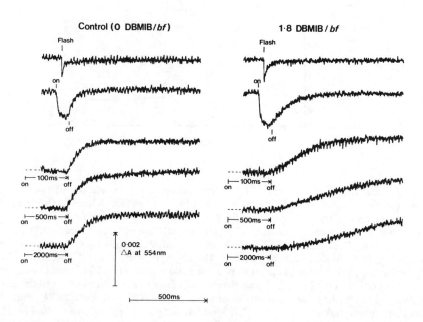

FIGURE 2. Light-induced onset of DBMIB inhibition of cytochrome f rereduction. Experiments were carried out as in fig. 1.b. except that the time of red (RG635) preillumination of dark-adapted chloroplasts was varied. Cytochrome f rereduction on cessation of this illumination was then assayed in control chloroplasts (left) or in chloroplasts which contained 1.8 DBMIB/bf monomer (right).

It is well known that HQNO raises the midpoint potential(s) of haem(s) b of the mitochondrial bc_1 complex [12]. It was therefore necessary to determine whether HQNO sterically inhibited the mitochondrial quinone reduction site directly or simply prevented the forward reaction because of the raised E_m values. This was tested by its effect on: (a) duroquinol or ubiquinol reduction of haem b in the presence of the Q_o-site inhibitor, myxothiazol; (b) the quinol-quinone transhydrogenase activity of the quinone reduction site. In both of these cases, raising of the midpoint potentials of the haems b might have been expected to stimulate activity. However, HQNO was found to potently inhibit both of these reactions, demonstrating that it did indeed directly inhibit the quinone reduction site, a result commensurate with its inhibitory effect on steady state flux through the enzyme.

Unfortunately, it is not possible to carry out directly analogous experiments with the bf complex since they do not possess a transhydrogenase activity and have b haems which are not reducible by plastoquinol or duroquinol via the Q_r site [13]. This is because of the low midpoint potentials of the bf complex b haems. Several other observations, however, strongly indicate that

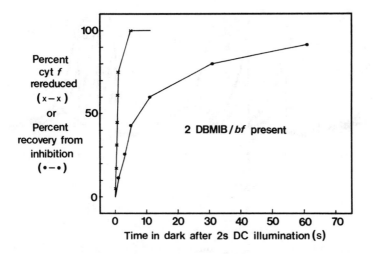

FIGURE 3. Dark recovery from DBMIB inhibition. Chloroplasts as in figure 1.b. and with 2 DBMIB/bf monomer were subjected to 2s continuous (RG635) illumination. At different dark times after this, the degree of inhibition (●) was monitored by measuring the rate constant of cytochrome f rereduction after a single saturating flash. f rereduction kinetics (✗) were monitored with a weak, non-actinic, measuring beam.

although NQNO (and HQNO) raise the midpoint potentials of the b haems of the bf complex [14] the Q_r site itself is not prevented from turning over. These include the following:-

(a) stigmatellin-insensitive reduction of haems b of isolated bf complex by anthraquinol sulphonate, which presumably occurs via the Q_r site, is stimulated by NQNO (data not shown);

(b) stigmatellin-insensitive oxidation of prereduced haem b_H by duroquinol in the isolated complex, again presumably via the Q_r site, is not inhibited by NQNO (data not shown);

(c) a continued electrogenic reaction associated with turnover of NQNO-liganded enzyme in chloroplasts occurs during a series of closely spaced flashes (Fig. 4). If NQNO had inhibited the Q_r site, then although the first flash would have a partial electrogenic reaction associated with haem b_H reduction [10], turnover of the enzyme on subsequent flashes would have been expected to have had zero or even a negative electrogenic reaction;

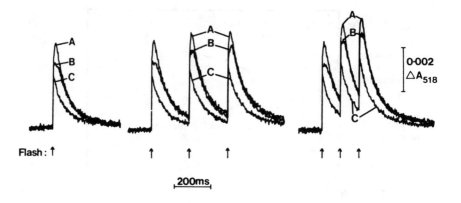

Flash: ↑   ↑   ↑   ↑   ↑ ↑ ↑

|200ms|

FIGURE 4. The extent of P-518_{SLOW} during multiple turnover flashes in the presence of NQNO. Chloroplasts were resuspended to 25 μg/ml in buffer as in fig. 1.b., but at pH 7.8 and containing 3mM NH_4Cl, 50μM MeV, 10μM DCMU and 1mM duroquinol. Saturating red (BG635) flash(es) were given after 10 s dark adaptation and each trace is the average of five recordings. A, control: B, + 500nM NQNO: C, +2μM stigmatellin and 1μM PMS. The P-518_{SLOW} of control chloroplasts is represented by the difference between traces (A - C); the NQNO-insensitive P-518_{SLOW} is given by the difference between traces (B - C). It can be seen that the NQNO-insensitive P-518_{SLOW} is at least as large, and possibly faster, on the third flash.

(d) NQNO does not prevent proton uptake associated with activity of the Q_r site [7];

(e) it has never proved possible to cause oxidant-induced reduction of more than one haem *b* per complex by oxidant-induced reduction in the presence of NQNO or HQNO [15]. This is in contrast to their action on the mitochondrial enzyme where full reduction of both haems *b* is possible by this means.

It would appear then from these results that NQNO does not inhibit electron transfer through the Q_r site of the *bf* complex, a result in contrast to its action on the mitochondrial enzyme. The reason for this surprising difference is not clear. At present, models which involve binding of NQNO to a site other than the Q_r site or the possible reduction of bound NQNO by the *b* haems are being considered.

3.3 A non-electrogenic reaction cycle of the *bf* complex?
I have previously argued that data taken to indicate a non-electrogenic reaction cycle of the *bf* complex are equivocal [15]. These arguments have been strengthened by recent direct measurements of the proton uptake associated with an electrogenic reaction cycle [7] which showed that such uptake occurred under all conditions tested. The above results which indicate that NQNO may not inhibit throughput of the Q_r site, when viewed in conjunction with these studies, suggest that the Q_r site may not be facultative and that the proton translocating reaction cycle may be operative under most, if not all, physiological conditions.

Under oxidising conditions, the kinetics of quinol oxidation are expected to be rather unusual since half of the original quinol is regenerated with each cycle of the enzyme. Such unique kinetics, which have large slow components, might best be termed "Zeno's paradox kinetics" and may be the cause of the difficulties in identifying the electrogenic reaction and associated proton uptake associated with turnover of the enzyme under oxidising conditions.

4.   ACKNOWLEDGEMENTS
This work is supported by the United Kingdom SERC (grant no. GR/E53941) and by the benefactors of the Glynn Research Foundation Ltd. Expert technical assistance was provided by S. Madgwick, electronic developments by Mr. A. Jeal and figures were produced by Mr. R. Harper.

5.   REFERENCES
 1 Rich, P.R., Moody, A.J. and Mitchell, R. (1989) in Charge and Field Effects in Biosystems (Allen, M.J., ed.) Plenum, *in press*
 2 Graan, T. and Ort, D.R. (1986) Arch. Biochem. Biophys. 248, 445-451
 3 Cramer, W.A., Black, M.T., Widger, W.R. and Girvin, M.E. (1987) in The Light Reactions (Barber, J., ed.) pp. 447-493, Elsevier, Amsterdam

4 Moss, D.A. and Bendall, D.S. (1984) Biochim. Biophys. Acta 767, 389-395

5 Rich, P.R., Heathcote, P. and Moss, D.A. (1987) Biochim. Biophys. Acta 892, 138-151

6 Hurt, E. and Hauska, G. (1981) Eur. J. Biochem. 117, 591-599

7 Hope, A.B. and Rich, P.R. (1989) Biochim. Biophys. Acta 975, 96-103

8 Moody, A.J. and Rich, P.R. (1989) Biochim. Biophys. Acta 973, 29-34

9 Rich, P.R. and Bendall, D.S. (1981) in Vectorial Reactions in Electron and Ion Transport in Mitochondria and Bacteria (Palmieri, F., Quagliariello, E., Siliprandi, N. and Slater, E.C., eds.), pp. 187-190, Elsevier/North Holland, Amsterdam

10 Jones, R.W. and Whitmarsh, J. (1988) Biochim. Biophys. Acta 933, 258-268

11 Jones, R.W. and Whitmarsh, J. (1985) Photobiochem. Photobiophys. 9, 119-127

12 Kunz, W.S. and Konstantinov, A.A. (1983) FEBS Lett. 155, 237-240

13 Rich, P.R. (1989) Highlights of Modern Biochemistry (Kotyk, A., Skoda, J., Paces, V. and Kostka, V., eds.) pp. 903-912. VSP, Zeist, Holland

14 Clark, R.D. and Hind, G. (1983) Proc. Natl. Acad. Sci. USA 80, 6249-6253

15 Rich, P.R. (1988) Biochim. Biophys. Acta 932, 33-42

ELECTRON TRANSFER BETWEEN PRIMARY AND SECONDARY DONORS IN
PHOTOSYNTHETIC BACTERIA : EVIDENCE FOR "SUPERCOMPLEXES".

P. JOLIOT*, A. VERMEGLIO** AND A. JOLIOT*. *IBPC, 13, rue P-et-M. Curie
75005 PARIS France. **SRA, CEN CADARACHE, 13108 Saint-Paul-lez-Durance
Cedex, France.

1. INTRODUCTION
    Most of the carriers of the photosynthetic electron transfer chain
are included in large transmembrane protein complexes, two in the case
of bacterial photosynthesis and three for oxygenic photosynthesis. On a
time-scale of several seconds, these complexes can be considered as
immobilized in the membrane. Two types of soluble electron carriers
establish a link between the membrane complexes : ubiquinone or
plastoquinone diffuse in the lipid phase of the membrane, while cyt c2
or plastocyanin which are hydrosoluble, diffuse in the periplasmic
space or the internal aquous phase of the thylakoid. In a classical
view of the photosynthetic apparatus, the soluble carriers are supposed
to diffuse rapidly over long distances ; therefore, we can expect that
in the dark or under weak illumination, the carriers of the electron
transfer chain are close to thermodynamic equilibrium. In such
circumstances, the localization of the different electron carriers
within the membrane should be of little functional importance.
    Equilibrium constants between redox carriers are easily computed
from their midpoint potentials, determined by conventional redox
titrations. Equilibrium constants may be also determined _in situ_ by
measuring the redox state of the carriers, either in the dark or in
conditions where the rate of the photosynthetic process is light-
limited. Surprisingly enough, the value of the apparent equilibrium
constants of electron transfer reactions between the primary PSII
acceptor and the primary PSI donor measured in the absence of mediators
[1,2] was found much lower than expected from the redox potential
titrations. The equilibrium constants were slowly increasing during a
dark adaptation of several minutes. No satisfying interpretation has
been proposed for these paradoxical results.

2. RESULTS AND DISCUSSION
    We recently came back to the determination of equilibrium
constants and addressed the case of bacterial photosynthesis [3]. We
studied electron transfer reactions between primary and secondary
donors in the R26 mutant strain of Rhodobacter sphaeroides. The
positive charges formed on P870 are first transferred to soluble cyt c2

M. Baltscheffsky (ed.), Current Research in Photosynthesis, Vol. III, 247–253.
© 1990 Kluwer Academic Publishers. Printed in the Netherlands.

and then, transferred to the high potential chain of the cyt b/c1 complex which includes cyt c1 and the FeS center. Experiments were performed in the presence of myxothiazol, which blocks the rereduction of cyt c1 and FeS center. We used living cells or benzoquinone-treated cells. Benzoquinone treatment considerably slows down the reductive pathway of the ubiquinone pool ; redox conditions could be then easily modulated by adding various amounts of KCN, which inhibits the oxidases. The redox state of P and cyt c2 plus cyt c1 (cyt ct) were determined spectrophotometrically.

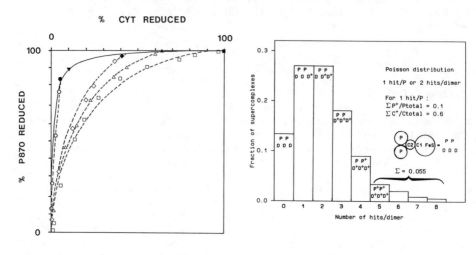

Fig. 1   Fig. 2
Fig. 1   Percentage of reduced P as a function of reduced Cytochromes during the course of a continuous illumination. Rb. sphaeroides R26.
Fig. 2   Distribution of positive charges among supercomplexes (see text)

The time-course of P and cyt ct oxidation were analyzed during the course of a weak illumination ($\approx$ 20 photons / center / second). In the presence of 2mM KCN, primary and secondary donors are fully reduced at the onset of illumination. The percentage of reduced P and cyt ct were plotted in Fig. 1, in order to estimate the equilibrium constants between these carriers during the course of illumination (open squares). The apparent equilibrium constant is close to 8, while on the basis of the midpoint potentials, we expected an equilibrium constant between 50 and 100. Starting from more oxidizing conditions (lower concentrations of KCN, open triangles and diamonds), the experimental data cannot be interpreted in terms of an equilibrium constant. Yet, an increase or a decrease of about a factor 4 in the intensity of illumination does not significantly affect the results; this shows that the rate of electron transfer is exclusively limited by the rate of the photochemical process. The redox state of the donors after 2 minutes-dark adaptation under various redox conditions are figured by the closed symbols. In this case, the experimental points fit the curve corresponding to an equilibrium constant of 70, in reasonable agreement

with the titration data. From this experiment, we conclude that
electron carriers are not in thermodynamic equilibrium during the
course of the weak illumination. We were able to interpret these data,
assuming that a limited number of reaction centers, cyt c2 and cyt b/c1
complexes are associated in structures that we called "supercomplexes";
within a supercomplex, electron transfer reactions are very fast and
during the course of a weak illumination, all the carriers included in
a same supercomplex are close to thermodynamic equilibrium. These
supercomplexes appear as isolated entities and electron exchange
between them occurs only in the minute time-range. During the course of
a continuous illumination, the photons are randomly distributed among
the supercomplexes and the number of positive charges stored will be
variable from one supercomplex to the other. Consider a supercomplex
that includes 2 reaction centers P, 1 cyt c2 and 1 cyt b/c1 complex and
assume, on one hand that the midpoint potentials of the three secondary
donors are equal and on the other hand, that the equilibrium constant
between primary and secondary donors is infinite. At a given time of
continuous illumination, the distribution of positive charges among the
supercomplexes can be computed from a Poisson law. Fig. 2 shows the
state of the supercomplexes when an average of one photon has been
trapped per reaction center. There is already 9% of the supercomplexes
with 4 positive charges (thus, one oxidized primary donor) and 5.5%
which have 5 positive charges (thus, two oxidized primary donors). In
this situation, the fractions of oxidized P and oxidized cytochrome are
≈ 0.1 and ≈ 0.6 respectively, which would correspond to an equilibrium
constant of 13, in spite of our assumption of an infinite equilibrium
constant. One short saturating flash will induce the same number of
charge separations as considered above, but now all the supercomplexes
are put in the (P P D^+D^+D) state : the fraction of oxidized P will be
then equal to zero. If cyt c2 is a diffusible carrier, the fraction of
oxidized P will remain equal to zero, provided that the number of
photons absorbed per photocenter is lower than 1.5.

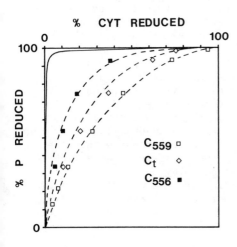

Fig. 3 Percentage of reduced P as a
function of reduced Cytochromes
during the course of a continuous
illumination. R. viridis.

A theoretical analysis of charge distribution within supercomplexes (or clusters in which the movement of diffusible carriers is restricted) has been developed by Lavergne et al [4]. This theory predicts the evolution of the redox state of the carriers under continuous illumination or flash excitation for any cluster stoichiometry. The predictive power of this treatment is illustrated by the analysis of the light-induced oxidation of primary and secondary donors in isolated centers of Rhodopseudomonas viridis (Fig. 3). In this case, it is definitely established that the secondary donors (cytochromes) are irreversibly bound to the reaction center. In the absence of mediators, no electron exchange is expected to occur between photocenters. In the presence of 200µM ascorbate, only two of the four cytochromes (cyt 556 and cyt 559) are in their reduced state prior to the illumination. As expected, the apparent equilibrium constant between P and the cytochromes measured during the course of illumination is much lower than that computed from the value of the redox potentials (K = 50 for cyt 559 and K = 1500 for cyt 556). The fit between the experimental data and the theoretical simulation (dashed lines) is excellent and clearly demonstrates that the measurement of electron transfer reactions under weak illumination is a powerful tool to characterize the degree of structuration of a photosynthetic electron transfer chain.

If one applies the treatment of Lavergne et al. [4] to Rhodobacter sphaeroides, a satisfying fit (Fig. 1, dashed lines) is obtained, assuming two types of supercomplexes : ≈ 70% of the centers are included in supercomplexes consisting of a dimer of reaction centers, one cyt c2 and one cyt b/c1 complex (P-P/c2/c1-Fes) ; the remaining fraction of the centers are included in supercomplexes P-P/c2. It is worth mentioning that a discrimination between different structural models requires the analysis of the oxidation process both under weak continuous illumination and repetitive flash excitation [3]. A special feature of our model is that cyt c2 is trapped in the supercomplex and thus cannot mediate any long distance electron transfer reactions. Moreover, the fact that only one cyt c2 molecule can be present in a supercomplex suggests that anticooperative interactions occur between the three available sites of fixation.

Our structural model also readily explains the biphasic kinetics of reduction of the primary donor after a short flash of variable energy [3]. We determined the half-time of the various processes in the reactions between primary and secondary donors. As already shown [5], the half-time of electron transfer between P and bound cyt c2 is ≈3µs. From cyt c1 (or FeS) to cyt c2, the half-time is ≈110µs. The switching time of cyt c2 from one reaction center to the other one within the same dimer is ≈70µs. Electron exchange between supercomplexes occurs in the minute time-range and therefore does not play any significant role in physiological conditions. In the particular case of R26 mutant of Rb. sphaeroides, all the carriers of the electron transfer chain are included in a single structure. The diffusion of cyt c2 is restricted to a very small domain, which certainly favors fast electron transfer reactions.

We performed similar experiments with G9 mutant strain of Rs.

<u>rubrum</u>. According to Van Grondelle et al. [6], cyt c2 freely diffuses
in the periplasmic space and does not bind to reaction center. Although
we agree with Van Grondelle's conclusion, we are led to propose
additional structural hypotheses to take into account the complex
kinetic behavior observed upon flash excitation.

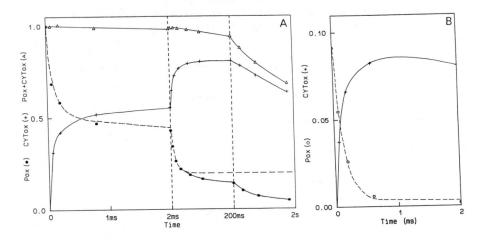

Fig. 4 Time-course of P reduction and cytochrome oxidation after a
short saturating flash (A) or a weak flash (B). Benzoquinone-treated G9
Rs. rubrum cells. 20μM myxothiazol.

Fig. 4A shows the time-course of P^+ reduction and cytochrome oxidation
after a saturating short flash. In less than 1 ms, 50% of P^+ is reduced
while the reduction of the second half occurs in a much longer time-
range. Conversely, after a weak flash (Fig. 4B), the reduction of P^+
approximately follows a first order kinetics. We determined that the
concentration of cyt c2 was equal or larger than 0.8 times the
concentration of the reaction centers ; therefore, the break observed
when half of the P^+ is reduced is not determined by the amount of
available cyt c2. The following structural hypothesis accounts for our
data :
1. Reaction centers are associated in dimers, as in <u>Rb. sphaeroides.</u>
2. For reaction centers including a reduced P, the affinity of cyt c2
is low when it is reduced, and high when it is oxidized.
3. For reaction centers including an oxidized P, the affinity of both
oxidized and reduced cyt c2 is low.
4. Only one cyt c2 molecule can be associated with a dimer of
photocenters. As in <u>Rb. sphaeroides,</u> anticooperative interactions must
occur between the two sites of the dimer.
    After a saturating flash, all the dimers have two oxidized primary
donors. A first P^+ is rapidly reduced by a soluble cyt c2. Then, the
oxidized cyt c2 remains bound to the reaction center and blocks the
access to the second oxidized donor (scheme 1). The reduction of this
donor should be limited by the time of exchange between bound and free

cyt c2. On the other hand, after a weak flash, the excited dimers have only a single P^+. Then, the reduction of P^+ will follow a pseudo first order kinetics, since the concentration of P^+ is low compared with the concentration of cyt c2. Lavergne developed computer simulations of this model which give an excellent fit with the experimental data (dashed line), whatever the initial redox poise.

The more cogent argument which favors our structural model is obtained by measuring the amplitude of the slow phase of the P reduction as a function of the flash energy. If f is the fraction of photocenters hit by the flash, the amplitude of the slow phase is proportional to f^2, i.e. to the fraction of dimers which were doubly excited during the flash.

It is noteworthy that in our hypothesis, the "product inhibition" by oxidized cyt c2, already proposed by Moser and Dutton [7], is of little functional consequence under strong continuous illumination, as the bound oxidized cyt c2 is immediately released when the primary donor is again oxidized.

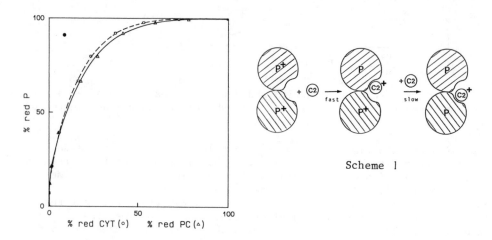

Scheme 1

Fig. 5 Percentage of reduced P700 as a function of reduced plastocyanin and reduced cytochrome during the course of a continuous illumination. S52 strain of <u>Chlorella sorokiniana</u>.

We underwent preliminary experiments with the S52 mutant strain of <u>Chlorella sorokiniana</u> lacking PSII and the major fraction of the chlorophyll antenna, in which we studied the electron transfer reactions between primary and secondary PSI donors. These experiments were performed in the presence of ascorbate, in benzoquinone-treated algae. In these conditions, the plastoquinone pool is oxidized while the donors (cyt f, plastocyanin and P700) are fully reduced. The relationship between the redox states of P700, cyt f and plastocyanin was studied during the course of a weak continuous illumination (Fig.5). The low apparent equilibrium constant we measured suggests that reaction centers, plastocyanin and cyt b/f complex are associated in supercomplexes. As a matter of comparison, we measured the redox state of cyt f and P700 after 2 minutes dark equilibration in more oxidizing conditions (Fig. 5, closed dot) ; in such conditions, the value of the equilibrium constant ($\approx$ 100) is in good agreement with the figure deduced from redox titrations. The supercomplexes very likely include monomers of PSI and of cyt b/f complexes. The stoichiometry of plastocyanin within these supercomplexes has to be precisely determined, but is very likely around 2.

Delosme [personal communication] measured the rate of electron transfer between P700 and cyt f after a short flash excitation. The half-time depends upon the physiological conditions and varies from 70μs to $\approx$ 600μs. These results suggest that formation and dissociation of supercomplexes are controlled by regulatory processes. On the basis of a biochemical and structural analysis, Wollman and Bulté [8] concluded that the cyt b/f complex could very likely be associated either with PSI or PSII centers. Supercomplexes between PSI center and cyt b/f complex favor cyclic electron flow around PSI, while supercomplexes between PSII and cyt b/f complex would favor the linear electron flow. The physiological processes which control the association of cyt b/f complex with the photocenters might present similarities with the processes which control the State I / State II transitions.

3. CONCLUSION

Analysis of the electron transfer reactions under weak continuous illumination shows that both in oxygenic and bacterial photosynthesis, electron carriers are far from thermodynamic equilibrium. Movements of so-called soluble carriers are often restricted to very small areas of the membrane. Surprisingly enough, this is also true in the case of the plastoquinone, the diffusion of which is limited to domains including 2 to 7 PSII centers [see poster summary by P. Joliot, J. Lavergne and D. Béal]. Therefore, the understanding of the mechanism of electron transfer requires a precise knowledge of the lateral organization of the carriers within the photosynthetic membrane.

REFERENCES
1. Joliot, P., Joliot, A. and Kok, B. (1968) Biochim. Biophys. Acta 153, 635-652.
2. Forbush, B. and Kok, B. (1968) Biochim. Biophys. Acta 162, 243-253.
3. Joliot, P., Verméglio, A. and Joliot, A. (1989) Biochim. Biophys. Acta. In press.
4. Lavergne, J., Joliot, P. and Verméglio, A. (1989) Biochim. Biophys. Acta. In press.
5. Overfield, R.E., Wraight, C.A. and Devault, D. (1979) FEBS Lett. 105, 137-142.
6. Van Grondelle, R., Duysens, L.N.M. and Van der Wal, H.N. (1976) Biochim. Biophys. Acta 440, 169-187.
7. Moser, C. and Dutton, P.L., (1988) Biochem. 27, 2450-2461.
8. Wollman, F-A. and Bulté, L. (1989) in Photocatalytic Production of Energy Rich Compounds. Elsevier Publishers, London, in press.

TOPOGRAPHY OF THE CHLOROPLAST CYTOCHROME b_6

A. SZCZEPANIAK and W. A. CRAMER, DEPARTMENT OF BIOLOGICAL SCIENCES, PURDUE UNIVERSITY, WEST LAFAYETTE, IN 47907 U.S.A.

1. INTRODUCTION

Cytochrome b_6 contains 4 His residues in membrane-spanning helices that are conserved in the cyt b of the b-c_1 complex of mitochondria from many phyla as well as in photosynthetic bacteria, cyanobacteria, and chloroplasts (1-3). The hydropathy plots for the amino acid sequences of these cytochromes were highly correlated mathematically (1,4). This led to the prediction that the four His residues used to coordinate the two hemes of the cytochrome are located on two of the membrane-spanning helices, with a His pair coordinated to a heme on each side of the membrane thereby crosslinking the two helices. The cyt b_6 protein of oxygenic photosynthesis which is ~$\frac{1}{2}$ the size of cyt b (b-c_1) constitutes the heme-binding domain of the latter.

Subsequent analysis of the location in the mitochondrial cyt b polypeptide of inhibitor-resistant mutations to DCMU and antimycin in yeast (5) and mouse (6) mitochondria, and to myxathiazol and stigmatellin in the photosynthetic bacteria (7), implied (i) that the heme binding domain of these b cytochromes contained eight membrane-spanning α-helices instead of the nine originally proposed. The segment removed from the bilayer and proposed to reside in the polar phase in the model inferred from the mutation work was helix IV in the original model (1,2). It does not contain His residues. Extrapolation of these results to the structure of the chloroplast cyt b_6 would imply that it has four membrane-spanning α-helices with the two heme-binding His residues on helices II and IV (Fig. 1), rather than the five originally proposed with the critical His residues on helices II and V. It was also predicted from the location of DCMU- and antimycin A-resistant mutants that the NH_2-terminus of the mitochondrial and bacterial cytochromes is on the n-side (stromal side) of the membrane, providing information on orientation that could not be obtained from considerations of hydropathy alone. These data for the mitochondrial and bacterial cytochromes, that rely on a specific sidedness of action of particular inhibitors, have not been checked by other methods of topographical analysis. The use of inhibitor-resistant mutants to study the topography of the cyt b_6 is more difficult because of the absence of n-side inhibitors (8).

2. MATERIALS AND METHODS (9)

Peptide Synthesis. Three decapeptides, (i) NH_2-D-W-F-E-E-R-L-E-I-Q-COOH, (ii) NH_2-A-V-K-J-V-T-G-V-P-D-COOH, and (iii) NH_2-I-R-K-Q-G-I-S-G-P-L-COOH, corresponding to epitopes spanning 5-14, 146-155, and 205-214, respectively, in the 214 amino acid cyt b_6 polypeptide from spinach chloroplasts were synthesized and coupled to BSA or KLH for the production of antibodies. The position of these epitopes in a four helix model for cyt b_6 folding in the membrane is shown (Fig. 1).

Proteolysis. Thylakoids (100 μl, 1 mg chl/ml) were incubated with DPCC-treated chymotrypsin-free trypsin, carboxypeptidase A (CpA) or *Staph. aureus* V8 protease at

M. Baltscheffsky (ed.), Current Research in Photosynthesis, Vol. III, 255–258.
© 1990 *Kluwer Academic Publishers. Printed in the Netherlands.*

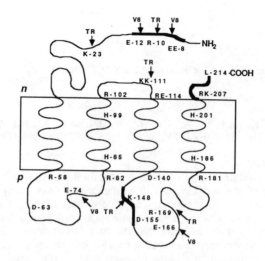

FIGURE 1. Four helix model of cyt b_6 in the membrane bilayer. The position is noted of the charged residues that are possible sites for the action of trypsin (on K,R) or V8 protease (on E), and of the epitopes (bold segments) to which antibodies were raised.

room temperature (ca. 20°). The trypsin and V8 protease reactions were terminated by addition of 5 mM PMSF, and CpA by 5 mM o-phenanthroline.

3. RESULTS AND DISCUSSION

3.1. *Shielding of Cytochrome b_6 at the Stromal Surface.* CpA has no effect on cyt b_6 (9), an expected result since the Pro residue at the penultimate position should block CpA (10). However, the efficacy of trypsin digestion was increased if the membranes were treated first with CpA. o-phenanthroline was added to inhibit CpA before trypsin treatment so that the two proteases did not act simultaneously. Reversing the order of protease addition had no effect, showing that the access of trypsin was increased by prior treatment with CpA. Similar results were obtained using antibodies (i) and (iii) to the NH$_2$- and COOH-termini (unpubl.). Thus, cyt b_6 on the stromal membrane surface is shielded by the COOH-termini of other thylakoid proteins.

3.2. *Products of Trypsin Proteolysis and Membrane Orientation of Cytochrome b_6.* Treatment of thylakoid membranes with trypsin resulted in generation of 1-2 detectable bands of slightly smaller molecular weight ($\Delta M_r \approx$ -1,000 and 2,500). The simultaneous decrease of the parental band and concomitant increase in the relative intensity of the cleaved polypeptide implies a parent-daughter relation (9). However, no daughter bands can be detected when antibody for the Western blot is used that is directed to the Asp-5—Gln-14 epitope at the NH$_2$-terminus (Fig. 2B) and Ile-205—Leu-214 at the COOH-terminus (unpubl.), indicating that trypsin acts on R-10 and/or K-23, and at RK-207, removing all or most of the regions with which the peptide-directed antibodies can react (Fig. 1). The loss of total intensity implies that the trypsin also acts on at least one other site that is a major epitope. These could be R-102, R-113, or KK-111 (Fig. 1). The existence of the latter double Lys residue on the stromal side may explain the extensive degradation of cyt b_6 seen in lanes 5 and 6 of Fig. 2A.

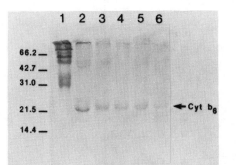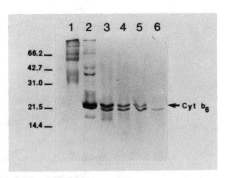

FIGURE 2. Immunodetection of trypsinolysis of cyt b_6 in thylakoids. (A) MW markers, untreated control, lanes 1,2; treatment with trypsin for 15 min, 20°C, (1:40, 1:20, 1:10 or 1:5 (w/w), trypsin:Chl), lanes 3-6; separation on 15% SDS-PAGE (10 μg Chl/lane) and detection on a Western blot using antibody to entire cyt b_6. For the conditions of lane 5 (15 min, 1:10, trypsin : Chl), the loss of cyt f, cyt b-559, and the 17 kDa OEC extrinsic protein was 25-30%, <20%, and 20-25%, respectively. (B) Trypsinolysis of cyt b_6 using antibody against the NH_2-terminal epitope, Asp-5—Gln-14 (9); lanes as in (A).

The sensitivity to trypsin of the epitopes from the entire cyt b_6 protein as well as those at the NH_2- and COOH-termini was measured in thylakoids and ISO membranes relative to that of proteins known to be located on the lumen side of the membrane. Cyt f, as well as the OEC 16 and 33 kDa proteins (not shown), were found to be more resistant in thylakoids to trypsin than the cyt b_6 epitopes (Fig. 3), whereas the trypsin-resistant epitopes in ISO membranes were those to the NH_2- and COOH-termini (not shown). Thus, epitopes from the NH_2- and COOH-termini show an accessibility to trypsin that is inversely related to that of cyt f and the OEC proteins, implying that the cyt b_6 termini are both exposed to the stroma, as in the model of Fig. 1.

3.3. *Relative Accessibility of Cyt b_6 and Cyt f on the Lumen Side to V8 Protease* Cyt b_6 is more sensitive to V8 protease than is cyt f in the presence or absence of SDS. A 15 min incubation (1:20, protease:Chl) causes the appearance of an M_r 15,800 (±250, n=4) product that also reacts with antibody directed against epitope (ii) Ala-146—Asp-155 (9). The M_r 15,800 product appears more quickly when the protease is added in the presence of SDS. An M_r 14,000 (±400, n=4) product appears clearly along with the M_r 15,800 band, with both of these bands having about twice the density in the presence of SDS. Both peptide fragments react with the antibody to the 146-155 epitope (9), but not to the COOH-terminal epitope (iii) (unpubl.). These data applied to the 4 helix model (Fig. 1) predict that the large V8 proteolysis product results from cleavage at Glu-166, and possibly Glu-74, on the p-(lumen) side.

The explanation of the extensive degradation of cyt b_6 at sites on the lumen side, by protease added on the stromal side, is that at high protease concentrations and/or prolonged incubation, the thylakoids are somewhat leaky to the protease. The degree of this leakiness, measured by degradation of cyt f, cyt b-559, and the 17 kDa OEC protein, is small, especially considering the large number of Glu residues in the latter

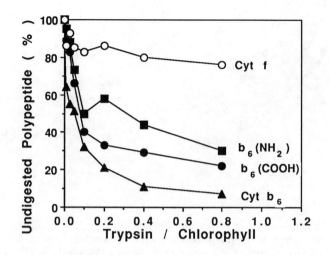

FIGURE 3. Relative sensitivity to trypsin added to thylakoid membranes of epitopes to cyt b_6 (▲), b_6 NH_2- (■) and COOH- (●) termini compared to cyt f (O).

two proteins, 17 in cyt f (11) and 11 in the 17 kDa protein (12). The greater sensitivity of cyt b_6 would imply that at least one of its lumen-side interhelix loops is more accessible to the aqueous phase than is cyt f, and may be involved in a lumen-skeletal structure that is important for function. The loop joining helices III and IV contains a segment that is highly conserved in chloroplasts and mitochondria, and in which myxathiazol- and stigmatellin-resistant mutations occur in the latter (6), implying that it is part of a quinone-binding site on the p-side of the bilayer.

REFERENCES

1 Widger, W.R., Cramer, W.A., Herrmann, R.G., and Trebst, A. (1984) Proc. Natl. Acad. Sci. U.S.A. 81, 674-678
2 Saraste, M. (1984) FEBS Lett. 166, 367-372
3 Hauska, G., Nitschke, W., and Herrmann, R.G. (1988) J. Bioenerg. Biomem. 20, 211-228
4 Shiver, J.W., Peterson, A.A., Widger, W.R., Furbacher, P.N., and Cramer, W.A. (1989) Meth. Enzymol. 172, 439-461, Academic Press, Orlando
5 di Rago, J.P. and Colson, A-M. (1988) J. Biol. Chem. 263, 12564-12570
6 Howell, N. and Gilbert, K. (1988) J. Mol. Biol. 203, 607-618
7 Daldal, F. (1987) in Cytochrome Systems: Molecular Biology and Bioenergetics (Papa, S., Chance, B. and Ernster, L., eds.), pp. 23-34, Plenum Press, NY
8 Furbacher, P.N., Girvin, M.E., and Cramer, W.A. (1989) Biochemistry 28, in press
9 Szczepaniak, A., Black, M.T, and Cramer, W.A. (1989) Zeit. für Naturforsch. 44c, 453-461
10 Ambler, R.P. (1967) in Meth. Enzymol. XI, pp. 436-445, Academic Press, NY
11 Alt, J. and Herrmann, R.G. (1984) Curr. Gen. 8, 551-557
12 Jansen, T., Rother, C., Steppuhn, J., Reinke, H., Beyreuther, K., Jansson, C., Andersson, B., and Herrmann, R.G. (1987) FEBS Lett. 216, 234-240
(Supported by NIH GM 38323.)

CHARACTERIZATION OF THE POLYPEPTIDE COMPONENTS OF THE CYTOCHROME BC_1 COMPLEX OF *RHODOBACTER SPHAEROIDES*

DAVID J. PURVIS, ROLF THEILER AND ROBERT A. NIEDERMAN, Department of Molecular Biology and Biochemistry, Rutgers University, Piscataway, NJ 08855-1059, USA

1. INTRODUCTION

The ubiquinol-cytochrome c_2 oxidoreductase (cytochrome bc_1 complex) of *Rhodobacter sphaeroides* is an integral component of the intracytoplasmic membrane (ICM) and functions in light-driven cyclic electron flow and the conservation of radiant energy as an electrochemical proton gradient. Previous studies on the assembly of electron transfer constituents in *R. sphaeroides* have demonstrated that complete cycles of electron flow do not occur merely upon insertion of newly synthesized reaction centers at sites of initiation of ICM growth, but instead, subsequent synthesis and assembly of redox centers of the bc_1 complex are required [1]. To further characterize the assembly process and for detailed structural investigations, the complex was purified and antibodies were raised against the isolated polypeptide constituents. In this report, results on the localization and levels of the bc_1 complex in various membrane fractions are presented; a detailed description of the structural work will appear elsewhere [2].

2. MATERIALS AND METHODS

Membranes were prepared from photoheterophically grown cells [2] by rate-zone sedimentation on sucrose density gradients as described in [3]. In this procedure, two pigmented membrane fractions are isolated; these consist of ICM-derived chromatophores and an upper pigmented band which contains partially developed membranes that arise from sites of initiation of ICM growth [1, 3]. The cytoplasmic and outer membranes were isolated from French-pressure cell extracts of chemoheterotrophically grown cells on a discontinuous sucrose gradient using a fixed angle rotor [2]. The cytochrome bc_1 complex was isolated from dodecyl-β-D-maltoside extracts of chromatophores essentially as described by Ljungdahl et al. [4], except that the final chromatography step was omitted. Attempts to isolate the bc_1 complex from the cytoplasmic membrane were not successful, but immunoblotting procedures (see below) demonstrated that the complex was present in these preparations.

Antibodies were raised in rabbits against the individual polypeptides components of the bc_1 complex that were purified by preparative SDS-polyacrylamide gel electrophoresis [2]. IgG was purified from the antisera by ammonium sulfate precipitation, and immunoblotting was performed as described by Towbin et al.[5] using peroxidase-labeled goat anti-rabbit IgG as the second antibody and 4-chloro-1-naphthol for the staining reaction. Assessment of the specificity of the antisera by this procedure indicated that of the four subunits, only the 14 kDa component was non-immunogenic. Antibody titers were measured by enzyme-linked immunosorbant assay. For the iron-sulfur protein, sera obtained 11 weeks after immunization exhibited a detectable reaction at dilutions up to ~10^{-6}.

M. Baltscheffsky (ed.), Current Research in Photosynthesis, Vol. III, 259–262.
© 1990 *Kluwer Academic Publishers. Printed in the Netherlands.*

3. RESULTS AND DISCUSSION

The polypeptide composition of the purified cytochrome bc_1 complex is shown in Fig. 1; bands near the top of the gel apparently represented aggregates of cytochrome b, including a major 88-kDa species. Aggregation of purified cytochrome b could be avoided by treatment with anhydrous trifluoroacetic acid prior to transfer to the electrophoresis sample buffer (not shown). Further characterization has indicated that the isolated bc_1 preparations were essentially homogeneous [2]. The fourth subunit of approximately 14 kDa has been observed in preparations of the *R. sphaeroides* bc_1 complex isolated by a variety of procedures [4, 7, 8]. Photoaffinity labeling has suggested a role for both the 14 kDa polypeptide and cytochrome b in Q binding [9]; in addition, the 14 kDa subunit has been implicated as a site for antimycin A interactions [8]. When the complex purified in the present studies was subjected to gel-permeation chromatography on a Sephadex G-150 column in the presence of 200 mM NaCl, the iron-sulfur protein was dissociated while the 14 kDa polypeptide remained tightly bound to the cytochrome constituents [2]. This suggested that the 14 kDa protein is an integral component of the *R. sphaeroides* bc_1 complex and not an artifact of the isolation procedure.

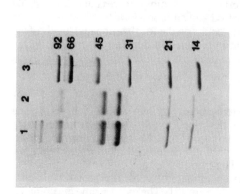 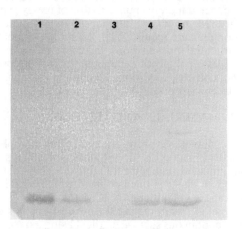

FIGURE 1 (left). Subunit composition of the purified cytochrome bc_1 complex from R. sphaeroides. Pooled fractions from DEAE column were concentrated by ultrafiltration and analyzed by SDS-poly-acrylamide gel electrophoresis on a Bio-Rad minigel apparatus by procedures described in [6]. Lanes 1, 2, bc_1 complex, 5 and 10 μg of protein, respectively; lane 3, protein standards (Bio-Rad): 14,400 Da, lysozyme; 21,500 Da, soybean trypsin inhibitor; 31,000 Da, carbonic anhydrase; 45,000 Da, ovalbumin; 66,200 Da, bovine serum albumin; 92,500 Da, phosphorylase B. The apparent molecular masses determined for the subunits of the complex were: cytochrome b, 43 kDa; cytochrome c_1, 37 kDa (33 kDa on 10-cm analyzing gel); Rieske iron-sulfur protein, 20 kDa; fourth polypeptide, 14.5 kDa. For determination of the molecular weight of the latter component, the purified polypeptide was dried under a stream of nitrogen and subjected to electrophoresis on an analyzing gel prepared with 18% (wt/vol) acrylamide. In addition to soybean trypsin inhibitor and lysozyme, molecular weight standards (Diversified Biotechnologies) included myoglobin, 16,950 Da; cytochrome c, 12,400 Da; myoglobin fragment III, 8,200 Da; myoglobin fragment II, 6,200 Da.

FIGURE 2 (right). Localization of cytochrome bc_1 complex in *R. sphaeroides* membrane fractions. Membranes were isolated as described in the text and subjected to SDS-polyacrylamide gel electrophoresis; each lane received 75 μg of protein. Protein bands were transferred to nitrocellulose and subjected to immunoblotting with a 1/1500 dilution of anti-iron sulfur protein IgG as described in the text. Lane 1, chromatophores; lane 2, bc_1 complex; lane 3, outer membrane from chemotrophically grown cells; lane 4, purified upper pigmented band; lane 5, cytoplasmic membrane from chemotrophically grown cells.

The cytochrome bc_1 complex was localized in the various membrane preparations isolated from *R. sphaeroides* by immunoblotting procedures using the anti-iron sulfur protein IgG (Fig. 2). The results confirmed that the bc_1 complex is present in the upper pigmented band and indicated that on a reaction center basis, the level of the iron-sulfur protein in this fraction was approximately equal to that in chromatophores. This was unexpected in view of estimates from EPR spectra which indicated that the Rieske iron-sulfur signal in the upper pigmented band was reduced 3 fold in comparison to that of chromatophores [1]; this was considered as a basis for the low rates of electron transfer in the bc_1 complex present in these immature membrane preparations. Moreover, studies on structural mutants of the yeast reductase have suggested that associations of this non-heme iron component with the other subunits of the complex is the final step in the assembly of the active holoenzyme [10]. It is possible that in *R. sphaeroides*, full development of the high potential iron-sulfur cluster requires post-translational modifications that occur subsequent to their insertion at sites of initiation of ICM growth. Fig. 2 also demonstrates that the cytochrome bc_1 complex is confined to the cytoplasmic membrane in chemohetero-trophically grown cells.

The 14 kDa component of the *R. sphaeroides* cytochrome bc_1 complex was of special interest since it has not been observed in the complexes isolated from other procaryotes [4, 11, 12]. A number of "extra polypeptides" have been demonstrated in oxidoreductase preparations from yeast and bovine heart mitochondria where they have also been implicated as Q-binding proteins [13, 14] and in interactions between the c-type cytochromes [15]. Studies in mutant yeast strains have indicated that several of these core subunits are essential for the maturation of apocytochrome b and that mutations in their structural genes cause pleiotropic defects in the assembly of the overall complex [10]. Moreover, gene inactivation procedures have revealed that a 17 kDa subunit may be necessary for proper assembly of both the cytochrome bc_1 and aa_3 complexes [16]. For further analysis, the *R. sphaeroides* 14 kDa subunit was purified to homogeneity by chromatography on a Biogel P-30 column in the presence of 50% aqueous formic acid and found to be rich in charged and polar amino acid residues [2]. Initial attempts to obtain sequence information on this protein proved unsuccessful since manual Edman degradation indicated that the N-terminus was blocked and not rendered accessible by deblocking procedures. Cyanogen bromide cleavage gave rise to a blocked N-terminal fragment and a C-terminal peptide which was found by gas-phase sequence analysis to comprise more than one-third of the protein. Within the sequence of 48 identified residues, an apparent transmembrane segment was located near the C-terminus [2]. Two further sequences comprising about 40 additional residues were determined from peptides isolated after cleavage of the blocked N-terminal fragment at tryptophan residues with BNPS-skatole. Portions of these sequences were confirmed with tryptic fragments from the intact protein. A preliminary search has failed to reveal significant homologies to any known or deduced protein sequences. Further studies are in progress to determine the complete primary structure and the structural and functional roles for this 14 kDa component.

ACKNOWLEDGEMENTS

These studies were supported by U.S. National Science Foundation grant DMB85-12587 and Biomedical Research Support grant PHS RR 07058-23. D. J. P. and R. T. were the recipients of fellowships from the Charles and Johanna Busch Memorial Fund Award to the Rutgers Bureau of Biological Research.

REFERENCES

1 Bowyer, J.R., Hunter,C.N., Ohnishi, T. and Niederman, R.A. (1985) J. Biol. Chem. 260, 3295-3304
2 Purvis, D.J., Theiler,R. and Niederman, R.A. Submitted for publication
3 Reilly, P.A. and Niederman, R.A. (1986) J. Bacteriol. 167, 153-159
4 Ljungdahl, P.O., Pennoyer, J.D., Robertson, D.E. and Trumpower, B. (1987) *Biochim. Biophys.* Acta 891, 227-241
5 Towbin, H., Staehelin, T. and Gordon, J. (1979) Proc. Nat. Acad. Sci. USA 76, 4350-4354
6 Broglie, R.M. and Niederman, R.A. (1979) J. Bacteriol.138, 788-798
7 Yu, L., Mei, Q-C. and Yu, C-A. (1984) J. Biol. Chem. 259, 5752-5760
8 Wilson, E., Farley, T.M. and Takemoto, J.Y. (1985) J. Biol. Chem. 260, 10288-10292
9 Yu, L. and Yu, C-A. (1987) Biochemistry 26, 3658-3664
10 Crivellone, M.D., Wu, M. and Tzagoloff, A.(1988) J. Biol. Chem. 263, 14323-14333
11 Yang, X. and Trumpower, B.L. (1986) *J. Biol. Chem.*261, 12282-12289
12 Wynn, R.M., Gaul, D.F., Chai, W-K., Shaw, R.W. and Knaff, D.B. (1986) Photosyn. Res. 9, 181-195
13 Yu, L., Yang, F-D. and Yu, C-A. (1985) J. Biol. Chem. 260, 963-973
14 Yu, L., Yang, F-D., and Yu, C-A., Tsai, A-L. and Palmer, G. (1986) Biochim. Biophys. Acta 848, 305-311
15 Kim, C.H. and King, T.E. (1983) J. Biol. Chem. 258, 13543-13551
16 Schmitt, M.E. and Trumpower, B.L. (1987) in Cytochrome Systems: Molecular Biology and Bioenergetics (Papa, S., Chance, B., and Ernster, L. eds), Plenum, New York

PREDICTION OF STRUCTURE FOR CYTOCHROME B FROM SEQUENCE DATA: WHAT INFORMATION IS AVAILABLE FROM SEQUENCE COMPARISON.

A.R. CROFTS, C.-H. YUN, R.B. GENNIS and S. MAHALINGHAM, Biophysics Division, U. of Illinois, 607 S. Goodwin, Urbana, IL 61801

1. INTRODUCTION

A preliminary model for the structure of the cytochrome b subunit of the UQH$_2$:cyt c$_2$ oxidoreductase of *R. sphaeroides* has been predicted (1,2) using a combination of methods; Chou-Fasman (3), Robson-Garnier (4) and Rao-Argos (5) prediction, hydrophobic analysis (6-8) using several hydrophobic indices, and amphipathic analysis (9). Further refinement has relied on comparison of subunits from mitochondria, chloroplast and bacteria by homologous alignment, mutability analysis, and comparative prediction. The model has eight transmembrane helices (1), and three amphipathic helices, which are strongly conserved. The main difference from previously accepted models (10,11) is in the removal of one transmembrane helix (helix IV) to an amphipathic situation. The most obvious structural consequence is that the sidedness of the sequence to the C-terminal end of helix IV has been reset, so that the liganding helices (II and V) are parallel in the new model. We have suggested (2) a new nomenclature in which the eight trans-membrane helices are lettered A-H, and the amphipathic helices are ab, cd (helix IV of refs. 10,11), and ef.

A model for the tertiary structure is discussed, in which six transmembrane helices are packed about the two heme prosthetic groups to allow for the putative His ligands, site-directed mutations of the His ligands, heme-modifying mutants, inhibitor resistance lesions, topological studies using *pho*A fusions, and extensive biophysical data.

2. METHODS

2.1. Information about structure from the sequence.

Several methods are currently used to extract information about secondary structure from sequence data. These have been developed primarily for use with soluble proteins, and are based on the existing structural data base derived from X-ray crystallography. We have used and developed methods more appropriate for predicting structure in membrane proteins.

2.1.1. Secondary structural prediction based on probability.

a)   Chou-Fasman (3); Robson-Garnier (4): based on aqueous proteins, and do not work well with membrane proteins. Extensions using neural-network learning algorithms are not much better.

b)   Rao-Argos membrane helix parameter (5): predicts membrane helices and termination, but not structure outside hydrophobic phase.

2.1.2.   Hydropathy analysis (6-8). Many hydropathy indices based on various physico-chemical principles. In general, some of these predict protein interiors well, and have been used with some success to predict membrane-spanning helices.

2.1.3.   Modified structural predictors, incorporating membrane helix prediction. The programs *MCF* and *MPREDICT* incorporate hydrophobic offset, or membrane helix prediction, to adjust the "standard" predictors to take account of the dif-

M. Baltscheffsky (ed.), Current Research in Photosynthesis, Vol. III, 263–266.
© 1990 *Kluwer Academic Publishers. Printed in the Netherlands.*

ferent properties of the hydrophobic phase.

2.1.4. Amphipathic analysis. The pattern of hydrophobicity along the sequence is a good predictor of secondary folding in known structures (9), and seems promising as a prediction method in membrane proteins. Alternating hydrophilic and hydrophobic spans at the helical repeat have been identified in the cytochrome b subunit, and are highly conserved. We suggest that at least three amphipathic helices can be identified in this way.

2.1.5. Mutability analysis. The importance of a residue in structure, function, ligation, etc. can be gauged from the degree to which it is conserved across species boundaries, as judged by sequence alignment and comparison. The pattern of mutability contains additional information about secondary and tertiary folding of the sequence (12). We have aligned sequences for cyt b subunits and scored each point in the sequence for mutability, using information theory (13). Changes in mutability at the helical repeat can be used to search for helices in which one side is involved in specific interactions (conserved) and the other in non-specific interactions (mutable). Such a pattern might indicate the orientation of a helix with respect to the rest of the structure. In membrane-spanning helices, the more mutable surface might be expected to be exposed to the lipid phase (12).

The set of programs used (the *SEQANAL* package) is available from the Biotechnology Center, University of Illinois.

3. STRUCTURE OF CYTOCHROME B SUBUNIT.

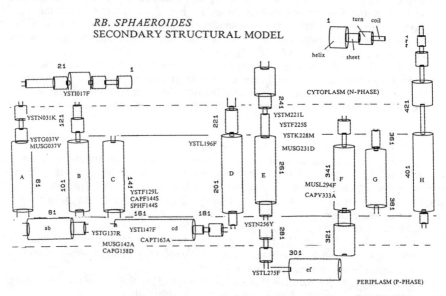

RB. SPHAEROIDES
SECONDARY STRUCTURAL MODEL

Fig. 1 shows the secondary structure predicted for the cyt b subunit of *Rb. sphaeroides*, using a "consensus" derived from the output of *MCF, MPREDICT*, amphipathic analysis, and sequence alignment and comparison. The structure has been folded in the membrane to take account of hydropathic and amphipathic analysis, to give the eight trans-membrane helix model previously proposed for the yeast cyt b subunit. Also shown are the locations of residues modified in inhibitor resistant strains, taken from refs. 14-16. To date, all lesions giving resistance to inhibitors at the antimycin site have mapped on the new model to the cytoplasmic (N-phase) side, and all those at the myxothiazol site to the periplasmic (P-phase) side. Similarly, data from *pho*A fusion experiments, and site directed mutation of putative heme ligands (C.-H. Yun, R.B. Gennis, and A.R. Crofts, unpublished) support the model.

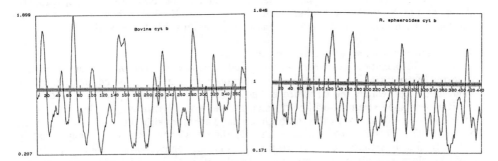

Fig. 2 shows profiles of amphipathy at the helical repeat (100° rotation at each residue, 9) for representative sequences, calculated using the Kyte-Doolittle hydropathy index (6), with a span of 11 in the running average, followed by smoothing with a span of 7. Helical amphipathy is consistently found at the relative positions indicated by the helices ab, cd, and ef in these and all other sequences tested. Helix cd showed a somewhat changeable character, with amphipathy varying inversely with hydrophobicity. Several transmembrane helices showed helical amphipathy at one or both ends which was conserved across species, and the hydrophilic span connecting B and C also always showed strong helical amphipathy. These spans may indicate that helices extend beyond the hydrophobic domain.

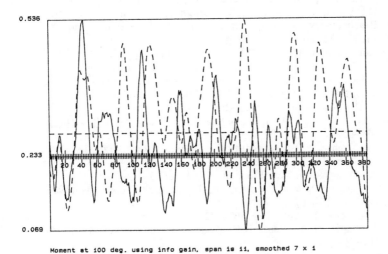

Moment at 100 deg. using info gain, span is 11, smoothed 7 x 1

Fig. 3 shows the mutability moment at the helical repeat of yeast cyt b (the data, except for inserted residues, is identical for all 15 sequences in the comparison). Helical wheels and cylinders show that helix A has a marked mutability moment, with one side of the helix consisting of highly conserved residues. We suggest that this side faces the protein, while the unconserved side faces the lipid. Residues modified in inhibitor resistant strains which map to the N-terminal end of the helix are at the "interface" between the protein and the lipid, and a similar pattern is found for residues at the C-terminal end of helix C. Amphipathic helices ab and cd contain substantial spans showing helical mutability. Several other putative helices (D, E, F, H) show helical mutability at one or both ends. The dashed line shows the membrane helix potential (5).

3.1.   Tertiary Structure of the cytochrome b subunit.

The information available provides useful constraints on preliminary models of the tertiary structure. As we have previously pointed out (1,2), based on the reaction center model for which the structure is known (cf. 13), residues which are modified in inhibitor resistance strains are likely to map in the tertiary structure to the same volume as the catalytic site at which the inhibitor binds. Together with the heme ligands, which fix the relative positions of helices B and D, the resistance mutations suggest that helices A,D and E should be close at the cytoplasmic ends, while helices C,E, and F should be close at their periplasmic ends. Amphipathic helix cd (at it's N-terminal end) has several mutations on the same side of the helix, and these need to interface with the same volume. Orientation of the helices is indicated by their mutability moment. A preliminary model including these constraints, with helices A-H vertical has been suggested (2), but will obviously need refinement as new information on spatial relationships becomes available.

ACKNOWLEDGEMENTS. Supported by PHS 5 RO1 GM26305 and 2 RO1 GM35438

REFERENCES
1   Crofts, A.R., Robinson, H.H., Andrews, K., Van Doren, S. and Berry, E. (1987) In "Cytochrome Systems: Molecular Biology and Bioenergetics", (Papa, S., Chance, B. and Ernster, L., eds.) pp. 617-624, Plenum Publ., New York.
2   Crofts, A.R., Wang, Z., Chen, Y., Mahalingham, S. Yun, C.-H. and Gennis, R.B. (1989) in "Biochemistry, Bioenergetics and Clinical Aspects of Ubiquinone", (Lenaz, G., ed.) Francis & Taylor, Ltd., London. In press.
3   Chou, P.Y. and Fasman, G.D. (1978) Adv.in Enzymology, 47, 45-148.
4   Robson, B., Douglas, G.M. and Garnier, J. (1983) in "Computing in Biology" (Geisow and Barret, eds.) pp.132-177. Elsevier Biomedical Press.
5   Rao, J.K.M. and Argos, P. (1986) Biochim. Biophys. Acta 869, 197-214.
6   Kyte, J. and Doolittle, R.F. (1982) J. Mol. Biol. 157, 105-132.
7   Engelman, D.M., Steitz, T.A. and Goldman, A. (1986) Ann. Rev. Biophys. Biophys. Chem. 15, 321-353.
8   Cornette, J.L., Cease, K.B., Margalit, H., Spouge, J.L., Berzofsky, J.A. and DeLisi, C. (1987) J. Mol. Biol. 195, 659-685
9   Eisenberg, D. (1984) Ann. Rev. Biochem. 53, 595-623.
10 Widger, W.R., Cramer, W.A., Herrmann, R. G. and Trebst, A. (1984) Proc. Natl. Acad. Sci. USA 81, 674-678.
11 Saraste, M. (1984) FEBS Lett. 166, 367-372.
12 Komiya, H. Yeates, T.O., Rees, D.C, Allen, J.P. and Feher, G. (1988) Proc. Natl. Acad. Sci. USA 85, 9012-9016.
13 Sarai, A. and Takeda, Y. (1989) Science, submitted.
14 di Rago, J.-P. and Colson, A.-M. (1988) J. Biol. Chem. 263, 12564-12570.
15 Howell, N., Appel, J., Cook, J.P, Howell, B. and Hauswirth, W.W. (1987) J. Biol. Chem., 262, 2411-2414.
16 Daldal, F. (1987) Personal Communication.

CHARACTERISATION OF A FULL-LENGTH cDNA CLONE ENCODING THE PEA
RIESKE Fe-S PROTEIN : IMPORT AND PROCESSING BY ISOLATED
CHLOROPLASTS.

A. Hugh Salter & John C. Gray
BOTANY SCHOOL, UNIVERSITY OF CAMBRIDGE, CAMBRIDGE CB2 3EA U.K.

1. INTRODUCTION

The cytochrome b-f complex of the chloroplast thylakoid membrane
operates as a plastoquinol-plastocyanin oxidoreductase and is thus
analogous to the mitochondrial cytochrome bc_1 complex with which it
bears a large amount of structural and functional similarity. It
consists in all higher plants of four components, which are
cytochrome f , cytochrome b-563, the Rieske Fe-S protein, and a 17kDa
protein (subunit IV)[1]. The cytochrome b-f complex has also been
reported to contain small polypeptides[1] and a chloroplast-encoded
5kDa polypeptide has recently been identified in maize and
spinach[2]. The 20 kDa Rieske Fe-S protein may be removed from the
isolated complex by hydroxyapatite chromatography in the presence
of Triton X-100[3].

The genes that encode the components of the complex are distributed
between the nucleus and the chloroplast. The chloroplast genes
$petA$, $petB$ and $petD$ encode cytochrome f, cytochrome b-563 and
subunit IV respectively[4]. The Rieske Fe-S protein has been
identified as the product of a nuclear gene. The protein is
synthesised from poly-A RNA as a 26kDa precursor which is processed
to the mature 20kDa protein, suggesting a cytoplasmic site of
synthesis[5]. The mRNA for the Rieske Fe-S protein can be hybrid-
selected using a cDNA clone and translated in rabbit reticulocyte
lysates to give the 26kDa precursor, which can be imported and
processed to the mature size in isolated spinach chloroplasts[6].
Although the nuclear gene itself has not yet been identified, cDNA
clones from spinach[6,7] and pea[8] have been isolated and shown to
encode the Rieske Fe-S protein by comparison of the derived amino
acid sequence with partial protein sequence.

The aim of the work described in this paper was to study the uptake
and assembly of the Rieske Fe-S protein in pea. An isolated full-
length cDNA[8] was used to direct transcription and translation *in
vitro*, in order to produce a precursor protein for uptake and
processing experiments.

M. Baltscheffsky (ed.), Current Research in Photosynthesis, Vol. III, 267–270.
© 1990 *Kluwer Academic Publishers. Printed in the Netherlands.*

2. METHODS AND MATERIALS

Rieske Fe-S protein was purified from isolated pea cytochrome b-f complex using published methods[3,10] and antibodies were raised in rabbits. These were used to screen a cDNA library in λgt11 as described previously[11]. A clone encoding the majority of the Rieske Fe-S protein was used to rescreen the cDNA library to obtain further clones. A full-length cDNA was thus obtained[8]. The insert from this clone was inserted into the expression vector pSP64. Following transcription *in vitro* using SP6 RNA polymerase and translation in a wheatgerm extract, ^{35}S-labelled translation products were incubated with isolated pea chloroplasts to study uptake and processing essentially as described by Bartlett *et al*[12]. The location and fate of the imported precursor was investigated by further subfractionation. The *N*-terminus of the mature pea Rieske Fe-S protein was determined by gas-phase sequencing of Rieske protein transferred to PVDF membranes.

3. RESULTS AND DISCUSSION

A full-length cDNA clone for the Rieske Fe-S protein encoding a precursor polypeptide of 228 amino acid residues, consisting of a presequence of 50 amino acids (5.3 kDa) and a mature protein 178 amino acids long (18.5 kDa) was isolated as previously described[8]. The deduced amino acid sequence is shown in Figure 1 together with that of spinach, and also with the *N*-terminal protein sequence of the pea protein. There is no significant similarity to the spinach nucleotide sequence upstream of the methionine shown as the start of the pea precursor in Figure 1.

There is little similarity of the pea presequence to the common amino acid framework which has been suggested for nuclear-encoded chloroplast proteins[13], and the presequence is not as well conserved between pea and spinach as the mature protein. The *C*-terminal region of the mature protein containing a cysteine-rich region is extremely well conserved between all known Rieske Fe-S proteins.This is presumed to be the active site where the 2Fe-2S prosthetic groups are bound. In particular the motifs CTHLGCV and CPCHGS are very strongly conserved, and the four cysteines are possible Fe ligands[14]. The histidine residues have also been implicated as possible ligands by ENDOR mearurements[15]. The *N*-terminal hydrophobic domain, underlined in Figure 1 is assumed to be the part of the protein that anchors the protein into the thylakoid membrane[16].

```
Ps(cDNA)                    MSSTIYLPQSPSQLCSGKSGISCPSIALLVKPTRTQMTG-RGNKGMKITCQ

So(cDNA)    MIISIFNQLHLTENSSLMASFTLSSATPSQLCSSKNGMFAPSLALAKAGRVNVLISKERIRGMKLTCQ

Ps(Prot)    ATSIPADRV

Ps(cDNA)    ATSIPADRVPDMSKRKTLNLLLLGALSLPTAGMLVPYGSFLVPPGLGSSTGGTVAKDAVGNDVVATEW

So(cDNA)    ATSIPADNVPDMQKRETLNLLLLGALSLPTGYMLLPYASFFVPPGGGAGTGGTIAKDALGNDVIAAEW

Ps(cDNA)    LKTHATGDVLYTGLKGDPAT-LVVGKDRTLATFAINAVCTHLGCVVPFNQAGNKFICPCHGSGTNDQG

So(cDNA)    LKTHAPGDRTLTQGLKGDPTYLVVESDKTLATFGINAVCTHLGCVVPFNAAENKFICPCHGSQYNNQG

Ps(cDNA)    RVVRGPAPLSLALAHCDVGVEDGKVVFVPWVGTDFRTGDAPWWS-

So(cDNA)    RVVRGPAPLSLALAHCDVD--DGKVVFVPWTETDFRTGEAPWWSA
```

Figure 1. Comparison of pea(Ps) and spinach (So) chloroplast
        Rieske Fe-S proteins
The derived amino acid sequences (shown as cDNA) from the cDNAs are
given together with the *N*-terminal protein sequence of the pea
protein (shown as Prot). The proposed Fe-S binding domains are
shown boxed and an *N*-terminal hydrophobic domain is underlined. The
arrow indicates the processing site between the mature protein and
the presequence.

Transcription of a pSP64 construct containing the full-length
Rieske cDNA followed by translation in a wheatgerm extract produces
a 27kDa polypeptide which corresponds well to the size obtained by
hybrid selection and translation of spinach mRNA[6].To investigate the
ability of isolated chloroplasts to import and assemble the Rieske
protein, ^{35}S-methionine labelled translation products were incubated
with isolated chloroplasts for 30 minutes in the light. At the end
of the incubation, chloroplasts were reisolated and fractionated to
give thylakoids and an octylglucoside fraction enriched in
cytochrome *b-f* complex[1], and the products analysed by SDS PAGE
(Figure 2).

This figure shows that the precursor protein produced by the
wheatgerm extract is correctly imported and assembled into the
cytochrome *b-f* complex. Track 1 shows the input from a wheatgerm
translation. There is a major band at 27kDa, and a minor band most
likely derived from initiation at the first internal methionine.
From the appearance within reisolated chloroplasts of a band of the
correct size (20kDa) in the total (Track 2), proteased (Track 3),
thylakoid (Track 4) and octylglucoside supernatant (Track 6)
fractions, we conclude that the precursor protein produced is
informationally sufficient to be imported and assembled correctly.
The processing would appear to occur in the stroma, since the
processed protein can also be found in this fraction (Track 5),
together with the imported precursor. The pathways of processing
and assembly are being further investigated.

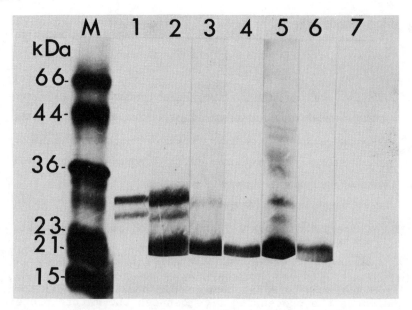

Figure 2. Uptake by isolated chloroplasts of translation products directed by the pea Rieske Fe-S cDNA.
Track 1, ^{35}S-Methionine-labelled wheatgerm translation products. Track 2, Reisolated chloroplasts. Track 3, Thermolysin treated and reisolated chloroplasts. Track 4, Thylakoid fraction. Track 5, Stromal fraction. Track 6, Octylglucoside extraction supernatant of thylakoid fraction. Track 7, Octylglucoside extracted thylakoid pellet. Track M is ^{14}C labelled marker proteins with sizes in kDa.

REFERENCES

1   Hurt, E. & Hauska, G.(1982) J.Bioenerg. Biomembr. 14,405-424
2   Haley, J. & Bogorad, L. (1989) Proc. Natl. Acad. Sci. USA. 86,1534-1538
3   Hurt, E. et al (1981) FEBS Lett. 134,1-5
4   Willey, D.L. & Gray J.C. (1988) Photosyn. Res. 17,125-144
5   Alt, J. et al (1983) EMBO J. 2,979-986
6   Tittgen, J. et al (1986) Mol. Gen. Genet. 204,258-265
7   Stepphun, J. et al (1987) Mol. Gen. Genet. 210,171-177
8   Salter, A.H. et al (1989) in Techniques and New Developments in Photosynthesis, (Malkin, R. & Barber, J. eds) pp. 473-476, Plenum, New York
9   Pfefferkorn, B. and Meyer, H.E. (1987) FEBS Lett. 206,233-237
10 Phillips, A.L. and Gray, J.C. (1983) Eur. J. Biochem. 137,553-560
11 Newman, B.N. and Gray, J.C. (1988) Plant Mol. Biol. 10,511-520
12 Bartlett, S.G. et al (1982) in Methods in Chloroplast Molecular Biology (Edelman, M., Hallick R. B. & Chua N.-H., eds.) pp. 1081-1092 Elsevier,Amsterdam.
13 Karlin-Neumann, G.A. & Tobin, E. (1986) EMBO J. 5,9-13
14 Harnisch, U. et al (1985) Eur. J. Biochem. 149,95-99
15 Cline, J.F. et al (1985) J. Biol. Chem. 260,3251-3254
16 Schagger, H. et al (1987) FEBS. Lett. 219,161-168

ON THE SITE OF ACTION OF NQNO IN THE CYTOCHROME b_6-f COMPLEX
AND THE QUESTION OF INTERHEME TRANSFER

P. N. FURBACHER, M. E. GIRVIN, and W. A. CRAMER
DEPT. OF BIOLOGICAL SCIENCES, PURDUE UNIVERSITY,
WEST LAFAYETTE, IN 47907 U.S.A.

INTRODUCTION

The increase in amplitude of cytochrome b_6 photoreduction and inhibition of the slow electrochromic phase by the compound NQNO was an important observation with regard to the understanding of function of the cytochrome b_6-f complex (1). The inferred analogy to the action of antimycin A provided support for a Q cycle mechanism. The basis of this analogy and the evidence supporting interheme transfer associated with the Q cycle is examined in this study.

RESULTS AND DISCUSSION (2)

Reduction of Half of Cytochrome b_6 by NADPH-Ferredoxin. Dithionite in the presence of anthraquinone as a lipophilic redox mediator caused the reduction of 1.95 ± 0.20 (four trials) hemes/600 Chl (Fig. 1A). The amplitude of the cyt b_6 heme reduction by NADPH in the presence of ferredoxin is approximately 1.08 ± 0.09 (three trials) heme equivalent/600 Chl, half of that obtained in the presence of dithionite (Fig. 1A). Reduction of cyt b_6 by NADPH requires ferredoxin (Fig. 1B), as noted previously by others (e.g., ref. 3).

NADPH-Ferredoxin Reduces Heme b_n. The pathway of cyt b_6 reduction by NADPH-ferredoxin is through the outside heme, since the reaction is not affected by the presence of the p-side inhibitor DBMIB. Therefore, the one-heme equivalent or 50% of the cyt b_6 that is reduced must be either (i) the stromal-side heme, b_n, in all complexes, or (ii) a 1:1 mixture of fully oxidized and fully reduced complexes, the latter perhaps because of thylakoid membrane heterogeneity. These two possibilities can be tested since the amplitude of flash reduction would be smaller by a factor of two if half of the complexes are fully reduced, but unaffected if b_n is initially reduced and b_p oxidized in all complexes. The amplitude of cyt b_6 reduction by a single turnover laser flash, measured in the absence and presence of NQNO, was not affected by pre-reduction with NADPH-Fd (Fig. 2A vs. 2B). This shows that there can be at most only a small fraction of b_6-f complexes in which both hemes are reduced by NADPH-Fd, so that heme b_n alone is reduced by NADPH-Fd in most complexes.

Site of Action of NQNO. In analogy to the proposed action of antimycin A in chromatophores and mitochondria, the effect of NQNO on cyt b_6 reduction was attributed to an inhibition of heme b_n oxidation that did not inhibit non-cyclic electron transport (1,4). The increase in amplitude of the flash-induced reduction of cyt b_6 caused by addition of NQNO also occurred, however, when heme b_n was pre-reduced by NADPH-Fd (Fig. 2A,B). Thus, NQNO caused an increase in the amplitude of heme b_p reduction and not heme b_n. The lack of effect on heme b_n is corroborated by a similar absence of inhibition of H^+ uptake associated with turnover of the b_6-f complex (5).

M. Baltscheffsky (ed.), Current Research in Photosynthesis, Vol. III, 271–274.
© 1990 *Kluwer Academic Publishers. Printed in the Netherlands.*

FIGURE 1. Comparison of (A) chemical (dithionite) and (B) enzymatic (NADPH-ferredoxin) reduction of cytochrome b6. Chloroplasts, 80 μg Chl/ml in a vertical cuvette, path length of 1.8 cm, with 1 μM DBMIB, 0.7 μM NADPH, 160 units glucose oxidase, 5 mM glucose, and 5 mM ascorbate. In (A) and (B), upper trace, dithionite and 10 mM anthraquinone were used to fully reduce both hemes. Lower traces in (A) and (B), NADPH added in the presence (A) and absence (B) of Fd. Temp, 20°C. Heme reduction calculated from ΔE_{mM} (563-572) = 17 (ref. 2).

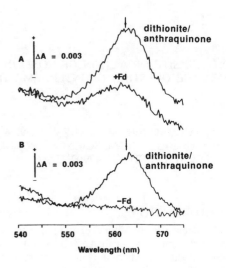

Cooperative Reoxidation of Cytochrome b_6. In the presence or absence of NQNO, the rate and extent of reoxidation following the flash-induced reduction was larger by a factor of 4-5, with $t_{1/2} \approx 30$ ms (Fig. 2B), when heme b_n was pre-reduced by NADPH-Fd. The effective $t_{1/2}$ for the oxidation in the absence of NADPH (Fig. 2A) was > 100 ms. The reoxidation is seen in Fig. 2B to extend below the original baseline. This has been observed only when heme b_n is initially reduced by NADPH. Since the faster reoxidation in the presence of NADPH-Fd occurs in the presence and absence of NQNO, the stimulation of the amplitude of b_6 reduction by NQNO is not a result of blocking reoxidation of heme b_p. The effect of NQNO might arise from an interaction of NQNO with the cytochrome and, in particular, elevation of the E_m of heme b_p (6). The faster reoxidation rate after pre-reduction of heme b_n implies a role of cyt b_6 in the pathway of Fd-dependent PSI cyclic electron transport. The pathway would involve a cooperative oxidant-induced reduction of heme b_p and Fd-dependent reduction of heme b_n, and a cooperative oxidation of the two hemes (Fig. 2A,B) by PQ.

The spectrum of the flash-induced reduction of cyt b_6 in the presence of NQNO is similar to that obtained by chemical and enzymatic reduction (compare Fig. 2C with Fig. 1A). Spectral data obtained in the presence of oxidized ferredoxin (open symbols) and ferredoxin reduced by NADPH (closed symbols) were not distinguishable. The maximum amplitude of the reduction induced by a saturating laser or xenon flash corresponded to 0.60 ± 0.09 heme/600 Chl (nine trials).

Multiple Flash Reduction of Cytochrome b_6. A Q cycle model involving interheme transfer implies that the two hemes of cyt b_6 should be reducible by successive light flashes (7) if their reoxidation is inhibited by NQNO, as was proposed for its mechanism of action. The effect of two successive saturating laser flashes, and of five xenon flashes (Fig. 3), on the amplitude of cyt b_6 reduction was tested in the presence and absence of NQNO, and at 9°C to slow the reoxidation, conditions that should allow the maximum cytochrome reduction. It was not possible to obtain an increase in the amplitude of b_6 reduction beyond 0.6-0.7 heme/flash on

A heme b_n oxidized

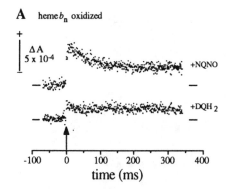

B heme b_n reduced by NADPH/ferredoxin

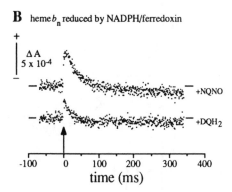

FIGURE 2. Effect of NADPH-ferredoxin on the amplitude of flash-induced reduction of cyt b_6. Reduction in the absence (A) and presence (B) of NADPH-Fd. Chloroplasts, 40 µg Chl/ml, 1 cm path, 4 µM DCMU, 5 µM gramicidin, 500 µM duroquinol, 5 µM Fd, 1 µM NQNO when present (upper traces, A and B), 5.5 mM glucose and 160 units glucose oxidase. Pre-reduction in (B) by 1 mM NADPH. Traces, average of 60 events (563 nm — 572 nm). Hash marks on the two sides indicate the position of the original baseline. (C) Spectrum of flash-induced absorbance change in the presence of Fd and NQNO, and in the absence (□) and presence (■) of NADPH (2).

C

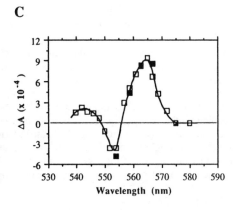

successive flashes (Fig 3). A similar result has been obtained by Rich *et al.* (8). As in the case of the single-flash experiment (Figs. 2A,B), the presence of NADPH did not affect the amplitude of the photoreduction (not shown).

It is concluded that it is predominantly only one heme, heme b_p, that is reduced by a light flash, and that interheme electron transfer was not observed under the conditions of these experiments. The quinone binding site that serves for reduction of heme b_p by $PQ^{\bullet-}$ can also serve in the green alga Chlorella as the site for DNP-INT-sensitive oxidation of pre-reduced cytochrome b_6 (9). The use of this pathway for the oxidation of heme b_p would be consistent with the conclusion that the electrogenic step under reducing conditions does not arise from interheme transfer (10). One should note that there has been a report of interheme electron transfer in vitro in the isolated cytochrome b_6-f complex (11).

Electrogenic H^+ translocation. A basic question is whether electrogenic H^+ translocation and an $H^+/e^- = 2$ ratio in the b_6-f complex are obligatory for non-cyclic electron transport at steady-state values of the ΔpH or $\Delta\bar{\mu}_{H^+}$. If so, then the H^+/e^- would be 3 for whole chain electron transport, and the ATP/2e⁻ ratio = 2. The observed maximum value of the maximum predicted ATP/2e⁻ ratio is approximately 1.25 (12) under conditions of non-cyclic electron transport, close to the value, 1.33, predicted if the $H^+/e^- = 1$ and 2 for the b_6-f complex and

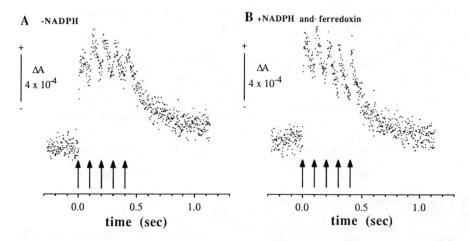

FIGURE 3. Multiple flash reduction of cytochrome b_6 in the absence of NADPH. Xenon flashes were spaced at 0.1 sec within a train, while repeated flash trains were spaced 10 sec apart. (2)

whole chain electron transport, respectively. A value of $H^+/e^- = 1$ for the b_6-f complex is also implied by the electrically neutral oxidation of PQH_2 in the steady-state (13). Thus, the issue of the mechanism of electrogenic H^+ translocation would appear to concern the small $\Delta\tilde{\mu}_{H^+}$ situation, or single flash experiment in the laboratory. In the latter case, it is our opinion that the direct evidence supporting a Q cycle in chloroplasts is not conclusive, and other mechanisms for electrogenic H^+ translocation should not be overlooked.

REFERENCES

1   Selak, M.A. and Whitmarsh, J. (1982) FEBS Lett. 150, 286-292
2   Furbacher, P.N., Girvin, M.E., and Cramer, W.A. (1989) Biochemistry 28, in press
3   Telfer, A. and Barber, J. (1981) in **Photosynthesis. II.** (Akoyunoglou, G., ed.), pp. 559-568, Balaban Int. Sci., Philadelphia
4   Jones, R.W. and Whitmarsh, J. (1988) Biochim. Biophys. Acta 933, 258-268
5   Hope, A.B. and Rich, P.R. (1989) Biochim. Biophys. Acta 975, 96-103
6   Clark, R.D. and Hind, G. (1983) Proc. Natl. Acad. Sci., U.S.A. 80, 6249-6253
7   Hladik, J., Snozzi, M., and Bachofen, R. (1987) Biochem. Biophys. Res. Comm. 148, 170-177
8   Rich, P., Heathcote, P., and Moss, D.A. (1987) Biochim. Biophys. Acta 892, 138-151
9   Delosme, R., Joliot, P., and Trebst, A. (1987) Biochim. Biophys. Acta 893, 1-6
10 Girvin, M.E. and Cramer, W.A. (1984) Biochim. Biophys. Acta 767, 29-38
11 Nitschke, W., Hauska, G., and Crofts, A.R. (1988) FEBS Lett. 232, 204-208
12 Hosler, J.P. and Yocum, C. (1985) Biochim. Biophys. Acta 808, 21-31
13 Graan, T. and Ort, D.R. (1983) J. Biol. Chem. 258, 2381-2836

(This research was supported by NIH GM-38323.)

Analysis of Cytochrome Absorption Changes in Spinach Chloroplasts

Elke Volz and Bernd Rumberg
Max-Volmer-Institut, Technische Universität Berlin,
D-1000 Berlin 12, FRG

1. Introduction

By spectral identification and kinetic characterization of three types of absorption changes in the spectral region between 390 and 450 nm, namely those of cytochrome-b_6, cytochrome-f and P-700, we give evidence for the concept of the Q-cycle as proposed by Mitchell [1] and get insight into the mechanism of the control of it. With this respect we resume our work on absorption changes of cytochrome-b_6 we put forward more than 20 years ago [2, 3]. The results presented here at the same time imply a profound theoretical basis for the understanding of the experimental results on the variability of the H/e ratio in [4].

2. Theory (Control of the Q-Cycle)

The theoretical concept is based on the following sequence of electron transfer steps, where C and P stand for the reaction centres of photosystem II and I, respectively, Q for plastoquinone, R for the Rieske-FeS-centre, Y for plastocyanin, and A for the terminal electron acceptor.

$$Cyt\text{-}b_{high} \underset{}{\overset{K_1}{\rightleftharpoons}} Cyt\text{-}b_{low}$$

$$H_2O \longrightarrow C \xrightarrow[k_o]{k_2} Q \xrightarrow[k_1]{} R \overset{K_2}{\rightleftharpoons} Cyt\text{-}f \overset{K_3}{\rightleftharpoons} Y \overset{K_4}{\rightleftharpoons} P \longrightarrow A$$

Activation of the Q-cycle depends crucially on the redox states of both Cyt-f and Cyt-b_{low}. This is explained in the following.

Plastoquinole (Q^{red}) after binding to R gives up its first electron obligatorily to R^{ox}, leaving the semiquinone behind, the lifetime of which compared to that of plastoquinole is short. The reaction route of the semiquinone in the first instance depends on the redox state of Cyt-f.

If Cyt-f is in the oxidized state a fast electron transfer from R^{red} to Cyt-f^{ox} takes place and the restored R^{ox} is re-reduced by electron transfer from the semiquinone. In this case the Q-cycle is not activated.

M. Baltscheffsky (ed.), Current Research in Photosynthesis, Vol. III, 275–278.
© 1990 Kluwer Academic Publishers. Printed in the Netherlands.

If Cyt-f is in the reduced state from the beginning, fast restoration of R^{ox} is not possible. In this case the electron acceptor of the semiquinone is Cyt-b_{low} pro-vided that it is in the oxidized state. Otherwise plastoquinole is restored by electron backreaction from Cyt-b_{low}^{red}. In this latter case Cyt-b_{low}^{red} lends its electron every second cycle to the semiquinone and the lifetime of Q^{red} at the binding site of R is prolonged by a factor of two.

The relative amount of R-Q^{red}-complexes is given by

$$RQ^{red} = Q^{red}/(Q^{red} + K_B^{-1} Q_t^{-1})$$

where K_B is the binding constant and Q_t the total amount of plastoquinone. Here and in the following the amount of all redox species, i.e. RQ^{red}, Q^{red}, b_l^{red}, b_h^{red}, C^{red}, R^{ox}, f^{red}, Y^{red}, P^{red} are given as fractional numbers, signifying the probability of the respective redox state. The absolute amounts of the protein complexes of photosystem I, photosystem II, and cytochrome-f-b_6 are denoted by z_I, z_{II}, and z_R, respectively.

The rates of non-cyclic electron transfer and that of cyclic electron transfer around the Q-cycle are then given by

$$\dot{e}_{nonc} = k_1 z_R RQ^{red} R^{ox} [2(1 - f^{red}) + f^{red}] = k_1 z_R RQ^{red} R^{ox} (2 - f^{red})$$
$$\dot{e}_{cyc} = k_1 z_R RQ^{red} R^{ox} f^{red} (1 - b_l^{red}) = k_1 z_R RQ^{red} R^{ox} f^{red} b_l^{ox}$$

Hence the H/e ratio is given by

$$H/e = (\dot{e}_{nonc} + \dot{e}_{cyc})/\dot{e}_{nonc} = 1 + f^{red} b_l^{ox}/(2 - f^{red})$$

The steady state amounts of C^{red}, Q^{red}, b_l^{red}, b_h^{red}, R^{ox}, f^{red}, Y^{red}, and P^{red} in dependence on the light intensity are computable from the following four steady state equations and four equilibrium equations. I_r and I_{fr} denote the intensity of red and far-red light, respectively, and α, β account for the absorbance of far-red relative to red light.

$$d(C^{red} z_{II}) = k_{II} z_{II}(I_r + \alpha I_{fr})(1 - C^{red}) - \dot{e}_{nonc} = 0$$
$$2d(Q^{red}Q_t)/dt = (k_o z_{II} C^{red} + k_2 z_R b_h^{red})(1 - Q^{red}) - (\dot{e}_{nonc} + \dot{e}_{cyc}) = 0$$
$$d(b_l^{red} z_R)/dt = \dot{e}_{cyc} - k_2 z_R b_h^{red}(1 - Q^{red}) = 0$$
$$d(P^{red} z_I)/dt = k_I z_I(I_r + \beta I_{fr}) P^{red} - \dot{e}_{nonc} = 0$$
$$K_1 b_l^{red}(1 - b_h^{red}) = (1 - b_l^{red}) b_h^{red}$$
$$K_2 (1 - R^{ox})(1 - f^{red}) = R^{ox} f^{red}$$
$$K_3 f^{red}(1 - Y^{red}) = (1 - f^{red}) Y^{red}$$
$$K_4 Y^{red}(1 - P^{red}) = (1 - Y^{red}) P^{red}$$

The measurable amount of Cyt-b_{low}^{red} in fact is only 50 % of the computable value b_l^{red} because of the electron backreaction to the semiquinone. Therefore, the measurable total amount of Cyt-b in the reduced state in the mean is

$$b\Sigma^{red} = b_h^{red} + 0.5 b_l^{red}$$

The number of electrons which are stored between the two light reactions is

$$n = C^{red} z_{II} + 2Q^{red} Q_t + (RQ^{red} + b\Sigma^{red} + R^{red} + f^{red})z_R + Y^{red} Y_t + P^{red} z_I$$

These electrons can be pumped out subsequent to actinic illumination by weak excitation of photosystem I preferentially which is realized by far-red light. This pumping is described by

$$dn/dt = d(P^{red} z_I)/dt = k_I z_I \beta I_{fr} P^{red} \quad \text{giving}$$

$$n = k_I z_I \beta I_{fr} \int_{t_d = 0}^{\infty} P^{red} dt$$

where t_d denotes the time period after actinic illumination was ceased. The value of the integral can be determined experimentally from the absorption change of P at 705 nm.

Fig. 1, below, left - Schematic time course of absorption changes at 433 nm induced by red actinic light in the presence of far-red background light. The actinic light intensity is 500 Wm⁻², producing approx. 90 % of the maximal electron transport rate.

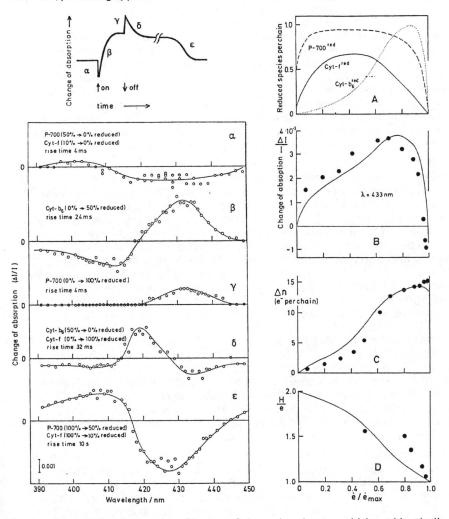

Fig. 2, right - Difference spectra of 5 types of absorption changes which are kinetically separable according to Fig. 1

Fig. 3, right - Amount of reduced P-700, Cyt-f and Cyt-b₆ (A), light-induced steady-state absorption change at 433 nm (B), light-induced change of the number of stored electrons (C), and H/e ratio at the Cyt-b₆-f-complex (D) in dependence on the electron transport rate as changed by change of the actinic light intensity. Standard value of $\dot{e}_{max}$ is 50 mM (mol Chl . s)⁻¹. Note that the results in A, B, C refer to a state of rest which is produced by far-red background illumination. Results in D (taken from ref. 4J) are obtained in the absence of far-red background illumination. All curves have been computed according to the theoretical model.

3. Experimental Conditions

The experimental procedure was essential the same as described earlier [2]. The experiments were performed with suspensions of envelope-free spinach chloroplasts under uncoupled conditions. The reaction medium contained
10 mM KCl, 10 mM tricine, 100 μM benzylviologen, 1 μM nigericin, and
10 μM chlorophyll. The reaction volume was 3 ml, temperature 20 °C, pH 8.0. The intensity of the monitoring beam was 300 mWm^{-2}. In order to overcome undefined starting conditions induced by the monitoring beam, the experiments were performed in the presence of a far-red background light (720 nm, 2.7 Wm^{-2}). Actinic light was red (630 - 700 nm) and duration was 250 ms (high intensity) up to 1 s (low intensity) which was sufficient to reach steady state conditions. The dimension of the rectangular cuvette was 15 x 15 mm. In order to obtain a homogeneous light intensity within the cuvette, actinic light was given simultaneously from two sides facing one another. The intensity was varied between 2 and 1500 Wm^{-2}. Up to ten signals were averaged in order to increase the signal to noise ratio.

4. Results

Fig. 1 gives a schematic drawing of the time course of the absorption changes which appear at 433 nm if actinic light of high intensity (500 Wm^{-2}) is applied. Five distinct kinetic phases can be separated from eachother which we signify by $\alpha, \beta, \gamma, \delta, \varepsilon$. Each of these five phases are associated with an individual difference spectrum as shown in Fig. 2. These difference spectra can be interpreted with respect to both the individual substances they are evoked of (cytochrome-b$_6$, cytochrome-f, P-700), and type and sequence of reactions these substances are involved in. This is outlined in Fig. 2. The results as far refer to special high intensity of actinic light and are in principal agreement with the theoretical concept outlined above. However, the redox states of the substances involved should change in a distinct manner if the intensity of the actinic light is changed. This is shown in Fig. 3A. In order to prove this prediction we measured in dependence on the intensity of the actinic light: (1) the steady state value of the absorption change at 433 nm (with cytochrome-b$_6$, cytochrome-f, and P-700 contributing, the extinction coefficients of which are related to each other as 1 : 0.67 : 0.36 at this wavelength according to the results in Fig. 2), (2) the number of stored electrons (as determined from the area of the absorption changes of P-700 at 705 nm), (3) the H/e ratio, (4) the electron transport rate. The results are presented in Figs. 3B, C, D.

For calculation according to the reaction scheme the following constants were taken from the literature: $z_I = z_{II}$, $= z_R = 2$ m mol/(mol Chl), $Q_t/z_{II} = 6$, $Y_t/z_I = 1$, $k_I/k_{II} = 1$, $k_0 = 1000$ s^{-1}, $K_1 = 100$, $K_2 = 30$, $K_3 = 1$, $K_4 = 10$. By adjustment according to the experimental conditions we define $k_1 = 15$ s^{-1}, $k_2 = 30$ s^{-1}, $K_B^{-1}/z_{II} = 1.2$, $\alpha = 0.13$, $\beta = 0.26$. The principal agreement between experimental and theoretical results gives evidence for the validity of the theoretical concept which also verifies all results on the variability of the H/e ratio presented in [4].

5. Literature

[1] Mitchell, P. (1976), J. Theor. Biol. 62, 327-367
[2] Rumberg, B. (1965), Biochim. Biophys. Acta 102, 354-360
[3] Rumberg, B (1966) in Currents in Photosynthesis (Thomas, J.B. and Goedheer, J.C., eds.) pp. 375-382, Ad. Donker-Publisher, Rotterdam
[4] Schubert, K., Liese, F., and Rumberg, B., this Proceedings

Analysis of the Variability of the H/e Stoichiometry in Spinach Chloroplasts

Karsten Schubert, Frank Liese and Bernd Rumberg
Max-Volmer-Institut, Technische Universität Berlin,
D-1000 Berlin 12, FRG

1. Introduction

Special interest in the variability of the H/e ratio comes from two sources:
(1) Mechanistic aspects regarding the function of the cytochrome-b_6-f-complex may be read out from changes of the H/e ratio as influenced by different parameters.
(2) The H/e ratio determines the number of H^+ which are available at the ATPase for the production of ATP. H/ATP ratios of 3 reported in the literature are mostly based on an assumed H/e ratio of 2 and any change of it would change the H/ATP ratio to the same extent.
The experimental studies presented here extend our previous work on this subject [1]. Evidence is given that the H/e ratio varies between 2 and 3.

2. Experimental procedure

The experiments were performed with suspensions of envelope-free chloroplasts isolated from spinach. The suspending medium contained 10 mM KCl, 10 mM MES, 100 µM ferricyanide, 400 nM valinomycin, 12 µM phenolred, chloroplasts containing 10 µM chlorophyll, and further additions as specified. The experiments were performed at 20 °C temperature. The initial pH was 8.0, change of pH did never exceed 0.05 units. Illumination was extended until steady state and lasted normally 45 s. In order to obtain homogeneous light intensity within the cuvette, actinic light was given simultaneously from two sides facing one another. The stationary light-induced H^+ flux was taken from the dark decay of the pH change in the external medium as described previously [1]. The changes of pH were monitored optically from the absorption changes of phenolred at 553 nm. Transmission changes caused by changes of light scattering were eliminated by subtraction of the signal obtained in the absence of indicator. Charge compensation during H^+ efflux in the dark was facilitated by addition of valinomycin. Electron flow was measured simultaneously with H^+ flux and was obtained from the linear pH decrease in the light (1 H^+ produced per electron transported).

3. Results

A typical recording of a H/e measurement is shown in Fig. 1. The H/e ratio is read out from the ratio of the slopes at the point of light-off. Identical H/e ratios are obtained if $NADP^+$ (with ferredoxin as cofactor) is used as electron acceptor instead of ferricyanide. If the optical pH detection is replaced by the

M. Baltscheffsky (ed.), Current Research in Photosynthesis, Vol. III, 279–282.
© 1990 *Kluwer Academic Publishers. Printed in the Netherlands.*

glass electrode measurement all the results presented here will be reproduced in principle. However, due to the sluggish response of the glass electrode the H/e values are depressed.
The H/e ratio as influenced by the intensity of the actinic light is shown in
Fig. 2. The experiments were performed under basal conditions, with uncoupler (nigericin) added and with DCMU added. The H/e ratio varies between three and two. A detailed valuation of the results is facilitated if we
discuss separately different regions of intensity which we define as regions of
low, intermediate, high and very high intensity (see also the Table). If the intensity is low (1 Wm^{-2}, 10 % e^--flow), the H/e ratio is high (near 3.0). If the intensity is intermediate (10 Wm^{-2}, 50 % e^--flow), the H/e ratio is intermediate
(approx. 2.5). If the intensity is high (100 Wm^{-2}, e^--flow nearly saturating), the
H/e ratio is low (near 2.0) in the case of basal conditions but intermediate
(approx. 2.5) in the case of nigericin or DCMU being added. If the intensity is
very high (1000 Wm^{-2}, maximal e^--flow), the H/e ratio is low (near 2.0) in any

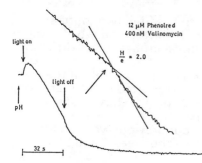

Fig. 1
Recording of the H/e measurement for basal conditions and
high actinic light intensity.

Table Correlation between H/e ratio and redox state of plastoquinone

actinic illumination (W/m²)	special addition	rate of e-flow (relative to sat. actinic ill.)	fraction of		H/e
			Q^{ox}	$Cyt\text{-}f^{red}$	
low (1)	-	10 %	0.9	0.9	2.9
intermediate (10)	-	50 %	0.6	0.8	2.6
high (100)	-	95 %	0.1	0.7	2.1
	Nigericin	80 %	0.4	0.8	2.5
	DCMU	60 %	0.6	0.5	2.5
very high (1000)	-	100 %	0	0	2.0
	Nigericin	100 %	0.1	0	2.1
	DCMU	100 %	0.5	0	2.0

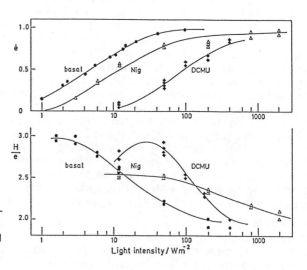

Fig. 2
e-flow and H/e ratio in dependence on the actinic light intensity for basal conditions with 8 nM
nigericin added and with 200 nM
DCMU added.

case. Most interesting is the effect of the increase of the H/e ratio from 2.0 to 2.5 upon addition of uncoupler or DCMU in the region of high intensity (100 Wm⁻²). This is shown in detail in Fig. 3A (nigericin) and Fig. 3B (DCMU). Nigericin may be exchanged for FCCP (Fig. 4). However, strange enough, if gramicidin was added, no effect was detectable (Fig. 4). An important finding is that increase of the H/e ratio in dependence on uncoupler (nigericin or FCCP) or DCMU never occurred if actinic light of very high intensity (1000 Wm⁻²) was employed. This is shown in Fig. 5 (FCCP) and Fig. 6 (DCMU).

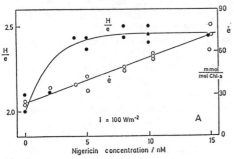

Fig. 3
e-flow and H/e ratio in dependence on the nigericin concentration (A) and the DCMU concentration (B) for actinic light of 100 Wm⁻² intensity.

Fig. 4
H/e ratio in dependence on the e-flow increase induced by addition of the uncoupling agents nigericin, FCCP, and gramicidin for actinic light of 100 Wm⁻² intensity.

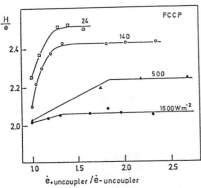

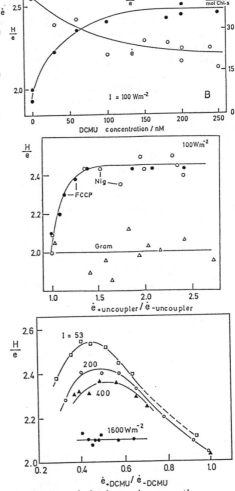

Fig. 5 H/e ratio in dependence on the e-flow increase induced by addition of FCCP for different actinic light intensities raging from 24 to 1600 Wm⁻².

Fig. 6 H/e ratio in dependence on the e-flow decrease induced by addition of DCMU for different actinic light intensities ranging from 53 to 1600 Wm⁻².

4. Discussion

The results reported here on the variability of the H/e ratio are in strict contrast to Rich's idea of an obligatory H/e value of 3 [2]. The variability reported here points to a special control mechanism at the level of the cytochrome-b_6-f-complex. Of importance with this respect are the redox states of the different components as influenced by the experimental conditions which may be estimated by computer simulation of the reaction kinetics of the electron transport system [3, 4]. Such an analysis points clearly to the paralellity between the H/e ratio and the fraction of oxidized plastoquinone. This is evident for all intensities as far as basal conditions are concerned (see Table). It makes sense if we interpret the variability of the H/e ratio on the basis of the Q-cycle as proposed by Mitchell [5] (see Fig. 7). Q^{ox} would indeed regulate the Q-cycle if we assume that the electron backreaction from Cyt-b_h into the plastoquinone pool is rate limiting. This assumption is verified by the increase of the H/e ratio upon the addition of uncoupler or DCMU which both, for complete different mechanistic reasons, induce an increased fraction of oxidized plastoquinone. However, this interpretation is opposed by the lack of increase of the H/e ratio by uncoupler or DCMU in the case of very high light intensity. Therefore, we have to assume that a second switch is in function which we attribute to the redox state of cytocrome-f for the following reasons. Plastoquinole passes the first of its two electrons obligatorily to the Rieske-FeS-centre. The lifetime of the reduced FeS-centre is short if Cyt-f is in the oxidized state. In this case the semiquinone passes the second electron also to the FeS-centre and the Q-cycle is not activated. If, however, Cyt-f is in the reduced state, the Rieske-FeS-centre remains reduced for a longer time and the semiquinone has the chance to activate the Q-cycle. Detailed computer simulation gives further strong evidence for this model mechanism [4].

Uncoupled conditions resemble those of activated ATP synthesis and therefore an increased H/e ratio of approx. 2.5 should also be observed in the case of activated ATP synthesis (supposed extreme high light intensity of 1000 Wm^{-2} is excluded). This means that H/ATP ratios of 3 which have been based on H/e values of 2 should be corrected towards 4. This conclusion indeed we were able to confirm [6].

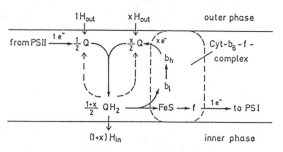

Fig. 7 Model of the e-flow events according to the Q-cycle

5. Literature

[1] Rathenow, M. and Rumberg, B. (1980) Ber. Bunsenges. Phys. Chem. 84, 1059-11062
[2] Rich, P.R. (1988) Biochim. Biophys. Acta 932, 33-42
[3] Liese, F. (1987), Thesis, Technische Universität Berlin
[4] Volz, E. and Rumberg, B. (1989) this Proceedings
[5] Mitchell, P. (1976) J. Theor. Biol. 62, 327-367
[6] Rumberg, B., Schubert, K., Strelow, F., and Tran-Anh, T. (1989) this Proceedings

A Q-CYCLE MECHANISM FOR ELECTRON TRANSFER IN CHLOROPLASTS

D.M. KRAMER and A.R. CROFTS, Biophysics Division, U. of Illinois,
607 S. Mathews, Urbana, IL 61801

1.   INTRODUCTION

Although a consensus has been established that mitochondrial and bacterial b/c_1 complexes operate through a modified Q-cycle mechanism (1-3), the operation of the b_6/f complex is still controversial. Rich and colleagues (4-6) and Hauska and colleagues (7,8) support a Q-cycle mechanism, but Cramer and colleagues (9,10) concluded that a Q-cycle does not operate, and Joliot and Joliot (11,12), while interpreting much of their data in terms of a modified Q-cycle, have suggested variants which might operate under reducing conditions. Whitmarsh and colleagues have suggested an alternative sequence of reactions at the Q_o- (Q_z-) site (13). These suggestions arise from substantial differences in interpretation of data, or in some cases in experimental result, between laboratories. Controversial areas are:

a)   The relative rates of reduction of cytochrome (cyt) b_6 and cyt f.

b)   Whether the two hemes have the same or different potentials.

c)   Whether the hemes are electronically connected.

d)   Measurement and interpretation of the kinetics of cyt b and electro-chromic changes at different ambient potentials.

e)   Inhibition by NQNO (HQNO) at the Q_c-site.

We report here our own studies of the kinetics of electron transfer and electro-chromic changes in chloroplasts, and the redox potential of cyt b.

2. PROCEDURES

2.1. Chloroplasts were isolated from market spinach in 0.4 M Sucrose, 50 mM HEPES pH 7.6, and 15 mM NaCl (SHN). The homogenate was centrifuged for 5 min at 3000 X g and the pellet resuspended in the same buffer.

2.2. Instrument. The spectrophotometer was designed and constructed in house, following the principals suggested by Joliot et al. (14). The actinic flash (through Kodak Wratten 70 filter) was found to be over 90% saturating. Preliminary experiments were made using the flash spectrophotometer of Joliot et al. (14); all data shown were obtained using our own instrument, which was equipped with redox poising facilities. The low actinic effect of the measuring beam in this instrument has enabled us to titrated the cyt b under essentially dark conditions, and to test the effect of a weak background illumination.

2.3. All experiments were carried out at 20°C in SHN with 2 uM of each of the following redox mediators, methyl viologen, benzyl viologen, 2-OH-1,4-napthoquinone, anthraquinone 1,5-disulfonate, pyocyanine, phenazine ethosulfate, and phenazine methosulfate. Redox poising was achieved by a redox poising system (Crofts and Wang, Photosynth. Res., in press) and, when needed, small amounts of either dithionite or sodium ferricyanide. The sample cuvette was kept under a stream of Ar gas. Kinetic traces were obtained on samples at 65 ug/ml chlo-

M. Baltscheffsky (ed.), Current Research in Photosynthesis, Vol. III, 283–286.
© 1990 *Kluwer Academic Publishers. Printed in the Netherlands.*

rophyll, and static redox titrations at either 150 or 250 ug/ml.

2.4.   Kinetic deconvolution of spectral components was achieved using the matrix algebra procedure suggested by Rich et al. (4-6).

3. RESULTS

3.1. Kinetics of cyt b changes at different ambient redox potentials.

At E_h values above 80 mV the cyt b_6 complement is completely oxidized, and goes transiently reduced on flash illumination. In the presence of NQNO, the extent of reduction is increased because the inhibitor slows the reoxidation. It has commonly observed that the rate of reduction if cyt b_6 is more rapid than the observed rate of reduction of cyt f (4-6,11,13). Similar observations in chromatophores had earlier lead us to point out that this behavior was not compatible with a Q-cycle. We subsequently demonstrated that the kinetic anomaly could be reconciled if account was taken of the role of the Rieske 2Fe.2S center (2). Selak and Whitmarsh (13) concluded that oxidation of plastoquinol led to reduction of cyt b_6 to produce $Q_Z^{\cdot-}$, followed by reduction of cyt f by this species to give plastoquinone, ie. a reversal of the more plausible sequence (1-3), but they did not take account of the "invisible" electron transfers of the 2Fe.2S center. The overlapping kinetic contributions of oxidation and reduction can be partially compensated by use of difference kinetics with appropriate inhibitors. By observing the differential reduction of cyt b and cyt f with and without NQNO and DBMIB or DNP-INP under moderately reducing conditions, it was possible to demonstrate that electron transport to the high potential chain was as rapid as that to cyt b in the presence of NQNO, with $t_{1/2}$ about 4 ms (Fig. 1).

As the ambient potential was lowered, the pattern of cyt b kinetics following flash oxidation changed. Reduction accelerated as the pool became reduced, and as the E_h was further lowered, the net reduction was replaced by a net oxidation. This titrated in with a midpoint around -15 mV. As the potential was lowered further, the reductive phase was lost, and a slower oxidation phase was seen (Fig. 2).

Under strongly reducing conditions, the first flash induced oxidation of cyt b with $t_{1/2}$ about 10 ms (Fig. 3), accompanied by a phase b 518 nm change, the rate and magnitude of which were reduced compared to the steady-state (not shown). A second flash induced a transient reduction followed by further oxidation. Subsequent flashes induced a small reduction-oxidation transient in cyt b, and a larger and faster 518 nm change, similar to the kinetics reported by Girvin and Cramer (9) as characteristic of the dark adapted state. These results are similar to those reported previously in other labs (4-6,11,12).

3.2. Redox titration of cyt b

Much of the controversy about the b_6/f complex revolves around the b-hemes;- do the two heme centers have different potentials, and are they in a common electron transfer chain? The literature is ambiguous, with titrations clearly showing two distinct potentials and spectra in isolated b_6/f preparations (7,8), but favoring only a single species in chloroplasts (9,10). This paradox might reflect the fact that in chloroplasts, the complex is connected to PS I, which can supply oxidant on illumination. Since measuring beams on conventional spectrophotometers deliver light at a rate sufficient to turn-over PS I every few seconds, it is possible that in some experiments, a low potential b-cyt was artifactually oxidized. Fig. 4 shows results from a redox titration using the flash measuring beam spectrophotometer. Spectra of cyt b were taken from differences on either side of the mid-point of the complete titration, and the inset shows the titration curve fit by one or two n=1 species. There are clearly two distinct components with E_m values around -15 mV (cyt b_H, A_{max} 563 nm) and -110 mV (cyt b_L, A_{max} 564.5 nm) at pH 7.6. These results agree closely with those using the isolated b_6/f

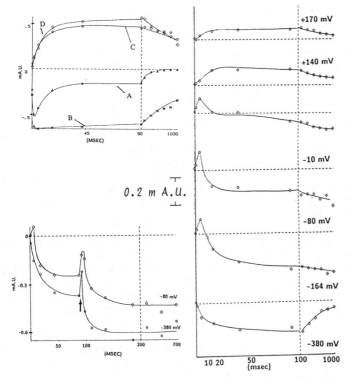

Fig. 1. (left) Kinetics
of cyt b and f after 1
flash. E_h was 80 mV.
A. cyt f, no additns;
B. A + 20uM DBMIB
C. A - B.
D. cyt b, 5uM NQNO

Fig. 2 (right) Kinetics
of cyt b at different
ambient potentials.

Fig. 3 (left) Kinetics
of cyt b with 2 flash-
es at the E_h values
shown.

Fig. 4 (below) Redox
titration of cyt b.
A. E_h(mV) -65 to 87
B. E_h -307 to - 87
(Inset, bottom). Points
from titration, with
theoretical curves.
(Inset, top). a. Dark;
b. 5 s light; c. 30 s
light; d. then 2 min
dark.

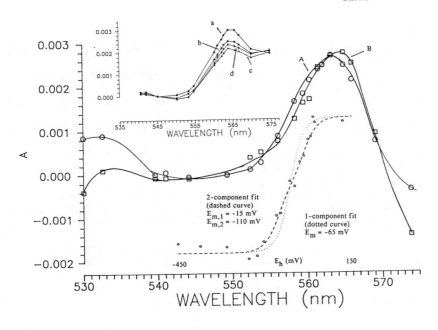

complex (7,8), or algae (12). The second inset shows the effect on the fully reduced system of illumination by 572 nm light at 0.6 $uE.m^{-2}.s^{-1}$ (the intensity of the measuring beam of our conventional spectrophotometer at 1.25 mm slit width). After 30 s, about half the cyt b had become oxidized, and the spectrum had shifted to that of cyt b_H. Oxidation of cyt b_L had $t_{1/2}$ of < 5 s, and recovered in the dark slowly.

DISCUSSION

Our results are consistent with a modified Q-cycle mechanism for the b_6/f complex. It is clear that the complex contains two b-heme centers of different redox potential, and that each can be reduced and oxidized during turn-over in reactions coupled to electrogenic events. There is no indication of any failure of electron transfer between b-hemes, or of inaccessibility of either heme to mediators (10). The slow reduction of heme b_L is likely a kinetic effect, as suggested by Joliot et al. (12). This, and the effect of the measuring beam may explain the apparent failure of reduction of cyt b_L by ferredoxin seen in the experiments of Cramer et al. (9,10). A remaining paradox is the behavior of NQNO, which fails markedly to inhibit cyt b oxidation in the low potential range (6,11). We feel that an interpretation of this behavior in terms of differential binding of the inhibitor under oxidizing and reducing conditions (P. Rich, personal commun.) is more plausible than schemes involving major modifications of the conventional mechanism, which imply structural features in the b_6/f complex which differ markedly from those of the b/c_1 complexes. Similarly, the slowed oxidation kinetics of cyt b on illumination from the fully reduced condition seem more adequately explained by a mechanism involving migration of neutral semiquinone from the Q_Z- to the Q_C-site as we have previously suggested (15, see also 6).

ACKNOWLEDGEMENTS. We are grateful for support from DOE PR#02-89ER13594. A.R.C. thanks the Joliots for hospitality, use of facilities, and many valuable discussions during a sabbatical visit to their lab, Spring 1986.

REFERENCES
1 Mitchell, P. (1976) J. Theoret. Biol. 62, 327-367.
2 Crofts, A.R., Meinhardt, S.W., Jones, K. and Snozzi, M. (1983) Biochim. Biophys Acta, 723, 202-218.
3 Crofts, A.R. (1985) in The Enzymes of Biological Membranes, 2nd. edn. (Martonosi, A. ed.) pp. 347-382. Plenum Press, New York.
4 Rich, P.R., Heathcote, P. and Moss, D.A. (1987) Biochim. Biophys. Acta. 892,138-151.
5 Rich, P.R., Heathcote, P. and Moss, D.A. (1987) Progress in Photosynthesis Research, (Biggins, J., ed.) Vol II, pp. 453-460.
6 Moss, D.A. and Rich, P.R. (1987) Biochim. Biophys. Acta, 894, 189-197.
7 Hurt, E.C. and Hauska, G. (1983) FEBS Lett. 153, 413-419.
8 Nitschke, W., Hauska, G. and Crofts, A.R. (1988) FEBS Lett. 232, 204-208.
9 Girvin, M.E. and Cramer, W.A. (1984) Biochim. Biophys. Acta, 767, 29-38.
10 Cramer, W.A., Black, M.T., Widger, W.R. and Girvin, M.E. (1987) In Electron Transfer Mechanisms and Oxygen Evolution (Barber, J., ed.) pp. 447-493. Elsevier, Amsterdam.
11 Joliot, P. and Joliot, A. (1984) Biochim. Biophys. Acta, 765, 210-218.
12 Joliot, P. and Joliot, A. (1986) Biochim. Biophys. Acta, 849, 211-222.
13 Selak, M.A. and Whitmarsh, J. (1982) FEBS Lett., 150, 286-292.
14 Joliot, P., Beal, D. and Frilley, B. (1980) J. Chim. Phys. 77, 209-216)
15 Crofts, A.R. (1986) J. Bioenerg. Biomemb. 18, 437-445.

OPERATION OF UQH_2:CYT C_2 OXIDOREDUCTASE OF *R. SPHAEROIDES* IN THE STEADY STATE

Yue Chen and Antony Crofts, Dept. of Physiology and Biophysics, University of Illinois, Urbana, Il 61801, USA.

1. INTRODUCTION

Measurement of the thermodynamic poise of redox components of electron transfer chains under coupled conditions has been used extensively in the mitochondrial field to analyze through "cross-over points" the contributions to different spans to the work required to drive ATP synthesis, or maintain the proton gradient. In the work described in this paper, a steady state approach has been developed by which the redox poise of the electron transfer chain, the electron flux and H^+-gradient could be simultaneously monitored, and the approach to the coupled steady-state (static head) could be followed kinetically on illumination of chromatophores from *Rhodobacter sphaeroides*.

a) In a complete steady-state profile for the electron transfer chain, the thermodynamically preferred pathway is consistent with the modified Q-cycle.

b) The measured steady-state flux and redox poise of b/c_1 are naturally explained by kinetic parameters suggested for the modified Q-cycle with modification to take account of membrane potential.

c) For b/c_1 at steady state, we have shown that:

i) The free energy drop calculated for every electron transfer step associated with the turnover is close to zero.

ii) The complex functions as an electrogenic H^+-pump at steady state close to static head.

iii) An almost symmetric balance between $E_h(Q\text{-pool})-E_h(b_L)$ and $(E_h(c_1)-E_h(Q\text{-pool}))$ is maintained as the chain approaches static head.

iv) Near static head, the driving force for electron transfer is close to the H^+-gradient of about 200 mV.

v) Electron transfer from b_L to b_H accounts for about 65%-70% of the total electrical span across the membrane.

d) The degree of coupling for the chain is > 0.96 and for b/c_1 > 0.98.

2. PROCEDURES

All experiments were performed using a single-beam spectrophotomoter linked to an LSI-11 computer through a Nicolet Explorer IIIA digital oscilloscope, and amplification, timing and control circuitry. Illumination was at 90° by either flash or continuous (Uniblitz shutter controlled). The cuvette was maintained anaerobic, and the redox potential poised by additions of ferricyanide or dithionite in the presence of mediators, as previously described (1). Cytochrome and carotenoid changes were measured at the wavelengths previously suggested (cyt c_2 at 550-554 nm; cyt c_1 at 552-548 nm; cyt b_H at 561-569 nm; cyt b_L at 566-575-0.5(561-569) nm; RC at 542nm, carotenoid change at 503 nm; refs. 1-3), and corrected for contributions from electrochromic changes by the method of Venturoli et al. (4). Maximal concentrations of redox centers accessible to the photosynthetic chain were assayed from the maximal change on multiple flash excitation

M. Baltscheffsky (ed.), Current Research in Photosynthesis, Vol. III, 287–290.

in the presence of antimycin (Fig. 1A). Redox poise was calculated from the Nernst-Peters equation. Proton gradient was estimated from the amplitude of the carotenoid change measured at 503 nm, scaled to a maximal voltage to match the work available from the redox drop between the quinol pool and cyt c_2 measured at the peak of the electrochromic change. Contributions from the pH gradient were minimised by inclusion of nigericin and KCl. The proton and electron fluxes were measured from the relaxation of the carotenoid change and of redox centers on turning off the light, or from the relaxation between flashes at the end of a train.

3.   RESULTS AND DISCUSSION
    In Fig. 1, typical traces show the approach to static head on flash or continuous illumination. Traces are shown at two values for initial redox poise. Points to note are the different rates at which the redox centers reach a steady poise, and the substantial reduction of cyt b_L, and oxidation of P870 (measured at 542 nm). Substantial displacements from the "uncoupled" poise are seen for the drop between cyt c_2 and P870, and between cyts b_L and b_H, and to a lesser extent, between cyt b_H and the quinone pool. These "cross-over" points indicate spans in which work is done against the membrane potential. Fig. 2 shows reduction of cytochrome b_L and b_H in the presence of myxothiazol, through "reversed electron flow" from quinol through the Q_C-site as a membrane potential is generated by electron transfer from added $DADH_2$ to the initially oxidized quinone pool. In the experiments of Figs. 1 and 2, the number of electrons flowing into the quinone pool could be calibrated from the reaction center turnover on each flash indicated by the carotenoid change, and this allowed calculation of the redox poise of the pool, and hence the "extra" work provided by the membrane potential to reduce the b-cytochromes. Fig. 3 shows profiles of redox poise and proton gradient as the system approaches static head. Examples show the development of redox gradients as the proton gradient develops. The Table shows values for the steady-state redox poise, current and proton gradient for the system poised at two values of initial E_h.

TABLE.
Steady State Redox Poise, Electron Flux and Proton Gradient

	Ambient E_h 100mV (continuous) mV (% reduced)	Ambient E_h 180mV (continuous) mV (% reduced)	Ambient E_h 180mV (flash) mV (% reduced)
$E_h(b_H)$	40 (60%)	72 (30%)	70 (32%)
$E_h(b_L)$	-100 (60%)	-74 (35%)	-80 (40%)
$E_h(c_1)$	283 (38%)	347 (5%)	347 (5%)
$E_h(c_2)$	335 (60%)	361 (35%)	365 (32%)
$E_h(RC)$	450 (50%)	468 (33%)	460 (40%)
$E_h(Q_{pool})$	100 (32%)	140 (2%)	140 (2%)
Electron flow (e⁻/s/cyt c_1)	40	40	50
Δp (mV)	200-235	210-221	220-225

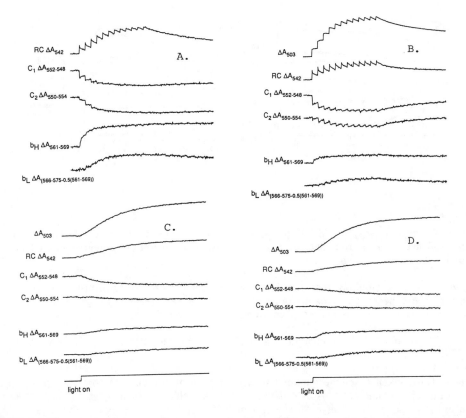

Fig.1. The approach to steady state on A, B: multiflash illumination. Standard reaction medium and mediators, E_b 180 mV, plus A, 0.01 mM antimycin to allow calibration of changes, time full scale = 500 ms
C, D: continuous illumination, conditions as above, but E_h in C=180 mV, in D=100 mV, time full scale = 100 ms.

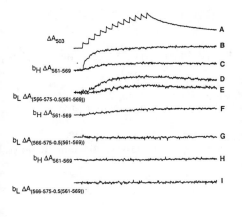

Fig. 2. Antimycin sensitive reduction of cyt b_H and b_L in the presence of myxothiazol. Standard reaction medium and mediators, plus:
A,C,E: Myxothiazol 0.01 mM, DADH$_2$ 1.5 mM, UHNQ 0.01 mM.
B,D: Maximal cyt b changes inpresence of antimycin 0.01 mM, valinomycin 0.02 mM.
F,G: As C, E, but plus valinomycin 0.02 mM.
H,I: As F, G, but with antimycin 0.01 mM.

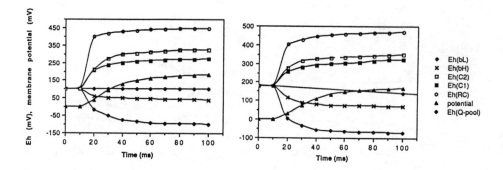

Fig. 3. Dynamic energy profile of the approach to static head. Initial E_h: left, 100 mV; right, 180 mV. Taken from data of Fig. 1. Steady state membrane potential of 200 mV assumed.

It will be obvious that the system approaches close to equilibrium as it approaches static head. The flux becomes low, and the net free-energy gradients in the system approach zero. The degree of coupling, as calculated from:

$$q = [1 - (\text{flux in static head})/ (\text{flux in level flow})]^{1/2}$$

has a value of about 0.98. In this calculation, a value of 1000 s^{-1} was used for the flux in level flow, taken from the maximal turn-over time of the enzyme (the slow phase of the carotenoid change has $t_{1/2}$ of 1-2 ms for the two-electron turn-over; cyt b_H reduction in the presence of antimycin has a $t_{1/2}$ of 0.5-1 ms for the one-electron process).

From the redox poise at static head, it is clear that the major fraction (65-70%) of electrical work of the b/c_1 complex is done on electron flow between the b-type cytochromes; oxidation of cyt b_H contributes 30-35%. There is no indication that reduction of cyt b_L or of cyt c involves work against the proton gradient. Cyts c_1 and c_2 are close to equilibrium poise, but a substantial effect of membrane potential on the differential poise of cyt c_2 and P870 is obvious, as previously noted (6).

ACKNOWLEDGEMENTS. We thank NIH for support from grant 5 RO1 GM26305

REFERENCES
1 Crofts, A. R., Meinhardt, S. W., Jones, K. R. and Snozzi, M.(1983) Biochim. Biophys. Acta, 723, 202-218.
2 Meinhardt, S.W. and Crofts, A.R. (1982). FEBS Lett., 149, 223-227.
3 Meinhardt, S.W. and Crofts, A.R. (1983). Biochim. Biophys. Acta, 723, 219-230.
4 Venturoli, G., Virgili, M., Melandri, B.A. and Crofts, A.R. (1986) FEBS Lett. 219, 477-484.
5 Cotton, N.P.J., Clark, A.J. and Jackson, J.B. (Eur. J. Biochem. 142, 193-198
6 Dutton, P.L., Petty, K.M., Bonner, H.S. and Morse, S.D. (1975) Biochim. Biophys. Acta 387,536-556.

THE MECHANISM OF QUINOL OXIDATION:
ACTIVATION BARRIERS IN UQH$_2$:CYT C$_2$ OXIDOREDUCTASE.

Z. Wang and A.R. Crofts, Biophysics Division, University of Illinois
407 S. Goodwin, Urbana, IL 61801, U.S.A.

1. INTRODUCTION

We have previously reported (1) a large apparent activation energy for the reduction of cytochrome b$_{50}$ (or b$_H$) in the chromatophores from *Rb. sphaeroides* Ga in the presence of antimycin, and suggested therefore that the diffusion of ubiquinone in the membrane was not a rate-limiting step in the quinol oxidation by the ubiquinol:cyt c$_2$ oxidoreductase (or cyt bc$_1$ complex). We could not rule out the possibility, however, that the activation barrier might actually arise from an obscure phase transition in the temperature range of our experiments. This scenario was also hinted by the apparent break in our Arrhenius plot. Here we present further studies of the temperature dependence of reduction of the b cytochromes. These experiments support the notion that the actual oxidation of the quinol at the Q$_z$ site of the bc$_1$ complex is the rate-limiting step. It is proposed that the semiquinone at the Q$_z$ site is the transient intermediate in the reduction of b cytochrome in the presence of antimycin.

2. MATERIALS AND METHODS

Chromatophores of *Rb. sphaeroides* stain Ga were prepared as described previously (2) and stored at -70°C in 50% glycerol until use. Kinetics were measured as in (3).

3. RESULTS
3.1   The Temperature Dependence of Midpoint Potentials

Redox titrations were performed at different temperatures between 520nm and 570nm as in (4), in the presence of antimycin (data not shown), and data were analyzed point by point by a computer program to obtain midpoint potentials for cyt c$_1$ and c$_2$, and the apparent two b cytochromes, b$_{150}$ and b$_{50}$. Assuming the midpoint potentials of the cytochromes have a linear dependence on temperature, best fitting temperature coefficients were found to be roughly -1mV/^{o}C for all the components. We also observed that the differential spectra of cytochromes c$_2$, c$_1$, b$_H$, and of the reaction center at pH7 resolved from kinetic traces showed little dependence on temperature in the range 10-35°C. Thus the wavelength pairs used to monitor redox status of these cytochromes should still be valid at least from 10-35°C.

3.2   Temperature Dependence of Kinetics of Oxidation Kinetics of C Cytochromes.

Fig. 1 showed oxidation of the c cytochromes in the presence of myxothiazol and UHDBT at 10 and 25°C. A slight increase of oxidation rate can be seen in both sets of traces. This is likely the indication that the rate of the slow phase of RC reduction by cyt c$_2$ was accelerated, since oxidation of the Rieske iron-sulfur protein by c$_1$ is very fast, as we have pointed out elsewhere (Crofts and Wang, in press).

3.3   Temperature Dependence of Reduction of Cytochrome b$_H$

In contrast to oxidation of c cytochromes, reduction of cyt. b$_H$ was strongly dependent on temperature, as shown in figure 2A. To obtain the temperature dependency of

M. Baltscheffsky (ed.), Current Research in Photosynthesis, Vol. III, 291–294.
© 1990 *Kluwer Academic Publishers. Printed in the Netherlands.*

rate constants of cyt b_H reduction, we have written an optimization program, to fit the traces with an integrated 2nd-order equation. One group of traces calculated from the fitting parameters obtained are plotted along the experimental data. The maximal derivatives of the theoretical curves were taken as the initial reaction rates, and gave the rate constants when divided by the initial concentrations of the reactants. The logarithm of the ratio of these rate constants at higher temperatures to that at 10^0C were plotted vs. $1/T$ in Fig. 2B.

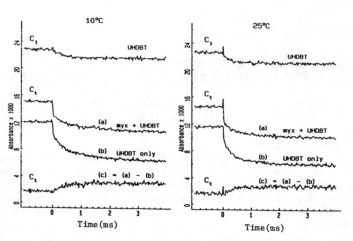

Fig.1 The Temperature Effect on Oxidation of C_1 and C_2

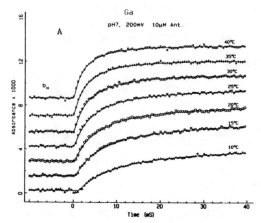

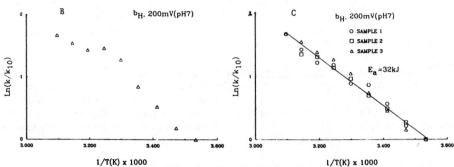

Fig. 2 The Temperature Dependence of Cyt b_H Reduction

A break around $35^{\circ}C$, which is somewhat variable from preparation to preparation, was evident in the figure. This is probably because the QH_2 production at RC varies with temperature, which is reflected by the extent of absorbance change at 561-569 used to monitor the cyt b_H. If the final extent of b_H reduction is taken as the initial concentration of QH_2, and the plots of Fig. 2B are corrected for this effect (see Fig. 2C), the curve does not show an obvious break. We used a single straight line to fit the data, and obtained an average of activation energy 7.6.

We have previously reported a break in similar Arrhenius plots at a lower temperature (1). Our previous analysis did not properly take into account the behavior of the iron-sulfur center as reductant to the c cytochromes. Furthermore, the rate constants calculated from the overall fitting were underestimates of the true values, especially below $20^{\circ}C$, since the initial rising phase of fitting curve had to be reduced to compensate for the lag period in the b_H reduction kinetics. Therefore the rate constants obtained from the overall fitting are hardly valid.

In the experiments shown here, it was observed that the ambient potential at which rate of cyt. b_H reduction reached maximum was about 100mV at $10^{\circ}C$, and shifted downward about 5mV for every $5^{\circ}C$, in agreement with the temperature dependency of midpoint potential of cyt. b_H. Therefore the redox potential was shifted accordingly in recording the kinetics. The same sort of Arrhenius plots as above were presented in figure 3A. Acceleration of b_H reduction appeared slowed down above $30^{\circ}C$. This is probably due to a) PES and PMS used as mediators begin to reduce c cytochromes appreciably at such low ambient potentials at high temperature; b) rate of oxidation of cyt c_1 (and hence FeS) becomes rate-limiting at high temperature. If the slope below $30^{\circ}C$ is taken to represent the activation energy, average of 7.4kcal from two experiments was obtained.

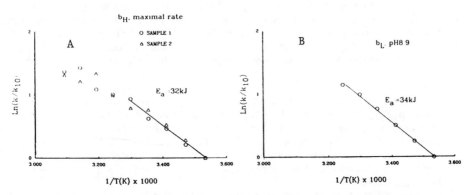

Fig.3 The Arrhenius Plots for Reduction of b_H and b_L at low potentials

3.4   Temperature Dependence of Reduction of Cytochrome b_{-90} (or b_L)
     We have also investigated the temperature dependence of reduction kinetics of cyt b_L. At high pH (e.g. pH9), b_H can be reduced before flash without significant reduction of the primary acceptor. Reduction of b_L is readily observed under such circumstances, since a significant portion of quinone pool is also reduced. We started at -10mV at 10^oC, and shifted -.6mV per degree centigrade, for the same reason as for b_H reduction. Kinetics for b_L reduction were recorded, and analyzed as above. An average 8.4kcal of activation energy from two experiments were computed (Fig.3B).

4. DISCUSSION
     The activation energy of 32 kJ.M^{-1} for UQH_2 oxidation was within experimental error the same for all states of the quinone pool. Our results demonstrate that the activation barrier is in the reaction by which UQH_2 at the catalytic site is oxidized. In order to better understand the rate determining processes, we have used a computer model to derive a set of kinetic and thermodynamic parameters which describe the kinetic behavior, and the way this varies with redox potential and temperature. The model includes forward and reverse rate constants for all reactions at the quinol oxidizing site, including binding and unbinding of quinone and quinol, and for the reactions of the antimycin inhibited b-cytochrome chain, and the components of the high potential chain. A computer program varies these kinetic parameters to fit the input data, which consists of the kinetic traces measured at different ambient redox potentials at a particular temperature. The kinetic constants output provide a minimal set of values which describe the kinetic behavior at that temperature. In contrast to our previous model (5), the mechanism takes account of the competition between Q and QH_2 at the Q_Z-site; a good fit to the variation of kinetics with E_h requires that binding of quinol should be 100-fold greater than that of quinone, and that all rates should be considerably faster than the rate determining step,- oxidation of bound quinol. The minimal kinetic model does not include the activation barrier identified above. The most probable step for this barrier is the reaction by which quinol is oxidized by the Rieske 2Fe.2S center, which is thought to generate a highly unstable semiquinone species (Q_Z^-) (6). The simplest scheme for this reaction would have the semiquinone intermediate at the energy level indicated by the activation barrier. A maximal value for the equilibrium constant for formation of Q_Z^- is 0.001 (6), and the minimal value that given by the activation barrier, 1.2×10^{-6}. We cannot exclude other barriers, such as "conformational" changes or states, but at present these would represent *ad hoc* additions to the simpler hypothesis.

5. REFERENCES
1. Wang, Z., Berry, E.A. and Crofts, A.R. (1987) In: Progress in Photosynthesis Research, Biggins, J. ed. pp 2:493-496, Martinus Nijhoff Publishers, Dordrecht.
2. Bowyer, J.R., Tierney, G.V. and Crofts, A.R.(1979) FEBS Lett. 101, 201-206.
3. Meinhardt, S.W. and Crofts, A.R.(1983) Biochim. Biophys. Acta 723, 219-230.
4. Crowther, D. (1977) Ph.D. Thesis, University of Bristol, Bristol.
5. Crofts, A.R., Meinhardt, S.W., Jones, K.R. and Snozzi, M.(1983) Biochim. Biophys. Acta 723, 202-218.
6. De Vries, S. (1983) Ph.D. thesis, University of Amsterdam, Amsterdam.

EFFECT OF CATIONS ON HEAT STIMULATION OF PHOTOSYSTEM I IN STROMA LAMELLAE PREPARATIONS

Nathalie Boucher, Johanne Harnois and Robert Carpentier, Centre de recherche en photobiophysique, Université du Québec à Trois-Rivières, C.P. 500, Trois-Rivières (Québec), G9A 5H7, Canada

1. INTRODUCTION

Higher plants are very sensitive to heat stress. The integrity of the thylakoid membrane constituents is first to be affected, well before other stromal or cellular components (1). Short exposure of photosynthetic membranes to temperatures in the range of 35-50°C results in a loss of grana stacking with concurrent dissociation of the peripheral antenna complex of PSII (2). However, the primary site of thermal damaging seems to be located at the PSII reaction center complex (3,4).

On the other hand, PSI mediated electron flow is stimulated by heat treatment with the same temperature threshold as for PSII inhibition (3,5). Recent studies (6) indicated that heat stress stimulation of PSI was not due to thermal uncoupling or to an increased PSI antenna size following the dissociation of PSII antenna complex as previously suggested (2,4). Rather, it was postulated that the stimulation originates from conformational modifications of the cytochrome b/f complex which results in the formation of new $DCIPH_2$ oxidation sites (6).

Phase separation of non-bilayer forming lipids could be responsible for initiating the modification in the thylakoid membrane structure which causes inhibition of PSII and stimulation of PSI during heat stress (4,7). However the exact nature of the changes responsible for the increased $DCIPH_2$ electron donation at the level of the cytochrome b/f complex are still undefined. To gain more information about the mechanism involved in heat stress stimulation of PSI we have analysed this phenomenum in a stroma lamellae preparation highly enriched in PSI core complex and cytochrome b/f complex (8). It was previously reported using whole thylakoid membranes that heat stimulation was enhanced by Mg^{2+} and Ca^{2+} (9). In this study we show that Mg^{2+}, Na^+, and K^+ but not Ca^{2+} and Mn^{2+} are efficient in that respect. Furthermore, it is demonstrated that the effect of salts is reversible upon prolonged incubation period. The role of cations in thermal stimulation of PSI is discussed.

M. Baltscheffsky (ed.), Current Research in Photosynthesis, Vol. III, 295–298.
© 1990 *Kluwer Academic Publishers. Printed in the Netherlands.*

2. RESULTS AND DISCUSSION

Oxygen uptake by a digitonin-derived PSI submembrane fraction (8) was monitored at 22°C with methylviologen as acceptor and DCIP/ascorbate as donor. Samples were preincubated for 5 min at various temperatures. In the PSI preparations, oxygen uptake increased with incubation temperature similarly to the case in whole thylakoid membranes (Fig. 1, ref. 3, 5-6). The occurrence of heat stress stimulation in a PSI submembrane fraction confirms the conclusion by Thomas et al. (6) to the effect that the enhanced PSI electron flow is not due to an increased PSI antenna size following thermal dissociation of the peripheral PSII antenna complex.

The incubation temperature to obtain the optimal PSI electron transfer rate was 50°C either in presence or absence of 10 mM $MgCl_2$. However, in the presence of $MgCl_2$, electron transfer increased to a larger extent at 40 and 50°C (Fig. 1), therefore indicating a positive effect of this salt. However, the decline of activity at temperature above 50°C was repetitively sharper with $MgCl_2$.

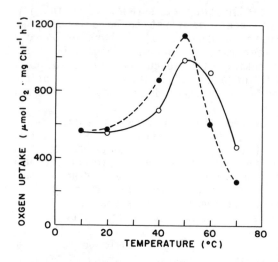

Figure 1: Oxygen uptake rates with PSI incubated 5 min at various temperature with (-●-) and without (-O-) addition of 10 mM $MgCl_2$. The samples were transfered to a Clark oxygen electrode cell and equilibrated at 22°C for 2 min before measurements. The reaction medium contained 11 µg Chl/ml, 0.2 mM DCIP, 1 mM sodium ascorbate, 0.5 mM methylviologen, 1 mM NaN_3, 20 mM Tricine-NaOH (pH 7.8)

To study these effects in more details, oxygen uptake was measured in samples preincubated either at 20 or 50°C with various $MgCl_2$ concentrations. The presence of $MgCl_2$ stimulated electron flow in samples treated at both 20 and 50°C. However, in samples incubated at 20°C, maximal activation was obtained at $MgCl_2$ concentrations below 1 mM whereas a larger activation was obtained for samples incubated at 50°C, but the $MgCl_2$ concentration required for maximal effect was around 10 mM. Therefore, even if a three fold stimulation of electron flow was produced by heat stress (50°C) in absence of salts, a four fold stimulation was obtained with 10 mM $MgCl_2$ in the incubation medium.

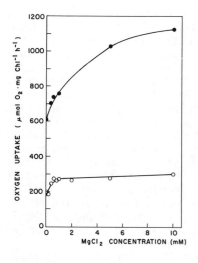 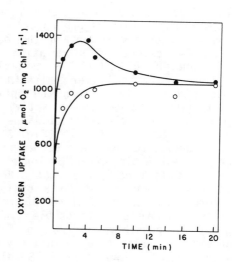

Figure 2: (left) Oxygen uptake rates with PSI incubated 5 min at 50°C (-●-) or at 25°C (-O-) with various MgCl₂ concentrations.

Figure 3: (right) Oxygen uptake rates with PSI incubated for various periods of time with (-●-) and without (-O-) addition of 10 mM MgCl₂.

TABLE 1. Effect of salt composition in the incubation medium on the extent of heat stimulation.

Salt	Concentration (mM)	Stimulation (%)
None	--	245
MgCl₂	10	330
Mg(NO₃)₂	10	367
MnCl₂	10	206
CaCl₂	10	215
NaCl	20	341
KCl	20	334

In Table 1, it is shown that Mg^{2+} but not Mn^{2+} or Ca^{2+} is the effective specie to enhance heat stress stimulation. $Mg(NO_3)_2$ was as effective as $MgCl_2$. The monovalent cations Na^{2+} and K^+ were also effective to a similar extent when they were used at a concentration of 20 mM.

The effect of the incubation period at 50°C (in presence or absence of $MgCl_2$) on the rate oxygen uptake is shown in Fig. 3. A 5 min incubation is necessary to obtain the optimal stimulation in absence of salts. The extent of stimulation is thereafter irreversible even after transfer to 22°C. The maximal electron flow in the presence of $MgCl_2$ is reached after only 3 min incubation and it represents a much higher activity than the optimal oxygen uptake rate obtained without salt. However, the activity declines during the next ten to fifteen min until it stabilizes at the same oxygen uptake rate obtained in absence of salt (Fig. 3). Thus, the portion of thermal stimulation induced by the presence of salts is only a transient effect which is reversible after prolonged heat stress exposure. On that respect, it is conceivable that a 5 min incubation at a temperature above 50°C is equivalent to a prolonged incubation period at 50°C. Therefore, the sharp decline of activity detected when increasing temperature above 50°C in samples incubated in the presence of $MgCl_2$ (Fig. 1) is possibly due to an inhibition of the cation induced enhancement of activity at relatively high temperature.

An increased stimulation of PSI electron flow with $DCIPH_2$ as donor in the presence of salts might be understood if screening of the thylakoid membranes surface charges can facilitate the conformational changes of the cytochrome b/f complex involved in the increased $DCIPH_2$ photooxidation. Thus, the weaker ability of cations to perform this function at relatively higher temperatures or after prolonged incubation period might be due to the dissociation of the ionic species from the thylakoid membrane under these conditions.

This research was supported by the National Sciences and Engineering Research Council of Canada, by the Fonds F.C.A.R. du Québec, and by program FODAR of Québec University.

REFERENCES
1 Santarius, K.A. (1976) J. Therm. Biol. 1, 101-107
2 Armond, P.A., Bjorkman, O. and Staehelin, L.A. (1980) Biochim. Biophys. Acta 601, 433-442
3 Armond, P.A., Schreiber, U. and Bjorkman, O. (1978) Plant Physiol. 61, 411-415
4 Gounaris, K., Brain, A.P.R., Quinn, P.J. and Williams, W.P. (1983) FEBS Lett. 153, 47-52
5 Stidham, M.A., Wribe, E.G. and Williams, G.T. (1982) Plant Physiol. 69, 929-934
6 Thomas, P.G., Quinn, P.J. and Williams, W.P. (1986) Planta 164, 133-139
7 Vigh, L., Gombos, Z., Horwath, I. and Joo, F. (1989) Biochim. Biophys. Acta 979, 361-364
8 Peters, F.A.L.J., Van Wielink, J.E., Wong Fong Sang, H.W., De Vries, S. and Kraayenhof, R. (1983) Biochim. Biophys. Acta 722, 460-470
9 Mohanty, P. (1987) in Progress in Photosynthesis Research (Biggins, J., ed.), Vol. II, pp. 597-604, Martinus Nijhoff Publishers, Dordrecht

Altered Anionic Nature of Cytochrome F After Carboxypeptidase
Treatment

Steven A. Molnar and Elizabeth L. Gross. Ohio State University,
Columbus, Ohio 43210, USA

1. INTRODUCTION

Willey et al. (1) have monitored carboxypeptidase digestion
of cytochrome f (Cyt f) in intact thylakoid membranes. They have
presented a model of the orientation of Cyt f in the thylakoid
membrane where residues 251-270 form a transmembrane alpha-helix,
residues 271-285 are in the stroma and the remainder of the
molecule resides in the intra-thylakoid space. It has been
postulated that the solubility of purified Cyt f, from members of
the Cruciferae, is due to the loss of the transmembrane alpha-helix
during purification. Turnip Cyt f is soluble and, upon
electrophoresis in the presence of SDS (SDS-PAGE), is resolved
into diffuse double bands with M_r of 28 and 32 Kd. The predicted
M_r of sequenced cytochromes f is 31 Kd and a loss of 4 Kd from
the C-terminus would include all of the presumed membrane
spanning alpha-helix. The remaining Cyt f would be more negative
by 2 units.

Using anion exchange fast protein liquid chromatography
(FPLC) we have resolved partially purified turnip cyt f into low
salt eluting (Cyt f_L) and high salt eluting (Cyt f_H) fractions.
Cyt f_L elutes at higher salt concentrations after extensive
treatment with carboxypeptidase. However, the carboxypeptidase
is known to contain amidase activity also.

2. PROCEDURE
2.1. Materials and Methods
2.1.1. Cyt f Purification and FPLC: Turnip Cyt f was
purified through the DEAE-cellulose step as previously described
(2). FPLC was performed using a mono-Q column with a flow rate
of 0.5 ml/min, buffer A= 10mM Tris (pH 7)+ .01% Trition X-100 and
buffer B= 10mM Succinate (pH 6)+ .01% Triton X-100 + 0.5M NaCl.
The pumps were programmed to produce a step from 0% to 4%B at
4min followed by three linear gradients with slopes of 2/3, 7/6
and 3/2 (%B/min) for 12, 12 and 22 min respectively.
2.1.2. Carboxypeptidase Digestion: Carboxypeptidases A, B
and Y were purchased from Sigma Chemical Company. Cyt f_L (175
nMoles in 1ml 10mM Tris pH 7 + .01% Triton X-100) was incubated
with carboxypeptidases A (20 units) and/or B (10 units) for 24
hr. at room temperature. Carboxypeptidases Y (20 units), A (40
units) and B (20 units) were incubated with Cyt f_L (120 nMoles)
at room temperature. Incubation products were purified using
FPLC.
2.1.3. Kinetics and Spectroscopy: Visible absorption
spectroscopy was done using an Aminco DW-2a spectrophotometer.
The extinction coefficients of Bendall et.al. were used (3).

M. Baltscheffsky (ed.), Current Research in Photosynthesis, Vol. III, 299–302.
© 1990 *Kluwer Academic Publishers. Printed in the Netherlands.*

Stopped flow kinetic measurements were made using a J4-9602
stopped flow accessory, a Keithley 427 current amplifier and a
Bascom-Turner Instruments 3120T recorder. Pseudo-first order
rate constants were measured for reduced cytochrome (0.5uM)
reacted with oxidized parsley plastocyanin (2.5uM) in 20mM sodium
phosphate at pH 7 + 300mM NaCl.
    2.1.4. <u>Electrophoresis</u>: SDS-PAGE was performed using the
method of Laemmli (4). Silver staining was done as described by
Morrissey (5).

3. <u>RESULTS</u>
3.1. FPLC of partially purified Cyt f yields two major peaks,
one eluting at 16 min (Cyt f_L) and the other at 28 min (Cyt f_H)
(fig.1a). The relative proportion of the peaks varies among
different preparations where Cyt f_L ranges form 20-80% of the
total Cyt f. The elution position of Cyt f_L may vary in the
range of 16-22 min with a shift to higher salt concentrations as
Cyt f_L/Cyt f_H >= 1. Occasionally three peaks are observed with
the additional peak intermediate between Cyt f_L and Cyt f_H.
Repeated FPLC purification of the additional peak gives
decreasing yields of Cyt f_H. Both Cyt f_L and Cyt f_H have stable
elution
characteristics (fig.1b&c).

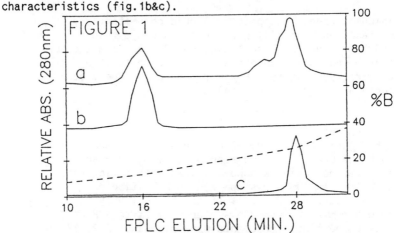

FIGURE 1.a) Elution profile of partially purified Cyt f. Cyt f_L
and Cyt f_H elute at 16 and 28 min respectively. b and c)
rechromatography of Cyt f_L and Cyt f_H respectively.

3.2. Incubation of Cyt f_L with carboxypeptidase A results in the
formation of a shoulder after the 16 min peak and a small peak at
25 min (fig.2a), Carboxypeptidase B incubation yields twin peaks
(at 16 and 25 min) each having a shoulder. The peak to shoulder
proportions are identical for each member of the set (fig.2b).
Incubation with both carboxypeptidases A and B results in a near
total loss of Cyt f_L with the formation of twin peaks at 24 and
26 min (fig.2c).

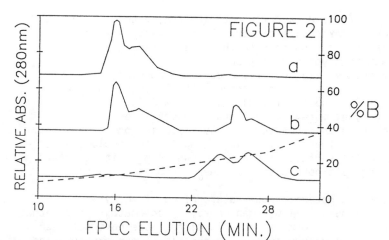

FIGURE 2.a) Elution profile of Cyt f_L incubated with
carboxypeptidase A. b) Cyt f_L incubated with carboxypeptidase B.
c) Cyt f_L incubated with carboxypeptidases A and B.

3.3. Extensive incubation of Cyt f_L with carboxypeptidases A,B
and Y results in the formation of material (Cyt f_{ABY}) which
elutes in a position identical to Cyt f_H (fig.3).

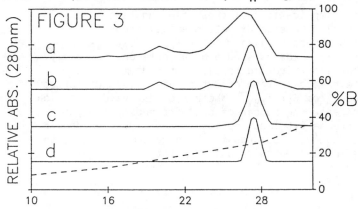

FIGURE 3.a) Elution profile of Cyt f_L after 24 hr. treatment with
1 aliquot of carboxypeptidases A,B and Y. b) Cyt f_L after 24
hr., with a second aliquot added after 12 hr. c) Cyt f_L after
36 hr., with an aliquot added every 12 hr. d) Elution
profile of Cyt f_{ABY}, ie. the rechromatographed peak from profile
c. Sample sizes were not equivalent.

3.4 Cyt f_L, Cyt f_H and Cyt f_{ABY} migrate as diffuse double bands
in SDS-PAGE with M_r of 28 and 32 Kd. Silver staining revealed
the digestion of contaminants that are routinely present.

Clearly the Cyt f_L 32Kd band was not digested, within the limits of resolution, by extensive exposure to carboxypeptidases A, B and Y. It is interesting to note that these preparations are also resistant to trypsin digestion.

3.5. The respective Pseudo-first order rate constants for Cyt f_L, Cyt f_H and Cyt f_{ABY}, when reacted with plastocyanin, are 1.4 (+-8%), 1.4 (+-5%) and 1.3 (+-6%) ($X10^7$ M^{-1} X S^{-1}). These rates deviate by no more than one standard deviation. The relatively more anionic character of Cyt f_{ABY} is not evident from the kinetic data. Therefore, it is reasonable to conclude that the changes on the surface of Cyt f_{ABY}, which give it stronger anionic binding, are not located at the plastocyanin binding site.

3.6. Although the heterogeneous nature of purified Cyt f preparations has been well documented (6,7), chromatographic methods for the separation of forms with ionic differences have not been reported. Cyt f_L exposure to amidase containing carboxypeptidase preparations results in a more anionic form of Cyt f without alterations in M_r. These observations indicate that amidase activity is responsible for the altered chromatographic nature of Cyt f_{ABY} and that carboxypeptidase digestion of Cyt f_L has not been detected. Cyt f_H is most likely the product of oxidative deamination of glutamine and/or asparagine residues on the surface of the protein.

3.7. The immediate implications of these findings are threefold. First, the additional dimension of heterogeneity needs to be explored. Chromatographic analysis of Cyt f_L incubated with deaminating amino acid oxidases should be undertaken. Secondly, it is expected that aspartic acid specific or glutamic acid specific endoproteinase digestion of Cyt f_L will yield different peptides than those from Cyt f_{ABY}. Whether oxidative deamination can be used to increase the number of specific endoproteolytic sites and thus increase Cyt f susceptibility to digestion should be investigated. Lastly, should deamination be demonstrated, the specific residues involved should be incorporated into the structural model of Cyt f.

REFERENCES

1. Willey, D.L., Auffret, A.D. and Gray, J.C. (1984) Cell 36, 555-562
2. Molnar, S.A., Anderson, G.A. and Gross, E.L. (1897) Biochim. Biophys. Acta 894, 327-331
3. Bendall, D.S., Davenport, H.E. and Hill, R. (1971) Methods Enzymol. 23, 327-344
4. Laemmli, U.K. (1970) Nature 277, 680-685
5. Morrissey, J.H. (1981) Analytical Biochm. 117, 307-310
6. Hurt, E. and Hasuka, G. (1982) J. Bioenergetics Biomembranes 14, 405-424
7. Bendall, D.S. (1982) Biochim. Biophys. Acta 683, 119-151

CHARACTERIZATION OF A COVALENTLY LINKED PLASTOCYANIN-CYTOCHROME F ADDUCT

L.Z. Morand[2], M. Frame[1], D.W. Krogmann[2], D.J. Davis[1] 1. Dept. of Chem. and Biochem, Univ. of Arkansas, Fayetteville, AR USA 72701   2. Dept. of Biochem., Purdut Univ. West Lafayette, IN USA 47907

1. INTRODUCTION
     Plastocyanin (PC) mediates electron transfer from the cytochrome f (cyt f) component of the cytochrome b6/f complex to the Photosystem I reaction center during photosynthetic electron transport. At the preceeding International Congress on Photosynthesis, predictions were made regarding regions on cyt f which might be likely candidates for the PC interaction site (1). To further examine this hypothesis, we have further characterized a covalently linked PC-cyt f adduct. This adduct was prepared by incubation of the two proteins in the presence of EDC, a water soluble carbodiimide, and has been demonstrated to have a 1:1 stoichiometry (2).

2. PROCEDURES
     PC was prepared from spinach by a previously described method (3). Turnip cyt f was prepared as described by Gray (4). Preparation and purification of the PC-cyt f adduct were done as described in the original report (2). Redox potentials were determined from spectral data collected after equilibration of the PC-cyt f adduct against ferri-/ferrocyanide couples having known redox potential. Correction was made for the absorbance of each component at the absorbance used to monitor the other. Heme accessibility was determined by solvent perturbation spectroscopy using 20% ethylene glycol as the perturbant. Measurements were made at the Soret band of the cyt f and heme accessibility calculated as described by Schlauder and Kassner (5). Methods for proteolysis, HPLC peptide mapping, and sequencing of peptide fragments to identify linkages within the PC-cyt f adduct are being described in a separate publication (6).

3. RESULTS
     Redox titrations of the PC, cyt f, and the PC-cyt f adduct are shown in Fig. 1. The redox potential for PC in the adduct (383 mV, n = 0.90) was not significantly different from that observed for free PC (381 mV, n = 0.95). In contrast, the redox potential of cyt f in the adduct (355 mV, n = 0.95) was shifted by about -20 mV relative to that of free cyt f (372 mV, n = 1.05). A similar shift in redox potential has been observed for the cytochrome component in a covalently linked PC-cyt c adduct (3).

M. Baltscheffsky (ed.), Current Research in Photosynthesis, Vol. III, 303–306.
© 1990 *Kluwer Academic Publishers. Printed in the Netherlands.*

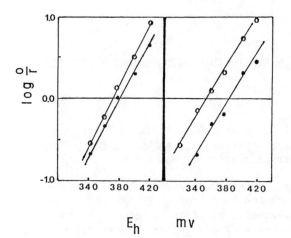

FIGURE 1.

REDOX TITRATION OF PC, CYT F, AND PC-CYT F ADDUCT. The open symbols show cyt f data and the closed symbols PC data. The data in the left panel is for the free proteins and that in the right panel for the PC-cyt f adduct.

Heme accessibility for free cyt f and cyt f in the PC-cyt f adduct was determined by solvent perturbation spectroscopy using 20% ethylene glycol as the perturbant. Cytochrome c was also examined as a control. The results are presented in Table 1.

	$\Delta A/A$	Exposure (%)	
Cyt f	0.0309	33.9	This study
PC-cyt f Adduct	0.0067	7.3	This study
Cyt c	0.0197	21.6	This study
Cyt c	0.0186	20.4	(5)

The heme exposure observed for cyt c was similar to that reported in the literature. Cyt f was also found to exhibit a substantial heme exposure, suggesting that it also has an exposed heme edge which may be involved in electron transfer to PC. The degree of heme exposure was greatly decreased in the PC-cyt f adduct, indicating that the exposed heme edge was partially buried at the interface between the two proteins in the adduct.

Detailed descriptions of proteolysis, HPLC peptide mapping, and sequencing of peptide fragments to identify the sites of covalent linkage within the PC-cyt f adduct are being published separately. These studies have shown that there are two sites at which PC is covalently linked to cyt f (Fig. 2).

FIGURE 2

SITES OF COVALENT LINKAGE IN
PC-CYT F ADDUCT

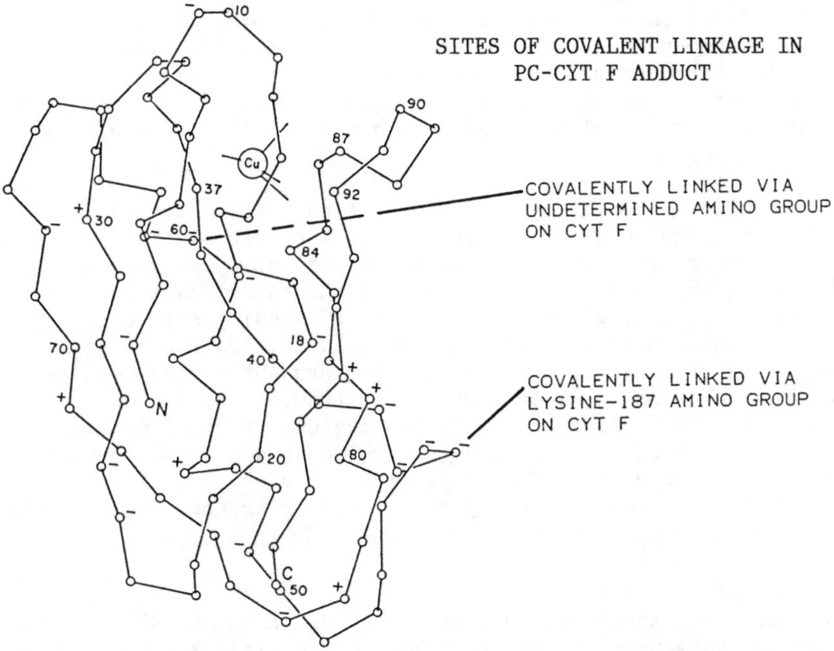

COVALENTLY LINKED VIA
UNDETERMINED AMINO GROUP
ON CYT F

COVALENTLY LINKED VIA
LYSINE-187 AMINO GROUP
ON CYT F

One of these sites has been identified as a covalent linkage
between Asp-44 of PC and Lys-187 of cyt f. The Lys-187 lies in one of
the regions previously predicted (1) as a candidate for participation in
the PC binding site. The second site of linkage involves Glu-60 (and
to a lesser extent, Glu-59) with as yet unidentified lysine residues of
cyt f.

4. DISCUSSION

The redox potentials, heme accessibility, and sites of covalent
linkage have been examined in a covalently linked 1:1 PC-cyt f adduct.
The redox potential of cyt f, but not of PC, was observed to be shifted
relative to that observed with the free protein, suggesting a possible
alteration of the heme environment. Although it is not known whether
this shift is physiologically relevant, it is interesting that it is in
the direction which would favor electron transfer from cyt f to PC.

Solvent perturbation experiments indicate the heme of cyt f to be
partially exposed to solvent as has been observed with other c-type
cytochromes (5). This observation refutes the suggestion made by
Siedow et al (7) that the high redox potential of cyt f might be due to
its heme being totally buried in the protein. The exposure of the cyt
f heme was greatly decreased in the PC-cyt f adduct. The exposed heme
edge of cyt f thus appears to be largely buried at the interface
between the two proteins in the adduct as might be expected if the
exposed heme edge is involved in electron transfer to PC.

Two sites of covalent linkage have been identified in the PC-cyt f adduct. The first involves covalent linkage of Asp-44 of PC to Lys-187 of cyt f and the second Glu-60 of PC to an as yet unidentified lysine on cyt f. It thus appears that both acidic patches (residues 41-45 and 59-61) of PC may be involved in interaction with cyt f, an observation consistent with the chemical modification studies of Anderson et al (8).

The identification of Lys-187 of cyt f as being involved in the covalent linkage to PC is of interest in that this residue lies in one of the three regions of the cyt f sequence previously suggested to be candidates for the PC binding site (1) and thus provides support for the hypothesis regarding the nature of the PC binding site on cyt f. In a recently published work involving chemical modification of arginyl residues on cyt f, Adam and Malkin (9) have presented evidence that Arg-88 and Arg-154 may also be involved in the interaction of cyt f with PC. Arg-154 also lies in one of the regions of cyt f proposed as candidates for the PC binding site (1) providing additonal support for the proposed nature of the PC binding site. However, Arg-88 lies outside of the proposed PC binding site, suggesting that regions other than those proposed initially (1) may also participate in PC binding.

ACKNOWLEDGEMENTS
This work was supported in part by NSF Grant No DCB-8722411 (D. Krogmann) and USDA Grant No 87-CRCR1-2310 (D. Davis). The authors also wish to thank Dr. M. Hermondson of Purdue University for his sequencing of the peptide fragments necessary for identification of the sites of covalent linkages.

REFERENCES
1. Davis, D.J. (1987) in Progress in Photosynthesis Research (J. Biggins, ed.), Vol. 2, pp.473-477, Martinus Nijhoff Publ., Dodrecht.
2. Davis, D.J. and Hough, K. (1983) Biochem. Biophys. Res. Commun., 116, 1000-1006.
3. Geren, L.M., Stonehuerner, J., Davis, D.J., and Millett, F., (1983), Biochim. Biophys. Acta, 724, 62-68.
4. Gray, J.C., (1978), Eur. J. Biochem., 82, 133-141.
5. Schlauder, G.G. and Kassner, R., (1979), J. Biol. Chem., 254, 4110-4113.
6. Morand, L., Frame, M., Colvert, K., Johnson, D., Krogmann, D., and Davis, D., (1989), Biochemistry, in press.
7. Siedow, J.N., Vickery, L.E., and Palmer, G., (1980), Arch. Biochem. Biophys., 203, 101-107.
8. Anderson, G.P., Sanderson, D.G., Lee, C.H., Durell, S., Anderson, L.B., and Gross, E.L., (1987), Biochim. Biopys. Acta, 894, 386-398.
9. Adam, Z. and Malkin, R., (1989), Biochim. Biophys. Acta, 975, 158-163.

CHEMICAL MODIFICATION OF THE LYSINE RESIDUES ON PLASTOCYANIN AND THE EFFECT ON CYTOCHROME f.

Elizabeth Gross and April Curtiss, Dept. of Biochemistry, The Ohio State University, Columbus, Ohio, USA, 43210.

Plastocyanin (1) (PC) is a 10.5 kD copper protein which is located in the lumen of the thylakoid where it shuttles electrons between cytochrome f (cyt f) and P700. PC contains two potential binding sites for reaction partners (2). Negatively-charged molecules bind at Site 1 is His 87 (Site 1) at the top of the PC molecule as depicted in Fig. 1. Site 2 is located in the vicinity of Tyr 83 (Site 2) which is surrounded by a patch of highly-conserved negatively-charged residues (3). Positively-charged molecules such as cobalt phenanthroline (3) and cytochrome c (4) bind to this site.

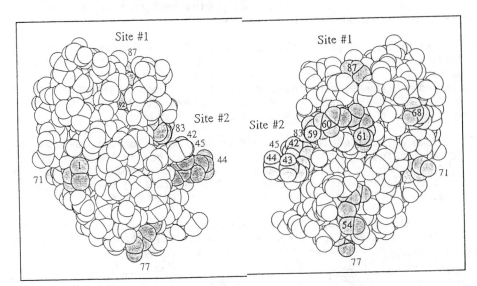

Fig. 1. Molecular graphics representation of spinach plastocyanin. X-ray coordinates of poplar plastocyanin (5) were obtained from the Brookhaven Protein Data Bank (6). 22 amino acid substitutions were made to convert poplar to spinach plastocyanin. The plastocyanin molecule is displayed using the Quanta program from Polygen Inc. which is available to us courtesy of the Ohio Supercomputer Center. The program was run on a Control Data-Silicon Graphics 4D/70 GT graphics

workstation. The ligands to the copper center, Tyr 83, the anion residues at residues #42-45, #59-61, #68, the amino terminus and lysines #54, #71 and #77 are shown. The two proposed binding sites on plastocyanin for reaction partners are also shown.

We have been using chemical modification techniques to determine which of the binding sites are used by PC's physiological reaction partners cyt f and P700 and also to determine the effects of both the net charge on the PC molecule and local charges on the interaction of PC with its reaction partners. Modification of carboxyl residues using ethylenediamine (EDA) + a water-soluble carbodiimide produced three singly-modified forms modified at residues #42-45, #59-61 and #68 (7). See Fig. 1 for the locations of the modifications.

Studies on the effect of modification on the rate of cyt f oxidation showed that cyt f binds at Site 2 near Tyr 83. However, it is not certain that electrons are actually donated at this site. Two other possibilities exist . First, after an initial binding at Site 2, cyt f may diffuse around the PC molecule to Site 1 and donate electrons to the copper via His 87. Second, cyt f being a large molecule (34kD), it may simultaneously bind at both binding sites and donate electrons at Site 1.

Cyt f has a net negative charge (8). However, chemical modification studies show that the binding for PC is positively-charged (7). Moreover, the interaction between the two molecules is governed by the electrostatic attraction between negatively-charged residues on PC and positively-charged residues at the binding site on cyt f rather than the net charge on the cyt f molecule.

However, all of the EDA modifications were located near one of the two binding sites. Therefore, we chose to modify the amino groups on PC in order to obtain forms modified at more remote locations on the PC molecule and to study the effect of increasing the net negative charge on the PC molecule on its interaction with cyt f.

For these studies, PC was modified using 4-chloro-3,5-dintro-benzoic acid (CDNB) which replaces a positively-charged amino group with a negatively-charged carboxyl group according to Eqn. 1 (9).

2. PROCEDURE

2.1 Preparation and separation of the CDNB-PC's.

PC was isolated from spinach as described by Anderson et al. (7). 0.4 ml of CDNB (5mg/ml) were added to 3.0 ml of reduced plastocyanin (0.4-0.6 mM) in 0.3 M carbonate buffer pH 9.0. The reaction was allowed to proceed for 24 hr. with a second aliquot of CDNB added after 7 hrs. The reaction was stopped by chromatography on a Bio-Gel P-10 column equilibrated with 25 mM Tris-Cl (pH 8.2). The mixture of modified plastocyanins was separated by FPLC using a mono-Q HR 5/5 anion exchange column.

Nine fractions were obtained. Fraction 1 consisted of unmodified PC. Fractions 2,3,4, and 6 (Fig. 2) were found to be singly-modified forms as determined by their incorporation of CDNB. The ratios of CDNB/PC were 0.8, 1.0, 1.2 and 1.3 for forms 2, 3, 4 and 6 respectively. The error in determining the incorporation was ±0.2. Each fraction was divided into two parts and purified using a second FPLC step. It was found that, in each case, the trailing halves of each peak were pure at least 90% pure.

3.2 Determination of the location of the label. The location of the CDNB moiety was determined for peaks F2, F3, F4 and F6. Each sample was treated with trypsin and the tryptic peptides were separated using reverse phase HPLC and eluted with a 9:1 acetonitrile/water gradient. In general, CDNB modification causes the loss of a tryptic cleavage site which results in the loss of two tryptic peptides accompanied by the appearance of a new tryptic peptide at another location. In each case, the new tryptic peptides were subject to amino acid analysis and sequencing of the first five amino acid residues. Each modified form was labelled in a different location on the plastocyanin molecule. The locations are shown in Table I and Fig 1.

2.3 Kinetics of the interaction of the modified PC's with cyt f, mammalian cytochrome c (cyt c) and potassium ferricyanide. The kinetics of the interaction of the CDNB-modified plastocyanins with cyt f, mammalian cyt c and potassium ferricyanide were measured using the stopped-flow attachment of the Aminco-DW2a spectrophotometer. In each case, second order rate constants were determined using pseudo first order conditions. The reactions were carried out in 25 mM succinate buffer, pH7.0, with sufficient NaCl added to attain an ionic strength of 0.300M. See Gross et al. (submitted to Biochim. Biophys. Acta) for further details concerning the experimental methods.

3. RESULTS AND DISCUSSION

Ferricyanide was chosen as a reaction partner because it is known to react at Site 1. No effect was observed (Table I.) which is consistent with the large distance between the sites of modification and His 87. Cyt c was chosen because it is known to bind at Site 2 (4) and has a net positive charge as well as positive charges surrounding the heme cleft (10). All of the CDNB-modified forms of PC showed a large increase in their rates of reaction with cyt c. This reflects the increase in negative charge on the PC molecule.

Cyt f also binds at Site 2 but has a net negative charge. Inhibition was observed for all of the modified forms indicating that the interaction with PC is controlled by the net negative charge on the cyt f molecule as opposed to the positive charge on the binding site.

Thus, the CDNB-PC results stand in contrast to those obtained for the EDA modifications. The two sets of experiments can be reconciled as follows. Charges at the binding site on cyt f interact with complimentary charges on PC. Changes in the charge on PC interfere with the complimentary interaction. In contrast, charges distant from

TABLE I.

Rate of Reaction of CDNB-plastocyanins with $K_3Fe(CN)_6$, Cyt c and Cyt f

Fraction	Residue Modified	Distance (A) to		k ($M^{-1}s^{-1}$ x 10^{-6})		
		Cu	Tyr 83	$K_3Fe(CN)_6$	Cyt c	Cyt f
Control	---	---	---	0.160±0.006	1.10±0.04	26.0±1.2
F1	---	---	---	0.176±0.008	1.2 ±0.1	31.9±3.6
F2	1	16.2	23.6	0.188±0.006	5.7 ±1.1	20.0±2.0
F3	71	15.0	22.1	0.176±0.016	5.8 ±0.8	28.7±3.6
F4	77	30.1	25.7	0.180±0.022	---	9.5±1.4
F6	54	25.0	19.1	0.174±0.012	5.7 ±0.5	20.8±3.5

the binding site only see the net charge on the cyt f molecule. Therefore, the CDNB modifications which are located far from the binding site, should cause inhibition, not stimulation of the reaction with cyt f.

These results do not explain why the EDA-modification at residue #68 caused inhibition of the interaction of PC with cyt f. Stimulation would be expected if net charge effects were controlling the interaction. These results suggest that residue #68 is within the interaction zone of cyt f (albeit possibly at the edge). Thus, cyt f may interact with Site 1 as well as Site 2. Thus, cyt f may approach the back of the PC molecule (Fig. 1) and have recognition sites at both locations.

REFERENCES

1   Freeman, H.C. (1981) Coord. Chem. 21, 29-51.
2   Sykes, A.G. (1985) Chem. Soc. Rev. 14, 283-315.
3   Boulter, D., Haslett, B.G., Peacock, D., Ramshaw, J.A.M. and Scawen, M.D. (1977) Int'l. Rev. Biochem. 13, 1-40.
4   King, G.C., Binstead, R.A. and Wright, P.E. (1985) Biochim. Biophys. Acta 806, 262-271.
5   Coleman, P.M., Freeman, H.C., Guss, J.M., Murata, M., Norris, V.A., Ramshaw, J.A.M. and Venkatappa, M. P. (1978) Nature 272, 319-324.
6   Bernstein, F.C., Koetzle, T.F., Williams, G.J.B., Meyer, Jr. E.F., Brice, M.D., Rogers, J.R., Kennard, O., Shimanouchi, T. and Tasumi, M. (1977) J. Mol. Biol. 112, 535-542.
7   Anderson, G.P., Sanderson, D.G., Lee, C.H., Durell, S., Anderson, L.B. and Gross, E.L. (1987) Biochim. Biophys. Acta 894, 386-398.
8   Gray, J.C. (1978) Eur. J. Biochem. 92, 133-141.
9   Brautigan, D.L., Ferguson-Miller, S. and Margoliash, E. (1978) J. Biol. Chem. 253, 130-139.
10 Margoliash, E. and Bosshard, H.R. (1983) TIBS 8, 316-320.

MODELING OF ELECTROSTATIC EFFECTS IN PLASTOCYANIN

S. Durell[*], E. Gross[*] and J. Labanowski[+], [*]Biophysics Program and Dept. of Biochemistry, The Ohio State University, Columbus, Ohio, USA, 43210 and [+]The Ohio Supercomputer Center, Columbus, Ohio, USA, 43212.

1. INTRODUCTION

Plastocyanin (PC) is a 10.5 kD copper protein which is located in the lumen of the thylakoid where it transfers electrons from cytochrome f (cyt f) to P700 (1). The interaction with both reaction partners is electrostatic in nature (2). The highly-conserved (3) patch of negatively-charged residues at positions #42-45 and #59-61 on PC (also called the East Face) (Fig. 1) is the initial recognition site on PC (2,). These negatively-charged residues interact with positively-charged residues on cyt f (2,).

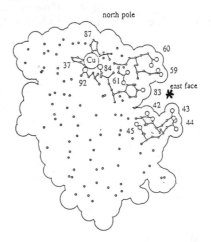

Fig. 1. Computer graphics representation of oxidized spinach PC. The atomic coordinates of oxidized poplar PC (4) were obtained from the Brookhaven Protein Data Bank. The atomic coordinates of spinach PC were derived from those of poplar PC by making the appropriate amino acid substitutions (22 out of 99 amino acid residues) using the computer drogram MOLEDT. The copper center, Tyr 83, and the negatively-charged residues at #42-45, #59-61 and #68 are highlighted. The cytf binding site is indicated by a *.

In order to understand this interaction, we have calculated the electrostatic potential field of plastocyanin. For our calculations, we chose the Del-Phi program of Klapper et al. (5) because it allows us to vary parameters such as dielectric constant, solvent ionic strength and Stern layer thickness. In addition, we were able to vary oxidation state of PC and the pH.

M. Baltscheffsky (ed.), Current Research in Photosynthesis, Vol. III, 311–314.
© 1990 Kluwer Academic Publishers. Printed in the Netherlands.

2. PROCEDURE

The Del-Phi program maps the atomic coordinates of PC onto a 3-dimensional grid. United atom van der Waals radii are assigned to the heavy atoms to define the surface of the protein. Fractional electrostatic charges are mapped onto the grid in such a way as to provide spherically symmetrical distributions around the charged atoms of the protein. The electrostatic potential field of the protein was then calculated by numerically solving the Poisson-Boltzmann equation by the finite difference method. The program was executed on a CONVEX C1 computer in the vector mode. See Durell et al. (submitted to Archives of Biochemistry and Biophysics) for details concerning the experimental methodology.

3. RESULTS AND DISCUSSION

3.1 The effect of oxidation state on electrostatic potential field surrounding PC. The electrostatic potential field of oxidized spinach PC (Fig. 2a) is positive at the top of the molecule (North Pole) in the region near His 87. His 87 is a ligand to the copper and a binding site for negatively-charged molecules such as ferricyanide (9) and Photosystem I (2). In contrast, the potential field is negative in the vicinity of Tyr 83 (the East Face) which is thought to be the binding site for positively-charged molecules such as cobalt phenanthroline (6) and cytochrome c (7) as well as cyt f (which has a positively-charged binding site (2)). Thus, there is agreement between the theoretical calcualtions and experimental findings.

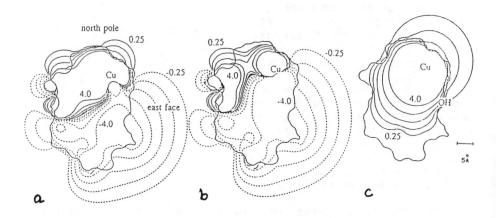

Fig. 2.   The effect of oxidation state on the electrostatic potential field surrounding spinach PC. The parameters used to calculate the electric field were: protein/solvent dielectric constants = 2/80; solvent ionic strength = 150 mM; Stern layer = 2 A. Isopotential lines are shown for kT/e of 4.0, 2.0, 1.0, 0.5, 0.25, -0.25, -0.5, -1.0, -2.0, -4.0.   a) Oxidized PC; b) Reduced PC; c) Oxidized - reduced PC (Ionic strength = 30 mM).

The electrostatic potential field of reduced PC is shown in Fig.

2b. The field was calculated by changing the charge on the copper atom form +2 to +1 without changing the location of any of the residues. This is justified since the crystals structures of oxidized and reduced PC are almost identical at pH 7.8 (1.) Reduction of the copper center increased the magnitude of the negative potential at the East Face (Fig. 2c.).

The predicted increase in the magnitude of the potential field will cause an of ca.0.3 pH units in the pK's of critical East Face residues. These predictions agree very well with experimental results obtained for the nitrotyrosine derivative of Tyr 83 (13) whose pK increases by 0.3±0.05 pH units upon reduction of the PC molecule. The redox-state dependent shifts in pK may be important in regulating the interaction of PC with cyt f, particularly at low pH.

3.2The effect of solvent ionic strength, protein dielectric constant and pH on the electrostatic potential field of plastocyanin. The effect of decreasing the ionic strength of the medium from 150 mM to 15 mM on the electrostatic potential field is shown in Fig. 3a. Two effects are observed. First, the magnitude of the negative potential at the East Face is increased, which will increase the attraction between PC and positively-charged reaction partners such as cyt f in aggreement with experimental results (2). The second effect is to decrease the magnitude of the positive field at His 87 which has the effect of decreasing the attraction of PC for negatively-charged reaction partners, which has also been observed.

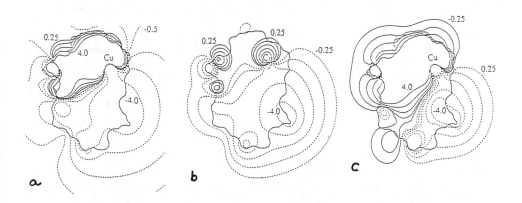

Fig. 3. The effect of solvent ionic strength, protein dielectric constant and pH of the medium on the electrostatic potential field for oxidized spinach PC. a) Ionic strength = 15 mM; b)Protein dielectric constant = 80; c) pH = 5.0

Fig. 3b shows the effect of increasing the protein dielectric constant of PC from 2 to 80. The positive field at His 87 is completely gone. The results show that if the internal dielectric constant were 80, the interactions of PC with its reaction partners would be quite different. Thus, it is very important to use a low dielectric constant for the interior of the protein. This is one of the problems with the results of Rush et al. (9) who used a dipole approach to model the interaction of PC with cyt c. The dipole approach presupposes an internal dielectric constant of 80. Another problem is that the electrostatic potential field of PC is too complex to be approximated by a dipole.

The effect of pH on the electrostatic potential field of PC is important, because it experiences a pH of ≤ 5 upon illumination of the thylakoids. Some of the carboxylic acid residues on PC should be protonated under these conditions, since pH 5 is close to their pK's. Protonation of these residues will change the magnitude of the electrostatic potential, and hence the interaction of PC with its reaction partners. We made a very simple approximation to the low pH case by decreasing the charge on all carboxylic residues on PC by 50 %. It can be seen (Fig. 3c) that the potential field around Tyr 83 is decreased while that at His 87 is increased. These results agree with known effects of pH on the interaction of PC with cyt f (6).

4. CONCLUSIONS

The Del-Phi program of Klapper et al. (5) was used to calculate the electrostatic potential field of PC. A region of positive potential was observed at His 87. The field at this site as the ionic strength is lowered decreasing the interction of PC with negatively-charged electron donors. It also decreases when the protein dielectric constant is increased from 2 to 80 due to increased shielding of the positively-charged copper center. In contrast, lowering the pH increases the magnitude of the positive field which is consistent with increases in the rate of reaction of PC with P700.

There is a negative potential region at the East Face which becomes even more negative upon reduction of the copper center. This results in an increase in the pK's of ionizable groups in the region. Decreasing the ionic strength increases the magnitude of this field whereas lowering the pH decreases it. Again, the calculations are consistent with experimental observations concerning the interaction of PC with cyt f.

REFERENCES
1 Freeman, H.C. (1981) Coord. Chem. 21, 29-51.
2 Anderson, G.P., Sanderson, D.G., Lee, C.H., Durell, S., Anderson, L.B. and Gross, E.L. (1987) Biochim. Biophys. Acta 894, 386-398.
3 Boulter, D., Haslett, B.G., Peacock, D., Ramshaw, J.A.M. and Scawen, M.D. (1977) Int'l. Rev. Biochem. 13, 1-40.
4 Coleman, P.M., Freeman, H.C., Guss, J.M., Murata, M., Norris, V.A., Ramshaw, J.A.M. and Venkatappa, M.P. (1978) Nature 272, 319-324.
5 Klapper, I., Hagstarom, R., Fine, R., Sharp, K. and Honig, B. (1986) Proteins, 1, 47-49.
6 Sykes, A.G. (1985) Chem. Soc. Rev. 14, 283-315.
7 King, G.C., Binstead, R.A. and Wright, P.E. (1985) Biochim. Biophys. Acta 806, 262-271.
8 Anderson, G.P., Draheim, J.E. and Gross, E.L. (1985) Biochim. Biophys. Acta 810, 123-131.
9 Rush, J.d., Levine, F. and Koppenol, W.H. (1988) Biochem. 27, 5876-5884.

TRIMETHYLAMINE N OXIDE RESPIRATION OF AEROBIC PHOTOSYNTHETIC BACTERIUM
ERYTHROBACTER SP. OCH 114

HIROYUKI ARATA, MINORU SHIMIZU, MASAKAZU MORITA AND KEN-ICHIRO
TAKAMIYA, DEPT OF BIOLOGY, FAC. OF SCIENCE, KYUSHU UNIV. 33 FUKUOKA
812, JAPAN

1. INTRODUCTION

Erythrobacter sp. OCh 114 is a photosynthetic bacterium which
adapts to aerobic environments (1-4). The amino acid sequence of its
cytochrome c_2 (cytochrome c_{551}) indicated close relation of this
species to the photosynthetic and non-photosynthetic species of the α-3
subdivision (5) of the purple bacteria (6).

OCh 114 is capable of anaerobic respiration. Trimethyl amine N-
oxide (TMAO) is one of the terminal oxidant (7). We have found tha the
electron transport chain of the TMAO respiration of this bacterium   is
differenct from that of the related facultative phototrophs at two
points (7): cytochrome $b-c_1$ complex is probably involved in OCh 114
while it is bypassed in Rhodobacter capsulatus (8); TMAO reductase of
OCh 114 does not reduce dimethylsulfoxide while a single enzyme reduces
both TMAO and dimethylsulphoxide in Rhodobacter sphaeroides (9) and R.
capsulatas (10).

Besides cytochrome c_2, OCh 114 has two soluble cytochromes with a
similar molecular weight. One of them increased when the bacteria were
grown in the presence of TMAO, and is possibly involved in the TMAO
respiration.

2. MATERIALS AND METHODS

Erythrobacter sp. OCh 114 was cultured at 28°C for 2 days in the
dark under vigorous aeration in the medium described in (7). Usually,
30 mM TMAO was added to the culture medium.

The bacteria were harvested and washed once with 50 mM Tricine-
NaOH (pH 8.0)/300 mM NaCl. To obtaine the soluble fraction, the
bacterial cells were broken by passing through a French pressure cell
and centrifuged at 500,000 g for 3 hrs. The supernatant was dialyzed
in 10 mM tricine-NaOH (pH 8.0). For SDS-PAGE, the soluble fraction was
further fractionated by adding ammonium sulfate to 75% saturation.
The supernatant contained most cytochromes having a low molecular
weight. It was dialyzed in 10 mM Tricine-NaOH (pH 8.0), concentrated
and used for SDS-PAGE.

SDS-PAGE was done according to Laemmli and Fevre (11), with a
linear gradient of polyacrylamide (13-18%). The concentration of SDS
in the gel was 0.1%. Heme proteins in the gel were stained by the
method of Thomas et al. (12).

Absorbance changes were measured with Shimadzu UV-240

M. Baltscheffsky (ed.), Current Research in Photosynthesis, Vol. III, 315–318.
© 1990 *Kluwer Academic Publishers. Printed in the Netherlands.*

spectrophotometer. Anaerobic conditions were obtained by flushing
the cuvett with oxygen-free argon gass.

For the pH change measurements, the bacterial cells was washed
with 300 mM KCl. pH changes were measured with a pH electrode. The
cell suspension was kept anaerobic for 30 min befor the measurement.

3. RESULTS AND DISCUSSIONS

3.1. Relative amount of soluble c-type cytochromes

This bacteria have three soluble cytochromes with a simmilar
molecular weight. Cytochrome c_{551} (cytochrome c_2) has been purified
(13) and its amino acid sequence has been determined (6). Cytochrome
c_{552}, which increases when the bacteria are grown under the light
aerobic condition, has been purified (Morita and Takamiya,
unpublished). Their properties were summerized on Table 1. We know
little about the third species, which has an appearent molecular wight
of 14,000 on SDS-PAGE.

TABLE 1. Properties of cytochromes c_2 and c_{552}

	molecular weight		E_{m7}	pI
	from the amino acid sequence	from the SDS-PAGE	(mV)	
c_2	13,235	14,500	250	4.9
c_{552}	–	13,500	215	5.6

FIGURE 1. SDS-PAGE of soluble fractions,
and purified cytochrome c_2 and
c_{552}. The photograph shows the
heme staining pattern. Lane 1,
cytochrome c_2; Lane 2,
cytochrome c_{552}; Lane 3, soluble
fraction from the cells grown in
the absence of TMAO; lane 4,
soluble fraction from the cells
grown in the presence of 30 mM
TMAO.

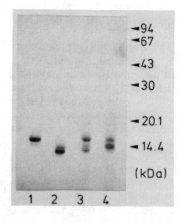

Fig. 1 shows the heme staining pattern of the fraction soluble
with 75 % saturation ammonium sulfate. Bacteria grown in the absence
(lane 3) and presence (lane 4) of TMAO were compared. Purified
cytochrome c_2 and c_{552} are also applied on the same gel. When the
bacteria were grown in the absence of TMAO, cytochrome c_2 was

predominant. In the presence of TMAO, the relative amount of the
medium-size species increased.

3.2. Oxidation of cytochromes by TMAO.
    Fig. 2A shows the absobance change due to the oxidation of c-type
cytochrome(s) in the soluble fraction by the addition of TMAO (trace
a). About 60% of total cytochrome was reduced by titrating with
dithionite befor the addition of TMAO. Most of cytochrome was oxidized
rapidly.
    We did the same experiments using purified cytochrome c_2 (trace b)
in the presence of the soluble fraction, which contained TMAO
reductase. The oxidation was very slow. We observed faster oxidation
with less pure cytochrome c_2 preparation, which contained small amount
of other cytochrome(s) (data not shown). Probably, cytochrome c_2 is
not the direct electron donnor to TMAO reductase. Cytochrome with
lower molecular weight, especially the one with the medium size, is
possibly the electron donner to the reductase.

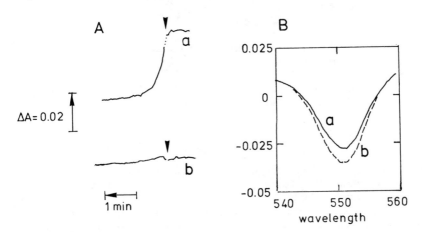

Fig. 2.A) Time courses of absorbance change at 550 nm due to the
        oxidation of c-type cytochromes by TMAO. a, the soluble
        fraction (5 mg protein/ml); b, cytochrome c_{551} (6.7 μM) and
        the soluble fraction (0.25 mg protein/ml). Cytochrome was
        reduced by titrating with dithionite under anaerobic
        condition. 0.5 mM TMAO was added at the times indicated by
        the arrows.
    B) Difference spectra befor and after the addition of 0.5 mM
        TMAO (a) or potasium ferricyanide (b) to the soluble
        fraction. The sample contained the soluble fraction at a
        concentration of 5 mg protein/ml.

3.3. Proton translocation accompanying the TMAO respiration.
    Fig. 3 shows pH change of the cell suspension caused by addition
of TMAO. In the presence of FCCP, TMAO induced increase of pH. This

is probably due to the uptake of extra proton by TMA:

$$(CH_3)_3NO + 2[H] + H^+ \rightarrow (CH_3)_3NH^+ + H_2O$$

In the absence of FCCP, temporary decrease of pH was observed besides the proton uptake. It was inhibited by antimycin or myxothiazol. The result support the idea that cytochrome $\underline{b}-\underline{c}_1$ complex is involved in the electron transfer of the TMAO respiration. Protons translocated by the Q-cycle mechanism probably contributed to the observed pH increase.

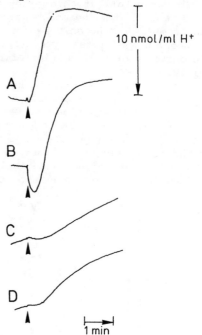

Fig. 3. pH change of the cell suspension by the addition of TMAO. The suspension contained 300 mM KCl, 10 mM sodium succinate and the bacterial cells (2.25 μM bacteriochlorophyll). A, 10 μM FCCP; B, no further addition; C, 10 μM antimycin; D, 10 μM myxothiazol.

REFERENCES
1 Shiba, T. (1989) in Anaerobic Photosynthetic Bacteria (Harashima, K., Shiba, T. and Murata, N. eds.), pp. 1-8, Japan Scientific Societies Press, Tokyo.
2 Shiba, T. (1984) J. Gen. Appl. Microbiol. 30, 239-244
3 Okamura, K., Takamiya, K. and Nishimura, M. (1985) Arch. Microbiol. 142, 12-17
4 Harashima, K., Kanazawa, K., Yoshida, I. and Kamata, H. (1987) Plant Cell Physiol. 28, 365-374
5 Woes, C.R. (1987) Microbiol. Rev. 51, 221-271
6 Okamura, K., Miyata, T., Iwanaga, S., Takamiya, K. and Nishimura, M. (1987) J. Biochem. 101, 957-966
7 Arata, H., Serikawa, Y. and Takamiya, K. (1988) J. Biochem. 1011-1015
8 King, G.F., Richardoson, D.J., Jackson, J.B. and Ferguson, S.J. (1987) Arch. Microbiol. 149,47-51
9 Satoh, T. and Kurihara, F.N. (1987) J. Biochem. 102, 191-197
10 McEwan, H., Wetzster, H. E., Meyer, O., Jackson, J.B. and Ferguson, S.J. (1987) Arch. Microbiol. 147, 340-345
11 Laemlli, U.K. and Favre, M. (1973) J. Mol. Biol. 80, 575-594
12 Thomas, P.E., Ryan, D. and Levin, W. (1976) Anal Biochem. 75,168-176
13 Okamura, K., Kisaichi, K., Takamiya, K. and Nishimura, M. (1984) Arch. Microbiol. 139,143-146.

EPR Spectra of Cytochrome c549 of <u>Anacystis</u> <u>nidulans</u>

Curtis W. Hoganson, Göran Lagenfelt, Lars-Erik Andréasson and Tore Vänngård, Department of Biochemistry and Biophysics, Chalmers University of Technology and the University of Gothenburg, S-412 96 Göteborg, Sweden

INTRODUCTION

A low-potential c-type cytochrome occurs in a number of blue-green algae [1-4]. The cytochrome contains one mesoheme [5] per 15500 Da polypeptide [3]. The function of the cytochrome is not known, but there is evidence suggesting a role in cyclic photophosphorylation [6].

We began to investigate cytochrome c549 after finding it in Photosystem II preparations from <u>Anacystis</u> <u>nidulans</u> and <u>Synechococcus</u>. A similar observation was made earlier [7]. The cytochrome is reported to be water-soluble and extractable with distilled water [1,2] or to be membrane-bound [2,4,8], requiring detergent or acetone [2] or 400 mM NaCl [4] to remove it from the membranes. The puzzle then appeared to be, are there are one or two low-potential cytochromes c549?

We report here that in our cultures of <u>A. nidulans</u> there are indeed two populations of cytochrome c549 that differ in their attachment to the membrane and appear to differ in their binding to an anion exchanger and in their EPR spectra.

The proposed functions for the cytochrome are all as electron carriers, so another puzzle involves its ability to bind carbon monoxide [5], which suggests that the cytochrome might be five-coordinate and that its function might involve binding an exogenous ligand. Many heme proteins that bind ligands have a 5-coordinate, high-spin iron in the absence of ligand, while many that carry electrons have 6-coordinate, low-spin iron [9]. Using EPR spectroscopy, we found that cytochrome c549 is of the low-spin type, and we conclude that it functions as an electron carrier.

MATERIALS AND METHODS

<u>A. nidulans</u> was grown and membranes and PSII extracts were prepared as described previously [10]. EPR samples of partially purified cytochrome were prepared from either the soluble proteins released by cell lysis or those washed off the photosynthetic membranes as outlined in the following paragraphs.

The solution from cell lysis was freeze-dried, redissolved, and fractionated by precipitation with $(NH_4)_2SO_4$. The 15%-55% fraction was dialyzed against 10 mM phosphate buffer (K$^+$, pH 7.0), concentrated, made 1 M in NaCl, and applied to a Sephadex G-75 column. Cytochrome fractions were dialyzed against 4 mM phospate buffer (K$^+$, pH 7.0) and passed through DEAE-cellulose. The cytochrome did not bind, whereas phycocyanin did. The eluate was concentrated and used for EPR in 400 mM sucrose, 50 mM MES (pH 6.0) and 15 mM NaCl.

M. Baltscheffsky (ed.), Current Research in Photosynthesis, Vol. III, 319–322.
© 1990 *Kluwer Academic Publishers. Printed in the Netherlands.*

Photosynthetic membranes were washed with 2 mM MES, pH 6.0 to remove phycocyanin and then washed with 1 M NaCl. This NaCl solution containing the cytochrome and residual phycocyanin was dialyzed against 1 mM Tris HCl, pH 7.5, and applied to a DEAE-cellulose column. The phycocyanin and cytochrome both bound, and were eluted in that order with a concentration gradient (potassium hydrogen phosphate, pH 6). Peak cytochrome fractions were used for EPR after changing the buffer.

EPR spectra were recorded with a Bruker ER 200 D-SRC X-band spectrometer equipped with a standard TE102 cavity and an Oxford Instruments ESR-10 helium-flow cryostat.

RESULTS AND DISCUSSION

Cytochrome c549 was always found in the photosynthetic membranes of Anacystis nidulans. The ratio of cytochromes in the phycocyanin-depleted membranes is about 2-3 cyt c549: 2 cyt b559: 1-2 cyt b563. Similar proportions have been reported [7]. Phycocyanin, the most abundant extrinsic membrane protein, can be released selectively by washing the membranes several times with a low ionic strength solution at -5°C. Freezing and thawing also releases phycocyanin. Membranes can then be washed with 1 M NaCl to release cytochrome c549. Table 1 illustrates one such experiment.

The mixture of cytosolic proteins also usually contains cyt c549. Too much is present to be simply the result of contamination by membrane fragments. This cytochrome failed to bind to DEAE-cellulose. Because all other reported examples of cytochrome c549 have bound to anion exchangers, we suspect that this protein has been modified during its isolation. SDS-PAGE (data not shown) revealed no obvious differences in molecular size between the two partially purified cytochrome samples; 16 kDa ± 1 kDa was determined for both. Three of the first five amino acids on the N-terminus are acidic residues [3], the loss of which might account for the alteration in binding to the ion exchanger without producing a large change in mobility on the gel. This question merits further investigation.

TABLE 1: Release of Extrinsic Membrane Proteins

wash number	ionic strength	phycocyanin (grams)	cytochrome (nmol)
1/thaw	low	3.7	nd
2	low	0.17	<8
3	low	0.21	<5
4	low	0.19	<6
5/thaw	low	0.38	<10
6/thaw	low	0.10	<10
7	high	0.06	55
8	high	0.01	19
9	high	0.004	13

low = 15 mM NaCl, 10 mM TrisHCl (pH 7.5), 10% glycerol; high = 1 M NaCl, 10 mM TrisHCl (pH 7.5); nd = not determined; thaw = sample was thawed before washing.

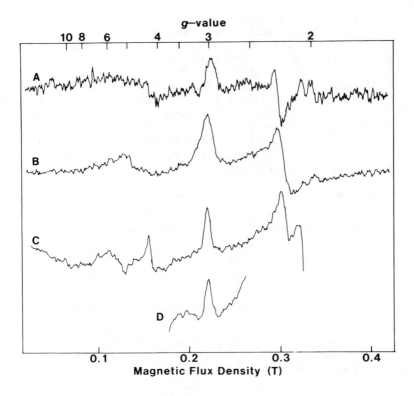

Figure 1. EPR spectra of cytochrome c549. A) partially purified cytosolic cytochrome, B) partially purified NaCl-solubilized cytochrome, C) detergent extract of thylakoid membranes, and D) whole membranes.

EPR spectra of the partially purified cytochromes were obtained (Fig. 1.) In addition, the spectra of cyt c549 in both unfractionated thylakoid membranes and in a detergent extract thereof were determined. These are presented as the difference spectrum between samples reduced with anthraquinol-2 sulfonate and with dithionite. All four spectra show peaks characteristic of a low spin heme. The principal $\underline{g}$-values for the four samples, determined from these spectra, are shown in Table 2. A weak feature at $\underline{g}$ = 1.4 (data not shown) has also been tentatively assigned as the $\underline{g}_x$ peak of the cytochrome.

Solubilization of the membrane-bound cytochrome has little effect on its spectrum. The cytosolic cytochrome, however, has a somewhat different set of $\underline{g}$-values. This difference may reflect heterogeneity in the cytochrome in vivo or heterogeneity induced by the different purification protocols.

The EPR spectra show a low-spin heme, indicating that cytochrome c549 is six-coordinate, supporting an electron-transfer function for it rather than a ligand-binding function. The ability of the cytochrome to bind CO [5] suggested five-coordinate iron. CO-binding can be reconciled to six-coordinate iron since the redox potential of a cytochrome depends on the extent to which its heme group is exposed to the aqueous environment, and a low potential indicates a high degree of exposure [11]. We have measured the midpoint potential of the NaCl-solubilized cytochrome to be about -300 mV, and the water-extractable cytochrome has a reported potential of -260 mV [5]. Thus, the exposure of the heme in cyt c549 may allow CO to approach the heme and to replace the endogenous sixth ligand.

TABLE 2. Principal g-values of cytochrome c549.

sample	g_z	g_y	g_x
Cytosolic	2.96	2.24	1.4
NaCl-solubilized	3.04	2.20	1.4
Detergent extract	3.05	2.19	nd
Thylakoid membranes	3.04	nd	nd

Acknowledgements
    This work was supported by a grant from the Swedish Natural Science Research Council. C.W.H. is the recipient of a fellowship from the American-Scandinavian Foundation.

REFERENCES
1 Holten, R.W. & Myers, J. (1967) Biochim. Biophys. Acta 131, 362-374
2 Ho, K.W., Ulrich, E.L., Krogmann, D.W. & Gomez-Lojero, C. (1979) Biochim. Biophys. Acta 545, 236-248
3 Alam, J., Sprinkle, J., Hermodson, M.A. & Krogmann, D.W. (1984)Biochim. Biophys. Acta 766, 317-321
4 Stewart, A.C. & Bendall, D.S. (1980) Biochem. J. 188, 351-361
5 Holten, R.W. & Myers, J. (1967) Biochim. Biophys. Acta 131, 375-384
6 Kienzl, P.F. & Peschek, G.A. (1983) FEBS Lett. 162, 76-80
7 Stewart, A.C. & Bendall, D.S. (1981) Biochem. J. 194, 877-887
8 Bricker, T.M. & Sherman, L.A. (1984) Arch. Biochem. Biophys. 235, 204-211
9 Wood, P.M. (1984) Biochim. Biophys. Acta 768, 293-317
10 Lagenfelt, G., Hansson, Ö & Andréasson, L.-E. (1987) Acta Chem. Scand. B41, 123-125
11 Stellwagen, E. (1978) Nature 275, 73-74

THE ACTIVE SITE OF RIBULOSE BISPHOSPHATE CARBOXYLASE / OXYGENASE

G. Schneider, Y. Lindqvist and T. Lundqvist
Swedish University of Agricultural Sciences
Uppsala Biomedical Center
Department of Molecular Biology
P.O. Box 590
S-751 24 Uppsala, Sweden

INTRODUCTION

Ribulose-1,5-bisphosphate carboxylase/oxygenase (Rubisco) has attracted a lot of interest due to its central role in the carbon metabolism of plants and photosynthetic microorganisms (for a review see (1)). The dual function of this enzyme, catalyzing the primary steps in both photosynthetic carbon dioxide fixation and photorespiration , makes it a challenging target for attempts to improve the efficiency of photosynthesis. Recombinant DNA-techniques provide a promising tool to modify the carboxylase/oxygenase ratio by genetic engineering. However, the application of these techniques requires a detailed knowledge of the catalytic mechanism of the enzyme and the structure of its active site.

The initial step in the photosynthetic CO_2 fixation consists of the addition of CO_2 to ribulose-1,5-bisphosphate. The intermediate six-carbon compound is subsequently cleaved into two molecules of phospho-glycerate. The latter is then partly recycled in the Calvin cycle, where it is used to regenerate ribulose bisphosphate and partly converted to starch.

Rubisco also catalyses the initial oxygenation step in photorespiration, during which a considerable amount of the stored energy is converted to heat thereby limiting crop yield. In this step, oxygen instead of carbon dioxide is added to ribulose bisphosphate, thus yielding one molecule of phospho-glycerate and one molecule of phospho-glycolate. The latter is metabolized in the glycolate pathway, where it is ultimately converted to CO_2. The reaction mechanism of the oxygenation reaction is much less understood than the mechanism of the carboxylation reaction.

The catalytic activities of Rubisco require an activation process, during which a lysine residue reacts with an activator CO_2 molecule (2), which is not the substrate CO_2. The labile carbamate formed in this reaction is stabilized by binding of a magnesium ion. The substrate ribulose-1,5-bisphosphate binds to the activated ternary complex and is subsequently either carboxylated by CO_2 or

M. Baltscheffsky (ed.), Current Research in Photosynthesis, Vol. III, 323–330.
© 1990 *Kluwer Academic Publishers. Printed in the Netherlands.*

oxygenated by O_2. All biochemical evidence indicates that these two reactions occur at the same site in the protein (1).

Rubisco from higher plants, algae and most photosynthetic microorganisms is a multisubunit complex built up of eight large (mol wt. 56 kd) and eight small (mol wt. 14 kd) subunits. The catalytic activities for both the carboxylation and oxygenation reaction reside on the large subunit. The primary structure of the large subunits of higher plants and algal carboxylases studied so far exhibit a high degree of amino acid homology, in the range of 70-90 % (1).

In contrast to these L_8S_8 type carboxylases, the enzyme from the photosynthetic bacterium *Rhodosprillium rubrum* differs considerably in primary and quaternary structure. This carboxylase is only a dimer of large subunits and lacks the small subunits (3). The overall amino acid homology to the large subunit of higher plant carboxylases is 25% (4,5). Despite this low overall amino acid homology, some peptide regions are highly conserved in all the carboxylases. Three of these conserved peptide regions have been identified as active site peptides (2,6,7), indicating a common active site and thus a similar three-dimensional structure for all the carboxylase large subunits.

In the following, we will describe the structure of the enzyme and correlate the structural information to biochemical and genetic data.

Overall structure of the enzyme

A number of crystallographic studies have focussed on Rubisco and structural information is now available for both the L_2 and the L_8S_8 type of the enzyme and for diffent complexes. Table 1 summarizes the Rubisco structures, which have been solved at present. From these studies, the following picture of the overall structure and assembly of the enzyme has emerged.

TABLE 1. Crystal structures of Rubisco

Source	Species	Resolution	Reference
Rh. rubrum	native	1.7 Å	8,11
Rh. rubrum	enzyme – phosphoglycerate	2.9 Å	9
Rh. rubrum	enzyme – CABP	2.6 Å	10
Rh. rubrum	enzyme – Mg(II) – CO_2	2.6 Å	unpublished
Rh. rubrum	enzyme – Mg(II) – CO_2 – CA1P	2.6 Å	unpublished
spinach	enzyme – Mg(II) – CO_2 – CABP	2.8 Å	11
tobacco	native	2.8 Å	12,13

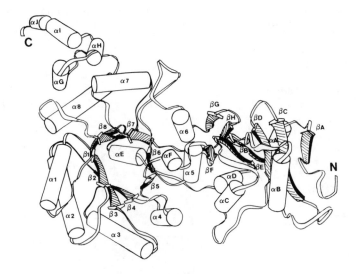

Figure 1:   Schematic view of the subunit of Rubisco from *Rh.*
                   rubrum. The secondary structural elements are
                   indicated (cylinders represent α-helices   and
                   arrows represent β-strands).

     The large subunit is divided in two domains, one smaller
N-terminal domain linked to a C-terminal domain which has an
eight-stranded barrel type structure (8). The domain arrangement and
the secondary structure of these domains is shown in Figure 1. The
two subunits interact tightly to form the functional L_2-dimeric
Rubisco molecule of *Rh. rubrum* (Figure 2). The core of this binding
area consists of interactions between the C-terminal domains around a
local twofold axis. In addition, two regions from the N-terminal
domain of one subunit interact with regions from the C-terminal
domain from the second subunit. These subunit interactions are of
functional importance as some of the residues involved occur in or
close to the active site region. Each active site of the L_2 dimer is
thus built up from residues of both subunits.

     The corresponding functional L_2 dimer occcurs as part of the L_8S_8
Rubisco molecule from spinach (11) and from tobacco (12,13). In the
higher plant type enzyme, four such dimers are arranged around a
fourfold axis, building up the L_8 core of the molecule.

     The active site of Rubisco is located at the carboxy-ends of the
eight β-strands in the barrel. The site is shaped like a funnel and
is mainly formed by the eight loop regions that connect the eight
β-strands with the corresponding helices in the barrel domain (figure
3). The N-terminal domain from the second subunit in the L_2 dimer

covers part of the top of the active site. In particular, two loop
regions of this domain provide residues to the active site.

Figure 2: A schematic view
of the subunit arrangement
in the L$_2$-dimer of Rubisco
from *Rh. rubrum*. The location
of the active sites are
indicated by the position
of the active site Mg(II) ion.
The distance between the two
active site metals is 36 Å.
(Drawing by U. Uhlin)

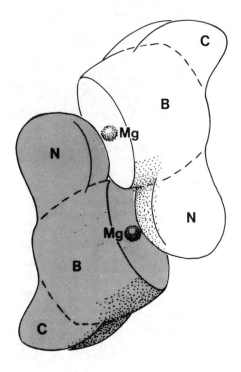

The activation process

The amino acid residue of central importance for activation is lys
191. Lys 191 is the last residue in β-strand 2 of the β/α-barrel and
is located at the bottom of the active site. The sidechain forms
hydrogen bonds to the main chain oxygen of Asn 192 and a water
molecule. The sidechains of residues Asp 193, His 287, Leu 261 and
Ile 164 are in van der Waals distance to the Lys sidechain.   The
addition of a CO_2 molecule to the ε-amino group of Lys 191 results in
the formation of a carbamate. The activation process thus changes a
positive charge, located at a central position in the active site to
a negative charge, which can now accomodate a positivly charged metal
ion. By binding Mg2+, the active site becomes poised to properly bind
and orient the substrate.

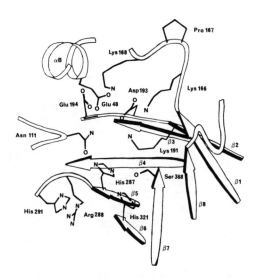

Figure 3: Schematic illustration of the active site in Rubisco.

Product and inhibitor binding

The binding of product and the inhibitor CABP has been studied in the non-activated and the activated form of the enzyme (Table 1). These studies have revealed the location of the active site and the mode of interaction of product and inhibitor respectively with groups on the enzyme. The product, 3-phospho-glycerate binds at the active site with the phosphate group interacting with residues Arg 288, His 321 and Ser 368 (Figure 4). The carboxyl group interacts with the side chains of His 287, Lys 191 and Asn 111. The inhibitor CABP binds in a rather extended conformation across the barrel. There are two distinct phosphate binding sites at opposite sides of the funnel, separating the two phosphate atoms of CABP by 9.7 Å. One phosphate site is identical to the one, observed in the binary complex of the enzyme with phospho-glycerate. The second phosphate binding site is formed by residues from loop 8, which form a one and a half turn helix. In addition, the sidechains of residues Lys 166 and Lys 329 interact with the phosphate group at this site (Figure 4).

The sugar bisphosphate molecule is thus anchored at its two ends on opposite sides of the funnel by the phosphate binding sites. In the activated quaternary complex, CABP is oriented in the middle region by coordination to the active site metal (11). The inhibitor is completely buried in the active site of the enzyme. Only some atoms of the P2 phosphate group and the 2- carboxy group are somewhat accessible to solvent.

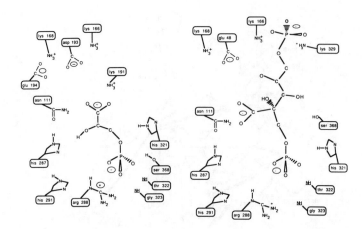

Figure 4:Binding of product and inhibitor to the active site of non-
           activated Rubisco. left: binding of phospho-glycerate
           right: binding of the inhibitor 2-carboxy-arabinitol -1,5-
           bisphosphate

In the non-activated enzyme, the inhibitor is bound 'the other
way around' at the active site as compared to the binding of CABP to
the activated enzyme (10,11). As a conseqence, the C-2 position,
which during carboxylation is attacked by a CO_2 molecule, is
different in the two species. The metal ion thus does not only play a
role in catalysis, but seems to be important for the proper
orientation of the substrate.

From these binding studies, a number of residues could be
identified which obviously are involved in the binding of the
substrate, ribulose-1,5-bisphosphate. Furthermore, a series of
conserved, polar residues within the active site, which might play a
catalytic role in the carboxylation reaction were located.

Site-directed mutagenesis

Several mutations at residues close to the metal binding site have
been constructed to study the functional role of the metal ion and
possible ligands both in the overall reaction and in partial
reactions (14). The structural information allows a correlation of
the results of these studies to the structure of the active site
(figure 5).

To determine whether the length or the charge of the lysine side
chain is the important feature of the activation process Lys 191 was
changed to Glu (15). The mutant was completely inactive and could not
form a stable complex with CABP. Model building experiments show that

the Glu side chain is too short to form a proper metal binding site instead of carbamylated Lys.

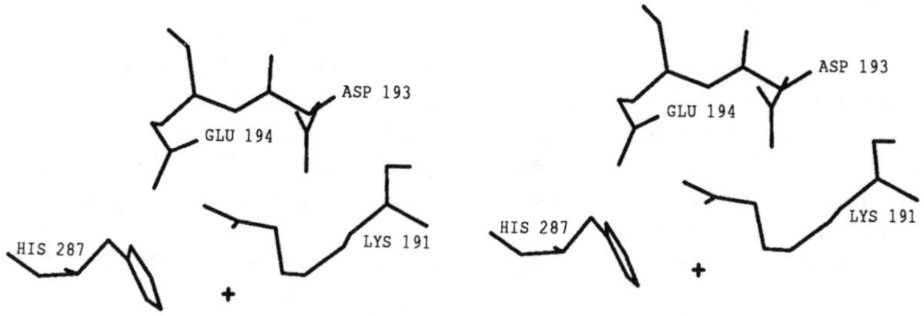

Figure 5: Stereo view of the environment of the Mg(II) binding site at the active site of Rubisco from *Rh. rubrum*. The metal position is indicated by a cross.

Mutation of the metal ligand Asp 193 to Asn abolishes the carboxylation reaction. At high concentrations of magnesium however, the mutant catalyzes the formation of the product when presented with the six-carbon intermediate. The mutant is thus deficient in the ability to catalyze the enolization of the substrate, ribulose-1,5-bisphosphate, an early step during catalysis. This step requires an intact metal binding site. Enzymatic studies of Rubisco where magnesium has been replaced with different metals show that the nature of the metal influences partitioning between carboxylation and oxygenation (16).

Mutants where the adjacent conserved residue Glu 194 has been changed to Gln or Val did not catalyze overall carboxylation, nor the partial enolization nor hydrolysis of the six-carbon intermediate (14). Clearly this residue has an important function, possibly as a metal ligand.

The structural information will allow both the further design of mutants, probing the function of certain amino acid residues in the catalytic cycle and aid the interpretation of the results obtained. This work will lead to a structural and functional mapping of the active site of Rubisco, which in turn is a prerequisite for the rational design of mutants with a changed carboxylation/oxygenation ratio.

Acknowledgements: This work was supported by grants from the Swedish research council NFR and the E.I. duPont de Nemours Company.

REFERENCES

(1) Andrews,T.J. and Lorimer,G.H. (1987) in The Biochemistry of
     Plants (Hatch,M.D.,ed.), Vol.10,pp.131-218, Academic
     Press,Orlando,FL
(2) Lorimer,G. (1981), Biochemistry 20, 1236 - 1240
(3) Schloss,J.V., Phores,E.F., Long,M.W., Norton,I.L., Stringer,C.D.
     and Hartman,F.C. (1979), J. Bacteriol. 137, 490 - 501
(4) Hartman,F.C., Stringer,C.D., Omnaas,J., Donnelly,M.I. and
     Fraij,B. (1982) Arch. Biochem. Biophys. 219, 422 - 437
(5) Nargang,F., McIntosh, L. and Somerville,C., Molec. gen. Genet.
     193,(1984) 220 - 224
(6) Herndon,C.S., Norton,I.C. and Hartman,F.C. (1982), Biochemistry
     21, 1380 - 1385
(7) Fraij, B. and Hartman,F.C. (1982), J. Biol. Chem. 257, 3501 -
     3505
(8) Schneider,G., Lindqvist,Y., Brändén, C.-I. and
     Lorimer,G.,(1986a) EMBO J. 5, 3409 - 3415
(9) Lundqvist,T. and Schneider,G. (1989a), J.Biol.Chem. 264, 3643 -
     3646
(10) Lundqvist,T. and Schneider,G. (1989b), J.Biol.Chem., 264, 7078 -
     7083
(11) Andersson,I., Knight,S., Schneider,G., Lindqvist,Y.,
     Lundqvist,T., Brändén, C.-I. and Lorimer,G. (1989), Nature 337,
     229-234
(12) Chapman,M.S., Se Won Suh, Curmi,P.M.G., Cascio,D., Smith ,W.W.
     and Eisenberg,D. (1987), Nature 329, 354 - 356
(13) Chapman,M.S., Se Won Suh, Curmi,P.M.G., Cascio,D., Smith ,W.W.
     and Eisenberg,D. (1988), Science 241, 71 - 74
(14) Lorimer,G., Gutteridge,S. and Madden,M. (1987), in Plant
     Molecular Biology (eds. D.v.Wettstein and N.-H. Chua) 31 -31
     (Nato ASI Series A, 140)
(15) Estelle,M., Hanks,J., McIntosh,L. and Somerville, C. , (1985),
     J. Biol. Chem. 260, 9523 - 9526
(16) Robison, P.D., Martin,N.N. and Tabita, F.R. (1979), Biochemistry
     18, 4453 - 4458

RUBISCO: SUBUNITS AND MECHANISM

T. John Andrews, Murray R. Badger, Daryl L. Edmondson,
Heather J. Kane, Matthew K. Morell and Kalanethee Paul

Research School of Biological Sciences, Australian National
University, PO Box 475, Canberra, ACT, 2601, Australia.

1. INTRODUCTION

D-ribulose-1,5-bisphosphate (ribulose-P_2) carboxylase-oxygenase (Rubisco) catalyses the initial reactions of the photosynthetic carbon reduction cycle and its photorespiratory appendage, the glycolate pathway, in all photosynthetic organisms. Except within the Athiorhodaceae, all Rubiscos are complex hexadecameric proteins composed of eight large (L) subunits, which bear the catalytic sites, and eight small (S) subunits, whose function is the subject of considerable current inquiry (1). Recently, this inquiry has been aided by the availability of structural information from crystallographic studies (2,3), by techniques for reversibly separating the large and small subunits of cyanobacterial Rubiscos (1) and by expression of the polypeptide products of cyanobacterial *rbc*L and *rbc*S genes in *Escherichia coli* (4,5). Insights into the interactions between the large and small subunits obtained by these approaches will be reviewed and the characteristics of the isolated subunits reported.

Rubisco's catalytic mechanism involves several enzyme-bound intermediates (1). These include the 2,3-enediol(ate) derived from ribulose-P_2 by abstraction of the proton at C-3 and the six-carbon, carboxylated intermediate, 2'-carboxy-3-keto-arabinitol-1,5-bisphosphate (keto-CABP). Both of these intermediates are unstable when released from the catalytic site (1). We here report evidence which suggests that the enediol intermediate is subject to misprotonation even while bound at the catalytic site, leading to the production of D-xylulose-1,5-bisphosphate (xylulose-P_2), and perhaps other pentulose bisphosphates, which remain bound and strongly inhibit catalysis. This provides an explanation for the long-standing observations (1,6) that purified, higher-plant Rubiscos slowly inactivate during catalysis.

2. SUBUNIT INTERACTION

2.1. <u>Obtaining separated subunits</u>: The large and small subunits of Rubisco from the cyanobacterium *Synechococcus* ACMM 323 may be separated by near-isoelectric precipitation at pH 5.2 (7). The large subunits precipitate leaving most of the small subunits in solution. The precipitated large subunits redissolve completely when returned to neutral pH and the procedure may be repeated, if necessary, until virtually all of the small subunits are removed. When applied to higher-plant (e.g. spinach) Rubisco, the procedure releases the small subunits in a similar manner but the precipitation of the large subunits is irreversible (8).

An alternative means for obtaining isolated subunits is provided by expression of the *rbc*L and *rbc*S genes from *Synechococcus* PCC 6301 in *E. coli*. These genes

M. Baltscheffsky (ed.), Current Research in Photosynthesis, Vol. III, 331–338.
© 1990 *Kluwer Academic Publishers. Printed in the Netherlands.*

comprise a simple bicistronic operon on the cyanobacterial chromosome and may be separated with restriction enzymes and cloned into separate *E. coli* expression plasmids (4). The properties of the subunits produced in this way appear to be identical to those of the subunits produced by the mild-acid procedure (5). However, expression in *E. coli* of the higher-plant *rbcL* gene gives rise to insoluble, denatured aggregates (9).

2.2. <u>Properties of isolated large subunits:</u> The isolated large subunits assemble predominantly to the octameric form (5,7). In *E. coli*, this assembly appears to be mediated by the products of the *groEL* and *groES* genes (10). However, the association between the large subunits in the octamer is much weaker than when the small subunits are also present (5). Thus the small subunits clearly supply some of the adhesive which stabilises the octameric structure of the large subunits and this is consistent with their position in the hexadecameric structure revealed in the crystallographic studies (2,3). However, the small subunits also exert a powerful stimulative effect on catalysis. In their absence, the large-subunit octamer is only 1% as active as in their presence and the substrate affinities are weaker (5). Addition of isolated small subunits to the large-subunit octamer *in vitro* leads to reconstitution of the hexadecamer with full recovery of activity (5,7). Even heterologous small subunits isolated from spinach Rubisco are effective in reconstitution and active hybrid Rubiscos may be produced in this way (8). The large-subunit octamer also binds 2'-carboxyarabinitol-1,5-bisphosphate (CABP), the analogue of the six-carbon reaction intermediate, keto-CABP, although less tightly than the intact hexadecamer does (5, 11).

Structural studies show that the small subunit interacts predominantly with the amino side (with respect to the ß strands) of the α/ß barrel domain of the large subunit at a position far removed from the catalytic site, which lies across the mouth of the α/ß barrel on the carboxyl side, at an interface with the aminoterminal domain of a companion large subunit (2,3). Therefore, the influence of the small subunit in promoting catalysis must be exerted by very indirect, conformational means. Strong synergism between binding of small subunits on one side of the α/ß barrel and binding of CABP at the active site on the other (5) indicates that conformational alterations induced by binding of the small subunit propagate through the barrel and may be instrumental in providing the essential complementarity of the catalytic site to the transition state leading to keto-CABP. This complementarity lies at the heart of Rubisco's catalytic efficiency.

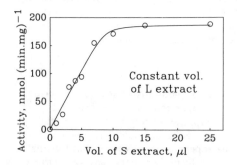 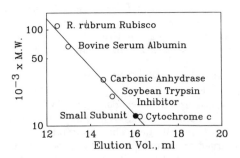

FIGURE 1 (left). Activation of large subunits from extracts of *E. coli* expressing *rbcL* by extracts of *E. coli* expressing *rbcS*.

FIGURE 2 (right). Determination of the molecular size of *E. coli*-expressed small subunits by gel filtration on Superose 12.

2.3. <u>Properties of isolated small subunits</u>: Small subunits expressed from the cyanobacterial *rbc*S gene in *E. coli* are catalytically functional when reconstituted *in vitro* with large subunits from extracts of cells expressing *rbc*L (Fig. 1). This provides a means of assaying small subunits which aids in their purification. The molecular size of isolated small subunits was measured by gel filtration, again using their promotion of Rubisco activity as a means of detection (Fig. 2). The value obtained indicated a molecular weight of 12,600, which is consistent with a monomeric structure.

Separate expression of the small subunit facilitates mutagenic studies of its role because it allows the binding ability of mutant small subunits to be distinguished from their ability to promote catalysis.

3. THE CAUSE OF SLOW INACTIVATION DURING CATALYSIS
3.1. The phenomenon:

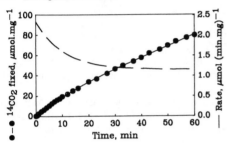

FIGURE 3. Slow inactivation of purified spinach Rubisco during carboxylation of ribulose-P_2. Data for ^{14}C fixed *vs* time (t) were fitted to the equation: product=$v_f \cdot t + [(v_i - v_f)(1 - e^{-kobs \cdot t})]/k_{obs}$ thus providing estimates of v_i and v_f, the initial and final rates, and the apparent first order rate constant, k_{obs}. The rate *vs* time curve (dashed line) was obtained as the first derivative of the above equation.

The decline in carboxylation rate observed when fully carbamylated higher-plant Rubiscos are exposed to ribulose-P_2 (Fig. 3) is an unexplained part of Rubisco's phenomenology (6,12-16). The inactivation does not proceed to completion but proceeds with a $t_{\frac{1}{2}}$ of approximately 7 min until, eventually, a linear rate (v_f) is achieved which, depending on conditions, may be as low as 20 % of the initial rate (v_i). Kinetic analysis of the fully inhibited form showed that only k_{cat} had changed. The affinities for both CO_2 and ribulose-P_2 were unaltered. While k_{obs} was not greatly affected by conditions, the extent of inactivation was greater at low pH and at low CO_2 concentrations (Fig. 4).

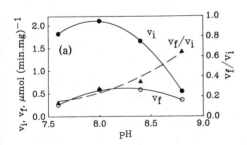
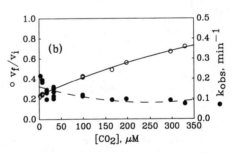

FIGURE 4. Effect of (a) pH and (b) CO_2 concentration on slow inactivation.

3.2. <u>Inactivation is not due to decarbamylation</u>: Lysine-201, within the active site on the large subunit, requires carbamylation by a non-substrate CO_2 molecule for activity. This carbamate is stabilised by binding of a divalent metal ion (1). Is the observed inactivation a result of decarbamylation induced by preferential binding of ribulose-P_2

to decarbamylated sites, as has sometimes been suggested (13,15)? Measurements of carbamylation levels during slow inactivation (Fig. 5) unequivocally ruled out this possibility. Clearly, it is the fully carbamylated enzyme that is being inactivated.

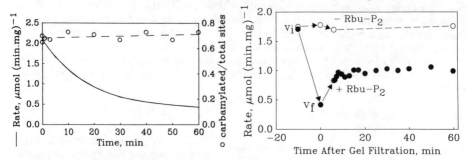

FIGURE 5 (left). Carbamylation levels during slow inactivation. Assays of the carboxylation rate were carried out with $^{14}CO_2$ as for Fig. 3 and aliquots were quenched at the indicated times by adding [^3H]CABP, together with an excess of unlabelled CO_2. The $^{14}C/^3H$ ratio of the high-M.W. fraction, isolated by gel filtration, indicated the carbamylation level.

FIGURE 6 (right). Partial recovery of inactivated enzyme after gel filtration. Activity was measured before (v_i) and after (v_f) complete consumption of 6 mM ribulose-P_2 and then at various times following isolation of the enzyme from the reaction mixture by gel filtration.

3.3. Characteristics of inactivated Rubisco: Isolation, by gel filtration, of inactivated Rubisco from the reaction mixture after exhaustion of the ribulose-P_2 led to only a partial recovery (Fig. 6). Neither a further 50-fold dilution nor a second gel filtration caused any further recovery. However, full activity could be recovered if the protein was gel filtered or dialysed in the presence of 0.2 M $(NH_4)_2SO_4$.

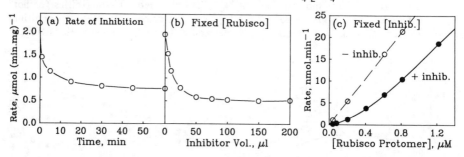

FIGURE 7. Inhibition of Rubisco by the isolated inhibitor. Supernatants of acidified inactivation reaction mixtures were mixed with fully carbamylated Rubisco in the presence of saturating CO_2 and Mg^{2+} concentrations at pH 8.3 for 60 min, unless otherwise indicated, before initiating 1 min assays by adding aliquots to otherwise complete assay mixtures containing 1 mM ribulose-P_2. (a), inhibition as a function of time; (b), inhibition as a function of inhibitor concentration; (c), titration of a constant inhibitor concentration by increasing concentrations of Rubisco. The curve in (c) is the best fit of the data to the equation (17):

$$v = k_{cat}\{E - I - K_D + [(E + I + K_D)^2 - 4.E.I]^{\frac{1}{2}}\}/2$$

where v is the measured reaction rate in the presence of inhibitor, k_{cat} is the rate in the absence of inhibitor, E is the Rubisco protomer concentration, I is the inhibitor concentration and K_D is the apparent enzyme-inhibitor dissociation constant.

3.4. <u>Isolation of the inhibitor responsible for inactivation</u>: Acidification of reaction mixtures after inactivation and exhaustion of the ribulose-P_2 released an inhibitor which could be used to inhibit fresh Rubisco. The inhibitor bound with a half-time of approximately 1 min (Fig. 7a) and it did not cause full inhibition even at long times or high concentrations (Fig. 7b), suggesting a strong degree of anticooperativity, i.e., the affinity for the inhibitor declined as site occupancy increased. The concentration of the inhibitor could be estimated by titrating a constant concentration of inhibitor with increasing concentrations of Rubisco (Fig. 7c). This procedure also estimated an apparent average value of the binding constant (K_D) (i.e., neglecting anticooperativity), which was 0.21±0.05 µM for seven such determinations.

3.5. <u>Identification of an inhibitor</u>: When slow inactivation proceeded in the presence of $^{14}CO_2$ and the Rubisco with bound inhibitor was isolated by gel filtration, no $^{14}CO_2$ was found attached to the enzyme. This indicated that, if the inhibitor was generated during catalysis, it must be derived from an intermediate prior to the carboxylated intermediate, keto-CABP. An obvious candidate is the enediol intermediate which might be suspected to be subject to misprotonation, giving rise to various pentulose-P_2 isomers which could remain bound to the catalytic site (Fig. 8)

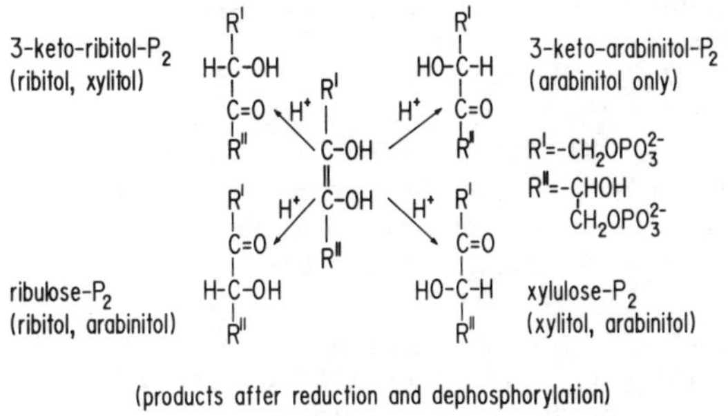

FIGURE 8. Alternative possibilities for protonation of the enediol intermediate. Only one of these possibilities correctly reproduces the substrate, ribulose-P_2. The others may be considered as misprotonations.

(products after reduction and dephosphorylation)

In order to test this possibility, inactivated Rubisco was isolated by gel filtration from a reaction mixture after exhaustion of ribulose-P_2 and the bound inhibitor was released by precipitation of the protein in 80% (v/v) methanol at pH 5. After evaporation of the supernatant, the residue was reduced with NaB^{3}H$_4$ at pH 8.5 and the products were resolved by anion-exchange chromatography and compared with the reduction products of ribulose-P_2 (Fig. 9a). Both samples showed several peaks of radioactivity but all but one of them, which eluted at the highest salt concentration, were also present in a blank containing no sample. These peaks represented acid-involatile contaminants originating from the commercial NaB^{3}H$_4$ preparation. The most anionic peak, not seen in the blank, occurred in the bisphosphate region of the gradient, with the inhibitor and ribulose-P_2 giving rise to identical peaks. Thus the inhibitor must be a bisphosphate. The contents of this peak were dephosphorylated with alkaline phosphatase and chromatographed on silica gel thin layers (solvent: propan-2-ol:ethyl acetate:water, 83:11:6 by vol., two ascents) and ^{3}H was detected with a radiochromatogram scanner (Berthold). The reduced, dephosphorylated forms of both the inhibitor and ribulose-P_2 resolved into two peaks. The former gave rise to arabinitol and xylitol and the latter to ribitol and arabinitol (Fig. 9b). These are the products expected from reduction and dephosphorylation of xylulose-P$_2$ and ribulose-P$_2$, respectively (see Fig. 8). Therefore, we conclude that the inhibitor preparation contained xylulose-P$_2$. Indeed, the rate and the severity of inhibition, as well as its anticooperative nature (Fig. 7), all strongly resemble previous observations of inhibition of Rubisco by xylulose-P$_2$ (18). Titration of authentic xylulose-P$_2$ with increasing amounts of Rubisco, as in Fig. 7c, estimated its apparent K$_D$ to be 0.15±0.06 µM.

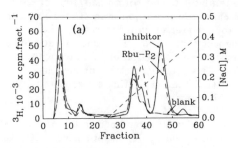 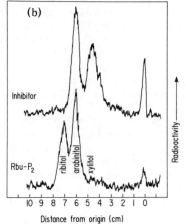

FIGURE 9. (a) Dowex 1-Cl⁻ chromatography (pH 2.5) of the products of NaB³H$_4$ reduction of the inhibitor and ribulose-P$_2$. (b) Thin-layer chromatography of the pooled fractions of the latest-eluting peak from (a) after dephosphorylation with alkaline phosphatase (radiochromatogram scan). The R$_f$ positions of the three pentitols, determined by co-chromatography with authentic standards, using alkaline permanganate visualization, are indicated. The origin peak in both samples varied in size in different experiments. It may reflect oxidative degradation of the pentitols during sample application or trailing of the earlier-eluting contaminants into the bisphosphate peak during anion-exchange chromatography.

3.6. <u>Enzymatic measurement of xylulose-P$_2$ in inhibitor preparations</u>: Xylulose-P$_2$ is a reasonably good substrate for aldolase, having a V$_{max}$/K$_m$ ratio approximately 20% of that for fructose-1,6-bisphosphate (19). The products are dihydroxyacetone phosphate and glycolaldehyde phosphate. Therefore, when coupled with glycerol-3-phosphate (glycerol-P) dehydrogenase and NADH, aldolase can be used to measure xylulose-P$_2$ spectrophotmetrically and this system may also be used to scavenge xylulose-P$_2$ from solutions. Using this assay, xylulose-P$_2$ was detected in the inhibitor preparation at a level of 0.25% of the ribulose-P$_2$ originally added to the reaction mixture (89% of the Rubisco protomer concentration).

3.7. <u>Xylulose-P$_2$ is produced during Rubisco catalysis</u>: Three lines of evidence support this contention. First, when the xylulose-P$_2$-scavenging system was present during the inactivation reaction, neither the extent nor the rate of inactivation was altered. The xylulose-P$_2$ level measured in the acidified supernatant after inactivation was reduced to 0.1% of the original ribulose-P$_2$ (36% of Rubisco sites). This level is 40% of that observed in the absence of the scavenging system. Presumably, the scavenging system removed any xylulose-P$_2$ which dissociated from the Rubisco catalytic site (as well as any xylulose-P$_2$ originally present in the ribulose-P$_2$) but it was ineffective in removing tightly bound xylulose-P$_2$. Second, the aldolase system mentioned above can be used to measure any xylulose-P$_2$ contamination present in the starting ribulose-P$_2$. Using artificial mixtures of xylulose-P_2 and ribulose-P_2, it was determined that a xylulose-P_2 contamination equal to 0.05% of the ribulose-P_2 could be detected with confidence. No xylulose-P_2 above this detection limit was observed. This reflects the purity of the ribulose-P_2 preparations which were synthesized enzymatically from ribose-5-phosphate (ribose-P) (20) and chromatographically purified without exposure to pH above 7 at any stage. Therefore, at most, only one-fifth of the xylulose-P_2 formed during inactivation could have originated from the starting ribulose-P_2 preparation. Third, when the inactivation reaction was conducted with ribulose-P_2 replaced by ribose-P, ATP, ribose-P isomerase and phosphoribulokinase, the level of inhibitor observed in the acidified supernatants was similar to that observed when ribulose-P_2, alone, was used. Moreover, this experiment was carried out with a limiting level of phosphoribulokinase and an excess of Rubisco, so that the steady-state pool size of ribulose-P_2 during inactivation was very small, thus minimizing the possibility of non-enzymatic isomerisation of ribulose-P_2 during the inactivation reaction.

3.8. <u>Another inhibitor in addition to xylulose-P_2?</u>: When inhibitor preparations were exposed to the aldolase/glycerol-P dehydrogenase/NADH scavenging system to remove xylulose-P_2, not all of the their inhibitory effect was lost (Fig. 10). Furthermore, exposure of the inhibitor preparation to pH 12.4 for 2 min also partially relieved the inhibition, whereas xylulose-P_2 was shown to have a half-life of several hours under these alkaline conditions. The combination of alkali treatment followed by aldolase treatment was required to completely destroy inhibitory potency (Fig. 10). Therefore, we must conclude that the inhibitor preparations contain at least one other strong inhibitor of Rubisco in addition to xylulose-P_2. It is sensitive to alkali but not to aldolase. Beyond this, we have no direct evidence as to its identity. However, we speculate that it may be one or both of the pent-3-ulose bisphosphates produced by protonation of the enediol intermediate at C-2, rather than C-3 (Fig. 8). Such compounds may be labile by virtue of the acidity of the protons alpha to the carbonyl group but could be stabilised when bound to the active site. In particular, one of them, namely, 3-keto-arabinitol-1,5-bisphosphate, would be formed by attack of a proton from the same direction that CO_2 attacks from during the carboxylation reaction. The lability of these compounds during work-up and under the mildly alkaline conditions required for borohydride reduction may have prevented their detection in the experiment shown in Fig. 9.

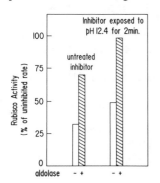

FIGURE 10. Effect of aldolase and alkali treatment on inhibitor(s). All assays contained glycerol-P dehydrogenase and NADH. Treated inhibitor preparations were mixed with fully carbamylated Rubisco for 60 min before initiating 1 min assays by adding ribulose-P_2. Separate experiments showed full recovery of ribulose-P_2 after exposure to the aldolase/glycerol-P dehydrogenase/NADH system at similar concentrations and for similar times. Therefore, phosphatase contamination of the scavenging enzymes is not a likely explanation for these observations.

4. A PHYSIOLOGICAL SIGNIFICANCE FOR SLOW INACTIVATION?

Formation of an inhibitor by misprotonation of the enediol intermediate is consistent with the greater extent of slow inactivation at lower pH (Fig. 4a). Furthermore, lower

CO_2 concentrations may result in a higher proportion of the enzyme being in the enediol form (21), also promoting slow inactivation (Fig. 4b). Both of these effects may be significant in regulating Rubisco's activity *in vivo*.

However, it is not likely that such extensive inhibition of Rubisco could be tolerated *in vivo* during active photosynthesis. Therefore, a mechanism must exist in the chloroplast for preventing or reversing this inhibition. Recently, it has been reported that the Rubisco activase system prevents slow inactivation and, furthermore, reverses it after it has occurred (22). No details about the mechanism by which activase achieves this effect are yet established. However, activase is light regulated via the stromal ATP/ADP ratio (23) and it is possible that, at low light levels, inhibitory pentulose bisphosphates may accumulate on Rubisco's catalytic site, thus modulating its activity to an appropriate level. A similar regulatory mechanism, also involving activase, has been postulated for the nocturnal Rubisco inhibitor, 2'-carboxyarabinitol-1-phosphate (CA1P), which occurs in a limited number of higher plants (24). Perhaps inhibitory pentulose bisphosphates formed by misprotonation of the enediol intermediate during catalysis perform a similar role, particularly in those species, such as spinach, which lack CA1P.

Obviously, chloroplasts would also require metabolic systems for disposing of these inhibitory pentulose bisphosphates. These may be fruitful targets for future study.

REFERENCES
1 Andrews, T.J. and Lorimer, G.H. (1987) in The Biochemistry of Plants, Vol. 10 (Hatch, M.D. and Boardman, N.K., eds.), pp.131-218, Academic Press
2 Chapman, M.S., Suh, S.W., Curmi, P.M.G., Cascio, D., Smith, W.W. and Eisenberg, D.S. (1988) Science 241, 71-74
3 Andersson, I., Knight, S., Schneider, G., Lindqvist, Y., Lundqvist, T., Brändén, C-I. and Lorimer, G.H. (1989) Nature 337, 229-234
4 van der Vies, S.M., Bradley, D. and Gatenby, A.A. (1986) EMBO J. 5, 2439-2444
5 Andrews, T.J. (1988) J. Biol. Chem. 263, 12213-12219
6 Yokota, A. and Kitaoka, S. (1989) Plant Cell Physiol. 30, 183-191
7 Andrews, T.J. and Ballment, B. (1983) J. Biol. Chem. 258, 7514-7518
8 Andrews, T.J. and Lorimer, G.H. (1985) J. Biol. Chem. 260, 4632-4636
9 Gatenby, A.A. (1984) Eur. J. Biochem. 144, 361-366
10 Goloubinoff, P., Gatenby, A.A. and Lorimer, G.H. (1989) Nature 337, 44-47
11 Andrews, T.J. and Ballment, B. (1984) Proc. Natl. Acad. Sci. USA 81, 3660-3664
12 Andrews, T.J. and Hatch, M.D. (1971) Phytochem. 10, 9-15
13 Laing, W.A. and Christeller, J.T. (1976) Biochem. J. 159, 563-570
14. Sicher, R.C., Hatch, A.L., Stumpf, D.K. and Jensen, R.G. (1981) Plant Physiol. 68, 252-255
15 McCurry, S.D., Pierce, J., Tolbert, N.E. and Orme-Johnson, W.H. (1981) J. Biol. Chem. 256, 6623-6628
16 Mott, K.A. and Berry, J.A. (1986) Plant Physiol. 82, 77-82
17 Williams, J.W. and Morrison, J.A. (1979) Meth. Enzymol. 63, 437-467
18 McCurry, S.D. and Tolbert, N.E. (1977) J. Biol. Chem. 252, 8344-8346
19 Mehler, A.H. and Cusic, M.E. (1967) Science 155, 1101-1103
20 Horecker, B.L., Hurwitz, J. and Weissbach, A. (1958) Biochem. Prep. 6, 83-90
21 Jaworowski, A., Hartman, F.C. and Rose, I.A. (1984) J. Biol. Chem. 259, 6783-6789
22 Robinson, S.P. and Portis, A.R. (1989) Plant Physiol., in press
23 Robinson, S.P. and Portis, A.R. (1988) Plant Physiol. 86, 293-298
24 Robinson, S.P. and Portis, A.R. (1988) FEBS Letts. 233, 413-416

RUBISCO FROM AMARANTHUS HYPOCHONDRIACUS

Xiang-yu Wu, Wei Gu and Guang-yao Wu
Department of Biology, Peking University, Beijing 100871
People's Republic of China

1. INTRODUCTION

Rubisco(ribulose 1,5-bisphosphate carboxylase-oxygenase E.C.4.1.1.39.) from C-4 plants have not yet been extensively studied. Badger and Andrews[1] have isolated rubisco from Zea mays and found it's $K_m(CO_2)$ higher than that from C-3 plants, but this is still in controversy[2].

Several species of Amaranthus are of potential economic importance, they could at least be used as fodder. They grow luxuriantly on poor soils which are unsuitable for crop plants. We have found Amaranthus hypochondriacus to be a good material for the study of rubisco in C-4 plants. The following is a description of our preliminary work on the isolation and characterization of rubisco from this plant, the separation of the large and small subunits of amaranth rubisco and their recombination. wheat rubisco was also isolated and in some instances used for comparison.

2. PROCEDURE
2.1. Materials and methods

2.1.1. Plant materials: Amaranth(Amaranthus hypochondriacus) and wheat(Triticum aestivum) were both grown in the field. The leaves were collected from both plants at their 5-leaf(amaranth) or 5-6 leaf(wheat) age and used for the isolation of their rubisco.

2.1.2. Isolation and purification of rubisco: The leaves were homogenized in a medium containing 100 mM Tris-HCl, 5 mM DTT(dithiothreitol), 10 mM $MgCl_2$, 1 mM EDTA, 12.5% glycerol, 10% PVP(polyvinylpyrrolidone), pH 7.8. The homogenate was filtered and centrifuged(10,000g, 15 min), fractionated with $(NH_4)_2SO_4$(35-55% saturation), the precipitate was taken up by buffer(10 mM Tris-HCl, 1 mM DTT, 1 mM $MgCl_2$, 0.1 mM EDTA, pH 7.8) and ran through Biogel A 1.5 column and eluted with the same buffer. The collected rubisco fraction was desalted by gel filtration and passed through DEAE-cellulose 52 column, the collected rubisco fractions were combined and applied again onto Sephacryl S-300 column.

M. Baltscheffsky (ed.), Current Research in Photosynthesis, Vol. III, 339–342.
© 1990 *Kluwer Academic Publishers. Printed in the Netherlands.*

Wheat rubisco was purified basically according to the literature(3).

2.1.3. Assay of the carboxylase and oxygenase activity: Carboxylase was assayed with carbon 14(4) and oxygenase with oxygen electrode(5).

2.1.4. Separation of large and small subunits of rubisco: They were separated with 3.5M urea(6) or with HCl(pH 5.4)(7).

3. RESULTS AND DISCUSSION

3.1. Purification and characterization of rubisco from amaranth and wheat: The amaranth leaves contained PEP carboxylase and a large amount of pigments. We have found it advisable to remove the pigments at first with Biogel 1.5, otherwise the later steps would be difficult. For the separation of rubisco from PEP carboxylase, DEAE cellulose 52 was found to be effective. For further purification of rubisco, gel filtration through Sephacryl S-300 was quite successful. The rubisco thus obtained showed only one band on natural PAGE and showed two bands with molecular weights 55kDa(large subunit) and 13kDa(small subunit) on 15% SDS-PAGE. The rubisco isolated from wheat was just the same as described in the literature(3).

TABLE 1. Some characteristics of rubisco isolated from amaranth and wheat

Rubisco from	Carboxylase			Oxygenase	
	$K_m(CO_2)$ $\mu mol/L$	$K_m(RuBP)$ $\mu mol/L$	V_{max} $\mu mol CO_2/min/mg$	$K_m(RuBP)$ $\mu mol/L$	V_{max} $\mu mol O_2/min/mg$
amaranth	9.5	25	1.02	42	0.136
wheat	15.5	35	0.68	33	0.230

The purified rubisco from both amaranth and wheat were assayed for their carboxylase and oxygenase activities. Their K_m values and V_{max} values are shown in table 1. From these data it could be seen that for carboxylation reaction, the affinity of amaranth rubisco to both CO_2 and RuBP were higher than those of wheat rubisco, while for oxygenation reaction, the reverse was true. As to the maximum velocity, amaranth rubisco seemed to prefer to carboxylation rather than oxygenation, but wheat rubisco, vice versa.

3.2. Separation of large and small subunits of amaranth and wheat rubisco: Treatment with 3.5 M urea could separate

the small and large subunits of amaranth rubisco completely. But in the case of wheat rubisco, complete
separation of these two subunits was unsuccessful with
urea, hence it was impossible to obtaine its large subunit free of small ones. The separated large subunit
of amaranth rubisco was soluble, different from that of
corn as described by Gatenby(8). With the treatment by
HCl(pH 5.4), small subunit preparation which was free
of large subunit could be obtained from both amaranth
and wheat rubisco, but not the large subunits.

3.3. Recombination of large and small subunits of amaranth
and wheat rubisco: The large and small subunits obtained by urea treatment or acid treatment and purified
separately by gel filtration on Sephadex G-100 were recombined in the following way. Definite amount(8 µg)

TABLE 2. Recombination of large(LSU) and small(SSU) subunits
of rubisco from amaranth.

Separation method	LSU µg	SSU µg	Specific activity $\mu mol CO_2$/min/mg	% of the holo-enzyme activity
Both LSU and SSU obtained with urea	8.0	0	0.017	11
	8.0	0.70	0.014	9
	8.0	1.75	0.063	40
	8.0	3.50	0.070	45
	8.0	7.00	0.085	55
	8.0	14.00	0.082	52
LSU obtained with urea SSU with HCl	8.0	0	0.017	11
	8.0	1.25	0.080	50
	8.0	2.59	0.096	61
	8.0	5.00	0.105	66
	8.0	7.50	0.109	69
	8.0	10.00	0.106	67

of large subunit and different amounts(0-14 µg) of
small subunit were mixed together in a buffer containing 100 mM Tris-HCl(pH 7.8), 10 mM $MgCl_2$, 5 mM DTT and
0.01 mM EDTA and incubated at 30-37 C for 5 hours.
The carboxylase activities were then assayed as described in Materials and Methods. For the calculation
of the % recovery of activity, one part of the rubisco
preparation which would be used for the separation of
large and small subunits was stored at 0-4 C for so
long as the separation and the recombination processes
took place. The carboxylase activities of the stored
holoenzyme and the recombined enzyme were then assayed
at the same time. In so doing the activity of the
holoenzyme became lower than that of the newly isolated

TABLE 3. Recombination of LSU from amaranth rubisco and SSU from wheat rubisco

LSU µg	SSU µg	specific activity µmol CO_2/min/mg	% of the holo-enzyme activity
8.0	0	0.017	11
8.0	1.25	0.079	50
8.0	2.50	0.088	56
8.0	5.00	0.091	58
8.0	7.50	0.089	57
8.0	10.00	0.097	62

one, that of amaranth rubisco became 0.15 µmol CO_2/mg/min and that of wheat rubisco became 0.11 µmol CO_2/mg/min. As shown in table 2, when LSU and SSU obtained by urea treatment were combined together, the recovery of activity might be as high as 55%, whereas when LSU obtained by urea treatment was combined with SSU obtained by acid treatment, the recovery of activity was even higher, up to almost 70%. Very interesting was that when SSU of wheat rubisco and LSU of amaranth rubisco were put together, the carboxylase activity was recovered up to 62%. This means that the subunits of rubisco have no species specificity. Comparing tables 2 and 3, it could be seen that the small subunit of amaranth rubisco seemed to be more potent in regulating the large subunit, probably due to the fact that amaranth rubisco was more active in carboxylation.

4. ADDENDUM

4.1. This project is supported by Chinese National Natural Science Foundation.

REFERENCES
1. Badger, M.R. & Andrews, T.J.(1974) Biochem. Biophys. Res. Commun. 60, 204-210.
2. Ragavendra, A.S. & Das, V.W.(1977) Z. Pflanzenphysiol. 82, 375-379.
3. Makino, A. et al.(1985) Plant Physiol. 79,57-61.
4. Wu, G.Y. et al.(1986) in "Zhiwu Shenghua Jishu he Fangfa" (Zhang, Z.L. & Wu, G.Y. ed.) pp 8-10. Nongye, Beijing.
5. Saluza, A.K. & McFadden, B.A.(1978) FEBS Lett. 96, 361-4.
6. Nishimura, M. & Akazawa, T.(1975) Biochemistry,14,46-51.
7. Andrews, T.J. & Lorimer; G.H.(1985) J. Biol. Chem. 260, 4632-4636.
8. Gatenby, A.A. (1985) Nature, 314,617-620.

FUNCTION OF ACTIVE-SITE RESIDUES OF RIBULOSE-BISPHOSPHATE CARBOXYLASE/OXYGENASE (RUBISCO)

FRED C. HARTMAN, EVA H. LEE, AND HARRY B. SMITH, Biology Division, Oak Ridge National Laboratory and University of Tennessee-Oak Ridge Graduate School of Biomedical Sciences, P. O. Box 2009, Oak Ridge, Tennessee 37831-8077

INTRODUCTION

Chemical modification [1], site-directed mutagenesis [2-5], and X-ray crystallography [6-11] have identified Lys166, Lys329, and Glu48 as active-site residues of the homodimeric Rubisco from *Rhodospirillum rubrum*. (In the L_8S_8 Rubisco from spinach, these residues correspond to Lys175, Lys334, and Glu60.) We have used two strategies to explore the function of these residues: (a) introduction of very subtle structural changes into their side chains by combining chemical modification with site-directed mutagenesis and (b) evaluation of the ability of mutant proteins, devoid in overall carboxylase activity, to catalyze the enolization of D-ribulose-1,5-bisphosphate (RuBP), *i.e.* the first step in the normal reaction pathway.

CONCERTED SITE-DIRECTED MUTAGENESIS AND CHEMICAL MODIFICATION

Subtle structural changes can be introduced by these two approaches in combination which cannot be achieved independently by either. Examples are conversion of a lysyl residue to an aminoethylcysteinyl residue and conversion of a glutamyl residue to carboxymethylcysteine:

$$>C_\alpha HCH_2CH_2CH_2CH_2NH_2 \longrightarrow >C_\alpha HCH_2SH \xrightarrow{\text{BrCH}_2\text{CH}_2\text{NH}_2} >C_\alpha HCH_2SCH_2CH_2NH_2$$

$$>C_\alpha HCH_2CH_2COOH \longrightarrow >C_\alpha HCH_2SH \xrightarrow{\text{ICH}_2\text{COOH}} >C_\alpha HCH_2SCH_2COOH$$

mutagenesis   modification

The overall structural change is the mere replacement of the lysyl γ-methylene by a sulfur atom in the former case [12] and insertion of a sulfur atom between the glutamyl β- and γ-methylenes in the latter case [13].

Treatment of the inactive K166C and K329C[1] mutant proteins with 2-bromoethylamine partially restores carboxylase activity (Fig. 1), presumably as a consequence of selective aminoethylation of the thiol group unique to each protein. Amino acid analyses, isoelectric focusing under denaturing conditions, slow inactivation of the wild-type

---

[1]The single-letter code for amino acids is used to designate mutants. The first letter denotes the amino acid present in the wild-type enzyme at the numbered position. The final letter denotes the amino acid present at the corresponding position in the mutant.

M. Baltscheffsky (ed.), Current Research in Photosynthesis, Vol. III, 343–346.
© 1990 *Kluwer Academic Publishers. Printed in the Netherlands.*

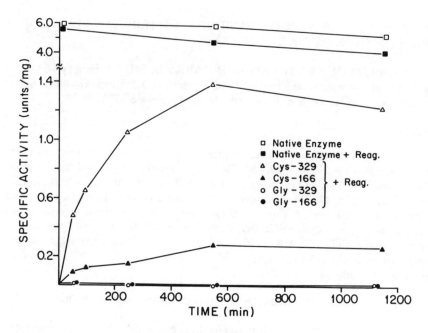

Figure 1. Carboxylase activity during treatment of wild-type Rubisco and mutant proteins (all at 0.4 mg/ml) with 2-bromoethylamine (100 mM).

carboxylase by bromoethylamine, and the failure of bromoethylamine to restore activity to the corresponding glycyl mutant proteins support this interpretation. The observed facile, selective aminoethylations are consistent with active-site microenvironments not dissimilar to that of the native enzyme. Catalytic constants of these novel carboxylases are significantly lower than that of the wild-type enzyme. The k_{cat} for aminoethylated K329C is 40% that of wild-type, while k_{cat} for aminoethylated K166C is reduced 5-fold relative to wild-type. These detrimental effects by such a modest structural change underscore the stringent requirement for lysyl side chains at positions 166 and 329. In contrast, the aminoethylated mutant proteins exhibit K_m values that are unperturbed relative to those for the native enzyme. Clearly, major reductions in k_{cat} with unaltered K_m values argue for direct roles of Lys166 and Lys329 in catalysis rather than in substrate binding.

Replacement of Glu48 with Gln [3], Asp, or Cys yields mutant proteins that retain < 0.05% of the wild-type carboxylase activity. However, activity is restored to 4% of the wild-type level upon treatment of the E48C protein with iodoacetate. Identical treatment of the E48Q and E48D proteins does not lead to any restoration of activity, and the wild-type enzyme actually undergoes ~15% loss of activity during incubation with iodoacetate. Thus, the restoration observed with E48C must be due to carboxymethylation of Cys48, which generates a glutamyl-like side chain. This novel carboxylase exhibits K_m value for RuBP and CO_2 that are only 2- or 3-fold greater than those of wild-type enzyme despite the 25-fold reduction in k_{cat}. These results illustrate a lack of tolerance to even slight relocation of the Glu48 γ-carboxylate, consistent with a discrete catalytic role -- either direct or indirect.

MUTANT PROTEINS AS CATALYSTS IN PARTIAL REACTIONS

The initial step in both carboxylation and oxygenation pathways as catalyzed by Rubisco is abstraction of the C3 proton of RuBP to form an enediol intermediate; this reaction can be monitored by transfer of tritium from solvent (T_2O) into RuBP or by loss of tritium from [3-^{3}H]ribulose-P_2.

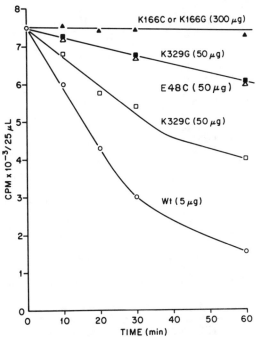

The dissection of partial reactions, if catalyzed by site-directed mutant proteins devoid of overall carboxylation activity, provides an avenue for ascribing the involvement of active-site residues to discrete steps. If the postulate that Lys166 serves as a base in the enolization of ribulose-P_2 is correct [1], position 166 mutant proteins should lack the proton exchange activity diagnostic of enolization. In contrast, the position 329 and 48 mutant proteins could be catalysts for the enolization, for by deduction Lys329 and Glu48 would function at some subsequent step [14]. These predictions are substantiated by data illustrated in Fig. 2. Even though K166G is essentially devoid of proton exchange activity, it is a catalyst for conversion of the six-carbon reaction intermediate to phosphoglycerate [15], a property expected of a protein deficient only in the initial step in the overall

Figure 2. Enolization of [3-^{3}H]ribulose-P_2 by wild-type Rubisco and mutant proteins as measured by the decrease in nonvolatile radioactivity. The μg-values denoted on the curves represent the amount of protein present in each 200-μl reaction mixture.

pathway. The demonstration that mutant proteins lacking Lys166, Lys329, or Glu48 are indeed enzymes, albeit not carboxylases, that act on a reaction intermediate or RuBP provides strong evidence of active-site topologies very similar to that of wild-type enzyme. Thus, the catalytic deficiency of these mutant proteins in overall carboxylation appears to reflect the absence of catalytic groups rather than conformational perturbations. Assignment of Lys166 to the initial proton abstraction step is clearly consistent with a wide variety of experimental observations. Although X-ray crystallography [8] shows the ϵ-amino group of Lys166 adjacent to the C1 bridge oxygen of bound carboxyarabinitol bisphosphate, it can be modeled to a location compatible with accepting the C3 proton of RuBP.

As the enolization activity of the position 329 mutant proteins requires both CO_2 and Mg^{2+}, Lys329 cannot be required for the activation process. Reversible enolization of RuBP is not accompanied by any net destruction nor decreased concentration of RuBP. The absence of dephosphorylation, isomerization, and/or epimerization shows that the enediol never dissociates from the enzyme but yet fails to react with either gaseous substrate. Perhaps the role of Lys329 is to enhance the reactivity of the enediol through polarization and development of the nucleophilic center at C2. This suggestion is not inconsistent with the position of the ϵ-amino group as revealed by X-ray crystallography [8].

ACKNOWLEDGMENTS

This research was sponsored by the Office of Health and Environmental Research, U.S. Department of Energy under Contract DE-AC05-84OR21400 with Martin Marietta Energy Systems, Inc.

REFERENCES

1 Hartman, F.C., Stringer, C.D., Milanez, S. and Lee, E.H. (1986) Philos. Trans. R. Soc. Lond. (Biol.) 313, 379-395

2 Hartman, F.C., Soper, T.S., Niyogi, S.K., Mural, R.J., Foote, R.S., Mitra, S., Lee, E.H., Machanoff, R. and Larimer, F.W. (1987) J. Biol. Chem. 262, 3496-3501

3 Hartman, F.C., Larimer, F.W., Mural, R.J., Machanoff, R. and Soper, T.S. (1987) Biochem. Biophys. Res. Commun. 145, 1158-1163

4 Larimer, F.W., Lee, E.H., Mural, R.J., Soper, T.S. and Hartman, F.C. (1987) J. Biol. Chem. 262, 15327-15329

5 Soper, T.S., Mural, R.J., Larimer, F.W., Lee, E.H., Machanoff, R. and Hartman, F.C. (1988) Protein Eng. 2, 39-44

6 Schneider, G., Lindqvist, Y., Brändén, C.-I, and Lorimer, G. (1986) EMBO Journal 5, 3409-3415

7 Chapman, M.S., Suh, S.W., Cascio, D., Smith, W.W. and Eisenberg, D. (1987) Nature (Lond.) 329, 354-356

8 Andersson, I., Knight, S., Schneider, G., Lindqvist, Y., Lundqvist, T., Brändén, C.-I. and Lorimer, G.H. (1989) Nature (Lond.) 337, 229-234

9 Chapman, M.S., Suh, S.W., Curmi, P.M.G., Cascio, D., Smith, W.W. and Eisenberg, D.S. (1988) Science 241, 71-74

10 Lundqvist, T. and Schneider, G. (1989) J. Biol. Chem. 264, 3643-3646

11 Lundqvist, T. and Schneider, G. (1989) J. Biol. Chem. 264, 7078-7083

12 Smith, H.B. and Hartman, F.C. (1988) J. Biol. Chem. 263, 4921-4925

13 Smith, H.B., Larimer, F.W. and Hartman, F.C. (1988) J. Cell Biol. 107, 830a

14 Hartman, F.C. and Lee, E.H. (1989) J. Biol. Chem. 264, 11784-11789

15 Lorimer, G.H. and Hartman, F.C. (1988) J. Biol. Chem. 263, 6468-6471

TOTAL SYNTHESIS OF A GENE FOR THE MATURE SMALL SUBUNIT OF RuBisCO (rbcS) FROM TOBACCO

Hai-bao Chen, Jie-min Weng and Jian-shao Bao, Shanghai Inst of Org Chem, Chinese Academy of Sciences, 345 Lingling Lu, Shanghai 200032, China

1. INTRODUCTION

As the bifunctional enzyme that catalyzes the competing reactions of ribulosebisphosphate with either CO_2 or O_2, the respective initinal steps in photosynthetic fixation of CO_2 and in photorespiration, ribulosebisphosphate carboxylase/oxygenase [abbreviated as RuBisCO, EC.4.1.1.39] is a major determitant of plant growth and yield. In plant, RuBisco has the structure of L_8S_8. To facilitate the study on structure-function relationship of rbcS by site-specific mutagenesis, we report here the total synthesis of a gene (Fig. 1) for the mature rbcS from tobacco.

```
                        15                  30                  45                  60                  75                  90
EcoRI
<------------------------------ 1 ----------------------------------->< ---------------------------- 3 ---
AATTC ATG CAA GTT TGG CCA CCT ATT AAC AAG AAA AAG TAC GAA ACT CTG TCT TAC CTG CCA GAT CTG TCT CAA GAA CAG CTG CTT TCC GAA GTT
    G TAC GTT CAA ACC GGT GGA TAA TTG TTC TTT TTC ATG CTT TGA GAC AGA ATG GAC GGT CTA GAC AGA GTT CTT GTC GAC GAA AGG CTT CAA
  <------------------------------- 2 ---------------------------------><----------------------------------
      Met Gln Val Trp Pro Pro Ile Asn Lys Lys Lys Tyr Glu Thr Leu Ser Tyr Leu Pro Asp Leu Ser Gln Glu Gln Leu Leu Ser Glu Val
                      5                  10                  15                  20                  25                  30

                  105                 120                 135                 150                 165                 180
--------------------------------------><---------------------- 5 ---------------------------------------><--------
GAG TAC CTT TTG AAG AAC GGT TGG GTA CCG TGC CTC GAG TTC GAA ACC GAG CAC GGC TTT GTC TAC CGT GAA AAC AAC AAG TCT CCA GGT
CTC ATG GAA AAC TTC TTG CCA ACC CAT GGC ACG GAG CTC AAG CTT TGG CTC GTG CCG AAA CAG ATG GCA CTT TTG TTG TTC AGA GGT CCA
---- 4 ------------------------------> <------------------------ 6 ------------------------------------------> <--
Glu Tyr Leu Leu Lys Asn Gly Trp Val Pro Cys Leu Glu Phe Glu Thr Glu His Gly Phe Val Tyr Arg Glu Asn Asn Lys Ser Pro Gly
                35                  40                  45                  50                  55                  60

                  195                 210                 225                 240                 255                 270
                                      HindIII
-------- 7 ---------------------------><------------------ 9 ---------------------><------------------------ 11 ----
TAC TAT GAT GGT CGT TAC TGG ACT ATG TGG AAG CTT CCG ATG TTC GGT TGC ACT GAT GCC ACT CAG GTG CTG GCT GAA GTT GAA GAA GCC
ATG ATA CTA CCA GCA ATG ACC TGA TAC ACC TTC GAA GGC TAC AAG CCA ACG TGA CTA CGG TGA GTC CAC GAC CGA CTT CAA CTT CTT CGG
---------------- 8 ------------------------><---------------- 10 -------------------------> <--------------------
Tyr Tyr Asp Gly Arg Tyr Trp Thr Met Trp Lys Leu Pro Met Phe Gly Cys Thr Asp Ala Thr Gln Val Leu Ala Glu Val Glu Glu Ala
                65                  70                  75                  80                  85                  90

                  285                 300                 315                 330                 345                 360
--------------------------------------><----------------------------- 13 -----------------------------------><--------
AAG AAG GCA TAC CCA CAG GCT TGG ATC CGT ATC ATC GGA TTC GAC AAC GTG CGT CAG GTC CAG TGC ATC AGT TTC ATT GCG TAC AAG CCG
TTC TTC CGT ATG GGT GTC CGA ACC TAG GCA TAG TAG CCT AAG CTG TTG CAC GCA GTC CAG GTC ACG TAG TCA AAG TAA CGC ATG TTC GGC
------- 12 --------------------------------><--------------------------- 14 -------------------------------------> <--
Lys Lys Ala Tyr Pro Gln Ala Trp Ile Arg Ile Ile Gly Phe Asp Asn Val Arg Gln Val Gln Cys Ile Ser Phe Ile Ala Tyr Lys Pro
                95                 100                 105                 110                 115                 120

                  375
                      Xba I
---- 15 ------------>
GAA GGC TAC TAA TAG T
CTT CCG ATG ATT ATC AGATC
------- 16 ------------->
Glu Gly Tyr
```

FIG. 1. The DNA sequence of a synthetic gene for tobacco mature rbcS

2. MATERIALS AND METHODS

2.1. Restriction endonuclease, T4 DNA ligase were purchased from new England Biolabs, Bst large fragment (1) of DNA polymerase I from Shanghai Inst. of Biochem., [$-^{32}P$]ATP from Amersham, [$-^{35}S$]ATP from Shanghai Inst of Nuclear Research, T4 PNKase was a gift from Chang-qin Chen (Shanghai Inst of Biochem), pWR13 and E. coli

M. Baltscheffsky (ed.), Current Research in Photosynthesis, Vol. III, 347–350.

strain JM83 were gifts from Li-he Gao (Shanghai Inst of Cell Biol)

2.2. Oligonucleotides were synthesized on an DNA synthesizer (Model ABI 381A), purified as described in (2) and [5'-^{32}]-Phosphorylated as (3).

2.3. T4 DNA ligase-catalyzed reactions of oligonucleotides were performed essentially as (3) with modification: Two adjacent duplexes formed by independent annealing (60 pmol in 20 ul) were coupled at 10 C overnifht. After aliquotes were taken from each reaction mixture, two ligation mixture were mixed and fresh ligase was added to promote the formation of desired half molecule.

2.4. Cloning of 5'- or 3'-half molecule into pWR13 was conducted as usual except that the crude product formed in procedure 2.1.3. was used directly. JM83 was used as the host cell.

2.5. DNA sequence analysis was performed using 'Dideoxy method' on a denatured double-stranded plasmid with Bst large fragment of DNA polymerase I and [-^{35}S]ATP at 65 C as (1).

3. RESULTS AND DISCUSSION

3.1. Design of DNA sequence for the synthetic gene was carried out on a computer VAX11/780 running the program of PSQ and NAQ afforded by NBRF of U.S.A. based on the known amino acids sequence of rbcS

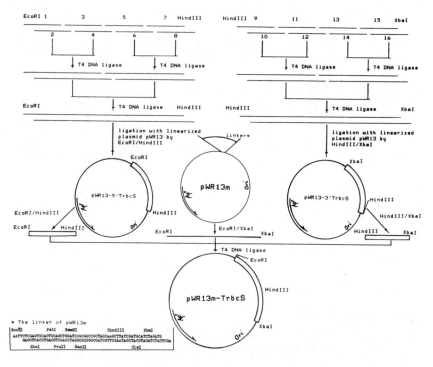

FIG. 2. Ligation of the chemically synthesized oligonucleotides to form the gene for the mature rbcS from tobacco

from tobacco. The synthetic gene was designed to contain 19 unique restriction sites throughout the whole gene (Table 1).

TABLE 1. Distribution of unique restriction sites in the synthetic gene

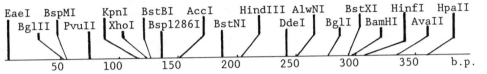

3.2. This gene was divided into two half molecules to be synthesized as shown in Fig. 2. To keep the right order in the ligation of duplexes and to ensure the proper cloning of each half molecule, oligomers 1, 8, 9 and 16 were not [5'-^{32}P]-phosphorylated. The ligation of oligonucleotides to form both the 5'- and 3'-half molecules in high yields as shown in Fig. 3. The resulted ligation mixture was directly used for cloning without further purification.

3.3. Two half molecules were cloned into plasmid pWR13 separately. Each chosen colony was characterized by several restriction enzyme digestions. The recombinant plasmid provedd by enzyme digestion were further sequence analysed. The sequence indicated in Fig. 4 corresponded exactly to that of designed gene.

3.4. To construct the synthetic gene in a vector suitable for future mutagenesis, plasmid pWR13 was modified: a synthetic polylinker EcorI-XbaI shown in Fig.2 was used to replace the polylinker

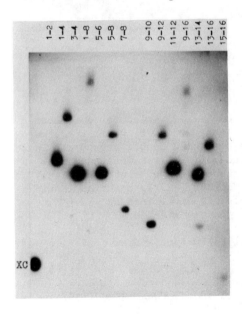

FIG. 3. Synthesis of 5'-half molecule and 3'-half molecule by stepwise T4 DNA ligase reaction of fragment 1 to 8 and 9 to 16 respectively. The aliquots from the ligation mixture were directly separated in a nondenaturing 12% poly-acrylamide electrophoresis slab gel and visualized by autoradiography.

EcoRI-XbaI shown in Fig. 2 was used to replace the polylinker
EcoRI-HindIII in pWR13. This plasmid was nominated as pWR13m.
The entire gene was constructed in a three component ligation
mixtures containing fragment I, II, which were excised at the
flanking restrition sites from the cloning vectors respectively,
and EcoRI/XbaI double digested pWR13m, then the ligation product
was used to transform JM 83 competent cell. Recombinant plasmids
pWR13m-TrbcS containing the whole synthetic gene were confirmed
by restriction enzyme digestion.

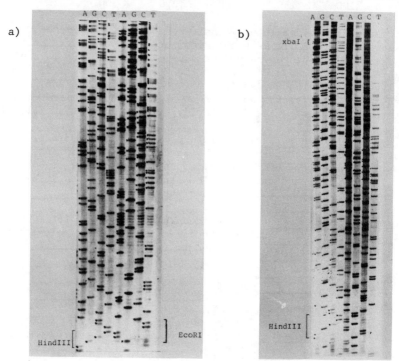

FIG. 4. a)The nucleotides sequence of 5'-half molecule, a synthetic
gene fragment from oligonucleotide 1 to 8, was determined
with 'Dideoxy method' on a denatured double stranded plasmid
pWR13-5'TrbcS in the presence of a 5'-terminal universal
primer of pWR13 for the sequencung of plus strand (right) and
of 3'-primer for the minus strand (left). b)the nucleotides
sequence of 3'-half molecule was determined as above.

REFERENCES
1 Ye, Sheng-yu and Hong, Guo-fan (1987) Scientia Sinica (Series B)
30, 503.
2 Lo, K.-m., Jones, S.S., Hackett, N.R. and Khorana, H.G. (1984)
Proc. Natl. Acad. Sci. USA 81, 2285.
3.Sekiya, T., Bresmer, P., Takeya, T. and Khorana, HH.G. (1976)
J. Biol. Chem. 251, 634.

SITE-DIRECTED MUTAGENESIS OF AMINO ACIDS ASSOCIATED WITH
THE ACTIVE SITE OF RUBISCO FROM *ANACYSTIS NIDULANS*

PARRY M. A., KETTLEBOROUGH C. A., HALFORD N., PHILLIPS A.
L., BRANDEN R. and KEYS A.J., DEPARTMENT OF
BIOCHEMISTRY,AFRC INSTITUTE OF ARABLE CROPS RESEARCH,
ROTHAMSTED EXPERIMENTAL STATION, HARPENDEN,
HERTFORDSHIRE,U.K. AL5 2JQ

1. INTRODUCTION
    The enzyme Rubisco is a target for genetic
manipulation because it catalyses a rate limiting step in
photosynthesis. Moreover Rubisco is inefficient in that
not only does it have a low catalytic rate but also
catalyses a wasteful reaction with oxygen. Consequently
researchers hope that by modification of genes for
Rubisco the enzyme's characteristics may be improved,
leading to a significant increase in photosynthetic
efficiency.
    Most work has been done on Rubisco from the
photosynthetic bacterium *R. rubrum* for which the genes
can be expressed in *E. coli* to produce polypeptide which
correctly assembles into an active dimer. This model
system is limited since the Rubisco produced has a much
simpler structure than the higher plant enzyme. However
the expression of the genes for Rubisco from higher
plants and the production of active enzyme in *E. coli* has
not yet been achieved.   Rubisco from *A. nidulans* has a
similar structure and 78% amino acid homology with
Rubisco from higher plants. The genes for both the large
and small subunits of Rubisco from *A. nidulans* have been
expressed in *E. coli* under the control of the *lac*
promoter to produce authentic active Rubisco (1).
    Gutteridge *et al* (2) demonstrated that the N-
terminus of the large subunit of wheat was important for
catalysis. Removal of a peptide (amino acids 9-14 in
wheat)resulted in a loss of catalytic activity without
disruption of carbamylation or the binding of the
transition state analog, 2-CABP. The position of this N-
terminal region in relation to the catalytic site has yet
to be determined by X-ray crystallographic analysis.
    Replacing the N-terminal 12 residues of the *A.
nidulans* large subunit with 6 unrelated *lacZ* residues
increased the Km (Ribulose-P$_2$) 12-fold and doubled the Km

M. Baltscheffsky (ed.), Current Research in Photosynthesis, Vol. III, 351–354.

CO_2 (3). Replacing the same region with the corresponding 15 residues from wheat or maize had no effect on the Km values. Although the amino acid sequences differ considerably from that of the N-terminus of the *A. nidulans* large subunit the role of the N-terminal region must be determined either by one of the few conserved residues or by the presence of residues with similar functional side chains (Table 1).

The functions of 2 conserved residues, threonine (T4) and lysine (K11) of *A. nidulans* (Table 1 ^), were investigated by site-directed mutagenesis. Changes were planned to determine whether the contribution of these residues was steric or due to their functional sidechains.

TABLE 1. Comparison of the N-terminal region of the large subunit of Rubisco in different species (4-9).

```
wheat*          .mspqteTka gvgfkAGVkd
maize           .mspqteTka svgfkAGVkd
potato          .mspqteTka svefkAGVkd
tobacco         .mspqteTka svgfkAGVke
Chlamydomonas   .mvpqteTka gagfkAGVkd
A. nidulans     ....mpkTqs aagykAGVkd
Anabaena        msyaqtkTqt ksgykAGVkd

CONSENSUS       -------T-- ----KAGVK-
                       ^         ^
```

* Wheat sequence (T. A. Dyer, personal communication).

2. METHODS AND RESULTS

Four oligonucleotides were made to change T4 of *A. nidulans* to serine and valine and K11 to glutamate and leucine. A 238 bp *Bam*H1-*Kpn*1 fragment was isolated from pAn938 construct (10), bearing the Rubisco genes, and subcloned into M13tg130. The ssDNA was isolated and the orientation of the insert checked.

Mutants were produced by the double primer method (11) using the M13 universal primer and phosphorylated mutagenic primer. The heteroduplex formed was introduced into BMH 71-18 *mutL* and plated out onto a lawn of *E. coli* BMH 71-18. Plaques were then gridded out onto 2*YT plates.

To identify colonies containing mutations, the colonies were immobolized on nitrocellulose and probed with ^{32}P labelled mutagenic primer. The filters were washed at progressively higher temperatures and strongly hybridizing colonies restreaked out and plaques used to prepare ssDNA for sequencing.

Mutant clones were introduced into *E. coli* TG2 and large scale M13 RF DNA isolations were made.

The 238 *Kpn*1-*Bam*H1 fragment bearing mutations was isolated from the RF and subcloned into pUC19 at the *Kpn*1 and *Bam*H1 sites. Both strands of the fragment were sequenced and those with no additional mutations ligated to a 4576bp *Kpn*1-*Bam*H1 fragment from pAn938. The construct was introduced into *E. coli* JM83 and clones of each mutant were sequenced.

Suspension cultures of *E. coli* JM83 expressing each of mutants, T4S, T4V, K11Q and K11L had carboxylase activities of 3.16-19.2 nmolCO$_2$ min^{-1} ml^{-1} OD$_{650}$$^{-1}$. Appropriate cell cultures were then grown in a 5 l. fermenter, harvested, and the mutant Rubiscos purified (3)

To investigate the catalytic properties of the enzymes they were activated by incubation for 5 minutes at 25°C in 50mM Bicine containing 20mM MgCl$_2$ 50mM NaHCO$_3$ and 10mM Na$_2$HPO$_4$. The activity was measured by adding 50ul containing 1-2ug of Rubisco protein to the reaction mix. At 30s the reaction was stopped with 10 N formic acid. The ^{14}C fixed into acid stable form was determined by scintillation counting. The specificity factor was determined as in (12)

TABLE 2. Kinetic parameters of wild type and mutant Rubisco.

Source of Rubisco	Km for Ribulose-P$_2$	CO$_2$	Specificity factor
Wild type pAN92	82 (11.4)	109 (9.4)	55
T4S	97 (7.3)	132 (23.4)	54
T4V	51 (3.9)	111 (16.7)	56
K11Q	84 (12.5)	85 (3.7)	56
K11L	190 (26.6)	84 (13.3)	52

3. DISCUSSION

As expected none of the mutant Rubiscos had a change in specificity factor.

Threonine has a hydroxyl group which can be involved in hydrogen bond formation. Replacement of T4 with serine which can also form hydrogen bonds or valine which has no

polar group had no significant effect on Ribulose-P_2
binding

The replacement of K11 with glutamate with its
negative rather than positive charge also had no
significant effect on Ribulose-P_2 binding. This may be
expected as this substitution occurs naturally in Rubisco
from Barley *(13) and T. urartu* (T. Dyer, personal
communication).

In contrast, replacement of K11 with leucine, which
has a side chain of similar size to lysine but is non
polar, increased the Km 3-fold. This suggests that the
polar properties of K11 are important in binding the
Ribulose-P_2. It is not clear from X-ray studies whether
the N-terminal residues extend into the catalytic site
and K11 is directly involved in substrate binding or
whether its effect is indirect by altering the geometry
at the active site.

4. REFERENCES

1 Gutteridge, S.,Phillips, A.L., Kettleborough,
C.A.,Parry, M.A.J. and Keys, A.J. (1986) Phil. Trans.
Roy. Soc. Lond. Ser. B 313, 433-445
2 Gutteridge, S., Millard, B. and Parry, M.A.J. (1986)
FEBS Lett. 196, 263-268
3 Kettleborough, C.A., Parry, M.A.J.,Burton, S.,
Gutteridge, S.,Keys, A.J. and Phillips, A.L. (1987) Eur.
J. Biochem. 170, 335-342
4 McIntosh, L., Poulsen, C. and Bogorad, L. (1980) Nature
288,556-560
5 Zurawski, G., Perrot, B., Bottomley, W. and Whitfeld,
P.R. (1981) Nucleic Acid Res. 9,3251-3270
6 Shinozaki, K. and Sigiura, M. (1982) Gene 20,91-102
7 Dron, M., Rahire, M. and Rochaix, J. D. (1982) J. Mol.
Biol. 162,775-793
8 Reichelt, B.Y. and Delany, S.F. (1983) DNA 2,121-129
9 Curtis, S.E. and Haselkorn, R. (1983) Proc. Natl. Acad.
Sci. U.S.A. 80,1835-1839
10 Kettleborough, C.A. (1989) PhD Thesis CNAA
11 Carter,P., Bedovelle, H. and Winter, G. (1985) Nucleic
Acid Res. 13,4431-4443
12 Parry, M.A.J., Keys, A.J. and Gutteridge, S. (1989) J.
Exper. Bot. 40,317-320
13 Zurawski, G., Clegg, M.T. and Brown, A.H.O. (1984)
Genetics 106,735-749

AN ESSENTIAL ARGININE IN THE LARGE SUBUNIT OF RIBULOSE BISPHOSPHATE CARBOXYLASE/OXYGENASE IDENTIFIED BY SITE-DIRECTED MUTAGENESIS

Robert L. Haining, Christopher L. Small, and Bruce A. McFadden, Dept. Biochemistry/Biophysics, Washington State University, Pullman, WA 99164-4660 U.S.A.

1. INTRODUCTION

Although major advances have been made in understanding the architecture of the active site of ribulose bisphosphate carboxylase/oxygenase (RuBisCO),[1] little is known about the catalytic function of active site residues aside from *lys*166 in the *Rhodospirillum rubrum* enzyme (and implicitly *lys*175 in spinach RuBisCO). This residue probably deprotonates RuBP.[2] In addition, the enzyme must protonate the developing anion generated by cleavage of the 6-carbon reaction intermediate in the carboxylation pathway, a requirement not evident in the oxygenation pathway.[3] The proton donor has not been identified nor have the residues been identified which participate in binding the anionic substrate RuBP.

Based on studies of chemical modification of RuBP carboxylase using phenylglyoxal,[4] we now characterize a critical *arg* in the L_8S_8 enzyme from *Anacystis nidulans* through directed mutagenesis of the L subunit gene for RuBisCO from *A. nidulans*. Specifically, replacement of highly conserved *arg*292 by *leu* or *lys* yields mutant enzymes with reduced binding of RuBP and greatly reduced catalytic activity.

2. MATERIALS AND METHODS

Bacterial Strains and Plasmids: *E. coli* JM105 was used for all mutagenesis and expression experiments. The plasmid pCS88[5] is an Ap^R lac$^-$ pUC19 derivative containing the tandemnly oriented large and small subunit genes of *A. nidulans* in their proper orientation for cotranscription.[6,7] It was constructed from the original pUC9-based expression plasmid, pCS75 with a minor deletion.[4]

Site-directed Mutagenesis and Plasmid Reconstruction: *Arg*292 of the *A. nidulans* L subunit was chosen for mutagenesis as described (see RESULTS; Fig. 1). Deoxyoligonucleotides of 27 and 30 bases were synthesized on a Pharmacia Gene Assembler. A computer search of M13 and *A. nidulans* RuBisCO gene fragment sequences using the FIND MISMATCH program of UWGCG was used to optimize synthetic deoxyoligonucleotide specificity. The mutagenesis and reconstruction procedures are shown in Fig. 2 (see RESULTS). Cotransfection with mutagenic deoxyoligonucleotides was performed based on published procedure.[9] Confirmation of base substitutions in pRH1L and pRH1K was accomplished by sequencing single-stranded phage DNA with the Sanger dideoxy method using the Klenow fragment of DNA polymerase and a universal M13 primer to sequence starting near the multiple cloning site, or the mutagenic primer to sequence downstream. Reconstructed plasmids

M. Baltscheffsky (ed.), Current Research in Photosynthesis, Vol. III, 355–358.

pRHR292L and pRHR292K were restriction-mapped to confirm orientation of the rbcLrbcS fragment and sequenced using the Sequenase I system (U.S. Biochemical).

Protein Purification and Assay after Site-directed Mutagenesis: Cultures of plasmid-containing cells were grown and induced as described.[4] A rapid two-step purification from extracts was developed for the wild-type and two mutant proteins after precipitation of each with $(NH_4)_2SO_4$[11] and subsequent dialysis.[4] Each step involved vertical sedimentation at 242,000 g at r_{max} for 2 hours at 5° C into a reoriented 0.2-0.8 M sucrose gradient run in a Beckman VTi-50 rotor.[10] The first gradient was linear and yielded mutant proteins which sedimented identically to wild-type RuBisCO and which could be detected in a standard assay[11] containing 13 mM RuBP. After pooling peak fractions and concentrating as necessary, each pooled fraction was subjected to sedimentation into a 4-step 0.2-0.8 M sucrose gradient.

3. RESULTS AND DISCUSSION

Selection of Amino Acid Substitutions in the L Subunit: A comparison of aligned RuBisCO L Subunits from the bacteria Alcaligenes eutrophus, A. nidulans, Anabaena, and R. rubrum, the eukaryotic green alga Chlamydomonas reinhardtii, and the higher plants Nicotiana tabacum and maize[6,12] was especially helpful in identifying conserved arg. In this comparison, it was found that only arg292 and 316 in L subunits of A. nidulans RuBisCO have been completely conserved. Moreover, the 10 residue stretches corresponding to lys313 through his322, and especially leu288 through val297, are highly conserved in the L subunit of RuBisCO from A. nidulans (Fig. 1).

FIGURE 1:

Amino acids that differ are shown.

```
               288      292     296            316      320
A. n.     L H I H R A M H A V    K C L R L S G G D H
A.                                   A
A. e.         L       G   G T    W       A     V
R. r.         Y       G   G A    M A     Q     A S G
C. r.                                A       M
N. t.                                A       M
maize     L H I H R A M H A V    K A L R M S G G D H
              291     295     299            319      323
```

Arginine 292 was of special interest because its counterpart in the spinach enzyme (arg295) is 3 residues removed from the completely conserved his298 which is known to be in the active site domain.[13] Accordingly, the codon for arg292 was selected for studies of mutagenesis and lys or leu, were introduced by directed mutagenesis at position 292 in the L subunit of A. nidulans RuBisCO (Fig. 2).

Crude Extract Assay: In Fig. 3, the response of crude extract fractions to RuBP is shown. One milli-unit of RuBisCO is that amount which catalyzes the RuBP-dependent fixation of 1.0 nmole of CO_2/minute at 30° C. Specific activity is expressed as milli-units/mg protein. As evident, both mutant enzymes were similarly saturated with RuBP in the 39-52 mM range. In contrast, wild-type RuBP carboxylase saturated in a lower concentration range of 13-26 mM. Quantitative comparisons were not possible because the K_m for RuBP markedly increases with increasing ionic strength. The major effect of the substitution of leu and lys for arg at position 292 was, however, upon the specific activity of the enzymes.

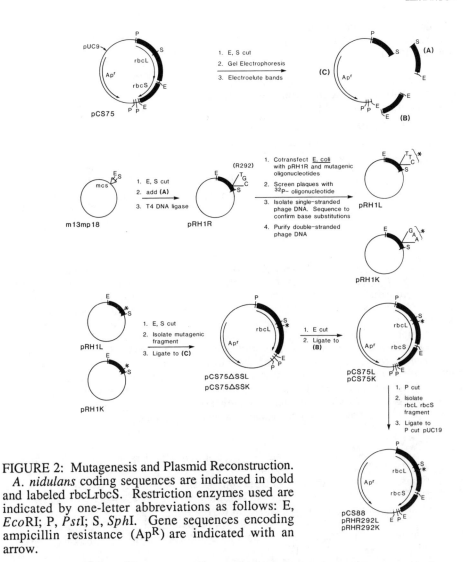

FIGURE 2: Mutagenesis and Plasmid Reconstruction.
A. nidulans coding sequences are indicated in bold
and labeled rbcLrbcS. Restriction enzymes used are
indicated by one-letter abbreviations as follows: E,
*Eco*RI; P, *Pst*I; S, *Sph*I. Gene sequences encoding
ampicillin resistance (Ap^R) are indicated with an
arrow.

Purification and Assay of Mutant Proteins: After the first sucrose gradient,
carboxylase activity could be detected in all three preparations, with the specific
activities of mutant enzymes reduced on the order of 100-fold in the case of the *lys*
variant as compared to wild-type and 2000-fold in the case of the *leu* variant (at 13 mM
RuBP). Only the wild-type enzyme was inhibited markedly by the potent RuBisCO
inhibitor CABP in assays of either crude extract preparations or sucrose fractions.[4] No
activity was measurable in peak fractions of either mutant from the second sucrose
gradient, although holoenzyme was detectable by western blot.

FIGURE 3: Saturation of mutant and wild-type RuBisCO by substrate RuBP.

Specific activities are shown for preparations in which the plasmids pCS88 (R; wild-type), pRHR292L (L; *arg*292 → *leu*) and pRHR292K (K; *arg*292 → *lys*) had been expressed.

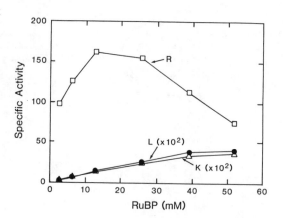

Implications of the Present Results: With rare exceptions, critical arginines have proven difficult to identify by traditional chemical modification and peptide isolation procedures. Here we present evidence for such an *arg*, first proposed on the basis of phenylglyoxal inactivation studies. Although large subunits of RuBisCO contain over 30 *arg* residues, upon stringent comparison, only two of these emerge as being completely conserved. *Arg*292 was chosen accordingly as stated.

Previous directed mutagenesis studies of active-site residues in RuBisCO have been limited to the dimeric form of the enzyme isolated from the purple-sulfur bacterium *R. rubrum*. We believe this to be the first mutagenesis study of a RuBisCO enzyme with the more complex L_8S_8 structure found in higher plants. Because of the power and ease of *in vitro* directed mutagenesis, we now suggest this as a general method of locating critical *arg* residues in a variety of enzymes.

REFERENCES
1 Andersson, I., Knight, L., Schneider, G., Linquist, T., Branden, C. and Lorimer, G. H. (1989) Nature 337, 229-234.
2 Lorimer, G. H. and Hartman, F. C. (1988) J. Biol. Chem. 263, 6468-6471.
3. Storrø, I. and McFadden, B. A. (1983) Biochem. J. 212, 45-54.
4. Haining, R. L. and McFadden, B. A. (in review).
5. McFadden, B. A. and Small, C. L. (1988) Photosynthesis Res. 18, 245-260.
6. Shinozaki, K., Yamada, C., Takahata, N., and Sugiura, M. (1983) Proc. Natl. Acad. Sci. USA 50, 4050-4054.
7. Shinozaki, K., and Sugiura, M. (1985) Mol. Gen. Genet. 200, 27-32.
8. Tabita, F. R. and Small, C. L. (1985) Proc. Natl. Acad. Sci. USA 82, 6100-6103.
9. Burke, D. T. and Olson, M. V. (1986) DNA 5, 325-332.
10. Berhow, M. A., Saluja, A. and McFadden, B. A. (1982) Plant Sci. Lett. 27, 51-57.
11. McFadden, B. A., Tabita, F. R. and Kuehn, G. D. (1975) Meth. Enz. 42, 461-472.
12. Andersen, K. and Caton, J. (1987) J. Bacteriol., 4547-4558.
13. Igarashi, Y., McFadden, B. A., and El-Gul, T. (1985) Biochemistry 24, 3957-3962.

PHOTOMODIFICATION OF A SERINE AT THE ACTIVE SITE OF SPINACH RuBisCO BY VANADATE

S. N. MOGEL AND B. A. McFADDEN, BIOCHEMISTRY AND BIOPHYSICS PROGRAM, WASHINGTON STATE UNIVERSITY, PULLMAN WASHINGTON 99164-4660

INTRODUCTION

The enzyme D-ribulose-1,5-bisphosphate carboxylase/oxygenase (RuBisCO) catalyzes the carboxylation and oxygenation of ribulose-1,5-bisphosphate (RuBP). While the former is the initial step in carbon fixation, the latter leads to photorespiration resulting in a net loss of carbon (1).

The enzyme in higher plants is a hexadecamer consisting of eight large subunits and eight small subunits. The active site is located within the large subunit and has been extensively studied, while the function of the small subunit is unknown. Various affinity labels and protein modification reagents have suggested that several important amino acids, including two lysines, are in the active site domain. The recent elucidation of the three dimensional structure of the enzyme has confirmed these observations (2). However serine had not been implicated at the active site previous to the crystal structure determination. We summarize here evidence to support UV-induced, vanadate dependent oxidation of a serine at the active site of spinach RuBisCO to an aldehyde which results in activity loss, and subsequent cleavage of the enzyme.

MATERIALS AND METHODS

Photomodification

Irradiation of spinach RuBisCO was performed in the presence of 0.3 mM Vi in 50 mM MOPS buffer at pH 7.5. The protein concentration was 0.3 mg/ml (4.3 μM active sites) at the time of irradiation which was performed on ice using a Hanovia 450-watt medium pressure Hg lamp (Ace Glass) at a distance of 9 cm. A glass filter was used to prevent surface heating and to screen out radiation below 330 nm. The samples were kept on ice during irradiation.

Reduction and RuBP Carboxylase Activity

After irradiation, an indicated amount of $NaBH_4$, prepared in 0.1 N NaOH, was added to the photomodified sample. The samples were incubated for one hour at 25° C. Fructose was then added to a final concentration of 23 mM to quench the remaining $NaBH_4$. The samples were allowed to react for an additional hour at 25° C. The samples were then activated and assayed for RuBP carboxylase activity (3).

M. Baltscheffsky (ed.), Current Research in Photosynthesis, Vol. III, 359–362.
© 1990 *Kluwer Academic Publishers. Printed in the Netherlands.*

Tritiation

The alkaline solution of [^{3}H]-NaBH$_4$ was added to irradiated samples to a final concentration of 0.6 mM (specific activity= 156 mCi/mMole). The samples were allowed to react for one hour at 25° C. The reaction was quenched with an equal volume of 12 N HCl and the samples were desiccated *in vacuo* (<0.1mm Hg) at room temperature to near dryness to remove volatile tritium. To each sample was then added 0.5 ml of 0.1 N HCl and the desiccation repeated. The samples were resuspended in 4% SDS and subjected to centrifugation through a 5-ml column of Sephadex G-50 as described by Penefsky (4). The samples were then counted for tritium in an aqueous counting scintillant (Amersham Corp.) using a Beckman LS9000 liquid scintillation counter.

RESULTS AND DISCUSSION

Vanadate rapidly inactivated RuBisCO when irradiated with UV light. The inactivation by vanadate displayed saturation kinetics and substrate protection indicating that an enzyme•Vi complex is formed and that modification resulting in loss of activity is probably occuring at the active site. Additional evidence for this was the

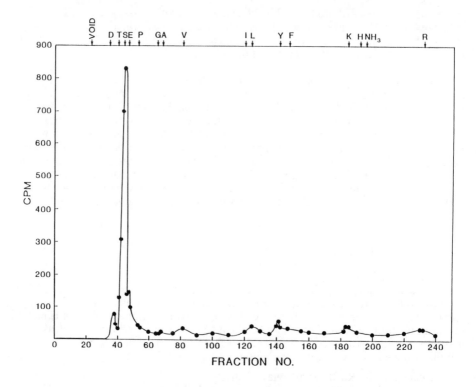

FIGURE 1: Amino acid analysis of 0.5 nmole of tritiated photomodified RuBisCO. The protein was hydrolysed in 6 N HCl for 22 hrs *in vacuo*. After separation of the ninhydrin-derivitized amino acids, the color of the fractions were allowed to fade for 14 hours at 25° C before counting for tritium.

observation that ribulose-1,5-bisphosphate and fructose-1,6-bisphosphate protected against inactivation (5). It was also observed that phosphate as well as bicarbonate partially protected against inactivation. Magnesium ion alone or with bicarbonate afforded no protection. Protection by phosphate may suggest that vanadate is binding to the phosphate binding site(s). However, vanadate readily forms oligomers, and the oligomeric state of vanadate which binds to the enzyme is currently under investigation. In the case of myosin, it has been shown using ^{51}V-NMR that tetravanadate is the form that binds to the enzyme (Cremo, personal communication).

Partial protection by bicarbonate may indicate that the carbamylated enzyme is more resistant to photoinactivation. Although non-substrate bicarbonate does bind to the active site, and actually competitively inhibits RuBP binding (6), anions such as formate, and perhaps acetate would be expected to behave similarly. The lack of protection by these compounds (5) suggests that the mode of bicarbonate protection may be due to carbamylation. The lack of any effect by Mg^{+2} suggests that it is the binding of CO_2 (or bicarbonate) that confers resistance to photomodification, and not the formation of the active ternary complex enzyme·CO_2·Mg^{+2}.

It was also observed that carboxylase activity could be partially restored by $NaBH_4$ treatment (5). This suggests the generation of an enzymic carbonyl group during photoinactivation by vanadate. This has been confirmed by tritiation of the modified enzyme with [^{3}H]-$NaBH_4$. The recovery of tritiated serine in the amino acid hydrolysate of RuBisCO (Fig. 1) confirms that the borohydride-reducible group introduced by photomodification is a "serine aldehyde" (Fig. 2). Because it has been established that reduction of the modified enzyme with unlabelled $NaBH_4$ partially restores activity, and the appearance of the borohydride-reducible group correlates with loss of activity (5), we conclude that this oxidation is responsible for much, if not all, of the activity loss.

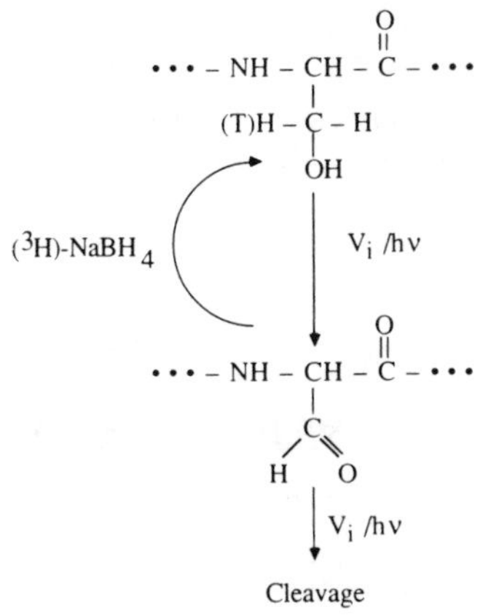

FIGURE 2: Serine is oxidized by vanadate and light to an aldehyde. Treatment with $NaBH_4$ restores serine, with tritium incorporated into the β-carbon if ^{3}H-$NaBH_4$ is used. Cleavage of the enzyme results, probably after modification of the serine aldehyde.

```
                              379
         Sp      Val – Ala– Ser– Gly– Gly–  Ile

         Mz        •    •    •    •    •    •

         Tb      Glu   •    •    •    •    •

         Cr      Val   •    •    •    •    •

         An        •    •    •    •    •    •

         Cv        •    •    •    •    •    •

         Ae        •    •    •    •    •    •

         Rr      Ile– Ile    •    •    •   Met
```

FIGURE 3: Sequence conservation around serine-379. The dots indicate sequence identity with the spinach enzyme. Sp; spinach. Mz; maize. Tb; tobacco. Cr; *Chlamydomonas reinhardtii*. An; *Anacystis nidulans*. Cr; *Chromatium vinosum*. Ae; *Alcaligenes eutrophus*. Rr; *Rhodospirillum rubrum*. (7).

We have also observed Vi-dependent photocleavage of the enzyme which appears to occur subsequent to inactivation (5).

The identity of the modified serine remains to be established. However the recent placement of serine-379 at the active site (2) and the surrounding sequence conservation (fig. 3) makes it an interesting candidate.

REFERENCES

(1) Miziorko, H. M. and Lorimer, G. H. (1983)   Annu. Rev. Biochem. 52, 507-535

(2) Andersson, I., Knight, S., Schneider, G., Lindquist, Y., Lindquist, T., Branden, C., and Lorimer, G.H. (1989) Nature 337, 229-234

(3) McFadden, B.A., Tabita, F.R., and Kuehn, G.D. (1975) Methods Enzymol. 42, 461-472

(4) Penefsky, H.S. (1977) J. Biol. Chem. 252, 2891-2899

(5) Mogel, S.N. and McFadden, B. A. (1989) Biochemistry 28, 5428-5431

(6) Pierce, J., Lorimer, G.H., and Reddy, G.S. (1986) Biochemistry 25, 1636-1643

(7) Viale, A.M., Kobayashi, H., and Akazawa, T. (1989) J. Bacteriol. 171, 2391-2400

PHOTOAFFINITY LABELING OF THE RUBISCO ACTIVE-SITE AND SMALL SUBUNIT
WITH 8-AZIDOADENOSINE 5'-TRIPHOSPHATE

MICHAEL E. SALVUCCI[a] AND BOYD E. HALEY[b], U.S.
DEPARTMENT OF AGRICULTURE–AGRICULTURAL RESEARCH SERVICE[a]
AND BIOCHEMISTRY DEPARTMENT[b], UNIVERSITY OF KENTUCKY,
LEXINGTON, KENTUCKY, 40546

1. INTRODUCTION
   The 8-azidopurine analogs have been used as probes for
identifying nucleotide-binding proteins in many biological systems
(1). Irradiation with UV light converts the azido moiety to a
reactive species that can bind covalently to residues in or near the
nucleotide site. In the present study, photoaffinity labeling was
used to probe for possible binding sites on the subunits of Rubisco.
The results presented herein provide evidence for distinct binding
sites on the Rubisco subunits by showing that $[^{32}P]8-N_3ATP$ labels
four active site peptides of the large subunit (LSu) and two peptides
from conserved regions of the small subunit (SSu).

2. PROCEDURES
2.1. Chemicals: The photoaffinity probes 8-azidoadenosine 5'-
   triphosphate ($8-N_3ATP$) and 8-azidoguanosine 5'-triphosphate
   ($8-N_3GTP$) were prepared as previously described (2) and
   radiolabeled with $32P$ by a modified exchange reaction (1).
2.2. Photoaffinity labeling in vitro: Rubisco was isolated from N.
   tabacum as described previously (3). Photoaffinity labeling of
   desalted leaf and stromal extracts and purified Rubisco was
   performed in porcelain spot plates at 4°C (4). Photolabeling in
   organello was performed using conditions for optimal adenylate
   uptake (5). Labeled polypeptides were separated by SDS-PAGE on
   10-18% polyacrylamide gradient gels and were visualized by
   autoradiography.
2.3. Isolation of photoaffinity labeled peptides: Photoaffinity
   labeled LSu tryptic peptides were isolated by a procedure
   involving ion-exclusion, ion-exchange, and reverse-phase HPLC
   (Salvucci, M.E., Kim, H. and Haley B.E., unpublished). Peptides
   were subjected to sequence analysis using a gas-phase sequencer
   (Applied Biosystem 470) and their positions in the intact enzyme
   were determined by comparison to the known sequence (6,7).
   Photoaffinity labeled SSu peptides were isolated from spinach
   Rubisco after separation of the subunits on Sephadex G-75.

M. Baltscheffsky (ed.), Current Research in Photosynthesis, Vol. III, 363–366.
© 1990 Kluwer Academic Publishers. Printed in the Netherlands.

3. RESULTS AND DISCUSSION

3.1. Photoaffinity labeling of Rubisco:

Several polypeptides were photolabeled with $[\alpha-32P]8-N_3ATP$ in desalted tobacco leaf and stromal extracts (Fig. 1). Two of the most heavily labeled were polypeptides with relative molecular masses that corresponded to the subunits of Rubisco. Incorporation of ^{32}P into both subunits of purified Rubisco occurred with either $\alpha-$ or $\gamma-$ labeled 8-N_3ATP. No incorporation occurred in samples that were not photolyzed (Fig. 1). These results indicated that labeling of the Rubisco subunits was due to irreversible covalent binding of $[^{32}P]8-N_3$ATP and not to protein phosphorylation. When $[\alpha-32P]8-N_3$GTP was used, photoincorporation into the SSu was less than 5% of that obtained with $[\alpha-^{32}P]8-N_3$ATP (Fig. 1).

Photoaffinity labeling with $[^{32}P]8-N_3$ATP was also performed with lysed pea chloroplasts. Whereas the Rubisco LSu was the predominant photolabeled polypeptide in freshly lysed extracts, there was no incorporation into the SSu either in the presence or absence of thylakoid membranes (Fig. 2). Ultrafiltration of the stromal extract increased the level of incorporation into all of the labeled polypeptides, and the Rubisco SSu was now one

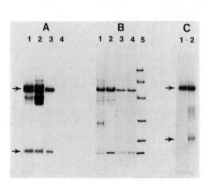 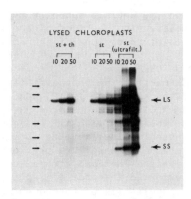

FIGURE 1. Photoaffinity labeling of tobacco leaf and chloroplast stromal extracts and purified Rubisco. A. Autoradiograph of photo-labeled polypeptides from tobacco leaves (lane 1), chloroplast stroma (lane 2) and purified Rubisco (lane 3). Lane 4 = no photolysis. B. Coomassie blue-stained gel of lanes 1-4. Lane 5 = molecular mass standards. C. Autoradiograph of stromal polypeptides photolabeled with $[\alpha-^{32}P]8-N_3$GTP (lane 1) and $[\alpha-^{32}P]8-N_3$ATP (lane 2).

FIGURE 2. Photoaffinity labeling of chloroplast stromal extracts containing thylakoids (st + th), extracts after removal of the thylakoid membranes by centrifugation (st) or centrifuged extracts that were ultrafiltered (st + ultrafilt.). $[\alpha-^{32}P]8-N_3$ATP was used at concentrations of 10, 20 & 50 µM.

of the more heavily labeled polypeptides (Fig. 2).

3.2. <u>Photoaffinity labeling of the Rubisco active-site</u>: Two lines of indirect evidence showed that binding of 8-N_3ATP to the LSu of Rubisco takes place in the active-site. First, covalent modification of Rubisco by incorporation of the photoprobe reduced enzyme activity by 14.4%, an amount equivalent to the amount of [^{32}P]8-N_3ATP incorporated into the LSu (data not shown). Second, phosphorylated effectors afforded a level of protection to the site which correlated with the apparent affinity of each for the active-site of Rubisco (data not shown). Photoaffinity labeling of the SSu was unaffected by active-site-directed effectors (data not shown).

The X-ray structure of spinach Rubisco identifies 10 loop regions in the active-site (8). The major photolabeled peptide isolated by ion-exclusion and ion-exchange chromatography, and reverse phase HPLC corresponded to the Rubisco LSu tryptic peptide Val-42 to Arg-79 (Table 1), an active-site peptide (9). Two portions of the tryptic peptide Asp-95 to Lys-128, the peptide which comprises loop B in the crystal structure (8) were also recovered. Also recovered were two peptides (Table 1) which include residues in two other loop regions of the Rubisco active-site (8). The peptide Asp-202 to Arg-213 (loop 2 in ref. 8) is adjacent to the activator lysine (10). The peptide Gln-259 to His-267 is the N-terminal fragment of Gln-259 to Arg-285 the tryptic peptide which encompasses loop 4. Thus, all four of the photoaffinity labeled LSu peptides have been previously shown to be active-site peptides based on X-ray crystallography or chemical modification or by both techniques.

TABLE 1. Tobacco Rubisco LSu peptides photolabeled with 8-N_3ATP

Peptide	Position in sequence	Comments, active-site loop (8)
1	Val-42 to Thr-63	active-site peptide (9), loop A
2	Asp-202 to Arg-213	peptide adjacent to the activator lysine (10), loop 2
3	Asp-106 to Asn-123	portion of a tryptic peptide, loop B
4	Asp-95 to Tyr-100	truncated tryptic peptide, loop B
5	Glu-259 to His 267	loop 4

3.3. <u>Photoaffinity labeling of specific sites on the Rubisco SSu</u>: For the isolation of SSu peptides, spinach Rubisco holoenzyme was photoaffinity labeled and the labeled subunits separated by gel-filtration chromatography in urea. Photolabeled SSu tryptic peptides were isolated by ion-exclusion and reverse phase HPLC.

TABLE 2. Spinach Rubisco SSu peptides photolabeled with 8-N$_3$ATP

Peptide	Position in sequence	Comments
1	Tyr-12 to Ala-28	Includes the highly conserved region Glu-13 to Leu-21
2	Leu-72 to Glu-90	Includes the highly conserved region Leu-72 to Asp-79

The sequences of the major photolabeled SSu peptides corresponded to SSu tryptic peptides Tyr-12 to Lys-36 and Leu-72 to Lys-91 (Table 2). These SSu peptides encompass two of the three highly conserved regions of the SSu (10).

3.4. Conclusions: Binding of 8-N$_3$ATP to the LSu of Rubisco is consistent with the propensity of Rubisco to bind phosphoesters at the substrate site (10). The isolation of only active-site peptides from the LSu showed that binding of 8-N$_3$ATP to the LSu was localized specifically in the active-site. Incorporation of 8-N$_3$ATP into specific regions of the SSu was unexpected and revealed a heretofore unknown binding site on this subunit. Photoaffinity labeling in organello (data not shown) and with undesalted chloroplast extracts demonstrated that the SSu site is inaccessible to 8-N$_3$ATP in situ. Since [^{32}P]8-N$_3$ATP was incorporated into the SSu in ultrafiltered and desalted extracts, it appears that the SSu site is blocked by a low molecular weight metabolite. Identification of the native ligand of this site may reveal a physiological function for the putative binding site on the SSu.

REFERENCES
1 Potter, R.L. and Haley, B.E. (1983) Meth. Enzymol. 91, 613-633
2 Czarnecki, J., Geahlen, R.T. and Haley, B.E. (1979) Meth. Enzymol. 56, 642-65
3 Crafts-Brandner, S.J., Salvucci, M.E. and Egli, D.B. (1989) Photosyn. Res., in press
4 Evans, R.K., Haley, B.E. and Roth, D.A. (1985) J. Biol. Chem. 260, 7800-7804
5 Robinson, S.P. and Wiskich, J.T. (1977) Plant Physiol. 59, 422-427
6 Shinozaki, K. and Sugiura, M. (1982) Gene 20, 91-102
7 Martin, P.G. (1979) Aust. J. Plant Physiol 6, 401-408
8 Andersson, I., Knight, S., Schneider, G., Lindqvist, Y., Branden, C.-I. and Lorimer, G.H. (1989) Nature 337, 229-234
9 Herndon, C.S. and Hartman, F.C. (1984) J. Biol. Chem. 259, 3102-3110
10 Andrews, T.J. and Lorimer, G.H. (1987) in The Biochemistry of Plants (Hatch, M.D., Boardman, N.K., eds.), Vol. 133, pp. 131-218,, Academic Press, New York.

IN VITRO STUDIES ON THE TENDENCY OF LARGE SUBUNIT FROM PLANT RUBISCO TO FORM INCORRECT AGGREGATIONS

E. RINTAMÄKI, Department of Biology, University of Turku, SF-20500 TURKU, FINLAND

1. INTRODUCTION

Ribulose-1,5-bisphosphate carboxylase-oxygenase (Rubisco) is the key enzyme both of photosynthesis and photorespiration in plants. The dual function of Rubisco makes it an important target enzyme for genetic engineering in attempts to improve the productivity of crop plants.

Plant Rubisco is an oligomeric protein comprised of eight large (L) and eight small (S) subunits. Recently the genes of both subunits have been cloned from many bacteria and higher plants but the attempts to produce an eukaryotic holoenzyme in Escherichia coli have failed (1). The higher plant Rubisco genes were expressed in E. coli but the subunits did not assemble into functional molecule. The same problem also exists in the reconstitution experiments in vitro (2,3).

In plant chloroplasts the newly synthesized L can bind to another chloroplast protein complex called large subunit binding protein (BP) (1). The intermediate steps of the assembly of higher plant Rubisco as well as the function of BP are still largely unknown.

The aim of this paper was to study in vitro the assembly and interactions of subunits of plant Rubisco. The inability of L subunit to reassemble is supposed to be caused by its insolubility. Therefore the effect of BP on the solubilization of L polypeptides was included in the studies.

2. MATERIALS AND METHODS

2.1. Purification of Rubisco and BP

Rubisco and BP were purified from young wheat leaves according to (4). BP fractions were further purified by Fast Liquid Chromatography in Superose ^{TM}6 column.

2.2. Dissociation of Rubisco molecule

Rubisco was dissociated according to (2) and (3). 1% SDS was used for dissociaton at pH 8.

2.3. Experimental procedure for studing the effect of BP on the solubilization of Rubisco L subunit

In control experiment wheat Rubisco in 10 mol m^{-3} phosphate buffer (= Rubisco solution in Table 1) was disso-

M. Baltscheffsky (ed.), Current Research in Photosynthesis, Vol. III, 367–370.

ciated into subunits by lowering the pH to 5. The precipitation was collected by centrifugation and the supernatant (= fraction 1) was neutralized to pH 8. The pellet was suspended with 40 mol m^{-3} Tris/acetate, pH 8 containing 10 mol m^{-3} DTT for dissolving the soluble material from the pellet (= fraction 2). The remaining pellet was solubilized in Tris buffer containing 4% SDS and 5% mercaptoethanol (= fraction 3).

In BP experiment the purified BP preparation was dissolved in phosphate buffer together with Rubisco (Rubisco + BP solution in Table 1). The protein and polypeptide composition of the solutions in Table 1 was studied with PAGE.

3. RESULTS AND DISCUSSION
3.1. Aggregation of plant Rubisco L subunits in vitro.

Wheat Rubisco was dissociated into subunits by extreme pH treatments. The separated subunits were unable to reassemble into functional holoprotein when the starting conditions were restored. Some of the separated wheat S subunits retained their ability to form functional heterologous Rubisco when mixed with L subunits from a cyanobacterial Rubisco indicating that the failure of the assembly was caused by the properties of plant L subunits.
Dissociation of Rubisco at acid pH: The acid treatment resulted in precipitation of L subunits together with some undissociated holoprotein (Table 1). The L subunits dissolved partly in neutral buffer containing 1% SDS at 40°C after long incubation, and completely if thiol reductant was also added into solution.
Dissociation of Rubisco molecule at alkaline pH: L subunits dissociated from the holoprotein did not precipitate in this treatment, even after neutralization of the solution. However, PAGE revealed that after complete neutralization the L subunits occurred as high molecular weight aggregations (Fig. 1A and 1B). Treatment with both SDS and thiol reductant was necessary to disrupt the aggregated structures (Fig. 1B, lanes 3 and 4), which indicates that the L subunits had been crosslinked by disulfide bridges. These interactions are incorrect, because oxidized sulfhydryl groups are not present in the functional Rubisco molecule (5). Since added thiol reductant did not prevent aggregation of the subunits during reconstitution, oxidation of the sulfhydryl groups apparently took place on contact faces sheltered by the secondary and tertiary structures of the polypeptides.
Dissociation of Rubisco at neutral pH: Aggregation of the subunits in nearly neutral buffer was tested by using SDS as the dissociating agent at pH 8.0. After removal of most of SDS from the solution by dialysis, disulfide crosslinked L oligomers appeared in the solution (Fig. 1B, lanes 7 and 8) indicating that sulfhydryl groups of wheat L subunits

are very sensitive to oxidation.

FIGURE 1. Native (A) and SDS-PAGE (B) of wheat Rubisco dissociated by alkaline or detergent treatment. The
pretreatments of Rubisco solution are listed below. Thick
arrow, aggregations of subunits; thin arrows, disulfide
crosslinked L; *, Rubisco holoprotein; ** aggregated
Rubisco; S_1, L_1, L_2, subunit monomers and a dimer.
A) NATIVE PAGE: 1. control Rubisco; 2. Rubisco after dissociation at pH 11 and neutralization to pH 8 by dialysis;
3. as lane 2 + 10 mM DTT; 4. Rubisco at pH 8.0 treated with
1% SDS and dialysed to remove SDS; 5. as lane 4 + 10 mM DTT
B) SDS-PAGE:
1. control Rubisco
heated with SDS and
thiol reductant;
2. control Rubisco;
3. Rubisco after dissociation at pH 11
and neutralization
to pH 8 by dialysis;
4. as lane 3 +
10 mM DTT;
5. control Rubisco;
6. control
Rubisco + 1% SDS;
7. Rubisco at
pH 8.0 treated with
1% SDS and dialysed
to remove SDS;
8. as lane 7 + 10 mM DTT.

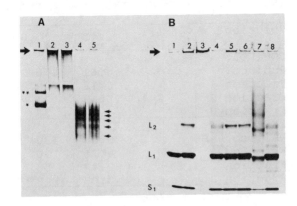

3.2. Solubilization of L subunit with BP

It has been proposed that the function of BP is to keep
L polypeptides soluble before the assembly of Rubisco (1).
This hypothesis was tested in the experiment presented in
Table 1. Dissociation of Rubisco was carried out at acid
pH, because this treatment results in quick separation of L
and S subunits (2).

In the control experiment S subunits remained in solution during dissociation of Rubisco (Table 1, fraction 1),
while L subunits and undissociated holoprotein precipitated. PAGE studies and the value of L/S molar ratio
revealed that undissociated holoprotein dissolved when the
pellet was suspended in neutral buffer (fraction 2). On the
other hand, L subunits were only soluble in neutral buffer
containing detergent and thiol reductant (fraction 3).

In the binding protein experiment BP was present during
the dissociation treatment of Rubisco solution and it pre-

cipitated together with L subunits and holoprotein. S sub-units and undissociated holoprotein followed the fraction-ation of the control experiment. In the presence of BP, however, L subunits were concentrated in fraction 2 being soluble in neutral buffer. This can be seen in high per-centage of L subunits and high L/S molar ratio of subunits of fraction 2 in the BP experiment (Table 1). This result indicated that under the experimental conditions BP was able to solubilize L subunits dissociated from holoprotein.

TABLE 1. The effect of BP on the solubility of Rubisco large subunit. Rubisco was dissociated into subunits in the absence (control) or presence of BP (experiment) (see Mate-rials and methods). The total amounts and the molar ratio of Rubisco subunits (L/S) are indicated. The theoretical value for the molar ratio of subunits in holoprotein is 1.

Solution	Total L		Total S		L/S
	mg	%	mg	%	mol/mol
CONTROL:					
Rubisco	0.61	100	0.16	100	1.05
Fraction 1	0.18	29	0.10	60	0.50
Fraction 2	0.19	31	0.05	30	1.09
Fraction 3	0.23	37	0.02	10	3.84
EXPERIMENT					
Rubisco + BP	0.84	100	0.22	100	1.07
Fraction 1	0.26	30	0.10	48	0.67
Fraction 2	0.47	56	0.07	32	1.89
Fraction 3	0.07	8	0.01	3	3.05

   The results of this paper indicate that L subunits of higher plant Rubisco have a high tendency to form incorrect self aggregations and this tendency was reduced by the presence of BP. I suggest that the function of BP is to act as a supporting column where newly synthesized L subunits bind to and this binding promotes the correct folding and association of the L subunits.

REFERENCES
1 Ellis, R.J. and van der Vies, S.M. (1988) Photosynth. Res. 16, 101-115.
2 Andrews, T.J., Lorimer, G.H. (1985) J. Biol. Chem. 260, 4632-4636.
3 Jordan, D.B. and Chollet, R. (1985) Arch. Biochem. Biophys. 236, 487-496.
4 Gutteridge, S., Parry, M.A.J. and Schmidt, C.N.G. (1982) Eur. J. Biochem. 126, 597-602.
5 Chollet, R., and Anderson, L. L., (1977) Biochim. Biophys. Acta, 482, 228-240.

STOPPED FLOW KINETICS OF THE Co^{2+}-ACTIVATED CYANOBACTERIAL RubisCO

Rolf Brändén[1], Nigel Halford[2], Alfred Keys[2] and Martin Parry[2]

[1]Department of Biochemistry & Biophysics, University of Göteborg, S-412 96 Göteborg, Sweden. [2]Department of Biochemistry, Rothamsted Experimental Station, Harpenden, Herts, AL5 2JQ England

INTRODUCTION: Decisions leading to a sucessful programme of muta-genesis in order to selectively change the active site of Rubisco thereby favouring the CO_2-fixation will probably require a rather good knowledge of the catalysis in relation to the structure of the catalytic site. The structure of the active site is known (1,2) and parts of the metal coordination sphere in presence of substrate, product and the inhibitor CABP have been found by EPR studies (3,4). However, in order to follow the subtle changes during catalysis transient kinetics must be made. Co^{2+}-activated Rubisco has absorp-tion properties suitable for these kind of studies (5) and have here been used to study altered catalytic properties of a mutant form of the enzyme from Anacystis nidulans.

MATERIALS AND METHODS: Preparation of the truncated enzyme form of A. nidulans, where the N-terminal region of the large subunit has been replaced by unrelated amino acids has been described earlier (6). The large subunit was prepared as described by Andrews and Ballment (7). The activation of the enzyme was made as before (5) and all experiments were carried out in a Hi-Tech SF-3 series stopped flow apparatus at 20°C in presence of 50 mM HEPES buffer at pH 8.2 containing 25 mM $NaHCO_3$.

RESULTS AND DISCUSSION: Fig. 1 shows the two distinct phases ob-served for the native A. nidulans Rubisco upon addition of RuBP.

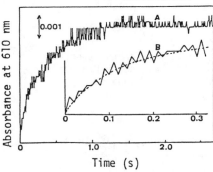

Fig. 1 Progress curves for Co^{2+}-activated Rubisco from A. nidulans upon addition of RuBP. After mixing, the concen-trations of enzyme (protomer), RuBP and Co^{2+} were 0.4 mM, 1.25 mM and 0.3 mM, respec-tively.

The half times for the approach to stationary states are independent of the RuBP concentration and 0.05s and 0.5s, respectively. For the truncated enzyme form only one single slow phase is seen (fig. 2b) which is independent of the RuBP concentration and has a half time of about 1.3s. Fig. 3 shows that half saturation of the total absorp-tion change obtained at steady state occurs at about 0.5 mM RuBP which is similar to the K_m for RuBP earlier found for the truncated enzyme form (6). The large subunit only gives one single slow phase with a half time of about 1.3s (fig. 2c) very similar to the truncated form.

M. Baltscheffsky (ed.), Current Research in Photosynthesis, Vol. III, 371–372.
© 1990 Kluwer Academic Publishers. Printed in the Netherlands.

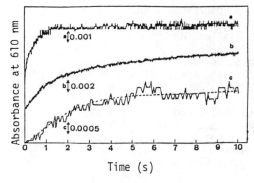

Fig. 2 Progress curves for different forms of Co^{2+}-activated Rubisco from A. nidulans. a) native form b) truncated form and c) the large subunit only. After mixing, the cons. of enzyme (protomer) and RuBP were in a) 0.3 mM and 1.25 mM, in b) 0.25 mM and 1.0 mM and in c) 0.20 mM and 1.0 mM, respectively.

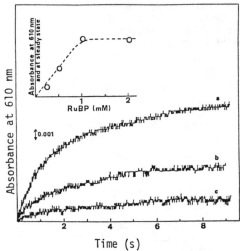

Fig. 3 The total absorption change at 610 nm and at steady state as a function of RuBP concentration. After mixing the concentration of of enzyme was 0.25 mM protomer and the concentration of RuBP were in a) 2 mM in b) 0.5 mM and in c) 0.25 mM. At 1 mM RuBP a trace nearly identical to that seen in a) was obtained.

The tenfold higher K_m and the normal V_{max} obtained for the truncated form of the enzyme (6) suggest that it is simply the binding properties for RuBP that is change for this species. We therefore suggest that the slow phase seen in fig. 2b and 2c reflects the initial coordination of RuBP to the metal ion at the active site.

REFERENCES

1. Andersson, I., Knight, S., Schneider, G., Lindqvist, Y., Lundqvist, T., Bränden, C.-I., Lorimer, G. (1989) Nature 337, 229-234
2. Lundqvist, T., & Schneider, G. (1989) J.B.C. 264, 7078-7083
3. Miziorko, H.M., & Sealy, R.C. (1984) Biochemistry 23, 479-485
4. Styring, S., & Bränden, R. (1985) Biochemistry 24, 6011-6019
5. Bränden, R., Janson, K., & Nilsson,P. (1989) Biochim. Biophys. Acta 995, 75-81
6. Kettleborough, C.A., Parry, M.A.J., Burton, S., Gutteridge, S., Keys, A., & Phillips, A. (1987) Eur. J. Biochem. 170, 335-342
7. Andrews, J., & Ballment, B. (1983) J.B.C. 258, 7514-7518

STRUCTURAL INVESTIGATIONS OF D-RIBULOSE 1,5-BISPHOSPHATE CARBOXYLASE/OXYGENASE FROM ZEA MAYS AND SPINACH

Joachim Vater[1], Lifen Ren[1], Johann Salnikow[1], Peter M. Abuja[2] and Ingrid Pilz[2]

INSTITUTE OF BIOCHEMISTRY AND MOLECULAR BIOLOGY, TECHNICAL UNIVERSITY OF BERLIN[1], D-1000 BERLIN (WEST) AND INSTITUTE OF PHYSICAL CHEMISTRY, UNIVERSITY OF GRAZ[2], A-8010 GRAZ, AUSTRIA.

1. INTRODUCTION

Appreciable progress has been achieved in the structural characterization of D-ribulose 1,5-bisphosphate carboxylase/oxygenase (Rubisco) during the past decade. The amino acid sequence of numerous Rubisco species has been elucidated both by proteinchemical and gene sequencing techniques. The quaternary structure of a few carboxylases has been investigated mainly by electron microscopy (1) as well as by X-ray and neutron small angle scattering (2-5). The structural analysis of some of these enzymes from microorganisms (6,7) and plants (8-10) is now reached near atomic resolution by X-ray diffraction methodology. In this publication we present data on the structure of the maize enzyme on the primary, secondary and quaternary structure level.

2. EXPERIMENTAL PROCEDURES

Purification of the maize carboxylase, enzymatic assays, preparation of the small subunit as well as cleavage and sequencing of this polypeptide were performed as described recently (11). The components of the heterogeneous moiety of the small subunit of the maize carboxylase were resolved by two-dimensional gel electrophoresis using the O'Farrell technique (12). Circular dichroism spectra of the spinach and maize Rubisco were recorded using a Jasco J-20 spectropolarimeter. Small angle X-ray scattering of the maize enzyme was measured as reported in (3,4).

3. RESULTS AND DISCUSSION

3.1.   Amino acid sequence and 2-dimensional gel electrophoresis of the small subunit of the maize Rubisco.

The small subunit of the maize carboxylase was digested with trypsin, chymotrypsin, *Staphylococcus aureus* protease or thermolysin. The peptides obtained were separated by reversed phase HPLC and sequenced by Edman degradation performed with the DABITC/PITC double coupling technique (13) as described recently (11). Our proteinchemically derived sequence is in complete agreement with the gene-derived sequence reported by Matsuoka et al. (14). However, the primary structure obtained by protein sequencing shows more than one amino acid in certain positions, when compared to the gene-derived sequence. Amino acid dimorphies are present in sixteen positions (boxed residues in Fig. 1 at positions 6,34,35,38,45,47,77,81,85,91,92,95, 106,107,116 and 118) as corroborated by at least two different peptide sets carrying either both amino acids or one of them. Furthermore, in nine positions (6,17,20,54, 84,90,115,117) additional substitutions have been observed

M. Baltscheffsky (ed.), Current Research in Photosynthesis, Vol. III, 373–376.
© 1990 *Kluwer Academic Publishers. Printed in the Netherlands.*

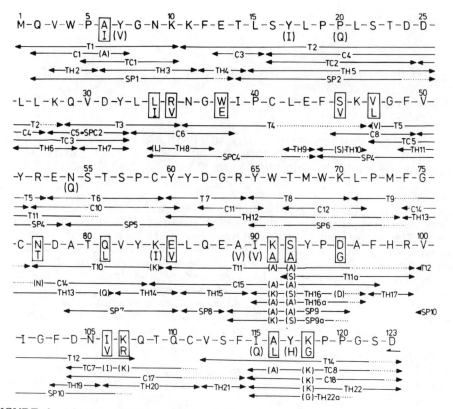

FIGURE 1. Amino acid sequence of the small subunit of the ribulose 1,5-bisphosphate carboxylase/oxygenase from maize.

T, tryptic peptides; C, chymotryptic peptides; TC, peptides obtained by digestion with trypsin and chymotrypsin; TH, thermolytic peptides; SP, peptides generated by the protease from Staphylococcus aureus; SPC, peptides obtained by digestion with S. aureus protease and chymotrypsin. Dotted lines correspond to residues not unequivocally identified by sequencing. Boxed amino acids are dimorphies corroborated by at least two different peptides, additional dimorphies (residues in parenthesis) have been observed only for one peptide fragment. C-terminal aspartic acid has been determined by hydrazinolysis.

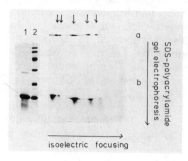

Figure 2. Two-dimensional gel electrophoresis of the small subunit of the maize Rubisco.

a) Isoelectric focusing tube gel; b) SDS-polyacrylamide gel. Lane 1: separated small subunit; lane 2: molecular mass standards (from top to bottom: 94;67;43;30;20 and 14,4 kDa).

(Fig. 1, residues in parenthesis) in one of the respective peptide fragments. Since here the assignment is less substantiated these dimorphies have to be considered as more tentative. These results indicate that the small subunit consists of at least two polypeptide chains due to the expression of two or more nuclear genes. In particular, Sheen and Bogorad (15) have demonstrated that at least three nuclear encoded genes are involved in the expression of the small subunit of the maize carboxylase. Two of them account for >80% of the SSU mRNS, while a third gene contributes approx. 10%. This pattern is also obvious on the protein level. Two-dimensional gel electrophoresis of the separated small subunit in Fig. 2 shows two dominant polypeptide species in combination with 2-3 minor gene products. The isoelectric points of these SSU variants are 7.23; 6.85; 6.3; 5.65 and 5.25 (from left to right in Fig. 2).

3.2 Secondary structure analysis of the spinach and maize carboxylase computed from circular dichroism spectra.

Circular dichroism spectra of the deactivated form of the Rubisco from spinach and maize were measured at 25°C in the range of 190-240 nm. For this purpose the proteins were dissolved in CO_2-depleted 10 mM phosphate buffer, pH = 7,2 oder 8,0 containing 50 μM dithioerythritol. A secondary structure analysis was performed using the method introduced by Provencher and Glöckner (16). In this procedure the CD-spectra of the carboxylases were analyzed with a computer programme by linear combination with the CD-spectra of 16 proteins the secondary structure of which is known from X-ray crystallography. The results obtained at pH 7,2 and 8 do not differ significantly. Therefore, the secondary structure data which are listed in Table 1 represent an average of all data computed for both pH-values. The α-helix content estimated for the spinach and maize Rubisco ranges between 20 and 30%, as reported by Tomimatsu and Donovan (17) for the carboxylases from alfalfa, spinach and tobacco. On addition of each 10 mM Mg^{2+} and HCO_3^- to the enzyme solutions changes in the CD spectra were induced indicating a lower helix content in the activated state. Under such conditions CD-data could be obtained only until 196 nm. Further experimental work is needed to extend the data range to 190 nm which is necessary for the secondary structure analysis with the computer programme of Provencher and Glöckner.

3.3. Investigation of the quaternary structure of the maize carboxylase by small angle X-ray scattering (SAXS).

Similar SAXS - profiles have been obtained for the active and inactive conformation of the maize carboxylase. Slight differences both in the I(h)- and p(r)-function are not significant. Therefore, in first approximation a model was constructed that fits both conformations equally well. The structural parameters are listed in Table 1. Model calculations were performed using the Multibody programme introduced by Glatter (18). The model exhibits the characteristic quaternary structure for the L_8S_8-type found in higher plants (3,4). The large subunits are arranged around a four-fold axis in two layers with the small subunits attached on top of them. There is a central channel through the whole molecule which contains the four-fold symmetry axis. The large subunit shows a deep groove facing the surroundings of the enzyme. It closely resembles the structure of the spinach Rubisco (3).

TABLE 1.Structural parameters of the Rubisco from spinach and Zea mays
I. Secondary structure analysis using CD data of the deactivated enzymes in the absence of Mg^{2+} and HCO_3

	α-Helix %	ß-sheet %	remainder %
spinach Rubisco	30	36	34
maize Rubisco	26	36	38

II. Quarternary structure of the maize Rubisco - Model parameters derived from a small angle X-ray scattering analysis:

Complete enzyme L_8S_8:

		large subunit:	
radius of gyration	4,91 nm	dimensions in x,y	6,82 nm
x	14,32 nm	z	3,42 nm
dimensions in y	15,41 nm	depth of groove	3,42 nm
z	10,93 nm	width of groove	1,36 nm
diameter of channel	1,36 nm		

REFERENCES

1 Eisenberg, D., Baker, T.S., Suh, S.W. and Smith, W.W. (1978) in Photosynthetic Carbon Assimilation (Siegelman, H.W. and Hind, G., eds.) pp. 271-281, Plenum Press, New York

2 Meisenberger, O., Pilz, I., Bowien, B., Pal, G.P. and Saenger, W. (1984) J. Biol. Chem. 259, 4463-4465

3 Pilz, I., Schwarz, E., Pal, G.P. and Saenger, W. (1987) Z. Naturforsch. 42c, 1089-1091

4 Abuja, P.M. and Pilz, I. (1988) Z. Naturforsch. 43c, 373-376

5 Donnelly, M.J., Hartman, F.C. and Ramakrishnan, V. (1984) J. Biol. Chem. 259, 406-411

6 Schneider, G., Lindqvist, Y., Brändén, C.-I. and Lorimer, G.H. (1986) EMBO J. 5, 3409-3415

7 Holzenburg, A., Mayer, F., Harauz, G., van Heel, M., Tokuoka, R., Ishida, T., Harata, K., Pal, G.P. and Saenger, W. (1987) Nature 325, 730-732

8 Chapman, M.S., Suh, S.W., Cascio, D., Smith, W.W. and Eisenberg, D. (1987) Nature 329, 354-356

9 Chapman, M.S., Suh, S.W., Curmi, P.M.G., Cascio, D., Smith, W.W. and Eisenberg, D.S. (1988) Science 241, 71-74

10 Andersson, I., Knight, S., Schneider, G., Lindqvist, Y., Lundqvist, T., Brändén, C.-I. and Lorimer, G.H. (1989) Nature 337, 229-234

11 Ren, L., Salnikow, J. and Vater, J. (1988) Biol. Chem. Hoppe-Seyler 369, 609-615

12 O'Farrell, P.H. (1975) J. Biol. Chem. 250, 4007-4021

13 Chang, J.-Y., Brauer, D. and Wittmann-Liebold, B. (1978) FEBS Lett. 93, 205-214

14 Matsuoka, M., Kano-Murakami, Y., Tanaka, Y., Ozeki, Y. and Yamamoto, N. (1987) J. Biochem. (Tokyo) 102, 673-676

15 Sheen, J.-Y. and Bogorad, L. (1986) EMBO J. 5, 3417-3422

16 Provencher, S.W. and Glöckner, J. (1981) Biochemistry 20, 33-37

17 Tomimatsu, Y. and Donovan, J.W. (1981) Plant Physiol. 68, 808-813

18 Glatter, O. (1980) Acta Phys. Austr. 52, 243-256

IMMOBILIZATION AS AN APPROACH TO STUDY THE QUATERNARY STRUCTURE OF RUBISCO FROM TOBACCO

Li Li-ren and Xu Ren-bang, Shanghai Institute of Plant Physiology, Academia Sinica, 300 Fonglin road, Shanghai, 200032, China.

1. INTRODUCTION

Ribulose-1,5-bisphosphate carboxylase/oxygenase (RubisCO,E.C.4.1.1. 39) is a key enzyme in both photosynthesis and phyotorespiration. this enzyme has been considered as a target for mutational changes involving genetic engineering to improve carboxylation. To achieve this, a more complete understanding of the enzyme molecular structure and of its relation to the catalytic mechanism are required. Both catalytic and activating sites of the enzyme reside on the large subunit. The function of small subunit remains unclear.

The dissociation and reconstitution of RubisCO subunits from prokaryotes(1,2) and eucaryotes(3) have been investigated recently. It has been demonstrated that the small subunit is a necessary component for RubisCO catalysis, and it is inferred that the role of the small subunit in maintenance of RubisCO activity is probably related to its spatial arrangment in the molecule. Up to now, insights into the quaternary structure of the L_8S_8 RubisCO are almost solely based on X-ray crystallographic and electron microscopic studies(4,5).

Previously we have conjectured(3) that the large subunits probably stretches over the small subunits, and that the small subunits are surrounded by the large subunits, based on dissociation and reconstitution experiments. In this paper, the concept has been further demonstrated by various biochemical evidences.

2. RESULTS
2.1. Hydrolysis of RubisCO by immobilized and soluble trypsin

The degradation of RubisCO by immobilized and soluble trypsin is compared in Fig.1. RubisCO was directly dissociated to large and small subunits by SDS(Fig.1A). By treating the enzyme with trypsin-Sepharose, the large subunit was broken in two bands(Fig.1B), but the small subunit was not affected. After RubisCO was treated by the trypsin, the large subunit band was greatly diminished(Fig.1C), while several other bands of lower molecule weight appeared. Similarly, the small subunit had was also diminished and there was a band under it.

This observation is consistant with the following. As the immobile trypsin-Sepharose particle was relatively large, it had access only to the surface of the Rubisco molecule. The large subunits appeared to be partially located on the outside of the RubisCO molecule,protecting any lysine and arginine sites of the small subunits from proteolysis by the immobilized trypsin. It should be indicated that the concentration of the soluble trypsin used in our experiment is much higher than previous report(6). In this case the hydrolysis of the small subunits might have occured following hydrolysis of the large subunits and exposure of the small subunits to trypsin action.

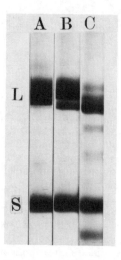

FIGURE 1

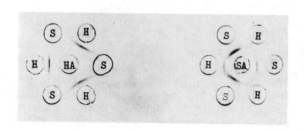

FIGURE 2
HA,Anti-small subunit serum.
HA,Anti-holoenzyme serum.
S,Small subunit.
H,Holoenzyme.

2.2. Immunochemical experiment of the holoenzyme and the small subunit

The immuno-double diffusion technique was used to examine the immuno-precipitation reactions of the anti-holoenzyme and the anti-small subunit sera against the holoenzyme and the small subunit. Anti-holoenzyme serum gave a single precipitin band with the small subunit holoenzyme(Fig.2A), but gave no precipitin band with the small subunit (or the reaction was very weak). This indicates that the determinant groups on anti-holoenzyme serum were directed against the large subunit. Anti-small subunit serum could combine with the small subunit, but only weakly with the holoenzyme.

The results were clearer when immobilized anti-small subunit IgG was used to study the immunoreaction(Fig.3). A band of small subunit could be observed on the stained gel(Fig.3A), when anti-small subunit IgG-Sepharose was incubated with small subunit. This indicates that small subunit can bind with anti-small subunit IgG-Sepharose. When the anti-small subunit IgG-sepharose was incubated with the holoenzyme, no bands either of the large or small subunits, were detected in the eluant as show on the stained gel(Fig.3B). This indicates that although small subunits were present in the holoenzyme, they were unaccessable to the immobilized anti-small subunit IgG. This is consistent with the immobilized anti-small subunit IgG particle being so large that it was unable to contact the small subunits because of steric hindrance and could only contact the large subunits at molecul ar surface. Fig.3C shows the eluant of anti-small subunit IgG-Sepharo se without with samll subunit or holoenzyme.

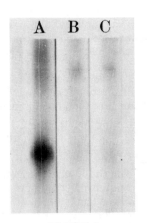

FIGURE 3

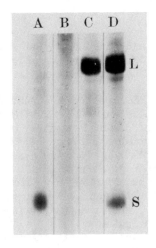

FIGURE 4

2.3. Dissociation of RubisCO-Sepharose by urea

The effects of various urea concentrations on the dissociation of RubisCO-sepharose have been shown in previous report(3), which indica ted that the small subunit was dissociated at 2-2.5 M urea, while the large subunit core, L_8 was dissociated into monomer above 3 M urea. In this paper, RubisCO-Sepharose was incubated and shaken with tris buffer containing 2 M urea, then washed repeatedly with 2 M urea until no more protein appeared in the supernatant. Under these condit ions a single peak of protein was observed. Further shake and wash of the RubisCO-Sepharose by 4 M urea was unable to remove further protein. If the concentration of urea was increased to 8 M, another protein peak was observed. Analysis by SDS-electrophoresis showed that the first peak, which appeared after washing with 2 M urea was the small subunit(Fig.4A). No protein band was detectable on the gel after treating with 4 M urea(Fig.4B). The second peak, which appeared after treating with 8 M urea was the large subunit(Fig.4C). SDS-elect rophoresis pattern of soluble RubisCO was given in Fig.4D.

If RubisCO-Sepharose was washed with 2 M urea once, only the small subunit was found on the gel. When the small subunits were partially removed by 2 M urea, and the RubisCO-Sepharose then treated with 4 M urea, both the large and small subunits were observed on the gel.

These results are consistent with the previous observation that RubisCO was covalently coupled to Sepharose by virtue of the epsilon amino on the large subunit(3). Thus, when part or all of the small subunits are present in the RubisCO-Sepharose, both the large and small subunit could be dissociated by 4 M urea. However, if all of the small subunits from the RubisCO-Sepharose are removed, 8 M urea but not 4 M urea was required to dissociate the large subunit core. This suggests that the binding between large subunits became tighter after the small subunits were completely removed from the RubisCO-Sep harose because of the strong hydrophobic interactions of the large subunits.

3. DISCUSSION

It has been conjuctured that the small subunit may indirectly partic ipate in catalysis, by probably playing a structure role. This resolut ion of the conjucture depends on elucidation of the quaternary structu re of RubisCO.

The model of the quaternay structure of RubisCO recently presented by Chapman et al. shows(4) that eight small subunits are clustered as two tetremers located at the top and bottom and eight extended large subunits bridge between. Chapman et al also indicated(5) that each large subunit has long COOH-terminal extension with 45 residues which run between and above small subunits to form the extreme top and bottom of the RubisCO molecule, each small subunit touches two other small subunits and three large subunits. In this way, our data appear consistent with the dirct evidence determined by X-ray crystall egraphy. But, we put emphasis on that the small subunits should be located at a protected position among the large subunits with only limited access to the outside surface of the enzyme.

Immobile trypsin-Sepharose and anti-small subunits IgG-Sepharose can fully interact with the large subunits, but not the small subunits, because the long COOH-terminal extensions of the large subunits run between and above small subunits. The small subunits appear largely covered by the large subunits. Perhaps the carboxyl-terminal tail of the small subunit is slightly exposed to the molecular surface, so the small subunits separated from the large subunit core can enter into solution when immobile holoenzyme is dissociated by 2 M urea.

When completely removing the small subunits the binding force between the large subunits appears to be further strengthened because of the strong hydrophobic interactions of the large subunits. So we suggest that the small subunit may be to sterically arrange the large subunit octamers loosely so that the spatial structure of the active site on the large subunit favors catalysis.

REFERENCES
1.Andrews,T.J. and Abel,K.M. (1981) J.Biol.Chem. 256,8445-51.
2.Jodan,D.B. and Chollet,R. (1985) Arch.Biochem.Biophys. 236, 487-96.
3.Li,Li-ren, Li,Cui-fang, and Xu,Ren-bang. (1988) Scientia Sinica(Seri es B), 31,1204-12.
4.Chapman,M.S. et al. (1987) Nature. 329, 354-56.
5.Chapman,M.S. et al. (1988) Science. 241,71-74.
6.Mulligan,R.M., Houtz,R.L. and Tolbert,N.E. (1988) Proc.Natl.Acad.Sci. 85,1513-17.

CHARACTERIZATION OF RuBP CARBOXYLASE/OXYGENASE OF N. TABACUM BY INHIBITION OF THE OXYGENASE FUNCTION BY MEANS OF SPECIFIC ANTIBODIES

M. Beuttenmüller, C. Nespoulous, A. Radunz and G.H. Schmid,
Lehrstuhl Zellphysiologie, Universität Bielefeld,
D-4800 Bielefeld 1, FRG

Introduction
In an earlier publication (1) we were able to show that an antiserum
to the bifunctional enzyme ribulose 1,5-bisphosphate carboxylase/oxygenase of the N. tabacum mutant Su/su which exhibits in comparison to
the wild type N. tabacum var. John William's Broadleaf (JWB) a higher
photorespiratory activity (references see (2)) causes, when used
against the homologous as well as against the non-homologous enzyme,
a 40 per cent higher inhibition of the oxygenase activity. From this
observation we conclude that structural differences must exist between
the enzymes of the two phenotypes of N. tabacum. These differences
cannot be detected with the usual immunological methods such as the
double immuno diffusion, the tandem crossed immuno electrophoresis or
the combined line rocket immuno electrophoresis (1,3). In all these
tests only fused precipitation bands are observed between the enzymes
of the wild type and the tobacco mutant Su/su to be compared.
In the present publication we compare the inhibitory effect of an antiserum to RuBP carboxylase/oxygenase of Spinacia oleracea on the oxygenase activity of the wild type enzyme of N. tabacum var. JWB with the
inhibitory effect of the homologous antiserum and that of the antiserum
to the above described N. tabacum mutant Su/su. Furthermore, we compare
the amount of antibodies bound out of the respective antisera. As shown
earlier, RuBP carboxylase/oxygenase from tobacco species shows only
partial immunochemical identity, when compared to the enzyme of Spinacia oleracea (1,3).

Results
Comparative immunological studies of RuBP carboxylase/oxygenase in the
tandem crossed immuno electrophoresis have shown that immunochemical
identity exists between the enzymes of the wild type N. tabacum var.
JWB and the mutant enzyme of N. tabacum Su/su, whereas only partial
identity between these two enzymes and the enzyme of Spinacia oleracea
is observed (Fig. 1). Determination of the maximal binding of antibodies onto the enzymes to be compared out of the homologous and non-
homologous monospecific antisera according to the methods of Heidelberger and Kendall (4,5) have led to the result that in the region of

M. Baltscheffsky (ed.), Current Research in Photosynthesis, Vol. III, 381–384.
© 1990 *Kluwer Academic Publishers. Printed in the Netherlands.*

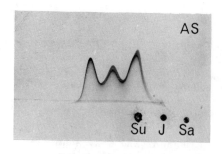

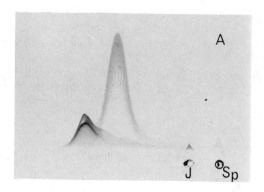

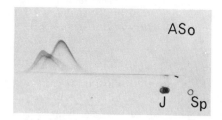

Fig. 1: Comparison of RuBP carboxylase/oxygenase of N. tabacum var. JWB with that of the tobacco mutant Su/su, Su/su var. Aurea, Spinacia oleracea by tandem crossed immuno electrophoresis.
Antigen: Chloroplast preparation of: J, N. tabacum var. JWB; Su, N. tabacum Su/su; Sa, N. tabacum Su/su var. Aurea; Sp, Spinacia oleracea.
Antiserum: AS, mixed antiserum to RuBP carboxylase/oxygenase of N. tabacum var. JWB and of N. tabacum Su/su, 1.4% serum in the gel; ASo, mixed antiserum to RuBP carboxylase/oxygenase of N. tabacum var. JWB and of Spinacia oleracea; A, antiserum to RuBP carboxylase/oxygenase of N. tabacum var. JWB

equivalence enzymes bind always the highest amount of antibodies out of these respective homologous antisera (Fig. 2). This result is understandable and demonstrates that the monospecific antisera used contain antibodies to all characteristic antigenic determinants of RuBP carboxylase/oxygenase. We can show that the enzymes of N. tabacum var. JWB and of Spinacia oleracea are able to bind approx. 9 antibody molecules, whereas the enzyme of the N. tabacum mutant Su/su clearly binds 3 antibody molecules more. This corresponds to a 30% higher antibody binding capacity. The same result is obtained, if the antibody binding onto the enzyme of the mutant N. tabacum var. Consolation is analysed (2). Only onto the enzyme of the phenotype with the highest photorespiratory activity 30% more antibodies were bound out of the homologous antiserum. If, however, antibody binding capacity is compared between non-homologous antisera, it is seen that the enzymes of the two tobacco phenotypes bind out of the antiserum to the spinach enzyme only half the amount of antibodies. The same is true for the reaction between spinach enzyme and the antisera to the tobacco enzymes (Fig. 2). This means that, taking into account the observed partial identity (Fig. 1), only half of the antigenic determinants are identical.

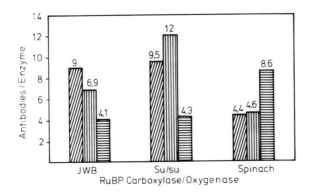

Fig. 2: Binding of antibodies onto RuBP carboxylase/oxygenase of N.t. var. JWB, of the mutant from N.t. Su/su and of Spinacia oleracea out of homologous and non-homologous antisera in the region of equivalence. The values give the number of antibody molecules bound onto one enzyme molecule.
Antiserum to RuBP carboxylase/oxygenase of N.t. var. JWB ⧄ , of N. tabacum Su/su ⫿⫿⫿ , of Spinacia oleracea ▤ .

Measurement of the oxygenase activity of RuBP carboxylase/oxygenase of N. tabacum var. JWB in dependence on the effect of homologous and non-homologous antisera shows that the enzyme is differently affected by the antisera with respect to its oxygenase activity (Fig. 3 A-C). Whereas the wild type enzyme is inhibited by 45% in the equivalence region by the homologous antiserum, its activity is inhibited by only 32%, if the antiserum to the Spinacia oleracea enzyme is used. The highest inhibitory effect, however, is caused by the antiserum to the enzyme of the mutant N. tabacum Su/su. It inhibits the oxygenase activity in the equivalence region by 72%. If the amount of bound antibodies out of the described antisera onto the wild type enzyme is compared, it can be readily seen that no proportionality exists between antibodies bound and the inhibitory effect. Whereas out of the antiserum to the mutant enzyme 23% less antibodies are bound, the antiserum nevertheless exerts an inhibitory effect on the oxygenase function which is twice as high as that caused by the homologous antiserum. This means that in the antiserum to the mutant enzyme which, as shown earlier, exhibits a higher oxygenase activity, more antibodies are present which are especially directed towards the oxygenase function.

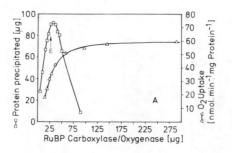

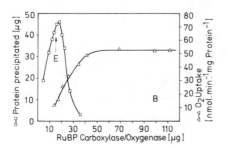

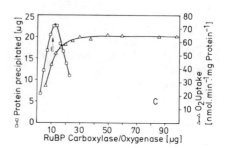

Fig 3: Dependence of oxygenase activity of RuBP carboxylase/oxygenase of N. tabacum var. JWB on the binding of antibodies out of the homologous and of the non-homologous antiserum.
A, treatment of RuBP carboxylase/oxygenase from N. tabacum var. JWB with the homologous antiserum and B, with the antiserum to the enzyme of N. tabacum Su/su and C, with the antiserum to the enzyme of Spinacia oleracea.
The curves with △-△ show the oxygenase activity of the enzyme incubated with antibodies whereas the curves with □-□ show the protein content of the enzyme-antibody precipitation. ↑ E, point of equivalence of the enzyme-antibody precipitation. ↑

References:
1. Nespoulous, C.,Fabisch, P., Radunz, A. and Schmid, G.H.(1988): Z. Naturforsch. 43c, 717-726
2. Georgi, S., Radunz, A. and Schmid G.H. (1989) these Proceedings
3. Radunz, A. and Schmid G.H. (1988): Z. Naturforsch. 43c, 554-562
4. Heidelberger, M. and Kendall, F. (1935) J. Exp. Med. 61, 563-571
5. Heidelberger, M. and Kendall, F. (1935) J. Exp. Med. 62, 697-702

IMMUNOLOGICAL DEMONSTRATION OF STRUCTURAL DIFFERENCES OF RuBP
CARBOXYLASE/OXYGENASE IN MUTANTS OF <u>NICOTIANA</u> <u>TABACUM</u>

Georgi, S., Radunz, A. and Schmid, G.H.,
Lehrstuhl Zellphysiologie, Universität Bielefeld,
D-4800 Bielefeld 1, FRG

INTRODUCTION

In <u>Nicotiana</u> <u>tabacum</u> mutants are known which differ with respect to
their rates of photorespiration (1-6). Thus, wild type <u>N.t</u>. var. John
William's Broadleaf (JWB), the aurea mutant <u>N.t</u>. Su/su var. Aurea and
the yellow-green phenotype of <u>N.t</u>. var. Consolation exhibit low rates
of photorespiration. On the other hand the tobacco aurea mutant Su/su
and <u>N.t</u>. var. Consolation green are the defective mutants which exhibit especially high rates of photorespiration. But also the yellow
phenotype of <u>N.t</u>. var. Consolation shows on the average a higher photorespiration than the yellow-green form and the wild type. A higher
oxygenase activity of the bifunctional stroma enzyme RuBP carboxylase/
oxygenase is responsible for this higher rates of photorespiration.
Earlier serological studies on RuBP carboxylase/oxygenase of the different tobacco plants have shown that no correlation exists between a
higher concentration of the enzyme and a higher photorespiratory activity (7). With one single antiserum to the wild type enzyme no differences with respect to the molecular structure between the enzymes of
the mutants and the wild type enzyme can be detected (8).
In this publication we first compare RuBP carboxylase/oxygenase of the
wild type and of the mutant series <u>N.t</u>. var. Consolation by means of
the double immuno diffusion test and the tandem crossed immuno electrophoresis. For this comparative study we do not only use an antiserum
to the wild type enzyme (7,8), but different mixtures of the antiserum
mentioned above and two monospecific antisera to the enzymes of the
mutants, exhibiting higher photorespiration (Fig. 1 and 2). Furthermore,
we analyse the quantitative binding of antibodies onto the enzymes of
the mutants out of homologous and non-homologous antisera according to
the method of Heidelberger and Kendall (9,10).
Okabe et al. (11) and Bhagwat et al. (12) have shown that hydroxylamine
specifically inhibits the oxygenase activity of RuBP carboxylase/oxyge-
nase. Moreover, Okabe et al. (11) have shown that a temperature treatment to 50°C increases both activities of the enzyme by about 60%. In
the following we investigate, whether chemical modifications of the
enzyme, induced by hydroxylamine or heat treatment, are immunochemically
characterizable.

M. Baltscheffsky (ed.), Current Research in Photosynthesis, Vol. III, 385–389.
© 1990 *Kluwer Academic Publishers. Printed in the Netherlands.*

RESULTS

In the double immuno diffusion test and in the tandem crossed immuno
electrophoresis (Fig. 1 and 2) the comparative study of RuBP carboxy-
lase/oxygenase of N.t. var. JWB and of the mutants N.t. var. Consolation
green, yellow-green and yellow yield only fusing precipitation bands,
although these studies were carried out with different mixtures of the
antisera to the enzymes of the wild type, of N.t. var. Consolation green
and that of N.t. var. Consolation yellow. This means that the tested
enzymes are immunochemically identical. Despite different rates of photorespiration these methods apparently cannot detect differences between
the molecular structure of the enzymes of these different tobacco
plants. The quantitative binding of antibodies onto the native untreated
enzymes of the mutants out of homologous and non-homologous antisera
(Table 1) shows that a difference exists between the molecular structure
of RuBP carboxylase/oxygenase of N.t. var. Consolation green, the mutant
with especially high photorespiration and the molecular structure of
the other analysed enzymes. Out of the homologous antiserum the enzyme
of the green tobacco mutant adsorbs approximately 40% more antibodies
than the other enzymes tested. This is valid in the region of equivalence as well as in the region of extreme antibody excess. It means that
the enzyme of N.t. var. Consolation green possesses either a larger number of homologous antigenic determinants or a different distribution
of these determinants. It should be noted that the enzyme of N.t. var.
Consolation yellow does not adsorb more antibodies out of the homologous
antiserum, although this mutant shows on the average higher photorespiration than the yellow-green form and the wild type. These results are
in agreement with experiments by Nespoulous et al. (13).

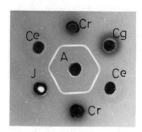 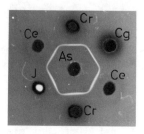 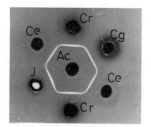

Fig. 1: Comparison of RuBP carboxylase/oxygenase of N.t. var. JWB with
that of the mutants of N.t. var. Consolation by means of the double
immuno diffusion test.
Antigen: Chloroplast preparations of: Cr, N.t. var. Consolation green;
Ce, N.t. var. Consolation yellow; Cg, N.t. var. Consolation yellow-
green; J, N.t. var. JWB.
Antiserum: As, mixed antiserum to RuBP carboxylase/oxygenase of N.t.
var. JWB and N.t. var. Consolation yellow; A, mixed antiserum to RuBP
carboxylase/oxygenase of N. t. var. JWB and N.t. var. Consolation green;
Ac, mixed antiserum to RuBP carboxylase/oxygenase of N.t. var. Consolation yellow and N. t. var. Consolation green.

Chemical modifications of RuBP carboxylase/oxygenase induced by hydroxylamine or heat treatment are immunochemically characterizable. Table 2 shows that the thus treated enzymes adsorb considerably less antibodies than the untreated enzymes, that is out of homologous and out of non-homologous antisera. The higher antibody binding capacity of the enzyme of N.t. var. Consolation green is maintained even after chemical modifications (Table 1 and 2). These treatments induce conformational changes which affect the accessibility of antigenic determinants or the antigenic determinants themselves in such a way that only a smaller number of antibodies can be bound. The largest molecular modification of the enzymes is caused by a simultaneous treatment with hydroxylamine and heat.

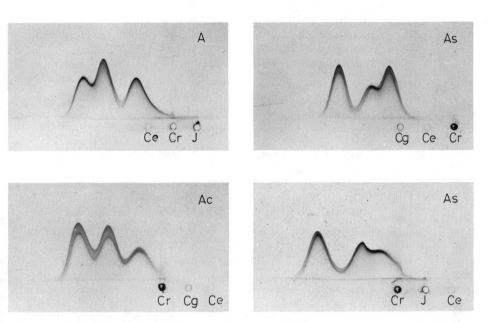

Fig. 2: Comparison of RuBP carboxylase/oxygenase of N.t. var. JWB with that of the mutants of N.t. var. Consolation by means of the tandem crossed immuno electrophoresis.
Antigen: Chloroplast preparations of: Cr, N.t. var. Consolation green; Ce, N.t. var. Consolation yellow; Cg, N.t. var. Consolation yellow-green; J, N.t. var. JWB.
Antiserum: As, mixed antiserum to RuBP carboxylase/oxygenase of N.t. var. JWB and N.t. var. Consolation yellow; A, mixed antiserum to RuBP carboxylase/oxygenase of N.t. var. JWB and N.t. var. Consolation green; Ac, mixed antiserum to RuBP carboxylase/oxygenase of N.t. var. Consolation yellow and N.t. var. Consolation green.

Table 1: Binding of antibodies onto untreated RuBP carboxylase/oxygenase of the mutants of N.t. var. Consolation out of homologous and non-homologous antisera in the region of equivalence. The values give the number of antibody molecules bound onto one enzyme molecule.

Antiserum to RuBP carboxylase/ oxygenase of	Enzyme of N.t. var. Consolation yellow	Enzyme of N.t. var. Consolation yellow-green	Enzyme of N.t. var. Consolation green
N.t. var. JWB	8.8	9.1	9.3
N.t. var. Cons. yellow	8.3	8.7	8.4
N.t. var. Cons. green	8.5	8.8	11.9

Table 2: Binding of antibodies onto RuBP carboxylase/oxygenase of the mutants of N.t. var. Consolation out of homologous and non-homologous antisera after various treatments in the region of equivalence. The values give the number of antibody molecules bound onto one enzyme molecule.
b. with 10 mM hydroxylamine treated enzyme
c. with heat treated enzyme
d. with heat treated enzyme which was thereafter treated with 10 mM hydroxylamine

Antiserum to RuPB carboxylase/ oxygenase		Enzyme of N.t. var. Consolation yellow	Enzyme of N.t. var. Consolation yellow-green	Enzyme of N.t. var. Consolation green
N.t. var. JWB	b	6.2	6.4	6.4
	c	3.0	3.2	3.4
	d	2.6	2.8	2.4
N.t. var. Consolation yellow	b	6.5	6.3	6.7
	c	3.2	3.7	3.3
	d	2.7	3.0	2.7
N.t. var. Consolation green	b	6.5	6.2	9.1
	c	3.6	3.7	4.7
	d	2.8	3.0	3.3

REFERENCES
1. Okabe, K. (1977) Z. Naturforsch. 32c, 781–785
2. Okabe, K., Schmid, G.H. and Straub, J. (1977) Plant Physiol. 60 150–156
3. Okabe, K. and Schmid, G.H. (1978) in: Proceedings of the Intern. Symposium on Chloroplast Development held on the Island Spetsai, Greece (Akoyunoglou,G. and Argyroudi-Akoyunoglou, J.H. eds.) pp. 501–506, Elsevier/North-Holland Biomedical Press, Amsterdam
4. Schmid, G.H., Bader, K.P., Gerster, R., Triantaphylides, C. and André, M. (1981) Z. Naturforsch. 36c, 662–671
5. Ishii, R. and Schmid G.H. (1982) Z. Naturforsch. 37c, 93–101
6. Ishii, R. and Schmid G.H. (1983) Plant & Cell Physiol. 24,1525–1533
7. Radunz, A. and Schmid, G.H. (1987) in: Progress in Photosynthesis Research III (Biggins, J. ed.) pp. 9617–9620, Martinus Nijhoff Publishers Dordrecht, The Netherlands
8. Radunz, A. and Schmid, G.H. (1988) Z. Naturforsch. 43c, 554–562
9. Heidelberger, M. and Kendall, F. (1935) J. Exp. Med. 61, 563–571
10. Heidelberger, M. and Kendall, F. (1935) J. Exp. Med. 62, 697–702
11. Okabe, K., Codd, G.A. and Stewart, W.D.P. (1979) Nature 279, 525–527
12. Bhagwat, A.S., Ramakrishna, J. and Sane, P.V. (1978) Biochem. Biophys. Res. Commun. 83, 954–962
13. Nespoulous, C., Fabisch, P., Radunz, A. and Schmid, G.H. (1988) Z. Naturforsch. 43c, 717–726

IMMUNOGOLD LOCALIZATION OF RIBULOSE-1,5-BISPHOSPHATE CARBOXYLASE IN SYNCHRONIZED CELLS OF EUGLENA GRACILIS Z

TETSUAKI OSAFUNE[1],SHUJI SUMIDA[1],AKIHO YOKOTA[2]AND EIJI HASE[3]

Dept.Microbiol., Tokyo Med. Coll., Tokyo 160[1]; Dept. Agri. Chem., Osaka Pref. Univ., Sakai 591[2]; Lab. Chem., Fac. Med., Teikyo Univ., Tokyo 192-03[3], Japan.

1. INTRODUCTION

The pyrenoid is a unique protein complex in the chloroplast stroma of most eukaryotic algae. Schiff(1) has provided some evidence that Euglena pyrenoids contain RuBisCO. Cook et al.(2) reported that the pyrenoid is recognized in the chloroplasts of synchronized cells of E. gracilis only in the first half of the light period. Recently, Kiss et al.(3) showed by immunofluorescence method that anti-spinach RuBisCO binds to the pyrenoid region of the chloroplasts of E. gracilis.

2. MATERIAL AND METHODS

Euglena gracilis Z cells were synchronized under the 14 h-light: 10 h-dark regimen at 25°C under photoautotrophic conditions(4). These cells were fixed in 2% glutaraldehyde in 0.1M phosphate-buffer(pH 7.2) for 60 min at 4°C, rinsed in same buffer and blocked in agar, followed by dehydration in ethanol series and then acetone. Samples were embedded in Epon 812 resin and serially sectioned. These sections were placed on nickel slit grids. These were floated section side down on drops of 0.1M phosphate-buffer saline (PBS) with 0.5% Bovine serum albumin for 30 min at room temperature, and then incubated in PBS containing antibody of Euglena RuBisCO(5-6) at 37°C for 10 min. The sections were washed twice in PBS, and incubated in PBS containing protein A-gold for 20 min. Sections were subsequently stained with uranyl acetate and viewed in an electron microscope. Serial cell sections were photographed at an appropriate magnification, and the distribution of gold particles(RuBisCO) and its structures in each section were drawn on a tracing paper. Using Nikon's Cosmozone S software, these data were entered on a digitizing table(5). The three-dimensional data in the computer were viewed on a colour display(NEC).

3. RESULTS AND DISCUSSION

Figure 1 shows time courses of changes in photosynthetic CO_2-fixation and the carboxylase activity of RuBisCO of Euglena cells(6) during the cell cycle in synchronized cultures. The carboxylase activity of RuBisCO extracted from those synchronized cells increased nearly double during the growth phase and decreased during the division phase(Fig. 1, middle). The photosynthetic CO_2-fixation of cells, measured at the same

M. Baltscheffsky (ed.), Current Research in Photosynthesis, Vol. III, 391–394.

light intensity and temperature as those in culture, showed the maximum level around the 10th h (Fig. 1, lower). Figure 2 shows a section through a cell from the culture showing the maximum photosynthetic CO_2-fixation (10 h-cell). Gold particles (RuBisCO proteins) are denser in the pyrenoid region (an arrow) than in the other area of chloroplasts. Three-dimensional localization of chloroplasts (C) and pyrenoid (arrows) in a cell are shown in Fig. 3. Figure 4 represents three-dimensional distribution of RuBisCO (gold particles). Figure 5 shows a section through chloroplasts in a 18 h-cell, and no pyrenoid structure is detectable in these chloroplasts. Gold particles are dispersed throughout the chloroplast. A section through chloroplasts in a 20 h-cell (Fig. 6) shows that gold particles are arranged in short lines in the narrow space between thylakoids. Subsequently, these gold particles gathered in the center of chloroplast (the pyrenoid region) in a 23 h-cell (Fig. 7). From comparison of photosynthetic CO_2-fixation with the total carboxylase activity of RuBisCO extracted from Euglena cells in the growth phase, it was strongly suggested that the carboxylase in the pyrenoid can be functioning in the CO_2-fixation in photosynthesis.

This work was aided by grants from the Ministry of Education, Science and Culture (No. 01540582 to T.O.), Japan.

4. REFERENCES
1 Schiff, J.A. (1973) Adv. Morphog. 10, 265-311
2 Cook, J.R., Haggard, S.S. and Triemer, R. (1976) J. Protozool. 23, 368-373
3 Kiss, J.Z., Vasconcelos, A.C. and Triemer, R.E. (1986) J. Phycol. 22, 327-333
4 Osafune, T., Mihara, S., Hase, E. and Ohkuro, I. (1975) Plant & Cell Physiol. 16, 313-326
5 Osafune, T., Sumida, S., Ehara, T. and Hase, E. (1989) J. Electron Microscopy 38(5), in press.
6 Yokota, A., Harada, A. and Kitaoka, S. (1989) J. Biochem. 105, 400-405

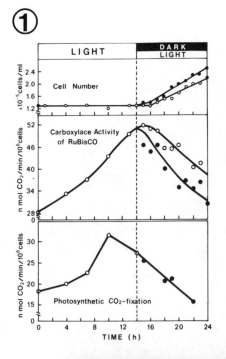

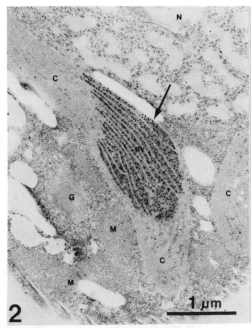

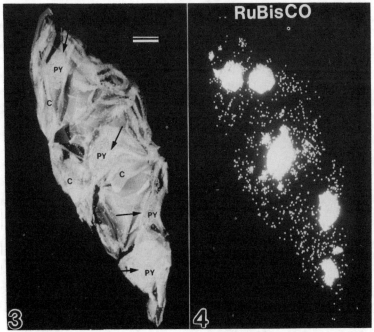

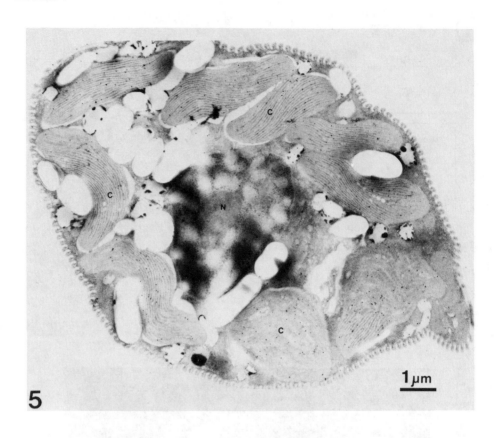

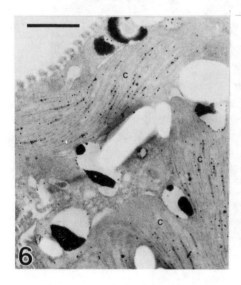

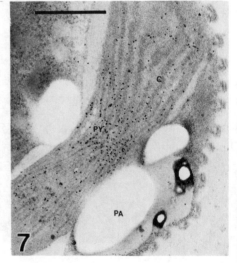

A SPECIFIC PHOSPHATASE FOR 2-CARBOXYARABINITOL-1-PHOSPHATE IN LEAVES.

ALFRED J. KEYS, ALISON H. KINGSTON-SMITH AND MARTIN A. J. PARRY,
DEPARTMENT OF BIOCHEMISTRY AND PHYSIOLOGY, AFRC INSTITUE OF ARABLE CROP
RESEARCH, ROTHAMSTED EXPERIMENTAL STATION, HARPENDEN, HERTFORDSHIRE,
U. K. AL5 2JQ.

1. INTRODUCTION

Diurnal variation in the activity of ribulose 1,5-bisphosphate carboxylase (Rubisco) in the leaves of some species of plants is explained by the accumulation at night of the tight-binding inhibitor 2-carboxy-D-arabinitol 1-phosphate (CA1P) (1,2). Leaves of french bean (*Phaseolus vulgaris, L.*) show the greatest inhibition of Rubisco activity at night (3,4). An attempt is reported to identify enzymes in the leaves of french bean that might be responsible for breaking down the inhibitor in the light. Preliminary experiments suggested that a phosphatase activity was present which removed the phosphate group from CA1P. An enzyme requiring NADPH was reported to breakdown CA1P in tobacco leaves (5); this has subsequently been shown to be a phosphatase that is activated by NADPH (6). The phosphatase in leaves of french bean has been partly purified and shown to be specific for the inhibitor. A similar enzyme is present in leaves of wheat. A major problem has been to separate the activity completely from phosphoglycollate phosphatase although the enzymes are quite clearly different.

2. METHODS

The first pair of leaves of french bean plants and leaves 2 and 3 of wheat plants were used as sources of enzymes 2 to 3 weeks after germination. The leaf material (100 g f. wt) was homogenized in 200 ml of Buffer A (20 mM Tris, 20 mM $MgCl_2$, 1mM $CaCl_2$ (pH 8.0), 2 g acid-washed insoluble polyvinylpyrrolidone, 1 mM p-aminobenzamidine, 1 mM phenylmethylsulphonylfluoride (PMSF) and 20 mM β-mercaptoethanol). The homogenate was filtered through 4 layers of muslin and the filtrate clarified by centrifugation at 100,000 xg for 30 min. Solid ammonium sulphate was added to the filtrate to precipitate most of the protein at 80 % saturation. The precipitated protein was resuspended in 70 ml of Buffer A, without the insoluble PVP. The solution was layered onto sucrose gradients in Buffer B (10 mM Tris, 10 mM $MgCl_2$, 10 mM $NaHCO_3$, 2 mM dithiothreitol and 1 mM EDTA pH 8.0) and centrifuged at 361,000 xg for 90 min. The solution above the sucrose was collected and desalted by passage through a Sephadex G 25 column (5 x 35 cm) previously equilibrated with 5 mM Bicine pH 8.0 containing 0.1 mM p-aminobenzamidine, 0.1 mM PMSF and 20 mM β-mercaptoethanol. The desalted

M. Baltscheffsky (ed.), Current Research in Photosynthesis, Vol. III, 395–398.
© 1990 *Kluwer Academic Publishers. Printed in the Netherlands.*

protein was adsorbed onto a column of Q-Sepharose (fast flow)(1.6 x 77 cm.) previously equilibrated with Buffer B. Proteins were eluted by increasing KCl in Buffer B in a total of 640 ml at a flow rate of 40 ml per hour. Fractions (10 ml) containing activity were pooled and the solution made to 80 % saturation with ammonium sulphate. The pelleted protein was taken up in 0.1M Bicine containing 20 mM dithiothreitol and desalted to the same buffer using a small column of Sephadex G 25 (1·2 x 15 cm.). The desalted, concentrated solution can be stored frozen at -25°.

2-Carboxyarabinitol-1,5-bisphosphate (CABP) (100 µmol) was made by cyanohydrin synthesis from ribulose 1,5-bisphosphate (7). The bisphophate was hydrolysed using either alkaline phosphatase from $E.$ $coli$ or the acid phosphatase from potato tubers (8) until half of the phosphorus present had been released as inorganic orthophosphate. The resulting CA1P was separated from the orthophosphate by chromatography on a DEAE Sephacel column (2.6 x 16.5 cm) in the bicarbonate form using a linear gradient of NH_4HCO_3 from 0 to 0.6 M in 700 ml. The fractions containing the CA1P were freed from most of the bicarbonate by successive evaporations of aqueous solutions under vacuum. The CA1P was converted to the sodium salt by ion-exchange and the solution (pH 7) was freeze-dried.

Inorganic orthophosphate was measured colorimetrically (9) using the complex of phosphomolybdate with malachite green. Organic phosphate was converted to orthophosphate by ignition with $Mg(NO_3)_2$ and acid hydrolysis (10).

Samples of column fractions (47.5 µl) were mixed with 2.5 µl of 10 mM CA1P or phosphoglycollate and incubated at room temperature. Reaction was stopped by the addition of 2.5 µl of trifluoroacetic acid. Precipitated protein was removed by centrifugation and the orthophosphate concentration in the supernatant liquid was measured. Disappearance of CA1P was measured in reaction mixtures of total volume 0.1 ml containing 0.9 nmol CA1P, 1 mM NADPH, 20 mM dithiothreitol (DTT) and 79 µl of the column fractions under test. After 30 min, Rubisco was added and after a further 30 min its activity was measured by the addition of $^{14}CO_2$ and ribulose 1,5-bisphosphate. The amount of carboxylation was measured from the ^{14}C remaining after evaporation of the acidified reaction mixture to dryness.

3. RESULTS AND DISCUSSION
Phosphatase activity with the greatest specificity for CA1P in whole leaf extracts was associated with the protein above the sucrose layer following density gradient centrifugation. Fig 1. shows that this activity was eluted from an anion exchange column at above 0.2 M KCl and coincided with activity destroying the inhibitory activity of added CA1P towards ribulose bisphosphate carboxylase. Tests of active fractions showed that these also had considerable phosphoglycollate phosphatase activity but little activity towards other phosphorylated substrates (Table 1.).

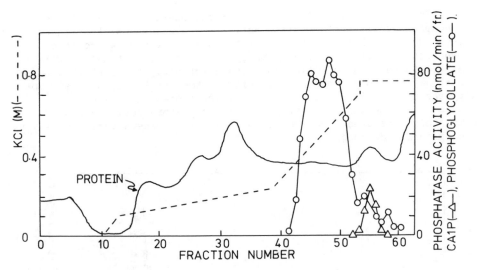

FIGURE 2. Fractionation of proteins from french bean leaves on a Q-Sepharose (fast flow) column. The protein had been previously partly purified as in FIGURE 1. Phosphoglycollate phosphatase activity and CA1P phosphatase acitivity are shown.

Wheat leaves contain a similar CA1P phosphatase activity to french bean. Activity was recovered from french bean leaves whether harvested at night or during the day.

REFERENCES
1 Gutteridge, S., Parry, M.A.J., Burton, S., Keys, A.J., Mudd, A., Feeney, J., Servaites, J. and Pierce, J. (1986) Nature 324, 274 - 276.
2 Berry, J.A., Lorimer, G.H., Pierce, J., Seemann, J.R., Meek, J. and Freas, S. (1987) Proc. Natl. Acad. Sci. 84, 734 -738.
3 Seemann, J.R., Berry, J.A., Freas, S.M. and Krump, M.A. (1985) Proc. Natl. Acad. Sci. 82, 8024 - 8028.
4 Servaites, J.C., Parry, M.A.J., Gutteridge, S. and Keys, A.J. (1986) Plant Physiol. 82, 1161 - 1163.
5 Salvucci, M.E., Holbrook, G.P., Anderson, J.C. and Bowes, G. (1988) FEBS Letters 231, 197 - 201.
6 Holbrook, G.P., Bowes, G. and Salvucci, M.E. (1989) Plant Physiol. 90, 673 - 678.
7 Pierce, J., Tolbert, N.E. and Barker, R. (1980) Biochemistry 19, 934 - 942
8 Gutteridge, S., Reddy, G.S. and Lorimer G.H. (1989) Biochem. J. 260, 711 - 716
9 Van Veldhoven, P.P. and Mannaerts, G.P. (1987) Analyt. Biochem. 161, 45 - 48
10 Ames, B.N. (1966) Methods in Enzymology, VIII, 115 - 116.
11 Verin-Vergeau, C., Baldy, P., Puech, J. and Cavalie, G. (1980) Phytochemistry 19, 763 - 767.

Fig. 2. shows the elution of CA1P phosphatase activity in relation to phosphoglycollate phosphatase activity. It is evident that there is little CA1P phosphatase activity at the peak of phosphoglycollate phosphatase activity but that phophoglycollate phosphatase activity trails into the peak of CA1P phosphatase activity; the distribution of phosphoglycollate phosphatase activity in the fractions is consistent with the report (11) that two isozymes are present in french bean leaves. In some experiments, the CA1P phosphatase activity was completely separated from the phosphoglycollate phosphatase activity by precipitation at pH 5.0.

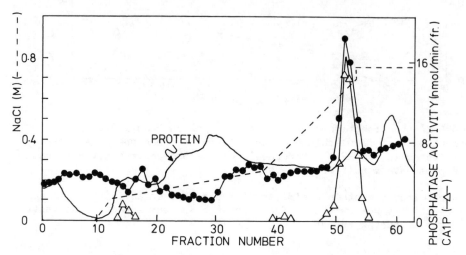

FIGURE 1. Fractionation of protein from french bean leaves on a Q-Sepharose (fast flow) column. The proteins had been precipitated from clarified extract at 80% saturation with $(NH_4)_2SO_4$ and freed from Rubisco and other proteins of high molecular weight by density gradient centrifugation. Release of orthophosphate (-△-) and release of inhibition of Rubisco activity (-o-) caused by incubating fractions with CA1P are shown

TABLE 1. Specificity

Substrate	Phosphatase activity (nmol. min. mg prot.)
CA1P	32
Phosphoglycollate	12
Ribulose 1,5-bisphosphate	5
3-phospho-D-glycerate	4
D-glucose-1-phosphate	2
D-glucose-6-phosphate	1.5
D-fructose-6-phosphate	0.4

TABLE 2. pH Dependence

pH	CA1P phosphatase (nmol. min. mg prot)
7.5	37
7.8	27
8.0	25
8.3	20
8.5	18
8.8	18
9.0	13

REGULATION OF RUBISCO ACTIVITY BY CARBOXYARABINITOL-1-PHOSPHATE AND ELEVATED ATMOSPHERIC CO$_2$ IN RICE AND SOYBEAN CULTIVARS

GEORGE BOWES[1], AMANDA J. ROWLAND-BAMFORD[2], and L. HARTWELL ALLEN JR.[2,3], Departments of Botany[1], and Agronomy[2], and United States Department of Agriculture/Agricultural Research Service[3], University of Florida, Gainesville, Florida 32611, U.S.A.

1. INTRODUCTION

The activity of ribulose bisphosphate carboxylase-oxygenase (rubisco) is influenced by environmental factors: light, temperature, and nutrients. Light, via rubisco activase, regulates the *in vivo* CO$_2$/Mg^{2+}-activation of rubisco (10). Light also effects the metabolism of carboxyarabinitol-1-phosphate (CA1P), an endogenous inhibitor of rubisco that exists to varying degrees in many, but not all species (6,13). The recent concern with increasing atmospheric CO$_2$ has led to studies of the effect of this nutrient on growth, photosynthesis, and rubisco activity (11,12). CO$_2$ acts as a substrate and activator for the rubisco reaction, but it also seems to have growth regulatory effects. Thus in some species the initial increase in photosynthesis at elevated CO$_2$ due to more substrate, is followed by a decline, as rubisco protein declines (9). Increasing atmospheric CO$_2$ will alter climatic temperatures, but little is known as to how these two variables may interact to affect photosynthesis and growth. This preliminary report suggests that in rice and soybean cultivars, rubisco activity, activation, and dark inhibition is regulated by these, and developmental, parameters.

2. PROCEDURES

2.1. Plant Material.

Rice (*Oryza sativa* L.) and soybean (*Glycine max* L. Merr.) cultivars were grown in a controlled environment chamber with a 16-h 25°C day/20°C night, a quantum irradiance of 500 μmol m^{-2}s^{-1}, and air CO$_2$. Rice was grown hydroponically, while the soybeans were in potting compost. In the CO$_2$ and temperature experiment, rice was grown in outdoor SPAR units (4) under solar irradiance at 330 or 660 μL CO$_2$ L^{-1}, and day/night dry bulb temperatures of 40/33, 34/27, or 28/21°C, with air dew point/paddy water temperatures of 18/37, 15/31, and 12/25°C, respectively. Leaf samples were rapidly excised and immersed in LN$_2$, 1 h before (dark), or in the middle of the light period. Powdered samples were stored in LN$_2$ (12).

2.2. Rubisco Extraction and Assay.

Rice tissue (1 g) in LN$_2$ was extracted, and the initial and total (CO$_2$/Mg^{2+}-activated) rubisco activity determined (7). Soybean rubisco was extracted, and assayed as described before (12). Assays were halted with glacial acetic acid after 30 s at 25°C. Activation in the light was calculated as: (initial/total activity) x 100; and dark inhibition as: [(total light activity - dark activity)/total light activity] x 100. Data are presented as the mean of 2-4 replicates ± S.E.

3. RESULTS AND DISCUSSION

The rice and soybean cultivars in Table 1 were grown under the same light, temperature, and CO_2 conditions, and were sampled after the same growth period. The total rubisco activity in the rice cultivars was generally lower, and more uniform than in soybean. All cultivars sampled in the dark exhibited less CO_2/Mg^{2+}-activated rubisco activity than in the light. In soybean and other species this is due to CA1P binding to the enzyme in the dark (2,6). Thus rice seems to belong to the group of species whose rubisco activity is CA1P-regulated. The degree of dark inhibition varied among the cultivars of both species by almost 50%. There was no correlation between total rubisco activity and dark inhibition, as Lemont and Davies with the highest activities, had the greatest and least dark inhibition, respectively. These data confirm an earlier report for soybean cultivars (1), and suggest that variation in CA1P-regulation may be common within, as well as between, species.

TABLE 1. Total light activity, and dark inhibition of rubisco in leaf extracts of rice and soybean cultivars. Samples of 3-4 rice or soybean trifoliate leaves (third leaf) were taken 20 days after planting.

Plant Cultivar	Total Rubisco Activity $\mu mol\ CO_2\ mg^{-1}\ protein.h^{-1}$	Rubisco Dark Inhibition %
Rice:		
Gulfmont	25.9 ± 0.7	29
Lebonnet	25.8 ± 0.1	30
Labelle	25.2 ± 0.9	37
IR-30	28.9 ± 0.5	41
Tebonnet	26.7 ± 2.3	48
Lemont	29.8 ± 0.5	54
Soybean:		
Davies	42.5 ± 3.1	21
Gordon	28.7 ± 0.7	28
Cobb	34.6 ± 3.3	37
Hardee	28.9 ± 1.0	39
Bragg	33.1 ± 3.0	40

From Table 2, it seems that the stage of leaf development influences more than just total rubisco activity. The basal section of the rice leaf, which was nearest the meristem, had the lowest total rubisco activity, and the least dark inhibition. Total rubisco activity, and the degree of activation increased towards the leaf tip, which was the oldest part. The percent dark inhibition was constant above 6 cm from the leaf base, but the low dark inhibition toward the leaf base may represent lower chloroplast concentrations or less synthesis of CA1P.

TABLE 2. Total light activity, activation, and dark inhibition of rubisco in extracts of leaf sections from different regions (base to tip) along the blade, for the rice cultivar Lemont, 26 days after planting.

Distance of Leaf Section from Base	Total Rubisco Activity	Rubisco Activation	Rubisco Dark Inhibition
cm	μmol CO_2 mg^{-1} protein.h^{-1}	%	%
0-3	12.6 ± 1.1	57	32
3-6	19.5 ± 0.6	55	49
6-9	20.5 ± 1.9	53	54
9-12	21.9 ± 0.9	69	54
tip	23.5 ± 0.5	74	53

The data in Table 3, for rice cultivar IR-30, were obtained with plants grown in outdoor chambers with natural sunlight, and thus at higher irradiance than the previous experiments. The total rubisco activity was not greatly influenced by the CO_2 regime, though CO_2 and temperature showed interactive effects. Rice plants sampled at a later

TABLE 3. Total light activity, activation, and dark inhibition of rubisco in leaf extracts of the rice cultivar IR-30 grown under various CO_2 and temperature regimes. Plants were grown in SPAR chambers with natural solar irradiance. Samples were taken 19 days after planting.

CO_2 Concentration	Day/Night Temperature	Total Rubisco Activity	Rubisco Activation	Rubisco Dark Inhibition
μL L^{-1}	°C	μmol CO_2 mg^{-1} protein.h^{-1}	%	%
330	40/33	26.6 ± 3.5	90	62
	34/27	27.6 ± 0.1	88	53
	28/21	26.1 ± 3.5	84	31
660	40/33	23.5 ± 2.2	70	45
	34/27	28.2 ± 1.0	73	55
	28/21	27.7 ± 2.0	84	50

growth stage do show a decrease in rubisco protein and activity under high CO_2 (9). The plants exposed to $40°C$-days died before completing their life cycle. Even though at this stage there were no visible effects of the high temperature, rubisco activity was lowest in the $40°C$/ high CO_2 treatment. At a moderate daytime temperature ($28°C$), rubisco activation was the same regardless of CO_2, but it declined in the higher CO_2/temperature regimes. Rubisco activation in wheat leaves declines when they are exposed for short periods to high temperatures (5). At air-CO_2, dark inhibition increased at high temperature, but the high CO_2 ameliorated the temperature-related variation. Rice photosynthesis shows an optimum between $25°$ and $35°C$, with a decline at $40°C$ (3,8). Also, rice productivity in the tropics is reduced at high temperature (8).

4. CONCLUSIONS

The degree of rubisco dark inhibition not only shows species, but also intercultivar, and development differences. As with total activity, rubisco activation is developmentally influenced; so for rice, assays of whole leaf extracts integrate various rubisco states. The growth CO_2 and temperature have interactive effects on the activity, activation, and dark inhibition of rice rubisco. Detrimental temperature effects on total rubisco activity may be compounded by elevated atmospheric CO_2.

5. REFERENCES

1   Bowes, G. and Holbrook, G.P. (1988) Plant Physiol. 86, S5
2   Holbrook, G.P., Campbell, W.J. and Bowes, G. (1987) *In* Progress in Photosynthesis Research (Biggins, J., ed.), Vol. 3, pp.399-402, Martinus Nijhoff Publishers, Dordrecht, The Netherlands
3   Ishii, R., Ohsugi, R. and Murata, Y. (1977) Jap. J. Crop Sci. 46, 516-523
4   Jones, P., Allen, L.H. Jr., Jones, J.W., Boote, K.J. and Campbell, W.J. (1984) Agron. J. 76, 633-637.
5   Kobza, J. and Edwards, G.E. (1987) Plant Physiol. 83, 69-74
6   Kobza, J. and Seemann, J.R. (1988) Proc. Natl. Acad. Sci. 85, 3815-3819
7   Makino, A., Mae, T. and Ohira, K. (1987) Plant & Cell Physiol. 28, 799-804
8   Osada, A. (1963) Proc. Crop Sci. Soc. Jap. 33, 69-76
9   Rowland-Bamford, A.J., Baker, J.T., Allen, L.H. Jr. and Bowes, G. (1988) Plant Physiol. 86, S103
10 Salvucci, M.E., Portis, A.R. Jr. and Ogren, W.L. (1986) Photosynthesis Res. 7, 193-201
11 Spencer, W. and Bowes, G. (1986) Plant Physiol. 82, 528-533
12 Vu, C.V., Allen, L.H. Jr. and Bowes, G. (1983) Plant Physiol. 73, 729-734
13 Vu, C.V., Allen, L.H. Jr. and Bowes, G. (1984) Plant Physiol. 76, 843-845

6. ACKNOWLEDGMENTS

Supported by DOE/USDA Interagency Agreement DE-AI01-81ER60001 to LHA, and NSF Grant No. DMB 8504856 to GB.

TRANSCRIPTIONAL REGULATION OF RUBISCO GENE EXPRESSION BY CO_2 IN RHODOSPIRILLUM RUBRUM

Xiang-yu Wu, Yong Xu and Guang-yao Wu
Department of Biology, Peking University, Beijing 100871
People's Republic of China

1. INTRODUCTION

Rubisco(E.C.4.1.1.39) in Rhodospirillum rubrum is very different from that of higher plants. It is L_2(composed of only two large subunits) instead of L_8S_8 as in higher plants, but it is still bifunctional, catalyzing both carboxylation and oxygenation(1). The rubisco gene rbcL in R. rubrum is located on the bacterial DNA(2).

R. rubrum can be grown both in the presence and in the absence of CO_2. In the former case, the rubisco content in the bacterial cell becomes much higher. The aim of the present work is to find out if there is any change in rbcL expression when R. rubrum is transferred from conditions without CO_2 to that with CO_2 and how the change happens.

2. PROCEDURE

2.1. Materials and Methods

2.1.1. Culture of Rhodospirillum rubrum: R. rubrum was cultured in Ormerod medium(4) with malate as C-source at pH 6.2-6.6, 28-30 C and under 27.8 umol/S/M^2 incandescent light and the cells were collected log phase. The condition with CO_2 was the same as without except 2%CO_2+98%H_2 was bubbled into the medium and malate omitted.

2.1.2. Assay of rubisco activity: with ^{14}C as in (3).

2.1.3. Purification of R. rubrum rubisco: The rubisco in the sonicated cells was purified by DEAE-52 and $(NH_4)_2SO_4$ fractionation(5). The purified rubisco was homogeneous on SDS-PAGE, the molecular weight was 56 kDa and specific activity was 0.524 $\mu mol CO_2$/mg protein/min.

2.1.4. Purification of DNA probe: The plasmid pRR2119 was transformed to E. coli DH5 and the rubisco gene fragment, the 2.4 kb EcoRI restriction fragment of pRR2119(6), was purified by freeze thaw method and recovered from agarose gel. The specific radioactivity of the DNA probe obtained by nick translation(7) was 10^7 cpm/μg DNA.

M. Baltscheffsky (ed.), Current Research in Photosynthesis, Vol. III, 403–406.

2.1.5. <u>Isolation of RNA</u>: The <u>R. rubrum</u> cells were broken by repeated freezing in liquid N_2 and thaw-
ing and the RNA was obtained in the aqueous
phase after successive extraction with phenol-
chloroform and chloroform-isoamyl alcohol(8).

2.1.6. <u>Northern blot hybridization and RNA dot blot</u>
<u>hybridization</u>: Both were performed as in (7,9).

3. RESULTS AND DISCUSSION

3.1. Rubisco contents in the R. rubrum cells grown under
different conditions: The rubisco activity of the
bacterial cells could be estimated by assaying it
in the culture medium after the cells have been spinned down. When the total soluble protein was isolated, the relative amount of rubisco could be estimated from the SDS-electrophoretogram after Coomassie
staining. The results are shown in table 1. It is
clear that the rubisco content in malate-grown cells
was less than 1% of the total soluble protein, but in
the CO_2-grown cells, the content became 29.6% or even
33.8% after successive culture with CO_2.

TABLE 1. The rubisco activities in the culture media and
the rubisco contents in the cells of <u>R. rubrum</u>
grown under different conditions

Growth condition	malate	CO_2	CO_2 (succe-ssive culture)
Rubisco activity (μmol CO_2/mg protein/min)	$1.15 \ 10^{-2}$	$23.5 \ 10^{-2}$	$35.5 \ 10^{-2}$
Relative rubisco acti-vity(medium)	1	20.4	30.9
Rubisco content(% of the total soluble protein)	1	29.6	33.8

3.2. Isolation and characterization of total RNA from R.
rubrum: The total RNA was isolated from cells grown
under different conditions and characterized by agarose electrophoresis and spectrophotometry. The
A_{260}/A_{230} was 2.15 and A_{260}/A_{280} was 2.1, and the
electtrophoretogram showed two distinct rRNA bands.
All these indicated that the RNA obtained had met
the requirements for molecular hybridization in both
purity and fragment size.

3.3. Nothern blot and dot blot hybridization of R. rubrum
RNA: Nothern blots of the RNA from R. rubrum cells
grown in different conditions when hybridized with
the cloned probe for rubisco gave the following

results: RNA from CO_2 grown cells showed significant positive hybridization, but there was practically no hybridization with RNA from malate grown cells. This was even
clearer when dot blot hybridization was conducted. Figure
1 is the autoradiograms of dot blot hybridizations and table 2 showed the countings of the hybridization dots. These

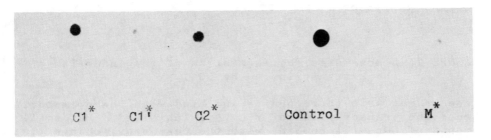

FIGURE 1. Autoradiograms of dot blot hybridization of R.
rubrum with cloned probe for rubisco. C1 and
C1': RNA from CO_2 grown cells(C1, inoculum 1:40;
C1', 1:20). C2: successive culture of CO_2 grown
cells. M:malate grown cells. Spots C1, C1'and
C2 contained 1 μg RNA, while spot M contained
4 μg RNA. Control contained 0.3 μg of 2.4 kb
EcoRI restriction fragment of plsmid pRR2119.

TABLE 2. Effect of different conditions on the level of
mRNA coding for rubisco in R. rubrum. M, C1,
C1'and C2 same as in fig. 1. The levels of mRNA
were estimated by dot hybridization and quantified
by scintillation counting of the filters.

Growth condition	M	C1	C1'	C2
Dot hybridization(cpm)	222	2402	2249	4392
Ralative amount	1	10.8	10.1	19.8

results clearly revealed that when R. rubrum was transferred from a growth condition with malate as the sole source
of carbon, the rubisco mRNA level rose significantly, indicating that CO_2 regulates rubisco synthesis on the transcriptional level.

3.4. How does CO_2 induce the transcription of rbc L?
Since R. rubrum is prokaryotic, this could be explained with operon hypothesis. As shown in Fig. 2, the
expression product of regulating gene, the repressor,
binds with the operating gene, so that theRNA polyme -

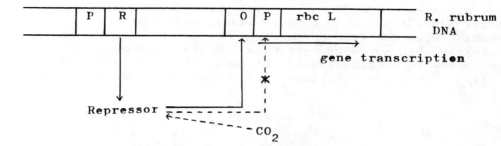

FIGURE 2. A schematic representation of the induction of
rbc L transcription by CO_2.

rase is not able to recognize and bind with the promotor,
hence the transcription of rbc L is inhibited. But small
amount of CO_2 will combine with the repressor, change its
conformation, and render it unable to bind with the operating gene. The result is the reversion of the inhibition
of the transcription of rbc L.

4. ADDENDUM

4.1. This project is supported by the Chinese National
     Natural Science Foundation.
4.2. The authors are indebted to Dr. Chen Zhang-liang for
     his help in performing molecular biological experi-
     ments, to Dr.B.B.Buchanan for providing R. rubrum
     culture and to Dr. C. R. Somerville for providing
     plasmid pRR2119.

REFERENCES
1. Whitman,W. B., et al. (1979) J. Biol. Chem. 254, 10184-
   10189.
2. Tabita, F. R. and McFadden,.B.A.(1974) J. Biol. Chem.
   249,3453-3458.
3. Wu Guang-yao et al.(1986) in "Zhiwu Shenghua Jishu he
   Fangfa"(Z.L.Zhang and G.Y.Wu ed.) pp.8-10. Nongye Chu-
   banshe, Beijing.
4. Ormerod,J.G. et al.(1961) Arch. Biochem. Biophys. 94,
   449-463.
5. Schloss, J.V. et al. (1979) J. Bacteriol. 137, 490-501.
6. Somerville,C.R. & Somerville,S.C.(1984) Mol.Gen.Genet.
   193,214-219.
7. Maniatis,T. ettal.(1982) Molecular Cloning. Cold Spring
   Harbor Laboratory.
8. Majundar,K.P. and McFadden,B.A.(1984) J. Bacteriol.
   157,795-801.
9. Davis,L.G. et al.(1986) Basic Methods in Molecular
   Biology. Elsevier.

REACTIVATION OF DARK-INACTIVATED RUBP CARBOXYLASE FROM PHASEOLUS VULGARIS IN VITRO

J.K. Sainis and N. Jawali. Molecular Biology & Agriculture Division, Bhabha Atomic Research Centre, TROMBAY, BOMBAY 400 085, INDIA.

1. INTRODUCTION

It has been proposed that light regulates the activity of RuBP carboxylase by two mechanisms. One is through Activase which has been shown to control the level of carbamylation of enzyme thus controlling the level of activation (1). The other mechanism involves binding of a phosphorylated inhibitor viz 2-carboxy-arabinitol 1-phosphate to the activated form of enzyme at low light intensities and in the dark. Thus after binding with this inhibitor, RuBP carboxylase remains in activated form but is unable to perform catalytic function (2,3,4). This inhibitor along with activase has been shown to match the activity of RuBP carboxylase with RuBP regenerating capacity in vivo (5).

We had predicted earlier that considering the protein and water content of stroma there is a possibility that RuBP carboxylase might be existing as a multienzyme complex (6,7,8). Later this finding was confirmed by Gontero et al (9) who showed that five enzymes of Calvin cycle exist as multienzyme complex. We have also observed that, the association of RuBP carboxylase with phosphoribulokinase and phospho-riboisomerase offers a catalytic advantage to RuBP carboxylase (8).

We report here that the dark inhibited enzyme from Phaseolus vulgaris can be reactivated in vitro in linked assay involving kinase and isomerase.

2. MATERIALS AND METHODS

Phaseolus vulgaris and Spinach plants grown in pots under natural illumination were used. Plants were kept covered for dark samples. Rest of the plants were exposed to natural sunlight up to 10a.m. The leaves from these plants were harvested and frozen for extraction of dark and light-extract.

Frozen leaves were extracted with twice the vol by wt of buffer containing 50 mM bicine (pH8), 20 mM $NaHCO_3$, 20 mM $MgCl_2$, 5 mM DTT, 1 mM EDTA and 5 mM Na ascorbate (10). This extract was used as such for testing RuBP carboxylase activity. The inhibitor was partially purified from dark—leaves by precipitating RuBP carboxylase with PEG and $MgCl_2$ and extracting the bound inhibitor with $HClO_4$. The acid extract was neutralysed with KOH, centrifuged and used.

M. Baltscheffsky (ed.), Current Research in Photosynthesis, Vol. III, 407–410.
© 1990 *Kluwer Academic Publishers. Printed in the Netherlands.*

RuBP carboxylase from Spinach was purified according to Hall and Tolbert (11) except that 0.01-0.33 M gradient of phosphate was used to elute RuBP carboxylase from DE-52 column.

Assay of activity: An aliqot of the crude extract was preincubated in 50 mM bicine buffer pH 8 with 20 mM $MgCl_2$, 20 mM $NaHCO_3$ (containing 10 u curies of radioactive bicarbonate), 10 mM DTT. Reaction was started with 2mM ATP and 10 mM R-5-P (Ribose-5-phosphate) or with 1 mM RuBP. Final reaction volume was 1 ml. Aliquots were taken out acidified to remove unreacted bicarbonate, dried and radioactivity counted by liquid scintillation spectrometry.

3.   RESULTS
When crude extracts from light and dark-samples of Phaseolus vulgaris were examined for their RuBP carboxylase activity the dark-samples showed only 50% specific activity as compared to light samples. If R-5-P + ATP dependent assay was carried out using the same extracts then dark-extracts show rates of CO_2 fixation which were 75 to 80% of the corresponding light controls in the linear phase of reaction (FIG-1). R-5-P + ATP dependent activity showed a comparatively higher lag in dark-extracts than corresponding light-extracts. This would be due to the presence of the bound inhibitor at the active site of the RuBP carboxylase in the dark-extracts which may be slowly getting released in this linked assay.

To further confirm this, crude extracts were activated with bicarbonate and $MgCl_2$ and DTT, and were preincubated with various substrates as given in Table 1. An aliquot was taken out at the end of 30 min and RuBP dependent activity was measured for one min. The results in TABLE 1 show that preincubation of RuBP carboxylase from dark-extracts with just R-5-P or ATP or RuBP could not reactivate the enzyme to the same extent as did the preincubation with R-5-P + ATP.

Earlier we had observed that RuBP carboxylase purified by the method of Hall and Tolbert (11) copurified with isomerase and kinase (8).

When RuBP carboxylase, isolated from spinach by the above procedure, was activated and treated with partially purified preparation of CA1P, it resulted in 67% inhibition of activity (data not given). When R-5-P + ATP dependent activity was measured on this extracts 75-80% of original RuBP dependent activity could be seen in the linear portion of the assays. This demonstrated that this process of reactivation occurs in the enzyme isolated from spinach also.

4.   DISCUSSION
It has been seen in Phaseolus vulgaris that when leaves kept in dark were exposed to light, the inactivated RuBP carboxylase gets activated (5). Several mechanisms have been put forward to explain this. Activase which has been shown to control the level of carbamylation of RuBP carboxylase has been implicated in release of nocturnal inhibitor in ATP + RuBP dependent reaction (12). A chloroplastic protein has been

shown to degrade this inhibitor in NADPH dependent reaction (13). We have observed that inactive RuBP carboxylase from dark-leaves can be reactivated in R-5-P + ATP dependent assay in vitro. It is less likely that the above mechanisms would be playing any part in this reactivation, observed in vitro because of the following reasons. 1. Reactivation with activase needs high concentration of RuBP, and ATP regenerating system. In our normal assays with R-5-P + ATP we do not have these conditions (FIG-1) and even after preincubation with RuBP and ATP the dark extracts showed 64% activity as compared to 79% obtained with R-5-P + ATP (TABLE-1). 2. We have not added NADPH in these assays therefore the question of role of the NADPH dependent chloroplastic protein does not arise. It is most likely that freshly synthesized RuBP in the multienzyme complex of RuBP carboxylase, kinase and isomerase must be getting channelled to the active site of RuBP carboxylase, replacing the inhibitor and there by reactivating the dark-inactivated enzyme. Since phosphoribulokinase has been shown to be activated by light the above mechanism of reactivation of dark-inhibited RuBP carboxylase would be important in vivo.

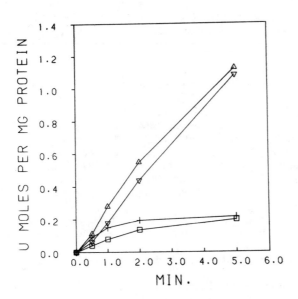

FIG-1: R-5-P + ATP and RuBP dependent activities in crude extracts of Phaseolus vulgaris exposed to light and dark. Light-extract,RuBP dependent activity, + — + ; Light-extract, R-5-P + ATP dependent activity △—△ ; Dark-extract,RuBP dependent activity, ☐— ☐ ; Dark-extracts, RSP + ATP dependent activity, ▽—▽ ;

TABLE 1. Reactivation of dark-inactivated RuBP carboxylase after preincubation with various substrates.

NO	CONDITIONS DURING PREINCUBATION	% SP. ACTIVITY
1.	LIGHT-EXTRACT(L-E)	100.0
2.	DARK-EXTRACT(D-E)	51.5
3.	L-E + R-5-P + ATP	108.5
4.	D-E + R-5-P + ATP	79.0
5.	L-E + RuBP	108.0
6.	D-E + RuBP	56.5
7.	D-E + R-5-P	55.0
8.	D-E + ATP	52.0
9.	D-E + RuBP + R-5-P	59.5
10.	D-E + RuBP + ATP	64.0
11.	D-E + RuBP + R-5-P + ATP	75.5

RuBP carboxylase present in crude extracts was activated with 20 mM $MgCl_2$ and 10 mM $NaHCO_3$ and 10 mM DTT in 50 mM Bicine buffer pH 8 for 15 min. The extracts were further treated with 10 mM R-5-P and/or 2 mM ATP and/or 1 mM RuBP as mentioned in Table for further 30 min. Aliquots were withdrawn and tested for RuBP dependent activity.

REFERENCES
1. Portis, A.R., Salvucci, M.E. and Ogren, W.L. (1986) Plant Physiol. 82, 967-971.
2. Servaites, J.C. (1985) Plant Physiol. 78, 839-843.
3. Seemann, J.R., Berry, J.A., Freas, S.M. and Krump, M.A. (1985) Proc. Natl. Acad. Sci. USA, 82, 8024-8028.
4. Gutteridge, S., Parry, M.A.J., Burton, S., Keys, A.J., Mudd, A., Feeney, J., Servaites, J.C. and Pierce, J. (1986) Nature. 324, 274-276.
5. Kobza, J., Seemann, J.R. (1989) Plant Physiol. 89, 174-179.
6. Sainis, J.K. and Harris, G.C. (1986) Biochem. Biophys. Res. Commun. 139, 947-954.
7. Sainis, J.K. and Harris, G.C. (1987) Prog. Photosynth. Res.6, 491-494.
8. Sainis, J.K., Merriam, K. and Harris, G.C. (1989) Plant Physiol. 89, 368-374.
9. Gontero, B., Cardenas, M.L. and Ricard, J. (1988) Eur. J. Biochem. 173, 437-443.
10. Berry, J.A., Lorimer, G.H., Pierce, J., Seemann, J.R., Meek, J. and Freas, S. (1987) Proc. Natl. Acad. Sci. USA. 84, 734-738.
11. Hall, N.P. and Tolbert, N.E.(1978) FEBS Lett. 96, 167-169.
12. Robinson, S.P. and Portis, A.R. (1988) FEBS Lett. 233, 413-416.
13. Salvucci, M.E., Holbrook, G.P.., Anderson, J.C. and Bowes, G. (1988) FEBS Lett. 231, 197-201.

ABBREVIATIONS
CA1P, 2-carboxy-D-arabinitol 1-phosphate; R-5-P, Ribose-5-phosphate; RuBP, Ribulose-1 5-bisphosphate.

RED OR BLUE LIGHT INDUCED DIFFERENT RUBISCO SMALL SUBUNITS IN FERN GAMETOPHYTES AFFECTING CARBOXYLATION RATES

HAVIVA EILENBERG[1] SVEN BEER[1], SHIMON GEPSTEIN[2], NURIT GEVA[1] AND AVIAH ZILBERSTEIN[1], DEPT OF BOTANY[1], TEL AVIV UNIV. 69978, TEL-AVIV, ISRAEL; DEPT OF BIOLOGY[2], TECHNION, 32000 HAIFA, ISRAEL

1. INTRODUCTION

Rubisco is a bifunctional enzyme, catalyzing carboxylation and oxygenation of ribulose 1,5-bisphosphate (RuBP) at the same catalytic site. It is a chloroplast stromal enzyme comprising of 8 chloroplast encoded large subunits (LSU), and 8 nuclear encoded small subunits (SSU) (1,2). The LSUs contain binding sites for the three substrates: CO_2, O_2 and RuBP and other features required for assembly, activation and catalytic activity (3,4). The LSU chloroplast gene, rbcL, is present in a single copy per genome and the amino acid sequences around the active sites are conserved in most photosynthetic organisms (5).

The SSUs are encoded by a genomic multi-gene family (rbcS) (2). Quantitative differences in transcription of the various members of the family have been observed (6). The expression of rbcSs is both light-regulated and tissue-specific (7); their presence is essential however their function remains still a mystery. It has been suggested that SSUs are required for maintaining the holoenzyme in a stable conformation since almost no catalysis can occur without them (8). Moreover, site-directed mutagenesis of one or two Trp residues in a conserved region of rbcS from Anacystis nidulans changed the catalytic rate of the enzyme, suggesting also an activating role for the SSU (9).

In the present study a differential appearance of two distinct SSU populations was observed in P. vittata gametophytes grown under red or blue light. A correlation between specific SSU type and catalytic properties of Rubisco was shown.

2. PROCEDURE

2.1 Materials and Methods

2.1.1. Germination and illumination of ferns: Fern (P. vittata) spores were germinated and synchronized as previously described (10). Following 48hr in the dark, the gametophytes were exposed to continuous red or blue light for different time periods.

2.1.2. Preparation of enzyme extract: Fern gametophytes were collected , ground and homogenized in a buffer containing 200mM Tris-HCl, pH=8.0; 0.2mM EDTA; 10mM $MgCl_2$, 10mM ascorbate, 2% PVP and 5mM DTT. All steps of the enzyme extract preparation were done at 4 °C. The homogenate was spinned at 12,000xg for 1 minute and the supernatant was used as the enzyme source. Total protein in the extract was determined according to Marder et al.(11), and it varied between 2-7mg protein/ml. The distribution of proteins in the enzyme extracts was analyzed using 5-15% SDS-acrylamide gels. The amount of specific Rubisco protein in each extract was estimated by ^{125}I-counting of LSU specific bands excised from immunoblots probed first with polyclonal antibodies raised in rabbit against SDS-treated spinach LSU and then with ^{125}I-donkey anti-rabbit IgG. Purified spinach Rubisco protein was used as standard.

2.1.3. Assay of Rubisco carboxylase: Rubisco carboxylase activity was assayed at 25 C by measuring RuBP-dependent incorporation of $^{14}CO_2$ into acid-stable products. The enzyme activity was measured in a volume of 0.55ml containing 0.3ml assay buffer (50mM Tris-HCl, PH=8.0; 1mM EDTA; 10mM MgCl$_2$ and 5mM DTT), 0.1ml of enzyme extract, NaH^{14}CO$_3$ and RuBP as indicated in Figure legends. Activation of the enzyme was achieved by incubating the enzyme extract for 10 minutes with 10mM NaHCO$_3$ on ice. Catalysis was initiated by addition of the activated enzyme to the reaction mix and the incubation was terminated after 0.5 minutes by addition of 0.1ml 6N HCl. Samples were dried for 2hr at 60 $\overset{\circ}{C}$ under a stream of air and then acid-stable disintegrations per minute were determined by liquid scintillation counter.

3. RESULTS AND DISCUSSION

3.1. Growth of P. vittata under blue or red light

Germinating haploid gametophytes of the homosporous fern Pteris vittata are easy to manipulate in axenic cultures and their growth can be controlled and synchronized by red (R) and blue (B) light (10). Figure 1 shows the different pattern of development of P. vittata gametophytes as a result of growth under continuous red (panel A) or blue (panel B) light for 8 days. The R-gametophytes are filamentous while the B-gametophytes exhibit the usual two-dimensional growth.

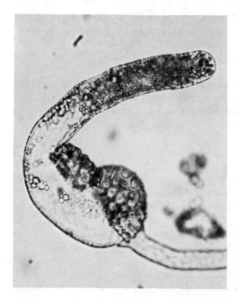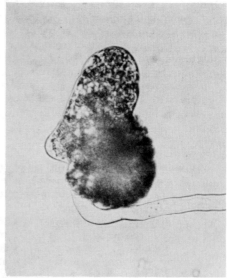

FIGURE 1. MORPHOLOGY OF FERN GAMETOPHYTES. Fern gametophytes grown under continuous red (panel A) or blue (panel B) light for 8 days.

3.2. Differences in immunodetection of red and blue SSUs

The light-induced morphological differences in gametophyte growth led us to question whether any significant variations in the Rubisco small subunit content could be observed. A Rubisco enriched enzyme extract was prepared from R- and B-gametophytes. Equal amounts of extract proteins were separated on a 5-15% acrylamide-SDS gel. No difference was observed in the pattern of protein distribution (data not shown). In order to specifically indentify the SSUs and LSUs in the extracts, the gel was blotted onto nitrocellulose filters and probed with anti-SSU or anti-LSU polyclonal antibodies. Figure 2 shows a typical immunoblot using anti-SSU as probe. It can be seen that R-induced SSUs are not recognized by antibodies raised against SSU from spinach, while the B-induced SSUs are well recognized (lane 2,3). Application of a double amount of extract protein (lane 1) did not improve detection of R-induced SSUs. However, cross-reactivity between the anti-SSU IgG and LSU bands indicated that the LSUs in extracts from both light treatments were equally recognized. This was also confirmed by immunoblots using anti-LSU IgG as a probe (data not shown). These results suggest that, in contrast to the homogenous appearance of LSUs, the SSU of Rubisco from the two photoinduced types of gametophytes belong to two different types of immunogenic epitopes.

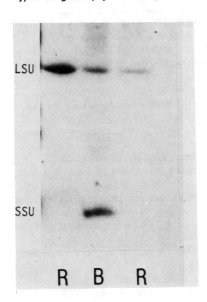

FIGURE 2. IMMUNODETECTION OR R- AND B-INDUCED SSUs. Total protein extracted from 8 days old R- or B-gametophytes were analyzed in Western blots using anti-SSU IgG specific antibodies. In lane 2 and 3 equal amounts of proteins were loaded while lane 1 has a double amount of proteins.

3.3. Comparison of R- and B-gametophyte Rubisco carboxylase activity

The presence of SSUs have been shown to be essential for catalysis. However, their exact function remains questionable. Thus, the natural occurrence of two distinct SSU populations in the same plant enabled us to study the possible role of SSUs in carboxylation activity. Maximal rate of carboxylation (Vmax) of Rubisco carboxylase was determined in the presence of increasing concentrations of either of the two substrates (CO_2 and RuBP). Table 1 shows that carboxylation activity in enzyme extracts of B-gametophytes is significantly higher than that of R-gametophytes. Approximately 3-fold (CO_2) and 2-fold (RuBP) higher maximal carboxylation rates were observed for the B-enzyme. Evidently, a certain correlation exists between SSU primary structure revealed by its antigenicity and the holoenzyme activity. Although the SSU role has been attributed primarily to be a structural one, our results suggest a possible regulatory role as well. Currently characterization of the fern rbcS gene-family is on the way in order to point out differences in rbcS exons.

TABLE I. COMPARISON OF Vmax VALUES OF R- AND B-GAMETOPHYTES

Extract source	Vmax (CO_2)	Vmax (RuBP)
	nmol min^{-1} (μ g Rubisco protein)$^{-1}$	
R-gametophytes	1.6 $\pm$ 0.9	5.6 $\pm$ 0.3
B-gametophytes	4.9 $\pm$ 0.2	11.4 $\pm$ 1.0

The Vmax values were determined in enzyme extracts of 24 [Vmax (CO_2)] and 18 [Vmax (RuBP)] days old R-and B-gametophytes. For Vmax (CO_2) estimation the assay was performed in the presence of 2mM RuBP while Vmax (RuBP) was determined in the presence of 18.2 mM $NaHCO_3$.

REFERENCES
1. O'Neal, J.K., Pokalsky, A.R., Kichne, K.L. and Shewmaker, C.K. (1987) Nucleic Acids Res. 15, 8661-8677.
2. Dean, C., Van den Elzen, P., Tamaki, S., Black, M., Dunsmuir P. and Bedrook J. (1987) Mol. Gen. Genet. 206, 465-474.
3. Miziorko, H.M. and Lorimer, G.H. (1983) Ann. Rev. Biochem. 52, 507-535.
4. Anderson, I., Knight, S., Schneider, G., Lindquist, Y., Lundquist, T., Branden, C.I. and Lorimer, G.H. (1989) Nature 337, 229-234.
5. Gutteridge, S. and Gatenby, A.A. (1987) Oxford Surveys of Plant Mol. and Cell Biol. 4, 95-135.
6. Dean, C., Van den Elzen, P., Tamaki, S., Dunsmuir P. and Bedbrook, J. (1985) EMBO J. 4, 3055-3061.
7. Kuhlemeir, C., Green P.J. and Chua, N.H. (1987) Annu. Rev. Plant Physiol. 38, 221-257.
8. Andrews, T.J. and Ballment, B. (1983) J. Biol. Chem. 258, 7514-7518.
9. Voordouw, G., De Vries, P.A., Van den Berg, W.A.M. and De Clerck, E.P.J. (1987) Eur. J. Biochem. 163, 591-598.
10. Zilberstein, A., Arzee, T. and Gressel, J. (1984) Zeit. Pflanzenphysiol. 114, 97-107.
11. Marder, J.B., Mattoo A.K. and Edelman, M. (1986) Methods in Enzymol. 118, 384-396.

ACKNOWLEDGMENT: This research is supported by the Israeli Ministry of Science and Development, National Council for Research and Development, under Grant 2694-1-87.

REGULATION OF THE ACTIVITY OF RIBULOSE BISPHOSPHATE CARBOXYLASE BY LIGHT AND CO_2

Juta Viil and Tiit Pärnik
Institute of Experimental Biology, Estonian Academy of Sciences, Harku, Estonia, 203051 USSR

1. Introduction

Ribulose 1,5-bisphosphate (RuBP) carboxylase (Rubisco) is known as being a light-regulated enzyme. If to express the carboxylation rate as

$$V = K * R * C \qquad (1)$$

(where K is the rate constant of the reaction, C is the intracellular CO_2 concentration, and R is the concentration of RuBP), activation and inactivation of Rubisco would manifest themselves as changes of K. We studied the kinetics of the rate constant at the illumination of leaves kept preliminarily in the dark for 10 to 20 s.

2. Materials and methods

Experiments were carried out with leaves of barley (the 3rd and the 4th leaf of 4 week old plants). Scheme of the exposure for the estimation of the parameters required for the calculation of K is given in Fig. 1.

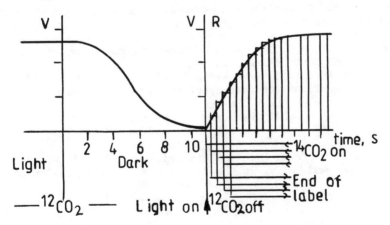

FIGURE 1. Scheme of the exposure for the estimation of the carboxyla- tion rate and of the content of RuBP in pre-darkened leaves.

Exposures were carried out in the fast-operating automatic chamber /1/. Methods have been described in detail in /2/.

M. Baltscheffsky (ed.), Current Research in Photosynthesis, Vol. III, 415–418.
© 1990 *Kluwer Academic Publishers. Printed in the Netherlands.*

3. Results and discussion

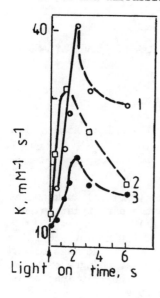

K, mM⁻¹ s⁻¹

Light on time, s

Fig. 2 gives the kinetics of K in leaves pre-illuminated under different conditions and thereafter darkened for 20 s. The activation of the enzyme reaches maximum in about 2 s. (The subsequent decrease in the calculated value of K is caused by R exceeding the concentration of carboxylation centres, E). High CO_2 concentration and low light intensity at preillumination decrease the maximum activity after the fast light activation.

FIGURE 2. Kinetics of K at the illumination of pre-darkened leaves. Condition before darkening: CO_2 300 ppm (curve 1,3) or 1000 ppm (curve 2); light 30 mW cm⁻² (curve 1,2) or 3 mW cm⁻² (curve 3).

K is an integrate parameter, which depends on rate constants of partial reactions constituting the whole carboxylation process /3/:

$$E_f + R_f \xrightarrow{k_1} ER \underset{CO_2}{\xrightarrow{k_2}} EC_6 \xrightarrow{k_3} 2 C_3 + E_f$$

where k_1, k_2 and k_3 are the rate constants, E_f represents unoccupied carboxylation centres, R_f means free RuBP molecules, ER is the enzyme-RuBP complex, EC_6 is the enzyme-bound 6C intermediate, and C_3 is 3-phosphoglyceric acid. The rates of these reactions, v_1, v_2, and v_3, respectively, may be expressed as:

$$v_1 = k_1 * E_f * R_f \quad (2); \quad v_2 = k_2 * ER * C \quad (3); \quad v_3 = k_3 * EC_6 \quad (4)$$

From these equations the rate constants may be expressed:

$$k_1 = \frac{v_1}{E_f * R_f} \quad (5); \quad k_2 = \frac{v_2}{ER * C} \quad (6); \quad k_3 = \frac{v_3}{EC_6} \quad (7).$$

As it follows from Eq. (5), in order to calculate k_1, one must estimate v_1, E_f, and R_f. v_1 is the derivative of the formation of ER:

$$v_1 = \frac{\Delta ER}{\Delta t} \quad (8); \quad v_1 = \frac{ER_2 - ER_1}{t_2 - t_1} \quad (9)$$

According to Eq. (3),

$$ER_1 = \frac{v_{2,1}}{k_2 * C_1} \quad (10); \quad ER_2 = \frac{v_{2,2}}{k_2 * C_2} \quad (11).$$

Replacing in (9):

$$v_1 = \frac{1}{k_2 (t_2 - t_1)} \left(\frac{v_{2,2}}{C_2} - \frac{v_{2,1}}{C_1} \right) \quad (12)$$

From the sequence of the partial reactions of carboxylation above it follows that the total concentration of active carboxylation centres
$$E_T = E_f + ER + EC_6 \quad (13)$$
In our experiments the leaves were illuminated (between darkening and labelling) in the CO_2 -free atmosphere, where $EC_6 = 0$. Therefore
$$E_f = E_T - ER \quad (14)$$
E_T may be found according to the following considerations. V obtains the maximum value, when $ER = E_T$, i.e. when the enzyme becomes saturated with RuBP. While binding of RuBP is an essentially irreversible reaction, in the CO_2 -free atmosphere one can estimate ER by RuBP at the moment of saturation. From Fig. 3
$$E_T = \frac{V_S}{k_2 * C_S} \quad (15)$$
where V_S is the maximum rate of carboxylation, C_S is the respective intracellular CO_2 concentration.

From Eq. (10), (11), (14), and (15) it follows that for the time period from t_1 to t_2 :
$$E_f = \frac{1}{k_2} * \left(\frac{V_S}{c_S} - 0.5 \left(\frac{v_{2,2}}{C_2} + \frac{v_{2,1}}{C_1} \right) \right) \quad (16)$$

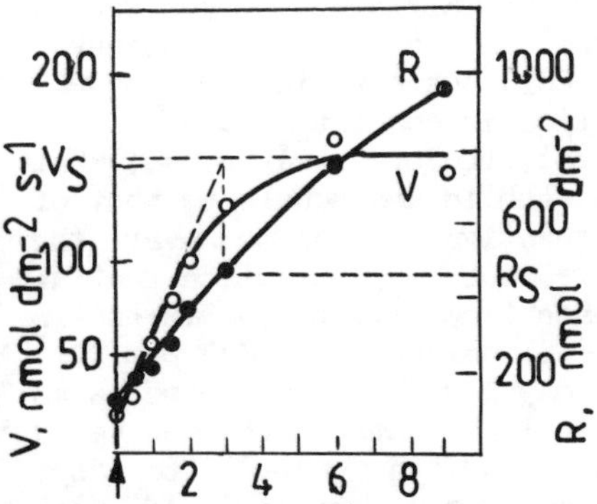

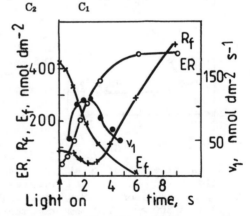

FIGURE 3. Kinetics of the carboxylations rate (V) and ribulose 1,5-bisphosphate content (R) in response to the illumination of darkened leaves. Conditions before darkening: CO_2 300 ppm, light 30 mW cm^{-2}, steady state photosynthesis 165 nmol dm^{-2} s^{-1}.

FIGURE 4. Kinetics of some parameters of the carboxylation reaction: concentration of the enzyme-RuBP complex (ER), unoccupied carboxylation centres (E_f), free RuBP (R_f) and the rate of the formation of the enzyme-RuBP complex (v_1). k =const =48.6 mM^{-1} s^{-1}. Pre-illumination as in Fig. 3.

As RuBP may be free or bound to the enzyme, its total concentration (R_T):
$$R_T = R_f + ER \quad (17)$$
It follows that from t_1 to t_2, according to Eq. (10), (11), and (17):
$$R_f = R_T - \frac{0.5}{k_2} \left(\frac{v_{2.1}}{C_1} + \frac{v_{2.2}}{C_2} \right) \quad (18)$$
From Eq. (5), (12), (16), and (18), k_1 may be calculated. All the parameters in those may be readily estimated, except k_2. This constant may be estimated for the light-activated enzyme from Eq. (15) replacing $E_T = ER = R_S$ (Fig. 3).

Values of k_2, obtained with leaves pre-illuminated under different conditions are given in the following table.

Exp.	Pre-illumination				k_2	
1	30 mW cm^{-2}		300	ppm CO$_2$	48.6 mM^{-1} s^{-1}	
	30 "		100	"	49.1	"
2	30 "		300	"	39.1	"
	3 "		300	"	19.9	"
	30 "		1000	"	26.3	"

Fig. 4 gives kinetics of some calculated parameters of the carboxylation reaction during the light activation of Rubisco.

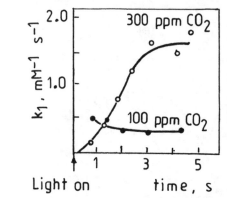

FIGURE 5. Kinetics of k_1 at the illumination of darkened leaves, if $k_2 = \text{const}$ (48.6 and 49.1 in 300 and 100 ppm CO$_2$, respectively).

If to apply tentatively these k_2 values to calculate k_1 over the whole activation period, the kinetics of k_1 is obtained as given in Fig. 5. A marked increase in the affinity of Rubisco to RuBP is seen in leaves pre-illuminated in 300 ppm CO$_2$, but not in 100 ppm CO$_2$. The activation is completed in 3 s. If to suggest, the other way round, that k_1 remains stabile and equals to that of the light-activated enzyme over the whole curve, one may calculate that k_2 must increase from 21.7 to 48.6 mM^{-1} s^{-1} in leaves pre-illuminated in 300 ppm CO$_2$. The data may also be interpreted as an increase in the number of activated centres from 90 to 460, if to adopt the light-activated values of both constants.

REFERENCES

1 Pärnik, T.R., Keerberg, O.F. and Jürismaa, E.J. (1987) Fiziol. Rastenij 34, 4, 837-845
2 Viil, J.A., Ivanova, H.N. and Pärnik, T.R. (1989) Fiziol. Rastenij 36, 3
3 Lane, M.D. and Miziorko, H.M. (1978) in Photosynthetic Carbon Assimilation (Siegelman, H.W. and Hind, G., ed.-s), pp 19-40, Plenum Publishing Corporation.

The role of the C-terminus of the large subunit of Rubisco investigated by mutagenesis.

B.Ranty[1], T.Lundqvist[2], G.Schneider[2], M.Madden[3], R.Howard[3] and G. Lorimer[3]

[1]Department of Plant Physiology, URA CNRS n°241, Paul Sabatier University, 118 route de Narbonne, 31062 Toulouse Cedex, France. [2]Department of Molecular Biology, Swedish University of Agricultural Sciences, Uppsala Biomedical Center, Box 590, 75124 Uppsala, Sweden. [3]Central Research and Development Department, E.I. DuPont de Nemours and Co., Wilmington, DE 19898, USA.

Introduction

Recent progress in in vitro genetic manipulations (1), and in the structural analysis of Rubisco (2,3) have provided the basis for a rationale mutagenesis of this key enzyme in the photosynthetic carbon metabolism, in attempts to define structure/function relationships. In combination with a better knowledge in the chemistry of the enzymatic reactions, studies of specific changes of highly conserved residues within the active site have been developed. So far, the role of at least two residues essential for activation (Lys 191 in Rhodospirillum rubrum Rubisco) or catalysis (Lys 166) have been defined (4,5). Another strategy consists to examine the functional importance of peptide regions of low homology. Construction of chimaeric genes by sequence replacement have indicated the critical requirement of some regions of the large subunit (i.e. N-terminus, bridge region between N- and C-terminal domains) for the assembly and/or function of the protein (6,7). A similar approach was used here to investigate the role of the C-terminus of the large subunit. Sequence deletion in the tail domain was performed on the gene coding for R.rubrum Rubisco. Mutation was designed to remove the last and pen-ultimate α-helices from the C-terminal extension (Fig.1).

...α_8...GVPVLDYAREHKELARAFESF [P] GDADQIYPGWRKALGVEDTRSALPA

Figure 1: Amino acid sequence at the C-terminus of Rubisco large subunit from R.rubrum (residue G_{420} to A_{466}). The α-helices are underlined. α_8 designates the last α-helice of the α/β barrel domain. Amino acid in box shows the position P_{441} where the sequence was stopped.

Procedure

Mutagenesis was performed on plasmid PL2, a derivative of pRR 2119 that contains the structural gene for R.rubrum Rubisco (7). Deletion

M. Baltscheffsky (ed.), Current Research in Photosynthesis, Vol. III, 419–422.

in the tail domain was constructed by <u>in vitro</u> techniques using synthetic, double-stranded oligonucleotides. The mutagenic oligonucleotide bears stop codons at position corresponding to P_{441} in the peptide sequence. The mutations were confirmed by sequencing the appropriate region of the double-stranded plasmid DNA.

Plasmid harboring the mutated gene for Rubisco was used to transform <u>E.coli</u> cells. Rubisco was isolated from cells grown on 2YT medium under selective conditions, and purified as previously described (5). Analysis of the mutant protein involved analytical gel filtration, electron microcopy of negatively stained samples with uranyl acetate. The enzymatic capability was assayed by RuBP dependent fixation of $^{14}CO2$ (8). The extent of activation of the enzyme by CO_2 and Mg^{2+}, and the ability to bind phosphorylated ligands were tested using 2-carboxy arabinitol bisphosphate, CABP (9).

Results and Discussion
Structural integrity of the mutant
The elution time of the mutant carboxylase by analytical gel filtration is significantly reduced, relative to that of the wild type enzyme, a dimer of large subunits (Fig.2). Analysis in denaturing conditions demonstrates that the mutant protein is a polymer of large subunits. Comparison with the elution profile of aggregates of L_2 crosslinked by disulphide bridges shows that the mutant elutes within the range of an octomer L_8 (Fig.2).

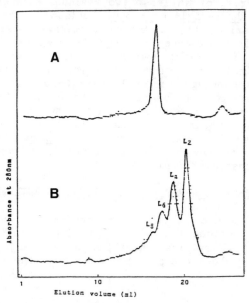

<u>Figure 2</u>: Gel filtration of the mutant Rubisco (A) and aggregates of <u>R.rubrum</u> Rubisco (B) on Superose 6 (Pharmacia).

The aggregated structure of the mutant was further solved by electron microscopic analysis. The images of negatively stained samples indicate that the mutant molecules have a ring like structure, similar to that previously reported for L_8S_8 Rubisco (Fig.3). A four fold radial symmetry was deduced from rotational analysis. All these data strongly suggest an L8 type for the mutant protein.

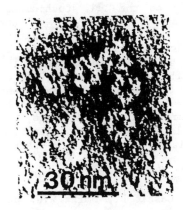

Figure 3: Electron microscopic view of the mutant Rubisco.

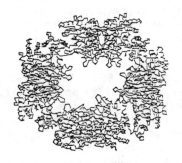

Figure 4: Stereodiagram of the L_8 mutant from R.rubrum Rubisco, built up by a collapsed arrangement of 4 truncated dimers.

Hydrophobic cluster analysis revealed that truncation of the large subunit increases the solvent accessibility for some residues such as L_{374} and L_{424}. The spatial proximity of these residues and their polar position in the 3-dimensional structure of the truncated dimer lead to the structural model proposed in Fig.4. The L_8 mutant consists of 4 dimers bound end to end by hydrophobic interactions. The effect of insertion of a polar amino acid in the hydrophobic patch ascertains the model. The substitution $L_{424}-N_{424}$ disrupts the L_8 assembly of the truncated protein and restores the dimeric structure (Ranty et al. in preparation). Truncation of the large subunit thus promotes the assembly of a L_8 type in which the arrangement of the dimers is different from that reported for the L_8 core of L_8S_8 Rubisco.

Catalytic activity of the mutant
Truncation of the large subunit is associated with a dramatic decline in the catalytic activity. The specific activity of the L_8 mutant is reduced to 1% in comparison of the wild type enzyme. Verification that the L_8 mutant undergoes carbamylation was provided by trapping the carbamate with CABP. The quaternary complex $(E.CO_2.Mg^{2+}.CABP)$ was isolated by gel filtration of the mutant protein pre-mixed with $^{14}CO2$, $MgCl_2$ and CABP. The binding of $^{14}CO2$ (0.83 mole/ mole of protomer) is close to the 1:1 stochiometry obtained with the wild type enzyme. However, the stability of the complex is greatly reduced relative to that of the native carboxylase. This suggests that the loss of activity in the L_8 mutant is due to a defect in binding phosphorylated ligands. The substitution $L_{424}-N_{424}$ does not improve the enzymatic capability of the truncated dimer. The tail domain is then a crucial requirement for the enzymatic ability, despite it is far from the active site. According to the crystallographic structure of R.rubrum Rubisco, the C-terminal region may be involved in maintaining the configuration of the active site through interactions with the α/β barrel structure.

References

1 Chapman M.S., Suh S.W., Curmi P.M.G., Cascio D., Smith W.W. and Eisenberg D.S. (1988) Science 141, 71-74.
2 Gutteridge S., Phillips A.L., Kettleborough C.A., Parry M.A.J. and Keys A.J. (1986) Phil. Trans. Soc. Lond.B 313,433-445.
3 Schneider G., Lindqvist Y., Branden C-I. and Lorimer G. (1986) EMBO J. 5, 3409-3415.
4 Estelle M., Hanks J., McIntosh L. and Somerville C. (1985) J. Biol. Chem. 260, 9523-9526.
5 Lorimer G.H. and Hartman F.C. (1988) J. Biol. Chem. 263, 6468-6471.
6 Kettleborough C.A., Parry M.A.J., Burton S., Gutteridge S., Keys A.J. and Phillips A.L. (1987) Eur. J. Biochem. 170, 335-342.
7 Gutteridge S., Lorimer G. and Pierce J. (1988) Plant Physiol. Biochem. 26, 675-682.
8 Lorimer G.H., Badger M.R. and Andrews T.J. (1977) Anal. Biochem. 78, 66-75.
9 Pierce J., Tolbert N.E. and Barker R. (1980) Biochem. 19, 934-942.

REGULATION OF PLASTID TRANSCRIPTION AND RNA ACCUMULATION DURING BARLEY LEAF DEVELOPMENT

John E. Mullet, Jeff C. Rapp, Brian J. Baumgartner, Tineke B. Sexton and Patricia E. Gamble, Department of Biochemistry and Biophysics, Texas A&M University, College Station, Texas 77843 USA

1. INTRODUCTION

Chloroplast development is coupled to leaf mesophyll cell development and is controlled, in part, by light (rev. 1, 2, 3). The extent of light control over chloroplast development varies considerably between plant species and leaf type. However, a common sequence of events can be discerned in most plants which leads from undifferentiated proplastids to photosynthetically active chloroplasts (1). This sequence of events has been studied extensively in monocots such as barley because of the spatial separation of stages in chloroplast development in these plants (4-7). Barley leaf cells are produced primarily by a meristematic zone located in the leaf base. These undifferentiated dividing cells contain 10 to 15 proplastids (5, 7). Proplastids accumulate 120 to 150 copies of plastid DNA but exhibit low overall transcription activity (7). Once cells in the leaf base stop dividing they are displaced toward the leaf apex due to cell enlargement and continued formation of cells in the leaf base. During the phase of cell enlargement, plastid transcription activity increases (7). The activation of plastid transcription is light-independent as is the accumulation of most soluble proteins and many membrane proteins found in chloroplasts (8). However, acquisition of photosynthetic competence and accumulation of chlorophyll and the chlorophyll-apoproteins requires light (9). When barley plants are illuminated, leaf chloroplasts become photosynthetically active and after 12 to 24 hrs of light, overall plastid transcription and translation activities decline (10).

In barley, two PSII chloroplast-encoded proteins, D_1 and D_2, are synthesized at relatively high rates in mature leaves (11). CP43 translation is also differentially maintained but to a lower extent. The need for continued synthesis of D_1 and D_2 is probably related to the relatively high turnover rates of these proteins in illuminated chloroplasts (12-14). Several mechanisms are involved in maintaining the capacity of D_1 and D_2 synthesis in chloroplasts. For example, D_1 mRNA is differentially accumulated in illuminated plants because transcription of the psbA gene (which encodes mRNA for D_1) is stimulated by light and because the psbA mRNA exhibits high stability (11, Klein and Mullet, unpublished). There are also nuclear-encoded proteins which help maintain synthesis of D_1 in mature chloroplasts (15-18). Likewise, D_2 mRNA levels are maintained in mature barley chloroplasts unlike other plastid mRNAs (psaA-psaB, rbcL, atpB) (11). In dark-grown plants, plastids accumulate six large mRNAs (5.7 to 1.7 kb) which hybridize to psbD-psbC (11). Upon illumination, the level of these six RNAs declines and two psbD-psbC RNAs which have a common 5'-end accumulate (11). The accumulation of these RNAs is controlled by a blue-light photoreceptor (19). In this paper, we provide evidence that differential accumulation of the light-induced psbD-psbC mRNAs is regulated at the levels of transcription and RNA stability.

M. Baltscheffsky (ed.), Current Research in Photosynthesis, Vol. III, 423–427.

2. PROCEDURE
2.1. Materials and Methods

Barley seeds *(Hordeum vulgare* L var Morex) were planted in vermiculite and grown in a dark chamber as previously described (15). Some plants were transferred to an illuminated chamber (350 $\mu\xi$/m^2/s, fluorescent plus incandescent bulbs) after 4.5 days of growth in darkness. Plastids were isolated from barley leaves and purified on Percoll gradients as described previously (10). Plastid concentration was determined using a hemocytometer. Total nucleic acid was isolated from plastids by SDS-phenol extraction as described (10). Northern blots were carried out by separating RNA from equal numbers of plastids on formaldehyde gels. This RNA was transferred to Gene Screen paper and probed as described previously (10). Transcription 'run-on' assays were carried out as described by Mullet and Klein (10) except that heparin was included in some assays to inhibit RNAse activity (20).

3. RESULTS AND DISCUSSION

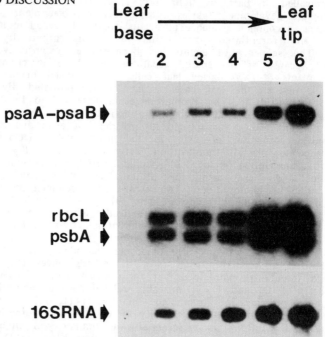

Fig. 1. Northern blot of plastid RNAs from sections of 6 day-old dark-grown barley leaves. Plastids were isolated from the following leaf segments; base to 1 cm (lane 1), 1 to 2 cm (lane 2), 2 to 3 cm (lane 3), 3 to 4.5 cm (lane 4), 4.5 to 6 cm (lane 5), 6 to 8 cm from the leaf base (lane 6). Total plastid nucleic acid extracted from an equal number of plastids was applied to nylon blots and probed with radiolabel DNA probes for RNA from *psaA-psaB, rbcL, psbA* and 16S rDNA as described previously (20).

3.1   Accumulation of plastid RNAs in dark-grown plants.

We have previously shown that plastid transcription activity increases in a light-independent manner shortly after cells of the barley leaf base stop dividing and enter the 1 to 3 cm zone of cell elongation near the leaf base.   Figure 1 shows that plastid RNA accumulation parallels the previously reported increase in plastid transcription activity.   Only very low levels of plastid RNAs are found in plastids isolated from a 1 cm region of the leaf base (Fig. 1, lane 1).   Plastids isolated from sections 1 to 2 cm from the barley leaf base contained detectable levels of 16S rRNA, and *psbA, psaA-psaB* and *rbcL* mRNA (Fig. 1, lane 2).   The levels of these RNAs per plastid increased further in cells 4.5 to 6 cm from the leaf base (Fig. 1, lane 5).   This increase begins where plastid division stops (7).   The build-up of RNA per plastid in this region probably reflects continued transcription of plastid genes and a decrease in the rate of dilution due to the shut down in plastid division activity.   Note also the near parallel build-up of RNA hybridizing to the 4 genes examined.   This is consistent with the global activation of plastid genes during this early phase of chloroplast development.

3.2   Light-induced transcription of *psbD-psbC*.

We have previously shown high levels of RNA hybridizing to *psbD-psbC* in barley plastids of 4.5 day-old dark-grown barley and that *psbD-psbC RNA* levels do not decline significantly when plants are illuminated for 72 hrs. If 4.5 day-old dark-grown plants are kept in darkness for an additional 72 hrs then *psbD-psbC* RNA levels decline 11% (11).   The maintenance of *psbD-psbC* levels in illuminated plants occurs because although six *psbD-psbC* transcripts decline when seedlings are illuminated, these RNAs are replaced by two different RNAs (11).   The two light-induced RNAs have a common 5'-end which could be generated by transcription initiation or RNA processing.   As a first attempt to distinguish between these possibilities plastid 'run-on' transcription assays were carried out.   Radiolabeled RNA transcribed from the *psbD-psbC* transcription unit was quantitated by hybridization to a 1.26 kbp EcoRI DNA fragment from this DNA region.   After hybridization, dots containing the hybridized RNA were excised and counted in a liquid scintillation counter.   These data are presented in Table I. The highest transcription activity from *psbD-psbC* was observed in plastids of 4.5 day-old dark-grown plants.   Plastids from 8 day-old dark-grown plants transcribed *psbD-psbC* at approximately 25% of the rate observed in plastids of 4.5 day-old seedlings.   A smaller decline in transcription of *psbD-psbC* was observed in 4.5 day-old dark-grown plants illuminated for 72 hrs (~50%).

To check if RNA turnover was influencing our assays, pulse-chase experiments were carried out (Table I, column II).   When 5 min pulse-labeling periods were followed by a 5 min chase, the amount of radiolabel in *psbD-psbC* transcripts declines significantly (13% to 53%).   *PsbD-psbC* RNAs transcribed in plastids of 8 day-old dark-grown plants were less stable than those from 72 hr illuminated seedlings.   To avoid the complication of RNA turnover in our assays, we added heparin which has been previously shown to inhibit plastid RNAse activity.   Heparin does not alter

Table I Transcription activity of the plastid-encoded *psbD-psbC* transcription unit in dark-grown and illuminated barley seedlings of different age.

	Transcription Activity, cpm/spot			
	-Heparin		+Heparin[a]	
	I.	II.	III.	IV.
Treatment	5-min pulse	5-min pulse + 5-min chase	5-min pulse	5-min pulse + 5-min chase
4.5-days-dark	1953	1400	2822 ± 98	2792 ± 45
4.5-days-dark + 72-h-dark	524	248	1242 ± 182	1235 ± 313
4.5-days-dark + 72-h-light	905	792	1378 ± 79	1297 ± 227

Plastids were isolated from 4.5-day-old dark-grown seedlings or from 4.5-day-old dark-grown seedlings kept in darkness for an additional 72 h or illuminated for an additional 72 h. Lysed plastids were pulse-labeled for 5-min using [^{32}P]-UTP in the presence or absence of heparin. The 5-min labeling period was followed by a 5-min chase period using unlabeled UTP (1.5 mM). Run-on transcripts from 4.0 x 10^6 plastids were hybridized to dot blots of EcoRI-digested plasmid DNA (1 pmol) containing a 1.26 kbp EcoRI fragment from *psbD-psbC*. After hybridization, the blots were washed and exposed to X-ray film. The radioactive spots were then excised from the filter and counted in a scintillation counter.

[a]Each data point represents the mean of two observations ± SD.

transcription from previously initiated RNA polymerase (10). Incorporation of ^{32}P-UTP into *psbD-psbC* RNA during a 5 min pulse-labeling period in the presence of heparin was greater than in its absence (Table I, compare column II to III). Furthermore, RNA formed during the 5 min pulse-labeling period was stable during subsequent chases in the presence of heparin. Assays done in the presence of heparin showed that transcription of *psbD-psbC* was reduced 50% in 8 day-old plants which had been illuminated for 72 hrs relative to plastids from 4.5 day-old seedlings. In contrast, the level of *psbD-psbC* mRNA in these plastids was not reduced (11). Therefore, the *psbD-psbC* RNAs which accumulate in illuminated plants must be approximately 2-fold more stable than the *psbD-psbC* RNAs in 4.5 day-old dark-grown seedlings. Furthermore, we have previously shown that transcription of rDNA, *rbcL* and *psaA-psaB* decline 4 to 8-fold when 4.5 day-old dark-grown seedlings are illuminated for 72 hrs. *psbD-psbC* transcription declined only 2-fold during this period suggesting that differential transcription of *psbD-psbC* contributes to the maintenance of *psbD-psbC* mRNA levels in illuminated plants.

4. ACKNOWLEDGMENTS
This research was supported by an NIH grant to JEM. The authors thank Mrs. Sharyll Pressley for her help in preparing this manuscript.

REFERENCES
1. Mullet, J.E. (1988) Ann. Rev. Plant Physiol. Plant Mol. Biol. 39, 475-502.
2. Harpster, M. and Apel, K. (1985) Physiol. Plant. 64, 147-152.
3. Tobin, E.M. and Silverthorne, J. (1985) Ann. Rev. Plant Physiol. 36, 569-593.
4. Smith, H. (1970) Phytochem. 9, 965-975.
5. Robertson, D. and Laetsch, W.M. (1974) Plant Physiol. 54, 148-159.
6. Apel, K. and Kloppstech, K. (1978) Eur. J. Biochem. 85, 581-588.
7. Baumgartner, B.J., Rapp, J.C. and Mullet, J.E. (1988) Plant Physiol. 89, 1011-1018.
8. Klein, R.R. and Mullet, J.E. (1987) J. Biol. Chem. 262, 4341-4348.
9. Klein, R.R., Gamble, P.E. and Mullet, J.E. (1988) Plant Physiol. 88, 1246-1256.
10. Mullet, J.E. and Klein, R.R. (1987) EMBO J. 6, 1571-1579.
11. Gamble, P.E., Sexton, T.B. and Mullet, J.E. (1988) EMBO J. 7, 1289-1297.
12. Schuster, G., Timberg, R. and Ohad, I. (1988) Eur. J. Biochem. 177, 403-410.
13. Mattoo, A.K., Hoffman-Falk, H., Marder, J.B. and Edelman, M. (1984) Proc. Natl. Acad. Sci. USA 81, 1380-1384.
14. Ohad, I., Kyle, D.J. and Arntzen, C.J. (1984) J. Cell Biol. 99, 481-485.
15. Gamble, P.E. and Mullet, J.E. (1989) J. Biol. Chem. 264, 7236-7243.
16. Leto, K.J., Keresztes, A. and Arntzen, C.J. (1982) Plant Physiol. 69, 1450-1458.
17. Kuchka, M.R., Mayfield, S.P. and Rochaix, J.-D. (1988) EMBO J. 7, 319-324.
18. Jensen, K.H., Herrin, D.L., Plumley, F.G. and Schmidt, G.W. (1986) J. Cell Biol. 103, 1315-1325.
19. Gamble, P.E. and Mullet, J.E. (1989) EMBO J. 8 (in press).
20. Klein, R.R., Mason, H.S. and Mullet, J.E. (1988) J. Cell Biol. 106, 289-301.

MOLECULAR BASIS OF PLASTOME MUTATIONS AND THEIR EFFECTS ON PHOTOSYNTHESIS

Rudolf Hagemann

Department of Genetics, Section Biosciences
Martin-Luther-University,   Domplatz 1
Halle (Saale), DDR-4020   German Dem. Rep.

ORIGIN OF PLASTOME MUTATIONS

Plastome mutations have been found and used in genetic experiments since the beginning of this century (1). There are three sources of plastome mutations for the experimenter: spontaneous, experimentally induced by mutagens, and nuclear-gene induced.

Spontaneous mutations: Spontaneous plastome mutations have been isolated from many plants. The frequency of the occurrence of variegated plants which are due to spontaneous plastome mutations is in the range of 0,02 - 0,06 %; however, higher values have also been re-ported (2). There is no doubt, that the mutation rate of the plastome is higher than the frequency of variegated mutant plants, because the mutation in a plastid DNA molecule does certainly not lead in every case to a variegation of the plant.

Mutations induced by chemical mutagens: In flagellates (Euglena, Chlamydomonas) several chemical mutagens for plastome mutations are available (3) . However, it took a rather long time to find out chemical mutagens which in-duce plastome mutations in higher plants. Between 1969 and 1974 it was shown that treatment of Helianthus annuus (4) and Saintpaulia ionantha (5, 6) with nitrosomethyl-urea leads to the occurrence of variegated plants which are due to plastome mutations. These results led us to perform mutation experiments with three standard objects of plastid genetics: Antirrhinum majus, Oenothera hookeri and Lycopersicon esculentum. We could prove that N-nitro-so-N-methyl-urea (NMU) and N-nitroso-N-ethyl-urea (NEU) act as effective mutagens for the induction of plastome mutations in higher plants (7, 8, 9, 10). With NMU and NEU geneticists have now chemical compounds at hand which enable them to induce experimentally plastome mutations in a wide range of higher plants (comp. 11).

M. Baltscheffsky (ed.), Current Research in Photosynthesis, Vol. III, 429–436.
© 1990 *Kluwer Academic Publishers. Printed in the Netherlands.*

Nuclear-gene induced plastome mutations: This is a very
special type of mutations. The basic genetic phenomenon
is as follows: A recessive mutant of a nuclear gene induces in homozygous condition the rather frequent occurrence of plastome mutations which lead to cells and
plants containing genetically different types of plastids:
wild type plastids developing into normal green chloroplasts and mutant plastids, which become white, yellow or
pale/light green. The sorting out of wild type and mutant
plastids results in the occurrence of variegated (dicots)
or striped (monocots) plants according to the special mode
of leaf growth. When the plastome mutations were induced
by the nuclear mutant gene, then they are inherited in a
typical non-Mendelian, extranuclear mode: They show uniparental inheritance (in most species) or biparental inheritance (in a minority of species). Cases of nuclear-
gene induced plastome mutations have in particular been
studied intensively in Hordeum vulgare, Zea mays, Oenothera hookeri and Arabidopsis thaliana, altogether in 10
different genera of angiosperms both dicots and monocots
(12, 13, 14).

MOLECULAR BASIS OF PLASTOME MUTATIONS
During the past decade insights have been obtained into
the molecular changes which characterize plastome mutations. They comprise several types: single base-pair
substitutions, frame shift mutations, deletions of parts
of a gene or of a complete gene or even of large parts
of the plastid genome.
Missense mutations: Single site mutations, resulting in a
base-pair substitution, can cause missense or nonsense
codons. Many independent missense mutations leading to
amino acid substitutions have been found in several lines
of weed plants as well as in cultivated flagellates which
gained resistance to s-triazines, including the widely
used herbicide atrazine. In agricultural areas of North
America, Europe and the Near East atrazine resistant lines descended from (at least) 38 different weed species.
Moreover, atrazine resistance has been obtained in selection experiments from Chlamydomonas reinhardtii and Euglena gracilis (also from several cyanobacteria). Many
atrazine resistant strains have been investigated in detail. The results are as follows: The atrazine resistance
of all eukaryotic plants is inherited in a non-Mendelian,
extranuclear mode. The extranuclear mutations leading to
atrazine resistance are plastome mutations. The plastid
gene psbA coding for the D1 (= Q_B) protein of the photosystem II complex is the site of these plastome mutations
in all atrazine resistant plants, studied so far. Obviously in populations of weeds and experimental plants.

TABLE **1.** Resistance against atrazine and compar.compounds
Mutations in psbA causing amino acid substitutions in protein D1 (= Q_B) of photosystem II

Species	Position of amino acid	Amino acid substitution	Reference
Amaranthus hybridus	264	Ser - Gly	(15, 16)
Brassica campestris	264	Ser - Gly	(16)
Chenopodium album	264	Ser - Gly	(38)
Nicotiana tabacum	264	Ser - Thr	(39)
Phalaris paradoxa	264	Ser - Gly	(16)
	(+238	Arg - Lys)	
Poa annua	264	Ser - Ala	(40)
Solanum nigrum	264	Ser - Gly	(17, 18, 16)
Chlamydomonas			
reinhardtii DCMU4	264	Ser - Ala	(41, 16)
" DR2	219	Val - Ile	(41, 16)
" MZ2	251	Ala - Val	(41, 16)
" Ar207	255	Phe - Tyr	(41, 16)
" BR202	275	Leu - Phe	(41)
" BR24	256	Gly - Asp	(41)
Euglena gracilis	264 resp. 265	Ser - Ala	(42)
	264 resp. 265	Ser - Thr	(43)

Which are intensely and continuously treated with the
herbicide, spontaneous mutations in the psbA plastid gene
are selected, which confer resistance against atrazine.
These plastome mutations are base-pair substitutions
leading to a codon for another amino acid (missense). As
shown in Table 1 the most frequently found change in D1
is the amino acid substitution at the position of amino
acid No. 264. But in the course of time amino acid substitutions have also been detected at other positions
(219, 251, 255, 256, 275). In Amaranthus hybridus and Solanum nigrum the amino acid serine at position 264 of D1
was changed in the spontaneous atrazine resistant mutants
to glycine; this is due to a single-site transition
mutation in psbA, changing the codon AGT (for serine) into GGT (for glycine). The amino acid substitution in D1
of Chlamydomonas reinhardtii from serine to alanine at
position 264 is the result of a transversion mutation
changing the codon TCT (for serine) into GCT (for alanine)
(15, 16, 17, 18, 19). The fact, that so many spontaneous
mutants in the psbA gene have been found, is simply due
to the continuous treatment of weed plants with atrazine
or other s-triazines over large areas of agriculturally
used land; this produces a very strong selection pressure

in favour of these mutants.

However, missense mutations take place also in other plastid genes. In a uniparentally inherited plastome mutant of Chlamydomonas reinhardtii (10-6C) an amino acid substitution in the large subunit (LS) of ribulose-1,5-bisphosphate carboxylase/oxygenase (= rubisco) from glycine (GGT) to aspartic acid (GAT) was found (20). This is due to a transition mutation GC - AT in the rbcL plastid gene. The mutation generates a full-length LS subunit of rubisco, which leads to a nonfunctional assembled carboxylase. (The nomenclature of plastid genes is outlined in (44) and (45).)

Nonsense mutations: Single-site mutations in plastid DNA can also lead to nonsense codons. The result of such a mutation was analysed in Oenothera hookeri. The mutant "I sigma" arose spontaneously and is deficient in rubisco activity. Transcription-translation of plastid DNA or translation of plastid RNA of the mutant both gave rise to a large subunit of rubisco with a molecular weight of about 30,000, whereas that of the wild type is 52,000. The authors suggest a mutational lesion within the coding region of the rbcL plastid gene, which causes a premature termination of translation and thus a truncated protein (21). In Chlamydomonas reinhardtii the effects of two nonsense mutations in the rbcL gene for the large subunit of rubisco have been studied (22). The plastid mutants 18-5B and 18-7G contain nonsense mutations close to the 3' and 5' ends of rbcL respectively. The mutation 18-7G has an amber (TAG) codon instead of TGG (Try) in codon 66 and blocks the synthesis of LS already after 65 amino acids. Mutation 18-5B changes a TGG codon (Try) to TGA (opal) and causes the synthesis of a truncated protein of about 450 amino acids, which, however, is unstable and degrades. Thus a rubisco holoenzyme does not form.

Frame shift mutation: In Chlamydomonas reinhardtii the plastome mutant FUD26 proved to be a frame shift mutation in the psaB gene, caused by a 4 base pair deletion. This frame shift leads to a truncated CP1 apoprotein, because polypeptide synthesis is terminated 7 codons (amino acids) behind the deletion site (23).

Deletions and rearrangements: Larger mutational changes in plastid DNA have also been found. Myers et al. (24) reported the isolation of mutants of Chlamydomonas reinhardtii with physical alterations in their plastid DNA. After treatment with 5-fluorodeoxyuridine alone or in combination with X-rays 15 mutants with plastid DNA alterations were found. The mutant ac-u-c-2-43 lacks one inverted repeat almost completely including an entire set of plastidal ribosomal RNA genes. The most dramatic rearrangements and deletion in plastid DNA have been found as a consequence of anther culture or microspore culture.

For a very long time it was difficult and laborious to
get haploids from cereal anthers or microspores. Moreover,
the great majority of the regenerated haploids have been
albinos, and only few cereal haploids were green (25, 26).
Day and Ellis (27, 28, 29) studied the plastid DNA of
such white cereal haploids and came to the surprising
result that the plastid genome of such albino plants has
obviously undergone a series of gross DNA rearrangements,
most of which are deletions. For a particular barley
albino plant it was shown that the white plastids contain
a linear double-stranded DNA of only 21 kb with a hairpin
structure (29). Monomers and dimers of this molecule were
found. This result leads to the assumption that a deletion of (about) 100 kb of the wild-type plastid DNA of
barley gave rise to the monomeric deletion form. Obviously, the stress conditions of an anther culture are able
to cause drastic changes, DNA rearrangements and deletions, in the plastid DNA of the microspores treated.

EFFECTS OF PLASTOME MUTATIONS ON PHOTOSYNTHESIS
On the whole, there are three types of phenotypic effects, caused by plastid mutations: (1) deficiencies in
the light and the dark reactions of photosynthesis and/
or changes in the leaf colour (light green, yellow,
creme, or white leaves), (2) antibiotic resistances and
(3) herbicide resistances.

(a) Deficiencies in photosynthetic reactions
There are plastid mutations in lower and higher plants,
which cause deficiencies in photosystem I or in photosystem II. These mutations lead to a loss, a reduction
or a change of particular thylakoid proteins, which are
part of the complex for photosystem I or photosystem II.
Several plastome mutants with defects in photosystem I
have been described and characterized in higher plants
as well as in Chlamydomonas. These mutants have lost the
activity of photosystem I, and simultaneously the major
chlorophyll-protein complex 1 - CP1 - is lacking (mutant alba-1 of Antirrhinum majus /30/; mutant "Mrs.
Pollock" of Pelargonium zonale /31/ or is drastically
reduced (mutant C_1 of Chlamydomonas reinhardtii /32/).
In Chlamydomonas reinhardtii seven plastome mutations
conferring a deficiency in photosystem I reaction centers
have been characterized. They map at four plastid loci,
which are scattered around the plastid genome. Three
mutations in the psaB (= psaA2) gene result in the absence
of CP1-related polypeptides and thus in a deficiency in
photosynthesis. One of these mutations (FUD26) is a 4 base
pair deletion resulting in a frame shift and a premature
termination of the protein, which is a truncated CP1
apoprotein (23).

A plastome mutant with a deficient photosystem II has
been described in Antirrhinum majus (mutant viridis-1
/33/). The deficiency in photosystem II is correlated
with a loss and a reduction respectively of thylakoid
bands associated with photosystem II. Moreover, it
should be kept in mind that all the different atrazine
resistant mutants (listed in Table 1) have alterations
in the protein D1 (= Q_B), which is a constitutive part
of the photosystem II complex. Most of them have a reduced photosynthetic capacity.
On the other hand, a plastome mutant (thm-u-1) has been
found in Chlamydomonas reinhardtii, which has a variant
thylakoid protein (polypeptide 5' is about 1000 dalton
larger than its wild type counterpart 5) and nevertheless
a normal photosynthetic capacity (34). Mutations in the
plastid gene rbcL, coding for the LS of rubisco, lead to
missense and nonsense codons, as referred to in the
preceeding paragraphs. They result in the synthesis of
unstable or truncated polypeptides, which arte nonfunctional and thus block the dark reactions of photosynthesis.
In Chlamydomonas reinhardtii a great many antibiotic
resistances have been induced and studied, which are
inherited in a non-Mendelian uniparental mode (3). They
represent plastome mutations which alter the molecular
structure of plastidal ribosomal proteins or ribosomal
RNA. Not much information is available whether or to what
extent such plastome mutations influence the photosynthetic
capacity of the Chlamydomonas cells.

(b) Atrazine resistances
In many higher and lower plants atrazine resistant plastome mutants have been found (Table 1). In almost all of
these mutants (including the DCMU mutants in Chlamydomonas
reinhardtii) the resistant phenotype is accompanied by a
reduced photosynthetic capacity. The changes, found in
these mutants in comparison to wild type, have been summarized by Hirschberg et al. (16) from many references as
follows: slower electron transport from Q_A to Q_B; a lower
quantum yield of CO_2 reduction; changes in lipid composition of the plastid membranes; lower chlorophyll a/b ratio;
changes in chloroplast ultrastructure; reduced fitness, as
measured by accumulation of dry matter, seed germination
etc. The slower electron transport from Q_A to Q_B was detected even after six generations of backcrossing indicating that this is a pleiotropic effect of the plastome mutation leading to atrazine resistance (comp. 35, 36).
However, recently a triazine resistant biotype of hood
cannarygrass (Phalaris paradoxa) has been found in Israel,
which proved to be equal or even superior to the susceptible biotype for several photosynthetik and growth para-

meters (37). The resistant line of P.paradoxa differs from
susceptible plants in position 264 of D1: serine is substituted by glycine, as in many other species (Table 1).
But P.paradoxa has in position 238 of D1 lysine instead of
arginine (as found in all other higher plants and algae).
The authors discuss the hypothesis that lysine in position
238 may reduce the detrimental effects of the serine to
glycine substitution in 264 outlined above (16).
Taking all findings together, atrazine resistant biotypes
obviously have a high positive selection value under conditions of continous atrazine usage in agricultural areas.
But in the absence of atrazine and other triazines their
(mostly) reduced photosynthetic capacity diminishes their
superiority.

REFERENCES
1 Hagemann,R. (1964) Plasmat.Vererbung, Fischer, Jena
2 Maly,R. (1958) Zschr.f.Vererbungslehre 89, 692-696
3 Gillham,N.W.(1978) Organelle Heredity, Raven, New York
4 Beletski,Y.D., Razoriteleva, E.K., Zhdanov,Y.A. (1969)
  Dokl. Akad.Nauk SSSR 186, 1425-1426
5 Hentrich,W., Beger,B. (1974) Arch.Zücht.f.4, 29-43
6 Pohlheim,F., Beger,B. (1974) Biol.Rundsch.12, 204-206
7 Hagemann,R. (1976) in Genetics and Biogenesis of Chloroplasts and Mitochondria (Bücher,Th. et al., eds.) p.
  331-338, Elsevier/North Holland, Amsterdam
8 Hagemann,R. (1979) Stadler Genetics Symp. 11, 91-115
9 Hagemann,R. (1982) in Methods in Chloroplast Molec. Biology (Edelman et al. eds.) p.119-127, Elsevier Biomedical, Amsterdam
10 Hagemann,R., Lindenhahn,M. (1983) Proc. XV Internat.
  Congr.Genetics, New Delhi, Abstr.Contrib.Papers,Part I,
  293, Oxford & IBH Publ. Corp., New Delhi
11 Hosticka,L.P., Hanson,M.R.(1984) Hered.75, 242-246
12 Tiley-Bassett,R.A.E. (1975) in Genetics and Biogenesis
  of Mitochondria and Chloroplasts (Birky,C.W. et al.,
  eds.) p.268-308, Ohio State Univ. Press, Columbus
13 Hagemann,R., Scholz,F. (1972)Züchter (=TAG) 32, 50-59
14 Hagemann,R. (1986) in Regulation of Chloroplast Differentiation (Akoyunoglou,G. and Senger,H., eds.) p.
  455-466, A.R. Liss, New York
15 Hirschberg,J., Bleecker,A., Kyle,D.J., McIntosh,L.,
  Arntzen,C.J. (1984) Z. Naturforsch. 39c, 412-420
16 Hirschberg,J., Yehuda,A.B., Pecker,I., Ohad,N. (1988)
  in Plant Molecular Biology (v.Wettstein, D., Chua,N.H.,
  eds.) p.357-366. Plenum, New York
17 Edelman,M., Goloubinoff,P., Marder,J.B., Fromm,H., De-
  vic, M., Fluhr,R., Mattoo,A.K. (1985) in Molecular Form
  and Function of the Plant Genome (Van Vloten-Doting,L.
  et al., eds.) p.1-10. Plenum, New York
18 Goloubinoff,P., Edelman,M., Hallick,R.B. (1984) Nucl.

Acids Res. 12, 9489-9496
19 Erickson,J.M., Rahire,M., Bennoun,P., Delepelaire,P., Rochaix,J.D.(1984)Proc.Natl.Acad.Sci.USA 81, 3617-3621
20 Dron,M., Rahire,M., Rochaix,J.D.(1983)Plasmid 9,321-324
21 Hildebrandt,J., Bottomley,W., Moser,J., Herrmann,R.G. (1984) Biochim. Biophys. Acta 783, 67-73
22 Spreitzer,R.J., Goldschmidt-Clermont,M., Rahire,M., Rochaix,J.D.(1985) Proc.Natl.Acad.Sci.USA 82, 5460-5464
23 Girard-Bascou,J ., Choquet,Y., Schneider,M., Delosme,M., Dron,M. (1987) Current Genetics 12, 489-495
24 Myers,A.M., Grant,D.M., Rabert,D.K., Harris, E.H., Boynton,J.E., Gillham,N.W.(1982) Plasmid 7, 133-151
25 Hu,H.(1984) Proc.XV Internat.Congr.Genetics New Delhi, Genetics: New Frontiers.Vol.IV,77-84.Oxford & IBH
26 Wenzel,G., Hoffmann,F., Thomas,E. (1977) Theoret.Appl. Genetics 51, 81-86
27 Day,A., Ellis,T.H.N. (1984) Cell 39, 359-368
28 Day,A., Ellis,T.H.N. (1985) Current Genetics 9,671-678
29 Ellis,T.H.N., Day,A. (1986) EMBO Journ. 5, 2769-2774
30 Herrmann, F. (1971) FEBS Letters 19, 267-269
31 Herrmann, F., Matorin,D., Timofeev,T., Börner,T., Rubin,A.B., Hagemann,R. (1974) Biochem.Physiol.Pflanzen 165, 393-400
32 Bennoun,P., Girard,J., Chua,N.H. (1977) Molec.Gen. Genetics 153, 343-348
33 Herrmann,F. (1972) Exptl. Cell Res. 70, 452-453
34 Chua,N.H. (1976) in Genetics and Biogenesis of Chloroplasts and Mitochondria (Bücher,T. et al., eds.) p. 323-330, Elsevier/North Holland, Amsterdam
35 Gressel,J. (1985) in Molecular Form and Function of the Plant Genome (Van Vloten-Doting,L. et al., eds.) p. 489-504. Plenum, New York
36 Ireland,C.R., Telfer,A., Covello, P.S., Baker,N.R., Barber,J. (1988) Planta 173, 459-467
37 Schonfeld,M., Yaacoby,T., Michael,O., Rubin,B. (1987) Plant Physiol. 83, 329-333
38 Bettini,P., McNally,S., Sevignac,M., Darmency,H., Gasquez,J., Dron,M. (1987) Plant Physiol. 84, 1442-1446
39 Sato,F., Shigematsu,Y., Yamada,Y. (1988) Molec.Gen. Genetics 214, 358-360
40 Barros,M.D.C., Dyer,T.A. (1988) Theor. Appl. Genetics 75, 610-616
41 Rochaix,J.D., Erickson,J. (1988) Trends Biochem. Sci. (TIBS) 13, 56-59
42 Johanningmeier,U., Hallick,R.B. (1987) Current Genetics 12, 465-470
43 Aiach,A., Ohmann,E., Johanningmeier,U.(1989) Pers.Comm.
44 Hagemann,R., Hagemann,M.M., Metzlaff,M.(1985) Progress in Botany 47, 208-228. Springer, Berlin Heidelberg
45 Hagemann,R., Hagemann,M.M., Metzlaff,M. (1987) Progress in Botany 49, 245-263. Springer, Berlin Heidelberg

STRUCTURE AND EXPRESSION OF THE CHLOROPLAST AND NUCLEAR GENES OF THE SUBUNITS OF PHOTOSYSTEM I IN CHLAMYDOMONAS REINHARDTII

J.D. ROCHAIX, L.G. FRANZEN, L. CARNOT, M. GOLDSCHMIDT-CLERMONT, Y. CHOQUET, J. GIRARD-BASCOU[+] and P. BENNOUN[+], Departments of Molecular Biology and Plant Biology, University of Geneva, 1211 Geneva 4, Switzerland; [+]Institut de Biologie Physico-chimique, 75005 Paris, France.

INTRODUCTION

Photosystem I (PSI) is one of the major complexes of the photosynthetic chloroplast electron transport chain. This multimolecular complex consists of at least three subunits I_A, I_B and an 8-9KDa protein encoded by the chloroplast genes psaA, psaB and psaC and of several nuclear encoded subunits whose number and size appear to vary between organisms. In the green unicellular alga Chlamydomonas reinhardtii these nuclear encoded subunits are called P20, P21, P28, P30, P35 and P37. P20, P21, P30 and P35 correspond to subunits II, III, IV and V of spinach as defined by Bengis and Nelson (1, cf. Table 1 for the correspondance between the C. reinhardtii and higher plant PSI subunits). PSI catalyzes the light-driven electron transfer from plastocyanin to ferredoxin (for review cf. ref. 2,3). Absorption of light by PSI results in an electron transfer from the reaction center chlorophyll P700 to the electron acceptors A_0, A1 and the iron-sulfur centers X, B and A. While P700 is reduced by plastocyanin, the electron on the PSI acceptor side is transferred to ferredoxin. The two larger chloroplast encoded subunits I_A and I_B appear to bind P700 and the first electron acceptors Ao and A1 and FeS_X. The chloroplast encoded 8-9 KDa subunit has been identified as an iron-sulfur protein and it is likely that it binds the iron centers A and B.

The function of the nuclear encoded subunits of PSI is not yet known. Recently the sequences of cDNA clones encoding several of these PSI subunits have been reported: subunit II (20-22KDa) from spinach (4) and tomato (5), subunits III, IV and V from spinach (6,7) and a 10.8KDa polypeptide from barley (8). Removal of subunit III (corresponding to P21 in C. reinhardtii) blocks, the electron transfer from plastocyanin to P700 (1) and a 19kDa subunit (subunit III)

M. Baltscheffsky (ed.), Current Research in Photosynthesis, Vol. III, 437–444.

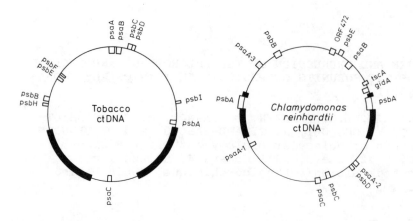

FIGURE 1. Arrangement of PSII and PSI genes on the chloroplast genomes of tobacco (13) and C. reinhardtii (22). The two dark segments indicate the chloroplast ribosomal inverted repeats. Genes that are transcribed clockwise and anticlockwise are depicted as inside and outside boxes, respectively. The direction of transcription of genes marked with centrally located boxes has not yet been determined in C. reinhardtii. psaA-1, psaA-2 and psaA-3 refer to the three exons of psaA. The product of tscA is involved in psaA exon 1-exon 2 splicing.

has recently been identified as the plastocyanin binding subunit (9).

We have examined the structure and expression of the chloroplast and nuclear genes of PSI in C. reinhardtii. Because photosynthetic function is dispensable when this alga is grown on acetate medium, mutants deficient in PSI activity can be isolated readily. We have used these mutants for studying the cooperation of the nuclear and chloroplast genomes in the assembly of the PSI complex.

RESULTS

Genes of chloroplast encoded PSI subunits

The sequences of the genes psaA and psaB encoding subunits I_A and I_B have been reported by Kück et al. (10). A surprising feature is that the psaA gene of C. reinhardtii is split into three parts that are widely separated on the chloroplast genome (fig. 1). The identities between the amino acid sequences of I_A and I_B from C. reinhardtii and

Table 1. Correspondance between PSI subunits

C. reinhardtii	spinach	pea	barley
P20	II (162, 179)	21kDa	18kDa
P21 (165,17.9)	III (154,17.3)	17	
P28 (100,11)		11	9.5
P30 (73,8.1)	IV (91,97)	13	16(101,10.8)
P35 (96,10)	V (98,10.8)	9	
P37 (87,8.4)			

All subunits indicated from C. reinhardtii (except P20) and spinach have been fully sequenced via cDNA cloning (6,7, 14, 15). The same is true for the 16kDa protein of barley (8). Subunits III and IV of spinach (formerly called subunits IV and III) have been redesignated (R.G. Herrmann, personal communication). Numbers in parenthesis indicate the number of amino acids and the real molecular mass. The other barley and pea subunits have been partially sequenced (16,19).

higher plants are 83 and 84% respectively. We have recently localized the psaC gene of C. reinhardtii on the chloroplast EcoRI fragment R23 using as probe a 42 nucleotide oligonucleotide derived from the tobacco psaC gene (kindly provided by Dr. M. Sugiura). This probe hybridizes to a 1.1 kb Sau 3A fragment of R23. Partial sequencing of this fragment provided the sequence of the C. reinhardtii psaC gene. This gene encodes a polypeptide of 81 amino acids with a sequence identity of 86 and 89% to its counterparts in tobacco and liverwort. This polypeptide resembles bacterial-type ferredoxins and contains 2 related clusters of 4 cysteine residues each that appear to bind the 2 (4Fe-4S) centers A and B of PSI (11,12).

It is apparent from fig. 1 that the organization of the PSI genes on the chloroplast genome is quite different between C. reinhardtii and higher plants. Note in particular the continuous organization of the psaA and psaB genes on the tobacco chloroplast genome and their dispersion in C. reinhardtii. This difference in organization has already been noticed previously with the genes of the PSII subunits (fig. 1).

```
P21
DIAGLTPCSE  SKAYAKLEKK  ELKTLEKRLK  QYEADSAPAV  ALKATMERTK  ARFANYAKAG
LLCGNDGLPH  LIADPGLALK  YGHAGEVFIP  TFGFLYVAGY  IGYVGRQYLI  AVKGEAKPTD
KEIIIDVPLA  TKLAWQGAGW  PLAAVQELQR  GTLLEKEENI  TVSPR

P28
KYGENSRYFD  LQDMENTTGS  WDMYGVDEKK  RYPDNQAKFF  TQATDIISRR  ESLRALVALS
GIAAIVTYGL  KGAKDADLPI  TKGPQTTGEN  GKGGSVRSRL

P30
EEVKAAPKKE  VGPKRGSLVK  ILRPESYWFN  QVGKVVSVDQ  SGVRYPVVVR  FENQNYAGVT
TNNYALDEVV  AAK

P35
ALDPQIVISG  STAAFLAIGR  FVFLGYQRRE  ANFDSTVGPK  TTGATYFDDL  QKNSTIFATN
DPAGFNIIDV  AGWGALGHAV  GFAVLAINSL  QGANLS

P37
DGFIGSSTNL  IMVASTTATL  AAARFGLAPT  VKKNTTAGLK  LVDSKNSAGV  ISNDPAGFTI
VDVLAMGAAG  HGLGVGIVLG  LKGIGAL
```

FIGURE 2. Sequences of five nuclear encoded PSI subunits from C. reinhardtii. Amino acids that are conserved in the corresponding subunits of spinach (P21, P30, P35; 6,7) and pea (N terminus of P28; 16) are darkened.

Nuclear encoded PSI subunits

To isolate cDNA clones encoding the other subunits of PSI we have purified these subunits and determined their N terminal amino acid sequences (14,15). Using the highly biased codon usage of C. reinhardtii nuclear genes, corresponding oligo-nucleotides were constructed and used as probes to isolate clones from a C. reinhardtii cDNA library. This allowed us to isolate full-length cDNA clones of the PSI subunits P21, P28, P30, P35 and P37 and to determine their sequences (14,15, fig. 2). P21 is 56% homologous to subunit III of spinach (6,14). The latter corresponds to the sequence published under the name "subunit IV" (R.G. Herrmann, personal communication). The overall amino acid sequence of P21 suggests that it is an extrinsic subunit. Based on its 63 aminoacid bipartite transit peptide typical for nuclear encoded lumenal proteins P21 appears to be localized on the lumen side of the thylakoid membrane (14, Table I). These data are compatible with the idea that subunit III is involved in the electron transfer from plastocyanin to P700 (1). There is a 69% identity in the 62 C-terminal residues of P30 with the corresponding part of the barley 16 kDa PSI subunit

(8,14). The N termini of these algal and higher plant
subunits are not conserved. It appears from its short basic
transit peptide and from its overall amino acid composition
that P30 is an extrinsic subunit located on the stromal
side of the thylakoid membrane. Similar conclusions can
also be reached for P28 and P35 (15). P28 is related to the
11kDa subunit of PSI from pea(16) whereas P35 corresponds
to subunit V of spinach PSI (7) and to the 9kDa subunit of
pea (16). The identity between P35 and subunit V of spinach
is only 35%, considerably less than the identity of P21 and
P30 with the corresponding higher plant subunits. No PSI
subunit related to P37 has yet been reported. Analysis of
its sequence and hydropathic profile suggests that it may
contain one membrane spanning domain (15). Southern
hybridizations of nuclear DNA with the cDNAs of P21, P28,
P30, P35 and P37 indicate that these subunits are encoded
by single copy genes (14, 15).

The function of the nuclear encoded PSI subunits is still
unknown. Mutants affected in the synthesis of these
subunits could provide valuable insights into this problem.
We have therefore screened 58 PSI mutants by Northern
hybridization using the cDNAs of P21, P28, P30, P35 and P37
as probes. No significant change in the transcript levels
of any of these subunits was found. A similar approach with
nuclear PSII mutants has identified mutations affecting the
transcription and/or stabilization of the mRNAs of the PSII
OEE1 and OEE2 proteins (17,18). One possibility is that the
absence of one of these nuclear encoded PSI subunits still
allows for partial PSI activity. Mutants of this sort would
be leaky in contrast to the mutants screened which were all
completely deficient in PSI activity. Another possibility
is that some of the mutants are affected at the
translational level. Antibodies against the individual
polypeptides are required to test this hypothesis.

Maturation of psaA mRNA depends on numerous nuclear encoded factors and on at least one chloroplast encoded factor

The three exons of psaA are far apart on the chloroplast
genome of C. reinhardtii with exon 1 and exon 2 oriented in
opposite direction (10,20, fig. 1). This rules out that the
psaA mRNA could result from the processing of a large
continuous chloroplast transcript. The data strongly
suggest that this mRNA results from two trans-splicing
reactions that fuse the transcripts of exon 1 and exon 2
and those of exon 2 and exon 3.

Analysis of several PSI mutants has revealed surprisingly
that about one quarter are affected in psaA mRNA

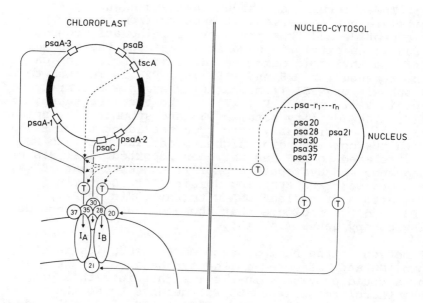

FIGURE 3. Scheme of PSI biosynthesis in C. reinhardtii. The chloroplast envelope is shown as a vertical double line that separates the chloroplast from the nucleo-cytosolic compartment. The chloroplast genome is shown as a circle with the two segments of the ribosomal inverted repeat shown as dark boxes. The chloroplast PSI genes psaA (split into the three exons psaA-1, psa A-2 and psA-3) psaB and psaC are indicated with open boxes. Their transcripts are translated on chloroplast ribosomes (T) and the products are inserted into the thylakoid membrane (marked with down ward arrows). The product of tscA is involved in psaA exon 1- exon2 trans-splicing. psa20, psa28, psa30, psa35 and psa37 and psa21 are nuclear PSI genes. Their transcripts are translated on cytoplasmic ribosomes (T) and the products are imported into the chloroplast. P21 appears to be localized on the lumenal side of the thylakoid membrane and has to cross therefore the thylakoid membrane. psa r1...rn denote nuclear genes whose products are involved in psa mRNA maturation and psaA and psaB mRNA translation.

production. These mutants can be grouped into three distinct classes based on the psaA mRNA precursors they accumulate (20). Class A mutants are affected in exon 2 exon 3 splicing, class C in exon 1 exon 2 splicing and class B mutants are deficient in both splicing reactions. Class A and B include only nuclear mutants while class C contains both nuclear and chloroplast mutants. These mutations appear to be specific for psaA splicing since other interrupted chloroplast genes such as psbA and the 23SrRNA genes produce wild-type levels of mature transcripts. A large number of nuclear complementation groups appear to be involved in the psaA splicing reactions: at least 5 for class A, 2 for class B and 6 for class C. These are only minimal estimates and it is likely that the real numbers are considerably higher.

The chloroplast PSI mutants FuD3 and H13 have the phenotype of class C mutants. Similar mutants were first described by Roitgrund and Mets (21) who noticed that their mutants had deletions removing part of the EcoRI fragment R12 and the adjacent chloroplast DNA region. We have also found deletions in the same region in the mutants FuD3 and H13 which are accompanied by large duplications of one chloroplast single copy region.

By bombarding these mutants in a particle gun with tungsten particles coated with DNA from a plasmid containing the R12 fragment we have been able to restore the photosynthetic activity of the mutants. These results indicate that the R12 fragment codes for a factor that is required for the splicing reaction of exon 1 and exon 2 transcripts. Whether this factor is a protein or an RNA remains to be seen.

CONCLUSIONS

The picture which emerges from these studies is that of a highly complex regulatory network between the chloroplast and nucleocytosolic compartments. (fig. 3). The number of nuclear factors involved in the expression of the two larger PSI subunits is impressive. At least 2 nuclear complementation groups are involved in the translation of the product of psaB and more than 13 nuclear genes and one chloroplast gene are required for psaA mRNA maturation. It is remarkable that these mutations appear to act specifically on the expression of one single chloroplast gene. The synthesis of other chloroplast gene products is unaffected in these mutants. A challenging task will be to identify the nuclear encoded factors defined by these mutations and to determine how they interact with the chloroplast.

ACKNOWLEDGEMENTS

We thank O. Jenni and F. Ebener for drawings and photography. This work was supported by grant 3.328-086 from the Swiss National Foundation.

REFERENCES

1 Bengis, C. and Nelson, N. (1977) J. Biol. Chem. 252, 4564-4569.
2 Malkin, R. (1987) in Topics in Photosynthesis (Barber, J., ed.) Vol. 8, pp. 495-525. Elsevier, Amsterdam.
3 Knaff, D.B. (1988) Trends Biochem. Sci. 13, 460-461.
4 Lagoutte, B. (1988) FEBS Lett. 232, 275-280.
5 Hoffman, N.E., Pickersky, E., Malik, V.S., Ko, K. and Cashmore, A.R. (1988) Plant Mol. Biol. 10, 435-445.
6 Münch, S., Ljungberg, U., Steppuhn., Schneiderbauer, A., Nechustai, R., Begreuther, K. and Herrmann, R.G. (1988) Curr. Genet. 14, 511-518.
7 Steppuhn, J., Hermans, J., Nechustai, R., Ljungberg, U., Thümmler, F., Lottspeich, F. and Herrmann, R.G. (1988) FEBS Lett. 218-224.
8 Okkels, J.S., Jepsen, L.B., Honberg, L.S., Lehmbeck, J., Scheller, H.V., Brandt, P., Hoyer-Hansen, G., Stummann, B., Henningson, K.W., von Wettstein, D. and Moller, B.L. (1988) FEBS Lett. 237, 108-112.
9 Wynn, R.M. and Malkin, R. (1988) Biochemistry 27, 5863-5869.
10 Kück, U., Choquet, Y., Schneider, M., Dron, M. and Bennoun, P. (1987) EMBO J. 6, 2185-2195.
11 Hoj, P.B., Svendsen, I., Scheller, H.V. and Lindberg Moller, B. (1987) J. Biol. Chem. 262, 12676-12684.
12 Oh-oka, H., Takahashi, Y., Wada, K., Matsubara, H., Ohyama, K. and Ozeki, H. (1987) FEBS Lett 218, 52-54.
13 Sugiura, M. (1987) Bot. Mag. Takyo 100, 407-436.
14 Franzén, L.G., Frank, G., Zuber, H. and Rochaix, J.D. (1989) Plant Mol. Biol. 12, 463-474.
15 Franzén, L.G., Frank, H., Zuber, H. and Rochaix, J.D. (1989) Molec. Gen. Genet. in press.
16 Dunn, P.P.J., Packman, L.C., Pappin, D. and Gray, J.C. (1988) FEBS Lett 228, 157-161.
17 Mayfield, S.P., Rahire, M., Frank, G. Zuber, H. and Rochaix, J.D. (1987) Proc. Natl. Acad. Sci. USA 84, 749-753.
18 Mayfield, S.P., Bennoun, P. and Rochaix, J.D. (1987) EMBO J. 6, 313-318.
19 Scheller, H.V., Hoj, P.B., Svendsen, I. and Moller, B.L. (1988) Biochem. Biophys. Acta 933, 501-505.
20 Choquet, Y., Goldschmidt-Clermont, M., Girard-Bascou, J. Kück, U., Bennoun, P. and Rochaix, J.D. (1988) Cell 52, 903-913.
21 Roitgrund, C. and Mets, L. (1988) Abstracts of Cell and Molec. Biology of Chlamydomonas. Cold Spring Harbor p. 34.
22 Rochaix, J.D. (1978) J. Mol. Biol. 126, 597-617.

REGULATION OF CYANOBACTERIAL GENE FAMILIES ENCODING PROTEINS OF PHOTOSYSTEM II

Susan S. Golden[1], Michael R. Schaefer[2], Silvia A. Bustos[1], Mark S. Nalty[1], and Dan-Sung C. Cho[1], Dept. of Biology[1] and Dept. of Biochemistry[2], Texas A&M University, College Station, TX, 77843 USA

Introduction

The genes *psbA* and *psbD*, which encode the photosystem II reaction center proteins D1 and D2, respectively, are unique genes in the chloroplast genomes of most plants. However, in cyanobacteria both genes are present as small multigene families. The three *psbA* genes of the cyanobacterium *Synechococcus* sp. strain PCC 7942 (also called *Anacystis nidulans* R2) encode two forms of D1 which differ primarily in their amino terminal amino acid sequences (1). This organism also has two *psbD* genes, designated *psbDI* and *psbDII*, which predict an identical D2 polypeptide (2). The *psbDI* gene, like chloroplast *psbD* genes, overlaps the open reading frame of *psbC*, the gene encoding the photosystem II CP43 protein (2). We are studying the photosystem II complex of *Synechococcus* at the level of regulation of the *psbA* and *psbD* gene families and expression of their protein products. A major goal is to identify the regulatory signals that modulate transcription and translation of the *psbA* and *psbD* genes in response to changes in the growth environment.

I. The three *psbA* genes respond differently to changes in light availability.

The *Synechococcus psbA* genes are highly conserved and share many restriction enzyme sites, although *psbAI* encodes a polypeptide (form I of D1) that differs at 25 of 360 amino acids from the product of *psbAII* and *psbAIII* (form II of D1) (Fig. 1). We have taken advantage of a common restriction site and the clustering of amino acid changes between the two forms at the amino termini of the proteins to construct translational gene fusions that served two functions in these studies: as *in vivo* reporters of *psbA* expression (3), and as a source of hybrid proteins carrying D1 form-specific antigen domains (4).

The gene fusions were made by ligating the *Escherichia coli lacZ* gene in frame at a conserved *Bst*EII site at amino acid 20 of each *psbA* open reading frame (Fig. 1). Each gene fusion was recombined into the chromosome of wild-type *Synechococcus* such that the resulting reporter strain had a specific *psbA* reporter gene and a full complement of wild-type *psbA* genes.

M. Baltscheffsky (ed.), Current Research in Photosynthesis, Vol. III, 445–451.

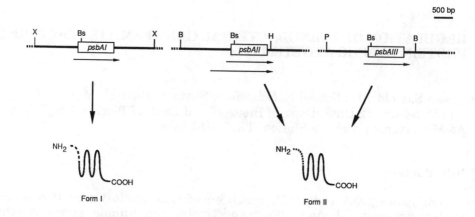

Figure 1. The *psbA* gene family of *Synechococcus* encodes two forms of the D1 protein. Open boxes indicate open reading frames of each of the *psbA* genes. Heavy solid lines represent flanking chromosomal DNA. The relative order and orientation of the genes, which are not closely linked on the chromosome, are depicted arbitrarily. Key restriction sites used for analysis are shown for the enzymes *Bam*HI (B), *Bst*EII (Bs), *Hin*dIII (H), *Pst*I (P), and *Xho*I (X). Wavy lines in the lower part of the figure represent the gene products; they are depicted with broken lines at the amino termini, emphasizing the distinctive domains between the two forms of D1.

Assays of β-galactosidase activity from the reporter strains showed that *psbAI* expression was much higher than that of other *psbA* genes, consistent with previous measurements of steady-state message levels (1). The *psbAI* reporter strain also showed higher expression in cells grown at lower light intensity (<50 $\mu E \cdot m^{-2} \cdot s^{-1}$) than in those exposed to higher light (>100 $\mu E \cdot m^{-2} \cdot s^{-1}$).

Time course experiments were performed in which large volume cultures were inoculated at low cell density and allowed to mature at a constant illumination of approximately 600 $\mu E \cdot m^{-2} \cdot s^{-1}$. As the cells divided, light penetrating the culture dropped continuously, until the light reaching the interior of the culture was approximately 5 $\mu E \cdot m^{-2} \cdot s^{-1}$. At intervals during culture growth, light intensity was measured at the center of the culture and β-galactosidase activity was assayed (Fig. 2). The *psbAI* reporter strain had its lowest level of β-galactosidase activity soon after the culture was inoculated, when light penetration was still high, and β-galactosidase activity continued to increase as the culture aged and light penetration decreased. Conversely, *psbAII* and *psbAIII* reporters showed significant β-galactosidase activity only in the first 24 hours and dropped to a low constant level when light reached ≤ 100 $\mu E \cdot m^{-2} \cdot s^{-1}$.

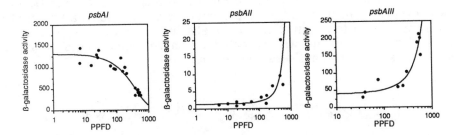

Figure 2. Expression of *psbA-lacZ* reporter genes as a function of light availability. Eight-liter cultures of each of the *psbA-lacZ* reporter strains were illuminated at a constant PPFD of 600 $\mu E \cdot m^{-2} \cdot s^{-1}$ and the light at the interior of the culture was measured at time points during the development of the culture. Samples of cells were collected at each point and assayed for β-galactosidase activity, which was plotted versus the light reading at the time of sampling. β-Galactosidase activity is expressed as specific activity (nmol ONPG·min^{-1}·mg protein^{-1}).

Experiments in which duplicate cultures were illuminated at different light intensities indicated that the observed *psbAI* reporter gene activities correlated with light availability and not with culture density or age; activity was higher in a culture illuminated at 250 $\mu E \cdot m^{-2} \cdot s^{-1}$ than in one illuminated at 500 $\mu E \cdot m^{-2} \cdot s^{-1}$, even though the cells grew faster at the higher light.

II. The ratio of the two forms of D1 in thylakoids changes at different light intensities as predicted by reporter genes.

The translational gene fusions to *psbAI* and *psbAIII* produced hybrid proteins containing the amino terminal regions of form I and form II of D1, respectively, attached to β-galactosidase (4). These proteins were expressed in *E. coli*, purified by anti-β-galactosidase affinity chromatography, and used to raise rabbit antisera that distinguished between the two forms of D1. Thylakoids were isolated from wild-type cells at time points representing different culture light environments as described above. Western analysis using the form-specific D1 antisera showed that the ratio of the forms in the thylakoid is altered among samples harvested at different light intensities, as predicted by reporter gene activities (Fig. 3). Form I was present in all samples, but was most abundant at lower light intensities. Form II was barely detectable in samples from light intensities below 100 $\mu E \cdot m^{-2} \cdot s^{-1}$, but was relatively abundant in the high-light samples; the autoradiogram detecting D1 form II was exposed longer than the other panels to detect the small amount of form II present at low light. Neither the absolute amounts nor the absolute ratios of the two forms was revealed by these experiments, since the sensitivities of the two antisera may differ.

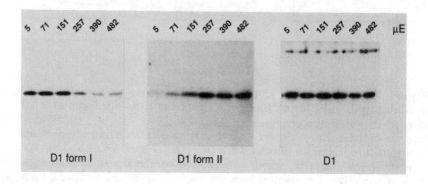

Figure 3. Changes in the ratio of the two forms of D1 in response to decreasing light availability. An 8-liter culture of wild-type cells was illuminated at a constant PPFD of 600 $\mu E \cdot m^{-2} \cdot s^{-1}$ and the light at the interior of the culture was measured at time points during the development of the culture. Samples of cells were collected at each point and thylakoid membranes were extracted. Solubilized membrane proteins (80μg) from each sample were separated by LiDS polyacrylamide gel electrophoresis, transferred to nitrocellulose membranes, and reacted with antisera directed against form I, form II or (combined) D1 as indicated. Each lane is marked with a number representing the light intensity, in $\mu E \cdot m^{-2} \cdot s^{-1}$, inside the culture at the time point used to prepare the sample in that lane.

III. Changes in *psbA* gene expression occur within a few minutes of transfer to different light environments.

The experiments described above measured changes in *psbA* expression over a period of several days. Although the *lacZ* reporter genes proved very useful in these analyses, the assayed product, β-galactosidase, is relatively stable; thus rapid changes involving decreases in reporter gene expression are difficult to detect with the gene fusions. To determine whether *psbA* gene expression changes rapidly in response to light, samples of wild-type cells from a culture receiving 125 $\mu E \cdot m^{-2} \cdot s^{-1}$ of light were transferred to conditions of 500, 250, 125, or 50 $\mu E \cdot m^{-2} \cdot s^{-1}$, and incubated for 5, 15, or 30 minutes. Total RNA extracted from the samples was subjected to gel electrophoresis and transferred to nylon membranes for Northern analysis. Gene-specific antisense RNA probes were used to detect the messages from each of the *psbA* genes.

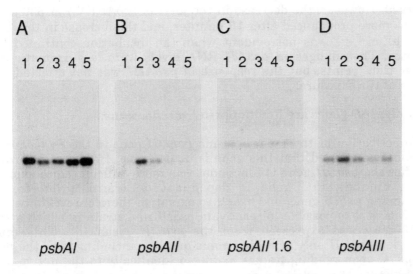

Figure 4. Rapid response of *psbA* message levels to changes in light intensity. Cells adapted to 125 μE·m^{-2}·s^{-1} of light were transferred to conditions of 500, 250, 125, or 50 μE·m^{-2}·s^{-1}, and incubated for 5 minutes. RNA was extracted from each sample, separated by agarose gel electrophoresis, transferred to charged nylon membranes, and probed with radiolabeled antisense RNAs specific for each transcript. Lanes contain RNA from cells in the original culture (lane 1) or from samples shifted to light intensities (in μE·m^{-2}·s^{-1}) of 500 (lane 2), 250 (lane 3), 125 (lane 4), or 50 (lane 5). Replicate blots were probed for the 1.2 kb transcripts from *psbAI* (panel A), *psbAII* (panel B),or *psbAIII* (panel D), or for an additional *psbAII* transcript that originates 400 nucleotides upstream of the 1.2 kb message (panel C).

Northern blots indicated changes in abundance of *psbA* transcripts after only 5 minutes of incubation at a light intensity different from that to which the cells were previously adapted (Fig. 4). The *psbAI* message level (panel A) dropped slightly after transfer to higher light intensities (lanes 2 and 3) and increased after transfer to lower light (lane 5). However, the *psbAII* message (panel B) was barely detectable in the control culture maintained at 125 μE·m^{-2}·s^{-1} (lane 1) but increased significantly after transfer to 500 μE·m^{-2}·s^{-1} (lane 2) or, to a lesser extent, to 250 μE·m^{-2}·s^{-1} (lane 3). A very low abundance messenger RNA that includes the *psbAII* open reading frame, but originates 400 bases further upstream than that shown in panel B, showed no response to changes in light intensity (panel C). The *psbAIII* message (panel D) showed the same pattern of expression as that of *psbAII*, except that the changes were less pronounced (panel D compared with panel B). When the incubations following the light shifts were extended to 15 or 30 minutes, the same general patterns were observed. However, the decrease in the level of *psbAI* RNA at 500 μE·m^{-2}· s^{-1} was more pronounced after 15 minutes, and the increase in this species at 50 μE·m^{-2}·s^{-1} was not evident when the incubation continued for 30 minutes. The changes in *psbAII* RNA levels were less dramatic at the longer time points, but the response of *psbAIII* was not affected by the length of the exposure.

IV. Both *psbD* genes are functional in *Synechococcus*.

Inactivation of the monocistronic *psbDII* gene in the *Synechococcus* chromosome showed that this gene is dispensable. However, determining whether the *psbDII* gene is functional was more difficult, since expression of the unique *psbC* gene is dependent on transcription from the overlapping *psbDI* gene, and *psbDI* inactivation therefore would be lethal. However, it was possible to inactivate *psbDI* in a strain in which a second *psbC* gene was expressed from the *psbDII* locus (5). This mutant expressed *psbDII* only as a dicistronic message including both the *psbDII* and *psbC* open reading frames arranged identically to the native *psbDI-psbC* operon.

Inactivation of the *psbDI* gene in the genetic background having two copies of *psbC* resulted in an increased steady-state level of message from the *psbDII-psbC* artificial operon (5). However, the increase in this message did not fully compensate for loss of the *psbDI* operon; the absolute level of *psbD-psbC* transcripts was still much lower than in wild-type cells. Although the *psbDI*-inactivated mutant grew well in liquid cultures, it consistently formed abnormally small colonies on plates even in the absence of antibiotics used to select the *psbC* duplication and *psbDI* inactivation events. When grown together with wild-type cells, or with other mutants in which the *psbDI-psbC* operon was active, the *psbDI*-inactivated strain was underrepresented in the population after several generations, indicating that it is less fit than the other strains. Analysis of thylakoid membranes from this mutant and other strains indicated that the *psbDI*-inactivated mutant had decreased amounts of both D2 and CP43 relative to strains having a wild-type *psbDI-psbC* operon (5).

V. How do photosystem II genes alter their expression in response to changes in the environment?

The experiments described above indicated that photosystem II genes alter their expression in response to environmental cues. In the *psbA* gene family, the genes respond to changes in light intensity; whether light is the direct stimulus is not addressed by the current experiments. Some evidence suggests that the transduction pathway is indirect, *i.e.* that the genes are signalled to alter expression by sensing changes in photosynthetic activity. Inactivation of one or more of the *psbA* genes affects the pattern of light response of the other related genes, even though the promoters and presumptive regulatory regions of the inactivated genes are still present (M. Schaefer *et al.*, this volume). The increase in *psbDII-psbC* messenger RNA level following inactivation of *psbDI* also suggests that deficiency in an essential photosystem II protein, and limited photosynthesis, can signal a gene to be up-regulated. This is also supported by experiments reported by Brusslan and Haselkorn (6), in which the photosystem II-inhibiting herbicide diuron enhanced the steady-state levels of transcripts from *psbDII* and the *psbA* genes. Elucidation of the molecular mechanisms that mediate environmental signal transduction to the photosystem II genes will be the major goal of our future experiments.

References

1 Golden, S.S., Brusslan, J. and Haselkorn, R. (1986) EMBO J. 5, 2789-2798
2 Golden, S.S. and Stearns, G. (1988) Gene 67, 85-96
3 Schaefer, M.R. and Golden, S.S. (1989) J. Bacteriol. 171, 3973-3981
4 Schaefer, M.R. and Golden, S.S. (1989) J. Biol. Chem. 264, 7412-7417
5 Golden, S.S., Cho, D-S.C. and Nalty, M.S. (1989) J. Bacteriol., in press
6 Brusslan, J.A and Haselkorn, R. (1989) EMBO J. 8, 1237-1245

LOCALIZATION OF THE *Rhodobacter capsulatus bchCA* OPERON OXYGEN-REGULATED PROMOTER

Cheryl L. Wellington[1], John J. Priatel[1], and J. Thomas Beatty[1, 2], Departments of Microbiology[1] and Medical Genetics[2], University of British Columbia, Room 300, 6174 University Boulevard, Vancouver, B.C., Canada, V6T 1W5.

1. INTRODUCTION

A distinguishing feature of the non-sulfur purple phototrophic bacteria is their ability to use anaerobic photosynthesis as a means of generating the energy required for growth. In addition to their photosynthetic capability, these Gram-negative organisms are often equipped with alternative mechanisms for ATP synthesis. In particular, the species *Rhodobacter capsulatus* is capable of five distinct modes of growth, making it one of the most metabolically versatile of living cells (1). This degree of metabolic flexibility among some members of the photosynthetic bacteria immediately raises the question of how these cells sense their surroundings and adjust their metabolism in order to fully exploit the potential of the environment.

The most obvious metabolic change these bacteria undergo is a dramatic increase in pigmentation as the cells switch from aerobic chemotrophic growth to photosynthetic growth. In a typical aerobic batch culture growing chemoheterotrophically, O_2 tension decreases steadily as a result of respiratory consumption. When O_2 tension drops below a threshold level of approximately 2% pO_2 (2), the cell induces the synthesis of an extensive intracytoplasmic membrane system (ICM) that contains components necessary for photosynthetic growth. These components include three pigment-protein complexes: two light harvesting (LH) complexes (B870 and B800-850) that are the primary sites of photon capture, and the reaction center (RC) complex which is the site of charge separation. All of these complexes have bound to them bacteriochlorophyll *a* (bchl; see refs. 3 and 4 for reviews).

The goal of much current research is to understand at the molecular level the mechanisms by which O_2 tension regulates the induction of the photosynthetic apparatus. One of the mechanisms operative in *R. capsulatus* consists of an increase in the frequency of transcription initiation of genes encoding peptides of the photosynthetic complexes, and of genes encoding carotenoid and bchl biosynthetic enzymes (5, 6, 7, 8, 9, 10).

We report here the isolation of the *R. capsulatus bchCA* operon oxygen-regulated promoter by in-frame fusion to a plasmid-borne *lacZ* gene (11). The DNA sequence of the *bchCA* operon transcriptional regulatory region was determined, and the 5' end of the *bchCA* mRNA was mapped by low resolution S1 nuclease protection analysis and high resolution primer extension experiments. Sequences with similarity to the *puf* operon promoter (7, 8) were identified immediately upstream of the *bchCA* mRNA 5' end.

2. MATERIALS AND METHODS

M. Baltscheffsky (ed.), Current Research in Photosynthesis, Vol. III, 453–459.
© 1990 *Kluwer Academic Publishers. Printed in the Netherlands.*

2.1.　Bacterial strains and plasmids

The wild type strain B10 of *R. capsulatus* has been described (12, 13), as have the *lacZ* fusion plasmid vectors pTB931 (11) and pXCA601 (7). Plasmids were conjugated from *Escherichia coli* hosts into *R. capsulatus* by triparental matings (14).

2.2.　Cell growth conditions

Cultures of *E. coli* were grown in LB medium (15) at 37° C, and plasmid-containing strains were grown in medium supplemented when appropriate with tetracycline (10 μg/ml) or kanamycin (10 μg/ml). Cultures of *R. capsulatus* were grown in RCV medium (16), supplemented with tetracycline (0.5 μg/ml) for strains containing plasmids. Growth with high or low aeration was done as described (5).

2.3.　Nucleic acid manipulations

Digestion of DNA fragments with restriction endonuclease enzymes, fragment purification by electroelution from electrophoresis gels, ligation and transformation procedures have been described (15). DNA sequence determination, S1 nuclease protection and primer extension experiments were done as described (7).

2.4.　Other procedures

The specific activity of ß-galactosidase in cell extracts was determined as described (5).

3.　RESULTS AND DISCUSSION

3.1.　Isolation of an *R. capsulatus* photosynthesis gene promoter by gene fusion

The 5.5 kb *Eco*RI-H fragment of pRPS404 (17), shown in Fig. 1, was partially digested with the restriction enzyme *Sau*3A 1, and resultant fragments less than 1.0 kb in size were purified and inserted into the unique *Bam*HI site of the broad host-range *lacZ* fusion vector pTB931. After transformation of the ligation products into *E. coli*, plasmids were mobilized into *R. capsulatus* strain B10 and tetracycline resistant recipients were screened for those that produced blue colonies on medium containing X-gal. One recombinant plasmid, pCW1, was isolated and found to contain an *R. capsulatus* insert of approximately 450 bp. Subsequent Southern blot analyses, mutagenesis, genetic complementation and DNA sequencing revealed that the amino terminus of the *bchC* gene was fused in frame to the *lacZ* gene in plasmid pCW1, and that the *bchC* and *bchA* genes form an operon (11). The DNA sequence of the *Sau*3A 1 fragment fused to the *lacZ* gene in plasmid pCW1 is shown in Fig. 2.

3.2.　Oxygen regulation of transcription from the *bchCA* promoter

Cultures of *R. capsulatus* strain B10 containing plasmid pCW1 were grown with either high

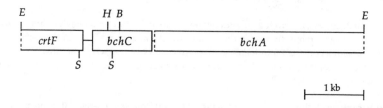

FIGURE 1.　Genetic map of the 5.5-kb *Eco*RI-H fragment of pRPS404 (17) showing the approximate locations of the genes that map partially (*crtF* and *bchA*) or completely (*bchC*) to the *Eco*RI-H fragment. Also shown are the *Eco*RI (E), *Sau*3AI (S), *Hind*III (H), and *Bam*HI (B) restriction sites of interest. The region between the two *Sau*3AI sites is the *R. capsulatus* insert in pCW1. The dotted genetic boundaries indicate uncertainty of the exact position of the start of the *bchA* gene, and that portions of DNA from the *crtF* and *bchA* genes extend beyond the *Eco*RI sites shown.

or low aeration and used for preparation of cell extracts for assay of ß-galactosidase specific activities. As can be seen in Table 1, oxygen starvation significantly increased the amount of ß- galactosidase activity present in these extracts. Because plasmid pTB931 had not been extensively characterized it was possible that some of the *lacZ* expression detected was due to transcriptional read-through from a promoter located on the plasmid vector. Therefore, the *EcoRI-Bam*HI segment of the *EcoRI-H* fragment containing the amino terminus of the *bchC* gene and upstream sequences (see Fig. 1) was fused to the *lacZ* gene of the better characterized plasmid pXCA601, which contains a transcriptional terminator upstream of *lacZ* fusion sequences and is known to have extremely low levels of *lacZ* expression in the absence of cloned promoter fragments (7). The resultant plasmid was designated pJP1. The absolute levels of ß-galactosidase activities measured in extracts of cells containing pJP1 were found to be quite different than the amounts obtained with pCW1 (Table 1), and oxygen starvation had less of an inductive affect on the pJP1 *lacZ* allele expression. This difference may be due to the different amount of *R. capsulatus* sequences 5' to the *bchC* gene present in the fusion plasmids (0.2 kb in pCW1 and approximately 1 kb in pJP1), or due to the different fusion points to the *bchC* gene in the two plasmids. Nevertheless, because oxygen regulation of ß-galactosidase activity was indeed observed in pJP1, we conclude that it was due to modulation of transcription initiation at the *bchCA* operon promoter.

```
        10        20        30        40        50        60        70
GATCGAGGCCGAACGCGGCTGACACGGCTGCGTTCGGACCCGGCTTTGACCCGGGGGTCAGAAAGTCGCA
Sau3A 1
        80        90       100       110       120       130       140
CATCCGTCTGTCGCAAAAGTGTCTAATCAAATTGACAGTCGGGCGTGTAAGTTCAATGATACACACAGGC

       150       160       170       180       190       200       210
                                  SD        m e t q v v i m s
GTGATCAGCCCGACTCTCCGGCCCGATCATACCGGGAGCAAGAAATGGAAACGCAAGTCGTCATAATGTC

       220       230       240       250       260       270       280
  g p k a i s t g i a g l t d p g p g d l v v d
CGGGCCCAAGGCCATCTCGACGGGCATCGCCGGTCTGACCGACCCCGGGCCGGGGGACCTCGTCGTGGAT

       290       300       310       320       330       340       350
  i a y s g i s t g t e k l f w l g t m p p f p g
ATCGCCTATTCCGGCATTTCGACTGGCACCGAGAAATTGTTCTGGCTCGGCACCATGCCACCCTTCCCGG

       360       370       380       390       400       410       420
  m g y p l v p g y e s f g e v v q a a p d t g
GCATGGGATATCCGCTTGTTCCCGGCTACGAAAGCTTCGGAGAGGTCGTTCAAGCCGCCCCCGACACCGG
                                  HindIII

       430       440       448
  f r p g d P V V L
CTTCCGACCGGGCGATCCCGTCGTTTTA...
           Sau3A 1
```

FIGURE 2. Nucleotide sequence of the *R. capsulatus* insert in pCW1 showing the fusion between the *bchC'* and *lac'Z* genes. The deduced amino acid sequence of the *bchC'/lac'Z* fusion gene is shown above the nucleotide sequence in single letter code; lower case letters represent the amino acids of the *bchC* gene, and upper case letters represent the amino acids of the *lacZ* gene. The two *Sau3A* I sites used for insertion of the N-terminus of the *bchC* gene in pCW1, and the *HindIII* site used in construction of the 5' end-mapping probe (section 3.3) are underlined. The potential ribosome binding site (SD) of the *bchC* gene is shown above the nucleotide sequence.

TABLE 1.   ß-galactosidase specific activities [a] of the *bchC'/lac'Z* fusions. Values are the average of four independent assays. Standard deviations are given in brackets.

Plasmid	Low O_2	High O_2	Low O_2/High O_2
pCW1	122.2 (26.2)	22.2 (1.8)	5.5
pJP1	57.0 (2.9)	36.2 (7.0)	1.6

[a] expressed as nmoles *o*-nitrophenylgalactopyranoside cleaved/min/mg protein

3.3.   Low resolution S1 mapping of the *bchCA* mRNA 5' end

The DNA probe for S1 nuclease end-mapping was prepared by radioactive labelling of pCW1 at the 5' ends generated by digestion with *Hind*III (within the *bchC* gene; see Figs. 1 and 2), followed by digestion of the labeled plasmid with *Fsp*I (located in the vector 15 bp from the junction to the *R. capsulatus* insert), and purification of the 415-bp *Hind*III-*Fsp*I fragment. Because this bipartite probe contained 15 bp of heterologous vector DNA as a tail, it allowed the distinction between protection from S1 nuclease digestion of the entire *R. capsulatus*-derived segment of the probe by an mRNA that would initiate upstream of the 5'-most nucleotide of the *R. capsulatus* segment, and self-protection of the whole chimeric probe by DNA-DNA reannealing.

Two bands that each resulted from protection of the probe by mRNA were observed in auto-radiograms of polyacrylamide gels of S1-protected hybrids (Fig. 3A). The predominant band of approximately 250 bases in length indicated a 5' end within the sequenced region, and a minor band of approximately 400 bases in length suggested readthrough into this region from an upstream promoter. Although this transcriptional readthrough evidently occurs on the chromosome of *R. capsulatus* (18), the results obtained with the *lacZ* fusions (Table 1) indicate that the segment of DNA cloned in pCW1 contains an oxygen-regulated promoter. Moreover, additional S1 nuclease protection experiments show that the predominant 5' end identified in Fig. 3 increases in abundance in response to oxygen starvation, just as the ß-galactosidase activities do in the *lacZ* fusions (Wellington and Beatty, manuscript in preparation). Therefore, we conclude that this 5' end results from transcription initiation approximately 50 nucleotides upstream of the proposed *bchC* start codon shown in Fig. 2.

3.4.   High resolution primer extension mapping of the *bchCA* mRNA 5' end

The exact position of the predominant 5' end observed in Fig. 3A was determined by use of a 24-mer antisense oligonucleotide as a primer to extend by reverse transcription to the 5' end of the *bchCA* mRNA. In Fig. 3B is shown an autoradiogram of a polyacrylamide gel on which the primer extension products were run alongside a dideoxy sequencing ladder that was generated by using the same oligonucleotide primer and a DNA fragment that contained the cloned promoter region as template. The band in lane 1 of Fig. 3B corresponds to the size of the major band detected in the 5' S1 nuclease protection experiment, and its position shows that this 5' end maps to nucleotide 137 of the sequence given in Fig. 2, 48 bp upstream of the proposed ATG start codon of the *bchC* gene.

3.5.   Sequence similarity between *bchCA* and *puf* promoter regions

In Fig. 5 is shown an alignment between the DNA sequence flanking the *bchCA* transcript 5' end and proposed oxygen-regulated *puf* operon promoter sequences (7, 8). Identical sequences are enclosed in boxes and consist of: (i) a conserved 5'-CGGGC-3' that is located 23 nt upstream of the *puf* +1 site and 19 nt upstream of the major *bchCA* 5' end; (ii) a 5'-TTCA-3' located 6 nt (*puf* promoter) or 7 nt (putative *bchCA* promoter) downstream of the 5'-CGGGC-

3' sequence; and (iii) a third conserved 5'-TACA-3' sequence found 6 nt (*puf* promoter) or 5 nt (putative *bchCA* promoter) downstream of the 5'-TTCA-3' sequence. Because the major 5' end maps to a region that has significant sequence similarity to *puf* operon promoter sequences, and because this region contains sufficient information to express the *lacZ* gene in an oxygen-dependent manner, we tentatively conclude that these sequences comprise part of an oxygen-regulated promoter at which transcription of the *bchCA* operon initiates.

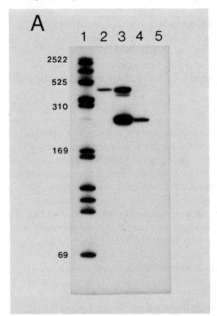
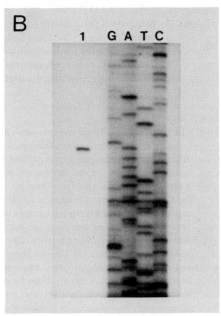

FIGURE 3. 5' end mapping of the *bchCA* operon. Panel A: S1 nuclease protection mapping of 5' ends of *bchC* mRNA. A double-stranded bipartite DNA probe was prepared by radioactively labelling pCW1 at the 5' ends generated by digestion with *Hind*III (containing the codon for amino acid 67 in the *bchC* gene), followed by digestion of the labeled plasmid with *Fsp*I (located in the vector 15 bp from the junction to the *R. capsulatus* insert), and purification of the 415-bp *Hind*III-*Fsp*I fragment. This probe (50 ng) was hybridized with 10 µg of *E. coli* tRNA (lane 2), or 10 µg of RNA extracted from R. capsulatus B10 (lanes 3, 4, and 5) at 51° C for 3 h. Hybrids were trimmed with 500 U (lanes 2 and 3), 1000 U (lane 4), or 1500 U (lane 5) of S1 nuclease as described (9). The sizes, in nucleotides, of *Hae*III fragments of single-stranded M13mp11 DNA (lane 1) are given on the left margin. Panel B: High-resolution primer extension mapping of the predominant *bchC* mRNA 5' end. A 24-mer oligodeoxynucleotide primer complementary to base positions 199 to 223 (Fig. 4) was radioactively labeled at the 5' end and hybridized to 10 µg of total RNA isolated from *R. capsulatus* B10. After extension with Moloney murine leukemia virus reverse transcriptase (7), the extension products (lane 1) were compared with a sequencing ladder generated by using the same primer and a 4.1-kb *Fsp*I double-stranded DNA fragment from pCW1 containing the *R. capsulatus* insert as template in chain-terminating reactions (lanes G, A, T, and C). To allow direct comparison with the sequences in Figs. 2 and 4, this autoradiogram was intentionally inverted and lanes labeled with the complementary base.

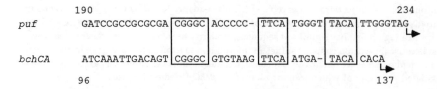

FIGURE 4. Alignment of *puf* operon promoter sequences with proposed promoter sequences from the *bchCA* operon. Numbers of the first and last nucleotides of these sequences correspond to the sequence positions given for the *puf* operon promoter region (7), and of the *bchCA* operon promoter region (Fig. 2). Identical sequences are boxed, and the nucleotides from which transcription is proposed to be initiated are marked by arrows.

3.6. Concluding remarks

The factors necessary for oxygen regulation in *R. capsulatus* are not yet known. In *E. coli* the *fnr* gene has been shown to encode an oxygen-responsive, CRP-like regulatory protein (19), and it is possible that oxygen-regulated photosynthesis gene promoters of *R. capsulatus* contain sequences that act in *cis* to modulate transcription intiation through interaction with a regulatory protein analogous to FNR. Although specific nucleotides of the *puf* operon promoter have been identified by site-directed mutagenesis (7), there has not yet been a report which identifies regulatory sequences distinct from an RNA polymerase binding site. However, it has been speculated on the basis of DNA sequence analysis that palindromic sequences in the 5' flanking regions of photosynthesis genes might be binding sites for a regulatory protein(s) (7, 8, 10). An alternative mechanism, again based on DNA sequence analysis, has been suggested in which an NTRA-like σ factor endows *R. capsulatus* RNA polymerase with different affinities for different promoters (8). The stage is now set for testing these various hypotheses, and our understanding of signal transduction will undoubtably be enhanced as a result of identification of *R. capsulatus* oxygen-responsive regulatory elements, and elucidation of how they convert an environmental signal into a genetic switch.

ACKNOWLEDGEMENTS

We thank D.A. Young and B.L. Marrs for valuable discussions and for sharing their unpublished data, W.R. Richards and B.R. Green for helpful comments. C.L.W. was supported by a Canadian N.S.E.R.C. postgraduate fellowship. This research was supported by Canadian N.S.E.R.C. operating grant A-2796 to J.T.B.

REFERENCES

1. Madigan, M.T. and Gest, H. (1979) Growth of the photosynthetic bacterium *Rhodopseudomonas capsulata* chemoautotrophically in darkness with H2 as the energy source. J. Bacteriol. 137, 524-530.
2. Clark, W.G., Davidson, E., and Marrs, B.L. (1984) Variation of levels of mRNA coding for antenna and reaction center polypeptides in *Rhodopseudomonas capsulata* in response to changes in oxygen concentration. J. Bacteriol. 157, 945-948.
3. Kiley, P.J., and Kaplan, S. (1988) Molecular genetics of photosynthetic membrane biosynthesis in *Rhodobacter sphaeroides*. Microbiol. Rev. 52, 50-69.
4. Drews, G. (1985) Structure and functional organization of light-harvesting complexes and photochemical reaction centers in membranes of phototrophic bacteria. Microbial. Rev. 49, 59-70.
5. Belasco, J.G., Beatty, J.T., Adams, C.W., von Gabain, A., and Cohen, S.N. (1985) Differential

expression of photosynthesis genes in R. *capsulatus* results from segmental differences in stability within the polycistronic *rxcA* transcript. Cell 40, 171-181.

6. Biel, A.J., and Marrs, B.L. (1983) Transcriptional regulation of several genes for bacteriochlorophyll biosynthesis in *Rhodopseudomonas capsulata* in response to oxygen. J. Bacteriol. 156, 686-694.

7. Adams, C.W., Forrest, M.E., Cohen, S.N and Beatty, J.T. (1989) Transcriptional control of the *R. capsulatus puf* operon: a structural and functional analysis. J. Bacteriol. 171, 473 - 482.

8. Bauer, C.E., Young, D.A., and Marrs, B.L. (1988) Analysis of the *Rhodobacter capsulatus puf* operon. Location of the oxygen-regulated promoter region and the identification of an additional *puf*-encoded gene. J. Biol. Chem. 263, 4820-4827.

9. Forrest, M.E., Zucconi, A.P., and Beatty, J.T. (1989) The *pufQ* gene product of *Rhodobacter capsulatus* is essential for formation of B800-850 light-harvesting complexes. Curr. Microbiol. 19, in press.

10. Armstrong, G.A., Alberti, M., Leach, F., and Hearst, J.E., (1989) Nucleotide sequence, organization, and nature of the protein products of the carotenoid biosynthesis gene cluster of *Rhodobacter capsulatus*. Mol. Gen. Genet. 216,254-268.

11. Wellington, C.L. and Beatty, J.T. (1989) Promoter mapping and nucleotide sequence of the *bchC* bacteriochlorophyll biosynthesis gene from *Rhodobacter capsulatus*. Gene, in press.

12. Weaver, P.F., Wall, J.D., and Gest, H. (1975) Characterization of *Rhodopseudomonas capsulata*. Arch. Microbiol. 105, 207-216.

13. Marrs, B. (1974) Genetic recombination in *Rhodopseudomonas capsulata*. Proc. Natl. Acad. Sci. USA 71, 971-973.

14. Ditta, G., Schmidhauser, T., Yakobson, E., Lu, P., Liang, X.-W., Finlay, D.R., Guiney, D., and Helinski, D.R. (1985) Plasmids related to the broad host range vector pRK290 useful for gene cloning and for monitoring gene expression. Plasmid 13, 149-153.

15. Maniatis, T., Fritsch, E.F., and Sambrook, J. Molecular Cloning. A Laboratory Manual. Cold Spring Harbor Laboratory, Cold Spring Harbor, NY, 1982.

16. Beatty, J.T., and Gest, H. (1981) Generation of succinyl-coenzyme A in photosynthetic bacteria. Arch. Microbiol. 129, 335-340.

17. Taylor, D.P., Cohen, S.N., Clark, W.G., and Marrs, B.L. (1983) Alignment of genetic and restriction maps of the photosynthesis region of the *Rhodopseudomonas capsulata* chromosome by a conjugation-mediated marker rescue technique. J. Bacteriol. 154, 580 - 590.

18. Young, D.A., Bauer, C.E., Williams, J.C., and Marrs, B.L. (1989) Genetic evidence for superoperonal organization of genes for photosynthetic pigments and pigment-binding proteins in *Rhodobacter capsulatus*. Mol. Gen. Genet., in press.

19. Spiro, S., Roberts, R.E. and Guest, J.R. (1989) FNR-dependent repression of the *ndh* gene of *Escherichia coli* and metal ion requirement for FNR-regulated gene expression. Molec. Microbiol. 3: 593-599

GENES FOR PHOTOSYSTEM II POLYPEPTIDES

J.C. GRAY, A.N. WEBBER, S.M. HIRD, D.L. WILLEY and T.A. DYER

Botany School, University of Cambridge, Downing Street, Cambridge CB2 3EA, UK, and Institute of Plant Science Research (Cambridge Laboratory), Trumpington, Cambridge CB2 2JB, UK.

1. INTRODUCTION

Photosystem II catalyses the light-driven transfer of electrons from water to plastoquinone, producing oxygen and generating a proton gradient across the thylakoid membrane. The complex may be regarded as made up of three assemblies of polypeptides: a light-harvesting complex (LHCII), an intrinsic membrane complex containing the reaction centre and two antenna chlorophyll proteins, and an extrinsic complex concerned with oxygen evolution. Photosystem II is structurally the most complex of the supramolecular assemblies of the thylakoid membrane and is currently recognised to be composed of at least 20 different polypeptides[1].

The genetic information for the polypeptides of photosystem II is distributed between the chloroplast and nuclear genomes in higher plants[1], and the genes for most of these polypeptides have been isolated and characterised in the last few years. This has generated a large amount of information on the primary structures of the polypeptides, which in turn has led to considerable speculation on the organisation and function of the polypeptides in the photosystem II complex. The aim of this article is to review the information available on the chloroplast-encoded polypeptides of photosystem II, particularly the low molecular weight polypeptides, and to discuss the organisation of the polypeptides in the thylakoid membrane.

2. CHLOROPLAST GENES

All chloroplast-encoded polypeptides of photosystem II appear to be intrinsic membrane proteins with one or more hydrophobic membrane-spanning regions. The reaction centre complex is composed exclusively of chloroplast-encoded polypeptides, and both the associated antenna chlorophyll *a*-proteins are encoded in the chloroplast genome. In addition, a number of smaller polypeptides associated with photosystem II preparations have recently been shown to be chloroplast-encoded, but the role of these polypeptides is unknown. The chloroplast genes for photosystem II polypeptides are listed in Table 1 and their locations in the chloroplast genomes of wheat (*Triticum aestivum*) and pea (*Pisum sativum*) are shown in Figure 1.

M. Baltscheffsky (ed.), Current Research in Photosynthesis, Vol. III, 461–468.
© 1990 *Kluwer Academic Publishers. Printed in the Netherlands.*

Table 1. Chloroplast genes for photosystem II polypeptides

Gene Designation	Gene Product	Codons
*psb*A	32kDa Q_B protein, D1	353
*psb*B	47kDa chlorophyll *a*-protein	508
*psb*C	44kDa chlorophyll *a*-protein	461
*psb*D	34kDa protein, D2	353
*psb*E	9kDa cytochrome *b*-559	83
*psb*F	4kDa cytochrome *b*-559	39
*psb*G	24kDa polypeptide	248
*psb*H	9-10kDa phosphoprotein	73
*psb*I	4.5kDa reaction centre polypeptide	36
*psb*J	hypothetical protein	53
*psb*K (*lhc*A)	3.9kDa polypeptide	37
*psb*L	4.8kDa polypeptide	38

The chloroplast genes *psb*A and *psb*D encode the reaction centre polypeptides D1 and D2. The genes encode related polypeptides of 353 amino acid residues which are predicted to form five membrane-spanning regions (Fig. 2) similar to the L and M subunits of the bacterial reaction centre[2]. However it is probable that the mature D1 polypeptide is smaller than the mature D2 polypeptide due to the removal of 12-16 residues at the *C*-terminus of D1[3]. Both polypeptides are modified at the *N*-terminus by the removal of *N*-formyl methionine and *N*-acetylation of the threonine residues[4]. Both the D1 and D2 polypeptides may be phosphorylated on the *N*-terminal threonine residue[4].

The chloroplast genes *psb*B and *psb*C encode the 47kDa and 44kDa chlorophyll *a*-proteins which function as antenna light-harvesting systems. The related polypeptides may each be predicted to fold with six hydrophobic membrane-spanning regions (Fig. 2) containing conserved histidine residues which may be involved in binding approximately 15 chlorophyll *a* molecules per polypeptide. The conserved histidine residues are located

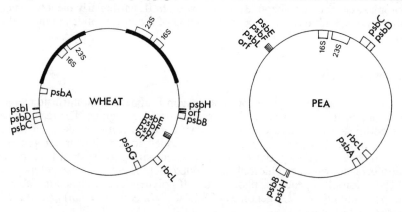

Figure 1.   Location of genes for photosytem II polypeptides in the chloroplast genomes of wheat and pea.

Table 2. *N*-terminal sequences of small polypeptides of wheat photosystem II
The longest sequence determined for each polypeptide is shown. Residues not
identified unambiguously are given as X.

Polypeptide	*N*-terminal sequence	Gene	Reference
10kDa	SGGKKIKVDKPLGLGGLTVXDXIDA	Nuclear	15, 16
9kDa	SGSTGERSFADIITS	*psb*E	14, 15
9kDa	ATQTVEDSSKPRPKRTGAGXL	*psb*H	15, 17
6.1kDa	LVDERMSTEGTGLSLGLSNN	Nuclear	15
4.8kDa	TQSNPNEQNVELNRTS	*psb*L	14, 15
5kDa	EVDPKKGSPEAKKKYAP	Nuclear	15, A.N. Webber
4.5kDa	XLTLPLFVYTIVIFFV	*psb*I	15
4.4kDa	TIDRTYPIFT	*psb*F	15
4.1kDa	ASPGLSPSLKNFL	Nuclear	15
3.9kDa	KLPEAYAIFNP	*psb*K	15

3. SMALL POLYPEPTIDES OF PHOTOSYSTEM II

The presence of small polypeptides in photosystem II preparations was first described by
Ljungberg et al.[10] They described the occurence of five polypeptides in the range 4kDa to
7kDa, and purified a hydrophilic 5kDa polypeptide. *N*-terminal amino acid sequencing in
several laboratories[11-15] has established that several of these polypeptides are encoded by
chloroplast genes. *N*-terminal sequences of small polypeptides of wheat photosystem II
preparations have been determined in two laboratories[14-17] and show excellent agreement.
The sequences are shown in Table 2. The only discrepancies between the laboratories are
the estimates of the sizes of the polypeptides sequenced. This is due to the use of different
high resolution polyacrylamide gel electrophoresis systems for the separation of the
polypeptides before transfer to polyvinylidene difluoride (PVDF) membranes[18]. These
electrophoresis systems generally give poor estimates of the size of small polypeptides.

The *psb*H gene for the 9-10kDa phosphoprotein was identified first by the correspondence
between the determined *N*-terminal amino acid sequence of the spinach protein[19] and the
deduced amino acid sequence of an open reading frame located downstream from the *psb*B
gene in tobacco, wheat and spinach chloroplast DNA[20-22]. The mature polypeptide of 72
amino acid residues is predicted to form a single membrane-spanning region with the
N-terminal threonine residue on the stromal side of the membrane where it may be
phosphorylated by a protein kinase[23]. The role of the 9-10kDa phosphoprotein is
unknown. It has been suggested that the protein is involved in the control of excitation
energy distribution[24] or is the chloroplast analogue of the H-subunit of the bacterial reaction
centre[25]. However neither of these suggestions has been fully substantiated.

The product of a gene designated *psb*I was first identified in photosystem II preparations
by antibodies raised against a synthetic peptide deduced from the sequence of an open

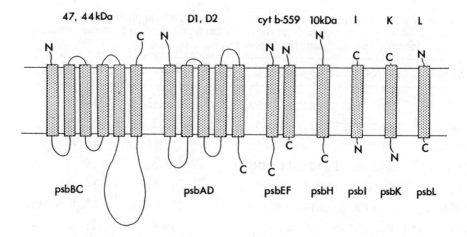

Figure 2. Proposed models for the topology of photosystem II polypeptides in the thylakoid membrane. Membrane-spanning regions are drawn as cylinders.

within the hydrophobic region of five of the proposed membrane spans, approximately one turn of an alpha-helix into the lipid bilayer. The phosphorylation of the N-terminal threonine residue of the 44kDa polypeptide[4] suggests that the N-termini of both polypeptides are located on the stromal side of the membrane, and this would place the large hydrophilic sequences between membrane spans V and VI of both polypeptides in the thylakoid lumen where they may interact with the extrinsic oxygen-evolving complex.

The coding region of the *psb*C gene overlaps the coding region of the *psb*D gene for the D2 polypeptide, but probably not by 50bp as reported previously[5,6]. Translation initiation at GUG is suggested for transcripts of the cyanobacterial *psb*C gene[7], and the conservation of this sequence and a putative ribosome-binding site GAGGAGG 10-16bases upstream from the GUG codon suggests a similar initiation site for chloroplasts. Initiation at GUG would produce a 14bp overlap with the *psb*D gene, and would require the removal of two residues, Met-Glu, to generate the N-terminal threonine residue that is modified by N-acetylation and O-phosphorylation[4].

The chloroplast genes *psb*E and *psb*F encode the 9kDa and 4kDa polypeptides of cytochrome b-559. Both polypeptides contain a single histidine residue located in a putative membrane-spanning region. The requirement for two histidine residues as ligands to the haem[8] indicates that cytochrome b-559 must consist of, at least, a dimer of polypeptides. The simplest model is a heterodimer of the 9kDa and 4kDa polypeptides with their N-termini on the same side of the membrane (Fig. 2). Recent immunochemical studies have established that the C-terminus of the 9kDa polypeptide is located on the lumenal side of the thylakoid membrane[9].

The genes *psb*A-F were the first six chloroplast genes for polypeptides of photosystem II to be described. The remaining authenticated chloroplast genes for photosystem II polypeptides were all identified by N-terminal amino acid sequencing of small polypeptides associated with photosystem II preparations.

reading frame in maize chloroplast DNA[26]. A polypeptide with an *N*-terminal amino acid sequence identical to the *psb*I gene product has been identified in the photosystem II reaction centre complex from spinach, pea and wheat[12,13,15]. This polypeptide therefore constitutes the fifth polypeptide of the reaction centre complex together with the products of the *psb*A, *psb*D, *psb*E and *psb*F genes. The polypeptide consists of 36 amino acid residues, retaining the *N*-terminal methionine residue blocked with a group, presumably formyl, which can be removed by acid treatment. The polypeptide contains a single hydrophobic region which may constitute a transmembrane span. The *C*-terminal region of the polypeptide is highly charged with basic and acidic residues, and in several respects the polypeptide is similar to the first 40 residues of the H subunit of the bacterial reaction centre[13]. If the *psb*I gene product fulfills a similar function to the H subunit, it might be expected that these charged residues would be located on the stromal side of the membrane. However, if so, the *psb*I gene product would be the only chloroplast-encoded polypeptide of photosystem II not to be oriented with its *N*-terminus on the stromal side of the membrane (see Fig. 2).

The *psb*L gene product was identified in an oxygen-evolving core complex of photosystem II by *N*-terminal protein sequencing[14,15]. The polypeptide, variously described as 3.2kDa[14] or 5kDa[15], consists of 37 amino acid residues, after the removal of the initiating *N*-formyl methionine residue, and is the product of open reading frame located just downstream of the *psb*E and *psb*F genes for the polypeptides of cytochrome b-559[14]. The polypeptide contains a single region of hydrophobic residues, sufficient to span the lipid bilayer as an alpha helix. The mature polypeptide has an *N*-terminal threonine residue, and has the same electrophoretic mobility as a small phosphoprotein recently identified in wheat etioplast membranes[14,17]. If the phosphoprotein represents the *psb*L gene product phosphorylated on the *N*-terminal threonine residue, this would suggest that the protein is arranged with the *N*-terminus on the stromal side of the membrane.

The *psb*K gene product is another small hydrophobic polypeptide predicted to contain a single membrane-spanning region[11,15]. The mature gene product appears to be a highly conserved polypeptide of 37 amino acid residues, although the open reading frames encoding the polypeptide differ markedly in different species. In tobacco an open reading frame of 98 or 61 codons encodes the sequenced polypeptide wich corresponds to the *C*-terminal 37 amino acid residues. In liverwort an open reading frame of 55 codons encodes a very similar *C*-terminal 37 residue polypeptide although there is little similarity between the *N*-terminal sequences predicted from the open reading frame but not present in the mature polypeptide. The similarity between the proteins deduced from the tobacco and liverwort genes starts precisely at the *N*-terminus of the mature polypeptide. The liverwort gene has been called *lhc*A because it shows limited sequence homology with the small light-harvesting polypeptides of photosynthetic bacteria[27].

4. *psb*G AND *psb*J

Two other open reading frames in chloroplast DNA have been suggested to be genes for photosystem II polypeptides. *psb*G is the designation of an open reading frame of 248 or 255 codons first identified in the maize chloroplast genome[28]. This open reading frame produced a protein of 24kDa which was identified in spinach photosystem II preparations with antibodies to a synthetic peptide predicted from the sequence of the open reading frame[28]. However it has not been possible to repeat this result with antibodies to the product of a gene-fusion including the analogous open reading frame from wheat

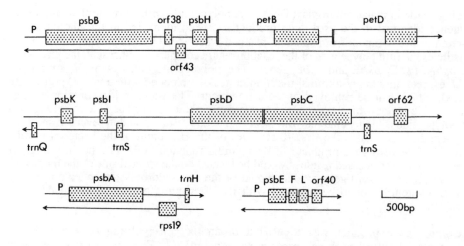

Figure 3. Transcription units of genes for photosystem II genes in wheat chloroplast
DNA. The location of promoters is denoted by P. The promoter for the *psb*DC
region has not been located precisely but is likely to be upstream of *psb*K.

(Nixon, P. and Barber, J., unpublished). As the *psb*G open reading frame overlaps the
putative *ndh*C gene for a component of NADH dehydrogenase[29], it is possible that *psb*G
does not constitute an authentic photosystem II gene.

The gene designation *psb*J has been suggested (Sugiura, M., personal communication) for
an open reading frame of 53 codons located on the opposite strand to *psb*G in maize
chloroplast DNA. The possibility that this was a gene for a photosystem II polypeptide was
raised by Kato et al.[26] A similar open reading frame is conserved in tobacco and liverwort
chloroplast DNA, but there is no published evidence that the product of this open reading
frame is associated with photosystem II. Further experimentation is necessary to
authenticate the products of the *psb*G and *psb*J genes as components of photosystem II.

5. TRANSCRIPTION OF *psb* GENES

The identified chloroplast genes for photosystem II polypeptides are transcribed in four or
five transcriptional units depending on the plant species. In all species *psb*A is located away
from the other *psb* genes (see Fig. 1) and is transcribed separately. The *psb*B and *psb*H
genes are transcribed as part of a large transcriptional unit including the *pet*B and *pet*D
genes for cytochrome *b*-563 and subunit IV of the cytochrome *bf* complex[30,31]. This
transcriptional unit also contains a highly conserved open reading frame of 33-38 codons
located between *psb*B and *psb*H in all chloroplast genomes examined (see Fig. 3). The
product of the open reading frame is predicted to form a hydrophobic membrane-spanning
region, with a highly charged *C*-terminal sequence. However, there is as yet no evidence
for the presence of a protein product derived from this open reading frame in chloroplasts.

The *psb*D and *psb*C genes overlap in all chloroplast genomes, and are co-transcribed as part of a complex transcriptional unit[6,32,33]. In cereals long transcripts of 5.8kb and 4.8kb initiate far upstream of *psb*D and probably include the coding regions of *psb*K and *psb*I (S.M. Hird, unpublished). The 5.8kb transcript also includes an open reading frame of 62 codons located downstream from *psb*C. This open reading frame potentially encodes a highly conserved protein which is predicted to fold with two hydrophobic membrane-spanning regions. However this putative protein has not yet been detected in chloroplasts. In other chloroplast genomes, the *psb*K and *psb*I genes are located separately from *psb*D and *psb*C, because of major sequence rearrangements with respect to the cereals, and are cotranscribed to produce transcripts of 1.2kb[11].

The *psb*E, *psb*F and *psb*L genes are cotranscribed to give a transcript of 1.1kb[14,34]. The transcriptional unit also contains an open reading frame of 40 codons located downstream of *psb*L. This open reading frame potentially encodes a highly conserved hydrophobic protein which is predicted to fold with a single membrane-spanning region. The presence of a good ribosome-binding site upstream from the open reading frame suggests that transcripts will be translated, but the protein has not yet been detected in chloroplasts.

6. CONCLUSIONS

Ten genes for photosystem II polypeptides have been located in chloroplast DNA from a number of green plants. Six genes, *psb*A-F, encode polypeptides whose functions have been relatively well described. The remaining four genes encode small polypeptides whose functions are not understood. These small hydrophobic polypeptides are all predicted to be intrinsic membrane proteins with a single alpha-helical membrane-spanning region. Two of these proteins, the products of the *psb*H and *psb*L genes, have *N*-terminal threonine residues which may be phosphorylated, although the functional significance of this is not clear. The product of the *psb*I gene is a component of the photosystem II reaction centre complex, where its charged *C*-terminal residues may have a similar function to those of the H subunit of the bacterial reaction centre. Two more small open reading frames, orf36 and orf40 in wheat, which are cotranscribed with *psb* genes, seem likely to encode small photosystem II polypeptides. If these polypeptides have blocked *N*-terminal residues they may have escaped detection by protein sequencing studies.

ACKNOWLEDGEMENTS

ANW was an SERC Postdoctoral Research Fellow, SMH was supported by an SERC-CASE research studentship and DLW is the Royal Society Rosenheim Research Fellow. The work was supported by grants from SERC, The Royal Society and The Nuffield Foundation.

REFERENCES

1   Gray, J.C. (1987) in Photosynthesis (Amesz, J., ed.), pp 319-342, Elsevier, Amsterdam
2   Deisenhofer, J., Epp, O., Miki, K., Huber, R. and Michel, H. (1985) Nature 318, 618-624
3   Marder, J.B., Goloubinoff, P. and Edelman, M. (1984) J. Biol. Chem. 259, 3900-3908

4   Michel, H., Hunt, D.F., Shabanowitz, J. and Bennett, J. (1988) J. Biol. Chem. 263, 1123-1130

5   Holschuh, K., Bottomley, W. and Whitfeld, P.R. (1984) Nucleic Acids Res. 12, 8819-8834

6   Alt, J., Morris, J., Westhoff, P. and Herrmann, R.G. (1984) Curr. Genet. 8, 597-606

7   Golden, S.S. and Stearns, G.W. (1988) Gene 67, 85-96

8   Babcock, G.T., Widger, W.R., Cramer, W.A., Oertling, W.A. and Metz, J. (1985) Biochemistry 24, 3638-3645

9   Tae, G.-S., Black, M.T., Cramer, W.A., Vallon, O. and Bogorad, L. (1988) Biochemistry 27, 9075-9080

10   Ljungberg, U., Henrysson, T., Rochester, C.P., Akerlund, H.E. and Andersson, B. (1986) Biochim. Biophys. Acta 849, 112-120

11   Murata, N., Miyao, M., Hayashida, N., Hidaka, T. and Sugiura, M. (1988) FEBS Lett. 235, 283-288

12   Ikeuchi, M. and Inoue, Y. (1988) FEBS Lett. 241, 99-104

13   Webber, A.N., Packman, L., Chapman, D.J., Barber, J. and Gray, J.C. (1989) FEBS Lett. 242, 259-262

14   Webber, A.N., Hird, S.M., Packman, L., Dyer, T.A. and Gray, J.C. (1989) Plant Mol. Biol. 12, 141-151

15   Ikeuchi, M., Takio, K. and Inoue, Y. (1989) FEBS Lett. 242, 263-269

16   Webber, A.N., Packman, L. and Gray, J.C. (1989) FEBS Lett. 242, 435-438

17   Hird, S.M., Webber, A.N., Dyer, T.A. and Gray, J.C. (1989) Curr. Genet., submitted

18   Matsudaira, P. (1987) J. Biol. Chem. 262, 10035-10038

19   Farchaus, J. and Dilley, R.L. (1986) Arch. Biochem. Biophys. 244, 94-101

20   Sugiura, M. (1987) Bot. Mag. (Tokyo) 100, 407-436

21   Hird, S.M., Dyer, T.A. and Gray, J.C. (1986) FEBS Lett. 209, 181-186

22   Westhoff, P., Farchaus, J. and Herrmann, R.G. (1986) Curr. Genet. 11, 165-169

23   Michel, H.P. and Bennett, J. (1987) FEBS Lett. 212, 103-108

24   Allen, J.F. and Holmes, N.G. (1986) FEBS Lett. 202, 175-181

25   Packham, N.K. (1988) FEBS Lett. 231, 284-290

26   Kato, K., Sayre, R.T. and Bogorad, (1987) Proc. Ann. Meeting Jap. Soc. Plant Physiol., Urawa, p 208.

27   Umesono, K., Inokuchi, H., Shiki, Y., Takeuchi, M., Chang, Z., Fukuzawa, H., Kohchi, T., Shirai, H., Ohyama, K. and Ozeki, H. (1988) J. Mol. Biol. 203, 299-331

28   Steinmetz, A.A., Castroviejo, M., Sayre, R.T. and Bogorad, L. (1986) J. Biol. Chem. 261, 2485-2488

29   Steinmüller, K., Ley, A.C., Steinmetz, A.A., Sayre, R.T. and Bogorad, L. (1989) Mol. Gen. Genet. 216, 60-69

30   Westhoff, P. and Herrmann, R.G. (1988) Eur. J. Biochem. 171, 551-564

31   Rock, C.D., Barkan, A. and Taylor, W.C. (1987) Curr. Genet. 12, 69-77

32   Oliver, R.P. and Poulsen, C. (1984) Carlsberg Res. Commun. 49, 647-673

33   Berends, T., Gamble, P.E. and Mullet, J.E. (1987) Nucleic Acids Res. 15, 5217-5240

34   Willey, D.L. and Gray, J.C. (1989) Curr. Genet. 15, 213-220

ORGANIZATION OF MONOCOT AND DICOT CHLOROPLAST GENOMES

Masahiro Sugiura

Center for Gene Research
Nagoya University, Nagoya 464-01, Japan

1. INTRODUCTION

The chloroplast genome is generally composed of single circular molecules, usually between 120 and 160 kbp in length. Most land plants possess a large inverted repeat of 10-76 kbp that contain rRNA genes and adjacent genes. Chloroplasts probably code for all of their own rRNA and tRNA species and some, but not all, of proteins required by their genetic system and for photosynthesis. This paper presents a summary of organization of the chloroplast genomes from dicot (tobacco) and monocot (rice) plants.

2. TOBACCO CHLOROPLAST GENOME

Tobacco was first used as a dicot plant for our study because it has been popular as an experimental plant for various studies. The clone bank of the entire tobacco (Nicotiana tabacum var. Bright Yellow 4) chloroplast DNA as a set of overlapping restriction endonuclease fragments was constructed (1) and the complete nucleotide sequence of tobacco chloroplast DNA was determined (2). The large and small single-copy regions (LSC and SSC, respectively) are 86,684 bp and 18,482 bp long, respectively. Both segments of the inverted repeat (IRa and IRb) were cloned and sequenced separately and found to be completely identical (25,399 bp). The entire genome is thus 155,844 bp long. The complete DNA sequence has been deposited with the EMBL database and presented in the special chloroplast sequence issue of the Plant Molecular Biology Reporter (3). Fig. 1 shows a circular gene map of the tobacco chloroplast genome. The DNA strand which codes for the large subunit of ribulose-1,5-bisphosphate carboxylase has been designated as A and the complementary strand as B. The nomenclature for genes followed the proposals of Hallick and Bottomley (4).

Four rRNA genes and thirty different tRNA genes have been identified in the DNA sequence. Six different tRNA genes have been shown to contain single introns (503-2,526 bp). Twenty five different sequences possibly coding for polypeptides homologous to E. coli ribosomal proteins, RNA polymerase subunits and initiation fuctor 1 have been found. Among them four ribosomal protein genes contain introns. The most striking feature is that rps12 consists of three

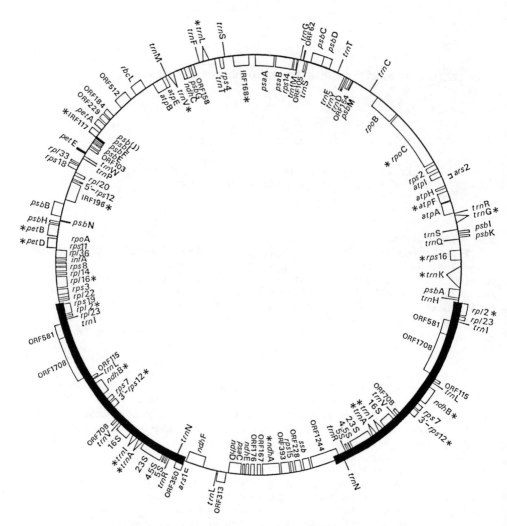

Fig. 1. Circular gene map of the tobacco chloroplast genome. IRa (right) and IRb (left) are shown by bold lines. Genes shown outside the circle are on the A strand and transcribed counterclockwise. Genes shown inside the circle are on the B strand and transcribed clockwise. Asterisks indicate split genes. Major ORFs are included.

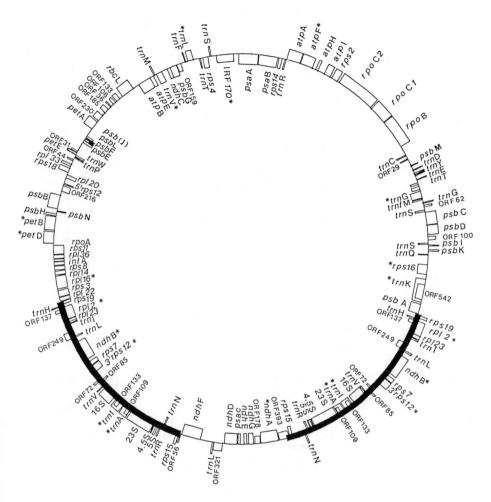

Fig. 2. Circular gene map of the rice chloroplast genome.
IRa (right) and IRb (left) are shown by bold lines.
Gene shown outside the circle are transcribed
counterclockwise and gene shown inside the circle are
transcribed clockwise. Asterisks indicate split genes.
Major ORFs are included.

TABLE 1. Genes for the photosynthetic apparatus

Genes[a]	Products	Rice[b]	Tobacco[b]	Homology(%)[c]
rbcL	RuBisCO, large subunit	477	477	93
psaA	PSI, P700 apoprotein A1	750	750	96
psaB	P700 apoprotein A2	734	734	97
psaC	9 kDa protein	81	81	95
psbA	PSII,D1-protein	353	353	99
psbB	47 kDa protein	508	508	97
psbC	43 kDa protein	473	473	97
psbD	D2-protein	353	353	98
psbE	cytochrome b559 (9 kDa)	83	83	98
psbF	cytochrome b559 (4 kDa)	39	39	100
psbG	G-protein	246	284	82
psbH	10 kDa phosphoprotein	73	73	90
psbI	I-protein	36	52	97
psbK	K-protein	61	98	72
psbL	L-protein	38	38	100
psb(J)	low MW protein	40	40	90
psbM(ORF34)	low MW protein	34	34	100
psbN(ORF43)	low MW protein	43	43	49
petA	b/f complex, cytochrome f	320	320	91
petB*	complex, cytochrome b6	215	215	99
petD*	complex, subunit IV	160	160	99
petE	complex, subunit V	37	37	100
atpA	H⁺-ATPase, subunit α	507	507	88
atpB	subunit β	498	498	92
atpE	subunit ε	137	133	73
atpF*	subunit I	180	184	79
atpH	subunit III	81	81	99
atpI	subunit IV	247	247	93
ndhA*	NADH dehydrogenase(?), ND1	362	364	76
ndhB*	ND2	510	387	96
ndhC	ND3	120	120	87
ndhD	ND4	500	509	82
ndhE	ND4L	101	101	83
ndhF	ND5	734	710	67
ndhG	ND6	176	176	76
(ndhH)(ORF393)	49 kDa protein	393	393	89
(ndhI)(ORF178)	18 kDa protein	178	167	81

a * split genes, putative genes (products not yet detected) are included.
b Numbers of amino acids
c Calculate by the GENETYX program HOMOGAPN and HOMOGAPP

exons and that its 5' exon (5'-rps12) is located 28 kbp downstream from the other exons (3'-rps12) in IRb on the same strand, or 86 kbp downstream from the 3'-rps12 in IRa on the opposite strand (5). We have designated this gene structure as a "divided" gene.

So far 27 genes for thylakoid polypeptides have been found (Table 1). The petB, petD and atpF genes contain single introns. The gene coding for low molecular weight proteins of the photosystem II (psbI-N) have recently been identified and mapped (6-10).

Six different sequences whose predicted amino acid sequences resemble those of components (ND1, 2, 3, 4, 4L and 5) of the respiratory-chain NADH dehydrogenase from human mitochondria have been found (3). As these sequences are actively expressed in tobacco chloroplasts, they are likely to be the genes for components of a chloroplast NADH dehydrogenase (ndhA, B, C, D, E and F) (11). Recently ndh-related sequences (ORF393 and ORF176) were also reported (12, 13).

3. RICE CHLOROPLAST GENOME

Rice was then chosen from the monocot plants to study because rice is a major food crop, especially in Asia. The clone bank of the entire rice (Oryza sativa L. var. Nihonbare) chloroplast DNA was constructed (14). The complete nucleotide sequence was determined by using this clone bank (15). The entire sequence has been deposited with the EMBL database. LSC is 80,592 bp long, SSC is 12,335 bp long and IR is 20,799 bp long. The total length of rice chloroplast DNA is therefore 134,525 bp. The genes for 4 different rRNA, 30 different tRNA and 62 different proteins have been mapped through their homology with the tobacco chloroplast genes (Fig. 2).

The rice genome is about 14% smaller than the tobacco genome and this is mainly due to missing long ORFs found in the tobacco genome; ORF1708 and ORF581 in IR and ORF1244 in SSC. Another big difference is that the 30 kbp region from trnR to trnfM found in the tobacco genome is rearranged in the rice genome.

ACKNOWLEDGEMENTS

I thank members of the Center for Gene Research, members of Mitsui Plant Biotechnology Research Institute, and Dr. A. Hirai and his coworkers for performing this work. This research was supported by grants from the Ministry of Education and from the Ministry of Agriculture.

REFERENCES

1 Sugiura, M., Shinozaki, K., Zaita, N., Kusuda, M. and Kumano, M. (1986) Plant Sci. 44, 211-216
2 Shinozaki, K., Ohme, M., Tanaka, M., Wakasugi, T., Hayashida, N., Matubayashi, T., Zaita, N., Chunwongse, J., Obokata, J., Yamaguchi-Shinozaki, K., Ohto, C., Torazawa, K., Meng, B.Y., Sugita, M., Deno, H., Kamogashira, T., Yamada, K., Kusuda, J., Takaiwa, F., Kato, A., Tohdoh, N., Shimada, H. and Sugiura, M. (1986) EMBO J. 5, 2043-2049

3 Shinozaki, K., Ohme, M., Tanaka, M., Wakasugi, T., Hayashida, N., Matubayashi, T., Zaita, N., Chunwongse, J., Obokata, J., Yamaguchi-Shinozaki, K., Ohto, C., Torazawa, K., Meng, B.Y., Sugita, M., Deno, H., Kamogashira, T., Yamada, K., Kusuda, J., Takaiwa, F., Kato, A., Tohdoh, N., Shimada, H. and Sugiura, M. (1986) Plant Mol. Biol. Rep. 4, 111-147

4 Hallick, R.B. and Bottomley, W. (1983) Plant Mol. Biol. Rep. 1, 38-43

5 Torazawa, K., Hayashida, N., Obokata, J., Shinozaki, K. and Sugiura, M. (1986) Nucl. Acids Res. 14, 3143

6 Ikeuchi, M. and Inoue, Y. (1988) FEBS Lett. 241, 99-104

7 Ikeuchi, M., Takio, K. and Inoue, Y. (1989) FEBS Lett. 242, 263-269

8 Ikeuchi, M., Koike, H. and Inoue, Y. (1989) FEBS Lett. in press

9 Webber, A.N., Hird, S.M., Packman, L.C., Dyer, T.A. and Gray, J.C. (1989) Plant Mol. Biol. 12, 141-151

10 Haley, J. and Bogorad, L. (1989) Proc. Natl. Acad. Sci. USA 86, 1534-1538

11 Matubayashi, T., Wakasugi, T., Shinozaki, K., Yamaguchi-Shinozaki, K., Zaita, N., Hidaka, T., Meng, B.Y., Ohto, C., Tanaka, M., Kato, A., Maruyama, T. and Sugiura, M. (1987) Mol. Gen. Genet. 210, 385-393

12 Wu, M., Nie, Z.Q. and Yang, J. (1989) Plant Cell 1, 551-557

13 Fearnley, I.M., Runswick, M.J. and Walker, J.E. (1989) EMBO J. 8, 665-672

14 Hirai, A., Ishibashi, T., Morikami, A., Iwatsuki, N., Shinozaki, K. and Sugiura, M. (1988) Theo. Appl. Genet. 70, 117-122

15 Hiratuka, J., Shimada, H., Whittier, R., Ishibashi, T., Sakamoto, M., Mori, M., Honji, Y., Kondo, C., Nishizawa, Y., Kanno, A., Hirai, A., Sun, C.R., Meng, B.Y., Li, Y.Q., Shinozaki, K. and Sugiura, M. (1989) Mol. Gen. Genet. 217, 185-194

AN EVOLUTIONARY GENETIC APPROACH TO UNDERSTANDING PLASTID GENE FUNCTION:
LESSONS FROM PHOTOSYNTHETIC AND NONPHOTOSYNTHETIC PLANTS

Jeffrey D. Palmer, Patrick J. Calie*, Claude W. dePamphilis, John M.
Logsdon, Jr., Deborah S. Katz-Downie, and Stephen R. Downie

Department of Biology, Indiana University, Bloomington, IN 47405
*Department of Biology, University of Michigan, Ann Arbor, MI 48109

1. INTRODUCTION

The biogenesis of chloroplasts and other plastid types requires
the coordinated expression of nearly a thousand different genes, most
of which now reside in the nucleus. The 90 or so protein genes and 34
ribosomal and transfer RNA genes that remain in the chloroplast genome
are compactly arranged in a small circular chromosome whose size is
typically about 150 kb (1). The prokaryotic, specifically cyanobacterial, ancestry of chloroplast DNA (cpDNA) is reflected in many of
the ways its genes are organized (often into operons), transcribed
(using eubacterial-like promoters and RNA polymerase), and translated
(on eubacterial-like 70S ribosomes) (1,2). Certain aspects of
chloroplast gene expression, however, appear to reflect the long period
of the organelle's existence within and adaptation to the environment
of the eukaryotic cell. These include the common occurrence of
introns, an extensive array of splicing and other kinds of RNA
processing, the long half-lives of chloroplast mRNAs, and a great
reliance on post-transcriptional processes, especially translational
mechanisms, for regulating the abundance of plastid proteins (1-3).
    The complete sequences of three chloroplast genomes have now been
determined - one from a bryophyte (Marchantia polymorpha; 4) and two
from flowering plants (tobacco and rice; 1). With the sequences of all
chloroplast genes known, several major challenges remain. First, the
identity of many chloroplast genes is only tentatively established
based on sequence similiarity to identified bacterial genes and without
any direct evidence from biochemistry or genetics. Second, many
chloroplast genes were initially identified only as open reading frames
(ORFs) of potentially significant length. The elucidation of the
biochemical function of these ORFs is currently limited to a few
components of the thylakoid membrane (1) and chloroplast RNA polymerase
(5). Of particular relevance to this challenge is the fact that the
metabolic diversity of plastids is belied by the apparent simplicity of
their gene products - limited thus far to components of the
photosynthetic and genetic apparatus (1). A further challenge is to
identify which parts of a given chloroplast gene are essential for its
product's function and which are dispensable.

M. Baltscheffsky (ed.), Current Research in Photosynthesis, Vol. III, 475–482.
© 1990 *Kluwer Academic Publishers. Printed in the Netherlands.*

We are taking an evolutionary genetic approach to address some of these issues. In one set of studies, we are exploiting the unusual instability of cpDNA in the photosynthetic plant geranium (Pelargonium hortorum) to provide a wealth of natural mutations affecting chloroplast gene structure and function. We describe several dramatically altered (fragmented and deleted) genes encoding components of the genetic apparatus. In a second set of studies, we are exploiting one of nature's grand experiments - the permanent loss of photosynthesis - as a means of unmasking the potential contribution of plastid genes to nonphotosynthetic processes within the plastid. Surprisingly, our results suggest that not only are most photosynthetic genes missing from the highly reduced plastid genome of the nonphotosyn-thetic parasite beechdrops (Epifagus virginiana), but that most of the ORFs and some of the genes encoding genetic functions are absent too.

2. CHLOROPLAST GENE MUTATIONS IN PELARGONIUM

Our initial study of the chloroplast genome of the garden geranium, Pelargonium hortorum, showed it to be highly rearranged in structure compared to most other land plant cpDNAs (6). Its structural alterations include a tripling in size (from 25 kb to 76 kb) of the large inverted repeat common to most cpDNAs, a series of large inversions, and the origin and dispersion of two families of novel repeated sequences. We now describe a fine-scale analysis of a region of the geranium genome that has undergone an unprecedented amount of gene-shattering deletion and fragmentation.

2.1. Massive fragmentation and deletion of the rpoA gene.

Figure 1 shows the gene arrangement, based on complete DNA sequencing, of a 21 kb region of the geranium chloroplast genome that is highly rearranged compared to tobacco (7) and most other land plants. The most drastic alterations are those affecting rpoA, the gene encoding the alpha subunit of chloroplast RNA polymerase (5). Only about 60% of the normally 1 kb long coding region of rpoA is present in the sequenced DNA of geranium and Southern hybridizations fail to detect any rpoA-like sequences elsewhere in the chloroplast genome. The retained 60% of rpoA is fragmented into three regions (labeled A-C in Figs. 1 and 2), whose locations relative to the intact rpoA gene of tobacco are shown in Fig. 2. Part or all of these three regions is present in multiple copies (Fig. 2) that are scattered over a 12 kb region of the chromosome (Fig. 1).

This massive fragmentation and deletion of a gene thought (5) to be a necessary component of the chloroplast RNA polymerase raises questions as to the location and nature of the gene for the alpha subunit polypeptide. Has the functional rpoA gene been transferred from the chloroplast to the nucleus? The answer appears to be no, because Southern hybridizations using an intact rpoA gene from a related genus (Geranium) to Pelargonium fail to detect homology to nuclear DNA from Pelargonium. Do the residual rpoA pieces in

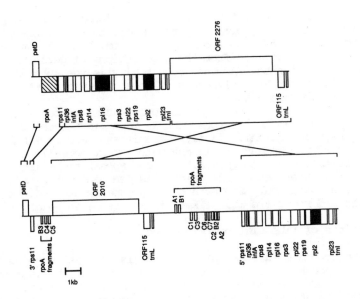

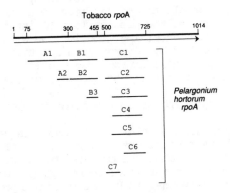

FIGURE 1. Gene rearrangement and fragmentation in a 21 kb segment of geranium cpDNA. The top map shows the standard arrangement (here represented by tobacco; 7) of a cluster of 17 chloroplast genes and the bottom map shows the highly altered arrangement of these genes in geranium cpDNA. "A1" through "C7" mark the 12 fragments of rpoA in geranium (cf. Fig. 2). Solid boxes within genes represent introns.

FIGURE 2. Location, relative to the intact rpoA gene of tobacco, of the fragments of rpoA that remain in the geranium chloroplast genome.

Pelargonium cpDNA produce a truncated but functional alpha polypeptide, perhaps through some newly created pattern of cis- and trans-splicing? We have little evidence to bear on this question; thus far we have failed to detect transcripts from the rpoA regions of geranium in Northern blot experiments. Another possibility is the substitution within the chloroplast RNA polymerase of an entirely different polypeptide for the alpha subunit.

The rearrangements of rpoA are not only extensive but also recent. As mentioned above, an intact rpoA gene is found in the chloroplast of another genus in the geranium family (Geraniaceae) and is flanked by intact copies of the genes - rpsll and petD - that normally flank it (Fig. 1). Furthermore, the rpoA alterations appear to be isolated events as far as the rest of the chloroplast-encoded subunits of RNA polymerase are concerned. Southern mapping experiments indicate that rpoB, rpoC1, and rpoC2 are most likely intact genes in Pelargonium.

2.2. Mutations of ribosomal protein genes.

In tobacco and most other plants, rpoA is the last gene of a 12-gene cluster thought to constitute an operon. Two of the 10 ribosomal protein genes that precede rpoA in this cluster show noteworthy changes in geranium. First, rpsll shows rpoA-like fragmentation and deletion, albeit on a smaller scale. Only 58% of the standard rpsll coding region is found in the 21 kb region of geranium cpDNA sequenced, and this is split into two segments (a 5' region of 44 codons and a 3' region of 37 codons) separated by 14 kb of other rearranged and transposed genes (Fig. 1). The function of the rpsll gene pieces is as unclear as for rpoA; we have yet to examine their possible expression in the chloroplast or to look for an rpsll-homolog in the nucleus.

Second, rpl16 of geranium has sustained a clean deletion of the 1 kb intron that characterizes the gene in all other plants examined (1,4,7), including all other genera in the geranium family. Although intron losses are not uncommon in nuclear genes, this is the first reported case for chloroplasts and has important implications. The best theory to account for the precise loss of introns is via gene conversion of an intron-containing genomic gene with an intron-lacking form of the gene generated by reverse transcription of its mature, spliced mRNA (8). Thus, this intron loss provides indirect evidence for the presence of a reverse transcriptase activity in chloroplasts.

2.3. Extreme size polymorphism in the largest chloroplast gene.

The largest gene in the chloroplast genome is an enigma. Not only is the identity of its product unknown, but it is also variable in size (2131-2276 codons in spinach, tobacco, and Marchantia; 4,7,9), even among isolates of a single strain of Oenothera hookeri (10). This gene is unusual in geranium in that it has become transposed from its normal location (as in tobacco) to a novel one (Fig. 1). In addition, the geranium gene, at 2010 codons, is considerably smaller than in any other plant examined as the result of a series of small deletions throughout the gene. Northern blot studies reveal that ORF2010 is transcribed in geranium, with some of the detected transcripts spanning the entire 6 kb gene. These observations dramatize the degree to which sequences in this gene are dispensable for the function of its (unknown) product and further delimit the potentially important sequences within the gene.

3. STRUCTURE AND FUNCTION OF PLASTID DNA IN NONPHOTOSYNTHETIC PLANTS

Nonphotosynthetic plants, most of which are parasitic on photosynthetic ones, have evolved repeatedly in flowering plants and algae (11). Although lacking chlorophyll, many or all of these nonphotosynthetic plants still contain plastids, at least some of which are known to store starch, pigments or lipids and contain plastid DNA and ribosomes (11). These plants provide important genetic systems in which to study the role of the plastid genome in processes other than photosynthesis. Below we describe our physiological and genetic characterization of the plastid of beechdrops, Epifagus virginiana, an obligate root parasite of its sole host, beech trees (Fagus americana), and then extend these findings to two other groups of parasitic plants.

3.1. Genetic and physiological loss of photosynthesis in the nonphotosynthetic parasite beechdrops.

Physiological and biochemical measurements reveal that beechdrops shoots are completely lacking in photosynthetic activity. Chlorophyll is undetectable and gas exchange measurements show an absence of any net CO_2 uptake. The plants lack any detectable Rubisco (ribulose-1,5-bisphosphate carboxylase/oxygenase) protein and activity, but do have measurable levels of PEPCase (phosphoenol pyruvate carboxylase) activity. However, carbon isotope composition studies show that beechdrops acquires its carbon via Rubisco rather than PEPCase. Moreover, the $\delta^{13}C$ value of beechdrops is essentially identical to that of its host beech tree. Taken together, these results indicate that beechdrops is incapable of net CO_2 fixation and that it acquires all of its carbon from its host.

Mapping studies of the beechdrops plastid genome show it to be a highly degenerate molecule that has lost most, if not all, of its photosynthetic genes (Table 1). The circular genome is only 71 kb in size, by far the smallest naturally occurring plastid genome known. Both single copy regions are highly reduced in size relative to related photosynthetic plants (the large and small single copy regions are 87 kb and 18.5 kb, respectively, in tobacco, but only 18 kb and 3.6 kb in beechdrops). Interestingly, beechdrops retains a full-sized inverted repeat of 25 kb. Overall, nearly two-thirds of the genetic complexity of tobacco (131 kb) is missing in beechdrops (46 kb). Figure 3 provides examples of hybridization experiments demonstrating that, under conditions in which total tobacco cpDNA hybridizes strongly to beechdrops DNA, tobacco probes specific to three photosynthetic genes (psbA, atpB, petA) fail to hybridize. We emphasize that the

TABLE 1. Genes found in cpDNA of tobacco and ones (indicated with *) partly or entirely deleted from cpDNA of beechdrops.

Probable function	Gene name*	Number of Genes[a]
Photosynthesis		17/26
photosystem I	psa A*,B*,C	2/3
photosystem II	psb A*,B,C*,D*,E*,F*,G,H*,I,K,L*	7/11
cytochrome b/f	pet A*,B*,C,E	2/4
ATP synthase	atp A*,B*,E,F*,H*,I*	5/6
Calvin cycle	rbc L*	1/1
chlorophyll synthesis	trn G	0/1
Transcription and Translation		8/59
RNA polymerase	rpo A,B*,C1*,C2*	3/4
ribosomal RNA	rrn 4.5S,5S,16S,23S	0/4
transfer RNA	trn 30 different (C*,K*,F*,L*)	4/30
ribosomal protein, 50S	rpl 8 different	0/8
ribosomal protein, 30S	rps 12 different (rps16*)	1/12
Miscellaneous		28/38
NADH dehydrogenase	ndh A*,B,C*,D*,E*,F*,G*,H*	7/8
other ORFs	at least 30	21/30

[a]Number of genes missing from beechdrops cpDNA (left of slash); number of genes present in tobacco cpDNA (right of slash).

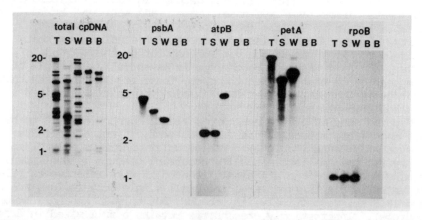

FIGURE 3. Absence of three photosynthetic genes and one RNA polymerase gene from beechdrops plastid DNA. Hybridization probes used are total cpDNA from tobacco and tobacco clones internal to the four indicated genes. Probes were hybridized to Southern blots containing BamHI digests of cpDNAs from tobacco (T), snapdragon (S), and witchweed (W), and ClaI and HindIII digests of beechdrops (B) total DNA.

negative hybridization results obtained in experiments like these have been confirmed by the mapping studies described above, which rule out the possibility of beechdrops having retained more than a small portion of these genes. The absence of most normally cpDNA-encoded genes from the plastid genome of beechdrops (Table 1) indicates that the physiological absence of photosynthetic activity discussed in the preceding paragraph reflects a permanent and irreversible loss of the genetic ability to produce a functional photosynthetic apparatus.

3.2. Deletions of nonphotosynthetic genes in beechdrops: A nonfunctional genome?

Plastids carry out a diversity of metabolism unrelated to photosynthesis, including certain steps of amino acid biosynthesis, lipid synthesis, nitrite and sulfate reduction, chlorophyll and terpenoid synthesis, carbon storage, and glycolysis, not to mention the maintenance of their own genome (DNA replication, repair, and recombination). Do any of these activities require plastid gene products? Our studies on beechdrops tentatively suggest that, at least in the physiological context of a parasitic plant that acquires carbon and other nutrients from its host, the answer may well be no. For not only are most of the photosynthetic genes missing from the beechdrop plastid genome, but so too are most of the NADH dehydrogenase genes and unidentified ORFs (Table 1). In fact, the possibility exists that the beechdrop plastid genome is completely nonexpressed and nonfunctional, in some sense a "pseudogenome". Evidence leading to this preliminary conclusion is of two types. First, beechdrops plastid DNA lacks genes for three of the four cpDNA-encoded subunits of RNA polymerase (e.g. Fig. 3) and probably, at a minimum, one ribosomal protein gene and four tRNA genes (Table 1). Second, we are thus far unable to detect any plastid transcripts, including ribosomal RNAs, in beechdrops.

3.3. Parallel trends in plastid genome reduction in different groups of nonphotosynthetic plants.

Are the highly reduced size and possibly nonfunctional nature of the beechdrops plastid genome unique to this particular plant, or have parallel reductions occurred in other, independently derived lineages of nonphotosynthetic plants? Hybridization studies similar to those shown in Fig. 3 suggest that the latter is the case. Most of the genes missing from beechdrops plastid DNA also fail to hybridize to plastid DNAs of two other nonphotosynthetic lineages (Cuscuta sp., Cuscutaceae, and Corallorhiza odontorhiza, Orchidaceae).

4. CONCLUSIONS

This paper is a first progress report of our efforts to apply an evolutionary genetic approach to understanding chloroplast gene function. The results reported here are promising for both the photosynthetic and nonphotosynthetic systems described. In the case of the photosynthetic plant geranium, we have identified two genes, one encoding an RNA polymerase subunit and the other a ribosomal protein, that were recently shattered by means of deletion and fragmentation. Although the full implications of these findings for the function of these genes and their products remain to be elucidated, it is clear that major changes must have taken place in either the coding site of these proteins (gene transfer), the identity of the gene producing them (gene substitution), or their expression and ultimate sizes (if the gene pieces within the chloroplast retain function). In the case of the nonphotosynthetic plant beechdrops, our results reveal that the plastid is physiologically and genetically incompetent to perform photosynthesis; indeed, most of the plastid photosynthetic genes have been lost entirely. Surprisingly, most other plastid genes are also missing in beechdrops, including ones encoding important components of the gene expression machinery. If future studies confirm our working hypothesis that the plastid genome in beechdrops is nonfunctional, then we will have to conclude that, in a parasitic plant at least, the plastid genome does not contribute to any of the diverse metabolic and biochemical processes that take place in plastids.

ACKNOWLEDGEMENTS

This work was supported by NIH RO1-GM35087 to JDP, NIH F32-GM11948 to PJC, NSF DCB-8710614 to CWD, and NSERC PDF to SRD. We are grateful to C. Cartwright for assistance with the geranium cpDNA sequencing studies, to M. Chase for helping to collect beechdrops, and to J. Teeri, J. Seeman, N. Bowlby, and C. Yocum for assistance with the physiological and biochemical studies of beechdrops.

REFERENCES

1 Sugiura, M. (1989) Ann. Rev. Cell. Biol. 5, 51-70
2 Gruissem, W. (1989) Cell 56, 161-170
3 Mullet, J.E. 1988. Ann. Rev. Plant Physiol. 39, 475-502
4 Ohyama, K., Kohchi, T., Fukuzawa, H., Sano, T., Umesono, K. and Ozeki, H. (1988). Photosyn. Res. 16, 7-22
5 Purton, S. and Gray, J.C. (1989) Mol. Gen. Genet. 217, 77-84
6 Palmer, J.D., Nugent, J.M. and Herbon, L.A. (1987) Proc. Natl. Acad. Sci. USA 84, 769-773
7 Shinozaki, K., Hayashida, N. and Suigura, M. (1988) Photosyn. Res. 18, 7-31
8 Fink, G.R. (1987) Cell 49, 5-6
9 Zhou, D.X., Massenet, O., Quigley, F., Marion, M.J., Moneger, F., Huber, P. and Mache, R. (1988) Curr. Genet. 13, 433-439
10 Blasko, K., Kaplan, S.A., Higgins, K.G., Wolfson, R. and Sears, B.B. (1988) Curr. Genet. 14, 287-292
11 dePamphilis, C.W. and Palmer, J.D. (1989) in Physiology, Biochemistry, and Genetics of Nongreen Plastids (Boyer, C.D., Shannon, J.C. and Hardison, R.C., eds.), in press, Amer. Soc. Plant Physiol., Rockville, Maryland

BIOGENESIS OF PHOTOSYSTEM II IN C3 AND C4 PLANTS - A MODEL SYSTEM TO STUDY DEVELOPMENTALLY REGULATED AND CELL-SPECIFIC EXPRESSION OF PLASTID GENES

PETER WESTHOFF, HANS SCHRUBAR, ANGELA OSWALD, MONIKA STREUBEL & KARIN OFFERMANN
Institut für Entwicklungs- und Molekularbiologie der Pflanzen, Heinrich-Heine-Universität Düsseldorf, D-4000 Düsseldorf 1, FRG

1. INTRODUCTION

Ordered plant development requires the coordinated, yet differential expression of functionally linked genes both in time and space. Differentiation thus is an inherent feature of all developmental processes. It is ultimately determined by the plant´s endogenous genetic programme, however, it may be initiated or modulated by external factors, with light being the most important one (1).

An intimate interplay between light and endogenous factors is characteristic for the biogenesis of the photosynthetic apparatus of higher plants (1). The acquisition of competence for photoautotrophic growth is a primary goal of the developmental programme of the germinating seedling. Therefore, the light-dependent differentiation of plastids in greening, etiolated seedlings is used as a paradigm for studying developmental control of gene expression in plants. Under normal light-dark regimes undifferentiated proplastids develop into green, mature chloroplasts, while growth in the dark leads to the formation of etioplasts. The transition into chloroplasts is arrested, until light is provided. Three photoreceptors, phytochrome, protochlorophyllide, and a blue-light-absorbing sensor system are involved in this process, their precise interaction in mechanistic terms is a matter of current interest (2,3).

Photosynthesis in higher plants is basically a cellular event, but it is also the attainment of a highly specialized organ, i.e. the leaf. While the parenchymatic leaf cells of C3 plants are able to carry out all partial reactions of photosynthesis, mesophyll and bundle sheath cells of C4 plants display a labour-sharing mode of organization. Photosynthesis in these plants, therefore, requires the close cooperation of two metabolically distinct cell types which are the result of divergent differentiation during leaf ontogeny (4,5).

In the present publication, our work on the biogenesis of photosystem II in C3 and C4 plants will be summarized. Photosystem II is composed of approximately twenty different subunits, the majority of which can be assigned to three functional domains: the reaction center, the water-splitting complex, and the light-harvesting assemblies (6). Photosystem II is a genetic mosaic, i.e. genes encoding its constituent polypeptides are spread between nuclear and plastid genomes (7,8). Its biogenesis, therefore, is expected to reveal typical

M. Baltscheffsky (ed.), Current Research in Photosynthesis, Vol. III, 483–490.
© 1990 *Kluwer Academic Publishers. Printed in the Netherlands.*

features of the regulatory mechanisms underlying chloroplast development in higher plants. Moreover, photosystem II genes are differentially expressed in mesophyll and bundle sheath cells of NADP malic enzyme type C4 species (9) Thus, this photosystem may also serve as a probe for studying the control of cell-specific gene expression in photosynthesis.

2. RESULTS AND DISCUSSION

2.1. Biogenesis of photosystem II during greening of etiolated spinach seedlings is a stepwise process and controlled post-transcriptionally

The biogenesis of photosystem II during light-induced greening of etiolated spinach seedlings is illustrated in Fig. 1. The chlorophyll-binding proteins of the reaction center, i.e. CP47, CP43, D2, and D1, as well as the 10 kDa polypeptide associated with the water-splitting activity cannot be detected in dark-grown seedlings. The appearance of these polypeptides is strictly dependent upon light. On the other side, the 33, 23, and 16 kDa proteins of the water-oxidation system and a 22 kDa photosystem II protein of unknown function are present in etioplasts. Light does not influence their accumulation significantly. Cytochrome b-559 shows an intermediate behaviour; a basal level accumulates already in the absence of light, but there is a substantial increase upon illumination.

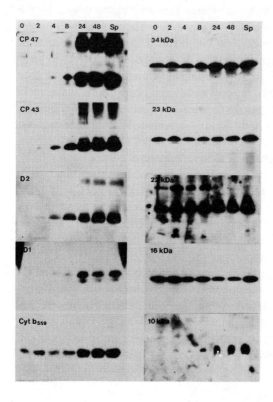

FIGURE 1. Photosystem II biogenesis in greening spinach seedlings. Etiolated spinach seedlings (6 days) have been illuminated for up to 48 hrs (indicated on top of the photographs). Protein samples equivalent to equal amounts of cotyledous tissue were analyzed by immunoblotting using ^{125}I-labelled protein A for detection of antigen-antibody complexes.

Thus, photosystem II biogenesis in greening spinach seedlings is a stepwise process. The extrinsic polypeptides of the water-splitting complex accumulate without being attached to a functional reaction center. Moreover, even the reaction center components cytochrome b-559, D1 and D2 are assembled in a non-coordinate manner.

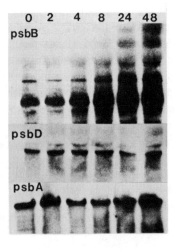

FIGURE 2. Accumulation of plastid transcripts encoding CP47 (psbB), D2 (psbD) and D1 (psbA) during greening of etiolated spinach. Northern blot analysis was performed as described in (18).

Northern blot experiments demonstrate that the absence of CP47, CP43, D1 and D2 cannot be explained by the lack of the corresponding mRNAs (Fig. 2). The expression of these genes, therefore, must be regulated post-transcriptionally (7). And indeed, recent reports have provided convincing evidence that the level of translation is the primary target (10,11).

2.2. Biogenesis of photosystem II in greening *Sorghum* seedlings: evidence for light-activated transcription of plastome-encoded genes

Etiolated *Sorghum* seedlings are characterized by tremendously enlarged mesocotyls, while overall leaf development is blocked. Even after prolonged periods of etiolation, i.e. 10 to 13 days of growth in the dark, leaves have hardly emerged from the coleoptile and remain unfolded. Thus leaf development in *Sorghum* is strongly dependent upon light. This is in contrast to other monocotyledous plants like barley or oats, whose primary leaves break through the coleoptile and increase in size under conditions of etiolation (3).

Electron microscopy of five days old dark-grown *Sorghum* seedlings reveals typical etioplasts with prolamellar bodies and rudimentary prothylakoids (G. Wanner, H. Schrubar & P. Westhoff, unpublished data). As inferred from this morphological criterium, plastid development is not arrested at the proplastid, amyloplast or amoeboplast stage, as might have been anticipated. But the investigation of protochlorophyllide oxidoreductase abundance shows a striking difference to other greening systems among monocotyledous plants. In barley and oats, protein as well as corresponding RNA levels drop within a few hours, as soon as the etiolated seedling is illuminated (12). In *Sorghum*, however, protochlorophyllide oxidoreductase levels do not change upon illumination for up to 48 hrs (Fig. 3) suggesting that greening of etiolated *Sorghum* differs from that of other monocotyledous plants analyzed so far.

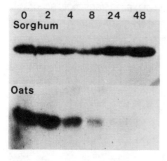

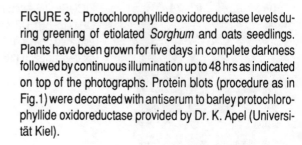

FIGURE 3. Protochlorophyllide oxidoreductase levels during greening of etiolated *Sorghum* and oats seedlings. Plants have been grown for five days in complete darkness followed by continuous illumination up to 48 hrs as indicated on top of the photographs. Protein blots (procedure as in Fig.1) were decorated with antiserum to barley protochlorophyllide oxidoreductase provided by Dr. K. Apel (Universität Kiel).

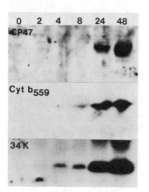

FIGURE 4. Photosystem II assembly in greening *Sorghum*. For growth of plants and methods see Fig. 3.

This view is supported by the mode of photosystem II assembly which, in greening *Sorghum*, does not occur stepwise as in spinach (Fig. 4). Polypeptides of the water-splitting apparatus and cytochrome b-559 cannot be detected in dark-grown plants, their accumulation is dependent upon light as is that of the chlorophyll apoproteins and the subunits of the cytochrome b/f complex. The biogenesis of photosystem II in *Sorghum*, therefore, is characterized by a coordinate appearance of its components, a process which is triggered by light.

The light-dependency is also observed for the accumulation of plastid transcripts encoding thylakoid membrane polypeptides. Steady-state levels of these RNAs are low in etiolated seedlings. A drastic increase occurs only upon illumination (Fig. 5, Panel A) indicating that the transcription of plastid genes is switched on or, at least, greatly stimulated by light. And indeed, the overall transcriptional activity per plastid as measured by run-off assays is very low in etioplasts, but increases more than five-fold in etiochloroplasts isolated from seedlings illuminated for 24 hrs (Fig. 5, Panel B; Schrubar & Westhoff, in preparation). This is in contrast to barley where light causes a rapid decline in the transcription activity of plastids after illumination (13). Thus *Sorghum* provides an easy-to-manipulate experimental system to analyze, how the transcription activity of plastids can be influenced by light and which controlling factors are involved in the modulation of this activity. Moreover, the coordinated and simultaneous establishment of the various plastid functions in greening *Sorghum* seedlings resembles the differentiation of proplastids to chloroplast as it occurs under normal light/dark regimes (14). It is to be expected, therefore, that regulatory mechanisms observed in this greening system may apply to chloroplast development under natural conditions, too.

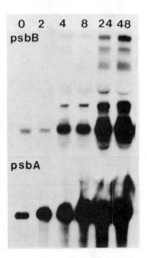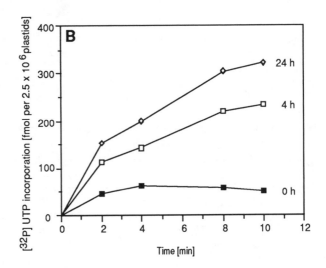

FIGURE 5. Transcription of plastid genes during greening of *Sorghum*. PANEL A: Northern blot analysis. PANEL B: Transcription run-on analysis. Intact plastids isolated from etiolated or greening (after 4 and 24 hrs of illumination) *Sorghum* seedlings were lysed and allowed to incorporate[^{32}P] UTP into elongating transcripts (13). Aliquots were removed at the indicated times and incorporation of [^{32}P] UTP into RNA was measured by liquid scintillation counting.

2.3. Differential expression of plastid genes encoding photosystem II proteins in mesophyll and bundle sheath cells of C4 plants

C4 plants of NADP malic enzyme type are characterized by dimorphic leaf chloroplasts, i.e. their bundle sheath chloroplasts are almost agranal, and are lacking or at least largely depleted in photosystem II activity (15). On the other side, grana structures and the capability of linear electron transport have been found in bundle sheath chloroplasts of developing leaves (16) implying that photosystem II and, concomitantly, its constituent polypeptides are lost, while the bundle sheath cells differentiate.

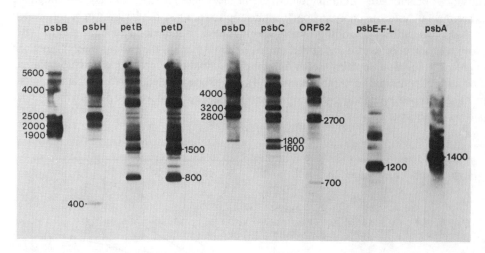

FIGURE 6. Transcript patterns of plastome-encoded photosystem II genes in *Sorghum*. Chloroplast RNA of *Sorghum* was analyzed by Northern blotting using appropriate probes from spinach. For the organization of the polycistronic psbB and psbD/C transcription units see Fig. 7.

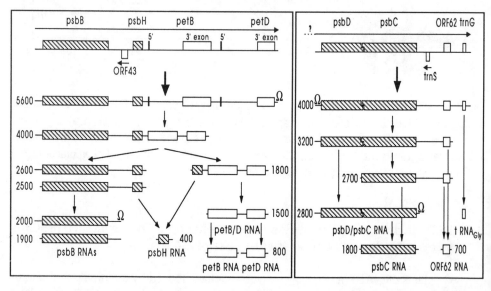

FIGURE 7. RNA processing pathways of the psbB and psbD/C transcription units in *Sorghum* chloroplasts. Transcript sizes are given in nucleotides. The Ω denotes stable stem and loop structures at RNA 5' and 3' ends. The transcription start point of the psbD/C transcription unit remains to be determined.

By immunoblot analysis, substantial amounts of the reaction centre subunits (D1, D2, cytochrome b-559) and the chlorophyll-binding proteins of the inner antenna complex (CP47, CP43) which are all encoded by plastid genes can be detected in bundle sheath chloroplasts of the NADP malic enzyme-type C4 plants maize, *Sorghum*, and *Pennisetum*. The levels of these proteins vary depending on the developmental stage of the plants. However, only trace amounts of the nuclear-encoded 23, 16 and 10 kDa lumenal proteins of the water-splitting apparatus are found in bundle sheath chloroplasts regardless their state of differentiation (A. Oswald, M. Streubel, U. Ljungberg, J. Hermans & P. Westhoff, manuscript in preparation). This might indicate that a reduced expression of the lumenal proteins of the water-splitting complex initiates the deregulation of photosystem II during bundle sheath differentiation and, moreover, that this differentiation process is under nuclear control. The abundance of the corresponding transcripts and, in addition, that of the 34 kDa protein mRNA is consistently low in bundle sheath cells (ibid.) suggesting that the expression of these genes is primarily controlled by transcription.

The control of expression of the plastid-encoded photosystem II proteins (CP47, CP43, D1, D2, and cytochrome b-559) seems to be more complex. First, all of these genes with the possible exception of psbA (D1) are parts of polycistronic transcription units whose primary transcripts are subjected to extensive processing events yielding mono- or oligocistronic RNA species (17,18). Second, the polycistronic transcription units encoding psbB (CP47) and psbD/C (D2 and CP43) have a heterogenous composition, i.e. their component cistrons encode for proteins or RNAs assembled in different functional entities (Fig. 6). Thus, the controlling mechanisms of gene expression in bundle sheath chloroplasts must ensure that transcriptionally linked genes can be expressed differentially.

Northern blot analyses of mesophyll and bundle sheath RNAs from maize, *Sorghum*, and *Pennisetum* revealed lower levels of photosystem II gene carrying transcripts in bundle sheath cells suggesting that their transcription has been blocked. But differences in RNA processing patterns are more intriguing. The steady state level of the monocistronic psbB RNA species is clearly reduced in bundle sheath cells, but the dicistronic petB/petD-RNA and the monocistronic petB and petD transcripts are present in almost equal amounts in mesophyll and bundle sheath cells (Fig. 6). Similarly, the levels of the processed dicistronic psbD/C and the monocistronic psbC RNA are drastically reduced in bundle sheath chloroplasts, while the polycistronic psbD-psbC-ORF62-trnG precursor transcripts do not show significant differences (P. Westhoff, A. Oswald, K. Offermann & K. Eskins, manuscript in preparation).

These data suggest that differential RNA stability is the dominant regulatory principle causing the observed differences in transcript ratios. After release from the polycistronic precursor individual RNA segments can exhibit different stabilities as has been shown in prokaryotic systems (19,20). Differential mRNA decay, therefore, may provide the basis for the cell-specific expression of plastid-encoded photosystem II genes in C4 plants. Moreover, differential mRNA decay may be of general importance for the regulation of plastid gene expression, since a heterogenous composition of polycistronic transcription units is a typical feature of plastid gene organization. The regulatory mechanisms underlying differential gene expression in mesophyll and bundle sheath chloroplasts are presently under study.

ACKNOWLEDGEMENTS

Work on the biogenesis of photosystem II in spinach was done, while P.W. was in the laboratory of Dr. R. Herrmann (University of Munich). The financial support of the Deutsche Forschungsgemeinschaft (SFBs 184 and 189) and Fonds der Chemischen Industrie is gratefully acknowledged. We thank Dr. K. Steinmüller for carefully reviewing the manuscript.

REFERENCES

1.   Mohr, H. (1987) Ann. Bot. 60, 139-155
2.   Nagy, F., Kay, S.A. and Chua, N.H. (1988) Trends Genet. 4, 37-42
3.   Mullet, J.E. (1988) Ann. Rev. Plant Physiol. Plant Mol. Biol. 39, 475-502
4.   Hatch, M.D. (1987) Biochim. Biophys. Acta 895, 81-106
5.   Nelson, T. and Langdale, J.A. (1989) Plant Cell 1, 3-13
6.   Miyao, M. and Murata, N. (1989) in Topics in Photosynthesis (Kyle, D.J., Osmond, C.B. and Arntzen, C.J., eds.), Vol. 9, Photoinhibition, pp. 289-307, Elsevier, Amsterdam
7.   Herrmann, R.G., Westhoff, P., Alt, J., Tittgen, J. and Nelson, N. (1985) in: Molecular Form and Function of the Plant Genome (van Vloten-Doting, L., Groot, G.S.P. and Hall, T.C., eds.), pp. 233-256, Plenum Publishing Corporation, New York
8.   Rochaix, J.D. and Erickson, J. (1988) Trends Biochem. Sci. 13, 56-59
9.   Schuster, G., Ohad, I., Martineau, B. and Taylor, W.C. (1985) J. Biol. Chem. 260, 11866-11873
10. Klein, R.R., Mason, H.S. and Mullet, J.E. (1988) J. Cell Biol. 106, 289-301
11. Laing, W., Kreuz, W. and Apel, K. (1988) Planta 176, 269-276
12. Santel, H.J. and Apel, K. (1981) Eur. J. Biochem. 120, 95-103
13. Mullet, J.E. and Klein, R.R. (1987) EMBO J. 6, 1571-1579
14. Leech, R.M. (1986) in Symp. Soc. Exp. Biol., Vol. 40, Plasticity in Plants (Jennings, D.H. and Trewavas, A.J., eds.), pp. 121-153, University of Cambridge, Cambridge
15. Woo, K.C., Anderson, J.M., Boardman, N.K., Downton, W.J.S., Osmond, C.B. and Thorne, S.W. (1970) Proc. Natl. Acad. Sci. USA 67, 18-25
16. Downton, W.J.S. and Pyliotis, N.A. (1971) Can. J. Bot. 49, 179-180
17. Westhoff, P., Grüne, H., Schrubar, H., Oswald, A., Streubel, M., Ljungberg, U. and Herrmann, R.G. (1988) in Photosynthetic Light-Harvesting Systems - Structure and Function (Scheer, H. and Schneider, S., eds.), pp. 261-276, Walter de Gruyter Verlag, Berlin
18. Westhoff, P. and Herrmann, R.G. (1988) Eur. J. Biochem. 171, 551-564
19. Belasco, J.G., Beatty, J.T., Adams, C.W., von Gabain, A. and Cohen, S.N. (1985) Cell 40, 171-181
20. Newbury, S.F., Smith, N.H. and Higgins, C.F. (1987) Cell 51, 1131-1143

THE ORGANIZATION AND EXPRESSION OF PHOTOSYNTHETIC AND NON-PHOTOSYNTHETIC OPERONS OF *EUGLENA GRACILIS* CHLOROPLAST DNA

Richard B. Hallick, David A. Christopher, Donald W. Copertino, Robert G. Drager, Ling Hong, Kristin P. Nelson, Catherine Radebaugh, Jennifer K. Stevenson, Noreen J. Sleator, and Gloria Yepiz-Plascencia.

Department of Biochemistry, University of Arizona, Tucson, AZ 85721 U.S.A.

1. INTRODUCTION

Euglena chloroplast DNA is a 145 kbp circular duplex genome that is very similar in gene content and gene order within transcription units to chloroplast genomes from many sources. By contrast, *Euglena* chloroplast DNA differs in the arrangement of operons around the circular genome, and in the number, location, and types of introns within operons for both photosynthetic and non-photosynthetic genes. The structure, coding capacity, and organization of the *Euglena gracilis* chloroplast DNA was recently reviewed by Hallick and Buetow (1). In the present overview, we will update this review, and describe some new results on the identification and structural analysis of *Euglena* chloroplast genes, including several genes for components of the photosynthetic membranes. We will describe the identification of a new category of cell organelle intron that is to date unique to *Euglena* chlroroplast genes. We will also describe features of some mRNA transcription and maturation pathways.

2. NON-PHOTOSYNTHETIC OPERONS

2.1.   tRNAs and rRNAs. The genes for the stable chloroplast RNA species, rRNAs and tRNAs, have been reviewed (1) Two additional tRNA genes, *trn*P-TGG and *trn*S-TGA have been characterized (2), bringing to 26 the total number of different *Euglena* chloroplast tRNA species known. There are single tRNA species for 15 of 20 amino acids, and isoaccepting species for leucine (3 species), serine (2), glycine (2), isoleucine (2), and methionine (2, initiator and elongator). We believe that these 26 species represent the complete set of chloroplast-encoded tRNAs. In addition, the DNA sequence of the 23S rRNA gene of ribosomal RNA operon C has now been determined (3), permitting the assembly with existing data of a composite sequence for an entire ribosomal RNA operon (EMBL accession X12890).

2.2.   A Large Ribosomal Protein Gene Cluster. Liverwort (4) and tobacco (5) chloroplast DNAs have a large cluster of ribosomal protein genes similar to the E. coli ribosomal protein operons *S10-spc-alpha*. This cluster encodes the *rpl23-rpl2-rps19-rpl22-rps3-rpl16-rpl14-rps8-infA-rpl36-rps11* chloroplast ribosomal protein genes, with single group II introns in the *rpl2* and *rpl16* genes (4,5). There is a similar operon in *Euglena* chloroplast DNA, located on the EcoRI map (1) on the fragments designated EcoC-U-Z-J-M-A. This operon begins as in higher plants with the five genes *rpl23-rpl2-rps19-rpl22-rps3* (6), followed by a gap of 2.8 kbp. This *rps3-rpl16* intercistronic region encodes two large open reading frames of 214 and 302 codons, respectively, each preceeded by a group II intron. These potential gene(s) are not similar to any other known genes, but are

M. Baltscheffsky (ed.), Current Research in Photosynthesis, Vol. III, 491–498.
© 1990 *Kluwer Academic Publishers. Printed in the Netherlands.*

transcribed, giving rise to a stable 1.4 kb RNA. Downstream from these genes is a second cluster of ribosomal protein genes, punctuated by one internal tRNA gene. The gene order is *rpl16-rpl14-rpl5-rps8-rpl36-trnI-rps14* (7,8). The *rpl5* is a new chloroplast gene not previously reported for any chloroplast genome. *rpl5* has also not been described as a nuclear-encoded, chloroplast protein gene. The derived *rpl5* amino acid sequence is 42% identical to *E. coli* ribosomal protein L5. Additional data on the 11 ribosomal protein genes is given elsewhere (6-8). The overall organization of 11 Euglena chloroplast ribosomal protein genes is shown in Figure 1.

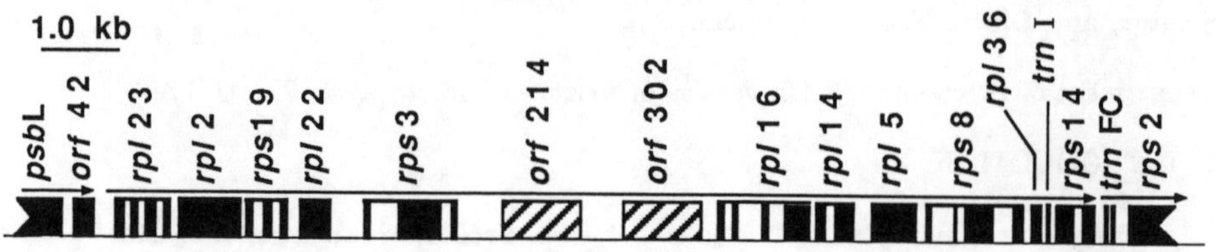

FIGURE 1. Organization of the large ribosomal protein gene cluster of *Euglena* chloroplast DNA, determined from complete DNA sequence analysis. Filled boxes are exons and open boxes are introns. Splice boundaries for *rpl16* introns 1-3, *rps8* introns 1-2, and *rps19* intron 1 were confirmed by primer-extension, cDNA sequence analysis. Gene nomenclature follows the convention of (9). Approximately 10% of the 145 kbp *Euglena gracilis* chloroplast genome is shown.

The number, position, and type of introns within the *Euglena* chloroplast ribosomal protein operon are distinct from their plant counterparts. The *rpl23*, *rps19*, and *rps3* loci are unique in that they contain 2-3 introns each. The *rpl16*, *rpl14*, *rps8*, and *rps14* genes contain 1-3 introns each. Of the 15 introns in this operon, the four introns *rps3*-intron 1, *rpl16* intron 2, and *rps8* introns 1 and 3 are in the group II category (10). The remaining 11 introns belong to a new category of chloroplast intron we have designated as "group III" (7). The properties of group III introns are as follows: (i) They are small and remarkably uniform in size, with a range of 93-111 nt; (ii) They have degenerate versions of the group II consensus boundary sequences (6); (iii) They lack the conserved secondary structure domains characteristic of group II introns (10); and (iv) They are located primarily, but not exclusively (see below) in genes for proteins involved in translation and transcription. One of the more novel juxtapositioning of introns occurs within *rps8*, where a group II and a group III intron flank an exon only 8 nt in length, the smallest yet characterized in a chloroplast gene. We believe that additional introns might be identified from cDNA sequencing within this operon in some of the intergenic spacers. There is precedent for this in the *rps4-rps11* (described below) and *rps7-tufA* (11) loci.

Transcripts arising from this operon have been characterized by Northern hybridization. Gene specific probes for each ribosomal protein, and for trnI, were employed. Each probe, beginning with the *rpl23* locus and ending with *rps14*, was found to hybridize to a common pre-mRNA of estimated size 8.3 kbp. This is the RNA size predicted for a full-length transcript of the entire operon after splicing of all 15 introns. It is noteworthy that the *trnI* gene is transcribed as an internal cistron in a polycistronic ribosomal protein operon. The most abundant transcripts detected by Northern hybridization were penta-, tetra- and tricistronic mRNAs, which are presumed to arise by stepwise processing of the 8.3 kb pre-mRNA. Numerous intermediates in this pathway were also evident. The ribosomal protein mRNAs were of very low abundance, approximately 1000-2000x less abundant than psbA mRNA in light grown cells.

2.3.   The *rps4-rps11* Operon. A small, dicistronic ribosomal protein operon has been identified in the EcoG-V region (1) of *Euglena* chloroplast DNA, flanked on either side by clusters of tRNA genes. The gene organization of this operon is shown in Figure 2. It was not possible to determine the splice boundaries within the *rps11* gene from DNA sequence data alone. Synthetic oligonucleotides complementary to the RNA like strand of *rps11* exon 3 and the template strand of *rps4* were used in the polymerase chain reaction (PCR) to synthesize a double strand cDNA copy of the internal region of the spliced *rps4-rps11* mRNA. From the cDNA sequence, two group III introns of 107 and 100 nt were identified within *rps11*, flanking a 13 nt exon. A third group III intron of 95 nt was identified within the *rps4-rps11* intercistronic spacer, located between the *rps11* ribosome binding site and initiator codon. The location of this later intron is similar to that of a small intron preceeding the Euglena chloroplast *tufA* locus (11). Transcripts from the *rps4-rps11* operon were analyzed by Northern hybridization with gene specific probes. The only RNA species detected in either dark or light grown cells was a 1.4 kb spliced, dicistronic mRNA. No precursors with the distal *trnL* cistron could be detected. Primer-extension cDNA sequence analysis was used to map the 5'-end of the dicistronic mRNA to a position at approximately -45 from the *rps4* start codon in the *rps4-trnY* intercistronic region.

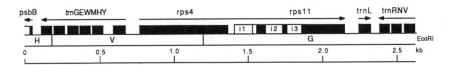

FIGURE 2. Organization of the *Euglena* chloroplast *rps4-rps11* Operon determined from chloroplast DNA and cDNA sequence analysis .

2.4.   The RNA Polymerase *rpoB-rpoC1-rpoC2* Operon. Genes for subunits of chloroplast DNA-dependent RNA polymerase have previously been located to the EcoF-R-G region (1,12) of Euglena chloroplast DNA, between the ribosomal RNA operons and a tRNA gene cluster. The DNA sequence of this entire region, spanning 12.7 kbp, has been determined. This region encodes an *rpoB-rpoC1-rpoC2* operon, similar in organization and gene products to the comparable operons from spinach (13), liverwort (4), and tobacco (5) chloroplast DNAs. The organization of this operon is shown in Figure 3. PCR-amplification, cDNA cloning and cDNA sequencing has been used to confirm the RNA splice boundaries for approximately half of the introns. The Euglena operon contains at least 22 introns, with 8 in *rpoB*, 12 in *rpoC1*, and 2 in *rpoC2*. There are four group II introns. These are rpoB-intron 8, rpoC1-intron 7, and rpoC2-introns 1 and 2. The remaining 18 introns are group III. By contrast, the three plant *rpoB-rpoC1-rpoC2* operons have a single group II intron within *rpoC1*. The Euglena *rpoB*, *rpoC1*, and *rpoC2* gene products are predicted to be 124.3 kDa, 68.2 kDa, and 94.6 kDa, respectively.

Transcripts from this RNA polymerase subunit operon have been characterized by Northern hybridization. *rpoB*, *rpoC1*, and *rpoC2* gene-specific probes all hybridize to the same 8.5 kb tricistronic, fully-spliced mRNA. The two possible dicistronic mRNAs, a 5.4 kb *rpoB-rpoC1* and a 4.7 kb *rpoC1-rpoC2* are also detected. Three possible monocistronic mRNAs, of 3.4 kb, 2.7 kb, and 1.8 kb for *rpoB*, *rpoC2*, and *rpoC1*, respectively, are also detected with the corresponding gene-specific probes. RNA processing sites have been localized by S1-nuclease mapping and primer extension cDNA sequencing to both the *rpoB-rpoC1* and *rpoC1-rpoC2* intercistronic regions. From these results, we conclude that all three cistrons are initially transcribed within the same polycistronic operon as an unspliced, pre-mRNA of approximately 12 kb in length. Splicing of the 22 introns yields the 8.5 kb tricistronic species, which is further processed by intercistronic RNA cleavage events. Post-transcriptional RNA processing events include not only splicing of group II and group III introns, but also RNA endonuclease processing at discrete, intercistronic sites. The role of these RNA processing events in regulating gene expression, if any, is unknown. There are no major differences in the spectrum of processed mRNA products between dark- and light-grown cells. Unspliced pre-mRNAs are not detected.

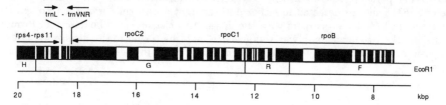

Figure 3. Organization of the Euglena chloroplast *rpoB-rpoC1-rpoC2* Operon determined from chloroplast DNA and cDNA sequence analysis. Location of this operon with respect to the EcoR1 cleavage map (1) is shown.

3. PHOTOSYNTHETIC OPERONS

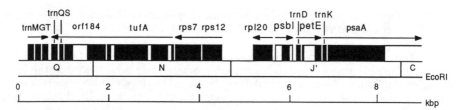

FIGURE 4. Organization of Euglena chloroplast *psbI*, *trnD*, *petE*, and *trnK* genes on the EcoJ' fragment of chloroplast DNA.

3.1. The *petE* Locus. Haley and Bogorad (14) characterized a 4-kDA subunit ("subunit V") associated with the cytochorme b6-f complex. They have shown that the polypeptide is a product of a maize chloroplast locus designated *petE*. We have identified the *petE* locus of *Euglena* chloroplast DNA within a previously reported DNA sequence between the *trnD* and *trnK* loci (15). The organization of this region is shown in Figure 4. The *Euglena petE* gene is interrupted by a single 373 nt group II intron after codon 5. The gene is 69 nt distal to *trnD*, and 48 nt proximal to *trnK*, in the same polarity as both tRNA genes. The derived amino acid sequence is 59% identical to the maize polypeptide, and

68% identical to the liverwort chloroplast "orf37" polypeptide (4). Multiple alignment of the Euglena, liverwort, and maize sequences is shown in Figure 5a.

A) *PETE*

```
                  *  *    *  **  *******   ***  ****** *
   EUGLENA      MVETLLSGIILGLIPITICGLFFTAYLQYMRSGNSFY
   MARCHANTIA   MVEALLSGIVLGLIPITLLGLFVTAYLQYRRGDQLDL
   MAIZE        MIEVFLFGIVLGLIPITLAGLFVTAYLQYRRGDQLDL
                        10        20        30
```

B) *PSBI*

```
                  ** **  ***      *****  **  *********
   EUGLENA      MLILKVFVYALILIFVSLFVFGLLSNDPGRNPYDDT
   MARCHANTIA   MLTLKLFVYTVVIFFVSLFVFGFLSNDPGRNPGRKE
   TOBACCO      MLTLKLFVYTVVIFFVSLFIFGFLSNDPGRNPGREE
                        10        20        30
```

FIGURE 5. Amino acid sequence alignments of Euglena a) *petE* and b) *psbI* gene products with corresponding plant and liverwort gene products. Asterisks (*) are amino acids conserved in all three species compared. The Euglena *psbI* sequence is internal to a longer orf of 116 codons.

3.2.   The *psbI* Locus. Ikeuchi and Inoue (16) have described a 4.8 kDa polypeptide component of photosystem II, and determined that it is the product of a chloroplast gene previously designated orf36 in liverwort (4), and orf52 in tobacco (5).This gene was renamed *psbI* (16). We have identified the *Euglena* chloroplast *psbI* locus, located immediately proximal to *trnD*. As shown in Figure 4, the Euglena chloroplast *psbI* coding region is internal to a longer orf of 116 codons. The *psbI*-like portion of the Euglena sequence is aligned with the liverwort and tobacco sequences in Figure 5b.

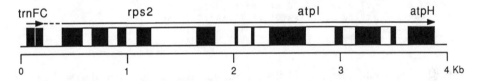

FIGURE 6. Organization of the Euglena chloroplast *rps2-atpI-atpH* genes determined from DNA sequence analysis.

3.3.   The *rps2-atpI-atpH-atpF-atpA* Operon. Chloroplast genomes from liverwort (4), tobacco (5), spinach (17), and other sources all have an operon for subunits of the ATP synthase complex encoding one subunit of CF-1, three subunits of CF-0 and the ribosomal protein S2. The gene organization of this operon is *rps2-atpI-atpH-atpF-atpA*. There is a single group II intron in the *atpI* locus of the plant operons (4,5,17). We have previously described the *Euglena* chloroplast *atpH* locus (18), and have located the *rps2* locus distal to the large cluster of ribosomal protein genes described above (Figure 1). The DNA sequence of the proximal 4 kbp of the *Euglena rps2-atpI* operon has been completed. The gene organization of this operon is shown in Figure 6. The distal regions, which are currently being analyzed, are believed to encode *atpF* and *atpA* as in higher plants. *Euglena* rps2 and atpI are interrupted by 4 and 5 introns, respectively. *atpH* is one of the rare *Euglena* chloroplast protein genes that lack introns. It is noteworthy that 4 of the *atpI* introns are in group III, with sizes of 102-111 nt. This is one of the examples of a gene for a component of the photosynthetic membranes that contains group III introns. The predicted amino acid sequence of the Euglena *atpI* gene product, pending confirmation by cDNA sequence analysis, is shown in Figure 7, aligned with the corresponding polypeptides from liverwort, tobacco, and E. coli. There are 73.6% and 73.2% identical residues with the liverwort and tobacco gene products, respectively, and 27.9% with *E. coli*. The polypeptide is considerably more conserved throughout evolution in the carboxyl terminal domains than at the amino terminal end.

```
EUGLENA      MFISGI--------F-----------LKIANVEVGQHFYWSILGFQIHGQVLINSWIVILI
MARCHANTIA   MSHTAKMASTFNNF-----------YEISNVEVGQHFYWQLGSFQVHAQVLITSWIVIAI
TOBACCO      MNVLSCSINTLKGL-----------YDISGVEVGQHFYWQIGGFQVHGQVLITSWVVIAI
E. COLI      MASENMTPQDYIGHHLNNLQLDLRTFSLVDPQNPPATFWTI---NIDS-MFFSVVLGLLF
                *            .                        .    *        .

EUGLENA      IGFLSIYTTKNLTLVPANKQIFIELVTEFITDISKTQIGEKEYSKWVPYIGTMFLFIFVS
MARCHANTIA   LLSLAVLATRNLQTIPMGGQNFVEYVLEFIRDLTRTQIGEEEYRPWVPFIGTMFLFIFVS
TOBACCO      LLGSATIAVRNPQTIPTGGQNFFEYVLEFIRDVSKTQIGEE-YGPWVPFIGTMFLFIFVS
E. COLI      LVLFRSVAKKATSGVPGKFQA-IELVIGFVNGSVKDMYHGKS-KLIAPLALTIFVWVFLM
               .      .  .    .  *    *    * * * .  *        . .  *  * *.  .

EUGLENA      NWSGALIPWKIIELPNGE---LGA----PTNDINTTAGLAILTSLAYFYAGLNKKGLTYF
MARCHANTIA   NWSGALFPWRVFELPNGE---LAA----PTNDINTTVALALLTSVAYFYAGLHKKGLSYF
TOBACCO      NWSGALLPWKIIQLPHGE---LAA----PTNDINTTVALALLTSVAYFYAGLTKKGLGYF
E. COLI      NLMD-LLPIDLLPYIAEHCLFLPALRVVPSADVNVTASMALGVFILILFYSIKMKGIGGF
               * .*.   ..         . .  * *  * . * * * ..... *     .   ** .. *

EUGLENA      KKYVQPTPIL----LPIN-ILED---FTKPLSLSFRLFGNILADELVVAVLVSLVPL---
MARCHANTIA   GKYIQPTPVL----LPIN-ILED---FTKPLSLSFRLFGNILADELVVAVLISLVPL---
TOBACCO      GKYIQPTPIL----LPIN-ILED---FTKPLSLSFRLFGNILADELVVVVLVSLVPL---
E. COLI      TKELTLQPFMHWAFIPVNLILEGVSLLSKPVSLGLRLFGNMYAGELIFILIAGLLPWWSQ
               *.    *     . * ***.   ..** .**.****** *.**   .. . *.*

EUGLENA      -IVPVPLIFLGLFTSGIQALIFATFYLNYIGEAMEGHH
MARCHANTIA   -VVPIPMMFLGLFTSAIQALIFATLAAAYIGESMEGHH
TOBACCO      -VVPIPVMLLGLFTSGIQALIFATLAAAYIGESMEGHH
E. COLI      WILNVPWAIFHILIITLQAFIFMVLTIVYLSMASE-EH
               .. .*   .. ..   ..**.**    *  .. .*
```

FIGURE 7. Multiple alignment of the atpI polypeptides of Euglena, liverwort (4), and tobacco (5) chloroplasts, and the E. coli F-0 alpha subunit. Residues that are identical across the comparison (*), or are conservative replacements (.) are marked. Alignment was via the CLUSTAL algorithm (19).

3.4.   *psbB*, *petB*, and *atpB* Genes. As shown in Figure 2, the *psbB* gene begins with a small exon of only 3 codons 62 nt downstream from the *trnG* locus in EcoH. In spinach (20), liverwort (4),tobacco (5), and other plants, this gene is in the *psbB-petB-petD* operon. Although the analysis of this region in *Euglena* is still in progress, we have determined that the *petB* locus is distal to *psbB* within the EcoD fragment, but *petD* does not follow *petB*. We find that the previously mapped atpB locus (1) begins 67 nt distal to *petB*.

4. SUMMARY.

4.1.   Group III Introns. Although group II introns are a well-known feature of both chloroplast and mitochondrial genomes, the newly described group III introns are novel. Small introns were first described in the *Euglena tufA* locus (21). We would now classify these *tufA* introns as group III introns. There are at least 42 group III Euglena introns. This includes 11 introns in the *rpl23* operon (Figure 1), 18 in the *rpoB-rpoC1-rpoC2* operon, 3 in *rps4-rps11*, 7 in *rps2-atpI*, and 3 in *tufA*. Additional group III introns occur in *psbB*, and most likely in numerous other loci. Group III introns appear to be more common in the operons that have low abundance transcripts. The chloroplast genes that give rise to the most abundant mRNA transcripts, *psbA* and *rbcL*, have only group II introns.

4.2.   Progress Toward a Complete DNA Sequencing of *Euglena* Chloroplast DNA. With the completion of the DNA sequence of the *rpoB-rpoC1-rpoC2* locus, 23S rRNA gene, and *rps4-11* operon, we have been able to assemble a continuous, composite DNA sequence of more than 37 kbp from new data and sequences in the EMBL and GenBank data bases for a segment of the chloroplast genome beginning in EcoB and ending in EcoH (1). This segment is continuous for the EcoRI restriction fragments EcoP1-EcoL1-EcoP2-EcoL2-EcoP3-EcoF-EcoR-EcoG-EcoV, accounting for 26% of the chloroplast genome. Another large block of continuous DNA sequence data has been assembled for the restriction fragments EcoQ-EcoN-EcoJ'-EcoC-EcoU-EcoZ-EcoJ-EcoM-EcoA that totals more than 33 kbp. This represents an additional 23% of the genome. Other smaller regions of known sequence add an additional 20-25 kbp to this total. At present, at least 90-95 kbp, or approximately two-thirds of the 145 kbp *Euglena* chloroplast genome has been sequenced. We hope that this review will help highlight some of the interesting aspects of *Euglena* chloroplasts as a model system for the study of the development of the photosynthetic apparatus.

Acknowledgements. This work was supported by the U. S. National Institutes of Health. We would like to recognize the many contributions of Erhard Stutz and his colleagues (cited in our earlier review (1)) to the detailed knowledge of the structure and organization of *Euglena* chloroplast DNA.

5. REFERENCES

1. Hallick, R.B. and Buetow, D.E. (1989) in The Biology of *Euglena*, Vol. IV (Buetow, D.E., ed.), pp. 351-414, Academic Press, New York.
2. Manzara,T. and Hallick, R.B. (1988), Nucleic Acids Res. 16, 9866.
3. Yepiz-Plascencia, G. M., Jenkins, M. E. and Hallick, R.B. (1988), Nucleic Acids Res. 16, 9340.
4. Ohyama, K., Fukuzawa, H., Kohchi, T., Shirai, H., Sano, T., Sano, S., Umesono, K., Shiki, Y., Takeuchi, M., Chang, Z., Aota, S., Inokuchi, H., and Ozeki, H. (1986), Nature 322, 572-574.
5. Shinozaki, K., Ohme, M., Tanaka, M., Wakasugi, T., Hayashida, N., Matsubayashi, T., Zaita, N., Chunwongse, J., Obokata, J, Yamaguchi-Shinozaki, K., Ohto, C., Torazawa, K., Meng, B. Y., Sugita, M., Deno, H., Kamogashira, T., Yamada, K., Kusuda, J., Takaiwa, F., Kato, A., Tohdoh, N., Shimada, H., and Sugiura, M. (1986) EMBO J. 5, 2040-2049.
6. Christopher, D. A., Cushman, J. C., Price, C. A., and Hallick, R. B. (1988), Current Genetics 14, 275-286.
7. Christopher, D. A., and Hallick, R. B. (1989), submitted for publication.
8. Nickoloff, J. A., Christopher, D. A., Drager, R. G., and Hallick, R. B. (1989), Nucleic Acids Res. 17, 4882.
9. Hallick, R. B. and Bottomley, W. (1983), Plant Mol. Biol. Reporter 1, 38-43.
10. Michel, F., and Dujon, B. (1983), EMBO J. 2, 33-38.

11. Montandon, P.-E., Knuchel-Aegerter, C., and Stutz, E. (1987), Nucleic Acids Res. 15, 7809-7822.
12. Little, M. C. and Hallick, R. B. (1988), J. Biol. Chem. 263, 14302-14307.
13. Hudson, G.S., Holton, T. A., Whitfeld, P. R. and Bottomley, W. (1988), J. Mol. Biol. 200, 639-654.
14. Haley, J. and Bogorad, L., (1989), Proc. Natl. Acad. Sci. USA 86, 1534-1538.
15. Manzara, T., Hu, J.-X., Price, C. A., and Hallick, R. B. (1987), Plant Mol. Biol. 8, 327-336.
16. Ikeuchi, M. and Inoue, Y. (1988), FEBS Lett. 241, 99-104.
17. Hudson, G. S., Mason, J. G., Holton, T. A., Koller, B., Cox, G. B., Whitfeld, P. R., and Bottomley, W. (1987), J. Mol. Biol. 196, 283-298.
18. Passavant, C. W., and Hallick, R. B. (1985), Plant Mol. Biol. 4, 347-354.
19. Higgins, D. G. and Sharp, P. M. (1988), Gene 73, 237-244.
20. Heinemeyer, W., Alt, J., and Herrmann, R. G. (1984), Curr. Genetics 8, 543-549.
21. Montandon, P.-E. and Stutz, E. (1983), Nucl. Acids Res. 11, 5877-5892.

THE MOLECULAR BIOLOGY OF SITE-DIRECTED MODIFICATION OF PHOTOSYSTEM II IN THE UNICELLULAR CYANOBACTERIUM SYNECHOCYSTIS SP. PCC 6803.

Paula Ravnikar, Idah Sithole, R. Debus, G. Babcock[*] and Lee McIntosh. D.O.E. Plant Research Laboratory; [*]Department of Chemistry, Michigan State University, East Lansing, Michigan, 48824, U.S.A.

1. INTRODUCTION AND BACKGROUND

1.1. Photosystem II

Ultimately, the majority of biological energy sources arise from the primary capture of light by photosynthetic organisms. Until relatively recently, it has only been possible to "observe" and to quantitate photosynthetic reactions and speculate on their mechanisms and potential limitations. With the advent of recombinant DNA techniques -coupled with suitable model photosynthetic/genetic systems- we may now approach the study of photosynthesis through interactive molecular modification. We may begin to propose theoretical models for photosynthetic mechanisms and proceed to directly test these hypotheses by altering the structure of the genes encoding photosynthetic reaction center components. These approaches have been made possible by great advances in our understanding of the structure of photosynthetic complexes.

Recently, the structures of the reaction centers from Rhodopseudomonas viridis and Rhodobacter sphaeroides have been solved at the atomic level (1,2). In both organisms the reaction center "core" polypeptides consist of the L and M subunits (responsible for charge separation), a cytochrome, and the H subunit (possibly required for stable assembly). It has become apparent that the bacterial reaction center, particularly the L and M subunits, can be directly compared to the reaction center polypeptides, D1 and D2, of Photosystem II (3).

In Photosystem II, an electron donor, a special chlorophyll $\underline{a}$, is photooxidized and in turn oxidizes a manganese complex $\underline{via}$ an intermediate electron donor "Z". The manganese complex accumulates four charges, extracts four electrons from water ("water splitting"), releases oxygen and forms a transmembrane proton gradient. Charge separation takes place with single electron transfer to a bound quinone "Q_A". In two separate reactions this acceptor transfers single electrons to another bound quinone "Q_B" which transfers two electrons (in a single reaction) to a membrane pool of plastoquinone. In turn, reduced plastoquinone transfers its electrons to the cytochrome b_6f complex. This complex, a plastoquinol:oxidized-

M. Baltscheffsky (ed.), Current Research in Photosynthesis, Vol. III, 499–507.
© 1990 Kluwer Academic Publishers. Printed in the Netherlands.

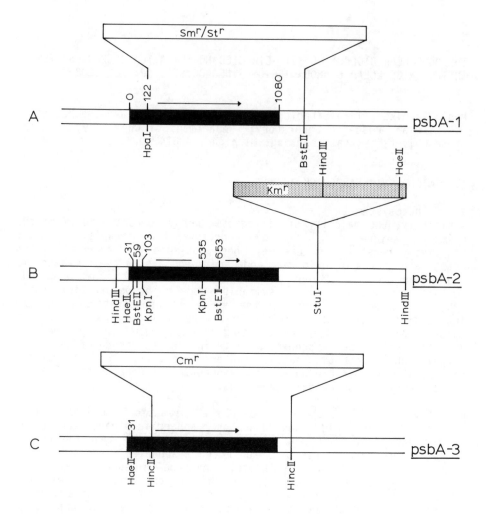

Figure 1. A schematic representation of the three copies of the psbA gene family in Synechocystis 6803. In order to facilitate mutagenesis of psbA-2 a strain was constructed where psbA-1 and psbA-3 were partially deleted and a drug resistance cassette was inserted downstream from the psbA-2 coding sequence.

plastocyanin oxidoreductase, mediates transfer of electrons from Photosystem II to Photosystem I. The Photosystem I reaction center, in which electron transfer takes place through three iron-sulfur centers, functions as a light-driven plastocyanin:ferredoxin oxidoreductase.

1.2. Synechocystis 6803.

A model system for the study of photosynthesis has been developed employing the cyanobacterium Synechocystis 6803 (4,5). Initially, we have employed this organism to study the reaction center of Photosystem II. In Photosystem II we have concentrated our experiments on the reaction center components D1 and D2, encoded by the psbA and psbD genes respectively. In Synechocystis 6803 there are two copies of psbD (6,7) and three copies of psbA (5,8; Figure 1). It is possible to transform Synechocystis 6803 with DNA directly and to recover transformants, through drug selection, that have foreign or altered DNA fragments integrated into the cyanobacterial genome through homologous recombination (4,5,7).

Synechocystis 6803 also possesses another property which makes it an excellent model system for the study of Photosystem II. It is possible to grow Synechocystis 6803 in the absence of Photosystem II; i.e., in the presence of 3-(3,4-dichlorophenyl)-1,1-dimethylurea (DCMU) and glucose (5,7). Under these conditions it is possible to obtain mutations within Photosystem II that may otherwise be lethal (8). It has also been shown that one can simply remove all active copies of one of the Photosystem II reaction center components and still recover viable cells in the presence of glucose (5). A strain of Synechocystis 6803 has also been made in which two copies of psbA, psbA1 and psbA3, have been functionally deleted (8; Figure 1).

2. PROCEDURE

2.1. Gene Replacement

Previously, we have employed this model system in conjunction with site-directed mutagenesis to make specific amino acid changes in the reaction center of Photosystem II. Deletion of a gene or its insertional merely requires the insertion of a bacterial drug-resistance cassette into a cloned Synechocystis gene or into sites which encompass the position previously occupied by the gene in question (Figure 1). The "modified" DNA is used to transform Synechocystis 6803 and mutants are selected for on agar plates containing the appropriate drug.

2.2. Site-specific mutations

Frequently, the mutation desired is one where a specific amino acid residue is changed and the mutant gene product expressed in the organism of choice. We have employed this approach to investigate Photosystem II function in Synechocystis 6803. However, this type of experiment requires a modified experimental design in comparison with

Selection/Screening of Site-directed Mutants

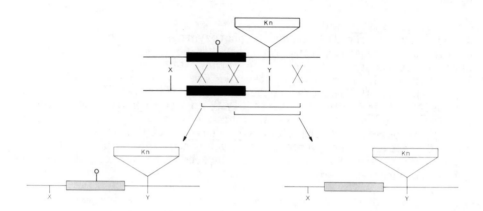

Figure 2. A diagram illustrating the possible homologous crossover events in a typical mutagenesis experiment for psbA in Synechocystis. The "O" represents a single site-directed mutation in the coding sequence (shaded area).

gene inactivation as described above. If we use psbA as a model it is possible to explain how a site-specific mutant is obtained. First, in this case there are three resident psbA genes and thus two of these genes must be removed in order that the mutations to be introduced later will not appear within a "wild-type" photosynthesis background. As described earlier, we deleted the major portions of both psbA1 and psbA3 for these experiments (7,8; Figure 1). This leaves one psbA copy, psbA2, for site-specific mutagenesis experiments (Figure 1.).

When specific amino acid changes are desired within a functional gene it is necessary to employ a drug-resistance marker that is not inserted with the gene of interest. This raises two problems. First, where is this gene to be placed? It is necessary to not interfere with the transcription of the gene of interest and also to not interrupt any nearby gene that may be required for cell viability. Due to the small genome size of Synechocystis 6803 (9), the spacing between genes in this organism is often observed to be quite close. Therefore, DNA sequencing is required in the areas

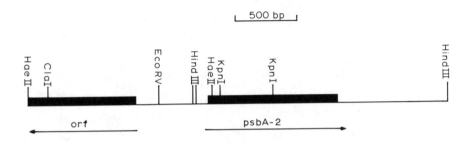

Figure 3. A restriction map showing psbA-2 and the upstream unidentified open-reading-frame (orf).

surrounding the gene to be mutated (see Results and Discussion). A second problem arises because the selectable marker is outside the gene such that selection of a drug-resistant mutant does not guarantee that the mutation is present within the functional gene. This is because the crossover events for homologous recombination may occur at two points which encompass the selectable marker, but which do not include the amino acid modification (Figure 2). Therefore, those mutants selected based upon drug resistance must be analyzed further. Synechocystis 6803 may also possess more than one copy of its genome (5,7) thus further complicating the analysis of potential mutants. Due to this potential problem, transformants are repeatedly streaked from single colonies in order to obtain stable isolates. In many cases it is possible to include a DNA restriction site modification along with the mutation that will allow for future analysis by DNA restriction endonuclease site mapping (7). Furthermore, all potential mutants are checked by DNA sequence analysis. In our experience, approximately 30-50% of our selected mutants will encompass the specific amino acid change.

3. RESULTS

Success in genetic modification may depend not only upon the

```
          10                    30                    50
GGCGTTTTGGGGGTTGAGAAGAGTTTACCTGGCGGTTTTTCGTGCGCCTTTACCATAGTT
          70                    90                   110
CTGGGCTGTGTAGAGGGGCGACACAACTGATTTTCAGGGACAATGGAGATGAAATAATGA
         130                   150                   170
AAAATAATGAAATTGATCACTGGGCCTTGCACGCCATTACTCTTAAGGTCAGTGGTCAGT
         190                   210                   230
CAGTTTAAGCAATAGTCGGGCATACAATTATGATCCATATACCTAATACTTATTGATATC
         250                   270                   290
CCTGAATTTTTTGGTCACATTGTCCCTGGGTTCCGCCACAATGTTTCATTAACCCCCAGC
         310                   330                   350
AAATATCCACTGGAACGCTAAAGCCGCAATCGTTGCTCACCATGGCGATCGCCAGAAGGC
         370                   390                   410
CTGCATCTGGGCAAGGATTCTGATATTTTTAGGGGGATGTATTTTGGGGCAATGGGGAAA
         430                   450                   470
AATTAACTAATGTCAAAGTCTAAAGTTGTTTTGCTGACAGGCATCACGGGGCAAGATGGC
              M  S  K  S  K  V  V  L  L  T  G  I  T  G  Q  D  G
         490                   510                   530
TCCTATCTGAGTGAATTGTTGTTGGAAAAGGGCTACCAAGTCCATGGCATCATTCGCCGA
  S  Y  L  S  E  L  L  L  E  K  G  Y  Q  V  H  G  I  I  R  R
         550                   570                   590
ACTTCTACCTTTAACACTGACCGCATTGATCATCTTTATGTTGATCCCCATGATCTTGAG
  T  S  T  F  N  T  D  R  I  D  H  L  Y  V  D  P  H  D  L  E
         610                   630                   650
GCGAAACTCCGACTTCATTATGGTGATCTGACCGACGGCACCACCCTGCGCCGCATTTTA
  A  K  L  R  L  H  Y  G  D  L  T  D  G  T  T  L  R  R  I  L
         670                   690                   710
GAAGATGTCAAACCGACGGAGATTTACAATCTGGGGGCCCAATCCCACGTGCGGGTGAGC
  E  D  V  K  P  T  E  I  Y  N  L  G  A  Q  S  H  V  R  V  S
         730                   750                   770
TTTGATTCTCCGGAATACACTGTAGATTCAGTGGCCATGGGGACGCTACGACTATTGGAA
  F  D  S  P  E  Y  T  V  D  S  V  A  M  G  T  L  R  L  L  E
         790                   810                   830
GCGATTCGGGATTATCAACATCGCACCGGCATCCAAGTAAGGTTCTATCAAGCCGGTTCT
  A  I  R  D  Y  Q  H  R  T  G  I  Q  V  R  F  Y  Q  A  G  S
         850                   870                   890
TCGGAAATGTTCGGCAAAGTGCAGGAGATTCCCCAAAAGGAAACCACCCCCTTTTATCCC
  S  E  M  F  G  K  V  Q  E  I  P  Q  K  E  T  T  P  F  Y  P
         910                   930                   950
CGCAGTCCCTACGCCTGTGCCAAGGTTTATGGCCATTGGCAAACGGTGAACTATCGGGAA
  R  S  P  Y  A  C  A  K  V  Y  G  H  W  Q  T  V  N  Y  R  E
         970                   990                  1010
TCCTATGACTTATTCGCCTGTAACGGCATTTTGTTCAACCACGAATCCCCCCGCCGGGGA
  S  Y  D  L  F  A  C  N  G  I  L  F  N  H  E  S  P  R  R  G
        1030                  1050                  1070
GAAACCTTTGTAACCAGGAAAATTACTAGGGCGATCGCCAGAATTGTGGCCGGCACCCAA
  E  T  F  V  T  R  K  I  T  R  A  I  A  R  I  V  A  G  T  Q
        1090                  1110                  1130
AAGAAATTGTATTTAGGCAATATCGATTCCAAGCGGGATTGGGGCTATGCCAAGGACTAT
  K  K  L  Y  L  G  N  I  D  S  K  R  D  W  G  Y  A  K  D  Y
        1150                  1170                  1190
GTACGGGCCATGTGGGCCATGTTGCAACAGGAACAGCCCGATGACTATGTGGTGGCCACG
  V  R  A  M  W  A  M  L  Q  Q  E  Q  P  D  D  Y  V  V  A  T
        1210                  1230                  1250
GGGGAAACCCACGAAGTGAAGGAATTTTTAGAAATTGCCTTTGGTTACGTCAACCTCAAC
  G  E  T  H  E  V  K  E  F  L  E  I  A  F  G  Y  V  N  L  N
        1270
TGGCAGAACTATGTGGCCTTTGATGAC
  W  Q  N  Y  V  A  F  D  D
```

Figure 4. The DNA sequence of the open-reading-frame upstream of psbA-2. The reduced amino acid sequence is shown below the DNA sequence. The arrow indicated the start of transcription and the underlined portions represent possible RNA polymerase recognition sites and a potential ribosome binding site.

fundamental proposals centered around specific genetic modifications of the gene(s) in question, but also on (1) gene copy number, (2) the potential regulatory sequences surrounding this gene, and (3) upon the close location of other genes whose products are required for growth of the organism. The psbA gene family in Synechocystis 6803 is a good example for all three of these concerns.

In higher plants there is usually a single copy of the psbA gene within the chloroplast DNA (10). However, in cyanobacteria there are small gene families of the psbA genes present (11,12,13). Thus, one must first characterize and possibly delete (see Materials and Methods) unwanted gene copies. Synechocystis 6803 has three copies of psbA (Figure 1) of which two, psbA2 and psbA3, are expressed and a third copy, psbA1, which is expressed at very low levels. Copies 2 & 3 are almost identical in coding sequence while copy 1 is much more divergent (Ravnikar and McIntosh, in preparation; 14,15). Apparently, copies two and three encode the major form of D1 polypeptide in Synechocystis 6803. A similar preference for a particular D1 protein has also been shown for Synechococcus sp. PCC 7942 (11). However, this was shown to vary somewhat with growth conditions.

psbA2 from Synechocystis 6803 has been the gene of choice for the genetic modification of the D1 polypeptide. Copy three was found to have another gene in close proximity which interferes with easy manipulation of the gene (Ravnikar and McIntosh, in preparation). The selectable marker employed for copy two mutagenesis, kanamycin resistance, was placed 3' to the coding sequence and outside the probable termination site of the transcript (8). There is no other gene present in this position. However, it is interesting to note that 5' to the amino terminus of psbA2 there is a large open-reading-frame (Figure 3, Figure 4). This open-reading-frame (ORF) is approximately 600 bp from the first ATG of psbA2 and is transcribed in the opposite direction. The open reading frame continues for 286 amino acids and runs off the cloned portion of DNA. The start-site for transcription is approximately 357 bp from the ATG of the ORF as determined by S1-nuclease protection experiments (Figure 4). The position of this transcript and open-reading-frame makes insertion of a marker for selection 5' proximal to the psbA2 gene problematic.

The identity of the open-reading-frame is as yet unknown, lacking convincing homology to any known sequence found in the EMBL and Genebank sequence data bases. If this open-reading-frame does encode a functional protein it is probably not a "chloroplast type" gene. However, since the S1-nuclease experiments (described above) demonstrate that this DNA fragment is transcribed in Synechocystis 6803 when grown under "normal" conditions (4,7), it is likely that this ORF is a gene.

4. DISCUSSION

Model cyanobacterial genetic systems such as Synechocystis 6803 have become more important in the continuing efforts to understand the mechanisms and limitations of photosynthetic reactions. While the ease with which these organisms may be manipulated has been proven, it is also necessary to understand the limitations still to be overcome. First among these, is a more complete understanding of the biology and molecular genetics of cyanobacteria. While we may sometimes employ these organisms in a similar capacity as Escherichia coli, our understanding of their biology and genetics is sadly lacking. In some cases, this may prove limiting to the type of experiments planned for the molecular modification of photosynthesis. Beyond the potential problems of interfering with resident genes described above, the growth conditions required for these photosynthetic manipulations may be one of the more difficult problems remaining to be solved. The best example of this is the application of similar approaches to the functional modification of Photosystem I. Conditions that will allow for growth in the absence of Photosystem I, and thus selection of Photosystem I functional mutants, must be defined. Photosystem I

5. ACKNOWLEDGMENTS

We would like to thank J. Sevrinck and P. Saetaert for their help in DNA sequence analysis, and K. Rorrer for technical assistance. This work was supported in part by DOE Contract DE-AC02-76ER01338 to L.M. and a McKnight Foundation Training Grant for Photosynthesis to Michigan State University and GM 37300 (G.B.).

REFERENCES

1. Allen, J.P., Feher, G., Yeates, T.O., Komiya, H. and Rees, D.C. (1987) Proc. Natl. Acad. Sci. USA 84, 5730-5734
2. Deisenhofer, J., Epp, O., Miki, K., Huber, R. and Michel, H. (1984) J. Mol. Biol. 180, 385-398
3. Michel, H. and Deisenhofer, J. (1988) Biochem. 27, 1-7
4. McIntosh, L., Williams, J.G.K., Somerville, C., and Gurevitz, M. (1985) in The Molecular Form and Function of the Plant Genome (L. van Vloten-Dotten, ed.), pp.335-346, Plenum, New York
5. Jansson, C., Debus, R.J., Osiewacz, H.D., Gurevitz, M. and McIntosh, L. (1987) Plant Physiol. 85, 1021-1025
6. Williams, J.G.K., and Chisholm, D.A. (1987) in Progress in Photosynthesis Research (Biggins, J., ed.), Vol. 4, pp.809-812, Martinus Nijhoff, Dordrecht, The Netherlands
7. Debus, R.J., Barry, B.A., Babcock, G.T., and McIntosh, L. (1988) Proc. Natl. Acad. Sci. USA 85, 427-430
8. Debus, R.J., Barry, B.A., Sithole, I., Babcock, G.T. and McIntosh, L. (1988) Biochem. 27, 9071-9074.

9. Herdman, M. (1985) in The Evolution of Genome Size
    (Cavalier-Smith, T., ed.), pp.37-68, J.Wiley & Sons, New York
10. Hirschberg, J. and L. McIntosh (1983) Science 222, 1346-1349
11. Schaefer, M.R. and Golden, S.S. (1989) J. Bact. 171, 3973-3981
12. Curtis, S.E. and Haselkorn, R. (1984) Plant Mol. Biol. 3, 249-258
13. Mulligan, B., Schultes, N., Chen, L. and Bogorad, L. (1984) Proc.
    Natl. Acad. Sci. USA 81, 2693-2697
14. Osiewacz, H.D. and McIntosh, L. (1987) Nucl. Acids Res. 15, 10585
15. Ravnikar, P.D., Debus, R.J., Sevrinck, J., Saetaert, P. and L.
    McIntosh (1989) Nucl. Acids Res. 17, 3991

MANIPULATING THE CHLOROPLAST GENOME OF CHLAMYDOMONAS
- - - MOLECULAR GENETICS AND TRANSFORMATION.

John E. Boynton, Nicholas W. Gillham, Elizabeth H. Harris, Scott M. Newman, Barbara L. Randolph-Anderson, Anita M. Johnson and Allan R. Jones, Departments of Botany and Zoology, Duke University, Durham, NC 27706 USA

In photosynthetic eukaryotes, genes encoding chloroplast proteins of multimeric complexes involved in photosynthesis and protein synthesis are partitioned between the cell's nuclear and chloroplast genomes. The chloroplast genome's relatively small size, high copy number and great evolutionary conservation have led to rapid progress in identifying and characterizing chloroplast genes. In fact, the entire chloroplast genomes of tobacco, liverwort and rice have been sequenced within the last three years (1-3). Somewhat less progress has been made in identifying the nuclear genes for the remainder of the chloroplast polypeptides, due to the larger number of genes and the much larger size and evolutionary diversity of the nuclear genomes themselves. However in many plant species, nuclear genes can be engineered in vitro, the constructs introduced by transformation, and their function studied in vivo.

While manipulation of cloned chloroplast genes in vitro has been possible for some time, until very recently there has been no way to introduce modified genes into the chloroplasts of plant cells to assess their function in vivo. Our initial success in transforming the chloroplast genome of the unicellular green alga Chlamydomonas (4) was made possible by development of a high velocity particle gun that delivers DNA-coated microprojectiles into the cell (5), the existence of stable nonphotosynthetic deletion mutants affecting the chloroplast atpB gene encoding the beta subunit of the ATP synthase (6,7) to serve as recipients, and the availability of the corresponding cloned wild type gene (8) to use as a donor. This allowed us to complement the mutant phenotype under conditions of stringent selection where rare photosynthetically competent cells were readily detected. This paper will summarize progress we have made since our initial report in increasing the frequency of transformation for point and deletion mutations at the chloroplast atpB locus, and results of transformation experiments with the chloroplast psbA gene encoding the D1 reaction center protein of photosystem II and the chloroplast 16S and 23S rRNA genes. Utilizing donor and recipient strains that differ in restriction fragment length polymorphisms, we are now able to determine the position of recombination events leading to integration of the donor fragments in individual transformants.

Further transformation studies with deletion and missense mutations affecting the chloroplast atpB gene: Using tungsten microprojectiles freshly prepared to minimize oxidation and the protocol described previously (4), we have now obtained transformation frequencies for the ac-u-c-2-21 mutant (CC-373) as high as 1.4 X 10^{-4}, about 50 fold greater than originally reported (4). This mutant recipient with a 2.5 kb deletion removing the 3' half of the atpB gene and extending downstream into the inverted repeat was complemented by a pBR313 plasmid (P-17) containing the 7.6 kb Bam 10 chloroplast fragment carrying the wild type atpB gene.

M. Baltscheffsky (ed.), Current Research in Photosynthesis, Vol. III, 509–516.
© 1990 *Kluwer Academic Publishers. Printed in the Netherlands.*

Transformation frequencies for this donor/recipient combination can be increased four fold by exposing the recipient cells immediately before bombardment to a low dose of UV irradiation (1.7×10^5 ergs/cm^2) followed by a 2 hr dark incubation after bombardment to prevent photoreactivation (Table 1). Lower UV doses have no effect on transformation frequencies and higher doses reduce transformation efficiency. While the mechanism of the UV effects on chloroplast transformation is not understood, UV irradiation is known to stimulate integration of heterologous donor sequences during transformation of cyanobacteria (9). Reducing the number of chloroplast genomes five to seven fold by growing the ac-u-c-2-21 mutant in 5 mM 5-fluorodeoxyuridine (FdUrd; 10) prior to transformation increases the frequency of transformation 20 to 280 fold (Table 1). This reduction in copy number very likely facilitates segregation of recipient cells homoplasmic for the integrated donor fragment. Experiments have not yet been done to determine if the UV and FdUrd treatments in combination are additive or synergistic.

Table 1. Attempts to increase the frequency of transformation for the chloroplast atpB deletion (ac-u-c-2-21) and missense (ac-u-c-2-29, ac-u-c-2-9) mutations.

Treatment of Recipient Cells	Increase in Transformation Frequency	
	deletion mutation	missense mutations
18 hour delay in replating cells on selective medium	0.4 fold	0.4 fold
Irradiation prior to bombardment with 1.7×10^5 ergs/cm^2 UV	4 fold	?
Pregrowth in 0.5 mM FdUrd to reduce genome copy number	20-280 fold	0.5 fold
Reduction of chloroplast protein synthesis with spectinomycin	?	2.6 fold
Reduction in chloroplast genome number and protein synthesis	?	13.7 fold

In our initial experiments (4), we found that ac-u-c-2-21 (CC-373) and ac-u-c-2-43 (CC-1015), deletion mutants lacking part or all of the atpB gene, yielded 4-15 fold higher frequencies of photosynthetically competent colonies than the ac-u-c-2-29 missense mutation (CC-440) in the same gene when all were transformed with the P-17 donor plasmid. Allowing additional time following bombardment for expression of the wild type donor gene prior to imposition of selection did not increase transformation frequencies for either ac-u-c-2-21 or ac-u-c-2-29 (Table 1). In an attempt to reduce the number of defective beta subunits made by the missense mutant recipient (11), we carried out transformation experiments on a strain (CC-707) containing the atpB missense mutation ac-u-c-2-9 (11), coupled with the chloroplast rRNA mutation spr-u-1-27-3. The latter mutation confers a low level of spectinomycin resistance on the chloroplast protein synthesizing system (12,13), and cells carrying it will grow in the presence of spectinomycin only on media containing acetate as a respirable carbon source, since they fail to synthesize photosynthetic polypeptides encoded by the chloroplast genome. Thus we predicted that growing ac-u-c-2-9 spr-u-1-27-3 in the presence of spectinomycin (40 ug/ml) and acetate for five to seven generations would reduce levels of defective atpB subunits and increase transformation frequencies compared to the same genotype grown in the absence of spectinomycin. Cells of this double mutant were also grown in 0.5 mM FdUrd for a similar number of generations to measure the effect of reducing chloroplast copy number on the frequency of transformation and in FdUrd + spectinomycin to determine whether the two agents acted additively or synergistically. We found that growth of the double mutant in spectinomycin prior to bombardment increased the transformation frequency 2.6 fold, whereas growth in FdUrd did not result in any increase (Table 1). The fact that a reduction in number of copies of the defective atpB gene did not increase transformation frequencies is consistent with our finding that a similar reduction in copy number of chloroplast genes in wild type cells has little or no effect on the amounts of photosynthetic polypeptides synthesized (14). However, when the double mutant was grown in spectinomycin + FdUrd, a 13.7 fold increase in transformants was seen. Thus reduction in genome number enhances the effect of reduction in chloroplast protein synthesis on the atpB missense mutation to increase the probability that the donor wild type DNA will be expressed sufficiently to restore photosynthetic competence to the recipient cells. Neither treatment alone or in combination produced a marked increase in the spontaneous reversion frequency of the recipient strain, which was 4-10 X 10^{-3} below the transformation frequency in each case.

The presence of defective beta subunits in the recipient missense mutant cell may interfere with wild type beta subunits encoded by the donor gene becoming assembled into a functional ATP synthase complex. This problem may also affect transformation of missense mutations in other chloroplast genes encoding polypeptides that are part of multi-component complexes. In collaboration with Dr. Robert Spreitzer, we found that bombardment of the 10-6C missense mutation in the rbcL gene encoding the RUBISCO large subunit (15) with a pUC8 donor plasmid carrying the 5.8 kb Eco 14 fragment containing the wild type gene yielded very few photosynthetically competent transformants (frequency 4-12 X 10^{-8}) but these were still 8 to 24 times more frequent than spontaneous reversions of the mutation. Since the defective large subunits of the 10-6C mutant assemble into a nonfunctional holoenzyme complex (15), we are testing the possibility that reducing the amount of the defective RUBISCO large subunit synthesized by this mutant prior to transformation will increase the transformation frequency.

We previously observed that the frequent size variation occurring in transformants of the 2.5 kb deletion mutation ac-u-c-2-21 was localized to a small Kpn I fragment in the inverted repeat region of the chloroplast genome downstream of the atpB gene that contains a 12 bp tandem repeat sequence (4). We now find by sequence analysis that this size variation results from duplication or deletion of this T T T A T T T T A C A C repeat module. In ac-u-c-2-21, 20 complete copies of the repeat occur in the fusion fragment immediately adjacent to the deletion breakpoint, whereas the wild type donor fragment contains 16 copies. A transformant with the smallest Kpn I fragment has 11 complete tandem copies and a transformant with the longest Kpn I fragment has 25 complete tandem copies. We do not know whether variation in length of these tandem repeats in the transformants results from unequal pairing and crossing over during the initial integration of the wild type donor fragment. The possibility that unequal pairing and crossing over may occur subsequently during replication of the initial transformed genome cannot be ruled out, since variability in the size of this Kpn fragment is also seen following transformation of ac-u-c-2-21 with a shorter donor fragment lacking the repeats (16).

To establish whether integration can occur within the atpB coding sequence with sufficient precision to permit synthesis of a functional beta subunit, the atpB missense mutation ac-u-c-2-29 was transformed with a pUC 8 plasmid carrying a 1.7 kb Eco-Pst insert containing the 5' half of the wild type atpB coding sequence plus upstream flanking sequence (Fig. 1). For a transformant to synthesize a functional beta subunit, a recombination event must occur within the atpB coding sequence, between the site of the AT -> GC missense alteration at bp 462 (11) and the Pst I site at bp 989 at the end of the donor fragment. However the frequency of transformants resulting from this intragenic integration event is five fold lower than for transformants obtained when the donor DNA was a pUC 8 plasmid carrying a 2.9 kb Eco-Kpn insert with the intact gene together

Fig. 1. Transformation of the atpB missense mutation ac-u-c-2-29 with pUC8 plasmids containing wild type sequences complementary to various segments of the coding sequence.

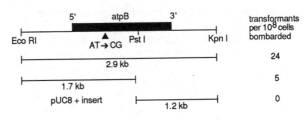

with upstream and downstream flanking regions. Since the smaller donor plasmid has ca. one third of the region of homology 3' to the missense mutation in which the integration event could take place compared to the longer plasmid, and yields about one fifth of the transformants of the larger fragment, the homologous pairing and recombination events within the atpB coding sequence leading to precise integration appear to be reasonably efficient.

Transformation of the psbA gene encoding the D1 reaction center polypeptide of photosystem II: A nonphotosynthetic mutation ac-u-β (CC-744) with symmetrical 9 kb deletions in the inverted repeat region of the chloroplast genome resulting in loss of both copies of the psbA gene (6) was used as recipient. These deletions are contained entirely within the partially homologous restriction fragments Xho 5 (17 kb) and Xho 8 (11 kb), resulting in mutant fusion fragments of 8 and 2 kb (Δ 5, Δ 8 in Fig. 2). The donor pUC18 plasmid provided by Drs. J. Erickson and J.-D. Rochaix carried a 10 kb Bam HI-Bgl II chloroplast fragment spanning the entire psbA gene and flanking regions from a DCMU resistant mutant Dr4 (17). The fragment had homology to one end of the fusion fragment in the recipient, but stopped about 200 bp short of the deletion breakpoint at the other end. All nine photosynthetically competent transformants isolated (frequency 0.18 X 10^{-6}) grew well on minimal medium and were herbicide resistant. In contrast to the homologous replacement events seen for atpB transformants, the eight psbA transformants examined were heteroplasmic, with similar complex patterns of mutant and wild type sequences.

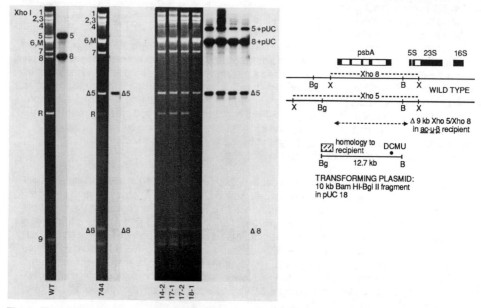

Fig. 2. Transformation of the symmetrical deletion mutation ac-u-β missing both copies of the psbA gene encoding the D1 reaction center polypeptide of photosystem II. Chloroplast DNA purified on NaI equilibrium gradients from wild type (WT), the nonphotosynthetic ac-u-β recipient (744) and four representative transformants was digested with Xho I, the fragments separated on 0.8% agarose gels, blotted to nitrocellulose and probed with ^{32}P nick translated pUC18 plasmid containing the 10 kb Bam HI-Bgl II fragment from the DCMU resistant mutant Dr4. The diagram at the right depicts the position of the psbA gene in the Xho 5 and Xho 8 fragments from the two copies of the inverted repeat of wild type, the location of the symmetrical deletion in the ac-u-β mutant and the location of the Bam-Bgl insert of the donor plasmid.

When the transforming plasmid was used as a probe, a minority of chloroplast genomes from these psbA transformants contained larger than normal restriction fragments derived from Xho 5 and Xho 8 with intact copies of the donor psbA gene (5+pUC and 8+pUC in Fig. 2). These same fragments in the transformants also hybridized to pUC 18 alone, indicating the presence of integrated pUC sequences. Both hybridizing bands correspond to faintly staining, substoichiometric bands on the ethidium bromide stained gel of purified chloroplast DNA. In each case, hybridization to 8+pUC is stronger than to 5+pUC, whereas equally strong hybridization to Xho 5 and 8 is seen in wild type (Fig. 2). This suggests that some copies of this minority fraction of chloroplast genomes in each transformant contain two copies of the restored psbA gene whereas others have only one. In contrast, the majority of chloroplast genomes in each transformant contain the 8 kb and 2 kb Xho I fusion fragments typical of the mutant recipient, in nearly stoichiometric amounts compared to the other stained restriction fragments.

When the psbA transformants were subcultured on acetate medium where photosynthesis was not required for growth, each segregated progeny subclones having chloroplast genomes identical to the original mutant recipient that contained only the 8 kb and 2 kb Xho I fusion fragments and no traces of the Xho fragments (5+pUC and 8+pUC) with the wild type psbA gene (Fig. 3). Thus the original transformants were being maintained as heteroplasmons under selective conditions that required them to photosynthesize. When the same original transformants were subcloned under photosynthetic conditions, all isolates maintained chloroplast genomes with the introduced psbA genes as well as both Xho I fusion fragments of the recipient (Fig. 3). Certain of these subclones lost the rarer psbA containing fragment derived from Xho 5 and maintained only the more common fragment derived from Xho 8. We postulate that incorrect insertion of the donor psbA gene has interrupted some nearby chloroplast gene whose product is required for cell survival, forcing the cells to maintain copies of the mutant recipient genome. This situation would be analogous to that described by Spreitzer and Chastain (18) where a chloroplast tRNA suppressor of a known nonsense mutation in the chloroplast rbcL gene is maintained as a permanent heteroplasmon under selective conditions.

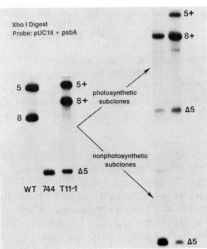

Fig. 3. Analysis of subclones of a typical photosynthetically competent psbA transformant (T11-1) selected under photosynthetic (top) and nonphotosynthetic (bottom) conditions. Total cell DNA from wild type (WT), the ac-u-β recipient (744), T11-1, and its subclones was digested with Xho I, the fragments separated on 0.8% agarose gels and probed with the transforming plasmid used in Fig.2. Only the top portion of the gels are shown; both the Δ5 and Δ8 fragments are present in the recipient and in all transformant subclones.

Using the 10 kb plasmid from the Dr4 mutant described above, pregrowing recipient cells on 0.5 mM FdUrd and selecting directly on DCMU, we have transformed a Chlamydomonas strain (CC-1852) whose chloroplast genome differs with respect to RFLP markers on either side of the psbA gene and lacks the third intron in the coding sequence. In this case, the donor plasmid has strong homology to both upstream and downstream flanks of the recipient psbA gene. In 9 of 10 putative transformants examined, the psbA gene has the RFLP pattern of the donor. We are now determining if these transformants result from homologous replacement events yielding chloroplast genomes that all contain two copies of the donor psbA gene.

Transformation of the wild type chloroplast 16S and 23S rRNA genes using a donor plasmid containing rRNA mutations conferring resistance to streptomycin, spectinomycin and erythromycin: Cells of strain CC-1852, with RFLP markers throughout the chloroplast genome, were also transformed with a donor pUC8 plasmid having the 7.0 kb Bam 11 chloroplast insert from strain CC-227 carrying the entire 16S rRNA gene with mutations conferring resistance to streptomycin (bp 474) and spectinomycin (bp 1123) and the 5' half of the 23S rRNA gene with a mutation conferring resistance to erythromycin (bp equivalent to E. coli 2058) (Fig. 4; 19). Transformants were selected simultaneously for streptomycin and spectinomycin resistance to preclude the possibility of isolating spontaneous mutations resistant to either antibiotic in the recipient strain. Reduction of the chloroplast genome copy number prior to bombardment by growing the recipient strain for five to seven generations in 0.5 mM FdUrd increased the frequency of cotransformation for streptomycin and spectinomycin resistance 10 fold, from 0.12×10^{-6} to 1.4×10^{-6}. No doubly resistant spontaneous mutants were detected on the control plates. About one fifth of the streptomycin-spectinomycin resistant transformants proved to be resistant to erythromycin, suggesting that they had received the entire 16S gene and the 5' half of the 23S gene from the donor plasmid (Fig. 4).

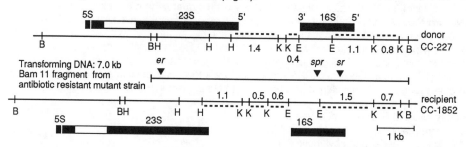

Fig. 4. Restriction maps showing RFLP variation in the inverted repeat region of recipient and donor strains used for rRNA gene transformation. Relative positions of streptomycin (sr), spectinomycin (spr) and erythromycin (er) mutations in the 16S and 23S genes within the 7 kb Bam 11 insert used for transformation are shown. Restriction sites for Bam HI (B), Eco RI (E), Kpn I (K) and Hind III (H) are indicated. The dotted lines indicate easily scored RFLPs.

Chloroplast DNA from these rRNA transformants is being analyzed for RFLP differences flanking the 16S genes to determine where specific exchange events have occurred during the integration process. Preliminary data (Fig. 5) show that 10 of 11 transformants contain the donor 1.4 kb Kpn-Hind fragment spanning the 5' end of the 23S gene (Fig. 4). Six transformants resistant to erythromycin resulted from an exchange event in the ca. 200 bp between the er locus and the Bam site 3' to this marker. In the erythromycin sensitive transformants, exchange presumably occurred between the er locus and the polymorphism in the Kpn-Hind fragment. One transformant contained a recombinant Kpn-Hind fragment that is longer than either parental form. Five of the 11 transformants analyzed contained the 0.8 kb Kpn fragment from the 5' flank of the 16S gene of the donor. In these transformants an exchange event occurred distal to this fragment, beyond the polymorphism in the 0.7/0.8 kb Kpn fragment or in the adjacent 0.2 kb Kpn-Bam fragment. In the six transformants that have the 0.7 kb Kpn fragment of the recipient, the integration event presumably occurred between the streptomycin resistance mutation in the 16S gene and the polymorphic region near the Kpn I sites. Since 10 of the 11 transformants are homoplasmic for either the donor or the recipient Kpn fragment, copy correction of the initial integration event to the opposite copy of the inverted repeat and segregation of the chloroplast genomes containing the resistance mutations must have occurred rapidly. The one transformant still heteroplasmic for this Kpn fragment, with approximately equal representation from the recipient and the donor, is homoplasmic for the 1.4 kb Kpn-Hind fragment from the opposite end of the donor DNA. Analysis of subclones of this transformant will be required to determine whether it segregates cells with two different types of resistant genomes, suggestive of two different integration events in the same recipient cell.

Fig. 5. Analysis of chloroplast DNA from streptomycin - spectinomycin resistant transformants for typical RFLP variation seen between recipient and donor sequences flanking the 16S rRNA gene. Total cell DNA was digested with Kpn I and Hind III (top) or Kpn I (bottom), the fragments separated on 1.0% agarose gels, blotted to nitrocellulose and probed with the ^{32}P labelled 1.4 kb Kpn-Hind fragment (top) located 3' to the 16S gene or the 2.0 kb Bam-Eco fragment (bottom) at the 5' end of the 16S gene (Fig. 4).

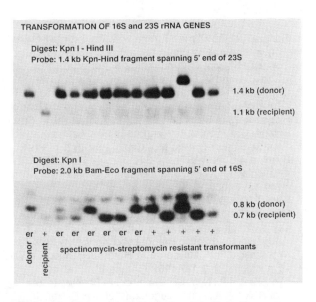

TRANSFORMATION OF 16S and 23S rRNA GENES

Digest: Kpn I - Hind III
Probe: 1.4 kb Kpn-Hind fragment spanning 5' end of 23S

1.4 kb (donor)
1.1 kb (recipient)

Digest: Kpn I
Probe: 2.0 kb Bam-Eco fragment spanning 5' end of 16S

0.8 kb (donor)
0.7 kb (recipient)

er   +   er   er   er   er   er   er   +   +   +   +   +

donor
recipient
spectinomycin-streptomycin resistant transformants

Additional characterization is required to pinpoint more precisely the sites of exchange events leading to homologous replacement of the rRNA gene sequences in these transformants. However, from the transformants examined thus far, we conclude that exchange events leading to integration of donor DNA into the recipient genome by direct replacement appear to occur very often near short repeat motifs marked by Kpn I and Aat II restriction sites that are ubiquitous in intergenic regions of the chloroplast genome of C. reinhardtii and account for much of the RFLP variation seen between different wild type strains (6). Also these exchanges very frequently take place near the ends of the donor fragment. In nearly all cases, the integrated donor sequences copy-correct efficiently to the other copy of the inverted repeat and the transformed genomes segregate rapidly to produce cells homoplasmic for the resistant chloroplast genomes.

In summary, we feel that chloroplast transformation in C. reinhardtii has been developed to a point where we can use it for site directed mutagenesis experiments on specific genes (e.g. atpB, psbA and rRNA) to learn in vivo more about their function and expression. We are also taking advantage of the transformation system to study chloroplast recombination with constructs where markers are flanked by varying configurations of short repeat motifs. Finally, we hope to develop a gene disruption vector with a heterologous selectable marker and to construct vectors for targeting foreign genes to particular sites in the chloroplast genome and maintaining foreign genes on nonintegrative plasmids that will replicate indefinitely in the chloroplast.

ACKNOWLEDGMENTS: We thank Dr. J.C. Sanford and his colleagues at Cornell University for providing the particle gun used in our initial transformation experiments and for their continuing advice, support and encouragement. We are also grateful to the North Carolina Biotechnology Center, which provided funds for Dr. S. Johnston to obtain the particle gun at Duke University that was used for most of the transformation experiments reported herein. We greatly appreciate the collaboration of Drs. J. Erickson at UCLA and J.-D. Rochaix at Geneva in the psbA experiments and Dr. R. Spreitzer at the University of Nebraska in the rbcL transformation experiments. This work was supported by grants from NIH (GM-19427) and AMOCO Technology Corporation. S.M.N. is supported by an NIH Postdoctoral Fellowship GM-12934.

REFERENCES

1 Shinozaki, K., M. Ohme, M. Tanaka, T. Wakasugi, N. Hayashida, T. Matsubayashi, N. Zaita, J. Chunwongse, J. Obokata, K. Yamaguchi-Shinozaki, C. Ohto, K. Torazawa, B.Y. Meng, M. Sugita, H. Deno, T. Kamogashira, K. Yamada, J. Kusuda, F. Takaiwa, A. Kato, N. Tohdoh, H. Shimada, and M. Sugiura (1986). EMBO J. 5, 2043-2049.

2 Ohyama, K., H. Fukuzawa, T. Kohchi, H. Shirai, T. Sano, S. Sano, K. Umesono, Y. Shiki, M. Takeuchi, Z. Chang, S. Aota, H. Inokuchi, and H. Ozeki (1986). Nature 322, 572-574.

3 Hiratsuka, J., H. Shimada, R. Whittier, T. Ishibashi, M. Sakamoto, M. Mori, C. Kondo, Y. Honji, C.-R. Sun, B.-Y. Meng, Y.-Q. Li, A. Kanno, Y. Nishizawa, A. Hirai, K. Shinozaki, and M. Sugiura (1989). Mol. Gen. Genet. 217, 185-194.

4 Boynton, J.E., N.W. Gillham, E.H. Harris, J.P. Hosler, A.M. Johnson, A.R. Jones, B.L. Randolph-Anderson, D. Robertson, T.M. Klein, K.B. Shark, and J.C. Sanford (1988). Science 240, 1534-1538.

5 Klein, T.M., E.D. Wolf, R. Wu, and J.C. Sanford (1987). Nature 327, 70-73.

6 Palmer, J.D., J.E. Boynton, N.W. Gillham, and E.H. Harris (1985). In: The Molecular Biology of the Photosynthetic Apparatus, eds. K.E. Steinback, S. Bonitz, C.J. Arntzen, and L. Bogorad, Cold Spring Harbor Laboratory, New York, pp. 269-278.

7 Woessner, J.P., A. Masson, E.H. Harris, P. Bennoun, N.W. Gillham, and J.E. Boynton (1984). Plant Mol. Biol. 3, 177-190.

8 Woessner, J.P., N.W. Gillham, and J.E. Boynton (1986). Gene 44, 17-28.

9 Dzelzkalns, V.A., and L. Bogorad (1986). J. Bacteriol. 165, 964-971.

10 Wurtz, E.A., J.E. Boynton, and N.W. Gillham (1977). Proc. Natl. Acad. Sci. USA 74, 4552-4556.

11 Robertson, D., J.P. Woessner, N.W. Gillham, and J.E. Boynton (1989). J. Biol. Chem. 264, 2331-2337.

12 Conde, M.F., J.E. Boynton, N.W. Gillham, E.H. Harris, C.L. Tingle, and W.L. Wang (1975). Mol. Gen. Genet. 140, 183-220.

13 Liu, X.-Q., J.P. Hosler, J.E. Boynton, and N.W. Gillham (1989). Plant Mol. Biol. 12, 385-394.

14 Hosler, J.P., E.A. Wurtz, E.H. Harris, N.W. Gillham, and J.E. Boynton (1989). Plant Physiol., in press.

15 Spreitzer, R.J., and L.J. Mets (1980). Nature 285, 114-115.

16 Blowers, A.D., L. Bogorad, K.B. Shark, and J.C. Sanford (1989). Plant Cell 1, 123-132.

17 Erickson, J.M., M. Rahire, P. Bennoun, P. Delepelaire, B. Diner, and J.D. Rochaix (1984). Proc. Natl. Acad. Sci. USA 81, 3617-3621.

18 Spreitzer, R.J., and C.J. Chastain (1987). Curr. Genet. 11, 611-616.

19 Harris, E.H., B.D. Burkhart, N.W. Gillham, and J.E. Boynton (1989). Genetics, in press.

STRUCTURAL COMPARISON BETWEEN RHODOSPIRILLUM RUBRUM PLASMID AND
CHLOROPLAST DNA

Tomisaburo Kakuno, Naoya Ichimura, Naruki Kaino, Takashi Ideguchi,
Hitoshi Namikawa, Bok-Hwan Kim, Hiroshi Nishise, Jinpei Yamashita and
Takekazu Horio

Division of Enzymology, Institute for Protein Research,
Osaka University, Suita, Osaka 565, Japan

1. INTRODUCTION
    Plasmids in photosynthetic bacteria have been isolated from
Rhodospirillum rubrum, Rhodobacter sphaeroides and Rhodobacter capsulatus (1-5). The sizes of their plasmids ranges from 40 to 200
kilobases. Kuhl et al. (3) have isolated the identical plasmids from
nine strains of R. rubrum. In addition, they have reported that the
plasmid-less mutants show different colors from the wild strain and
can not grow photosynthetically in the light (6). In order to elucidate
the biological roles of the plasmids in photosynthetic bacteria, it is
essential to determine their DNA sequences. The present study reports
the restriction map and the partial nucleotide sequences of R. rubrum
plasmid.

2. MATERIALS AND METHODS
2.1. Bacterium and culture: The non-sulfur purple photosynthetic
     bacterium, R. rubrum S-1, was photosynthetically grown in the
     light at 27 °C for 2 days in the minimum culture medium,
     which was the same as those of Ormerod et al. (7).
2.2. Restriction digestion of plasmid: R. rubrum plasmid was digested
     with restriction enzymes under their optimum conditions. In most
     cases, 25 μl of a reaction mixture contained 20 units of a
     restriction enzyme and 2 μg of a plasmid in an appropriate
     buffer for each enzyme. The digestion was carried out at 37 °C for
     3 h.
2.3. Southern cross hybridization: Southern cross hybridization was
     carried out by the method of Potter and Dressler (8) to construct
     the restriction map of the plasmid. An agarose gel with a wide
     sample well (11.5 x 0.2 cm) was placed on a cooling plate of a
     horizontal electrophoresis apparatus. The isotope-labelled and
     non-labelled restriction fragments of the plasmid were separately
     electrophoresed and blotted on the nylon membranes.
     After the treatments with a hybridization buffer, the non-labelled
     membrane was overlaid on the isotope-labelled membrane on a glass
     plate so that the DNA-binding surfaces could contact with each
     other in an orthogonal position as to the directions of
     electrophoresis. After the hybridization was completed, the upper

M. Baltscheffsky (ed.), Current Research in Photosynthesis, Vol. III, 517–520.
© 1990 *Kluwer Academic Publishers. Printed in the Netherlands.*

membrane was washed, air-dried and exposed to an X-ray film for
autoradiography.
2.4. DNA sequence analysis: DNA sequencing was based on dideoxy method
by the use of fluorescent-dye primers. Most of the sequences were
determined by a DNA Sequencing System Model 370A.

3. RESULTS AND DISCUSSION
3.1. Restriction digestion of plasmid: The plasmid from R. rubrum was
digested with the following restriction enzymes; EcoR I, Hind III,
Sma I, Sac I, Xba I, Xho I, Kpn I or BamH I. The digests were
electrophoresed on an agarose gel. The profiles of restriction
digestion were similar to those reported by Khul et al. (3). The
plasmid in this study, therefore, seems to be identical to pKY1.

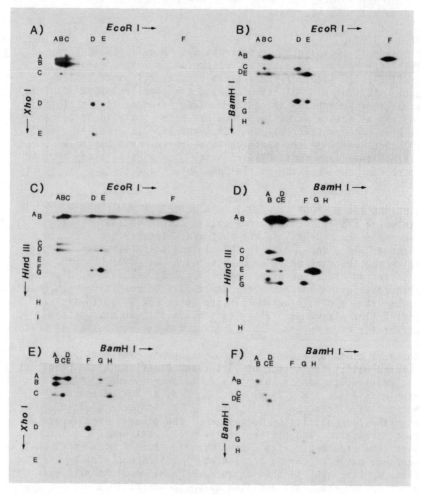

FIGURE 1. Autoradiograms of Southern cross hybridization

3.2. Southern cross hybridization on restriction fragments of pKY1:
Southern cross hybridizations between the Eco̲R I digest and the
three other other digests with X̲ho I, Hin̲d Ⅲ and Ba̲mH I were
carried out to construct the restriction map of pKY1. The crossing
points between the bands possessing common sequences are shown as
hybridized spots on X-ray films (Fig. 1). In view of five sets of
the cross hybridization, the restriction map for the four
restriction enzymes was successfully constructed (Fig. 2).

3.3. Nucleotide sequences of Hin̲d Ⅲ fragments:
Hind Ⅲ fragments F, E, D and G were sequenced by a DNA sequencer
utilizing four fluorescent-dye primers. The directions and loci
of these fragments were confirmed by polymerase chain reaction
(PCR). The GC content in the region sequenced was 50% that is
lower than that of R̲. rubrum chromosomal DNA but higher than those
of chloroplast DNAs. When possible reading frames were searched by
the method of Fickett , 60 open reading frames with more than
150 bases could be present.
Among them, 24 protein
reading frames were
probable.

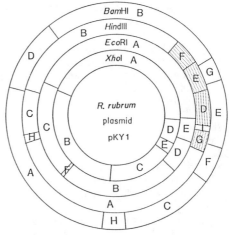

3.4. Homology between pKY1 and
chloroplast DNA:
The restriction fragments
of pKY1 were searched for
homology with N̲. tabacum
chloroplast DNA by GENETYX-
CD system (Table 1).

FIGURE 2. Restriction map of pKY1

TABLE 1 Homology between pKY1 and N̲. Tabacum chloroplast DNA

Region in pKY1	Homology	Gene
F 236 – 344	53% (110 bp)	5S rDNA (121 bp)
F 1657 – 1729	60% (74 bp)	4.5S rDNA (103 bp)
E 235 – 323	48% (89 bp)	ORF 38 (117 bp)
D 717 – 505	50% (218 bp)	rps 15 (264 bp)
G 802 – 985	47% (189 bp)	psb E(c) (252 bp)

```
1)  TGGCCTGGTGGTCA-TTGCGGGCTCGAAACACCCGATCCCGATCCCATCCCGAACTCGGCCG
    *** ******    **** *  ** *** * *   *  *** *   *   **
2)  TTGGACTGGTGCGGGCTTGCCGTACCGGTACAACACACATCCTGCCCGCCTGTAGT-ATGCAA
    *****  *  ** * **** ** ** **** **** ****   * ** *  **
3)     CTGGT--GTCCTAGGCGTAGAGGAACCACACCAATCCATCCCGAACTTGGTGGTTAAA

    -TGAAAGAGCC-CTGCGCCAATGGTACTGCGTCTTAA-GGCGTGGGAGAGTAGGTCGCCGCCAGGCCT
     * **  *     * **  *    *** ***    ** *     * *
    -ATTTA-TGCAACAAAAAGCCACAGAATGACTACCTG-GGCCACGGATCTAGAGTGGAAATGAACCAA
     * ** ***    * * *      **  **** **  *   * ** **     *
    -CTCTACTGCGGTGACGATACTGTAGGGGAGGTCCTGCGGAAAAATAGCTCGACGCCAGGAT

         1) R. rubrum 5S rDNA (10)
         2) pKY1 (F231-357)
         3) N. tabacum chloroplast 5S rDNA (11)
```

FIGURE 3. Comparison of sequences among 5S RNA genes and pKY1

The F fragment of Hind III digest showed 53% and 60% homology with the chloroplast 5S and 4.5S rDNAs, respectively (Table 1). On the other hand, the E, D and G fragments showed more than 47% homology rps 15, ORF 38 and psb E, respectively. The homology search with M. polymorpha chloroplast DNA gave lower values than those of N. tabacum. Comparison among the sequences of R. rubrum 5S rDNA, pKY1 and N. tabacum chloroplast 5S rDNA suggested their close relationship (Fig. 3).

4.1. REFERENCES

1 Suyama, Y. and Gibson, J. (1966) Biophys. Res. Commun. 24, 549-553

2 Saunders, V.A., Saunders, J.R. and Bennett, P.M. (1976) J. Bacteriol. 125, 1180-1187

3 Khul, S.A., Nix, D.W. and Yoch, D.C. (1983) J. Bacteriol. 156, 737-742

4 Fornari, C.S., Watkins, M. and Kaplan, S. (1984) Plasmid 11, 39-47

5 Hu, N.T. and Marrs, B.L. (1979) Arch. Microbiol. 121, 61-69

6 Kuhl, S.A., Wimer, L.T. and Yoch, D.C. (1984) J. Bacteriol. 159, 913-918

7 Ormerod, J. G., Ormerod, K. S. and Gest, H. (1961) Arch. Biochem. Biophys. 94, 449-463.

8 Potter, H. and D. Dressler, D. (1986) Gene 48, 229-239

9 Fickett, J.W. (1982) Nucleic Acids Res. 10, 5303-5313

10 Newhouse, N., Nicoghosian, K. and Cedergren, R.J. (1981) Can. J. Biochem. 59, 921-932

11 Sugiura et al. (1986) Plant Mol. Biol. Rep. 4, 110-147

CLONING, NUCLEOTIDE SEQUENCE AND EXPRESSION OF *RHODOBACTER SPHAEROIDES* Y THIOREDOXIN GENE

Sabine Pille, Annick M. Breton, Frederic Ampe and Jenny D. Clément-Métral
Groupe de Conception Moléculaire, Laboratoire de Technologie Enzymatique, BP 649, 60206 Compiègne, France.

Thioredoxin (1,2) are small (M_r 11-12,000) ubiquitous redox proteins with two half-cystine residues in the conserved active site structure :Trp-Cys-Gly-Pro-Cys. The oxidized form $Trx-S_2$ is reduced by NADPH and thioredoxin-reductase; the reduced form $Trx(SH)_2$ is a powerful protein disulfide oxido-reductase which regulates the activity of enzymes by thiol redox control; it serves as hydrogen donor for various reductive enzymes such as ribonucleotide reductase or enzymes reducing sulfate or methionine sulfoxide. Also, $Trx(SH)_2$ is essential for phage T7 DNA replication as a subunit of T7 DNA polymerase and assembly of filamentous phages (fl and M13), at least in *E. coli*.

Mutations in the *trxA* gene of *E. coli* are not lethal, therefore the precise cellular physiological functions of thioredoxin are yet unknown.
The first evidence of the existence of the thioredoxin system (NADPH, thioredoxin, thioredoxin-reductase) in a photosynthetic organism came from *Rhodobacter sphaeroides* (3). The presence of the thioredoxin system in a photosynthetic bacterium is of great interest, as the regulation of pigment synthesis of *Rb. sphaeroides* has been discussed for a number of years in terms of the existence of a regulatory substance sensitive to the oxido-reduction state of the cell; in addition 5-aminolevulinic acid synthetase, the first and key enzyme of the bacteriochlorophyll synthesis pathway is regulated *in vitro* by thiol redox control mediated by $Trx(SH)_2$ (4). As a first step toward the understanding of the regulation of pigment synthesis by oxygen in this bacterium, the amino-acid sequence of the *Rb. sphaeroides* Y thioredoxin and a three-dimensional model derived from the *E. coli* crystallographic structure have been previously reported (5).

In the present study, we have used synthetic oligodeoxynucleotide probes based on the amino-acid sequence to identify and clone the *Rb. sphaeroides* gene *trxA* from a genomic library of this bacterium. A restriction fragment, bearing this *trxA* gene, was ligated in the pKK233-2 expression vector in order to produce larger quantities of *Rb. sphaeroides* thioredoxin to further investigate structure-function relationships.

M. Baltscheffsky (ed.), Current Research in Photosynthesis, Vol. III, 521–524.
© 1990 *Kluwer Academic Publishers. Printed in the Netherlands.*

CLONING AND SEQUENCING OF THE GENE ENCODING *Rb. sphaeroides* thioredoxin.

EVRKSDVPVVVDFWAEWCGPCRQIGPALEELSKEYAGKVKIVKVNVDENPZSPAMLGVRGIPA

3' CTG AAG ACC CGG CTT ACC ACG CC 5'
                    T
OLIGONUCLEOTIDE SP1

3' TTT CAG TTG CAG CTG CTT TTG GG 5'
              T   T
OLIGONUCLEOTIDE SP2

Oligodeoxynucleotide (32P) probes SP1 and SP2 were hybridized witn a λ EMBL3 genomic library of *Rb. sphaeroides* Y.
One positive recombinant clone was isolated.

NUCLEOTIDE SEQUENCE OF THE *trxA* gene of *Rb. sphaeroides*

```
CCGGCAGGGGGCCATCCTTACTTTCCAAGCAAGCCTACGGATCAGGAGA
                                        =====
                                        RBS

ATTGAAT ATG TCC ACC GTT CCC GTG ACG GAC GCC ACC TTC
        M   S   T   V   P   V   T   D   A   T   F

GAC ACC GAG GTG CGC AAG TCC GAC GTG CCC GTC GTC GTC
D   T   E   V   R   K   S   D   V   P   V   V   V

GAT TTC TGG GCC GAA TGG TGC GGC CCC TGC CGG CAG ATC
D   F   W   A   E   W   C   G   P   C   R   Q   I

GGC CCG GCG CTC GAG GAG CTC TCG AAG GAA TAT GCC GGC
G   P   A   L   E   E   L   S   K   E   Y   A   G

AAG GTG AAG ATC GTG AAG GTC AAT GTC GAC GAG AAC CCC
K   V   K   J   V   K   G   N   V   D   E   N   P

GAG AGC CCG GCG ATG CTG GGC GTT CGC GGC ATC CCG GCG
E   S   P   A   M   L   G   V   R   G   I   P   A

CTG TTC CTC TTC AAG AAC GGT CAG GTC GTG TCG AAC AAG
L   F   L   F   K   N   G   Q   V   V   S   N   K

GTC GGC GCT GCG CCG AAG GCC GCG CTG GCC ACC TGG ATC
V   G   A   A   P   K   A   A   L   A   T   W   I

GCT TCG GCG CTC TGA GATCCTCTGCCATAGCAGAGACCGGACGGGG
A   S   A   L   *                              ———

CGCCTTCGGGCGCCCTTTTCCTTGAGCAAGCGACCGACCGCGACGGGCGAG
——→        ←——
   -18.4Kcal

GATCC
```

EXPRESSION OF THE *Rb. sphaeroides* *trxA* gene in *E. coli*.
-Subcloning in an expression vector : construction of pUTC3

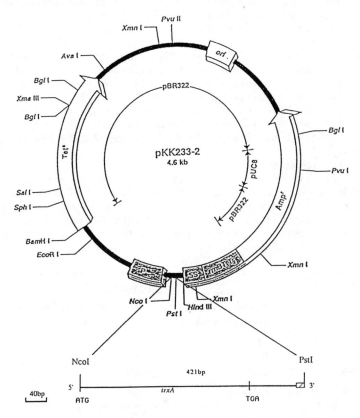

Thin line represents *R.sphaeroides* DNA and hatched line M13mp18 DNA.

A NcoI restriction site was created at the "ATG" translation initiation
codon of the *trxA* gene by oligonucleotide directed-mutagenesis. A 425
bp NcoI-PstI fragment was ligated into the pKK233-2 vector. Plasmid
pUTC3 was used to transform the *E. coli* thioredoxin deficient strain
BH16.

Bacterial Strains	relevant characteristics
Rhodobacter sphaeroides Y	wild type
Escherichia coli:	
MV1190	*trxA*+, (F':*tra* , *pro*, *lacI^Q*)
BH216	*trxA2*, *metE46*,
BH216 F'	*trxA2*, *metE46*, (F':*pro*, *lacI^Q*, Tc^R)
1843	*trxA*+, *met*,
SH250	*trxA*+, *metE46*,

- Complementation tests

a) Methionine sulfoxide test

Clones BH216(pUTC3) grew well with 30 µg/ml of methionine sulfoxide as a methionine source on minimal medium M9, whereas the parent strain BH216 was unable to use methionine sulfoxide.

b) Sensitivity to phage M13

Thioredoxin is required in *E. coli* for filamentous phage assembly. When BH216F' is infected, no plaque was observed, while when BH216F'(p UTC3) is infected by M13 turbid plaques appear that represent 10% of the pfu(plaque forming units) on a lawn of MV1190. It is to note that F', necessary for phage adsorption, is unstable and that besides *trxA* BH216 and MV1190 are not isogenic. Nevertheless, the *Rb. sph. trxA* gene complements, at least partially, the *E. coli trxA2* mutation for M13 phage assembly.

c) Sensitivity to phage T7

In *E. coli*, thioredoxin is a subunit of T7 DNA polymerase, therefore a *trxA2* strain is resistant to T7 infection. T7 plaques BH216(pUTC3) as well as a TrxA$^+$ strain (1843): the same amount of pfu were recovered with both strains (100% efficiency). Unlike *Anabaena* PCC 7119 and *Corynebacterium nephridii* C-2 thioredoxins, the *Rb. sph.* protein can replace the *E. coli* thioredoxin in the growth of T7 phage.

d) Thioredoxin assay

Strains	Coupled enzyme	
	E. coli	*Rhodobacter sphaeroides*
	Thioredoxin reductase	Thioredoxin reductase
SH250	0,117	0,016
BH216	0,022	0,004
BH216 (pUTC3)	0,322	0,565

The assay was performed as previously described (6) with thioredoxin-reductase and coupled to the reduction of DTNB (5,5'-dithiobis(2-nitrobenzoic acid)). The reaction mixture contained 10µM thioredoxin-reductase from either *E. coli* or *Rb. sph.* corresponding respectively to 185 U/mg and 53 U/mg and was followed at 412 nm. The activities are expressed in units/A_{280}. Units = ΔA_{412} / min.

REFERENCES

1)- Holmgren, A. (1985) Ann. Rev. Biochem. 54, 237-271

2)- Gleason, F.K. and Holmgren, A. (1988) FEMS microbiol. Lett. 54, 271-298

3)- Clément-Métral, J.D. and Holmgren, A. (1983) in Thioredoxins, structure and functions. (Gadal, P. ed.) p. 59-68, CNRS, Paris.

4)- Clément-Métral, J.D. (1979) FEBS Lett. 101, 116-120

5)- Clément-Métral, J.D., Hlomgren, A., Cambillau, C., Jörnvall, H., Eklund, H. Thomas, D. and Lederer, F. (1988) Eur. J. Biochem. 172, 413-419.

6)- Slaby, I. and Holmgren, A. (1975) J. Biol. Chem. 250, 1340-1347.

NUCLEOTIDE SEQUENCE OF THE GENES ENCODING THE TWO MAJOR PROTEINS IN THE CYTOPLASMIC MEMBRANE OF SYNECHOCOCCUS PCC 7942

Tatsuo Omata[1], Teruo Ogawa[1], Thomas J. Carlson[2] and John Pierce[3]
[1]Solar Energy Research Group, The Institute of Physical and Chemical Research (RIKEN), Wako, Saitama 351-01, Japan; [2]Central Research & Development Department and [3]Agricultural Products Department, E.I. DuPont de Nemours & Co., Wilmington, DE 19880-0402

1. INTRODUCTION

Cells of Synechococcus PCC 7942 contain 45-kD and 42-kD proteins as major proteins in the cytoplasmic membrane when grown under low CO_2 conditions with nitrate as the nitrogen source [1]. Ammonium-grown cells lack the 45-kD protein [2,3,4], while high CO_2-grown cells lack the 42-kD protein [5]. Insertional mutation of the gene for the 45-kD protein resulted in inactivation of nitrate transport, indicating that the protein is an essential component of the nitrate-transporting mechanism [4]. The 42-kD protein, on the other hand, was once supposed to be involved in the transport of inorganic carbon (CO_2 or HCO_3^-) [5]. However, inactivation of the gene for this protein did not affect the activities of CO_2/HCO_3^- transport in Synechococcus [6], and the role of the 42-kD protein remains unclear.

In this study, we determined the nucleotide sequences of the genes encoding the 45-kD and 42-kD proteins. The deduced amino acid sequences revealed strong homology of these two proteins.

2. MATERIALS AND METHODS

DNA fragments containing a part of the genes for the 45-kD and 42-kD proteins were obtained from a genomic library of Synechococcus PCC 7942 constructed in λ gt11 phage. The cloned gene fragments were used for construction of the mutants M45 [4] and M42 [6], which carry an aminoglycoside 3'-phosphotransferase gene (the "kanamycin resistance cartridge") inserted in the structural gene for the 45-kD protein and the 42-kD protein, respectively. Gene libraries of M45 and M42 DNA were constructed in pUC119 and the plasmids containing the entire nucleotide sequences of the genes for the 45-kD and 42-kD proteins were obtained by selecting the clones carrying the kanamycin resistance marker. Nucleotide sequences of the genes were determined using the dideoxy chain-termination method.

M. Baltscheffsky (ed.), Current Research in Photosynthesis, Vol. III, 525–528.
© 1990 *Kluwer Academic Publishers. Printed in the Netherlands.*

```
TAGAGCCCACTCTTCACCTAGACCGAACCCGAACAATTTCCACCCTTTTCTCCACTTCCA      60
AACATCATGAGTCAATTTTCTCGGCGCAAATTCCTGTTGACGGCGGGCGGAACTGCAGCA     120
GCAGCCCTCTGGCTCAATGCCTGCGGTAGCAACAACAGCTCCACTGATACGACTGGTTCG     180
ACTTCAACCCCGGCTCCCAGCGGTACGAGTGGCGGCGATGCGCCAGAAGTCAAAGGTGTG     240
ACCTTGGGCTTCATTGCCCTGACCGATGCAGCGCCGGTGATCATCGCCCTCGAAAAAGGT     300
TTGTTCGCCAAGTACGGCCTACCCGACACCAAGGTCGTCAAGCAAACCTCTTGGGCTGTC     360
ACCCGCGACAACCTTGAGTTGGGCAGCGATCGCGGCGGCATCGACGGTGCCCACATCCTT     420
AGCCCAATGCCCTACTTGCTGACGGCGGGCACGATCACCAAGTCGCAGAAGCCGCTGCCG     480
ATGTACATCTTGGCGCGACTCAATACCCAAGGTCAGGGCATTTCGCTTTCCAACGAGTTT     540
CTGGCTGAAAAGGTTCAGATTAAGGATCCAAAACTGAAGGCGATCGCCGACCAGAAGAAA     600
GCCTCAGGCAAACTGCTGAAAGCAGCAGTCACTTTCCCTGGCGGTACCCACGACCTCTGG     660
ATGCGCTACTGGCTGGCAGCCAATGGCATTGATCCCAACAATGACGCCGACCTGGTGGTG     720
ATTCCGCCGCCACAGATGGTCGCCAACATGCAGACCGGTACCATGGACACCTTCTGTGTG     780
GGTGAGCCGTGGAATGCACGCTTGGTCAACAAAAAACTCGGTTACACCGCTGCTGTGACT     840
GGCGAACTCTGGAAGTTCCACCCCGAAAAAGCGCTGACGATTCGCGCAGATTGGGCAGAC     900
AAAAATCCCAAAGCAACAATGGCACTGCTCAAGGCTGTGCAAGAAGCCCAAATCTGGTGC     960
GAAGATCCCGCCAACTTGGATGAGCTCTGCCAAATCACTGCTCAAGACAAATACTTCAAA    1020
ACCAGCGTCGAAGACATCAAACCCCGCCTCCAAGGCGACATCGACTATGGCGATGGCCGG    1080
TCGGTCAAAAACTCTGACCTGCCGGATGCGCTTCTGGAGTGAAAACGCCTCCTTCCCCTAC    1140
AAGAGCCATGATCTCTGGTTCCTGACTGAGGACATTCGCTGGGGTTATCTGCCCGGCTTCG    1200
ACCGATACAAAAGCCTTGATCGAGAAGGTCAACCGTAGCGATCTCTGGCGCGAAGCTGCT    1260
AAGGCGATTGGTCGCGAGCAAGATATTCCGGCTAGCGATTCCCGGGGGGTAGAGACCTTC    1320
TTTGACGGTGTCACCTTCGACCCTGAAAATCCCCAGGCCTATCTCGACGGTCTCAAGTTC    1380
AAAGCCATCAAAGCCTAAGTCGTCCTGTTCACGCCTGCGATCGCGCGATCGCAGGCACTC    1440
ACCCCGCCCCTGTCATGACTGTCACGCTTCGCCCCCCCAGTTCTGTCCGTCGCTCTGCTT    1500
GGGTTAAAAATCCAAAGCTCAAGCCCTTTCTGCCCTACGTTGT                    1543
```

Fig. 1 Nucleotide sequence of a 1543-bp fragment from <u>Synechococcus</u> PCC 7942 DNA, containing the gene for the 45-kD protein (<u>nrt</u> A). The initiation and termination condons are underlined.

3. RESULTS AND DISCUSSION

The nucleotide sequence of the gene for the 45-kD protein is shown in Fig. 1 and that for the 42-kD protein in Fig. 2. The gene for the 45-kD protein (<u>nrt</u> A) encoded a 443 amino acid polypeptide with a calculated molecular weight of 48424 (Fig. 3, lower line), and the gene for the 42-kD protein (<u>cmp</u> A) encoded a 450 amino acid polypeptide with a molecular weight of 49108 (Fig. 3, upper line). The nucleotide sequence of the gene for the 42-kD protein was identical with that for the "carotenoid-binding protein" of the same cyanobacterium recently reported by another group of workers [7].

Comparison of the amino acid sequences of the 45-kD and 42-kD proteins revealed that the two proteins are homologous, 47% of the amino acid residues being identical (Fig. 3). Taking conservative replacement of amino acid residues into account, the homology of the two proteins is 86%. No proteins having homology with these two proteins were found in recent databases of published sequneces (Wilbur-

```
GGTTATCAGCCTTATCGGTCTGGAATAACCAGTTGGCCTAAAGTCATGCAGACAGAGCGT      60
TTCTGCGCCTCTCGTGAAGCAATTCGCACAACTTGTCCATCTTTAGAGGCATCTCCTGTT     120
GTGGGATGTAGGGGAGACGTATGAACGAATTTCAACCAGTCAATCGTCGTCAGTTTCTGT     180
TCACGCTCGGAGCAACCGCTGCTAGCGCTATTTTGCTGAAGGGTTGCGGTAATCCTCCTT     240
CCAGTAGCGGCGGCGGGACTTCTAGTACAACTCAGCCAACTGCTGCAGGGGCGAGTGATC     300
TGGAAGTCAAGACAATCAAATTGGGCTACATCCCCATCTTTGAAGCGGCTCCACTGATCA     360
TTGGCCGCGAAAAAGGCTTTTTTGCCAAATATGGCTTGGATGTTGAAGTCTCGAAACAAG     420
CCAGCTGGGCAGCTGCTCGCGATAACGTCATTCTCGGTTCTGCTGGTGGCGGCATCGATG     480
GCGGTCAGTGGCAAATGCCGATGCCTGCCTTGCTAACGGAAGGTGCGATCAGCAACGGTC     540
AAAAAGTTCCCATGTATGTCTTGGCTTGCTTGAGCACCCAAGGCAATGGCATCGCTGTTT     600
CCAATCAGCTCAAGGCCCAAAATCTGGGCTTGAAGCTAGCGCCCAACCGCGACTTTATCC     660
TCAACTACCCGCAAACTAGCGGCCGGAAGTTCAAAGCATCCTACACCTTCCCGAACGCCA     720
ACCAAGACTTCTGGATTCGCTATTGGTTTGCAGCTGGCGGTATCGATCCTGATAAAGACA     780
TTGAACTCTTGACCGTTCCCAGCGCAGAAACTCTACAAAATATGCGCAATGGCACGATCG     840
ATTGCTTCAGTACCGGCGATCCCTGGCCGTCGCGGATTGCCAAAGATGACATCGGCTATC     900
AAGCTGCGCTGACAGGTCAAATGTGGCCTTACCACCCCGAGGAATTCTTGGCGCTGCGAG     960
CAGACTGGGTAGACAAACATCCGAAAGCTACGCTCGCCTTGCTGATGGGCTTGATGGAAG    1020
CGCAGCAATGGTGCGATCAGAAAGCAAATCGGGCAGAGATGGCCAAGATCCTCTCCGGTC    1080
GCAACTTCTTTAACGTGCCGGTTTCGATCCTGCAGCCGATTCTGGAAGGTCAAATCAAAG    1140
TTGGAGCAGACGGAAAAGATCTCAACAACTTTGATGCCGGCCCGCTCTTCTGGAAGAGTC    1200
CGCGCGGCAGTGTCTCCTATCCCTACAAAGGGCTCACCCTCTGGTTCTTGGTGGAGTCGA    1260
TCCGCTGGGGCTTCAACAAGCAAGTGCTACCTGACATTGCAGCCGCCCAGAAACTCAACG    1320
ATCGCGTGACTCGTGAAGACCTCTGGCAAGAGGCAGCCAAGAAATTAGGGGTGCCCGCTG    1380
CGGATATCCCAACCGGATCGACTCGCGGTACCGAGACCTTCTTTGATGGCATCACCTACA    1440
ACCCAGACAGTCCGCAAGCTTATCTCCAAAGCTTGAAGATTAAACGCGCATAAGTAGGGG    1500
CTTCAATCATCAACCTTAGTTCAGTCACTATCAGGAGATAGACAGACCATGGTTACTGCA    1560
CGGGAAACAAGACGAAACGGAAGTCGTCCTTCTGGCTTAAAAAAAATGGCGTCAGAAACTC    1620
```

Fig. 2   Nucleotide sequence of a 1620-bp fragment from <u>Synechococcus</u>
PCC 7942 DNA, containing the gene for the 42-kD protein (<u>cmp</u> A).

Lipman search of the NBRF Protein Sequence Database-Release 20).
      The 42-kD protein is synthesized in the cytoplasmic membrane of
<u>Synechococcus</u> when cells are exposed to carbon-limited conditions [5].
The good correlation of the amount of the protein with the activity of
inorganic carbon transport [5] suggested that the protein was involved
in transport of CO_2 or HCO_3^-. However, this was not the case since the
M42 mutant could transport inorganic carbon as efficiently as the wild-
type cells [6]. The other group of workers reported that the 42-kD
protein was synthesized when cells were exposed to high light conditions (1.9 mW cm^{-2}) [8]. Since M42 grew quite well under these light
conditions [6], it is unlikely that the protein is required for growth
under these light regimes. The strong homology of the 42-kD protein
with the 45-kD protein (Fig. 3) may suggest a role for the 42-kD protein in transport of some ion(s) or nutrients, or may represent a
common structure of the proteins localized in the cytoplasmic membrane
of the cyanobacterium.

```
42-kD protein       MNEFQPVNRRQFLFTLGATAASAILLKGCG--NPPSSSGGG      39'
                    ** ** * * *** *  *  * ** *        *
45-kD protein           MSQFSRRKFLLTAGGTAAAALWLNACGSNNSSTDTTGS    38"

TSSTTQPTAAGASDLEVKTIKLGYIPIFEAAPLIIGREKGFFAKYGL-DVEVSKQASWAA    98'
**        *   ***  ** *  *** ** *** ****** *  * ** ***
TSTPAPSGTSGGDAPEVKGVTLGFIALTDAAPVIIALEKGLFAKYGLPDTKVVKQTSWAV    98"

ARDNVILGSAGGGIDGGQWQMPMPALLTEGAISNGQK-VPMYVLACLSTQGNGIAVSNQL   157'
*** *** *****  *** *** * *   ** *** ** * *** ** **
TRDNLELGSDRGGIDGAHILSPMPYLLTAGTITKSQKPLPMYILARLNTQGQGISLSNEF   158"

KAQNLGLKLAPNRDFILNYPQTSGRKFKASYTFPNANQDFWIRYWFAAGGIDPDKDIELL   217'
 *   *  * *    ** *** **  *** * ** **** ** **** *  *
LAEKVQIK-DPKLKAIADQKKASGKLLKAAVTFPGGTHDLWMRYWLAANGIDPNNDADLV   217"

TVPSAETLQNMRNGTIDCFSTGDPWPSRIAKDDIGYQAALTGQMWPYHPEEFLALRADWV   277'
    *  ** ** ** * *  *      ** ** ** * *** *  ****
VIPPPQMVANMQTGTMDTFCVGEPWNARLVNKKLGYTAAVTGELWKFHPEKALTIRADWA   277"

DKHPKATLALLMGLMEAQQWCDQKANRAEMAKILSGRNFFNVPVSILQPILEGQIKVGAD   337'
** ***** ***   *** **  ** * * *      *  *    * ***  *  * *
DKNPKATMALLKAVQEAQIWCEDPANLDELCQITAQDKYFKTSVEDIKPRLQGDIDYG-D   336"

GKDLNNFDAGPLFWKSPRGSVSYPYKGLTLWFLVESIRWGFNKQVLPDIAAAQKLNDRVT   397'
*   * * **   *** **** * ****          **       *  *
GRSVKNSDLRMRFW---SENASFPYKSHDLWFLTEDIRWGY----LPASTDTKALIEKVN   389"

REDLWQEAAKKLGVPAADIPTGSTRGTETFFDGITYNPDSPQAYLQSLKIKRA         450'
* *** **** *   *** ** ****** *  ***** ** *
RSDLWREAAKAIG-REQDIPASDSRGVETFFDGVTFDPENPQAYLDGLKFKAIKA       443"
```

Fig. 3   Alignment of the amino acid sequences of the 42-kD and 45-kD proteins.   Asterisks indicate identical amino acids.

REFERENCES

1   Omata, T. and Ogawa, T. (1987) in Progress in Photosynthesis Research   (Biggins, J., ed.) Vol. 4, pp.309-312, Nijhoff, Dordrecht
2   Madueño, F., Vega-Palas, M.A., Flores, E. and Herrero, A. (1988) FEBS Lett. 239, 289-291
3   Sivak, M.N., Lara, C., Romero, J.M., Rodríguez, R. and Guerrero, M.G. (1989) Biochem. Biophys. Res. Comm. 158, 257-262
4   Omata, T., Ohmori, M., Arai, N. and Ogawa, T. (1989) Proc. Natl. Acad. Sci. (USA), in press
5   Omata, T, and Ogawa, T. (1986) Plant Physiol. 80, 525-530
6   Omata, T., Carlson, T.J., Ogawa, T. and Pierce, J., submitted
7   Reddy, K.J., Masamoto, K., Sherman, D.M. and Sherman, L.A. (1989) J. Bacteriol. 171, 3486-3493
8   Masamoto, K., Riethman, H.C. and Sherman, L.A. (1987) Plant Physiol. 84, 633-639

CHIMERIC RESCUE OF *RB. CAPSULATUS* REACTION CENTER GENES WITH SEQUENCES FROM *RB. SPHAEROIDES*

AILEEN K. TAGUCHI AND NEAL W. WOODBURY
Arizona State University and the Center for the Study of Early Events in Photosynthesis, Tempe, AZ 85287, USA

JONATHAN W. STOCKER AND STEVEN G. BOXER
Department of Chemistry, Stanford University, Stanford, CA 94305, USA

1. INTRODUCTION

Site-directed mutagenesis is becoming a very important technique in the study of photosynthetic reaction center structure-function relationships. However, there are certain disadvantages associated with this approach. First, it relies very heavily on the intuition of the investigator to select particular mutations that will give rise to interesting phenotypes; many times, mutagenesis can result in very little change in photosynthetic function, in complete loss of function, or in lack of assembly. Second, it is difficult to use specific mutagenesis to detect the concerted effect of several amino acids.

Here we describe methodology for generating, selecting, and rapidly screening large numbers of mutants in specific regions of the reaction center genes. One can generate mutants involving changes in both small and large numbers of amino acids and the mutant phenotypes always include stable reaction centers that are at least partially functional.

2. METHODS

2.1 <u>Strains and Plasmids</u>. *Rhodobacter capsulatus* strain U43 containing a deletion of the *puf* operon was generously provided by Dr. Douglas Youvan, as were plasmids pU29 and pU2922 (1, 2). pJW1 (3) was generously provided by Dr. George Feher. The M gene deletion used in this work is missing 48 bp between the *Bst*EII and *Sac*II restriction sites of M.

2.2 <u>Chimeric Rescue</u>. A detailed description of these procedures will be presented elsewhere.

2.3 <u>Fluorescence Decay Measurements</u>. The single photon counting instrument will be described in detail elsewhere. All measurements were made on whole cells using 870 nm excitation and 900 nm emission detection.

3. RESULTS

3.1 <u>Mutagenesis via Chimera Rescue</u>. We have developed a new form of mutagenesis to study the effects of interspecies differences on reaction center structure and function. In this approach, we select for recovery of photosynthetic activity in deletion mutants of the host gene (usually the *Rb. capsulatus* reaction center operon) by recombination with a donor gene from an organism with a related reaction center. For these experiments, we have constructed pCR, a derivative of pU2922 containing the *puf* operon of *Rb. capsulatus* as well as unique *Bam*HI and *Xho*I sites for insertion of donor genes into the plasmid.

We have used this system to repair a 48 bp deletion in the M gene of the *Rb. capsulatus* operon by recombination with sequences from the 4.5 kb *Pst*I fragment from the *sphaeroides puf* operon of pJW1 (Fig. 1). Even though most of the *sphaeroides* operon is present, the starting plasmid does not produce spectroscopically detectable amounts of reaction centers. The two operons were placed in the plasmid with opposite orientations to allow single, homologous

M. Baltscheffsky (ed.), Current Research in Photosynthesis, Vol. III, 529–532.
© 1990 *Kluwer Academic Publishers. Printed in the Netherlands.*

recombinational events between the two operons to occur without loss of sequence following inversion. When this plasmid was conjugated into U43 and put under photosynthetic selection, photosynthetic activity was recovered with a frequency of approximately 10^{-7}.

In initial studies, two photosynthetically competent chimeric reaction center genes were isolated and sequenced. In one case, repair of the deletion in the M gene of *capsulatus* resulted in the replacement of *capsulatus* gene sequence between position M669 and M780 with *sphaeroides* sequence. In the other case, positions M559 through M747 were replaced. Reaction centers isolated from these mutants had steady state absorbance spectra and P^+Q^- recombination kinetics comparable to wild type reaction centers. More recently, we have partially characterized 44 independently isolated mutations resulting in restoration of photosynthetic activity. Through restriction mapping, we have identified at least three classes of mutants: 1) single inversions in which some or all of the M gene and all sequence downstream of M in the *Rb. capsulatus* operon has been reciprocally exchanged with the analogous section of the *sphaeroides* operon 2) conversion events in which a section of the coding sequence of the *capsulatus* M gene has been replaced by *sphaeroides* sequences nonreciprocally (i.e., *sphaeroides* sequences do not appear to be altered) and 3) events which have resulted in photosynthetic rescue without repair of the lesion in the M gene of *Rb. capsulatus*. We suspect that the third class, which represents nearly half of the mutants analyzed to date, is due to conversion of the 5' sequences of the *sphaeroides* operon resulting in expression of the *sphaeroides* B875 and reaction center genes. In support of this, deletion of the *capsulatus* operon from the recombined plasmid and reintroduction of the plasmid back into U43 results in photosynthetic activity. This implies that the *sphaeroides* L and M genes can assemble with the *capsulatus* H gene and that it is possible to express the B875 antenna complex of *sphaeroides* in the *capsulatus* photosynthetic membrane at least in the presence of *sphaeroides* L and M reaction center subunits. Schematic representations of each class of mutation are shown in Fig. 1. Sequence analysis of these mutants is ongoing.

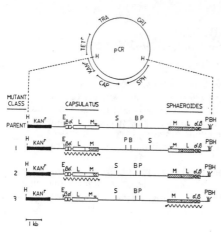

Fig. 1. Schematic diagram of pCR with the *sphaeroides* operon as a donor. Three of the classes of recombinants that arose from the chimera rescue experiments are also shown. The hatched boxes represent *sphaeroides* sequences; the open boxes represent *capsulatus* sequences. Only the *Pst*I sites that define the subclone of pJW1 (3) used in this experiment are shown. Restriction sites: B = *Bam*HI; E = *Eco*RI; H = *Hin*DIII; P = *Pst*I; S = *Sac*I.

3.2 <u>Screening of Mutants Using Time-Resolved Fluorescence Spectroscopy</u>. In order to screen many mutants quickly for potentially interesting phenotypes, we have employed time-resolved single photon counting techniques using whole cells directly from liquid culture. To avoid build-up of the long-lived P^+Q^- state, the quinone is chemically reduced with dithionite (approximately 20 mM). The fastest component of the decay is associated with the excitation trapping time and in simple antenna systems is thought to be proportional to the initial electron transfer rate in the reaction center (4). When the quinone is reduced, the initial radical pair state, P^+Bphe^-, lives for about 10 nanoseconds and back electron transfer from this state gives rise to nanosecond delayed fluorescence which is usually easy to distinguish from the much faster excitation trapping. The amplitude of the delayed fluorescence varies with the free energy difference between the states P* and P^+Bphe^- (5). Thus, this technique allows one to quickly measure parameters that are sensitive to both the kinetics and thermodynamics of the initial electron transfer in the reaction center and in this way identify mutants in which this reaction may be altered.

Representative fluorescence decays from whole cells in the presence of dithionite are shown in Fig. 2. The decay curve shown in the top panel is from cells harboring a plasmid that encodes wild type *capsulatus* reaction center and antenna proteins. The bulk of the decay occurs with a time constant of 40-45 ps, followed by a much lower amount of longer-lived delayed fluorescence with a multiexponential decay. The delayed fluorescence includes the 10 ns lifetime of P^+Bphe^-. The mutants examined thus far show one of two phenotypes with regard to their fluorescence decay curves. The decay kinetics from one group of mutants are similar to the parent strain (Fig. 2, middle panel). The other mutants tested all had emission decays that were very similar to each other but different from the decay of either the parent strain or the mutants described above. An example of one of these decays is shown in the bottom panel of Fig. 2. The biggest difference between this trace and those above it is the large increase in fluorescence on the 100 ps - 1 ns timescale.

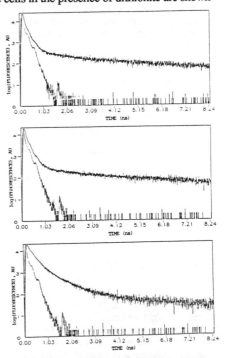

Fig. 2. Time-resolved fluorescence decays of whole cells of *Rb. capsulatus*. In each sample, the reaction center quinones were reduced with sodium dithionite. Excitation was at 870 nm, detection at 900 nm. For each decay, the instrument response function is also shown. Top decay: wild type reaction center operon. Middle decay: chimera #15 (very similar decays were observed for #4 and #32 as well). Bottom decay: chimera #5 (very similar decays were observed for #1 and #2 as well).

4. DISCUSSION

4.1 Chimeric Reaction Centers Can Be Used to Study Sequence Differences Between Homologous Reaction Center Genes.

We have shown that it is possible to use chimeric rescue as a method for generating functional reaction center genes that utilize sequences from two different organisms. One can use this technique both to determine which homologous sequences between two reaction center genes perform similar roles and to identify the homologous regions that play different roles. Once regions with important differences are identified, specific mutagenesis techniques can be used to investigate the detailed sequence requirements further. We intend to expand this technique to compare more distantly related reaction centers (such as *capsulatus* and *viridis*) as well as to generate functional chimeric reaction center subunits with sequence from both the homologous L and M polypeptides.

4.2 A Subset of the Chimeras Show Altered Fluorescence Decays.

The proper interpretation of the fluorescence increase we have observed in a number of the chimeras (Fig. 2, bottom panel) is not yet clear. Depending on how the data is fit to a series of exponentials, one either finds that the trapping time for the excitation has increased by about a factor of three, or one finds a smaller increase in the trapping time (50%) with a large increase in the amount of fluorescence decaying on a 100 ps to 1 ns timescale. It appears that there has been a significant change either in the rate that excitations reach the reaction center or in the kinetics or thermodynamics of the initial electron transfer reaction. The biochemical and spectroscopic properties of these mutants are being investigated in more detail.

It is interesting to note that those mutants that apparently express both the reaction center and antenna genes of *sphaeroides* also display the altered fluorescence decay kinetics shown in the bottom panel of Fig. 2. This suggests that the difference in the fluorescence decay is probably not due to an altered interaction between the chimeric reaction centers and the antenna. Possibly, the change is due to the interaction between the chimeric L and/or M subunits of the reaction center and the H subunit which in all cases is provided by the *capsulatus* genome.

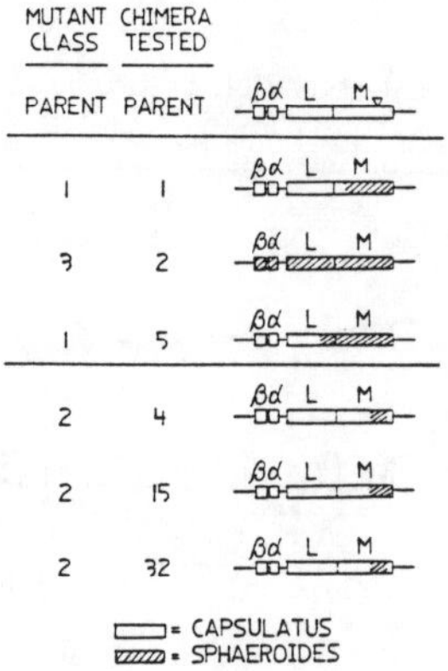

Fig. 3. Schematic diagrams of six *capsulatus/sphaeroides* chimeric *puf* operons generated by the chimera rescue technique described in the text. "Mutant class" refers to the three classes of mutants identified in the text. "Chimera tested" refers to the identification number of the specific mutant. The approximate boundaries between *capsulatus* and *sphaeroides* sequences was determined by restriction mapping.

4.3 The Fluorescence Decays are Correlated with Primary Structure. The effects of these mutations on excitation trapping and/or initial electron transfer events are correlated with their structure. Chimera mutants 4, 15 and 32 each show fluorescence decays very similar to the wild type (Fig. 2, top and middle panels). Mutants 1, 2 and 5 show the altered fluorescence decay (Fig. 2, bottom panel). This correlates quite well with the preliminary structures for these rearrangements determined by restriction mapping (Fig. 3). Mutants 4, 15 and 32 contain changes that are probably all confined to the 3' portion of M, while 1, 2 and 5 appear to extend through most or all of the 5' half of M as well. As we analyze a larger number of mutants in this way and obtain more detailed sequence data on the precise end-points of these rearrangements, it should be possible to locate the region of sequence responsible for the phenotypic variation. Directed mutagenesis techniques can then be used to determine exactly which amino acids are involved.

5. ACKNOWLEDGEMENTS

This is publication #19 from the Arizona State University Center for the Study of Early Events in Photosynthesis. The Center is funded by U.S. Department of Energy grant #DE-FG02-88ER13969 as part of the USDA/DOE/NSF Plant Science Centers program. N. Woodbury acknowledges support from an NSF Plant Molecular Biology Postdoctoral Fellowship #DMB-8508973 and a Faculty Grant in Aid from Arizona State University. S.G. Boxer acknowledges support from the NSF Biophysics Program. J.W. Stocker received support from a NSF predoctoral fellowship.

BIBLIOGRAPHY
1 Youvan, D.C., Ismail, S. and Bylina, E.J. (1985) Gene 38, 19-30
2 Bylina, E.J., Ismail, S. and Youvan, D.C. (1986) Plasmid 16, 175-181
3 Williams, J.C., Steiner, L.A., Ogden, R.C., Simon, M.I. and Feher, G. (1983) Proc. Natl. Acad. Sci. USA 80, 6505-6509
4 Sundstrom, V., van Grondelle, R., Bergstrom, H., Akesson, E. and Gilbro, T. (1986) Biochim. Biophys. Acta 851, 431-446
5 Woodbury, N.W. and Parson, W.W. (1986) Biochim. Biophys. Acta 850, 197-210

ANALYSIS OF NITRATE REDUCTION GENES IN CYANOBACTERIA

Xanja Andriesse, Hans Bakker, Gerard van Arkel and Peter Weisbeek. Department of Molecular Cellbiology, University of Utrecht, Padualaan 8, 3584 CH Utrecht, The Netherlands

1. INTRODUCTION

Cyanobacteria are a very divergent group of unicellular or filamentous micro-organisms, which constitute one of the largest subgroups of Gram-negative prokaryotes. They have very few growth requirements due to their capacity to carry out a plant-like oxygen-evolving photosynthesis, so only carbon dioxide and nitrogen are needed in more than trace amounts.

Nitrate reduction in cyanobacteria is tightly coupled to photosynthesis by ferredoxin, which provides both nitrate reductase (NR) and nitrite reductase (NiR) with electrons. In contrast to higher plant NR, cyanobacterial NR consists of only a single polypeptide of about 80 kD with one $[Fe_4S_4]$ or two $[Fe_2S_2]$ clusters and a molybdenum cofactor.

Nitrate reduction mutants of Anacystis nidulans R2 (Synechococcus PCC7942) are obtained after chemical and transposon mutagenesis. The NR activity of the mutants is less than 1% of the wildtype. With the aid of these mutants three wildtype nitrate reduction genes have been cloned using phenotypical complementation (1,2). The exact function of the genes is not known, but they can code a). for the NR itself (apoenzyme structural gene; comparable with the nia genes from higher plants, b). for regulatory proteins or c). for molybdopterin synthesis and insertion proteins (comparable with higher plant cnx genes).

At present the mutants and the corresponding wildtype genes are being analyzed in physiological, biochemical and genetic experiments. In here, we describe the analysis of one of the cloned genes, the narB gene.

M. Baltscheffsky (ed.), Current Research in Photosynthesis, Vol. III, 533–536.
© 1990 *Kluwer Academic Publishers. Printed in the Netherlands.*

2. RESULTS

To determine the localization of the narB gene on the cloned fragment the sites of the chromosomal mutations were mapped by transformations with subclones of the narB containing DNA fragment. The mutations were supposed to map on the smallest overlapping fragment of the subclones responsible for transformation to phenotypical wildtype cells. One mutation mapped in the 0.7 kb Bgl II fragment, two in the 0.5 kb Bgl II/Nco I fragment and three in the 1.0 kb Nco I/Hind III fragment (fig. 1A). To check the results chromosomal DNA of transposon mutants and the wildtype was digested with several restriction enzymes, which had no recognition sites in the transposon. NarB subclones were used as probes on Southern blots and hybridization patterns were compared. The transposon mutations mapped on the restriction fragments with shifted molecular weights due to the presence of the transposon. The results obtained with this method correspond with those obtained with the transformations.

The sequence of the narB gene was determined in both directions using the dideoxy-method. For stretches without suitable restriction sites oligo-nucleotides were used as primers.

From the sequence analysis it was learned, that the narB gene codes for a protein of 715 or 729 aminoacids with a molecular weight of about 80 kD. There are two possible startcodons, the first having a truncated Shine-Delgarno sequence, the second having non at all (fig. 1C).

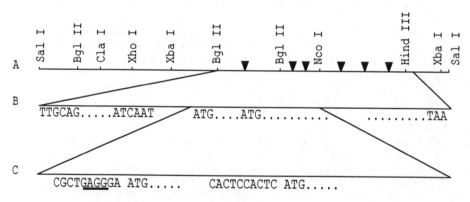

Fig. 1. Restriction map of the narB containing DNA fragment. (1A).The sites of the transposon insertions in the mutants are marked by arrows. (1B).Promoter sequence and open reading frame with two possible startcodons. (1C).Sequences upstream of startcodons. The possible ribosome bindingsite is underlined.

The nucleotide sequence and the deduced aminoacid sequence were compared with the EMBL sequence library. Two other genes were found with homology with the narB gene. Both genes code for formate dehydrogenase, the first for FDH_H from E. coli (3), the second for FDH_A from Methanobacterium formicicum (4). At the level of the proteins there is a similarity of 30.1% between NAR_B and FDH_H and 33.8% between NAR_B and FDH_A, while the similarity between the two formate dehydrogenases 39.9% is. Dot matrix comparisons (fig. 2) show, that the similarity is spread over the complete proteins, but also that there are boxes with very strong similarity. The similarity starts with the second possible startcodon and not the first one.

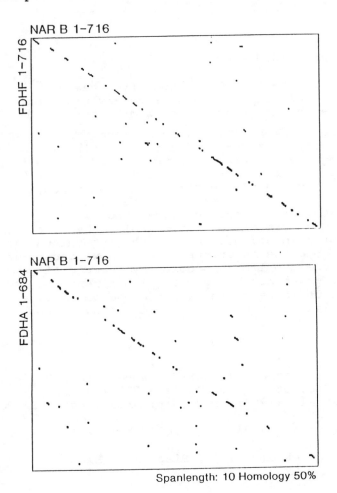

Spanlength: 10 Homology 50%

Fig. 2. Dot matrix comparisons between NAR_B and FDH.

5' of the coding region, a possible promoter was found with an E. coli consensus sequence (fig. 1B). The sequence differs from the predicted Synechocystis 6803 psbB promoter (5) by two AT conversions (table 1).

TABLE 1. Promotersequences

(Possible) promoter	-35 region	space	-10 region
E. coli consensus	TTGACA	16-18	TATAAT
Synechocystis 6803 psbB	TTGCAG	17	TACAAT
A. nidulans R2 narB	TTGCAG	17	ATCAAT

3. CONCLUSION AND DISCUSSION

One of the nitrate reduction genes from the cyanobacterium A. nidulans R2 shows a remarkable similarity with two formate dehydrogenases from two bacteria, the FDH_H from E. coli and the FDH_A from M. formicicum. There are two possible startcodons for NAR_B and the similarity with the formate dehydrogenases starts with the second one, although there is no ribosome bindingsite in front of it. The Shine-Delgarno sequence of the first startcodon consists of only four nucleotides at a site two bases upstream. From these results it is not clear yet, what the right startcodon is. The most direct way to solve the problem, purifying the protein and determining the N-terminus, is very laborious, because NR exists in very low amounts in the cell. Now, the problem is studied by the use of chimeric genes, which are being made with a reporter gene cloned exact at the site of the first or second ATG. The new constructs will be used in regulation studies too.

REFERENCES

1. Kuhlemeier, C.J. et al. (1984) J. Bacteriol. 159, 36-41.
2. Kuhlemeier, C.J. et al. (1984) Gene 31, 109-116.
3. Zinoni, F. et al. (1987) Proc. Natl. Acad. Sci. USA 83, 4650-4654.
4. Shuber, A.P. et al. (1986) J. Biol. Chem. 261, 12942-12947.
5. Vermaas, W.F.J. et al. (1986) Plant Mol. Biol. 8, 317-326.

STRUCTURE OF THE GENES FOR LHC-II IN SCOTS PINE (*Pinus sylvestris* L.)

Stefan Jansson[1] Petter Gustafsson[1] and Ivar Virgin[2]
[1]Dept of Plant Physiology, University of Umeå, 901 87 Umeå, SWEDEN
[2]Dept of Biochemistry, University of Stockholm, 106 91 Stockholm, SWEDEN

INTRODUCTION

Pines are in contrast to angiosperms capable of forming chlorophyll and probably all photosynthesis-associated proteins in the dark. However, the thylakoids of dark-grown ("etiolated") pine seedlings differ from light-treated material in at least two ways: We and others has shown that the chlorophyll *a/b* ratio is higher, which indicates that the antenna size is smaller. PSII activity is also affected, there is a limitation on the water-splitting side of PSII in the dark-grown seedlings. In order to study the structure and regulation of pine photosynthetic genes, we wanted to isolate cDNA clones encoding LHC-II polypeptides from Scots pine.

ETIOLATED THYLAKOIDS ARE DEPLETED IN LHC-II

To study whether different PSII polypeptides showed different stoicheometry in "etiolated" and light-treated Scots pine seedlings western blotting was performed. Thylakoids were prepared from "etiolated" seedlings and seedlings which had been exposed to light continuous white light for 48 hrs. Thylakoid proteins were subjected to SDS-PAGE and analyzed by immunoblotting using antibodies against different PSII polypeptides. All polypeptides except LHC-II apo-proteins were present in equal amounts in "etiolated" and light treated pine seedlings.

Table 1. Relative amounts of PSII polypeptides in "etiolated" and light-treated Scots pine thylakoids.

	"Etiolated"	Green
D1 32 kD	1	1
D2 32 kD	1	1
$cytb_{559}$	1	1
OEC 33 kD	1	1
OEC 23 kD	1	1
OEC 16 kD	1	1
LHCP	0.2	1
10 kD	1	1
22 kD	1	1

M. Baltscheffsky (ed.), Current Research in Photosynthesis, Vol. III, 537–540.
© 1990 *Kluwer Academic Publishers. Printed in the Netherlands.*

CLONING OF PINE *cab* GENES

A cDNA library was constructed in λgt10 out of RNA prepared from Scots pine seedlings
grown in the dark and exposed to light for three days. The library was screened with a
pea *cab* cDNA clone (pAB96) as probe and 17 clones were isolated and sequenced. 8
different sequences were obtained and based on sequence homology it was concluded that
the clones originated from 3 genes, *cab*-II/1A, *cab*-II/1B and *cab*-II/2. Some of the
other clones had other polyadenylation sites. Some clones had also point mutations
compared to the three genes, and are probably alleles of those.

TYPE I AND TYPE II *cab* GENES

In angiosperms two types of genes encoding LHC-II apoproteins are found, Type I and
Type II genes. The proteins encoded by the Type I and Type II genes are ≈90 %
homologous. The differences between the Type I and Type II LHC-II are conserved, and
there exists 11 "Type I/Type II-specific" amino acids, indicated in Fig 1. Two of the
sequenced Scots pine *cab* cDNA clones (LHC-II/1A and LHC-II/1B) encoded polypeptides
highly homologous (89 and 92 %) to the consensus Type I LHC-II, and one (LHC-II/2)
was 92 % homologous to the consensus Type II LHC-II. The "Type I/Type II-specific"
amino acids were also conserved.

```
              10        20        30        40        50        60        70
1A       ...ATG.KSVAASID.........L........P.........................................S......
1B       ...AT..KLTA.A.T.........L........P..............................N................
TypeI    MRKtatkakpvs sgSPWyGpDRVkYLGPfSGEsPSYLTGEFpgDYGWDTAgLSADPeTFakNReLEVIHcRWaMLGA
             !          ! !       !      !!!
TypeII   MRRTv KsvP   qSIWYGeDRPKyLGPFSEQTPSYLTGEFPGDYGWDTAGLSADPETFArNRELEVIHcRWAMLGA
2

              80        90       100       110       120       130       140       150
1A       .......................A.............S.Q.I..............I....I..............T..
1B       .......................A..........................I...........I.........T..
TypeI    LGCVFPELLaRNGvKFGEAvWfKaGSQIFseGGLdYLGNPSLvHAQSiLAIWAcQVvLMGAVEGYRvAGgPLGevvDp
             !                          !        !                  !        !!
TypeII   LGCvFPEiLsKNGVtFGEAVWFKAGsQIFseGGLDYLGNPNLvHAQSILAIWAtQVVLMGfvEGYRVGGGPLGEGLDk
2        .L.V....K..........A...................I...........C......LI..............P

             160       170       180       190       200       210       220       230
1A       I....N.........D.......................I.................Y......
1B       I............E........................I.................Y......
TypeI    LYPGGSFDPLgLAddpeAFaELkVKEiKnGRLAMfSMFGFFvQAiVTGKGPlenLADHlaDPVNNNAwafATNFVPgK
             !                                                         !
TypeII   iYPGGAFDPLGLAdDPEAFAELKVKEIKNGRLAMfSMFGFFvQAIVTGKGPIENLsDHiADPVANNAWAfATNFVPGK
2        L...D...........K....................Y..L...........Y.....
```

<u>Fig 1.</u> Comparison of pine and angiosperm Type I and Type II LHC-II protein sequences.
1A, 1B and 2 are the deduced amino acid sequence of the pine cDNA clones
LHC-II/1A, LHC-II/1B and LHC-II/2, respectively, and Type I and Type II the
consenus amino sequence deduced from all published Type I and Type II genes,
respectively.

TRANSIT PEPTIDE OF SCOTS PINE preLHC-II

The transit peptide of the Scots pine preLHC-II/1A and pre-LHC-II/1B had homology to angiosperm LHC-II transit peptides. The three blocks of homology previously identified in other chloroplast-directing peptides was present in the pine sequences. The pine transit peptide were longer than other LHC-II transit peptides (44 and 40 amino acids) and although originating from Type I genes they did more resemble transit peptides from Type II genes of other plants.

```
Lemna ab30      MAAS MA    LSS PSLVG K AVKLAPAASE      VF GEGRVS
Wheat ab1.6     MAATTMS    LSS SSFAG K AVKNLPS  L      I  GDARVN
Petunia cab2    MAAATMA    ISS SSFAG K AVNV PSSSQ      IT GNGKAT
Tomato cab1B    MAAATMA    LSS PSFAG Q AVKLSPSASE      IS GNGRIT

Pine cab-II/1A  MATT MASCGIGSR CAFAGAQ LSSVKPQNNQLLGVG GAH GQARLT
Pine cab-II/1B       MASCGIGS  CAFAGGQ ISSLKPHTNQLLGVGAGVH GEARVT

Lemna ab19      MAASAIQS SAFAG QTA LK QRD ELVRKVGV SDGRFS
Petunia cab37   MATSAIQQ SAFAG QTA LKSQN  ELVRKIGS G GRAT
Tomato cab4     MATCAIQQ SAFVG Q AVGKSQN  EFIRKVGNF GEGRIT

         I            II                          III
```

Fig 2. Comparison of pine and angiosperm LHC-II transit peptides. The upper four sequences are from Type I LHC-II and the lower three from Type II LHC-II. Boxes are regions of homology identified by Karlin-Neumann an Tobin (2)

C+G BIAS AND CpG ISLANDS

Monocots and dicots differ in nucleotide frequencies at the third codon position. In all dicot genes and some monocot genes the G+C frequency is around 50% at the wobble base position, whereas the corresponding values of many monocot genes are close to 100%. The pine *cab* genes had a moderately strong bias (70-75%) for G+C in codon position three.

In nuclear DNA of higher plants, cytosine in the sequences CpG (CG) and CpXpG (CXG) is normally methylated, and those sequences are avoided. However certain areas in the genome (CpG islands) are found where cytosine methylation is suppressed in all stages of development. In the CpG islands, the CpG dinucleotide is not avoided. Our data indicate that the pine *cab*-II/1A, and *cab*-II/1B, but not the *cab*-II/2 gene, lies within CpG islands (Fig 3).

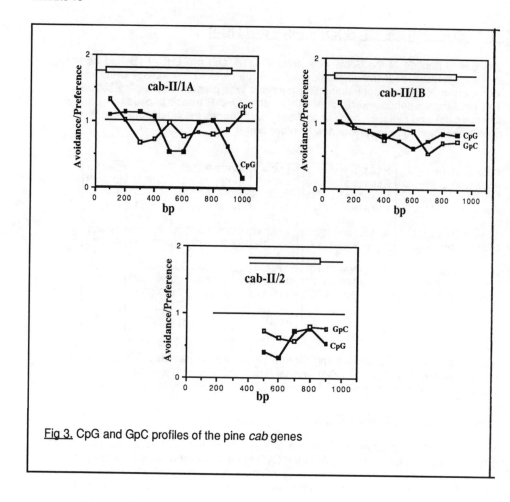

Fig. 3. CpG and GpC profiles of the pine *cab* genes

CONCLUSIONS:

☞   "Etiolated" thylakoids are depleted in LHC-II
☞   Both Type I and Type II *cab* genes are present in Scots pine
☞   The encoded proteins are ≈90% homologous to their angiosperm counterparts
☞   Transit peptide sequences are conserved between angiosperns and gymnosperms
☞   The pine *cab* genes show a bias for G+C in codon position 3
☞   Two of the pine *cab* genes lie within CpG islands

REFERENCES

1   Jansson, S. and Gustafsson P. (1989) Plant. Mol. Biol. In press
2   Karlin-Neumann, G.A. and Tobin E.M. (1985) EMBO J. 5, 9-13

SEQUENCE HOMOLOGY BETWEEN LIGHT HARVESTING POLYPEPTIDES OF PLANTS AND THE DIATOM *Phaeodactylum tricornutum*.

Annamaria Manodori and Arthur R. Grossman, Carnegie Institution of Washington, Department of Plant Biology, Stanford, California

1. INTRODUCTION

Many proteins of the photosynthetic apparatus are evolutionarily conserved. Regions of the chlorophyll (chl) *a, b* binding (Cab) light harvesting (LH) proteins in higher plants and green algae are highly conserved and probably have similar functions (1). Both the PS I and PS II Cab polypeptides have molecular masses generally of between 21 and 29 kDa and bind chl *a, b* and xanthophylls. Recently, the major LH complex from the diatom *Phaeodactylum tricornutum* was isolated and characterized (2,3). It is associated with PS II and contains three polypeptides of molecular masses 18, 19 and 19.5 kDA that bind chl *a, c* and fucoxanthin. The polypeptides of the complex are translated on 80S cytoplasmic ribosomes as higher molecular weight precursors (3), as are Cab polypeptides of higher plants. The presequence is probably required for the transport of the polypeptides into the plastid. To test for similarities among LH proteins from diverse photosynthetic organisms, polyclonal antibodies to the fucoxanthin, chl *a,c* binding (Fac) proteins of *P. tricornutum* (3) were reacted with LH proteins of several different photosynthetic organisms, and used to isolate *fac* genes. A region of approximately 60 amino acids is homologous between Fac and Cab polypeptides.

2. MATERIALS AND METHODS

2.1. Materials: All chemicals were of reagent grade. Restriction enzymes and enzymes for cloning and sequencing were from Pharmacia, Boehringer Mannheim and U.S. Biochemical Corporation. Radioactive nucleotides were from Amersham.

2.2. Growth conditions: *Phaeodactylum tricornutum* Bohlin (Utex 646) was grown at 25°C in continuous illumination at 200 $\mu Em^{-2}s^{-1}$. Cultures were bubbled with air supplemented with 3% CO_2 in ESAW artificial seawater medium enriched by ten times for the normal levels of nitrate and phosphate and buffered at pH 7.7 with 10 mM Tris-HCl.

2.3. Electrophoresis and immunology: Proteins were resolved by SDS-PAGE on 7.5-15% polyacrylamide gradient gels. For Western blots proteins were transferred to nitrocellulose paper and stained immunologically with antibodies to Fac polypeptides and Protein A-conjugated horseradish peroxidase.

2.4. RNA isolation and preparation of genomic library: RNA was isolated as previously described (3) and electrophoresed on a 1%

M. Baltscheffsky (ed.), Current Research in Photosynthesis, Vol. III, 541–544.

formaldehyde agarose gel, transferred to nitrocellulose paper, and probed with DNA fragments labeled by random oligonucleotide priming. A library of *P. tricornutum* genomic DNA (inserts 3-6 kb) was constructed in λZAP (Stratagene, La Jolla, CA). Sequencing was by the dideoxy chain termination method after subcloning fragments into the phage M13.

3. RESULTS AND DISCUSSION

An immunological relationship among the LH proteins from various photosynthetic organisms was established using the antibodies raised to the Fac polypeptides of *P. tricornutum*. As shown in Fig.1, these antibodies react with PSII LH polypeptides of spinach, and the

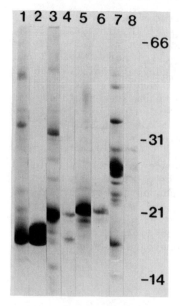

chromophytic algae *Amphidinium* and *Botridiopsis*. These results confirm and extend a similar analysis by Plumley and Schmidt (4) in which antibodies to the higher plant LH polypeptides were shown to cross react with those of diatoms. This is surprising considering the differences in pigment composition among the complexes.

To determine the organization and the sequences of genes encoding the LH polypeptides in the diatoms and examine their relationship to functionally analogous genes from other photosynthetic organisms, we used Fac antibodies to screen a library of *P. tricornutum* genomic DNA in the expression vector λZAP. The inserts from two recombinant clones (IZ1A and IZ6A) were mapped by digestion with restriction enzymes (Fig.2) and shown to have strong homology to each other based on hybridization studies and nucleotide

Fig.1. Stained gel (lanes 1,3,5,7) and Western blot (lanes 2,4,6,8) showing reactivity of antibodies raised to Fac polypeptides of *P. tricornutum* with LH proteins of membrane preparations of *P. tricornutum* (lanes 1,2), *Botrydiopsis* (lanes 3,4) *Amphidinium* (lanes 5,6), and spinach (lanes 7,8).

---

sequencing. A fragment of the insert from IZ1A (see Fig.2) was purified and hybridized back to both genomic DNA and RNA. It hybridized to abundant transcripts of approximately 1,000 bases in preparations of total RNA and poly A + RNA (Fig.3). Similar results were obtained using the inserts from each of the three clones presented in Fig.2. We often observe higher molecular weight RNA species (indicated with an arrow in Fig.3) suggesting that the primary transcripts undergo processing. Genomic Southern blot analyses suggest that in *P. tricornutum* the LH

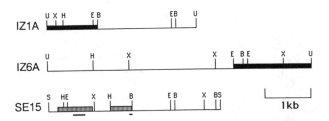

Fig.2. Restriction maps of *P. tricornutum* clones IZ1A, IZ6A and SE15. The shadowed regions indicate fragments isolated for hybridization studies and crosshatched regions are open reading frames with homology to Cab polypeptides. The restriction enzymes used for mapping were *HindIII* (H), *BamHI* (B), *EcoRI* (E), *SalI* (S) and *XhoI* (X).

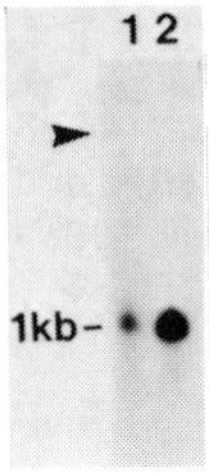

1 2

1kb-

Fig.3. Northern blot analysis of *P. tricornutum* total RNA (lane 1) and poly A+ RNA (lane 2) probed with a fragment from IZ1A.

sequences represent a family of genes on the nuclear genome. This is shown in Fig.4 where at least eleven different *EcoRI* fragments hybridize to a 500 bp *EcoRI* fragment of clone IZ1A at a stringency allowing 40% mismatch. The 500 bp *EcoRI* fragment was used to obtain additional members of the *fac* gene family. One clone, SE15 (Fig.2), contains two regions that are homologous to the probe. The nucleotide sequence of one of these revealed a region of 67 amino acids (present in the middle of an open reading frame of 246 residues) which exhibits considerable homology to a sequence located in the middle of PS II Cab proteins from petunia, cucumber, tomato, pea, wheat, *Euglena* and *Lemna*, and to a PS I Cab protein from tomato (Fig.5). We conclude that we have isolated genes encoding LH proteins of *P. tricornutum*. To clearly establish the coding region of *fac* genes and determine whether the genomic sequences contain introns, we are constructing a cDNA library and will use the characterized genomic clones to isolate analogous cDNAs.

The Cab proteins have been shown to have highly conserved regions. Models for the native conformation of mature Cab proteins predict that each of these regions consist of a membrane spanning portion and a hydrophilic sequence. The sequence of the *P. tricornutum* Fac polypeptide that is presented is homologous to the hydrophilic region, probably located on the stromal side of the thylakoid membranes between membrane spanning domains two and three (5) of CAB polypeptides. Residues conserved between Cab and Fac polypeptides may have a common functional importance in LH proteins, such as chlorophyll binding. Basic residues such as histidine, asparagine and glutamine are thought to be capable of coordinating chlorophyll molecules. The region of the Fac protein shown in Fig.5 has two histidine and three glutamine

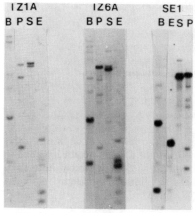

IZ1A   IZ6A   SE1
B P S E   B P S E   B E S P

residues. In CAB polypeptides one of these histidines (position 114) is replaced by asparagine, which may be functionally equivalent. Of the three glutamines in the Fac sequence only one is conserved among the different light harvesting polypeptides; it lies within the third membrane spanning region. To test for functional or structural significance, these residues would be interesting targets for site directed mutagenesis once appropriate systems are developed.

Fig.4. Southern blot analysis of *P. tricornutum* DNA cut with restriction enzymes *BamHI* (B), *PstI* (P), *SalI* (S) and *EcoRI* (E) and probed with fragments from IZ1A (Panel A), IZ6A (Panel B) and SE15 (Panel C).

	61	1	1	1	V 1	1	1	127

```
Phaeodactylum  LRLSRLPALRSPEHGVRERTVAQAPLGFYDPLGLVADGDQEKFDRLRYVEIKHGRISMLAVAGYLAQ
Petunia        L-MGAVEGYRVAGGPLGEVIDPLYPGGSFDPLGL-AD-DPEAFAELKVKEIKNGRLAMFSMFGFFVQ
Wheat          L-MGAVEGYRIAGGPLGEIVDPLYPGGSFDPLGL-AE-RPQAFAELKVKEIKNGRLAMFSMFGFFVQ
Euglena                          PGGPFDPLGL-AD-DPDTFPELKVKEIKNGRLAMSGMLGFYAQ
Tomato PSI     LAIEFLAAFVEHQRSMKDSEKKKYPGGAFDPLGY-SK-DPAKFEELKVKEIKNGRLALLAIVGFCVQ
```

Fig.5. Comparison of amino acid sequence of residues 61-127 of an open reading frame in clone SE15 to regions of PSII Cab polypeptides of petunia, wheat, *Euglena* and a PSI Cab polypeptide of tomato (1). Identical residues are boxed.

ACKNOWLEDGEMENT
We wish to thank Glenn Ford and Loretta Tayabas for technical assistance. This is a CIW-DPB publication no. 1055.

REFERENCES
1 Chitnis, P.R. and Thornber, J.P. (1988) Photosynthesis Res. 16, 41-63
2 Alberte, R.S, Friedman, A.L., Gustafson, D.L., Rudnick, M.S. and Lyman, H. (1983) Biochem. Biophys. Acta 635, 304-316
3 Fawley, M.W. and Grossman, A.R. (1986) Plant Physiol. 81, 149-155 Sci. U.S.A. 86, 1949-1954
4 Plumley, F.G. and Schmidt, G.W. (1984) J. Phycol. Suppl. 20, 10
5 Peters, G.F. and Thornber, J.P. (1988) Photosynthetic light-harvesting systems. Walter de Gruyter & Co., Berlin, N.Y.

MOLECULAR STUDIES OF THE LIGHT HARVESTING COMPLEX OF THE CHROMOPHYTIC ALGA, *PAVLOVA LUTHERII*

C.D. SCARAMUZZI[*], R.G. HILLER[*] AND J. SPEIRS[+]
[*]School of Biological Sciences, Macquarie University, N.S.W., Australia, 2109
[+]CSIRO, Division of Horticulture (Sydney Lab.), P.O. Box 52, North Ryde N.S.W., Australia, 2113

1. INTRODUCTION

The major accessory light harvesting pigment-protein complex of the chromophytic alga, *P. lutherii* is a chlorophyll a/c/fucoxanthin pigment-protein complex (acf complex) which is a 21 kDa thylakoid bound polypeptide. Polyclonal antibodies raised against this polypeptide are monospecific and display strong cross reactivity with the 26 - 28 kDa chlorophyll a/b proteins (CAB proteins) of higher plants (spinach) but no cross reactivity to the chlorohyll a/c$_2$ light harvesting complexes of the cryptophyte alga, *Chroomonas sp* (Hiller *et al.*, 1988). These findings imply a degree of evolutionary relatedness between the acf complexes of the Prymnesiophyta and the CAB proteins but little or no homology to the chlorophyll a/c proteins of the Cryptophyta. However, partial amino acid sequence data for the chlorophyll a/c complex of the cryptophytic alga, *Cryptomonas maculata* shows homology to the CAB proteins of pea (Sidler *et al.*, 1988). There is no information at the molecular level for the acf complex in *P. lutherii*. It is not known whether it is nuclear encoded or chloroplast encoded. These areas are being investigated for the acf complex of *P. lutherii* using cDNA gene probes for the CAB proteins of pea and *Lemna gibba* and synthetic oligonucleotides constructed from the chlorophyll a/c amino acid sequence data.

2. MATERIALS AND METHODS

2.1. Pigment-Protein Complexes

The protein complexes of *P. lutherii* were separated from thylakoid membranes on a digitonin (0.1%), sucrose gradient (10-40%). Fractions were collected and the polypeptides separated under denaturing conditions on a 15-20% gradient polyacrylamide gel and stained with silver stain. Polypeptides from other gels were transferred electrophoretically to nitrocellulose membrane and reacted with antisera to the acf complex of *P. lutherii*.

M. Baltscheffsky (ed.), Current Research in Photosynthesis, Vol. III, 545–548.
© 1990 *Kluwer Academic Publishers. Printed in the Netherlands.*

2.2. DNA Probes used
2.2.1. cDNA gene probes

pFab31: 600 bp coding for CAB protein of pea, courtesy of Smith, S.M., Dunsmuir, P. and Bedbrook, J. Division of Plant Industry, CSIRO, Canberra (pers. comm.).

FAB19: Complete chlorophyll a/b protein coding region and 5' and 3' flanking nucleotides for the aquatic monocot *Lemna gibba*, courtesy of Dr. Elaine M. Tobin (Karlin-Neumann,G A., *et al.*, 1985).

pGR407: 766 bp coding for pea Rubisco SSU (Bedbrook, J.R., Smith, S.M. and Ellis, R.J., 1980).

PW512: 641 bp coding for wheat Rubisco SSU (Smith, S. M., Bedbrook. J. and Speirs, J., 1983).

pZmc37: 2500bp coding for maize Rubisco large subunit (LSU) (Bedbrook *et al.*, 1979).

2.2.2. Synthetic oligonucleotide sequence

32 mer constructed from partial amino acid sequence of chlorophyll a/c protein (Sidler *et al.*, 1988).

2.3. Separation of nuclear and chloroplast DNA

Genomic DNA was sheared by a passage through a fine syringe needle and subjected to CsCl centrifugation using conditions outlined by Rochaix (1982). Fractions were collected and absorbance at 260 nm was recorded. Ten ul of each fraction was treated with 0.5 ml 10 mM NaOH and the DNA bound to nylon membrane. These filters were hybridised to several gene probes.

2.4. Isolation, cloning and screening of 5.7 kb DNA fragment

Genomic DNA was isolated from whole cells in the presence of SDS and Proteinase-K, digested to completion with Hind III and fractionated on a 10 - 40% glycerol gradient. Aliquots of each fraction were electrophoresed on a 0.5% agarose gel and transferred to nylon membrane. Filters were hybridised to ^{32}P labelled cDNA CAB gene probes, washed and exposed to Xray film for two days with two intensifying screens. Size selected DNA was ligated to pUC19. *E. coli* strain JM101 was transformed with 100-150 ng of recombinant DNA and positive transformants selected and screened by colony hybridisation using ^{32}P labelled insert DNA. Plasmid DNA was isolated from the positive transfomants, digested with HindIII, electrophoresed on 1% agarose gels and transferred to nylon membrane. Filters were hybridised to ^{32}P end labelled 32 mer, a synthetic oligonucleotide for the chlorophyll a/c protein of *Cryptomonas*, washed and exposed to Xray film for 4 days with two intensifying screens.

3. RESULTS AND DISCUSSION

3.1. Pigment-Protein complexes

The pigment protein complexes of *P. lutherii* separated into three distinct regions on the sucrose-digitonin gradient. An upper band which is orange brown in colour, a central greenish brown band and a lower green band. Polyacrylamide gel electrophoresis demonstrate that all three fractions contain the acf complex (21 kDa polypeptide) with the central and lower fractions containing the polypeptides of PSII and PSI respectively (Fig. 1A). Western blotting with the 21 kDa antiserum shows that the 21 kDa polypeptide is monospecific and that the uppermost fraction is abundant in acf complex (Fig. 1B)

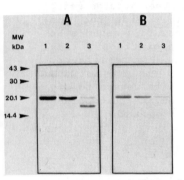

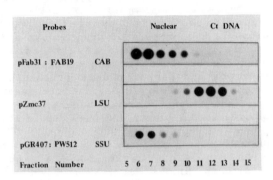

FIGURE 1. a) Polyacrylamide gel electrophoresis and b) Western blot: Pigment-protein complexes of *P. lutherii*, cross reactivity of antisera raised against the 21 kDa polypeptide of the chlorophyll a/c/fucoxanthin complex.

FIGURE 2. Screening of *P. lutherii* with cDNA gene probes.

3.2. Separation of nuclear and chloroplast DNA

The elution profile of *P. lutherii* DNA from the CsCl gradient has one major peak with a minor shoulder on the light side. The major peak has a buoyant density of approximately 1.720 g cm^{-1} whereas the smaller peak has a buoyant density of approximately 1.690 g cm^{-1} measured against *Micrococcus lysodeikticus* DNA (1.731 g cm^{-1}) and *E. coli* DNA (1.695 g cm^{-1}). These results are consistent with nuclear and chloroplast DNA buoyant densities (Rochaix, 1982), and correspond to approximately 67 and 37% G+C content. Hybridisation to the DNA fractions with CAB gene probes confirms that the two peaks of DNA are predominantly nuclear and chloroplastic (Fig.2).

3.3. Hybridisation studies

A DNA fragment of approximately 5.7 kB hybridised to both CAB gene probes but the hybridisation was weak. The 5.7 kB fragment did not hybridise to ^{32}P labelled *P. lutherii* chloroplast DNA indicating a nuclear origin for this DNA fragment. From cells transformed with the 5.7 kb fragment ligated into pUC19 three clones have been selected which hybridised to the 32 mer for the chlorophyll a/c of *Cryptomonas*. Sequencing of this fragment of DNA is proceeding.

4. CONCLUSIONS

Results tentatively suggest that the gene coding for the chlorophyll-caroteno complex in *P. lutherii* has been located using CAB gene probes and a synthetic oligonucleotide for the chlorophyll a/c protein of *Cryptomonas* and that this gene is on the nuclear genome. These results infer an evolutionary link between the light harvesting complexes of the Prymnesiophyta, Cryptophyta and higher plants (Chlorophyta). The nuclear and chloroplast DNA of *P. lutherii* differ vastly with regard to G+C content and amount. The LSU gene is located on the chloroplast genome, as in all plants and the SSU is nuclear encoded.

REFERENCES

1. Hiller, R.G., Larkum, A.W.D. and Wrench, P.M. (1988) **Biochim. Biophys. Acta** 932: 223-231
2. Sidler, W., Frank, G., Wehrmeyer, W. and Zuber, H. (1988) **Experentia** 44: A1-A98
3. Smith, S.M., Dunsmuir, P. and Bedbrook, J. (pers. comm.)
4. Karlin-Neumann, G.A., Kohorn, B.D., Thornber, J.P. and Tobin, E.M. (1985) **J. Mol. Appl. Gen.** 3: 45-61
5. Bedbrook, J.R., Smith, S.M. and Ellis, R.J. (1980) **Nature** 287: 692-697
6. Smith, S.M., Bedbrook, J. and Speirs, J. (1983) **Nucl. Acids Res.** 11: 8719-8733
7. Bedbrook, J.R., Coen, D.M., Beaton, A.R., Bogorad, L.and Rich, A. (1979) **J. Biol. Chem.** 254: 905-910
8. Rochaix, J.D. (1982) in **Methods in chloroplast molecular biology** (Edelman et al.) pp 295-300 Elsevier Biomedical Press

CHLOROPLAST DEVELOPMENTAL-STAGE SPECIFIC CONTROLS ON LHCP II GENES IN CULTURED SOYBEAN CELLS

GEZA ERDOS,[1] HOU-QI CHEN[1] AND DENNIS E. BUETOW[1,2], DEPARTMENT OF PHYSIOLOGY AND BIOPHYSICS[1] AND OF PLANT BIOLOGY[2], UNIVERSITY OF ILLINOIS, URBANA, ILLINOIS 61801, USA

1. INTRODUCTION

Ideal conditions to study the expression of genes for plastid proteins occur when dark-grown plant seedlings, higher plant cells in culture, or algae are exposed to light which induces the massive formation of functional chloroplasts (ct) (1). The plant system used here is the soybean cell-line SB-P (2) which is highly chlorophyllous and capable of photoautotrophic growth. We devised a reproducible "greening" system using this soybean cell-line (3). Best conditions for greening consist of growing the cells in the dark on a defined medium containing 3% sucrose for two weeks, subculturing them in the dark for another two weeks, subculturing them again in the dark for one week more and then placing them in the light (white, 180 µE/m^2/sec). At the time of light-exposure, the medium contains 0.3% sucrose, an amount which does not repress subsequent chlorophyll synthesis.

We used this soybean "greening system" to study light-induced ct development (3) and to determine molecular controls that regulate the expression of nuclear genes that code ct proteins. Reported here are studies on expression of the nuclear gene(s) coding the polypeptides of the light-harvesting chlorophyll a/b-binding protein (LHCPII) complex of photosystem II.

2. PROCEDURE

2.1 Materials and methods

2.1.1. Soybean cells, SB-P (<u>Glycine</u> <u>Max</u> L. Merr. Var. (Corsoy) were grown in KT medium in the dark and greened as described (3). Chlorophylls were measured as described (4). Total cell protein extract were prepared as described (3) and total protein was measured as Lowry <u>et</u> <u>al</u>. (5). LHCPII proteins were quantitated by a dot-blot radioimmunoassay (6) with polyclonal antibodies. Total RNA was isolated from harvested cells (which were frozen in liquid nitrogen and ground in a motor with a pestle) and then separated into poly (A$^+$)-and poly (A$^-$)-fractions by oligo-dT cellulose chromatography. The poly (A$^+$)-fraction was translated in a cell-free wheat-germ system (7). Resultant products were immunoprecipitated with polyclonal antibodies to the 28.5 kd LHCPII protein followed by absorption on <u>Staphylococcus</u> protein A-Sepharose CL4B

M. Baltscheffsky (ed.), Current Research in Photosynthesis, Vol. III, 549–552.
© *1990 Kluwer Academic Publishers. Printed in the Netherlands.*

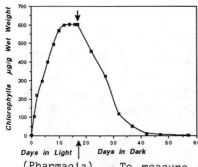

FIGURE 1. Light-induced accumulation of total chlorophyll during greening of previously dark-grown SB-P cells and the reversible loss of total chlorophyll when the cells are re-exposed to darkness. The vertical arrows mark the transition between light and dark.

(Pharmacia). To measure total LHCPII-mRNA, total RNA was dot-hybridized (8) on a Zeta-Probe membrane (Biorad) to a ^{32}P-labeled LHCPII gene-probe from pea.

3. RESULTS AND DISCUSSION

3.1 The Soybean Greening System is Reversible. During greening of dark-adapted soybean cells, chlorophylls start to accumulate per g wet weight at about 2 to 4 hr and reach a maximal level by 10 to 12 days (Fig. 1). When the cells are returned to the dark, their chlorophyll content gradually decreases reaching the previous dark level in 25 to 35 days (Fig. 1). During greening, the plastid develops from amyloplast to immature plastid to chloroplast without an etioplast stage (9) as described for plants growing under normal light-dark regimes (10).

3.2 Dark-Grown Cells. Dark-grown cells contain a large amount of LHCPII-mRNA (65% of that in control green cells) but this mRNA is less active in in vitro translation by 50% compared to the same

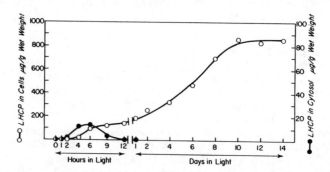

FIGURE 2. Accumulation of total LHCPII proteins during light-induced greening of SB-P cells. Accumulation per g wet weight of cells (o-o); accumulation in the cytosol per g wet weight of cells (●-●). Dark-grown cells were exposed to continuous white light at 0 hr.

mRNA from control cells. Only a trace amount of LHCPII-proteins is detected in the dark-grown cells.

3.3 First two days of light-induced chloroplast development. LHCPII proteins increase in amount 194-fold during the first two days of ct development (Fig. 2, Table 1). During the same time, the increase in translatable LHCPII-mRNA is about 12-fold (Fig. 3, Table 1) while the amount of total LHCPII-mRNA increased only 4-fold (Fig. 3, Table 1). Thus, during early ct development (first two days) at least, multiple controls regulate LHCPII gene-expression. A relatively weak control (possibly transcriptional) results in an increased amount (4x) of LHCPII-mRNA, a second control in an increasing translatibility (12x) of this mRNA, and a third control (likely posttranscriptional) in a greatly increased amount (194x) of accumulated LHCPII-proteins.

3.4 Two to 16 days of light-induced chloroplast development. LHCPII-proteins (Fig. 2) continue to accumulate up to 10-12 days of greening. In contrast, the relative amount and translatability of LHCPII-mRNA peak by two days of greening and then decline

Table 1. Relative Increase in Total and Translatable LHCPII mRNA and Total LHCPII-Proteins During Light-Induced Greening of SB-P Cells

Relative increase over the level in dark-grown cells

Time of Greening	LHCPII-mRNA		LHCPII-Proteins[*]
	Total	Translatable	
0 hr	1.0	1.0	trace
1	1.3	1.7	1.0
2	1.7	2.7	2.6
4	1.9	3.1	12
6	1.9	3.5	71
9	2.3	4.1	93
12	2.6	4.7	107
24	3.2	6.0	142
2 days	4.2	12.3	194
4	2.4	7.5	246
6	2.2	3.9	363
8	1.6	3.1	537
10	1.5	3.4	657
12	1.7	3.3	629
14	1.6	2.6	655
16	1.6	3.2	---

[*]Values are shown relative to the 1 hr value which is standardized at 1.0. Only trace amounts of LHCP-II protein were detected in the dark (0 hr.).

becoming stable by eight days at levels found in control green cells (Fig. 3). Therefore, the above controls on LHCPII gene expression during early ct development which lead to an increased amount and translatability of LHCPII-mRNA must be modulated or changed during later ct development.

The data indicate that LHCPII gene-expression is regulated by multiple and ct development-stage specific controls.

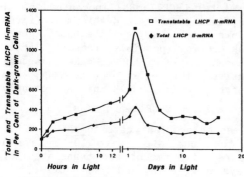

FIGURE 3. Relative amounts of total and translatable LHCPII-mRNA during light-induced greening of SB-P cells. Values for dark-grown cells (0 hr) are standardized at 100 percent.

4. ACKNOWLEDGMENT
Supported by grants from SOHIO and the McKnight Foundation.

REFERENCES
1. Ohad, I. and Drews, G. (1982). In: Photosynthesis (Govindjee, ed.), Vol. II, pp. 89-140, Academic Press, New York.
2. Horn, M. E., Sherrard, J. H. and Widholm, J. (1983) Plant Physiol. 72, 426-429.
3. Erdös, G., Shinohara, K. and Buetow, D. E. (1986). In: Regulation of Chloroplast Differentiation (Akoyunoglou, G. and Senger, H. eds.), pp. 505-510, Alan R. Liss, New York.
4. Lichtenthaler, H. K. and Wellburn, A. R. (1983). Biochem. Soc. Trans. 603, 591-592.
5. Lowry, O. H., Rosenbrough, N. J., Farr, A. L. and Randall, R. J. (1951). J. Biol. Chem. 193, 265-275.
6. Jahn, R., Scheibler, W. and Greengard, P. (1984). Proc. Natl. Acad. Sci. USA 81, 1684-1687.
7. Marcu, K. and Dudock, B. (1974). Nucleic Acids Res. 1, 1385-1397.
8. Zeta-Probe Blotting Membranes, Instruction Manual, p. 2, Bio-Rad Laboratories, Richmond, California.
9. Erdös, G., Shinohara, K., Chen, H.-Q., Lee, S., Gillott, M. and Buetow, D. E. (1987). In: Progress in Photosynthesis Research (Biggins, J., ed.), vol. IV, pp. 539-542, M. Nijhoff Pub., Dordrecht, The Netherlands.
10. Wellburn, A. R. (1982). Int. Rev. Cytol. 80, 133-191.

THE EXTENDED FAMILY OF CHLOROPHYLL A/B-BINDING PROTEINS OF PSI AND PSII

ERAN PICHERSKY[1] and BEVERLEY R GREEN[2], Biology Dept[1], University of Michigan, ANN ARBOR MI 48109 USA and Botany Dept[2], University of British Columbia, VANCOUVER, BRITISH COLUMBIA V6T 2B1 Canada.

1. INTRODUCTION

The chlorophyll a/b-binding complexes are the major light-harvesting antennas of higher plants and green algae. Recent work has revealed a diversity of molecular species among the chlorophyll a/b-binding (CAB) proteins [reviews 1,2], suggesting functional specialization. There are several types of CAB polypeptides in each photosystem. In PSI, the light Harvesting Complex I (LHCI) can be isolated as a single complex with four polypeptides, or as two separate complexes. In PSII, there are three distinct chlorophyll-protein complexes: LHCII (the major antenna, external and physiologically adjustable), CP29 (the internal antenna) and CP24 (a minor external antenna). Not surprisingly, the protein diversity is brought about by the expression of a large set of different genes. Recent work from our lab [3] and others has demonstrated that in higher plants the nuclear genes encoding the different CAB proteins are structurally related to each other. Furthermore, there are both closely-related and distantly-related members of this family, i.e. the process of gene duplication and divergence has been going on in the CAB gene family throughout the evolution of plants.

2. THE GENES

2.1. The tomato system

Work in Dr. Pichersky's lab has concentrated on the dicotyledonous plant species *Lycopersicon esculentum* (tomato) as a model system to investigate the composition and genomic organization of the CAB gene family, the mechanisms involved in the regulation of expression of individual CAB genes and the entire CAB gene family as a whole, and the mechanisms involved in the evolution of these genes. We chose tomato because it is a diploid species with a relatively small genome size. These attributes facilitate the construction of complete genomic libraries and the isolation of genes, and they give one a more correct impression of the "basic" number of genes in each of the branches of the CAB gene family (as compared with number of genes in polyploid species). In addition, because of the extensive genetic map of tomato, the localization of the CAB genes in the genome was easily accomplished by using the newly-developed method of restriction fragment length polymorphism (RFLP) mapping in conjunction with previously identified and assigned markers.

2.2. The LHCII genes

The genes for the major polypeptides of LHCII are the "classic CABs" of plant molecular biology literature, and are often referred to as "CAB genes" or "LHCP genes" without any additional designation. They are now divided into Type I (7 or 8 copies in tomato, copy number ranges from 3-16 in other species; these genes contain no introns), and Type II (2 copies in tomato, 1 in petunia; these genes contain a single intron) [4]. Two clusters of genes (in locus *Cab*1 and locus *Cab*3) encode the tomato Type I PSII CAB polypeptides (Table 1). The tomato Type I PSII CAB proteins are >97% identical to each other in the mature part of the polypeptide. PSII Type I protein sequences are also strongly conserved among species, with >90% identity among angiosperms [2,4]. The two unlinked PSII Type II CAB genes in tomato, *Cab4* and *Cab5*, encode proteins which are 98% identical to one another but are significantly different from Type I CABs from any

M. Baltscheffsky (ed.), Current Research in Photosynthesis, Vol. III, 553–556.

species, including tomato (85% identity) [4]. The tomato Type II CAB proteins show higher sequence identity (>90) to the Type II CAB sequences from both monocots and dicots, suggesting that the Type I and Type II PSII CAB genes represent two lineages which had split prior to the monocot-dicot split [4].

2.3 The CP29 Gene

We have recently isolated the gene encoding the CP29 polypeptide of tomato [5]. The sequence reveals an unmistakable homology to the other CAB sequences, including those of PSI (Fig. 1). The CP29 protein shares two regions of high homology with both LHCII and LHCI, accounting for about 40% of the sequence; and is slightly more related to LHCII than to LHCI CABs. However, it is overall quite different from the LHCII CAB polypeptides, in keeping with its distinctive chlorophyll a/b ratio (4-5 vs. 1.2) and apparent role as a non-mobile internal antenna in PSII [6]. The CP29 gene has five introns, the largest number of any CAB gene characterized to date (Table 1).

2.4 The LHCI genes

Genes for three of the four LHCI polypeptides of tomato have also been isolated [3,7,8]. They are much more divergent from each other than the LHCII genes. They have been designated PSI Types I, II and III (Table 1). Type I is represented by two closely-linked genes, Cab6A and Cab6B, which encode identical polypeptides. Types II and III are single genes, Cab7 and Cab8, which code for the higher molecular weight polypeptides of LHCI. The latter are slightly more related to each other than to the Type I LHCI CAB genes.

2.5 Introns

An interesting feature of the tomato CAB genes is that the different types each contain different number of introns, ranging from none (PSII Type I) to five (CP29) (Table 1). The position of one of these introns, within one of the highly-conserved regions is conserved within a few nucleotides in all of them (except for the LHCII genes, which do not have this intron). The other introns do not occur at the same position in any CAB genes (with one possible exception).

TABLE 1) SUMMARY OF GENETIC DATA ON TOMATO CAB GENES

CHL-PROTEIN COMPLEX	CATEGORY	TOMATO GENES ISOLATED	# OF GENES	# OF INTRONS	CHROMOSOMAL LOCATION
LHCII	Type I	Cab1A,1B,1C,1D	4	0	chr. 2(tightly-linked cluster)
		Cab3A,3B,3C	3	0	chr. 3(tightly linked cluster)
	Type II	Cab4	1	1	chr. 7
		Cab5	1	1	chr. 12
CP29	-	Cab9	1	5	chr. 6
LHCI	Type I	Cab6A,B	2	3	chr. 5(tightly-linked pair)
	Type II	Cab7	1	4	chr. 10
	Type III	Cab8	1	2	chr. 10 >not closely linked

3. PROTEIN SEQUENCE and STRUCTURE

It was initially thought that CAB proteins are strongly conserved, because the first few CAB protein sequences obtained from the sequence of the cloned genes showed greater than 90% sequence identity between monocots and dicots. However, our recent work in which a large number of CAB gene sequences have been determined now makes it clear that sequence conservation is limited to the same type of CAB polypeptides. Thus, the Type I and Type II PSII CAB polypeptides are indeed over 90% identical in monocots and dicots *within the type*, but are only 85% identical to each other even within the same species (the first few CAB genes obtained all belonged to the PSII Type I branch of the family). A third type of PSII CAB protein, CP29, is substantially more divergent from either PSII Type I or Type II (only 40% sequence identity with either) than they are from each other. The PSI CAB polypeptides are even more divergent; the highest overall sequence homology observed in pairwise comparisons of the three types of PSI CAB proteins is 35%-40%, which is only marginally greater than their homology to PSII CAB sequences (30%). The comparisons among the different CAB sequences are shown in Fig. 1. Thus, the range of variation observed among CAB polypeptides is in fact quite large. These differences might reflect their different functions in the photosynthetic apparatus; alternatively, it might simply be a reflection of their phylogenetic distance.

```
                               10        20        30        40
Type III PSI:           MATQALISSSSISTSAEAARQIIGSRISQSVT-RKASFVVRAASTPPVK
Type II  PSI:       MASACASSTIAAVAFSSPSSRRNGSIVGTTKASFLGGRRLR.SKYSTTPTA.S.TTVC.A
Type I   PSI:      MASNTLMSCGIPAVCPSFLSSTKSKFAAAMPVSVGATNSMSRFSMSA-------------
Type I   PSII:          MATSTMALSSSTFAGKAVKLSPSSSEITGNGR..M..TATKAKP..SGSPW
Type II  PSII:          MATCAIQQSAFVGQAVGKSQNEFIRKVGNFGEGRI..M.RTVKSA-PQ.---IW
CP29:       MAAATSLYVSEMLGSPVKFSGVARPAAPSPSSSATFKTVALFKKKAAAAPAKA..AA.SP.DDELAKW
                           50        60        70        80        90       100
Type III PSI  QGANRQ--LWFAS---KQSLSYLDGSLPGDFGFDPLGLS-DPEGTGGFIEPKWLAYGEVING
Type II  PSI  ADPD.P--...PG---STPPPW.................AS...------SLR.NQQA.LVHC
Type I   PSI  --------D.MP.---QPRP......A..........GEV.A------NLERYKES.L.HC
Type I   PSII Y.PD.VKY.GPF.---GE.P...T.EF...Y.W.TA...A...------TFAKNREL...HC
Type II  PSII Y.ED.PKY.GPF.---E.TP...T.EF...Y.W.TA...A...------TFARNREL...HC
CP29          YGPD.RIF.PEGLLDRSEIPE..NGEV...Y.Y..F...KK..------DFAKYQAY.L..A
                          110       120       130       140       150       160
Type III PSI  RFAMLGAAGAIAPEILGKAGLIPQETALAWFQTGVIPPAG-TYNYWADNYTLFVLEMALMGF
Type II  PSI  .W......IFI..L.T.I.ILNTP---------SWYT..-EQE.FT.TT.L.IV.LV.I.W
Type I   PSI  W...AVP.I.V..A..LGNWVKAQ-EW.AIPG.QATYL.-QPVP.GTLP.ILAI.FLAIAF
Type I   PSII W.....L.CVF..L.ARN.VKFG.--AV..KA.SQIFSE-GGLDYLG.PS.VHAQSI.AIW
Type II  PSII W.....L.CVF....S.N.VKFG.--AV..KA.SQIFSE-GGLDYLG.PN.VHAQSI.AIW
CP29          W.......F.I..AFN.F.ANCGPE-AP..K..ALLLD.N.L..FGK---.IPINLI.AVV
                          170       180       190       200       210       220
Type III PSI  AEHRRFQDWAKPGSMGKQYFLGLEKGLGGSGDPAYPGGPLFNPLGFG-KDEKSMKELKLKEI
Type II  PSI  ..G..WA.II...CVNTDPIFPNN.LT.T--.VG....LW.D...W.SGSPAKI...RT...
Type I   PSI  V..Q.SME------------------KD.EKKK....A-.D...YS-..PAKFE...V...
Type I   PSII .CQVVLMGAVEGYRIA-------GGP..EVV..L....S-.D...LA-D.PEAFA...V...
Type II  PSII .CQVVLMGFVEGYRV.-------GGP..EGL.KI....A-.D...LA-D.PEAFA...V...
CP29          AE-VVLVGG.FYYRII--------N..-DLF.KLH.S..-.D...LA-..PDQAAI..V...
                          230       240       250       260       270
Type III PSI  KNGRLAMLAILGYFIQ-ALVTGVGPYQNLLDHLADPVNNNVLTSLKFH       (Cab8)
Type II  PSI  .........VM.AWF.-HIY...ID..FA.....GHATIFAAFSPK         (Cab7)
Type I   PSI  ......L..FV.FCV.QSAYP.T..LE..AT.....WH..IGDVIIPKGIFPN  (Cab6)
Type I   PSII .......FSMF.F.V.-.I...K..LE..A...........AWAFATNFVPGK (Cab1,3)
Type II  PSII .......FSMF.F.V.-.I...K..IE..S..IN...A..AWAYATNFVPGK (Cab4,5)
CP29          .......FSM..F..-.Y...Q..VE..AA..S..FG..L..VIGGASERVPTL (Cab9)
```

Figure 1) Comparisons of tomato CAB protein sequences. In the mature part of the proteins (from app. position 30), only the Type III PSI CAB sequence is shown in full. A dot in the other sequences represents identity, a dash represents a gap introduced to maximize homology.

The large variation in sequences among the different types of CAB polypeptides must mean that the functions shared by them are localized to the two highly-conserved regions (about 20% of the sequence each) and perhaps a few isolated residues elsewhere. As can be seen in Fig. 1, there are no residues outside the two conserved regions which are invariable, and only a few which are almost invariable. Using algorithms for predicting secondary structure [9], all the CAB polypeptides are predicted to have three membrane-spanning helices (MSHs), as first proposed for LHCII by Karlin-Neumann et al [10], and a fairly large mass exposed on the stromal side (Fig. 2). The alignment of sequences in Fig. 1 was aided by super-imposing the hydropathy plots, and supports a model with 3 rather than 4 MSHs, although there may be a small amphipathic helix on the C-terminal lumenal surface (see Fig. 2).

Considering these divergent but related sequences, we propose a "Generic CAB" structure (Fig. 2). The regions of high homology include most of the first and third

MSHs as well as two stroma-exposed regions predicted to have two beta-turns (a Type I and a Type II) each. The conserved regions are drawn with heavy lines in Fig. 2. These two exposed regions (negatively charged, high Pro, Gly, Asp content) are probably responsible for the fact that antibodies to one CAB complex cross-react with polypeptides of the others [11]. The middle MSH is somewhat conserved between CP29 and LHCII, but has very little sequence identity with the middle MSH of the LHCI CABs. This suggests that this helix may not be involved in binding chlorophyll but could be involved in PSII-specific interactions. There are not enough conserved His, Asn and Gln to accommodate the amount of chlorophyll (7-13/polypeptide chain). This could mean that some chlorophylls are liganded by backbone carbonyls or water. However, different complexes have different chl a/b ratios and possibly different numbers of chlorophyll molecules, so it may not be necessary for all the chl-binding side chains to be conserved. We have not been able to detect any significant homology to the light-harvesting antennas of photosynthetic bacteria.

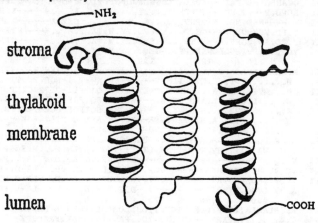

Figure 2) A model for a "generic" CAB protein orientation and configuration in the thylakoid membranes. A similar model was first proposed by Karlin-Neumann et. al. [10]. Heavy line indicates regions of significant primary sequence conservation among all tomato CAB proteins.

REFERENCES
1. Green, B.R. (1988) *Photosyn. Res.* **15**, 3-32.
2. Chitnis, P.R. & Thornber, J.P. (1988). *Photosyn. Res.* **16**, 41-63.
3. Pichersky, E., Brock T.G., Nguyen, D., Hoffman, N.E., Piechulla, B., Tanksley, S.D. & Green, B.R. (1989) *Plant Mol. Biol.* **12**, 257-270.
4. Pichersky, E., Hoffman, N.E., Malik, V.S., Bernatzky, R. Tanksley, S.D., Szabo, L. & Cashmore, A.R. (1987) *Plant Mol. Biol.* **9**, 109-120.
5. Pichersky, E., Subramanian, R., White, M.J., Reid, J., & Green, B.R. In preparation.
6. Camm, E.L. & Green, B.R. (1989) *Biochim. Biophys. Acta* **974**, 180-184.
7. Hoffman, N.E., Pichersky, E., Malik, V.S., Castresana, C., Ko, K., Darr, S.C., & Cashmore, A.R. (1987) *Proc. Natl. Acad. Sci.* (USA) **84**, 8844-8848.
8. Picherky, E., Tanksley, S.D., Piechulla, B., Stayton, M.M., & Dunsmuir, P. (1988). *Plant Mol. Biol.* **11**, 69-71.
9. Green, B.R. in *Current Research in Protein Chemistry*, (Villafranca, J., ed.), Academic Press, in press.
10. Karlin-Neumann, G.A., Kohorn, B.D., Thornber, J.P. & Tobin, E.M. (1985) *J. Mol. Appl. Genet.* **3**, 45-61.
11. White, M.M. & Green, B.R. (1987) *Eur. J. Biochem* **165**, 531-535.

IDENTIFICATION OF A psbG-HOMOLOGOUS GENE IN SYNECHOCYSTIS
SP. PCC6803

KLAUS STEINMÜLLER* AND LAWRENCE BOGORAD** * INSTITUT FÜR
ENTWICKLUNGS- UND MOLEKULARBIOLOGIE DER PFLANZEN, HEINRICH-
HEINE-UNIVERSITÄT DÜSSELDORF, UNIVERSITÄTSSTRASSE 1, 4000
DÜSSELDORF, FRG ** THE BIOLOGICAL LABORATORIES, HARVARD
UNIVERSITY, 16 DIVINITY AVENUE, CAMBRIDGE, MA 02138, USA

1. INTRODUCTION

The chloroplast DNAs of higher plants contain several
open reading frames (ORFs) of as yet unknown functions (1).
In the plastid DNAs of tobacco, maize and the liverwort
Marchantia polymorpha three genes are cotranscribed: ndhC-
psbG-ORF159 (maize)/158 (tobacco)/159 (M. polymorpha).
We have recently demonstrated, that in the cyanobacterium
Synechocystis sp. PCC6803, the three genes occur in the same
order and are cotranscribed as well (2).
PSII-G, the gene product of psbG, has been identified with
the help of antibodies against a synthetic oligopeptide as
an additional component of photosystem II preparations (3).
We report here, that the cyanobacterium Synechocystis sp.
PCC6803 contains a gene that has 64 % amino acid sequence
similarity to psbG and we provide evidence that this gene is
located on a plasmid.

2. MATERIALS AND METHODS

For the isolation of psbG2, HindIII
digested total DNA was separated on a 10 -
30 % sucrose gradient. Fractions enriched
in fragment sizes of 5 - 6 kb were
subcloned in Bluescript KS. About 700
colonies were screened by Southern blot
analysis with a psbG specific probe under
low stingency conditions and six positive
clones were identified.

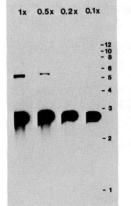

FIGURE 1.
Total DNA was isolated from Synechocystis,
cut with HindIII and separated on a 0.75 %
agarose gel. Four identical Southern
blots were hybridized with a psbG specific
probe and washed under conditions of
different stringency (1x, 0.5x, o.2x and
0.1x SSC at 62 C).

M. Baltscheffsky (ed.), Current Research in Photosynthesis, Vol. III, 557–560.
© 1990 Kluwer Academic Publishers. Printed in the Netherlands.

Two clones, carrying a 5.2 kb insert in inverse orientations were isolated and mapped by restriction enzyme analysis. The two clones were used to construct deletion clones with the exonuclease III/mung bean nuclease system. Deletion clones containing the psbG-homologous region were sequenced.

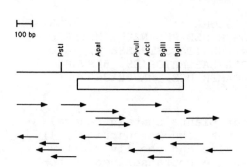

FIGURE 2.
Restriction map and
sequencing strategy of psbG2.

3. RESULTS AND DISCUSSION
    After hybridization of Southern blots of HindIII digested total Synechocystis DNA with a psbG specific probe and washings under conditions of different stringency, an additional hybridization signal was detected at about 5.2 kb (Fig. 1). This fragment was isolated, subcloned and partially sequenced. A restriction map and the sequencing strategy are presented in Fig. 2.
The sequence analysis reveals an open reading frame of 219 amino acids of which 141 (64 %) are at identical positions as in psbG. The ORF was therefore named psbG2.
Sequence analysis of the upstream and downstream regions of psbG2 indicates, that there are no reading frames homologous to ndhC or ORF157 adjacent to psbG2.

MSPNPANPTDLERVATAKILNPSARSQVTQDLSENVILTTVDDLYNWAKLSSLWPLLYGT
..---------TSTHALTLQ..IQAP...KE........CL..I....R..T.Y.MMF..

ACCFIEFAALIGSRFDFDRFGLVPRSSPRQADLIITAGTITMKMAPALVRLYEEMPEPKY
....M..M..F.P...LE...SI..AT......M.........Y.....Q...QI.....

VIAMGACTITGGMFSSDSTTAVRGVDKLIPVDVYIPGCPPRPEAIFDAIIKLRKKVANES
..........A....A..P.........................VI.G.........G..

IQERAITQQTHRYYSTSHQMKVVAPILDGKYLQQGTRSAPPRELQEAMGPVPPALTTSQ
R.DYTEDL....FHAVR.R..P.S...T.Q..RHHEDLT.HHDPLLIK

QKEQLNRG   psbG   FIGURE 3.
              psbG2   Amino acid sequence comparison
                                between psbG and psbG2

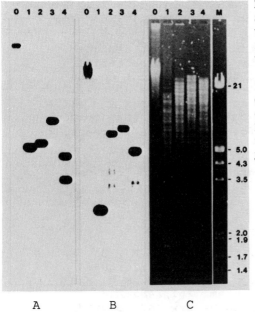

A   B   C

FIGURE 4.
Southern blot analysis of
undigested (0) and
restriction enzyme digested
total Synechocystis DNA
(1: HindIII, 2: EcoRI,
3: KpnI, 4: AccI)
C: ethidium bromide stained
gel (0.6% agarose)
B: and A: hybridization
with specific probes for
psbG (B) and psbG2 (A)

Undigested as well as restriction enzyme digested total DNA
was separated on a 0.6 % agarose gel. The ethidium bromide
stained gel shows that the bulk of the undigested genomic
DNA is sheared and runs as a broad band above 20 kb (Fig.4
C, lane 0). Southern blots were prepared from two identical
gels and hybridized with specific probes for psbG and psbG2.
As expected, the psbG probe hybridizes to the broad band of
undigested DNA (Fig. 4 B, lane 0). The psbG2 probe instead
recognizes a sharp band of significantly higher molecular
weight than the sheared genomic DNA (Fig. 4 A, lane 0). This
suggests, that psbG2 is located on a megaplasmid which has
remained intact during the DNA isolation procedure.

The presence of multiple copies of genes for the photosynthetic apparatus in cyanobacteria has been demonstrated
for psbA (4,5), psbD (6) and the phycocyanin genes (7).
For these genes, the amino acid sequence similarities among
the members of a multigene family range between 80 and 99 %.
The similarity between psbG2 and psbG of Synechocystis is
significantly smaller (64 %) and is comparable with the
similarity between the psbG genes from Synechocystis and
higher plants (f.e. maize, 52 %, reference 2).
The physiological functions of multigenes in cyanobacteria
are not understood. The psbA gene family of Anacystis
nidulans R2 contains three members and one gene alone is
sufficient for survival of the cells (5). Recent experiments
show, that the genes are expressed differentially under low

and high light conditions (8). Thus, additional gene copies
might be necessary for growth in nature under suboptimal
growth conditions in a changing environment.
So far, no physiologcial functions have been assigned to
cyanobacterial plasmids (9). By analogy to bacterial
systems, it has been suggested that they might encode
functions for heavy metal or drug resistance, bacteriocin
production or degradation of organic compounds etc. (10).
The location of psbG2 on a plasmid suggests that cyanobacterial plasmids also code for photosynthetic genes.

ACKNOWLEDGEMENTS
This work was supported by a grant to K. St. from the
Deutsche Forschungsgemeinschaft (SFB 189).

REFERENCES
1. Ohyama, K., Kohchi, T., Sano, S. and Yamada, Y. (1988)
   TIBS 13,19-22
2. Steinmüller, K., Ley, A.C., Steinmetz, A.A., Sayre, R.T.
   and Bogorad, L. (1989) Mol. Gen. Genet. 216,60-69
3. Steinmetz, A.A., Castroviejo, M., Sayre, R.T. and
   Bogorad, L. (1986) J. Biol. Chem. 261,2485-2488
4. Mulligan, B., Schultes, N., Chen, L., and Bogorad, L.
   (1984) Proc. Natl. Acad. Sci. USA 81,2693-2697
5. Golden, S.S., Brusslan, J. and Haselkorn, R. (1986) EMBO
   J. 5,2789-2798
6. Williams, J.G.K. and Chrisholm, D.A. (1987) in Progress
   in Photosynthetic Research (Biggins, J., ed.), Vol. IV,
   pp.809-812, Nijhoff, Dordrecht
7. Conley, P.B., Lemaux, P.G. and Grossman, A.R. (1988) J.
   Mol. Biol. 199,447-465
8. Schaefer, M.R. and Golden, S.S. (1989) J. Bacteriol.
   171,3973-3981
9. Tandeau de Marsac, N. and Houmard, J. (1987) in The
   Cyanobacteria (Fay, P. and Van Baalen, C., eds.), pp.251-
   302, Elsevier, Amsterdam
10.Van den Hondel, C.A.M.J.J., Keegstra, W., Borrias, W.E.
   and van Arkel, G.A. (1979) Plasmid 2,323-333

ISOLATION AND SEQUENCE ANALYSIS OF THE PSBA GENE FROM SCENEDESMUS OBLIQUUS

CHRISTOPHER TODD[1], BRUCE DINER[2] and JOHN BOWYER[1], Department of Biochemistry, Royal Holloway and Bedford New College, Egham Hill, Egham, Surrey TW20 0EX, U.K.   [2]CR&D, E.I. DuPont de Nemours Co., Wilmington, Delaware 18173, U.S.A.

1.   INTRODUCTION

It is now generally accepted that a heterodimer of the D1 and D2 proteins of Photosystem II binds the primary photoreactants (1,2). This heterodimer is also believed to provide at least some of the Mn ligands for the assembly of an active oxygen evolving complex (3).

A low-fluorescence mutant (LF-1) of Scenedesmus obliquus has been isolated and partially characterised (4-8). LF-1 lacks the ability to evolve oxygen but PS II activity is restored by artificial donors. The absence of oxygen evolving activity results from a failure to bind Mn correctly at the catalytic site (9); this in turn is associated with a failure to post translationally process D1, which normally leads to removal of a carboxyl terminal extension (8).

Although our results suggest that the LF-1 mutant lacks the processing protease activity (10), we also set out to determine whether there were any sequence changes within the psbA gene encoding the D1 protein, which could lead to amino acid substitutions affecting D1 processing. Both wild type and mutant psbA genes have to be sequenced; some of the results of the wild type gene sequencing are presented here.

2.   PROCEDURE

Scenedesmus obliquus strain D3 was grown under high light (100Wm^{-2}) at 25°C in NGY medium (11) and harvested by centrifugation in late logarithmic phase of growth. The cell pellet was frozen in liquid N_2 and lyophilized. The dry cells were ground to a very fine powder before nucleic acid extraction with CTAB (12). The various nucleic acid components were separated by CsCl density gradient centrifugation in the presence of bisbenzimide (Hoechst dye No. 33258). This fluorescent dye binds strongly to A-T rich regions of DNA and significantly reduces the buoyant density of such DNA (13). This reduction in buoyant density enables the resolution of the A-T rich chloroplast DNA (cpDNA) from other contaminants.

The purified cpDNA was examined by restriction enzyme digestion, agarose gel electrophoresis and Southern blot analysis with the heterologous psbA gene from Poa annua (a gift from M.D.C. Barros). A single Bgl II restriction fragment of 9.6 kb hybridised to the

M. Baltscheffsky (ed.), Current Research in Photosynthesis, Vol. III, 561–564.
© 1990 *Kluwer Academic Publishers. Printed in the Netherlands.*

heterologous probe. This fragment was ligated in to the Bam HI site of pBR322 to produce the 14 kb plasmid pSWT37. This plasmid was mapped and fragments produced by Eco RI digestion were subcloned into the vector pUC118 (an M13 phagemid derivative of pUC18). The psbA gene regions of the subclones were sequenced by the dideoxy chain-termination method primed with custom made oligonucleotides and oligonucleotides homologous to Synechocystis 6803 psbA (a gift from J.G. Metz).

3. RESULTS AND DISCUSSION

The sequence analysis of the subcloned fragments revealed a unique psbA gene structure of 4 exons separated by 3 introns (Fig. 1). The exon-intron boundaries of the Scenedesmus psbA gene were determined by comparison of the amino acid sequence deduced from this psbA gene with the sequence of Chlamydomonas psbA and the uninterrupted spinach psbA.

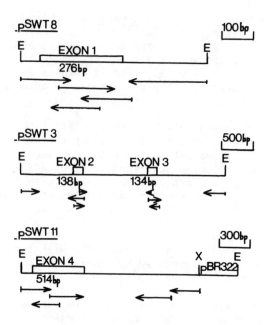

FIGURE 1. Strategy for sequencing Eco RI subclones of the Scenedesmus wild type 9.6 kb Bgl II cpDNA fragment with homology to the psbA gene of Poa annua

The deduced amino acid sequence for the compiled coding region is 93.2% homologous to Chlamydomonas reinhardii (14), 92.7% homologous to soybean (15), 92.4% homologous to spinach, tobacco and mustard (16-18), 87.3% homologous to Prochlorothrix hollandica (19), 86.2% homologous to Euglena gracilis (20) and 85.9% homologous to copy 1 of

Anacystis nidulans (21) psbA genes. This high homology of the D1 protein is consistent with the strong structural and functional constraints placed on a protein with such a central role in the energy capturing systems of photosynthetic organisms.

The deduced sequence of D1 from _Scenedesmus obliquus_ is more closely related to the sequences found in _Chlamydomonas_ and higher plants than to members of other photosynthetic groups. However _Scenedesmus_ appears to have retained a feature of Cyanobacteria and Prochlorophyta which is the lysine residue at position 238; this residue is arginine in most known higher plant sequences. This lysine residue was predicted in _Scenedesmus_ because of the susceptibility of the D1 protein to digestion by the endoprotease lys-c (5,7).

Codon usage in _Scenedesmus_ psbA involves only 38 of the 61 possible amino acid coding triplets. Codons ending in G account for only 8.76% of the total whereas those ending in T 38.42%, C 26.84% and A 25.99% of the total. This codon usage is very similar to that found in _Chlamydomonas_ psbA. All psbA genes sequenced to date terminate with TAA; _Scenedesmus_ is no exception. The entire sequence will be published elsewhere and is available on request.

The carboxyl terminal region of the wild type psbA gene has the predicted cleavage site (ala 344) for carboxyl terminal processing (22). However the 10 codons which code for the removed portion of the D1 protein are quite different from those of _Chlamydomonas_ (Figure 2). This appears to be because _Chlamydomonas_ is unusual; the _Scenedesmus_ sequence is homologous to higher plants in this region.

FIGURE 2. Deduced carboxyl-terminal sequences of the D1 protein

			344																
Synechocystis 6803 i	FPLDLA	S	G	D	A	Q	M	V	A	L	N	A	P	A	I	E	G	*
Synechocystis 6803 iii	FPLDLA	S	G	E	Q	A	P	V	A	L	T	A	P	A	V	N	G	*
Amaranthus hybridus	FPLDLA	A	I	E							A	P	S	T	N	G	*
Alfalfa	FPLDLA	A	V	E							A	P	S	I	N	G	*
Anacystis nidulans 1	FPLDLA	A	G	E	A	T	P	V	A	L	T	A	P	S	I	N	G	*
Anacystis nidulans 2	FPLDLA	A	G	E	A	T	P	V	A	L	T	A	P	A	I	N	G	*
Anacystis nidulans 3	FPLDLA	A	G	E	A	T	P	V	A	L	T	A	P	A	I	N	G	*
Chlamydomonas reinhardii	FPLDLA	S	T	N							S	S	S	N	N	*
Euglena gracilis	FPLDLA	*
Nitella	FPLDLA	A	I	E							A	P	S	T	N	G	*
Petunia	FPLDLA	A	I	E							A	P	S	T	N	G	*
Solanum nigrum	FPLDLA	A	I	E							A	P	S	T	N	G	*
Soybean	FPLDLA	A	I	E							A	P	S	I	N	G	*
Spinach	FPLDLA	A	I	E							A	P	S	T	N	G	*
Tobacco	FPLDLA	A	I	E							A	P	S	T	N	G	*
Scenedesmus obliquus D3	FPLDLA	S	V	E							A	P	S	V	N	A	*

REFERENCES

1 Nanba, O. and Satoh, K. (1987) Proc. Natl. Acad. Sci. USA 84, 109-112
2 Barber, J. (1987) Trends Biochim. Sci. 12, 123-124
3 Mei, R., Green, J.P., Sayre, R.T. and Frasch, W.D. (1989) Biochemistry 28, 5560-5567
4 Metz, J.G., Wong, J. and Bishop, N.I. (1980) FEBS Lett. 114, 61-66
5 Metz, J.G., Pakrasi, H.B., Seibert, M. and Arntzen, C.J. (1986) FEBS Lett. 205, 269-274
6 Diner, B.A., Ries, D.F., Cohen, B.N. and Metz, J.G. (1988) J. Biol. Chem. 263, 8972-8980
7 Taylor, M.A., Nixon, P.J., Todd, C.M., Barber, J. and Bowyer, J.R. (1988) FEBS Lett. 235, 109-116
8 Taylor, M.A., Packer, J.C.L. and Bowyer, J.R. (1988) FEBS Lett. 237, 229-233
9 Seibert, M., Noriaki, T. and Inoue, Y. (1989) Biochim. Biophys. Acta 974, 185-191
10 Packer, J., Taylor, M., Gerrish, C. and Bowyer, J.R. (1989) Proc. VIIIth Intl. Congr. Photosynth., Stockholm, Kluver Academic Publishers, Dordrecht, in press
11 Bishop, N.I. (1971) Methods Enzymol. 23, 372-408
12 Murray, M.G. and Thompson, W.F. (1980) Nuc. Acids Res. 8, 4321-4325
13 Manuelidis, L. (1977) Anal. Biochem. 78, 561-568
14 Erickson, J.M., Rahire, M. and Rochaix, J.D. (1984) EMBO J. 3, 2753-2762
15 Spielmann, A. and Stutz, E. (1983) Nuc. Acids Res. 11, 7157-7167
16 Zurawski, G., Bohnert, M.J., Whitfield, P.R. and Bottomley, W. (1982) Proc. Natl. Acad. Sci. USA 79, 7699-7703
17 Sugita, M. and Sugiura, M. (1984) Mol. Gen. Genet. 195, 308-313
18 Link, G. and Langridge, U. (1984) Nuc. Acids Res. 12, 945-958
19 Morden, C.W. and Golden, S.S. (1989) Nature 337, 382-385
20 Keller, M. and Stutz, E. (1984) FEBS Lett. 175, 173-177
21 Golden, S.S. and Haselkorn, R. (1985) Science 229, 1104-1107
22 Takahashi, M., Shiranishi, T. and Asada, K. (1988) FEBS Lett. 240, 6-8

TRANSCRIPTIONAL LIGHT REGULATION OF psbA GENE EXPRESSION IN SYNECHOCYSTIS 6803

Abdallah Mohamed and Christer Jansson

Department of Biochemistry, Arrhenius Laboratories, University of Stockholm, S-106 91 Stockholm, Sweden

INTRODUCTION

Assembly-disassembly of photosystem (PS) II is a dynamic process that is regulated by light at the transcriptional, translational and post-translational levels. Although there is ample evidence for light-regulated expression of PSII-specific genes [1-3], it is not clear how these regulatory mechanisms operate. In the present work we describe the influence of light on steady-state transcript levels of the psbA, psbD, psbD-C and rbcL-S genes in the cyanobacterium Synechocystis 6803 [4]. psbA, psbD and psbC encodes the PSII polypeptides D1, D2 and CP43, respectively, and rbcL and rbcS encodes the large and small subunit, respectively, of 1,5-ribulose-bisphosphate carboxylase. Transcript levels were also studied in constructed mutants of S. 6803 with only one intact psbA gene.

RESULTS AND DISCUSSION

Illuminated cultures of S. 6803 accumulated high levels of psbA, psbD, psbD-C and rbcL-S transcripts (Figs. 1-3, wildtype panels). When the light intensity was increased from the normal light conditions of 50 $\mu E \cdot m^{-2} \cdot s^{-1}$ to 1500 $\mu E \cdot m^{-2} \cdot s^{-1}$ the transcript levels for psbA, psbD and psbD-C became higher while those for rbcL-S became lower. The PSII activity, measured as oxygen evolution under saturating light conditions, in cells incubated at 1500 $\mu E \cdot m^{-2} \cdot s^{-1}$ showed an approximately 200-fold increase over cells incubated at 50 $\mu E \cdot m^{-2} \cdot s^{-1}$. This suggests that S. 6803 cells could adapt to high light irradiances and it is possible that the higher levels of psbA and psbD transcripts under such conditions were required to meet an accelerated trunover rate of the D1 and D2 polypeptides.

M. Baltscheffsky (ed.), Current Research in Photosynthesis, Vol. III, 565–568.
© 1990 *Kluwer Academic Publishers. Printed in the Netherlands.*

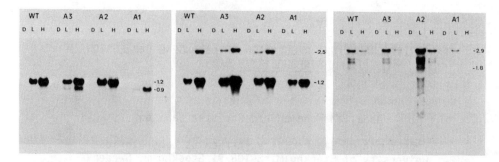

Figure 1 (left). Northern blot analysis of RNA isolated from S. 6803 wildtype (wt) and mutants (A3-A1). The probe was a mixture of psbA-1 and psbA-2 from S. 6803. D = 48 hours in darkness; L = 20 hours in low light (50 $\mu E \cdot m^{-2} \cdot s^{-1}$); H = 20 hours in high light (1500 $\mu E \cdot m^{-2} \cdot s^{-1}$).

Figure 2 (middle). Northern blot analysis. Conditions as in Fig. 1, with the exception that the probe was the psbD-2 gene from S. 6803 (provided by R. Debus). The presence of the 2.5 kb transcript shows that the overlapping psbD1 and psbC genes in S. 6803 [6] are cotranscribed.

Figure 3 (right). Northern blot analysis. Conditions as in Fig. 1, with the exception that the probe was a 5' portion of the rbcL gene from S. 6803 [7]. The presence of the 2.9 kb transcript suggests that the rbcL and rbcS genes are cotranscribed in S. 6803.

No psbA, psbD, psbD-C or rbcL-S transcripts could be detected in dark cultures of S. 6803 (Figs. 1-3). Prolonged exposure of the X-ray films showed that the psbA probe sometimes hybridized to a 0.6 kb transcript from both dark and illuminated cultures, as well as to a 0.8 and 1.8 kb transcript from illuminated cultures. The 0.8 kb transcript was most consistently seen in RNA from older cultures.

In contrast to the lack of psbA transcripts in dark cultures, thylakoid isolated from such cultures contained high amounts of the D1 polypeptide (Fig. 4).

The different S. 6803 mutants with only one intact psbA gene are briefly described in Table 1. The mutants were constructed by insertional mutagenesis using gene cartridges conferring antibiotic resistance. Analyses of RNA from the mutants showed that both psbA-2 and psbA-3 could produce high levels of transcript (Fig. 1). Morover, no significant reduction in the relative abundance of total psbA transcript could be observed after inactivation of either psbA-2 or psbA-3. No psbA transcript could be detected from the psbA-1 gene.

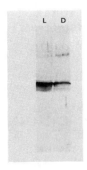

Figure 4. Western blot analysis of thylakoids isolated from wildtype cells incubated either for 48
hours in the dark (D) or for 20 hours in low light
($50\mu E \cdot m^{-2} \cdot s^{-1}$). The antibody was directed against
the D1 polypeptide.

This is consistent with the finding that mutant A1 lacked oxygen
evolving activity and had to be grown photoheterotrophically.
Complementation of mutant A1 with either intact psbA-2 or psbA-3
resulted in photoautotrophic transformants. This shows that the perturbed PSII activity in mutant A1 was correlated to lack of intact
psbA-2 and psbA-3 genes, and not to a secondary effect introduced
during construction of the mutant. The lower psbA transcript observed
in RNA from mutants A3 and A1 is a truncated psbA-2 transcript terminated by transcription termination signals in the Ω fragment [5] in
the inactivated psbA-2 gene [4].

All mutants, including A1, produced wildtype levels of psbD, psbD-C
and rbcL-S transcripts under illuminated conditions, although the
level of psbD-C transcripts in mutant A1 was comparatively low (Figs.
2 and 3).

Table 1. Constructed mutants of S. 6803 containing only one intact
psbA gene.

Mutant	Antibiotic resistance	Inactivated psbA genes	Active psbA genes
A1	Str, Spc, Cm	psbA-2 and psbA-3	psbA-1
A2	Kn, Cm	psbA-1 and psbA-3	psbA-2
A3	Kn, Str, Spc	psbA-1 and psbA-2	psbA-3

III.12.**568**

Acknowledgements: This work was supported by the Swedish Natural Science Research Council and the Carl Trygger Foundation for Scientific Research.

REFERENCES

1 Schaefer, M.R. and Golden, S.S. (1989) J. Bact. 171, 3973-3981
2 Klein, R.R. and Mullet, J.E. (1987) J. Biol. Chem. 262, 4341-4348
3 Hughes, J.E. and Link, G. (1988) Photosynth. Res. 17, 57-73
4 Jansson, C., Debus, R.J., Osiewacz, H.D., Gurevitz, M. and McIntosh, L. (1987) Plant Physiol. 85, 1021-1025
5 Prentki, P. and Krisch, H.M. (1984) Gene 29, 303-313
6 Chisholm, D. and Williams, J.G.K. (1988) Plant Mol. Biol. 10, 293-301
7 Reiss, T., Jansson, C. and McIntosh, L., these Proceedings

REGULATION OF TRANSLATION OF TWO CHLOROPLAST mRNA's BY THYLAKOID MEMBRANES

STEFAN LEU AND ALLAN MICHAELS, DEPARTMENT OF BIOLOGY, BEN GURION UNIVERSITY OF THE NEGEV, BEER-SHEVA, ISRAEL.

1. INTRODUCTION

The expression of chloroplast encoded genes is regulated at different stages. Transcriptional, translational and posttranslational regulation of chloroplast gene expression have been described (1). Several mRNAs for chloroplast made proteins are abundant in proplastids as well as in mature chloroplasts in the dark, even though no translation of these messages is observed (2).

Rough thylakoids contain mRNA's for soluble and membrane proteins (3, 4, 5). They form rapidly upon illumination and show maximal abundance during periods of highest protein synthesis (5, 6). The thylakoid association specifically influenced the translation of different mRNAs. It was, therefore, proposed that the chloroplast regulates its translation by thylakoid associated factors (3, 4).

We have studied the translational control of ps1A2 (reaction center protein 2 of Photosystem I) and LS (large subunit of ribulose bisphosphete carboxylase) by chloroplast factors, using mRNAs produced in vitro from the corresponding genes cloned into vectors containing the T7 RNA polymerase promotor.

2. MATERIAL AND METHODS

The genes for ps1A2 and LS were resected from the cloned EcoRI fragment 15 of Chlamydomonas chloroplast DNA (7) and cloned into pGem and pT7-1 plasmid. RNA from the different plasmids was produced with T7 RNA-polymerase (BRL) according to the manufacturer, using plasmids linearized with restriction endonucleases as templates.

In vitro translations were carried out according to the manufacturer (Promega Biotech) with [35S] methionine (1000 Ci/ml). After 1 hour incubation at 30°C, 1 μl-aliquots of the translation mixtures were used to determine hot trichloroacetic acid (TCA) precipitable incorporation of [35S] methionine. Products were analized by SDS-electrophoresis (SDS PAGE)(4). Gels were stained and dried, and labelled bands were detected by autoradiography.

M. Baltscheffsky (ed.), Current Research in Photosynthesis, Vol. III, 569–572.
© 1990 *Kluwer Academic Publishers. Printed in the Netherlands.*

Thylakoid membranes used in the translation mixtures were isolated as described (8). The membranes were washed three times with R-buffer (reticulocyte translation buffer: 120 mM KAc, 1.2 mM MgAc2, 25 mM HEPES/KOH; pH 7.8), and resuspended in R-buffer to 1 mg/ml of chlorophyll. E. coli membranes were prepared by ultrasonication of log phase cells, centrifugation at 5000 x g and afterwards at 30000 x g. The 30000 x g pellet was washed, resuspended in R-buffer and used for translation assays.

3. RESULTS AND DISCUSSION

The mRNA for LS was obtained by digesting LS-pT7 at the BamHI site of the polylinker. The full length ps1A2 mRNA was obtained from plasmid linearized with XbaI. Digestion of the plasmid containing the gene for ps1A2 with BamHI and MboII resulted in truncated mRNA's: PS B encoding for the first 93 amino acids; and PS M encoding for the first 43 amino acids of ps1A2. These in vitro produced mRNAs were translated in the reticulocyte lysate in the absence or presence of Chlamydomonas thylakoid membranes. The effect of membranes on the translations of these mRNA's was quantified and standardized by dividing the incorporation above background in the absence of membranes by the one obtained in the presence of membranes. LS translation was inhibited by 20 - 25 percent in the presence of thylakoid membranes (Figure 2). The inhibitory effect of thylakoids on LS translation could be washed from the membranes (9). Membranes from lettuce chloroplasts also inhibited LS mRNA translation by about 25%, while E. coli membranes, slightly stimulated LS mRNA translation. The inhibitory activity seems therefore to be specific for chloroplast membranes.

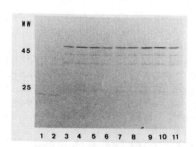

Figure 1: Products of LS mRNA translation in the presence of 1 μl gradient fractions obtained by ultracentrifugation of chloroplast extract through a sucrose gradient (10 - 30%, SW50, 4 hours 50000 rpm). 1,2) fractions 20, 28 in 5 μl translation mix without added RNA; 3-12) fractions 1,3,4,5,6,8,12,20,28, each in 5 μl translation mix containing 25 μg/ml LS mRNA.

An inhibitory factor was extracted from isolated Chlamydomonas chloroplasts with 0.5 M KCl. The extract was desalted by chromatography through Sephadex G-25 and fractionated by ultracentrifugation on a sucrose gradient. Maximal inhibitory activity was found in the fractions 4 - 6, containing polypeptides of 40 - 70 kDa (Figure 1). The activity was heat labile and not a proteolytic enzyme since posttranslational incubation does not reduce the amount of incorporation into LS, as determined by autoradiography of dried gels or by scintillation counting (Table 1).

Addition		Relative Incorporation
-		100%
Membranes		78%
Gradient fraction Nr:		
2		37%
6		26%
14		95%
2		103%
6	boiled for 5 min	114%
14		120%
2	posttranslational	61%
6	incubation (45 min,	91%
14	30 C, 20 ug/ml CHI)	100%

Table 1: Effect of: fresh thylakoid membranes; three fractions of KCl extract separated by sucrose gradient ultracentrifugation (see figure 1); the same fractions boiled before incubation; the same fractions added after translation was stopped with cycloheximide (20 μg/ml); on the radioactivity incorporated by LS mRNA translation.

Translation of ps1A2 mRNA was stimulated about 2-fold in the presence of thylakoid membranes (9). It was also stimulated by lettuce chloroplast membranes and E. coli membranes. Translation of PS B mRNA, encoding for the first 11 kD of ps1A2, was stimulated 2.7-fold in the presence of thylakoid membranes. PS M, which in contrast to PS B does not contain the first hydrophobic domain of ps1A2, showed a reduced incorporation in the presence of membranes (Figure 2).

These results are the first direct evidence for the regulation of chloroplast mRNA translation by interaction with thylakoid associated chloroplast factors. LS translation seemed to be subject to regulation by a thylakoid-associated factor which inhibited run-off and in vitro translation of LS mRNA (3, 4, 9). Translation of ps1A2 was stimulated by the interaction of the first hydrophobic domain of this protein with the added membranes. These results confirm previous results obtained by runoff translations of membrane bound or triton solubilized chloroplast polysomes in the reticulocyte lysate (4).

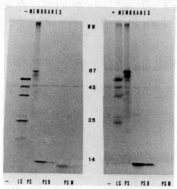

Figure 2: Translation products of in vitro translations of RNAs in the absence and presence of thylakoid membranes (0.3 mg/ml) in the reticulocyte lysate: (-) no message control; LS: 25 μg/ml LS-RNA; PS: 25 μg/ml PS-RNA; PSB: 100 or 33 μg/ml of PSB-RNA; PSM: 100 and 33 μg/ml PSM-RNA.

4. REFERENCES:

1. Gruissem W. (1989) Cell 56, 161 - 170.
2. Mullet J.E. (1988) Annu. Rev. Plant Physiol. 39, 475 - 502.
3. Minami E.I. and Watanabe A. (1984) Arch. Biochem. Biophys. 235, 562 - 570.
4. Leu S., Bolli R., Mendiola-Morgenthaler L. and A. Boschetti (1984) Planta 160, 204 - 211.
5. Breidenbach E., Jenni E. and Boschetti A. (1988) Eur. J. Biochem. 177, 225 - 232.
6. Chua N.H., Blobel G., Siekevitz P. and Palade G. (1976) J. Cell. Biol. 71, 497 - 514.
7. Dron M., Rahire M. and Rochaix J.D. (1982) J. Mol. Biol. 162, 775 - 793.
8. Herrin D., Michaels A. and Hickey E. (1981) Biochim. Biophys. Acta 281, 399 - 405.
9. Leu S., Herrin D. and Michaels A. (1989) In: Proceedings of the Braunschweig Symposium of Applied Plant Mol. Biol. (G. Galling editor), 22 - 37.

ACKNOWLEDGEMENT:
This work was supported by a grant from NSF.

TISSUE SPECIFIC ACTIVITY OF ARABIDOPSIS THALIANA PLASTOCYANIN AND FERREDOXIN PROMOTER ELEMENTS IN TRANSGENIC TOBACCO PLANTS.

SJEF SMEEKENS, OSCAR VORST AND PETER WEISBEEK
DEPARTMENT OF MOLECULAR CELL BIOLOGY, UNIVERSITY OF UTRECHT, PADUALAAN 8, 3584 CH UTRECHT, THE NETHERLANDS.

1. INTRODUCTION

Plastocyanin (PC) and ferredoxin (FD) are two nuclear-encoded chloroplast proteins which are functional in photosynthetic electron transport. In higher plants the expression of the PC and FD genes is light controlled, most likely by a phytochrome-dependent mechanism (1, 2). In addition, expression of these genes is mostly confined to green tissue.

We are interested in the expression regulation of these genes and want to identify the cis- and trans-acting factors involved in the light-mediated and tissue-specific regulation. For this purpose we have constructed and analysed transgenic plants which contain chimeric genes consisting of the Arabidopsis thaliana PC and FD promoters fused to a reporter gene.

2. PROCEDURE

The cloning and analysis of the A. thaliana strain Columbia PC and FD genes has been described (3, 4). For the gene transfer experiments a Xba1 site was introduced 5 bp in front of the FD and PC initiator ATG codon. This Xba1 site was used for fusion of promoter fragments with beta-glucuronidase (GUS) in vector pBI101 (5). Transgenic plants were regenerated and transferred to soil in a growth chamber (10h/14h light dark cycle, 25°C at 55 % relative humidity. Leaf segments (10-12 cm) and roots were harvested 25 days after transfer and frozen on dry ice. Frozen tissue (stored at -70°C) was ground in 50 mM sodium phosphate (pH 7.0), 10 mM EDTA, 0.1% Triton X-100, 0.1% sarkosyl and 10 mM ß-mercaptoethanol. Enzymatic reactions were incubated at 37°C in the same buffer, containing 1 mM 4-methylumbelliferyl-ß-D-glucuronide as a substrate, and were stopped by adding 100 µl of the reaction mixture to 2 ml 0.2 M Na_2CO_2. Formation of 4-methylumbelliferone was quantified by measuring fluoresence at 450 nm (under excitation at 365 nm).

M. Baltscheffsky (ed.), Current Research in Photosynthesis, Vol. III, 573–575.
© 1990 *Kluwer Academic Publishers. Printed in the Netherlands.*

3. RESULTS AND DISCUSSION
The genes encoding <u>A. thaliana</u> PC and FD were isolated from a genomic library screened with the PC and FD cDNA probes from <u>Silene pratensis</u>.

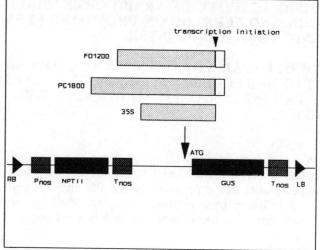

Figure 1 Promoter elements ligated in front of the GUS gene in binary vector pBI101.1.

These genes were sequenced and the transcription initiation site determined by S1 nulcease experiments (3, 4).

The promoter regions of the FD (1.2 kb) and PC (1.8 kb) genes, including the 5'-noncoding sequences, were fused to the reporter gene GUS in the binary vector pBI101.1 (Fig. 1; 5). The resulting vectors were transferred to <u>Agrobacterium tumefaciens</u> and tobacco leaf discs transformed. Kanamycin resistant tobacco plants were regenerated and tested. Similarly, a promoterless GUS gene (pBI101) and a 35S-GUS fusion gene (pBI121) were transferred into plants. For each construct the GUS activity of 10-30 independent transformants was determined.

To test whether the activity of FD and PC promoters is tissue-specific we measured reporter gene activity in leaves and roots of the transgenic plants. Both FD and PC are active almost exclusively in leaves (Fig. 2). The level of leaf-specific expression is 4-5 times higher for FD and PC than for the 35S promoter. Moreover, the 35S promoter

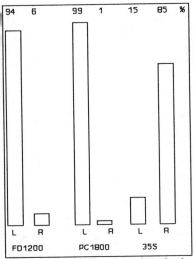

Figure 2 Expression levels in leaves (L) and roots (R) of the transgenic tobacco plants.

is very active in roots when compared to leaves. The GUS activity of the promoterless construct was comparable to untransformed plants.

In conclusion 1.2 kb of the <u>A. thalianana</u> FD promoter and 1.8 kb of the PC promoter give high level, tissue specific expression in transgenic tobacco plants.

4. REFERENCES

1. Kaufman, L., Roberts, L., Briggs, W. and Thompson, W. (1986) Plant Physiol. 81, 1033-1038.
2. Haslett, B. and Cammack, R. (1974) Biochem. J. 144, 567-572.
3. Vorst, O., Oosterhoff-Teertstra, R., Vankan, P., Smeekens, S. and Weisbeek, P. (1988) Gene 65, 59-69.
4. Vorst, O., van Dam F, Oosterhoff-Teertstra, R., Smeekens, S. and Weisbeek, P., submitted for publication.
5. Jefferson, R., Kavanagh, T. and Bevan, M. (1987) EMBO J. 6, 3901-3907.

STRUCTURE OF THE GENES FOR PHOSPHOENOLPYRUVATE CARBOXYLASE AND PYRUVATE Pi DIKINASE FROM MAIZE.

Makoto Matsuoka and Muneaki Samejima

National Institute of Agrobiological Resources, Tsukuba, Ibaraki, Japan.

1. INTRODUCTION

Phosphoenolpyruvate carboxylase (PEPC) and pyruvate Pi dikinase (PPDK) play significant roles in the photosynthetic fixation of carbon in C_4 and CAM plants. PEPC catalyzes the fixation of atmospheric CO_2 to phosphoenolpyruvate (1), and PPDK catalyzes the formation of phosphoenolpyruvate, the substrate for PEPC (2).

We have been conducting biochemical and molecular-biological comparisons of C_4 photosynthetic enzymes between C_3 and C_4 plants because these enzymes can be used in the study of changes in gene expression during the evolution of C_3 to C_4 photosynthesis (3,4,5). The comparison of genes for C_4 photosynthetic enzymes between C_3 and C_4 plants provides a useful method for elucidating the way in which C_4 plants have gained the unique properties associated with the regulation of expression of these enzymes. Here we report the isolation and structural characterization of genomic clones that contain the PEPC and PPDK genes from maize. We discuss the putative regulatory sequence in the 5'-flanking region of the gene.

2. EXPERIMENTAL PROCEDURES

Genomic DNA from maize (Zea mays L. cv. Golden Cross Bantam) was isolated from etiolated leaves as previously described (6).

Cloning and screening of the genomic DNA were performed as described elsewhere (7). The nucleotide sequence of the genomic clone was determined by the dideoxynucleotide chain-termination method (8).

3. RESULTS AND DISCUSSION

Isolation and Characterization of the PEPC gene.

Fig. 1 shows the restriction map and the strategy for sequencing of the PEPC gene. The analyzed sequence comprises 2910 bp which cover the coding region, all introns and the 5'- and 3'-flanking regions, for a total of 6781 bp. The sequence of the coding region is quite similar to previously reported cDNA sequence for maize C_4-type PEPC (9). The high degree of similarity indicates that the isolated genomic clone correspondents to the gene that encodes the C_4-type PEPC.

The PEPC gene contains ten exons which are separated by nine introns (Fig 1). The sizes of both the exon and intron regions vary considerably: exons range between 85 and 999 bp, while introns range between 92 and 897 bp in length. In the all introns, typical GT/AG donor-acceptor sites are present, and the sequences surrounding these splice junctions are similar to the plant consensus sequence but are not identical.

The primary extension analysis indicates that the cap site is 84 nucleotides upstream from the first residue of the initiation codon.

M. Baltscheffsky (ed.), Current Research in Photosynthesis, Vol. III, 577–580.
© 1990 *Kluwer Academic Publishers. Printed in the Netherlands.*

The sequence around the site, TTGATCA, is homologous with the consensus cap sequence of plant genes (10). The 5'-untranslated region of the longest PEPC cDNA is 82 bp in length (11), confirming the result of the primer-extension analysis. In the 5'-flanking sequence of the PEPC gene no typical TATA element is found around -30 position but a homologous sequence, TATTT, is found at positions -28 to -24. A typical CCAAT element or a homologous sequence is not found around position -80. Another characteristic sequence, CCGCCC, is found twice: at positions -47 to -52 and -79 to -84. The sequence is also found in the first intron at positions 282 to 287. The hexanucleotide sequence is known as the binding site for SV40 Sp1 protein (12). An unusual feature of the 5'-flanking region is that there are six long, direct repeat sequences (Table I). These six direct repeat sequences contain many cytidine residues (more than 50%) and are located at positions between -548 and -30. It is possible that the six direct repeat sequences in the PEPC gene may have a function(s) that is involved with the expression of the PEPC enzyme in maize mesophyll cells.

Isolation and Characterization of the PPDK gene.

Overlapping genomic clones containing PPDK gene were isolated and characterized. Fig. 2 shows the restriction map and the strategy for sequencing of the PPDK gene. The analyzed sequence comprises 2844 bp which cover the coding region, all introns and the 5'- and 3'-flanking regions, for a total of about 13 kb. The sequence of the coding region is quite similar to previously reported cDNA sequence for maize C_4-type PPDK (6); suggesting that the isolated genomic clones correspondent to the gene that encodes the C_4-type PPDK.

The PPDK gene contains nineteen exons which are separated by eighteen introns (Fig 2). The sizes of both the exon and intron regions vary considerably: exons range between 57 and 431 bp, while introns range between 78 bp and about 5.9 kb in length. In the all introns except the 14th intron, typical GT/AG donor-acceptor sites are present, and the sequences surrounding these splice junctions are similar to the plant consensus sequence but are not identical (13). The donor site of the 14th intron contains no-conforming splice site, GC. This type of 5'-splice junction is a rare case and have been observed in several eucaryotic genes.

The primary extension analysis indicates that the cap site is 211 nucleotides upstream from the first residue of the initiation codon. The sequence around the site, TTCACCC, is homologous with the consensus cap sequence of plant genes (10). In the 5'-flanking sequence of the PPDK gene typical TATA element is found around -30 position. A typical CCAAT element is not found around position -80, but an inverted homologous sequence of CCAAT element (ATAGG) is found around position -70. The sequence of the binding site for SV40 Sp1 protein is found at position -51 to -41. It is noteworthy that there are three long, direct repeat sequences in the 5'-flanking region (Table II). These sequences contain 14 bp-direct repeats and the first (-286 to -258) and the third sequences (-216 to -172) also contain another 13 bp-direct repeats but the second (-257 to -224) does not contain this repeat. The second and the third sequence contain one more 12 bp-direct repeats which are similar to SV40 enhancer core

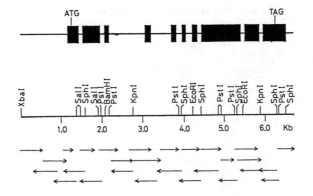

Fig. 1   Structure of the PEPC gene and sequencing strategy.
Locations of exon and intron regions are presented as boxes and lines between boxes, respectively. ATG and TAG indicate the locations of the initiation and the termination codons of the PEPC gene, respectively. A restriction map of the gene is also presented. The directions and lengths of the sequences determined are shown by horizontal arrows.

Table I. Putative regulatory elements found in the PEPC gene.

Element	Position	Sequence
TATA box	-24 to -28	TATTT
CCAAT box	-367 to -371	CCAAT
Sp-1 binding site	-80 to -85	CCGCCC
	-48 to -53	CCGCCC
	275 to 280(intron 1)	CCGCCG
	281 to 286(intron 1)	CCGCCC
light-responsive element	-653 to -661	CCTTATCCT
direct repeated sequence	-536 to -550	CCCTCAACCACATCCTGC
	-510 to -527	GACACCCTCG-CCACATCC
	-453 to -470	GACGCCCTCT-CCACATCCTGC
	-378 to -395	GACGCCCTCT-CCACATCCTGC
	-201 to -214	CCCTCT-CCACATCC
	-30 to -39	CT-CCCCATCC

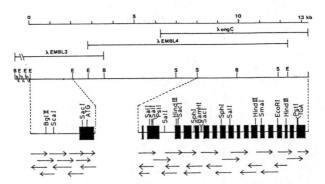

Fig. 2   Structure of the PPDK gene and sequencing strategy.
Symbols are the same as those described in Fig. 1.

Table II. Putative regulatory elements found in the PPDK gene.

Element	Position	Sequence
TATA box	-32 to -29	TATAA
	(consensus)	(TATAA)
CCAAT box	-1233 to -1229	CCAAT
	(consensus)	(CCAAT)
Inverted CCAAT	-72 to -68	ATAGG
	(consensus)	(ATTGG)
Sp1-binding site	-51 to -42	GTCGCGCCCC
	(consensus)	$GTC_{ACT}CCGCCC_{A}^{C}$
direct repeated sequence	-780 to -766	GGAGGTGGAAGGCCT
	-307 to -298	GTGGA-GTCGT
	-286 to -258	CTGTAGCCACTCGTACGCTACAGCCCAAG
	-257 to -224	CGCTAGAGCCCAAGAGGCCGGAGGTGGAAGGCGT
	-216 to -172	CTATAGCCACTCGC-CGCAAGAGCCCAAGAGGCCGGAGCTGGAAGG
	-108 to -99	GTGGA-GACGT
SV40 enhancer core sequence	(consensus)	$GTGG_{TTT}^{AAA}G$
PEPC element	46 to 62	ACCCCCTCTCCAGCTCC
	(consensus)	ACGCCCTCTCCACATCC

sequence. Three other enhancer core like sequences are also found at other positions in the 5'-flanking region. The enhancer core sequence is known to be important in the light regulation of pea genes encoding the small subunit of ribulose 1,5-biscarboxylase (14). Thus, the sequences may have regulatory activity by light in maize cells.

4.   REFERENCE

1 Andreo, C.S., Gonzalez, D.H. and Iglesias, A.A. (1987) FEBS Lett. 213, 1-8

2 Edwards, G.E., Nakamoto, H., Burnell, J.N. and Hatch, M.D. (1985) Annu. Rev. Plant Physiol. 36, 255-286

3 Matsuoka, M. and Hata, S. (1987) Plant Physiol. 85, 947-951

4 Hata, S. and Matsuoka, M. (1987) Plant Cell Physiol. 28, 635-641

5 Matsuoka, M. and Yamamoto, N. (1989) Plant Cell Physiol. 30, 479-486

6 Matsuoka, M., Ozeki, Y., Yamamoto, N., Hirano, H., Kano-Murakami, Y. and Tanaka, Y. (1988) J. Biol. Chem. 263, 11080-11083

7 Matsuoka, M. and Minami, E (1989) Eur. J. Biochem. 181, 593-598

8 Sanger, F., Micklen, S. and Coulson, A.R. (1977) Proc. Natl. Acad. Sci. USA 74, 5463-5467

9 Izui, K., Ishijima, S., Yamaguchi, Y., Katagiri, F., Murata, T. Shigesada, K., Sugiyama, T. and Katsuki, H. (1986) Nucl. Acids Res. 14, 1615-1628

10 Joshi, C.P. (1987) Nucl. Acids Res. 15, 6643-6653

11 Yanagisawa, S., Izui, K., Yamaguchi, Y., Shigesada, K. Katsuki, H. (1988) FEBS letter 229, 107-110

12 Kadonaga, J.T., Jones, K.A. and Tjian, R. (1986) Trends Biochem. Sci. 11, 20-23

13 Hanley, B.A. and Shuler, M.A. (1988) Nucl. Acids Res. 16, 7159-7176.

14 Kuhlemeier, C., Fluhr, R., Green, P.J. and Chua, N.H. (1987) Genes Dev. 1, 247-255

REQUIREMENT FOR PHOSPHOENOLPYRUVATE CARBOXYLASE IN A CYANOBACTERIUM

I. LUINENBURG and J. R. COLEMAN, Centre for Plant Biotechnology, Botany Dept., University of Toronto, Toronto, Ont. CANADA. M5S 3B2

1. INTRODUCTION

Although cyanobacteria are known to assimilate inorganic carbon by the C_3 photosynthetic pathway, they also fix large amounts of carbon in the light as C_4 acids (1). These C_4 acids, primarily aspartate and malate, may represent as much as 20% of the total carbon fixed and have been shown to be the product of phosphoenolpyruvate (PEP) carboxylase [EC 4.1.1.31] activity (1,2,3). PEPCase catalyzes the irreversible carboxylation of PEP, utilizing HCO_3^- to form oxaloacetate (OAA) and P_i with the rapid amination or reduction of OAA producing aspartate or malate, respectively (4). In cyanobacteria, PEPCase activity is thought to play an anapleurotic role by generating carbon skeletons (5). Cyanobacteria as a group are characterized by possessing an incomplete TCA cycle lacking both α-ketoglutarate dehydrogenase and NADH oxidase (6). Metabolic energy cannot be derived from this pathway and the cycle is incapable of regeneration (7). The C_4 acids synthesized by PEPCase activity could be used to replenish the TCA cycle intermediates which are in turn utilized for biosynthetic reactions. The synthesis of C_4 acids may also be required for the production of cyanophycin, a nitrogen storage compound accumulated by cyanobacteria (8). The apparent central role of PEPCase in cyanobacterial carbon metabolism has stimulated efforts to isolate the gene for this enzyme and characterize the regulation of expression. Complementation of E. coli PEPCase deficient mutants has led to the cloning of a PEPCase gene (*ppc*) from Anacystis nidulans (Synechococcus 6301) (9) and Anabaena variabilis (10). As an initial step in determining the role of this enzyme in cyanobacterial carbon metabolism, we have isolated *ppc* from the transformable, unicellular Synechococcus 7942 and have attempted to generate PEPCase-deficient mutants by insertional inactivation of *ppc*.

2. METHODS AND MATERIALS

Growth of bacteria, manipulation of plasmids pUC18 and pHP45Ω, and Southern blot analysis were carried out as previously described (11,12,13). Cultures of Synechococcus PCC 7942 were maintained on BG-11 medium and grown in batch culture at 28 C in an illuminated shaker (14). Isolation of

M. Baltscheffsky (ed.), Current Research in Photosynthesis, Vol. III, 581–584.
© 1990 *Kluwer Academic Publishers. Printed in the Netherlands.*

cyanobacterial genomic DNA was performed as previously described (15). Segregation events were selected on media containing: 40 µg/ml spectinomycin and 25 mM glutamate; 40 µg/ml spectinomycin, 25 mM glutamate, 0.5 mM acetate, 0.1 mM malate; or 40 µg/ml spectinomycin and 0.1 mM proline, arginine, aspartic acid, lysine, threonine, methionine, serine, glycine, alanine, valine, leucine, isoleucine; 50 µM tyrosine, tryptophan, phenylalanine, histidine; 0.5 mM cysteine, glutamic acid,succinic acid, citric acid, pyruvate, acetate, ammonium chloride; 0.1mM malate. PEPCase assays were performed essentially as described (16).

3. RESULTS AND DISCUSSION

For isolation of the *ppc* gene, plasmid libraries of Synechococcus genomic DNA, inserted into pUC18, were screened by Southern blot analysis using oligonucleotide probes derived from a published cyanobacterial *ppc* sequence (9). Partial sequence analysis of a 4.4 kb BamHI fragment revealed complete homology to the known cyanobacterial *ppc* sequence and allowed the orientation of the gene on the cloned fragment to be determined. The sequence similarity between the two Synechococcus strains is in agreement with other research which has also shown a close genetic relationship between Synechococcus strains 7942 and 6301 (17). As our initial intent was to determine whether PEPCase activity is essential for the survival of this cyanobacterium, a series of inactivated *ppc* constructs were made (Fig. 1). This was accomplished by the insertion of a DNA fragment, containing a spectinomycin / streptomycin resistance cartridge flanked by transcriptional and translational stop signals (11), into the cyanobacterial *ppc* coding and flanking regions (Fig. 1). These plasmids were then used to transform Synechococcus by recombination of the homologous DNA on either side of the drug resistance cassette with genomic DNA (19). In this way, it is possible to specifically interrupt a known region of genome with a selectable marker. As cyanobacteria are considered to be polyploid, segregation during a number of subsequent divisions is required to obtain a homogeneous population of inactivated genomes within an individual (15).

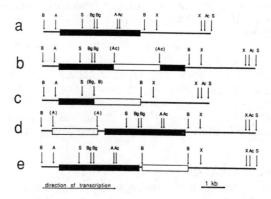

Figure 1. Inactivation of Synechococcus *ppc* gene. a) Restriction map of *ppc* gene. b) Inactivating construct placing Sm/Stp cassette within *ppc*. c) Inactivating construct

placing Sm/Stp cassette within *ppc* and deleting a portion of *ppc* concurrently.   d) Upstream control DNA construct placing Sm/Stp cassette upstream of *ppc* coding region.   e) Downstream control DNA construct placing Sm/Stp cassette downstream of *ppc* . Solid line: noncoding DNA. Solid bar: *ppc* sequence. Open bars: Intervening Sm/Stp encoding cassette (11). Vertical arrows: Restriction enzyme sites abbreviated as A (Ava 1), Ac (Acc 1), B (BamHI), Bg (Bgl 11), S (Sac 1), X (Xho 1).

Transformation of Synechococcus 7942 with the *ppc* coding region interrupted with the drug resistance cassette (Fig. 1b) produced a number of transformants that after segregation were spec^r and amp^s, however PEPCase activities were near wild type (data not shown).   Southern blot analysis of the genomic DNA from these transformants revealed the presence of both wild type and insertionally inactivated *ppc* genes (Fig 2). Numerous attempts to segregate these genotypes were unsuccessful. Transformation using a deletion mutant (Fig. 1c) in which a portion of the *ppc* coding region has been removed and replaced with the drug resistance cassette generated similar results (data not shown).   Control insertions (Fig.1d,e), where regions of the cyanobacterial DNA immediately 5' and 3' of the *ppc* coding sequence were interrupted, resulted in the predicted homogeneous genome (Fig. 2) and wild type PEPCase activities (data not shown).

It has been possible to inactivate specific genes in cyanobacteria using the protocol described above (19,20,21).   Attempts to inactivate other genes have resulted in merodiploid formation and the subsequent inability to segregate the genome types (19).   As there is no evidence for multiple PEPCase genes in Synechococcus 7942, it would appear that a functional PEPCase is essential for this cyanobacterium.

Attempts to bypass this metabolic requirement by nutritional complementation, and thus isolate a *ppc-* mutant from the merodiploid cells, were unsuccessful.   Limited entry of various TCA cycle intermediates and amino acids or an unknown requirement for PEPCase activity may explain the inability to produce a *ppc-* cyanobacterium.

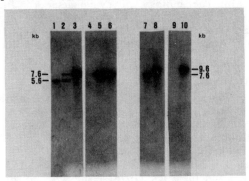

Figure 2.   Southern analysis of cyanobacterial chromosomal DNA after inactivation of *ppc* and control insertion in upstream and downstream regions. Chromosomal DNA was isolated from wild type Synechococcus (lanes 1,4,7,9) and from cells transformed with: pUC 18 containing the inactivating construct b (lanes 2,5);   pUC 18 containing the upstream insertional control construct d (lanes 8,10);   pUC 18 containing the

downstream insertional control construct e (lanes 3,6).   After digestion with Sac 1 (lanes 1-6) or Xba 1 (lanes 7-10), agarose gel electrophoresis and transfer to nitrocellulose, the DNA blots were probed with a Sac 1/Acc 1 (lanes 1-3) or BamHI (lanes 7,8) fragment containing a portion of the *ppc* coding region, or a BamHI fragment containing the Sm/Stp resistance cassette (lanes 4-6 and 9,10).   The positions and molecular size (kb) of the hybridizing DNA fragments are indicated.

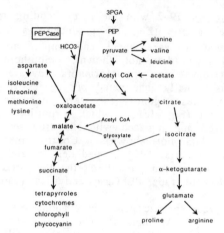

Figure 3. Cyanobacterial TCA Cycle.

4. REFERENCES

1.   Coleman JR Colman B (1980) Planta **149**: 318-320.
2.   Coleman JR Colman B (1981) Plant Cell Environ. **4**: 285-290.
3.   Owttrim GW Colman B (1984) Adv. Photosyn. Res. **3**: 549-552.
4.   Maruyama H Easterday RL Chang HC Lane MD (1966) J. Biol. Chem. **241**: 2405-2412.
5.   Owttrim GW Colman B (1987) Biochem. Cell. Biol. **66**: 93-99.
6.   Smith AJ London J Stanier RY (1967) J. Bacteriol. **94**: 972-983.
7.   Smith AJ (1982) **In:** The biology of cyanobacteria.   Blackwell, Oxford, U.K., pp. 47-85.
8.   Weathers PJ Allen MM (1978) Arch. Microbiol. **116**: 231-234.
9.   Kodaki T Katagiri F Asano M Izui K Katsuki H (1985) J. Biochem. **97**: 533-539.
10. Harrington TR Glick BR Lem NW (1986) Gene **45**:113-116.
11. Prentki P Krisch HM (1984) Gene **29**: 303-313.
12. Miller JH (1972) **In:** Experiments in Molecular Genetics, Cold Spring Harbor Laboratories, Cold Spring Harbor, New York p 433.
13. Maniatis T Fritsch E Sambrook J (1982) **In**: Molecular Cloning: A Laboratory Manual, Cold Spring Harbor, New York.
14. Allen MM (1968) J. Phycol. **4**: 1-4.
15. Golden SS Brusslan J Haselkorn R (1987) Methods Enz. **153**: 215-231.
16. Colman B Cheng KH and Ingle RK (1976) Plant Sci. Lett. **6**: 123-127.
17. Golden SS Nalty MS Cho DC (1989) J. Bacteriol. **171**: 24-29.
18. Williams JGK Szalay AA (1983) Gene **24**: 37-51.
19. Golden SS Brusslan J Haselkorn R (1986) EMBO **5**: 2789-2798.
20. Vermaas WFJ Williams JGK Arntzen CJ (1987.) Plant Mol. Biol. **8**: 317-326.
21. Williams JGK (1988) Methods Enz. **167**: 766-778.

THE GLUTAMATE 1-SEMIALDEHYDE AMINOTRANSFERASE OF BARLEY: PURIFICATION OF THE PROTEIN, c-DNA CLONING, SEQUENCING AND CHARACTERISATION OF THE mRNA

Bernhard Grimm, Simon P. Gough and C. Gamini Kannangara
Department of Physiology, Carlsberg Laboratory, Gamle Carlsberg Vej 10, DK-2500 Copenhagen Valby, Denmark.

1. INTRODUCTION

Chlorophyll synthesis in plants is regulated at steps converting glutamate into δ-aminolevulinate (ALA). The stromal protein glutamate 1-semialdehyde (GSA) aminotransferase catalyzes the last reaction in the synthesis of ALA. We identified and sequenced a c-DNA clone encoding the GSA-aminotransferase in order to study the expression of this enzyme and its catalytic mechanism of transamination.

2. MATERIALS AND METHODS

Barley seedlings were grown in darkness for 5 days and illuminated for various lenghts of time. Growth and identification of *tigrina* mutants of barley have been described in (1). The GSA-aminotransferase was purified from greening barley seedlings by isolating chloroplast stromal proteins and passing these through a size filtration column and thereafter through a series of affinity columns (2). The run-through fraction, which contains the aminotransferase was separated in non-denaturing gels and the band identified by enzymatic activity and in a Western blot (Fig. 1) with an antibody against the enzyme. Separation of the fraction by SDS-PAGE (Fig. 1) revealed the enzyme to be a homomeric dimer with a subunit mass of 46 kDa (3). The NH$_2$-terminal amino acid sequence of the aminotransferase and of a 17 kDa cyanogen bromide fragment were obtained (3) (Fig. 2). Corresponding oligonucleotides were synthesized and used as primers in a polymerase chain reaction (PCR) with the Taq-polymerase (4). DNA fragments amplified by PCR from a c-DNA library were cloned into p-GEM-72f(+). A 460 bp clone encoding the aminotransferase peptides was

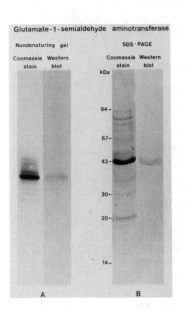

Glutamate-1-semialdehyde aminotransferase

Nondenaturing gel | SDS-PAGE

Coomassie stain | Western blot | Coomassie stain | Western blot

kDa
94 –
67 –
43 –
30 –
20 –
14 –

A | B

Figure 1. Identification of purified GSA-aminotransferase from barley separated in non-denaturing and SDS-gels by Western blotting with an antibody against the aminotransferase

Mature protein

```
         A   V   S   I   D   E   K A Y T V N K S E E I F N A
5'                               3'
 CAGCTTG GCA GTA TCA ATA GAC GAA
         G   G   G   C   T   G
Hind III C   C   C   T
         T   T   T
```

17 kDa peptide

```
 G A L R L V R A F T G R   E   K   I   L   K   F   E
                       3'                               5'
                         CTC TTC TAA AAA TTC AAA CCTTAAGG
                             T   T   GGC T   G
                                     T   G       Eco RI
                                     T
```

Figure 2. Amino-terminal amino acid sequences of the barley aminotransferase and of the internal cyanogen bromide fragment. Also given are the oligonucleotide primers used for the polymerase chain reaction

identified by dideoxy-nucleotide sequencing. With the aid of these clones a lambda gt 11 library prepared from poly(A) RNA of 6 hr illuminated barley leaves was screened and a c-DNA clone containing the entire coding region for the aminotransferase obtained. For Northern hybridization poly(A) RNA was prepared, separated on formaldehyde-agarose gels and blotted onto nitro-cellulose. Probing of the Northern blots and of Southern blots of restriction fragments of barley DNA was carried out using the cloned fragments prepared by PCR.

3. RESULTS AND DISCUSSION

A Southern blot of barley DNA digested with restriction enzymes revealed only one or two genes for the aminotransferase (Fig. 3). Northern blot analysis of poly(A) RNA from barley probed with the DNA fragment obtained by PCR predicts a 1800 b mRNA for the aminotransferase. Analysis of equal amounts of poly(A) RNA obtained during greening indicates that the steady state aminotransferase mRNA level is approximately the same in dark grown and in 10 hour illuminated plants (Fig. 4). The amount of this mRNA decreases after 16 hours illumination and at 24 hours only traces of the specific RNA are detected. The level of m-RNA in the dark grown tigrina mutants, which overproduce protochlorophyllide, is identical to the wild-type control (Fig. 5). Feeding ALA to dark grown leaves of the wild-type possibly decreases the level

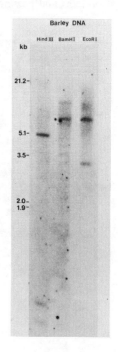

Figure 3. Southern blot of restriction nuclease digests of barley DNA hybridized with a probe for the aminotransferase

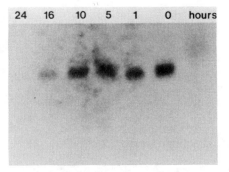

Figure 4. Northern blot of Poly(A) RNA from 5d dark grown barley leaves and leaves illuminated for different times. The RNA was probed with the DNA fragment specific for the aminotransferase

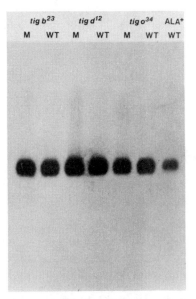

Figure 5. Northern blot analysis of Poly(A) RNA of dark grown *tigrina* mutants (M) and their wild-types (WT) with a DNA fragment specific for the aminotransferase

of mRNA for the aminotransferase. Thus transcription of mRNA for the aminotransferase is not enhanced on illumination. Earlier experiments have shown a stimulation of ALA forming activity during greening (5). Further studies will show whether this is due to an increased translation of the aminotransferase or an activation of the enzyme. It seems certain that the overproduction of protochlorophyllide in *tigrina* mutants is not due to an enhanced transcription of the gene encoding aminotransferase. The decline in ALA-synthesizing activity after 12 h of greening(s) is correlated with a reduction in mRNA encoding the aminotransferase.

REFERENCES
1. Gough, S.P. & Kannangara, C.G. (1979) Carlsberg Res. Commun. **44**, 403-416
2. Kannangara, C.G., Gough, S.P., Oliver, R.P. & Rasmussen, S.K. (1984) Carlsberg Res. Commun. **49**, 417-437
3. Grimm, B., Bull, A., Welinder, K.G., Gough, S.P. & Kannangara, C.G. (1989) Carlsberg Res. Commun. **54**, 67-79
4. Saiki, R.K., Gelfand, D.H., Stoffel, S., Scharf, S.J., Higuchi, R., Horn, T.T., Mullis, K.B. & Erlich, H.A. (1988) Science **239**, 487-491
5. Kannangara, C.G. & Gough, S.P. (1979) Carlsberg Res. Commun. **44**, 11-20

PHOTOSYNTHETIC CHARACTERIZATION OF MUTANTS OF *ZEA MAYS* INDUCED BY THE DNA TRANSPOSABLE ELEMENT, *MUTATOR*

DONALD MILES and WILLIAM COOK, Biology Division, Tucker Hall, University of Missouri, Columbia, MO 65211 USA

Fourteen new photosynthesis mutants were isolated from *Zea mays L.* (maize) stocks which were outcrossed to lines containing active *Mutator* elements. This outcrossing causes replication and translocation of the DNA elements leading to new insertion into genes at random and mutation (transposon mutagenesis). After two generations of self-pollinations (M_2 generation) new mutant genes which were induced segregate in a 1:3 ratio. Photosynthesis mutants were screened and isolated by monitoring the increased level of chlorophyll fluorescence in the intact plant. Mutant genes which cause a visibly high chlorophyll fluorescence are termed *hcf*. Upon standard analysis of the state of photosynthetic electron transport, several different types of photosynthesis mutants were discovered which cause sufficient limitation in photosynthesis to increase whole plant visual fluorescence yield.

All 14 mutations are inherited in a manner to indicate a single nuclear recessive gene is altered which causes the limitation in chloroplast electron transport. Mutants exhibit instability through small somatic reversions (small areas of green tissue) characteristic of *Mutator* induced genes. Upon genetic analysis of the 14 mutants one was allelic to the previously described PS-II mutant *hcf3*, which is located on chromosome 1S (1). Five of the others mutant loci were mapped to chromosome arm. *hcf101* is on 7L, *hcf102* is on 8L, *hcf104* on 7L, *hcf108* on 5S, and *hcf113* is located on chromosome 9S.

Photosynthetic electron transport was measured by standard techniques leading to an assessment of the rate or quantity of PS-I, PS-II, cytochrome b_6/f complex, coupling factor CF_1, plastoquinone, and P-700. Table 1. summarizes electron transport in PS-II, PS-I, and PS-II + PS-I for these 14 mutants.

M. Baltscheffsky (ed.), Current Research in Photosynthesis, Vol. III, 589–592.
© 1990 *Kluwer Academic Publishers. Printed in the Netherlands.*

TABLE 1. Photosynthetic electron transport of maize *hcf* mutants

Mutant	PS-II	PS -I	PS-II + PS-I[1]
Control	100[2]	100	100
*hcf*3MU	18	107	5
*hcf*103	18	143	0
*hcf*114	15	150	6
*hcf*102	81	128	16
*hcf*109	100	130	4
*hcf*110	97	101	11
*hcf*105	57	37	0
*hcf*111	91	66	12
*hcf*101	126	72	84
*hcf*104	76	41	40
*hcf*112	112	31	24
*hcf*113	58	76	38
*hcf*107	59	104	98
*hcf*108	73	75	61

[1] Electron donors and acceptors for PS-II: 0.4 mM phenylene diamine, 2.0 mM $K_3Fe(CN)_6$; for PS-I: 2.0 mM Na ascorbate, 0.5 mM diaminodurene, 0.1 mM methyl viologen, 8.0 uM DCMU; for PS-II + I: 0.1 mM methyl viologen, 10 mM methyl amine as uncoupler. Reaction contained 40 mM Tricine at pH 8.0, 60 mM NaCl and 4 mM $MgCl_2$.

[2] Expressed as percent of sibling controls. Control value: PS-II 259, PS-I 849, PS-II + I 136 umol O_2/mg chl/h evolved or consumed. Average of 3 experiments.

Analysis of the data shows some mutants to be blocked in PS-II (*hcf*103MU, 103, 114), others blocked in the cytochrome b_6/f complex (*hcf* 102, 105, 109, 110, 111), and another class blocked in PS-I (*hcf* 101, 104). Upon further analysis mutants *hcf* 107 and 108 showed a reduction of the proton translocating ATPase CF_1, while the two remaining mutants were not clearly defined. Analysis of leaf fluorescence induction kinetics (Kautsky effect) supported the above characterization of the mutants.

SDS PAGE was performed on thylakoid membranes prepared

from all mutants. In most cased the loss of electron transport was correlated with the loss of the multi-subunit protein membrane complex associated with that electron transport. Unlike most previous reports of photosynthesis mutants (2), two of the PS-II mutants (*hcf* 103, 114) were not depleted in PS-II polypeptides even though there was a substantial loss of electron transport. Variable fluorescence indicated that Q_A was functional though no usual electron acceptor would function to accept elections from the Q_B site. Extraction and chromatography of plastoquinone indicated a complete loss of PQ9 and the presence of an apparent modified quinone. We suggest that this modified quinone functions in the Q_A site but not as effectively at the Q_B binding site.

TABLE 2. Biochemical characteristics of *hcf*101, *hcf*104

	Normal	*hcf*101	*hcf*104
Leaf pigmentation	green	pale-green	green
chlorophyll a:b	3.4	2.7	3.3
CPI	100%[1]	15%	40%
P-700	100%[2]	15%	40%
PS-I e- transport	100%[3]	72%	40%
PS-I + II	100%	84%	41%
H_2O to HCO_3^-	100%	71%	---
PS-II	100%	126%	76%

[1] SDS PAGE; percentage of normal siblings.
[2] Oxidized-reduced, chemically, for P-700 content.
[3] O_2 consumption or evolution as in TABLE 1; H_2O to HCO_3^-: 2 mmol/liter NaHCO$_3$, 160 mg leaf tissue at 16 uE/M^{-2} s^{-1} light. Control rate of 28 umol O_2/mg chl/h.

Polypeptide analysis of one of the PS-I mutants (*hcf*104) showed a very good correlation in the quantity of CPI, 68kDa and other PS-I polypeptides, P-700 and the rate of PS-I electron transport. *hcf*104 has lost 60% of all of these PS-I components and demonstrated the same 60% loss of the PS-I election transport

(Table 2). When the other PS-I mutant (*hcf*101) was analyzed there was little correlation between the PS-I components and the rate of election transport. *hcf101* retains 15% of the CPI, the PS-I polypeptides, and 15% of the P-700 (oxid-redu). However, the rate of PS-I electron transport measured by a variety of different methods all show about 72% of the control sibling plants. This was not expected.

There is a dramatic difference between these two PS-I mutants. *hcf*104 shows the same characteristic of all previous PS-I mutants isolated from the green algae or higher plants. That is, the direct relationship of the PS-I complex and the rate of PS-I electron transport *hcf*101 shows a 'free running' rate of PS-I with the existing quanity of P-700 turning over at near its maximum rate. The mutations in these two cases are clearly different with *hcf101* altering those PS-I complexes which remain in the thylakoid to function at an enhanced rate, possibly by providing optimal access to the PS-I electron donor pool.

The other series of mutations, including those altering coupling factor, appear to have the more usual characteristics of previously isolated mutants. These studies appear to show that more unusual mutants can be isolated by transposon mutagenesis than with chemical mutagenesis.

Mutants which identify nuclear-encoded functions essential to chloroplast development are valuable resources. Transposon mutagenesis using the *Mutator* system may provide access to some of the nuclear loci which are essential to chloroplast development and, in so doing, reveal patterns of interaction between the nucleus and organelle in eukaryotic systems. The work presented here lays a foundation for the isolation of nuclear loci essential to the assembly of the major components of the photosynthetic apparatus associated with the chloroplast thylakoid membrane.

This research was supported by United States Department of Agriculture Grants SE86 CRCR 1-2028 and 88-37234-3705.

REFERENCES
1. Cook, W. B. and Miles, D. (1988) Photosynthesis Res. 18, 33-59
2. Miles, D. (1982) in Methods in Chloroplast Molecular Biology, (Edelman. M., Hallick, R. B. and Chua, N-H eds) pp.75-107. Elsevier, Amsterdam

TRANSCRIPTION OF SOME CHLOROPLAST GENES COULD BE UNDER PHYTOCHROME
CONTROL: A COMPUTER PREDICTION AND ANALYSIS OF LIGHT-RESPONSIVE
SEQUENCES

VICTOR E. SEMENENKO, DMITRY A. LOS, Plant Physiology,
Institute USSR Academy of Sciences. Botanicheskaya ul.,35,
Moscow, USSR

INTRODUCTION
It has been shown that expression of some photosynthetic plant
nuclear genes is regulated via phytochrome (1,2,3). It was also found
that phytochrome-activated transcription of these genes is determined by
upstream cis-acting DNA sequence elements (4,5,6), called LREs. Provided
that, 1) transcription of these genes is activated by light in
chloroplast-containing cells (4,7), 2) the expression of both nuclear
and chloroplast genomes is tightly coordinated and 3) transcription of
some chloroplast genes was shown to be under phytochrome control (1,8),
we have suggested that phytochromeinducible transcription in
chloroplasts could be directed by the same mode as the nuclear one.
Thus, in order to find the genes under phytochrome control and to define
the genetic mechanisms of light response in chloroplasts, it seems
reasonable to search nucleotide sequences homologous to nuclear LREs. We
distinguish two groups of LREs: the first one, with CCTTATCAT motif, was
revealed by computer comparison of the known positive regulated
light-induced sequences (9), and the second one was obtained from
experimental data and corresponds to binding sites for plant nuclear
protein factor GT-1 (10,11). Thus, the computer analysis was performed
to find chloroplast sequences homologous to both types of
LREs.Chloroplast LRE-like sequences, their location, structure of
flanking region and possible mechanisms of function are discussed here.

HARDWARE AND SOFTWARE
The analysis was performed on a IBM PC/AT computer with IBI/Pustell
Sequence Analyses Programs. Sequence data were obtained from GenBank
Genetic Sequence Data Bank R.48.0, The EMBL Nucleotide Sequence Data
Library and also from our own chloroplast gene library.

RESULTS AND DISCUSSION
1. LRE-like sequences in chloroplast genome
We have examined two complete chloroplast genome sequences
(Nicotiana tabacum (12) and Marchantia polymorpha (13)) and some
individual chloroplast genes searching for LRE-like matrices homologous
to the light responsive elements found in plant nuclear light-inducible

M. Baltscheffsky (ed.), Current Research in Photosynthesis, Vol. III, 593–596.

2. Chloroplast sequences homologous to binding sites for plant nuclear protein factor GT-1.

It was shown that GT-1 factor interacts with short concervative sequences within light responsive elements upstream of rbcS-3A (10,11). Thesesequences,called boxesII, II*, II**,III,III*, III**, are required for light-dependent transcription activation. We have found a number of chloroplast sequences homologous to GT-1 binding boxes. The degree of homology varied from 100% to 71% (with 4 nucleotides difference).

BOX II	GTGTGGTTAATATG
BOX II*	GTGAGGTAATATCC
BOX II**	TATGGGTAACATTT
BOX III	TAGTGAAAATGATA
BOX III*	GAGTGTAAATGTGT
BOX III**	TTGTGAAGTAACAG
Consensus	GA AA AAA
	--GTG--AA---nn
	TT GT TGT

FIGURE 2. Nuclear GT-1 boxes which were used for homology search (10,11).

Core nucleotides did not differ from consensus in more than one point. GT-1 chloroplast boxes were basically localized in 5`-ends of genes encoding ATPase subunits, PSII and NADH-dehydrogenas polypeptides and numerous nonidentfied polypeptides (ORFs). It was found that ndhA intron, carring 100% LRE consensus, included four boxes homologous to GT-1 BOX II consensus and one box homologous to III* BOX. In addition, two BOX III* like sequences were located inside the gene(fig.3).Some gene 5'-ends were "saturated" with GT-1-like boxes.

atpB	aTGgGAAtTAgCAcTC*	-112	BOX III**
	TatTGAAtTAACcGat	-94	BOX III**
atpE	GgtAGGTAATATCg	-65	BOX II*
atpF	TTaTGAAcTAACgaaC	-210	BOX III**
	agGgGGTAAaATCC	intron	BOX II*
atpH	cTGTGGcTAAaAaG	-169	BOX II
	TGTATcGtTAACcaTT	-43	BOX II**
psbA	GaGAGGTtATtTtC	3`-end	BOX II*
	TtTAaGatTAACATTT	-297	BOX II**
	TAcaGAAAATtAgA*	-199	BOX III
psbB	TTcgGAAaTAAtcGaC	-290	BOX III**
	gTaTGAAtTAgCgGTt	-61	BOX III**
psbD	gACTGAAAATGAaA*	-256	BOX III
	taaTGGTTcATATG	-218	BOX II
psbH	TAGcGAAAAaaATt*	-374	BOX III
ndhA	aAaTGTAtATGTGa	intron	BOX III*
	GAGTGTgAAaGatT	ins	BOX III*
	GgGTGgAAATtTcT	ins	BOX III*
ndhB(B)	aAGaGAAAAaGAaA	-617	BOX III
	GTtAcGgAATcTCC*	-431	BOX II*
	GTttGGaAATtTCC*	-91	BOX II*
ndhB(A)	GTtAcGgAATcTCC*	-340	BOX II*
	GTttGGaAATtTCC*	-107	BOX II*
ndhF	GAagGTcAATaTGT	-694	BOX III*
	TAcTGgAAATaAaA	-611	BOX III
	TcaTGAAGTAAaAaTg	-291	BOX III**

FIGURE 3.GT-1-like boxes associated with some tobacco chloroplast genes.

genes (9). 23 and 14 LRE-like elements were found with 88% homology in tobacco and liverworth, respectively. One 100% homology was found in tobacco ndhB-intron. The LREs found are described to be upstream, downstream, inside genes or located in introns. Such positions coincided with those found in nuclear genes (9). Most of LRE downstream regions were found to be AT-rich and involved "TATA"-like boxes. Chloroplast LREs were distributed into groups, preferably associated with psb- and ndhgene families, encoding photosystem II and NADH-dehydrogenase complex polypeptides, respectively. Some chloroplast LRE-like regions are likely to be structural elements of the genome and do not have any functional significance. However, a few of them being characterized by some universal features may participate in light regulation of expression.

1.1 LREs associated with the psbD-psbC operon

It was reported that red light resulted in two-fold increase of psbD/C mRNA in pea (14). psbD was found to carry LRE-like sequences upstream and inside the gene. Thus, psbD could be under phytochrome control.We have analyzed the structure of LRE flanking regions in five different species (12,13,15,16,17). The genes examined demonstrated a highly conservative structure around LREs. LRE upstream regions of psbD included short inverted repeats, which seemed to be able to generate cross-like structures (fig.1) As reported, such sequences are typical of prokaryotic operators and eukaryotic enhancers (18,19).

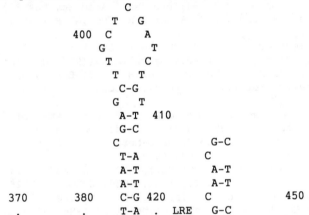

FIGURE 1. LRE-region in psbD-gene. Potential cross-like structures in LRE-region located in tobacco psbD gene. Numbering of sequences begins from the first base of psbD.

It seems likely, that if LREs located inside psbD functioned as regulatory elements and had any role in phytochrome response they would control not psbD itself but psdC, spliced with psbD in all species studied, except Chlamydomonas. C.reinhardtii psbD and psbC genes exist as individual transcription units.It seems interesting that no LREs have been found in Chlamydomonas psbD gene, although amino acids composition of D2-proteins was similar in all five species (17).

```
aaGAGGTAAgATCC          -56    BOX II*
TGaATcGGaAACAaTT        -39    BOX II**
```

In the attempts to define the molecular mechanisms of phytochrome or light response in chloroplast on the level of transcription we have used the computer search and comparison of the known plant nuclear LRE sequences with chloroplast genes. As a result a number of homologous sequences was found.

We suggest that the chloroplast genome carries specific sequences for phytochrome response similar to nuclear ones. The transcription regulation in plastids could be connected not only with site-specific recognition of light-responsive elements but also with topology changes in LRE flanking regions. It is possible that the revealed palindromic sequences could form cross-like structures due to light-induced torsional stress of cpDNA molecules, attached to thylakoid membranes. These structures could enhance or depress the formation of DNA-protein complexes in LRE-regions and regulate transcription. This scheme implies that LRE-containing sequences act as protein-binding sites which could attach hypothetic or known (GT-1) polypeptides - mediators of phytochrome response.

REFERENCES
1. Tobin,E.M.,Silverthorn,J.(1985) Annu.Rev.Plant Physiol. 36, 569-593
2. Silverthorn,J.,Tobin,E.M.(1984) Proc.Natl.Acad.Sci.USA 81, 1112-1116
3. Morelli,G.,Nagy,F.,Fraly,R.T.,Roger,S.R.,Chua,N.-H.(1985) Nature, 315, 200-204
4. Fluhr,R.,Kuhlemeier,C.,Nagy,F.,Chua,N.(1986) Science 232, 1106-1112
5. Simpson,J.,VanMontagu,M.,Herrera-Estrella,L.(1986) Science 233,34-38
6. Nagy,F.,Boutry,M.,Hsu,M.,Wong,M.,Chua,N.(1987) EMBO J 6, 2537-2542
7. Fluhr,R.,Moses,P.,Morelli,G.,Coruzzi,G.,Chua,N.-H.(1986) EMBO J 5, 2063-2071
8. Grebenier,A.,Steinback,K.,Bogorad,L.(1979) Plant Physiol.63,436-439
9. Grob,U., and Stuber,K.(1987) Nucleic Acids Res. 15, 9957-9973
10. Green,P.J.,Yong,M.-H.,Cuozzo,M.,Kano-Murakami,Y.,Silverstain,P., Chua,N.-H.(1988) EMBO J. 7, 4035-4044
11. Green,P.J.,Kay,S.A.,Chua,N.-H.(1987) EMBO J. 6, 2543-2549
12. Shinozaki,K.,Ohme,M.,Tanaka,T.,et.al.(1986) EMBO J.5,2043-2049
13. Ohyama,K.,Fukuzawa,H.,Kohchi,T.et.al.(1986) Nature 322,572-574
14. Glick,R.E.,McCauly,S.W.,Gruissem,W.,Melis,A.(1986) Proc.Natl.Acad. Sci.USA 83, 4287-4296
15. Rassmunsen,O.F.,Bookjans,G.,Stummann,B.M.(1984) Plant Mol.Biol. 3, 191-199
16. Holschuh,K.,Bottomley,W,Whitfield,P.R.(1984) Nucleic Acids Res. 12, 8819-8834
17. Erickson,J.M.,Rahire,Malnoe,P.,Girard-Bascou,J.,Pierre,Y.,Bennoun,P. Rochaix,J.-D.(1986) EMBO J. 5, 1745-1754
18. Dickson,R.C.,Abelson,J.,Barnes,N.M.,Resnikoff,W.S.(1977)J.Mol.Biol., 111, 65-71
19. Oxender,D.L.,Zurawski,G.,Yanofsky,C.(1979) Proc.Natl.Acad.Sci.USA 76,5524-5528

VARIATION IN CHLOROPHYLL SYNTHESIS IN HEXAPLOID WHEAT
Division of Genetics and Plant Physiology, Indian Agricultural
Research Institute, New Delhi 110012, India

DALMIR SINGH, K.C. BANSAL AND Y.P. ABROL

1. INTRODUCTION
The attainment of a high yield potential depends on the rapid
rates of photosynthesis (1). Crop photosynthesis is the function of
leaf area and the rate of photosynthesis per unit leaf area. In
northern India, drought during anthesis and grain filling periods
reduces the rate of photosynthesis and accelerates leaf senescence
particularly in crops like wheat and gram. The accelerated leaf
senescence is associated with the loss of chlorophyll and proteins.
Since chlorophyll is an essential pigment involved in the absorption
of radiant energy, the rate of photosynthesis gets affected due to its
loss. Recently, it has been reported that the genetic variation in
photosynthetic rate in different species of wheat is more closely
associated with leaf chlorophyll content than other physiological
characteristics (2). Moreover, the wild diploid and tetraploid
species of wheat with high rates of flag leaf photosynthesis have been
suggested as genetic source for yield improvement (3). The present
investigation was, therefore, carried out to exploit the chlorophyll
synthetic gene efficiency from diploid, tetraploid and hexaploid
species of wheat, in the genetic background of cv. Pb C591 where a
single gene located on chromosome 3A has been reported to be controlling chlorophyll synthesis in cv.Pb C591 (4). In the present communication, we report the results obtained with T.sphaerococcum (6x)
as the test material.

2. PROCEDURE
2.1 Materials and methods
Monosomic series of cv. Pb C591, a hexaploid (2n=42) Indian
wheat variety and a strain of T.sphaerococcum (2n=42) were
grown in the field. At appropriate stage of meiosis, monosomic
(2n=41) plants were identified cytologically at first meiotic
metaphase. Monosomic identified plant for chromosome 3A, was
used as female parent and crossed with T.sphaerococcum (2n=42).
The crossed seeds obtained from this cross were planted in the
field and the F_1 hybrid plants were analysed cytologically to
determine their chromosomal constitution at meiosis. Two types
of plants were found. One with chromosome constitution of
2n=41 (deficient for chromosome 3A of cv. Pb C591) and another
with 2n=42 (with presence of chromosome 3A of cv.Pb C591).

M. Baltscheffsky (ed.), Current Research in Photosynthesis, Vol. III, 597–599.
© 1990 *Kluwer Academic Publishers. Printed in the Netherlands.*

The chlorophyll contents were estimated at the time of anthesis and grain filling from all the F_1 hybrid plants in their flag leaves. Method used for estimation was that of Hiscox and Israelston (5).

3. RESULTS AND DISCUSSION

The chlorophyll contents a, b and their total, estimated at the time of anthesis, are presented in Table 1. The results indicated that chlorophyll a, b and their total are little higher in T.sphaerococcum than monosomic 3A of cv Pb C591. The F_1 hybrids (i.e. 2n=41) deficient for chromosome 3A of cv. Pb C591 and 2n=42, possessing chromosomes 3A of cv.Pb C591 and T.sphaerococcum possess significantly higher chlorophyll content than both the parents. The differences among these hybrids, however, were not much. The presence of higher amount of chlorophyll in the F_1 hybrids (deficient for chromosome 3A of cv.Pb C591, where chlorophyll synthetic gene has been located as well as with the presence of 3A) suggest that the chlorophyll synthetic gene(s) of T.sphaerococcum is/are much more efficient in the genetic background of cv.Pb C591 in producing about 13 per cent more chlorophyll than T.sphaerococcum, the highest parent.

TABLE 1. Chlorophyll content (mg g^{-1} dry wt) in flag leaves of cv.Pb C591 (mono 3A), T.sphaerococcum and their F_1 hybrids at anthesis (21.3.1989)

Genotype	Chromosome No.	Chl a	Chl b	Total Chl	Chl a/b
PARENTS					
Pb C591 (mono 3A)	41	1.3	0.9	2.2	1.44
T.sphaerococcum	42	1.4	1.0	2.4	1.40
F_1 HYBRIDS					
32-1	41	1.4	1.1	2.5	1.27
32-5	41	1.5	1.1	2.6	1.36
32-3	42	1.4	1.1	2.5	1.27
32-4	42	1.5	1.1	2.6	1.36
32-8	42	1.5	1.1	2.6	1.36

Results obtained at the time of grain filling are presented in Table 2. It is clear from the table that the F_1 hybrids (2n=41) deficient for chromosome 3A of cv.Pb C591 possess more chlorophyll than the disomic (2n=42) hybrids where chromosome 3A of cv.Pb C591 is present. It suggests that the chlorophyll contributed by T.sphaerococcum has the capability to senescence at lower rate than the chlorophyll of cv.Pb C591.

TABLE 2. Chlorophyll content (mg g^{-1} dry wt) in flag leaves of cv.Pb C591 (mono 3A), T.sphaerococcum and their F$_1$ hybrids during grain filling (19.4.1989)

Genotype	Chromosome No.	Chl a	Chl b	Total Chl	Chl a/b
PARENTS					
Pb C591(mono 3A)	41	1.4	1.5	2.9	0.93
T.sphaerococcum	42	1.6	1.8	3.4	0.89
F$_1$ HYBRIDS					
32-1	41	1.6	1.7	3.3	0.94
32-5	41	1.6	1.8	3.4	0.89
32-3	42	1.5	1.6	3.1	0.94
32-4	42	-	-	-	-
32-8	42	1.4	1.6	3.0	0.88

- not determined

The study clearly indicates the possibility of an enhanced efficiency of chlorophyll synthetic gene in the background of different genotypes. Consequently, it would be worthwhile to incorporate the chlorophyll synthetic genes from diploid and tetraploid wheat species with high rate of photosynthesis to the modern cultivars.

REFERENCES
1   Austin, R.B. (1986) Molecular Biology and Crop Improvement, Cambridge University Press, Cambridge
2   Bansal, K.C. and Abrol, Y.P. (1989) VIII Int.Cong.Photosynthesis Sweden
3   Austin, R.B., Morgan, C.L., Ford, M.A. and Bhagwat, S.G.(1982) Ann. Bot.49, 177-189
4   Singh, D. and Joshi, B.C. (1979) Wheat Inf.Serv.50, 45-46
5   Hiscox, J.D. and Israelston, G.P. (1979) Can.J.Bot.57,1332-1334

GENETIC CONTROL OF PHOTOSYNTHATE METABOLISM

Tristan A. Dyer[1], Christine A. Raines[2], Marian Longstaff[3], Julie C. Lloyd[1], Shiaoman Chao[1], Peter J. Sharp[1], Michael D. Gale[1], Eileen M. McMorrow[4], J William Bradbeer[4], [1]IPSR Cambridge Laboratory, Cambridge CB2 2JB; [2]University of Essex, Colchester CO4 3SQ; [3]Sainsbury Laboratory, Norwich NR4 7UH; [4]King's College London, London W8 7AH, U.K.

1.   INTRODUCTION
        The complexity of the control of metabolic processes involved in photosynthesis is becoming increasingly apparent. The plant is able to respond rapidly to changes environmental conditions and, superimposed on this, there are inherent developmental patterns which lead to long-term changes in enzyme levels. The overall objective of our research is to obtain a comprehensive understanding of how the various controls operate.
        In order to achieve our objective we are isolating and characterising the coding sequences of key enzymes involved in photosynthetic carbon metabolism and are using these sequences to:

(a)   make transgenic plants with altered amounts of the enzymes to evaluate the contribution of each to the control of metabolic flux;
(b)   determine how the encoded proteins are controlled by allosteric changes in their structure;
(c)   use the sequences for the isolation of genomic sequences for promoter analysis and as probes for gene quantitation and chromosomal location;
(d)   evaluate, by Northern hybridisation, changes in mRNA levels at different stages in development and as a result of different treatments.

We describe here some of our results.

2.   PROCEDURE
2.1.   Materials and methods
2.1.1.   cDNA library construction and screening: Double-stranded cDNA was synthesised from wheat leaf polyA+ RNA using the RNase H method of Gubler and Hoffman (see 1). The cDNA was then cloned in a λgt11 vector. The resulting library was screened using polyclonal antibodies and positive plaques purified to homogeneity.
        The largest inserts were subcloned into a plasmid and sequenced using a double-stranded plasmid method.

M. Baltscheffsky (ed.), Current Research in Photosynthesis, Vol. III, 601–604.
© 1990 *Kluwer Academic Publishers. Printed in the Netherlands.*

2.1.2. <u>Analysis of mRNA levels and chromosomal location of genes</u>: Isolated polyA+ RNA was electrophoresed under denaturing conditions and transferred to a nylon membrane filter. Restricted genomic DNA was fractionated in agarose gels and also transferred to a nylon membrane (2). Probes were labelled with ^{32}P using a random priming method.

2.1.3. <u>Analysis of protein levels</u>: Total soluble leaf proteins were fractionated in SDS-polyacrylamide gels and transferred to nitrocellulose. Immunodetection was performed using antibodies followed by horse-radish peroxidase-conjugated goat anti-rabbit antiserum and the peroxidase activity detected by staining with chloro-1-naphthol.

3.   RESULTS

We have isolated and sequenced cDNAs for wheat phosphoribulokinase (PRK), for chloroplast fructose-1, 6-bisphosphatase (FBP) and for both the chloroplast and cytosolic versions of phosphoglycerate kinase (PGK). We are at present sequencing a putative cDNA clone for sedoheptulose-1,7-bisphosphatase (SBP) and isolating the coding sequence of cytosolic FBP. For the sake of comparison, we have also sequenced the <u>E coli</u> gene for FBP (3).

3.1.   <u>Light activation of FBP and PRK</u>

Our results are perhaps of greatest interest with respect to what they can tell us about the regulation of the activity of these enzymes by light. From the deduced amino acid sequence of the chloroplast FBP it can be seen that it contains an extra block of amino acids near its mid-point which is not found in any other of the FBP so far examined. These include sequences from mammals, yeast and <u>E coli</u>. This block is not found either in the plant cytosolic FBP (U. Ladror and F. Marcus, unpublished results). Sequences flanking this block are highly conserved so that there is no doubt that they all had a common progenitor. The extra block of amino acids in the chloroplast FBP contains two cysteine residues and it seems highly probable that these form a disulphide bridge in the less active form of the enzyme (1,4). The enzyme probably becomes fully activated when this disulphide bridge is broken on reduction by reduced thioredoxin generated in the light. Some idea of where this block is in the enzyme may be obtained by examining the corresponding regions in the 3D molecular structure which has been determined for the pig kidney enzyme (5). It would appear to be in a connection between two β-sheets and on the surface of the molecule. This region is somewhat distant from the active site which seems to be in a pocket formed by two neighbouring monomers.

In contrast to FBP, the cysteines involved in the light regulation of PRK are located far apart, near the amino terminus, and are associated with the ATP-binding site (6). PRK is found only in photosynthetic organisms so there are not the same possibilities for sequence comparison of homologues, as there are for FBP. However, it seems probable from the available data that the way in which the PRK is light activated is rather different from that of FBP. SBP regulation, on the other hand, may be much more like that of FBP because its substrate is very similar. It shares immunological epitopes with FBP which supports this idea.

3.2. Developmental and light activation of he PRK, FBP and chloroplast PGK genes

The wheat leaf has a developmental gradient along its length with a zone of cell division at its base and oldest tissue at its tip. We have used this feature to study the developmental expression of the genes for these enzymes. The mRNA levels for each are highest below the middle of leaf and decrease towards the tip (1,6,7). None was found in the roots or in etiolated tissues. Even a very brief illumination resulted in the accumulation of a detectable amount in the etiolated leaves. In contrast, mRNA for the cytosolic PGK was found in about the same amount in all tissues examined. Accumulation of the FBP follows the same pattern as that of its mRNA but, in contrast, its levels do not decline again in older tissues suggesting that the protein is relatively stable.

3.3. Chromosomal location and copy member of the genes

Whereas there are about 12 genes for the small subunit of Rubisco, the genes for PRK, FBP and PGK are found only in single copies per haploid genome of wheat (2). Furthermore, the enzymes are encoded by loci dispersed on different chromosomes. This was a somewhat surprising find in view of the fact that wheat has a large genome size and a very high proportion of repeated sequences. This suggests that there may be a mechanism selecting for low copy number, especially for genes encoding enzymes important in basic metabolic pathways.

3.4. Possible recombination between the genes for chloroplast and cytosolic PGK

A comparison of these coding sequences reveals a higher than expected level of similarity between the sequences and between the proteins which they encode (7). Analysis of this data in relation to that for PGK sequences of mammals, prokaryotes and yeasts suggests that the genes for these enzymes have recombined so that they are now more similar to each other than would be predicted if the chloroplast gene had evolved from a prokaryotic progenitor and the cytosolic gene had evolved from the eukaryotic progenitor. Particular conserved features of the enzyme structure may have made this possible.

4. DISCUSSION

By isolating and sequencing the coding sequences of enzymes involved in photosynthetic carbon reduction we are getting insights at a molecular level into how these enzymes are regulated. Furthermore, isolation of these sequences makes it possible for us to determine how developmental and environmental factors affect enzyme synthesis. Having these sequences also provides a means of making transgenic plants with altered enzyme levels, so that their contribution to the control of metabolic flux can be determined as outlined by Kacser and Porteous (8).

ACKNOWLEDGEMENTS

We are indebted to Professors N-H. Chua and Bob Buchanan for providing us with antibodies, and to Professor F. Markus and Dr U. Ladror for unpublished FBP sequence data. AFRC research grant no. PG 29/49 to J.W.B. is gratefully acknowledged. C.A.R., M.L. and S.C. were supported by AFRC New Initiatives grants and J.C.L. by D.T.I. finance.

REFERENCES

1   Raines C.A., Lloyd, J.C., Longstaff, M., Bradley, D., Dyer, T.A., (1988) Nucleic Acids Res. 16, 7931-7942.
2   Chao, S., Raines, C.A., Longstaff, M., Sharp, P.J., Gale, M.D., Dyer, T.A., (1989) Mol. Gen. Genet, in press.
3   Hamilton W.D.O., Harrison, D.A., Dyer, T.A., (1988) Nucleic Acids Res 16, 8707.
4   Markus, F., Moberly, L., Latshaw, S.P., (1988) Proc. Natl. Acad. Sci. U.S.A 85. 5379-5383.
5   Ke, H., Thorpe, C.M., Seaton, B.A., Marcus, F., Lipscomb, W.N., (1989) Proc. Natl. Acad. Sci. U.S.A 86, 1475-1479.
6   Raines, C.A., Longstaff, M., Lloyd, J.C., Dyer, T.A., (1989) Molec. Gen. Genet, in press.
7   Longstaff, M., Raines, C.A., McMorrow, E.M., Bradbeer, J.W., Dyer, T.A., (1989) Nucleic Acids Res, in press.
8   Kacser, H., Porteous, J.W., (1987) TIBS 12, 5-14

IN-VITRO TRANSLATION AND PROCESSING OF COMPARTMENT-SPECIFIC GLUCAN
PHOSPHORYLASE ISOZYMES FROM PISUM SATIVUM L.

Martin Steup, Jochen van Berkel and Jutta Conrads-Strauch
Botanisches Institut der Westfälischen Wilhelms-Universität Münster,
D-4400 Münster, FRG

1. INTRODUCTION

Glucan phosphorylase (1,4 α-D-glucan: orthophosphate α-D-glucosyl-
transferase, E.C. 2.4.1.1) catalyzes the reversible transfer of a glu-
cosyl residue between α-D-glucose-1-phosphate and a non-reducing end
of an α-1,4-linked oligo/polyglucan. By linking the cellular mono- and
polysaccharide metabolism the enzyme is thought to play often a central
role in the carbon flux of a cell. It is widely distributed among pro-
karyonts, plants, and animals.

Comparative studies on phosphorylases isolated from evolutionary
distant sources showed that the enzymes possess both striking similarities (which strongly suggest a common evolutionary origin) and distinct
kinetic dissimilarities. In a native state, all phosphorylases studied
so far occur as dimers or tetramers composed of identical monomers.
Each monomer contains one pyridoxal phosphate and a highly conserved
primary structure in the vicinity of the cofactor binding site. The
enzymes follow the same catalytic mechanism, a rapid equilibrium random
Bi Bi mechanism. However, unlike animal phosphorylases, the microbial
and plant enzymes are not subjected to covalent or allosteric control.
Within the group of higher plant phosphorylases two types of enzyme
have been distinguished which differ in monomer size, peptide pattern,
glucan specificity, and intracellular location (1-3). Based on immunochemical studies on leaf tissues (4-5), one enzyme form has been localized in the cytosol whereas the other one resides in the chloroplast.
Thus, the two plant phosphorylase types represent non-interconvertible
proteins which presumably have entirely different metabolic functions.

In the present study, biosynthesis of both enzyme forms has been
studied using heterotrophic tissues of Pisum sativum L. For this purpose, cotyledons of germinating or developing seeds were chosen. Polyadenylated RNA was isolated and translated in vitro. Phosphorylase isozymes were identified by immunoprecipitation and SDS-PAGE. Following
in-vitro translation, the size of the cytosolic isozyme was indistinguishable from that of the mature protein. In contrast, the plastidic
isozyme was synthesized as a precursor which was processed to its final
size by a stromal fraction of isolated pea chloroplasts.

2. PROCEDURE

2.1 Materials and Methods

2.1.1. Plant material: Pea plants (Pisum sativum L. var. 'Kleine
Rheinländerin) were grown under controlled conditions (6) or
in the Botanical Garden of the Institute.

M. Baltscheffsky (ed.), Current Research in Photosynthesis, Vol. III, 605–608.
© 1990 Kluwer Academic Publishers. Printed in the Netherlands.

2.1.2. <u>Enzyme purification</u>: The cytosolic phosphorylase form was purified from pea leaflets (5). For purification of the plastidic enzyme form see (7).

2.1.3. <u>Antibodies</u>: Polyclonal antibodies directed against the cytosolic or the plastidic phosphorylase form were raised in rabbits. IgG were isolated from the antisera as previously described (5).

2.1.4. <u>Nucleic acid isolation</u>: Total RNA was prepared by the procedure of Cashmore (8). Polyadenylated RNA was isolated by affinity chromatography on poly U-Sepharose.

2.1.5. <u>In-vitro translation and immunoprecipitation</u>: Polyadenylated RNA was translated using rabbit reticulocyte lysate (Amersham N 90). Immunoprecipitation was performed essentially as described by Chua and Schmidt (9) or according to von Figura et al. (10).

2.1.5. <u>Detection</u>: Following immunoprecipitation, samples were subjected to SDS-PAGE. Radioactivity was detected by fluorography or by autoradiography. In the latter case proteins were transferred to nitrocellulose.

3. RESULTS AND DISCUSSION

Cotyledons of developing or germinating pea seeds contain two forms of glucan phosphorylase which are electrophoretically and immunologically identical with the cytosolic (isozyme I) and the plastidic (enzyme III; cf. 6) phosphorylase form from pea leaflets. For pea cotyledons the dual intracellular location of phosphorylase was ensured by indirect immunofluorescence. Using this technique, isozyme I was localized in the cytosol of parenchyma cells of cotyledons whereas the other isozyme was visualized in the stromal space of amyloplasts or proplastid-like organelles (data not shown).

For in-vitro synthesis of the compartment-specific phosphorylase forms polyadenylated RNA (mRNA) was isolated from cotyledons of either developing or germinating seeds and was used to program a reticulocyte lysate. When varying amounts of a mRNA preparation were applied to the translation mixture a decrease of the rate of total protein synthesis was observed at higher mRNA concentrations (Fig. 1). Although the mRNA concentration applied did not affect the size distribution of the translation products, for each mRNA preparation the optimal concentration was determined empirically.

Following in-vitro translation, the two compartment-specific phosphorylase forms were precipitated using antibodies directed against either form I or form III. When mRNA isolated form germinating pea seeds (6 days after imbibition) was used to program in-vitro translation, the anti-cytosolic phosphorylase-IgGs precipitated the homologous antigen as a heavily labeled band of radioactivity (Fig. 2A lane a). The apparent size of the labeled protein was indiscernible from that of purified form I. For a further identification of this translation product, purified cytosolic (or plastidic) phosphorylase was added to the translation mixture prior to immunoprecipitation (Fig. 2B). The non-labeled homologous antigen did compete with the in-vitro synthesized protein (Fig. 2B lane b) but the non-labeled plastidic isozyme did

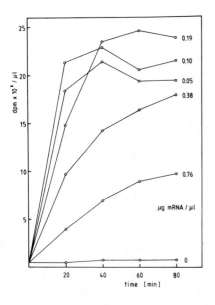

FIGURE 1. Effect of varying concentrations of polyadenylated RNA isolated from cotyledons of germinating
pea seeds on the rate of in-vitro
translation (total protein synthesis)

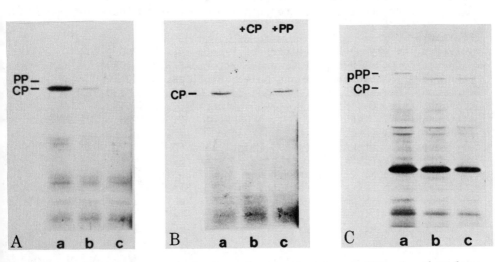

FIGURE 2 A–C. In-vitro translation of compartment-specific phosphorylase
forms. A: In-vitro translation of mRNA isolated from cotyledons of germinating seeds. Immunoprecipitation was performed using anti-cytosolic
(lane a) or anti-plastidic (lane b) phosphorylase-IgG. Lane c: preimmune
control. The position of the mature cytosolic (CP) and plastidic (PP)
enzyme form is marked. B: Immunoprecipitation in the presence of an excess of purified cytosolic (lane b) or plastidic (lane c) phosphorylase.
Lane a: no addition. Immunoprecipitation was performed using anti-cytosolic phosphorylase IgG. Details as in 2 A lane a. C: Processing of the
precursor of the plastidic phosphorylase form by a stromal fraction of
isolated chloroplasts. For details see text. pPP: Precursor of the plastidic enzyme; CP: cytosolic enzyme form

not (Fig. 2B lane c). In contrast, immunoprecipitation performed with anti-plastidic phosphorylase-IgG resulted in a weak band of radioactivity with an apparent size of 116 kD which exceeds that of the authentic enzyme form by approximately 11 kD (Fig. 2A lane b). In addition, a small amount of cytosolic phosphorylase was coprecipitated which is due to a limited cross-reaction between the antibody preparation used and the heterologous isozyme. The results shown in Fig. 2A and B concur with the previously observed striking increase in activity of the cytosolic phosphorylase isozyme during germination (1).

When in-vitro translation was performed using polyadenylated RNA from developing pea seeds the plastidic phosphorylase form (in its high molecular weight state) was the predominantly translated phosphorylase isozyme whereas the cytosolic counterpart was recovered as a very weak band of radioactivity (data not shown). Again, the apparent molecular weight of the labeled plastidic phosphorylase was lager by 11 kD than that of the purified enzyme form (Fig. 2C lane a). A complete conversion of the precursor to the size of the mature isozyme was achieved when the translation mixture (prior to precipitation with anti-plastidic phosphorylase IgG) was incubated with a stromal fraction (precipitate between 40-70% saturation of ammonium sulfate) of isolated pea chloroplasts (Fig. 2C lane b: 50 µl stromal fraction per translation mixture, lane c: 100 µl stromal fraction). The identity of the precursor was further confirmed by competition experiments (data not shown).

REFERENCES
1. Steup, M. (1988) Biochemistry of Plants 14, 255-296
2. Newgard, C.B., Hwang, P.K. and Fletterick, R.J. (1989) CRC Critical Reviews in Biochemistry and Molec. Biol. 24, 69-99
3. Nakano, K., Fukui, T. (1986) J. Biol. Chem. 261, 8230-8236
4. Schächtele, C., Steup, M. (1986) Planta 167, 444-451
5. Conrads, J., van Berkel, J., Schächtele, C. and Steup, M. (1986) Biochim. Biophys. Acta 882, 452-463
6. Steup, M., Latzko, E. (1979) Planta 145, 69-75
7. Conrads, J. (1987) Ph.D. thesis Münster (FRG)
8. Cashmore, A.R. (1982) in Methods in Chloroplast Molecular Biology (Edelman, M. et al., eds.) pp. 387-392, Elsevier, Amsterdam
9. Chua, N.-H., Schmidt, G.W. (1978) Proc. Natl. Acad. Sci. 75, 6110-6114
10. von Figura, K., Gieselmann, V. and Hasilik, A. (1985) Biochem. J. 225, 543-547

CHARACTERIZATION OF A cDNA CLONE FOR THE *PsaE* GENE FROM BARLEY AND PLASMA DESORPTION MASS SPECTROMETRY OF THE CORRESPONDING PHOTOSYSTEM I POLYPEPTIDE PSI-E.

HENRIK VIBE SCHELLER, JENS SIGURD OKKELS, *PETER ROEPSTORFF, LARS BÆK JEPSEN, AND BIRGER LINDBERG MØLLER.

DEPARTMENT OF PLANT PHYSIOLOGY, ROYAL VETERINARY AND AGRICULTURAL UNIVERSITY, DK-1871 FREDERIKSBERG C AND *DEPARTMENT OF MOLECULAR BIOLOGY, ODENSE UNIVERSITY, DK-5230 ODENSE, DENMARK.

1. INTRODUCTION.

Photosystem I (PS I) preparations from barley contain polypeptides with apparent molecular masses of 82 (PSI-A and PSI-B), 18 (PSI-D), 16 (PSI-E), 14, 9.5 (PSI-H), 9 (PSI-C), 4, and 1.5 kDa (PSI-I) as determined by sodium dodecyl sulfate polyacrylamide gel electrophoresis (1, 2). The nomenclature used for the subunits is described in more detail by Møller et al. (3). In this paper we report the characterization of a cDNA clone for the *PsaE* gene encoding the 16-kDa polypeptide PSI-E. The molecular mass of the mature polypeptide is 10,821 Da when deduced from the nucleotide sequence. To test whether the discrepancy between the molecular mass determinations could be due to post-translational modification of the polypeptide, the isolated polypeptide was analyzed by plasma desorption mass spectrometry. It has previously been established that the N- and C-terminal amino acid residues of the PSI-E polypeptide are not modified (4).

2. MATERIALS AND METHODS.

The techniques used for cloning and sequencing of the *PsaE* gene have been described elsewhere (5). Northern blotting analysis was carried out with Zeta-Probe (Bio-Rad) according to the manufacturer. Prior to plasma desorption mass spectrometry, the isolated PSI-E polypeptide (1) was additionally purified by high performance liquid chromatography using a C_4 column (Vydac) and elution with a linear gradient of 2-propanol in the presence of 0.1% trifluoroacetic acid. Samples were prepared for spectrometry according to Jonsson et al. (6). The plasma desorption spectrometer used was a Bio-Ion Bin 10K instrument (Bio-Ion Nordic AB) which is similar to the instrument described by Sundqvist et al. (7).

3. RESULTS AND DISCUSSION.

The nucleotide sequence and deduced amino acid sequence for the PSI-E polypeptide is shown in Fig. 1. The open reading frame codes for a precursor protein with a calculated molecular mass of 15,457 Da. The N-

M. Baltscheffsky (ed.), Current Research in Photosynthesis, Vol. III, 609–612.
© 1990 *Kluwer Academic Publishers. Printed in the Netherlands.*

and C-terminal amino acid sequences of the mature polypeptide were determined previously (4) and it was therefore possible to calculate a molecular mass of 10,821 Da for the mature polypeptide. The open reading frame has three in-frame ATG codons upstream of the maturation site. We assume that the first ATG codon is the initiation site because translation is normally initiated at the first ATG codon (8-9). However, sequences similar to the consensus sequence for initiation codon regions in plants (10) are present at both the first and the second ATG codon. Northern blot hybridization indicates that only one transcript is formed (Fig. 2).

```
                              CTAGCTAGCACCCACAAACAGCACCTGCTGCCGTCCCG
                                      -38   -33                     -1
met ala ser thr asn met ala ser ala thr ser arg phe met leu ala ala gly ile pro
ATG GCG AGC ACC AAC ATG GCG TCG GCC ACC TCC AGA TTC ATG CTG GCG GCG GGC ATC CCC
1                                                                           60
ser gly ala asn gly gly val ser ser arg val ser phe leu pro ser asn arg leu gly
AGC GGC GCC AAC GGC GGC GTG AGC AGC CGT GTC AGC TTC CTC CCG TCC AAC CGG CTC GGC
                                                                           120
leu lys leu val ala arg ala glu glu pro thr ala ala ala pro ala glu pro ala pro
TTG AAG CTC GTG GCC CGG GCC GAG GAG CCG ACT GCC GCC GCG CCG GCG GAA CCA GCA CCG
                                                                           180
ala ala asp glu lys pro glu ala ala val ala thr lys glu pro ala lys ala lys pro
GCG GCG GAC GAG AAA CCG GAA GCC GCC GTG GCC ACC AAA GAG CCC GCC AAA GCC AAG CCG
                                                                           240
pro pro arg gly pro lys arg gly thr lys val lys ile leu arg arg glu ser tyr trp
CCG CCG AGG GGA CCC AAG AGG GGC ACC AAG GTG AAG ATC CTG AGG AGG GAG TCC TAC TGG
                                                                           300
tyr asn gly thr gly ser val val thr val asp gln asp pro asn thr arg tyr pro val
TAC AAC GGG ACT GGA TCC GTC GTC ACG GTT GAT CAG GAT CCC AAC ACC CGT TAC CCG GTG
                                                                           360
val val arg phe ala lys val asn tyr ala gly val ser thr asn asn tyr ala leu asp
GTG GTG CGT TTC GCC AAG GTG AAC TAC GCC GGC GTG TCG ACC AAC AAC TAC GCC CTG GAC
                                                                           420
glu ile lys glu val ala ala STOP
GAG ATC AAG GAG GTT GCT GCT TGA ACGATCGAGGCTGCCGCGTGCTCAATCCAATGTTTGTATCAGTAGCT
                                                                           491
CGTCAAGTGGCGATGTGAATGTTAGCCTCACAAATCTTATGTGTAATACCTCTGCGATTATATGTATTTGCCTGCTTCC
                                                                           570
TC(A)₂₄
```

FIGURE 1. Nucleotide sequence of the cDNA clone and deduced amino acid sequence. The maturation site is indicated with an arrowhead. The wavy lines indicate predicted (11) α-helices. The helices are hydrophilic and therefore not predicted to be membrane-spanning.

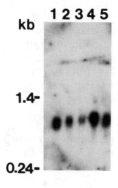

FIGURE 2. Northern blot of total RNA isolated from 5 days old barley seedlings hybridized with a *PsaE* probe. The seedlings were grown in the dark and illuminated prior to harvesting for 0 h (lane 1), 2.8 h (lane 2), 5.5 h (lane 3) and 8 h (lane 4) or were grown with continuous illumination (lane 5).

```
              1             10            20            30            40            50
Barley        A-E-E-P-T-A-A-A-P-A-E-P-A-P-A-A-D-E-K-P-E-A-A-V-A-T-K-E-P-A-K-A-K-P-P-P-R-G-P-K-R-G-T-K-V-K-I-L-R-R-
Spinach       A-A-E-E-A-A-A-A-P-A-A-A-S-------------P-E-G-E-A-P-K-------A-A-A-K-P-P-P-I-G-P-K-R-G-S-K-V-R-I-M-R-K-
Pea           A-S-E-D-T-A-E-A-A-A-P-S-A-....
Chlamydomonas                                   E-E-V-K-A-A-P-K-K-E-V----------------G-P-K-R-G-S-L-V-K-I-L-R-P-
Synechococcus                                                         A-I-A-R-G-D-K-V-R-I-L-R-P-

              60            70            80            90            100
Barley        E-S-Y-W-Y-N-G-T-G-S-V-V-T-V-D-Q-D-P-N-T-R-Y-P-V-V-V-R-F-A-K-V-N-Y-A-G-V-S-T-N-N-Y-A-L-D-E-I-K-E-V-A-A
Spinach       E-S-Y-W-Y-K-G-V-G-S-V-V-A-V-D-Q-D-P-K-T-R-Y-P-V-V-V-R-F-N-K-V-N-Y-A-N-V-S-T-N-N-Y-A-L-D-E-I-Q-E-V-A
Chlamydomonas E-S-Y-W-F-N-Q-V-G-K-V-V-S-V-D-Q---S-G-V-R-Y-P-V-V-V-R-F-E-N-Q-N-Y-A-G-V-T-T-N-N-Y-A-L-D-E-V-----V-A-A-K
Synechococcus E-S-Y-W-F-N-E-V-G-T---V-A-S-?-D-E-S-G-I-K-Y-P-V-?-?-?-F-E-K-..
```

FIGURE 3. **Comparison of the amino acid sequence of the PSI-E polypeptide from barley with those obtained in other species.** The sequences from spinach (12) and *Chlamydomonas* (13) were deduced from nucleotide sequences. The sequences from pea (14) and *Synechococcus* (15) were determined by N-terminal amino acid sequencing.

Deduced amino acid sequences or N-terminal amino acid sequences have now been reported for five species (Fig. 3). It was previously noted that the barley sequence contains a possible glycosylation site (Asn-X-Thr) although glycosylation of the protein was thought to be unlikely (5). Comparison with the other species shows that the site is not conserved.

The PSI-E polypeptide does not contain hydrophobic stretches long enough to represent likely membrane-spanning segments. Therefore the polypeptide is concluded to be a peripheral membrane protein. The structure of the transit peptide of the PSI-E polypeptide indicates that it is probably located on the stromal side of the thylakoid membrane. This conclusion has been substantiated by antibody-binding, chemical cross-linking, and protease digestion studies (16 and unpublished). Münch et al. (12) have suggested that the PSI-E polypeptide has a luminal location and is identical to 'subunit III' which is thought to interact with plastocyanin. The results obtained in barley are in clear disagreement with a luminal location of PSI-E. We find that subunit III is identical to PSI-F and the possible function of this subunit is discussed elsewhere (17).

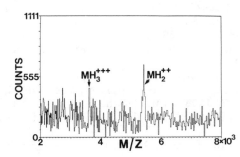

FIGURE 4. **Plasma desorption mass spectrum of the isolated PSI-E polypeptide.** The peaks at 3605.8 and 5412.4 correspond to the triple and double charged molecular ions. Correcting for the protons, an average molecular mass of 10,819 ± 5 Da is calculated. Analysis of a different preparation of the isolated PSI-E polypeptide yielded a mass of 10,820 ± 5 Da (not shown).

The calculated molecular mass of 10,821 for the mature polypeptide is much lower than the apparent molecular mass of 16 kDa. In contrast, the PSI-D and PSI-F polypeptides which have similar amino acid compositions show little difference between apparent and calculated molecular masses.

Therefore, it was of interest to determine if the high apparent molecular mass of the PSI-E polypeptide could be due to post-translational modifications. The isolated PSI-E polypeptide was analyzed in a plasma desorption mass spectrometer (Fig. 4). Analysis of two different preparations of the polypeptide showed the presence of a component with molecular mass 10,819 ± 5 and 10,820 ± 5 Da. Thus, it was clearly established that the PSI-E polypeptide is not post-translationally modified apart from the cleavage of the peptide bond at the maturation site. The spectrometrical mass determination also shows that the deduced amino acid sequence must be correct. A single erroneously deduced amino acid residue will nearly allways lead to a discrepancy in molecular mass which would be revealed by the spectrometrical analysis. The unusual electrophoretic migration of the PSI-E polypeptide in sodium dodecyl sulfate-polyacrylamide gels must be due to a special conformation of this polypeptide even under the highly denaturing conditions in the gels.

REFERENCES.

1 Høj, P.B., Svendsen, I., Scheller, H.V. and Møller, B.L. (1987) J. Biol. Chem. 262, 12676–12684
2 Scheller, H.V., Svendsen, I. and Møller, B.L. (1989) J. Biol. Chem. 264, 6929–6934
3 Møller, B.L., Scheller, H.V., Okkels, J.S., Koch, B., Andersen, B., Nielsen, H.L., Olsen, I., Halkier, B.A. and Høj, P.B., these proceedings
4 Scheller, H.V., Høj, P.B., Svendsen, I. and Møller, B.L. (1988) Biochim. Biophys. Acta 933, 501–505
5 Okkels, J.S., Jepsen, L.B., Hønberg, L.S., Lehmbeck, J., Scheller, H.V., Brandt, P., Høyer-Hansen, G., Stummann, B., Henningsen, K.W., Wettstein, D.v. and Møller, B.L. (1988) FEBS Lett. 237, 108–112
6 Jonsson, G.P., Hedin, A.B., Håkansson, P.L., Sundqvist, B.U.R., Säve, B.G.S., Nielsen, P.F., Roepstorff, P., Johansson, K.-E., Kamensky, I. and Lindberg, M.S.L. (1986) Anal. Chem. 58, 1084–1087
7 Sundqvist, B., Håkansson, P.L., Kamensky, I., Kjellberg, J., Salehpour, M., Widdiyasekera, S., Fohlman, J., Peterson, P. and Roepstorff, P. (1984) Biomed. Mass Spectrom. 11, 242–254
8 Kozak, M. (1984) Nucleic Acids Res. 12, 857–872
9 Cigan, A.M. and Donahue, T.F. (1987) Gene 59, 1–18
10 Lütcke, H.A., Chow, K.C., Mickel, F.S., Moss, K.A., Kern, H.F. and Scheele, G.A. (1987) EMBO J. 6, 43–48
11 Chou, P.Y. and Fasman, G.D. (1974) Biochemistry 13, 222–245
12 Münch, S., Ljungberg, U., Steppuhn, J., Schneiderbauer, A., Nechushtai, R., Beyreuter, K. and Herrmann, R.G. (1988) Curr. Genet. 14, 511–518
13 Franzén, L.-G., Frank, G., Zuber, H. and Rochaix, J.-D. (1989) Plant Mol. Biol. 12, 463–474
14 Dunn, P.P.J., Packman, L.C., Pappin, D. and Gray, J.C. (1988) FEBS Lett. 228, 157–161
15 Alhadeff, M., Lundell, D.J. and Glazer, A.N. (1988) Arch. Microbiol. 150, 482–488
16 Andersen, B., Koch, B., Scheller, H.V., Okkels, J.S. and Møller, B.L., these proceedings.
17 Scheller, H.V., Andersen, B., Okkels, J.S., Svendsen, I. and Møller, B.L., these proceedings

CHARACTERIZATION OF A cDNA CLONE FOR THE *PsaH* GENE FROM BARLEY AND mRNA LEVEL OF PS I GENES IN LIGHT-INDUCED BARLEY SEEDLINGS.

JENS SIGURD OKKELS, HENRIK VIBE SCHELLER, LARS BÆK JEPSEN, BIRGITTE ANDERSEN AND BIRGER LINDBERG MØLLER.
Department of Plant Physiology, Royal Veterinary and Agricultural University, DK-1871 Frederiksberg C, Denmark.

1. INTRODUCTION.

Photosystem I (PS I) catalyzes the coupled photoreduction of ferredoxin and photooxidation of plastocyanin. PS I core preparations from plants and cyanobacteria has been shown to contain a number of polypeptides encoded by both chloroplast and nuclear genes. So far four different chloroplast genes, designated *psaA*, *psaB*, *psaC*, and *psaI*, and cDNA clones for four different nuclear genes, designated *PsaD*, *PsaE*, *PsaF*, and *PsaG* have been characterized from various plants and cyanobacteria. The composition of PS I and the nomenclature used is discussed in detail by Møller et al. (1). A cDNA clone encoding a fifth nuclear encoded PS I polypeptide, designated PSI-H, has now been identified. We here report the nucleotide sequence of the cDNA clone and show that the corresponding gene *PsaH* and two other PS I genes are induced by light.

2. MATERIALS AND METHODS.

Total RNA for Northern blotting were electrophoresed in formaldehyde/formamide agarose gels and transferred to Zetaprobe membranes (Bio-Rad Laboratories, Inc.,Richmond, CA, U.S.A.) with 10 mM NaOH as transfer liquid for 6 to 8 hours. Hybridisation and all other methods were as previously described (2).

3. RESULTS AND DISCUSSION.

The nucleotide sequence of the two cDNA clones obtained from immunological screening of the cDNA libary is shown in Fig. 1A. Clone 1.4 is a partial cDNA clone starting with the 5'-end at nucleotide 316 of clone 1.6 and with identical sequence except for an extra 9 basepair (bp) at the poly-A tail.

The deduced amino acid sequence corresponding to bp 145-195 of the single open reading frame found in clone 1.6 is identical to the amino acid sequence obtained by N-terminal sequencing of the mature 9.5-kDa polypeptide. The residues determined by amino acid sequencing are underlined in Fig. 1A. The open reading frame codes for a precursor polypeptide with a calculated molecular mass of 14,882 Da. The molecular mass of the mature polypeptide can be calculated to be 10,193 Da which is in good agreement with the predicted molecular mass of 9.5 kDa based on the migration in SDS-polyacrylamide gels.

M. Baltscheffsky (ed.), Current Research in Photosynthesis, Vol. III, 613–616.
© 1990 *Kluwer Academic Publishers. Printed in the Netherlands.*

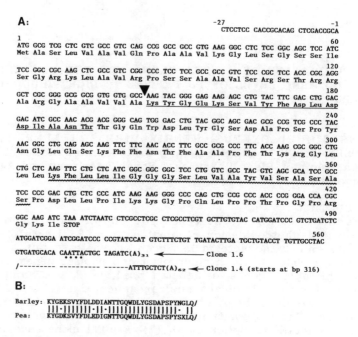

Figure 1: A. DNA sequence of the *PsaH* cDNA clone encoding the precursor for the 9.5-kDa polypeptide. The amino acid sequence obtained by sequencing of the isolated 9.5-kDa polypeptide is underlined. The maturation site (▼), the polyadenylation site (······), and the predicted (4) membrane-spanning α-helix (∿) are indicated.
B. Comparison of the N-terminal amino acid sequence of an 11-kDa PS I polypeptide from pea (3) and the amino acid sequence derived from the barley *PsaH* cDNA clone. A vertical line indicates an amino acid identity and a dot represents a conservative replacement.

Comparision of the amino acid sequence of the 9.5-kDa polypeptide of barley with a reported N-terminal sequence (35 amino acid residues) of an 11-kDa polypeptide from pea (3) reveals that these two polypeptides are homologous (Fig. 1B). We have named the gene for the 10.2-kDa polypeptide *PsaH*.

A transmembrane location of the 9.5-kDa polypeptide is suggested from the hydropathy plot (Fig. 2), which shows a hydrophobic area of 19 amino acids (residue number 103 to 121) sufficiently long to represent a membrane spanning region. Using parameters for membrane-buried helices (4), the hydrophobic region was predicted to have the α-helix conformation typical of membrane spanning segments.

Figure 2: Hydropathy plot of the 14.9-kDa PSI-H precursor polypeptide. The predicted membrane-spanning α-helix (〰), the maturation site (▼), and the distribution of positively (+) and negatively (-) charged amino acid residues are indicated.

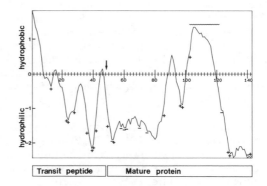

Northern blot hybridization indicates that the size of the transcript for the *PsaH* gene is approximately 0.7 kb (Fig.3A). The hybridization also shows that the *PsaH* gene is transcribed in dark-grown barley seedlings followed by a decrease in the relative amount of *PsaH* transcript during the first 5.5 hours of illumination. After 8 hours of illumination an increase in the *PsaH* transcript is observed (Fig. 3A). Equal amounts of total RNA was loaded in each lane of the gel. Thus the relative amount of *PsaH* RNA at different illumination times can be compared. The decrease in *PsaH* mRNA during the first 5.5 hours of illumination can be explained by an increase in the total amount of RNA upon illumination without any change in the amount of *PsaH* mRNA. Only after 8 hours of illumination is the relative amount of *PsaH* mRNA increased compared to the amount in dark-grown seedlings. In seedlings grown under continuous light, the transcript level of *PsaH* is slightly lower than in seedlings illuminated for 8 hours, but higher than in dark-grown seedlings.

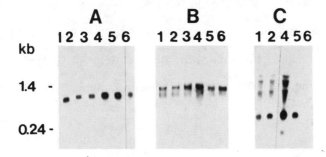

Figure 3: Northern blot of total RNA isolated from 5-days-old barley seedlings and hybridized with **A.** *PsaH*, **B.** *PsaD* or **C.** *psaI* barley DNA probes. The seedlings were grown in the dark and illuminated prior to harvesting for 0 hrs (lane 1), 2.75 hrs (lane 2), 5.5 hrs (lane 3), 8 hrs (lane 4), and continuous light for 5 days (lane 5). Lane 6 contains poly(A⁺) RNA from barley seedlings illuminated for 5.5 hrs.

Figure 3B shows a similar Northern blot hybridized with a barley *PsaD* probe. The transcript size for *PsaD* can be estimated to be approximately 1.0 kb. Again a slight decrease in the relative amount of the *PsaD* mRNA can be observed after 2.75 hours of illumination compared to the dark-grown seedlings. However, at 5.5 hours a slight increase is observed, which is further increased at 8 hours of illumination. In seedlings grown under continuous light, the level of *PsaH* mRNA is lower than in the light-induced seedlings, but slightly higher than in the dark-grown seedlings.

The chloroplast encoded *psaI* gene of barley produces a transcript of approximately 350 bp (Fig. 3C). Therefore this gene which has a 111 bp coding region is most likely transcribed as a monocistronic transcript. The larger bands observed in Fig. 3C represents unspecific hybridization to ribosomal RNA. The relative level of the *psaI* transcript is already increased after 2.75 hours of illumination compared to the level in dark-grown seedlings. After 8 hours of illumination the relative transcript level is further increased. In seedlings grown under continuous light, the transcript level of *psaI* is lower than in the light-induced seedlings.

Dark-grown barley seedlings contain a transcript for all three PS I genes investigated in this paper. Since these dark-grown seedlings have not been exposed to light, the three PS I genes must have been transcribed in the dark at some stage. Whether the transcripts present in dark-grown seedlings are due to a continuous transcription in the dark of the three genes or reflects an accumulation of stable transcripts has to await further analysis. All three genes increase the relative amount of transcript upon illumination. However, this increase is induced at different illumination times. Run-on transriptional analysis can reveal whether this relative increase reflects an increase of the transcription rate.

REFERENCES.
1 Møller, B.L., Scheller, H.V., Okkels, J.S., Koch, B., Andersen, B., Nielsen, H.L., Olsen, I., Halkier, B.A. and Høj, P.B., these proceedings
2 Okkels, J.S., Scheller, H.V., Jepsen, L.B. and Møller, B.L. (1989) FEBS Lett. 250, 575–579
3 Dunn, P.P.J., Packman, L.C., Pappin, D. and Gray, J.C. (1988) FEBS Lett. 228, 157–161
4 Rao, J.K. and Argos, P. (1986) Biochem. Biophys. Acta, 869, 197–214

STUDIES ON THE psbH, woxA, ndhC AND psbG LOCI IN THE CYANOBACTERIUM SYNECHCOSYSTIS 6803

S.R. MAYES, K.M. COOK and J. BARBER
AFRC Phototsynthesis Group, Department of Biochemistry, Imperial College, London SW7 2AY, UK

ABSTRACT
Southern blots using heterologous DNA probes suggest Synechocystis 6803 has one copy of the psbH, woxA and ndhC genes but two distinct copies of the psbG gene which we denote psbG-1 and psbG-2. In this poster we summarise the progress made in characterising these loci and present Southern blot data for studies on the Synechocystis 6803 psbG gene cluster. This data is contrasted with the situation in another cyanobacterium Anacystis nidulans UTEX 625 (also known as Synechococcus leopoliensis or Synechococcous PCC 6301).

INTRODUCTION
We are using the cyanobacterium Synechocystis 6803 as a convenient genetic system for studying photosystem II (PSII) through targeted mutagenesis of its constituent polypeptides. Since PSII architecture is relatively conserved throughout oxygenic photosynthetic organisms, any interesting manipulations may be applied to higher plants.

The chloroplast psbH gene encodes for the 8-10kD phosphoprotein of PSII. It co-purifies with PSII-enriched preparations but is absent from core preparations (1). This small polypeptide has one predicted membrane-spanning helix. It is known to be reversibly phosphorylated in the chloroplast on the conserved residue Thr-2 which protrudes into the stroma (2). However the protein function is not well understood.

The woxA or psb1 gene product is the 33 kD extrinsic "manganese-stabilising protein" (MSP). It is situated in close proximity to the reaction centre polypeptides D1, and D2 and the manganese cluster of the water oxidation machinery on the lumenal side of the thylakoid membrane.

The psbG gene is flanked by the ndhC gene and an open reading frame of approximately 158 residues in all the chloroplast genomes studied. The three genes are apparently co-transcribed in tobacco (3). At the time these studies were initiated, the psbG gene product was reported to be a PSII component. Subsequently Nixon et al have shown that not to be the case and have suggested that it is a component of a NAD(P)H/plastoquinone oxidoreductase residing in the thylakoid membrane (4). The ndhC gene is thought to encode another subunit of this postulated complex. It exhibits good sequence homology to the mitochondrial ND3 gene which encodes a subunit of the mitochondrial respiratory NADH/ubiquinone oxidoreductase complex. The role of the ORF158 product remains uncertain though it could possibly be another subunit of this proposed complex.

METHODS
Low stringency Southern blots were performed essentially as described in ref. 5 using characterised genes from wheat (Triticum aestivum) or Anacystis nidulans R2 as radiolabelled probes. Hybridisation conditions were chosen to obtain maximum clarity of signal and were dependent on the length and degree of

M. Baltscheffsky (ed.), Current Research in Photosynthesis, Vol. III, 617–620.
© 1990 *Kluwer Academic Publishers. Printed in the Netherlands.*

cross-homology to Synechocystis 6803 DNA of the probe used. For the psbG cluster Southern blots shown here the hybridisation conditions were 5 x SSPE, 5 x Denhardts solution, 0.2% SDS, 1 mM ATP at 55°C. Carrier E. coli tRNA, final concentration 70 μg/ml, was included. The final filter wash was 2 x SSPE, 0.2% SDS at room temperature. The specific probes are shown in Fig.2. For the psbH, woxA and psbG studies a λEMBL3 partial Sau3A Synechocystis 6803 genomic library was screened and clones isolated and characterised. (The library was a kind gift from Dr J.G.K. Williams, E.I. Dupont de Nemours Co., Wilmington DE.)

SUMMARY OF PROGRESS

Our results to date are presented in Fig.1. As this work overlaps with that of other groups, their data has been included for completeness. The detailed mapping and sequence data are to be published elsewhere.

Fig.1

Gene	Source of Heterologous DNA Probe	Detected Gene Copy no. in Syn. 6803	Isolation Status	Predicted no. of Polypeptide Residues
psbH	Wheat (Triticum aestivum)	1	gene sequenced over 20 kb mapped	64[*]
woxA	Anacystis nidulans R2	1	gene partially sequenced over 23 kb mapped	246 mature form (6)
psbG	Wheat	2	psbG-1 gene sequenced, over 20 kb mapped	242[*]?
			psbG-2 ( )	248[*] (7)
ndhC	Wheat	1	not attempted	see (7)

[*] includes N-terminal methionine

RESULTS OF THE ndhC AND psbG SOUTHERN EXPERIMENTS

Steinmuller et al recently reported the sequencing of the ndhC-psbG ORF 15? operon from Synechocystis 6803 (7). This is seen as the 2.7 kb HindIII 7.2 kb EcoRI hybridization bands on the genomic DNA Southern blots shown in Figs 3a,4a. We have designated the psbG gene copy in this cluster psbG-2. The additiona 5.7 kb Hind III/6.1 kb Eco R1 signals in Fig.4a reveal psbG gene copy psbG$_{-1}$. We have further characterised this copy (see Fig.1). Examination of the cloned psbG$^-$ indicates it is not linked to ndhC or ORF 158 gene copies. This is consistent with Fig. 3a where only one ndhC gene is detected.

The results from A. nidulans UTEX 625 although not definitive, suggest a contrasting situation. Again there is conserved ndhC-psbG linkage. This resides in a genome region defined by the 6.3 kb Hind III, > 25 kb Eco R1 restriction fragments seen in Figs. 3b and 4b. A second psbG gene is not detectable whilst ndhC again appears to be single copy.

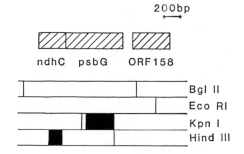

Fig. 2 Restriction map of the wheat chloroplast psbG cluster redrawn from reference (8). Indicated in black are the restriction fragments isolated as ndhC and psbG probes.

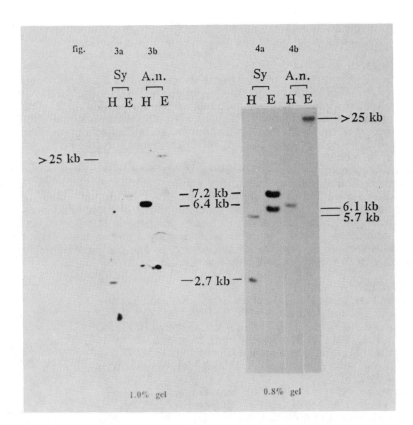

Figs. 3,4. Autoradiograms of ndhC (fig.3) and psbG (fig. 4) Southern blots. Code:- Sy: Synechocystis 6803 genomic DNA, A.n: A nidulans UTEX 625 genomic DNA restricted with H: HindIII, or E: EcoRI.

Fig. 5. Comparison of the deduced Synechocystis 6803 H protein sequence to the wheat sequence (10). Performed using PALIGN program, PC Gene software distributed by Genofit.

```
The character to show that two aligned residues are identical is '|'
The character to show that two aligned residues are similar is '.'
Amino acids said to be 'similar' are: A,S,T; D,E; N,Q; R,K; I,L,M,V;
                                                                F,Y,W


PSBH_SYN   - MA------------QRTRLGDILRPLNSEYGKVVPGWGTT -28
              ||            ||  |  .|.||||||||| |||||
PSBH_WHEAT- MATQTVEDSSKPRPKRTGAGSLLKPLNSEYGKVAPGWGTT -40


PSBH_SYN   - PVMGVFMALFLVFLLIILQIYNSSLILEGFSVDWAG -64
              | ||| |||| .|| ||| |||||--|.|        -
PSBH_WHEAT- PFMGVAMALFAIFLSIILEIYNSSVLLDGI---LTN -73
```

Identity : 41 (64.1%)
Similarity: 7 (10.9%)

CONCLUSIONS

The Synechocystis 6803 psbH gene is shorter than its chloroplast counterpart (Fig. 5). Our data agrees with the reported 6.5 kD sizing and N-terminal sequencing of the Synechococcus vulcanus psbH polypeptide (9). The amino terminus appears truncated and lacks the Thr-2 phosphorylation site. It is doubtful that this polypeptide is phosphorylated in Synechocystis 6803. In addition psbH is not situated 3' to psbB in Synechocystis 6803 as is the conserved case in chloroplast genomes.

Partial sequencing of our woxA clone confirms it is the same gene already characterised by Philbrick and Zelinskas (6).

The data presented here shows there are two distinct psbG genes in Synechocystis 6803, psbG-1 and psbG-2. Comparison of these sequences reveals strong homology in the central portion of each polypeptide but marked divergence at both amino and carboxy termini. psbG copy number may vary between cyanobacterial species as we have evidence for only one psbG copy in A. nidulans UTEX 625. In both species there is only one ndhC gene.

REFERENCES

1.   Millner, P.A. et al (1986) Biochim. Biophys. Acta 852, 30-57
2.   Michel, H.P. and Bennett, J. (1987) FEBS Lett. 212, 103-108
3.   Matsubayashi, T. et al (1987) Mol. Gen. Genet. 210, 385-393
4.   Nixon, P.J. et al (1989) J. Biol. Chem. in press
5.   Maniatis et al (1982) in Molecular Cloning pp 382-389
6.   Philbrick, K. and Zelinskas, B.A. (1988) Mol. Gen. Genet.
     212, 418-425
7.   Steinmuller, K. et al (1989) Mol. Gen. Genet. 216, 60-69
8.   Nixon, P.J. (1988) Ph.D. Thesis, University of London
9.   Koike, H. et al (1989) FEBS Lett. 244, 391-396
10. Hird, S.M. et al (1986) FEBS Lett. 209, 181-186

ACKNOWLEDGEMENTS

Warm thanks to Drs. S.M. Hird (psbH), T. Kuwabara (woxA) and P.J. Nixon (psbG, ndhC) for providing the DNA probes.

A CIRCULAR 73 KBP DNA FROM THE COLOURLESS FLAGELLATE ASTASIA LONGA THAT RESEMBLES THE CHLOROPLAST DNA OF EUGLENA

GERHARD SIEMEISTER, CHRISTIANE BUCHHOLZ and WOLFGANG HACHTEL
Botanisches Institut der Universität Bonn,
Kirschallee 1, D-5300 Bonn 1, FRG

1. INTRODUCTION

Astasia longa is a colourless unicellular flagellate that was isolated from natural material by Pringsheim (1). It is virtually indistinguishable by light microscopy from artificially bleached mutants of Euglena gracilis. Distinct biochemical, physiological and ultrastructural differences between Euglena and Astasia require the designation of the latter as a separate genus (2). It was shown (3) that small proplastid-like bodies are present in most but not all of the artificially bleached Euglena strains, and are absent in Astasia longa.

Recently, we reported on the isolation and on restriction and gene mapping of a circular 73 kbp DNA from an organellar fraction from Astasia longa (4). Our data indicate that this 73 kbp DNA is a truncated form of a plastid DNA that resembles the chloroplast DNA (cpDNA) of Euglena. Here, we present our present knowledge concerning the organization and expression of the genes encoded on the 73 kbp DNA of Astasia longa with particular regard to the rbcL gene.

2. MATERIALS AND METHODS

Cell culture, preparation of organelles and DNA from Astasia longa (strain 1204-17a) were performed as described (4). Cloning of DNA fragments, preparation of RNA from the organelles, electrophoresis and blotting of glyoxylated RNA, Northern hybridization, and nuclease S1 mapping followed standard procedures (5). Nucleotide sequence was determined as described in (6, 7). Analysis of sequence data was performed using the Amersham Staden plus software package and the FASTP program (8). Electrophoresis of proteins on polyacrylamide gels and transfer of proteins to nitrocellulose followed by immunodetection was as described in (9) and in (10), respectively.

3. RESULTS

3.1. Identified genes on the 73 kbp DNA

Genes for the rRNAs, elongation factor Tu, and large subunit of ribulose-1,5-bisphosphate carboxylase have been localized previously by Southern hybridization (4). Now we sequenced the regions containing

M. Baltscheffsky (ed.), Current Research in Photosynthesis, Vol. III, 621–624.
© 1990 *Kluwer Academic Publishers. Printed in the Netherlands.*

TABLE 1. Identified genes on the 73 kbp DNA from <u>Astasia longa</u>.
Split genes are indicated by an asterisk.

Gene	Percentage homology of		DNA species compared	Ref.
	nucleotide sequence	amino acid sequence [a]		
23S rRNA	81		<u>Euglena</u> cpDNA	(11)
16S rRNA	83		" "	(12)
5S rRNA	68		" "	(13)
<u>trn</u>V (UAC)	68		" "	(14)
ORF456		56 / 84	" " (ORF458)	(15)
<u>trn</u>R (UCU)	55		<u>Marchantia</u> cpDNA	(16)
<u>trn</u>T (UGU)	90		<u>Euglena</u> cpDNA	(17)
<u>trn</u>M (CAU)	73		" "	(17)
<u>trn</u>G (GCC)	82		" "	(17)
<u>trn</u>S (GCU)	79		" "	(17)
<u>trn</u>Q (UUG)	82		" "	(17)
<u>tuf</u>A *		86 / 99	" "	(18)
<u>rps</u>7		50 / 88	" "	(19)
<u>rps</u>2 *		38 / 75	<u>Marchantia</u> cpDNA	(16)
<u>rps</u>14 *		62 / 87	" "	(16)
<u>rpl</u>36		58 / 89	" "	(16)
<u>rps</u>8 *		41 / 76	" "	(16)
<u>rpl</u>5		44 / 86	<u>E. coli</u> DNA	(20)
ORF50		45 / 77	<u>Marchantia</u> cpDNA (ORF69)	(16)
<u>rbc</u>L *		82 / 97	<u>Euglena</u> cpDNA	(21)
<u>rpo</u>B * (5'-end)		32 / 74	<u>Marchantia</u> cpDNA	(16)

[a] Amino acid identity / identity plus conservative replacements

these genes as well as their surroundings. By comparison of the
nucleotide sequences and the derived amino acid sequences of potential
open reading frames with data from <u>Euglena</u>, <u>Nicotiana</u>, and <u>Marchantia</u>
cpDNAs and from <u>E. coli</u> we were able to identify the genes listed in
Table 1. The arrangement of these genes is given in Fig. 1. Note that
sequences homologous to the chloroplast genes <u>psaA</u>, <u>psbA</u>, <u>psbD</u>, <u>psbE</u>,
and <u>atpA</u> that code for components of the photosystems and the ATPase,
respectively, are missing on the 73 kbp DNA of <u>Astasia</u>.

3.2. Analysis of the <u>rbc</u>L gene

3.2.1. Sequence and gene organization

The <u>rbc</u>L gene encoding the large subunit of ribulose-1,5-bisphos-
phate carboxylase is a continuous gene in the cpDNA of higher plants
but is interrupted by nine introns in <u>Euglena</u> (21). The <u>Astasia</u> rbcL
gene covers a region of 3924 bp and contains seven introns. Coding
sequences as well as the positions of the introns within the gene are

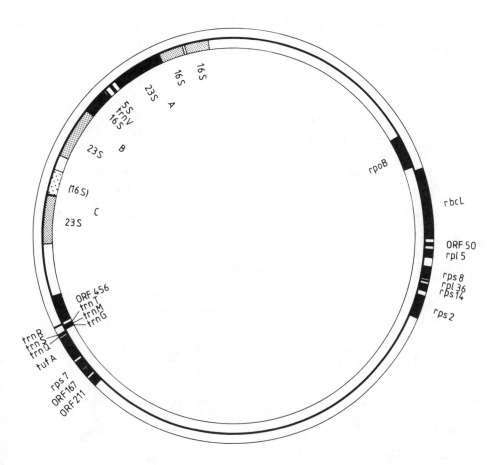

FIGURE 1. Gene map of the circular 73 kbp DNA from Astasia longa.
Genes were identified by Southern hybridization (shadowed
boxes) or by nucleotide sequence (filled boxes).

highly conserved as compared with the Euglena gene despite the absence
of two introns in Astasia.

3.2.2. Gene expression
    The transcription of the Astasia rbcL gene into a 1.5 kb mRNA was
revealed by Norhtern blot analysis using RNA extracted from the
organellar fraction. The transcription start point was localized by
nuclease S1 mapping. The question arose whether the gene product is
present in the heterotrophic Astasia. Immunoblot analysis using antisera against the ribulose-1,5-bisphosphate carboxylase holoenzyme from

rye (J. Feierabend, personel communication) identified the gene product of the rbcL gene of Astasia as a 53 kD polypeptide. This is exactly the same size as in Euglena chloroplasts.

4. CONCLUSIONS

Genes for components of the chloroplast transcriptional and translational systems that are encoded by chloroplast DNA in higher plants and algae are highly conserved on the 73 kbp DNA of Astasia longa. From the ability of Astasia to synthesize the large subunit of the carboxylase one may conclude that these genes are expressed and their products build up functional intact systems. In addition, mechanisms of mRNA splicing must be at work. Typical chloroplast genes for components of the photosystems are absent. We conclude that the genes of the circular 73 kbp DNA resembling the chloroplast DNA of Euglena play an indispensable but unknown role in the heterotrophic habit of Astasia.

REFERENCES
 1 Pringsheim, E.G. (1942) New Phytol. 41, 171-205
 2 Blum, J.J., Sommer, J.R. and Kahn, V. (1965) J. Protozool. 12, 202-9
 3 Kivic, P.A. and Vesk, M. (1973) Can. J. Bot. 52, 695-699
 4 Siemeister, G. and Hachtel, W. (1989) Curr. Genet. 15, in press
 5 Maniatis, T., Fritsch, E.F. and Sambrook, J. (1982) Molecular cloning: a laboratory manual. Cold Spring Harbor Laboratory Press, New York
 6 Sanger, F., Nicklen, S. and Coulson , A.R. (1977) Proc. Natl. Acad. Sci. U.S.A. 74, 5463-5467
 7 Chen, E.Y. and Seeburg, P.H. (1985) DNA 4, 165
 8 Lipman, D.J. and Pearson, W.R. (1985) Science 227, 1435-1441
 9 Chua, N.H. (1980) in Methods in Enzymology (Colowick, S.P. and Kaplan, N.O., eds.), Vol. 69, pp. 434-446, Academic Press, New York
10 Towbin, H., Staehelin, T. and Gordon, J. (1979) Proc. Natl. Acad. Sci. U.S.A. 76, 4350-4354
11 Yepiz-Plascencia, G.M., Jenkins, M.E. and Hallick, R.B. (1988) Nucleic Acids Res. 16, 9340
12 Graf, L., Roux, E., Stutz, E. and Kössel, H. (1982) Nucleic Acids Res. 10, 6369-6381
13 Karabin, G.D., Narita, J.O., Dodd, J.R. and Hallick, R. B. (1983) J. Biol. Chem. 258, 14790-14796
14 Orozco, E.M. and Hallick, R.B. (1982) J.Biol. Chem. 257, 3265-3275
15 Montandon, P.E., Vasserot, A. and Stutz, E. (1986) Curr. Genet. 11, 35-39
16 Ohyama, K., Fukuzawa, H., Kohchi, T., Shirai, H., Sano, T., Sano, S., Umesono, K., Shiki, Y., Takeuchi, M., Chang, Z., Aota, S., Inokuchi, H. and Ozeki, H. (1986) Nature 322, 572-574
17 Karabin, G.D. and Hallick, R.B. (1982) J. Biol Chem. 258, 5512-5518
18 Montandon, P.E. and Stutz, E. (1983) Nucleic Acids Res.11, 5877-5892
19 Montandon, P.E. and Stutz, E. (1984) Nucleic Acids Res.12, 2851-2859
20 Ceretti, D.P., Dean, D., Davis, G.R., Bedwell, D.M. and Nomura, M. (1983) Nucleic Acids Res.9, 2599-2616
21 Gingrich, J.C. and Hallick, R.B. (1985) J. Biol. Chem. 260, 16156-16161

EXPRESSION OF A PEA GENE FOR FERREDOXIN-NADP+ OXIDOREDUCTASE IN TRANSGENIC TOBACCO PLANTS.

P. DUPREE AND J. C. GRAY
BOTANY SCHOOL, UNIVERSITY OF CAMBRIDGE, DOWNING STREET, CAMBRIDGE CB2 3EA, U.K.

1. INTRODUCTION

Ferredoxin-NADP+ oxidoreductase (FNR) catalyses the final step of the linear electron transfer chain by mediating the passage of electrons from reduced ferredoxin to NADP+. There is also some evidence that FNR is involved in cyclic electron flow around photosystem I (1,2). Thus FNR may play a key role in regulating the relative amounts of electrons moving through the cyclic and non-cyclic pathways, and hence may adjust the synthesis of ATP and reducing power to meet the demands of the plant.

FNR is distributed between the stroma and the thylakoid membrane of higher plants. Estimates of the proportion bound to the spinach thylakoid membrane vary from 40 to 80% (3,4). FNR is probably attached to the membrane by a specific binding protein of 17 kDa (5). Both stromal and bound forms often show considerable heterogeneity when analysed by SDS and non-denaturing polyacrylamide gel electrophoresis. Indeed, up to 8 forms of spinach FNR have been separated by isoelectric focussing(6). The significance, if any, of these variants is not yet clear.

Clones of cDNAs have been isolated from pea (7), spinach (8) and *Mesembryanthemum crystallinum* (9). The deduced amino acid sequences are approximately 90% identical, a high level of similarity. A small gene family, probably two or three copies (7,8,9), encodes the FNR precursor. This 43 kDa precursor, of 360 amino acids in peas, is processed after import by the chloroplast to its mature size of 35kDa by removal of a 52 amino acid transit peptide (7).

The aim of the work described here was to isolate a gene encoding FNR from pea and to express it in transgenic tobacco plants. This would allow the expression of the gene to be studied, and enable the source of the variation and cause of the dual location of FNR to be investigated.

2. MATERIALS AND METHODS

The λEMBL3 library of *Bam*H1-digested pea genomic DNA was provided by D.I. Last (10). Growth of λ and λDNA preparations were as described by Last and Gray (10). DNA transferred onto the membrane Hybond-N (Amersham) and probed as described by Newman and Gray (7). For the purpose of sequence determination, deletion subclones were generated by exonuclease III digestion of the full-length 5kbp *Bam*H1-*Hind*III clone in pUC18 according to Henikoff (11). The nucleotide sequences

M. Baltscheffsky (ed.), Current Research in Photosynthesis, Vol. III, 625–628.
© 1990 *Kluwer Academic Publishers. Printed in the Netherlands.*

of the full-length insert and truncated fragments were determined by the dideoxynucleotide chain-termination method of Sanger (12).

Constructs of pBin19 (13) in *Escerichia coli* TG1 were mobilised into *Agrobacterium tumefaciens* LBA4404 (14) by triparental mating with *E. coli* HB101 carrying pRK2013 (13). Tobacco leaf discs (*Nicotiana tabacum* var. Samsun) were transformed by co-cultivation with these *Agrobacterium* strains for 48 hours (15). Transformants, selected by resistance to kanamycin, were transferred to soil and grown to maturity.

Protein samples were prepared as follows. Leaves (100 mg approx.) were ground in an Eppendorf microfuge tube in 300µl 10mM Tricine-NaOH pH 8, 5mM EDTA. After removal of cell debris by low-speed centrifugation, 2.3 volumes of acetone were added to the supernatant to precipitate the proteins. After incubation for five minutes on ice, proteins were pelleted by centrifugation at 10 000g for three minutes. The pellet was dried in a vacuum desiccator to remove acetone and then resuspended in 200µl of loading buffer (10% glycerol, 50 mM Tris-HCl pH8, 0.001% bromophenol blue). Proteins separated by electrophoresis in 15% polyacrylamide gels in the buffer system of Davis (16), were stained for diaphorase activity by incubation in 1mM nitro-blue tetrazolium (NBT, Sigma) 100mM Tris-HCl pH 7.5 for 10 minutes followed by a further incubation for 10-30 minutes in 2mM NADPH, 100mM Tris-HCl pH 7.5 at 25°C.

3. RESULTS AND DISCUSSION

A full-length pea cDNA clone for FNR was used to screen a λEMBL3 library of *Bam*H1-digested pea genomic DNA. Two plaques containing different inserts were purified. The pea cDNA was used to probe Southern blots of restriction digests of the inserts. The hybridising insert of one clone, a 3.7kbp *Bam*H1 fragment, contained two exons corresponding to the central region of the cDNA bordered by non-coding regions of 800 and 1700bp. This clone was not investigated further because the gene was both incomplete and the nucleotide sequence of the exons showed significant differences to that of the cDNA. The 13kbp insert of the other clone contained a 3.5kbp region which strongly hybridised with the cDNA. The nucleotide sequence of a 5kbp *Bam*H1-*Hind*III fragment containing this region was determined and this indicated the presence of a complete gene for FNR. The gene contains 9 exons of between 65 and 290bp and 8 introns of between 87 and 577bp (see Fig. 1.). The transit peptide is encoded by the first exon and a substantial part of the second. The exon sequence was identical to the cDNA sequence indicating that this gene and the cDNA were of the same origin.

The 5kbp*Bam*H1-*Hind*III fragment, containing 930bp of upstream sequence and 1kbp of downstream sequence was cloned into pBin19 and then introduced into tobacco leaf discs by *Agrobacterium*-mediated transformation. Regenerated plants were analysed for the presence of pea FNR in their leaves. FNR displays high levels of diaphorase activity (17). Therefore total leaf extracts subjected to non-denaturing polyacrylamide gel electrophoresis were stained with NBT and NADPH for diaphorase activity. Wild-type tobacco plants gave two equally staining bands, whereas pea plants gave a single major band of lower mobility. Extracts of some transgenic plants were found to contain a protein with diaphorase activity of similar mobility to pea FNR in addition to the two tobacco forms (see Fig. 2.). This suggests that these plants are expressing the introduced gene for pea FNR. The activity of pea FNR in these transgenic plants is approximately half that of the endogenous tobacco FNR. The presence of active pea FNR in these transgenic tobacco plants suggests that the prosthetic group FAD was correctly associated with the FNR polypeptide. Moreover, the identical electrophoretic mobility of pea FNR in pea and transgenic tobacco plants suggests that the FNR precursor was also correctly processed in the transgenic tobacco plants. These plants provide suitable material for investigation of the cause and significance of the dual location of FNR in chloroplasts, and also to determine the source of FNR heterogeneity.

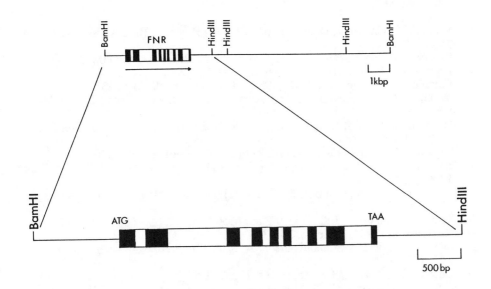

FIGURE 1. Map of a pea genomic clone containing the gene for ferredoxin-NADP$^+$ oxidoreductase. Coding regions are shown as filled boxes.

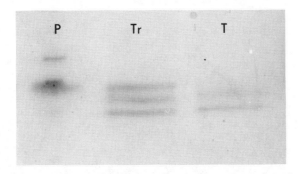

FIGURE 2. Expression of the pea FNR gene in transgenic tobacco plants. NADPH - nitro blue tetrazolium reductase activity was detected after non-denaturing polyacrylamide gel electrophoresis of leaf extracts from pea (P), transgenic tobacco (Tr) and wild-type tobacco (T).

4. ACKNOWLEDGEMENTS

We wish to thank B. J. Newman for the pea FNR cDNA and R. Slatter for helpful advice.
P.D. is supported by an SERC studentship.

5. REFERENCES

1   Shahak, Y., Crowther, D. and Hind, G. (1981) Biochim. Biophys. Acta 636, 234-243
2   Hosler, J. P. and Yocum, C. F. (1985) Biochim. Biophys. Acta 808, 21-31
3   Böhme, H. (1978) Eur. J. Biochem. 83, 137-141
4   Carrillo, N. and Vallejos, R. H. (1982) Plant Physiol. 69, 210-213
5   Vallejos, R. H., Ceccarelli, E. and Chan, R. (1984) J. Biol. Chem. 259, 8048-8051
6   Hasumi, H., Nagata, E. and Nakamura, S. (1983) Biochem. Biophys. Res. Comm. 110, 280-286
7   Newman, B. J. and Gray, J. C.(1988) Plant Mol. Biol. 10, 511-520
8   Jansen, T., Reiländer, H., Steppuhn, J. and Herrmann, R. G. (1988) Curr. Genet. 13, 517-522
9   Michalowski, C.B., Schmitt, J. M. and Bohnert, H. J. (1989) Plant Physiol. 89, 817-822
10 Last, D. I. and Gray, J. C. (1989) Plant Mol. Biol. 12, 655-666
11 Henikoff, S. (1984) Gene 28, 351-359
12 Sanger, F., Nicklen, S. and Coulson, A. R. (1977) Proc. Natl Acad. Sci. (USA) 74, 5463-5467
13 Bevan, M. (1984) Nucleic Acids Res. 12, 8711-8721
14 Ooms, G., Hooykaas, P. J., Moolenaar G. and Schilperoot, R. A. (1981) Gene 14, 33-50
15 Horsch, R. B., Fry, J. E., Hoffman, N., Eicholtz, D., Rogers, S. G. and Frayley, R. T. (1985) Science 227, 1229-1231
16 Davis, B. J. (1964) Ann. N. Y. Acad. Sci. 121, 404-427
17 Avron, M. and Jagendorf, A. T. (1956) Biochim. Biophys. Acta 808, 21-31

BEHAVIOR OF CHLOROPLAST NUCLEOIDS DURING THE CELL CYCLE OF
CHLAMYDOMONAS REINHARDTII IN SYNCHRONIZED CULTURE

TOMOKO EHARA[1], YUTAKA OGASAWARA[2], TETSUAKI OSAFUNE[1] AND
EIJI HASE[3]

Dept. Microbiol., Tokyo Medical College, Tokyo 160[1]; Dept.
of Biology, Konan Univ., Kobe 657[2]; Lab. Chem., Fac. Med.,
Teikyo Univ., Tokyo 192-03[3], Japan.

INTRODUCTION

Since the introduction of the technique of staining of chloroplast
(cp) nucleoids in algae with 4',6-diamidino-2-phenylindole (DAPI), the
DNA fluorochrome, most algae have been classified into two major groups
on the basis of shape and distribution of nucleoids in the chloroplasts,
(i) cp-nucleoids scattered in the chloroplast and (ii) those forming a
ring lying inside the girdle lamellae (1-4). Kuroiwa et al. (3) followed changes in number, size and shape of cp-nucleoids in synchronized
cells of Chlamydomonas reinhardtii. Ovoid cp-nucleoids increased in
size and divided, showing dumbell-shaped form.

In this work, an adequate concentration of glutaraldehyde used for
fixation of cells before DAPI-staining was selected, because the concentration was found to affect profoundly the shape and distribution
of cp-nucleoids.

MATERIAL AND METHODS

Chlamydomonas reinhardtii cells were synchronized under the 12 h
light: 12 h dark regimen at 25°C, the light intensity being 6,000 lux
at the surface of culture container (5). These cells were mixed with
0.1% (w/v) glutaraldehyde (final conc.) and immediately centrifuged
for 7 min at 4°C. The sedimented cells were washed with culture medium
to remove glutaraldehyde. Procedures of DAPI-staining were the same
as those used by Kuroiwa et al. (3).

When the concentration of glutaraldehyde was higher than 0.3% (w/v),
the shape of cp-nucleoids was always granular, without giving the profiles characteristic of various stages of the cell cycle.

RESULTS AND DISCUSSION

Figure 1 is a schematic illustration of the behavior of cp-nucleoids
in the Chlamydomonas cell cycle observed. About ten granular nucleoids
were dispersed in the chloroplast at the beginning of the light period
(I in Fig. 1), and they soon gathered around the pyrenoid conjoining
with each other, and temporarily surrounded it (II). The association
of conjoined nucleoids with the pyrenoid was observed again later in
the light period (III in Fig. 1). Toward the end of the light period
these nucleoids were changed into the form of threads interconnected

with fine fibrils spreading throughout the chloroplast, and only faintly fluoresced (IV). Subsequently, the fluorescence of some parts of the thread-like form became brighter, and these nucleoids were apportioned into daughter chloroplasts in the chloroplast division (V). Soon after the chloroplast division, these thread-like nucleoids were transformed into about 20 granular forms (VI), which were gradually combined to form about 10 larger granular bodies in zoospores immediately prior to the liberation from mother cells.

When cells containing conjoined cp-nucleoids (II or III in Fig. 1) were fixed with 0.5% (w/v), in place of 0.1%, granular profiles of cp-nucleoids were observed near the pyrenoid. When the same cells were treated with 0.1 mg protenase (Sigma, type XIV)/ml for 30 min at 37°C, their cp-nucleoids became swollen and blurred. When the cells containing thread-like cp-nucleoids (IV in Fig. 1) were fixed with 0.5% (w/v) glutaraldehyde before DAPI-staining, fairly many small and brighter granules interconnected with fine threads were observed (Fig. 2). When those cells were treated with 0.05 mg protenase/ml for 30 min at 37°C, the originally faint DAPI-fluorescence of this type of cp-nucleoids became much more weaker and the profile blurred.

The gathering of cp-nucleoids around or near the pyrenoid has been observed in various algae (1, 3, 4, 6, 7).

The profiles of DAPI-stained cp-nucleoids were greatly modified by fixation of cells with glutaraldehyde of higher concentrations or treatment with protenase before staining with DAPI. These results strongly suggest that the various morphologies of cp-nucleotides observed in synchronized Chlamydomonas cells are determined mostly by different configurations of protein components associated with cp-DNAs. For instance, DNA molecules in thread-like nucleoids (IV in Fig. 1) may be spread over a network of their protein components. The protein network may be coagulated into grosser aggregates on treatment with glutaraldehyde of high concentrations, and concomitant gathering of DNAs on the protein aggregate could give granular profiles of brighter DAPI-fluorescence (Fig. 2: left, fixed with 0.1% glutaraldehyde, and right, with 0.5%). Goodenough (7) could not observe cp-nucleoids in dividing cells of Chlamydomonas reinhardtii, while the nucleoids in interphase cells were detectable. Coleman (1) also described that cp-nucleoids in Chlamydomonas cells could not be observed when cells entered mitosis. The above interpretation of the thread-like cp-nucleotides seems to be compatible with those previous observations.

The conjoined form of cp-nucleotids (II or III in Fig. 1) is probably the result of compact aggregation of protein components, but not connection of DNA molecules, and on treatment with protenase, the proteins may be separated into smaller aggregates carrying DNA, giving granular profiles of cp-nucleotids. Kuroiwa (3)et al. observed by DAPI-fluorescence microscopy that cp-nucleoids of Nitella became dispersed in situ upon protease treatment.

Possible relations of morphological changes of cp-nucleoids in the Chlamydomonas cell cycle with such biochemical events as synthesis and replication as well as transcription of cp-DNA remains to be worked out.

This work was aided by grants from the Kazato Research Foundation
(1988, to T. E.) and the Ministry of Education, Science and Culture
(NO. 62304007, to T. O.).

REFERENCES
1 Coleman, A.W. (1978) Exp. Cell Res. 114, 95-100
2 Coleman, A.W. (1979) J. Cell Biol. 82, 299-305
3 Kuroiwa, T., Suzuki, T., Ogawa, K. and Kawano, S. (1981) Plant Cell
  Physiol. 22, 381-396
4 Coleman, A.W. (1985) J. Phycol. 21, 1-16
5 Mihara, S. and Hase, E. (1971) Plant Cell Physiol. 12, 225-236
6 Ris, H. and Plaut, W. (1962) J. Cell Biol. 13, 383-391
7 Goodenough, U.W. (1970) J. Phycol. 6, 1-6

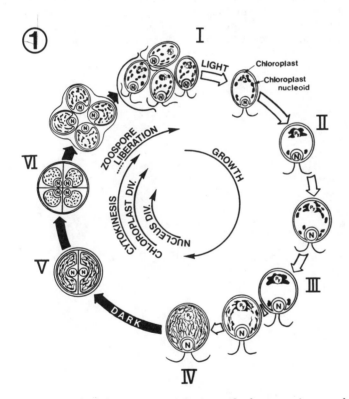

Fig. 1.   A schematic representation of changes in morphology
          of DAPI-stained cp-nucleoids during the cell cycle
          of Chlamydomonas reinhardtii in synchronized culture.
          White arrows show processes in the light, and dark
          ones those in the dark.

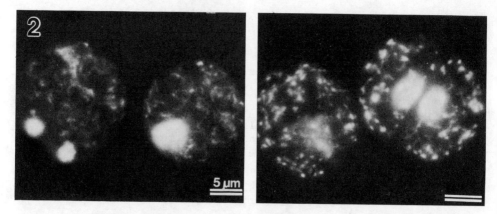

Fig. 2. DAPI-fluorescence photomicrographs of cells containing
O-type cp-nucleoids (left), and a modified morphology
(right) observed when fixed with glutaraldehyde of a high
(0.5%, w/v) concentration. Note that one of two cells in
each figure has two nuclei.

HEAT SHOCK RESPONSE IN THE CHLOROPLAST GENOME

A.GNANAM and S.KRISHNASWAMY, UNIVERSITY OF MADRAS, CHEPAUK, MADRAS 600005, INDIA

1.   INTRODUCTION
A wide range of organisms and cells in culture, respond to elevated temperatures with an induction of a set of new proteins called Heat Shock Proteins (HSPs) (1). Reports are available on the number and nature of HSPs associated with the organelles like nuclei, mitochondria, chloroplasts and ribosomes (2,3-6). Since chloroplasts and mitochondria are thought to have been derived from prokaryotic organisms (7), it is logical to expect that in the eukaryotic organisms besides the nuclear coded HSPs, there may be certain HSPs coded by the organelle genome and synthesized by their own protein synthetic machinery. Contrary to this expectation, there are no evidences to indicate the involvement of the genomes of these organelle in the induction of HSPs except for some indirect evidences recently (8). Our results on the studies of the heat shock response of the plastids obtained from *Vigna sinensis* seedlings indicate that the plastid genome does have a heat shock response and the induction of this response depends on the mode of heat shock treatment (rapid or gradual) given to the leaves.

2.   PROCEDURE
2.1. Materials and methods
2.1.1. Plant materials: Seven day old *vigna sinensis* seedlings grown in growth chambers at 25°C with a 12-h light/dark cycle, except for raising etiolated seedlings which were grown in continuous dark conditions. Intact chloroplasts were isolated as described earlier (9).
2.1.2. Protein synthesis by Leaf segments: About 500 mg of leaves were cut and transferred to a 25-ml conical flask containing 3 ml of sterile water and kept in a thermostated water bath shaker at specified temperature. Illumination was provided at a photon flux density of 37.2 uE/M /s. for gradual heat shock, the temperature was increased at the rate of 3°C/h. After incubating the leaf segments at a specified temperature for 30 min, 50 uCi of ^{14}C-chlorella protein hydrolysate (26 mCi/m atom of C) was added. After 90 min of incubation the leaf segments were homogenized and chloroplasts were isolated.
2.1.3. Protein synthesis by chloroplasts and etioplasts: Light dependent protein synthesis by isolated chloroplasts and etioplasts was carried out as described earlier (9). SDS-PAGE was carried out as described by Laemmli (8) with modifications. The gel contained a linear 9-18% acrylamide concentration gradient with 5-10% glycerol co-gradient. Electrophoresis was carried out at 20°C for 12 h at 17 mA with initial 1 h at 5 mA. Fluorography was carried out at -90°C with Screen type x-ray film.

M. Baltscheffsky (ed.), Current Research in Photosynthesis, Vol. III, 633–636.
© 1990 *Kluwer Academic Publishers. Printed in the Netherlands.*

3. RESULTS AND DISCUSSION

3.1. Effect of temperature on protein Synthesis by isolated Chloroplasts: Intact chloroplasts of *V.Sinensis* mediated protein synthesis in a light-dependent reaction without the requirement for ATP. No protein synthesis was seen in the dark. Fig.1 shows the fluorographic profile of the proteins synthesized at various temperatures. The general profile of the polypeptides synthesized was not altered very much by the change in incubation temperature. However, at 35 C and above, there was a distinct increase in the synthesis and/or accumulation of four polypeptides in the molecular sizes of 85,70,60 and 23 kDa. All four polypeptides could be observed, at least as faint bands, even at 25 C. The synthesis of HSPs at 40 C in the isolated chloroplasts were completely inhibited by chloramphenicol but not by cycloheximide. The transcriptional inihibitors like actinomycin-D and rifamycin were also inihibitory to the HSP synthesis (Fig 2).

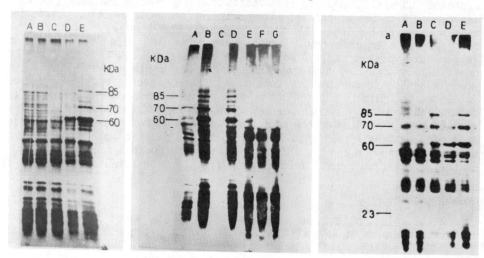

Fig.1 Profile of the chloroplast protein synthesized at different temperatures. Lanes A,B,C,D & E represent 25,30,35,38 and 40°C respectively. In Fig.2, Lane A, chloroplasts incubated at 25°C, Lanes B through G, at 40°C, but with different inihibitors. B-none,C-chloramphenicol, D-cycloheximide, E-actinomycin-d, F-rifamycin and G-ethidium bromide. Fig.3. Same as in Fig.1 but of isolated etioplasts.

In order to establish the localization of these HSPs, chloroplasts incubated with ^{14}C-amino acids at 25° and 40°C were fractionated into stroma and thylakoids and their flurographic profiles were compared. All four HSPs seen in the intact chloroplasts were detectable only in the thylakoid membrane and not in the stromal fraction. Another interesting observation is the complete absence of 85 and 60 kDa HSPs in the thylakoid membranes of the chloroplasts labeled at 25°C, while the 70 and 23 kDa could be detected as a faint band. In contrast in the fluorographic profile of the total chloroplast proteins, all four heat-induced polypeptides could be detected as faint band at 25°C. From these two observations, it can be concluded that the 60 and 85-kDa polypeptides associated with the thylakoid membranes are newly synthesized only at the elevated temperatures, while the 70 and 23 kDa are synthesized in small amounts even at 25°C. As in the case of chloroplasts, in the etioplast preparations incubated at elevated temperatures, there was an induction of synthesis of a set of HSPs (85,70 and 60 kDa). Although the HSPs detectable in the etioplasts incubated at the elevated temperature are comparable to the HSPs observed in the chloroplasts, there was a significant difference in the temperature range for the induction of HSPs between chloroplasts and etioplasts. While it was 35°C for the induction of HSPs in the chloroplasts, it was 40°C for the etioplasts.(Fig.3)

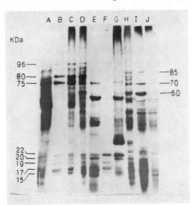 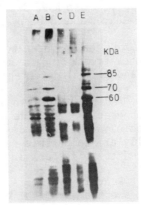

Fig.4. Protein profile of whole leaf subjected to rapid or gradual heat shock and of the chloroplast fraction. Lanes A and E, total leaf homogenate and chloroplast fraction incubated at 30°C. B and F, rapid heat shock given at 40°C for 30 min., C and G rapid heat shock given at 40°C for 5 min. D and H, gradual heat shock given from 30° to 40°C. I, isolated chloroplasts heat shock at 40°C and J, Control of I at 25°C. Fig.5. Protein profile of the chloroplasts derived from the leaves subjected to rapid heat shock. A-control, 25°C., B-leaf incubated at 25°C but chloroplasts labeled at 40°C. C-leaves incubated for 2 h and chloroplasts labeled at 40°C. D-leaves incubated for 15 min. at 40°C and chloroplasts labeled at 40°C. E-chloroplasts isolated from leaves subjected to gradual Heat Shock.

3.2. Effect to Heat Shock on Protein Synthesis by Vigna leaf Segments: In order to see whether the HSPs synthesized by the isolated chloroplasts and etioplasts *in vitro* can be synthesized *in vivo*, young green leaves were subjected to rapid or gradual heat shock treatments and labeled with ^{14}C-amino acids. Chloroplast preparations were made from these heat-shocked leaves and fluorographic analysis of the polypeptides associated with these chloroplast preparations as well as with that of the total leaf homogenate was made. Fig.4 illustrates the heat shock response of the young green leaves subjected to rapid heat shock. At temperatures higher than 35°C, most of the normally occuring polypeptides were not synthesized and only a set of HSPs (96,80,75,22 and

15 kDa) made their appearance in the fluorographic profile of the total leaf homogenate. The 75 kDa protein is synthesized in considerable amounts even at 25°C suggesting its constitutive expression. The fluorographic profile of chloroplasts isolated from leaves heat shocked at 35°C was closely comparable to that of the chloroplasts isolated from leaves at 25°C (Fig.1). At the incubation temperature of 40° and above, most of the high molecular weight polypeptides associated with the chloroplast fraction decreased and only five low molecular mass polypeptides (22,20,19,17 and kDa) of which one polypeptide (20 kDa) appeared only as a faint band. These chloroplast-associated low molecular weight HSPs are not synthesized *in vivo* in leaves infiltrated with chloramphenicol. It is thus possible that the 22 kDa and other low molecular mass HSPs detectable in chloroplasts obtained from heat-shocked leaves could be of nuclear origin.

In the total leaf homogenate of the Vigna leaves subjected to a gradual heat shock treatment, in addition to three high molecular mass HSPs (96,80 and 70 kDa) detectable in the rapid heat-shocked leaves, a 60-kDa HSP was detected as a distinct band in the fluorographic profile (Fig.4). Furthermore, two new HSPs in the size of 85 and 70 kDa were also detectable as a faint band. These three HSPs (85,70 and 60 kDa) detectable in the total leaf homogenate of the leaves heat shocked gradually are comparable to the HSPs detectable in the chloroplasts subjected to heat shock *in vitro*.

3.3. In vitro Protein Synthesis in the Chloroplasts isolated from the Preheat-shocked Leaves: In vitroprotein synthesis at 40°C was performed with the chloroplast preparations obtained from the leaves subjected to rapid and gradual heat shock treatments. In chloroplast preparations from leaves subjected to rapid hat shock either for 2 h or for 15 min, the synthesis of all three high molecular weight HSPs was not detectable, while the synthesis of chloroplast proteins could be seen atleast as faint bands. However, in chloroplast preparations from leaves subjected to gradual heat shock treatment all three high molecular weight polypeptides were synthesized as in the case of chloroplasts isolated from control leaves(Fig.5).

REFERENCES
1. Schlesinger,M.J., Aliperti, .& Keely, P.M.(1982) Trends Biochem. Sci. 7, 222-225
2. Tanguay.R.M.(1983) Can.J.Biochem.Cell.Biol. 61, 387-394
3. Lin,C.Y., Roberts,J.K. & Key, J.L.(1984) Plant Physiol. 74, 152-160
4. Velazquez, J.M., DiDomenico, B.J. & Lindquist, S. (1980) Cell 20, 679-689
5. Vincent, M & Tanquay, R.M.(1979) Nature 281, 501-503
6. Kloppstech, K., Meyer, G., Schuster, G. & Ohad, I. (1985) EMBO J. 4, 1901-1909
7. Yamamori, T., Ito, K, Nakamura, Y. & Yura, T. (1978) J. Bacteriol. 134, 1133-1140
8. Laemmli,, U.K. (1970) Nature 227, 680-685
9. Daniell, H., Ramanujam, P., Kirshnan, M., Gnanam,A & Rebeiz.C.A (1983) Biochem. Biophys.Res.Commun. 111, 740-749.

CLONING OF THE psbK GENE FROM THE CYANOBACTERIUM SYNECHOCYSTIS 6803

Z.H. Zhang, S.R. Mayes and J. Barber
AFRC Photosynthesis Research Group, Department of Biochemistry,
Imperial College, London SW7 2AY, UK

INTRODUCTION

Recent studies have shown that several low molecular weight proteins are associated with the photosystem II (PSII) complex in higher plants and cyanobacteria (1,2,3). Of these, two have been identified by N-terminal sequencing to be the products of the psbK and psbI genes (3,4,5,6). Depending on the species as well as the gel system, the psbK gene product (K protein) has an apparent molecular weight of 2-3.9 kDa as judged by SDS-PAGE and the psbI product of about 4.8 kDa (5,3,6).

The K protein has been shown to be present in PSII preparations but not in purified oxygen-evolving spinach PSII core preparations (5). However it has been detected in oxygen-evolving preparations from the cyanobacterium Synechococcus vulcanus (3). The mature form of the K protein is shorter than would be predicted from the gene, which suggests processing. Sequence comparisons between liverwort and tobacco indicate that both proteins are well conserved.

The psbI gene product is present in PSII complexes and is retained in purified pea reaction centre preparations (6). A similar sized protein has also been observed in Synechocystis 6803 reaction centre preparations (K. Gounaris, personal communication). The psbK and psbI genes are linked in the chloroplast genomes of liverwort, tobacco and rice (7,8,9). On the complementary strand, this locus is flanked by two tRNA genes, $tRNA^{set}$ and $tRNA^{gln}$. However, in wheat the psbI gene is upstream of the psbD and psbC (10). We aimed to isolate and sequence the psbK gene from Synechocystis 6803 with the view to investigate the functions of its product in PSII activity.

Synechocystis 6803 is a convenient organism for genetically manipulating PSII. It can be readily transformed with exogenous DNA and is capable of photoheterotrophic growth on media supplemented with glucose when PSII function is impaired. Due to the similarities of the structures of the PSII components, any conclusions drawn from work on Synechocystis 6803 are applicable to higher plants.

MATERIALS AND METHODS

The Synechocystis 6803 and a partial Sau 3A λEMBL3 genomic library were a kind gift from J.G.K. Williams (E.I. du Pont de Nemours Co., Wilmington DE). The nitrocellulose used in Southern blot and library screening is from Schleicher and Schuell. Southern blot and library screening were performed essentially as in reference 11. DNA was immobilized onto nitrocellulose and low stringency hybridisation conditions were as in S.R. Mayes et al., this proceedings. The DNA probes, as shown in figure 1, were a gift from Professor K. Ohyama. Radio-labelling of probes was carried out by the primer extension reaction using random oligonucleotides (12).

M. Baltscheffsky (ed.), Current Research in Photosynthesis, Vol. III, 637–640.
© 1990 *Kluwer Academic Publishers. Printed in the Netherlands.*

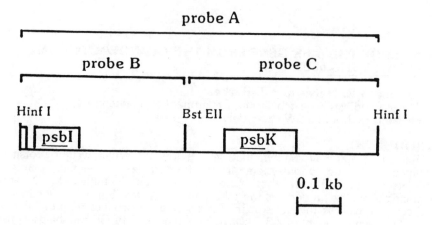

Figure 1 Liverwort (<u>Marchantia</u> <u>polymorpha</u>) chloroplast DNA probes used in this experiment.

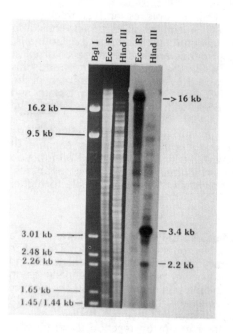

Figure 2 Hybridisation of liverwort (<u>Marchantia</u> <u>polymorpha</u>) chloroplast DNA probes to Southern blot of <u>Synechocystis</u> 6803 DNA.

RESULTS

When restricted genomic DNA from Synechocystis 6803 was probed with region A (Fig.1), two hydridisation bands, sized 3.4 kb and 2.2 kb, were detected in the Hind III digested lane and one band of >20 kb, in the EcoR1 digested lane (Fig.2). The 3.4 kb Hind III and >20 kb EcoR1 bands were also observed when the genomic DNA was hydridized to labelled probe C (fig.1), however the 2.2 kb Hind III band was not present (data not shown). This suggests that the hybridization of probe C is to a unique region of the Synechocystis 6803 genome.

Using probe C, the Synechocystis 6803 genomic library was screened and a clone was isolated. Figure 3 shows the preliminary restriction map of this clone, designated λZZKI. It does contain a 3.4 kb Hind III fragment, but does not have any EcoR1 sites. The hybridisation signal was localized to a 1.8 kb SmaI fragment, which was subcloned into a pUC18 vector. Further restriction analysis of this subclone indicated that the region of homology to probe C was within a 0.4 kb HpaII fragment. Preliminary sequencing of this fragment has been carried out.

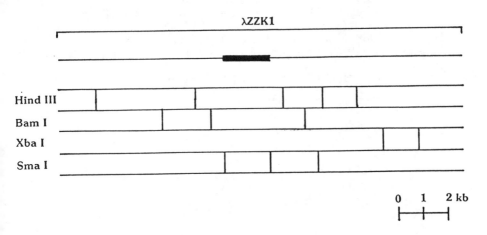

Figure 3 Preliminary restriction map of clone λZZK1. The fragment which is highlighted in the diagram hybridises to psbK probe.

The 2.2 kb Hind III fragment in a genomic λEMBL3 clone was obtained by screening the genomic library. This fragment was subcloned into a pUC18 vector from which the hybridisation signal to probe B (fig.1) was located to a BamH1/Hinc II fragment, sized 0.67 kb. Sequencing of this fragment showed it not to contain psbI but 16 bp of tRNA^{ser} which were also included in probe B. During this work it was noted that a Hind III fragment, sized 3.6 kb, showed a weak hybridisation to probe B in genomic DNA and from the genomic clone containing the 2.2 kb Hind III fragment. Sequencing identified this signal as being due to tRNA^{ser} too.

CONCLUSIONS

We have isolated the psbK gene from Synechocystis 6803 and have located it to a 0.4 kb Hpa II fragment within a 1.8 kb Sma I fragment, which has been inserted into a pUC18 vector. We have shown that this gene is probably a single copy. However we have been unable to detect the psbI gene. The reason for the latter is unclear but could be due to a low homology between the psbI gene in liverwort and the cyanobacterial gene.

ACKNOWLEDGEMENTS

We are grateful to Miss Katie Cook and Dr Niki Gounaris for valuable discussion during this work and help in writing this article. This research is supported by the Agriculture & Food Research Council. Mr Z.H.Zhang is financed by the Sino-British Friendship Scholarship Scheme.

REFERENCES

1. Ljingberg, U. et al. (1986) Biochim. Biophys. Acta 849, 112-120
2. Ikeuchi, M. and Inoue, Y. (1988) Plant Cell Physiol. 29, 1233-1239
3. Koike, H. et al. (1989) FEBS Lett. 244, 391-396
4. Ikeuchi, M. and Inoue, Y. (1988) FEBS Lett 241, 99-104
5. Murata, N. et al. (1988) FEBS Lett. 235, 283-288
6. Webber, A.N. et al. (1989) FEBS Lett. 242, 259-262
7. Umesono, K. et al. (1988) J. Mol. Biol. 203, 299-331
8. Deno, H. and Sugiura, M. (1983) Nucl. Acids. Res. 11, 8407-8414
9. Hiratsuka, J. et al. (1989) Mol. Gen. Genet. 217, 185-194
10. Hird, S.M. (1988) Ph.D. Thesis, University of Cambridge
11. Maniatis et al. (1982) in: Molecular Cloning, Publ. Cold Spring Harbor Labs. pp 382-389
12. Feinberg, A.P. et al. (1983) Anal. Biochem. 132, 6-13

ADDITIVITY IN THE CONTRIBUTION TO HERBICIDE BINDING OF AMINO ACID RESIDUES IN THE D1 PROTEIN OF PHOTOSYSTEM II

YAEL EISENBERG, NIR OHAD, AMNON HOROVITZ AND JOSEPH HIRSCHBERG, DEPARTMENT OF GENETICS, THE HEBREW UNIVERSITY OF JERUSALEM, JERUSALEM, 91904 ISRAEL

1. INTRODUCTION

Photosystem II herbicides inhibit electron transfer from Q_A to Q_B by binding to the D1 protein thus causing a displacement of the plastoquinone Q_B [1,2]. Competition between the herbicides and Q_B for the same binding site has been demonstrated [2,3]. Different amino acid substitutions in the D1 protein have been previously found to reduce herbicide binding thereby conferring herbicide-resistance [4,5].

The effects of an amino acid substitution in the D1 protein of photosystem II on the binding of different herbicides to D1 has been previously successfully predicted [6]. This was done by assuming additivity in the contributions to the binding energy of the amino acids at positions 255 and 264 in D1. Additivity in this case implies that the free energy change due to a substitution at one site did not depend on which amino acid is occupying the second site.

A thermodynamic cycle, for the alternative binding of four homologous protein inhibitor molecules to a proteinase, that consists of two parallel and identical changes, was previously put forward [7], as follows:

$$\Delta G^{\circ}(2)\ EI_{a_n d_{n+i}} \xrightarrow{\beta|\alpha} EI_{b_n d_{n+i}}\ \Delta G^{\circ}(4)$$

$$\alpha \uparrow \qquad \uparrow \alpha|\beta \qquad\qquad (1)$$

$$\Delta G^{\circ}(1)\ EI_{a_n c_{n+i}} \xrightarrow[\beta]{} EI_{b_n c_{n+i}}\ \Delta G^{\circ}(3)$$

In this diagram a,b,c and d represent different amino acids of the inhibitor, and the subscripts n and n+i denote their position in the homologous sequences, all other amino acids being identical. α and β indicate the amino acid replacements $c_{n+i} \to d_{n+i}$ and $a_n \to b_n$, respectively. $\alpha|\beta$ and $\beta|\alpha$ indicate the temporal order of the replacements. $\Delta G^{\circ}(1)$, $\Delta G^{\circ}(2)...\Delta G^{\circ}(4)$ stand for the free energies of binding of the respective inhibitor to the proteinase. A measure for non-additivity is given by:

$$\Delta G^{\circ}(I) = \Delta G^{\circ}(\alpha|\beta)-\Delta G^{\circ}(\alpha) = \Delta G^{\circ}(\beta|\alpha)-\Delta G^{\circ}(\beta) \qquad (2)$$

where $\Delta G^{\circ}(I)$ is the coupling or interaction of free energy.

By applying the principle of free energy conservation and assuming additivity one obtains:

M. Baltscheffsky (ed.), Current Research in Photosynthesis, Vol. III, 641–644.
© 1990 Kluwer Academic Publishers. Printed in the Netherlands.

$$\frac{K_2}{K_1} = \frac{K_4}{K_3} \qquad\qquad (3)$$

where K_1, K_2 ...K_4 are the binding constants of the respective inhibitors to the enzyme. From Eqn. 3 one may calculate any one of the four binding constants provided the remaining three in that equation are known.

2. MATERIALS AND METHODS

2.1. Strains and growth conditions. Cell cultures of Synechococcus PCC7942 were grown in BG11 medium at 35° c as described [8]. Selection of the herbicide resistant mutants Di1, D5, Tyr5 and G264, has been previouly described [6,8,9]. A new double mutant, TG, was constructed by site-directed mutagenesis of psbAI, following the procedure described in ref 9. In this mutant phenylalanin at position 255 was changed to tyrosin and serine at 264 was replaced by glycin.

2.2. Measurement of PSII-dependent electron transfer. PSII-dependent electron transfer from H_2O to DCPIP was analysed in isolated membranes by measuring the rate of photochemical reduction of DCPIP [8]. I_{50} was determined as the concentration of herbicide that inhibited the rate of DCPIP reduction by 50%.

3. RESULTS

Mutations in psbAI of the cyanobacterium Synechococcus PCC7942, that confer herbicide resistance, have been previously described [5-9]. We have constructed a new double mutant, TG, in which Phe at position 255 of the D1 protein was changed to Tyr, and Ser at position 264 was changed to Gly (data not shown). Amino acids in these positions of D1 are known to contribute to the binding of various herbicides [5,10].

Two thermodynamic cycles, similar to that in scheme 1, for the alternative binding of a herbicide to different variants of the D1 protein, can be postulated (Fig. 1).

Predictions, using Eqn. 3, were made for I_{50} concentrations of 22 different herbicides with respect to D1 protein of the mutant Tyr5 (cycle A) and were compared with actual

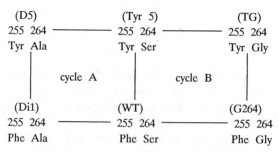

FIGURE 1: Amino acid substitutions in the D1 protein of herbicide resistant mutants of Synechococcus PCC4972. Name of mutants are given in parentheses and the amino acid residues that occupy positions 255 and 264 in each mutant are indicated.

experimental results. I_{50} values of different PSII herbicides, as determined by in-vitro assays under identical conditions, correspond to their binding constants [11,12]. A plot of the experimental vs. calculated values is given in Fig. 2A. In the case of a perfect fit all of the points would be expected to fall on the dashed line with a slope of 1. As may be seen, most of the predictions (16 out of 22), fall very close to this line, within the limits of experimental error. Only two predictions, clearly do not fit the experimental results.

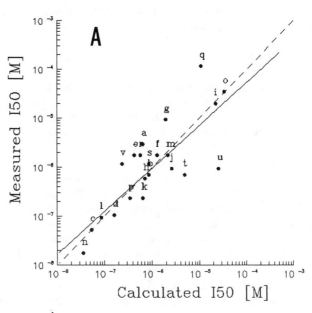

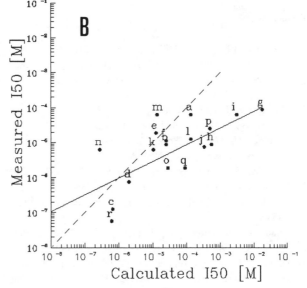

FIGURE 2: Correlation between experimental and predicted I_{50} values of the different herbicides with respect to mutant Tyr5 (A) and mutant TG (B). Average experimental error in log I_{50} is about ±0.15. Herbicides used were: fenuron (a); monuron (b); diuron(c); linuron (d); tebuthiuron (e); ethidimuron (f); atrazine (g); ametryne (h); propazine (i); prometryne (j); terbutryne (k); metribuzine (l); metamitron (m); bromacyl (n); cyanoacrylate-s (o); cyanoacrylate-r (p); bromoxynil (q); ioxynil (r); dinoseb (s); phenmedipham (t); fluometuron (u); simazine (v)

A similar analysis was done to examine additivity in the thermodynamic cycle B in Fig. 1. Experimental data on mutants G264, Tyr5 and the wild-type were used for calculating the I_{50} values of mutant TG, according to Eqn.2. The plot in Fig. 2B shows the correlation of these results to the actual measured ones.

As shown in Fig. 2B, no additivity was found for the contribution of the amino acid replacements in cycle B when all herbicdes were included in the calculation. However, treating the urea herbicides and triazines separately, demonstrated that a correlation does exist between measured and calculated I_{50} values of the urea herbicides but not of triazines (data not shown).

4. DISCUSSION

Additivity in the contributions to the binding of herbicides, of amino acids in positions 255 and 264 of the D1 protein, was demonstrated in the case of amino acid substitutions in cycle A of figure 1. This result reflects an apparent lack of intramolecular interactions between amino acids Phe or Tyr at position 255 and Ser or Ala at position 264 of the D1 protein. In addition, the interactions between Phe or Tyr at 255 with herbicides are not affected when Ser at 264 is replaced by Ala.

In contrast, only a weak additivity was found in the case of mutants G264 and TG in cycle B of Fig. 2B. The single mutations in Tyr5 [6] and in G264 [9] strongly reduce the binding of triazines to D1, but binding of urea herbicides in these mutants is only slightly affected. It has been speculated [9] that the Ser to Gly change in D1 causes a significant structural rearrangement of the D1 protein. Such an effect on the polypeptide backbone can lead to various alterations in the interaction between the inhibitors and amino acids in the herbicide-binding niche in D1. It is possible that additivity in the contribution to the binding of herbicides is distorted in cases of allosteric effects or loss of the rigid structure of the polypeptide inflicted by the amino acid substitutions.

REFERENCES

- [1]   Velthuys, B.R. (1981) FEBS Lett. 126, 277-281.
- [2]   Lavergne, J. (1982) Biochim. Biophys Acta 679, 12-18.
- [3]   Vermaas, W.F.G., Artnzen, C.J., G.V., L.-Q. and Yu, C.A. (1983) Biochim. Biophys. Acta 723, 266-275.
- [4]   Hirschberg, J. and McIntosh, L. (1983) Science 222, 1346-1348.
- [5]   Hirschberg, J., Ben-Yehuda, A., Pecker, I. and Ohad, N. (1987) in Plant Molecular Biology NATO ASI Series Vol. 140 (von Wettstein, D. and Chua, N.-H., eds.) pp. 357-366. Plenum Press, New York.
- [6]   Horovitz, A., Ohad, N. and Hirschberg, J. (1989) FEBS Lett. 243, 161-164.
- [7]   Horovitz, A. (1987) J. Mol. Biol. 196, 733-735.
- [8]   Hirschberg, J., Ohad, N., Pecker, I. and Rahat, A. (1987). Z. Naturforsch. 42C, 758-761.
- [9]   Ohad, N, and Hirschberg, J. (1989) Photosynthesis Res. (in press).
- [10] Trebst, A. (1987) Z. Naturforsch. 42C, 742-750.
- [11] Tischer, W. and Strotmann, H. (1977) Biochim. Biophis. Acta 460, 113-125.
- [12] Thiel, A. and Boeger, P. (1984) Pestic. Biochem. Physiol. 22, 232-242

CLONING AND FUNCTIONING OF CHLOROPLAST PROMOTERS IN E.COLI AND
SYNECHOCYSTIS

DMITRY A. LOS, NADEZHDA V. LEBEDEVA, IRINA V. ELANSKAYA* ,
SERGEY V. SHESTAKOV*, VICTOR E. SEMENENKO. Plant Physiology
Institute, USSR Academy of Sciences, Botanicheskaya ul., 35,
127176 Moscow, USSR.   *Moscow State University, Department
of Biology, Moscow, USSR

INTRODUCTION
The investigation of light and dark regulation mechanisms of
chloroplast genome expression is of paramount interest for molecular
biology and genetic engineering of photosynthesis. Much attention is
focused on the study of chloroplast DNA (cpDNA) regulatory sequences:
promoters, terminators, silencers (1,2,3). Unfortunately, there are no
direct data concerning location and functioning of the cpDNA sequences
responsible for light regulation of genes activity. In this work we
describe the experiments on chloroplast promoters cloning in E.coli,
measurement of their activity and construction of promoter-selection
vector for cyanobacterium Synechocystis. The latter vehicle was
produced for direct studying of the light-dependent expression from
chloroplast and/or cyanobacterial promoters. The chloroplast promoters
obtained can also be used for biotechnological purposes.

STRAINS AND METHODS
The cultures of green halophilic unicellular alga Dunaliella
salina Teod. strain 9 and cyanobacterium Synechocystis PCC6803 were
obtained from The Unicellular Algae Culture Collection of Plant
Physiology Institute, Moscow, USSR. E.coli straines used were DH1 and c
925. Chloroplast DNA was prepared as described in (4). Molecular
cloning was performed according to Maniatis et al.(5). Trascription and
translation reactions in E.coli minicells were performed according to
Stouker et al.(6). Transformation of Synechocystis was described
earlier in (7).

RESULTS AND DISCUSSION
D.salina cpDNA was digested by restriction endonuclease Bam HI and
ligated into the promoter selection vector pML4 (8). We have selected
seven clones carrying different cpDNA insertions. CpDNA promoter
active fragments which were inserted upstream CAT-gene, having no
promoter of its own, directed CAT expression. Thus, these E.coli clones
acquiring chloramphenicol (Cm) resistance, grew on Cm-containing medium
(300 ug/ml). E.coli clones carrying recombinant plasmids, called pDSc
(table 1) were characterised by a different rate of growth on Cm-media

(fig.1). It seems, that chloroplast promoters of pDSc6 and pDSc29 plasmids were more active in E.coli, than the intrinsic pBR328 CAT-promoter. pDSc20 had the same DNA fragment inserted in opposite directions. The promoter activity of cpDNA fragments was tested by the expression of recombinant plasmids in E.coli minicells. The results are shown in fig.2. We have observed only CAT expression. No chloroplast genes localized in the DNA fragments were expressed in minicells system. One may see the residual expression of CAT-gene pML4 line due to incomplete RNA I termination in pML4 ORI locus (8). We have used the most active chloroplast promoter from pDSc6 in our further work connected with the vectors construction for E.coli and cyanobacteria. The latter fragment was subcloned using Sau 3A restriction enzyme, and the deletion variant of pDSc6 plasmid was produced. pDSc6-46 contained only pML4 ORI and CAT-gene, directed by 100 bp chloroplast sequence. As a result, we have obtained cpDNA fragments, which are recognized by E.coli RNA-polymerase. However, we do not know whether these fragments have any promoter activity in organello, because of the difference shown between chloroplast and E.coli RNA-polymerases recognition (9,10).

TABLE 1.The molecular weight of cpDNA promotor-active fragments cloned in pML4		
Plasmid	cpDNA fragment MW, kb	
pDSc2-1	4.6	
pDSc3	1.3	
pDSc6	3.4	
pDSc8-1	4.0	
pDSc15-2	6.3	
pDSc20-2	9.5	
pDSc29-2	9.5	

Moreover, the E.coli expression systems do not allow direct study of light activated chloroplast promoters and sequences. To create the adequate light-dependent system for the investigation of prokaryotic-like chloroplast light-regulated promoters, we have chosen cyanobacterium Synechocystis PCC 6803. The gene cloning system is currently being developed for the strain (11), and this cyanobacterium can exist in either autotrophic or heterotrophic conditions. We have used the plasmid pSE76 , produced from Synechocystis cryptic plasmid (11), to construct a promoter selection vector for cyanobacteria. The promoterless NPT II-gene was inserted into the unique SalI-site of pSE76 (fig.3). The final construction carried the active Cm-resistance gene and the nonactive Km- resistance gene. To check the efficiency of our vector in cyanobacteria we have recloned the chloroplast promoter-active fragment from pDSc6 into pSE-PKm and transformed Synechocystis by the latter recombinant plasmid. The clones obtained became resistant to chloramphenicol and kanamycin and could exist in both E.coli and Synechocystis. The efficiency of transformation was 100 clones per ug DNA and coincided with that, described for pSE76.

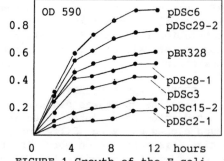

FIGURE 1.Growth of the E.coli clones containing pDSc plasmids on Cm-medium (300 ug/ml)

pDSc15-2 pDSc3 pDSc6 pDSc8-1 pDSc29-2 pML4 pDSc2-1

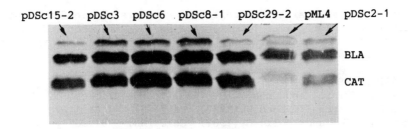

BLA

CAT

FIGURE 2. The CAT-gene expression in E.coli minicells under control of chloroplast DNA promoter-active fragments S-Methionine was used in experiments.

Thus, we have constructed the promoter selection vector for light-dependentstrain Synechocystis which is usable for the cloning of prokaryotic and chloroplast promoters. This construction could be used not only in fundamental research of light and dark control of gene expression but also for biotechnological purposes, e.g., constructing expression vectors. Expression vectors for cyanobacteria are still to be developed, and the promising approach to maximum expression is the insertion of usable regulatory elements, such as promoters could be effectively used in cyanobacteria and provide high efficiency of

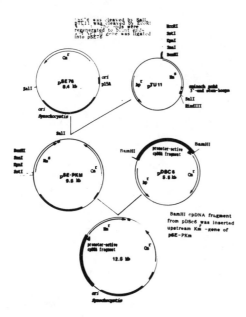

FIGURE 3. The scheme of cyanobacterial promoter-selection vector construction and the chloroplast promoter cloning in Synechocystis

expression. The D.salina chloroplast promoters obtained are used for constructing chloroplast transformati on vectors for Dunaliella - a commercially important genus, which has no cell wall and thus, can be used in transformation experiments.

REFERENCES

1. Hanley-Bowdoin,L. and Chua,N.-H.(1987) Trends Biochem.Sci.12,67-70
2. Stern,D.B. and Gruissem,W.(1987) Cell 51, 1145-1157
3. Thompson,R.J. and Mosig,G.(1987) Cell 48, 281-287
4. Los,D.A.,Lebedeva,N.V.,Semenenko,V.E.(1989) Sov.Plant Physiol.36,754
5. Maniatis,T.,Fritsch,E.,Sambrook,J.(1982) The Molecular Cloning.480p.
6. Stoker,N.G.,Pratt,J.,Holland,B.(1984) in: Transcription and Translation. A Practical approach, IRL Press Ltd. 400 p.
7. Shestakov,S.,Elanskaya,I.,Bibikova,M.(1985) Proc.V Int.Symp.on Photosynthetic Prokaryotes. Grindelwald, Swizerland,p.109
8. Mashko,S.V.,Lebedeva,M.I.,Podkovyrov,S.M.(1985) Sov.Mol.Biol.19,1194
9. Zech,M.,Hartley,M.R.,Bohnert,H.J.(1981) Current Genet. 4, 37-46
10. Hanley-Bowdoin,L.,Orzco,E.M.,Chua,N.-H.(1985) in: Mol.Biol. of
    Photosynth.Appar. N.Y., Cold Spring Harbor p.311
11. Elanskaya,I.V.,Bibikoma,M.V.,Bogdanova,S.L.,Babykin,M.M.,Shestakov,
    S.V.(1987) Proc.Acad.Sci.USSR 293,716-719

INSERTION OF A CHLOROPLAST psbA GENE INTO THE CHROMOSOME OF THE CYANOBACTERIUM SYNECHOCYSTIS 6803

Thomas Reiss[1], Christer Jansson[2] and Lee McIntosh[1]

[1]MSU-DOE Plant Research Laboratory and Department of Biochemistry, Michigan State University, East Lansing, MI 48824, USA
[2]Department of Biochemistry, Arrhenius Laboratories, University of Stockholm, S-106 91 Stockholm, Sweden

INTRODUCTION

Photosystem (PS) II in the procaryotic cyanobacteria is structurally similar to that in higher plants and contains around 20 different polypeptide subunits [1]. The reaction center of PSII, harboring the key components for the charge separation, consists of the D1 and D2 polypeptides [2,3]. Our studies concern the biogenesis of PSII in the cyanobacterium Synechocystis 6803. We are particularly interested in the role of the D1 polypeptide in the assembly process. We have previously described [4] the construction of a S. 6803 mutant where synthesis of the D1 polypeptide has been inactivated by insertional mutagenesis of the psbA gene family, encoding the D1 polypeptide. A preliminary functional characterization of that mutant showed that the PSII activity was severely perturbed while PSI activity was unaffected [4,5]. The structural analysis revealed that despite the lack of the D1 and D2 polypeptides, mutant thylakoids still retained several intrinsic PSII polypeptides [1].

To increase our understanding of how the D1 polypeptide interacts with other polypeptide subunits during PSII biogenesis we decided to test whether a D1 polypeptide from a higher plant could functionally and structurally replace the cyanobacterial D1 polypeptide in S. 6803. In the present work we describe the insertion of the chloroplast psbA gene from Amaranthus hybridus into S. 6803 and we also give a brief account of the expression of this foreign gene.

RESULTS AND DISCUSSION

To construct an expression vector for integration of foreign genes into the chromosome of S. 6803 we fused a synthetic polylinker to the 3' end of a 1 kb fragment of S. 6803 DNA harboring 5' flanking, promoter and ~200 nt coding sequences of the rbcL gene. To allow for homologous recombination with the S. 6803 chromosome the construct

M. Baltscheffsky (ed.), Current Research in Photosynthesis, Vol. III, 649–652.
© 1990 *Kluwer Academic Publishers. Printed in the Netherlands.*

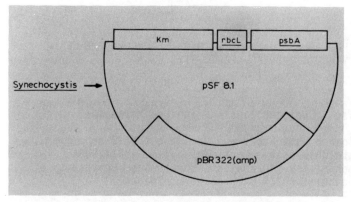

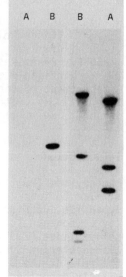

Figure 1 (left). Plasmid pSF8.1 used for integration of the chloroplast psbA gene from A.
hybridus into the chromosome of S. 6803.

Figure 2 (right). Southern blot analyses of
Hind III-digested DNA isolated from S. 6803
wild type (A) and mutant S. 6803 SF (B). The
probe in the left panel was the psbA gene
from A. hybridus and in the right panel a
mixture of the psbA-1 and psbA-2 genes from
S. 6803.

was cloned into plasmid pkW 1188 [7] which contains a segment of
S. 6803 DNA and the nptII gene from Tn 903 conferring kanamycin resistance. Cloning of a 2 kb fragment bearing the psbA gene from A. hybridus [8] into this expression vector resulted in plasmid pSF8.1
(Fig. 1).

Following transformation of mutant S. 6803 T-1,2,3 [4] with plasmid
pSF8.1 colonies were selected for photoautotrophic growth. DNA from
potoautotrophic transformants were then analyzed by Southern blot
hybridization to confirm the insertion of the A. hybridus psbA gene.
Fig. 2 shows the results from one selected transformant, S. 6803 SF.

Northern blot analysis demonstrated that the A. hybridus psbA gene
was highly expressed in S. 6803 SF (Fig. 3). No expression could be
detected from the S. 6803 genes in S. 6803 SF. The psbA transcript
in S. 6803 SF was ~1.3 kb in size, slightly larger than the transcript from the S. 6803 genes. To examine whether the 1.3 kb transcript contained any rbcL mRNA a Northern blot was probed with the
rbcL fragment from pSF8.1. As is indicated in Fig. 3 the psbA transcript in S. 6803 SF did not hybridize to the rbcL probe, suggesting
that it is not a fusion product. The lower transcript in S. 6803 SF
originates from the inactivated psbA-2 gene [6].

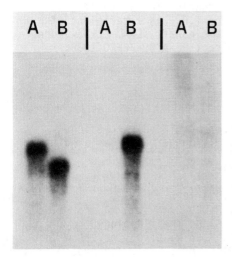

Figure 3. Northern blot analyses of RNA isolated from S. 6803 wild type (A) and mutant S. 6803 SF (B). In the left panel the probe was a mixture of the psbA-1 and psbA-2 genes from S. 6803, in the middle panel the psbA gene from A. hybridus and in the right panel the 5' region of the rbcl gene from S. 6803.

Western blot analysis (Fig. 4) and a partial functional characterization suggested that the A. hybridus psbA gene in S. 6803 SF produced a D1 polypeptide that could assemble with S. 6803 polypeptides to form a functional chimeric PSII complex. This is particularly interesting in view of the differences in the carboxy-terminus between chloroplast and cyanobacterial D1 polypeptides [9]. As deduced from the psbA gene sequence, cyanobacteria contain a ~7 amino acid addition near the end of the carboxy-terminus. The function of this extra sequence is unknown. The data presented here suggest that it is not crucial for proper insertion of the D1 polypeptide in the thylakoid membrane, or for PSII activity.

Figure 4. Western blot analysis of thylakoids isolated from S. 6803 wildtype (A), mutant T-1,2,3 (B) and mutant S. 6803 SF (C). The antibody was directed against the D1 polypeptide from A. hybridus [10].

Acknowledgements: C.J. acknowledges the support by the Swedish Natural Science Council, the Carl Trygger Foundation for Scientific Research and the Magnus Bergvall Foundation. T.R. was a recipient of a fellowship from the Deutsche Forschungsgemeinshaft. L.M. acknowledges the support of Department of Energy Contract DE-AC02-76ERO-1338.

REFERENCES

1 Nilsson, F., Andersson, B. and Jansson, C. These Proceedings
2 Michel, H., Weyer, K.A., Gruenberg, H., Dunger, I., Oesterhelt, D. and Lottspeich, F. (1986) EMBO J. 5, 1149-1158
3 Trebst, A. (1986) Z. Naturforsch. 41c, 240-245
4 Jansson, C., Debus, R.J., Osiewacz, H.D., Gurevitz, M. and McIntosh, L. (1987) Plant Physiol. 85, 1021-1025
5 Jansson, C., Debus, R.J., Osiewacz, H.D., Gurevitz, M. and McIntosh, L. (1987) in Plant Gene Systems and their Biology (Key, J.L. and McIntosh, L., eds.) pp. 371-381, Alan R. Liss, Inc., New York
6 Mohamed A. and Jansson, C. (1989) Plant Mol. Biol., in press
7 Williams, J.G.K. (1988) Meth. Enzymol. 167, 766-778
8 Hirschberg, J. and McIntosh, L. (1983) Science 222, 1346-1349
9 Morden, C.W. and Golden, S.S. (1989) Nature 337, 382-384
10 Ohad, I., Kyle, D.J. and Hirschberg, J. (1985) EMBO J. 4, 1655-1659

STRUCTURE OF TARGETING PEPTIDES FOR ORGANELLAR PROTEIN IMPORT

Gunnar von Heijne, Department of Molecular Biology, Karolinska Institute, NOVUM, S-141 52 Huddinge, Sweden

Introduction

The intracellular sorting of newly synthesized proteins from the cytosol to their final locations inside or outside the cell is carried out by a complex system of cytosolic and organellar proteins that recognize specific "signals" in the nascent protein, route it into the appropriate sorting pathway, ensure its translocation across one or more membranes, and deliver it to its site of function. In the plant cell, four major sorting pathways lead to the extracellular medium, to the nucleus, to mitochondria, and to chloroplasts. In this paper, the "signals" that serve to route proteins into the last two pathways will be discussed; the reader is referred to other reviews for details on the secretory and nuclear import pathways[1-3].

From the biochemical point of view, import into chloroplasts and mitochondria share a number of similarities, but there are also some notable differences. "Chaperones", i.e. proteins that prevent premature folding, or even bring about the unfolding, of other proteins seem to be involved in the early phase of targeting, keeping the nascent protein in a "translocation competent" state[4]. Receptors on the surface of the appropriate organelle then apparently recognize some critical feature(s) of the "signal" (targeting or transit peptide); it is possible that membrane lipids are also involved in this step[5]. Finally, the nascent protein is translocated into the organelle, but the details of this most interesting event are not yet known.

Chemical energy in the form of ATP hydrolysis is required to keep the protein in the translocation competent state and possibly also during the translocation step. Import into mitochondria also requires an electrical potential across the inner mitochondrial membrane; in contrast, chloroplast import has no such requirement[6].

Most proteins that are imported into mitochondria and chloroplasts are made as pre-proteins with amino-terminal extensions that contain the targeting information. For mitochondrial proteins, the term "targeting

M. Baltscheffsky (ed.), Current Research in Photosynthesis, Vol. III, 653–660.
© 1990 *Kluwer Academic Publishers. Printed in the Netherlands.*

peptide" seems to be most frequently used, whereas for chloroplast proteins one mostly meets the term "transit peptide". Here, I will refer to these two classes of signals as mTPs and cTPs, and in what follows I will review the characteristic features of mTPs ands cTPs as we understand them today.

Statistical studies of mTPs

Thanks to the rapid advances in DNA sequencing, the amino acid sequences of more than 100 mTPs are known today. In many cases, however, the precise point of cleavage between the mTP and the mature protein has not been determined. When trying to extract the consensus features of these sequences, one also has to avoid including highly homologous proteins into one's sample. In a recent study[7], we were able to collect 37 non-homologous mTPs with known cleavage sites from the literature; the analysis of this sample, as well as that of an earlier, smaller sample[8], allows some conclusions to be drawn about both the overall structure of mTPs, as well as about their mode of processing.

In terms of the overall amino acid composition, mTPs stand out by virtue of their high content of positively charged residues (particularly Arg) and their almost complete lack of negatively charged Asp and Glu residues. In addition, hydrophobic moment analysis[8] indicates that mTPs can be folded into highly amphiphilic α-helices with an apolar face and a polar, positively charged face, Fig.1.

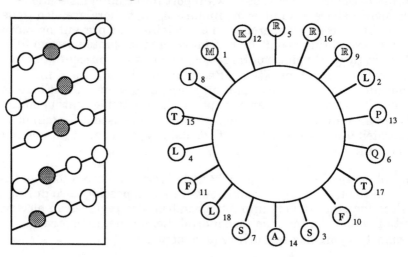

Fig.1 A typical mTP (COX IV from yeast) plotted in helical net (left) and helical wheel (right) projections. Positively charged residues are shaded (left) or outlined (right)

When mTPs are aligned from their point of cleavage and the amino acid distribution is calculated for each individual position in the aligned sample, highly significant deviations from the average mTP amino acid frequencies are found in positions -2 and -10. In both cases, Arg is highly over-represented[7]. Further, mTPs with Arg in position -2 do not as a rule have Arg in -10, and *vice versa*. Also, an Arg in -10 is almost invariably followed by a hydrophobic residue in position -8 and by a Ser or Thr in -5[7,9].

One-step processing:

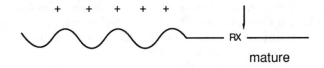

Two-step processing:

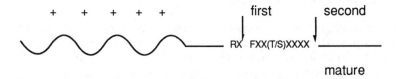

Fig.2 One-step vs. two-step processing of mTPs

This suggests that there may be two classes of mTPs: one class that is cleaved by a matrix-localized protease with a preference for cleaving one residue downstream of an Arg, and another class that is cleaved first by this protease and then by a second protease that removes an additional eight residues, Fig.2. The functional significance of one-step vs. two-step processing is not known.

Experimental studies of mTPs

Aside from early studies aimed at demonstrating that an mTP grafted onto a normally cytosolic protein would suffice to target the hybrid molecule into mitochondria[10,11], most of the experimental work has been focussed on testing the amphiphilic helix-concept. Two major lines of enquiry have been pursued: mutational analysis of real mTPs, and biophysical studies on the interaction between synthetic mTPs and model membranes.

Although most of the work on the effects of point-mutations and small deletions in mTPs can be rationalized in terms of the positively charged amphiphilic helix model, a particularly convincing study was recently reported by Bedwell et al[12]. The minimal portion of the yeast $F_1\beta$-ATPase mTP required for efficient import *in vivo* and *in vitro* was first defined by deletion analysis. This "core" segment was then subjected to saturation mutagenesis using degenerate oligonucleotide primers, and the import efficiency of more than 100 different mutations was measured. When these mutations were plotted on the helical-wheel representation of the "core" segment, all of the "down"-mutations turned out to either introduce a negatively charged residue on the positively charged face of the α-helix, or to introduce a charged residue on the apolar face. Mutations that had no effect on the import efficiency were such that they did not perturb the amphiphilic character of the helix.

Biophysical studies of synthetic mTPs also tend to reinforce the amphiphilic helix idea. Such peptides adopt a helical conformation in the presence of lipids[13], bind strongly to lipid monolayers with the helical axis parallel to the surface of the membrane[14], and disrupt liposomes even at low concentrations and in a potential-dependent manner (a negative-inside potential enhances the lytic effect)[13].

Finally, when segments of "random" DNA were placed in front of the gene for a cytosolic marker protein that allowed selection for mitochondrial import of the hybrid molecule, a surprisingly large proportion of the clones turned out to be positive for import[15]. When the sequences of the import-active hybrids were determined, the overall impression was that of slightly degenerate amphiphilic helices with an excess of positively over negatively charged residues.

Taken together, these observations all agree with the notion that a positively charged amphiphilic helix is the most important defining characteristic of mTPs, although it has recently been suggested that an amphiphilic ß-sheet like structure might also work[16].

Statistical studies of cTPs

Since much fewer cTPs are known from DNA sequencing, the results from statistical analyses are less detailed than for the mTPs. Nevertheless, some regularities have been noted[7,17]. cTPs are highly enriched for Ser, and to some extent also for Thr. Like mTPs, they almost completely lack negatively charged residues. Positively charged residues seem to be tolerated, but are not enriched in comparison to their frequency in soluble proteins in general.

cTPs seem to have a three-domain structure, with an uncharged amino-terminal region of some 10 residues that also lacks turn-promoting Gly and Pro residues, Fig.3; a central region that is mainly characterized by a high incidence of Ser and a lack of Asp and Glu; and a carboxy-terminal domain that often contains one or more Arg residues.

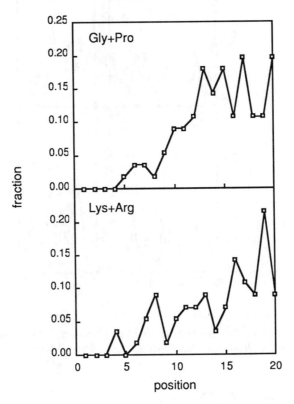

Fig.3. Distribution of Gly+Pro (top) and Lys+Arg (bottom) in a sample of 56 amino-terminally aligned cTPs

Closer examination of the carboxy-terminal domain reveals a tendency for it to be able to form an amphiphilic ß-strand. There are also strong amino acid preferences in positions -3 to +1 (shaded in Fig.4): these positions contain very few turn-promoting residues (Gly, Pro, Asn); have a rather low Ser-content, and acidic residues start appearing in abundance only in position +2. Conversely, Ala is very frequent in positions -1 and +1, and the branched hydrophobic residues Ile and Val are frequently found in position -3, Fig.4.

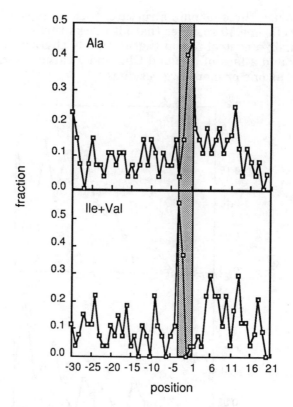

Fig.4. Distribution of Ala (top) and Ile+Val (bottom) in a sample of 26 cTPs aligned from their cleavage sites. Positions -3 to +1 are shaded.

Experimental studies of cTPs

So far, cTPs have not been as extensively studied as mTPs. No conserved secondary structure similar to the amphiphilic helix of mTPs is apparent from the theoretical analysis, and biophysical studies of synthetic cTPs have not been performed so far.

Deletion analysis has also failed to provide a clear answer to the question of what constitutes a functional cTP; it does seem that the central region is less sensitive to deletions or insertions than the amino- and carboxy-terminal domains[18,19], but this conclusion is based on very little data.

mTPs and cTPs: similarities and differences

In summary, matrix-targeting mTPs seem to have a two-domain structure with a positively charged amphiphilic α-helix providing the targeting function followed by a short region defining the cleavage site. With few exceptions, all mTPs are cleaved by a matrix protease that apparently recognizes an Arg two residues upstream from the cutsite; a subset of the mTPs go on to be cleaved a second time eight to nine residues further downstream, probably by a distinct processing activity[21].

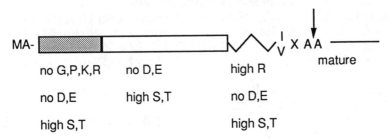

Fig.5. Basic design of a cTP

Stroma-targeting cTPs are similar to mTPs in that they lack negatively charged residues, but beyond this they are different, Fig.5. They do not seem to be built according to the amphiphilic helix model, and they have an uncharged amino-terminal region that one does not see in mTPs. Their cleavage site is also different: there is no "Arg$_{-2}$ signal" but rather a pattern of (Ile,Val)-X-Ala↓Ala. A partial match to this pattern is found in most cTPs, but some cleavage sites are completely different. This raises the interesting possibility that two-step cleavage might take place also for some cTPs, but experimental data on this point is lacking.

References

1. von Heijne, G (1988) Biochim.Biophys.Acta **947**, 307-333.
2. von Heijne, G (1988) ISI Atlas of Science **1**, 205-209.
3. Dingwall,C., & Laskey,R.A. (1986) Ann.Rev.Cell Biol. **2**, 367-390.
4. Deshaies,RJ, Koch,BD, Werner-Washburne,M, Craig,EA, & Schekman,R (1988) Nature **332**, 800-805.
5. Hartl,FU, Pfanner,N, Nicholson,DW, & Neupert,W (1989) Biochim.Biophys.Acta **988**, 1-45.
6. Eilers,M. & Schatz,G. (1988) Cell **52**, 481-483.
7. von Heijne,G., Steppuhn,J., & Herrmann,R.G. (1989) Eur.J.Biochem. **180**, 535-545.
8. von Heijne,G. (1986) EMBO J. **5**, 1335-1342.

9. Hendrick,J.P., Hodges,P.E., & Rosenberg,L.E. (1989)
   Proc.Natl.Acad.Sci.USA **86**, 4056-4060.
10. Hurt,E.C., Peshold-Hurt,B., & Schatz,G. (1984) FEBS Lett. **178**, 306-310.
11. Horwich,A.L., Kalousek,F., Mellman,I., & Rosenberg,L.E., (1985)
    EMBO J. **4**, 1129-1135.
12. Bedwell,D.M., Strobel,S.A., Yun,K., Jongeward,G.D., & Emr,S.D.
    (1989) Mol.Cell.Biol. **9**, 1014-1025.
13. Roise,D., Horvath,S.J., Tomich,J.M., Richards,J.H., & Schatz,G. (1986)
    EMBO J. **5**, 1327-1334.
14. Tamm,L.K. (1986) Biochemistry **25**, 7470-7476.
15. Allison,D.S., & Schatz,G. (1986) Proc.Natl.Acad.Sci.USA **83**, 9011-9015.
16. Roise,D., Theiler,F., Horvath,S.J., Tomich,J.M., Richards,J.H.,
    Allison,D.S., & Schatz,G. (1988) EMBO J. **7**, 649-653.
17. Keegstra,K., Olsen,L., & Theg,S. (1989) Ann.Rev.Plant Physiol. **40**, in
    press.
18. Smeekens,S., Geerts,D., Bauerle,C., & Weisbeek,P. (1989)
    Mol.Gen.Genet. **216**, 178-182.
19. Ostrem,J.A., Ramage,R.T., Bohnert,H.J., & Wasmann,C.C. (1989)
    J.Biol.Chem. **264**, 3662-3665.
20. Reiss,B., Wasmann,C.C., Schell,J., & Bohnert,H.J. (1989)
    Proc.Natl.Acad.Sci.USA **86**, 886-890.
21. Kalousek,F., Hendrick,J.P., & Rosenberg,L.E. (1989)
    Proc.Natl.Acad.Sci.USA **85**, 7536-7540.

THE BIOGENESIS AND ASSEMLY OF THE MAJOR ANTENNA COMPLEX OF PHOTOSYSTEM II (LHCIIb) IN BARLEY.

SHAUL YALOVSKY AND RACHEL NECHUSHTAI. DEPARTMENT OF BOTANY, THE HEBREW UNIVERSITY OF JERUSALEM, JERUSALEM 91904, ISRAEL.

1. INTRODUCTION

The biogenesis of sub-cellular organelles is a challenging field of cellular biology, concerned with the coordinated assembly of the various constitutents of the organelle, which results in a functional entity. In the present work we describe studies on the in-organello events in the biogenesis of the major light-harvesting complex of photosystem II (LHCIIb). The LHCIIb is a well characterized pigment-protein complex situated mainly in grana-thylakoids (1-3). Its precursor (pLHCP) is a nuclear-encoded protein postranslationally imported by the plastid (4-6). It has been shown that following importation into isolated plastids, pLHCP is inserted into the thylakoid membrane, incorporated into the pigmented LHCIIb, and processed to its mature form (7,8). Furthermore, it was demonstrated that pLHCP can be inserted into isolated thylakoids in the presence of MgATP and a stromal protein factor (9-12). It was claimed that 80-85% of pLHCP inserted into thylakoids, was located in grana-lamellae, and that the insertion and processing are restricted to this membranal fraction (11). In the present study, we suggest a different path taken by pLHCP from its insertion into thylakoids until its arrival to grana-lamellae where it is assembled into the pigmented LHCIIb complex.

2. PROCEDURE

2.1. Barley (Hordeum vulgare L. cv. Naomi) seedlings were grown in vermiculite and thylakoids were isolated and fractionated into grana- and stroma-lamellae as described in Ref (13).

2.2. The ab30 gene of Lemna gibba cloned in psp65 was in vitro expressed as described in Ref (14,15).

2.3. The pLHCP was inserted into isolated thylakoids in an in vitro system described in Ref (9,10,13,15).

2.4. Chlorophyll and protein deteminations were carried out according to standard methods described before (16). The thylakoid proteins were analyzed by fully denaturing PAGE (17).

3. RESULTS AND DISCUSSION

Insertion of labeled pLHCP into isolated thylakoids at 25°C followed by their fractionation into grana- and stroma-lamellae was

M. Baltscheffsky (ed.), Current Research in Photosynthesis, Vol. III, 661–664.

carried out as described in Ref (15). The proteins of these fractions were analyzed on a fully denaturing gel (Fig. 1). Most of the pLHCP that was inserted into thylakoids, was localized in the grana, while only traces were found in the stroma-lamellae. Moreover, It is likely that the precursor was inserted correctly since it was resistant to washing with NaBr (Fig. 1-b).

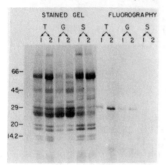

FIGURE 1. Barley thylakoids (T) were incubated with labeled pLHCP. Following incubation of 30 minutes at 25C, the thylakoids were fractionated into grana (G)- and stroma (S)-lamellae, or left intact. The three membranal fractions were then washed with either 2M NaBr (1), or buffer (2). Equal amounts of membranes from each fraction (10 μg Chl) and the translation products (tp) were analyzed by SDS-PAGE followed by protein staining (a) and fluorography (b).

Since traces of pLHCP were found in stroma-lamellae it was tempting to determine the capability of purified grana- and stroma-lamellae to insert the precursor. Isolated thylakoids were therefore fractionated into their grana- and stoma-lamellae and insertion reaction was carried out with each fraction seperatly as well as with unfractionated thylakoids see Ref (13). The capability of purified grana- and stroma lamellae to insert pLHCP was similar. Both showed greater capability to insert pLHCP than unfractionated thylakoids (Fig. 2-b). The high purity of grana- and stroma-lamellae (Fig. 2-a and Ref. 13) excludes the possibility that the observations resulted from cross-contamination between the two fractions.

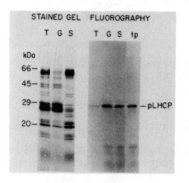

FIGURE 2. Barley thylakoids (T) were separated into grana (G) and stroma (S) lamellae and incubated seperately with labeled pLHCP. The different fractions were then washed with 2M NaBr and equal amounts of membranes (10μg of Chl) were analyzed by SDS-PAGE followed by protein staining (a) and fluorography (b)

Since grana- and stroma-lamellae demonstrated similar capability to insert pLHCP, it is unlikely that insertion in vivo is restricted to grana. Two hypothesis are possible: either the precursor inserts

into both fractions, or into stroma lamellae subsequently migrating
to grana. To determine which hypothesis is correct, we carried out
insertion of labeled pLHCP into thylakoids at 10C followed by chase
with excess of unlabeled pLHCP at 25C as described in Ref (15). The
level of pLHCP found in stroma-lamellae reduced gradually during
chase at 25C, while it gradually accumulated in grana (Fig. 3). This
indicates that the precursor was inserted into stroma-lamellae and
then migrated to grana lamellae.

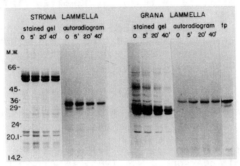

Figure 3. Insertion of labeled pLHCP into isolated thylakoids was
carried out for 30 minutes at 10C. The labeled precursor was then
chased with excess of unlabeled pLHCP at 25C. Fractions of 700 µl
were removed and fractionated into grana (G)- and stroma (S)-lamellae
immediatly after application of unlabeled precursor, zero time, or
after 10, 20, and 40 minutes. Equal amounts of the two membranal
fractions (10 µg Chl) were analyzed by SDS-PAGE followed by protein
staining (a) and fluorography (b).

It was further shown that in the stroma-lamellae pLHCP was "free" and
thus able to move to the grana thylakoids where it was found in the
monomeric and trimeric forms of the pigmented LHCIIb (15). Based on
these finding the following model is suggested, for the path taken by
pLHCP after it is translocated into the plastid (Fig. 4).

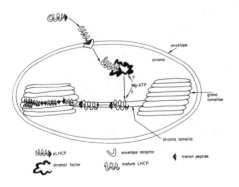

FIGURE 4. A model
describing the path taken
by pLHCP after it is
translocated into the
chloroplast.

The study presented in this paper demonstrates that the path taken by pLHCP is different than what was previously suggested (11), showing that insertion of pLHCP into thylakoids occurs mainly into the stroma-lamellae rather than being restricted to the grana. The path taken by pLHCP to the grana-lamellae is similar to that found for the 32 kDa protein of the reaction center of photosystem II. The precursor form of this protein is also inserted into stroma thylakoids where it is processed and palmitoylated before migrating to its location of activity in the grana-lamellae (18).

AKNOWLEDGEMENT. The research described here was supported by a grant from The Bat-Sheva de-Rothchild Foundation to R. Nechushtai. We would like to thank Prof. E. Tobin from The Department of Biology, University of Califonia, Los-Angeles, CA, for her kind gift of the ab30 gene.

REFERENCES
1 Thornber, J.P. (1986) in Enc. Plant Physiol. New Series 19, (Steahelin, L.A. and Arntzen, C.J. eds.) pp. 98-142, Springer-Verlag, Berlin
2 Bennet, J. (1983) Biochem. J. 212, 1-13
3 Andersson, B. and Anderson, J.M. (1985) in Modern Methods of Plant Analysis, New Series I, (Linskens, H.F. and Jackson J.F. eds.) pp. 231-258, Springer-Verlag, Berlin
4 Dunsmuir, P. Smith, S.M. and Bedbrook, J. (1983) J. Mol. Appl. Genet. 2, 285-300
5 Grossman, A. Bartlett, S. and Chua, N-H. (1980) Nature (Lond.) 285, 625-628
6 Schmidt, G.W. Bartlett, S.G. Grossman, A.R. Cashmore, A.R. and Chua, N-H. (1981) J. Cell Biol. 91, 468-478
7 Chitnis, P.R. Thornber, J.P. (1988) Photosynthesis Res. 16, 41-63
8 Chitnis, P.R. Morishige, D.T. Nechushtai, R. and Thornber, J.P. (1988) Plant Mol. Biol. 11, 95-107
9 Chitnis, P.R. Nechushtai, R. Harel, E. and Thornber, J.P. (1987) in Progress in Photosynthesis Research, IV, (Biggins,J.ed.) pp. 573- 576, Martinus Nijhoff, Dordrecht
10 Chitnis, P.R. Nechushtai, R. and Thornber, J.P. (1987) Plant Mol. Biol. 10, 3-11
11 Cline, K. (1988) Plant Physiol. 86, 1120-1126
12 Fulsom, D.R. and Cline, K. (1988) Plant Physiol. 88, 1146-1153
13 Yalovsky, S. Schuster, G. Ne'eman, E. Harel, E. and Nechushtai, R. (1989) Plant Mol. Biol. Submitted
14 Kohorn, B.D. Harel, E. Chitnis, P.R. Thornber, J.P. and Tobin, E.M. (1986) J. Cell Biol. 102, 972-981
15 Yalovsky, S. and Nechushtai, R. (1989) Plant Mol. Biol. Submitted
16 Chitnis, P.R. Harel, E. Kohorn, B.D. Tobin, E.M. Thornber, J.P. (1986) J. Cell Biol. 102, 982-988
17 Laemmli, U.K. (1970) Nature (Lond.) 277, 680-685
18 Matoo, A.K. and Edelman, M. (1987) Proc. Natl. Acad. Sci. USA. 84, 1497-1501

TRANSPORT AND PROCESSING OF CYTOPLASMICALLY-SYNTHESISED THYLAKOID PROTEINS

RUTH MOULD, PETER ELDERFIELD, JAMIE SHACKLETON and COLIN ROBINSON. DEPARTMENT OF BIOLOGICAL SCIENCES, UNIVERSITY OF WARWICK, COVENTRY, CV4 7AL

1. INTRODUCTION

The biogenesis of thylakoid proteins is a complex issue since these proteins are synthesised by two distinct genetic systems. Of particular complexity and interest is the biogenesis of cytoplasmically-synthesised thylakoid lumen proteins, since these proteins must cross three membranes to reach their sites of function. Previous work on one such protein, plastocyanin, indicated that the import of this protein can be divided into two phases. Plastocyanin is initially synthesised as a precursor, which is post-translationally imported across the double-membrane envelope and processed to an intermediate form by a stromal processing peptidase, SPP. The intermediate is then transferred across the thylakoid membrane and processed by a second thylakoidal processing peptidase, TPP (1-3). TPP is an integral thylakoid membrane protein with the active site on the lumenal face of the membrane; the enzyme is located exclusively in non-appressed, "stromal" lamellae (4.5).

2. RESULTS

2.1. Biogenesis of the photosynthetic oxygen-evolving complex.

A major question arising from the plastocyanin work concerns the biogenesis of other lumenal proteins: do these undergo a similar, two-step import mechanism? We addressed this question by analysing the import and processing of two prominent lumenal proteins, the 33 kDa and 23 kDa proteins of the oxygen-evolving complex of photosystem II. These are hydrophilic proteins which are loosely attached to the lumenal face of the thylakoid membrane (6,7). Full-length clones were isolated from a wheat cDNA expression library, and the precursor proteins were expressed by in vitro transcription/translation. In collaboration with the group of R G Herrmann (Munich) we also analysed the biogenesis of the same proteins from spinach.

Figure 1 shows that the precursors of the spinach and wheat 33 kDa proteins, and wheat 23 kDa protein (pre-33 K, pre-23 K) are all processed to intermediate-size forms by partially purified pea SPP, and to the mature sizes by pea TPP. In some cases, stromal intermediate-size forms are also detected during the import of the precursors into isolated intact chloroplasts (not shown). We conclude from these data that these precursors are transported

M. Baltscheffsky (ed.), Current Research in Photosynthesis, Vol. III, 665–669.
© 1990 Kluwer Academic Publishers. Printed in the Netherlands.

into the thylakoid lumen <u>via</u> stromal processing intermediates. The pre-sequences of lumenal proteins thus appear to consist of two consecutive, separate targeting signals, specifying "envelope transfer" and "thylakoid transfer" respectively.

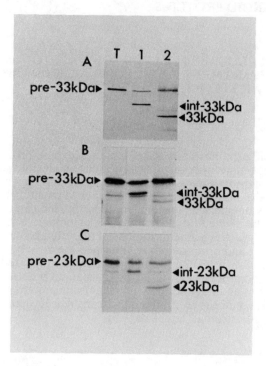

FIGURE 1. Processing of spinach pre-33 K (A) wheat pre-33 K (B) and wheat pre-23 K (C). Precursors (lanes T) were incubated with partially purified SPP (lanes 1) or TPP (lanes 2) SPP and TPP were partially purified as described (3,4).

2.2.   Reaction mechanism of TPP

Analysis of the second, thylakoid transfer domains from a number of precursors of lumenal proteins has shown that they share several common features. These include a hydrophobic "core" region, and a terminal processing site in which residues -1 and -3 are small-chain amino acids, often Ala (8). These are features which are also found in the leader (signal) peptides which direct proteins through the bacterial plasma membrane or eukaryotic endoplasmic reticulum. These similarities prompted us to compare the reaction specificities of the processing peptidases involved in the maturation of these proteins; Figure 2 shows that precursors of two higher plant thylakoid lumen proteins, pre-33 K and pre-23 K are processed to the mature size by either partially purified TPP, or purified <u>E.coli</u> leader peptidase. We have also found that TPP is capable of cleaving leader (signal) peptides of both prokaryotic and eukaryotic origin. We conclude that the reaction specificities of TPP, E.coli leader peptidase, and eukaryotic signal peptidase are identical.

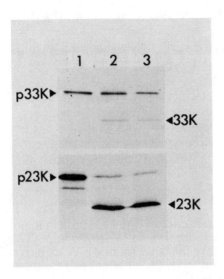

FIGURE 2. Processing of lumenal proteins by TPP and E.coli leader peptidase. Wheat pre-33 K and pre-23 K (lanes 1) were incubated with pea TPP (lanes 2) or leader peptidase (lanes 3).

2.3.   Protein import by isolated thylakoids

A detailed examination of the mechanism of protein transport across the thylakoid membrane requires an assay system in which this event can be studied independently of protein transport across the envelope. This was achieved by incubation of wheat pre-33 K with isolated pea thylakoids, stroma and ATP. Under these conditions, pre-33 K is processed to the intermediate form by SPP and mature size 33 K protein appears inside the thylakoids (9). Figure 3 shows the dependence of 33 K import on the concentration of ATP added; optimal import is achieved with ca. 10 mM ATP. Under these conditions, a significant proportion of the 33 K translation product is imported into the thylakoids (probably as the intermediate) and processed to the mature size. The mature 33 K is resistant to protease digestion of the thylakoids after the import incubation.

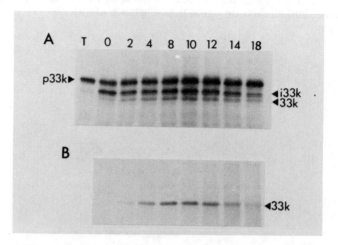

FIGURE 3. ATP-dependence of thylakoid protein import pre-33 K was incubated with thylakoids, stroma and ATP at concentrations given above the lanes (in mM). After incubation, samples were analysed directly (A) or after protease treatment of the thylakoids (B).

More recent results have shown that efficient import of pre-33 K and pre-23 K can be achieved in the absence of added ATP if the incubation mixtures are illuminated in suitable buffer conditions in the presence of stromal extracts.

3.   SUMMARY

Nuclear-encoded thylakoid lumen proteins are imported by a complex pathway involving the operation of two protein translocation systems and two distinct processing peptidases. All of these elements of the import pathway can now be assayed and studied independently, and future work will aim to probe the mechanisms involved at each stage. It will be particularly interesting to determine how closely the thylakoidal protein import/maturation system resembles the well-studied E.coli system, since the emerging evidence suggests that this a prokaryotic-type system operating within a eukaryotic organelle.

REFERENCES

1.   Smeekens, S., Bauerle, C., Hageman, J., Keegstra, K. and Weisbeek, P. (1986) Cell 46, 365-375.

2.   Hageman, J., Robinson, C., Smeekens, S. and Weisbeek, P. (1986) Nature 324, 567-569.

3.   Robinson, C. and Ellis, R.J. (1984) Eur. J. Biochem. 142, 337-342.

4. Kirwin, P.M., Elderfield, P.D. and Robinson, C. (1987) J. Biol. Chem. 262, 16386-16390.

5. Kirwin, P.M., Elderfield, P.D., Williams, R.S. and Robinson, C. (1988) J. Biol. Chem. 263, 18128-18132.

6. Miyao, M. and Murata, N. (1985) FEBS Lett. 180, 303-308.

7. Andersson, B., Larsson, C., Jansson, C., Ljungberg, U. and Akerlund, H.E. (1984) Biochim. Biophys. Acta 766, 21-28.

8. Von Heijne, G., Steppuhn, J. and Herrmann, R.G. (1989) Eur. J. Biochem. 180, 535-545.

9. Kirwin, P.M., Meadows, J.W., Shackleton, J.B., Musgrove, J.E., Elderfield, P.D., Mould, R., Hay, N.A. and Robinson, C. (1989) EMBO J. 8, 2251-2255.

MOLECULAR CHAPERONES AND CHLOROPLAST BIOGENESIS

R.JOHN ELLIS, SASKIA VAN DER VIES AND SHARON ALLDRICK,
DEPARTMENT OF BIOLOGICAL SCIENCES, UNIVERSITY OF WARWICK,
COVENTRY, U.K. CV4 7AL

1. INTRODUCTION
    It is now two years since it was first proposed that
many cellular processes require the mediation of a family
of proteins termed molecular chaperones (1). During these
two years evidence supporting the concept that molecular
chaperones mediate universal cellular functions has grown
(2-4). More and more proteins are being identified which
carry out chaperone roles in a growing variety of cellular
processes. In this article we briefly discuss the concept of
molecular chaperones, and speculate on their possible roles
in chloroplast biogenesis in the hope of stimulating
research in this area. It is particularly appropriate to
discuss the chaperone concept at this Congress, since its
origin springs from research on the assembly of the
photosynthetic enzyme Rubisco carried out at the University
of Warwick since 1979 (5).

2. THE MOLECULAR CHAPERONE CONCEPT
2.1 Definition
    Molecular chaperones are currently defined as
proteins which mediate the correct folding of other
proteins, and in some cases their assembly into
oligomeric structures, but which are not components
of those final structures (3). It is proposed that the
essential function of molecular chaperones is both
to prevent the formation of incorrect structures
and to unscramble any that do occur e.g. as a result
of heat shock. The prevailing paradigm concerning
protein folding and assembly supposes that these
processes occur spontaneously without the assistance
of extrinsic factors; this paradigm is based solely
on in vitro studies (6). The normal environment most
relevant to protein folding and assembly is that
which is encountered within the cell, and it is
intuitively acceptable that folding pathways for
newly synthesized proteins may have evolved which
rely upon interactions with pre-existing proteins.
Why might this be the case?

M. Baltscheffsky (ed.), Current Research in Photosynthesis, Vol. III, 671–678.
© 1990 *Kluwer Academic Publishers. Printed in the Netherlands.*

There are a number of fundamental cellular processes which involve the transient exposure of interactive surfaces, such as charged regions or hydrophobic domains, to the environment. These processes include protein synthesis, protein transport, the operation of complexes such as those involved in DNA replication or clathrin cage formation, the assembly of organellar complexes from subunits made in more than one subcellular compartment, and recovery from stresses such as heat shock. The self-assembly hypothesis assumes that all interactions between such exposed surfaces are totally specific i.e.are both necessary and sufficient to produce the functional conformation (7). It seems more likely to us that during a given folding and assembly process there is a certain probability that non-specific interactions will occur that lead to the formation of incorrect structures that are non-functional. Where this probability is low, molecular chaperones may not be required, but where it is high, they could be obligatory for the formation of functional structures. Support for this idea comes from observations on the assembly of structures as diverse as nucleosomes, phage particles and oligomeric enzymes such as Rubisco, where incorrect structures form in the absence of extrinsic factors (3). It is the extrinsic factor nucleoplasmin, required for the correct assembly of nucleosomes, for which the term ' molecular chaperone' was first proposed (8). Recent findings made in our own and other laboratories prompted our suggestion that this term be extended to a wider range of proteins (1,3).

2.2   Mode of action

The term 'molecular chaperone' is appropriate to describe the action of this group of proteins because the traditional role of the human chaperone, if described in biochemical terms, is both to prevent improper interactions between potentially complementary surfaces and to disrupt any improper liaisons that do occur. Our present limited knowledge suggests that known chaperones do not possess steric information, any more than the human chaperone does. Rather their function appears to be to inhibit unproductive folding and assembly pathways. The role we propose for molecular chaperones is thus a subtle one, and can best be described as assisting self-assembly. Nothing is known about how chaperones identify the relevant interactive surfaces, but recognition is followed by non-covalent binding. In some cases e.g. Rubisco assembly, this binding is reversed by ATP

hydrolysis, and we imagine that in the cell this
reversal occurs under circumstances which permit
the correct folding and assembly pathways to take
place. The mode of action of molecular chaperones is
a total mystery, and the resolution of this mystery
will require the successful completion of structural
studies which have commenced in several laboratories.

2.3   Examples of molecular chaperones
Table 1 lists proteins that we regard as molecular
chaperones, together with their proposed roles. Two
recently discovered examples are of especial interest
because these chaperones are attached covalently to
the molecules whose assembly they control, viz. the
pro-sequence of subtilisin(12) and the ubiquitin
sequence present at the aminoterminus of two ribosomal
precursor proteins in yeast and other eukaryotes (13).
The advantage of these cotranslational chaperones
is that they can bind their ligands without requiring
a specific recognition site in these ligands.

TABLE 1.Molecular chaperones

Name	Proposed roles	Reference
1.Nucleoplasmins	Nucleosome assembly Transcription?	8,9
2.Chaperonins	Protein folding Oligomer assembly Protein transport DNA replication? mRNA turnover?	2,3
3.BiP - hsp 70	Protein transport Oligomer assembly Oligomer disassembly	2,3,10
4.SRP	Protein transport	11
5.Pro-sequence	Subtilisin folding	12
6.Ubiquitinated ribosomal proteins	Ribosomal assembly in eukaryotes	13
7.Trigger factor	Protein transport	14
8.SecB protein	Protein transport	14,15

In the remainder of this article we discuss the chaperones
most relevant to chloroplast biogenesis - the chaperonins.

3.   THE CHAPERONINS
3.1   Properties
      The chaperonins are defined as a group of sequence-
      related molecular chaperones found in all bacteria,
      mitochondria and plastids (4). Table 2 lists some
      of the properties of the chaperonins. They are all
      abundant constitutive proteins that increase in
      amount after heat shock. In the case of E.coli and
      S.cerevisiae they are essential for cell viability at
      all temperatures. The bacterial chaperonins are major
      immunogens in human bacterial diseases because of
      their accumulation during the stress of infection.

TABLE 2. Some properties of the chaperonins

Origin	Name	Subunit Mr	Oligomer
Bacteria	groEL	57,259 (E.coli)	14-mer
	65 kDa antigen	56,686 (M.leprae)	
	groES	10,368 (E.coli)	6 to 8-mer
Mitochondria	hsp 60	60,830 (yeast)	14-mer
	mitonin or		
	HuCha60	57,939 (human)	
Plastids	Rubisco subunit		
	binding protein:		14-mer
	alpha subunit	57,393 (wheat)	
	beta subunit	56,453 (rape)	

References: groEL,(16); 65 kDa antigen,(17); groES,(18);
            hsp 60,(19,20); HuCha60,(21); Rubisco subunit
            binding protein,(3-5).

      There are two types of chaperonin that we term large
      and small. The large members have Mr values in the
      range 56-61,000 with amino acid sequence identities
      in the range 43-54%. The small chaperonins (Mr about
      10,000) have so far been found only in bacteria, but
      since all the evidence suggests that the large and
      small chaperonins function together in bacteria, it
      is probable that homologues to the groES protein
      occur in mitochondria and plastids. The large plastid
      chaperonin, like the other large chaperonins, occurs
      as a 14-mer in crude extracts. When this oligomer is
      purified to homogeneity and analysed on denaturing
      polyacrylamide gels, two similar polypeptides are
      resolved termed alpha and beta, which show 50% amino
      acid sequence identity. It is not yet clear whether
      alpha and beta subunits occur also in the bacterial
      and mitochondrial chaperonins. Genes for the alpha

and beta subunits of the plastid chaperonin from
Pisum sativum have been cloned and are currently
being sequenced (S.P.Alldrick and R.J.Ellis,
unpublished).

3.2   Functions
The best-studied chaperonin is the product of the
groEL gene in E.coli. This protein, together with
the smaller chaperonin (groES) encoded in the same
operon, were first identified as bacterial products
required for the assembly of the head of phage lambda
and T4 and the tail of phage T5. The role of these
proteins in the case of phage lambda is to mediate
the assembly of the oligomeric structure which joins
the head to the tail of the phage (16). But what is
the role of these proteins in the uninfected bacterial
cell? Increasing evidence suggests that these proteins
serve multifunctional roles in bacteria, and by
extension in mitochondria and plastids as well. These
roles include protein folding, the assembly of
oligomers, transport across membranes, DNA replication,
mRNA turnover and recovery from stress. Table 3
summarises the evidence for the roles of the
chaperonins in bacteria, mitochondria and plastids.
There is good evidence that the mitochondrial
chaperonin is required for the assembly of complexes
such as ATP synthase in yeast, while the evidence that
the plastid chaperonin is required to mediate the
assembly of Rubisco has improved recently. The query
marks in Table 3 represent areas where published
evidence is currently lacking, but we predict that
these will be replaced by affirmation marks in most
cases.

TABLE 3. Multifunctional roles of the chaperonins

Role	Bacteria	Mitochondria	Plastids
Protein folding	?	?	?
Oligomer assembly	Yes (16)	Yes (20)	Yes (5)
Protein transport	Yes (14,22)	?	Yes (27)
DNA replication	Yes (23)	?	?
Stress response	Yes (24)	Yes (26)	Yes (28)
mRNA turnover	Yes (25)	?	?

Numbers in brackets indicate the relevant references.

3.3   A potential reversed nucleotide binding site
        The plastid and bacterial chaperonins respond to
        added MgATP by releasing the bound ligand as the ATP
        is hydrolysed, and in the case of the plastid
        chaperonin by also dissociating into the monomeric
        subunits (5). Searches for known consensus sequences
        involved in the binding of ATP were unsuccessful.
        However a good match to the dinucleotide binding site
        consensus sequence of Wierenga et al (29) is seen in
        all the available chaperonin sequences provided the
        comparison is made by scanning the latter from the
        carboxyterminus to the aminoterminus (Table 4).
        This remarkable finding raises the possibility that
        a given binding site can be constructed from the same
        set of amino acid residues running in either direction
        along the polypeptide chain; this possibility is
        currently being tested for the chaperonins. Moreover
        this observation suggests that searches for consensus
        sequences in proteins, e.g. for active sites, should
        be run in both directions in case this phenomenon has
        a more general occurrence.

TABLE 4.   A potential reversed nucleotide binding site

```
                                                              N
                         C C            C C           C  CQ
     Reversed            M M            M M           M  MT
     dinucleotide        V V            V V           V  VS
     binding             L L            L L           L  LH
     site             E  I I            I I           I  IR
     consensus        D  A A            A A      G  G G A  AK
     (29)            C36.................................1 N
                        *  *  ^        *   *      *   * * * **
     M1  N VLKVGGTSDVEVNEKKDRVTDALNATRAAVEEGIVLGGGCALLRCIPALDSC
     M2    VIRVGGASEVEVGEKKDRYDDALFATRAAVEEGILPGGGTALVKASRVLDE

     P1    VIKVGAATEVEMKEKKARVEDALHATRAAVEEGVVAGGGVALIRVASKLAD
     P2    VIKAGAATEVELKERKHRIEDAVRNAKAAVEEGIVAGGGVTLLQAAPALDK
     P3    VIKAGAATEVELKERKHRIEDAVRNAKAAVEEGIVAGGGVTLLQAAPTLDE
     P4    VIKVGAATEVEMKEKKARVEDALHATRAAVEEGVVPGGGVALIRVLKSLDS

     C1    VIKVGAATETELEDRKLRIEDAKNATFAAIEEGIVPGGGAALVHLSTVVPA
     C2    VIKVGATTETELEDRQLRIEDAKNATFAAIEEGIVPGGGAAYVHLSTYVPA
     C3    VIKVGAATETELEDRKLRIEDAKNATFAAIEEGIVPGGGATLVHLSTVIPA
     C4    VIQVGAQTETELKEKKLRVEDALNATKAAVEEGIVVGGGCTLMCLASKVDA
```

Symbols for chaperonins: mitochondria, human (M1), yeast
(M2); bacteria, Mycobacterium leprae (P1), Mycobacterium
tubercolosis (P2), E.coli (P3), Coxiella burnetii (P4);
plastid, Ricinus communis leucoplast (C1), Triticum
aestivum chloroplast alpha (C2), Brassica napus chloroplast
alpha (C3), Brassica napus chloroplast beta (C4). The
Brassica sequences are by courtesy of S.M.Hemmingsen.

.   POSSIBLE ROLES OF MOLECULAR CHAPERONES IN THE
    BIOGENESIS OF CHLOROPLASTS
    The concept of molecular chaperones carries
    implications for those researchers studying the
    biogenesis of chloroplasts. It is obvious that all the
    processes believed to be mediated by the chaperonin
    group occur in plastids (Table 3), but evidence
    of the involvement of the chaperonins in some of these
    processes is lacking for the chloroplast. It is
    likely in our view that the plastid chaperonins, as
    well as other as yet unidentified chaperones, are
    involved in mediating the folding of those proteins
    which are made by chloroplast ribosomes, but which
    are not subsequently assembled into oligomers or
    transported across the thylakoid membrane. Indeed,
    the control of the folding of proteins during their
    synthesis may well be the basic function of all
    chaperones, but evidence on this point is lacking for
    chloroplasts, as well as for bacteria and mitochondria.
    The role of the bacterial chaperonin in DNA replication
    and mRNA turnover suggests functions in the analogous
    processes in chloroplasts. The function of the
    mitochondrial chaperonin in mediating the assembly
    of membrane complexes such as ATP synthase suggests
    that it could be worth searching for similar roles
    in chloroplasts. Protein transport both into and
    within the thylakoid lumen is another promising area
    where chaperones are likely to be involved, especially
    because thylakoid proteins are inserted into non-
    appressed lamellae but some then travel laterally
    within the thylakoid lumen to the appressed regions
    (30).

    The best way to look for chaperones is to search for
    proteins that are transiently associated with the
    early steps of the process under study. In many cases,
    but not all, the chaperone is attached to its protein
    ligand by non-covalent bonds so that non-denaturing
    techniques should be used in the search for such
    associations. Where genetic approaches are possible i.e.
    in Chlamydomonas or in transgenic plants, strains
    carrying mutations in the chaperone genes or
    antisense constructs could be used to examine the
    consequences for chloroplast biogenesis.

EFERENCES
    Ellis,R.J. (1987) Nature 328, 378-79
    Ellis,R.J., van der Vies,S.M. and Hemmingsen,S.M.(1989)
    Biochem.Soc.Symp. 55, 145-153
    Ellis,R.J. and Hemmingsen,S.M.(1989) Trends in Biochem.
    Sci. 14, 339-343

4   Hemmingsen,S.M., Woolford,C., van der Vies,S.M., Tilly,K. Dennis,D.T., Georgopoulos,C.P., Hendrix,R.W. and Ellis, R.J. (1988) Nature 333, 330-334
5   Ellis,R.J. and van der Vies,S.M. (1988) Photosyn.Res. 16, 101-115
6   Creighton,T.E. (1984) in Proteins, p.312, W.H.Freeman
7   Pain,R. (1987) Trends in Biochem.Sci. 12, 309-312
8   Laskey,R.A.,Honda,B.M., Mills,A.P. and Finch,J.T. (1978) Nature 275, 416-420
9   Dilworth,S.M. and Dingwall,C. (1988) Bioessays 9,44-49
10 Pelham,H.R.B. (1986) Cell 46,959-961; (1986) Nature 332, 776-777
11 Walter,P. and Lingappa,V.R. (1986) Ann.Rev.Cell Biol. 2, 499-516
12 Zhu,X., Ohta,Y., Jordan,F. and Inouye,M. (1989) Nature 339, 483-484
13 Finley,D., Bartel,B. and Varshavsky,A. (1989) Nature 338,394-401
14 Lecker,S. et al, (1989) manuscript submitted
15 Weiss,J.B., Ray,P.H. and Bassford,P.J. (1988) Proc. Natl.Acad.Sci.USA 85, 8978-8982
16 Kochan,J. and Murialdo,H. (1983) Virology 131,100-115
17 Young,D. et al, (1988) Proc.Natl.Acad.Sci.USA 85,4267-70
18 Chandrasekhar,G.N. et al (1986) J.Biol.Chem.261, 12414-19
19 Reading,D.S., Hallberg,R.L. and Myers,A.M. (1989) Nature 337, 655-659
20 Cheng,M.Y. et al, (1989) Nature 337, 620-625
21 Jindal,S. et al (1989) Mol.Cell.Biol. 9,2279-2283
22 Bochkareva,E.S., Lissin,N.M. and Girshovich,A.S. (1988) Nature 336, 254-257
23 Jenkins,A.J. et al, (1986) Molec.Gen.Genet. 202, 446-454
24 Lindquist,S.(1986) Ann.Rev.Biochem. 55, 1151-1191
25 Chanda,P.K. et al, (1985) J.Bact. 161, 446-449
26 McMullin,T.W. and Hallberg,R.L. (1987) Mol.Cell Biol. 7, 4414-4423
27 A.A.Gatenby (personal communication)
28 E.Vierling and S.M. Hemmingsen (personal commmunication)
29 Wierenga,R.K., Terpstra,P. and Hol,W.G.J. (1986) J.Mol.Biol. 187,101-107
30 Anderson,J.M. and Andersson, B. (1988) Trends in Biochem. Sci. 13,351-355

ACKNOWLEDGEMENTS   Thanks are due to the Science and Engineering Research Council for financial support.

INFLUENCE OF 5-AMINOLEVULINATE AND COMPLEXING AGENTS UPON CHLOROPHYLL ACCUMULATION

URSULA KITTSTEINER[1], AGNIESZKA MOSTOWSKA[2], HEIKE MALINOWSKI[1] AND WOLFHART RÜDIGER[1]

[1]Botanisches Institut, Universität München, 8000 München 19, FRG; [2]Department of Plant Physiology II, University of Warsaw, 00-927 Warsaw, Poland

INTRODUCTION

Increased accumulation of chlorophyll precursors in dark-grown angiosperms cannot only be observed after feeding plants with 5-aminolevulinate (ALA) but also with complexing agents like 1,10-phenanthroline (Phe), 2,2`-bipyridyl (2;2) or 8-hydroxyquinoline (8H) (see 2, 4, 10, 12). As one explanation, the lack of heme formation due to complexation of iron ions has been discussed; this leads to missing feed-back inhibition by heme of the tetrapyrrole pathway. Several authors found a requirement for iron in enzymic steps of chlorophyll synthesis, e.g. coproporphyrinogenase reaction (6), conversion of magnesium protoporphyrin monomethyl ester to protochlorophyllide (pchlide) (13), and esterification of chlorophyllide (chlide) (9). In combination, these points explain the increased accumulation of chlorophyll precursors in the dark as well as the reduced rate of greening in the light. This effect is analysed in more detail in pretreated cress seedlings.

MATERIALS AND METHODS

Seeds of *Lepidium sativum* L. were sown in petri dishes on wet filter paper and germinated for 3,5 days in darkness at 25°C. Seedlings were incubated under green dim light with ALA [5mM], Phe [2mM], 2;2 [2mM] and 8H [3mM] for 12h and 17h, respectively. The treated plants were illuminated with white light. Continuous incandescent light (2h and 12h) was obtained from fluorescent tubes with an intensity of 5 W/m^2 at the height of the leaves. A photographic flash lamp (Metz Mecablitz) was used in the experiments concerning photoconversion and esterification. For pigment analysis the cotyledons were cut by razor-blades and immediately frozen in liquid nitrogen. Analysis and calculation of pigment content were performed according to (3). The concentration of total carotenoids was determined at their main absorbancy after deduction of the relative absorption of pchl(ide) and chlorophyll a and b (chl a, chl b), respectively (7). Light-harvesting chlorophyll a/b protein (LHCP) was detected by SDS gel electrophoresis of the membrane fraction and immunoblotting.

M. Baltscheffsky (ed.), Current Research in Photosynthesis, Vol. III, 679–682.

RESULTS

After a dark pretreatment with ALA or metal chelators etiolated cress plants show an increase of pchl(ide) synthesis under our experimental conditions to 214% (ALA), 119% (Phe), 146% (2;2) and 136% (8H) of the water control (Fig.2). The chlorophyll content of ALA-fed seedlings is found to be diminished (80% chl a, 43% chl b of water control) after exposure to white light for 12h. A similar, but stronger effect can be seen after incubation with metal chelators (Fig.1). The reduced rate of greening concerns chl b to the same extent as chl a, but not carotenoids (see Table I).

Tab.I: Pigment analysis of cress cotyledons after incubation with various compounds. 0h = immediately after dark incubation, 2h and 12h = after irradiation for 2h and 12h. Percentages are related to water dark control (100% = 30.4 µg/g fw).

Com-	total carotenoids [%] after			chla+b/car	chl a/b
pound	0 h	2 h	12 h	12 h	12 h
H$_2$O	100	141	147	2.2	3.9
ALA	102	125	146	1.6	7.1
Phe	112	116	126	0.9	4.6
2;2	106	120	155	0.1	–
8H	103	110	139	0.4	4.2

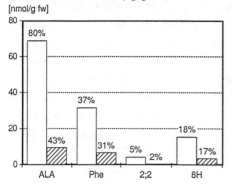

Fig.1: Pigment analysis after 12h light; H$_2$O control [nmol/g fw]: chl a 86.8; chl b 22.2; □ chl a; ▨ chl b;

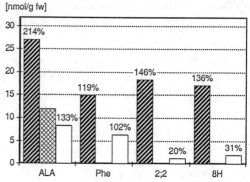

Fig.2: Pigment analysis dark/2h light; H$_2$O control [nmol/g fw]: pchl(ide)/dark 12.7; chl a/2h light 6.3; ▨ pchl(ide)/dark; ▨ pchl(ide)/2h light; □ chl a/2h light;

Fig.2 shows the situation after 2h illumination in more detail. Nonphotoconverted pchl(ide) is only observed in ALA-treated plants. Apparent loss of chlorophyll occurs after pretreatment with 2;2 and 8H (80% and 70%, respectively), but not with Phe.

Pigments could directly be detected in intact seedlings by fluorescence microscopy. Intensity of red fluorescence in the cotyledons coincides with accumulation of chlorophyll precursors in the dark and disappearance after 2h irradiation (see Fig.2). The site of photodynamic damage, however, does not coincide with the place of accumulation of red fluorescence: We find a typical turgor loss in the upper part of hypocotyl after prolonged illumination of cress plants which were preincubated with 2,2 or Phe. No loss of turgor or other cell damage can be observed in the cotyledons.

Flash irradiation of intact seedlings and gathered cotyledons (Fig.3) reveals that photoconversion of preincubated cress does not differ considerably from that of controls. Esterification, however, shows remarkable decrease. Only about 30% of chlide were transformed to chl a after 2;2- and 8H-treatment. Control plants present about 90% esterified chlide within the same period (60 min). The total pigment content after flash irradiation of detached cotyledons (Fig.4) does not significantly change in this time range, so that an increased turnover of newly formed or esterified chlide due to preincubation with chelators can be excluded. Pchl(ide) levels are also determined to be rather constant during the dark period after flash light. This can be explained that reaccumulation of pchl(ide) is slow in garden cress or that a putative degradation of pchl(ide) is compensated by its *de novo* synthesis.

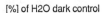

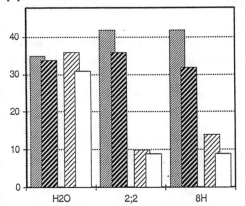

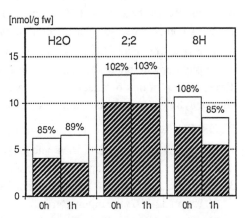

Fig.3: Photoconversion of gathered cotyledons (▨) and intact plants (▨); esterification of gathered cotyledons (▨) and intact plants (□); percentages are related to H2O dark control: 7.4 nmol/g fw pchl(ide)

Fig.4: Total pigment content after flash irradiation of gathered cotyledons related to corresponding dark control (pchl(ide) in nmol/g fw): H2O: 7.4; 2;2: 12.8; 8H: 9.9;
□ photoconverted,
▨ nonphotoconverted;

Fig.5: Western Blot of LHCP. In addition to pigment analysis, we tested cress plants for presence of LHCP after 12h irradiation. LHCP levels decreased after incubation with complexing agents. This seems to be in parallel with the chlorophyll content (Fig.1) after the same illumination time.

H2O ALA Phe 2;2 8H

DISCUSSION

Etiolated cress seedlings incubated with ALA or chelators confirm the increase of pchl(ide) (Fig.2) in the dark (2, 12). In accordance to earlier data (1), the chlorophyll content of ALA-fed plants is slightly higher in the lag phase of chlorophyll synthesis (2h light), whereas after 12h illumination (Fig.1) the chlorophyll content is diminished (14).

The effect of chelators in the light is known to inhibit chlorophyll synthesis (5). We corroborate and extent the observation of (9) that one possible site of inhibition of chlorophyll synthesis is the esterification of chlide. We do not agree, however, with (9) that chlorophyllase is the attacked enzyme. According to (11), chlorophyll synthetase is responsible for phytylation of chlide. Here we report the first evidence that esterification of chlide is a real target of metal chelator action.

Chloroplast protein levels in iron-deficient plants were examined by (8). Reduction of chlorophyll-protein complexes was interpreted to be typical for iron deficiency. We confirm the reduction in the case of LHCP levels (Fig.6) after incubation of etiolated cress with chelating compounds and subsequent illumination.

In summary, treatment of cress seedlings with chelators leads to increased accumulation of chlorophyll precursors in the dark, but decreased accumulation of chlorophylls in the light. Two possible points of attack are indicated by the present results: decreased activity of chlorophyll synthetase and diminished accumulation of chlorophyll proteins, e.g. LHCP.

REFERENCES

1   Castelfranco, P.A., Rich, P.M. and Beale, S.I. (1974). Plant Physiol. 53, 615-618
2   Duggan, J.and Gassman, M. (1974). Plant Physiol. 53, 206-215
3   French, C.S. (1960) in "Handbuch der Pflanzenphysiologie" (W. Ruhland, Ed.), Bd. V/1, pp.252-297, Springer, Berlin
4   Granick, S. (1959). Plant Physiol. 34, XVIII
5   Hendry, G.A.F. and Stobart, A.K. (1978). Phytochemistry 17, 671-674
6   Hsu, W.P. and Miller, G.W. (1970). Biochem. J. 117, 215-220
7   Lichtenthaler, H.K. (1987). Methods Enzymol. 148, 350-382
8   Machold O.(1971). Biochim. Biophys. Acta 238, 324-331
9   Rao, S.R., Sainis J.K. and Sane P.V. (1981). Phytochemistry 20, 2683-2686
10 Rebeiz, C.A., Montazer-Zouhoor, A., Hopen, H.J. and Wu, S.M. (1984). Enzyme Microb. Technol. 6, 390-401
11 Rüdiger W., Benz, J. and Guthoff, C. (1980). Eur. J. Biochem. 109, 193-200
12 Ryberg M. and Sundqvist C. (1976). Physiol. Plant. 36, 356-361
13 Spiller, S.C., Castelfranco, A.M. and Castelfranco, P.A. (1982). Plant Physiol. 69, 107-111
14 Sundqvist, C. (1969). Physiol. Plant. 22, 147-156

GABACULINE EFFECT ON CHLOROPHYLL ACCUMULATION IN Pinus nigra SEEDLINGS

GORDANA JELIĆ and MILA BOGDANOVIĆ, University of Belgrade, INEP, Department of Biotechnological Research, Banatska 31b, 11080 Zemun, Yugoslavia.

Chlorophyll accumulation in the presence of gabaculine was measured in Pinus nigra seedlings. Depending on its concentration and the stage of embryo development, gabaculine, an inhibitor of transaminases), inhibits Chl synthesis in the light. Gabaculine had no effect on Chl synthesis in the dark, even at such a concentration as 500 μM. The results suggest that, in pine seedlings, the ALA-synthetase-mediated pathway of Chl synthesis operates in the dark.

INTRODUCTION

Black pine cotyledons accumulate chlorophyll during development of intact seedlings in the light or in the dark. It may be assumed that in the case of pine seedlings, two systems for the regulation of Chl synthesis may exist, one operating in the light as in angiosperm greening tissue, and another operating in the dark (1,2,3). In order to check this assumption, gabaculine effects on the accumulation of Chl in black pine seedlings were followed up during development in the light and in the dark. Gabaculine strongly inhibits ALA formation via the five-carbon path whose efficiency is rate limiting for Chl synthesis (4,5,6).

MATERIAL AND METHODS

Seeds of Pinus nigra were soaked in distilled water at room temperature for 24 h. Whole seedlings were developed in Petri dishes with filter paper moistened in nutrient solution (7). Embryos of a designated age were incubated in the presence of gabaculine under the same light conditions as those during the development, being 12 h each day/night photoperiod, 24°C/16°C temperature, light intensity 220 μA m^{-2}s^{-1}; dark - same chamber, under Al foil. Chl was measured according to Moran (8).

RESULTS

Black pine embryos accumulate Chl when seedlings grow in the light or in the dark. Under our experimental conditions, the rate of Chl accumulation tended to change around the 7th day of development. Gabaculine slowed down Chl accumulation in the light, but had no effect in the dark (Fig. 1). The amount of Chl synthesised in GAB-treated embryos exposed to light is in agreement with that synthesised in the dark, regardless of the presence of the inhibitor.

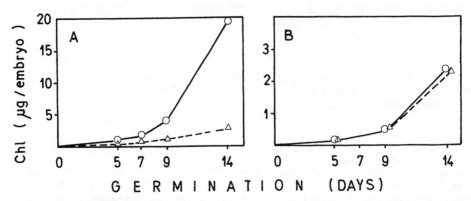

FIGURE 1 The effect of gabaculine on Chl accumulation in pine seedlings growing for 14 days (A) in the light, and (B) in the dark. O no inhibitor, △ 100 μM GAB.

Seven (eight) days old Pinus nigra embryos respond to GAB. The extent of such a response depends on GAB concentration and the length of incubation (Fig. 2A) in the light. In the dark, however, there was no Chl accumulation inhibition, even at very high GAB concentrations (500 μM) and long incubation (7 days) (Fig. 2B). Pine seedling response to GAB also depends on the stage of embryo development. A relatively stronger inhibition of Chl synthesis is likely to occur at earlier stages when synthetic processes are dominant for the rate of Chl accumulation (Fig. 3). Gabaculine, however, has no effect whatsoever, on Chl accumulation in the dark, regardless of the stage of embryo development.

When embryos were isolated from megagametophyte immediately after imbibition, and then developed in nutrient media, Chl synthesis was possible only in the light. GAB inhibits this process stronger than in the whole seedlings, which may be explained by the absence of a certain factor from megagametophyte which otherwise stimulates Chl accumulation in the embryo.

DISCUSSION
One of the points to regulate Chl synthesis is the formation of 5-ALA. GAB has been reported to inhibit Chl and phytochrome synthesis in leaf tissues and some photosynthetic cyanobacteria (5,6). In Euglena GAB would block ALA formation via the 5 carbon path in the light (4), but had no effect on ALA-dehydrogenase. In barley leaves ALA is formed by the ALA synthetase reaction only in the dark, while greening leaves utilize another pathway (9). ALA formation is the point where phytochrome regulates Chl biosynthesis in the light in Pinus silvestris, but in the dark ALA formation is not rate limiting for Chl accumulation (2).

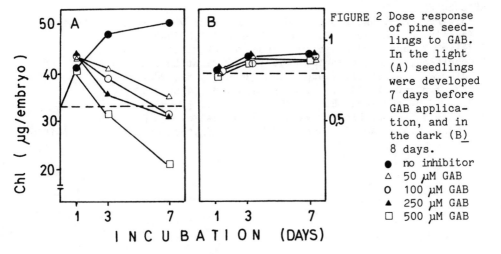

FIGURE 2 Dose response of pine seedlings to GAB. In the light (A) seedlings were developed 7 days before GAB application, and in the dark (B) 8 days.
● no inhibitor
△ 50 μM GAB
○ 100 μM GAB
▲ 250 μM GAB
□ 500 μM GAB

FIGURE 3 Influence of embryo age on GAB effect on Chl accumulation in whole pine seedlings grown in the light (□), whole seedlings grown in the dark (■), and isolated embryos developed in the light (△). Incubation was in 100 μM GAB during 72 h.

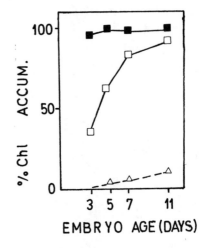

Assuming that Chl biosynthetic pathway is universal and controlled by regulators specific to different tissues, our results suggest that pine seedlings have two pathways developed for Chl synthesis. In the light they operate both, only 5-carbon path is more efficient and controlled by the phytochrome. In the dark, however, only a path via ALA synthetase would operate. It is an evolutionary older and less efficient a path whose activity is regulated by some other factors.

ACKNOWLEDGEMENTS
This study was supported by a grant from the Republic Fund for Science, Serbia.

REFERENCES
1 Wolwertz, M.R. and Brouers, M. (1980) Photosynth. Res. 1, 105-113
2 Kasemir, H. and Mohr, R. (1981) Planta 152, 369-373
3 Jelić, G. and Bogdanović, M. (1988) Plant Sci. 61, 197-202
4 Corriveau, J.L. and Beale, S.I. (1986) Plant Sci. 45, 9-17
5 Guikema, J.A. et al. (1986) Plant Physiol. 82, 280-284
6 May, T.B. et al. (1987) Plant Physiol. 84, 1309-1313
7 Reid, P.H. and York, E.T. (1958) Agron. J. 50, 63-67
8 Moran, R. (1982) Plant Physiol. 69, 1376-1381
9 Hendry, G.A.F. and Stobart, A.K. (1977) Phytochemistry 16, 1567-1570

EVIDENCE FOR A LIGHT-INDEPENDENT CHLOROPHYLL BIOSYNTHETIC PATHWAY IN ANGIOSPERM SEEDS GERMINATED IN DARKNESS.

Heather Adamson, Martin Lennon, Ke-li Ou, Nicolle Packer and Jane Walmsley. School of Biological Sciences, Macquarie University, 2109, N.S.W. Australia

1. INTRODUCTION

It is not generally recognised that during the course of evolution of seed plants, many angiosperms and gymnosperms have retained the capacity for light-independent (dark) chlorophyll (Chl)[*] synthesis exhibited by cyanobacteria, algae, bryophytes and pteridophytes (1,2,3). As a consequence the view that when greening or mature angiosperm leaves are transferred from light to darkness, Chl(ide) formation ceases immediately because of the cessation of Pch(lide) photoreduction, is still widely held (4). It is reinforced by the visual contrast between etiolated dark grown angiosperm seedlings and the bright green cotyledons of dark grown gymnosperms. This important phenotypic difference in the two groups of seed bearing plants is usually interpreted in terms of an absolute reqirement of angiosperms for light for Pch(lide) reduction, whereas in gymnosperms Chl is formed in light as well as darkness (5). In this context it is not surprising that early reports of trace amounts of Chl in dark grown angiosperm seedlings (6,7) and the accumulation of Chl by wheat embryos grafted onto pine megagametophytes (8) attracted little attention.

Since the ability of angiosperms grown in photoperiodic environments to continue synthesising Chl for hours (9) and sometimes days (10) after transfer to darkness is now well documented it is clear that the essential difference between angiosperms and gymnosperms, with respect to Chl formation, is not whether there is one (light-dependent) Chl pathway or two (light-independent and light-dependent). It is that angiosperms need to be exposed to light during development before they are able to accumulate Chl in darkness: gymnosperms do not.

The aim of this study was to check on previous reports of trace amounts of Chl in dark grown angiosperm seedlings. Are they the result of poor experimentation (light leakage) ? Do they stem from carryover of Chl from the seed? Or do they reflect limited dark synthesis of Chl in angiosperms which have not been preilluminated ?

[*] Abbreviations: ALA, amino levulinic acid; Chl, chlorophyll; Chlide, chlorophyllide; Chl(ide), Chl and Chlide; Pchlide protochlorophyllide;

2. PROCEDURE

Total darkness was achieved by growing plants (Triticum vulgare, Pinus pinea) in a specially constructed inner dark growth room separated

M. Baltscheffsky (ed.), Current Research in Photosynthesis, Vol. III, 687–690.
© 1990 *Kluwer Academic Publishers. Printed in the Netherlands.*

from the general space by a dark laboratory and two intervening light
locks. Estimates of the intensity of ambient actinic light and point
source leaks in the dark growth and work rooms were made by means of an
(S1) Photoemissive Device (I.T.T. Fort Wayne, Ind. USA) amplified
through a Rikadenki chart recorder. The device was calibrated against a
Li-Cor Integrating Quantum /Radiometer Photometer. The proportion of
actinic light was estimated as a fraction of red light in the ambient
light outside the dark room complex. Maximum Chl formation due to light
leakage was estimated from the calculated ambient actinic light
intensity in the growth and work rooms, the surface area of 5 day old
wheat shoots, an exposure time of 5 days and a theoretical yield of 2
Chlide molecules per light quantum (11). As an added precaution, wheat,
but not pine seedlings were grown in the dark room under a black cloth
which transmitted 5% of any possible incident light and were harvested
and extracted in total darkness (ie. without benefit of the Ilford 909
green safelight which was used when working with pine). Low temperature
(77°K) fluorescence emission (Ex. 443 nm) and excitation (Em. 671 nm)
spectra of pigment extracts (85% acetone into diethyl ether) were
recorded on a Perkin-Elmer MPF-44B fluorescence spectrophotometer.
Chl(ide) a and b spectra were corrected for Pchl(ide) and the pigments
estimated relative to the fluorescence intensity of Chl a and b
standards. Chl(ide) and Pchl(ide) were estimated by absorbance, when
appropriate, as previously described (3).

3. RESULTS

The light-tight quality of the dark growth room complex used for
this work is demonstrated in Table 1. Stray light was minimal and the
maximum amount of Chl(ide) which could be formed as a result of
photoreduction was well below that measured in any extracts. Wheat
seedlings grown and manipulated under these stringent conditions
contained small amounts of Chl(ide) a and b. This is evident when
typical emission and excitation ·spectra are compared with Chl a, b and
Pchl(ide) standards (Fig 1). The 677 nm peak in the extract emission
spectrum is consistent with Chl(ide) a, as is the secondary 421 nm peak
in the excitation spectrum. Due to its spectral properties Chl(ide) b
is more easily detected than Chl(ide) a and is obvious at 476nm in the
excitation spectrum. In some extracts phaeophytin is seen (417 nm in
excitation spectrum). Since at no stage during growth, harvesting and
extraction, were these seedlings exposed to light there are only two
possible explanations for these results. Either Chl(ide) was present in
the seeds and was translocated to the shoots during the dark growth
period or it was synthesised in complete darkness without any prior
exposure to light.

Table 1. Dark work and growth room specifications.

	Work room	Growth room
Actinic light ($Em^{-2}s^{-1}$)	10^{-19}	10^{-20}
Expected Chl (mol shoot^{-1})	10^{-17}	10^{-17}

Traces of Chl(ide) in ungerminated wheat seeds were not sufficient to account for the amount present in 5 day old dark grown seedlings (Tab. 2). We believe the only explanation is that Chl(ide) was synthesised via a light-independent route during germination and early growth, without prior exposure of the imbibed seeds to light. This conclusion is strengthened by the time course of Chl(ide) and Pchl(ide) changes in dark grown and dark manipulated wheat shoots following a single 60 msec light flash (Fig.2). After phototransformation of accumulated Pchlide to Chlide, the Chl a level increased 3 fold (9.7 to 27.8 p mol shoot $^{-1}$) during the interval from 1 min 30 sec to 7 min 50 sec after the flash. This can only be accounted for by reduction of Pchl(ide) by a light-independent enzyme. Evidence for such an enzyme in angiosperms has been presented previously, but only in greening tissues (2,3,12).

In contrast to dark grown wheat seedlings which contain only trace amounts of Chl(ide), dark grown pine seedlings accumulate approx 600 nmol Chl(ide) g fresh weight^{-1}.

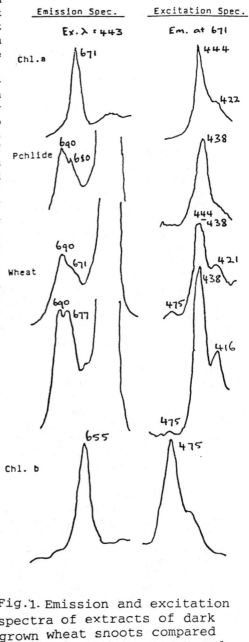

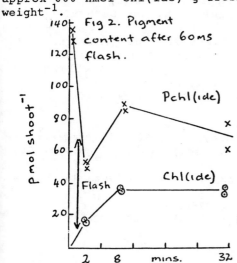

Fig 2. Pigment content after 60ms flash.

Fig. 1. Emission and excitation spectra of extracts of dark grown wheat snoots compared with chlorophyll a and b and protochlorophyllide standards.

Tab. 2. Mean Chl(ide) content (pmol shoot or seed $^{-1}$ and (SEM) of dark treated wheat, calculated from emission and excitation spectra.

	Chl(ide) a		Chl(ide) b
	Em. spec.	*Ex. spec.*	*Ex. spec.*
pmol/shoot	1.42 (0.46)	4.26 (1.37)	1.14 (0.24)
pmol/seed	0.63	-0.02	0.02

4. DISCUSSION

These findings are consistent with previous reports (6,7) of trace amounts of Chl in dark grown angiosperm seedlings. Since rigorous steps were taken to ensure the validity of our results, it is most unlikely that Chl in 5 day old dark grown wheat seedlings was due to either stray light or translocation of pre-existing Chl from the seed.The importance of this finding is that it indicates that the distinction usually made between angiosperms and gymnosperms, namely that the latter have two pathways for Chl biosynthesis while angiosperms have only one is incorrect. Since dark grown angiosperms and gymnosperms apparently contain both light dependent and light independent Pchlide reductases we suggest that the essential distinction between the two great lines of seed plants is that they have evolved different ways of regulating Chl synthesis via essentially the same pathways. This in turn, may well be linked to differences in the control of Chl accumulation.

REFERENCES
1 Castelfranco,P.A. and Beale, S.I. (1983) Ann. Rev. Plant Physiol. 34, 241-278
2 Popov, K. and Dilova, S. (1963) In Progress in Photosynthesis Research (H. Metzner, ed.), Vol. 2, pp.606-609, IUBS, Tubingen
3 Adamson, H., Griffiths, W.T., Packer, N. and Sutherland, M. (1985) Physiol. Plant. 64, 345-352
4 Kasemir, H. (1983) In Encycl. Plant Physiol. (A.Pirson, M. Zimmermann, eds.) Vol 16B, pp 662-668, Springer Verlag, Berlin
5 Kasemir, H. and Mohr, H. (1981) In Photosynthesis V Chloroplast Development (G. Akoyunoglou ed.) Balaban Sci. Serv. Phil. Pa.
6 Goodwin, R.and Owens, O. (1946) Plant Physiol. 22, 197 -200
7 Robbelen, G. (1956) Planta 47, 532-546
8 Bogdanovic, M. (1973) Physiol. Plant. 29, 17-18
9 Packer, N., Adamson, H. and Walmsley, J. (1987) in Progress in Photosynthetic Research (Biggins, J., ed.), Vol. 4, pp.487-490, Martinus Nijhoff, Dordrecht
10 Adamson, H., Hiller, R.G. and Vesk, M. (1980) Planta 150, 269-274
11 Sironval, C. (1972) Photosynthetica 6, 375-380
12 Packer, N. and Adamson, H. (1986) Physiol. Plant. 68, 222-230

PHOTOCHEMICAL RING-OPENING IN 20-CHLORO-CHLOROPHYLLS

STRUCK, A.[1], CMIEL, E.[2], SCHNEIDER, S.[2,3], and SCHEER, H.[1]
1) Botanisches Institut der Universität München, Menzinger Str. 67, D-8000 München 19, 2) Institut für Physikalische Chemie der Technischen Universität München, Lichtenbergstr. 4, D - 8046 Garching, 3) Institut für Physikalische und Theoretische Chemie der Universität, D-8520 Erlangen, FRG

1. INTRODUCTION

Chlorophyll (Chl) derivatives are readily and regiospecifically chlorinated at C-20, the free methine-bridge next to the reduced ring D (1-3). The interest in chlorinated chlorophylls has recently been renewed after their isolation from extracts of various green plants, algae and cyanobacteria (4-9) and a suggested relation to photosystem I of oxygenic photosynthesis (4, 5). This relation, and hence the involvement in photosynthesis, has been met with criticism and now been disproved (8, 10-12).

The status of 20-chloro-chlorophylls as natural pigments is still under debate (8, 12). During a systematic investigation of the chemistry of chlorinated chlorophylls, we have now observed a photochemical degradation of these pigments leading eventually to open chain tetrapyrroles, e.g. bile pigments. This raises the possibility that chlorinated chlorophylls may be components of plant tetrapyrrole degradative pathways, on which very little is known to date (13, 14).

2. MATERIALS AND METHODS

Pigments: 20-chloro-pheophorbides of the a-series have been synthesized by the method of (2) from the respective pheophorbides (6). Insertion of magnesium was done according to (15).

Photochemistry: A solution of the pigments in acetone ($5-10\mu M$) was irradiated with white light (150 W cold light source, 2 cm distance, ambient temperature). The reaction was followed spectrophotometrically. After conversion to the intermediate ($\lambda_{max} \approx 686$ nm), the solution was kept in the dark for 24 hrs and then worked up. Products were isolated by chromatography on silica gel.

^1H-*nmr spectra of the photoproduct:* A solution of 20-Cl-chlorophyll a (I) was irradiated in the nmr tube in acetone-d_6. Spectra were recorded at increasing irradiation times up to a total of 20 min.

M. Baltscheffsky (ed.), Current Research in Photosynthesis, Vol. III, 691–694.

3. RESULTS

Irradiation of 20-chloro chlorophyll a in acetone results in the progressive formation of a red-shifted pigment. In the difference spectrum,
pronounced extrema are observed at 432 and 667 nm (-) and 686 nm (+),
with a small net increase in oscillator strength in the red spectral
region, and a decrease in the Soret region. If the solution is kept in
the dark afterwards, the red-shifted absorption of the photoproduct
disappears, with a concomitant broad absorption increase in the 500-600
nm region. The oscillator strength of the red band (Q_y) is decreased
during this reaction. The spectroscopic changes upon treatment of other
20-chloro-chlorophylls were similar. By contrast, demetalated chlorinated pheophorbides, showed only a slow, irreversible bleaching.

Chromatography of the final product mixture yielded a blue pigment
showing under neutral conditions a weak, broad absorption in the red
spectral region, and more intense band around 320 nm, and no fluorescence. With acid, the red absorption band is reversibly increased, and
shifted from 590 to 696 nm, this form is very weakly fluorescent. The
pigment is unstable towards prolonged exposure to alcaline conditions.

The formation of the intermediate photoproduct was followed by *in situ*
proton nmr spectroscopy. The most informative changes occured in the
low-field region, where all signals of the photoproduct are shifted to
higher fields.

4. DISCUSSION

Structure of products: From its absorption properties, the photoproduct still appears to be a cyclic-conjugated tetrapyrrole. The nmr
spectrum indicates a reduced ring-current. Since only two methine
signals appear in both the educt and the photoproduct, the C-20 position
lacks a hydrogen substituent in the product, too. The spectra are compatible with a 20-oxonia-chlorophyll (17).

I   II

R_1 = H, R_2 = COOCH$_3$, R_3 = C$_{20}$H$_{39}$ (Phytyl)

The final product of the subsequent dark reaction is a bile pigment. The reversible changes upon protonation show the absence of a Mg-ligand, and the wavelength maxima are indicative of a dihydrobilindione (18). The spectral data are compatible with the bilin (II) obtained previously (19) in a non-photochemical reaction from chlorophyll. The ring-opening of oxa-porphyrins to bilins is well documented (20).

The only other photochemical reaction converting a chlorin to an open-chain tetrapyrrole, is the photooxygenation of the bacteriomethyl-pheophorbides c and e, which are methylated at C-20 (21,22). The common structural feature of the latter and the 20-chloro-chlorophylls is the presence of a bulky substitutent at the C-20 methine bridge, which may be responsible for the facilitated cleavage at this bridge. A noticeable difference is that in the 20-chlorinated pigments, the Mg-complexes are the reactive species, and the metal-free pheophorbides are unreactive; the situation is just opposite in the 20-methylated-pigments.

Significance to chlorophyll breakdown: Several pigments of the cyclic tetrapyrrole-type have been identified in ageing or darkened photosynthetic organisms, including chlorophyllides lacking the esterifying C-17^4 alcohol, pheophorbides lacking the central Mg, pyro-compounds lacking the 13^2 carbomethoxy-group, and pigments showing a combination of the above modifications (see 13, 14). It is unclear at present if any of them are intermediates of natural chlorophyll breakdown, e.g. in leaves before shedding in the fall. There is no chemical evidence which qualifies these pigments as intermediates preparing the macrocycle for degradation, because they are chemically or photochemically at least as stable as the parent chlorophylls, and are highly fluorescent and hence potential sensitizers for photodynamic damage.

Chlorinated chlorophylls would principally offer certain advantages. Their fluorescence yield is lower and we have now demonstrated their easy photodegradation. Chlorination is thus a chemically reasonable, preparatory step for further degradation, and chlorinating enzymes are well known from several sources (23). We, therefore, suggest to keep looking for such pigments *in situ* in spite of their negative correlation with PSI. Since chlorine-containing compounds are abundant in marine plants (24), chlorination may also be involved in the generation of bile pigments involved in bioluminescence (25).

REFERENCES:
1 Fischer,H. (1940) In Die Chemie des Pyrrols. (Edited by H. Fischer and H. Orth), Vol. II,2. Hälfte, pp. 389-397, Akademische Verlagsgesellschaft, Leipzig.
2 Woodward, R. B. and V. Skariç (1961) J. Amer. Chem. Soc. 83,4676-4677
3 Hynninen,P. H. and S. Lötjönen (1981) Tetrahedron Lett. 22,1845-1846
4 Dörnemann,D. and H. Senger (1981) FEBS Lett. 126,323-327
5 Dörnemann,D. and H. Senger (1986) Photochem. Photobiol. 43,573-582
6 Scheer,H., E. Gross, B. Nitsche, E. Cmiel, S. Schneider, W. Schäfer,

H.-M. Schiebel, and H.-R. Schulten (1986) Structure of Methylpheo-phorbide-RCI. Photochem. Photobiol. 43,559-571

7 Watanabe, T., M. Kobayashi, M. Nakazato, I. Ikegami, and T. Hiyama (1986) Progress in Photosynthesis research, Vol.1 (Edited by J. Biggins), pp. 303-306, Martinus Nijhoff, Dordrecht

8 Kobayashi,M., T. Watanabe, A. Struck, and H. Scheer (1988) FEBS Lett. 235,293-297.

9 Senge, M. and H. Senger (1988) Photochem. Photobiol. 48,711-717

10 Fajer,J., E. Fujita, H. A. Frank, B. Chadwick, D. Simpson, and K. M. Smith (1986) In Progress in Photosynthesis research, Vol.1 (Edited by J. Biggins), pp. 307-310, Martinus Nijhoff, Dordrecht.

11 Katoh,T. and K. Yasuda (1987) Plant Cell Physiol. 28, 1529-1536.

12 Senge, M., D. Dörnemann, and H. Senger (1988) FEBS Lett. 234,215-217.

13 Rüdiger,W. and S. Schoch (1989). In Chemistry and Biochemistry of plant pigments (Edited by T. W. Goodwin), pp. 1-59, Academic Press, London

14 Hendry,G. A. F., J. D. Houghton, and S. B. Brown (1987) New Phytol. 107,255-302.

15 Isenring,H. P., E. Zass, K. Smith, H. Falk, J. Louisiér, and A. Eschenmoser (1975) Helv. Chim. Acta 58,2357.

17 Fuhrhop,J.-H., P. Krüger, and W. S. Sheldrick (1977) Liebig's Ann. Chem. 1977, 339.

18 Scheer (1976) Z. Naturforsch. 31c, 413-418

19 Huster, M., S. and K. M. Smith (1988) Tetrahedron Lett. 29,5707-5710.

20 Fuhrhop,J.-H. and P. Krüger (1977) Liebig's Ann. Chem. 1977,360.

21 Brown, S.B., K.M. Smith, K.M., G.M.F. Bisset, and R.F. Troxler (1980) J. Biol. Chem. 255, 8063

22 Brockmann,H. jr. and C. Belter (1979) Z. Naturforsch. 34,127-128.

23 Champion,P. M., R. Chiang, E. Münck, P. Debrunner, and L. P. Hager (1975) Biochemistry 14,4159-4164.

24 Moore, R.E. (1978) In Marine Natural Products (Edited by P.J. Scheuer), Academic Press, New York, 44-124.

25 Shimomura, O. (1988) J. Amer. Chem. Soc. 110, 2683-2685

THE SYNTHESIS OF RADIOACTIVE PHOTOAFFINITY LABELS CONTAINING MAGNESIUM TETRAPYRROLE INTERMEDIATES OF CHLOROPHYLL AND BACTERIOCHLOROPHYLL BIOSYNTHESIS.

WILLIAM R. RICHARDS, ALAN K. BAGGOO, ANDREW J. BIRO, RATHINDRA C. BHATTACHARJEE, FREYA E. HORY, AND MUNJI S. KEBIRE, DEPARTMENT OF CHEMISTRY, SIMON FRASER UNIVERSITY, BURNABY, BRITISH COLUMBIA, CANADA V5A 1S6.

1. INTRODUCTION

The application of photoaffinity labeling techniques to a wide variety of biological tissues has increased greatly in recent years (1,2). Photoaffinity analogues of quinones have recently been employed to study the binding sites for the primary electron acceptor quinones in the photosynthetic reaction centers of a cyanobacterium (3) and *Rhodobacter sphaeroides* (4), and also the quinone binding sites in the cytochrome b-c$_1$ complex of *R. sphaeroides* (5). Similar studies have employed photoaffinity analogues of retinal to study the chromophore binding site in bacteriorhodopsin (6). Corresponding photoaffinity analogues of chlorophylls or chlorophyll precursors have not yet been reported. We have synthesized a radioactive photoaffinity label which contains the substrate of S-adenosyl-L-methionine: magnesium protoporphyrin methyltransferase (EC 2.1.1.11), an early enzyme in the magnesium branch of the biosynthetic pathways of both chlorophyll a and bacteriochlorophyll. Magnesium protoporphyrin IX (MgP) was chosen as the first affinity ligand for study because the methyltransferase has been purified (7) and its subcellular location is known in both higher plants (7,8) and photosynthetic bacteria, where it is bound to the chromatophore membrane of both *R. sphaeroides* (7) and *Rhodobacter capsulatus* (B.S. Hundle and W.R. Richards, unpublished). In this paper, we report procedures used during a pilot project for the synthesis of a small amount of the MgP-photoaffinity label. It is planned to use it with chromatophores from the parent strain, and cell membrane fractions from mutants of *R. capsulatus* unable to synthesize bacteriochlorophyll. Proteins radioactively labeled by treatment with various concentrations of the photoaffinity label will be examined by sodium dodecyl sulfate-polyacrylamide gel electrophoresis and autoradiography. The procedure for the synthesis of the photoaffinity label allows for the substitution of magnesium tetrapyrrole substrates for other enzymes of chlorophyll and bacteriochlorophyll synthesis, and a photoaffinity label containing chlorophyllide a has also been prepared for use in detection of the enzyme, chlorophyll synthetase, in higher plants (9). Other photoaffinity labels are currently in preparation.

M. Baltscheffsky (ed.), Current Research in Photosynthesis, Vol. III, 695–698.
© 1990 *Kluwer Academic Publishers. Printed in the Netherlands.*

2. METHODS AND MATERIALS

2.1. Preparation of a Photoaffinity Label Containing Magnesium
Protoporphyrin. MgP was prepared as described by Hinchigeri *et
al.* (10), and was covalently attached to Thiopropyl-Sepharose 6B
(Pharmacia) by a modification of the diazo-coupling procedure
originally developed by Suttnar *et al.* (11). The gel contained
21.5 μmol mL^{-1} of activated thiol groups, as determined by the
release of 2-thiopyridone upon treatment of the gel with 0.5 M 2-
mercaptoethanol plus 1 mM EDTA in 0.3 M NaHCO$_3$, pH 8.4. Approx.
6.5 mL of the swollen gel was reacted for 45 min with a 1.4 molar
excess (0.016 mM) cysteamine in 12 mL of 0.1 M sodium acetate, pH
4.0, containing 1 mM EDTA. Under these conditions, 14.6 μmol mL^{-1}
of 2-thiopyridone was released from the gel. Amide formation
between the bound cysteamine residues and the N-t-butoxycarbonyl
(N-t-BOC) derivative of p-aminobenzoic acid [prepared by the
method of Itoh *et al.* (12) using a 1.1 molar excess of N-(t-
butoxycarbonyl)oxyimino-2-phenylacetonitrile (Sigma) and a 1.5
molar excess of triethylamine in dioxane-water (1:1, v/v)] was
carried out as described by Sharma and Brown (13) by the careful
addition of solid 1-ethyl-3-(3-dimethylaminopropyl)carbodiimide
(Sigma) over a period of 2 h, to a final concentration of 0.1 M,
maintaining the pH between 4.5-6.0. The reaction was allowed to
proceed for another 24 h; the N-t-BOC protecting group was then
removed with 0.5 M HCl. Diazotization of the p-amino group was
accomplished in 0.3 M NaNO$_2$ in 0.5 M HCl for 7 min at 4°C.
Titration of a small amount of the gel with a solution of α-
naphthol in ethanol-water (1:1, v/v), and measurement of A_{475} due
to the formation of a red diazo pigment, indicated that 10.9 μmol
mL^{-1} of diazonium ions had formed. The diazotized gel was then
reacted with MgP in methanol-water (1:1, v/v) containing 0.4 mM
Triton X-100. Based on the reduction of the concentration of the
MgP, approx. 3.0 μmol mL^{-1} of MgP had coupled. The disulfide of
the cystamine side chain was reduced by treatment with a solution
of 0.5 M 2-mercaptoethanol plus 1 mM EDTA, 0.4 mM Triton X-100,
and 0.05 M NaHCO$_3$, pH 9.4, mixed with methanol (1:1, v/v). The
MgP-containing derivative was then eluted with the same solvent,
which was removed *in vacuo*. The side chain of the MgP derivative
was extended by reaction of the thiol group with a 25-fold molar
excess of N-(2-iodoethyl)trifluoroacetamide (Sigma) in 0.2 M Tris-
Cl, pH 8.1, containing 10 mM dithiothreitol, by the method of
Schwartz *et al.* (14). The resulting product (in which the -SH had
been extended to a -SCH$_2$CH$_2$NH$_2$ group) was absorbed onto a column
of powdered polyethylene (Polysciences), washed with distilled
water, and eluted with methanol. The final step was the reaction
of the amino group of the extended product with 0.1mM N-[*benzoate*-
3,5-^{3}H]succinimidyl-4-azidobenzoate (New England Nuclear; 1.0 Ci
mmol^{-1}) for 24 h in dioxane-0.4 M NaHCO$_3$ by the method of Galardy
et al. (15) to yield the completed photoaffinity label. The
product was purified as above by chromatography on powdered
polyethylene .

2.2. Preparation of a Photoaffinity Label Containing Chlorophyllide *a*.
Chlorophyllide *a* was prepared from chlorophyll *a* extracted from
spinach and purified by powdered sucrose column chromatography by
the method of Strain and Svec (16). An acetone powder of
chlorophyllase was prepared from spinach by the method of Tanaka
et al. (17) and used to hydrolyze the purified chlorophyll *a*. The
product was extracted with acetone:0.01 M ammonia (9:1) and washed
with n-hexane to remove unreacted chlorophyll. It was then
covalently attached to Sepharose CL-4B (Pharmacia) after
activation of the gel with CNBr by the method of Richards *et al.*
(18), followed by reaction with a solution of 0.5 mM cystamine in
0.4 M NaHCO$_3$, pH 10.0, for 12 h at 4 °C. The remainder of the
coupling procedure was identical to that used for MgP above.

3. RESULTS AND DISCUSSION

Photoaffinity labels may be classified as either endo or exo,
depending upon whether they covalently bind inside or outside the area
of affinity ligand binding. The photoaffinity label synthesized in
this work (Figure 1) is of the exo type, and consists of three parts:
(a) MgP, the specific affinity ligand (S); (b) a bridge (B), linked
(via a 4-diazo group on a benzoyl on one end of the bridge) to a *meso*-
position of the MgP; and (c) a photoreactive 4-azido group (X) and two
tritium atoms on the benzoyl on the other end of the bridge.

X	B	S
(Photochemically) reactive group	(Bridge)	(Specific) ligand

Figure 1. A photoaffinity label containing magnesium protoporphyrin IX

Several metalloporphyrins, including hemin and MgP (10), and both
magnesium and zinc 2,4-divinylpheoporphyrin a$_5$ (18), have been linked
to Sepharose gels for the affinity chromatographic purification of
enzymes of chlorophyll synthesis. The method employed for both these
and the present study was based on the diazonium ion coupling procedure of hemin to agarose columns developed by Suttnar *et al.* (11) for
the affinity chromatographic purification of serum hemopexin. The
procedure takes advantage of the reactivity of the *meso*-positions of
porphyrins and metalloporphyrins towards electrophilic substitution.
It was found that as many as 20% of the available diazonium groups had
reacted with MgP, presumably by exchange of the diazonium ion for H$^+$
on one or more of its four *meso*-positions; however, it was not
possible to know whether coupling had occurred via only one, or more

than one, diazonium ion, and also which *meso*-position(s) of the MgP had reacted (one possibility is shown in Figure 1). Based on the extinction coefficient for unaltered MgP, the yield of the penultimate product was 28.5 nmol. Compared with the spectrum of MgP, the Soret band in the spectrum of the penultimate product (in methanol) was shifted ca. 7 nm to shorter wavelengths: λ_{max} (in nm) = 412 (1.00), 547 (0.06), and 585 (0.04). The final product had a specific activity of 0.8 Ci $mmol^{-1}$. After more substantial amounts are made, it will be more thoroughly characterized and its properties investigated.

4. ACKNOWLEDGEMENTS

Supported by Grant A5060 of the NSERC of Canada. We wish to thank James Wieler for the preparation of chlorophyllide *a*.

REFERENCES

1. Bayley, H. (1983) Photogenerated Reagents in Biochemistry and Molecular Biology, Elsevier, Amsterdam.
2. Schuster, D.L., Probst, W.C., Erlich, G.E. and Singh, G. (1989) Photochem. Photobiol. 49, 785-804.
3. Satoh, K., Katoh, S., Dostatni, R., and Oettmeier, W. (1986) Biochim. Biophys. Acta 851, 202-208.
4. Theiler, R. (1986) Biol. Chem. Hoppe-Seyler 367, 1197-1208.
5. Yu, L. and Yu, C.-A. (1987) Biochemistry 26, 3658-3664.
6. Huang, K.-S., Radhakrishnan, R., Bayley, H. and Khorana, H.G. (1982) J. Biol. Chem. 257, 13616-13623.
7. Richards, W.R., Fung, M., Wessler, A.N., and Hinchigeri, S.B. (1987) *in* Progress in Photosynthesis Research, (Biggens, J., ed.), Vol. IV, pp. 475-482, Martinus Nijhoff Publ., Dordrecht.
8. Ellsworth, R.K. and Dullagham, J.P. (1972) Biochim. Biophys. Acta 268, 327-333.
9. Rüdiger, W. (1987) *in* Progress in Photosynthesis Research, (Biggens, J., ed.), Vol. IV, pp. 461-467, Martinus Nijhoff Publ., Dordrecht.
10. Hinchigeri, S.B., Chan, J.C.-S. and Richards, W.R. (1981) Photosynthetica 15, 351-359.
11. Suttnar, J., Hrkal, Z. and Vodrazka, Z. (1977) J. Chromatogr. 131, 453-457.
12. Itoh, M., Hagiwara, D. and Kamiya, T. (1975) Tetrahedron Lett. 49, 4393-4394.
13. Sharma, S.K. and Brown, S.A. (1978) J. Chromatogr. 157, 427-431.
14. Schwartz, W.E., Smith, P.K. and Royer, G.P. (1980) Anal. Biochem. 106, 43-48.
15. Galardy, R.E., Craig, L.C., Jamieson, J.D. and Printz, M.P. (1974) J. Biol. Chem. 249, 3510-3518.
16. Strain, H.H. and Svec, W.A. (1966) *in* The Chlorophylls, (Vernon, L.P. and Seely, G.R., eds.), pp. 21-66, Academic Press, New York.
17. Tanaka, K., Kakuno, T., Yamashita, J. and Horio, T. (1982) J. Biochem. (Tokyo) 92, 1763-1773.
18. Richards, W.R., Walker, C.J., and Griffiths, W.T. (1987) Photosynthetica 21, 462-471.

INHIBITION OF CAROTENOID BIOSYNTHESIS AND LHC II ASSEMBLY IN METHYL PARATHION TREATED WHEAT SEEDLINGS*

ANBUDURAI, P.R., MOORTHY, P., SIVAGURU, M., BALAKUMAR, T., JAMES, M.R. AND [2]SANTHANAM,R., [1]Unit of Stress Physiology and Plant Biochemistry, Department of Botany, The American College, Madurai 625 002, India, [2]Department of Plant Sciences, Madurai Kamaraj University, Madurai 625 021, India.

INTRODUCTION

Methyl parathion (MP) (O,O-dimethyl O-p-nitrophenyl phosphoro-thioate), a widely used organophosphorous insecticide and photosystem (PS II) inhibitor (1), inhibited the chlorophyll and carotenoid contents, photosystem II activity and LHC II accumulation. The results are discussed in terms of the amount of carotenoids and the accumulation of LHC II.

PROCEDURE

Wheat seedlings (**Triticum vulgare**) were grown at laboratory conditions, over three layers of filter paper in petri plates, in the absence (control) and in the presence of various concentrations (40,60,80,100 & 120μM) of Methyl parathion (MP). After 10 days various parameters were analysed.

RESULTS AND DISCUSSION

In wheat seedlings both total chlorophyll and carotenoid contents decreased with increase in concentration of MP treatment (Fig.1). The inhibition of carotenoid content was more as compared to the total chlorophylls. The chl a/b ratio increased gradually with increasing concentration of MP (Table 1).

The analysis of chlorophyll-protein complexes shows a drastic reduction in CP IIa and CP IIb bands (associated with LHC II) in the thylakoids of MP treated seedlings (Plate.1). The reduction in LHC II could be either due to the direct interaction of MP with the synthesis of LPC II proteins or due to the failure in the assembly of the LHC II proteins.

The increase in chl a/b ratio indicated the reduction in the amount of LHC II. The observed decrease in absorption around 685 nm indicates the reduction in chlorophyll forms associated with LHC II and PS II (Fig.2).

Supported by American College, R & D.

Baltscheffsky (ed.), Current Research in Photosynthesis, Vol. III, 699–702.
1990 Kluwer Academic Publishers. Printed in the Netherlands.

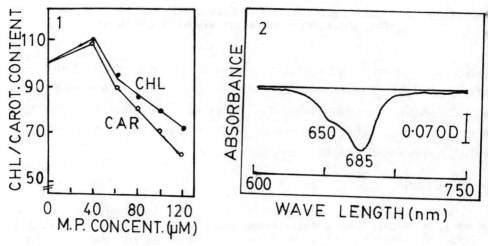

FIGURE 1. Chlorophyll and carotenoid contents in ten-day old wheat seedlings, grown in the presence of various concentrations and absence of MP. Values are expressed as percent of control. The chlorophyll and carotenoid contents were 1.25 ± 0.15 mg/g FW and 0.4 ± 0.08 n moles/g FW respectively.

FIGURE 2 Absorption difference spectrum of thylakoids of contro minus 120µM methyl parathion treated wheat seedlings.

TABLE.1. Changes in the Chl a/b ratio in control and various concentrations of MP treated plants.

Methyl Parathion concentration (µM)	Chlorophyll a/b ratio
0	2.560
40	2.600
60	2.740
80	2.750
100	2.800
120	2.810

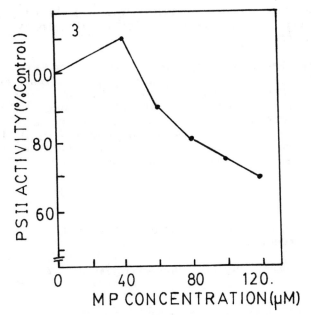

FIGURE 3. The PS II activity (DCIP reduction) in the isolated thylakoids of control and various concentrations of methyl parathion treated wheat seedlings. The DCIP reduction was measured spectrophotometrically. The control rate was 165 μ moles of DCIP reduced/mg Chl/hr.

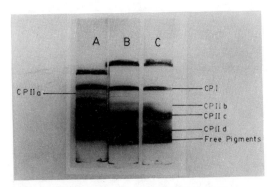

PLATE 1: POLYACRYLAMIDE GEL ELECTROPHORESIS

Analaysis of chlorophyll protein complexes in control (A), 80 (B) and 120 (C) μM methyl parathion treated seedlings.

The decrease in PS II activity ($H_2O \longrightarrow$ DCIP) (Fig.3) could be due to the decrease in the number of PS II units/chloroplast in MP treated seedlings.

In MP treated seedlings the extent of reduction in carotenoid content is more than that of the chlorophylls. As shown in the previous work (2), the drastic reduction in the carotenoid content may be the reason for the reduction in the LHC II level (functional assembly of LHC II). However, a significant decrease in the absorption around 685 nm in MP treated thylakoids reveals that the PS II unit **per se** has decreased due to MP treatment, which is evident from the decrease in PS II activity at saturating light conditions.

REFERENCES

1. Anbudurai,P.R., R.Mannar Mannan and Salil Bose (1981), **J. Biosciences, 3,** 23-25.

2. Dahlin,C.(1988), **Physiol. Plantarum, 74,** 342-348.

ACCUMULATION OF CHLOROPHYLL AND LHCP mRNA IN ETIOLATED OAT LEAVES UPON INFILTRATION OF CHLOROPHYLLIDE

SCHOCH, S., LEMPERT, U., SCHOBER, M., RUDIGER, W.
Botanisches Institut der Universität, Menzinger Str. 67,
D-8000 MÜNCHEN 19, FRG

1. INTRODUCTION

It is well known that the transformation of etioplasts into choloroplasts in higher plants is light dependent. This implicates an intimate interaction of both pigment and protein synthesis. Many plastidic membrane proteins are nucleus-encoded. One of the most prominent examples is the light-harvesting chlorophyll a/b protein (LHCP). The mRNA encoding the apoprotein of LHCP can be induced by phytochrome [1]; however, other plastid derived factor(s), in addition to phytochrome, have been discussed to be required for the accumulation of LHCP mRNA [2]. The LHCP protein fails to accumulate under conditions where LHCP mRNA is present but chlorophyll (chl) is absent or decreased [3,4]. The synthesis of chl in higher plants requires light to photoconvert protochlorophyllide (pchlide) into chlorophyllide (chlide). The last step, the enzymatic esterification to chl is light independent. The enzyme, chl synthetase, is located in the plastid [5]. Chl can also be synthesized from exogenous chlide after being infiltrated into etiolated oat leaves in darkness [6]. We took advantage of this technique in order to supply chl in the dark and thus, study the accumulation of LHCP mRNA independently from chl synthesis.

2. RESULTS

In seedlings which during the growing period were watered occasionally in green light (= green light pretreatment), twice as much chl was synthetisized from infiltrated chlide as in leaves kept in absolute darkness. The results of esterification by infiltration either by vacuum or by transpiration are the same (tab.1). The amount of ^{14}C-chl produced in leaves infiltrated with ^{14}C-labeled chlide but illuminated after dark incubations, is somewhat reduced compared to the amount of esterified pigment formed without illumination. Thus may be due to photooxidation of newly synthesized chl. Although the greening process does not appear to be inhibited in these experiments, only 0.2 - 0.4 % of the esterified pigment is derived from the infiltrated labeled chlide (tab.2).

M. Baltscheffsky (ed.), Current Research in Photosynthesis, Vol. III, 703–706.
© 1990 *Kluwer Academic Publishers. Printed in the Netherlands.*

Table 1. Esterification of infiltrated chlide. 0.5g samples of 2 cm-peaces of primary leaves of etiolated oat seedlings which had occasionally received green light (2×10^{-3} W/m^{2}s), were immersed in a solution of 100 nMol/ml chlide according to [6]. After infiltration for 5 min, the samples were incubated in the dark for various time periods (0.5-4 h). Infiltration by transpiration was supported by blowing a stream of air over the primary leaves. Chl was separated from not esterified pigments on DE 52 and calculated from absorption spectrum ($\varepsilon = 90200$). Controls were vacuum infiltrated without chlide, total incubation time 70 min.

Infiltration	green light pretreatment	number of experiments	Chlorophyll [nM/g FW]
Vacuum	+	34	3.5 +/- 1.5
Vacuum	-	7	1.3 +/- 0.4
Transpiration	-	6	1.5 +/- 0.6

Tab.2. Vacuum infiltration of ^{14}C-chlid (from labeled chlamydomonas, a gift from Prof. Ohad, Israel) into leaves grown in absolute darkness. After infiltration, the samples were incubated for 1 or 2 h in darkness, than illuminated for 16 to 18 h with white light of 3000 lux (sample 1) or 300 - 400 lux (samples 2, 3). The esterified pigment was separated on silicagel (CCl$_4$: acetone = 88:12) and calculated from absorption spectra. The recovery was more than 80 %. C = etiolated leaves were illuminated for 18 h, to the acetone extract labeled ^{14}C-chlide solution was added and proceeded as usual.

Sample	Applied pigment		Esterified pigment	Separation by TLC of labeled esterified pigment	
	activity [dpm]	chlide [nM/g FW]	[nM/g FW]	[dpm]	[nM/g FW]
1	188000	186	238	428	0.42
2	1.174000	249	304	3165	0.67
3	1.496000	332	241	3888	0.86
C	407000	4.2	278	50	<0.01

The accumulation of LHCP mRNA in leaves treated with green light is
shown in fig. 1. The results may indicate a positive effekt of vacuum
infiltration with chlide on LHCP mRNA accumulation, on the other hand,
infiltration with or wthout chlide had no effect in leaves kept in
complete darkness. It is known that phytochrome controls LHCP mRNA
accumulation in etiolated seedlings [1]. Therefore, the seedlings were
illuminated by far-red light before chlide infiltration and the leaves
kept for 3 to 6 h in the dark. Apparently, the infiltration of chlide
by transpiration does not affect LHCP mRNA levels, whereas after
vacuum infiltration LHCP mRNA pools are drastically reduced (fig. 2).

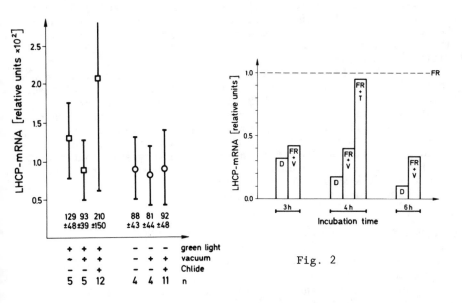

Fig. 2

Fig.1. Level of LHCP mRNA in primary leaves of etiolated oat seedlings
after infiltration of chlorophyllide. For conditions see tab 1.
LHCP mRNA was determined according to [9]. Mean values for 0.5 - 4 h
incubation after infiltration. Values are based on control experiments
where the not infiltrated leaves were incubated for 1 - 2 h. Control:
the leaves were immersed immediately in liquid nitrogen without
incubation.

Fig.2. Level of LHCP-mRNA in primary leaves of etiolated oat seedlings
after FR irradiation and followed by infiltration. Values are based on
FR irradiated leaves without infiltration = 1.0. No photoconversion
was detected under these conditions. D = dark controls, FR = 10 min
far-red irradiated leaves, V = vacuum infiltration with chlide, T =
infiltration by transpiration with chlide.

3. DISCUSSION

In agreement with data published for rye seedlings [7] we found 1-3 nM /gFW chl after chlid infiltration into etiolated oat leaves (tab.1). This corresponds to 5-20 % of the amount of chl which accumulates in vivo during the first 1-2 h after illumination of etiolated oat seedlings. The chlide esterifying enzyme chl synthetase has been localized in the inner membranes of plastids [5,8] and therefore, we assumed that at least 5-20 % of the infiltrated chlide penetrated into the inner membranes of the etioplasts. The leaves illuminated after infiltration of chlide accumulated 200-300 nM /g FW chl but only 0.2-0.4 % is derived from the labeled infiltrated chlide. Although presumably enough infiltrated chlide is available in the leaves, it is not used for further esterification (tab.2). One possible explanation is that the infiltrated chlide does not get into the plastid at all, but is esterified by an enzyme located in the cytoplasm. Plastid derived factor(s) appear to be required for the accumulation of nuclear encoded LHCP mRNA [2]. To examine whether chlide or chl could be one of these factor(s), the accumulation of LHCP mRNA was determined after infiltration of chlide. It seems that although for esterification the vacuum and transpiration infiltration were similar (tab.1), the vacuum method had an destructive effect on LHCP mRNA already accumulated after a far-red pulse (fig.2). No effect was found in leaves without previous stimulation of LHCP mRNA accumulation by phytochrome (fig.1). Thus, infiltration by transpiration rather than vacuum should be the technique of choice when studying gene expression.

REFERENCES

1. Horwitz, B.A. ,Thompson, W.F. and Briggs, W.R. (1988) Plant Physiol. 86, 299-305
2. Batschauer, A., Moesinger, E., Kreuz, K., Doerr, I. and Apel, K. (1986), Eur. J. Biochem. 154, 625-634
3. Bennett, J. (1981), Eur. J. Biochem. 118, 61-70
4. Cuming, A.C. and Bennett, J. (1981), Eur. J. Biochem. 118, 71-80
5. Rüdiger, W., Benz, J. and Guthoff, C. (1980), Eur. J. Biochem. 109, 193-200
6. Rudoi, A.B., Vezitskii, A.Y. and Shlyk, A.A. (1982) Biokhimiya 47, 733-739
7. Vezitskii, A.Y. and Walter, G. (1981), Photosynthetica 15 (1), 104-108
8. Benz, J., Hampp, R. and Ruediger, W. (1981), Planta 152 54-58
9. Paulsen, H. and Bogorad, L. (1988), Plant Physiol. 88, 1104-1109

THE COORDINATION OF SYNTHESES OF BACTERIOCHLOROPHYLL AND BACTERIOCHLOROPHYLL-BINDING PROTEINS IN *RHODOBACTER CAPSULATUS*

Debra A. Young and Barry L. Marrs, CR&D Dept., E. I. du Pont de Nemours & Co., Inc., Experimental Station, Wilmington, Delaware 19880-0173, USA

1. INTRODUCTION

Although bacteriochlorophyll (Bchl) synthesis has been studied for many years, very little is known about the mechanisms that coordinate the synthesis of Bchl with the availability of proteins to bind it. This is an important regulatory point, since Bchl is a potent sensitizer for photodynamic killing, but when Bchl is properly complexed with proteins and carotenoids that aid in the efficient conversion of excitation energy into electrochemical energy, Bchl can be safely accumulated to high levels. One obvious means of limiting the accumulation of free Bchl would be through feedback inhibition of Bchl synthesis, but Lascelles (1) was unable to find evidence for such a regulatory pathway. Lascelles eventually proposed that Bchl was synthesized as a Bchl-protein complex. We have recently revived that hypothesis as an explanation for the mode of regulation observed for a new Bchl-regulatory gene, *pufQ* (2).

2. RESULTS AND DISCUSSION

2.1 PufQ Coordinates Bchl and Bchl-binding Protein Synthesis.

Prior work has shown that there is a gene in the *puf* operon that is required for Bchl synthesis (Bauer and Marrs, 1988). Since this gene is part of the *puf* operon, it serves the function of coordinating Bchl synthesis with the synthesis of the LH-1 and reaction center proteins that are encoded by that operon. This would ensure that Bchl synthesis could not proceed in the absence of synthesis of those Bchl-binding proteins, and thus these organisms can avoid making Bchl, a dangerous photosensitizer, in the absence of proteins that can bind it in a relatively safe form.

2.2 PufQ May Act as a Mg-Tetrapyrrole Carrier Protein

Lascelles (1968) had earlier postulated that Bchl synthesis in *Rhodobacter* might require a carrier protein, and Richards, first working with Lascelles and later with his own students, showed that Bchl precursors are complexed with a 9 kDa polypeptide in mutants that are blocked in Bchl synthesis. Before the existence of the 9 kDa protein was known, the reasons for suggesting a carrier protein were that exogenous protoporphyrin IX seemed to be incorporated by cells into heme but not into Bchl and that concurrent protein synthesis was required for Bchl synthesis. Furthermore, although Lascelles could demonstrate feedback inhibition of tetrapyrrole synthesis by heme, no similar effect by Bchl or its precursors could be demonstrated.

We have suggested the hypothesis that the PufQ protein might be the carrier protein envisioned by Lascelles. The evidence supporting this is far from conclusive, but we know of no data that are inconsistent with this hypothesis.

M. Baltscheffsky (ed.), Current Research in Photosynthesis, Vol. III, 707–709.
© 1990 *Kluwer Academic Publishers. Printed in the Netherlands.*

PufQ is clearly needed for normal levels of synthesis of Bchl and all its Mg-containing precursors. We have shown that transcription of the *puf* operon and several *bch* genes are independent of the PufQ status of the cell, so we rule out transcriptional control as the mode of action for PufQ. The amount of Bchl synthesized seems to be proportional to the amount of PufQ, which is consistent with a stoichiometric role for PufQ in Bchl synthesis, but does not rule out a catalytic role if one assumes substrates are present in excess. Substrate excess is unattractive, because no tetrapyrrole is accumulated to excess in the absence of PufQ, but it is conceivable that PufQ plays a catalytic role in some related, yet unidentified, process. The amount of PufQ is controlled by oxygen tension, since it is a product of the *puf* operon that has been shown to be strongly regulated by pO_2 (Bauer et al, 1988). This is in contrast to the operons containing the known genes for Bchl synthetic enzymes, since they are only weakly regulated by oxygen.

The gene for PufQ has been sequenced (Bauer et al, 1988), and we know the molecular weight is 8,556. This is the same as the molecular weight reported by Richards et al (1975) for a protein they found complexed with Bchl precursors excreted from *Rhodobacter sphaeroides.*. Furthermore, the amino acid sequence of PufQ shows about 40% similarity to the Bchl-binding region of the reaction center genes, *pufL* and *pufM*. These bits of evidence are consistent with the proposed carrier protein role for PufQ.

An interesting property of the protein isolated by Richards et al is that when it was mixed with pure Bchl, it appeared to convert the Bchl to bacteriopheophytin (Bphe). In the next section we shall describe attempts to characterize a *pufQ*-dependent pigment-protein complex we have identified in specially constructed strains of *R. capsulatus* . Although we had anticipated a Bchl-protein complex, the material we found seems to be a Bphe-protein.

2.3　Youvan et al (1985) had examined the spectra of mutants lacking all known reaction center, light harvesting 1 and light harvesting 11 proteins, but these mutants were also lacking PufQ, so they would not have been expected to make Bchl in sufficient quantity for easy spectral detection. When we learned about PufQ, we decided to construct new strains that had deletions of the pigment-binding *puf* and *puc* genes, and see what happened when PufQ was present. The results showed the accumulation of a new pigment-protein complex, P855, in the presence of PufQ. This complex has been partially purified. It appears to contain Bphe as its only pigment. The IR absorption maximum is thus, red-shifted more than 100 nm. The Soret peak is at 384nm. The position of the IR peak is pH dependent, but is not shifted by excess dithionite or ferricyanide. The complex is easily dissociated by many detergents, releasing Bphe that absorbs at 750 nm. The complex does not appear to be membrane-associated, since it sediments through 60% sucrose. We have not yet succeeded in purifying the complex sufficiently to determine whether the protein in the complex is PufQ.

We entertain two alternative hypotheses concerning P855. We are obviously attracted to the idea that P855 might be the hypothetical PufQ-Bchl complex predicted by the carrier protein model for PufQ function. In the absence of the normal Bchl-binding proteins, this complex might be expected to accumulate in cells. On the other hand, we wonder why P855 appears to contain Bphe instead of Bchl. It seems possible that this is an artifact of accumulation, and that normally Bchl is transferred to RC and LH proteins before Mg is lost. But it also seems possible that P855 is not an accumulated precursor but rather a disposal product, which functions to sequester unused Bchl or Mg-tetrapyrroles as a protection against photodynamic killing. If we find that the protein in P855 is actually PufQ, this latter hypothesis would become unattractive, because one would not expect the absence of the waste removal system to shut down biosynthesis as observed in mutants lacking PufQ. If the protein in P855 is not PufQ, the waste disposal hypothesis might be correct.

REFERENCES

1 Lascelles, J. (1968) in Advances in Microbial Physiology (Rose, A. H., and Wilkinson, J. F., ed.), Vol. 2, pp. 1-42, Academic Press, Inc., New York

2. Bauer, C. E., and Marrs, B. L. (1988) Proc. Nat. Acad. Sci. USA. 85: 7074-7078

3. Richards, W. R. & Lascelles, J. (1969) Biochemistry, 8: 3473-3482

4. Richards, W. R., Wallace, R. B., Tsao, M. S. and Ho, E. (1975) Biochemistry , 14, 5554-5561

5. Bauer, C. E., Young, D. A., and Marrs, B. L. (1988) J. Biol. Chem. 263, 4820-4826

6. Youvan, D. C., Ismail, S. and Bylina, E. J. (1985) Gene 38, 19-30

PHYSIOLOGICAL FACTORS AFFECTING THE ACCUMULATION OF PLASTOCYANIN, CYTOCHROME c-552, AND A 30-kD SOLUBLE PROTEIN IN *Chlamydomonas reinhardtii*.

Gregg Howe*, Sally Kutsunai, and Sabeeha Merchant. Departments of Biology*, and Chemistry & Biochemistry, UCLA, Los Angeles, CA 90024.

1. INTRODUCTION

The accumulation of several proteins involved in photosynthesis is controlled by physiological factors which are generated either internally by ongoing developmental programs or externally by the environment. The dependence of photosynthesis on metal ions such as Cu, Mn, and Fe is well documented [1]. The suggestion that these ions might serve as regulators of the assembly of some components of the photosynthetic apparatus follows the early work of Wood [2] who demonstrated that, depending on the availability of Cu in the growth medium, either the Cu-protein plastocyanin (PC) or the heme-protein cytochrome c-552 of *Chlamydomonas reinhardtii* can function as electron carriers between the cyt b_6/f complex and PSI. Cells of *C. reinhardtii* supplemented with physiological concentrations of Cu accumulate PC but lack cyt c-552 (Figure 1). In Cu-deficient medium, alternatively, cyt c-552 accumulates concomitantly with a decrease in PC levels. Previously we have shown that at least two different Cu-responsive mechanisms govern the reciprocal expression of these two proteins [3]. PC accumulation is controlled at the post-translational level by a mechanism involving the rapid degradation of apoPC [4]. In contrast, the accumulation of cyt c-552 in response to Cu is managed at the level of stable cyt c-552 messenger RNA [3,5].

Here we report that the expression of cyt c-552 is controlled at the transcriptional level by Cu and that this response, which is highly specific for Cu as the regulatory ion, can be titrated by varying the ratio of available Cu per cell. We also show that the accumulation of a 30 kD soluble protein, in addition to being Cu-responsive, is regulated by other physiological factors relating to cell density/growth phase.

2. PROCEDURE

Cells were maintained in either Cu-supplemented or Cu-deficient tris-acetate-phosphate (TAP) medium as described previously [3]. Preparation and analysis of protein and RNA from *Chlamydomonas reinhardtii* have also been described [3-5]. The analysis of RNA synthesized by isolated nuclei is described by Keller et al. [6].

3. RESULTS

That the expression of PC and cyt c-552 in *Chlamydomonas reinhardtii* can be experimentally manipulated by varying the availability of Cu in the growth medium is shown in Figure 1. In experiments designed to examine the role of cell density on the cellular perception of total medium Cu we have determined

M. Baltscheffsky (ed.), Current Research in Photosynthesis, Vol. III, 711–714.
© 1990 *Kluwer Academic Publishers. Printed in the Netherlands.*

that the switch in accumulation of PC vs. cyt c-552 in *C. reinhardtii* is titratable by nanomolar concentrations of total medium Cu (3 to 300 nM) and occurs at a constant ratio of medium Cu to cells (10^6/cell; data not shown). The steady-state level of cyt c-552 mRNA decreases rapidly upon addition of Cu to Cu-deficient cells (Figure 2). This suggests a Cu-regulated control mechanism capable of modifying either the stability of the cyt c-552 message and/or the transcription rate of the cyt c-552 gene. This response was not elicited by Ag(I), a good bioelectronic analog of Cu(I) [7, 8]. The transcriptional activity of the cyt c-552 gene in nuclei isolated from cells grown in either the presence or absence of Cu show that only nuclei isolated from Cu-deficient cells are able to elongate pre-initiated cyt c-552 transcripts (Figure 3). The transcription of genes whose transcript levels are not Cu-dependent (*e.g.* PC or tubulin) is not affected by Cu. These results indicate that the expression of cyt c-552 is controlled at the level of transcript initiation.

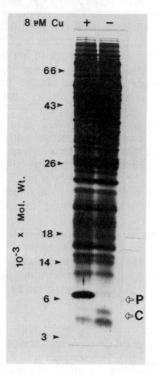

FIGURE 1. Total soluble protein from cells grown in the presence (+) or absence (-) of 8 uM CuSO$_4$ were analyzed by SDS-PAGE and visualized by silver staining. The positions of migration of plastocyanin (P) and cyt c-552 (C) are shown.

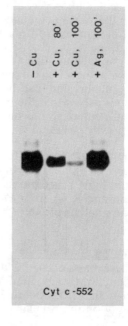

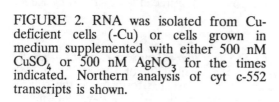

FIGURE 2. RNA was isolated from Cu-deficient cells (-Cu) or cells grown in medium supplemented with either 500 nM CuSO$_4$ or 500 nM AgNO$_3$ for the times indicated. Northern analysis of cyt c-552 transcripts is shown.

In addition to cyt c-552 we have observed other proteins which accumulate only in Cu-deficient cells. One such conspicuous example is a 30 kD polypeptide which is the product of a nuclear gene [5]. Maximal accumulation of the 30 kD polypeptide occurs in logarithmically-growing cultures maintained under Cu-deficient conditions (Figure 4). Unlike cyt c-552 accumulation, levels of the 30 kD protein in Cu-deficient cells decrease to the basal level found in Cu-supplemented cells once the cultures attain stationary phase (Figure 4). This result shows that the synthesis and/or stability of this 30 kD polypeptide is subject to regulatory physiological factors in addition to its regulation by Cu.

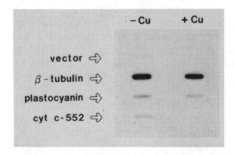

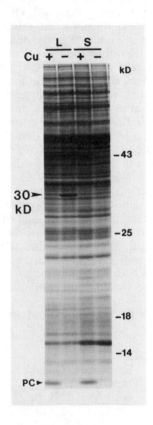

FIGURE 3. Nuclei were isolated from Cu-deficient (-Cu) or Cu-supplemented (Cu+) cells. Transcripts were elongated in the presence of ^{32}P-(C+G)TP. Hybridization of these transcripts to immobilized DNAs containing sequences for tubulin, plastocyanin, and cytochrome c-552 is shown.

FIGURE 4. Total soluble protein from cells grown in the presence (+) or absence (-) of 8 uM CuSO$_4$ was obtained from cultures in log-phase (L, ~ 10^6 cells/ml) or from the same cultures which had attained stationary-phase (S, ~10^7 cells/ml). Protein was separated by SDS-PAGE and visualized by Coomassie Blue. The positions of migration of plastocyanin (PC) and the 30 kD polypeptide are shown.

4. DISCUSSION

We have shown that the accumulation of PC, cyt c-552, and a 30 kD polypeptide is dependent on Cu availability and, in the latter case, also on cell density. We find that synthesis of PC or cyt c-552 is responsive to nM concentrations of chelated medium Cu, and that the switch between utilization of PC vs. cyt c-552 depends on the ratio of medium Cu to cells rather than on the concentration of total Cu. Northern analysis of cyt c-552 mRNA steady-state levels show that the maximal message levels observed under Cu-deficient conditions decrease rapidly in response to added Cu. Other metals tested including Ag(I) which is an electronic analog of Cu(I) are ineffective in repressing the levels of cyt c-552 mRNA. Nuclear run-on experiments further indicate that Cu-dependent decreases in the cyt c-552 mRNA levels result from decreased transcription of the cyt c-552 gene. These data taken together suggest the existence of a Cu-titratable cellular factor which can alter cyt c-552 expression by interacting with regulatory sequences on the cyt c-552 gene. To our knowledge this represents the first example of a metal-regulated plant promoter.

Recently it has been shown that Cu(I), as well as its analog Ag(I), can activate metallothionein gene transcription in yeast by binding directly the ACEI trans-activator protein [8]. Our experiments with the Ag(I) ion show that it does not appear to mimic the effect of Cu on the accumulation of cyt c-552 mRNA. This could indicate either that the active metalloregulator of the cyt c-552 gene is Cu(II) rather than Cu(I) or that the sensory molecule that responds to Cu is exquisitely specific for Cu (vs. other metals) as the regulator. This level of specificity combined with the extreme sensitivity of the response, < 100 nM total (chelated + free) Cu, suggest that the cyt c-552/Cu-response system could find practical application as a metal ion biosensor.

The finding of proteins other than cyt c-552 and PC whose accumulation is affected by Cu suggests that this ion might regulate the expression of a network of different proteins involved in Cu metabolism. We have identified a 30 kD protein that accumulates differentially in response to both Cu as well as to cell density. Whether this latter response is attributed directly to cell senescence or indirectly to other changes, e.g. shading, remains to be established. Certain features of the 30 kD polypeptide including its molecular weight and its apparent high content of cysteine and methionine as shown by its rapid labelling by ^{35}S in vivo [4] are reminiscent of the properties of the yeast mitochondrial cyt c/heme lyase [9]. We suggest that the 30 kD polypeptide might be a plastidic cyt c-552/heme lyase which catalyzes the covalent attachment of heme to apocyt c-552. We are currently purifying the 30 kD protein to test this idea and to further explore the unique regulatory controls of this protein.

This work was supported by the USDA and the Searle Scholars Program / Chicago Community Trust.

REFERENCES
1   Sandmann, G. and Boger, P. (1983) In Encylopedia of Plant Physiology New Series. Inorganic Plant Nutrition (Lauchli, A. and Bieleski, R. L., eds.) Vol. 15B, pp. 563-596.
2   Wood, P. M. (1978) Eur. J. Biochem. 87:9-19.
3   Merchant, S. and Bogorad, L. (1986) Mol. Cell. Biol. 6:462-469.
4   Merchant, S. and Bogorad, L. (1986) J. Biol. Chem. 261:15850-15853.
5   Merchant, S. and Bogorad, L. (1987) J. Biol. Chem. 262:9062-9067.
6   Keller, L. R., Schloss, J. A., Silflow, C. D., and Rosenbaum, J. L. (1984) J. Cell Biol. 98:1138-1143.
7   Winge, D. R., Nielson, K. B., Gray, W. R., and Hamer, D. H. (1985) J. Biol. Chem. 260:14464-14470.
8   Furst, P., Hu, S., Hackett, R., and Hamer, D. (1988) Cell 55:705-717.
9   Dumont, M. E., Ernst, J. F., Hampsey, D. M., and Sherman, F. (1987) EMBO J. 6:235-241.

MECHANISM AND CONTROL OF THE INACTIVATION OF CYT b6/f COMPLEXES DURING GAMETOGENESIS IN C. REINHARDTII.

Laurence Bulté and Francis-André Wollman. Institut de Biologie Physico-Chimique, 13, rue Pierre et Marie Curie, 75005 Paris, France.

Vegetative cells of C. reinhardtii differentiate in gametes upon nitrogen starvation. Crosses between gametes of opposite mating type then lead to zygote formation and subsequent meiosis.

Disappearance of cyt b6/f complexes from thylakoid membranes in gametes cells.

A major change in the organization of the photosynthetic apparatus in gametes from the WT strain of C. reinhardtii is the disappearance of cyt b6/f complexes (Fig. 1) which is completed after 60 hours in our experimental conditions.

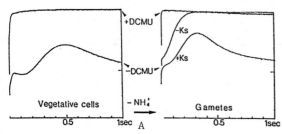

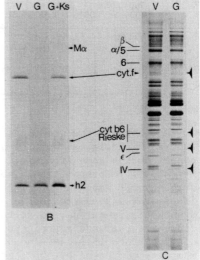

Fig. 1 : A) Fluorescence of WT gametes is similar to that of cyt b6/f mutants reaching Fmax in the absence of DCMU ; B) TMBZ staining indicates the absence of cyt f and b6 and the presence of a poorly stained band Mα ; C) the five subunits of cyt b6/f complexes (1) are lacking in gametes (silver staining of thylakoid membrane polypeptides). Kasugamycin (Ks) 1mg/ml prevents cyt b6/f disappearance.

M. Baltscheffsky (ed.), Current Research in Photosynthesis, Vol. III, 715–718.
© 1990 *Kluwer Academic Publishers. Printed in the Netherlands.*

We observed no decrease in the rate of synthesis of the chloroplast-encoded subunits of the cyt b6/f complex relative to that of
other membrane polypeptides in the gametes (results not shown).
Therefore the loss of cyt b6/f complex must be due to an increased
turnover of its subunits in the membrane and not to a block in their
synthesis. That it would be caused by abnormal membrane insertion is
unlikely, since these subunits showed the same pattern of trypsin
sensitivity as in vegetative cells (results not shown).

Control of the disappearance of cyt b6/f complexes.
    WT gametes have therefore lost their ability to survive in photo-
trophic conditions and depend on mitochondrial ATP production. Table I
shows that inhibition of mitochondrial activity prior to gametogenesis
prevents cyt b6/f disappearance. Cyt b6/f complexes are also maintained
in the thylakoid membranes from WT gametes differentiated in darkness
and in gametes from PSI mutants. In these cases, both linear and cyclic
photosynthetic electron flows are inactive. In contrast, the absence
of PSII activity, which preserves cyclic electron flow around PSI, does
not prevent cyt b6/f disappearance. Thus both mitochondrial and photosynthetic linear as well as cyclic activities control the presence
cyt b6/f complexes in the thylakoid membranes from the gametes. These
observations suggest that the rate of ATP synthesis in the gametes is
a key factor in this metabolic process.

Table 1:   PRESENCE OF cyt b6/f COMPLEXES IN GAMETES 60 HOURS OLD.

| | PHOTOPHOS. + OXIDATIVE PHOS. | OXIDATIVE PHOS. INACTIVATED | | OXIDATIVE PHOS. AND: | | | |
| | | | | INACTIVE PHOTOPHOS. | | CYCLIC PHOTOPHOS. ONLY | |
	WT (light)	mutants (DUM, Dk34)	WT + AA or Mixo	WT (dark)	PSI mutants	WT + DCMU + light	PSII mutants
cyt b6/f	-	+	+	+	+	-	-
M	+	ε	ε	ε	ε	+	+

    A change in the accuracy of translation has been described in
several differenciation processes (2). There is evidence for such a
change during gametogenesis in C. reinhardtii (3, Bulté and Bennoun,
manuscript in preparation). Since the accuracy of translation is
strongly ATP dependent (4), the disappearance of cyt b6/f complexes
in gametes may be controlled by inaccuratly translated proteins. This
hypothesis is further supported by the effect of Kasugamycin, which
increases the accuracy of translation (5) and prevented cyt b6/f
disappearance (Fig. 1). In addition, we note that the decrease in the
membrane amount of cyt b6/f complexes starts in 20 hours old gametes,
concurrently with the decrease in translation accuracy (Bulté and
Bennoun, manuscript in preparation).

The M protein.

A 70 Kda polypeptide Mα (app. M.W. after SDS-PAGE) appears in all instances where cyt b6/f complexes disappear from the gametes but is absent when cyt b6/f complexes remain in the thylakoid membranes (Table I). Its synthesis and accumulation are CAP insensitive but cycloheximide sensitive, which is indicative of a nuclear control. It shows the highest rate of synthesis among the proteins produced in gametes, 25 hours old, and becomes a major component of the cells after 60 hours (Fig. 2).

Mα is part of a high M.W. complex, the M protein (> 7 10^5 Da), which dissociates upon heating in the presence of SDS in the major 70 kDa component (Mα) and a minor component high M.W. (Mβ). None of them show DTT sensitivity. Mα is immunodetected by α-cytf (Fig.2) but not by α-Rieske protein and is slightly haeme stainable (Fig.1). Last, the M protein is associated neither with the thylakoid membranes (Fig.3) nor with smaller vesicles (Table II). It behaves like a genuine soluble protein complex.

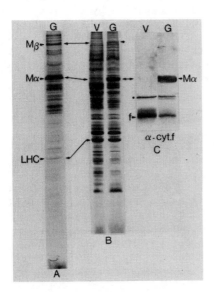
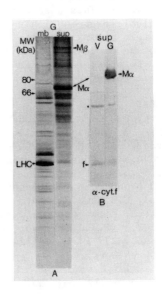

Fig. 2 : A) Mα shows high rates of synthesis in gametes, 25 hours old, pulse labelled with $^{35}SO_4$ in the presence of CAP. B) Mα is a major component in gametes, 60 hours old. C) Immunodetection of Mα by α-cyt f in gamete whole cells. Immunodetection of cyt f is much higher in vegetative than in gamete cells. Note the presence of another band (*) both in vegetative and gamete cells.

Fig. 3 : A) Thylakoid membrane proteins and soluble proteins from gametes, 60 hours old. The M protein is not found in the thylakoid membrane fraction but is retained in the 150 000 g supernatant (45 min. centrifugation). B) Mα is immunodetected by α-cytf among the soluble proteins from the gametes.

Table 2:   PROPERTIES OF THE M PROTEIN.

APP. M.W. In native state	SED. COEF.	DENSITY g/cm3	MAIN SUBUNITS upon SDS-PAGE				SYNTHESIS		LOCALISATION		IMMUNODETECTION		
			NH		H		CAP	Cyclo	mb prot.	sol. prot.	α-cyt f	α-cyt b6	α-Rieske
			+DTT	-DTT	+DTT	-DTT							
$7 \, 10^5 <$ M.W.$< 1.6 \, 10^6$	24 S	1.28	$>3 \, 10^5$	$>3 \, 10^5$	$7 \, 10^4$ $>8 \, 10^4$	$7 \, 10^4$ $>8 \, 10^4$	+	-	-	+	+	?	-

CONCLUSION

Cyt b6/f complexes are withdrawn from the thylakoid membranes in gametes. This process is under a dual mitochondrial and chloroplast control, most likely through the intracellular ATP level. The inactivation of photosynthesis at the cyt b6/f level further contributes to a limitation in ATP synthesis in the gametes. Thus low ATP levels may be required at some stages of the sexual cycle in C. reinhardtii.

The disappearance of cyt b6/f complexes does not originate from an arrest in the synthesis of their individual subunits. Thus it must arise from a destabilization of the complex in the thylakoid membrane of the gametes. This disappearance is accompanied by the formation of a new soluble protein of high M.W. which contains epitopes of cyt.f. This protein may participate in a proteolytic degradation process or in a storage process of some subunits of the cyt b6/f complex. Its relation to other regulation proteins (heat shock proteins, ubiquitin, chaperonin) deserves further study.

REFERENCES

1 Lemaire, C., Girard-Bascou, J., Wollman, F-A. and Bennoun, P. (1986) Biochim. Biophys. Acta 851, 229-238.
2 Picard-Bennoun, M., Coppin-Raynal, E. and Dequard-Chablat, M. (1983) in Protein synthesis, Abraham et al. eds. Humana Press Inc., pp. 221-232.
3 Picard-Bennoun, M. and Bennoun, P. (1985) Curr. Genet. 9, 239-243.
4 Kurland, C.G. and Gallant, J.A. (1986) in Accuracy in molecular processes, Kirkwood et al. eds., Camb. Univ. Press, pp. 136.
5 Van Buul, C.P.J.J., Visser, W. and van Knippenberg, P.H. (1984) FEBS Lett. 177 (1), 119-124.

BIOSYNTHESIS OF PHOTOSYSTEM I AND CYTOCHROME b6/f
COMPLEXES

Teruhiro Takabe, Takashi Hibino, and Hiroshi Ishikawa
Department of Chemistry, Faculty of Science and Technology,
Meijo University, Tenpaku, Nagoya 468, Japan

1. INTRODUCTION
    The effect of light on chloroplast development and
plant gene expression has been extensively investigated.
However, little is known about the mechanisms by which
nuclear and chloroplast gene expression is coordinated
during the formation of Photosystem I (PSI) and Cyt b6/f
complexes. It may be reasonable to postulate that assembly
of PSI and Cyt b6/f complexes is mediated by protein
interactions that take place in the lipid phase after
delivery of the subunits into the membrane. At present, it
is not possible to specify whether there is an obligately
order in which subunit contacts are made. In previous
papers (1,2), we have studied changes of amount of PSI
complex, plastocyanin, and Cyt b6/f complex during greening
of pea, wheat, barley, and rice leaves by an immunochemical
quantification method. The accumulation levels of proteins
are depend on the rates of transcription and translation as
well as the stabilities of protein and mRNA. Therefore,
information concerning the protein synthesis and the levels
of corresponding mRNAs is important to understand the
control mechanisms regulating the appearance of functional
PSI and Cyt b6/f complexes in the thylakoid membranes, which
is not yet studied.
    In this paper, we have studied the protein synthesis
and mRNA accumulation of Cyt b6/f complex during chloroplast
development in cucumber cotyledons. We will show that the
significant amounts of pet A and pet B transcript products
are present during the greening period, but their
translation are severely blocked in the dark-grown cotyledon.
We have also isolated clones encoding the subunit 2 of PSI
complex and determined the nucleotide sequence. The
structure and regulation of this gene will be discussed.

2. MATERIALS AND METHODS
    The cucumber seedlings were grown in darkness for 3
days at 28°C, then illuminated with white fluorescent light

M. Baltscheffsky (ed.), Current Research in Photosynthesis, Vol. III, 719–722.
© 1990 *Kluwer Academic Publishers. Printed in the Netherlands.*

of approx. 10 J·m⁻¹·s⁻¹. Cotyledons were frozen in liquid
N₂, powdered by Waring blendor, and used for protein and
mRNA extraction.

The relative amounts of polypeptides in the cotyledons
were determined by a Western blotting analysis. The
relative synthesis rates of proteins were determined by in
vivo labeling with [³⁵S]-Met and the immunoprecipitation
method. The relative amounts of hybridizable mRNA were
determined by a Northern hybridization method.

A cucumber cDNA library was constracted from a size
fractionated poly(A)⁺RNA by vector-primer and linker method.
DNA sequencing was carried out by the dideoxy chain-
termination method.

3. RESULTS AND DISCUSSION
3.1. Accumulation of Protein and Chl during the Greening of
Cucumber Cotyledons. The time course of Chl and
protein accumulation during light-induced chloroplast
development is represented in Fig. 1. When expressed
on a wet weight cotyledon basis, the Chl contents
rapidly increased during the first 2-days of
illumination followed by a slight decrease. The
protein content of the soluble fraction rapidly
decreased during the illuminated time although that of
the membrane fraction was almost constant.

3.2. Accumulation of Cyt b6/f Complex during Chloroplast
Development. The time course of polypeptide
accumulation for Cyt b6/f complex during light-induced
development was studied by using an immunochemical
quantification method. Antigens aginst Cyt f, Cyt b6,
and chloroplast Rieske proteins did not cross-react

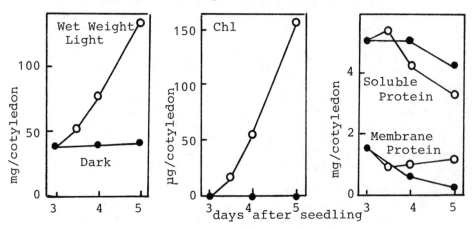

Fig.1. Wet weight, Chl content, and protein content

with the mitochondrial membrane fraction, although these antigens did cross-react with the chloroplast membrane fraction as well as total membrane fraction of dark-grown and illuminated cotyledons (data not shown). Therefore, under the present conditions, we can ignore the contribution of the mitochondrial Cyt b/c_1 complex to the levels of chloroplast Cyt b6/f complex. As shown in Fig. 2, very small amount of polypeptides for Cyt f, Cyt b6 and Rieske Fe-S proteins were observed in the dark-grown cotyledons. The amounts of polypeptides for Cyt f, Cyt b6, and Rieske proteins increased about

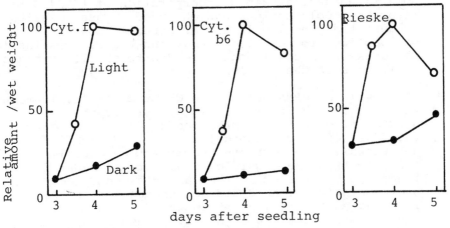

Fig. 2. Accumulation of Cyt b6/f complex polypeptides

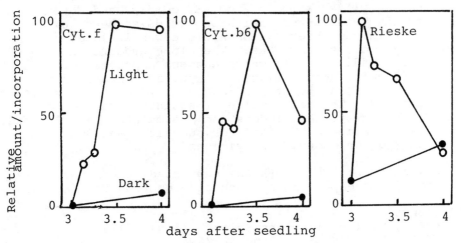

Fig. 3. Synthesis of Cyt b6/f complex polypeptides

5, 15, and 5-fold, respectively during the greening period of cucumber cotyledons.

3.3. Synthesis of Cyt b6/f Complex during Chloroplast Development. The incorporation of $[^{35}S]$-Met into the polypeptide chains of soluble and membrane fractions were almost linear up to 2 h (data not shown), so all the data were the results of 2 h labeling. As shown in Fig. 3, the incorporation of $[^{35}S]$-Met into the polypeptide chains of Cyt f, Cyt b6, and Rieske proteins was very low in the dark-grown cotyledons. Upon illumination, rapid incorporation of $[^{35}S]$-Met into these polypeptides was observed. These results suggest that the low levels of accumulation of polypeptides for Cyt f, Cyt b6, and Rieske proteins in the dark-grown cotyledons were due to the low synthetic activities of these polypeptides.

3.4 The Levels of mRNA during the Chloroplast Development. The specificity of DNA probe (pet A) for the hybridization with the mRNA coding Cyt f and not with the mRNA coding mitochondrial Cyt c_1 was confirmed (data not shown). The northern hybridization experiments indicate that the significant amounts of mRNAs for Cyt f and Cyt b6 present in the dark-grown cotyledons and their relative amounts did not change during the illuminated time (data not shown). These results indicate that the low levels of accumulation of Cyt f and Cyt b6 are not due to the block of transcription.

3.5. Cloning and Sequencing of Subunit 2 of PSI Complex. We have purified subunit 2 of PSI complex and determined twenty three N-terminal amino acids sequence by a gas-protein sequencer. A cDNA clone was isolated by oligonucleotide probes. The clone predicts a single open reading frame, which encodes a protein of 22720 Da (207 amino acid residues). Typical feature of subunit 2 is the long stretch of basic residues from Arg 140 to Lys 148. The polypeptide of subunit 2 was not detected in ethiolated cotyledons and accumulated rapidly after illumination. The mRNA for subunit 2 was detected in dark-grown cucumber cotyledons.

Acknowledgement; This work was supported in part by a Grant-in-Aid of Japan Private School Promotion Foundation.

REFERENCES
1 TAKABE, T. (1986) Plant Science 43, 193-199
2 TAKABE, T., TAKABE, T. and AKAZAWA, T. (1986) Plant

ASPECTS OF ASSEMBLY OF CHLOROPHYLL A/B-PROTEIN COMPLEXES

J. Kenneth Hoober, Margaret A. Maloney and Dawn B. Marks

Department of Biochemistry, Temple University School of Medicine, Philadelphia, PA 19140

1. INTRODUCTION
    Yellow cells of Chlamydomonas reinhardtii y1 green at 38°C sufficiently rapidly that chloroplast development can be examined kinetically over a time span of minutes (1,2). Chlorophyll (Chl) and the Chl a/b-binding (Cab) polypeptides accumulate at linear rates after exposure to light (3,4). To gain information on the process by which these components come together to form the major light-harvesting Chl a/b-protein complexes, we measured the kinetics of accumulation of the major Cab polypeptides and of the Chls that accumulate during the initial period of greening. We also investigated the difference in accumulation of Cab polypeptides in the light or dark.

2. PROCEDURE
2.1. Materials and Methods
    Degreened C. reinhardtii y1 cells were preincubated 2 h at 38°C in the dark and then exposed to incandescent light (2). Chl was analyzed by HPLC (3). Energy transfer was assayed by exciting membranes with 472 nm light, the absorption maximum of Chl b, and measuring the emission spectrum of the sample between 600 and 700 nm (3). Accumulation of Cab polypeptides was determined by immunoprecipitation of extracts of cells that were labeled with [^{14}C]arginine (2,4). Proteolytic activity was assayed by the absorbance change at 410 nm that accompanies hydrolysis of amino acyl-p-nitroanilides (4,5).

3. RESULTS AND DISCUSSION
    Degreened cells incubated in the dark at 38°C for 2 h contained a full complement of translatable mRNA for the major Cab polypeptides (2), but the polypeptides did not increase, relative to other cellular proteins, until cells were exposed to light. When cells were labeled with [^{14}C]arginine, ^{14}C accumulated in Cab polypeptides at a linear rate in the light in parallel with Chl. The rate of accumulation was 5- to 10-fold greater in the light than in the dark (Fig. 1). Newly-synthesized Cab polypeptides were recovered quantitatively with membranes. Thermolysin cleaved about 2kDa from two of the three Cab polypeptides

in membranes from greening yl cells (4), which indicated that these polypeptides were integrated into the membrane structure (6).

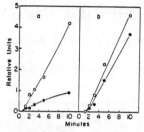

Fig. 1. Accumulation of ^{14}C in (a) Cab polypeptide 11 and (b) the small subunit of ribulose 1,5-bisphosphate carboxylase in the (o) light or (•) dark.

The residual Chl in degreened cells was enriched in Chl b, with an a/b ratio of 0.6-0.8 (Fig. 2.a.). Analysis by reverse-phase HPLC of Chl synthesized during the first hour of light revealed that geranylgeranyl esters of Chl b (Fig. 2.b., peak 1) and Chl a (Fig. 2.b., peak 5) were the predominant forms during rapid greening. Phytyl forms of Chl b (Fig. 2.b., peak 4) and Chl a (Fig. 2.b., peak 8) increased slowly at first and then at an increasing rate

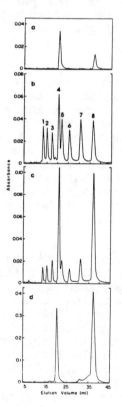

Fig. 2. HPLC analysis of Chls in yl cells (a) grown 3 d in the dark at 25°C, (b) after 1 h in light at 38°C, (c) as in (b) but treated with gabaculine for an additional 60 min, and (d) grown in the light for 2 d at 25°C. Peaks 1 and 5, geranylgeranyl esters of Chlides b and a, respectively; peaks 2 and 6, dihydrogeranylgeranyl esters of Chlides b and a, respectively; peaks 3 and 7, tetrahydrogeranylgeranyl esters of Chlides b and a respectively; peaks 4 and 8, phytyl esters of Chlides b and a, respectively.

with time in the light (3). When synthesis of Chl was inhibited with gabaculine (Fig. 2.c.) or by transfer of cells to dark (not shown), the sidechains were further reduced and the phytylated Chlides became the principle forms. Essentially all Chl in green cells was recovered as the phytyl esters (Fig. 2.d.)

To determine whether these Chls were integrated into Chl-protein complexes, transfer of energy from Chl b to Chl a was assayed. As shown in Fig. 3, very little fluorescence from Chl b was detected with membranes prepared from greening cells, which implied that essentially all Chl b was sufficiently near molecules of Chl a for efficient energy transfer. Thus, we conclude that the Chl b was integrated into light-harvesting complexes. From the data shown in Fig. 2.b., we conclude that these complexes form rapidly regardless of the extent of reduction of the Chl sidechains.

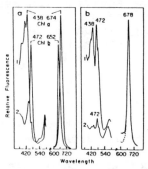

Fig. 3. Energy transfer from Chl b to Chl a in newly formed membranes. (a) Membranes were dissociated with Triton X-100 to show excitation and emission spectra of Chls. (b) Excitation spectra (emission: curve 1, 678 nm; curve 2, 650 nm) and emission spectra (excitation: ———, 472 nm; - - -, 438 nm) of intact membranes.

Cab polypeptides did not accumulate in y1 cells in which Chl synthesis was inhibited (4). To search for the reason for this observation, we studied cells of the pg113 mutant strain of C. reinhardtii, which retain nearly full levels of Cab polypeptides even though Chl b is undetectable (7). In contrast to the situation with membranes from y1 cells, the Cab polypeptides associated with purified thylakoid membranes of pg113 cells were completely digested by thermolysin. Thus in pg113 cells, Cab polypeptides seem to be associated with the stromal surface of thylakoids and not integrated into the membrane.

No difference in incorporation of [^{14}C]arginine into Cab polypeptides was found in pg113 cells incubated in the dark or light at 38°C. Thus there seems to be no effect of light on translation of Cab mRNA. The possibility exists that pg113 cells also are deficient in a proteolytic activity that normally degrades those Cab polypeptides not associated with Chl b. To test this possibility, we assayed proteolytic activities associated with membranes.

After resolution of cellular membranes on sucrose gradients, an active peptidase that hydrolyzed leucyl-p-nitroanilide was found associated with membranes with a buoyant density slightly lower than that of thylakoids. The specific activity of this membrane-bound enzyme in pg113 cells (Fig. 4.b.) was 10-15% of that in membranes from yl cells (Fig. 4.a.). Because of its high activity in yl cells, this membrane-bound peptidase may provide an explanation for the lack of accumulation of the Cab polypeptides in yl cells in the dark.

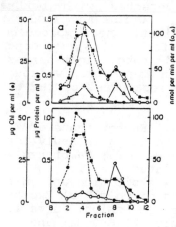

Fig. 4. Analysis of membrane-bound peptidase activity on 0.5-1.4 M sucrose gradients. (a) Membranes were obtained from greening yl cells. (b) Membranes were obtained from dark-grown pg113 cells. Peptidase activity was assayed with (o) Leu-p-nitroanilide and (△) Ala-p-nitroanilide. (●), Chl; (■), protein.

A transient, rapidly degraded pool of Cab polypeptides could not be detected in yl cells in the dark. We propose that proteolysis of Cab polypeptides occurs either concomitantly with transport into the chloroplast or immediately thereafter if Chl, in particular Chl b, is not available. Chl seems to rescue these polypeptides from degradation.

This research was supported by NSF grant 8613585.

REFERENCES
1 Hoober, J.K. and Stegeman, W.J. (1976) J. Cell Biol. 56, 1-12
2 Hoober, J.K., Marks, D.B., Keller, B.J. and Margulies, M.M. (1982) J. Cell Biol. 95, 552-558
3 Maloney, M.A., Hoober, J.K. and Marks, D.B. (1989) Plant Physiol., in press.
4 Hoober, J.K., Maloney, M.A., Asbury, L.R. and Marks, D.B. Plant Physiol., submitted.
5 Tuppy, H., Wiesbauer, U. and Wintersberger, E. (1962) Hoppe-Seyler's Z. Physiol. Chem. 329, 278-288
6 Chua, N.-H. and Blomberg, F. (1979) J. Biol. Chem. 254, 215-223
7 Michel, H., Tellenbach, M. and Boschetti, A. (1983) Biochim. Biophys. Acta 725, 417-424

RECONSTITUTION OF CHLOROPHYLL A,B-CONTAINING COMPLEXES FROM LHCP
OVERPRODUCED IN BACTERIA

H. PAULSEN AND W. RÜDIGER, Botanisches Institut III der Universität, Menzinger
Str. 67, D-8000 MÜNCHEN 19, WEST GERMANY

INTRODUCTION
    PSII-associated light-harvesting complexes (LHCII) are essential for the efficiency
of photosynthesis in higher plants. Basic questions concerning the structure of LHCII,
such as the interaction between pigments and apoprotein, as well as the assembly of the
complex, are still unsolved. An experimental approach to answering these questions is
to reconstitute LHCII in vitro. Plumley and Schmidt (1) succeeded in reconstituting
pigment-protein complexes from acetone-extracted pea thylakoids and pigments. The
resulting complexes had spectroscopic properties closely resembling those of native
LHCII. We set out to reconstitute pigment-containing complexes from pea LHCP
overexpressed in bacteria. Using bacteria-produced LHCP offers several advantages:
(i) large amounts of LHCP can be made; (ii) the protein is homogenous, i.e. it is not
modified post-translationally and it originates from a single gene instead of a cab gene
family; (iii) the primary structure of the protein is easily changed by specifically
mutating the gene. The latter possibility should enable us to identify structural
elements of the LHCP molecule that are functionally important for the assembly of the
complex and for the light-harvesting process.

RESULTS AND DISCUSSION
    We constructed plasmids that allow the overexpression of a light-harvesting
chlorophyll a/b-binding protein (LHCP) in bacteria. Starting out from the pea cab
gene AB 80 (genomic clone pPAR4, ref. 2), the 5' region of the gene including the
initiation codon and, in some cases, further parts of the coding region (up to 15
codons), was deleted (H. Paulsen and L. Bogorad, in preparation). The resulting gene
fragments were cloned into expression vectors of the pDS series (3).

E. coli (strain JM 101) transformed with these vectors produce a protein of the
expected molecular weight that immuno-reacts with LHCP antibodies. Under optimal
conditions, bacteria produce up to 20 % of their total protein as LHCP derivatives
(Fig. 1, lane T). These LHCP derivatives correspond, according to the gene construct
used for expression, to pLHCPs with two or three amino acids changed and/or added
at their N termini and to deletion mutants including one missing its transit peptide
and 15 N-terminal amino acids of the mature protein.

M. Baltscheffsky (ed.), Current Research in Photosynthesis, Vol. III, 727–730.
© 1990 *Kluwer Academic Publishers. Printed in the Netherlands.*

Bacteria overproducing these LHCP derivatives accumulate the protein as insoluble inclusion bodies that are pelletable and can be separated from most bacterial debris in a few subsequent washing and centrifugation steps (4). This way, LHCP from bacteria can be purified to 95 % (Fig. 1).

FIGURE 1: Purification of overexpressed LHCP from bacteria.

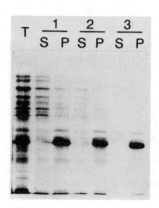

Bacteria harboring a pLHCP expression plasmid were induced to accumulate pLHCP. An aliquot of the cell suspension was withdrawn (T). The bacteria were pelleted, lysed with lysozyme and deoxycholic acid/Nonidet P40, and centrifuged. Aliquots of supernatant (1s) and pellet (1p) were saved. The pellet was washed two times (2,3) with a buffer containig 0.5 % Triton X 100. Aliquots of supernatants (s) and pellets (p) from steps 1 to 3 as well as of total bacteria (T) were denatured in 1 % SDS and loaded onto PAGE (0.1 % SDS). The gel was stained with Coomassie.

FIGURE 2: Reconstitution of LHCP overproduced in bacteria with a pigment extract from pea thylakoids.

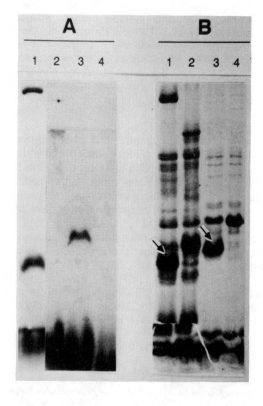

Pea thylakoids before (1) and after (2) denaturing (1% SDS, 1 min, 100°C) and reconstitution mixtures with pLHCP and a total pigment extract from pea thylakoids, also before (3) and after (4) heat-denaturing, were electrophoresed on PAG under partially denaturing conditions (0.1 % LDS, 4°C). A: "Green gel", aside from free pigment on the bottom of each lane, only those protein bands are visible that contain chlorophyll. B: Stained gel. The protein bands corresponding to the green bands in A are marked by arrows.

Reconstituting pLHCP from bacteria with the acetone-soluble fraction of pea thylakoids results in the formation of a chlorophyll-containing complex that is stable in partially denaturing poyacrylamide gel electrophoresis (PAGE) (Fig. 2, lane 3). In the gel, the complex forms a well-defined sharp band that has a somewhat higher mobility than the free protein (lanes 3 and 4). This is also characteristic of native LHCII as compared to free LHCP (lanes 1 and 2). The reconstituted pLHCP-pigment complex migrates more slowly than LHCII, presumably because of the transit peptide still present in the reconstituted protein. Using an   excess amount of

Various versions of pLHCP and LHCP produced by bacteria can be reconstituted with pigments, including the one missing its transit peptide as well as 15 N-terminal amino acids (not shown). It is concluded that the N terminus does not play an important role in pigment binding.

Spectroscopic properties of reconstituted complexes, such as absorption spectra, fluorescence excitation and emission spectra and energy transfer from Chl a to Chl b, are very similar to those of LHCII isolated from thylakoid membranes (not shown). The resemblance between the CD spectra also suggests a very similar arrangement of pigments in the reconstituted complex as compared to native LHCII (Fig. 3).

FIGURE 3: CD spectra of native LHCII (A) and complexes reconstituted from pLHCP overexpressed in bacteria and pigments extracted from pea thylakoids (B). LHCII and reconstituted complexes were isolated on a partially denaturing PAG (see Fig. 2). The green bands were excised and used directly for recording CD spectra.

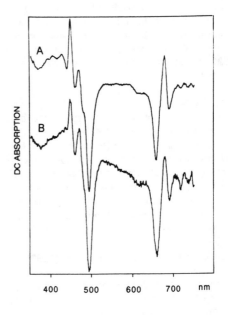

FIGURE 4: Reconstitution of pLHCP with various mixtures of isolated pigments. pLHCP (3 ug) was reconstituted with the following pigment mixtures: 1, Chl a and b (50 ug each); 2, Chl a (100 ug) + xanthophylls (4 ug); 3, Chl a (75 ug) + Chl b (25 ug) + xanthophylls (4 ug); 4, Chl a and b (50 ug each) + xanthophylls (4 ug); 5, Chl a (25 ug) + Chl b (75 ug) + xanthophylls (4 ug); 6, Chl b (100 ug) + xanthophylls (4 ug). The reconstitution mixtures were applied to partially denaturing PAGE (see Fig. 2). The gel was photographed without staining ("green gel"). The lower bands in lanes 1 to 6 represent free pigment, the upper bands in lanes 3 to 5 represent chlorophyll-containing complexes of pLHCP.

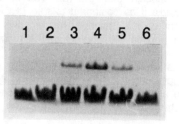

Reconstitution can also be achieved with isolated pigments instead of total pigment extracts. The pigments were isolated using several chromatographic steps (5) and were virtually free of lipids. Chl a and b as well as carotinoids are reqired for complex formation in vitro (Fig. 4). Complex yields are highest when Chl a:b ratios are about 1. Irrespectively of the Chl a:b ratio in the reconstitution mixture, Chl a:b ratios in the reconstituted complex are always 1.1 ± 0.1. The xanthophylls lutein, neoxanthin and violaxanthin are sufficient as carotinoid components. Among these, violaxanthin can be omitted without significantly affecting complex formation, omitting neoxanthin decreases complex formation by 50 % whereas lutein is essential (not shown).

CONCLUSIONS

Using LHCP or pLHCP overproduced by bacteria, pigment protein complexes can be reconstituted in vitro that, spectroscopically, closely resemble LHCII. Thus, one species of unmodified LHCP is sufficient for pigment-LHCP complex formation. The N-terminal region of the protein can be varied without affecting complex formation and therefore, does not seem to be involved in pigment binding. As pigment components, Chl a and b and at least two out of three xanthophylls are required. Varying the Chl a:b ratio in the reconstitution mixture changes the yield of complex formed but not the Chl a:b ratios in the complex.

REFERENCES

1 Plumley, F.G. and Schmidt, G.W. (1987) Proc. Natl. Acad. Sci. U.S.A. 84, 146-150
2 Cashmore, A. (1984) Proc. Natl. Acad. Sci. U.S.A. 81, 2960-2964
3 Bujard, H., Gentz, R., Lanzer, M., Stueber, D., Mueller, M., Ibrahimi, I., Haeuptle, M.T. and Dobberstein, B. (1987) Methods Enzymol. 155, 416-433
4 Nagai, K. and Thøgersen, H.C. (1987) Methods Enzymol. 153, 461-481
5 Britton, G. and Goodwin, T.W. (1971) Methods Enzymol. 18, 654-701

OPTIMIZATION OF AN ORGANELLE-FREE PROCESSING REACTION FOR
THE CHLOROPHYLL A/B BINDING PROTEIN PRECURSOR

Mark Abad, Steven Clark, and Gayle Lamppa
Dept. of Molec. Genet. and Cell Biol., The University of Chicago,
Chicago, IL USA 60637

1. INTRODUCTION

The chlorophyll a/b binding protein (LHCP) associated with photosystem II is a major
component of the thylakoid membranes (1). Its synthesis, maturation, localization and
assembly into the light harvesting complex are key events in the development of the
chloroplast. Intact pea chloroplasts import a 31 kD precursor synthesized in vitro from
a wheat gene and process it to two mature forms of ~26 kD and 25 kD that integrate
into the thylakoid membranes (2). We have identified a proteolytic activity in soluble
extracts of lysed pea chloroplasts that processes the precursor protein at its N-terminus
to the 25 kD form found upon processing during import (2). This activity was a)
retained in the supernatant after ultracentrifugation, which removes membrane
vesicles, b) selectively ammonium sulfate precipitable, and c) sensitive to boiling,
indicating that it is conferred by a soluble, denaturable enzyme. The inhibition of the
enzyme by divalent metal ion chelators suggests that it is a metalloprotease. We have
described the basic physical properties of this enzyme and have partially purified it by
gel filtration chromatography. The Rubisco small subunit precursor (pS) is processed
by the identical peak of activity that cleaves pLHCP. These results are reviewed below
and have recently been presented (3).

2. PROCEDURE
2.1. Materials and methods

2.1.1. In vitro expression of pLHCP: A wheat genomic clone encoding
pLHCP (4) was used to direct an in vitro transcription/translation
system (via SP6 RNA polymerase and reticulocyte translation
lysates) to synthesize radiolabelled pLHCP.

2.1.2. Preparation of active chloroplast processing extracts: Intact pea
chloroplasts were isolated from homogenized, 9 day old, leaf
tissue using Percoll gradients, and hypotonically lysed. The
membranes were removed by centrifugation and the soluble extract
was recovered as the supernatant.

2.1.3. Organelle-free processing assay: Aliquots of soluble extract were
incubated with radiolabelled pLHCP in an organelle-free reaction
under various conditions to establish optimal cleavage. The
reaction products were analysed by SDS-PAGE followed by
fluorography.

M. Baltscheffsky (ed.), Current Research in Photosynthesis, Vol. III, 731–734.
© 1990 *Kluwer Academic Publishers. Printed in the Netherlands.*

3. RESULTS

3.1. Our results indicate that the processing enzyme for pLHCP resides in the soluble, stromal phase of the chloroplast. Intact pea chloroplasts were hypotonically lysed using increasing amounts of 50 mM Hepes KOH, pH 8.0. Extracts prepared by lysing at a final concentration of 400 or 800 μg chlorophyll/ml contained potent processing activity, whereas, extracts prepared by lysing at 200 μg chlorophyll/ml did not effectively cleave pLHCP. The processing activity was retained after membrane vesicles were removed by ultracentrifugation. The resuspended membrane pellets from this separation did not process pLHCP and the membrane residue added directly to pLHCP translation products resulted in their degradation. It should be noted that a crude extract, before ultracentrifugation, is stable as long as 7 months at -20°C.

3.2. The LHCP precursor is processed to two smaller forms during import, however, only the smaller form is produced during organelle-free processing. Import experiments using intact chloroplasts and radiolabelled pLHCP yielded both a 26 kD and 25 kD form of mature LHCP that were both inserted into the thylakoid membranes. Organelle-free processing of the same pLHCP substrate produced only the 25 kD form (see Fig. 1. A). A time course of organelle-free processing showed that the 25 kD polypeptide of LHCP gradually accumulated over the course of one hour and no intermediate size species were observed. On the other hand, a time course of pLHCP import into chloroplasts showed that the 26 kD and 25 kD forms of LHCP are both produced within 3 minutes.

3.3. We have demonstrated that processing occurs by proteolytic cleavage of pLHCP at its N-terminus. The pLHCP gene was restructured to yield templates that directed the synthesis of mutant precursors that lacked 13, 27, or 91 amino acids at their C-termini. When compared to the wild type precursor, organelle-free processing of the mutants pΔ13 and pΔ27 yielded progressively smaller forms of mature LHCP that were proportional to the size of the C-terminal deletion. This provides strong evidence that processing occurs at the N-terminus since C-terminal processing of these mutants would have yielded mature forms of LHCP that are identical in size. Unexpectedly, pΔ91 was not cleaved, indicating that it had undergone a major conformational change.

3.4. The processing activity can be selectively precipitated by ammonium sulfate and is sensitive to boiling. The processing enzyme is precipitated between 40% and 70% ammonium sulfate saturation of the crude extract. The enzyme is inactivated if the extract is boiled for one minute, whereas mock reactions without added extract show no specific cleavage or protein degradation.

3.5. Organelle-free processing reactions were performed over a pH range from 6 to 9.5 and over a temperature range of 4°C to 42°C. Optimal processing occurred at pH 8-9 and at 26°C. The divalent metal ion chelators EDTA and 1,10-phenanthroline inhibited cleavage at 2 mM and 0.4 mM respectively. The crude extract was fractionated by Sephacryl S-300 gel filtration chromatography and the processing activity eluted as a single peak. We estimate that the processing enzyme has a M_r of ~240,000. To establish if fractions eluted from the Sephacryl S-300 column would cleave pS, the same fractions used to size the pLHCP processing enzyme were again assayed using pea pS as a substrate. We found that pS was converted to its mature form by the identical fractions that processed pLHCP, and furthermore, the peak of both activities was identical.

4.   DISCUSSION

A processing activity has been identified in the soluble fraction of pea chloroplasts that cleaves the N-terminus of the precursor of the wheat chlorophyll a/b binding protein (pLHCP) in an organelle-free assay. Cleavage was also found when pea pLHCP is used as a substrate (M.S. Abad, unpublished, Fig. 1. lanes 1 and 2). A 25 kD polypeptide is released that comigrates with the smaller of the two mature forms produced during in vitro import of pLHCP into chloroplasts. The 26 kD polypeptide is not a processing intermediate, as demonstrated by pLHCP mutagenesis, which was used to independently disrupt each processing site (5). The processing enzyme has the properties of a metalloprotease. This enzyme has a molecular weight of about 240,000, and optimal processing occurs at pH 8-9 and at 26°C. Processing of pS to the mature form also occurs by the enzyme fraction prepared under our conditions that cleaves pLHCP. The properties of this enzyme are very similar to those of the protease described by Robinson and Ellis (6) that cleaves pS and the plastocyanin precursor. Thus, the enzyme may be a general transit peptidase that releases the functional forms of most nuclear encoded proteins, synthesized as precursors which are imported into the chloroplast. Alternatively, it may be a member of a family of closely related proteases. As a working hypothesis, we propose that the protease selectively cleaves pLHCP at a secondary site to produce a subpopulation of LHCP that is localized to the thylakoids and assembled into the peripheral light harvesting complex of PS II (see Fig. 1. B). To determine if these possibilities exclude one another, we are purifying the pLHCP processing enzyme to homogeneity to establish its substrate specificity and role in the maturation and localization of LHCP to the thylakoid membranes.

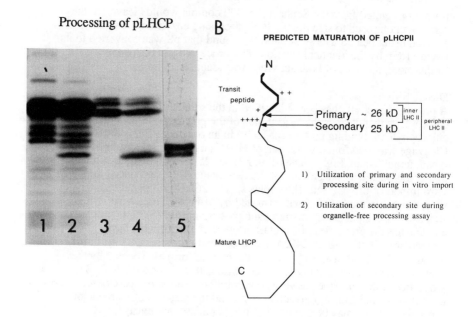

Processing of pLHCP

B

Figure 1. A) In vitro translation products of pLHCP were analyzed after organelle-free or in organello processing by SDS-PAGE followed by fluorography. Lane 1-pea pLHCP translation products, lane 2-products of organelle-free processing of pea pLHCP, lane 3-wheat pLHCP translation products, lane 4-products of organelle-free processing of wheat pLHCP, lane 5-Products of in organello processing during import of wheat pLHCP. B) A diagram is presented showing the cleavage sites predicted to give the two mature forms of pLHCP.

REFERENCES

1 Schmidt, G.W., Bartlett, S.G., Grossman, A.R., Cashmore, A.R. and Chua, N.-H. (1981) J. Cell Biol. 91, 468-478
2 Lamppa, G.K. and Abad, M.S. (1987) J. Cell Biol. 105, 2641-2648
3 Abad, M.S., Clark, S.E. and Lamppa, G.K. (1989) Plant Physiol. 90, 117-124
4 Lamppa, G.K., Morelli, G. and Chua, N.-H. (1985) Mol. Cell. Biol. 5, 1370-1378
5 Clark, S.E., Abad, M.S. and Lamppa, G.K., J. Biol. Chem. (in the press)
6 Robinson, C. and Ellis, R.J. (1984) Eur. J. Biochem. 142, 337-342

IMMUNOLOCALIZATION OF LHCP II APOPROTEIN IN THE GOLGI OF EUGLENA

TETSUAKI OSAFUNE[1], JEROME A. SCHIFF[2] AND EIJI HASE[3]

Dept.Microbiol.,Tokyo Med. Coll., Shinjuku, Tokyo 160,Japan[1];Photobiol.Group,Biology Dept.,Brandeis Univ.,Waltham,MA 02254 USA[2] ; Lab. Chem. Fac.Med. Teikyo Univ.,Hachiouji,Tokyo 192-03, Japan[3]

The photosynthetic antenna system of Euglena contains a light-harvesting chlorophyll a/b complex (LHCP II) which yields a major polypeptide of 26.5 kD(1). This poly-peptide is low or undetectable in mutants low in chloro-phyll b and in wild-type cells grown in darkness(1) or in dark-grown non-dividing wild-type cells exposed to low intensities of light at the developmental threshold (7 ft-c) (2). On shifting cells at 7 ft-c to a morer normal intensity for chloroplast development (80~150 ft-c) there is a rapid and selective accumulation of chlorophyll b and the 26.5 LHCP II apoprotein(2). The LHCP II apoprotein is transcribed in the nucleus and is translated in the cyto-plasm of a number of organisms including Euglena(3~5) resulting in the formation of a precursor protein con-taining a transit sequence. The precursor attaches to the chloroplast and on entry the transit sequence is detached and the mature apoprotein is incorporated into the photo-synthetic apparatus. In the course of work on the photo-control of the formation of the 26.5 kD LHCP II apoprotein in Euglena using a highly specific antibody, we observed a clear antibody reaction in the Golgi apparatus; this is the subject of the present report.

Dark-grown resting cells of Euglena gracilis Klebs var. bacillaris Cori or strain Z Pringsheim were obtained as described previously(2,6) and were exposed to 7 ft-c of light for up to 144 hrs. Some cultures at 7 ft-c were moved to normal saturating light (80 ft-c) after 72 hrs. Dark-grown resting cultures were exposed to 80 ft-c di-rectly to induce normal chloroplast development(2,6). The preparation and properties of highly-specific antibody to the 26.5 kD LHCP II apoprotein and preimmune serum has been described(1). For electron microscopy, cells were fixed in glutaraldehyde, washed, dehydrated in an ethanol series followed by acetone and embedded in Epon 812 resin. Thin sections on nickel slit grids were floated, section side down, on drops of 0.1M phosphate buffer (pH 7.0) con-taining 0.85% (w/v) NaCl (PBS) and, additionally, 0.5%

M. Baltscheffsky (ed.), Current Research in Photosynthesis, Vol. III, 735–738.
© 1990 Kluwer Academic Publishers. Printed in the Netherlands.

(w/v) bovine serum albumin, for 30 min, at room temperature. They were then floated on PBS containing antiserum
or preimmune serum at 600 fold dilution for 10 min. at 37
℃.   After two washes in PBS by flotation, they were
floated on PBS containing a 20 fold dilution of protein A-
gold for 20 min. and then on 3% (w/v) uranyl acetate for
10-20 min. and after drying were viewed in an electron
microscope.

Dark-grown resting cells of Euglena gracilis var.
bacillaris or dark-grown resting cells exposed to 7 ft-c
of light for up to 168 hrs. show little reaction with
LHCP Ⅱ antibody as determined by deposition of particles
of protein A-gold (not shown). When cells that had been
incubated for 72 hrs. at 7 ft-c are shifted to 80 ft-c for
8 hrs. considerable gold deposition is found over the
Golgi apparatus and the thylakoids of the plastids indicating a strong reaction with LHCP Ⅱ antibody (Fig.1). No
gold deposition is seen with preimmune serum in place of
anti-serum (Fig.2). Serial sections through two Golgi complexes show that the gold label in the antibody-treated
material is present at all levels regardless of their
orientation (Figs.3~5). The same pattern of reaction of
LHCP Ⅱ antiserum is seen in dark-grown resting cells
exposed to 80 ft-c of light to induce normal chloroplast
development (not shown) indicating that the reaction in
the Golgi and plastids is not unique to cells undergoing a
shift up in light intensity. The 26.5 kD LHCP Ⅱ apoprotein
is known to be transcribed as an unusually large message
which is translated as a large polypeptide(5~8).   Presumably, this large polypeptide contains multiple copies of
precursor polypeptides of more normal size. It is tempting
to speculate that the processing of the large polypeptide
into the smaller precursor polypeptides takes place in the
Golgi and that the more normal-sized precursors are then
taken up by the plastids in the usual way. However, other
explanations are possible and further experiments will be
necessary to explain the presence of an antibody reaction
to LHCP Ⅱ apoprotein in the Golgi apparatus.

REFERENCES

1   Cunningham, Jr., F.X. and Schiff, J.A. (1986)
    Plant Physiol. 80, 231-238
2   Spano, A.J., Ghaus, H. and Schiff, J.A. (1987)
    Plant Cell Physiol. 28, 1101-1108
3   Schmidt, G.W. and Mishkind, M.L. (1986)
    Ann. Rev. Biochem.55, 879-912
4   Keegstra, K. and Olsen, L.J. (1989) Ann. Rev. Plant
    Physiol. Plant Mol. Biol. 40, 471-501
5   Rikin, A., Schiff, J.A. and Schwartzbach, S.D. (1988)
    Plant Physiol. 86, S-18
6   Rikin, A. and Schwartzbach, S.D. (1988) Proc. Natl.
    Acad.Sci. USA 85, 5117-5121
7   Rikin,A. and Schwartzbach,S.D.(1989) Planta 178,76-85
8   Houlne,G. and Schantz, R.(1987) Curr.Genet.12,611-616

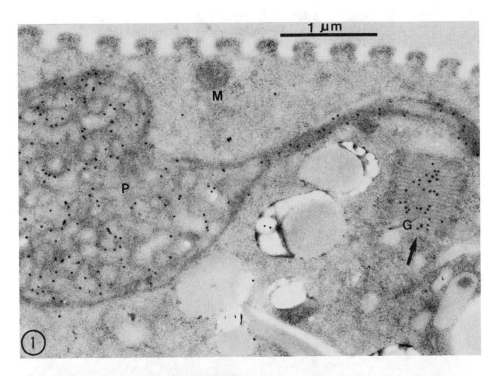

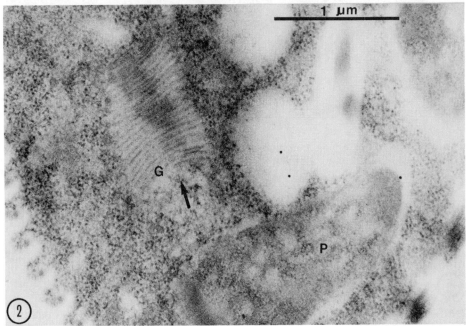

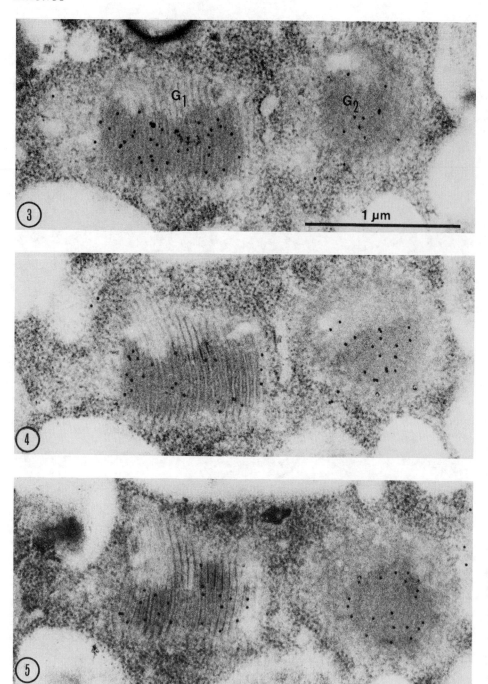

DEVELOPMENTAL CONSEQUENCES OF CHLOROPHYLL DEPRIVATION ON THE LIGHT HARVESTING SYSTEM OF SOYBEAN

Ralph L. Henry, Maolin Li, Xiaoyin Cai, and James A. Guikema, Division of Biology, Kansas State University, Manhattan, KS 66506, USA

1. INTRODUCTION

Regulation of development, with the assembly of multimeric complexes, often requires the integration of diverse biosynthetic pathways. Thylakoid biogenesis is a notable example, since it requires cytosolic and chloroplastic protein synthesis, chlorophyll (Chl) production, iron-sulfur center biosynthesis, etc. Two biochemical probes, gabaculine (3-amino-2,3-dihydro-benzoic acid) and AHA (4-amino-hexynoic acid), permit the study of thylakoid assembly when one of these pathways, Chl biogenesis, is restricted by inhibition at the level of aminolevulinic acid synthesis (1,3).

2. MATERIALS AND METHODS

Soybean (Glycine max L. cv Henderson) seedlings were grown in darkness for 6 d. On day 5, aqueous gabaculine (0-150 uM) or AHA (0-1 mM) were provided in place of the normal watering. On day 6, plants were shifted to continuous light, and were harvested on day 8.

3. RESULTS

When administered 24 h before the shift of etiolated soybean seedlings to light, neither gabaculine nor AHA caused changes in root size, shoot height, leaf area, or total leaf protein/g fwt. However, both treatments modulated the leaf Chl content in a dosage-dependent manner. A 5-fold higher concentration of AHA than gabaculine was required for similar inhibition. Fig. 1, in

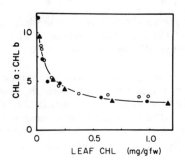

Fig. 1. Chl a:b ratios as a function of total leaf Chl. Chl was modulated using gabaculine in lima bean (▲) and soybean (●), and using AHA in soybean (o).

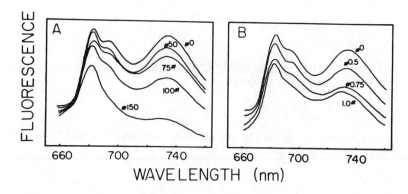

Fig. 2. Chl fluorescence emission at 77K of thylakoid membranes from gabaculine (A) and AHA (B) treated soybean. The values denote the inhibitor dosage (uM for gabaculine in [A], mM for AHA in [B]).

which the Chl a:b ratios of treated leaves are plotted as a function of total leaf Chl, shows two prominent effects: [a] gabaculine and AHA reduced total leaf Chl, and [b] increased Chl a:b ratios when the leaf Chl was below a threshold of 250 ug/g fw.

Thylakoid membranes were isolated, and Chl fluorescence examined at 77K (Fig. 2). Gabaculine and AHA had two salient effects. We noted a loss in the relative contribution of F735, with a blue-shift to about 730 nm. In addition, the abundance of F695 decreased, relative to F685.

Taken together, these data suggest that restricting protoporphyrin biosynthesis not only modulated Chl accumulation, but also altered the Chl microenvironment --perhaps by an altered complement of Chl-binding proteins. This possibility prompted our examination of thylakoid composition by Western blot analysis.

In Fig. 3, we quantify several proteins in whole-leaf extracts. Certain peptides (such as one at 53 kDa) were unchanged by gabaculine or AHA. In contrast, LHC2 did not accumulate in treated tissue. Since LHC2 binds most of the leaf Chl b, loss of LHC2 is consistent with an increase in a:b ratios (Fig. 1). Furthermore, LHC1 also did not accumulate in treated tissue. Our LHC1 antibody recognized three of four LHC1 peptides, and these responded differently to inhibitor treatment. One LHC1 peptide at 25 kDa (barely visible in 2 d thylakoids) increased 4-5 fold.

Peptides of the reaction center cores were nearly impossible to quantify from whole-leaf extracts. In Table 1, we quantify the P700-apoprotein of PS1 and CPa1-apoprotein of PS2 (4) from thylakoid preparations. These are presented relative to LHC2, for comparison to Fig. 3.

Our results show that, by restricting porphyrin synthesis, we change thylakoid structure. The implication is that, when Chl is limiting, reaction center proteins (which bind Chl a) are preferentially assembled, thus restricting synthesis of Chl b and/or the stable assembly of LHCs which bind both Chl a and b. Reaction center activity would be preserved at the expense of the light harvesting cross-section, provided by antenna proteins. However, loss of Chl also hinders core assembly, monitored by P700-apoprotein, CPa1-apoprotein, and fluorescence signals at F735.

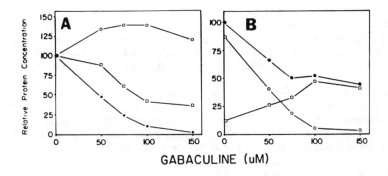

GABACULINE (uM)

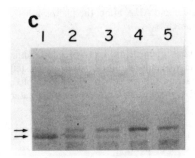

Fig. 3. Quantification of proteins in whole leaf extracts by Western blot analysis. A. LSU of RuBPCase (□); LHC2 (●); protein at 53 kDa (○). B. Total LHC1 (●), 25 kDa LHC1 species (□); total LCH1 minus 25 kDa peptide (○). C. Western blot showing the accumulation of the 25 kDa LHC1 species (top arrow). Gabaculine treatments of 0 (lane 1), 50 uM (lane 2), 75 uM (lane 3), 100 uM (lane 4), and 150 uM (lane 5).

Table 1. Analysis of thylakoid membrane preparations.

Inhibitor	Conc.	Leaf Chl	Ratio of Chl a:b	Ratio of apoCPa1:LHC2	Ratio of apoP700:LHC2
	(uM)	(ug/g FW)	(ug/ug)	(rel. peak area)	
none	--	959	3.38+/-0.28	1	1
gabaculine	50	570	3.73+/-0.34	1.24	1.33
	100	202	5.20+/-0.34	0.77	0.78
AHA	250	500	3.59+/-0.07	0.76	0.33
	750	94	5.92+/-0.83	1.20	1.35

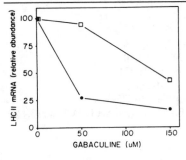

GABACULINE (uM)

Fig. 4. Quantification of LHC2 message levels in the total mRNA fraction (□) and in the mRNA fraction associated with polysomes (●). Quantification was by Northern blot analysis.

One alternative interpretation merits discussion: phytochrome is a product of protoporphyrin synthesis, and is an intimate component of plastid greening. Light stimulation of phytochrome triggers transcription of LHC genes. Since our treatment regime may reduce leaf phytochrome (5,6), lowered LHC accumulation may stem from a loss of LHC message. To rule out this possibility, we measured mRNA levels using a cDNA probe for soybean LHC2 (7).

At gabaculine levels which reduce LHC2 by more than 50%, total LHC2 message was unchanged (Fig. 4). Significantly, however, the LHC2 message in the polysomal pool was dramatically reduced. Clearly, a loss of LHC2-gene transcription did not cause our results, suggesting that gabaculine (and AHA), perhaps owing to their effects on Chl availability or on pool sizes of Chl intermediates, imposes a translational restriction on LHC production.

In summation, our data show these important points:

[1] When applied in low dosages to seedling roots, gabaculine and AHA affect the photosynthetic apparatus, without observable changes in other growth parameters.

[2] These inhibitors limit Chl accumulation and, as a consequence, an array of Chl-binding proteins. Recent studies, using chlorina mutants and/or pulsed illumination, suggested biosynthesis models of PS2 (8-10) and PS1 (8) in which reaction center cores are first assembled, then a stabilization of LHC antennas. Gabaculine and AHA, by limiting Chl, may have a greater impact on the later biosynthetic steps.

[3] One LHC1 peptide was present 5-fold after inhibitor treatment. We are monitoring this peptide during greening, since it may be important early in development.

[4] Measurements of LHC2 mRNA suggest a translational block of LHC2 synthesis.

ACKNOWLEDGMENTS

This work was supported by NASA (NAGW-1197) and the USDA Competitive Research Grants Program. AHA was a gift of the Merrell Dow Research Institute. Anti-LHC2 antibody was obtained from Dr. ME Duysen, the antibody against CPa1 from Dr. T Bricker (4), and cDNA probe for LHC2 from Dr. DE Buetow (7).

REFERENCES

1.   Corriveau JL, Beale SI. Plant Sci 1986; 45:9-17.
2.   May TB, Guikema JA, Henry RL, Schuler MK, Wong PP. Plant Physiol 1987; 84:1309-1313.
3.   Elich TD, Lagarias JC. Plant Physiol 1988; 88:747-751.
4.   Bricker TM, Frankel LK. Arch Biochem Biophys 1987; 256:295-301.
5.   Elich TD, Lagarias JC. Plant Physiol 1987; 84:304-310.
6.   Gardner G, Gorton HL, Brown SA. Plant Physiol 1988; 87:8-10.
7.   Hsiao K, Erdos G, Buetow DE. Plant Mol Biol 1988; 10:473-474.
8.   Glick RE, Melis A. Biochim Biophys Acta 1988; 934:151-155.
9.   Morrissey PJ, Glick RE, Melis A. Plant Cell Physiol 1989; 30:335-344.
10. Glick RE, McCauley SW, Gruissem W, Melis A. Proc Nat Acad Sci USA 1986; 83:4287-4291.

ASSOCIATION OF EXTRINSIC PROTEASES WITH SPINACH PHOTOSYSTEM II
MEMBRANES

TOMOHIKO KUWABARA and KENJI SHINOHARA[1]
Department of Biomolecular Science, Toho University, Funabashi 274,
Japan, and Forestry and Forest Product Research Institute, Ibaragi
305, Japan

1. INTRODUCTION
   It is certain that thylakoid-bound proteases play an essential role
in the processing and turnover of thylakoidal proteins. Nevertheless,
the research on the thylakoidal proteases has not much progressed. In
a previous study [1], we revealed that latent proteolytic activity was
extracted from the spinach PSII membranes with 1 M NaCl, and that the
dialysis of the extract activated the protease. Here, we further
characterized the proteolytic activity in the extract.

2. MATERIALS and METHODS
2.1. Extraction of proteases from PSII membranes
   PSII membranes were prepared from spinach thylakoids as in [1]
except that the Triton X-100/chlorophyll ratio in the detergent
treatment was 20/1 (w/w) instead of 25/1 (w/w). The membranes were
suspended in 1 M NaCl/25 mM Mes-NaOH (pH 6.5) at a chlorophyll
concentration of 2 mg/ml to extract membrane-bound proteases together
with the 18- and 23-kDa proteins of PSII water-oxidation complex [1].
The suspension was centrifuged at 35,000 x g for 10 min at 4°C. The
supernatant was the extract.
2.2. Partial purification of the 17.4- and 22.1-kDa fragments
   Solid NaCl was added to the extract to raise the NaCl concentration
to 4.5 M. The extract was loaded on a butyl-Toyopearl 650M (Toso)
column equilibrated with 4 M NaCl/40 mM Na phosphate buffer (PB) (pH
6.5). Following rinsing the column with 3 M NaCl/40 mM Na PB (pH 6.5),
the proteins were eluted with 1 M NaCl/40 mM Na PB (pH 6.5). Upon
dialysis of the eluate against 20 mM Na PB (pH 7.0), the 18- and
23-kDa proteins partially degraded to polypeptides of 17.4 and 22.1
kDa, respectively. These fragments were co-purified with the
respective native proteins by the method described in [1].
2.3. Proteolytic reaction by dialysis
   Proteolytic reaction of the proteases in the extract was performed
by dialyzing the extract against 10 mM Hepes-NaOH (pH 6.7) at 7°C for
16 h. Degradation products generated from the 18- and 23-kDa proteins
were detected by urea-SDS-PAGE, which was performed modifying the
Laemmli's system [2] as follows. The separation and stacking gels

contained 15% polyacrylamide/4 M urea/0.1% SDS/0.5 M Tris-HCl (pH 8.8) and 5% polyacrylamide/4 M urea/0.1% SDS/0.125 M Tris-HCl (pH 6.4), respectively. The electrode buffer consisted of 0.1% SDS/50 mM Tris/384 mM glycine.

RESULTS AND DISCUSSION

3.1. N-terminal amino acid sequences of the 17.4- and 22.1-kDa fragments

The 17.4- and 22.1-kDa fragments were well separated from the respective native proteins by urea-SDS-PAGE (Fig. 1). These fragments were analyzed for the N-terminal amino acid sequence following blotting onto a polyvinylidene difluoride membrane [3]. The N-terminal sequence of the 17.4-kDa fragment was very similar to that from the fifth residue of the 18-kDa protein, and indicative of the proteolysis between Pro-4 and Ile-5 (Fig. 2). In the previous study [1], we had shown that the 18-kDa protein was cleaved between Pro-12 and Leu-13 by a protease in the extract to generate the 16.5-kDa fragment (Fig. 2, previously termed 17-kDa fragment). The cleavages at these post-proline sites suggest the involvement of prolyl endopeptidase (PEPase, E.C. 3.4.21.26). The 17.4-kDa fragment may be an intermediate of the degradation of the 18-kDa protein to the 16.5-kDa fragment. The sequence of the N-terminal 15 residues of the 22.1-kDa fragment was the same as that from the tenth residue of the 23-kDa protein (Fig. 2). The deduced cleavage site, between Phe-9 and Gly-10, suggests the presence of a protease other than the putative PEPase.

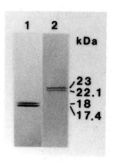

Fig. 1. Urea-SDS-PAGE of the 17.4-kDa fragment co-purified with the 18-kDa protein (lane 1) and the 22.1-kDa fragment co-purified with the 23-kDa protein (lane 2).

```
                         1               10                 20
18-kDa protein    E-A-R-P-I-V-V-G-P-P-P-P-L-S-G-G-L-P-G-T-E-N-S-D-
17.4-kDa fragment         I-V-V-G-P-P-P-P-L-S-X-G-L-P-G-X-E-N-
16.5-kDa fragment                       L-S-G-G-L-P-G-T-E-N-S-D-

23-kDa protein    A-Y-G-E-A-A-N-V-F-G-K-P-K-K-N-T-E-F-M-P-Y-N-G-D-
22.1-kDa fragment                   G-K-P-K-K-N-T-E-F-M-P-Y-N-G-D-
```

Fig. 2. Alignments of the N-terminal amino acid sequences of the 18-kDa protein and 17.4- and 16.5-kDa fragments, and the 23-kDa protein and 22.1-kDa fragment. The sequences of the 18-kDa protein [1], 16.5-kDa fragment [1] and 23-kDa protein [4] are from the literature.

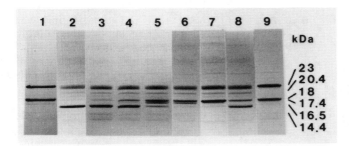

Fig. 3. Effects of the pretreatment of the extract. Prior to the reaction, the extract (lane 1) was not pretreated (lane 2) or pretreated with 10 mM Hepes-NaOH (pH 6.7) containing 0.1 M $CaCl_2$ (lane 3), 0.4 M $CaCl_2$ (lane 4), 0.7 M $CaCl_2$ (lane 5), 1.0 M $CaCl_2$ (lane 6), 1.0 M $BaCl_2$ (lane 7) or 1.0 M $MgCl_2$ (lane 8), or with 1.0 M Tris-HCl (pH 9.3)(lane 9) by dialysis at $7^\circ C$ for 26 h.

3.2. Pretreatment of the extract with divalent cation or alkaline Tris

The proteolytic reaction of the extract by the dialysis against 10 mM Hepes-NaOH (pH 6.7) degraded the 18- and 23-kDa proteins and generated polypeptides of 22-23, 20.4, 16.5, and 14.4 kDa (Fig. 3, lane 2). The polypeptides larger than 18 kDa are likely to be the fragments of the 23-kDa protein. The 16.5-kDa fragment is a degradation product of the 18-kDa protein [1], whereas the origin of the 14.4-kDa protein is unidentified. When the extract was pretreated with increasing concentration of $CaCl_2$ (0.1 to 1 M), the 17.4-kDa fragment came to be accumulated instead of the 16.5-kDa fragment with decreasing degradation of the 18-kDa protein (lanes 3-6). This observation reinforces the inference from the structure that the 17.4-kDa fragment is an intermediate. Failure to detect the 17.4-kDa fragment in the reaction without the pretreatment (lane 2) suggests that the cleavage between Pro-12 and Leu-13 is faster than that between Pro-4 and Ile-5. The former seems to be more severely affected than the latter by the pretreatment with $CaCl_2$. The pretreatment with 1 M $BaCl_2$ was more effective in suppressing the degradation of the 18-kDa protein than 1 M $CaCl_2$ (lane 7), whereas that with 1 M $MgCl_2$ was less effective (lane 8). The pretreatment with 1 M monovalent cation salt (KCl and LiCl) was ineffective (data not shown). None of the above pretreatments could suppress the degradation of the 23-kDa protein (lanes 3-8), suggesting the involvement of a different protease(s). The pretreatment with 1 M Tris-HCl (pH 9.3) almost completely suppressed the degradation of both 18- and 23-kDa proteins (lane 9). This treatment seems to be useful for the purification of thylakoidal proteins susceptible to the thylakoidal proteases.

3.3. Effects of protease inhibitors

Neither 18- or 23-kDa protein degraded by the dialysis against the medium containing 0.5 M NaCl (Fig. 4, lane 2). This suggests that all the proteases in the extract are inactive in the high salt medium. Interestingly, inclusion of 2 mM dithiothreitol (DTT) in the dialysis

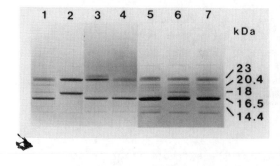

Fig. 4. Effects of protease inhibitors on the degradation of the 18- and 23-kDa proteins. The extract was dialyzed against 10 mM Hepes-NaOH (pH 6.7) containing none (lane 1, control), 0.5 M NaCl (lane 2), 2 mM DTT (lane 3), 2 mM DFP (lane 4), 2 mM NEM (lane 5), 2 mM 1,10-phenanthroline (lane 6) or 2 μM Z-Thiopro-thiazolidine (lane 7).

medium specifically inhibited the generation of the 20.4- and 14.4-kDa fragments, accumulating degradation products at the 22-23-kDa region (lane 3). This finding suggests that the 20.4- and 14.4-kDa fragments are formed by a DTT-sensitive protease(s). A possible mechanism of the inhibition by DTT is a conformational change of the protease by the reduction of disulfide bond(s). 2 mM diisopropyl fluorophosphate (DFP, an inhibitor of serine protease), 2 mM N-ethylmaleimide (NEM, an inhibitor of cysteine protease), and 2 μM N-benzyloxycarbonyl-L-thiopropyl-thiazolidine (Z-Thiopro-thiazolidine, an inhibitor of PEPase) were not inhibitory at all (lanes 4,5 and 7, respectively). 2 mM 1,10-phenanthroline (an inhibitor of metal protease) slightly inhibited the degradation of the 18-kDa protein (lane 6). Since DFP and Z-Thiopro-thiazolidine are potent inhibitors of the PEPases ever studied [5,6], the ineffectiveness of these reagents to the generation of the 16.5-kDa fragment suggests that the responsible protease is a new type of PEPase.

ACKNOWLEDGEMENTS
    We thank Mr. Y. Hashimoto for preliminary experiments, and Prof. T. Yoshimoto of Nagasaki University for providing Z-Thiopro-thiazolidine. This work was supported by Grants-in-Aid for Scientific Research (62540515) and Scientific Research on Priority Areas of the Molecular Mechanism of Photoreception (62621001) from the Ministry of Education, Science and Culture, Japan, to T.K.

References
1. Kuwabara, T., Murata, T., Miyao, M. and Murata, N. (1986) Biochim. Biophys. Acta 850, 146-155
2. Laemmli, U.K. (1970) Nature 227, 680-685
3. Matsudaira, P. (1987) J. Biol. Chem. 262, 10035-10038
4. Murata, N., Kajiura, H., Fujimura, Y., Miyao, M., Murata, T., Watanabe, A. and Shinozaki, K. (1987) in Progress in Photosynthesis Research (Biggins, J., ed.), Vol. 1, pp.701-704, Martinus Nijhoff Publishers, Dordrecht
5. Wilk, S. (1983) Life Sci. 33, 2149-2157
6. Tsuru, D., Yoshimoto, T., Koriyama. N and Furukawa, S. (1988) J. Biochem. 104, 580-586

DEVELOPMENTAL GRADIENTS OF GENE EXPRESSION IN THE EMERGING FOURTH LEAF OF LOLIUM TEMULENTUM

T. G. EMYR DAVIES and HELEN J. OUGHAM, Plant and Cell Biology Department, IGAP-WPBS, Aberystwyth, Dyfed SY23 3EB, UK.

1. INTRODUCTION
    The growing leaf of a graminaceous plant represents a linear gradient of cell age and differentiation. Cellular function modulates from growth and elongation at the enclosed basal region to photosynthesis in the leaf blade. The comparatively small cell division and elongation zone is the region which controls the rate of leaf expansion, and is thus an important determinant of plant productivity [1]. We have previously speculated that a common regulatory mechanism may turn off growth processes and activate chloroplast assembly. In order to gain a deeper understanding of the factors regulating chloroplast biogenesis, the development of photosynthetic function in fourth leaves of Lolium temulentum has been examined using both Northern and Western analysis.

2. MATERIALS AND METHODS
    Plant growth conditions and the immunological detection of proteins by Western blotting have been described previously [2]. For the purposes of Northern analysis, total RNA was extracted from leaf tissue by a modification of the method of Malik [3]. RNA samples (8ug) were subjected to formamide/formaldehyde agarose gel electrophoresis and subsequently transferred to nylon membranes. Membranes were then prehybridised for 6h. Inserts used as DNA probes were isolated from the following plasmids: pCABIIa, containing a 1.6 kilobase (kb) Pst1 insert of Triticum aestivum genomic DNA including the gene for chlorophyll a/b binding protein of photosystem II [4]; pI27, containing a 1.1 kb EcoR1 insert complementary to the mRNA for protochlorophyllide reductase from Hordeum vulgare (T. Griffiths, unpublished); pTac39, containing a 1.1 kb HindIII insert from the T. aestivum chloroplast cytochrome f gene [5]; prbcL, containing a 1.9 kb HindII insert from the Triticum urartu ribulose bisphosphate carboxylase large subunit gene (T.A. Dyer, R.S. Barker, C.M. Bowman, unpublished); pPND1, containing a 1.2 kb insert including the whole psb A gene from Poa annua [6]. The radiolabelled probes were heat-denatured, added to the prehybridisation mix, and hybridisation carried out overnight. Following stringent washing regions of hybridisation were detected by autoradiography.

2. RESULTS AND DISCUSSION
    Transcripts of the three plastid genes (psb A, pet A and rbc L) and the nuclear cab gene at first increased in relative abundance with increasing

M. Baltscheffsky (ed.), Current Research in Photosynthesis, Vol. III, 747–750.
© 1990 *Kluwer Academic Publishers. Printed in the Netherlands.*

distance from the leaf base (Fig. 1.a-d).

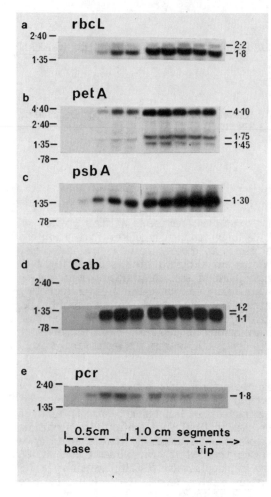

FIGURE 1. Northern analysis of individual messages along the age gradient of fourth leaves of L. temulentum. The analyses were carried out on blots in which each track contained an equal amount of total RNA.

The rbc L probe identified a minor and a major band of approximately 2.2 and 1.8 kb respectively; in other monocots the presence of multiple transcrips of rbc L has been accounted for by specific processing at the 5' end. The pet A gene is usually co-transcribed with adjacent open reading frames [7], the largest product being a primary transcript which requires further processing before it can be translated. Western analysis (Fig. 2.a) revealed that the major antigenic zone consists of at least two components of ca 32 and 33kDa. Only the 1.3 kb psb A transcript was faintly detectable in the basal 0.5 cm of the Lolium fourth leaf; its level increased up to 5 cm from the base, while those for the other two genes plateaued at 3 cm from the base. The wheat cab probe hybridised with an apparent doublet of RNA species of 1.1 and 1.2 kb; as in wheat, it is likely that this size class may include more than one gene product [4]. The transcript(s) were not detected in the basal 0.5 cm; were present at a low level in the next 0.5 cm segment; and thereafter were present at an apparently steady level along the entire length of the leaf. This pattern reflects the gradual transition from non-green, dividing cells to mature photosynthetic leaf tissue. Previous work on rbc L and psb A gene expression in monocots has shown that light is not required for synthesis of their transcripts, although it affects levels of these mRNAs. It is therefore unlikely that progressive exposure to light is in itself sufficient to account directly for increases in levels of plastid gene transcripts; it is also important that the developmental stage of the cells and plastids is such as to permit light-induction of gene expression [8]. Distribution of PCR along the morphogenetic gradient in the fourth leaf is of interest as a pace-setting factor in chloroplast assembly. Western analysis (Fig. 2.b) revealed that developing fourth leaves of L. temulentum contain two immunologically-distinct forms of PCR: a 39 kDa polypeptide which is present in the first 4 cm of the leaf and gradually disappears as the tissue emerges into full light; and a 41 kDa form which is present throughout the leaf length.

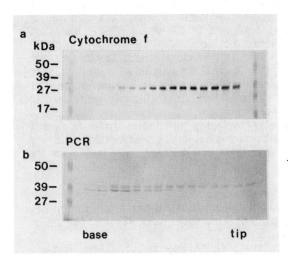

FIGURE 2. Western immunoblots of (a) cytochrome f and (b) PCR, extracted from consecutive 0.5 cm segments of the developing fourth leaf of L. temulentum. Outer tracks are prestained protein standards.

Figure 1.e shows that a single mRNA size class (1.8 kb) from Lolium is recognised by a barley PCR probe. This RNA is barely detectable in the basal 0.5 cm; its abundance is maximal from 1 to 4 cm from the base, and thereafter declines gradually. This distribution correlates well with that of the PCR protein if the abundances of the two molecular weight species in a given segment are combined. It therefore appears that both protein forms may be translation products of a single RNA species, but arise by differential processing or proteolysis during extraction [9]. Alternatively there may be more than one PCR RNA of the same or similar size, in which case the results could be accounted for by invoking tissue-specific translational-level regulation of gene expression. Unlike dark-grown tissue exposed to light, normally-developing Lolium leaves do not exhibit a precipitous decrease in PCR protein or message content as cells move from the sheath environment into full light. It is likely that the gradual differentiation of proplastids into fully-photosynthetic chloroplasts, which occurs with increasing cell age and exposure to light funnelled down the sheath, permits the attainment of a balance between protochlorophyllide synthesis and reduction which stabilises PCR (and its message) at a fairly low level. The persistance of PCR in tissue where it is not required for new chlorophyll biosynthesis seems unlikely, but Dehesh et al. [10] showed that in maize, while PCR within the plastid was subject to rapid loss upon illumination of dark-grown tissue, the extra-plastidic PCR (by immunological and size criteria an identical molecule) was comparatively stable.

4. CONCLUSIONS

The steep gradient of gene expression in the developing fourth leaf of Lolium temulentum, which is manifested in the spectrum of total polypeptides [11], in vivo labelling patterns [12] and individual proteins, is not fully reflected in the profile of translatable mRNA species (Ougham and Davies, manuscript submitted), suggesting that post-transcriptional regulation may play an important part in controlling the metabolic activities of grass leaf cells at different levels of differentiation. As cells move from the zone of division and elongation at the base, the acquisition of photosynthetic competence is reflected in a co-ordinated increase in the levels of transcripts of a nuclear and three plastid genes encoding components of the photosynthetic apparatus. None of these messages shows a marked decline in level towards the tip of the leaf. In the case of the psb A RNA, this probably relates to the very high turnover rate of the gene product (the D1 or 32 kDa protein). The persistence of cab and protochlorophyllide reductase mRNA throughout the length of the leaf blade suggests that they are either long-lived, or continuously synthesised to participate in the turnover of photosynthetic polypeptides and chlorophyll. Results with this and other normally-developing leaf systems differ in several respects from those obtained with dark-grown tissue, emphasising that the effects of light on etioplasts cannot always be taken as valid models for the corresponding processes in developing plastids.

REFERENCES

1 Pollock, C.J. and Eagles, C.F. (1988) in Plants and temperature (Long, S.P. and Woodward F.I. eds), Symp. Soc. Exp. Biol. Vol. 42, The Company Of Biologists Ltd., Cambridge, pp.157-179

2 Davies, T.G.E., Ougham, H.J., Thomas, H., and Rogers, L.J. (1989) Physiol. plantarum 75, 47-54

3 Malik, N.S.A. (1987) Physiol. plantarum 70, 438-446

4 Lamppa, G.K., Morelli, G. and Chua, N-H. (1985) Mol. Cell Biol. 5, 1370-1378

5 Willey, D.L., Howe, C.J., Auffret, A.D., Bowman, C.M., Dyer, T.A. and Gray, J.C. (1984) Mol. Gen. Genet. 194, 416-422

6 Nixon, P.J., Dyer, T.A., Barber, J. and Hunter, C.N. (1986) in Progress in Photosynthesis research (Biggins, J. ed.), Vol. III. Martinus Nijhoff, New York, pp.779-782

7 Willey, D.L. and Gray, J.C. (1988) Photosynthesis Research 17, 125-144

8 van Grinsven, M.Q.J.M. and Kool, A.J. (1988) Plant Mol. Biol. Reporter 6, 213-239

9 Griffiths, W.T. and Walker, C.J. (1987) in Progress in Photosynthesis Research, (Biggins, J. ed.), Vol. IV pp.469-474, Nijhoff, Dordrecht

10 Dehesh, K., van Cleve, B., Ryberg, M. and Apel, K. (1986) Planta 19, 172-183

11 Ougham, H.J. (1987) Physiol. Plant. 70, 479-484

12 Ougham, H.J., Jones, T.W.A. and Evans M.Ll. (1987a) J. Exp. Bot. 38, 1689-1696

DEVELOPMENT OF PS II PHOTOCHEMISTRY AFTER A SINGLE WHITE FLASH IN ETIOLATED BARLEY LEAVES.

F. FRANCK
Laboratoire de Photobiologie, Département de Botanique B 22, Université du Sart-Tilman, B-4000 LIÈGE (Belgium).

INTRODUCTION.

Smith (1) showed that etiolated barley leaves subjected to two short (5 min) periods of illumination separated by a dark interval longer than 25 min were able to evolve oxygen in the light. This result was confirmed by the detection of the Kok-Joliot sequence in plastids isolated after the second illumination (2). However the precise time-course of the synthesis or assembly of active PS II reaction centers after protochlorophyllide photoreduction is not established.
We use here the 77 K variable fluorescence as a probe for measuring PS II photochemistry and we follow its development after a first and second short illumination of etiolated barley leaves.

MATERIAL AND METHODS.

Barley seedlings were grown in darkness on vermiculite at 26°C during the indicated number of days.
For 77 K fluorescence variations measurements, two leaves were applied against a multibranched optical guide which was then immersed in liquid nitrogen. Excitation light was from a He-Ne laser (632.8 nm, 12 mW.cm^{-2}) The fluorescence was measured through a broad (30 nm bandwidth) interference filter at 695 nm using an EMI photomultiplier.
Fluorescence spectra were recorded using a home-made fluorimeter.

RESULTS.

Etiolated leaves first irradiated with one ms white flash and then kept in darkness for 120 min at 26°C exhibited the 77 K fluorescence induction curve shown in Fig. 1. The fluorescence intensity increased from a F_o level to a F_M level with a half-time of 100-120 ms. The relative amplitude of the variable fluorescence F was calculated using the formula $F_v = (F_M - F_o)/F_M$.

M. Baltscheffsky (ed.), Current Research in Photosynthesis, Vol. III, 751–754.
© 1990 *Kluwer Academic Publishers. Printed in the Netherlands.*

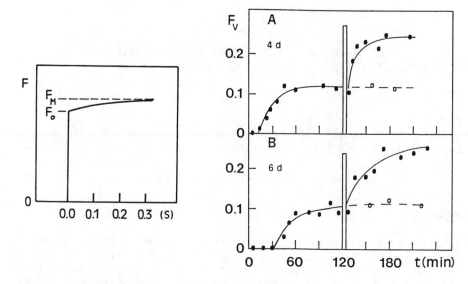

FIGURE 1 (left). 77 K fluorescence variations in a 6-day-old leaf immersed in liquid nitrogen 120 min after one ms white flash.
FIGURE 2 (right). Changes in F_v as a function of time during leaf treatment : 1 ms flash - 120 min dark - 5 min continuous light - dark.
The values in open circles are those of leaves which only received the initial flash. A : 4-day-old leaves. B : 6-day-old leaves.

Fig. 2,A shows F_v as a function of the dark time in 4-day-old leaves. At time 120 min after the flash, leaves which had been kept in darkness were illuminated again with 5 min white light and F_v was measured during the second dark period. Variable fluorescence could be detected already at time 15-20 min after the initial flash. Before that time, the 77 K fluorescence intensity was constant. F_v increased then up to time 60-80 min after the flash and reached a stable value. After the 5 min illumination a second increase phase of F_v was observed.
In 6-day-old leaves (Fig. 2,B), the same processes were observed but F_v appeared later after the initial flash. The duration of the lag phase was increased to about 30 min. After the second illumination, $\bar{F}_v$ increased more slowly than in 4-day-old leaves.

Fluorescence spectra were recorded at 77 K at different moments of the same treatment of the leaves in order to detect spectral changes which might be associated with the development of F_v . Fig. 3 shows the fluorescence spectra of 6-day-old leaves at time 20 and 90 min after the initial flash, thus before and after the development of F_v . The increase of the 657 nm band was due to the regeneration of the active protochlorophyllide. At the same time, a slight but reproducible shift of the chlorophyll(ide) band towards longer wavelengths was observed.

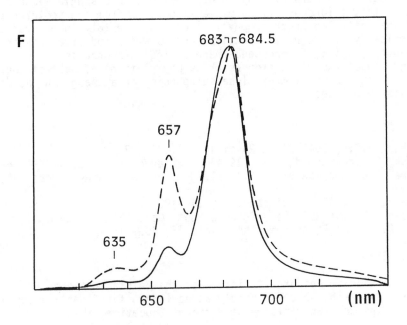

FIGURE 3. 77 K fluorescence spectra of 6-day-old leaves frozen 20 min (full line) or 90 min (broken line) after one ms flash.

The 683 nm chlorophyll(ide) band in the 20 min spectrum was that of the final product of the Shibata shift (4) whose duration was approx. 15 min (data not shown). In the 90 min spectrum, the emission maximum was sifted to 684-685 nm and the shape of the band became assymetric.

DISCUSSION.

It was found previously (1,2) that two short illumination periods spaced by a sufficiently long interval were necessary in order to detect oxygen evolution in etiolated leaves. Since the 77 K variable fluorescence appears already during the dark period after a single ms flash, PS II reaction centers capable of photochemistry must be synthesized or assembled during the dark period, whereas oxygen evolution requires an activation by continuous light. Thus the situation found here after one flash is very similar to the situation found after a large number of flashes (5,6) in the sense that a photoactivation of the water-splitting system is needed for oxygen evolution to occur. In addition here, a large amount of regenerated protochlorophyllide is reduced during the 5 min illumination. This leads to a rapid increase of the amount of PS II reaction centers reflected by the increase of F_v.

The fact that F_v appears already in darkness afer one single flash demonstrates that chlorophyll(ide) pigments derived from the photoreduction of the initial protochlorophyllide pool are rapidly incorporated in photochemically active PS II reaction centers. The modifications in the 77 K chlorophyll(ide) fluorescence band during this process may have different causes:a modification (such as phytylation) of part of the pigments, a change in pigment close surrounding or a change in the energy transfer processes.

REFERENCES.

1. Smith, J.H.C. (1954) Plant Physiol. 29, 143-148
2. Franck, F. and Schmid, G.H. (1984) Z. Naturforsch. 39c, 1091-1096
3. Thorne, S.W. and Boardman, N.K. (1970) Biochim. Biophys. Acta 234, 113-125
4. Shibata, K. (1957) J. Biochem. 44, 147-173
5. Strasser, R.J. (1973) Ber. Schweiz. Bot. Ges. 83(1), 1-13
6. Rémy, R. (1973) Photochem. Photobiol. 18, 409-416

ACKNOWLEDGEMENTS.

F. Franck is Senior Research Assistant of the Belgian National Fund for Scientific Research, which is kindly acknowledged for financial support, as well as the Belgian Ministry of National Education.

PHOTOREDUCTION OF THE PROTOCHLOROPHYLLIDE INTO CHLOROPHYLLIDE IN ETIOLATED LEAVES AND COTYLEDONS FROM PHASEOLUS VULGARIS CV COMMODORE.

Benoît Schoefs and Fabrice Franck, Dept. of Botany; Lab. of Photobiology, Univ. of Liège, B-4000 Liège, Belgium

1. INTRODUCTION.

The kinetics of the photoreduction of protochlorophyllide (Pchlide) into chlorophyllide (Chlide) has generally been studied in 10-15-d dark-grown bean leaves (1-3) or in Pchlide holochromes of such leaves (4). We have detected Pchlide photoreduction in very young etiolated leaves and cotyledons of Phaseolus vulgaris. The reaction kinetics has been compared during their first 10 days of growth. The question of the reaction order has been reinvestigated by computer analysis of the data.

2. MATERIAL AND METHODS.

Seedlings of Phaseolus vulgaris cv Commodore were grown on tap water in a dark room at 298 K. Light-induced absorbance variations at 440 nm were recorded with a home-made apparatus adapted from the Fork spectrophotometer (5-6). The actinic illumination was provided by a He-Ne laser (632.8 nm, 12 mW m^{-2}). Fluorescence variations at 690 nm were obtained the same actinic excitation conditions than for absorbance measurements. All calculations were performed with a computer, using Poisson law.

3. RESULTS.

During the photoreduction of Pchlide, the absorbance at 440 nm decreased due to the lower molar extinction coefficient of Chlide compared to that of the Pchlide (7-8), while the fluorescence at 690 nm increased due to the formation of the Chlide emitting at 688 nm (9).

Figure 1 shows typical absorbance and fluorescence kinetics obtained in 8-day old leaves. Since these measurements could be performed on a rapid time-scale (1-2 s), the influence of the rapid Chlide bathochromic shift (10) could be neglected.

M. Baltscheffsky (ed.), Current Research in Photosynthesis, Vol. III, 755–758.

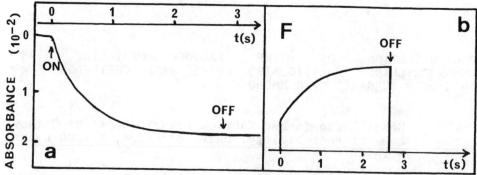

Figure 1.   Absorbance (a)   and fluorescence   kinetics (b)
during photoreduction of Pchlide in 8-day old leaves.

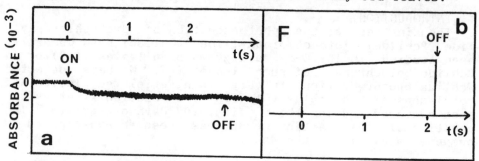

Figure 2.   Absorbance (a)   and fluorescence   kinetics (b)
during photoreduction of Pchlide in 1-day old leaves.

Figure 2   shows that the photoreduction could be detected
through such absorbance and fluorescence recordings already
one day after sowing. In cotyledons, the photoreduction
could sometimes be detected at the 2nd day, and always from
the 3rd day (data not shown).

The amplitude of the absorbance and fluorescence kinetics
increased with the age of the samples.

Absorbance and   fluorescence values   (around 25 points/s)
were introduced in the computer after normalization
using the equation : $\delta A_t^{norm.} = - \delta A_t/\delta A_{max}$ and $\delta F_t^{norm.} = \delta F_t/\delta F_{max}$

Average kinetics   were calculated from 3 absorbance at 10
fluorescence recordings   for each   day and   the best fitting
curves found.

The results   of normalisation   and modelization are shown
in fig 3 for 8 day old leaves.

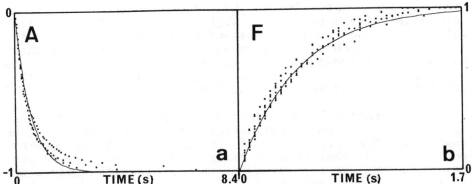

Figure 3. Modelization of absorbance (a) and fluorescence kinetics (b) during photoreduction of Pchlide in 8-day old leaves.

Good fits were obtained at all ages using monoexponential equations : $\delta A_t^{norm.} = e^{-kt}$ and $\delta F_t^{norm.} = e^{-k't}$.

At 5 % level of signifiance k and k' were found equal and constant during the first 10 days of growth. The slight apparent deviation of the fitting curves may be due to the occurence of an additionnal exponential component. However, calculations showed that its relative contribution would be rather small (< 20 %) and that its rate constant would not be very different than the rate constant of the main component. In cotyledons, measurements were less reliable due to the difficulty of sample preparation and large variability, but k and k' values of the same order than in leaves were found.

4. DISCUSSION.
    The kinetics of Pchlide photoreduction was previously reconstitued through 77 K fluorescence spectra measured after illumination at room temperature. Such kinetics were interpreted as a second order reaction (10) or as a sum of two first order reaction (11-12) These fluorescence measurements were influenced by the energy transfer from Pchlide to Chlide which has been shown to be very efficient at 77 K (13-14). Absorbance kinetics were also recorded (2,4,10) but on a very extended time scale (up to 1h) during which spectral shifts of Chlide and Pchlide regeneration occur.
    In this report, absorbance and fluorescence kinetics were measured at room temperature in the time scale. In our conditions, good fitting was obtained using simple monoexponential equations. Moreover, rate constants calculated from absorbance or fluorescence kinetics were not significantly different. This shows that energy transfer

from Pchlide into Chlide has low efficiency at room temperature. The absence of significant transfer tallies well with the quasi-monoexponential character of the kinetics. The occurrence of an additionnal exponential phase may not be excluded due to experimental error, but its relative amplitude would be much smaller than that calculated earlier in different conditions (11,16).

The fact that we can observe photoreduction already in 1-day old leaves with similar kinetics as in older leaves shows that the formation of the active Pchlide does not require long etiolation periods and is not correlated directly with the formation of the prolamellar body since the latter is only detected after 3 days (17).

REFERENCES.
1. Thorne, S.W. (1971) Biochim. Biophys. Acta 226, 113
2. Thorne, S.W. and Boardman, N.K. (1972) Biochim. Biophys. Acta 267, 104
3. Michel, JM. and Sironval, C. (1977) Plant Cell Physiol. 18, 1223
4. Boardman, N.K. (1962) Biochim. Biophys. Acta 64, 2798
5. de Kouchkowsky, Y. and Fork, D.C.(1964) Proc. Natl. Acad. Sci. 52, 232
6. Jouy, M. and Sironval, C. (1979) Planta 147, 127
7. Kahn, A. (1983) Physiol. Plant. 59, 99
8. Michel-Wolwertz, M.R. and Brouers, M. (1983) Photosynth. Res. 4, 265
9. Sironval, C. and Kuyper, Y. (1972) Photosynthetica 6(3) 254
10. Gassman, M., Granick S. and Mauzerall, D. (1968) Biochem. Biophys. Res. Commun. 32, 295
11. Smith, J.H.C. and Benitez, A. (1954) Plant Physiol. 29, 135
12. Sironval, C., Brouers, M., Michel, J.M. and Kuiper, Y. (1968) Photosynthetica 2, 268
13. Nielsen, O.F. and Kahn, A. (1973) Biochem. Biophys. Acta 292, 117
14. Brouers, M., Kuyper, Y. and Sironval, C. (1972) Photosynthetica 6(2), 169
15. Brouers, M. and Sironval, C. (1974) Plant Sc. Lett. 2, 67
16. Vaughan, G.D. and Sauer, K. (1974) Biophys. Acta 347, 383
17. Klein, S. and Schiff, J.A. (1972) Plant Physiol. 49, 619

AKNOWLEDGEMENTS.
The autors are grateful to Dr. Garnir H.P. from the Nuclear Physics Laboratory of the Liège University for his help for the computer calculations. Franck F. is a Senior Research Assistant of the FNRS (Belgium).

PURIFICATION AND CHARACTERISATION OF THE CARBOXYL-TERMINAL PROCESSING PROTEASE OF THE D1 PROTEIN OF PHOTOSYSTEM II FROM SCENEDESMUS OBLIQUUS AND PISUM SATIVUM

JEREMY PACKER, MARK TAYLOR, CHRISTOPHER GERRISH AND JOHN BOWYER, Department of Biochemistry, Royal Holloway and Bedford New College, Egham Hill, Egham, Surrey TW20 0EX, U.K.

1. INTRODUCTION

The LF-1 mutant of S. obliquus has been identified as lacking a specific protease activity responsible for the C-terminal processing of the D1 protein of the photosystem II reaction centre (1). This results in a failure to process the C-terminus of D1 (2), giving rise to a phenotype in which the D1 protein is 1-2 kDa larger than in the wild type and the oxygen evolving complex of PS II is non-functioning (3). A partial purification of the D1 processing protease from spinach has been reported (4). Here we report the purification to homogeneity of the enzyme from S. obliquus wild type and a partial purification from pea leaves.

2. PROCEDURE

Thylakoids and PSII membranes were prepared from S. obliquus as described in (5). Pea thylakoids were prepared as in (6). A thylakoid lumenal extract was prepared from thylakoids washed as in (1) which were sonicated (8 x 30 sec bursts) and the membranes removed by centrifugation (120,000 x g, 45 mins). The supernatant was then dialysed against 4 x 1 l of 10mM Tricine pH 7.0 for 3 hours. Anion exchange chromatography of the extract was carried out on Fractogel TSK-DEAE 650 (21 x 230 mm). Proteins were eluted by a 120 ml, 0-0.5M gradient of NaCl in 10mM Tricine pH 7.0. After concentration (Centricon 10) the active fractions were loaded on to an HPLC size exclusion column (TSK-2000 SWG, 21.5 x 600mm) and eluted with 10mM Tricine pH 7.0, 100mM NaCl. Active fractions from this step were pooled and desalted (Pharmacia PD10) and loaded on to an HPLC DEAE column (TSK DEAE-5PW, 7.5 x 75mm). Elution was with a linear 0-0.5M NaCl gradient in 10mM Tricine pH 7.0 over 120 mins. The flow rate was 1.0 ml/min in all cases. Activity was measured in the fractions as described in (1).

3. RESULTS AND DISCUSSION

The extracts from sonicated thylakoids were subjected to a series of chromatographic steps as described in Materials and Methods. Fig. 1A, B show polyacrylamide gels of active fractions at each stage of the chromatography of the S. obliquus extract.

After the final DEAE step a well resolved band can be detected (arrowed in Fig. 1B) which titrates with protease activity and has a

M. Baltscheffsky (ed.), Current Research in Photosynthesis, Vol. III, 759–762.
© 1990 *Kluwer Academic Publishers. Printed in the Netherlands.*

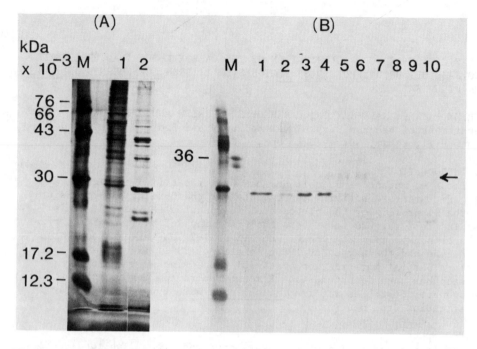

FIGURE 1. SDS-polyacrylamide gel electrophoresis of active fractions from purification of the D1 protease from S. obliquus. Proteins were detected by silver staining. (a) M, molecular weight markers; lane 1, crude soluble extract from sonicated thylakoids; lane 2, eluate from Fractogel TSK DEAE-650 column (b) M; molecular weight markers as in (a), with 36 kDa marker; lane 1, eluate from TSK G2000 SWG column; lanes 2-5, fractions eluting (right to left) from TSK DEAE-5PW column. Fraction 6 is the fraction from the middle of the elution profile of D1 processing activity. The putative protease band is arrowed.

MW of 33-34 kDa. This concurs with an apparent MW of 35 kDa from the elution profile during size exclusion chromatography (not shown). The purest fractions containing protease activity are contaminated by a minor component of 40 kDa, but this does not co-elute with protease activity. A gel showing purification of the protease from pea leaves is shown in Fig. 2. In this case there are several bands in the purest preparation, none of which can be readily identified as the protease. The apparent MW of the pea enzyme from size exclusion chromatography was also 30-35 kDa. The spinach enzyme has a MW of 34 kDa as judged from size exclusion chromatography (4).

The partially purified protease from S. obliquus was incubated with thylakoids from LF-1 in which D1 had been labelled in vivo incubation with ^{35}S-methionine (Fig. 3). Processing of D1 to the mature size did not occur unless the labelled thylakoids were sonicated in the presence of the protease, allowing the protease to have access to the lumen of the thylakoids. No degradation of other labelled proteins can be seen.

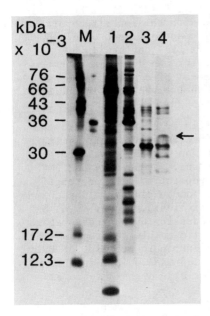

FIGURE 2. SDS-polyacrylamide gel electrophoresis of active fractions from purification of the D1 protease from pea. Proteins were detected by silver staining. M, molecular weight markers; lane 1, crude extract from sonicated thylakoids; lane 2, eluate from Fractogel TSK DEAE-650 column; lane 3, eluate from TSK G2000 SWG column; lane 4, eluate from TSK DEAE-5PW column. The putative protease, based on its apparent molecular weight from size exclusion chromatography, is arrowed.

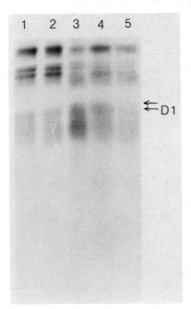

FIGURE 3. Membrane topology of the D1 carboxyl terminal processing site. Thylakoids labelled in vivo with [^{35}S]-methionine were mixed with partially purified (after size exclusion chromatography) protease from S. obliquus, sonicated as indicated, and then incubated for 1 hour. Samples were electrophoresed and the gel fluorographed. Lane 1, wild type thylakoids, no additions; lane 2, wild type thylakoids, sonicated with protease; lane 3, LF-1 thylakoids, no additions; lane 4, LF-1 thylakoids with protease but not sonicated; lane 5, LF-1 thylakoids sonicated with protease. The positions of processed and non-processed D1 are indicated.

Previous reports of D1 processing in vitro have involved the preparation of a crude thylakoid extract by solubilisation with Triton X-100 (1,4). This study demonstrates that Triton X-100 is not required to release the protease from the thylakoid. It might there-fore be soluble in the lumen or associated with the inner face of the membrane. In the absence of detergent, processing is not observed unless access is provided to the interior of LF-1 thylakoids by sonication. This supplies direct evidence for the hypothesis that the C-terminus of D1 is located on the lumenal side of the membrane. This was previously supposed by analogy with the bacterial reaction centre (7).

The enzyme from S. obliquus has been partially characterised. The pH optimum for processing has been determined using the PSII membrane assay (1). It is rather sharp at pH 6.5. None of the usual protease inhibitors tested have inhibited D1 processing. These were 2mM PMSF, 10mM iodoacetamide, 20mM EDTA and 10μg/ml pepstatin. The protease cannot therefore be assigned to any of the common classes. The enzyme was inhibited by 1-10mM concentrations of divalent cations: Cu,Zn>Mn> Ca,Mg. Divalent cations also inhibited processing by a crude prepara-tion in Triton X-100 (4). The enzyme was also unable to process ^{35}S-labelled precursors of the 23kDa and 33kDa extrinsic proteins of PSII from wheat prepared by in vitro translation of mRNA. This further confirms the specificity of the protease for D1 and the absence of non-specific proteolytic activity.

The inability of the protease to N-terminally process nuclear encoded lumenal proteins, and its lack of detergent requirement distinguish it from the previously studied N-terminal processing peptidase from pea thylakoids (8). Although removal of the C-terminal extension of D1 appears to be an essential prerequisite for formation of a complete water-splitting complex (1), the function of the extension remains a mystery. DNA sequence data suggest that D1 is not synthesised with an extension in Euglena gracilis (9). The extension may therefore not be required for assembly of D1 into PSII but may provide a more subtle selective advantage.

REFERENCES
1 Taylor, M.A., Packer, J.C.L. and Bowyer, J.R. (1988) FEBS Lett. 237, 229-233
2 Taylor, M.A., Nixon, P.J., Todd, C.M., Barber, J. and Bowyer, J.R. (1988) FEBS Lett. 235, 109-116
3 Metz, J.G., Wong, J. and Bishop, N.I. (1980) FEBS Lett. 114, 61-66
4 Inagaki, N., Fugita, S. and Satoh, K. (1989) FEBS Lett. 246, 218-222
5 Metz, J.G. and Seibert, M. (1984) Plant Physiol. 76, 829-832
6 Bowyer, J.R., Camilleri, P. and Stapleton, A. (1984) FEBS Lett. 172, 239-244
7 Trebst, A. (1986) Z. Naturforsch 41c, 241-245
8 Kirwin, P.M., Elderfield, P.D. and Robinson, C. (1987) J. Biol. Chem. 262, 16386-16390
9 Keller, M. and Stutz, E. (1984) FEBS Lett. 175, 173-177

PURIFICATION AND PROPERTIES OF A THYLAKOIDAL ENZYME OF SPINACH INVOLVED IN THE PROCESSING OF D1 PROTEIN OF PS II REACTION CENTER

N. Inagaki, S. Fujita and K. Satoh
Dept. Biol., Okayama Univ., Okayama., Japan

1. INTRODUCTION

It is generally believed that D1 and D2 proteins constitute the RC of PSII in a similar manner to the L and M subunits forming the purple bacterial RC (1-3). On the other hand, the D1 protein is also recognized as one of the most unstable proteins in thylakoid membranes in the light and is known to be recovering rapidly through a light-regulated de novo synthesis (4). The protein is synthesized as a precursor 1-2 kDa greater in size than that of the mature form. The maturation process of the newly synthesized precursor protein is predicted to occur through a C-terminal cleavage at Ala-344 of the amino acid sequence deduced from spinach psbA gene (5,6). The processing seems to be essential for the assembly of the catalytic center for water cleavage, but not for the primary photochemistry of PSII (7,8). The enzyme has recently been solubilized from wild-type strain of Scenedesmus obliquus (8).

In the present study, we have succeeded in extracting the D1-specific processing enzyme from spinach thylakoids by Triton X-100 treatment. The purification and properties of this enzyme will be presented in this paper.

2. PROCEDURE

2.1. Preparation of D1 precursor protein

High-MW RNAs were extracted from spinach chloroplasts. The RNAs were translated to proteins by a wheat germ cell-free system containing [^{35}S]-methionine.

2.2. Assay of protease activity

The in vitro translated protein described above was added to enzyme in 50 mM Tris-HCl buffer (pH 7.2) and 0.05 % Triton X-100, then incubated at 25 °C for 2 h. Proteins were separated by SDS-PAGE and visualized on fluorograms and densitometrically monitored.

3. RESULTS AND DISCUSSION

3.1. Extraction

In the experiment shown in Fig. 1., fractions obtained from spinach chloroplasts by different treatments were incubated with in vitro translated D1 precursor protein. The specific break down of the

M. Baltscheffsky (ed.), Current Research in Photosynthesis, Vol. III, 763–766.
© 1990 Kluwer Academic Publishers. Printed in the Netherlands.

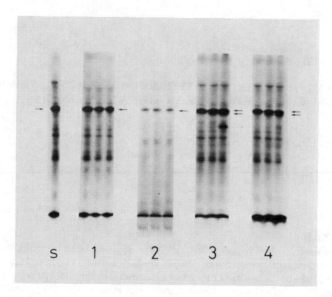

Figure 1
Extraction of D1 specific processing
enzyme. Samples obtained by procedures
indicated in the flow chart were
incubated with *in vitro* translation
products.
In each column (fluorogram)
  Left lane :   0 min
  Center lane : 60 min
  Right lane : 120 min incubated

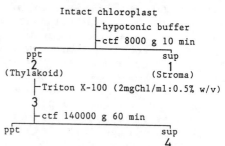

precursor protein to the mature size was observed only after
Triton-X100 treatment and the activity remained in the supernatant
after centrifugation.
3.2. Purification
Processing enzyme in the supernatant can be purified by gel-
filtration chromatography using Sephadex G-75 (9). Using MW
standards, the size of the enzyme was estimated to be about 34 kDa
in its active state. The enzyme was further purifified by an
anion-exchange chromatography using QAE-Toyopearl (Fig. 2). CBB-
staining of the proteins separated by SDS-PAGE in the active
fractions exhibited two bands of about 34 kDa. These two proteins
were separated by hydroxylapatite chromatography.
3.3. Properties
    3.3.1. <u>Activators</u> <u>and</u> <u>inhibitors</u>: The enzymatic activity was
          inhibited by chelators such as 1,10-phenanthroline and 2,2-
          dipyridyl and reducing agents such as DTT and 2-
          mercaptoethanol, but not by protease inhibitors as PMSF, NEM,
          leupeptine, antipain, cymostatin, pepstain A, phospholamidon,
          bestatin and amastatin.

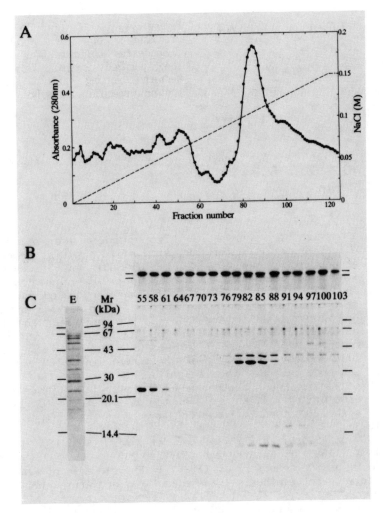

Figure 2
Purification of processing enzyme by anion-exchange chromatography using QAE-Toyopearl.
A) Elution profile of QAE-Toyopearl column chromatography. (0.05 % Triton X-100 ,50 mM Tris-HCl pH 7.5 at 4°C).
B) Enzyme activity of each fraction (fluorogram).
C) SDS-PAGE analysis of each fraction (CBB-staining).

3.3.2. Cleavage of LF-1 D1 : In the experiment shown in Fig. 3, the purified spinach enzyme was incubated with PSII enriched membranes prepared from LF-1 mutant of Scenedesmus. The D1 protein of LF-1 mutant was cleaved to the size of mature protein in the wild type, suggesting that the processing enzyme is common between higher plant and algae.

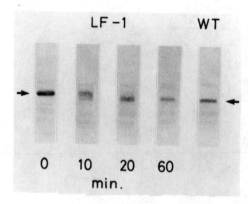

Figure 3
Processing of D1 protein of *Scenedesmus obliquus* LF-1 mutant by the purified enzyme from spinach. Western blotting analysis using D1 protein specific antibody.

3.3.3. <u>Cleavage</u> <u>of</u> a <u>synthetic</u> <u>oligopeptide</u> : When a synthetic oligopeptide, COOH-terminal side of D1 protein deduced from spinach psbA gene (Asn-325 to Gly-353), was incubated with the purified enzyme, two components appeared during incubation period. Based on the amino acid sequence analysis of two products,larger one was Ala-345 to Gly-353 and smaller one was Asn-325 to Arg-334. It is concluded that (1) the cleavage takes place at the predicted processing site of native D1 protein (COOH-side of Ala-344); (2) the oligopeptide consisting of the COOH-terminal 29 amino acids sequence provides the recognition domain for the processing enzyme; and (3) another cleavage also takes place at COOH-side of Arg-334, but not for the native state. (collaboration with T. Ono and Y. Inoue)(10).

REFERENCES
1 Nanba, O. and Saoth, K. (1987) Proc. Natl. Acad. Sci. USA 84, 109-112
2 Trebst, A. (1986) Z. Naturforsch 41C, 240-245
3 Michel, H. and Deisenhofer, J. (1986) In Encyclopedia of Plant Physiology : Photosynthesis (Staehelin L. A. and Arntzen, C. J. eds) vol.19 (new series), 371-381, Spriger, Berlin
4 Mattoo, A. K., Marder, J. B. and Edelman, M. (1989) Cell 56, 241-246
5 Takahashi, M., Shiraishi, T. and Asada, K. (1988) FEBS Lett. 240, 6-8
6 Takahashi, Y., Nakane, H. and Satoh, K. (1989) submitted
7 Diner, B. A., Ries, D. F., Cohen, B. N. and Metz, J. G. (1988) J. Biol. Chem. 263, 8972-8980
8 Taylor, M. A., Packer, J. C. L. and Bowyer, J. R. (1988) FEBS Lett. 237, 229-233
9 Inagaki, N., Fujita, S. and Satoh, K. (1989) FEBS Lett. 246,218-222
10 Fujita, S., Inagaki, N., Ono, T., Inoue, Y. and Satoh, K. (1989) FEBS Lett. In press

NUCLEAR-CODED SUBUNITS OF PSI IN <u>NICOTIANA</u>

Junichi Obokata[1], Kohki Mikami[1], Nobuaki Hayashida[2], and
Masahiro Sugiura[2].
Research Center for Molecular Genetics, Hokkaido University,
Sapporo 060 [1], Center for Gene Research, Nagoya University,
Nagoya 464[2], Japan.

1. INTRODUCTION

The PSI complex in thylakoid membranes contains subunits encoded
each by the nuclear and chloroplast genomes. A few years ago we
initiated research on PSI biogenesis with a special emphasis on the
contribution of the nuclear genome. In this article we would like to
summarize our recent work briefly, and then discuss the role of the
nuclear genome in relation to the evolution of photosynthetic apparatus.
The details of our recent work will be described elsewhere.

2. CONTRIBUTION OF THE NUCLEAR GENOME ON PSI BIOGENESIS.

For the first step of the analysis of PSI biogenesis, we determined
which subunits of PSI are nuclear-encoded. PSI complex was prepared from
several species of <u>Nicotiana,</u> and each subunit was separated by high
resolution LDS PAGE. Partial amino acid sequences were determined for
each subunit, and compared with the amino acid sequences deduced from
tobacco chloroplast DNA sequence in order to determine which subunits
are chloroplast-encoded. As far as the PSI subunits having mol. wt.
from 5.6 kDa to 20 kDa are concerned, it was only psaC protein that was
proved to be of chloroplast origin. All the others, some of which are
blocked at their N-termini, are not coded for by chloroplast DNA,
indicating that they are of nuclear origin.
    Considering that most of the PSII subunits are of chloroplast
origin, it is a characteristic of the PSI complex that its biogenesis is
largely dependent on the nuclear genome.

3. SUBUNIT POLYMORPHISM CAUSED BY ALLOPLOIDY.

Comparative analysis of the PSI subunits among pure line and
alloploid species in <u>Nicotiana</u> revealed that an alloploid genome brings
about polymorphism of nuclear-encoded subunits (Obokata et al.
submitted). This implies that polyploidy and interspecific hybrids have
complicated the subunit composition of the photosynthetic apparatus
during the plant evolutions.

M. Baltscheffsky (ed.), Current Research in Photosynthesis, Vol. III, 767–770.
© *1990 Kluwer Academic Publishers. Printed in the Netherlands.*

Table 1. Amino acid sequence homology (%) of the PSII subunits encoded by chloroplast DNA.

	psbA	psbB	psbC	psbD	psbE	Ref.
tobacco	100	100	100	100	100	1.
spinach	100	96.5	97.9	98.3	98.8	2.3.4.5.
barley	98.3	95.5		96.6	95.2	6.7.8.9.
liverwort	96.9	91.5	96.0	96.6	88.0	10.
Chlamydomonas	92.9			94.1		11.12.

4. DIVERSITY OF NUCLEAR-ENCODED SUBUNITS.

Chloroplast-coded subunits of PSII are listed in Table 1, showing they are highly conserved over a wide range of plant species. This conservative nature of chloroplast-encoded subunits is also true to PSI. Fig.1 represents the frequency of amino acid substitution, insertion, and/or deletion in the PSI proteins of chloroplast-origin (psaA, psaB, and psaC) and nuclear-origin (psaE) among several plant species. Using the tobacco protein as a control, the frequencies of amino acid alteration for the psaA subunit are 2.1%, 3.9%, and 7.3% in spinach, maize, and liverwort, respectively. Similar values are obtained for the psaB and psaC subunits, indicating that chloroplast-encoded subunits of

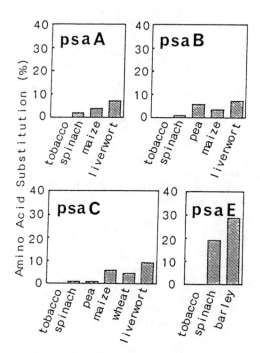

Fig. 1. The diversity of the PSI subunits. The Frequency of amino acid substitution, insertion, and/or deletion is caluculated on chloroplast-coded subunits (psaA, psaB, and psaC) or the mature protein of the nuclear-coded subunit (psaE), using the tobacco proteins as controls.
References:
psaA;1,10,13,14,
psaB;1,10,13,14,15,
psaC;16,17,18,19,20,
psaE;Obokata et al. un-
published, 21,22.

PSI are highly conserved. As for the psaE subunit which is nuclear-encoded, the alteration frequency turns out to be 18.5% and 29.3% in spinach and barley respectively, which are considerably higher than the values for chloroplast-encoded subunits. These results clearly show that the extent of sequence conservation during plant evolutions is quite different between nuclear-encoded subunits and chloroplast-encoded subunits.

Another aspect of the diversity is the heterogeneity of the subunit encoded by the haploid genome. It is well known that the apoproteins of LHCP are coded for by the multigene family, manifesting multiformity. As for the PSI complex, we found the evidence that the haploid genome of Nicotiana codes for two types of psaD proteins (Obokata et al. in preparation). Since the chloroplast genome does not code for a multigene family as far as we know, this type of diversity is also a characteristic of the nuclear-encoded subunits.

5. DOES THE NUCLEAR GENOME ENDOWS PHOTOSYNTHETIC APPARATUS PLASTICITY ?

It appears that the nuclear genetic system has introduced the diversity into PSI proteins by mechanisms such as the polyploidy, intersecific hybrids, multigene family, and the mutations on the genes. On the other hand, the chloroplast system has highly conserved the integral subunits of the reaction center during plant evolutions. Considering these points, we would like to propose a model of the PSI complex as in Fig. 2. According to this model, nuclear-encoded proteins which have plasticity during speciation surround the reactioncenter core, and have generated the diversity of the photosynthetic apparatus

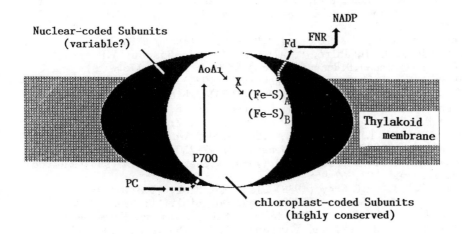

Fig.2. A model of the PSI complex explaining the relationships among the extent of sequence conservation, the site of biosynthesis, and the function of the subunits.

during plant evolutions. This diversity may have enabled plants to adapt various physiological environment.

This wark was supported by Grant-in-Aid for Scientific Research on Priority Areas of the Molecular Mechanism of Photoreception (62621501, 63621001,01621501) from the Ministry of Education, Science and Culture, Japan.

References
1. Shinozaki,K., M.Ohme, M.Tanaka, T.Wakasugi, N.Hayashida, T.Matsubayashi, N.Zaita, J.Chunwongse, J.Obokata, K.Yamaguchi-Shinozaki, C.Ohto, K.Torazawa, B.Y.Meng, M.Sugita, H.Deno, K.Kamogashira, K.Yamada, J.Kusuda, F.Takaiwa, A.Kato, N.Tohdoh, H.Shimada, and M.Sugiura (1986) EMBO J. 5:2043-2049
2. Zurawski,G., H.J.Bohnert, P.R.Whitfeld, and W.Bottomley (1982) Proc.Natl.Acad.Sci.USA 79:7699-7703
3. Morris,J., R.G.Hermann (1984) Nucleic Acid Res. 12:2837-2850
4. Holschuh,K., W.Bottonley and P.R.Whitfeld (1984) Nucleic Acid Res. 12:8819-8834
5. Hermann,R.G., J.Alt, B.Schiller, W.R.Widger and W.A.Cramer (1984) FEBS Lett. 176: 239-244
6. Boyer,S.K., J.E.Mullet (1988) Nucleic Acid Res.16:8184
7. Reverdatto,S.V., A.V.Andreeva, A.A.Buryakova, O.G.Chakhmakhcheva and V.A.Efimov (1989) Nucleic Acid Res. 17:2859
8. Efimov,V.A., A.V.Andreeva, S.V.Reverdatto, R.Jung and O.G.Chakhmakhcheva (1988) Nucleic Acid Res. 16:5686
9. O.G.Chakhmakhcheva, A.VAndreeva, A.A.Buryakova, S.V.Reverdatto and V.A.Efimov (1989) 17:2858
10. Ohyama,K., H.Fukuzawa, T.Kohchi, H.Shirai, T.Sano, S.Sano, K.Umesono, Y.Shiki, M.Takeuchi, Z.Chang, S.Aota, H.Inokuchi and H.Ozeki (1986) Nature 322:572-574
11. Erickson,J.M., M.Rahire and J.D.Rochaix (1984) EMBO J. 3:2753-2762
12. Erickson,J.M., M.Rahire, P.Malnoe, J.Girard-Bascou, Y.Pierre, P.Bennoun and J.D.Rochaix (1986) EMBO J. 5:1745-1754
13. Kirsch,W., P.Seyer and R.G.Herrmann (1986) Current Genet. 10:843-855
14. Fish,L.E., U.Kuck and L.Bogorad (1985) J.Biol.Chem. 260:1413-1421
15. Lehmbeck,L., O.F.Rasmussen, G.B.Bookjans, B.R.Jepsen, B.M.Stummann and K.W.Henningsen (1986) Plant Mol.Biol. 7:3-10
16. Hayashida.N., T.Matsubayashi, K.Shinozaki, M.Sugiura, K.Inoue and T.Hiyama (1987) Current Genet. 12:247-250
17. Oh-oka,H., Y.Takahashi, K.Kuriyama, K.Saeki and H.Matsubara (1988) J.Biochem. 103:962-968
18. Dunn,P.P.J., J.C.Gray (1988) Plant Mol Biol. 11:311-319
19. Schantz,R., L.Bogorad (1988) Plant Mol Biol. 11:239-247
20. Kochi,T., H.Shirai, H.Fukuzawa, T.Sano, T.Komano, K.Umesono, H.Inokuchi, H.Ozeki and K.Ohyama (1988) J.Mol.Biol. 203:353-372
21. Munch,S., U.Ljunberg, J.Steppuhn, A.Schneiderbauer, R.Nechshtai, K.Beyreuther an R.G.Herrmann (1988) Curr.Genet. 14:511-518
22. Okkels,J.S., L.B.Jepsen, L.S.Honberg,J.Lehmbeck, H.V.Scheller, P.Brandt, G.Hoyer-Hansen, B.Stummann, K.W.Henningsen, D.Wettstein and B.L.Møller (1988) FEBS Lett. 237:108-112

LIGHT-INDUCED ACCUMULATION OF PS II PROTEINS AND EXPRESSION
OF OXYGEN EVOLUTION ACTIVITY IN EUGLENA

A. MIZOBUCHI, H. HIRAMATSU AND Y. YAMAMOTO
DEPT. OF BIOL., OKAYAMA UNIV., OKAYAMA 700, JAPAN

1. INTRODUCTION
    Analysis of biogenesis of oxygen evolution system in
chloroplast is one of the promising ways for elucidating
its structure and function. During the development of
chloroplasts under illumination, the constituents of the
oxygen evolution system have to be synthesized and
organized properly in the thylakoid membrane to enable an
efficient reaction. So far the process of assembly of the
oxygen evolution system in thylakoid membrane has not been
studied extensively, and information on this problem is
quite limited. In the present study, we investigated the
assembly of the PS II components in greening process of
cells of Euglena gracilis Z mainly with SDS-PAGE and
Western-blotting analysis. The results suggest that
accumulation of the extrinsic 30 kDa protein in the
thylakoid primarily determines the organization of the
oxygen evolution system and expression of its activity in
Euglena.

2. MATERIALS AND METHODS
    The dark-adapted Euglena cells grown in Hutner's
heterotrophic medium and being at early stationary phase
were transferred to light condition (1,500 lx, provided by
white fluorescent lamps). After illumination for given
periods, the cells were collected by centrifugation at
5,000 x g for 3 min, and washed once with a medium
containing 50 mM potassium phosphate (pH 7.0) and 0.33 M
sorbitol.
    SDS-PAGE and Western-blotting were done as previously
described (1,2). Proteins from 4 x 10[5] cells were analysed
in each lane of the gel. Preparation of the antibodies
against the extrinsic 33-kDa protein, the reaction center-
binding D1, D2 proteins, the apoprotein of LHC was
described previously (2,3). The protein bands in the
nitrocellulose membranes in Western-blotting were analyzed
by a Shimazu dual-wavelength TLC scanner CS-930. Density
of the proteins on the nitrocellulose membranes developed
by the reaction of peroxidase-conjugated anti-rabbit goat
IgG, peroxide and reduced 4-chloro-1-naphthol was measured

M. Baltscheffsky (ed.), Current Research in Photosynthesis, Vol. III, 771–774.
© 1990 Kluwer Academic Publishers. Printed in the Netherlands.

at 510 nm. Before the quantitation of the density, linear relationship between the amount of protein and the density was ascertained.
Measurement of DCIP photoreduction, assay of chlorophyll and carotenoid, and in organello translation were carried out as described elsewhere(4).

3. RESULTS AND DISCUSSION

By the dark-light transition of Euglena cells, chloroplasts are developed and photosynthetic activity appears. To see the effect of light illumination on the biogenesis of PS II, we first carried out SDS-PAGE for the proteins of dark- and light-grown Euglena cells, and compared their polypeptide profile each other (Fig. 1). After illumination of the cells, proteins with relative molecular mass ranging from 20,000-40,000 were induced, and among them the apoprotein of LHC (a relative molecular mass of about 27,000) was most prominent. As to photosynthetic pigments, carotenoid was the major pigment in the dark-grown cells. At the early stage of greening, chlorophyll a to b ratio was high (15-20), but the ratio decreased to the value of 3 as the greening proceeded, which probably shows that the reaction center and antenna chlorophyll a molecules are synthesized firstly and syntheis of chlorophyll a/b in LHC follows it.

Light-induced accumulation of D1 protein, LHC apoprotein and extrinsic 30 kDa protein in the thylakoid membrane of Euglena was assayed by SDS-PAGE and Western blotting with specific antibodies prepared against proteins from spinach (Fig. 2).
In the dark-grown cells, no PS II protein was detected by the immuno-blotting analysis. D1 protein, LHC apoprotein and 30 kDa protein were accumulated under illumination but

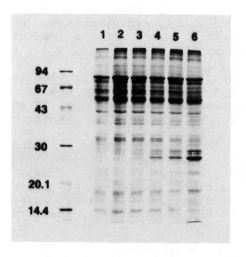

Fig. 1. A SDS-polyacrylamide gel showing the total proteins of Euglena cells in the greening process. The far left lane is the molecular weight markers. Lane 1; the dark-grown cells. Lanes 2-6; the cells illuminated by white fluorescent lamps (1,500 lx) for 8, 17, 26, 29 and 55 h, respectively after dark incubation. The cell number in each lane was 4 x 10^5.

their accumulation did not occur simultaneously. Compared with D1 and LHC apoprotein, appearance of the 30 kDa protein was delayed considerably.

The specific delay of accumulation of the 30 kDa protein in the membrane seems to be critical for the expression of oxygen evolution activity in chloroplasts. By measuring the electron transport activity of Euglena chloroplasts in greening process, it was shown that DCIP photoreduction activity with water as an electron donor developed later compared with DPC as a donor. Apparently the former activity appeared in parallel with the accumulation of the 30 kDa protein in the membrane (Fig. 3).

These results suggest the following scheme for the assembly of the PS II complex in Euglena. Illumination of the dark-grown cells induces synthesis of the core components of PS II, i.e., D1, D2, CP43, CP47 and cytochrome b559 (synthesis of CP43, CP47 and cytochrome b559 were not shown here). All these components are known to be encoded by chloroplast DNA (5). On the other hand, the extrinsic 30 kDa protein and the apoprotein of LHC are encoded by nuclear DNA (6, 7), and it is possible that their expression is regulated differently from that of the core components (8). These nuclear encoded proteins are synthesized in the cytoplasm and their precursors are transported through chloroplast envelope membrane (9). In

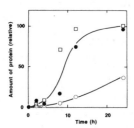 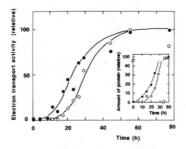

Fig. 2. The amount of PS II proteins accumulated in Euglena cells in the greening process. ●; D1 protein. o; the extrinsic 30 kDa protein. □; apoprotein of LHC. The amount of each protein in 4 x 10^5 cells is shown.

Fig. 3. Electron transport activity and accumulation of PS II proteins in thylakoid during the greening process of Euglena cells. ●; DCIP photoreduction with DPC as an electron donor. o; DCIP photoreduction with water as an electron donor. In the inset, closed and open circles show the amount of LHC apoprotein and the extrinsic 30 kDa protein in the thylakoid, respectively.

the case of the 30 kDa protein it must cross the thylakoid membrane also. In the earlier stage of development of Euglena, protein transport system is probably not fully functional, which may be a cause for the delay of the assembly of the specific proteins. In that case, expression of ATPase activity and the specific enzymes responsible for the processing may limit the assembly of the proteins in chloroplasts. Transport of the 30 kDa protein across the envelope and thylakoid membrane should be most affected under these conditions.

As the 30 kDa protein is shown to be responsible for stabilization of Mn atoms in the catalytic center of oxygen evolution system (10), coordination of Mn atoms to the appropriate protein and formation of a stable cluster structure of Mn atoms in the presence of the 30 kDa protein may be required for the expression of oxygen evolution activity in Euglena chloroplasts. Probably light plays some crucial role in ligation of Mn to PS II complex and that should be elucidated in the greening process of Euglena. Under the present condition, Euglena cells were grown in an enriched culture medium and Mn is not limiting the growth of the cells. Further analysis of the organization of oxygen evolution system has to be carried out in an Mn-limited growth condition to reveal the role of Mn in the assembly of PS II polypeptides and expression of oxygen evolution activity.

REFERENCES
1 Yamamoto, Y. (1988) J. Biol. Chem. 263, 497-500
2 Yamamoto, Y. (1988) Biochim. Biophys. Acta 993, 165-171
3 Aoki, K., Ideguchi, T., Kakuno, T., Yamashita, J. and Horio, T. (1986) J. Biochem. 100, 875-882
4 Mizobuchi, A. and Yamamoto, Y. (1989) Biochim. Biophys. Acta, in the press
5 Shinozaki, K., Ohme, M., Tanaka, M., Wakasugi, T., Hayashida, N., Matsubayashi, T., Zaita, N., Chunwongse, J., Obokata, J., Yamaguchi-Shinozaki, K., Ohto, C., Torazawa, K., Meng, B. Y., Sugita, M., Deno, H., Kamogashira, T., Yamada, K., Kusuda, J., Takaiwa, F., Kato, A., Tohdoh, N., Shimada, H., and Sugiura, M. (1986) EMBO J. 5, 2043-2049
6 Westhoff, P., Jansson, C., Klein-Hitpass, L., Berzborn, R., Larsson, C. and Bartlett, S. G. (1985) Plant Mol. Biol. 4, 137-146
7 Coruzzi, G., Broglie, R., Cashmore, A. and Chua, N.-H. (1983) J. Biol. Chem. 258, 1399-1402
8 Tobin, E. M. and Silverthorne, J. (1985) Ann. Rev. Plant Physiol. 36, 569-593
9 Lubben, T. H., Theg, S. M. and Keegstra, K. (1988) Photosynthesis Res. 17, 173-194
10 Yamamoto, Y. (1989) Bot. Mag. Tokyo, in the press

THE DEVELOPMENT OF THE PHOTOSYNTHETIC APPARATUS IN PHASEOLUS VULGARIS L.
AND NICOTIANA TABACUM L.. METHODOLOGICAL ASPECTS OF THE ELECTRON TRANS-
PORT.

R.Valcke (1), K.Van Loven (1,2), S.Beinsberger (1,2), H.Van Onckelen (2)
& H.Clijsters (1).
(1) Dept S.B.M., Limburgs Universitair Centrum, Universitaire Campus,
    B-3610 Diepenbeek, Belgium.
(2) Dept Biologie, Universitaire Instelling Antwerpen, Universiteits-
    plein, B-2610 Wilrijk, Belgium.

1. Introduction

The study of the development of the photosynthetic apparatus may
involve the measurement of the capacity of the electron transport by
polarographic methods. This can be done by using the classical Rank
Brother Oxygen Electrode(1).
Depending on the system under study, oxygen production or consumption
is measured. In both cases the use of artificial electron acceptors and
electrondonors is necessary (2). The classical electron acceptor for the
whole electron transport chain with water as electron donor is methylviologen. The same acceptor is used when one measures the photosystem I
(PSI) electron transport but now with different artificial electron
donors after inhibition of photosystem 2 (PS2) with DCMU (2). In both
cases an oxygen consumption is registered due to the auto-oxidation of
the reduced methylviologen (3).
PS 2 activity is measured as an oxygen production with water as electron
donor and with artificial electron acceptors who withdrawn the electrons
somewhere between PS 2 and PS 1(4).

In this report we present a systematic study of some of the known electron acceptors and donors in their use to measure the electron transport
capacity of the photosynthetic redox chain.

2. Procedure

2.1. Plant material: Phaseolus vulgaris cv. Limburgse Vroege was cul-
     tivated on vermiculite under a 12h day (25°C)/ 12h night (21°C)
     regime for 8 days. Relative humidity was 65%. A photon flux den-
     sity of 150 molm s was obtained using Cool White 20 SA, Universal
     White 25 SA (Osram) and Phillinea (Phillips) Lamp.
     Nicotiana tabacum cv Petit Havanna SR1 was cultivated in pot gr
     ground for 6 weeks under the same conditions as described above.
2.2. Thylakoidmembranes were isolated in 400mM sucrose, 10mM NaCl, 10
     mM EDTA, 50mM Tricine-NaOH pH 8.5 and 0.2% BSA. After filtration
     through nyloncloth and miracloth and centrifugation, the pellet

M. Baltscheffsky (ed.), Current Research in Photosynthesis, Vol. III, 775–778.
© 1990 *Kluwer Academic Publishers. Printed in the Netherlands.*

was resuspended in 400mM sucrose, 10mM NaCl, 50mM Tricine-NaOH pH 8.0 and kept on ice.

2.3. <u>Photosystem 2</u> activity was measured using water as electron donor and with DCPIP, TMQ, DAD, PD, TMPD, BQ and DMBQ as electron acceptors. The reaction medium contains 2mM NaCl, 5mM $MgCl_2$, 2mM K_2HPO_4 10mM Tricine-NaOH pH 7.8, 48mM $K_3Fe(CN)_6$.

2.4. <u>Photosystem 1</u> activity was measured using methylviologen as electron acceptor. As electron donor we use the same series as above but now reduced with $NaBH_4$ (3).

2.5. <u>Chlorophyll</u> measurements were performed as described by Lichtenthaler and Wellburn (5).

3. Results and discussion.

The value of the photochemical activity of PS 2, expressed as mol O_2 produced (mol O_2 mg chl h) depends on the electron acceptor used (table 1).

Electron acceptor	PS 2 activity in μmol O_2/mgchl/h	
	Phaseolus	Nicotiana
DCPIP	154 + 2	40 + 2
BQ	250 + 20	82 + 1
DMBQ	190 + 20	48 + 8
TMQ	110 + 20	46 + 1
PD	210 + 70	98 + 6
DAD	180 + 10	62 + 2
TMPD	180 + 30	47 + 3

Table 1: PS 2 activity in μmol O_2/mgchl/h of the primary leaf of Phaseolus and of the 5th leaf of Nicotiana as a function of the electron acceptor.

The highest values were obtained with BQ and PD. Within the quinone series, the value of PS 2 activity decreases with increasing number of methyl substitution of the benzene ring. This can be due to a better solubility of the substituted quinones in the hydrophobic region of the thylakoid membranes. This may result in a lower transfer to the final electron acceptor, $K_3Fe(CN)_6$ which is very hydrophilic. A possible saturating reduction of the quinone pool excerts a feedback pressure on the PS 2 complex leading to a reduced oxygen production. An other explanation may be a partial detioration of the electron transfer chain at both sites of the PS 2 complex. Moreover the redox potential of a compound depends strongly on its environment (6). In an aprotic medium, the expected forms of quinone are Q, $Q^{\cdot-}$ and Q^{2-} with Q^{2-} less stable due to charge

delocalisation. The electrochemical behaviour in a protonic medium is
is much more complicated due to different intermediate forms (4). The
activity with DCPIP, an hydrophilic electron acceptor is somewhere in
between.

Within the PD series there is only a slight decrease in activity between
the unsubstituted and the substituted forms. Moreover there is no difference between DAD and TMPD. This observation is only true for Phaseolus
but not for Nicotiana.

Table 1 shows also a marked difference in electron transport activity
between the two species used.

The photochemical activity of PS1 with MV as electron acceptor and
with different electron donors reduced with $NaBH_4$ is shown in table 2.

Electron donor	PS 1 activity in µmol O_2/mgchl/h	
	Phaseolus	Nicotiana
DCPIP(H)	50 + 2	70 + 10
BQ(H)	37 + 4	40 + 3
DMBQ(H)	*	*
TMQ(H)	34 + 2	32 + 5
PD(H)	264 + 10	90 + 10
DAD(H)	850 + 40	200 + 30
TMPD(H)	428 + 9	130 + 30

Table 2: PS 1 activity in µmol O_2/mgchl/h of the primary
leaf of Phaseolus and of the 5th leaf of Nicotiana
as a function of the electron donor.
(H) reduced form.
* : negative values.

Within the quinone series there is no significant difference in the electron donating capacity of the different molecular forms. The negative
result of the DMBQ(H) cannot be explained at the moment. The PD series
results in much higher values. The unsubstituted form has the lowest
activity. Under the conditions used (pH 7.8) TMPD is an electron donor
and DAD(H) as well as PD(H) are electron and proton donors.Moreover the
primary amines PD (H) and DAD(H) are stronger acids than TMPD(H). The
higher activity of DAD(H) compared to PD(H) can be explained by a better
solubility of DAD(H) in the hydrophobic interior of the membrane. The
difference between DAD(H) and TMPD(H) can be explained by the fact that
DAD(H) is a much stronger acid than TMPD(H) and as such a stronger reducing compound.

In summary, the variability in electron transport activity expressed as μmol O_2/mg chl/h using different electron acceptors and donors are due to the differences in solubility (hydrophobicity), redox potential and redox forms of the compounds. An accurate definition of the methodology used, not only of the description of the measuring system (composition) but also of the extraction procedure and of the plant material used is a prerequisite to study the activity of the electron transport chain under different conditions.

References

1 Delieu, T. and Walker, D.A. (1972) New Phytol., 71, 201–225
2 Bögert, P and Kunert, K.J. (1978) Z. Naturforsch., 33c, 688–694
3 Allen, J.F. and Holmes, N.G. (1986) in Photosynthesis–Energy Transduction. A Practical Approach. (Hipkins, M.F. and Baker, N.R., ed.) pp. 103–141, IRL Press.
4 Danks, S.M., Evans, E.H. and Whittaker, P.A. (1983) Photosynthetic Systems– Structure, Function and Assembly. pp. 44, Wiley J. & Sons.
5 Lichtenthaler,H.K. and Wellburn, A.R. (1983) Biochem. Soc. Trans., 11, 591–592
6 Rich, P.R. and Moss, D.A. (1987) in The Light Reactions (Barber, J., ed.), pp. 421–445, Elsevier Science Publ. B.V.

Abbreviations

DCPIP: 2,6-dichlorophenol indophenol
BQ: p-Benzoquinone
DMBQ: 2,5-dimethyl-p-benzoquinone
TMQ: 2,3,5,6-tetramethyl-p-benzoquinone (duroquinone)
PD: p-phenylenediamine
DAD: 2,3,5,6-tetramethyl-p-phenylenediamine
TMPD: N,N,N',N'-tetramethyl-p-phenylenediamine
DCMU: 3-(3,4-dichlorophenyl)-1,1-dimethylurea
(H): reduced form

Acknowledgement

The authors want to thank the technical assistance of Mrs. G. Clerx. This work was supported by the F.K.F.O. of Belgium, research grant n° 29.00009.87.

TRANSPORTING PROTEINS INTO THE THYLAKOID LUMEN.

K. KO, A.R. CASHMORE, PLANT SCIENCE INSTITUTE, DEPT. OF BIOLOGY, UNIVERSITY OF PENNSYLVANIA, PHILADELPHIA, PA., USA 19104

1. INTRODUCTION
Thylakoid lumen proteins such as the 33 kD subunit of the oxygen-evolving complex (OEE1) are synthesized as precursors in the cytoplasm and must transverse three distinct membranes to assemble into their functional sites. Various chimeric precursors and deletions of the OEE1 transit peptide were constructed to study how chloroplast proteins are imported and targeted to the thylakoid lumen.

2. PROCEDURE
2.1. Construction of chimeric genes:The 1,200 bp cDNA insert coding for the OEE1 precursor of *Arabidopsis thaliana* and various gene fusions were subcloned into the transcription vectors, pGEM4 or pBLUESCRIPT, using standard cloning techniques.
2.2. *In vitro* transcription and translation:Templates were transcribed and translated as described (1,2).
2.3. Chloroplast import and fractionation:*In vitro* import assays were carried out using pea chloroplasts as described (3) and suborganellar fractionation was done according to (4). Thermolysin treatment of reisolated intact chloroplasts and subfractionated thylakoids was employed to differentiate bound and imported products.

3. RESULTS AND DISCUSSION
3.1. Import and localization of the OEE1 precursor
The native OEE1 precursor was imported, processed and translocated to the thylakoid lumen (Fig. 1), as demonstrated by isolating thylakoids and showing that imported OEE1 protein was resistant to treatment with thermolysin but became sensitive subsequent to sonication. The translocation characteristics of OEE1 were demonstrated to be dependent on the OEE1 transit peptide. In the absence of the transit peptide, OEE1 neither imported, nor did it bind to isolated chloroplasts (data not shown).

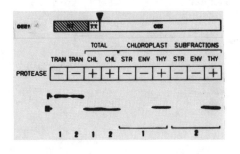

FIGURE 1. Importing the OEE1 precursor. Labels within the bar depict parts of OEE1: CT, putative chloroplast importing domain; TT, putative thylakoid lumen targeting domain; OEE, mature body. The triangle represents the cleavage site. Sonication and protease-treatment are indicated in the squares. Translation profiles are in lanes marked TRAN; total chloroplast protein profiles are marked CHL; stromal, envelope and thylakoid subfractions are marked STR, ENV and THY, respectively. Precursor and mature forms are indicated as P and M, respectively.

3.2. The RBCS transit peptide redirects OEE1 protein to the stroma
To determine if the OEE1 protein could be targeted to the stromal compartment instead of the lumen, we replaced its transit peptide with the presequence of the stromal RBCS protein. The

resulting fusion protein, SSOEE1, was capable of redirecting OEE1 to the stromal compartment (Fig. 2). The redirected OEE1 protein was correctly processed to the mature form and appeared to be stable in the stroma. The data indicate that sequences within the OEE1 transit peptide are primarily responsible for targeting to the lumen.

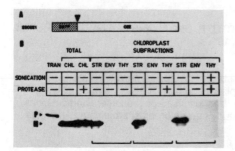

FIGURE 2. Import of OEE1 directed by the RBCS transit peptide. The polypeptide is represented in A (SSOEE1) The RBCS transit peptide is designated SSTP. The treatments and legends are explained in Fig. 1. The import data are shown in B.

3.3. Import directed by an RBCS-OEE1 chimeric transit peptide

The C-terminal region of the OEE1 transit peptide contains a series of residues which give rise to a hydrophobic peak in a hydropathy plot. It was of interest to determine if insertion of this putative thylakoid lumen targeting domain behind the RBCS transit peptide would reinstate the ability to target OEE1 to the thylakoid lumen. The resulting polypeptide, STOEE1, (Fig. 3A) made by fusing the RBCS transit peptide to the C-terminal 27 amino acids of the OEE1 presequence, was imported, processed to the mature form and localized in the lumen (Fig.3B).

A second fusion was prepared in which the C-terminal 27 residue domain of the OEE1 presequence was fused to the first 7 amino acids of the RBCS transit peptide. This chimeric precursor (OETP4A) was imported (Fig. 3C) and was resistant to subsequent thermolysin treatment. Approximately 60% of the imported OETP4A remained as the precursor form in the stromal compartment. A portion of the imported protein was processed to the mature form and localized in the thylakoids where it was resistant to protease degradation. The mature form represented about 40% of the imported products. Although the integration of OEE1 into the thylakoids was far less efficient than OEE1 and STOEE1, the OETP4A transit peptide, which contained only the hydrophobic domain of the OEE1 presequence and the first 7 residues of the RBCS transit peptide, possessed the capability to import OEE1 into chloroplasts and to target it to the lumen.

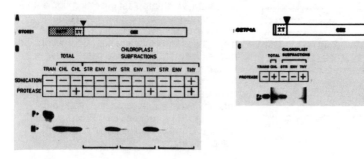

FIGURE 3. Importing with the RBCS-OEE1 chimeric transit peptide. The polypeptide is represented in A as STOEE1. The import results are shown in B. In panel C, the import results of OETP4A.

3.4. The OEE1 transit peptide contains separate domains for importing and thylakoid targeting

To examine the possible existence of other functional domains within the OEE1 transit peptide, three truncated presequences representing successive thirds of the N-terminal putative chloroplast import domain were constructed (Fig. 4A). Import was observed only with the longest truncated transit peptide, which contains the entire 58 residue segment (OETP3A) (Fig. 4B). OETP3A was processed to the mature form and was resistant to thermolysin treatment. The suborganellar location of OEE1 was in the stroma. None of the imported protein was integrated in a protease-protected fashion into the thylakoids. We have demonstrated that the 85 residue long OEE1 presequence contains separate signal domains for importing and for targeting to the thylakoid lumen. The importing domain, which mediates translocation across the two membranes of the chloroplast envelope, is present in the N-terminal 58 amino acids and the thylakoid lumen targeting domain, which mediates translocation across the thylakoid membrane, is located within the C-terminal 27 residues. From our studies it is clear that the C-terminal hydrophobic domain is both sufficient and necessary to direct translocation of OEE1 from the stroma to the lumen.

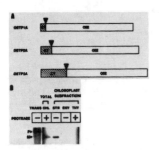

FIGURE 4. Truncated OEE1 transit peptide import experiments. The truncated polypeptides are illustrated in A. The polypeptides OETP1A and OETP2A were not imported into chloroplasts (data not shown). Only OETP3A was an import competent protein. The import data is shown in B.

3.5. The OEE1 transit peptide directs import and targeting of foreign proteins to the thylakoid lumen

One chloroplastic and two nonchloroplast chimeric precursors were constructed using the OEE1 transit peptide and assayed for import and suborganellar targeting (Fig.5A). The OEE1 presequence was shown to redirect a stromal protein (RBCS) to the lumen (Fig. 5B). Most of the imported RBCS were processed to a lower MW intermediate form and rendered thermolysin resistant. This intermediate form was located in the stroma and represented about 80-90% of the imported RBCS. A portion of the processed intermediates were translocated across the thylakoid membrane. The integrated product was further processed to a lower MW form corresponding to mature RBCS. This protease-resistant RBCS represented approximately 10% of the imported product. Both foreign chimeric precursors (OETPGO and OETPDHFR) were imported into chloroplasts and processed to lower MW forms (Fig 5C&D). However, only DHFR was translocated to the lumen and rendered resistant against subsequent exposure of isolated thylakoids to thermolysin. Imported glycolate oxidase remained in the stromal compartment as a form larger than the relative size of native GO but smaller than OETPGO precursor. A portion of the GO intermediate forms were associated with the thylakoids but they were sensitive to protease indicating that these molecules were exposed on the stromal face of the membrane. In contrast, most of the DHFR was integrated and processed to a form similar in relative size to native DHFR. The mature form was located inside the lumen and represented about 60-70% of the imported DHFR. Approximately 30-40% of imported OETPDHFR remained in the stromal compartment as an intermediate form.

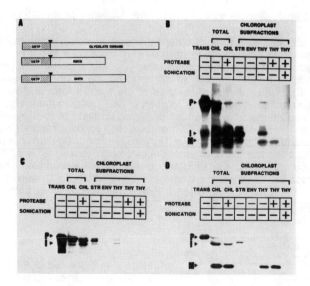

FIGURE 5. Targeting foreign proteins to the thylakoid lumen. The OEE1 transit peptide was fused to glycolate oxidase (GO), RBCS and dihydrofolate reductase (DHFR) (A). The import results are shown for RBCS (B), GO (C) and DHFR (D). Intermediate forms are marked by I.

REFERENCES
1 Melton, P.A., Krieg, P.A., Rebagliati, M.R., Maniatis, T., Zinn, K., Green, M.R.(1984) Nucl. Acids Res. 12, 7035-7056
2 Erickson, A.H., Blobel, G. (1983) Methods in Enzymol. 96, 38-50
3 Bartlett, S.G., Grossman, A.R., Chua, N.-H. (1982) In: Methods in Chloroplast Molecular Biology (eds., M. Edelman, R.B. Hallick,N.-H.Chua). Elsevier , Amsterdam.
4 Smeekens, S., Bauerle, C., Hageman, J., Keegstra, K., Weisbeek, P. (1986) Cell 46, 365-375.

ACKNOWLEDGEMENTS
The authors would like to thank Zdenka Ko for her assistance. This research was funded by NIH grant GM38409 to ARC.

PRESENT ADDRESS: K.K. - Dept. of Biology, Queen's University, Kingston, Ontario, Canada. K7L 3N6

EXPERIMENTS TO INCORPORATE IN - VITRO SYNTHESIZED PHOTOSYSTEM I COMPO-
NENTS INTO THYLAKOIDS OF THE BARLEY MUTANT *viridis - zb* [63]

PETER BRANDT[1], GUNILLA HØYER-HANSEN[2] AND DITER VON WETTSTEIN[1],
[1] CARLSBERG LABORATORY, DEPARTMENT OF PHYSIOLOGY, GAMLE CARLSBERG VEJ
10, DK - 2500 COPENHAGEN-VALBY, DENMARK
[2] FINSENLABORATORIET, STRANDBOULEVARDEN 49, DK - 2100 COPENHAGEN-ØSTER-
BRO, DENMARK

1. INTRODUCTION

Photosystem I is one of four multisubunit complexes of thylakoid
membranes involved in the photosynthetic electron transport. The PSI of
barley contains eight polypeptides (1). Three of these polypeptides are
plastid - encoded. These polypeptides include the chlorophyll a - binding proteins (gene products of psaA and psaB) (2) and the Fe-S - containing PSI subunit VII (gene product of psaC) (3). The remaining PSI
polypeptides are nuclear - encoded including the chlorophyll a/b - binding proteins of the light - harvesting complex (gene products of cabI)
(ref. 4), the subunit II (gene product of psaD) (5,6) and the subunit
III (gene product of psaE) (7). Thus, the synthesis and assembly of the
PSI complex requires coordination between nuclear and chloroplast gene
expression.

The nuclear gene mutant *viridis-zb*[63] has been shown to lack completely PSI activity (8) and the associated EPR signals (9). In the polypeptide pattern of the mutant the Chl_a - protein 1 and the PSI subunits
II and III (18.3 kda and 15.2 kda respectively) are below the level of
detection. Subunits II and III are, however, present in small amounts
as shown by immunoblotting assay using monoclonal antibodies (10). But
the Chl_a - apoprotein 1 of *viridis - zb* [63] is not detectable.

We therefore choose the barley mutant *viridis-zb*[63] to elucidate the
mechanisms governing the synthesis and/or the assembly of PSI-subunits
during the greening of etiolated seedlings.

2. PROCEDURE

Seeds of wild-type bonus (*Hordeum vulgare* L.,cv. Svalöfs Bonus) and
the recessive nuclear gene mutant *viridis-zb*[63] were germinated as described before (11). The isolation of mRNA, *in-itro* translation,immuno-
precipitation and SDS-PAGE was performed according to (11,12). Chloroplasts were isolated by the method of (13).*In-organello* translation was
performed according to (14). Construction of expression vectors for the
psaD gene or the psaE gene and analysis of the products obtained by in-
vitro transcription/translation were done according to (12) and to the
procedure supplied by Promega.

M. Baltscheffsky (ed.), Current Research in Photosynthesis, Vol. III, 783–786.
© 1990 *Kluwer Academic Publishers. Printed in the Netherlands.*

3. RESULTS AND DISCUSSION

3.1 Detection of the mRNA for the Chl$_a$ - apoprotein 1, the PSI-subunit II and the PSI-subunit III in *viridis - zb* 63

The polypeptide patterns of greening barley indicate that these PSI - polypeptides are synthesized during the first six hours of greening(15). Therefore, poly-A$^+$ and plastid RNA were isolated and the presence of the transcripts for SUII, the SUIII and the Chl$_a$ - apoprotein 1 was studied by *in-vitro* translation and following immunoprecipitation with monoclonal antibodies. In the wild - type as well as in the mutant these transcripts are present (FIG.1a-c). The translation products for the SUII and SUIII show an apparent M$_r$ of about 23 and 30 kD respectively and for the Chl$_a$ -apoprotein 1 an apparent M$_r$ of about 69 kD.

(a)   (b)   (c)

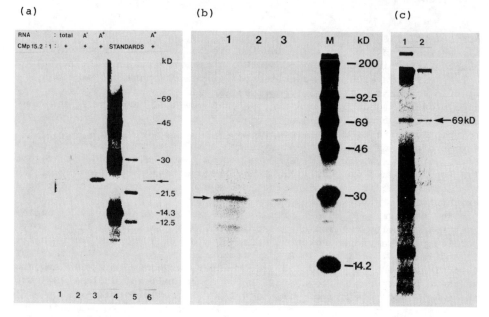

FIGURE 1. Products of *in-vitro* translation in reticulocyte lysate (a), in wheat germ extract (b) or in S-30 extract from *E..coli* (c) primed with total RNA (a,1), ptRNA (a,2;b,2;c,1) or poly-A$^+$ RNA (a,3;b,1) from the wild-type or primed with poly-A$^+$ RNA (a,6;b,3) or ptRNA (c,2) from the mutant followed by immunoprecipitation with CMp15.2:1 (a), CMXVII 3G4 (b) or CMpChl$_a$ -P1:1 (c).

3.2 Construction and expression of pGEM-SUII and pGEM-SUIII

The gene construct pGEM-SUIII was obtained by ligation of a cDNA clone encoding the SUIII of barley (7) into the EcoRI site of pGEM-7Zf. The gene construct pGEM-SUII was obtained either by ligation of a cDNA clone encoding the SUII of spinach (5) into the EcoRI site of pGEM-7Zf or of a cDNA clone encoding the SUII of tomato into the EcoRI/XbaI site of pGEM-4 (6; kind gift of Dr.N.E.Hoffman). These two heterologous subunits II were used, because their amino acid sequences are homologous to the partial determined amino acid sequence of the PSI-SUII of barley (16).

The relative orientation of the DNA-inserts in the multiple cloning site of these expression vectors was determined by RsaI digestion and identification of the length of the resulting DNA-fragments. Purified plasmid DNA was linearized with XbaI (pGEM-SUIII, pGEM-SUII-tomato) or with HindIII (pGEM-SUII-spinach) and transcribed with SP6 RNA polymerase (pGEM-SUIII, pGEM-SUII-tomato) or with T7 RNA polymerase (pGEM-SUII-spinach). $m^7G(5')ppp(5')G$ was added to the assay for synthesis of capped mRNA. The transcripts were translated either in reticulocyte lysate or in wheat germ extracts and the translation products were identified by SDS-PAGE (FIG.2). pGEM-SUIII was successfully transcribed and afterwards translated in the reticulocyte lysate without capping (FIG.2b). For the expression of pGEM-SUII-tomato capping was essential. Its mRNA was translated in the wheat germ extract only (FIG.2a). pGEM-SUII-spinach, however, was never be expressed. The M_r of the precursor polypeptides correspond to the M_r of the immunoprecipitated polypeptides, which were translated *in-vitro* before using isolated poly-A^+ (Fig.1a,b).

(a) (b)

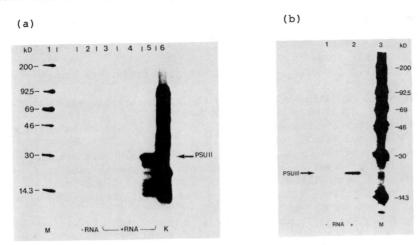

FIGURE 2. Products from pGEM-SUII (tomato)(a) or pGEM-SUIII (barley)(b) after coupled in-vitro transcription/translation and SDS-PAGE. Translation was performed either in reticulocyte lysate (a,1 and 2; b,3) or in wheat germ extract (b, 2 and 4 - 6). For details see text.

3.3 Isolation of chloroplasts and *in- organello* translation

Chloroplasts were isolated from the wild - type or from the mutant by leaf-homogenization (13) and fractionation in discontinuous Percoll gradients. The recommended gradients for the wild - type chloroplasts or the mutant chloroplasts contain in 30 ml - tubes: 10 ml 94%(v/v) and 12 ml of either 40% (v/v)(wild - type chloroplasts)or 26% (v/v) (mutant chloroplasts) Percoll-buffer-solution. After purification these isolated chloroplasts show different *in-organello* translation capacity. The pattern of *in - organello* synthesized polypeptides show, that the mutant chloroplasts are able to synthesize three different polypeptides in the MWG - range of 69 kD. One of these three polypeptides will be a good candidate for the missing Chl_a - apoprotein 1. On the other hand two polypeptides of about 32-35 kD are only present in the wild-type, but missing in the mutant.

4. Conclusion

The results clearly demonstrate, that (a) the transcripts for the questioned PSI - polypeptides are present in the mutant, (b) the nuclear encoded PSI-subunits are imported into the mutant chloroplasts (11) and (c) that the mutant is able to synthesize the core-polypeptides of PSI. Further experiments will demonstrate wether feeding of isolated mutant chloroplasts with *in - vitro* translated SUII and SUIII will stimulate the synthesis of the Chl_a - apoprotein 1 and will stabilize the assembly of the PSI - complex.

REFERENCES

1 Scheller, H.V., Svendsen,I. and Møller, B.L. (1989) J.Biol.Chem. 264, 6929-6934

2 Høj, P.B., Svendsen, I., Scheller, H.V. and Møller, B.L. (1987)J.Biol Chem. 262,12676-12684

3 Scheller, H.V., Svendsen, I. and Møller, B.L. (1989) Carlsberg Res. Commun. 54,11-15

4 Glazer, A.N. and Melis,A. (1987) Ann.Rev.Plant Physiol. 38,11-45

5 Lagoutte, B. (1988) FEBS Lett. 232,275-280

6 Hoffman, N.E., Pichersky, E., Malik, V.S., Ko, K. and Cashmore, A.R. (1988) Plant Mol. Biol. 10,435-445

7 Okkels, J.S., Jepsen, L.B., Hønberg, L.S., Lehmbeck, J., Scheller, H.V., Brandt, P., Høyer-Hansen, G., Stummann, B., Henningsen, K.W., von Wettstein, D. and Møller, B.L. (1988) FEBS Lett. 237,108-112

8 Hiller, R.G., Møller, B.L. and Høyer-Hansen, G. (1980) Carlsberg Res. Commun. 45,315-328

9 Møller, B.L., Nugent, J.H.A. and Evans, M.C.W. (1981) Carlsberg Res. Commun. 46,373- 382

10 Høyer-Hansen, G., Hønberg, L.S. and Simpson, D.J. (1985) Carlsberg Res. Commun. 50,23-35

11 Høyer-Hansen, G., Hønberg, L.S. and Høj, P.B. (1985) Carlsberg Res. Commun. 50,211-221

12 Neumann, E. (1988) Carlsberg Res. Commun. 53,395-409

13 Klein, R.R. and Mullet, J.E. (1986) J. Biol. Chem. 261,11138-11145

14 Gamble, P.E., Sexton, T.B. and Mullet, J.E.(1988)EMBO J. 7,1289-1297

15 Høyer-Hansen,G. and Simpson,D.J.(1977)Carlsberg Res. Commun.42,379

16 Scheller, H.V., Høy, P.B., Svendsen, I. and Møller, B.L.(1988) Biochim. Biophys. Acta 933,501-505

ABSORBANCE CHANGES AT 520 NM INDUCED BY 700 NM LIGHT IN SHORTLY PREILLUMINATED ETIOLATED BEAN LEAVES

Bertrand M, F Franck and E Dujardin - Laboratory of Photobiology, B22 - 4000 Liège, Belgium.

1. INTRODUCTION

Etioplasts isolated from 14 day-old etiolated bean seedlings can photoreduce $NADP^+$ already after three minutes of illumination (1). Such an early PSI activity asks the question of the presence of P700 at a greening stage when the mean green pigment is chlorophyllide. Jouy (2) discovered that 30s-red preilluminated etiolated leaves exhibit a light-induced absorbance increase between 500 and 550 nm. In green leaves, it is known that absorbance changes in that region reflect the photochemistry of reaction centers (3). We report here the efficiency of red and far-red light to produce this change in order to detect a photoactive long-wavelength absorbing pigment - similar to P700 - in etiolated and shortly greened leaves.

2. MATERIAL AND METHOD

14 day-old etiolated bean leaves were used as such or etioplasts were isolated from the leaves according to a procedure described elsewhere (1).

Light-induced absorbance variations at 520 nm were registered at room tempereature with a home-made apparatus adapted from the Fork spectrophotometer (4). The wavelengths of the actinic light were selected with interference filters with a maximum transmission at 670 nm (R light) or 703 nm (FR light) and a bandwidth of 16 nm. The photon fluxes were measured using an optical multichannel analyser (OMA II, Princeton instruments) calibrated with a Li-Cor LI-200SB quantum meter.

3. RESULTS

When preilluminated etioplast suspensions were subjected to R or FR light, we never observed any change in absorbance

On the contrary, an absorbance increase at 520 nm ($+\delta520$) occurs upon excitation by R or FR light in etiolated leaves

M. Baltscheffsky (ed.), Current Research in Photosynthesis, Vol. III, 787–790.
© 1990 Kluwer Academic Publishers. Printed in the Netherlands.

which were or were not preilluminated by 1 ms intense white
flash (fig. 1 a and b). The absorbance increases slowly and
reaches a plateau after 2-3 min. The kinetics obtained with
green leaves (fig. 1c) exhibit a rapid initial phase and are
more complex. Similar kinetics as in fig. 1b have been
obtained with leaves subjected to greening for 1 to about 15
min of continuous white irradiation. Then the amplitude of
the changes decreases with the duration of greening (fig. 2
a and c).

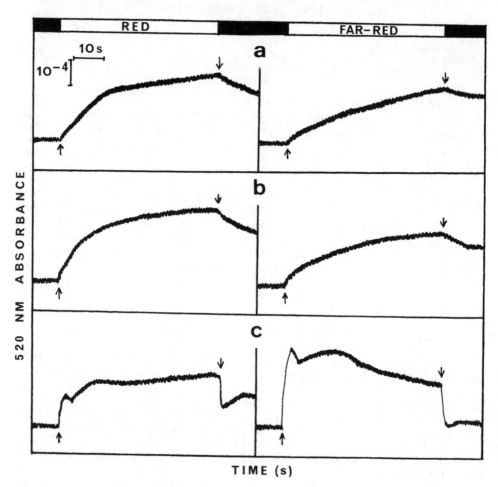

Figure 1. Red or far-red light-induced 520 nm absorbance
changes in etiolated leaves (a), in 1 ms-flashed etiolated
leaves (b) or in green leaves (c).

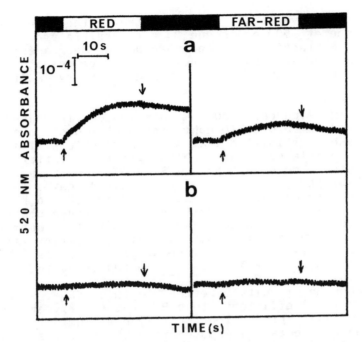

Figure 2. Red or far-red light-induced 520 nm absorbance changes in etiolated leaves which have been greened for 30 min (a) or 90 min (b).

We have measured the $+\delta A520$ initial velocity (V_R or V_{FR}) under either R or FR actinic light. With 1 ms-flashed etiolated leaves, the average V_{FR}/V_R ratio obtained for 30 measurements was 0.54 ± 0.12. The absorbed photon fluxes F_R and F_{FR} of R and FR light were calculated on the basis of the incident photon fluxes and the room temperature absorbance spectrum of the leaves. The F_{FR}/F_R ratio was 0.22. Therefore FR light is more efficient than R light for inducing the $+\delta A520$. This is true whatever the stage of greening between 0 and 30 min.

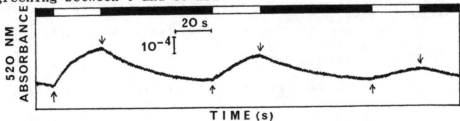

Figure 3. Reproducibility of the $+\delta A520$ increase in a 1 ms-flashed etiolated leaf at dark/red light transitions.

Two observations indicate that the increase in absorbance at 520 nm is due to a reversible process : 1) at light/dark transitions, the absorbance decreases; 2) the light-induced absorbance increase can be repeated several times with the same leaf at 1 min dark intervals (fig. 3).

4. DISCUSSION

The light-induced 520 nm absorbance increase is not correlated to protochlorophyllide photoreduction since 1) a 1 ms-flashed etiolated leaf shows a kinetic similar to that of an etiolated leaf, although the latter has not regenerated more than 15% of the amount of protochlorophyllide present in etiolated leaves (5); 2) the absorbance change is reversible both under R and FR light.

It is also unlikely that the $+\delta 520$ change observed with etiolated or greening leaves reflects normal P700 photochemistry as it does in green leaves, since its amplitude decreases with greening time, whereas it is known that the rate of PSI activity increases during the same period (6).

Anyhow the results reported in this paper show that FR light is more efficient than R light to trigger the $+\delta A520$ increase. This proves that shortly preilluminated etiolated bean leaves contain a photoactive receptor sensitive to wavelengths around 700 nm.

The authors thank the CGRI, the B. Comans Foundation and the National Ministry of Education (Belgium) for financial support. F. Franck is Senior Research Assistant of the FNRS.

REFERENCES
1 Bertrand, B., Bereza, B. and Dujardin, E. (1988) Z. Naturforsch. 43c, 443-448
2 Jouy, M.(1981) In Photosynthesis (Akoyunoglou, G. ed.), Vol. V, pp. 253-260, Balaban International Science Services, Philadelphia, Pa
3 Chua, N.H. and Levine, R.P. (1969) In Progress in Photosynthesis Research (Metzner, H. ed.), Vol II, pp. 978-990, Tubingen, Germany
4 De Kouchkovshy, Y. and D.C. Fork (1964) Proc Natl. Acad. Sci. 52, 232-239
5 Granick, S. and Gassman, M. (1970) Plant Physiol. 45, 201-205
6 Oelze-Karow H. and Butler, W.L. (1971) Plant Phyiol. 48, 621-625

PROTEIN SYNTHESIS IN CHLOROPLASTS

ERIC BREIDENBACH, REGULA BLÄTTLER and ARMINIO BOSCHETTI, Institut für Biochemie, Universität Bern, Freiestr. 3, CH-3012 BERN, SWITZERLAND

1. INTRODUCTION
In the algae Chlamydomonas reinhardii cell division and synthesis of individual proteins is induced by a diurnal light/dark regime. To study the regulation of protein synthesis in chloroplasts we compared the labeling of the 32 kDa herbicide-binding protein (D1), the large subunit (LS) of the ribulose-bisphosphate carboxylase (rubisco) and the chloroplast elongation factor EF-Tu during the cell cycle and in different translation systems. i.e. in vivo labeling of cells in the presence of cycloheximide (CHI), in organello labeling of isolated intact chloroplasts and labeling in a chloroplast lysate.

2. METHODS
Chlamydomonas reinhardii was grown with 10 h dark/14 h light cycles (1). Chloroplasts were isolated as described (2). Cytoplasmic S-100: Cells (31 mg chlorophyll) were broken in the Yeda press. Intact cells, chloroplasts and membranes were gently sedimented (6000xg). The clear soluble fraction was centrifuged (100,000xg, 3 h). The supernatant (23 ml) was taken as the cytoplasmic S-100. Labeling of cells in vivo in the presence of CHI with [35S]sulfate was done as described (3). Labeling of intact chloroplasts (in organello) with [^{35}S]methionine was assayed as described (2). In organello labeling with cytoplasmic S-100 contained 9 parts of assay medium with cytoplasmic S-100 and 1 part of isolated intact chloroplasts (500 g chlorophyll/ml). Labeling in a homologous system: Isolated chloroplasts were osmotically lysed and supplemented with an energy regenerating system. Electrophoretic analysis of proteins: Pobes were solubilized and separated on a 10-20% SDS/polyacrylamide gel (SDS PAGE). Immunological detection of EF-Tu: Western blots were treated with antisera raised against EF-Tu of E.coli (gift of Erik Vijgenboom, Leiden, Netherlands).

3. RESULTS AND DISCUSSION
3.1 Comparison of different translation systems
In vivo only proteins synthesized in the chloroplast were labeled in the presence of CHI (3). We identified D1, LS and EF-Tu as the predominantly labeled proteins (3, Fig.1 and 3). We previously showed that in organello D1 and LS were strongly labeled (2). However, the ratio of the labeling of D1 and LS in vivo and in organello differed significantly (Fig.1). In vivo the ratio of labeling of D1 and LS was about 1. In organello the ratio of labeling of D1 and LS was determined as about 3-4. The same ratio of labeling was found in pro-

M. Baltscheffsky (ed.), Current Research in Photosynthesis, Vol. III, 791–794.

tein synthesis of lysed chloroplasts (Fig.1).
The addition of cytoplasmic S-100 to intact chloroplasts before in organello synthesis restored the ratio of labeleing of D1 and LS. We do not know if the "true" ratio of labeling of D1 and LS in this system is due to the prolonged incubation period or due to "cytoplasmic" influence. The preincubation of cells in the presence of CHI for various times before labeling in vivo showed that the rates of synthesis of LS and D1 were nearly independent of duration of CHI treatment. Therefore synthesis of the small subunit of rubisco seems not to be necessary for the LS synthesis.

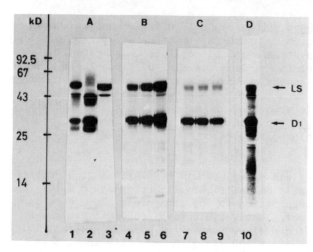

FIGURE 1.
Fluorographs of SDS-PAGE of four different systems of chloroplast protein synthesis. A: in vivo labeling in presence of CHI, cells (lane 1), membranes (lane 2), soluble fraction (lane 3). B: simulated in vivo labeling (in organello in the presence of cytoplasmic S-100) incubated for 15 min (lane 4), 30 min (lane 5) and 45 min (lane 6). C: in organello incubated for 15 min (lane 7), 30 min (lane 8) and 45 min (lane 9). D: [^{35}S]methionine labeled proteins of a homologous system incubated for 30 min.

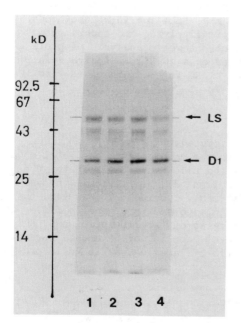

FIGURE 2.
Autoradiograph of in vivo labeled cells after various preincubation times with CHI. Labeling was done for 1h in the presence of CHI, lane 1-4: 15, 30, 60 min and 120 min of preincubation.

3.2 Identification of EF-Tu

The very high homology of EF-Tu of <u>E.coli</u> and chloroplast EF-Tu (4) made it possible to identify this protein immunologically as single sharp band in the soluble fraction of whole cells and chloroplasts, respectively (Fig.3). The molecular weight of 45 kDa corresponds well to data of EF-Tu from spinach and <u>Euglena</u> (5).

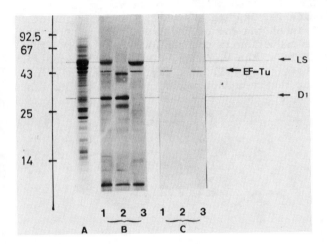

FIGURE 3.
Identification of the elongation factor EF-Tu. **A:** Coomassie Blue staining after SDS-PAGE.
B: Autoradiographs of Western blot:
C: Immunological identification of EF-Tu. 1: chloroplasts; 2: thylakoids; 3: soluble fraction.

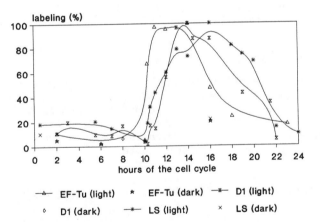

FIGURE 4. Rate of synthesis of EF-Tu, D1 and LS during the cell cycle.
After SDS-PAGE of <u>in vivo</u> labeled cells the radioactivity in the bands corresponding to D1, LS or EF-Tu was measured. For protein, the highest incorporation during the cell cycle was taken as 100%.

3.3 Rate of synthesis during the cell cycle.

During the cell cycle the synthesis of distinct chloroplast proteins are regulated individually i.e. synthesis of D1, LS and EF-Tu (Fig.4). In cells harvested during the dark period these proteins were not labeled without light and only faintly labeled when incubated for 1 hour in the light. This findings point to a cell cycle-dependent competence for protein synthesis. The highest rate of EF-Tu synthesis preceded the highest rate of synthesis of D1 and of LS and also the peak of maximal chloroplast protein synthesis (Fig.5). Therefore, synthesis of EF-Tu, which is involved in chloroplast protein synthesis, could be a regulatory factor for protein synthesis in chloroplasts. Dilution of EF-Tu relative to the chloroplast volume in growing cells leads to a significant reduction of the concentration of EF-Tu at the end of the light period (Fig. 5). This decline preceds the reduction in chloroplast translation. The high concentration of EF-Tu at the beginning of the light, when chloroplast protein synthesis is still low, argues against the role of EF-Tu in regulation of the translational activity in chloroplasts

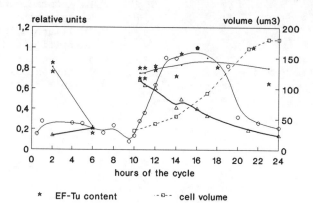

FIGURE 5. Cell volume, rate of chloroplast protein synthesis, content and concentration of EF-Tu. The EF-Tu content was determined by immunostaining on a Western blot of an equivalent number of cells and quantified photometerically. The concentration of EF-Tu was calculated by dividing the relative EF-Tu content with the relative cell volume, determined electronically with a Coulter counter.

4. ACKNOWLEDGEMENTS
This work was partly supported by Swiss National Foundation.

5. REFERENCES
1 Bolli R., Mendiola-Morgenthaler L. and Boschetti A. (1981) Biochim. Biophys. Acta 653, 276-287
2 Mendiola-Morgenthaler L., Leu S. and Boschetti A. (1985) Plant Science 38, 33-39
3 Breidenbach E., Jenni E. and Boschetti A. (1988) Eur. J. Biochem. 177, 225-232
4 Spremulli G.H. and Spremulli L.L. (1987) Biochem. Biophys. Res. Comm. 148, 1490-1495
5 Sreedharan S., Beck C.M. and Spremulli L.L. (1985) J. Biol. Chem. 260, 3126-3131

VARIATION IN NET PHOTOSYNTHESIS, RUBISCO ACTIVITY AND CHLOROPLAST ULTRASTRUCTURE AMONG SOMATIC HYBRIDS OF SOLANUM TUBEROSUM AND S. BREVIDENS

PEHU*, E., NURMI**, A. AND M.A.J. PARRY*

* Dept. of Biochemistry, Institute of Arable Crops Research,
  Rothamsted Experimental Station, Harpenden, Herts. AL5 2 JQ,U.K.
** Dept. of General Botany, University of Helsinki, Viikki,
  00710 Helsinki, Finland

1. INTRODUCTION

In the production of somatic hybrids by chloroplast fusion, both nucleus and cytoplasm are combined. Moreover, the occurrence of somaclonal variation during culture and assortment of the cytoplasmic organelles can result in a wide range of hybrid types regarding their nuclear and cytoplasmic constitutions. Somatic hybrids therefore provide unique opportunities for investigating the effect of parental genome dosage, ploidy and nuclear and cytoplasmic interaction on physiological traits.

2. MATERIALS AND METHODS

Five somatic hybrids of S. brevidens and dihaploid S. tuberosum were included in this study. In addition to the hybrids, two non-hybrid plants, diagnosed in the molecular characterization to contain DNA of one parent only were included as ploidy comparisons.

Three individual plants of each genotype were established from in vitro shoots in the greenhouse. The plants were grown in under 16h daylength maintained by supplemental lights of 150uEin/m intensity. The minimum day and night temperatures were maintained at 18 C and 13 C, respectively.

Photosynthesis (Pn) was measured at saturating light levels. Most recent, fully expanded leaves at the peak of the vegetative growth stage were included in this study. Net photosynthesis (Pn) rates were measured as described by Lawlor et al. (1). Leaf area was measured by Li-Cor LI-3050A leaf area meter.

Sample preparation for Rubisco activity measurements was conducted according to Servaites (2) and assay of the carboxylase activity was carried out as described in Gutteridge et al. (3).

M. Baltscheffsky (ed.), Current Research in Photosynthesis, Vol. III, 795–798.
© 1990 Kluwer Academic Publishers. Printed in the Netherlands.

The leaf samples for ultrastructural examination were collected and immediately fixed in 2.5% glutaraldehyde in 0.1M sodium phosphate buffer, pH 7.4. Postfixation and staining was carried out according to Aro et al. (4).

3. RESULTS AND DISCUSSION

A positive effect of increased nuclear ploidy on Pn rate has been demonstrated for S. brevidens and S. tuberosum and their somatic hybrids (Table 1).

TABLE 1. Means and standard deviations for net photosynthesis, Rubisco activity and specific leaf weight of the fusion parents, isogenic parental lines and the somatic hybrids.

Geno-type	Chromo-some number	Nuclear genome dosage 1=S. tub. 2=S. brev.	CP DNA-type 1=S. tub. 2=S. brev.	SLW g/mm mean std		Rubisco activity umol CO/min/mm mean std		Photo-synthesis uMol CO m s mean std	
Fusion parents:									
PDH40	24	1	1	0.018	0.001	0.20	0.001	8.57	1.42
S.brev.	24	2	2	0.018	0.001	0.16	0.001	4.79	1.41
Isogenic parental lines:									
84199	46	22	2	0.013	0.001	0.09	0.007	10.94	1.01
81058	72	111	1	0.019	0.001	0.06	0.007	14.40	0.43
Somatic hybrids, tetraploids:									
70064	48	12	2	0.020	0.002	0.16	0.007	9.40	0.75
65013	48	12	1	0.018	0.002	0.10	0.001	4.63	0.57
Somatic hybrids, hexaploids:									
81158	72	112	1	0.023	0.001	0.19	0.014	11.45	0.07
81136	72	221	1	0.022	0.002	0.10	0.001	8.78	0.15
84155	72	112	2	0.020	0.004	0.16	0.007	11.80	3.12

Both of the two hybrids having the lowest Pn value, 65013 and 81136, had large starch granules in the chloroplasts (Table 1., Fig. 1.a). The accumulation of starch is probably due to the absence of an efficient sink in these hybrids as 81136 does not tuberize and 65013 produces only swollen stolons (5).

Further electron microscopic examination of chloroplast ultrastructure revealed great variation between the fusion parents
and among the hybrids regarding the size of the chloroplasts,
starch granules and plastoglobuli, as well as in grana stacking
and ratio of appressed to non-appressed thylakoids (Fig. 1.a,b).
Large grana stacks were associated with low Pn rates, which
confirms the findings of Vapaavuori et al. (6) and Aro et al. (4).

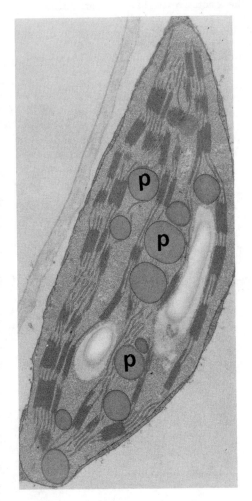 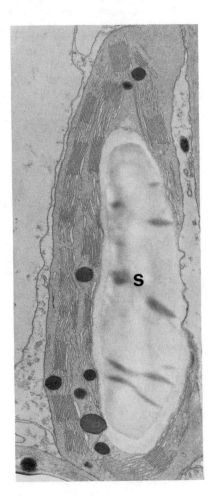

FIGURE 1. Electron micrographs of mesophyll chloroplasts
of somatic hybrids.

1.a. Tetraploid 70064 with   1.b. Hexaploid 81136 with
very large plastoglobuli (P).   hudge starch granules (S).

Genotype had a pronounced effect on the Rubisco activity, however, none of the hybrids exceeded the activity measured for PDH40 (Table 1.). The parental chloroplast type, as such, did not influence the Rubisco activity, however, our results indicated that Rubisco activity was affected by nuclear-organelle genome incompatibility. At the tetraploid level the most affected hybrid had tuberosum cpDNA. Among the hexaploid hybrids the parental nuclear dosage effect supported the incompatibility hypothesis. The presence of two parental nuclear genomes together with cpDNA from the same species resulted in an enzyme of higher catalytic activity. Again the hybrid having tuberosum cpDNA was most affected. It seems that there is stronger incompatibility between tuberosum cpDNA with brevidens nuclear genome. Interestingly, there was a positive correlation between Rubisco activity and Pn rate among the hybrids, which indicates that assembly of the chloroplast-nuclear hybrid proteins might be a limiting component characteristic in photosynthesis of somatic hybrids.

REFERENCES
1 Lawlor, D.W., Kontturi, M. and Young, A.T. (1989) J. Exp. Bot. 40, 43-52
2 Servaites, J.C. (1985) Arch. Biochem. Biophys. 238, 154-160
3 Gutteridge, S., Parry, M.A.T. and Schmidt, N.G. (1984) Eur. J. Biochem. 126, 597-602
4 Aro, E.M., Rintamäki, E., Korhonen, P. and Mäenpää, P. (1986) Plant, Cell and Environment 9, 87-94
5 Pehu, E., Karp, A., Moore, K., Steele, S., Dunckley, R. and Jones, M.G.K. (1989) Theor Appl Genet, in press
6 Vapaavuori, E.M., Nurmi, A., Vuorinen, A.H. and Kangas, T. (1989) Tree Physiol., in press

AMPHIPATHIC β-SHEET DOMAINS IN CHLOROPLAST TRANSIT PEPTIDES

W. A. CRAMER[1], J. W. SHIVER[1], P. N. FURBACHER[1], AND K. KEEGSTRA[2],
[1]DEPARTMENT OF BIOLOGICAL SCIENCES, PURDUE UNIVERSITY, WEST LAFAYETTE, IN 47907, AND [2]DEPARTMENT OF BOTANY, UNIVERSITY OF WISCONSIN, MADISON, WI 53706, U.S.A.

INTRODUCTION

The amino acid sequences of many hundreds of signal sequences are known from animals, plants, bacteria, and viruses. The development of general concepts for the mechanism of interaction of signal sequences with the membrane and for the targeting of the mature protein has been complicated by the variability of the primary sequences. Therefore, correlations has been sought in predicted secondary structures (1-4). A role for amphipathic α-helical structures have been emphasized in the literature for transit peptides of imported mitochondrial proteins (1,2). It is shown in the present work that amphipathic β-sheets are more prominent than such α-helices in predicted secondary structures for chloroplast transit peptides. There is a tendency for such structures to appear near the cleavage site for stromal-targeted proteins (5) and often also in the region upstream that would be expected to lead the translocation across the chloroplast envelope membranes.

METHODS

Hydrophobic moment analysis. A search can be made for amphipathic segments using the periodic nature of the segregation between polar and nonpolar residues. The periodic difference in residue hydrophobicity creates a hydrophobic moment,

$$\mu_H = \sum_{n=1}^{N} h_n S_n$$

for a peptide segment with N amino acids, where h_n is the hydrophobicity (consensus indices of ref. 6) of the nth amino acid and S_n is a unit vector extending from its α carbon to the center of the side chain. N=9 was chosen for calculations involving residues that may span a membrane bilayer in the β-conformation (7), and was used in all calculations presented here. For an α-helix or β-sheet, the distribution of the hydrophobic moment through the sequence can be written as a Fourier sum (8), for which the magnitude of the moment may be calculated using the relationship:

$$\mu_H = \left\{ \left[\sum_{n=1}^{N} h_n \sin(\delta n) \right]^2 + \left[\sum_{n=1}^{N} h_n \cos(\delta n) \right]^2 \right\}^{\frac{1}{2}}$$

M. Baltscheffsky (ed.), Current Research in Photosynthesis, Vol. III, 799–802.
© 1990 *Kluwer Academic Publishers. Printed in the Netherlands.*

where δn is the angle, in radians, at which successive side chains emerge with a periodicity, δ, of 100° for α-helix, or 160°-180° for twisted and straight (180°) β structures. A hydrophobic moment-angle profile in which μ_H is plotted versus the periodicity (μ_H versus δ), using h_n values from ref. (6), indicates the preferred secondary structure of a segment if the peptide of length N maximizes the value of μ_H.

RESULTS AND DISCUSSION

The distribution of μ_H for $\delta = 170°$ (β) and $\delta = 100°$ (α) is shown in Fig. 1 for selected members of the families of chloroplastic precursors. The amino acid sequences of the transit peptides are shown in the bottom panel. The plots are aligned according to the cleavage site at the end of the transit peptide. Proteins destined for the thylakoid lumen (i.e., plastocyanin and the polypeptides of the oxygen evolving complex) must traverse the thylakoid membrane in addition to the envelope membranes. For these precursors, the first 40-60 amino acids comprise the stromal targeting domain, whereas the last 20-25 residues form the thylakoid transport domain (9). Thus, it is the first domain that is relevant for comparison with the other transit peptides.

The overall hydrophobic character of chloroplast transit peptides is low (4). It can be seen that most transit peptides show a propensity for at least one amphipathic β-structure region close to the cleavage site, as proposed in (5). Considering a set of stroma-targeted proteins, the corn Cab peptide (panel A) showed a single prominent peak near the cleavage site in the 170° plot. This pattern was observed in all 21 other Cab sequences that were investigated (unpubl.). The transit peptide of acyl carrier protein (panel B) showed several peaks in the β-plot, including one near the cleavage site. A similar pattern was observed in 6 other acyl carrier protein sequences that were examined. For some precursors, different patterns were seen when sequences from different species were examined. For example, when pea and *Silene* ferredoxin were investigated, the *Silene* sequence showed a prominent peak near the cleavage site and a smaller peak upstream (panel C) whereas the pea sequence shows two small peaks (panel D). Only these two ferredoxin sequences were examined. Rubisco SS transit sequences also showed different patterns. Some sequences showed prominent peaks in the β-plot (e.g., wheat, panel E) whereas others showed only weak peaks (e.g., cucumber, panel F). Thirty-five different SS sequences were investigated and the dichotomy shown in Fig. 1 (panels D and E) is representative.

For many lumen-targeted proteins (panels G, H, and I), the amphipathic β character tends to be localized within the stromal targeting domain of the transit peptide. The sequences often contain two regions of high μ_H, with the most prominent peak being the one closest to the cleavage site between the stromal targeting domain and the thylakoid transport domain. For *Silene* plastocyanin, the prominent peak is near residue -30 with a smaller peak near residues -50. Similar patterns were seen with plastocyanin from pea, spinach, and *Arabidopsis*. The spinach OEC 33 kDa and 16 kDa proteins also showed a somewhat similar pattern (panel H). On the other hand, the 23 kDa protein of the spinach oxygen evolving complex did not show this pattern (panel J). Regions of high μ_H for β structures were not found in the thylakoid transfer domain of lumenal precursors nor in the signal sequences of cyanobacterial lumen proteins (data not shown). The maximum amplitude of the μ (170°) peaks found in our studies was 1.0 for pea plastocyanin relative to a maximum μ value of 2.0 ($\delta = 180°$) for a repeating sequence of Arg-Ile. The maximum μ_H of the β sheet segments of the *omp*F protein of the *E. coli* outer membrane, that is known from structural data to be predominantly in the β structure (10), is 0.8. The chloroplast transit peptides also show a significant tendency toward amphipathic α-helices (right-hand panels), but the μ (100°)

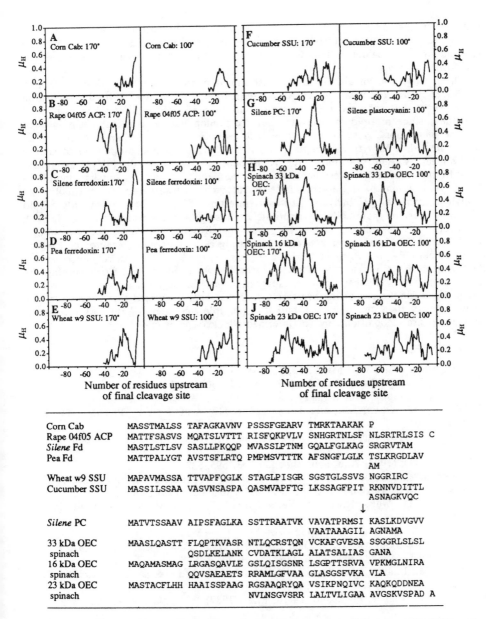

Corn Cab	MASSTMALSS TAFAGKAVNV PSSSFGEARV TMRKTAAKAK P
Rape 04f05 ACP	MATTFSASVS MQATSLVTTT RISFQKPVLV SNHGRTNLSF NLSRTRLSIS C
Silene Fd	MASTLSTLSV SASLLPKQQP MVASSLPTNM GQALFGLKAG SRGRVTAM
Pea Fd	MATTPALYGT AVSTSFLRTQ PMPMSVTTTK AFSNGFLGLK TSLKRGDLAV
	AM
Wheat w9 SSU	MAPAVMASSA TTVAPFQGLK STAGLPISGR SGSTGLSSVS NGGRIRC
Cucumber SSU	MASSILSSAA VASVNSASPA QASMVAPFTG LKSSAGFPIT RKNNVDITTL
	ASNAGKVQC
	↓
Silene PC	MATVTSSAAV AIPSFAGLKA SSTTRAATVK VAVATPRMSI KASLKDVGVV
	VAATAAAGIL AGNAMA
33 kDa OEC	MAASLQASTT FLQPTKVASR NTLQCRSTQN VCKAFGVESA SSGGRLSLSL
spinach	QSDLKELANK CVDATKLAGL ALATSALIAS GANA
16 kDa OEC	MAQAMASMAG LRGASQAVLE GSLQISGSNR LSGPTTSRVA VPKMGLNIRA
spinach	QQVSAEAETS RRAMLGFVAA GLASGSFVKA VLA
23 kDa OEC	MASTACFLHH HAAISSPAAG RGSAAQRYQA VSIKPNQIVC KAQKQDDNEA
spinach	NVLNSGVSRR LALTVLIGAA AVGSKVSPAD A

FIGURE 1. Hydrophobic moment of transit peptides for periodicity, $\delta = 170°$ (left) and 100° (right), as a function of residue position from the cleavage site, stromal (A-E) and thylakoid (G-J) as described in text. Sequences are shown, along with possible intermediate stromal cleavage site in *Silene* PC (↓).

peaks are neither as pronounced nor as conserved in their locations. We note that an examination of 25 mitochondrial presequences (not shown) reveals that many of them have one or more regions that show a propensity to form at least one region of β structure with a high μ_H.

The β structure domains in chloroplast transit peptides may have three functions: *(a) Direct interaction with the surface of the envelope membrane.* Circular dichroism studies show that bacterial leader peptides adopt a β conformation when associated with the surface of lipid monolayers, and are predominantly α-helical when inserted into the membrane (3). *(b) Interaction with receptor proteins that mediate transloca-tion.* The chloroplast transit peptide has little thermodynamic propensity to span a lipid bilayer by itself. Of course, the leader peptide would cross the bilayer membrane an odd number of times, presumably once, if the peptide is to carry out its function to "lead." At least one of the β-structure segments in each transit peptide is usually long enough to span the lipid bilayer. However, insertion of a single β segment into a lipid bilayer is thermodynamically unfavorable because of the unsaturated H bonds (11). Therefore, the peptide is presumably translocated across the envelope membranes through an ATP-dependent mechanism (12) using a proteinaceous receptor or translo-cator protein (13). *(c) Recognition by a processing protease.* In most sequences exam-ined, a prominent β structure is close to the known cleavage site for removing the transit sequences. This has led to the suggestion that this segment is part of the recog-nition signal for the processing protease (5). It has been suggested that processing may occur in more than one step (14), and it is possible that some of the less prominent peak of μ_H are recognition sites for intermediate cleavage events.

REFERENCES

1 von Heijne, G. (1986) EMBO J. 5, 1335-1341

2 Verner, K. and Schatz, C. (1988) Science 241, 1307-1313

3 Gierasch, L. (1989) Biochemistry 28, 923-930.

4 Keegstra, K., Olsen, L.J., and Theg, S.M. (1989) Ann. Rev. Pl. Physiol. Mol. Biol. 40, 471-501

5 Von Heijne, G., Steppuhn, J., and Herrmann, R.G. (1989) Eur. J. Biochem. 180, 535-345

6 Eisenberg, D. (1984) Ann. Rev. Biochem. 53, 595-623

7 Shiver, J.W., Peterson, A.A., Widger, W.R., Furbacher, P.N., and Cramer, W.A. (1989) in Meth. Enzymol. 172, pp. 439-461, Academic Press, Orlando

8 Eisenberg, D., Weiss, R.M., and Terwilliger, T.C. (1984) Proc. Natl. Acad. Sci. 81, 140-144

9 Keegstra, K. and Bauerle, C. (1988) BioEssays 9, 15-19

10 Nabedryk, E., Garavito, R.M., and Breton, J. (1988) Biophys. J. 53, 671-676

11 Engelman, D.M. and Steitz, T.A. (1981) Cell 23, 411-422

12 Theg, S.M., Bauerle, C., Olsen, L.J., Selman, B.R., and Keegstra, K. (1989) J. Biol. Chem. 264, 6730-6736

13 Singer, S.J., Maher, P.A., and Yaffe, M.P. (1987) Proc. Natl. Acad. Sci. 84, 1015-1019

14 Robinson, C. and Ellis, R.J. (1984) Eur. J. Biochem. 142, 343-346

Acknowledgment. This research was supported by NIH grant GM-38323 (WAC) and DOE grant 86ER13526 (KK). The authors thank G. von Heijne for a preprint of ref. 5 that is the first published report of prominent β-structure in chloroplast transit pep-tides.

CONTROL OF THYLAKOID GROWTH TERMINATION

J. H. Argyroudi-Akoyunoglou and G. Tzinas
NRC "Demokritos", Institute of Biology, Athens, Greece

1. INTRODUCTION

Etiolated plants exposed to intermittent light (ImL) accumulate Chl$\underline{a}$ in low amount and PSU core complexes; they lack Chl$\underline{b}$ and LHC complexes. Transfer of such plants to continuous light (CL) results in accumulation of Chla, Chlb and LHCs in levels similar to those of plants directly exposed to CL; this occurs, however, only in young plants briefly preexposed to ImL or in old plants irrespective of duration of ImL preexposure. In contrast, no Chl nor LHCs accumulate in CL after prolonged preexposure to ImL in young etiolated plants, inspite their deficiency in these components, and their unimpaired LHC-gene transcription[1-6].

To see what controls their accumulation in thylakoids under conditions where Chl synthesis is not expected to be limited (in CL), we exposed etiolated plants to a variety of ImL regimes to induce formation of thylakoids with different composition/stoichiometry[7], and determined prior to or after transfer to CL the activity and composition of thylakoids.

We found that only in cases where the preexisting (in ImL) PSII unit content (activity/g fr w)-irrespective of unit size-, and the H_2O-MV rate reach those of fully green plants, further changes in thylakoid composition cease in CL. Moreover, in plants preexposed to ImL with very long dark intervals (where the cytf/Chl or cytf/PSII is in excess of that in green controls) transfer to CL stimulates PSII unit formation in excess of that in controls (so that the desired PSII/cytf ratio may be attained)

Our results suggest that the accumulation of Chl and LHCs depends on the developmental stage of the thylakoid and the plant's need to attain full photosynthetic competence. Thylakoid growth is terminated when maximum electron flow is reached (irrespective of thylakoid composition).

2. MATERIALS AND METHODS

Six-day old etiolated bean leaves (red kidney var) grown and handled as in (1), exposed to cycles of 2 min light alternating with dark intervals of either 28 min, 98 min or 4 h (2-28;2-98;2-4h), were transferred to CL at 2,000 lux for up to 70h. Isolation of plastids and thylakoids, Chl, PSI, PSII, cytf content determinations and electrophoretic analyses were as in (7), H_2O-MV rates were determined as in (8).

M. Baltscheffsky (ed.), Current Research in Photosynthesis, Vol. III, 803–806.
© 1990 *Kluwer Academic Publishers. Printed in the Netherlands.*

Table 1. Chl, PSI, PSII, cytf, P700 content and stoichiometries in 6-day etiolated bean plants exposed to 1mL with dark intervals of varying duration, and then transferred to CL for 70 h.

Sample	Chl (ug) /g fr w	Chla/b ratio	ACTIVITY (Vmax, umoles)					/mole Chl /g fr w (mmoles)	cytf /g fr w (nmoles)	P700 ug /g fr w	t½ (ms)
			/mg Chl x h		/g fr w x h						
			PSI	PSII	PSI	PSII	PSII+PSI				
2'L-28'D											
2d-96 LDC	670	6.0	345	500	231	335	31.5	3.63	2.63	1.91	85
+70h CL	2730	2.2	220	192	601	524	65.5	1.15	3.39	5.70	25
6d-288 LDC	1177	3.5	250	370	294	435	54.0	1.89	2.41	2.70	50
+70h CL	1463	3.3	230	333	336	487	59.1	1.85	2.93	2.98	50
2'L-98'D											
2d-28 LDC	218	high	550	1150	120	251	6.3	5.90	1.31	1.18	230
+70h CL	2750	2.7	220	192	605	528	66.0	1.15	3.41	5.58	25
6d-86 LDC	630	12.1	530	1050	334	662	55.0	5.90	3.81	3.30	180
+70h CL	1230	3.3	230	445	283	547	66.4	2.15	3.60	2.54	65
2'L-4h D											
2d-12 LDC	113	high	645	1290	73	146	2.1	12.10	1.48	0.64	240
+70h CL	2750	2.2	220	303	605	833	82.5	1.75	5.21	5.65	35
6d-36 LDC	320	high	645	1176	206	376	43.2	11.80	4.00	1.90	190
+70h CL	1195	3.5	476	710	569	849	77.7	3.65	4.73	4.76	95
Control (70h CL)	2750	2.2	220	192	605	528	60.5	1.14	3.39	5.72	25

+70 h CL →

Sample	PSII/cytf/PSI	PSII/PSI	PSI (% of green)	PSII (% of green)	PSII/cytf/PSI	PSII/PSI	PSI (% of green)	PSII (% of green)
2'L-28'D								
2d-96 LDC	0.8/1/0.48	1.65	38	63	1/1/1	1.0	99	99
6d-288 LDC	1.1/1/0.65	1.69	48	82	1/1/0.6	1.66	55	92
2'L-98'D								
2d-28 LDC	1.1/1/0.48	2.35	20	47	1/1/1	1.0	100	100
6d-86 LDC	1.1/1/0.48	2.27	55	125	1/1/0.45	2.2	47	103
2'L-4h D								
2d-12 LDC	0.6/1/0.26	2.30	17	27	1/1/0.6	1.58	100	158
6d-36 LDC	0.6/1/0.28	2.30	34	71	1.2/1/0.7	1.70	95	161

3. RESULTS AND DISCUSSION

Fig.1 and Table 1 show the Chl accumulation and PS activities in plastids of ImL leaves prior to or after transfer to CL. Chl accumulation in CL diminishes as preexposure to ImL is prolonged and so is the decrease in Chl a/b ratio and LHC accumulation. Similarly, the half rise time of the fluorescence induction kinetics ($t\frac{1}{2}$) is reduced in plants transferred to CL after brief preexposure to ImL (reflecting the growth of the PSII unit), but not after prolonged ImL treatment. The PSII unit growth in CL, therefore, is inhibited in plants preexposed to prolonged ImL.

The PSI and PSII content (PS activity/g fr w) in ImL plants prior to or after transfer to CL, expressed also as % of that found in green controls, is shown in Table 1. The PSII content increases gradually in ImL and reaches that in controls -or overexceeds it in 2-98 ImL plants) (Fig. 2). Transfer to CL of plants briefly preexposed to ImL, where the PSII content is still lower than that in controls, induces accumulation of new PS units until the PSII unit content reaches that of the control. The PS units formed in CL are large in size and thus Chl and LHC accumulate. However, transfer of plants to CL after prolonged ImL preexposure, where the PSII unit content has already reached that in the control, does not induce further PSII unit formation -actually in 2-98 ImL plants, transfer to CL reduces the PSII unit content-. Thus, in spite the deficiency in Chl and LHC content and the small PS unit size in ImL thylakoids, no PSII units accumulate in CL, as long as the PSII activity/g fr w has reached that in green controls. To this conclusion lead also the results with old and young (2-98) ImL plants[6]. The PSII content in young plants reaches that of controls after long preexposure to ImL; so, transfer to CL in this case does not stimulate accumulation of PSII, Chl nor LHCs[4]; in contrast, the PSII content in old ImL plants never reaches that of the green control during exposure to ImL; so, irrespective of duration of ImL preexposure, new PSII units, Chl and LHCs accumulate after transfer to CL[5].

As soon as the PSII units stop to accumulate, the PSI units also stop.

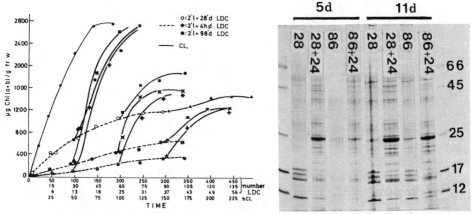

FIGURE 1. (a): Chl accumulation in 2-28, 2-98, and 2-4h ImL plants prior to (---) or after their transfer to CL (——). (b): SDS-PAGE of thylakoid polypeptides obtained from 6d and 11d old etiolated bean leaves exposed to 28 or 86 cycles of 2-98 ImL, and then transferred to CL for 24 hours.

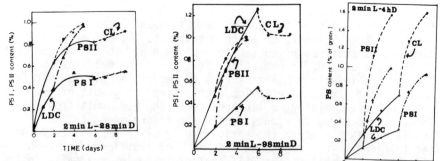

FIGURE 2. PSI and PSII content/g fr w (% of that in green controls) in plastids of etiolated bean leaves exposed to 2-28, 2-98 or 2-4h ImL (LDC, —) and then transferred to continuous light (CL, ----).

Thus, the high PSII/PSI ratio in ImL plants decreases in CL only after brief preexposure to ImL, but it is not affected after long preexposure.

In the case of plants preexposed to 2-4h ImL, where the cytf/Chl or cytf/PSII ratio overexceeds that of green controls (cytf synthesis occurs in the dark) (see fig 3), the accumulation of PSII units after transfer to CL is overstimulated and activities higher than in controls are reached (reflecting the need of the plant to attain the required stoichiometry - PSII/cytf=0.6 in 2-4h ImL; PSII/cytf=1.0 in the control-, or the excessive formation of RC apoproteins in ImL, that are fully accomodated with Chl after transfer to CL).

Finally, in all cases, irrespective of duration of preexposure to ImL, and of preexisting thylakoid composition, the H$_2$O-MV whole electron transport/g fr w attains that of the controls, reflecting the dynamic modulation of thylakoid composition (larger PSIIU/more PSIU -PSII/PSI=1.0 in CL, or smaller PSIIU/fewer PSIU - PSII/PSI=2.5 in ImL).

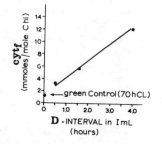

FIGURE 3. The cytf/Chl Molar ratio in thylakoids, as affected by the duration of the dark interval in ImL. 6 day etiolated bean leaves were exposed to ImL cycles of 2 min light alternating with 28 min, 98 min or 4 h dark intervals for 2 days.

REFERENCES
1. Argyroudi-Akoyunoglou and Akoyunoglou (1970) Plant Physiol. 46, 247.
2. Argyroudi-Akoyunoglou and Akoyunoglou (1979) FEBS Lett. 104, 78-84.
3. Akoyunoglou, G. (1977) Arch. Biochem. Biophys. 183, 571-580.
4. Akoyunoglou and Argyroudi-Akoyunoglou (1978) Plant Physiol. 61, 834.
5. Tsakiris, S. and Akoyunoglou, G. (1984) Plant Sci Lett 35, 97-102.
6. Argyroudi-Akoyunoglou (1989) In:Techniques and New Developments in Photosynthesis Research (Barber, Malkin, eds), Plenum. N.Y. (in press).
7. Tzinas, Argyroudi-Akoyunoglou, Akoyunoglou (1987) Photos. Res. 14, 241.
8. Armond, P.A. et a/(1976) Arch. Biochem. Biophys. 175, 54-63.

δ-AMINOLEVULINATE (ALA) SYNTHESIS IN SYNECHOCOCCUS 6301: REQUIREMENT FOR tRNA[Glu] AND PYRIDOXAMINE PHOSPHATE.

Alan D. Bull[1], Volker Breu[2], Arnold J. Smith[1] and C. Gamini Kannangara[2]
[1]*Department of Biochemistry, University College of Wales. Aberystwyth SY23 3DD, Dyfed Wales.*
[2]*Department of Physiology, Carlsberg Laboratory, Gamle Carlsberg Vej 10, DK-2500 Valby, Denmark.*

1. INTRODUCTION:

In plants, algae, cyanobacteria and some other bacterial species 5-aminolevulinate (ALA) is synthesized from glutamate (1-6). This reaction sequence involves ligation of glutamate to a tRNA[Glu] species and subsequent reduction to glutamate-1-semialdehyde (GSA) (7). The conversion of GSA to ALA is then catalysed by GSA-aminotransferase (E.C. 5.4.3.8.) (2,8). Dependent on the requirement of pyridoxamine-phosphate (PAMP) or pyridoxal-phosphate (PALP) for activity, either 4,5-diaminovalerate (8-10) or 4,5-dioxovalerate (DOVA) (5,11,12) are proposed as intermediates.

We have separated the ALA-synthesizing enzyme system of *Synechococcus PCC 6301* into three different fractions by gel-filtration and subsequent affinity chromatography (7) and studied the cofactor requirement of GSA-aminotransferase.

2. MATERIALS AND METHODS:

2.1. Chemicals: glutamate-1-semialdehyde (GSA) was prepared by ozonolysis of vinyl γ-aminobutyric acid (13). L-glutamate-U-[14]C (275 mCi mmole^{-1}) and ^{3}H-glutamate (22 Ci mmole^{-1}) were obtained from Amersham, UK. B_6 cofactors and 5-aminolevulinate were obtained from Sigma (Poole, UK), 3-amino-2,3-dihydrobenzoic acid hydrochloride (gabaculine) was from Fluka AG (Switzerland).

2.2. Preparation of crude cell-free extracts: *Synechococcus PCC 6301* was grown photoautotrophically (14) and cells were broken using a French press at 86.25 MPa. in 0.1 M Tricine buffer pH 9.0, containing 0.3 M glycerol, 25 mM $MgCl_2$ and 1 mM dithiothreitol (DTT). After centrifugation at 200,000 g (20 min) the supernatant was used for further purification.

2.3. Gel-filtration and affinity chromatography: For separation of the ALA-synthesizing components we used gel-filtration on Sephacryl S-300 and subsequent affinity chromatography as a sequential system of Blue-Sepharose, Red Agarose and Chlorophyllin Sepharose (7).

2.4. Enzyme assays: Ligase activity was measured as described previously (7). Dehydrogenase activity was measured in combination with the ligase. The assay-mixture contained 0.1 M Tricine-buffer (pH 7.9), 0.3 M glycerol, 25 mM $MgCl_2$, 1 mM DTT, 1 mM ATP, 1 mM NADPH, 5 μCi ^{3}H-glutamate and 1-2 OD_{260} units of soluble RNA. The products were analysed by HPLC as described earlier (7). GSA-aminotransferase was measured at pH 7.2 to avoid chemical conversion of GSA to ALA (9).

M. Baltscheffsky (ed.), Current Research in Photosynthesis, Vol. III, 807–810.
© 1990 *Kluwer Academic Publishers. Printed in the Netherlands.*

3. **RESULTS AND DISCUSSION:**
On Sephacryl S-300 (Fig 1) GSA-aminotransferase and tRNAGlu-ligase (fraction 30-55) were separated from membrane fragments (fraction 1-20), low molecular weight components (fraction 60-100). The elution profile and activity-pattern of gel-filtration on Sephacryl S-300 was very similar to that of the unicellular green alga *Scenedesmus obliquus* (15) and barley (16).

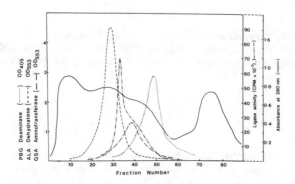

Fig 1: Separation of a soluble extract from the cyanobacterium *Synechococcus 6301* on Sephacryl S-300. The UV-pattern, measured at 280 nm and the activities for PBG-deaminase, ALA-dehydratase, GSA-aminotransferase and glutamyl-tRNAGlu-Synthase are given.

When the fractions 30 to 55 were passed sequentially through Blue Sepharose, Red Agarose and Chlorophyllin Sepharose, then the components of the ALA-synthesizing system were differentially adsorbed by the affinity materials. Table 1 shows that only the Blue Sepharose bound fraction is able to ligate glutamate to $tRNA^{Glu}$ in an ATP dependent reaction.

Table 1:

Fraction	ATP	RNA	CPM (^{3}H-glutamyl tRNA)
Blue Sepharose bound	+	+	217087
Blue Sepharose bound	-	+	1347
Blue Sepharose bound	+	-	1187
Run-off	+	+	1232
Red Agarose bound	+	+	1117

A second $tRNA^{Glu}$-ligase, binding to Red Agarose, which had been described for *Scenedesmus obliquus* (15) could not be detected. This is of current interest, because this enzymatic step has recently been described to be controlled by Pchlide inhibition (17). The eluate from Blue-Sepharose also contains the dehydrogenase, which uses glutamate loaded to $tRNA^{Glu}$ as substrate and reduces it to GSA in an NADPH dependent reaction (Fig 2A). The GSA-aminotransferase, which produces ALA using GSA as substrate is located in the unbound fraction (Fig 2B). In the presence of Blue-Sepharose bound protein, RNA, ATP, NADPH and unbound fraction we can therefor reconstitute the complete ALA-synthesizing activity.The same distribution of enzymes was found for barley (7) and *Scenedesmus obliquus* (15). In these organisms the ALA-dehydratase and PBG-deaminase are located in the unbound fraction together with GSA-aminotransferase and DOVA-Transaminase. In contrast using *Synechococcus 6301* the ALA-dehydratase and PBG-deaminase binds to Red-Agarose. This fraction would therefore be a good starting material for purification of these enzymes.

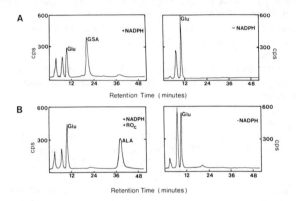

Fig 2: Reconstitution assay for ALA-synthesis *in vitro* using HPLC analysis of ^{14}C-labelled products:
A: Blue Sepharose bound fraction + soluble RNA
B: Blue Sepharose bound fraction + Run off fraction (RO$_C$) + soluble RNA.

The soluble RNA fraction, which was prepared from the Chlorophyllin-Sepharose bound material was separated by HPLC as described (7). Only one tRNA^{Glu} could be detected using the ligase from the Blue-Sepharose fraction (Fig. 3). This tRNA^{Glu} could be used to reconstitute ALA-synthesis. The same result has been described for barley (3) whereas *Methanobacterium thermoautotrophicum* (19) and *Scenedesmus obliquus* (16) possess two different tRNAs^{Glu} which can both be used to reconstitute ALA synthesis.

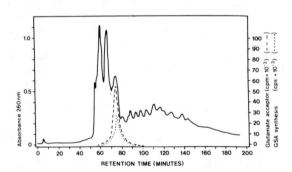

Fig 3: Separation of soluble RNA by HPLC. Only one tRNA acts as glutamate acceptor (– –). This tRNA^{Glu} can also be used to reconstitute ALA-synthesis (·····).

The GSA-aminotransferase activity could be stimulated by pyridoxamine-phosphate (PAMP) from 5.3 nmol ALA mg protein^{-1} min^{-1} to 8.2 nmol ALA mg protein^{-1} min^{-1}. The enzyme was almost completely inhibited by 5 μM gabaculine (Fig. 4). This inhibition had already been demonstrated by *in vivo* experiments (20). The *in vitro* inhibition was not observed when

0.75mM PAMP added together with the gabaculine (10).

The following conclusions are made from the present study:

1.) In *Synechococcus 6301* ALA is made from glutamate using a ligase, a dehydrogenase, an aminotransferase and a tRNA^{Glu} as catalytic components.

2.) Unlike *Synechocystis 6803* (18) and *Scenedesmus obliquus* (15), *Synechococcus 6301* uses only one tRNA^{Glu} for protein and ALA-synthesis, indicating that it is an important point of regulation.

3.) The GSA-aminotransferase of *Synechococcus 6301* is different to that of barley (8), *Scenedesmus obliquus* (15) and *Chlorella* (21) in that it functions optimally in the presence of pyridoxamine-phosphate.

4. **REFERENCES:**

1   Castelfranco, P.A. and Beale, S.I. (1983) Annu. Rev. Plant Physiol 34, 241-278
2   Kannangara, C.G. and Gough, S.P. (1978) Carlsberg Res. Commun. 43, 185-194.
3   Kannangara, C.G., Gough, S.P., Bruyant, Ph., Hoober, J.K., Kahn, A. and v. Wettstein, D. (1988) TIBS 13, 139-143.
4   Smith and Rogers (1988) In: Proceedings of the Phytochemical Society of Europe. Biochemistry of the algae and cyanobacteria. (Rogers, L.J. and Gallon, J.R., eds.), Clarendon Press, Oxford, pp. 69-96.
5   Breu, V. and Dörnemann, D. (1988) Biochim. Biophys. Acta 967, 135-140.
6   Avissar, Y.J., Ormerod, J.G. and Beale, S.I. (1989) Arch. Microbiol. 151, 513-519.
7   Kannangara, C.G., Gough, S.P., Oliver, R.P. and Rasmussen, S.K. Carlsberg Res. Commun. 49, 417-437.
8   Grimm, B., Bull, A., Welinder, K.G., Gough, S.P. and Kannangara, C.G. (1989) Carlsberg Res. Commun. 54, 67-79.
9   Hoober, J.K., Kahn, A., Ash, D.E., Gough, S. and Kannangara, C.G. (1988) Carlsberg Res. Commun. 53, 11-25
10 Bull, A.D., Grimm, B., Breu, V. Kannangara, C.G., Rogers, L.J. and Smith, A.J. (in preparation)
11 Dörnemann, D. and Senger, H. (1980) Biochim. Biophys. Acta 628, 35-45.
12 Breu, V., Kah, A. and Dörnemann, D. (1988) Biochim. Biophys. Acta 964, 61-68.
13 Gough, S.P. and Kannangara, C.G. (1989) Carlsberg Res. Commun. (in press)
14 Smith, A. J., London, J. and Stanier, R.Y. (1967) J. Bacteriol. 94, 972-983.
15 Breu, V. (1988) In: Wissenschaftliche Forschungsbeiträge Biologie, Biochemie, Chemie (Ch. Intemann and A. Intemann, eds.) Intemann Verlag, München.
16 Kannangara, C.G., Gough, S.P. and Girnth, C. (1981), In: Photosynthesis V. Chloroplast Development (G. Akoyunoglou, ed.), Balaban Int. Sc. S., Philadelphia.
17 Dörnemann, D., Kotzabasia, K., Richter, P., Breu, V. and Senger, H. (1989) Botanica Acta 102, 112-115.
18. O'Neill, G.P., Peterson, D.M., Schön, A. Chen, M.-W. and Söll, D. (1988) J. of Bact. 170, 3810-3816.
19 Friedmann, H.C., Thauer, R.K., Gough, S.P. and Kannangara, C.G. (1987) Carlsberg Res. Commun. 52, 363-371.
20 Bull, A.D., Pakes, J.F., Hoult, R.C. Rogers, L.J. and Smith, A.J. (1989) Biochem Soc Trans (in press)
21 Avissar, Y. J. and Beale, S.I. (1989) Plant Physiol. 89, 852-859.

SYNTHESIS AND ASSEMBLY OF A CHLOROPLAST ATP SYNTHASE SUBUNIT IN VITRO

ALLAN MICHAELS, DVORAH WEINBERG, AND STEFAN LEU, DEPARTMENT OF BIOLOGY , BEN-GURION UNVIERSITY OF THE NEGEV, BEER-SHEVA, ISRAEL.

1. INTRODUCTION

Chloroplast ATP synthase couples proton translocation across the thylakoid membrane to synthesis or hydrolysis of ATP. The extrinsic part of this complex, CF1, can be extracted from the membrane and shows Ca^{++} and Mg^{++} dependent ATPase activity (1). CF1 is composed of 5 subunits, three of which are synthesized and encoded in the chloroplast (2). Subunits α and β of Cf1 have been shown to be synthesized on membrane bound ribosomes in <u>Chlamydomonas</u>, but by soluble and membrane bound ribosomes in peas (3, 4). Enzymatic properties of CF1 and of the closely related mitochondrial and bacterial F1 complexes have been extensively studied. A heterodimer alpha3/beta3 has been shown to bind nucleotides and have ATPase activity. This trimer contains one active site, while the other binding sites have regulatory functions (5, 6). Recently, a Mg^{++} dependent ATPase activity has been found in isolated β-subunit of spinach CF1 (7).

In this paper we describe the in vitro transcription/ translation of the cloned atpB gene and its insertion into CF1. The in vitro assembly of beta subunit into CF1 may provide more evidence for the formation of CF1 by self-assembly.

2. MATERIAL AND METHODS

The gene encoding the beta subunit of CF1 was resected with KpnI and Hind III from plasmid pB7 (obtained from N. Gillham) (8). The resulting fragment was ligated to pT7-2. Recombinant colonies were identified by antibiotic selection on solid media. Plasmids isolated from recombinant clones were analysed by restiction endonuclease digestion for the correct insert and orientation. Plasmid containing the atpB gene was purified by CsCl gradient centrifugation, linearized with restriction endonuclease EcoRI, phenol extracted, precipitated and used as template to produce RNA in vitro with T7 RNA polymerase. After

M. Baltscheffsky (ed.), Current Research in Photosynthesis, Vol. III, 811–814.

digestion with RNAase free DNAaseI the in vitro transcribed RNA was phenol extracted, precipitated by addition of two volumes of ethanol and analyzed by electrophoresis to determine concentration and homogeneity of each preparation (9).

Translation of the in vitro transcribed RNA was done according to the supplier (Promega) with the Mg^{++} and K^+ concentrations adjusted to 1.5 and 120 mM, respectively. Incorporation of radioactivity into hot TCA insoluble material was determined by liquid scintillation. Both agarose and acrylamide gel electrophoresis was done as described (9, 10). Chloroplast membranes were prepared from synchronous cultures of Chlamydomonas as previously published (3). CF1 was isolated by sucrose gradient centrifugation essentially as published (3); the membranes were solubilized in 1%Triton, 1 mMEDTA, 10 mMTris pH 8, centrifuged at 12000 x g for 5 minutes and directly applied to the gradient.

3. RESULTS

Translation of the atpB mRNA in the reticulocyte extract showed synthesis of polypeptides with a maximum Mr of about 52 kDa. Translation was neither stimulated nor inhibited in the presence of isolated photosynthetic membranes. atpB mRNA directed synthesis of a doublet polypeptide. Analysis of recovered, washed membranes showed that the beta subunit was associated with thylakoids (Fig 1).

We wanted to determine if the membrane-associated beta was part of the CF1 complex or unspecifically bound to thylakoids. Membranes were recovered from translation reactions, solubilized in detergent and analyzed as described in Methods. The position of CF1 was determined by coomassie staining. Some labelled beta subunit as well as lower molecular weight products of the translation were found at the top of the gradient, while radioactivity in the beta subunit of CF1 peaked at fraction 9 - 10, coincident with the position of stained CF1 subunits alpha and beta in the gradient (Fig 1).

4. DISCUSSION

Our previous results indicated that the alpha and beta subunits of CF1 were translated by rough thylakoids. We postulated that after synthesis the chloroplast translated subunits of CF1 may exist in a transient manner unassembled in the membrane (3). In this publication we show that beta CF1 produced from in vitro transcription/translation of the atpB gene is capable of assembly into isolatable CF1, either by exchange with existing CF1 or by assembly of new CF1 from pools of the other subunits present in the membrane, as postulated in our previous work.

Point mutations in the atpB gene are deficient in CF1 assembly. These mutations prevented assembly of subunits α and ε to the membrane. The mutated β-subunit was translated, but not accumulated on the membrane. The authors concluded, that subunit beta is necessary for CF1 assembly and binding to the membrane (11). However, these results also permit the conclusion, that the mutated β-subunit prevents CF1 assembly and therefore induces high turnover of the unassembled subunits. There can still be small unassembled pools of CF1 subunits in normal membranes, allowing assembly of in vitro synthesized beta subunit.

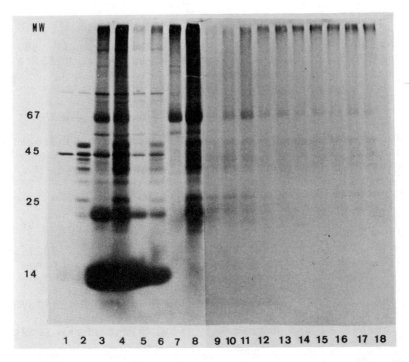

Figure 1: Assembly of in vitro labelled subunit beta of CF1: 1) translation products without added RNA; 2) translation products of atpB mRNA; 3) translation products without added RNA in the presence of thylakoid membranes (0.3 mg/ml of chlorophyll); 4) translation products of atpB mRNA in the presence of thylakoid membranes; 5,6) translation products in the supernatants after centrifugation of the total reactions 3 and 4 (5 min; 12000x g); 7,8) translation products in the washed thylakoid membrane fraction recovered from total reactions 3 and 4; 9 - 18) Translation products in gradient fractions 1 - 10.

We have measured assembly of subunit beta of CF1 in a heterologous system. The translation of chloroplast mRNAs in the reticulocyte lysate results in a product pattern comparable to that of in vivo pulse labelling (10). In spite of the heterologous nature of the translation conditions, it was possible to insert functional D1 protein into thylakoids isolated from photoinhibited cells and restore PSII function (12). Here, we demonstrate the assembly of in vitro synthesized beta subunit into CF1. Starting from the cloned gene, this model system will allow studies of CF1 assembly with altered atpB genes.

5. REFERENCES

1. Shavit, N. (1980) Ann. Rev. Biochem. 49, 111-138.
2. Merchant S., Shaner S.L. and Selman B.R. (1983) J. Biol. Chem. 258, 1026-1031.
3. Herrin D. and Michaels A. (1985) Arch. Biochem. Biophys. 237, 224 - 236.
4. Bhaya D. and Jagendorf A.T. (1985) Arch. Biochem. Biophys. 237, 217 - 223.
5. Walker J.E., Saraste M. and Gay N.J. (1984) Biochim. Biophys. Acta 768, 164 - 200.
6. Ysern X., Amzel L.M. and Pedersen P.L. (1988) J. Bioeneg. Biomembr. 20, 423 - 450.
7. Frasch W.D., Green J.D., Caguiat J. and Mejia A. (1989) J. Biol. Chem. 264, 5064 - 5069.
8. Woessner J.P., Gillham N.W. and Boynton J.E. (1986) Gene 44, 17 - 28.
9. Maniatis T., Fritsch E.F. and Sambrook J. (1982) in: Molecular Cloning, Cold Spring Harbor Laboratory.
10. Leu S., Bolli R., Mendiola-Morgenthaler L. and Boschetti A. (1984) Planta 160, 204 - 211.
11. Robertson D., Woessner J.P., Gillham N.W. and Boynton J.E. (1989) J. Biol. Chem. 264, in press
12. Michaels A. and Herrin D. (1989) Plant Physiol. 89, 100 - 103.

ACKNOWLEDGEMENTS

This work was supported by a grant from NSF.

SPECIFICITY OF IN VITRO IMPORT IN SPINACH LEAF MITOCHONDRIA AND CHLOROPLASTS

J. WHELAN[*], C. KNORPP, M.A. HARMEY[*] AND E. GLASER
DEPARTMENT OF BIOCHEMISTRY, ARRHENIUS LABORATORIES, UNIVERSITY OF STOCKHOLM, S-106 91 STOCKHOLM, SWEDEN
[*]BOTANY DEPT., U.C.D., DONNYBROOK, DUBLIN 4, IRELAND

INTRODUCTION

In a plant cell, two organelles provide the cells energy requirement, the chloroplast and the mitochondrion. Both organelles have a limited coding capacity and must import more than 90% of their proteins from nuclear coded precursors in the cytoplasm. Import into mitochondria and chloroplasts have been studied for some time but import into plant mitochondria and the sorting phenomenon in a plant leaf cell is a rather new topic for investigations. There has been reports of mis-sorting (1). Post-translational import is believed to follow a similar theme for both mitochondria and chloroplasts. The ATP synthase is present in both chloroplasts and mitochondria. The chloroplast ATP synthase $CF_1\beta$-subunit is encoded by the chloroplast while the mitochondrion $F_1\beta$-subunit is nuclear coded. In photosynthetic tissue, chloroplasts have greater relative surface area and thus the mitochondrial F_1 precursor has to be effectively directed to the mitochondrion. We investigated the sorting properties for the β-subunit of the F_1-ATP synthase by using in vitro transcribed/translated the mitochondrial Nicotiana plumbagnifolia $F_1\beta$ and Neurospora crassa $F_1\beta$. The sorting phenomenon was investigated on two levels, import and processing ability of both organelles for the $F_1\beta$-subunit.

MATERIALS AND METHODS

The Nicotiana $F_1\beta$ and Neurospora $F_1\beta$ were transcribed in linearized pTZ 18U and pGem3 respectively, translated in a rabbit reticulocyte lysate giving (^{35}S)-methionine labeled precursor proteins. Spinach mitochondria were prepared according to Hamasur et al. (2). Processing with mitochondrial matrix extract was carried out according to Hawlitschek et al. (3). Processing and import with chloroplasts was carried out according to Robinson et al. (4). Import into spinach mitochondria was carried out according to Whelan et al. (1989).

M. Baltscheffsky (ed.), Current Research in Photosynthesis, Vol. III, 815–818.
© 1990 *Kluwer Academic Publishers. Printed in the Netherlands.*

RESULTS

The <u>Nicotiana</u> F$_1$β is imported into spinach mitochondria (Fig. 1, lane 2). The 59 kDa precursor is processed to a 51 kDa protein which was insensitive to externally added protease. The <u>Neurospora</u> F$_1$β gives one major translation product of 56 kDa (Fig. 2, lane 1) which was imported and processed to 54 kDa (Fig. 2, lane 2). The import of the <u>Neurospora</u> F$_1$β needs a membrane potential which is shown in Fig. 2, lane 4 and 5. Addition of valinomycin and oligomycin inhibits th0 formation of the membrane potential, no imported products are present.

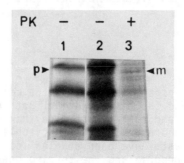

Fig. 1. Import of <u>Nicotiana</u> F$_1$β into spinach leaf mitochondria. Lane 1, <u>in vitro</u> translation product. Lane 2, import. Lane 3, import followed by protease K treatment. Precursor 59 kDa (p) and mature form 51 kDa (m) indicated.

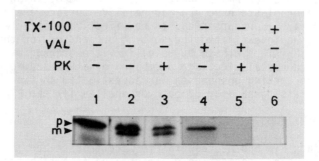

Fig. 2. Import of the <u>Neurospora</u> F$_1$β into spinach leaf mitochondria. Lane 1, <u>in vitro</u> translation product. Lane 2, import. Lane 3, import followed by protease K treatment. Lane 4, import in the presence of valinomycin and oligomycin. Lane 5, import in the presence of valinomycin and oligomycin and protease K treatment. Lane 6, import, Triton X-100 treated prior to protease K treatment. Precursor of 56 kDa (p) and mature form of 54 kDa (m) indicated.

When we studied cross import into chloroplasts we found that the Neurospora $F_1\beta$ binds weakly to the chloroplast membrane (Fig. 3, lane 2). No import of the Neurospora $F_1\beta$ can be seen into spinach chloroplasts, all proteins are acessible to added protease (Fig. 3, lane 3). The chloroplasts can process the Neurospora $F_1\beta$ to about 54.5 kDa. The smaller form does not bind to the membrane (Fig. 3, lane 2) but is seen in the supernatant together with the complete precursor form (Fig. 3, lane 5). All protein in the supernatant are sensitive to added proteases (Fig. 3, lane 6). This processing activity is found in the stroma compartment of the chloroplast (Fig. 4, lane 2). The thylakoid fraction seems to give several breakdown products with the Neurospora $F_1\beta$ (Fig. 4, lane 3).

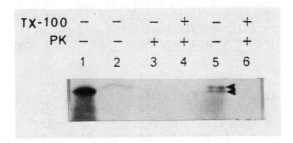

Fig. 3. Import of Neurospora $F_1\beta$ into spinach chloroplasts. Lane 1, in vitro translation product. Lane 2, import. Lane 3, import followed by protease K treatment. Lane 4, import into chloroplasts lysed with Triton X-100 prior to protease K treatment. Lane 5, supernatant after import (lane 2). Lane 6, supernatant after import followed by protease K treatment (lane 3).

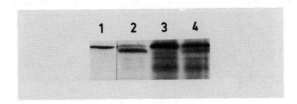

Fig. 4. Processing of Neurospora $F_1\beta$ with stroma and thylakoid extracts. Lane 1, in vitro translated Neurospora $F_1\beta$. Lane 2, Neurospora F_1 processed with stroma. Lane 3, Neurospora $F_1\beta$ processed with thylakoid extract. Lane 4, Neurospora $F_1\beta$ processed with stroma and thylakoid extract.

DISCUSSION

Spinach leaf mitochondria can import <u>Nicotiana</u> and <u>Neurospora</u> $F_1\beta$ precursors. The mitochondria seems to be able to import the <u>Neurospora</u> $F_1\beta$ faster than they process it. This might be due to poor processing efficiency of heterologous import. The processing protein in spinach mitochondria does not seem to process incomplete precursor, which would suggest a strict conformational requirement in processing.

The precursor of <u>Neurospora</u> $F_1\beta$ binds to the chloroplast membrane, this may be an unspecific binding of the amphiphilic presequence to a lipid membrane. The chloroplast does not import the <u>Neurospora</u> $F_1\beta$ but it is able to process it to a size of 54.5 kDa. The processing activity is found in the stroma. The processing which can be seen in the import using intact chloroplasts might be due to some lysed chloroplasts in the import reaction. No import or processing of the Fe-S protien is observed. Our studies indicates that the specificity of import is high, and no mis-sorting could be seen of a mitochondrial precursor into the chloroplast. However we did detect a reproducable specific processing of <u>Neurospora</u> $F_1\beta$ by the stroma fraction.

Acknowledgements

We are grateful to Prof. M. Boutry for a generous gift of the cDNA clone of $F_1\beta$ of <u>Nicotiana plumbagnifolia</u> and to Prof. W. Neupert for a generous gift of cDNA clones of $F_1\beta$ and Fe-S protein from <u>Neurospora crassa</u>. We are also grateful to Prof. Bertil Andersson for stimulating discussions and general support.

REFERENCES

1 Hurt, E.C., Soltanifer, N., Clermont, M.G., Rochaix, S.D. and Schatz, G. (1986) EMBO J. 5, 1343-1350
2 Hamasur, B., Birgersson, U., Eriksson, A.C. and Glaser, E., submitted
3 Hawlitscheck, G., Schneider, H., Schmidt, B., Tropschug, M., Hartl, F.-U. and Neupert, W. (1988) Cell 53, 795-806
4 Robinson, C.R. and Ellis, R.J. (1984) Eur. J. Biochem. 142, 337-342

NADPH:PROTOCHLOROPHYLLIDE OXIDOREDUCTASE IN BARLEY
(HORDEUM VULGARE) SEEDLINGS

SAVCHENKO G.E., ABRAMCHIK L.M., KLYUCHAREVA E.A.,
CHAIKA M.T., INSTITUTE OF PHOTOBIOLOGY, BELORUSSIAN SSR
ACADEMY OF SCIENCES, MINSK, USSR

1. INTRODUCTION

The quantitative aspects of changes in various intracellular pools of NADPH:protochlorophyllide oxidoreductase
(POR) are important for understanding the principles of
operation of the multienzyme system of chlorophyll biosynthesis which proteins are encoded by nuclear DNA and
synthesized in the cytoplasm. The application of immunochemical methods /1,2/ allowed to detect loss of POR in
the system of intraplastid membranes of etiolated leaves
under illumination. In this work the enzyme-linked immuno-
sorbent assay (ELISA) was employed for quantification of
POR in different intracellular compartments of postetio-
lated and green barley seedlings.

2. PROCEDURE
2.1. Materials and methods
2.1.1. Plant material: Barley (Hordeum vulgare) seedlings
were grown at 23 C in darkness and irradiated with
white light of 3800 lux. Green plants were grown
under the same illumination. Upper parts of the
leaves were analyzed (excised 0.5 cm below the
top): 3-cm-long segments of seedlings older than 3
days and 2-cm-long segments of 3-day-old ones. The
latter had no coleoptile.
2.1.2. Intracellular fractions: Homogenates for the determination of total POR in leaf tissue were obtained
by grinding the material frozen in liquid nitrogen
to powder. Phosphate buffer (pH 7.2) containing
1 mM EDTA, 1 mM MgCl$_2$, 0.3 mM NADPH and 4 mM protease inhibitor phenylmethyl sulfonylfluoride was
added. The homogenates were filtered through two
layers of nylon cloth. The membrane-free POR fraction was obtained by centrifugation of homogenate
at 144 000 g for 1 h. In another series of experiments chloroplasts were prepared from homogenates
without grinding in liquid nitrogen. After osmotic

M. Baltscheffsky (ed.), Current Research in Photosynthesis, Vol. III, 819–822.
© 1990 *Kluwer Academic Publishers. Printed in the Netherlands.*

shock photosynthetic membranes were sedimented by centrifugation at 9 000 g. Stroma and cytoplasm were centrifuged at 144 000 g for 1 h. Procedures with etiolated and darkened plants were performed under dim green light.

2.1.3. POR visualization: POR was quantified with an ELISA technique /3/. 100 μl portions of the suspension containing no detergent were applied on the wells of a polysterene plate. The adsorption of the antigene and antibodies proceeded overnight at +4 C. Horse-radish peroxidase conjugate with antirabbit antibodies (Sigma) and o-phenylenediamine were used. Each analytical measurement was repeated at least three times. The suspensions were diluted several times which allowed to plot concentration curves of antigene binding (by total protein content) (Fig.1). We encountered, however, certain problems with the photosynthetic membranes. Stored in the cold without detergent, they turned into poorly resuspendable aggregates. The latter, therefore, were ultrasonicated prior to the immunoenzymatic analysis to obtain a homogeneous suspension. On this account it was difficult to prepare suspensions of photosynthetic membranes with a predetermined protein content. The latter was measured according to Markwell /4/.

2.1.4. Antibodies to POR: Rabbits were immunized with the enzyme isolated from prolamellar bodies of 7-day-old etiolated barley leaves and purified by chromatography on DEAE-cellulose in the presence of exogenous NADPH and protochlorophyllide (Pchlde) /5/. For ELISA, either rabbit antiserum diluted in the ratio of 1:8 (Fig.1) or the fraction of immunoglobulin G isolated from the antiserum on DEAE-cellulose and diluted several times (Fig.2) were used.

3. RESULTS AND DISCUSSION

Fig.1 a,b presents data on changes in relative POR content in homogenates prepared from etiolated seedlings of different age. The behaviour of the curves testifies to an appreciable increase in the total content of the enzyme in 10-day-old seedlings. It is possibly due to the addition of NADPH. Without NADPH a decrease of POR was observed even in 6-day-old seedlings. Apparently, during irradiation of 3- and 7-day-old etiolated seedlings neither total POR content in tissue nor the membrane-free POR content changed significantly: the experimental points for non-illuminated or illuminated seedlings of the same age concentrated near one curve (Fig. 1, a,b,d,e). The most noticeable deviation from it was observed in 7-day-old seedlings after 4.5 h of illumination (Fig.1 b).

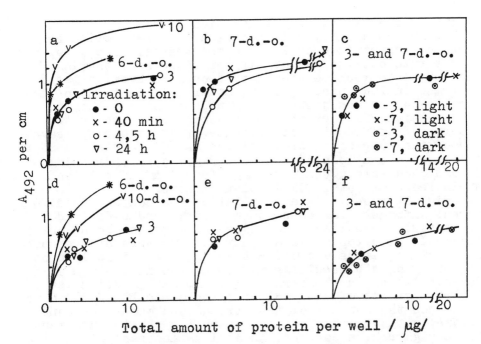

FIGURE 1. The total (a,b,c) and membrane-free (d,e,f)
        pools of POR in etiolated (•,*,ⱽ –a,b,d,e), post-
        etiolated (×, ○,▽ –a,b,d,e) and green (•, ×, ⊙,
        ⊗ –c,f) barley leaves.

POR in intracellular compartments of green barley leaves

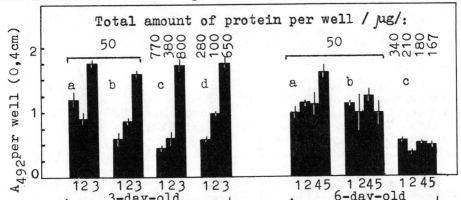

FIGURE 2.a) Cytoplasm. b) stroma. c) photosynthetic mem-
        branes. d) small intraplastid membranes. Illumina-
        ted green leaves (1), seedlings darkened for 24 h
        (2) and 96 h (3), cut leaves darkened for 24 h
        without (4) and with ALA (5).

Thus as a result of illumination of etiolated seed-lings, POR apparently does not decay but redistributes among different intracellular compartments. Of course, one cannot rule out the possibility of rapid resynthesis of the enzyme to replace the decayed one. However, a rapid decrease in POR-encoding m-RNA after illumination /6/ may testify to the absence of new synthesis of the enzyme.

Relative POR content in the homogenates and in the membrane-free fraction of proteins of green barley leaves was of the same order of magnitude as POR content in post-etiolated and etiolated tissues (Fig.1 c,f). Darkening of 3- and 7-day-old green seedlings for 24 h did not lead to an increase of total POR in plant tissue.

Fig. 2 presents data on relative POR content in dif-ferent intracellular compartments of 3- and 6-day-old green barley seedlings including the membrane-bound ones. The pools of cytoplasmic and stromal POR were of the same order of magnitude and did not change significantly upon darkening of the seedlings for 24 h. The incubation of 6-day-old leaves in the dark on a 20 mM ALA solution led to a marked growth of the pool of cytoplasmic POR but did not influence the content of the stromal and membrane-bound enzyme, although the fraction of photosynthetic membranes had a high Pchlde content. An obvious increase of the POR level in all intracellular compartments was only observed upon prolonged darkening of 3-day-old green seedlings (Fig. 2, a-d). ELISA detected POR in small membrane frag-ments sedimented from stroma (Fig. 2,d). It increased upon prolonged darkening. The immunocytochemical method allowed to detect especially large amounts of POR in small mem-brane fragments of green bean leaves in the absence of darkening /7/. As suggested by Shlyk /8/, the light mem-brane fragments may contain centres of chlorophyll bio-synthesis - a system of multienzyme complexes performing the assembly of the pigment molecule.

REFERENCES
1 Ryberg, M., Dehesh, K. (1986) Physiol. Plant. 66,616-624
2 Dehesh, K., Ryberg, M. (1985) Planta 164, 396-399
3 Stocker, J., Malawassi, F., Trucco, M. (1983) in Immunological Methods (Lefkovits, I., Pernis, B., ed.),
  pp.329-338, Mir, Moscow
4 Markwell, M., Haas, S., Bieber, L., Tolbert, N. (1978)
  Analyt. Biochem. 87, 206-210
5 Apel, K., Santel, H., Redlinger, T., Falk, H. (1980)
  Eur. J. Biochem. 111, 251-258
6 Apel, K. (1981) Eur. J. Biochem. 120, 89-93
7 Savchenko, G.E., Abramchik, L.M., Serduchenko, E.V.,
  Chaika, M.T. (1989) Dokl. Acad. Nauk BSSR 33, 660-663
8 Shlyk, A.A. (1980) in Biogenesis and Function of Plant
  Lipids (Mazliak P., ed.), pp. 311-320,Elsevier,Amsterdam

PROTEIN IMPORT INTO CHLOROPLASTS OF CHLAMYDOMONAS REINHARDTII

CHANA GABAI, STEFAN LEU, DVORAH ISH-SHALOM*, ITZAK OHAD* AND ALLAN MICHAELS, DEPARTMENT OF BIOLOGY, BEN GURION UNIVERSITY OF THE NEGEV, BEER-SHEVA AND *DEPARTMENT OF BIOCHEMISTRY, HEBREW UNIVERSITY, JERUSALEM, ISRAEL

1. INTRODUCTION

The chloroplast DNA encodes about 150 proteins which are translated by the chloroplast 70S ribosomes. The other chloroplast proteins are encoded in the nucleus, translated by the cytoplasmic 80S ribosomes as soluble precursors and imported into the chloroplast (1). During this import, the precursor peptides are cleaved and the proteins are immediately assembled with their target complexes (2).

The procedure for the isolation of chloroplasts from cell wall mutants of Chlamydomonas yields relatively pure, active chloroplasts. These chloroplast were photosynthetically active (3) and synthesized proteins in organello (4). They also imported, processed and assembled in vitro synthesized precursors for the small subunit of ribulose bisphosphate carboxylase and for the light harvesting chlorophyll a/b proteins (5, 6, 7).

In every organism analysed so far, a sub-lethal heat shock induced expression of several nuclear genes encoding a set of proteins ranging in molecular weight from 18 - 94 Kd. It is assumed that these proteins confer temporary protection against heat damage (8).

The nuclear encoded 22 kDa heat shock protein (hsp22) of Chlamydomonas is transported into the chloroplast, where it was localized in the grana thylakoids (9) and apparently protected PSII from photoinhibition (10). In contrast to most other imported proteins, hsp22 was not detected as a high molecular weight precursor in vitro. Therefore it does not have a precursor peptide and seems not to be processed during import in vivo (8).

In this study we isolated chloroplasts of normal and heat shocked Chlamydomonas reinhardtii cells. PolyA-RNA was purified from heat shocked cells. In vitro translation products of this RNA were used to investigate import into chloroplasts derived from normal and heat-shocked cells.

M. Baltscheffsky (ed.), Current Research in Photosynthesis, Vol. III, 823–826.
© 1990 *Kluwer Academic Publishers. Printed in the Netherlands.*

2. MATERIALS AND METHODS

Chlamydomonas reinhardii cc124 was cultivated synchronously (14 hours light - 10 hours dark) in a high salt medium (3). The culture was divided into two parts after 5 hours light at a cell density of about 5 - 10 million cells/ml. Growth was continued under regular conditions or at 42°C for 2 hours. Cells were then harvested and used for chloroplast preparation as described (3). Purity and intactness of the chloroplasts was analysed by light driven protein synthesis in the presence of chloramphenicol or cycloheximide (4), or by electrophoretic analysis of extracted chloroplast and cell RNA (11).

PolyA RNA from heat shocked Chlamydomonas reinhardtii was isolated as described (8). This RNA was translated in vitro in a reticulocyte lysate. Translation products were identified by indirect immunoprecipitation as described (12).

Import incubations were as previously described (5, 6). Translations (50 μl) were diluted with 950 μl import medium (250 mM sorbitol, 35 mM HEPES/KOH pH 7.8; 1mM MgCl2; 1mM MnCl2, 2 mM K-EDTA, 5 mM methionine; 0.4 mM other amino acids). Chloroplasts isolated from normal and heat shocked cells were resuspended in the diluted translation mixture to 0.3 mg/ml of chlorophyll and incubated in the light for 45 min at 25°C. Chloroplasts were treated with trypsin (0.25 mg/ml), washed and recovered as described (5, 6).

Chlorophyll was determined according to Vernon (13), and polyacrylamid gelelectrophoresis (in 9 - 18 % linear gradients) was according to Laemmli (14).

3. RESULTS AND DISCUSSION

Intactness and purity of the isolated chloroplasts was checked by in organello translation in the presence of inhibitors. No translation products were observed in the dark and in the presence of chloramphenicol (50 μg/ml) while cycloheximide did not inhibit light stimulated in organello translations in control or heat shocked chloroplasts (Figure 1).

Translation of polyA RNA from heat shocked cells showed two major products of 22 and 24 kDa (Figure 1B). The products were identified with specific antibodies as 22 kDa heat shock protein and the 24 kDa precursor protein of SS. These in vitro translation products were diluted in import medium and incubated with chloroplasts isolated from control or heat shocked cells. The small subunit of rubcase was imported and processed in both chloroplast preparations and was protected from trypsin. The 22 kDa heat shock protein only associated with the chloroplasts, but was not imported in a trypsin protected form into chloroplasts from heat shocked or control cells (figure 1B).

Since the hsp22 was recently identified as extrinsic grana thylakoid component of heat shocked <u>Chlamydomonas</u> (9), these results may indicate a different mechanism for hsp22 import, which may be temperature or stress related.

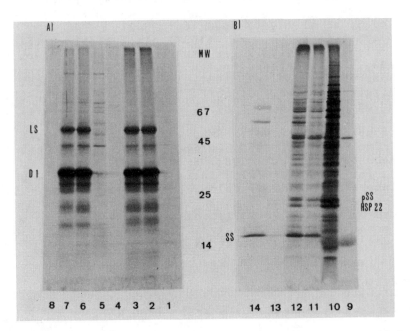

Figure 1 A: Proteins labelled by light dependent in organello protein synthesis by normal (1 - 4) and heat shock chloroplasts (5 - 8), analysed by SDS electrophoresis and autoradiography of the dried gel: 1, 5) incubations in the dark; 2, 6) incubations in the light; 3, 7) incubations in the light in presence of 20 μg/ml cycloheximide; 4, 8) incubations in the light in the presence of 50 μg/ml chloramphenicol.

Figure 1 B: Uptake of products from in vitro translation of polyA RNA from heat shocked <u>Chlamydomonas</u> in the reticulocyte lysate: 9) products of control incubation without added RNA; 10) translation products of polyA-RNA from heat shocked <u>Chlamydomonas reinhardtii</u>; 11) in vitro translation products of polyA-RNA associated with washed control chloroplasts; 12) in vitro translation products associated with chloroplasts isolated from heat shocked cells. 13) products in recovered, trypsin treated control chloroplasts; 14) products in trypsin treated heat shock chloroplasts.

4. REFERENCES

1. Hoober J.K. (1984) Chloroplasts (Siekevitz P. ed.) Plenum Press.
2. Chua N-H. and Schmidt G.W. (1979) J. Cell Biol. 81: 461 - 483.
3. Mendiola-Morgenthaler L. et al (1984) Plant Sci. 38: 33 - 39.
4. Leu S. et al (1984) FEBS 166: 23-27.
5. Boschetti A. et al (1987) In: Algal Development (Molecular and Cellular Aspects), Wiesner, W. et al. eds., Springer, Berlin, p. 114-122.
6. Boschetti A. et al (1987) In: Prog. Photosynth. Res., Biggins, J., ed., Nijhoff, Norwell MA, p. 585-588.
7. Goldschmidt Clermont M. et al (1989) Plant Phys. 89, 15 - 18.
8. Kloppstech K. (1985) EMBO Jour. 4: 1901-1909.
9. Grimm B. et al (1989) Eur. J. Biochem. in press.
10. Schuster G. et al (1988) EMBO J. 7, 1 - 6.
11. Maniatis, T. et al, In: Molecular cloning - a laboratory manual. Cold Spring Harbor Press, Cold Spring Harbor N.Y., p. 202 (1982).
12. Leu S. et al (1984) Planta 160, 204 - 211.
13. Vernon L.P. (1960) Analyt. Chemie 32, 1144 - 1150.
14. Laemmli U.K. (1970) Nature 227, 680 - 685.

ACKNOWLEDGEMENTS:

This work was supported by a grant from NSF.

BIOSYNTHESIS OF CHLOROPLAST CAROTENOIDS

GEORGE BRITTON, DEPARTMENT OF BIOCHEMISTRY, UNIVERSITY OF LIVERPOOL, P.O. BOX 147, LIVERPOOL L69 3BX. U.K.

1. INTRODUCTION:DISTRIBUTION AND FUNCTIONS OF CAROTENOIDS

The photosynthetic pigments of higher plants comprise not only the chlorophylls (a and b) but also a range of carotenoids. The main ones of these are ß-carotene (usually 25-30% of the total carotenoids) and the xanthophylls lutein (45-50%), violaxanthin (ca. 15%) and neoxanthin (ca. 15%), though small amounts of others, e.g. α-carotene, zeaxanthin, antheraxanthin, lutein-5,6-epoxide and α-cryptoxanthin, may also be detected. The carotenoids, like the chlorophylls, are located in the pigment-protein complexes (PPC) of the thylakoid membrane, and show differential distribution among the complexes [1]. Thus, reaction centre-core complexes are enriched in, and may contain only, ß-carotene, whereas the xanthophylls are characteristic of the light-harvesting complexes, in which neoxanthin is particularly tightly bound. α-Carotene, which may in occasional species constitute up to 50% of the total carotene, is found with ß-carotene in the reaction centre-core complexes. Some xanthophylls, especially violaxanthin, have been found in the chloroplast envelope. The overall carotenoid compositions of algae may be more complex and a wider range of structures may be encountered, but the general situation is similar, with carotene in the reaction centre-core complexes and xanthophylls in the light-harvesting complexes, where their light absorption properties may be substantially modified so that they absorb maximally at up to 540nm.

Within the complexes, the carotenoids have different functions [2,3]. The xanthophylls serve as accessory light-harvesting pigments, absorbing light in the range 400-500nm and passing energy on to chlorophyll by singlet energy transfer. The carotenes, on the other hand, play a vital protective role by harmlessly quenching the energy of triplet chlorophyll (^{3}Chl) which may be formed in conditions of high light intensity, and hence preventing formation of the destructive species, singlet oxygen, $^1O_2$. The carotene can also quench any $^1O_2$ that may be produced.

M. Baltscheffsky (ed.), Current Research in Photosynthesis, Vol. III, 827–834.
© 1990 *Kluwer Academic Publishers. Printed in the Netherlands.*

2.   CAROTENOID BIOSYNTHESIS
2.1. General features
     The carotenoids are located, and function, in the PPC, and their biosynthesis is an important part of the construction of the PPC and chloroplast development. The overall process of chloroplast development, including carotenoid biosynthesis, is under direct nuclear control by a block of genes which is switched on as a unit. The supply of the various components, including carotenoids, as required, is regulated by control mechanisms operating on the individual biosynthetic pathways. The regulatory factors which control the formation of carotenoids in the chloroplast and their deposition in the thylakoid PPC are thus at least as important as the reactions and pathways of carotenoid biosynthesis, about which much more is known.
2.2 Pathway
     The carotenoids are biosynthesized by a specialized branch of the isoprenoid pathway which is used by plants for the biosynthesis of a wide variety of important compounds, including the C_{20} sidechain (phytol) of chlorophyll. The main stages of carotenoid biosynthesis are outlined in Fig. 1.

     The early stages of carotenoid biosynthesis are common to the biosynthesis of all isoprenoids. The characteristic isoprenoid precursor, mevalonic acid (MVA) is converted into the C_5 compound isopentenyl diphosphate (IDP), some of which is isomerized to dimethyallyl diphosphate (DMADP). The isoprenoid chain is then built from these precursors by means of prenyl transferase enzymes to give, successively, the C_{10} geranyl diphosphate, precursor of monoterpenes, the C_{15} farnesyl diphosphate, the precursor of sesquiterpenes, and also of triterpenes and steroids, and then the C_{20} geranylgeranyl diphosphate (GGDP) which is the immediate precursor not only of the carotenoids but also of phytol and other diterpenes, and of longer chain isoprenoid compounds. The first C_{40} hydrocarbon, phytoene, is formed from two molecules of GGDP via the C_{40} intermediate, prephytoene diphosphate.

     Phytoene undergoes a series of sequential desaturation reactions to give phytofluene, ζ-carotene, neurosporene and finally lycopene. In each of these steps, two hydrogen atoms are removed by trans-elimination from adjacent positions to introduce a new double bond and extend the conjugated chromophore by two double bonds. The phytoene that has been isolated from most plant tissues and cell-free systems is the (15$\underline{Z}$) or (15-$\underline{cis}$)

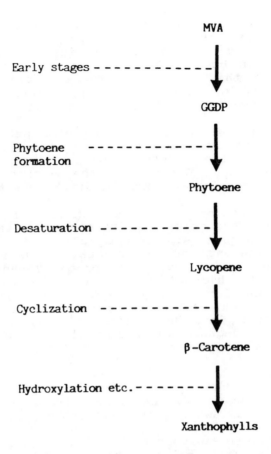

Fig. 1. Summary of the main stages of carotenoid biosynthesis.

isomer, whereas the final fully desaturated carotenoids that accumulate are mainly all-_trans_ (all-_E_), so it is generally assumed that the 15,15' double bond must be isomerized at some, as yet undetermined, stage of the desaturation sequence. The cofactor requirements for desaturation have not been established, but the involvement of some kind of simple electron transport system related to cytochrome P_{450} has been suggested. Desaturation is easily inhibited and is a major target site for bleaching herbicides. The short chromophore acyclic intermediates such as phytoene which accumulate are unable to quench the energy of ^3Chl or $^1O_2$, and thus cannot protect the plant against photosensitized oxidation.

Arguments still persist about whether the acyclic intermediate that is cyclized is lycopene or neurosporene, although the mechanism of the cyclization reaction would be the same in both cases. It is more satisfactory to consider that the requirement for cyclization is simply that one half of the carotenoid molecule should have reached the lycopene level of desaturation.

Cyclization is initiated by proton attack at C-2 of the folded acyclic precursor, to give a transient C-5 carbonium ion which is stabilized by alternative loss of hydrogen from C-6 or C-4 to give the ß- or ε-ring. The ß- and ε-rings, once formed, are not interconverted.

Oxygen functions and other structural modifications in carotenoids are generally introduced at the end of the biosynthetic sequences. Hydroxylation at C-3 occurs by direct replacement of H by OH, with retention of configuration. Thus lutein is formed by hydroxylation of α-carotene. The hydroxylation is believed to be catalysed by a mixed-function oxidase enzyme, requiring cytochrome-P_{450}. The 5,6-epoxide groups, present in violaxanthin and neoxanthin, are introduced after the hydroxylation, and the allenic end-group of neoxanthin is believed to be formed by rearrangement of a 3-hydroxy-5,6-epoxy-ß-ring end-group.

Details of the pathways and reactions of carotenoid biosynthesis may be obtained from some of the comprehensive reviews that are available [4,5].

2.3 Carotenogenic enzymes

It is generally believed that carotenoid biosynthesis takes place on a multienzyme complex which is bound to, or may be an integral part of, a membrane. Phytoene synthetase appears to be peripheral to the membrane and is easily dissociated from it by detergent, but the later enzymes, i.e. desaturases, cyclases, hydroxylases, are tightly associated in the membrane and are difficult to solubilize without destroying their activity. The organization of the enzymes, and any associated electron transport systems, in the membrane is crucial for carotenoid biosynthesis to proceed.

3. REGULATION OF CAROTENOID BIOSYNTHESIS
3.1 Carotenoid biosynthesis and chloroplast development

Light is the main regulatory requirement for chloroplast development and hence for carotenoid biosynthesis. The major stimulus is red light, acting via both phytochrome and chlorophyll [6]. The reaction centre complexes, including their carotenoids, are made first, followed by the light-harvesting complexes containing the xanthophylls. Plants that are grown or maintained in the dark become etiolated, i.e. yellow in colour and have etioplasts instead of normal chloroplasts. The etioplasts are normally devoid of chlorophyll but contain substantial amounts of carotenoids, almost entirely xanthophylls. On illumination, etiolated plants develop normal chloroplasts, acquire normal chloroplast pigments and become green. The greening of etiolated seedlings has provided a convenient system for studying chloroplast development, but results from such a system should be considered with caution since the normal course of plant growth does not involve etiolation and etioplasts. Under a normal light regime, chloroplasts are formed de novo, from proplastids.

Chloroplast pigment compositions are influenced by light, and the relative amounts of the various PPC, especially the light-harvesting complexes, may change in response to changes in light conditions. Thus many plants, when grown in strong or dim light, respectively, develop 'sun' or 'shade' chloroplasts with different PPC distributions and pigment compositions [7]. Shaded leaves of some trees have a significantly higher xanthophyll : carotene ratio than do sunlit leaves because they develop larger amounts of light-harvesting complexes.

3.2 Site of carotenoid biosynthesis
The chloroplast carotenoids are certainly biosynthesized within the chloroplast, but there are conflicting views about whether the organelle is completely autonomous and can synthesize its own precursor molecules, especially MVA, or whether it needs to import the later intermediate, IDP. There is also some dispute about where the later stages of carotenoid biosynthesis are located within the chloroplast, i.e. in the envelope or thylakoid membrane.

Because there are several different carotenoids, and these are localized and function in different PPC within the chloroplast, many questions arise about the intricate regulatory mechanisms that determine the different carotenoid compositions of the individual PPC [4]. Is there, for example, only one site at which all the carotenoids are biosynthesized or is each individual compound made at a different site by a dedicated collection of enzymes? What then directs the flow of substrates into any particular carotenoid and the utilization of that carotenoid molecule for a particular PPC?

The time courses of xanthophyll synthesis (especially lutein) and bulk carotene synthesis in the same developing system appear to be different [8]. Thus when either dark-grown or light-grown seedlings are incubated, in the light, with [^{3}H]-MVA and $^{14}CO_2$ simultaneously, lutein and ß-carotene show different ^{3}H:^{14}C ratios, reflecting the different kinetics of their synthesis. Since ß- and ε-rings are not interconverted, the final stages of lutein and ß-carotene synthesis must be independent, but it is not known at which stage the two pathways diverge.

3.4 Phases of carotenoid biosynthesis

The carotenoids destined for each PPC appear not to be made independently. Labelling experiments indicate that newly formed carotenoid molecules enter a labile pool from which they are either taken for incorporation into the PPC or rapidly destroyed. Obviously, many intricate and interesting regulatory mechanisms remain to be elucidated.

The situation is complicated even further because several different phases of carotenoid biosynthesis must be considered, (i) bulk synthesis during the initial construction of the photosynthetic apparatus; (ii) synthesis in the mature leaf as part of turnover; (iii) synthesis in response to changes in environmental conditions, especially light intensity; (iv) synthesis by the enzymes that were present in etiolated tissues, and may continue to function in the light; (v) synthesis of abnormal compounds in response to stress.

Each of these phases may have its own distinct regulatory factors and mechanisms.

The choice of system for study is also important. Substantial differences can be expected in the characteristics of chloroplast development and its associated carotenoid biosynthesis in different plant species and even varieties of the same species. The age of the plant or tissue and the growth and environmental conditions used are very important. Cotyledons or first leaves may behave quite differently from true leaves, even of the same plant. Results obtained with a greening etiolated system are not necessarily relevant to a plant developing normally in the light.

4. CAROTENOID BIOSYNTHESIS IN GREENING ETIOLATED LEAVES: A DEUTERIUM LABELLING EXPERIMENT

Etiolated barley seedlings, grown in the dark for 6 days, contained no chlorophyll, very little ß-carotene or neoxanthin, but substantial amounts of lutein, violaxanthin and antheraxanthin. On illumination, the seedlings rapidly became green (24 hours), chlorophylls a and b were made, ß-carotene and neoxanthin accumulated, but little change was observed in the levels of lutein and violaxanthin. An experiment which used deuterium labelling from D_2O was used to investigate whether any of the carotenoids that were present in the etiolated leaves were retained during greening and could be incorporated into the developing chloroplasts [9]. In this experiment, excised, etiolated barley shoots were allowed to green in $H_2O:D_2O$ (1:1) for 24 hours, and the carotenoids from sections of the green shoots were extracted, purified and assayed by mass spectrometry. The lutein and violaxanthin contained no deuterium, therefore no new synthesis of these xanthophylls had occurred, and the molecules that were present in the etiolated leaves must have been retained and incorporated into the PPC of the developing thylakoids. ß-Carotene was heavily enriched with deuterium, showing that it was made by new synthesis, in two phases, first from existing fixed C-H substrates and later from small molecules (CO_2) and D_2O. In contrast to this, however, neoxanthin, which also appeared in substantial quantity only after greening, contained virtually no deuterium, showing that it was not synthesized de novo during chloroplast development, but must have been formed from an existing carotenoid pool, probably from antheraxanthin, the level of which decreased substantially. This confirms the very different behaviour of the individual carotenoids during chloroplast development in this greening etiolated leaf system.

Different labelling patterns were also observed for pigments isolated from different regions of the shoot, reflecting the different metabolic activities of these regions.

Experimental procedures such as this, which allow 'old' and 'new' molecules of the same compound to be distinguished, promise to be extremely useful in further, detailed studies of chloroplast development.

REFERENCES
1.   Siefermann-Harms, D. (1985) Biochim. Biophys. Acta 811, 325-355.
2.   Siefermann-Harms, D. (1987) Physiol. Plantarum 69, 561-568.
3.   Cogdell, R.J. (1988) in Plant Pigments (Goodwin, T.W., ed.), pp. 183-230, Academic Press, London.

4. Britton, G. (1986) in Regulation of Chloroplast Differentiation (Akoynoglou, G. and Senger, H., eds.), pp. 125-134, A.R. Liss, New York.
5. Britton, G. (1988) in Plant Pigments (Goodwin, T.W., ed.), pp. 133-182, Academic Press, London.
6. Oelmuller, R. and Mohr, H. (1985) Planta 164, 390-395.
7. Grumbach, K.H. and Lichtenthaler, H.K. (1982) Photochem. Photobiol. 35, 209-212.
8. Sergeant, J.M. and Britton, G. (1984) in Advances in Photosynthesis Research (Sybesma, C., ed.), Vol. IV, pp. 779-782, Martinus Nijhoff/Dr. W. Junk, Dordrecht, The Netherlands.
9. Barry, P. (1988). Ph.D. Thesis, University of Liverpool.

SPECTRAL PROPERTIES AND MOLECULAR STRUCTURE OF PROTOCHLORO-
PHYLL, PROTOCHLOROPHYLLIDE AND CHLOROPHYLLIDE-A FORMS IN
MODELS AND IN ISOLATED ETIOPLAST MEMBRANE FRAGMENTS

BÖDDI, B. EÖTVÖS UNIVERSITY, DEPARTMENT OF PLANT PHYSIOLOGY,
MUZEUM KRT 4/A, BUDAPEST, H-1088. HUNGARY

INTRODUCTION
Pioneering investigations of the chlorophyll biosynthesis have shown that the knowledge of the primary chemical
structure of chlorophylls and their precursors is not nearly
enough for understanding of the process of this biosynthesis. This is especially true for the final steps of this
process; a large body of data has been accumulated about the
complicated spectral phenomena during the phototransformation of protochlorophyllide (PChlide) into chlorophyllide-a
(Chlide-a) and the phytilization process (see for review 1).
This, together with the spectral multiplicity of PChlide
must be in connection with the differencies in the molecular
interactions of the PChlide molecules and with the changes
of these interactions (2,3).
In etiolated leaves the majority of PChlide is connected
to the PChlide reductase enzyme which, according to the
ternary complex model, bounds NADPH molecule(s), too (4).
This complex is an integral unit of prolamellar bodies (PLB)
and in vivo can be characterized with a 650 nm absorption
and 657 nm low-temperature fluorescence emission maximum (5).
However, PChlide or PChl molecules must be connected to
other components of the etioplast inner membranes, these
molecules can regenerate the phototransphormed PChlide or
cannot be phototransformed at all (2). These molecular
complexes have absorption maxima at 628-630 and 635-637 nm
(6).
The newly-formed Chlide-a molecules must be connected to
the PCR-complexes just after the photoconversion and after
the decomposition of PLB-s the pigment molecules have to be
transferred to the phytilizing enzyme (3). This process
needs basic structural transformations of the membranes
which includes the changes of the molecular interactions of
the pigments and thus can be followed with spectroscopic
methods (7).

MATERIALS AND METHODS
For the model experiments, PChl was isolated from pump-
kin seed coats and purified by column chromatography (8).
PChlide was purified from cell-free medium of Rhodobacter

M. Baltscheffsky (ed.), Current Research in Photosynthesis, Vol. III, 835–842.
© 1990 *Kluwer Academic Publishers. Printed in the Netherlands.*

cultures (9). Chlide-a was extracted from spinach leaves and purified by column chromatography (10).

Solid films were prepared on glass surfaces from ether solution of the pigments by evaporating the solvent with high vacuum. Then the films were treated with vapours of acetone or dioxane (11).

Micellar solutions were prepared with Triton X-100 with a concentration of 3×10^{-4}M (12).

The etioplast inner membrane preparates were isolated from dark-grown wheat leaves, the isolation procedure included differential and sucrose-gradient centrifugation (5,13).

The absorption spectra of the solid films and micellar solutions were recorded with a Perkin Elmer 554 spectrophotometer, the absorption spectra of the membrane fragments were detected with Aminco DW 2a spectrophotometer. The fluorescence spectra were recorded with a Perkin Elmer MPF-44B and an SLM Aminco 8000C spectrofluorimeter. The CD spectra were measured with Jasco J40 and Jasco J500-A spectropolarimeters (11,13). The spectra were processed with computer programmes including baseline correction, smoothing, derivate and Gaussian component calculating programmes (13).

RESULTS AND DISCUSSION

PChl forms in solid films: After preparation, the red absorption maximum of the films was between 632 and 640 nm. The acetone vapour treatment of the films with 640 nm absorption maximum caused first a blue-shift in the absorption spectrum as a result of which the main band appeared at 632 nm. During further treatment a shoulder appeared there at 650 nm and then gradually this band became the main maximum of the spectrum. In the fluorescence spectra of films with 650 nm absorption band a maximum at 655-657 nm was observed. The CD spectra showed interesting changes under the acetone vapour treatment: in the first minutes an intense couplet with negative band at 651 nm was found. Then this signal decreased and disappeared and later on a CD couplet with positive band at 654 nm appeared (11). The dioxane vapour treatment resulted in the appearance of the 650 nm absorption an 655 nm emission peaks in the spectra of the films but the CD signal of these films were identical to those of water/dioxane solutions containing PChl dimers connected via dioxane molecules. Consequently, there was no CD signal belonging to the 650 nm absorption band in these, dioxane treated films (Fig.1.). Similar spectral phenomena were found in the case of PChlide solid films.

The strong red shifts of the absorption and fluorescence maxima and the position and the presence of induced CD signals (CD couplets) indicated the presence of pigment aggregates in the films. The differencies of the CD signals

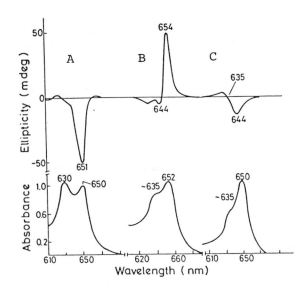

FIGURE 1. Absorption and CD spectra of protochlorophyll
solid films. A: Film treated with acetone vapour
for 1 min, B: the same film after 45 min acetone
vapour treatment, C: film treated with dioxane
vapour for 5 min.

(despite of the similarities of the absorption and fluorescence spectra) showed that aggregates can be formed with
different types of interactions - in the case of acetone
vapour treatment keto-C=O--Mg interactions (15), while in
case of dioxane vapour π-π overlaps (16) are formed- and
also the intrinsic geometry of the aggregates can be
different.

　　To get information about the size of the 650 nm absorbing PChl form, micellar solution of Triton X-100 was prepared
with a concentration of 3×10^{-4}M. Different amounts of PChl
was added to these micellar solutions. In parallel with the
increasing PChl concentration - which means the increasing
number of PChl molecules in the micelles - a gradual absolute
and relative increase of the 650 nm absorption and 655 nm
emission band was observed (12). The absorption spectra were
resolved into Gaussian components and the ratio of the 650
nm to the 634 nm Gaussian component was calculated. These
values were plotted against the number of PChl molecules
per micelle. The CD spectra of the micellar solutions had
CD couplets around 650 nm. The CD spectra were normalized
for the same PChl concentration and the area under the CD

signals were calculated and plotted in the function of the number of PChl molecules/micelle. Both curves had a sudden increase at the PChl molecule number of 10 (Fig.2.).

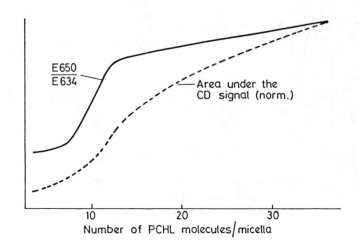

FIGURE 2. The formation of the 650 nm absorbing protochlo-
       phyll form in micellar solutions of Triton X-100:
       the relative increase of the 650 nm absorption band
       (continuous line) and the increase of the normalized
       CD signals (dotted line) in the function of the
       number of protochlorophyll molecules in the micelles.

The same experiment was carried out with Chlide-a. In the micellar solution this pigment exhibited a 684 nm absorption and 696 nm emission band. The CD spectrum of these solutions contained CD couplet around 690 nm. The above described calculations resulted in a 9.6 molecule per micelle, in average.

The measurements with the micellar solutions of Triton X-100 proved that at least 10 molecules of PChl are needed for the formation of the 650 nm absorbing PChl form and the same number of Chlide-a molecule for the formation of the 684 nm absorbing Chlide-a form. This agrees with the in vivo results that the 650 nm PChlide form transforms into the 684 nm Chlide-a form during the photoconversion.

Four different etioplast inner membrane fragments were isolated and characterized with spectroscopic methods. The PLB fraction (B11) in the presence of NADPH exhibited practically the same spectral properties than the intact leaves. In the low-temperature fluorescence emission spectra a 659 nm band was the most intense, two bands of low intensity was found at 633 and 643 nm (Fig.3.).

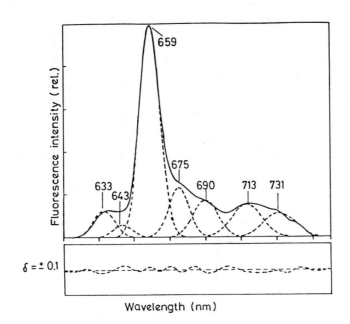

FIGURE 3. Low-temperature fluorescence emission spectrum of
PLB-s isolated from etiolated wheat leaves in the presence of NADPH. The spectrum was resolved into
Gaussian components (dotted line), the error of
resolution is shown at the bottom of the figure.

In the absorption spectrum of this fraction the 650 nm band
was the main peak in the red region. Less intense peaks
were found at 625 and 638 nm.
    In the prothylakoid (PT) fraction (B22) the 638 nm
absorbing and 643 nm emitting form was dominating. Two
mixed fractions designated as B12 and B21, were also collected which had the same absorption and fluorescence emission bands as the above descrebed PLB and PT fraction but
in different ratios.
    Large CD couplets were found in the CD spectra of the
membrane fractions. The most striking property of these
spectra is the positive signal at 655 nm. The zero crossing
was at 643 nm and negative bands were found at 623-636 nm
(13). The complexity of the negative band is probably due
to the contribution of the CD signal of the shorter wavelength absorbing PChlide form and can correspond to the
signals observed in CD spectra of PChlide-holochrome pre-

parates (17). The position and the shape of these CD signals
and also their similarity to the CD signals of models (Fig.
1. spectrum B) are evidences for the PChlide-PChlide interactions. The PChlide aggregates must be bound to units of
the PCR. NADPH stabilizes this complex: when the NADPH was
washed out, a blue shift in the absorption and fluorescence
spectra took place in parallel with the disappearance of
the CD signals. Fluorescence polarization measurements indicated a decrease of the unit size in the preparates which
means a disaggregation of the PCR into smaller units.

The irradiation of the membrane fragments resulted in
phototransformation of PChlide into Chlide-a which was indicated by the appearance of the main low-temperature fluorescence emission band at 696 nm. Gaussian components were
found at 693 and 675 nm (Fig. 4.).

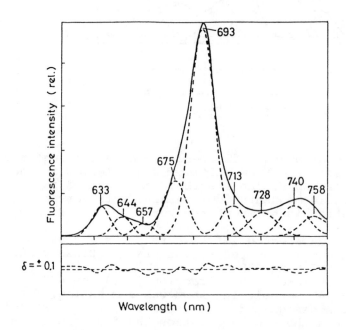

FIGURE 4. Low-temperature fluorescence emission spectrum of
an irradiated etioplast inner membrane preparate.
The spectrum was resolved into Gaussian components
(dotted lines), the error of the resolution is indicated at the bottom of the figure.

Corresponding to these two new fluorescence bands also the
CD signal showed a complexity. After irradiation positive

bands appeared at 682 and 686-688 nm. Studying partially phototransformed samples, the kinetics of the PChlide phototransformation was also studied. This indicated that two photoactive PChlide forms transformed into two Chlide-a forms. The shorter wavelength absorbing PChlide form is more sensitive, its transformation took place first.

On the basis of these results a model has been constructed about the possible structure of the etioplast inner membrane units (PChlide forms) and the phototransformation of PChlide. In this model several units of PCR keep together an aggregate (probably larger than dimer) of PChlide molecules. NADPH is also connected in this complex it stabilizes the structure of unirradiated samples. These larger PCR-complexes can be integral components of PLB-s and are the 650 nm absorbing PChlide forms. Smaller PCR complexes having smaller PChlide aggregates can occur on the edge of PLB-s which are the photoactive, shorter wavelength (638 nm) absorbing PChlide forms. Under irradiation, the smaller units transform first and then the 650 nm form. The newly-formed Chlide-a is first connected to the PCR complexes but without an excess of NADPH these complexes disintegrate, resulting in also the disaggregation of the Chlide-a aggregates.

REFERENCES
1 French, C.S. (1984) in Protochlorophyllide Reduction and Greening (Sironval, C. and Brouers, M., eds.), pp. 7-16, Martinus Nijhoff/Dr W. Junk Publishers, The Hague
2 Virgin, H. (1981) Ann. Rev. Plant Physiol. 32, 451-463
3 Van Der Cammen, J.C.J.M. and Goedheer (1984) in Protochlorophyllide Reduction and Greening (Sironval, C. and Brouers, M., eds.), pp. 191-194.
4 Oliver, R.P. and Griffiths, W.T. (1982) Plant Physiol. 70, 1019-1025
5 Ryberg, M. and Sundqvist, C. (1988) Physiol. Plant. 73, 218-226
6 Virgin, H.(1975) Photosynthetica 9, 84-92
7 Ryberg, M. and Dehesh, K. (1986) Physiol. Plant. 66, 616-624
8 Houssier, C. and Sauer, K. (1969) Biochim. Biophys. Acta 172, 492-502
9 Shioi, Y. and Beale, S.I. (1987) Anal. Biochem. 162, 493-499
10 Holt, A.S. and Jacobs, E.E. (1954) Am. J. Bot. 41, 710--717
11 Böddi, B., Soós, J. and Láng, F. (1983) Biochim. Biophys. Acta 593, 158-165
12 Böddi, B., Kovács, K. and Láng, F. (1983) Biochim. Biophys. Acta 722, 320-326
13 Böddi, B., Lindsten, A., Ryberg, M. and Sundqvist, C. (1989) Physiol. Plant. 76, 135-143

14 Zenkevitsh, E.I. and Losev, A.P. (1972) Mol. Biol. 6, 824-832
15 Bystrova, M.I., Safronova, I.A. and Krasnovsky, A.A. (1982) Mol. Biol. 16, 291-301
16 Böddi, B. and Láng, F. (1981) Photobiochem. Photobiophys. 2, 321-328
17 Henningsen, K.W., Kahn, A. and Houssier, C. (1973) FEBS Lett. 37, 103-108

The experiments with isolated etioplast inner membranes were carried out as a teamwork with Christer Sundqvist, Margareta Ryberg and Agneta Lindsten, University of Göteborg, Department of Plant Physiology, Sweden.

THE PHASE STRUCTURE OF GALACTOLIPIDS AND THEIR ROLE IN THE FORMATION
OF THE PROLAMELLAR BODY

EVA SELSTAM[1], INGVAR BRENTEL[2] AND GÖRAN LINDBLOM[2], Dept of Plant
Physiology[1] and Physical Chemistry[2], Univ. of Umeå, S-901 87 Umeå, Sweden.

1. INTRODUCTION

In leaves of dark grown plants, proplastids differentiate to etioplasts.
In this plastid, two different membrane systems are formed, the normal
planar prothylakoid (PT) membrane and the regulary branched crystalline
prolamellar body (PLB) membrane (Fig. 1). Despite beeing heterogenous in
structure these membranes are continuous. The structure of the PLB membrane has been extensively studied by electron microscopy, for summaries
see 1 and 2. The PLB membrane is a unit membrane (3) where the crystalline
lattice is formed by 4- or 6-armed units (Fig. 2). The 4-armed unit is a tetrapod
where 4 tubes meet in one point with equal angles. Tetrapods are arranged in
different networks analogous to the crystal structures in wurtzite and
zincblende (= diamond). The PLB can be formed by either the wurtzite or the
zincblende type or by a combination of the two types in one PLB. The 6-armed
unit is a cubic structure where the 6 tubes meet at right angles.

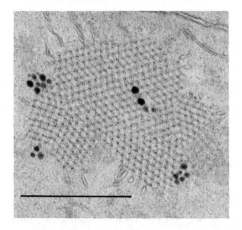

Figure 1. Electron micrograph of a PLB from an etioplast of wheat. The
structure of this PLB is of the zincblende type. The bar represents 1 μm.

M. Baltscheffsky (ed.), Current Research in Photosynthesis, Vol. III, 843–848.

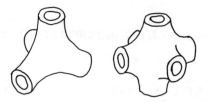

Figure 2. 4- and 6-armed units of the tetrapodal and cubic PLB structures (4).

The crystalline structure in both the tetrapodal and the cubic PLB are similar to the structures formed by infinite periodic minimal surface (IPMS). IPMS is a mathematical description of curved surfaces, where a minimal surface is defined to have a mean curvature of zero (5). Curvatures described by minimal surfaces have the free energy of the curvature at a minimum. Several IPMS structures have been described. The D-type (diamond) is formed by tetrapodal units and similar to the PLB structure of zincblende type (Lindstedt and Liljenberg, manuscript) and the P-type (primitive) has a cubic symmetry which is similar to the 6-armed PLB structure (6).

IPMS has also been a useful tool in the description of the structure of bicontinuous reversed cubic phases of lipids (7). The symmetries of bicontinuous cubic phases are classified by their space group, which is determined by X-ray diffraction. Three different symmetries, of interest here, are known for bicontinuous cubic membrane lipids namely., Ia3d, Pn3m and Im3m. These symmetries correspond to different networks with 3-, 4- and 6-armed units. The exact form of the lipids and water in these symmetries are not clear but there are some experimental evidence for that a description by principals of IPMS give a good picture (7). The 3-, 4- and 6-armed symmetries will thus correspond to the minimal surface of the G, D and P type. Described by an IPMS the cubic phase is formed by an infinite lipid bilayer which is arranged so that the minimal surface is 'draped' on each side with lipid monolayers, whose terminal methyl end touch the minimal surface. The curved lipid bilayer separates the water into two independent water channels. An example can be taken from the well known phase equilibrium of monoolein and water. In the monoolein-water system two cubic phases are formed (8). At low water content the space group of the cubic phase is Ia3d and at high water content it is Pn3m. The Ia3d structure is of the G-type (gryoid) and the Pn3m is of the D-type (diamond) (9). A cubic symmetry with even higher water content has the space group Im3m, having a minimal surface of the P-type (primitive) (7).

Due to the similarities between the structure of the PLB and the bicontinuous reversed cubic phases PLB has been suggested to be of a cubic structure. This hypothesis is supported by the findings that the PLB lipid components are able to form a bicontinuous reversed cubic phase with water (10; Fig. 3, Fig. 4).

TABLE 1. Lipid composition of PLB, PT and thylakoid (THYL) membranes.
n.d. - nondetectable, t.-traces. (Widell-Wigge and Selstam, unpublished).

membrane	mol % lipid							
	MGDG	DGDG	SQDG	PG	PC	PI	PS	MGDG/DGDG
PLB	50.8	28.7	7.7	9.5	3.3	n.d.	n.d.	1.8
PT	45.0	32.0	6.2	8.9	6.2	1.6	n.d.	1.4
THYL	49.2	30.9	8.6	9.7	1.1	t.	t.	1.6

2. PHASE STRUCTURES OF THE PLB MEMBRANE LIPIDS

The PLB is composed of chloroplast lipids and mainly one protein (11, 12). The lipid content is higher (1.26 nmol μg^{-1} protein) in the PLB than in the PT membrane (0.97 nmol μg^{-1} protein), respectively. The lipid composition has many similarities with both the prothylakoids and the thylakoids (Tab. 1). It is dominated by the galactolipids, monogalactosyl diacylglycerol (MGDG) and digalactosyl diacylglycerol (DGDG) and it also contains minor amounts of sulfoquinovosyl diacylglycerol (SQDG), phosphatidyl glycerol (PG) and phosphatidyl choline (PC). The high content of MGDG is interesting since this lipid forms a reversed hexagonal phase (H_{II}) with water contrary to a lamellar phase (L_α) as the other plastid membrane lipids do. To investigate to what extent the reversed hexagonal forming lipid MGDG can influence the plastid membrane lipids to form cubic phases, a phase diagram of the ternary system MGDG/DGDG/^2H_2O, and a phase equilibria of a mixture containing ^2H_2O and MGDG:DGDG:SQDG:PG, 52:26:10:10 (by mol) was determined. The phase structures were investigated by nuclear magnetic resonance (NMR) methods (10).

In the tentative ternary phase diagram of ^2H_2O and MGDG/DGDG three different phase structures are present, lamellar, reversed hexagonal and a cubic phase (Fig. 3, 10). The lamellar phase occurs in all pure DGDG/^2H_2O mixtures and also in mixtures of MGDG/DGDG/ ^2H_2O at low MGDG contents. The reversed hexagonal phase present in all pure MGDG/^2H_2O mixtures and in mixtures of MGDG/DGDG/^2H_2O at high MGDG contents. In between the lamellar and reversed hexagonal phase areas a cubic phase is found. The structure of the cubic phase was determined by small angle X-ray diffraction and measurement of the translational diffusion coefficient of the lipids and led to the conclusion that the found to be a bicontinuous reversed cubic phase (I_2)is bicontinuous and of the space group Ia3d. The length of the unit cell was 102 Å. The single cubic phase occurs only at low water contents and no cubic phase was found in equilibrium with water. On the other hand presence of MGDG in a mixture with DGDG will result in the formation of nonlamellar phases (H_{II} and/or I_2). The more MGDG in the mixture the more of the nonlamellar phase areas is formed as can be seen in the phase diagram. The cubic phase formed of low water contents is not of the same symmetry as the structure of the PLB membrane.

In figure 4 the tentative pseudobinary phase equilibria of ^2H_2O and MGDG/DGDG/SQDG/PG 52:26:10:10 (by mol) is shown. The phase equilibria has been studied in the low water region from 2-12 mol ^2H_2O/mol lipid and it is found to be rather similar to the phase equilibria determined for ^2H_2O and MGDG/DGDG 1,2:1 (by mol) (10). Also at low water contents a single reversed cubic phase is found. At higher water contents the MGDG/DGDG/SQDG/PG mixtures a lamellar phase is formed in equilibrium with an isotropic phase. This latter phase area starts from 13 mol ^2H_2O/mol lipid or approximately 23 % ^2H_2O and extends up to approximately 85 % ^2H_2O, where it is in equilibrium with free water. For the MGDG/DGDG 1.2:1 mixture a lamellar phase is in equilibrium with free water at 14 mol ^2H_2O/mol lipid. The reason for the MGDG/DGDG/SQDG/PG mixture to be able to take up a large amount of water is the presence of negatively charge lipids in the mixture. The isotropic phase formed at high water content of this lipid mixture is at present not analysed, but it seems probable to assume it to be a bicontinuous cubic phase. The cubic phase formed at a ^2H_2O content of approx 5 mol ^2H_2O/mol lipid is of the Ia3d type. As mentioned above several cubic phase structure may occur depending on water content. Thus, the cubic phase, found at high water contents for the MGDG/DGDG/SQDG/PG mixture is probably of the Pn3m structure and may be changing to an Im3m structure at the higher water contents (Pn3m and Im3m are the two types of symmetry that is found for the PLB membrane).

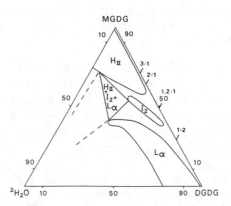

Figure 3. Tentative ternary phase diagram of the ^2H_2O/MGDG/DGDG system. $L\alpha$, lamellar phase; H_{II}, reversed hexagonal phase; I_2, bicontinuous reversed cubic phase.

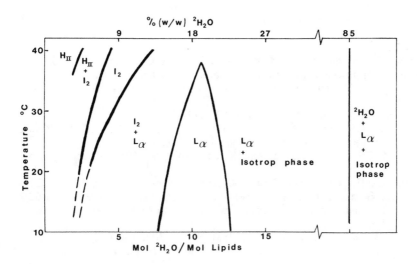

Figure 4. Tentative pseudobinary phase equilibria of the ^2H_2O and
MGDG/DGDG/SQDG/PG 52:26:10:10 (by mol). For abbreviations see Fig. 3.

3. DISCUSSION

From the studies of the phase structures of the ^2H_2O and MGDG/DGDG/
SQDG/PG mixture it can be concluded that the membrane lipids of the PLB, by
themselves, are able to form a cubic phase at high water content and also in
equilibrium with free water. Thus the membrane lipids could be responsible
for the formation of the crystalline structure of the PLB membrane. The PLB
membrane also contain one dominating protein, the protochlorophyllide
oxidoreductase (PCR) (13,14,15,16). In the etioplast, PCR is concentrated in the
PLB membrane (17,18). It is a hydrophilic membrane protein (19) impossible
to wash off the membrane by salt treatments (20, Grevby, C., Engdal, S.,
Ryberg, M. and Sundquist, C., personal communication). In the PLB
membrane the PCR is present in a specific protochlorophyllide-NADPH-PCR
complex with a large number of aggregated proto-chlorophyllide molecules
(21,22). We therefore hypothesises that this complex together with the lipids
spontaneously form a membrane curvature with the lowest free energy
leading to the observed cubic structure. Most probably the formation of the
PLB membrane is due to the interaction between the membrane lipids and the
protochlorophyllide-NADPH-PCR complex and it can be expected that this
lipid protein complex will have a higher free energy in a planar bilayer
than in a curved cubic structure. It may therefore be suggested that the
assembly of the specific protochlorophyllide NADPH PCR complex in the
membrane spontaneously will lead to the formation of the cubic phases. The
dimensions of the cubic structure Ia3d, is 102 Å, which is smaller than the
structure of PLB. However, the Ia3d symmetry has the lowest water content of
the cubic phases and increasing the water content will also increase the

dimensions of the cubic structure. Also the dimensions of the cubic structure will increase in presence of a hydrophilic protein (23).

REFERENCES
1. Gunning, B.E.S. and Steer, M.W. (1975) in Plant Cell Biology an Ultra-structural Approach, pp. 254-257, Arnold Publishers, London
2. Murakami, S., Yamada, N., Nagano, M. and Osumi, M. (1985) Protoplasma 128, 147-156
3. Gunning, B.E.S. (1965) Protoplasma 60, 111-130
4. Gunning, B.E.S. and Steer, M.W. (1975) in Ultrastructure and the Biology of Plant Cells, pp. 111-116, Arnold Publishers, London
5. Andersson, S., Hyde, S.T., Larsson, K. and Lidin, S. (1988) Chem. Rev. 88, 221-242
6. Larsson, K., Fontell, K. and Krog, N. (1980) Chem. Phys. Lipids 27, 321-328
7. Lindblom, G. and Rilfors, L. (1988) Biochim. Biophys. Acta 988, 221-256
8. Hyde, S.T., Andersson, S., Ericsson, B. and Larsson, K. (1984) Z. Kristallogr. 168, 213-219
9. Longley, W. and MacIntosh, T.J. (1983) Nature 303, 612-614
10. Brentel, I., Selstam, E. and Lindblom, G. (1985) Biochim. Biophys. Acta 812, 816-826
11. Ryberg, M., Sandelius, A.S. and Selstam, E. (1983) Physiol. Plant. 57, 555-560
12. Selstam, E. and Sandelius, A.S. (1984) Plant Physiol. 76, 1036-1040
13. Ryberg, M. and Sundqvist, C. (1982) Physiol. Plant. 56, 125-132
14. Ikeuchi, M. and Murakami, S. (1983) Plant Cell Physiol. 24, 71-80
15. Selstam, E. and Widell, A. (1986) Physiol. Plant. 67, 345-352
16. Selstam, E., Widell, A. and Johansson, L.B.-Å. (1987) Physiol. Plant. 70, 209-214
17. Shaw, P.J., Henwood, J.A., Oliver, R. and Griffiths, W.T. (1985) Eur. J. Cell Biol. 39, 50-55
18. Ryberg, M. and Dehesh, K. (1986) Physiol. Plant. 66, 616-624
19. Selstam, E. and Widell-Wigge, A. (1989) Physiol. Plant., submitted
20. Widell-Wigge, A. and Selstam, E. (1989) Planta, in press
21. Ryberg, M. and Sundqvist, C. (1988) Physiol. Plant. 73, 218-226
22. Böddi, B., Lindsten, A., Ryberg, M. and Sundqvist, C. (1989) Physiol. Plant. 76, 135-143
23. Ericsson, B., Larsson, K. and Pontell, K. (1983) Biochim. Biophys. Acta 729, 23-27.

SEPARATION OF STROMAL, THYLAKOID, INNER AND OUTER ENVELOPE MEMBRANE
PROTEINS OF SPINACH CHLOROPLASTS INTO HYDROPHILIC AND HYDROPHOBIC
FRACTIONS

Nicole Dumont, Paul-André Siegenthaler, Laboratoire de
Physiologie végétale, Université de Neuchâtel, CH-2000
Neuchâtel, Switzerland

INTRODUCTION
The chloroplast contains about 400 structural or functional
polypeptides, out of which up to 20 to 30% could be coded for and
synthesized in the plastid (1). They are distributed between the
stroma, the thylakoid, and the envelope membrane (lumen, inner and
outer membranes) and give, when separated on SDS-PAGE, characteristic
but very complex profiles. Due to this complexity, two (or more)
otherwise different polypeptides may comigrate and thus contribute to a
single Coomassie band. We have used Triton X-114 (TX-114) phase
partition, essentially as described by Bordier (2), so as to obtain a
preliminary separation of the polypeptides according to their
hydrophobic/hydrophilic properties. Additional techniques such as
proteosynthesis in organello in the presence of ^{35}S-methionine (3), 2D-
electrophoresis (4) and immunology (5) were used to go further into the
identification of specific proteins that could have been otherwise
mistaken for other comigrating ones.

RESULTS AND DISCUSSION
After isolation of intact spinach chloroplasts, four fractions were
obtained mostly according to (6): thylakoid, inner and outer envelope
membranes and stroma. The polypetides belonging to the envelope lumen
should now be found in the stroma and/or the inner and outer envelope
membranes, depending on the interactions involved. These four fractions
were submitted to TX-114 phase partition and then separated by SDS-PAGE
(fig.1). As expected, all but four of the stroma polypeptides
partitioned in the aqueous phase and the recovery was excellent. The
recovery was also quite good in the membranes when strongly hydrophobic
or hydrophilic polypeptides were concerned: the thylakoid 32 and 23
kDa, the inner membrane 34 kDa were exclusively recovered in the
organic phases, while the outer membrane 109, 40, 16 and 14 kDa
partitioned in the aqueous phase. Therefore, by discriminating between
hydrophobic and hydrophilic polypeptides, TX-114 enhances the SDS-PAGE
resolution. However, Coomassie bands often have a counterpart with
identical Mr in the other phase, in which case, we may be dealing
either with two or more different polypeptides or with peripheral ones

M. Baltscheffsky (ed.), Current Research in Photosynthesis, Vol. III, 849–852.

that are not totally separated from the membrane (ie: T15; IM72, 25; OM72). Furthermore, a unique hydrophobic or hydrophilic Coomassie band may still contain more than one polypeptide. Three cases of comigration (T15, S72, S,IM,OM 54) will be discussed below.

Fig. 1 SDS-PAGE of the four fractions after TX-114 phase partition

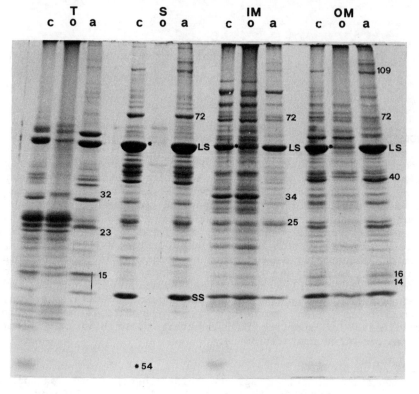

T: thylakoid S: stroma IM: inner membrane OM: outer membrane
c: untreated control (30 g) o: organic phase a: aqueous phase
LS: RubisCO large subunit SS: RubisCO small subunit
100 g of each fraction were submitted to TX-114 phase partition
(one third of the stroma aqueous phase was loaded)

Case 1: Thylakoid 15 kDa
As seen in Fig.1, the 15 kDa Coomassie band partitioned unequally in the two phases, the aqueous band being much more important than the corresponding one in the organic phase. To determine whether there was more than one polypeptide, the separation was repeated after proteosynthesis. The autoradiograph indicated that the hydrophobic polypeptide was labelled while the hydrophilic comigrating one was not. Therefore, the Coomassie band which, before TX-114 treatment, appeared

as unique was in fact composed of two polypeptides of different genomic
origin and different hydrophobic/hydrophilic properties.

Case 2: <u>Stroma 72 kDa</u>
Fig.1 shows that the stroma 72 kDa was clearly hydrophilic. On 2D-
electrophoresis, it was resolved into two spots with pI ~6.5 and
~6.3 respectively, which might be charge isomeres of a unique
polypeptide. We have raised a polyclonal antibody against the aqueous
72 kDa polypeptide and tested it on 2D-electrophoresis. Only the
polypeptide with pI ~6.3 gave a positive reaction. 2D-electrophoresis
was then repeated with ^{35}S-methionine-labelled material. The
autoradiograph showed that the polypeptide with pI ~6.5 (which was not
immuno-reactive) was labelled. Therefore, the single Coomassie aqueous
band in 1D-electrophoresis (7) was composed of two different
comigrating polypeptides with different genomic origin but identical
behaviour toward TX-114 phase partition.

Case 3: <u>Stroma, Inner and Outer envelope membranes 54 kDa</u>
After proteosynthesis and TX-114 phase partition, a radioactive 54 kDa
band was found in the organic phases of the stroma, the inner and outer
envelope membranes at the level of the RubisCO large subunit (LS)
(fig.1). The RubisCO is a known contaminant of the envelope membrane
and has been, so far, impossible to eliminate. As the TX-114 partitioning was shown to be reliable, we tried to find out whether this 54
kDa Coomassie band was the LS or not. First, an antibody against the
RubisCO (kindly provided by Dr. A. Radunz) was tested on the three
treated fractions as well as on their respective controls (fig.2).

Fig. 2: Immunoblot of the three fractions after TX-114 treatment

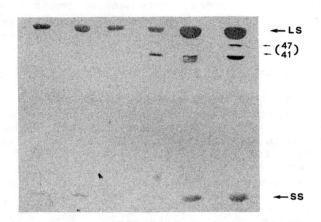

Symbols as in Fig.1 (only the relevant part of the immunoblot is shown)

Fig.2 shows that a positive reaction was found only in the controls and the aqueous phases of the three fractions. No reaction was seen on any organic phase. Furthermore, a polyclonal antibody was raised in our laboratory against the polypeptide found in the stromal organic phase. When tested, it did not react with LS in any of the aqueous phases but reacted with all three organic phases. There is therefore a fair probability that the hydrophobic polypeptide, uncovered in the three fractions by TX-114 treatment, was not the large subunit. If so, the RubisCO, known to resist sonication and other drastic treatments (8), could be eliminated from the envelope membranes by TX-114 phase partition.

CONCLUSIONS

Owing to the ability of Triton X-114 to bind to integral hydrophobic polypeptides by replacing most of the lipid molecules and together with temperature-induced phase partition, it is possible to separate membraneous polypeptides having close electrophoretic mobility but different behaviour towards TX-114 phase partition as well as possible stromal contaminants. Indeed, as the separation is excellent when one deals with either very hydrophobic or very hydrophilic polypeptides, any soluble stromal contaminant will be recovered in the aqueous phase. Furthermore, the organic phase polypeptides are exclusively of membrane origin while those from the aqueous phase may have a double origin, namely stroma and membrane. However, comigration may still exist in one of the two phases and furthermore, in some cases, the phase partition is not clear cut. The latter may be due either to unfavorable hydrophilic/hydrophobic balance or to incomplete solubilization and may therefore be indicative of peripheral or extrinsic polypeptides. It is then necessary to use other criteria, such as those illustrated here, to differentiate between polypeptides with similar electrophoretic mobility but with identical or ambivalent behaviour towards TX-114 phase partition. Taken together, these methods represent a valuable preparative step towards the isolation, purification and characterization of membraneous spinach chloroplast polypeptides (9).

REFERENCES:
1 Gnanam, A., Subbaiah, C.C. & Mannar Mannan, R. (1988) Photosynth. Res. 19, 129-152
2 Bordier, C. (1981) J. Biol. Chem. 156, 4, 1604-1607
3 Dumont, N. & Siegenthaler, P.A. (1987) Experientia 43, 660
4 Dunbar, B.S. (1987) in Two-Dimensional Electrophoresis and Immunological Techniques (Plenum Press, New York) pp. 217-222
5 Towbin, H., Staehelin, T. & Gordon, J. (1979) Proc. Natl. Acad. Sci. USA 76, 4350-4354
6 Keegstra, K. & Yousif, A.E. (1986) Methods in Enzymology 118, 316-324
7 Laemmli, U.K. (1970) Nature 227, 680-685
8 Werner-Washburne, M., Cline, K. & Keegstra, K. (1983) Plant Physiol. 73, 569-575
9 Siegenthaler, P.A. & Dumont, N., in preparation

AEROBIC AND ANAEROBIC PHOTOSYNTHESIS AND BACTERIOCHLOROPHYLL
FORMATION IN RHODOBACTER SULFIDOPHILUS

Yuzo Shioi and Michio Doi
Division of Biology, Miyazaki Medical College,
Kiyotake, Miyazaki 889-16, Japan

1. INTRODUCTION

Rhodobacter sulfidophilus was first isolated by Hansen and Veldkamp (1) in 1973 from marine mud flats of the Netherlands as a new species of facultative anaerobic photosynthetic bacteria belonging to the Rhodospirillaceae. This bacterium has unique characteristics regarding the utilization of hydrogen sulfide and a remarkably high sulfide tolerance for a member of the Rhodospirillaceae. However, little research has been done on this bacterium, except for studies on sulfate metabolism (2).

Recently, we reported that R. sulfidophilus grew and synthesized bacteriochlorophyll a (Bchl a) aerobically under both dark and light conditions in addition to the typical anaerobic light conditions (3). Furthermore, this bacterium is capable of photosynthesis under both anaerobic and aerobic light conditions which is different from the already known facultative anaerobic and aerobic photosynthetic bacteria. We have therefore concluded that R. sulfidophilus is a link between the facultative anaerobic and aerobic photosynthetic bacteria.

The versatile chracteristics of growth in this bacterium are unique and physiologically significant to merit investigation of the regulatory mechanism of its photosynthetic energy transducing systems using oxygen. In this report, we have new evidence to further confirm the aerobic growth and photosynthesis of R. sulfidophilus.

2. MATERIALS AND METHODS

Three bacterial species, Rhodobacter sullfidophilus (W4), Rhodobacter sphaeroides and Erythrobacter sp. (OCh 114) were grown aerobically or anaerobically in the light (6,000 lux) or dark at 28 C for the indicated period of time in the medium described previously (4). R. sphaeroides was grown in a medium described by Bose (5). The details of the growth conditions and analytical procedures were described in a previous report (3).

3. RESULTS AND DISCUSSION

Growth and Bchl formation of R. sulfidophilus were compared with those of the facultative anaerobic photosynthetic bacterium, R. sphaeroides, and the aerobic photosynthetic bacterium, Erythrobacter sp. OCh 114 (Table 1). R. sulfidophilus grew and synthesized Bchl a

M. Baltscheffsky (ed.), Current Research in Photosynthesis, Vol. III, 853–856.
© 1990 Kluwer Academic Publishers. Printed in the Netherlands.

both under aerobic conditions in either the dark or light and also under anaerobic conditions in the light, but not under anaerobic or semianaerobic conditions in the dark. The amount of Bchl in aerobically dark-grown cells of R. sulfidophilus was several fold higher than that of Erythrobacter sp. OCh 114 and comparable to that of anaerobically grown cells of both this bacterium and also R. sphaeroides. In comparison, R. sphaeroides grew and synthesized Bchl a mainly under anaerobic conditions in the light. The growth of R. sphaeroides was reduced 60% and only a small amount of Bchl formed when it was grown aerobically in the dark. Erythrobacter sp. OCh 114 grew and synthesized Bchl a only under aerobic conditions in the dark or light. The suppression of pigment accumulation by light was commonly observed in aerobically grown cells of R. sulfidophilus and Erythrobacter sp. OCh 114 (6). R. sulfidophilus could not grow anaerobically under dark conditions in the presence of nitrate which indicated that R. sulfidophilus lacked denitrifying activity, unlike the Erythrobacter sp. OCh 114.

The exogenously administered Bchl precursor, 5-aminolevulinic acid (ALA), inhibited the Bchl biosynthesis in Erythrobacter sp. OCh 114 (7). This was due to the conversion of ALA to the metabolite, 4-hydroxy-5-aminovaleric acid, which caused the inhibition of porphobilinogen synthase in the porphyrin synthetic pathway (7). In R. sulfidophilus, there was no inhibition, but rather a 1 to 6% increase by the addition of 1 to 10 mM ALA which suggested that the formation of 4-hydroxy-5-aminovaleric acid did not occur. The effect of ALA was quite different among the three species of bacteria used.

The absorption spectra of intact cells of R. sulfidophilus grown under various conditions are shown in Fig. 1. These spectra clearly show the presence of Bchl in aerobically grown cells in the light and dark, in addition to the usual anaerobically grown cells in the light. This bacterium contains Bchl-protein complexes that absorb at 802 nm, 860 nm and shoulder around 885 nm in the near infrared region. The carotenoid composition of R. sulfidophilus was different between anaerobically and aerobically grown cells as reported for Erythrobacter sp. OCh 114 (7). These facts suggested that in these

TABLE 1. Effect of growth conditions on growth and bacteriochlorophyll formation in three species of photosynthetic bacteria.

Growth conditions	Species					
	R. sulfidophilus		R. sphaeroides		Erythrobacter sp.	
	Growth	Bchl	Growth	Bchl	Growth	Bchl
Anaerobic light	1.61	15.0	1.88	15.6	0.084	0.23
Anaerobic dark	0.14	0.42	0.14	0.55	0.078	0.23
Semianaerobic light	1.73	14.2	1.60	12.1	0.26	0.27
Semianaerobic dark	0.21	0.61	0.14	0.44	0.23	0.51
Aerobic light	1.91	1.52	1.14	0.35	1.28	0.56
Aerobic dark	1.80	11.1	1.09	0.89	1.23	4.63

Growth: mg protein/ml; Bchl: nmol/ml.
The bacteria were grown at the indicated conditions in the dark or light (6,000 lux) at 28 C for 24 h.

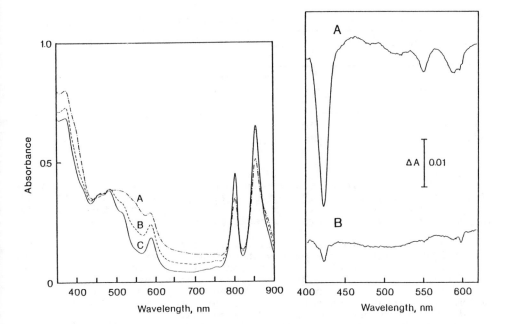

FIG. 1. Absorption spectra of intact cell suspension of R. sulfidophilus. The cells were grown anaerobically in light (A), semianaerobically in the light (B), and aerobically in dark (C) at 28 C for 24 h.

FIG. 2. Light-minus-dark difference spectra of the membrane fraction from aerobically dark- (A) and light- (B) grown cells of R. sulfidophilus. The same protein concentration was used (0.95 mg/ml). The difference spectrum was measured immediately after the off-set of actinic light by rapid scanning mode.

two species of bacteria, a common mechanism may be involved in the metabolic change from aerobic to anaerobic conditions. Absorption spectra of cell extracts were shown in a previous report (3).

The light-minus-dark difference spectrum of a membrane fraction obtained from aerobically dark and light-grown cells of R. sulfidophilus showed the photooxidation of cytochrome (Fig. 2). The light-induced oxidation of cytochrome was reversible, although the reverse reaction was slow. These results showed that aerobically grown cells of this bacterium have a photosynthetic system which can operate their electron transport system even under aerobic conditions in the light as in the case of anaerobically grown cells.

Table 2 shows the effect of light on the aerobic growth. Irradiation increased the cell yield of R. sulfidophilus 135% as compared to cells grown 36 h in the dark or 12 h in the dark followed 24 h in the light. A low light effect during continuous light growth was due to a low content of Bchl which was necessary for

TABLE 2. Effect of light on the aerobic growth of R. sulfidophilus.

Growth conditions	Growth (mg/ml)	%	Bchl (nmol/ml)	%
36 h dark	2.43	100	12.38	100
36 h light	2.59	106	1.60	13
12 h dark + 24 h light	3.28	135	5.96	48

The cells were grown aerobically in the dark or light
(6,000 lux) at 28 C for 36 h.

photosynthetic reactions as discussed previously (3). The stimulation
of growth by light indicated that R. sulfidophilus evidently obtained
energy from a photosynthetic system, and light was used for growth as
in the case of photosynthetic bacteria grown aerobically (4, 7).

The results of this study confirmed our previous results (3) on
R. sulfidophilus in that a photosynthetic system was obviously present
and that light-driven electron flow occurs in aerobically grown cells
as well as the usual anaerobically grown cells as evident by the
photooxidation of cytochrome and enhancement of aerobic growth by
light. The versatile chracteristics of growth in R. sulfidophilus are
unique and significant considering the evolutionary relationship
between the facultative anaerobic and aerobic photosynthetic bacteria.

Acknowledgements

This study was supported in part by a Grant-in-Aid for Scientific
Research (01304003) from the Ministry of Education, Science and
Culture, Japan.

REFERENCES

1. Hansen, T. A. and Veldkamp, H. (1973) Arch. Mikrobiol. 92,
   45-58.
2. Imhof, J. (1982) Arch. Microbiol. 132, 197-203.
3. Shioi, Y. and Doi, M. (1989) submitted.
4. Shioi, Y. (1986) Plant Cell Physiol. 27, 567-572.
5. Bose, S. K. (1963) in Bacterial Photosynthesis (H. Gest, A. San
   Pietro and L. P. Vernon, eds.), Antioch Press, Yellow Springs,
   Ohio.
6. Shioi, Y. and Doi, M. (1988) Arch. Biochem. Biophys. 266,
   470-477.
7. Shioi, Y. and Doi, M., Tanabe, K. and Shimokawa, K. (1988) Arch.
   Biochem. Biophys. 266, 478-485.
8. Harashima, K., Kawazoe, K., Yoshida, I. and Kamata, H. (1987)
   Plant Cell Physiol. 28, 365-374.

PLASTIDIC ISOPRENOID SYNTHESIS CHANGES FROM AN AUTONOMOUS TO A
DIVISION-OF-LABOR STAGE DURING CHLOROPLAST MATURATION

Adolf Heintze, Petra Hoppe, Petra Hagelstein, Jörn Görlach and
Gernot Schultz, Botanisches Institut, Tierärztliche Hochschule,
D-3000 Hannover 71, F.R.G.

1. INTRODUCTION

Carotenoids, plastoquinone, tocopherols and the phytyl moiety of
chlorophyll are generally known as isoprenoids synthesized in the
chloroplast. The origin of IPP to form these plastidic compounds is,
however, still under debate. We are able to demonstrate that the basal
region of leaves from 10-d old barley seedlings containing developing
chloroplasts forms plastidic isoprenoids predominantly from photosynthetically fixed CO_2 and only to a lesser extent from added mevalonate
(Mev). The conditions totally changes during chloroplast maturation.
The ability to form these compounds from CO_2 disappears at the apical
region of the leaves containing mature chloroplasts. In this region
IPP, formed from added Mev, is effectively used for isoprenoid synthesis. Developing and mature chloroplasts isolated from leaf protoplasts
conform in behavior with the corresponding leaf regions.

As demonstrated earlier (1, 2) the isoprenoid formation is tightly
linked to photosynthetic carbon metabolism and 3-PGA → PEP → pyruvate
pathway in developing chloroplasts. The results of isotopic dilution
experiments presented in this paper suggest that two independent substrate pools, a pyruvate and an acetate pool, are needed to synthesize
the introductory compound of plastidic Mev pathway.

2. MATERIAL AND METHODS

$NaH^{14}CO_3$ (2.0 GBq $mmol^{-1}$), /2-^{14}C/D,L-Mev, DBED salt (1.63
GBq $mmol^{-1}$), /2-^{14}C/acetate, sodium salt (1.96 GBq $mmol^{-1}$) were
from Amersham Buchler, Braunschweig, FRG, and /2-^{14}C/pyruvate, sodium
salt (462 MBq $mmol^{-1}$) from NEN, Dreieich, FRG. Experiments using leaf
parts from light grown barley seedlings (3) were done as in (4).
Isolation of chloroplasts from protoplasts were carried out as in A.
Heintze et al., in preparation. For analytical work see (5).

3. RESULTS AND DISCUSSION

3.1. Incorporation of $NaH^{14}CO_3$ or /2-^{14}/Mev into isoprenoids of
different regions of leaves from barley seedlings
3.1.1. Experiments using leaf parts: As shown in Fig. 1A for different
parts cut from the first leaf of barley seedlings, rates of incorporation of $NaH^{14}CO_3$ into plastidic isoprenoids are highest in the basal

M. Baltscheffsky (ed.), Current Research in Photosynthesis, Vol. III, 857–860.
© 1990 Kluwer Academic Publishers. Printed in the Netherlands.

region of the leaf containing developing chloroplasts (incomplete
thylakoid stacking though photosynthetically active; see legend to Fig.
1). The situation totally changes towards the apical region of the

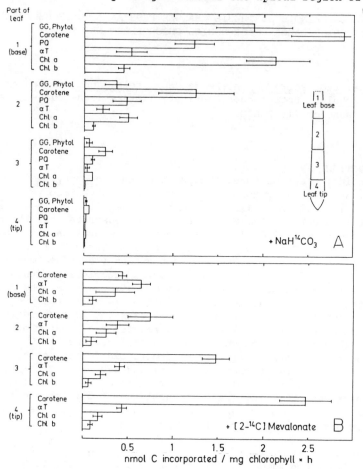

FIGURE 1. Incorporation of $NaH^{14}CO_3$ or $/2-^{14}C/Mev$ into isoprenoids
of different parts cut from the first leaf of barley seedlings (5 independent experiments with 40 leaves each). Each part of the leaf (region
1 (leaf base), 2, 3 and 4 (leaf tip)) was supplied with $NaH^{14}CO_3$
(5.7 KBq; Fig. 1A) or $/2-^{14}C/Mev$ (1.85 KBq; 1 mol Mev = 5 mol incorporated C; Fig. 1B). The photosynthetic CO_2-fixation rates , in umol
CO_2 (mg chl)$^{-1}$ h^{-1} , were 118 for protoplasts obtained from regions
1 + 2 and 150 for those from regions 3 + 4. The values for mg chl (g
fresh weight)$^{-1}$ for the regions 1 - 4 were: 0.38, 0.79, 1.03, 1.31
and for chloroplast size in um: 2.6, 3.4, 3.7, 4.0. Based on fresh
weight, the incorporation rates into sterols, in nmol C incorporated
fresh wt^{-1} , were for regions 1 - 4; by applying $NaH^{14}CO_3$: 0.24,
0.13, 0.49, 0.31; by applying $/2-^{14}C/Mev$: 1.99, 1.64, 2.11, 2.36.

leaf. The mature chloroplasts in this region, having maximal capacity for photosynthetic CO_2 fixation (legend to Fig. 1), become unable to form isoprenoids from $NaH^{14}CO_3$ (Fig. 1A). These findings provide strong evidence for a plastidic Mev pathway in developing chloroplasts which, independently from ER-cytosolic Mev pathway, supplies the plastidic isoprenoid formation (6). When $/2-^{14}C/Mev$ is applied, the opposite occurs. The incorporation rates into plastidic isoprenoids rise considerably from basal to apical region (Fig. 1B) whereas the rates for the sterol formation largely remains on the same level (legend to Fig. 1). This indicates that the plastidic IPP forming system in the mature chloroplast disappears and is replaced by an import of IPP (7) formed from added Mev at the cytosolic face of the ER. The formation of carotene from $/4-^{14}C/IPP$ by isolated spinach chloroplasts was shown by us in (4).

3.1.2. Experiments using chloroplasts: The above described changes in the formation of plastidic isoprenoids from CO_2 could also be shown in chloroplasts, isolated from protoplasts of different regions of barley leaves, in the presence of $NaH^{14}CO_3$ in the light (K. Meereis and U. Schwanke, unpublished; Table 1). The strong decrease of fatty acid formation but not of aromatic amino acid and valine formation during chloroplast maturation indicates a diminution of the activity at the pyruvate $\rightarrow$ acetyl-CoA step.

3.2. Studies on the introductory step of Mev pathway in developing
       chloroplasts

The tight linkage of carotene formation to photosynthetic CO_2 fixation (1) suggests a direct synthesis of the introductory compound of the Mev pathway from C_2-units. In isotopic dilution experiments in Fig. 2, no decrease of labeling of carotene and PQ was observed when increasing amounts of acetate were added to $NaH^{14}CO_3$ (Fig. 2A) or $/2-^{14}C/pyruvate$ (Fig. 2B). On the other hand, when 3-PGA was added to

TABLE 1. Formation of carotene, plastoquinone, 16:0- and 18:1-fatty acids, valine and aromatic amino acids from $NaH^{14}CO_3$ by intact chloroplasts isolated from different regions of the first leaf of barley seedlings. Chloroplasts (60 µg chl ml^{-1}) were illuminated for 30 min (see Material & methods) adding 5 mM $NaH^{14}CO_3$ (406 KBq). The photosynthetic CO_2-fixation rate, in µmol CO_2 $(mg \ chl)^{-1} \ h^{-1}$, was 19 for chloroplast isolated from basal part of leaves, 25 for those of the middle part and 27.5 for those of the apical part.

Product formed from $NaH^{14}CO_3$	Chloroplasts isolated from		
	basal part	middle part of the leaf	apical part
	nmol C incorporated $(mg \ chl)^{-1} \ h^{-1}$		
Carotene	16.5	9.1	4.6
Plastoquinone	11.7	6.4	4.2
16:0	57	35	n.d.
18:1	94	59	37
Valine	37	24	27
Aromatic amino acids	15	16	15

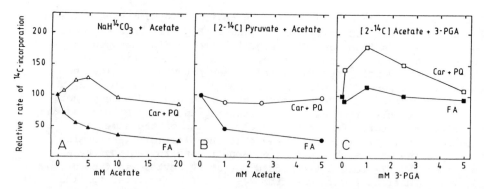

FIGURE 2. The pyruvate and the acetate pool are both needed for the formation of the introductory compound of plastidic Mev pathway. Isoprenoid (Car + PQ) and fatty acid (16:0 +18:1) formation in developing chloroplasts was studied in an isotopic dilution experiment. Chloroplasts (31 - 38 µg chl ml^{-1} ; vol 1 ml) were supplied with the labeled precursor and increasing amounts of unlabeled substrate in the following combinations. Absolute values of ^{14}C-incorporation into isoprenoids and fatty acids, in nmol C incorporated (mg chl)$^{-1}$ h^{-1} = 100, are indicated by brackets //. FIG. 2A: 5 mM NaH^{14}CO$_3$ (540 KBq) + 0 - 20 mM acetate; $\triangle$ Car + PQ formed /3.8/; $\blacktriangle$ fatty acids formed /5.1/. FIG. 2B: 0.7 mM /2-^{14}C/pyruvate (259 KBq) + 0 - 5 mM acetate; $\bigcirc$ Car + PQ formed /1.39/; $\bullet$ fatty acids formed /5.77/. FIG. 2C: 70 µM /2-^{14}C/acetate (137 KBq) + 0 - 5 mM 3-PGA; $\square$ Car + PQ formed /0.126/; $\blacksquare$ fatty acids formed /13.56/.

/2-^{14}C/acetate (Fig. 2C) a labeling of isoprenoids were found. The fatty acid formation serves as isotopic dilution control. The mutual non-competition of pyruvate (including precursors) and acetate but the effective labeling by both substrates provides conclusive evidence that both substrates are needed to supply the introductory reaction of plastidic Mev pathway. We suggest that developing chloroplasts form the assumed acetoacetyl-CoA from acetyl-CoA and another activated decarboxylation product of pyruvate.

Acknowledgements: Supported by the Deutsche Forschungsgemeinschaft and a grant from the Verband der Chemischen Industrie.

REFERENCES
1 Schulze-Siebert,D. and Schultz,G. (1987) Plant Physiol. 84, 1233-1237
2 Schulze-Siebert,D. and Schultz,G. (1989) Plant Sci. 59, 167-174
3 Homeyer,U. and Schultz,G. (1988) Planta 176, 378-382
4 Schultz,G. and Schulze-Siebert,D. (1989) in Biological Role of Plant
  Lipids (Biacs,P.A., Gruiz,K., Kremmer,T., eds), pp.313-319,
  Akadémiai Kiadó, Budapest and Plenum Publishing Corp., New York
5 Schulze-Siebert,D., Heintze,A. and Schultz,G. (1987) Z. Naturforsch.
  42c, 570-580
6 Goodwin,T.W. (1965) in Biosynthetic Pathways in Higher Plants
  (Pridham,J.B. and Swain,T., eds.), pp. 57-71, Academic Press, London
7 Kreuz,K. and Kleinig,H. (1984) Eur. J. Biochem. 141, 531-535

LOW TEMPERATURE EFFECT ON PCR AND CHLOROPHYLL ACCUMULATION IN RYE
SEEDLINGS

M. Krol and N.P.A. Huner, Dept. of Plant Science, University of
Western Ontario, London, Canada N6A 5B7

1. INTRODUCTION

During the development of angiosperm seedlings in the dark proplastids develop into etioplasts. The major pigment which accumulates
in etioplasts is protochlorophyll(ide) Pchl(ide). Etioplasts contain
two different membrane systems prolamellar bodies (PLBs) and prothylakoids (PTs). PLBs breakdown in light and Pchl(ide) is photoconverted
to chlorophyllide(Chlide) which is then estrified to chlorophyll. The
photoconvertion of Pchl(ide) to Chlide is catalyzed by NADPH-proto-
chlorophyllide-oxidoreductase (PCR). The enzyme is a major polypeptide of etioplast membrane (1,2). The enzyme is stable in darkness
and forms a ternary complex with NADPH and Pchl(ide) (3). These two
substrates protect the PCR from degradation by proteolitic enzymes(3).
PCR is present as a single peptide of 36 kD mol.wt. (4).

2. PROCEDURE
2.1. Materials and methods
Seeds of winter rye were grown in the dark for 5 days at 20°C or
21 days for 5°C. Subsequently 20°C and 5°C etiolated seedlings
were exposed to IML (2 min light followed by 118 min of dark),
CL, or normal day/night (16 h/8 h) conditions at 20 or 5°C
respectively.

2.2. Isolation of etioplast and thylakoid membranes
Etioplast and thylakoid membranes were isolated in 50 mM Tricine
(pH 7.6) containing 17% sucrose, 2 mM MgCl2 and 1 mM EDTA. The
membrane pellets were applied to the linear sucrose gradient
(20-60 % w/v). The plastid band was removed and osmotically
shocked with isolation buffer minus sucrose.

2.3. Electrophoresis of membrane polypeptides
Etioplast and thylakoid membranes were solubilized with SDS
(SDS:protein = 8:1) according to (5).

M. Baltscheffsky (ed.), Current Research in Photosynthesis, Vol. III, 861–863.

2.4. Western blot analysis

The polypeptides separated by gel electrophoresis were transferred to nitrocellulose membranes at a constant voltage using the
method available from the ABN Poly Blot Manual. After washing,
the PBS membranes were placed in a solution of PBS +1% BSA
containing antibody (anti PCR). After 8 h of incubation,
membranes were transferred to the secondary antibody solution
consisting of goat anti-rabbit IgG. The colour reaction was
developed by incubating membranes with 4 chloro-1-naphtol
saturated in methanol + 10 ul H_2O_2/10 ml of solution. The
membranes were stored at 5°C.

3. RESULTS AND DISCUSSION

We show that 5°C and 20°C etiolated rye seedlings exhibited etioplasts containing PLBs. After exposure of 5°C etiolated seedlings to
5°C of IML (48 cycles) plastids still exhibited the presence of PLBs
as well as thylakoid membranes. Exposure of the 5°C IML seedlings to
24 h of continuous light at 5°C caused the PLBs to disappear and the
stroma lamellae to develop. We observed a low, but detectable level
of PCR by Western blot analysis. The protein composition of IML
thylakoids showed the presence of PCR proteins. As a consequence of
this process chl a levels were higher at 5°C than at 20°C under IML.

In angiosperms the amount of PCR is controlled by light (3).
Illumination of etiolated plants at 20°C caused a rapid decrease in
PCR activity associated with the decrease in the amount of enzyme protein (6). High levels of PCR in the seedlings greening under IML at
5°C could be explained by the presence of PLBs. Another possibility
is that PLBs exist because low temperature reduces the synthesis of
membrane proteins and consequently not enough proteins exist to force
the production of thylakoids. Alternatively, biogenesis at 5°C limits
the membrane protease activity required for further development.

Plastids developed at 5°C in the presence of CL did not show the
presence of PLBs after 30 h of illumination. Using immunoblot analyses we detected the presence of PCR in thylakoids isolated after 30 h
of illumination. This data supports previous results (7) that PCR is
translocated from PLBs to the developing thylakoids during greening.

Why does CL and 5°C delay chlorophyll accumulation, in spite of
the presence of high levels of PCR (Table 1)? Is the dark period
important for chlorophyll accumulation at low developmental
temperature?

After exposure to a 16 h photoperiod the amount of chlorophyll
increased and amount of PCR remained stable after 3 days of
illumination. The photoconvertible PCR was not affected by light at
low temperature until biogenesis of the chloroplast had reached a
certain developmental stage.

TABLE 1. Effect of low temperature and L/D 16 h photoperiod Cl, and
IML on the chlorophyll accumulation.

	Chlorophyll accumulation ug/g fresh weight		
	CL 72 h	IML 48 cycles	L/D 3d
5°C	169	679	579
20°C	1500	405	1760

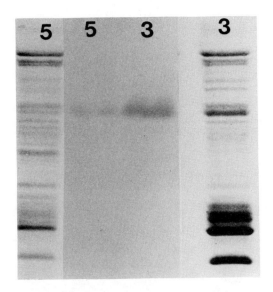

FIGURE 1. Polypetide composition and Western blot analyses of
chloroplast membranes isolated from rye seedling exposed to
a 16 h photoperiod for 3 or 5 days at 5 C.

REFERENCES
1 Griffiths, W.T. (1975) Biochem. J. 152, 623-635.
2 Selstam, E. and Sandelius, S. (1984) Plant Physiol. 76, 1036-1040.
3 Griffiths, W.T. (1978) Biochem. J. 174, 681-692.
4 Oliver, R.P. and Griffiths, W.T. (1980) Biochem. J. 191, 277-280.
5 Chua, N.H. (1980) in Method in Enzymology (San Pietro, H. ed.),
   Vol. 69C, pp. 434-446, Academic Press, New York
6 Mapleston, R.E. and Griffitns, W.T. (1980) Biochem. J. 1989,
   125-133.
7 Ryberg, M. and Dehesh, K. (1986) in Regulation of Chloroplast
   Differentiation (Akoyunoglou, G. and Senger, H., ed.), Vol. 2, pp.
   87-91, Alan R. Liss, Inc.

REGULATION OF PLASTID GENE EXPRESSION DURING FRUIT RIPENING IN TOMATO.
GENE AND TRANSCRIPTION MAP OF THE PLASTID CHROMOSOME.

María Rosa Marano and Néstor Carrillo
Department of Biological Sciences, Universidad Nacional de Rosario.
Facultad de Ciencias Bioquímicas y Farmacéuticas. Suipacha 531. (2000)
Rosario. ARGENTINA.

1. INTRODUCTION

Plastids undergo a series of differentiation processes in the course
of plant development. In ripening fruits, chloroplasts (cp) are transformed in non-photosynthetic chromoplasts (cr), a transition that is
accompanied by chlorophyll breakdown and carotenoid accumulation (1).
Changes in both nuclear and plastid (pt) gene expression are involved in
the process (1-4). Messenger RNAs for pt genes encoding photosynthetic
peptides are absent or strongly diminished in chromoplasts (2,3). The
role of transcriptional control in this lowered gene expression has been
a matter of some controversy. Run-on experiments showed little change in
the overall transcriptional activity of different plastids (4,5), whereas dramatic variations in translation occurred. Akazawa et al., on the
other hand, observed transcriptional inactivation due to extensive methylation of ptDNA, not only in tomato chromoplasts (6) but also in
other types of non-photosynthetic plastids (7,8).

So far, expression experiments have been confined to a limited number
of representative genes. In this note we extend those studies to most of
the pt chromosome. Complete gene map of the tomato pt genome is presented, together with the transcription map (steady-state RNA levels). The
role of methylation was also studied with isoschizomers that recognize
methylated bases in their target sequences. No evidence was found of
pt DNA methylation during chromoplast differentiation.

2. EXPERIMENTAL PROCEDURES

Tomato (Lycopersicon esculentum cv Platense) chloroplasts (9) and
chromoplasts (3) were isolated by previously published procedures. Pt
DNA and total RNA were prepared as described in Ref. 3 and 9, respectively. Conditions for agarose electrophoresis of DNA restriction fragments, electrophoresis of RNA in formaldehyde/formamide/agarose gels
Southern and Northern hybridizations were esentially those of Ref. 10.

3. RESULTS AND DISCUSSION

Fig. 1 depicts a restriction map for the tomato (cv Platense) chromoplast DNA with several restriction endonucleases. A physical map obtained for chloroplast DNA of tomato leaves was identical (not shown),

M. Baltscheffsky (ed.), Current Research in Photosynthesis, Vol. III, 865–868.
© 1990 *Kluwer Academic Publishers. Printed in the Netherlands.*

illustrating the lack of recombinational events in pt DNA during the cp-cr transition. The locations of several genes on the crDNA molecule were determined by hybridization of blotted fragments against heterologous probes representing about 90% of the tobacco chloroplast genome (11). Results are summarized in Fig. 1. Gene order is similar to that of tobacco and other <u>Solanaceae</u>. Most restriction sites are conserved.

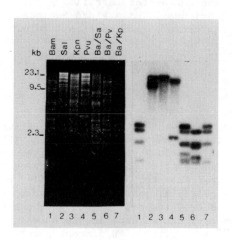

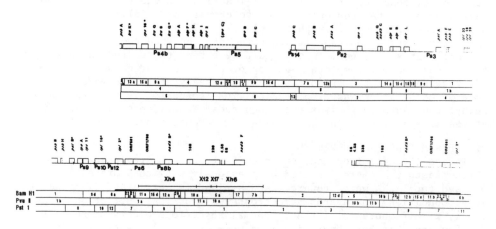

FIGURE 1. Restriction and gene maps of tomato chromoplast DNA. Tobacco cpDNA probes used, their sites of hybridization and gene content (11) are given in the upper parts. Insert, typical Southern hybridizations of single- and double-digested restriction fragments against probe Xh4.

Steady-state levels of pt-derived transcripts were determined for both tomato leaves and mature red fruits. Northern blots were hybridized against the same tobacco cpDNA probes depicted in Fig. 1 and the resulting patterns are shown in Fig. 2.

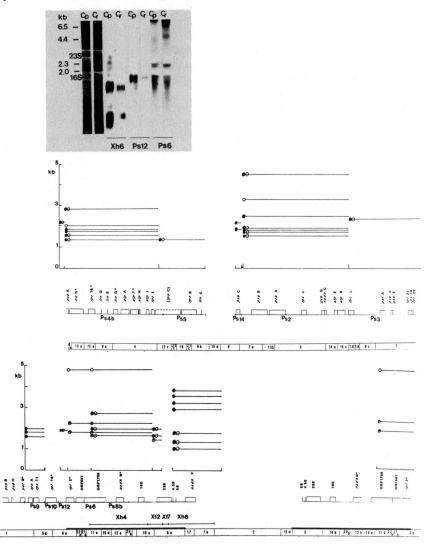

FIGURE 2. Transcription map of tomato ptDNA. Transcripts are shown in the upper parts with their sizes (kb) in the ordinates. Lengths of the lines correspond to those of the probes used and the relative hybridization intensities are indicated: ●, cp-specific; ●●, cp more than cr; ●, similar levels in cp and cr; o, cr-specific. Insert, typical Northern hybridizations. Probes are described in Figure 1.

The amounts of most RNAs are strongly diminished or absent in chromoplasts as compared to chloroplasts, in good agreement with previous results (2-4). Other transcripts, most remarkably those of rRNAs show comparable amounts in both types of plastids. Finally, some chromoplast specific transcripts were detected that hybridized to probes Ps2, Ps4b and Ps6 (Fig. 2). Ps6 contains genes for rpl23 and trnI, and for open reading frames (orfs) of 1708 and 581 kDa eventual polypeptides. Specific RNAs related to orfs were also observed in Capsicum chromoplasts (3). The question of whether the cr-specific transcripts are really new mRNAs or the result of a different processing of primary transcripts has yet to be established.

Different mechanisms have been proposed to explain the lower amounts of certain transcripts in cr, notably those related to photosynthetic peptides (4-6). The role of ptDNA methylation was investigated with pairs of restriction enzymes that are able to discriminate the presence of methylated bases in their recognition sequences: MboI/Sau3AI, MspI/HpaII and BstNI/EcoRII. Restriction patterns obtained with both cp and crDNA looked identical (not shown). Moreover, hybridization of the restriction fragments against most of the tobacco chloroplast genome also failed to reveal any difference between the two types of plastid DNA (data not documented).

4. CONCLUDING REMARKS
   -Physical and gene maps of tomato cp and crDNAs are identical and
   well conserved with respect to those of other Solanaceae.
   -Most RNA molecules found in chloroplasts are absent or very decreased in chromoplasts. Some cr-specific transcripts do exist,
   mostly related to open reading frames of unknown function.
   -Methylation of ptDNA appears not to be involved in the regulation
   of gene expression during chromoplast formation.

REFERENCES
1 Grierson D. (1986) Oxford Surveys Plant Mol. Cell. Biol. 3, 363-383
2 Piechula, B., Pichersky, E., Cashmore, A. and Gruissem, W. (1986) Plant Mol. Biol. 5, 373-384
3 Gounaris, I. and Price, C. (1987) Curr. Genet. 12, 219-224
4 Kunz, M., Evrard, J-L., d'Harlingue, A., Weil, J-H. and Camara, B. (1989) Mol. Gen. Genet. 216, 156-163
5 Deng, XW. and Gruissem, W. (1987) Cell 49, 379-387
6 Ngernprasirtsiri, J., Kobayashi, H. and Akazawa, T. (1988) Plant Physiol.
7 Ngernprasirtsiri, J., Kobayashi, H. and Akazawa, T. (1988) Proc. Natl. Acad. Sci. USA 85, 4750-4754
8 Ngernprasirtsiri, J., Kobayashi, H. and Akazawa, T. (1989) J. Biol. Chem.
9 Bathgate, B., Purton, M.E., Grierson, D. and Goodenough, P. (1985) Planta (Berlin) 165, 197-204
10 Maniatis, T., Fritsch, E.F. and Sambrook, J. (1982) Molecular Cloning, a Laboratory Manual, Cold Spring Harbor Laboratory
11 Shinozaki, K. et al. (1986) EMBO J. 5, 2043-2049

STRUCTURE AND REGULATION OF A RAPIDLY LIGHT INDUCED NUCLEAR ENCODED THYLAKOID PROTEIN.
University of Hannover, Fed. Rep. of Germany, August 6-11, 1989

UWE KÜHNE, UDO CRONSHAGEN, AND FRANK HERZFELD, Dept of Biology; Institute of Botany, D-3000 Hannover, Fed. Rep. of Germany

1. INTRODUCTION

We are dealing with a nuclear encoded protein with an uncommon mRNA induction kinetics not yet described for another protein. The transcription is rapidly induced after illumination of dark grown pea seedlings. During continuous light the mRNA level decreases in a remarkable short time. At cytoplasmic 80S ribosomes the mRNA is translated into a 24 kDa precursor. After in vitro transport into chloroplasts a processed form of this early light induced protein (ELIP) of 17 kDa is found in the thylakoid fraction (1,2).

2. MATERIALS AND METHODS

Pea seedlings (Pisum sativum cv. Rosa Krone) were grown in total darkness. They were either harvested as etiolated plants or illuminated as indicated.
Poly(A)$^+$mRNA was prepared by oligo(dT)cellulose chromatography (3).
The isolation of nuclei, the transcription experiments and the isolation of mRNA is described at Kolanus et al.(4).
The ELIP specific coding region of a cDNA-clone was cloned into the bacterial expression vector pEX1 (5, 6). Antibodies were raised against the fusionprotein expressed by this expression clone.
SDS-PAGE was performed according to Neville (7) on a 6% stacking gel and a 12.5% resolving gel.
For western blotting procedure the proteins were transferred from the gels to nitrocellulose papers by elektrotransfer with a semi dry blotting system. Immunedetection of ELIP was carried out in general as described by Towbin et al (8) with a horse-radish-peroxidase-conjugated secondary antibody to visualize the antigen-antibody-complex on the nitrocellulose sheets.
Pea seedlings were grown under different illumination conditions as indicated.
Chloroplasts and etiochloroplasts, respectively, were isolated by methods previously described (2). Broken plastids were centrifuged at 100 000 x g for 30 minutes to pellet the thylakoid membranes. For SDS-PAGE the pelleted thylakoids and in some cases the supernatant were suspended in an appropriate sample buffer and stored frozen until use.
Thylakoid fractionation was done according to Steinback et al (9). The different fractions were analyzed by SDS-PAGE and western blotting.

M. Baltscheffsky (ed.), Current Research in Photosynthesis, Vol. III, 869–872.
© 1990 *Kluwer Academic Publishers. Printed in the Netherlands.*

3. RESULTS AND DISCUSSION

3.1. mRNA Kinetics

In dark grown pea seedlings there is no detectable ELIP-mRNA. The transcription is induced by light and the maximum level of poly(A)$^+$mRNA appears already after 2-4 h illumination of etiolated seedlings with white light (Fig.1). During this period, the mRNA of ELIP is one of the most abundant mRNA-species as shown by in vitro translation. Continued illumination leads to a decrease of mRNA. Seedlings being more than 16 h illuminated contain no traceable ELIP-mRNA in hybridization experiments.

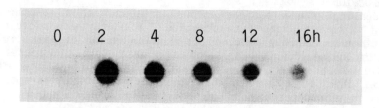

Fig. 1 Kinetics of light induction of ELIP mRNA. Etiolated pea seedlings were illuminated as indicated. Poly(A)$^+$mRNA was isolated, dotted onto nitrocellulose filters and hybridized to ^{32}P-labelled ELIP cDNA.

The results of run-off-transcription experiments show the regulation being located at the transcription level (Fig.2).

Fig.2 Southern hybridization of ELIP cDNA and two reference clones to run-off-transcripts. The DNA fragments from three replica gels were transferred to nitrocellulose and hybridized to ^{32}P-labelled transcripts isolated from nuclei from pea seedlings illuminated as indicated. The arrow indicates the signal of ELIP.

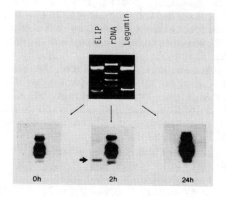

3.2. Protein Kinetics

The protein kinetics shows a rapid increase of the content of ELIP after illumination of dark grown pea seedlings with a maximum after 16 h. Continued illumination leads to a slow but constant decrease of the ELIP content (fig.3). Because of the rapid mRNA and the slow protein decrease ELIP seems to be a quite stable transient membrane protein in etiolated pea seedlings. Even after 48 h of illumination of etiolated pea seedlings ELIP could be detected in the thylakoid membranes.

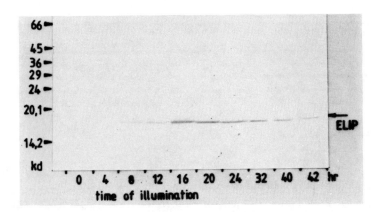

Fig. 3 Detection of ELIP after different periods of illumination. Pea seedlings were grown in total darkness for six days and then illuminated as indicated. Thylakoid membrane proteins were isolated, resolved on a 12.5 % SDS-gel and transferred to a nitrocellulose sheet by a semy dry blotting system. ELIP was immunodetected with an ELIP specific primary antibody and a horse radish peroxidase conjugated secondary antibody.

3.3. Protein Structure

The hydropathic plot of ELIP shows three hydrophobic domains (fig.4a). One of them is predicted to be transmembrane. The respective plots of the chlorophyll a/b binding (cab) proteins are quite similar. An example is shown in fig.4b.

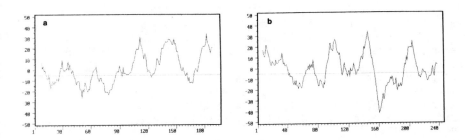

Fig. 4 Hydropathic indices of ELIP (a) and cab6A (b)(9) using a computation interval of 15 amino acids.

3.4. Thylakoid Fractionation

Five fractions were obtained from a sucrose density gradient as indicated in fig.5a . The results of the western blot analysis are shown in fig.5b . Only in the lowest fraction of the gradient, corresponding to the PS I (10), ELIP is detectable.

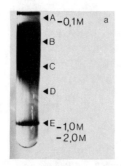 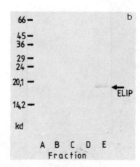

Fig. 5 Thyladoid fractionation on a 0.1 to 0.7 M sucrose density gradient with a 2 M sucrose cushion after centrifugation for 16 h on 100 000 g (a). The designated fractions were analysed by SDS-PAGE and western blot (b).

3.5. Discussion

ELIP is a nuclear encoded chloroplast protein. The mRNA is regulated at the transcription level by light. The protein itself appears after illumination of etiolated pea seedlings during transition of etioplasts to chloroplasts. The hydropathic plot resembles that of cab-proteins with its three hydrophobic helices, one of them being transmembrane. Therefore we suggest that ELIP has a function in the assembly of a thylakoid membrane component. The results of the fractionation experiment point to the fact that the role of ELIP is associated with PS I. Further experiments concerning the regulation and the function of the protein are in progress.

4. REFERENCES

1 Meyer, G., Kloppstech, K. (1984) Eur.J.Biochem 138, 201-207
2 Meyer, G. (1986) PhD thesis, Hannover
3 Apel, K., Kloppstech, K. (1978) Eur.J.Biochem 85, 581-588
4 Kolanus, W., Scharnhorst, C., Kühne, U., Herzfeld, F. (1987) MGG 209, 234-239
5 Stanley and Luzio (1984) EMBO Journal 3 , 1429-1434
6 Scharnhorst, C. (1987) PhD thesis, Hannover
7 Neville G.M. (1971) J.Biol.Chem. 246, 6328-6334
8 Towbin H., Staehlin T., and Gordon J. (1979) Biochemistry Vol.76, No.9 , 4350-4354
9 Hoffman, N.E., Pichersky, E., Malik, V.S., Castresana, C., Ko, K., Darr, S.C., and Cashmore A.R. (1987) Proc. Natl. Acad. Sci. USA Vol. 84, 8844-8848
10 Steinback K.E., Mullet J.E., Arntzen C.J. (1982) in "methods in chloroplast molecular biology" p863ff M.Edelmann et al, Elsevier Biomedical Press, Amsterdam

LIGHT AND SUBSTRATE CONTROL OF RADISH 5-AMINOLEVULINATE
DEHYDRATASE

Claude Huault, Simo J. Tchuinmogne, Jean D. Blondel and
Alain P. Balangé, Laboratoire de Photobiologie, CNRS, Unité
Associée 203, Faculté des Sciences, BP 118, 76134 Mont Saint
Aignan Cedex, FRANCE

1. INTRODUCTION
   Porphyrin biosynthesis is a major biochemical event which leads in
higher plants, to hemes and chlorophylls, and to important hemoproteins
such as phytochrome. Thus, this pathway controls the cellular energetics
through respiration and photosynthesis, and photomorphogenesis as well.
Work from our laboratory was devoted to regulation of 5-aminolevulinate
dehydratase (5-ALAD; EC 4.2.1.24), the second enzyme of the
porphyrin pathway which condenses two molecules of 5-aminolevulinic
acid (ALA) into the monopyrrole porphobilinogen (PBG). In radish
seedlings, 5-ALAD is encoded by the nuclear genome (1) under phytochrome
control (2) during the early growth of radish seedling. 5-ALAD is then
translocated into etiochloroplasts (3), and bound to prothylakoids as
shown recently (4).
One main interest in the study of 5-ALAD is its central position in the
metabolism at the cross-road between the Shemin pathway and the Beale
pathway leading to ALA, and the branched metabolism producing hemes and
chlorophylls. Another interest is related to the evolution of energetics
in radish seedlings from sowing, which depend, first of the
differentiation of mitochondrias, and in later steps, of the development
of chloroplasts, when the cotyledons have turned into leaves.
We have demonstrated recently that the treatment of the radish seedlings
with gabaculine (GAB), during the late steps of development (i.e. 48 h
or 96 h after sowing) leads to an important decrease of 5-ALAD activity
measured in the extracts (5). The 5-ALAD inhibition by GAB, which is
known to inhibit ALA formation through the Beale pathway, is overcome by
the supply of ALA, but not by glutamic acid which is its chloroplastic
precursor. From these facts, we have assumed that ALA, which is the
substrate of 5-ALAD, may control the maturation of this oligomeric
enzyme (5), at least during the latest steps of germination which
coincide with the differentiation of plastids and with the development
of the Beale pathway.
No work has been devoted, till now, on the regulation of 5-ALAD during
the early phase of seedling development just after sowing. This report
deals with the effect of GAB and actinomycine D supplied at sowing.

M. Baltscheffsky (ed.), Current Research in Photosynthesis, Vol. III, 873–876.
© 1990 *Kluwer Academic Publishers. Printed in the Netherlands.*

2. PROCEDURE

2.1. Seedling growth and light conditions

Radish seeds (*Raphanus sativus L.*, cv national, Vilmorin, Le Ménitré 49250, Beaufort en vallée, France) were sown on distilled water either in the dark or under continuous standard far-red light as described elsewhere (1).

For experiments using inhibitors, aqueous solutions were added to replace normal watering. GAB (3-amino-2,3-dihydrobenzoic acid; SERVA No. 12677) was used at concentration of 0.1 mol m^{-3}. Actinomycin D (SERVA No 10710) was applied at a final concentration of 0.1 mol m^{-3}. All the solutions were neutralized to pH 7. The manipulations of seedlings were performed under dim green safelight.

2.2. Extraction and measurements of 5-ALAD activity

Extraction and measurements of enzyme activity was achieved as described previously (1). 5-ALAD activity was expressed in nanomole of PBG formed per second and per cotyledon.

3. RESULTS AND DISCUSSION

3.1. Effect of gabaculine

As previously reported (5), GAB has no effect on 5-ALAD activity *in vitro*. GAB, supplied at sowing, does not affect germination (data not shown).

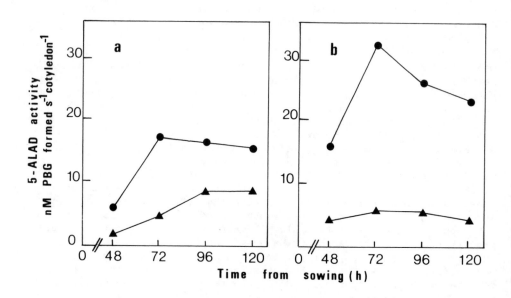

FIGURE 1. Effect of the supply of gabaculine on 5-ALAD activity. a) in cotyledons grown in complete darkness. b) in cotyledons grown under continuous far-red light (●——●, control; ▲——▲, gabaculine-treated cotyledons).

As shown on Fig. 1, GAB reduces only partially the increase of
5-ALAD activity. In dark-grown cotyledons (see Fig. 1.a.),
5-ALAD activity is reduced (25 % of the control 72 h after sowing
and 55 % of the control 120 h after sowing). In far-red grown
cotyledons (see Fig. 1.b.), 5-ALAD activity is also reduced (28 %
of the control after 48 h of germination, and about 20 % after
120 h).
We have shown, in a previous report, that 5-ALAD protein is not
present in seeds (6). Thus, it is possible that the GAB-insensitive
5-ALAD should be a protein which is only formed during the early
step of germination.

3.2. Effect of actinomycin D

As for GAB, actinomycine D was supplied at sowing and does not
limit germination.
Fig. 2 represents the effect of Actinomycine D on the time-course
of 5-ALAD activity in cotyledons.

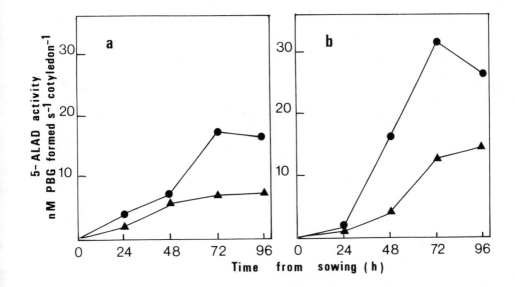

Figure 2. Effect of the supply of actinomycine D on 5-ALAD activity.
    a) in cotyledons grown in complete darkness. b) in
    cotyledons grown under far-red light (●——●, control;
    ▲——▲, actinomycine D-treated cotyledons).

In dark-grown cotyledons (see Fig. 2.a.), 5-ALAD activity is
reduced (40 % of the control 72 h after sowing). In far-red grown
cotyledons (see Fig. 2.b.), 5-ALAD activity is also reduced (60 %
of the control 72 h after sowing).
Previous experiments have shown that cycloheximide prevents
completely the increase of 5-ALAD activity in the early step of

germination, both in dark-grown and in far-red grown cotyledons
(2). Immunoquantification of 5-ALAD does not reveal any 5-ALAD
protein 24 h after sowing (data not shown). Preformed mRNA have
been detected in radish seeds (7). Therefore, it is possible that
the stored mRNA present in the earlier step of germination contain
mRNA specific of 5-ALAD which may be translated immediately after
sowing. We postulate that this 5-ALAD species which is formed
despite the actinomycine D treatment corresponds to the
GAB-insensitive 5-ALAD and that it could participate to the
synthesis of hemes and cytochromes in extrachloroplastic
compartments. The 5-ALAD species sensitive to treatment by GAB and
actinomycine D could be related to etiochloroplasts whose
differentiation takes place during the latest steps of
germination (3,8).

REFERENCES
1 Balangé, A.P. and Rollin, P. (1979) Physiol. Vég. 17, 153-166
2 Huault, C., Bruyant, P. and Balangé, A.P. (1984) Physiol. Plant. 81,
469-473
3 Balangé, A.P. and Lambert, C. (1980) Phytochemistry, 19, 2541-2545
4 Nasri, F., Huault, C. and Balangé, A.P. (1988) Phytochemistry, 27,
1289-1295
5 Tchuinmogne, S.J., Huault, C., Aoues, A. and Balangé, A.P. (1989)
Plant Physiol. in press
6 Huault, C., Aoues, A. and Colin, P. (1987) Plant Physiol. Biochem.
25, 723-728
7 Aspart, L., Meyer, Y., Laroche, M. and Penon, P. (1984) Plant Physiol.
76, 664-673
8 Brangeon, J., Balangé, A.P. and Forchioni, A. (1983) Physiol. Plant.
58, 249-256

DEVELOPMENT OF PHOTOSYNTHETIC APPARATUS IN CALLUS CULTURES DERIVED FROM A C_4 PLANT MAIZE.

SHIKHA ROY AND ASHWANI KUMAR, DEPARTMENT OF BOTANY,
UNIVERSITY OF RAJASTHAN, JAIPUR, 302004. INDIA.

1. INTRODUCTION

There has been considerable speculation regarding connection between "Kranz" anatomy and the physiology of C_4 type carbon assimilation(1). Plant tissue culture offers an opportunity to study the mechanism of photosynthesis at cellular level. Development of photosynthetic apparatus has been studied in several dicot callus cultures(2). However it has been relatively difficult to induce greening in callus cultures derived from monocot C_4 plants (3). The present investigations were undertaken with an object to study the chloroplast development in the callus cultures, derived from a monocot C_4 plant maize, in relation to "Kranz" anatomy and chloroplast dimorphism.

2. PROCEDURE

2.1. Materials and methods

2.1.1. The callus was isolated from the apical portion of epicotyl of the germinating seeds, on modified MS medium(4). These cultures were maintained in a light bank providing continuous fluorescent light mixed with incandescent light in the ratio of 4:1 at Ca 21 W m^{-2}. Ultrastructural investigations were conducted on the green callus cultures excised from the peripheral layers of the callus cultures. The ultrastructural investigations were carried out following the method of Kumar et al (2). The callus tissue was fixed overnight in three percent glutaraldehyde followed by one percent osmium tetraoxide solution for 3 h. Both fixatives were dissolved in Sodium cacodylate (0.02M) buffer. The fixed tissues were dehydrated in acetone/water series. After passage through the acetone series the tissues were passed in propylene oxide for half an hour followed by Epon mixture series and finally embeded in Epon mixture (5). The resin was cured for 72 h at $45°C$. The blocks were sectioned with LKB ultratome, using a glass knife. The sections were mounted on formvar coated copper grids and stained with Lead citrate and examined under Philips 300 EM with an acceleration of voltage of 60 KV.

3. RESULTS AND DISCUSSION

3.1. Under the experimental conditions employed, cells proliferated

M. Baltscheffsky (ed.), Current Research in Photosynthesis, Vol. III, 877–880.
© 1990 Kluwer Academic Publishers. Printed in the Netherlands.

from the explants and greened. In general, the cells contained densely filled central vacuole and a band of parietal cytoplasm appressed to the cell wall. The cytoplasm contained large number of free and bound ribosomes, polysomes, mitochondria and golgi bodies. The chloroplasts occur within this narrow band of thin cytoplasm with the tonoplast on one side and the plasma-lemma on the other (Fig, 1-3).A broad variation in the plastidial structures was recorded in these cultured tissues. The extent of organisation of the internal membrane system was used as an indicator for the developmental stage of the inidividual plastid

3.2. The stage 1 was characterised by lack of internal membrane system which represented the proplastids (Fig, 1a).They also contained plastoglobuli.Stage 2 is represented by young chloroplasts with an envelope consisting of two membranes which contain a few stroma thylakoids and with formation of vesicles in the peripheral region (Fig, 1b,c).

3.3. According to Laetsch and Price (6) proplastids of bundle sheath as well as, mesophyll cells look alike. Therefore from this stage 2, possibly there two lines of development: one which ultimately leads to the formation of bundle sheath type of chloroplasts, which is more elongated in size (1.5 to 2.0 X 6.0 to 7 um); having well developed stroma thylakoids, running across the entire length of the plastid with very poor stacking. They broadly resembled the "Bundle sheath" plastids of the maize plant. This can be represented by stage 3A (Fig,2).

3.4. According to Johnson (7), bundle sheath chloroplasts in maize do not loose all their grana and similarly many grasses have rudimentary grana. It is felt that the development and then loss of grana in the bundle sheath cell chloroplast is a reasonable example of ontogeny providing some hint of phylogeny. It is difficult to ascertain whether this stage is a transient stage towards next successive stage or a final stage in itself. However, the shape and size of chloroplasts of the next successive stage does not reveal its ontogeny. It has been speculated that the lack of grana in the bundle sheath chloroplasts is due to reduction rather than to a unique type of chloroplast development which completely bye passes the formation of grana(6). Second line of further development of the chloroplasts from the stage 2 can be represented by stage 3B, having sufficient development of the stroma, as well as grana thylakoids (Fig, 3). These chloroplasts contained starch grain and plastoglobuli. They were relatively oval and measured between 1.5 to 2.0 X 3 to 4.5 um. These plastids reveal the developmental stage of mesophyll chloroplasts.

3.5. Cut leaves of maize fed with sucrose for 78 h resulted in accumulation of starch in mesophyll plastids. Similarly in tissue culture also the culture medium contained sucrose and that might have caused starch accumulation in the mesophyll type of chloroplasts.

3.6   In stage 4. the chloroplasts have well developed stroma and
       grana thylakoids (Fig, 4), measuring 1.5 to 2.0 X 3.0 to 5.0 um.
       They represent the mature mesophyll type of chloroplasts. Hence
       in the present study although the callus cells do not show
       "Kranz" anatomy but still there may be separate two types of cells
       representing bundle sheath and mesophyll cells, which have two
       respective types of chloroplasts from a common origin. Because
       the ontogeny of these chloroplasts reveals their common origin
       (6), the contention is supported by this fact. Proplastids in
       meristematic tissue cannot be seggregated into two classes.
       Even in tissues which is essentially mature, the chloroplasts
       demonstrate their ability to follow similar developmental steps
       (6). Another paper presented at this conference (8) deals with
       the functional aspects of chloroplast differentiation and
       largely supports the contention that structural differentiation
       regulated the functional abilities with respect to different
       enzyme patterns also.

4. Acknowledgement: The award of USDA-ICAR grant to Dr. Ashwani Kumar
   and valuable suggestions of Prof. R.A.Kennedy , USA are
   gratefully acknowledged.

REFERENCES
1   Kennedy,R.A. (1976) Plant Physiol.58, 573-575.
2   Kumar, A. Bender, L. Pauler, B. Neumann, K.-H, Senger,H.and Jeske, L.
    (1983) Plant cell tissue and organ culture 2, 161-177
3   Laetsch, W.M. and Kortschak, H.P. (1972) Plant Physiol.49, 1021-1023.
4. Roy,S.and Kumar,A.(1986) In Proc.VI International Congress of
    plant tissue and cell culture. Minneapolis, USA p 400.
5. Luft, H.J.(1961) J.Biophys. Biochem. Cytol. 9, 409-414.
6. Laetsch, W.M. and Price, I.(1969) Am. J.Bot. 56, 77-87.
7   Johnson, Sr. M.C. (1964) Ph.D. thesis, Univrsity of Texas, Austin,
    USA.
8   Kumar, A. Roy, S.and Neumann, K.-H. (1989) In Proc. VIII th
    International Congress on Photosynthesis, Stockholm, Sweden.

FIGURE 1-4. Stages of chloroplast development in maize callus
       1a. Proplastid with plastoglobuli (PG).1b and 1c. Young
       plastids (Stage 2). 2. "Bundle sheath" type of chloroplast
       (Stage 3A). 3. Young "Mesophyll" type of chloroplast with
       starch grain (ST) (Stage 3B).4. Mature mesophyll type of
       chloroplast (Stage 4) showing grana stackings.

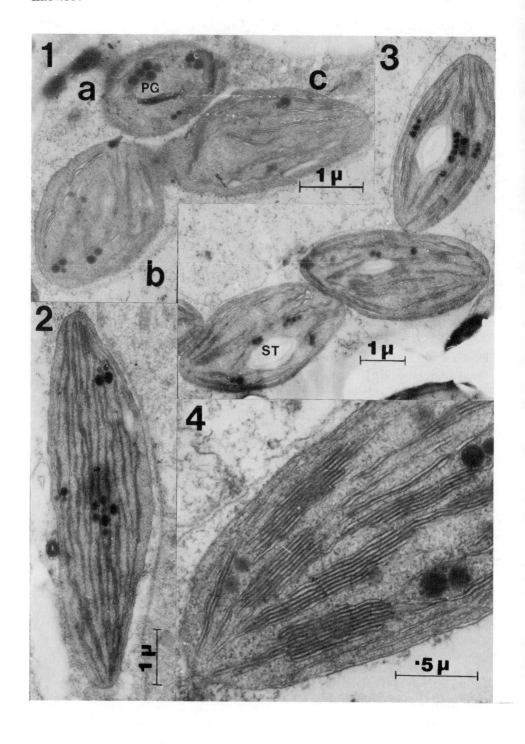

DIVERSITY OF THE PATHWAYS FROM PROTOCHLOROPHYLLIDES TO
CHLOROPHYLLS *A* AND *B*.

Kiriakos Kotzabasis and Horst Senger
Fachbereich Biologie/Botanik, der Philipps Universität
Marburg, Lahnberge, 3550 Marburg, FRG.

INTRODUCTION
It is well established that the last two steps for the
biosynthesis of chlorophyll (Chl) are a fast photoreduction of protochlorophyllide (PChlide) to chlorophyllide (Chlide) (1,2) and a rather slow esterification of
Chlide to Chl (3). The fast reduction of PChlide to
Chlide is light dependent in angiosperms and some
mutants of algae (4,5).- Chl *b* is an integral pigment
of the photosynthetic apparatus of higher plants and
green algae. Its mode of biosynthesis is still a matter
of debate. Most reports favor the direct formation of
Chl *b* from Chl *a* (6,7). However, there are a few
reports on the existence of Chlide *b* (8,9,10).- In
this paper we present new results about the pathways
from PChlides to Chl *a* and Chl *b* .

MATERIALS AND METHODS
Organism and growth
Pigment mutant C-2A' of *Scenedesmus obliquus* (11) was
grown heterotrophically in the dark as described (12).
Isolation of pigments The pigments were extracted with
hot methanol. PChlides were isolated and separated by a
TLC-system with the method of (10). Chlide *b* was
isolated with the method of (13). The PChl isolation
and the determination of PChl/Chl and PChlide/Chlide
photoconversion were carried out as described (14).
Preparation of membrane particles The preparation of
membrane fraction from C-2A' mutant cells of *Scenedesmus obliquus* followed the modified method of (15,16).
Spectroscopic methods Absorption spectra were recorded
with a Kontron dual beam spectrophotometer (Uvikon
820). Fluorescence data were obtained with a Shimadzu
spectrofluorophotometer RF-540.

RESULTS AND DISCUSSION
Pigment mutant C-2A' of *Scenedesmus obliquus* synthesi-

M. Baltscheffsky (ed.), Current Research in Photosynthesis, Vol. III, 881–884.
© 1990 *Kluwer Academic Publishers. Printed in the Netherlands.*

zes only small amounts of PChlide and PChl during the initial phase of heterotrophic growth in darkness (5). Three different PChlides were separated and characterized. They show distinct differences in polarity, absorption and fluorescence (17). Until further characteristics are established we consider them to be monovinyl- and divinyl- PChlide and a third PChlide (PChlide-1) with different side groups.

PChl(ides)	absorption maxima (in methanol)	Fluorescence maxima (in acetone)
PChlide-1	626/435	F631/E434
DV-PChlide	629/438	F633/E437
MV-PChlide	628/432	F632/E429
PChl	624/432 (in acetone)	F629/E429

Tab. 1.: The absorption and fluorescence (F:emission; E:excitation) maxima of the three separated PChlides and PChl.

Some of the PChlide is phytilated to protochlorophyll (PChl). The data of absorption, fluorescence emission and excitation of the extraced pigments are given in Tab. 1. They are in accordance with those reported in the literature (18,19). The PChl is photoconvertible to Chl a , when dark grown cells were exposed for 2min to light of 652nm (3Wm^{-2}) (14). The kinetics of PChl and PChlide photoreduction are identical (Fig. 1). After photoreduction of all photoconvertible PChlide (1h white light of 20 wm^{-2}) Chlide b could be extracted and characterized by absorption and fluorescence measurements. The absorption in 80% acetone showed two maxima at 459 and 648nm, a fluorescence emission and excitation maximum in acetone at 653 and 450nm respectively. The hydroxylamine test (20) confirmed, that this Chlide b possesses an aldehyde group. This Chlide b is a physiological intermediate in Chl b synthesis. In vitro experiments demonstrated that Chlide b can only be synthesized by free, i.e. not protein-bound Chlide a and the photoconversion can only take place in membrane fractions. All Chlide b can be phytilated to Chl b .- In vitro experiments revealed that Chl b can also derive from Chl a (16).
In addition to the above mentioned in vitro experiments, Chl(ide) b formation was studied in intact cells. Aliquots of a culture of C-2A', grown for 20h in the dark, were either immediately extracted with methanol or first illuminated for 5min (3Wm^{-2},650nm) and then incubated for 5min in the dark before extraction. Each extract was separated with TLC, the Chlide b and

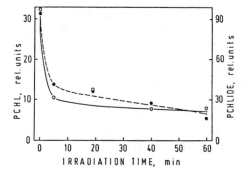

Fig. 1.: Kinetics of PChlide (——) and PChl (---) photoreduction in cells of mutant C-2A' of *Scenedesmus*, grown in the dark, upon irradiation with white light (20 Wm⁻²).

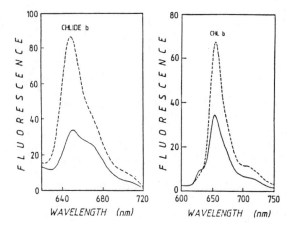

Fig. 2.: Fluorescence spectra of extracted and separated Chlide *b* (left) and Chl *b* (right) before (——) and after (--) exposure to red light (650nm, 3 Wm⁻², 5 min) with 5min additional dark incubation. The spectra were recorded in 80% and 100% acetone respectively.

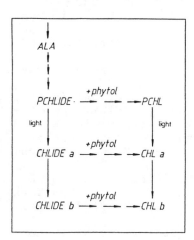

Fig. 3.: Scheme of Chl *a* and *b* biosynthesis in the pigment mutant C-2A' of *Scenedesmus obliquus*.

Chl *b* fractions were scraped off separately and determined quantitatively by fluorescence emission spectroscopy (Fig. 2). The levels of Chlide *b* and Chl *b* increased considerably.

<u>In vitro</u> experiments with membrane fractions demonstrated that the enzyme catalysing this reaction accepts both, Chlide *a* and Chl *a* as substrate, is membrane-bound and specific for a 17,18 dihydroporphyrin structure (reduced pyrrole ring IV).

Our data show that Chl *b* is formed from Chlide *b* as well as from Chl *a* in mutant C-2A' of *Scenedesmus*.

Fig. 3 summarises these data and presents an updated model for the biosynthesis of Chl *b* in *Scenedesmus.*

REFERENCES

1 Griffiths, W.T. (1975) Biochem. J. 152, 623–635
2 Griffiths, W.T. (1978) Biochem. J. 174, 681–692
3 Rüdiger, W., Benz, J. and Guthoff, C. (1980) Eur. J. Biochem. 109, 193–200
4 Oh-hama, T. and Hase, E. (1980) Plant Cell Physiol. 21, 1263–1272
5 Senger, H. and Brinkmann, G. (1986) Physiol. Plant. 68, 119–124
6 Duranton, J. (1966) Physiol. Veg. 4, 75–88
7 Virgin, H. (1977) Physiol. Plant. 40, 45–49
8 Aronoff, S. (1981) Biochem. Biophys. Res. Commun. 102, 108–112
9 Bednarik, D.P. and Hoober, J.K. (1985) Science 230, 450–453
10 Kotzabasis, K. and Senger, H. (1986) Naturwiss. 73, 681–682
11 Bishop, N.I. (1971) Methods Enzymol. 23, 130–143
12 Bishop, N.I. and Wong, J. (1971) Biochim. Biophys. Acta 234, 433–445
13 Kotzabasis, K. and Senger, H. (1989) Bot. Acta 102, 173–177
14 Kotzabasis, K., Schüring, M.P. and Senger, H. (1989) Physiol. Plant. 75, 221–226
15 Senger, H. and Mell, V. (1977) in Methods in Cell Physiology (Prescott, D.M., ed.), Vol.XV, pp 201–218, Academic Press, New York 16 Kotzabasis, K. and Senger, H. (1989) Physiol. Plant. (in press)
17 Kotzabasis, K. and Senger, H. (1986) Z. Naturforsch. 41c, 1001–1003
18 Svec, W.A. (1978) in The Porphyrins, (Dolphin, D., ed.), Vol. V, pp. 341–399, Academic Press, New York
19 Belanger, F.C. and Rebeiz, C.A. (1980) J. Biol. Chem. 25, 1266–1272
20 Ogawa, T. and Shibata, K. (1965) Photochem. Photo biol. 4,193–200

Protochlorophyllide Reduction and Pyridine Nucleotide Redox State During Greening of Protoplasts and Etioplasts from Avena sativa L.

G. Peine, K. Bahnsen, G. Walter and P. Hoffmann

Humboldt-University of Berlin, Dept. Bot., Sect. Biol. Reinhardtstr. 4, 1040 Berlin, G.D.R.

1. INTRODUCTION

Photoconversion of protochlorophyllide (PChlide) into chlorophyllide (Chlide) is due to the enzym protochlorophyllide oxidoreductase (PCR; EC 1.6.99.1) and requires light and NADPH + H^+ as hydrogen donor. Active PChlide, fluorescing at 657 nm, is assumed to be a complex consisted of PCR, 2-3 molecules of PChlide and NADPH + H^+ whereas photoinactive PChlide should be PChlide molecules, separated from NADPH + H^+ and PCR, with a fluorescence maximum at 633nm. But, at present the effect and the role of NADPH + H^+ in the photoconversion process in vivo is not fully understood. Additionally, there are only less informations about the intracellular redox state of the pyridine nucleotides during photoconversion including the regulatory possibilities of the energy metabolism. Therefore, the following questions were to be answered:

1. Does photoconversion occur in isolated protoplasts and etioplasts, derived from protoplasts, after the isolation procedure?

2. If so, does the illumination influence the internal redox state of pyridine nucleotides in both systems?

2. MATERIAL AND METHODS

Protoplasts were isolated enzymatically from primary leaves of 7-day-old oat seedlings (Avena sativa L.) grown in hydroponic culture in complete darkness at 21 °C.
The purified protoplasts were separated into etioplasts and a cytoplasmic supernatant by silicon oil-sucrose step gradient centrifugation through a 24 μm-aperture nylon net (1).
Isolated protoplasts and etioplasts were illuminated with weak white light (10 W/m^2) for 0.5, 2 or 30 min and, thereafter, assayed for pyridine nucleotides by enzymatic cycling measurements (2).
Pigments were determined spectrophotometrically in 80 % acetone(3).

M. Baltscheffsky (ed.), Current Research in Photosynthesis, Vol. III, 885–887.
© 1990 *Kluwer Academic Publishers. Printed in the Netherlands.*

3. RESULTS AND DISCUSSION
PChlide Photoconversion in Protoplasts and Etioplasts

Low temperature fluorescence emission spectra (77 K; excitation
wavelength: 436 nm) showed clearly the occurence of photoactive
P 657 photoconversion into Chlide (see Fig. 1).
But, protoplasts and etioplasts have a large portion of photoinac-
tive PChlide, fluorescing at 634-637 nm.
As verified by pigment content determination, about 48% of the
PChlide were transformed into Chlide, only, compared with 85% in
intact leaves (data not shown).

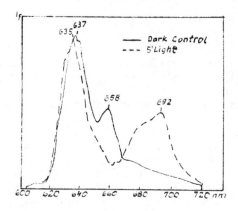

FIGURE 1. Low temperature fluorescence emission spectra (77 K) of
etiolated and illuminated protoplasts after excitation
with polychromatic light (maximum at 436 nm; n=8)

Pyridine Nucleotide Contents and Redox State

Both in protoplasts and etioplasts, NADPH + H$^+$ and NAD$^+$ predomi-
nate among the four nucleotide forms. After 0.5 min of illumination, the NADPH + H$^+$, NAD$^+$ and NADH + H$^+$ amounts decreased for
25-30%. Further illumination provoked an increase of the nucleotide contents above the initial level at which they remained stable.
In etioplasts, the NADH + H$^+$ content rose after 0.5 min to 2 min
of illumination and decreased slowly, thereafter.
The other nucleotide forms dropped similarly as in protoplasts
within the first 2 min.
The redox state of the pyridine nucleotides, expressed as ARC
(NADPH/NADP$^+$ + NADPH) and CRC (NADH/NAD$^+$ + NADH) showed a similar
range for each couple during the whole treatment (Table 1).

TABLE 1. Redox state of pyridine nucleotides in isolated oat
protoplasts and etioplasts, derived from protoplasts,
after illumination (10 W/m^2; n=8; s= 20-30 %)

Light	Protoplasts		Etioplasts	
(min)	ARC	CRC	ARC	CRC
0	0.77	0.45	0.66	0.45
0.5	0.72	0.38	0.72	0.58
2.0	0.69	0.47	0.71	0.54
30.0	0.68	0.48	0.66	0.57

Fully etiolated protoplasts and etioplasts contain a large amount
of NADPH + H^+ reflecting a high reduction power.
The redox state of the $NADP^+/NADPH$ + H^+ system did not change
drastically during photoconversion.
The maintenance of an reduction level of this couple at 66-77%
over at least 30 min of illumination underlines the high buffering
capacities to provide NADPH + H^+ on the basis of internal reser-
ves, only.
Otherwise, the 77-K fluorescence emission spectra showed large
peaks originating from photoinactive PChlide.
This could mean:
a.) the presence of photoinactive PChlide fluorescing at 633 nm
does not correspond to the endogenuous NADPH + H^+ level, or

b.) the NADPH + H^+ content in the stroma of etioplasts does not
reflect a possible local absence of NADPH + H^+ bound to the
pigment-protein-complex.

REFERENCES
1 Robinson, S.P. and Walker, D.A. (1979) Arch.Biochem.Biophys.
196, 319-323
2 Peine, G.; Hoffmann, P.; Seifert, G. and Schilling, G. (1985)
Biochem. Physiol. Pflanzen 180, 1-14
3 Lichtenthaler, H.K. and Wellburn, A.R. (1983) Biochem. Soz.
Transaction, 603rd Meeting Liverpool 603, 591-592

Index of Names

894

896

898